SAP® ABAP™

Handbook

The Jones and Bartlett Publishers SAP® Book Series

SAP® R/3® FI Transactions
V. Narayanan (978-1-934015-01-8) © 2007

Upgrading SAP®
Maurice Sens (978-1-934015-15-5) © 2008

SAP® FI/CO Questions and Answers
V. Narayanan (978-1-934015-22-3) © 2008

SAP® ABAP™ Handbook
Kogent Learning Solutions, Inc. (978-0-7637-8107-1) © 2010

SAP® ABAP™ Questions and Answers
Kogent Learning Solutions, Inc. (978-0-7637-7884-2) © 2010

SAP® MM Questions and Answers
Kogent Learning Solutions, Inc. (978-0-7637-8144-6) © 2010

SAP® SD Questions and Answers
Kogent Learning Solutions, Inc. (978-0-7637-8198-9) © 2010

SAP® ERP® Financials and FICO Handbook
Surya N. Padhi (978-0-7637-8080-7) © 2010

For more information on any of the titles above, please visit us online at http://www.jbpub.com/. Qualified instructors, contact your Publisher's Representative at 1-800-832-0034 or info@jbpub.com to request review copies for course consideration.

SAP® ABAP™

HANDBOOK

Kogent Learning Solutions, Inc.

JONES AND BARTLETT PUBLISHERS
Sudbury, Massachusetts
BOSTON TORONTO LONDON SINGAPORE

World Headquarters
Jones and Bartlett Publishers
40 Tall Pine Drive
Sudbury, MA 01776
978-443-5000
info@jbpub.com
www.jbpub.com

Jones and Bartlett Publishers
Canada
6339 Ormindale Way
Mississauga, Ontario L5V 1J2
Canada

Jones and Bartlett Publishers
International
Barb House, Barb Mews
London W6 7PA
United Kingdom

Jones and Bartlett's books and products are available through most bookstores and online booksellers. To contact Jones and Bartlett Publishers directly, call 800-832-0034, fax 978-443-8000, or visit our website www.jbpub.com.

Substantial discounts on bulk quantities of Jones and Bartlett's publications are available to corporations, professional associations, and other qualified organizations. For details and specific discount information, contact the special sales department at Jones and Bartlett via the above contact information or send an email to specialsales@jbpub.com.

Production Credits
Publisher: David Pallai
Editorial Assistant: Molly Whitman
Production Assistant: Ashlee Hazeltine
Associate Marketing Manager: Lindsay Ruggiero
V.P., Manufacturing and Inventory Control:
Therese Connell

Composition: diacriTech
Art Rendering: diacriTech
Cover and Title Page Design: Kate Ternullo
Cover Image: © Kenton/Dreamstime.com
Printing and Binding: Malloy, Inc.
Cover Printing: Malloy, Inc.

Library of Congress Cataloging-in-Publication Data
SAP ABAP handbook/Kogent Learning Solutions, Inc.
p. cm.
Includes index.
ISBN-13: 978-0-7637-8107-1 (hardcopy)
ISBN-10: 0-7637-8107-X (ibid.)
1. ABAP/4 (Computer program language) I. Kogent Learning Solutions, Inc.
QA76.73.A12S265 2009
005.13'3–dc22

2009021645

6048
Printed in the United States of America
13 12 11 10 09   10 9 8 7 6 5 4 3 2 1

Trademark Acknowledgment

This publication contains references to the products of SAP AG. SAP, R/3, xApps, xApp, SAP NetWeaver, Duet, PartnerEdge, ByDesign, SAP Business ByDesign, and other SAP products and services mentioned herein are trademarks or registered trademarks of SAP AG in Germany and in several other countries all over the world.

Business Objects and the Business Objects logo, Business Objects, Crystal Reports, Crystal Decisions, Web Intelligence, Xcelsius and other Business Objects products and services mentioned herein are trademarks or registered trademarks of Business Objects in the United States and/or other countries.

SAP AG is neither the author nor the publisher of this publication and is not responsible for its content, and SAP Group shall not be liable for errors or omissions with respect to the materials.

Contents at a Glance

Introduction		*xxi*
Chapter 1	A Gateway to SAP Systems	1
Chapter 2	The Logon Process of the SAP System	27
Chapter 3	SAP Easy Access	55
Chapter 4	Understanding ABAP Workbench	89
Chapter 5	ABAP Dictionary	123
Chapter 6	ABAP Programming in ABAP Editor	227
Chapter 7	Internal Tables	299
Chapter 8	Accessing Data in the SAP System	411
Chapter 9	Modularization Techniques	497
Chapter 10	ABAP User Dialogs	549
Chapter 11	The BDC and LSMW Tools	645
Chapter 12	Forms in mySAP ERP: SAPscript and SAP Smart Forms	735
Chapter 13	Reports	817
Chapter 14	Business Add-Ins (BADIs)	847
Appendix A	Object Orientation in ABAP	881
Appendix B	Introducing Cross-Application Technologies	907
	Glossary	927
	Index	943

Table of Contents

Introduction **xxi**

About This Book xxi
How to Use This Book xxii
Conventions xxii
Other Resources xxiv

Chapter 1 A Gateway to SAP Systems **1**

Explaining the Concept of an ERP System 2
History of SAP Systems 4
Need for ABAP 6
Exploring the Architecture of SAP R/3 8
The Logical View 9
The Software-Oriented View 10
The User-Oriented View 13
Explaining the Architecture of the Application Server 14
Dispatching Dialog Steps 22
Describing the User Context and Roll Area in the SAP System 24
The Client-Dependency Feature 26
Summary 26

Chapter 2 The Logon Process of the SAP System **27**

Starting the SAP System 28
Maintaining the SAP Logon Screen 31
Adding a New Entry 31
Modifying the Entry 35
Deleting the Entry 36
Creating and Using SAP Shortcuts 37
Creating SAP Shortcuts 37
Configuring the SAP Logon 47

	Changing the Password	50
	Logging Off of the SAP System	52
	Summary	53
Chapter 3	**SAP Easy Access**	**55**
	Explaining the SAP Easy Access Screen	56
	Exploring the GUI of the SAP System	60
	The Screen Header	60
	The Screen Body	67
	Customizing the SAP GUI	70
	Managing Favorites	72
	Adding an Item	75
	Inserting Folders	76
	Moving Favorites and Folders	78
	Renaming Favorites and Folders	80
	Deleting Favorites and Folders	82
	Adding a Web Address	82
	Handling SAP Sessions	84
	Creating a New Session	84
	Displaying a List of All Sessions	86
	Ending a Session	87
	Summary	88
Chapter 4	**Understanding ABAP Workbench**	**89**
	Overview of ABAP Workbench	90
	Exploring the ABAP Workbench Tools	91
	ABAP Dictionary	92
	ABAP Editor	94
	Front-End Editor (New)	95
	Front-End Editor (Old)	96
	Back-End Editor	98
	Class Builder	99
	Function Builder	101
	Screen Painter	102
	Menu Painter	103

Object Navigator 105
Message Maintenance 109
ABAP Text Elements 110
Maintain Transaction 111
Describing Package Builder 112
Types of Packages 113
Testing Tools in ABAP Workbench 114
ABAP Debugger 114
ABAP Runtime Analysis 115
Performance Analysis 116
Describing Web Services 117
Web Application Builder for ITS 118
Web Application Builder for BSP 119
Describing XSLT Editor 120
Summary 121

Chapter 5 ABAP Dictionary 123

Overview of ABAP Dictionary 124
Exploring Domains 125
Describing Fixed Values for Domains 126
Exploring Conversion Routines for Domains 127
Creating a Domain 128
Modifying the Existing Domain 133
Deleting a Domain 138
Exploring Data Types 138
Data Elements 138
Structures 144
Table Types 144
Exploring Type Groups 145
Exploring Database Tables 146
Types of Tables 148
Types of Table Fields 152
Technical Settings of a Table 154
Creating Tables 158
Relating Tables by Using Foreign Keys 174

Exploring Views 180
Relating Database Tables Using Relational Operators 181
Creating Different Types of Views 184
Deleting Views 211
Exploring Search Helps 212
Elementary Search Help 212
Collective Search Help 213
Append Search Help 214
Exploring Lock Objects 215
Describing Lock Arguments 217
Exploring the Lock Mode and the Lock Table 218
Describing the Lock Mechanism 220
Creating Lock Objects 222
Summary 226

Chapter 6 ABAP Programming in ABAP Editor 227

Structure of an ABAP Program 228
Introductory Program Part 229
Declaration Part for Global Data, Class Definitions, and Selection Screens 229
Processing Blocks 230
ABAP Editor 231
Types of ABAP Programs 236
ABAP Syntax 238
Inserting Comments into ABAP Programs 239
Exploring Types and Objects 241
Data Types 242
Object Types 245
Objects in ABAP 246
Variables in ABAP 248
The `DATA` Statement 248
The `PARAMETERS` Statement 252
Constants in ABAP 256
The `TABLES` Statement 258
Assignment Statements 259
The `MOVE` Statement 259
The `MOVE-CORRESPONDING` Statement 263

The `WRITE TO` Statement 265
The `CLEAR` Statement 266
Formatting Options 268
The `WRITE` Statement 268
The `FORMAT` Statement 271
Exploring System Variables 278
Dynamic Assignment 278
Describing Flow Control Statements 279
The `IF...ENDIF` Control Statement 280
Looping 289
Terminating Loops 294
Summary 297

Chapter 7 Internal Tables 299

Overview of Internal Tables 300
Data Types of an Internal Table 303
Types of Internal Tables 303
Standard Tables 304
Sorted Tables 304
Hashed Tables 305
Creating Internal Tables 305
Creating Internal Tables as Data Types 306
Creating Internal Tables as Data Objects 313
Performing Operations on an Entire Internal Table 316
Moving and Assigning Internal Tables 316
Initializing Internal Tables 319
Refreshing Internal Tables 320
Releasing the Memory of Internal Tables 320
Comparing Internal Tables 322
Performing the Sort Operation in Internal Tables 325
Determining the Attributes of Internal Tables 333
Operations on Individual Lines 335
Inserting Lines in Internal Tables 337
Inserting Summarized Lines in Internal Tables 346
Appending Lines to Internal Tables 348
Reading the Lines of Internal Tables 356
Modifying the Lines of Internal Tables 364

Deleting Lines 373
Searching Table Entries 386
Maintaining Internal Tables 390
Control Break Processing 392
The AT FIRST and AT LAST Statements 392
The AT NEW and AT END OF Statements 395
The SUM Statement 401
The ON CHANGE OF Statement 403
Summary 410

Chapter 8 Accessing Data in the SAP System 411

Accessing Database Tables 412
Open SQL 413
Reading Data Using the SELECT Statement 416
The SELECT Clause 417
The INTO Clause 428
The FROM Clause 437
The WHERE Clause 446
The GROUP BY Clause 459
The HAVING Clause 462
The ORDER BY Clause 463
Subqueries 465
Examples of Subqueries 467
Inserting Data into a Database Table 471
Examples of Data Insertion 472
Updating Data in a Database Table 477
Examples of Updating Data in Tables 479
Deleting the Data from a Database Table 483
Examples of Deleting Data 485
Modifying the Lines of Database Tables 488
Using Cursors to Read Data 490
Opening and Closing Cursors 491
Retrieving Data 491
Committing Database Changes 494
Summary 495

Chapter 9 Modularization Techniques 497

Working with Subroutines 498
- Working with Formal and Actual Parameters 503
- Handling Data in Subroutines 505
- Using Local Field Symbols 510
- Making Internal and External Calls 513
- Passing Parameters to Subroutines 518
- Terminating Subroutines by Using `EXIT` and `CHECK` Statements 524

Function Modules 526
- Creating Function Modules 528
- Calling Function Modules from ABAP Programs 540

Source Code Modules 543
- Macros 544
- Include Programs 545

Summary 548

Chapter 10 ABAP User Dialogs 549

Introducing Dialog Programming 550

Screen Painter 552
- Learning About Attributes 555
- Flow Logic 559
- Learning About the Layout Editor 561
- The Tabstrip Control in Graphical Layout Editor 568
- Creating a Table Control by Using Graphical Layout Editor 590

Menu Painter 599
- Working with Menu Painter 600

Working with Selection Screens 620
- Defining a Selection Screen 620
- Calling a Selection Screen 638
- Processing Selection Screens 643

Summary 643

Chapter 11 The BDC and LSMW Tools 645

The Data Transfer Techniques 646
The Batch Input Technique 646
The Direct Input Technique 649
The BAPI Technique 649
Data Transfer Methods 649
The Direct Input Method 650
The Call Transaction Method 650
The Batch Input with Session Method 651
Data Transfer by Using the `BDCDATA` Structure 652
The BDC Tool 653
Creating a BDC Program by Using the Call Transaction Method 653
Transferring Data by Using the Batch Input with Session Method of BDC 675
The LSMW Tool 697
Updating Records by Using the Batch Input Recording Method 698
Summary 733

Chapter 12 Forms in mySAP ERP: SAPscript and SAP Smart Forms 735

Exploring the SAPscript Tool 736
Components of the SAPscript Tool 738
Structure of an SAPscript Form 739
Managing Tools 743
Accessing the Form Painter Tool 747
Form Subobjects 751
The SAPscript Runtime Environment 762
Print Program 763
SAPscript Function Modules 771
Controlling the SAPscript Forms 787
SAPscript Control Commands 789
SAPscript Symbols 791
The SAP Smart Forms Tool 793
Overview of the SAP Smart Forms Tool 794
SAP Smart Form Components 795

Explaining the Smart Form Process 798
Advantages of Smart Forms 800
Important Objects for Form Development 800
Creating and Maintaining Smart Forms 801
Style Builder 806
Comparing SAPscript and Smart Forms 808
Migrating SAPscript Forms to Smart Forms 810
Individual Migration 811
Mass Migration 812
Converting a Style 814
Summary 816

Chapter 13 Reports 817

Working with Classical Reports 818
Creating a Classical Report 820
Interactive Reports 827
Creating an Interactive Report 829
Comparing Classical and Interactive Reports 839
ALV Reports 839
Creating an ALV Report 840
Summary 846

Chapter 14 Business Add-Ins (BADIs) 847

Concept of BADIs 848
Enhancement Framework 849
Overview of Enhancement 851
The Enhancement Builder Tool 854
Enhancement Techniques in Enhancement Framework 854
Structure of a BADI 856
Definition of BADIs 858
Defining a BADI 860
Displaying, Changing, or Deleting a BADI Definition 869
Implementation of BADIs 870
Calling BADIs 875
Differences Between Classic and New BADIs 875
Filter-Dependent BADIs 876

Function Code Enhancements 878
Screen Enhancements 879
Summary 880

Appendix A Object Orientation in ABAP 881

Overview of ABAP Objects 882
Explaining the Basic Concepts of OOP in ABAP 883
Objects 884
Classes 885
Interfaces 885
Encapsulation 885
Inheritance 886
Polymorphism 887
Defining and Implementing a Class 887
Exploring the Components of a Class 889
Visibility Sections in a Class 892
Handling the Objects 893
Declaring and Implementing Interfaces 895
Declaring and Calling Methods 898
Declaring and Calling Constructors 901
Working with Events in ABAP Objects 902
Triggering an Event 903
Handling an Event 904

Appendix B Introducing Cross-Application Technologies 907

Introducing IDoc 908
Exploring the Uses of IDoc 909
EDI Technique 909
ALE Technique 910
Legacy System Integration 910
Third-Party Product Integration 910
Workflow Integration 911
SAP R/2 System 911
Internet and XML Integration 911
OCR Integration 912
ICR Integration 912

Benefits of the IDoc Interface 912
Describing the IDoc Structure 913
IDoc Runtime Components 917
    Control Record 917
    Data Records 918
    Status Records 918
ALE 919
    ALE Architecture 920
RFC 924
    RFC Interface 924
    Types of RFC 926

Glossary 927

Index 943

INTRODUCTION

Congratulations on buying the *SAP® ABAP™ Handbook*! This book features comprehensive content on the various concepts of the SAP system and ABAP language. SAP technology was introduced by SAP AG, Germany. For over thirty years, SAP technology has formed an indispensable part of many business enterprises with respect to enterprise resource planning (ERP). The pace of technological enhancements is getting faster day by day, and this has been particularly true with SAP. Today, most companies using SAP software employ it to build applications that have more to do with cross-platform reliability.

ABOUT THIS BOOK

The *SAP® ABAP™ Handbook* covers hundreds of topics, theoretically as well as practically, related to the SAP ABAP programming language. The book also covers the SAP R/3® release, the functionalities of the ABAP/4 language, various tools to develop ABAP programs in SAP systems, data access in the SAP system, system architecture, and system administration. A few chapters of this book also provide implementation-ready program code to help you understand different concepts.

This book is ideal for beginners who intend to familiarize themselves with the SAP ABAP technology because it begins with the very basics and then moves on to more complex topics. An added advantage to this book is that it also suits professionals who are already familiar with SAP technology and want to enhance their skills. It describes the techniques and procedures that are employed most frequently by users working with SAP R/3.

This book is divided into easy-to-understand sections, with each topic addressing different programming issues in SAP ABAP, such as:

- Introduction of the SAP system and ABAP
- The logon process
- The GUI
- ABAP Workbench
- ABAP Dictionary

- ABAP programming in ABAP Editor
- Internal tables
- Data access
- Modularization techniques: subroutines, function modules, and source code modules
- Dialog programming in ABAP
- Data transfer techniques: BDC and LSMW
- SAPscript and Smart Forms
- Creating reports in the SAP system
- Defining and implementing BADIs
- Object orientation in ABAP
- Cross-application technologies: IDoc, ALE, and RFC

This is just a partial list of all of the valuable information in this book. The book provides special coverage of the SAP ABAP technology implemented in mySAP ERP, more than any other book dedicated to the subject.

Our sole intent has been to provide a book with in-depth and sufficient information so that you enjoy reading and learning from it. Happy reading!

HOW TO USE THIS BOOK

In this book, we have employed the mySAP ERP software to run the code. You must, therefore, install mySAP ERP on your system to use and implement the applications provided in the book. This book begins with the basics of SAP software and makes you familiar with its user interface. After that, it discusses ABAP/4 commands and programming. This book consists of 14 chapters and 2 appendices to explain the concepts and techniques of ABAP/4 programming.

CONVENTIONS

There are a few conventions followed in this book that need to be introduced. For example, the code in this book is given in the form of code listings. The code with a listing number and caption appears as follows:

```
REPORT  ZINTERNAL_TABLE_DEMO.
*/declaring table type by using the TYPES statement

TYPES: BEGIN OF DataLine,
                S_ID TYPE C,
                S_Name(20) TYPE C,
                S_Salary TYPE I,
       END OF DataLine.
TYPES MyTable TYPE SORTED TABLE OF DataLine WITH UNIQUE
KEY S_ID.
WRITE:/'MyTable is an internal table. It is a sorted type
of table with a unique key defined on the S_ID field.'.
```

LISTING 7.1 **Declaring a table type with the TYPES statement**

The *SAP® ABAP™ Handbook* also provides you with additional information on various concepts in the form of notes, as follows:

> **Note:** *To know more about the* MOVE *statement, refer to the "Moving and Assigning Internal Tables" section of this chapter.*

Every figure contains a descriptive caption to enhance clarity, as follows:

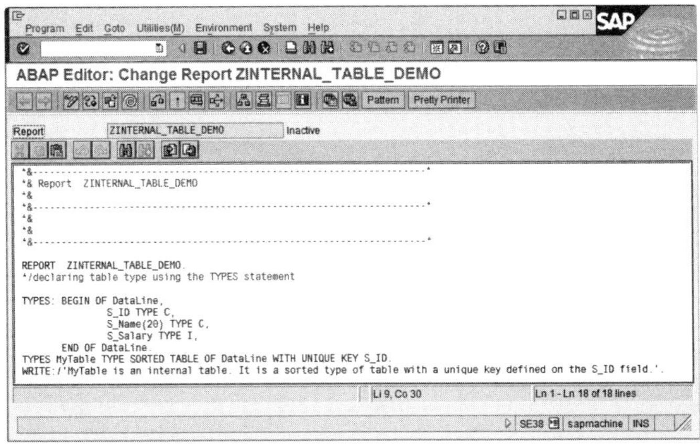

FIGURE 7.7 **Adding code in the ABAP editor: change report screen**

In this book, tables are placed immediately after their first callout. An example of a table is below.

Table Type	Description
INDEX TABLE	Creates a generic table type with index access
ANY TABLE	Creates a fully generic table type
STANDARD TABLE or TABLE	Creates a standard table
SORTED TABLE	Creates a sorted table
HASHED TABLE	Creates a hashed table

TABLE 7.1 List of table types

OTHER RESOURCES

Here are some other useful HTML links where you can find texts related to SAP ABAP and some helpful tutorials:

- http://help.sap.com/
- http://sapbrainsonline.com/

Chapter 1 A Gateway to SAP Systems

If you need information on:	*See page:*
Explaining the Concept of an ERP System	2
History of SAP Systems	4
Need for ABAP	6
Exploring the Architecture of SAP R/3	8
Explaining the Architecture of the Application Server	14
Dispatching Dialog Steps	22
Describing User Context and Roll Area in the SAP System	24
The Client-Dependency Feature	26

Systems Applications and Products in Data Processing (SAP) is business software that integrates all applications running in an organization. These applications represent various modules on the basis of business areas, such as finance, production and planning, and sales and distribution, and are jointly executed to accomplish the overall business logic. SAP integrates these modules by creating a centralized database for all the applications running in an organization. You can customize SAP according to your requirements by using the Advanced Business Application Programming (ABAP) language. ABAP, also referred to as ABAP/4, is the technical module of SAP and the fourth-generation programming language used to create applications related to SAP.

The SAP system was introduced as an Enterprise Resource Planning (ERP) software designed to coordinate all the resources, information, and activities to automate business processes, such as order fulfillment or billing. Nowadays, the SAP system also helps you to know about the flow of information among all the processes of an organization's supply chain, from purchases to sales, including accounting and human resources.

Integration of different business modules is a key factor that separates SAP from other enterprise applications. Integration of business modules helps to connect various business modules, such as finance, human resources, manufacturing, and sales and distribution, so that the data of these modules can be easily accessed, shared, and maintained across an enterprise. Integration also ensures that a change made in one module is reflected automatically on the other modules, thereby keeping the data updated at all times.

In this chapter, you learn about SAP and its need in today's businesses. This chapter also deals with the importance of ERP and its implementation in SAP. The chapter provides a comprehensive history of SAP, focusing on the circumstances that necessitated its development, and, finally, on how its introduction helped to improve system performance and business efficiency. In addition, this chapter describes the need for the ABAP/4 language in SAP and also explains the architecture of the SAP system, including its three views: logical, software-oriented, and user-oriented. It also explores the various components of the application servers that are used in SAP, such as work processes, the dispatcher, and the gateway, and describes the structure and types of work processes. You also learn how to dispatch a dialog step, a procedure that helps a user to navigate from one screen to another in the SAP system, as well as two important concepts: user context and roll area, which are memory areas that play an integral role in dispatching dialog steps and in implementing a work process. This chapter also explains the client-dependency feature of SAP. The chapter concludes with a brief discussion on the integrated environment of SAP.

EXPLAINING THE CONCEPT OF AN ERP SYSTEM

A system that automates and integrates all modules of business areas is known as an ERP system or simply ERP. An ERP system is used to integrate several data sources and processes, such as manufacturing, control, and distribution of goods in an organization. This integration is achieved by using various hardware and software components. An ERP system is primarily module-based, which implies that it consists of various modular software applications or modules. A software module in an ERP system automates a specific business area or module of an enterprise, such as finance or sales and distribution. These software modules of an ERP system are linked to each other by a centralized database.

A centralized database is used to store data related to all the modules of the business areas. Using a centralized database ensures that the data can be accessed, shared, and maintained easily. Combined with the module-based implementation, an ERP system improves the performance and efficiency of business processing.

Before the advent of the ERP system, each department of a company had its own customized automation mechanism. As a result, the business modules were not interconnected or integrated, and updating and sharing data across the business modules was a big problem. Let's use an example to understand this concept better. Suppose the finance and sales and distribution modules of an enterprise have their respective customized automation mechanisms. In such a setup, if a sale is closed, its status would be updated automatically in the sales and distribution module. However, the updated status of the sale of an item would not be updated in the finance module automatically. Consequently, the revenue generated from the sale of an item would need to be updated manually in the finance module, resulting in a greater probability of errors and an asynchronous business process. The problem was fixed with the help of the integration feature built into the ERP system.

Another benefit of the ERP system is that it helps synchronize data and keep it updated. Ideally, an ERP system uses only a single, common database to store information related to various modules of an organization, such as sales and distribution, production planning, and material management.

Despite the benefits of the ERP system, the system has certain drawbacks. Some of the major drawbacks of the ERP system are:

- Customization of ERP software is restricted because you cannot easily adapt ERP systems to a specific workflow or business process of a company.
- Once an ERP system is established, switching to another ERP system is very costly.
- Some large organizations may have multiple departments with separate, independent resources, missions, chains-of-command, etc., and consolidation into a single enterprise may yield limited benefits.

SAP was introduced to overcome the drawbacks of the contemporary ERP systems. The introduction of SAP systems not only removed the preceding bottlenecks but also led to improved system performance and business efficiency by integrating individual applications. In other words, an SAP system ensures data consistency throughout the system, in addition to removing the drawbacks of the contemporary ERP systems.

Next, let's explain why and how an SAP system is introduced in business processing.

HISTORY OF SAP SYSTEMS

SAP is a translation of the German term Systeme, Anwendungen, und Produkte in der Datenverarbeitung. It was developed by SAP AG, Germany. The basic idea behind developing SAP was the need for standard application software that helps in real-time business processing. The development process began in 1972 with five IBM employees: Dietmar Hopp, Hans-Werner Hector, Hasso Plattner, Klaus Tschira, and Claus Wellenreuther in Mannheim, Germany. A year later, the first financial and accounting software was developed; it formed the basis for continuous development of other software components, which later came to be known as the SAP R/1 system. Here, R stands for real-time data processing and 1 indicates single-tier architecture, which means that the three networking layers, Presentation, Application, and Database, on which the architecture of SAP depends, are implemented on a single system. SAP ensures efficient and synchronous communication among different business modules, such as sales and distribution, production planning, and material management, within an organization. These modules communicate with each other so that any change made in one module is communicated instantly to the other modules, thereby ensuring effective transfer of information.

The SAP R/2 system was introduced in 1980. SAP R/2 was a packaged software application on a mainframe computer, which used the time-sharing feature to integrate the functions or business areas of an enterprise, such as accounting, manufacturing processes, supply chain logistics, and human resources. The SAP R/2 system was based on a two-tier client-server architecture, where an SAP client connects to an SAP server to access the data stored in the SAP database. SAP R/2 was implemented on the mainframe databases, such as DB/2, IMS, and Adabas. SAP R/2 was particularly popular with large European multinational companies that required real-time business applications, with built-in multicurrency and multilanguage capabilities. Keeping in mind that

SAP customers belong to different nations and regions, the SAP R/2 system was designed to handle different languages and currencies. The SAP R/2 system delivered a higher level of stability compared to the earlier version.

Note: Time-sharing implies that multiple users can access an application concurrently; however, each user is unaware that the operating system is being accessed by other users.

SAP R/3, based on a client-server model, was officially launched on July 6, 1992. This version is compatible with multiple platforms and operating systems, such as UNIX and Microsoft Windows. SAP R/3 introduced a new era of business software—from mainframe computing architecture to a three-tier architecture consisting of the Database layer, the Application layer (business logic), and the Presentation layer. The three-tier architecture of the client-server model is preferred to the mainframe computing architecture as the standard in business software because a user can make changes or scale a particular layer without making changes in the entire system.

The SAP R/3 system is a customized software with predefined features that you can turn on or off according to your requirements. The SAP R/3 system contains various standard tables to execute various types of processes, such as reading data from the tables or processing the entries stored in a table. You can configure the settings of these tables according to your requirements. The data related to these tables are managed with the help of the dictionary of the SAP R/3 system, which is stored in an SAP database and can be accessed by all the application programs of SAP.

The SAP R/3 system integrates all the business modules of a company so that the information, once entered, can be shared across these modules. The SAP R/3 system is a highly generic and comprehensive business application system, especially designed for companies of various organizational structures and different lines of business.

The SAP R/3 system runs on various platforms, such as Windows and UNIX. It also supports various relational databases of different database management systems, such as Oracle, Adabas, Informix, and Microsoft SQL Server. The SAP R/3 system uses these databases to handle the queries of the users.

With the passage of time, a business suite that would run on a single database was required. This led to the introduction of the mySAP ERP application as a follow-up product to the SAP R/3 system. The mySAP ERP application is one of the applications within the mySAP Business Suite. This suite includes mySAP ERP, mySAP Supply Chain Management (SCM), mySAP Customer Relationship Management (CRM), mySAP Supplier Relationship Management (SRM), and mySAP Product Lifestyle Management (PLM). The latest release of the mySAP ERP application is SAP ERP Central Component (ECC6.0). The mySAP ERP categorizes the applications into the following three core functional areas:

- Logistics
- Financial
- Human resources

> **Note:** The book focuses on the latest release of the mySAP ERP application, i.e., ECC6.0.

As stated earlier, the runtime environment and integrated suite of application programs within the SAP R/3 system are written in a fourth-generation language, ABAP/4.

NEED FOR ABAP

ABAP, or ABAP/4, is a fourth-generation programming language first developed in the 1980s. It was used originally to prepare reports, which enabled large corporations to build mainframe business applications for material management and financial and management accounting.

ABAP is one of the first programming languages to include the concept of logical databases, which provides a high level of abstraction from the centralized database of the SAP system. Apart from the concept of logical databases, you can also use Structured Query Language (SQL) statements to retrieve and manipulate data from the centralized database. To learn more about working with databases with the help of the SQL statements, refer to Chapter 8.

The ABAP programming language was used originally to develop the SAP R/3 system. That is, the runtime environment and application programs in the SAP R/3 system are written in the ABAP language. The SAP R/3 system provides the following set of applications, also known as functional modules, functional areas, or application areas:

- Financial Accounting (FI)
- Production Planning (PP)
- Material Management (MM)
- Sales and Distribution (SD)
- Controlling (CO)
- Asset Management (AM)
- Human Resources (HR)
- Project System (PS)
- Industry Solutions (IS)
- Plant Maintenance (PM)
- Quality Management (QM)
- Workflow (WF)

These functional modules are written in the ABAP language. In addition, you can use the ABAP language to enhance the applications that you create in the mySAP ERP system. For instance, besides the available reports and interfaces in the mySAP ERP system, you can create your own custom reports and interfaces.

The ABAP language environment, which includes syntax checking, code generation, and the runtime system, is a part of SAP Basis. SAP Basis, a component of an SAP system, acts as a technological platform that supports the entire range of SAP applications, now typically implemented in the framework of the SAP Web Application Server. In other words, the SAP Basis component acts as an operating system on which SAP applications run.

Similar to any other operating system, the SAP Basis component contains both low-level services, such as memory management and database communication, and high-level tools, such as SAP Smart Forms and log viewers, for end-users and administrators. You learn more about these concepts later in this book.

The ABAP language provides the following features:

- **Data sharing**—Enables you to store data in memory at a central location. Different users and programs can then access the data without copying it.

- **Exception handling**—Helps define a special control flow for a specific error situation and provide information about the error.
- **Data persistency**—Enables you to store data permanently in relational database tables of the SAP R/3 system.
- **Making enhancements**—Enables you to enhance the functionality of programs, function modules, and global classes, without modifying or replacing the existing code.

EXPLORING THE ARCHITECTURE OF SAP R/3

As stated earlier, the SAP R/3 system evolved from the SAP R/2 system, which was a mainframe. The SAP R/3 system is based on the three-tier architecture of the client-server model. Figure 1.1 shows the three-tier architecture of the SAP R/3 system:

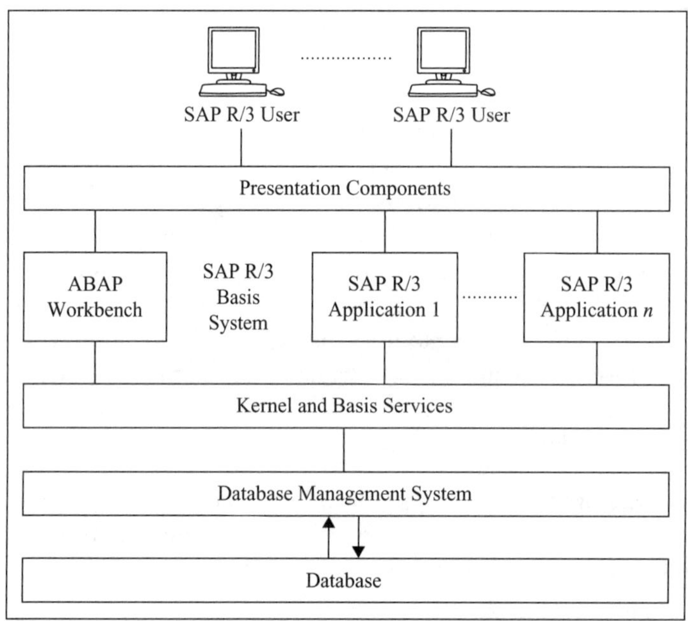

FIGURE 1.1 **SAP R/3 architecture**

Figure 1.1 shows how the R/3 Basis system forms a central platform within the R/3 system. The architecture of the SAP R/3 system distributes the workload to multiple R/3 systems. The link between these systems is established with the help of a network. The SAP R/3 system is implemented in such a way that the Presentation, Application, and Database layers are distributed among individual computers in the SAP R/3 architecture.

The SAP R/3 system consists of the following three types of views:

- Logical view
- Software-oriented view
- User-oriented view

The Logical View

The logical view represents the functionality of the SAP system. In this context, the R/3 Basis component controls the functionality and proper functioning of the SAP system. Therefore, in the logical view of the SAP R/3 system, we describe the services provided by the R/3 Basis component that help to execute SAP applications.

The following is a description of the various services provided by the R/3 Basis component:

- **Kernel and Basis services**—Provide a runtime environment for all R/3 applications. The runtime environment may be specific to the hardware, operating system, or database. The runtime environment is written mainly in either C or C++, though some parts are also written in the ABAP programming language. The tasks of the Kernel and Basis services are as follows:
  - Executing all R/3 applications on software processors (virtual machines).
  - Handling multiple users and administrative tasks in the SAP R/3 system, which is a multiuser environment. When users log on to the SAP system and run applications within it, they are not connected directly to the host operating system, since the R/3 Basis component is the actual user of the host operating system.
  - Accessing the database in the SAP R/3 system. The SAP R/3 Basis system is connected to a database management system (DBMS) and the database itself. R/3 applications do not communicate with the database directly; rather, these applications communicate with the database through the administration services provided by the R/3 Basis system.

- Facilitating communication of SAP R/3 applications with other SAP R/3 systems and with non-SAP systems. You can access SAP R/3 applications from an external system by using the Business Application Programming Interfaces (BAPI) interface.
- Monitoring and controlling the SAP R/3 system when the system is running.

- **ABAP Workbench service**—Provides a programming environment to create ABAP programs by using various tools, such as the ABAP Dictionary, ABAP Editor, and Screen Painter.
- **Presentation Components service**—Helps users to interact with SAP R/3 applications by using the presentation components (interfaces) of these applications.

The Software-Oriented View

The software-oriented view displays various types of software components that collectively constitute the SAP R/3 system. It consists of SAP Graphical User Interface (GUI) components and Application servers, as well as a Message server, which make up the SAP R/3 system. Since the SAP R/3 system is a multitier client-server system, the individual software components are arranged in tiers. These components act as either clients or servers, based on their position and role in a network. Figure 1.2 shows the software–oriented view of the SAP R/3 architecture:

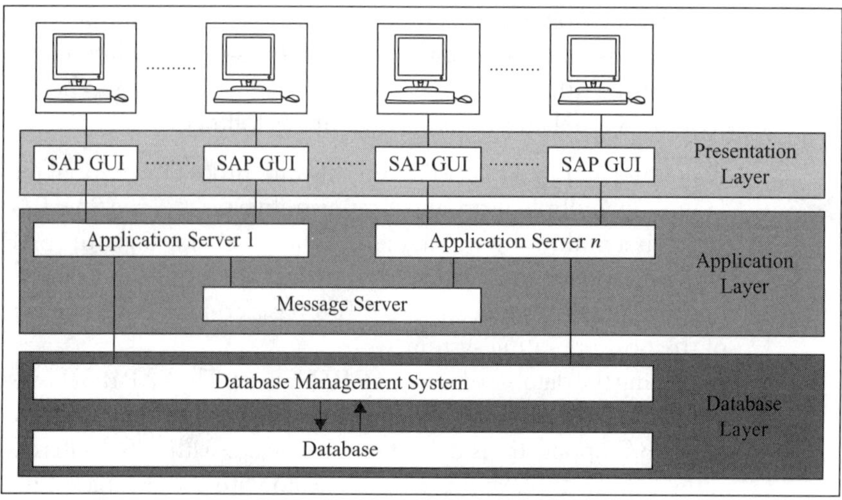

FIGURE 1.2 **Software-oriented view**

As shown in Figure 1.2, the software-oriented view of the SAP R/3 system consists of the following three layers:

- Presentation layer
- Application layer
- Database layer

Presentation Layer

The Presentation layer consists of one or more servers that act as an interface between the SAP R/3 system and its users, who interact with the system with the help of well-defined SAP GUI components. For example, using these components, users can enter a request, to display the contents of a database table. The Presentation layer then passes the request to the Application server, which processes the request and returns a result, which is then displayed to the user in the Presentation layer. While an SAP GUI component is running, it is also connected to a user's SAP session in the R/3 Basis system.

> **Note:** The servers in the Presentation layer have been referred to as Presentation servers in this chapter.

Application Layer

The Application layer executes the application logic in the SAP R/3 architecture. This layer consists of one or more Application servers and Message servers. Application servers are used to send user requests from the Presentation server to the Database server and retrieve information from the Database server as a response to these requests. Application servers are connected to Database servers with the help of the local area network. An Application server provides a set of services, such as processing the flow logic of screens and updating data in the database of the SAP R/3 system. However, a single Application server cannot handle the entire workload of the business logic on its own. Therefore, the workload is distributed among multiple Application servers. Figure 1.3 shows the location of the Application server between the Database and Presentation servers:

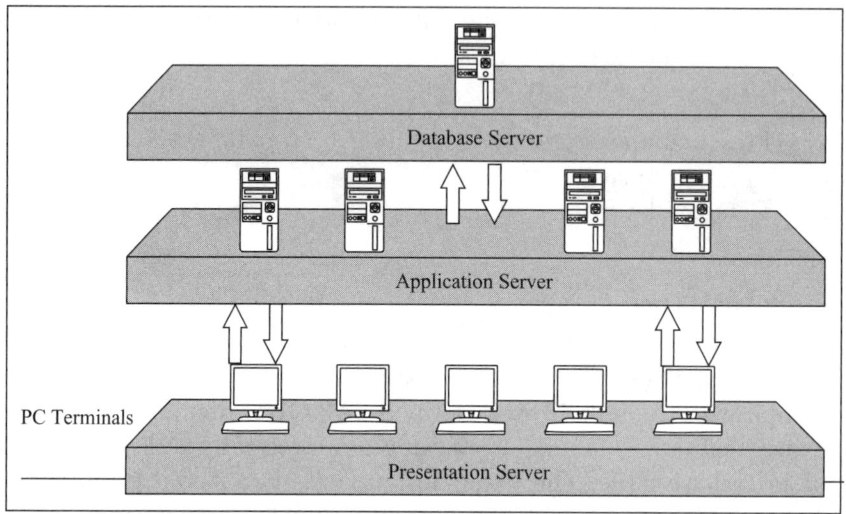

FIGURE 1.3 **Application server**

The Message server component of the Application layer (shown in Figure 1.2) is responsible for communicating between the Application servers. This component also contains information about Application servers and the distribution of load among these servers. It uses this information to select an appropriate server when a user sends a request for processing.

The separation of the three layers of the SAP R/3 system makes the system highly scalable, with the load being distributed among the layers. This distribution of load enables the SAP R/3 system to handle multiple requests simultaneously. The control of a program moves back and forth among the three layers when a user interacts with the program. When the control of the program is in the Presentation layer, the program is ready to accept input from the user, and during this time the Application layer becomes inactive for the specific program. That is, any other application can use the Application layer during this time. As soon as the user enters the input on the screen, the control of the program shifts to the Application layer to process the input and the Presentation layer becomes inactive, which means that the SAP GUI (the user interface of the SAP R/3 system) cannot accept any kind of input. In other words, until the Application layer completes processing the input and calls a new screen, the SAP GUI does not become active. The procedure in which a new screen is presented before the user is known as a dialog step. Dialog steps are processed in the Application layer, as shown in Figure 1.4:

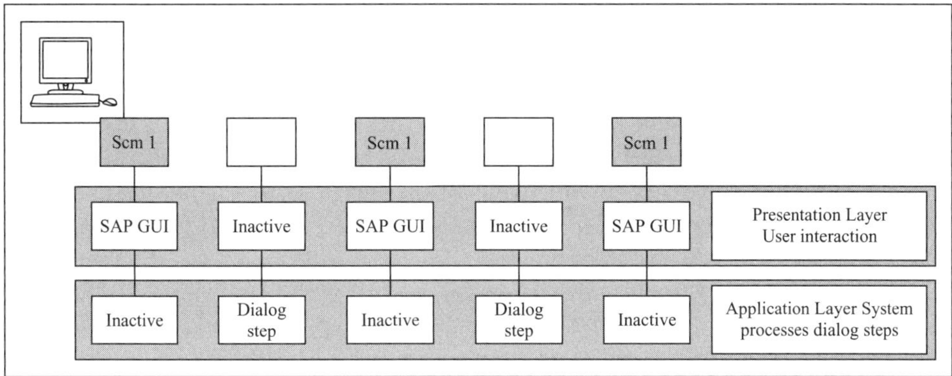

FIGURE 1.4 **A dialog step**

Database Layer

The Database layer of the SAP R/3 architecture comprises the central database system. The central database system has two components, DBMS and the database itself. The SAP R/3 system supports various databases, such as Adabas D, DB2/400 (on AS/400), DB2/Common Server, DB2/MVS, Informix, Microsoft SQL Server, Oracle, and Oracle Parallel Server.

The database in the SAP R/3 system stores the entire information of the system, except the master and transaction data. Apart from this, the components of ABAP application programs, such as screen definitions, menus, and function modules, are stored in a special section of the database, known as Repository, also known as Repository Objects. The database also stores control and customized data, which govern how the SAP R/3 system functions. Distributed databases are not used in the SAP R/3 system because the system does not support them.

Note: Master data is the core data, which is essential to execute the business logic. Data about customers, products, employees, materials, and suppliers are examples of master data. Transaction data refers to information about an event in a business process, such as generating orders, invoices, and payments.

The User-Oriented View

The user-oriented view displays the GUI of the R/3 system in the form of windows on the screen. These windows are created by the Presentation layer.

To view these windows, the user has to start the SAP GUI utility, called the SAP Logon program, or simply SAP Logon. After starting the SAP Logon program, the user selects an SAP R/3 system from the SAP Logon screen. The SAP Logon program then connects to the Message server of the R/3 Basis system in the selected SAP R/3 system and retrieves the address of a suitable Application server; i.e., the Application server with the lightest load. The SAP Logon program then starts the SAP GUI connected to the Application server.

The SAP GUI starts the logon screen. After the user successfully logs on, the initial screen of the R/3 system appears. This initial screen starts the first session of the SAP R/3 system. Figure 1.5 shows the user-oriented view of the SAP R/3 system:

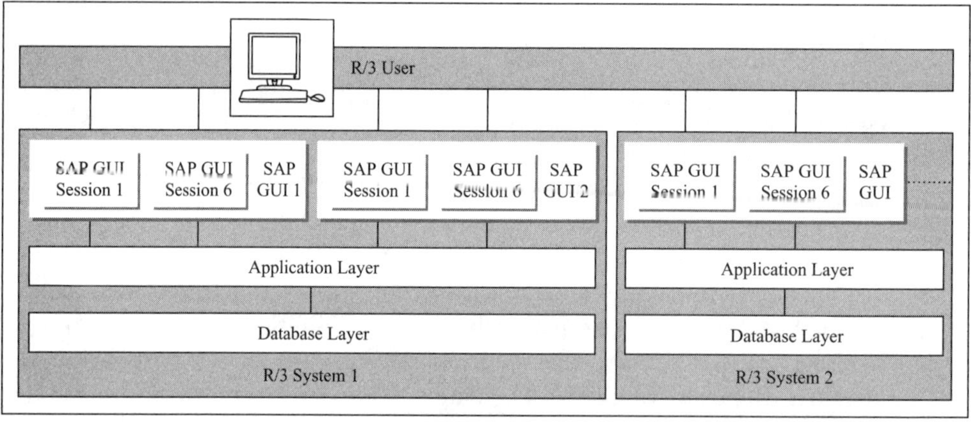

FIGURE 1.5 **User-oriented view**

A user can open a maximum of six sessions within a single SAP GUI. Each session acts as an independent SAP GUI. You can simultaneously run different applications on multiple open R/3 sessions. The processing in an opened R/3 session is independent of the other opened R/3 sessions.

EXPLAINING THE ARCHITECTURE OF THE APPLICATION SERVER

One of the most important components of the SAP R/3 system is the Application server, where ABAP programs run. The Application server handles the business logic of all the applications in the SAP R/3 system. The Application layer consists of Application servers and Message servers. Application servers communicate with the Presentation and Database layers. They also communicate with each other through Message servers. Application servers consist of dispatchers and various work processes, discussed later in this chapter. Figure 1.6 shows the architecture of the Application server:

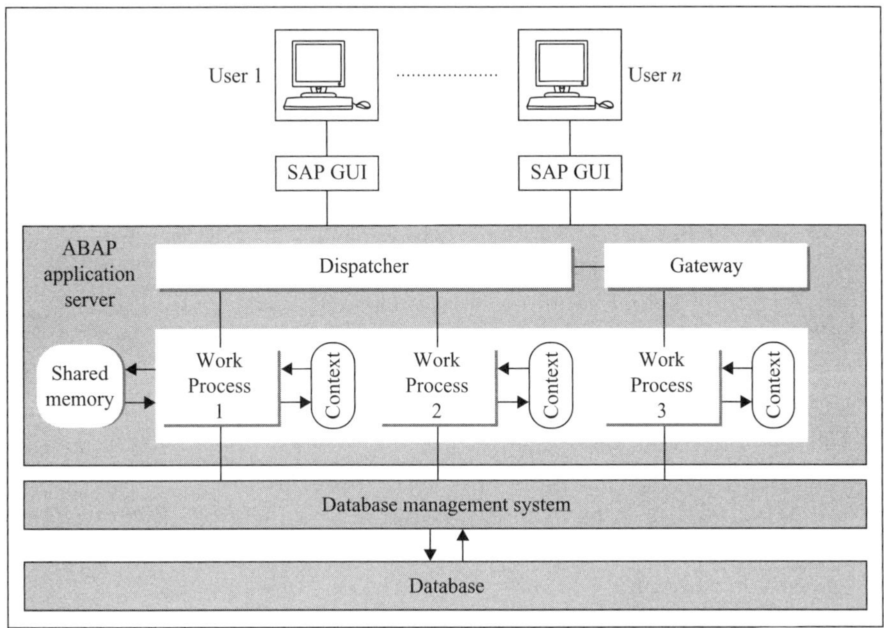

FIGURE 1.6 **Architecture of the application server**

Figure 1.6 shows the following components of the Application server:

- **Work processes**—Represents a process used to execute the user request. An Application server contains multiple work processes that are used to run an application. Each work process uses two memory areas, the user context and the roll area. The user context contains information regarding the user, and the roll area contains information about program execution.

- **Dispatcher**—Acts as a bridge to connect different work processes with the respective users logged on to the SAP R/3 system. The requests received by Application servers are directed first to the dispatcher, which enrolls them to a dispatcher queue. The dispatcher then retrieves the requests from the queue on a first-in, first-out basis and allocates them to a free work process.
- **Gateway**—Acts as an interface for R/3 communication protocols, such as a Remote Function Call (RFC). RFC is the standard SAP interface used to communicate between SAP systems.
- **Shared Memory**—Represents the common memory area in an Application server. All work processes running in an Application server use shared memory. This memory is used to save the contexts (data related to the current state of a running program) or buffer data. Shared memory is also used to store various types of resources that a work process uses, such as programs and table content.

Describing a Work Process

A work process is a component of the Application server that is used to run individual dialog steps used in an SAP R/3 application. Each work process contains two software processors, the Screen processor and the ABAP processor, and one database interface. A work process uses two special memory areas whenever it processes a user request. The first memory area is known as user context, which holds information regarding the user logged on to the SAP R/3 system. This information consists of user authorization as well as the names of currently running programs. The second memory area is known as the roll area, which holds information about the current program pointer (the location in which data of the program is stored), dynamic memory allocations, and the values of the variables needed to execute the program.

Exploring the Structure of a Work Process

In this section, we discuss the structure of a work process that is used in the R/3 system. Figure 1.7 shows the components of a work process:

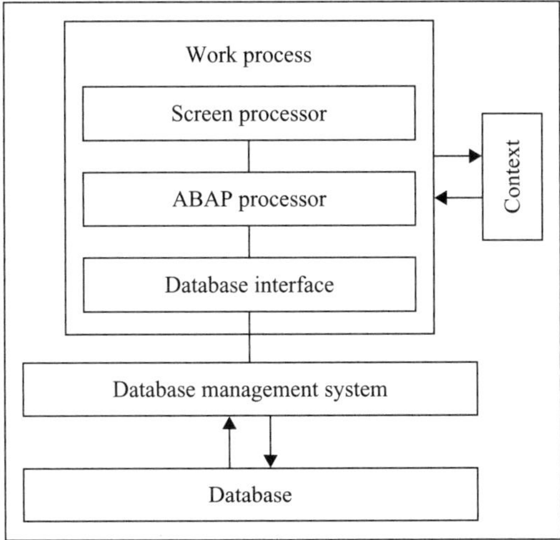

FIGURE 1.7 **The components of a work process**

As shown in Figure 1.7, the three components of a work process are:

- Screen processor
- ABAP processor
- Database interface

The Screen Processor

In R/3 application programming, user interaction and processing logic are different operations. From the programming point of view, user interaction is controlled by screens consisting of flow logic. The screen processor executes screen flow logic and also controls a large part of the user interaction. This flow logic helps a work process to communicate with the SAP GUI through a dispatcher. The screen flow logic also includes some modules, such as `PROCESS AFTER INPUT` (PAI) and `PROCESS BEFORE OUTPUT` (PBO), which explain the flow of data between the screens.

The ABAP Processor

The ABAP processor executes the processing logic of an application program written in the ABAP language. The ABAP processor not only processes the logic but also communicates with the database interface to establish a connection between a work process and a database. The screen processor informs the ABAP processor of the module of the screen flow logic that will be processed. Figure 1.8 shows the communication between the screen processor and ABAP processor, when an application program is running:

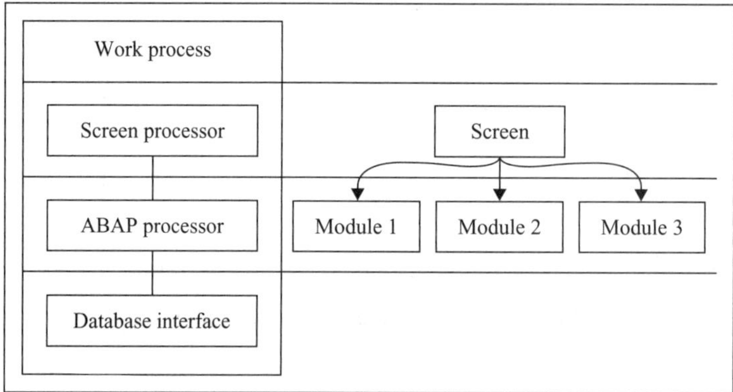

FIGURE 1.8 **The screen processor and the ABAP processor at work**

The Database Interface

The database interface performs the following tasks in a work process:

- Establishing or terminating the connection between the work process and the database
- Accessing database tables
- Accessing the R/3 Repository Objects, such as ABAP programs and screens
- Accessing catalog information (the ABAP Dictionary)
- Controlling transactions (commit and rollback handling)
- Managing table buffering on an Application server

Figure 1.9 shows the different components of the database interface:

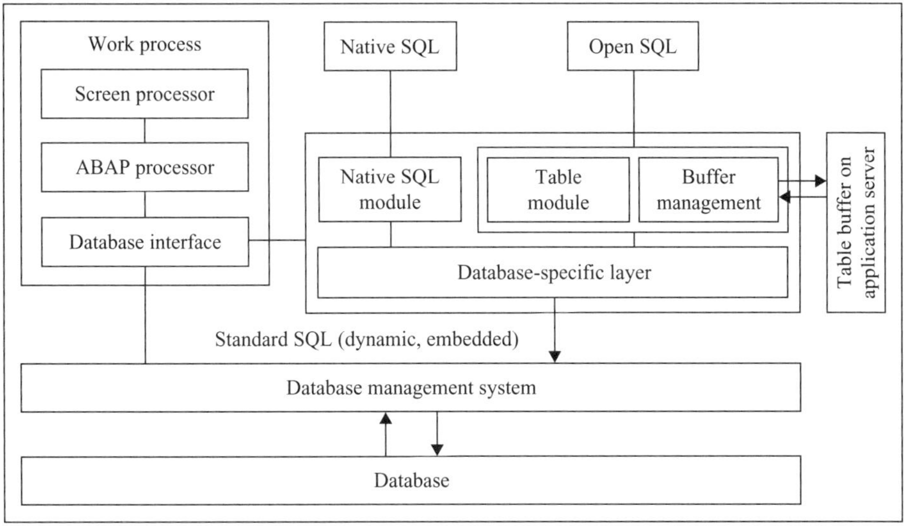

FIGURE 1.9 **Components of the database interface**

As shown in Figure 1.9, databases can be accessed in two ways: using `Open SQL` statements and using `Native SQL` statements.

Open SQL provides statements that, in conjunction with other ABAP constructions, can simplify or speed up database access. Native SQL statements, on the other hand, are a subset of standard SQL that is not integrated with the ABAP language code. To learn more about Open and Native SQL statements, refer to Chapter 8.

The Database-specific layer (Figure 1.9) hides the differences between database systems from the rest of the components of the database interface.

Now, let's describe the various types of work processes.

Types of Work Processes

All work processes can be categorized into five basic types on the basis of the tasks they perform: dialog, update, background, enqueue, and spool. In the Application server, the type of the work process determines the kind of task for which it is responsible. The dispatcher starts a work process, and depending on the type of work process, assigns tasks to it. This means that you can distribute work process types to optimize the use of resources in the Application servers. Figure 1.10 shows different types of work processes within an ABAP Application server:

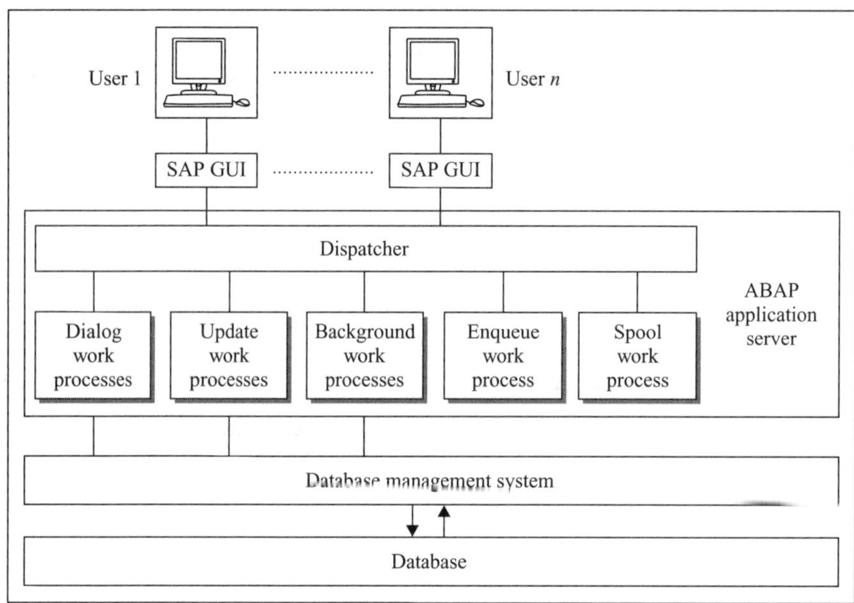

FIGURE 1.10 **Types of work processes**

In Figure 1.10, you see the different types of work processes, including the dialog work process, update work process, background work process, enqueue work process, and spool work process.

Table 1.1 describes the types of work processes:

Work Process	Description	Settings
Dialog work process	Deals with requests to execute dialog steps triggered by an active user. The dialog work process is not used for requests that take long to execute and lead to high central processing unit (CPU) consumption. The default time for a dialog work process is 300 seconds. If the	The maximum response time of a dialog work process can be set by specifying the time in the rdisp/max_wprun_time parameter.

Continued

Work Process	Description	Settings
	dialog work process does not respond in this time period, it is terminated.	
Update work process	Executes database update requests. There must be at least one update work process per SAP system, but there can be more than one update work process per dispatcher. An update work process is divided into two different modules, V1 and V2. The V1 module describes critical or primary changes, for example, creating an order or making changes to the material stock in the SAP R/3 system. The V2 module describes less critical secondary changes. These are pure statistical updates, for example, calculating the sum of the values of certain parameters. V1 modules have higher priority than the V2 modules.	The rdisp/wp_no_vb profile parameter is used to control the number of update work processes of V1 modules, and the `rdisp/wp_no_vb2` parameter is used to control the number of update work processes of V2 modules.
Background work process	Executes the programs that run without the involvement of the user, such as client copy and client transfer. There must be at least two background work processes per SAP system, but more than one background work process can be configured per dispatcher. Usually, background work processes are used to perform jobs that take a long time to execute.	The number of background work processes can be changed by specifying the value in the `rdisp/wp_no_btc` parameter.
Enqueue work process	Handles the lock mechanism. It administers the lock table, which is the main part of a Logical Unit of Work (LUW). The lock table stores the locks for logical databases in the SAP R/3 system. Only one enqueue work process is required for each SAP R/3 system.	The number of enqueue work processes can be specified in the `rdisp/wp_no_enq` parameter.
Spool work process	Passes sequential data flows on to printers. Every SAP system requires at least one spool work process. However, there can be more than one spool work process for a dispatcher.	The parameter to set the number of spool work processes is `rdisp/wp_no_spo`.

TABLE 1.1 Different types of work processes

> **Note:** In Table 1.1, all the parameters related to different types of work processes are specified in the Maintain Profile Parameters screen of the SAP system. You can access the Maintain Profile Parameters screen by entering the RZ11 transaction code in the Command field. To learn more about the Command field, refer to Chapter 3.

Now, let's discuss how dialog steps are executed by a work process.

DISPATCHING DIALOG STEPS

The dispatcher distributes the dialog steps among the various work processes on the Application server. A dialog step is a procedure in which a new screen appears in the SAP R/3 system for user interaction. Dispatching of dialog steps means navigating from one screen to another screen, where one screen accepts a request from the user and the other screen displays the result of the request.

It is very important for a programmer in SAP to understand how dialog steps are processed and dispatched, because the process is completely different from the processing involved in executing an ABAP program.

> **Note:** A dialog step is an SAP R/3 screen, which is represented by a dynamic program called a dynpro. The dynpro program consists of a screen and all the associated flow logic. It contains field definitions, screen layout, validation, and flow logic. A flow logic explains the sequence in which the screens are processed. When users navigate the SAP R/3 system from screen to screen, they are actually executing dialog steps. A set of dialog steps make up a transaction.

Often, the number of users logged on to an ABAP Application server is many times greater than the number of available work processes. In addition, each user can access several applications at a time. In this scenario, the dispatcher performs the important task of distributing all the dialog steps among the work processes on the ABAP Application server. Figure 1.11 shows an example of how dialog steps are dispatched in an ABAP Application server:

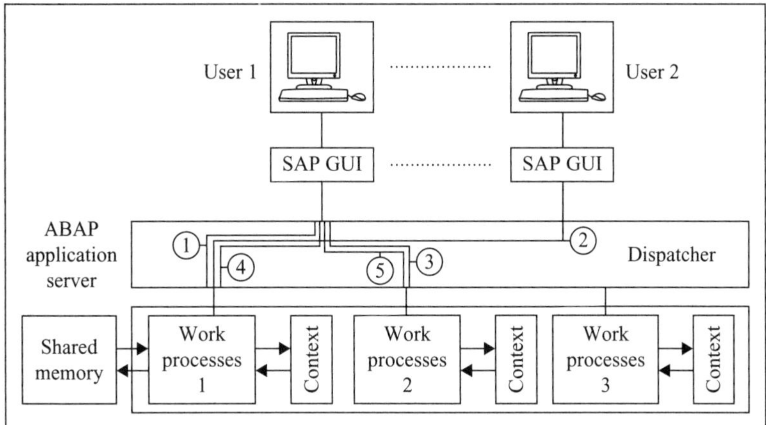

FIGURE 1.11 **Dispatching dialog steps**

Figure 1.11 shows two users, User 1 and User 2. The dispatcher receives a request to execute a dialog step from User 1 and directs it to work process 1, which is free. Work process 1 addresses the context of the application program (in shared memory), executes the dialog step, and becomes free again. Now, the dispatcher receives a request to execute a dialog step from User 2 and directs it to work process 1. Work process 1 executes the dialog step in the same way that it did in the case of User 1. However, while work process 1 is in progress, the dispatcher receives another request from User 1 and directs it to work process 2 because work process 1 is not free. After work processes 1 and 2 have finished processing their respective dialog steps, the dispatcher receives yet another request from User 1 and directs it to work process 1, which is now free. When work process 1 is in progress, the dispatcher receives another request from User 2 and directs it to work process 2, which is free. This process continues until all the requests of the users are processed.

From the preceding example, we can conclude that a program assigns a single dialog step to a single work process for execution. The individual dialog steps of a program can be executed on different work processes, and the program context must be addressed for each new work process. Moreover, a work process can execute dialog steps of different programs from different users.

An ABAP program is always processed by work processes, which require the user context for processing. A user context represents the data specifically assigned to an SAP user. The information stored in the user context can be changed by using the roll area of the memory management system in SAP.

DESCRIBING THE USER CONTEXT AND ROLL AREA IN THE SAP SYSTEM

All user contexts are stored in a common memory area of the SAP system. The memory management system of SAP comprises the following three types of memory which can be assigned to a work process in SAP:

- **SAP Roll Area**—Specifies a memory area with a defined size that belongs to a work process. It is located in the heap of the virtual address space of the work process.
- **SAP Extended Memory**—Represents a reserved space in the virtual address space of an SAP work process for extended memory. The size of the extended memory can be set by using the `em/initial_size_MB profile` parameter of the `Maintain Profile Parameters` screen in the SAP system.
- **Private Memory**—Specifies a memory location that is used by a work process if a dialog work process has used up the roll area memory and extended memory assigned to it.

Roll area memory is used as the initial memory assigned to a user context. Roll area memory is allocated to a work process in two stages. In the first stage, memory is allocated by specifying the `ztta/roll_first` parameter in the `Maintain Profile Parameters` screen. However, if this memory is already in use by the work process, additional memory is allocated in the second stage. The size of the additional memory area is equal to the difference between the `ztta/roll_area` and `ztta/roll_first` parameters. Here, the `ztta/roll_area` parameter specifies the total size of the roll area, in bytes. Figure 1.12 shows the structure of the roll area memory:

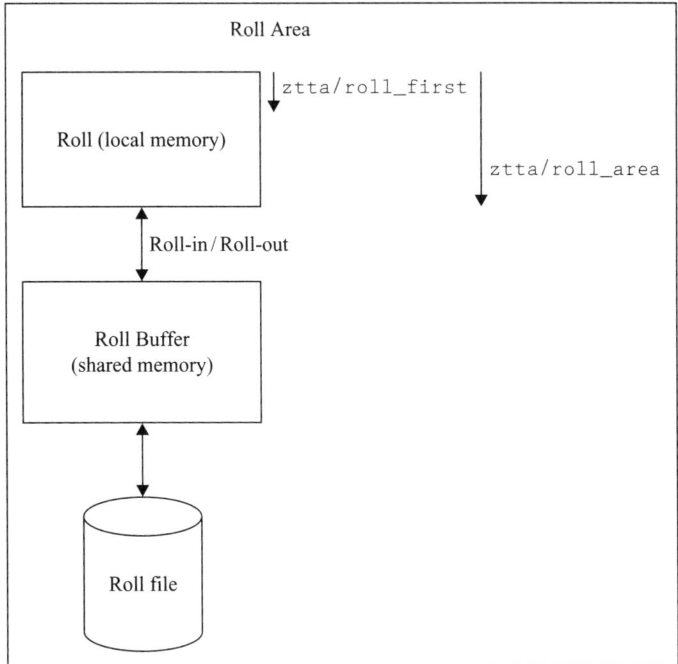

FIGURE 1.12 **Structure of the roll area memory in SAP**

As shown in Figure 1.12, whenever a dialog step is executed, a roll action occurs between the roll buffer in the shared memory and the roll local memory, which is allocated by the `ztta/roll_first` parameter. The area in the shared memory, which belongs to a user context, is then accessed. Note that when the context of a work process changes, its data is copied from the local roll area to a common resource called the roll file through the roll buffer (a shared memory).

As shown in Figure 1.12, the following roll processes are performed by the dispatcher:

- `Roll-in`—Copies user context from the roll buffer (in shared memory) to the roll local memory
- `Roll-out`—Copies user context from the roll local memory to the roll buffer

THE CLIENT-DEPENDENCY FEATURE

The SAP R/3 system provides an important feature called client-dependency, which means that a change made by a client in the SAP system is reflected on the other client. Let's take an example of R/3 database tables to illustrate this. Some tables in the SAP R/3 system are client-dependent, while others are client-independent. A client-dependent table has its first field or column of the `CLNT` type. The length of this field is always of three characters, and by convention, this field is always named `MANDT` and contains the client number as its content. A client-independent table, on the other hand, does not have the `CLNT` type as its first field. Now, if any data is updated in the rows of a client-independent table, the change is not reflected on the other clients of the SAP R/3 system.

The client-dependency feature can also be explained in terms of `SAPscript` forms and Smart Forms. An SAP script form is a template that simplifies the designing of business forms. On the other hand, `SAP Smart Forms` is a tool used to print or send business forms through e-mail, the Internet, and faxing. In the SAP R/3 system, `SAPscript` forms are client-dependent, while the SAP Smart Forms are not.

Now, let's assume that a user generates two forms by using `SAPscript` forms with two different client logins, client 800 and client 000. In this case, any changes made in client 800 will not be reflected in the form designed in client 000. On the other hand, in the case of Smart Forms, any changes made to one client will be reflected in the other client as well.

Note: SAPscript and Smart Forms are described in detail in Chapter 12.

SUMMARY

This chapter has explored the concept of SAP and its importance as leading business software. The chapter has also described the concept of ERP and its implementation in SAP. In addition, it has described the architecture of SAP R/3 system and the role and function of its three layers: Presentation, Application, and Database, and the various components of the Application server, such as work processes, the dispatcher, and the gateway. In addition to these topics, the text has explored memory management in SAP. Finally, the chapter concludes with a discussion on the client dependency feature of SAP.

Chapter 2

The Logon Process of the SAP System

If you need information on:	*See page:*
Starting the SAP System	28
Maintaining the SAP Logon Screen	31
Creating and Using SAP Shortcuts	37
Configuring the SAP Logon	47
Changing the Password	50
Logging Off of the SAP System	52

Similar to any application software or system, the mySAP ERP system provides an authorization mechanism to ensure that only authenticated and authorized users access the system. The authentication mechanism of the mySAP ERP system requires you to log on to the system using your login name and password before you can start working on the mySAP ERP system. This process of verifying the users based on the login names and passwords is called user authentication. With a mySAP ERP system, the login name and the password are provided by the system administrator. However, you can change the password afterwards for security purposes.

You can log on to the mySAP ERP system by using the SAP Logon Screen. This screen also allows you to perform various activities related to the SAP logon process. For example, you can add and configure SAP servers that you need to connect to during the logon process. You can also create and manage shortcuts to various functions of the mySAP ERP system. While creating these shortcuts, you can specify the logon settings for these functions. In addition, you can customize or change your password to log on to the mySAP ERP system.

In this chapter, you learn about the logon process in the mySAP ERP system. The chapter starts by explaining the steps to start the mySAP ERP system through the SAP Logon screen. Next, you learn how to maintain the SAP Logon screen by adding, modifying, and deleting one or more mySAP ERP systems. You also explore how to create and manage shortcuts, which facilitate you to access a transaction screen, report, or a system command directly in the SAP system. Then, you learn how to configure the settings in the SAP Logon screen, such as the language in which you want the screen of SAP Logon to appear and whether you want to display the SAP Logon screen with wizard. In addition, you explore how to change the password to log on to the mySAP ERP system. Finally, the chapter discusses various ways to log off of the mySAP ERP system.

STARTING THE SAP SYSTEM

The SAP Logon screen can be accessed by either selecting the SAP Logon option from the start menu or double-clicking the SAP Logon shortcut ( ) icon from the desktop. Perform the following steps to start an SAP system from the Start menu from your Windows OS:

1. `Start>All Programs>SAP Front End>SAP Logon` ( ), as shown in Figure 2.1:

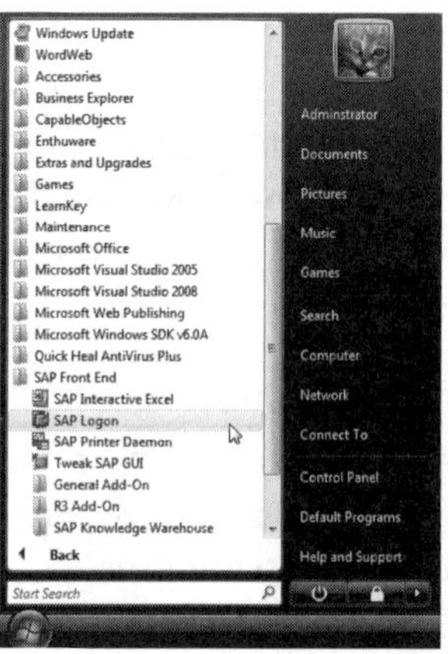

FIGURE 2.1 **Selecting the SAP logon option**

The SAP Logon screen appears, as shown in Figure 2.2:

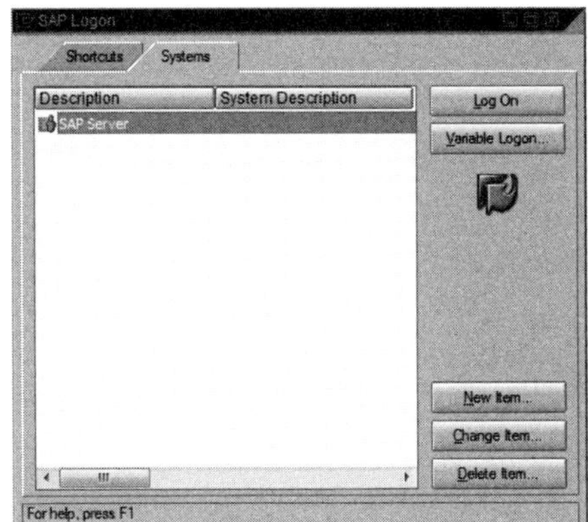

FIGURE 2.2 **The SAP logon screen**

2. Click the Log On button on the SAP Logon screen (see Figure 2.2).

The SAP screen (first screen of the SAP system) to enter the logon details appears, as shown in Figure 2.3:

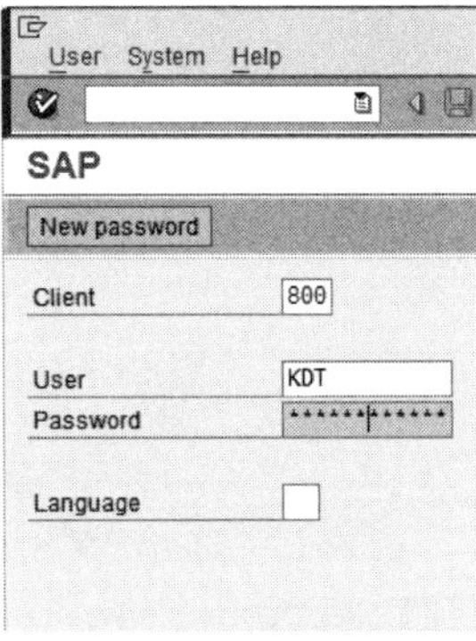

FIGURE 2.3 **The SAP screen for entering the logon details**

The SAP screen comprises the following fields:

- **Client**—Enter the client number.
- **User**—Enter the user ID.
- **Password**—Enter the password provided by your system administrator.
- **Language (optional)**—Set the language in which you want to display screens, menus, and fields.

> **Note:** Notice that as you enter the password, asterisks appear in the field rather than the characters that you type. As a security measure, the system does not display the value entered in the Password field.

3. Enter the values in all the fields of the SAP screen; for instance, we have entered the client ID as 800, user name as KDT, and the password as sapmac, as shown in Figure 2.3. Now, press the ENTER key. The SAP Easy Access screen appears, as shown in Figure 2.4:

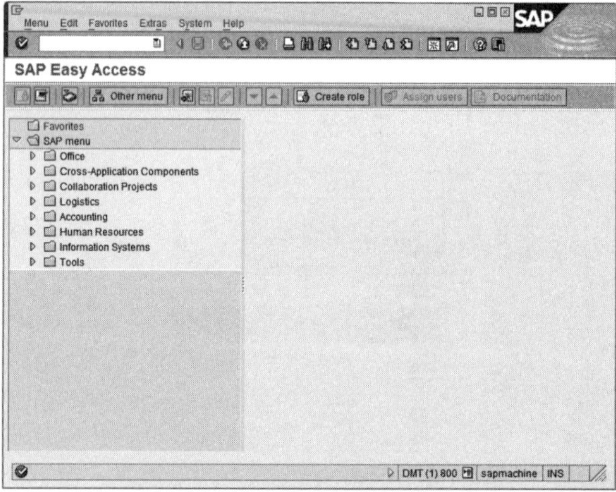

FIGURE 2.4 **The SAP easy access screen**

The SAP Easy Access screen serves as a gateway to work in SAP and contains all the development tools provided by SAP. However, before starting to work in this screen, you need to understand that the SAP Logon screen (see Figure 2.2) of an SAP system can be modified on the basis of user requirements. It has to be noted that the changes done on the SAP Logon are not reflected at the front end; they affect only the internal processing of the SAP system.

MAINTAINING THE SAP LOGON SCREEN

The SAP Logon screen is used to log on to an SAP system. It is a window-based program, which acts as a mediator between the SAP system and the SAP GUI interface. By default, the SAP Logon screen contains the following two tabs (see Figure 2.2):

- **Systems**—Allows the user to add a SAP server or a group of servers as well as edit or delete an existing server in the list of servers.
- **Shortcuts**—Allows you to create, delete, or edit the shortcut of a particular screen in the list of shortcuts.

The SAP Logon screen, within the Systems tab, is maintained by performing the following operations:

- **Adding a New Entry**—Adds a new server to the list of servers.
- **Modifying the Entry**—Modifies the properties of a server.
- **Deleting the Entry**—Deletes a server.

Now, let's discuss each operation in detail, one by one.

Adding a New Entry

In the SAP Logon screen, the Systems tab displays a list of servers. You can add a single instance of a server as well as a group of servers in this list. Perform the following steps to add a single server:

1. Click the New Item (New Item...) button on the SAP Logon screen (see Figure 2.2). The Create New System Entry Wizard appears, as shown in Figure 2.5:

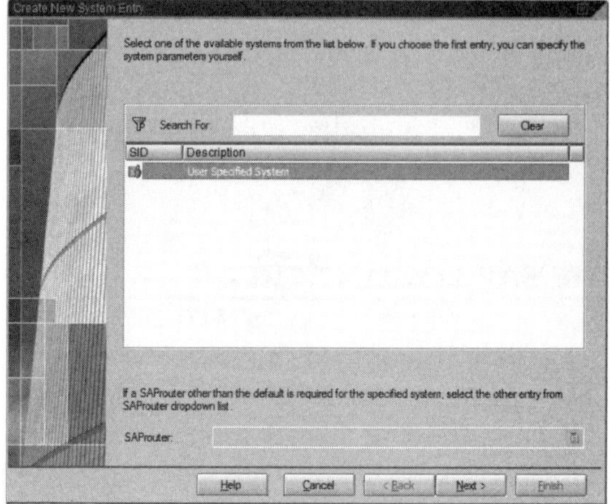

FIGURE 2.5 **The create new system entry wizard**

The `Create New System Entry wizard` contains a list of all the SAP servers. In our case, only a single instance of the server is displayed. Note that in the case of multiple servers, the first entry in the list appears as selected by default.

2. Select the server that you want to add and click the `Next` button (see Figure 2.5). A screen that accepts the system connection parameters appears, as shown in Figure 2.6:

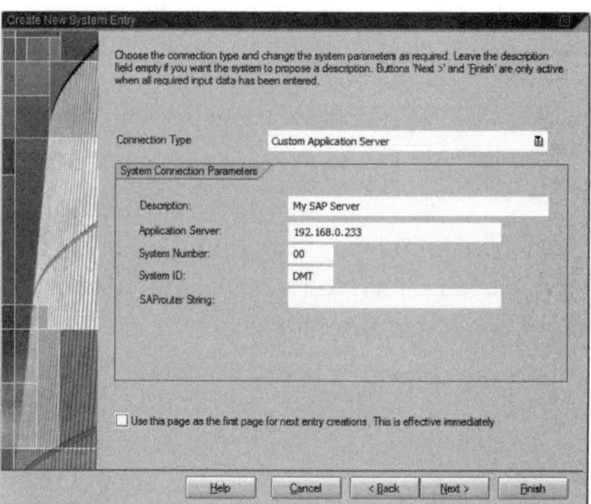

FIGURE 2.6 **Showing system connection parameters**

3. Select Custom Application Server or Group/Server Selection from the drop-down list of the Connection Type field. In this case, we have selected the Custom Application Server option.

In addition, the System Connection Parameters group box contains the following fields:

- **Description**—Specifies a short description of the system entry. It is an optional field.
- **Application Server**—Specifies the name of the host computer on which the required server is hosted.
- **System Number**—Specifies the system number.
- **System ID**—Specifies the system ID of the SAP system that you want to connect to.
- **SAProuter String**—Specifies an SAProuter string if an SAProuter is required. It is an optional field.

4. Enter the values in all the fields of the System Connection Parameters group box. For instance, we have given the Description as My SAP Server, Application Server as 192.168.0.233, System Number as 00, and System ID as DMT, as shown in Figure 2.6.
5. Click the Next button (see Figure 2.6). The Choose Network Settings screen in the Create New System Entry Wizard appears, as shown in Figure 2.7:

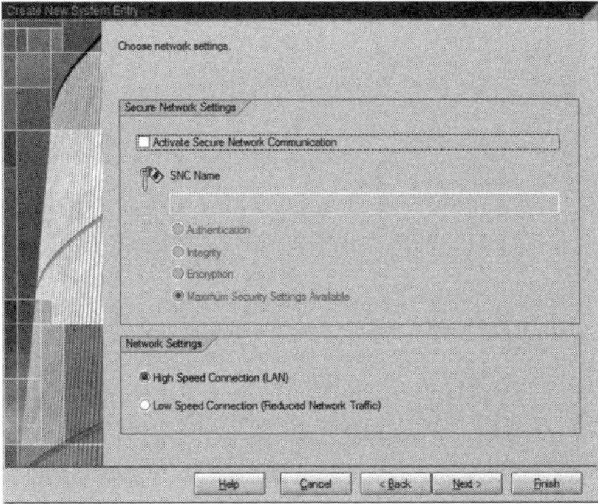

FIGURE 2.7 **The choose network settings screen**

6. Click the `Next` button (see Figure 2.7) in the `Choose Network Settings` screen. The screen to specify the Language Settings and Upload/Download Encoding appears, as shown in Figure 2.8:

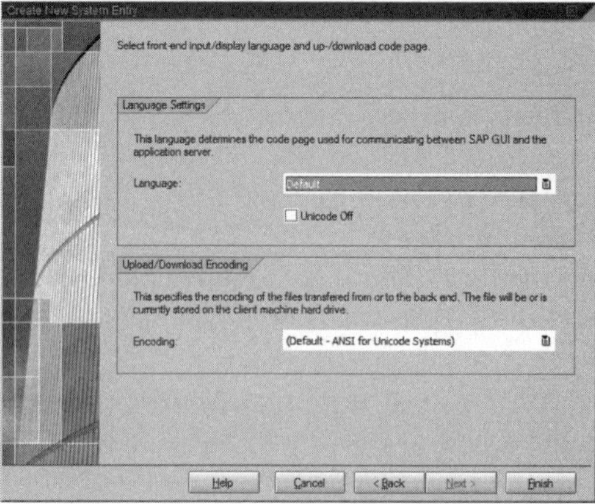

FIGURE 2.8 **The language settings and upload/download encoding screen**

7. Click the `Finish` button to complete the process (see Figure 2.8).

A new item, My SAP Server, is added in the Systems selection list, as shown in Figure 2.9:

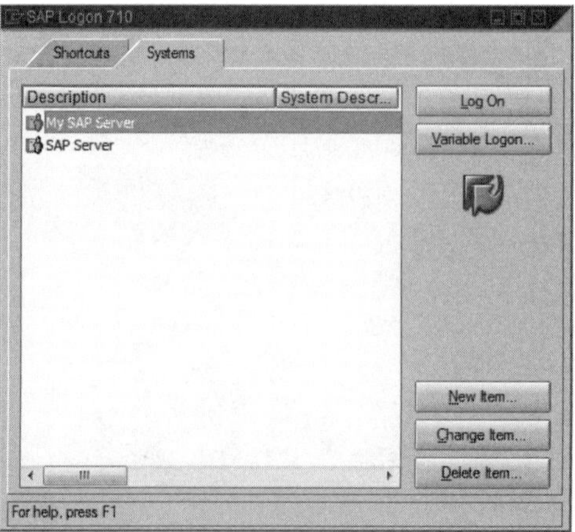

FIGURE 2.9 **Showing the new server entry**

Modifying the Entry

In the `SAP Logon` screen, you can modify the configuration settings of an existing SAP server entry, such the description and the address of the server. Perform the following steps to modify the configuration settings of an SAP server:

1. Select an SAP server whose properties you want to change. Here, we are using the My SAP Server, which is already selected in the servers list of the `SAP Logon` screen (see Figure 2.9).
2. Click the `Change Item` button (see Figure 2.9). The `System Entry Properties` dialog box appears (Figure 2.10).
3. Enter "New link to SAP Server" in place of My SAP Server in the `Description` field, as shown in Figure 2.10:

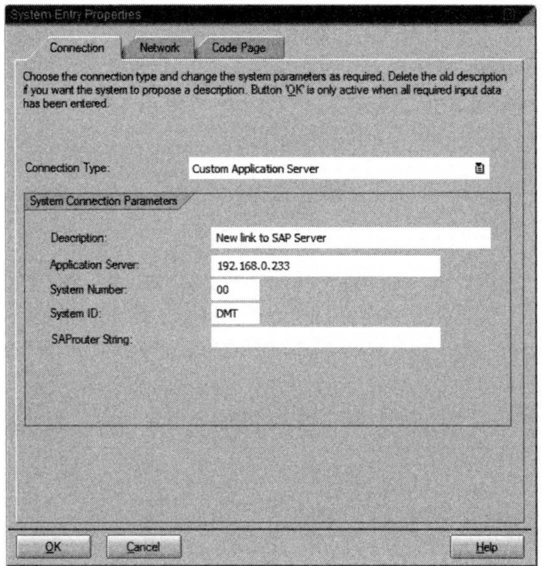

FIGURE 2.10 **The system entry properties dialog box**

4. Click the `OK` button (see Figure 2.10) or press the ENTER key to complete the process.

Notice that the name of the item My SAP Server is changed to New link to SAP Server, as shown in Figure 2.11:

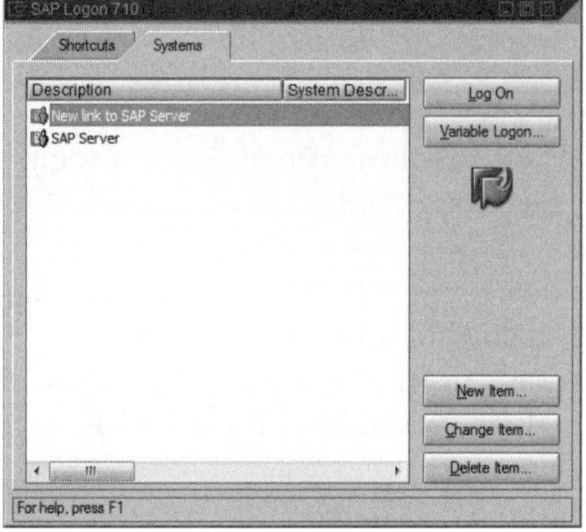

FIGURE 2.11 **Showing the modified description**

Deleting the Entry

Perform the following steps to delete an item from the servers list:

1. Select the SAP server that you want to delete. Here, we proceed with the already selected item "New link to SAP Server" (see Figure 2.11).
2. Click the `Delete Item` button (see Figure 2.11). The `Saplogon API` dialog box appears, asking for confirmation, as shown in Figure 2.12:

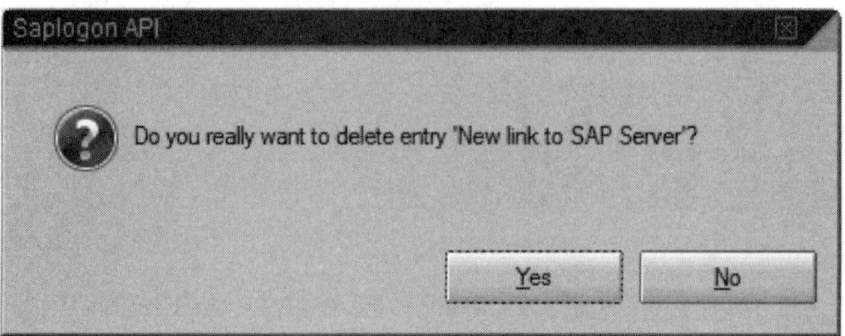

FIGURE 2.12 **The Saplogon API dialog box**

3. Click the `Yes` button (see Figure 2.12) to delete the selected item. Notice that the New link to SAP Server item is now deleted from the SAP selection list.

Now, let's learn how to create and use various shortcuts to open different screens of the SAP system.

CREATING AND USING SAP SHORTCUTS

Shortcuts are components of the SAP GUI and are used to access the most frequently used functions or transactions directly. In actuality, you can use SAP shortcuts to start an SAP transaction, view a report, or perform system command execution directly from your Microsoft Windows desktop or the `SAP Logon` screen. Afer the shortcuts are created, they appear as regular icons on the desktop of your computer.

Creating SAP Shortcuts

An SAP shortcut can be created only on computers running on the Windows operating system. The SAP shortcut file type is registered automatically in the Windows registry after the successful installation of an SAP GUI. The basic requirements to create an SAP shortcut are as follows:

- An SAP user ID from your system administrator
- A password
- The transaction code for the screen for which you want to create an SAP shortcut

The following are the three ways to create an SAP shortcut:

- Creating an SAP shortcut from the desktop
- Creating an SAP shortcut from a specific screen
- Creating an SAP shortcut in the SAP Logon screen

Creating an SAP Shortcut from the Desktop

Perform the following steps to create an SAP shortcut from the desktop:

1. Right-click anywhere on the desktop. A context menu appears. Select `New > SAP GUI Shortcut`.

An SAP shortcut icon, `New SAP GUI Shortcut`, appears on the desktop, as shown in Figure 2.13:

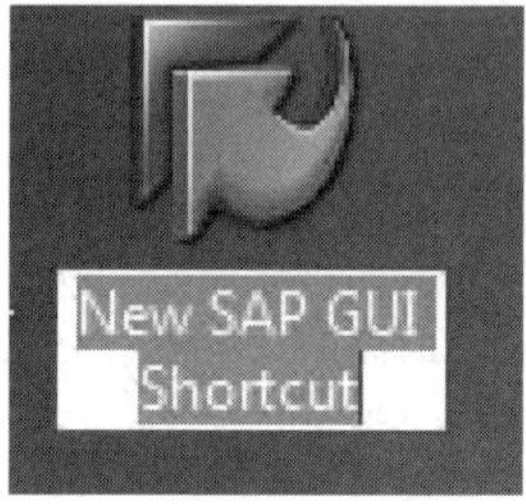

FIGURE 2.13 **New SAP GUI shortcut icon**

2. Enter a name for the shortcut (for instance, MySAPLogon), and press the `ENTER` key. A new shortcut to the SAP Logon file is created on the desktop with the name `MySAPLogon`.

Now, let's edit the properties of the shortcut to the SAP Logon file.

1. Right-click the shortcut file (`MySAPLogon`) and select the `Edit` option.

The `SAP Shortcut Properties` dialog box appears, as shown in Figure 2.14:

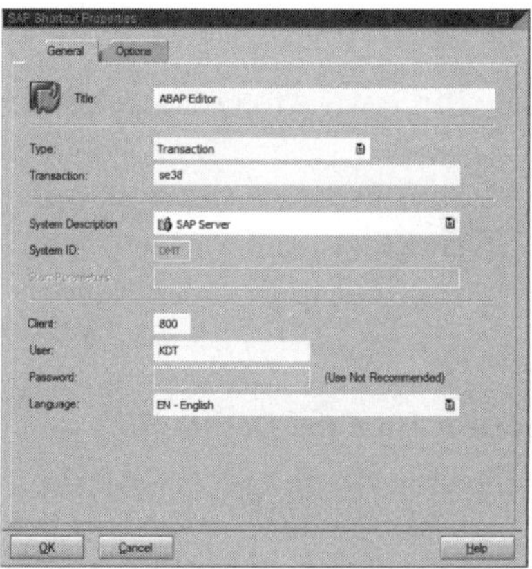

FIGURE 2.14 **The SAP shortcut properties dialog box**

2. Enter a title in the `Title` field. In Figure 2.14, we have entered ABAP Editor.
3. In the `Type` field, select the type of shortcut from the following options:
   - `Transaction`
   - `Report`
   - `System` command

In this case, we have selected `Transaction` (see Figure 2.14).

4. Enter a transaction command (for instance, se38) in the `Transaction` field, as shown in Figure 2.14.
5. In the `SystemDescription` field, select `SAP Server` from the drop-down list, as shown in Figure 2.14.

> **Note:** In this case, the default System ID is DMT.

6. Now, enter the client number in the `Client` field, say, 800 (see Figure 2.14).
7. Enter the name of the user (for instance, KDT) in the `User` field and the desired language (for instance, EN-English) in the `Language` field, as shown in Figure 2.14.

> **Note:** The system automatically uses your Windows user ID if you leave the User field blank. The Password field is deactivated for security reasons. This field can be activated by administrators only.

8. Finally, click the `OK` button and the desired shortcut is placed on your desktop.

Creating an SAP Shortcut from a Specific Screen

Perform the following steps to create an SAP shortcut from a specific screen in the SAP system:

1. Open the screen in which you want to create an SAP shortcut. In this case, we have opened the initial screen of Screen Painter (by using the `SE51` transaction code), as shown in Figure 2.15:

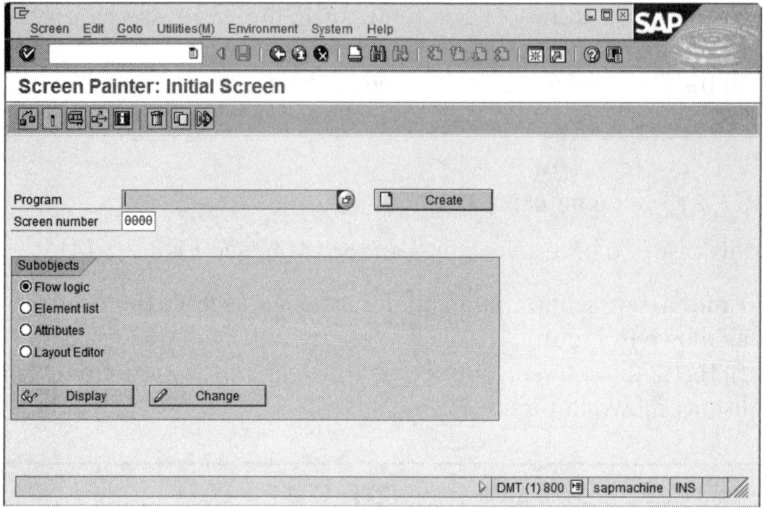

FIGURE 2.15 **Initial screen of screen painter**

Note: Use the SE51 transaction command to open Screen Painter.

2. Click the `Customize Local Layout` (icon) icon on the standard toolbar and then select the `Create Shortcut` option, as shown in Figure 2.16:

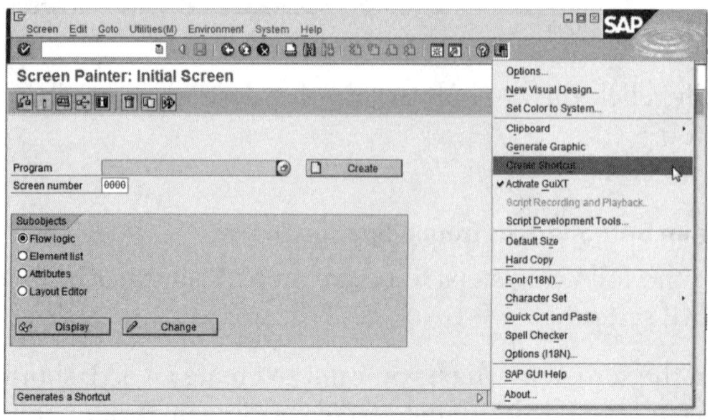

FIGURE 2.16 **Selecting the create shortcut option**

The Create New SAP Shortcut Wizard appears, as shown in Figure 2.17. Ensure that the information filled in the Title, Type, Transaction, Client, User, and Language fields is correct. You can also modify the values specified in these fields. Here, we have modified the System Description field.

3. Select the System Description as SAP Server, as shown in Figure 2.17:

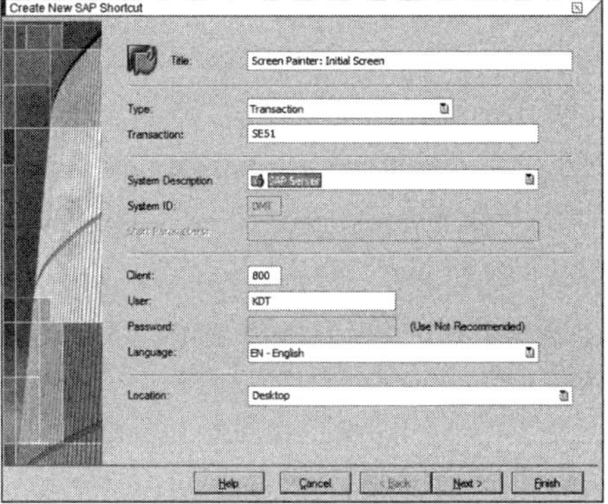

FIGURE 2.17 **Modifying the system description field**

4. Click the Next button. The next screen appears, as shown in Figure 2.18:

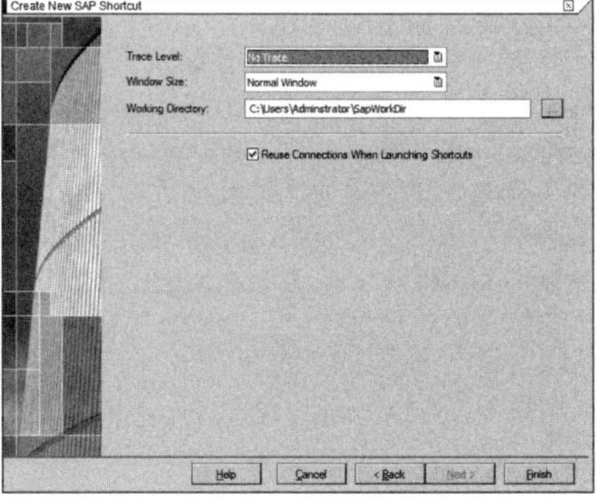

FIGURE 2.18 **Showing the properties of the new shortcut**

5. Click the `Finish` button. The `SAP GUI Shortcut` dialog box appears, as shown in Figure 2.19:

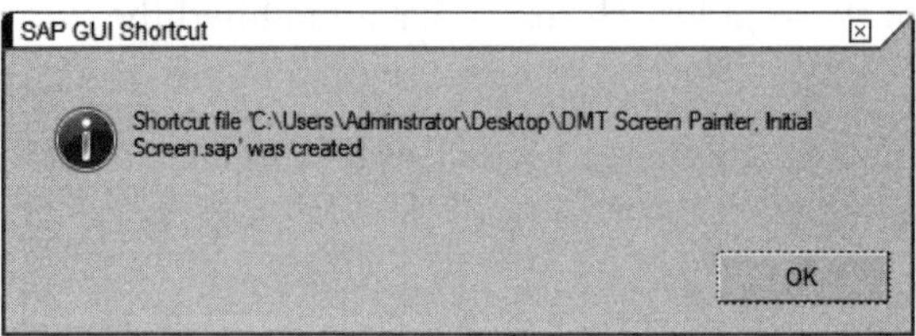

FIGURE 2.19 **The SAP GUI shortcut information box**

6. Click the `OK` button, as shown in Figure 2.19, to complete the process.

   The DMT Screen Painter shortcut appears on your desktop.

> **Note:** The system automatically saves the shortcut file with the .sap extension in the desktop directory.

Creating an SAP Shortcut in an SAP Logon Screen

We can also create an SAP shortcut in an SAP Logon screen. The `Shortcuts` tab of the `SAP Logon` screen allows us to create, edit, or delete a shortcut with the help of the following buttons:

- **New Item**—Helps create shortcuts that allow you to start SAP transactions, run reports, or execute system commands directly after logging on to the defined system.
- **Change Item**—Edits an existing shortcut in the shortcuts list.
- **Delete Item**—Deletes an existing shortcut from the shortcuts list.
- **Log on**—Allows to log on to an SAP system through the created SAP shortcut.

The user can log on to an SAP system in the following ways:

- By selecting an entry in the shortcuts list and pressing the `Log On` button
- By selecting an entry in the shortcuts list and pressing the ENTER key
- By double-clicking an entry in the shortcuts list

Perform the following steps to create a new shortcut in the SAP Logon screen:

1. Click the `Shortcuts` tab on the `SAP Logon` screen, as shown in Figure 2.20:

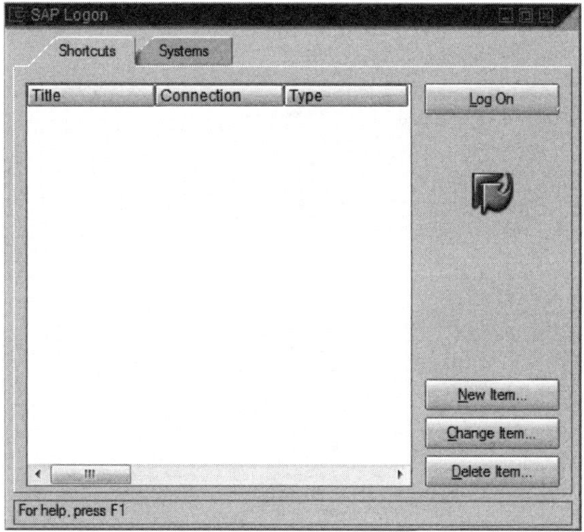

FIGURE 2.20 **The shortcuts tab**

> **Note:** You can add already created SAP shortcuts (present on your desktop) to the shortcuts list just by dragging and dropping their icons in the SAP Logon screen.

2. Click the `New Item` button, as shown in Figure 2.20. The `Create New SAP Shortcut` dialog box appears (see Figure 2.21).

3. Enter "Menu Painter Shortcut" in the `Title` field, "`System` Command" in the `Type` field, "`/nSE41`" system command in the `Command` field, "SAP Server" in the `System Description` field, "800" in the `Client` field, and "KDT" in the `User` field. Click the `Next` button of the `Create New SAP Shortcut` dialog box, as shown in Figure 2.21:

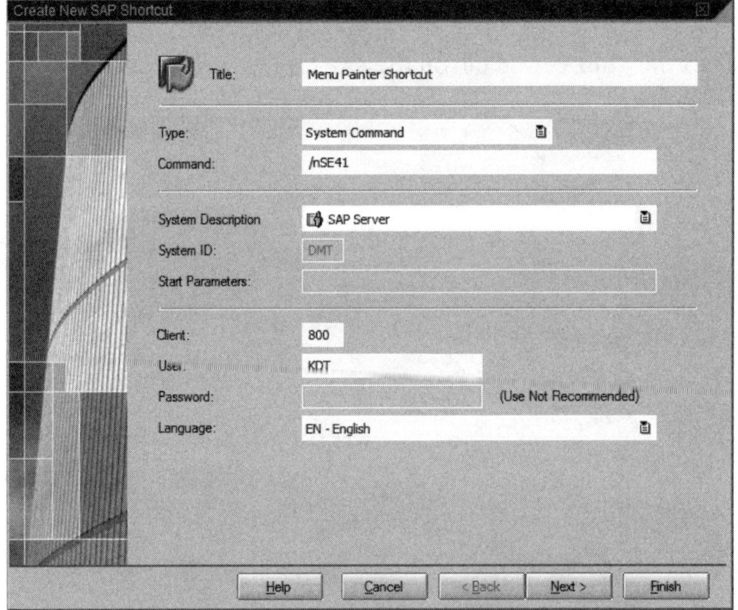

FIGURE 2.21 **The create new SAP shortcut wizard**

Note that the `Create New SAP Shortcut Wizard`, shown in Figure 2.21, is similar to the `Create New SAP Shortcut Wizard`, shown in Figure 2.17. Therefore, on clicking the `Next` button, you get a screen similar to that shown in Figure 2.18.

4. Click the `Finish` button. A new shortcut is displayed in the `Shortcuts` tab, as shown in Figure 2.22:

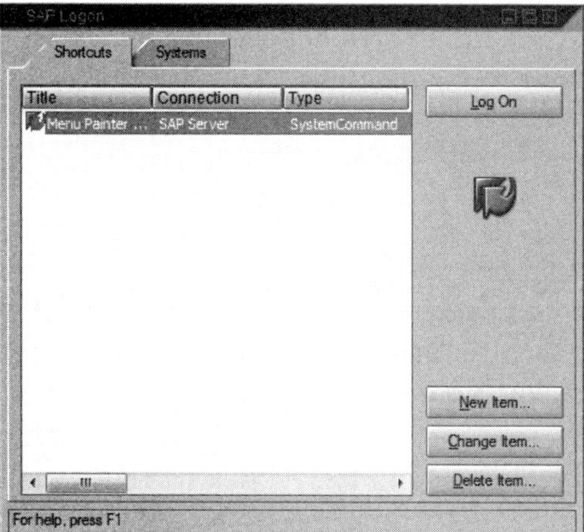

FIGURE 2.22 **Showing the new shortcut**

The user can modify the properties of this shortcut by using the `Change Item` button or delete it by using the `Delete Item` button.

Using SAP Shortcuts

Once an SAP shortcut is created, it can be used easily by just double-clicking it. Note that to be able to work on an SAP system, the user must have an SAP user name and password provided by the system administrator. An SAP shortcut can be used in the following contexts:

- With no SAP session running
- With an SAP session running

A session is an SAP system instance opened by a user. Multiple sessions can be started when the user has to work on more than one task at a time. All these sessions (screens) of SAP can be kept active or open simultaneously; consequently, the user saves time navigating from one screen to another. Each session is independent of the others, that is, an operation performed on one session does not affect the other sessions.

> **Note:** The system administrator specifies the maximum number of sessions (up to 6) that can be opened at a single time.

Now, let's see how to use an SAP shortcut, both with and without a session running.

With No SAP Session Running

If no SAP session is running on the computer, the SAP system displays a dialog box requesting the user name and password for security purposes if you access a shortcut. A dialog box with the name corresponding to the created shortcut appears.

Perform the following steps to use a shortcut when an SAP session is not running:

1. Double-click the SAP shortcut assigned to any specific screen. In this case, we have used the shortcut (Menu Painter Shortcut) that we created in the "Creating an SAP Shortcut in SAP Logon" section.

The `Menu Painter Shortcut` dialog box appears, as shown in Figure 2.23.

2. Enter the user name and password given by the system administrator in the `User Name` field and `Password` field, respectively. In this case, the user name is KDT and the password is sapmac. However, for security reasons, the password is encrypted, as shown in Figure 2.23:

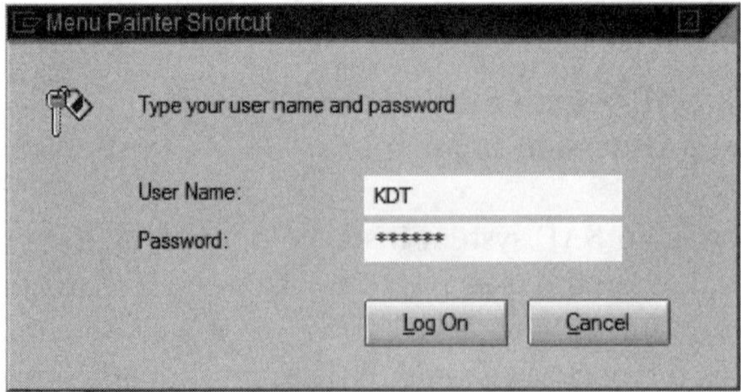

FIGURE 2.23 **The screen painter dialog box**

3. Click the `Log On` button or press the `ENTER` key to start the SAP session.

To change or view your shortcut definition, right-click in the opened dialog box (Figure 2.23), outside the title bar, input fields, or buttons. A context menu appears. Click the `Open` option to view and the `Edit` option to make changes in the .sap shortcut file.

> **Note:** If you have not entered the password, only the `Edit` option is activated. However, after you enter even the first character of the password, both the `Open` and `Edit` options are activated.

With an SAP Session Running

To use a shortcut when an SAP session is already running, double-click the SAP shortcut for the task that you want to perform. If an application is already running, a new SAP session is started; otherwise, the current SAP session starts the task. The following are the ways to use a shortcut while an SAP session is running:

- **Drag and drop the shortcut from your desktop to the currently running SAP session**—The SAP system displays the defined transaction or report.
- **Drag and drop the shortcut, while pressing the CTRL key, from your desktop to the currently running SAP session**—The SAP system displays the defined transaction or report in a new session.
- **Drag and drop the shortcut, while pressing the SHIFT key, from your desktop to the currently running SAP session**—The SAP system displays the properties of the shortcut.

> **Note:** If an SAP shortcut is created using the System command `/NTCD (/N` plus the transaction code), the task is executed only in the current SAP session.

CONFIGURING THE SAP LOGON

In this section, we discuss how to configure various settings of the `SAP Logon` screen, such as the language of the `SAP Logon` screen and the path of configuration files, within the `SAP Logon Configuration` dialog box. For that, click the (icon) icon present at the top-left corner of the `SAP Logon` screen and select `Options`, as shown in Figure 2.24:

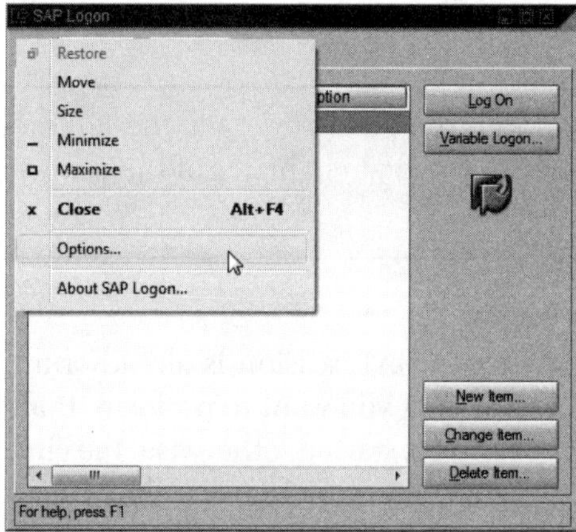

FIGURE 2.24 **Selecting options**

The `SAPLogonConfiguration` dialog box appears, as shown in Figure 2.25:

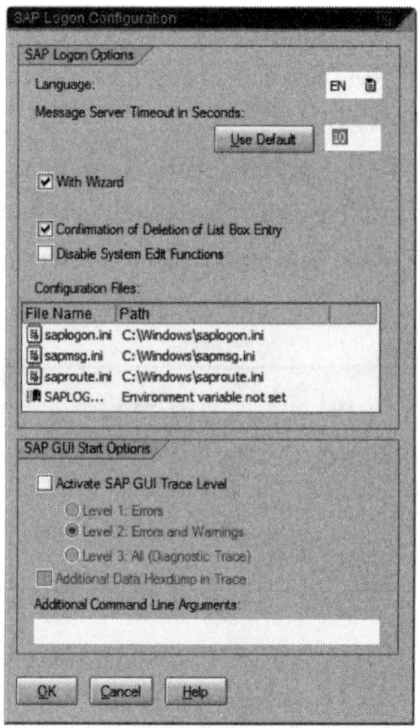

FIGURE 2.25 **The SAP logon configuration dialog box**

In the `SAP Logon Configuration` dialog box, you can specify or change various setting options.

Table 2.1 describes the options of the `SAP Logon Configuration` dialog box:

Option	Description
Language	Helps select the language in which the user needs to display the SAP logon. To use this option, the SAP Logon language file must be installed by the system administrator.
Message Server Timeout in Seconds	Specifies the time the `SAP Logon` screen waits for a response from the R/3 Message Server. The default value is 10 seconds.
With Wizard	Specifies whether or not you want to work in SAP Logon with the wizard. The `SAP logon` screen needs to be restarted for the settings to be effective.
Confirmation of Deletion of List Box Entry	Specifies whether you want to display a warning before deleting a system or logon group from the SAP Logon.
Disable System Edit Functions	Specifies whether you want to prevent logon entries from being changed.
Configuration Files	Shows a list of configuration files (.ini files) that can be opened by double-clicking.
Activate SAP GUI Trace Level	Specifies whether you want to define and activate a network trace (SAP GUI trace). Selecting this check box enables the user to select the level of tracing. If the user selects level 2 or 3, an additional log file is generated that records all incoming data in an encrypted binary code.
Additional Data Hexdump in Trace	Specifies whether you want to list additional memory areas in the SAP GUI trace. This check box is activated only when level 2 or 3 is selected.
Additional Command Line Arguments	Specifies additional SAP GUI command line arguments, for instance, /WAN is used when a low-speed connection is required for all your SAP systems.

TABLE 2.1 Settings of the SAP logon configuration dialog box

After setting the properties in the SAP Logon Configuration dialog box, click the OK button to return to SAP Logon screen.

CHANGING THE PASSWORD

Initially, the system administrator provides you with a password to log on to the SAP system. However, it is recommended to change your password when you log on for the first time for security purposes. You can even set the time interval after which you would like to change your SAP password. The SAP system itself prompts you to change your password after the specified period of time. Perform the following steps to change the password:

1. Open the SAP screen by clicking the Log On button of the SAP Logon screen.
2. Enter the data in the Client, User, and Password fields on the SAP Logon screen (shown previously in Figure 2.3).
3. After entering the values in the required fields, click the New password button on the application toolbar, as shown in Figure 2.3, or press the F5 key. The SAP dialog box appears, as shown in Figure 2.26:

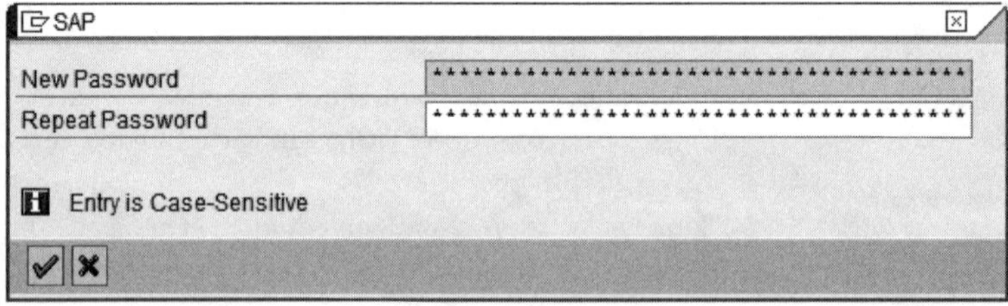

FIGURE 2.26 **Displaying the SAP dialog box**

4. Enter the new password in the New Password field and retype it in the Repeat Password field (see Figure 2.26).
5. Click the Confirm (✔) icon to save your new password, as shown in Figure 2.26.

The following are some rules and restrictions that one must follow while creating a password:

- A password should not exceed eight characters and should not be less than three characters.
- A password should not begin with any of the following characters:
  - A question mark (?)
  - An exclamation mark (!)
  - A blank space
  - Three identical characters, such as 333
  - Any sequence of three characters contained in your user ID (for instance 'man' if your word user ID is Friedman)
- A password can have a combination of the following letters and numbers:
  - The letters a through z
  - The numbers 0 through 9
  - Punctuation marks
- While creating a password, do not use the following:
  - The words pass or init as your password
  - Any of the last five passwords you have used

> **Note:** If SAP, passwords are not case-sensitive. For example, the password blueSky is the same as Bluesky or BLUESKY.

Table 2.2 lists some examples of valid and invalid passwords:

Valid Password	Invalid Password
Kashvi	!exercf (begins with an invalid character)
Tanu=8	Sssb (contains three identical characters)
6yuto	Ap (contains less than three characters)

TABLE 2.2 Valid and invalid passwords

LOGGING OFF OF THE SAP SYSTEM

After completing your work on the SAP system, you need to save the necessary data and log off of the system. Perform the following steps to log off of the SAP system:

1. Click the `Log off` icon on the standard toolbar, as shown in Figure 2.27:

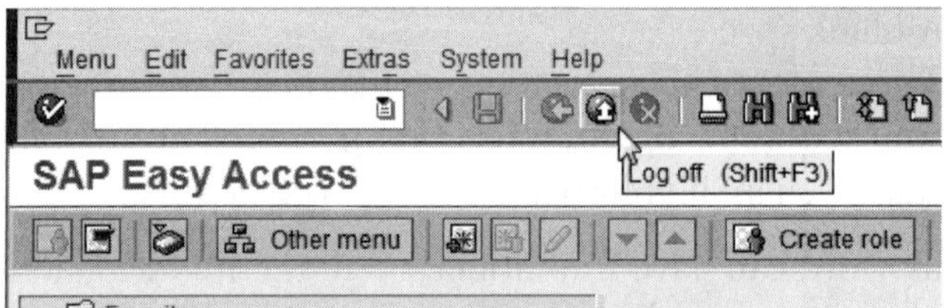

FIGURE 2.27 **Clicking the log off icon**

If there is any unsaved data, a dialog box appears, asking for confirmation, as shown in Figure 2.28:

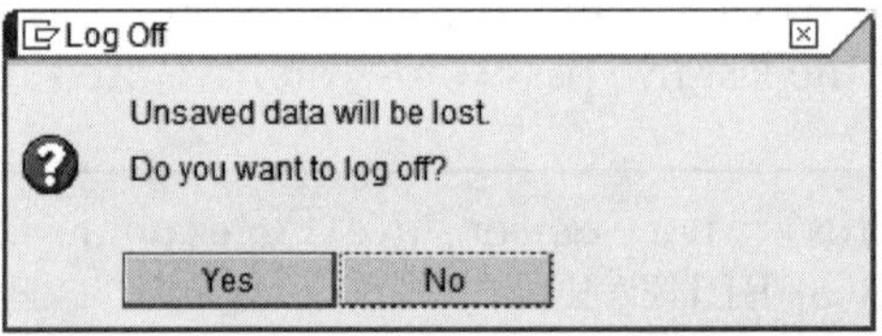

FIGURE 2.28 **The log off dialog box**

2. Click the `Yes` button if you want to log off without saving the unsaved data; otherwise, click the `No` button.

There are two other alternate methods to log off of the SAP system. One of them is by selecting the `Log off` option from the `System` menu, as shown in Figure 2.29:

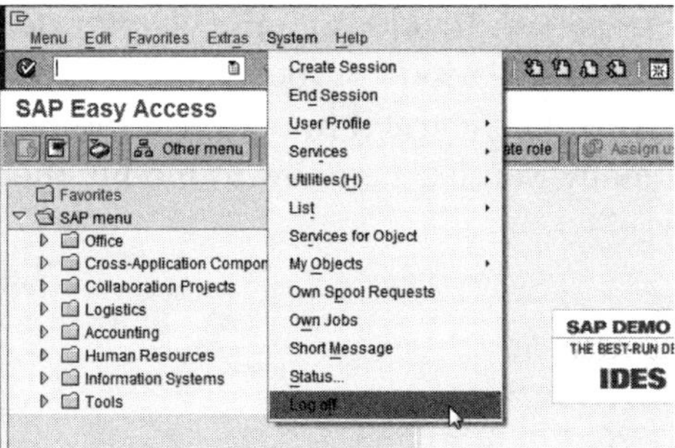

FIGURE 2.29 **Log off option on the system menu**

The `Log off` dialog box appears (see Figure 2.28).

In the second method, you can exit directly from the SAP system, without any confirmation, by typing the `/nex` transaction command in the command field and pressing the `ENTER` key, as shown in Figure 2.30:

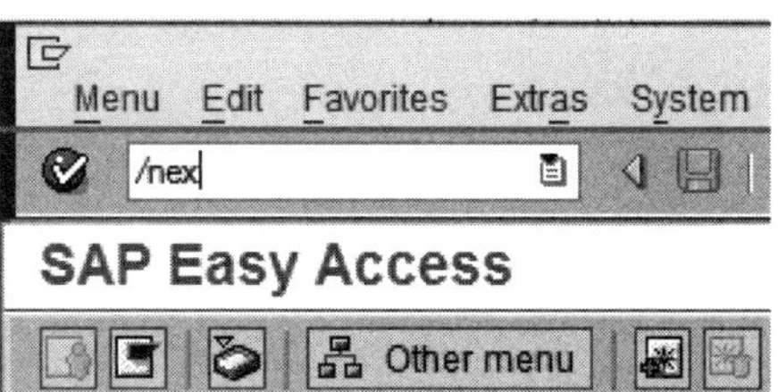

FIGURE 2.30 **Logging off using the transaction code**

The `SAP` screen immediately disappears.

SUMMARY

In this chapter, you have learned how to log on to the SAP R/3 system. You have also explored the steps to open the initial screen of an SAP system and maintain the SAP logon information by adding, changing, and deleting the instances of the SAP server. In addition, the chapter described how to create and use the shortcuts for various purposes, such as to log on or to open a particular screen. Next, you learned how to edit the configuration settings of the SAP system. Finally, you learned how to modify the password and log off of the SAP system.

Chapter 3 SAP Easy Access

If you need information on:	*See page:*
Explaining the SAP Easy Access Screen	56
Exploring the GUI of the SAP System	60
Customizing the SAP GUI	70
Managing Favorites	72
Handling SAP Sessions	84

SAP GUI is the software that displays a graphical interface to enable users to interact with an SAP system. This software acts as a client in the three-tier architecture of an SAP system, which contains a database server, an application server, and a client. SAP GUI can run on a variety of operating systems, such as Microsoft Windows, Apple Macintosh, and UNIX.

You can access the complete SAP GUI only after successfully logging on to an SAP system. When you have successfully logged on to an SAP system, you get the first screen of the system, named SAP Easy Access. The opening of this screen represents a new session in the SAP system. Consequently, each screen of the SAP GUI that you open creates a new session. You may open a maximum of six sessions simultaneously. The SAP Easy Access screen displays a user menu that displays the options to perform your tasks, such as creating and modifying transactions, reports, and web addresses. The menus of the navigational user menu can be expanded or collapsed. Moreover, you can create and maintain favorites for those transactions and reports that you commonly use.

In this chapter, you learn about the first screen of the SAP system, i.e., SAP Easy Access, after you have logged on to the SAP system. The chapter starts by explaining the SAP user menu that appears on the SAP Easy Access screen. Next, you explore the SAP GUI by discussing its three main components: the screen header, screen body, and status bar. You also learn how to customize the layout and settings of the screens displayed in the SAP system, such as modifying the color, text size, and window size of the screen. You learn how to navigate within the workplace menu and manage favorites by adding, modifying, and deleting items such as transactions, web address, and folders. Finally, you learn how to handle one or more sessions and navigate from one session to another.

EXPLAINING THE SAP EASY ACCESS SCREEN

The first screen that appears after logging on to the SAP system is SAP Easy Access. This screen is the SAP user menu screen, also known as the SAP window. As we learned earlier, when we log on to an SAP system, a new session begins. The status bar displayed at the bottom of the screen shows the number of sessions opened by a user. The SAP user menu enables you to perform multiple tasks by allowing you to work on multiple sessions simultaneously. For example, suppose your manager asks you to generate a report when you are processing a new customer order. In such a situation, there is no need to stop processing the order. You can leave the previous session (the screen to process the new order) open on your computer and begin a new session to create the report. Moreover, you can customize the SAP user menu screen to fit the requirements. You learn more about customizing the SAP user menu screen later in this chapter.

The mySAP ERP system is designed as a client system, i.e., you can operate the system from any computer that has the SAP GUI installed and is connected to the SAP database. For example, if you are visiting your distribution plant and later realize that you forgot to perform a task at your plant, then you can perform the same job right at the distribution plant, because SAP recognizes you on the basis of your user name and password.

The SAP user menu consists of the following two folders:

- **Favorites**—Stores the list of favorites, i.e., frequently visited transaction codes or web addresses.

- **SAP menu**—Enables a user to work on the SAP system according to the roles and authorization provided by the administrator.

Figure 3.1 shows the `SAP Easy Access` screen containing the `Favorites` and `SAP Menu` folders:

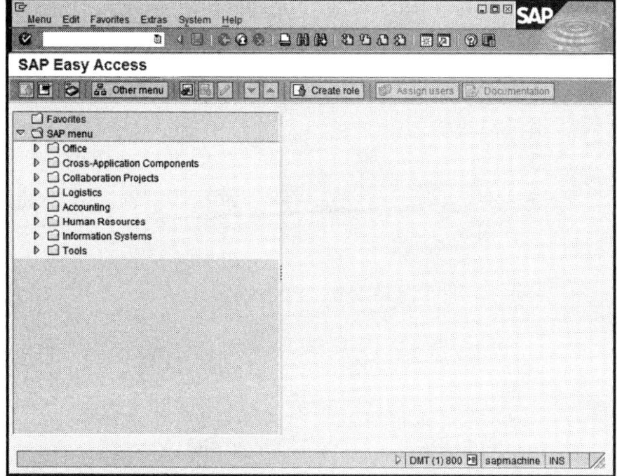

FIGURE 3.1 **The SAP easy access screen**

As shown in Figure 3.1, the `SAP Menu` folder contains the following eight subfolders:

- Office
- Cross-Application Components
- Collaboration Projects
- Logistics
- Accounting
- Human Resources
- Information Systems
- Tools

Note: The number and names of subfolders displayed in the SAP Menu folder may be different from those displayed in your SAP Easy Access screen, as they appear according to the settings configured by the system administrator.

You can modify various settings for the SAP Easy Access screen in the Settings dialog box. The Settings dialog box is opened by selecting the Settings option in the Extras menu bar (the Extras menu bar will be discussed later in the chapter). Figure 3.2 shows the Settings dialog box:

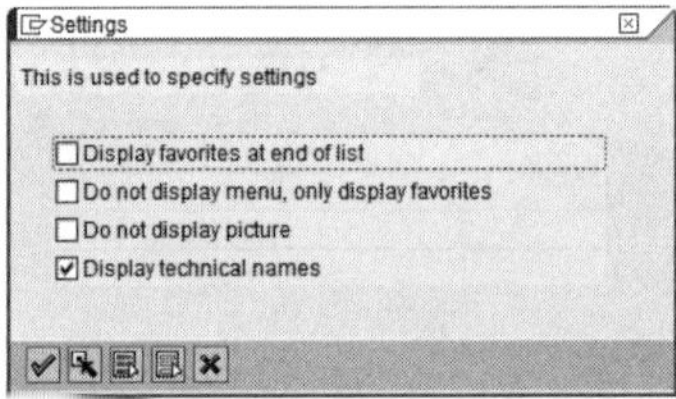

FIGURE 3.2 **The settings dialog box**

As shown in Figure 3.2, the Settings dialog box has several check boxes with the following options:

- Display favorites at end of list
- Do not display menu, only display favorites
- Do not display picture
- Show technical name

You can select one or more options from the available options by selecting the corresponding check box. Note that when the Do not display picture check box is unchecked, the SAP Easy Access screen also shows a graphic that appears on the right side of the screen, as shown in Figure 3.3:

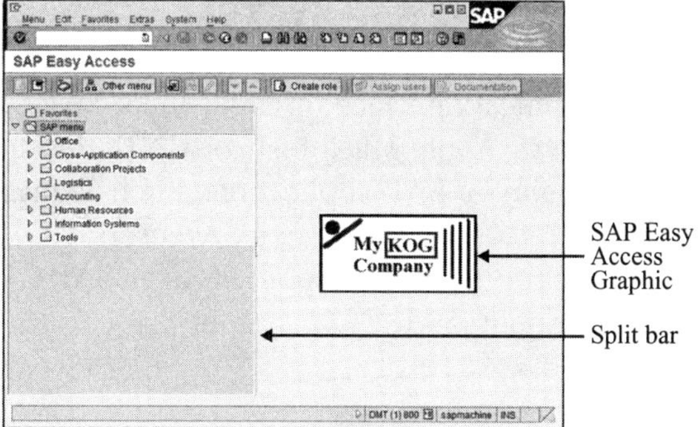

FIGURE 3.3 **The graphic and split bar in the SAP easy access screen**

As shown in Figure 3.3, the `SAP Easy Access` screen consists of a graphic and a split bar. You can hide or deactivate this graphical image by selecting the `Do not display picture` check box in the `Settings` dialog box (Figure 3.2). Another way to hide or deactivate the graphic is by dragging the split bar from the center to the right side of the `SAP Easy Access` screen, as shown in Figure 3.4:

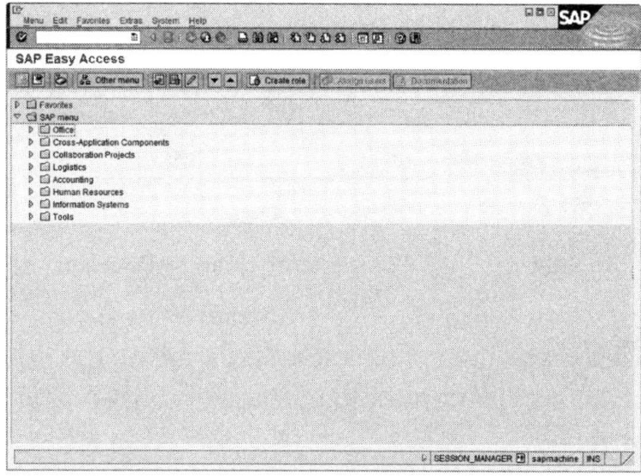

FIGURE 3.4 **Dragging the split bar to hide the graphic**

EXPLORING THE GUI OF THE SAP SYSTEM

SAP GUI is the graphical interface or client in an SAP system. It is software that runs on a Windows, Apple Macintosh, or UNIX desktop, and allows you to access SAP functionality in SAP applications, such as mySAP ERP. SAP GUI also helps exchange information between SAP users.

Figure 3.5 shows the general components of an SAP GUI screen of the SAP ERP Central Component (SAP ECC) system:

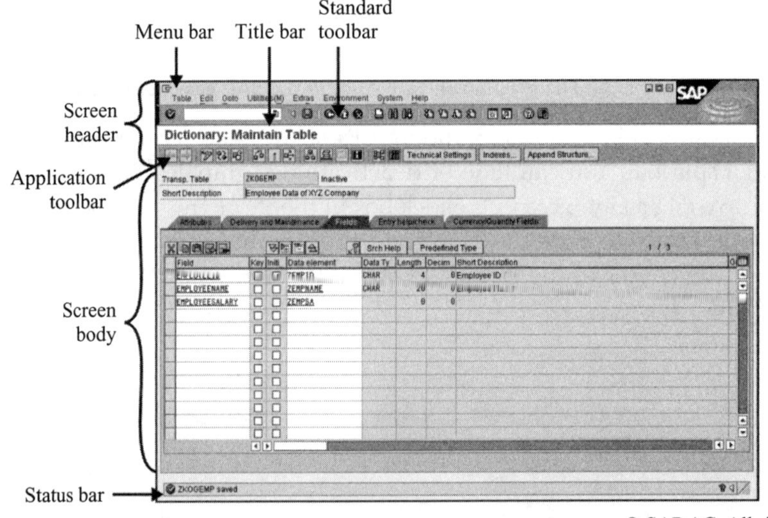

FIGURE 3.5 **Components of an SAP screen**

Figure 3.5 shows a menu bar, a standard toolbar, the title bar showing the title of the screen, an application toolbar, the working area, and the status bar.

The Screen Header

The screen header is located at the top of the main screen (see Figure 3.5). It includes the screen banner, along with other toolbars. Figure 3.6 shows the screen header:

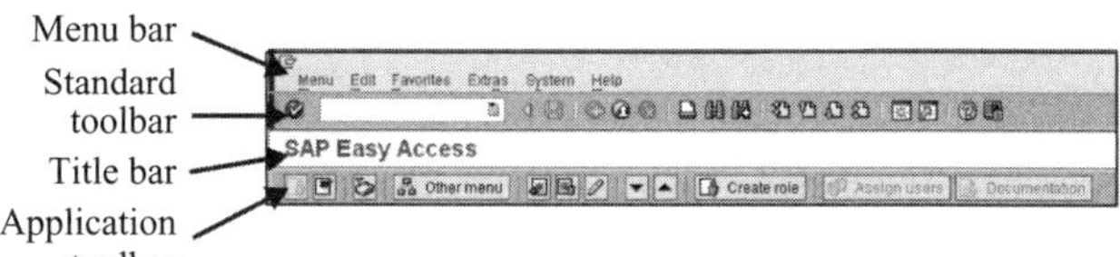

FIGURE 3.6 **Various toolbars in the screen header of the SAP screen**

As shown in Figure 3.6, the screen header of any screen in SAP GUI consists of the following elements:

- Menu bar
- Standard toolbar
- Title bar
- Application toolbar

Let's discuss each of these elements in detail.

The Menu Bar

The menu bar contains menus to perform functional and administrative tasks on the SAP system. For example, generating reports is a functional task, and assigning passwords is an administrative task. The menus in the menu bar appear according to the opened screen or transaction. In the `SAP Easy Access` screen, the menu bar contains six menus: `Menu`, `Edit`, `Favorites`, `Extras`, `System`, and `Help`. In addition, it contains a small icon (▭) at the extreme upper-left corner, as shown in Figure 3.7:

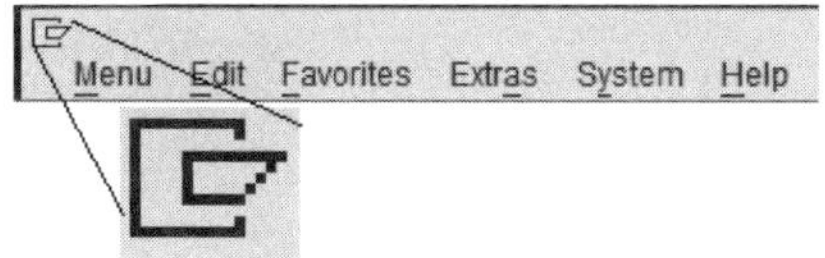

FIGURE 3.7 **Icon displayed at the upper-left corner**

Using the ( ) icon, you can control SAP GUI by performing various tasks, such as creating a new session and closing a transaction. When the ( ) icon is clicked, a drop-down menu appears, as shown in Figure 3.8:

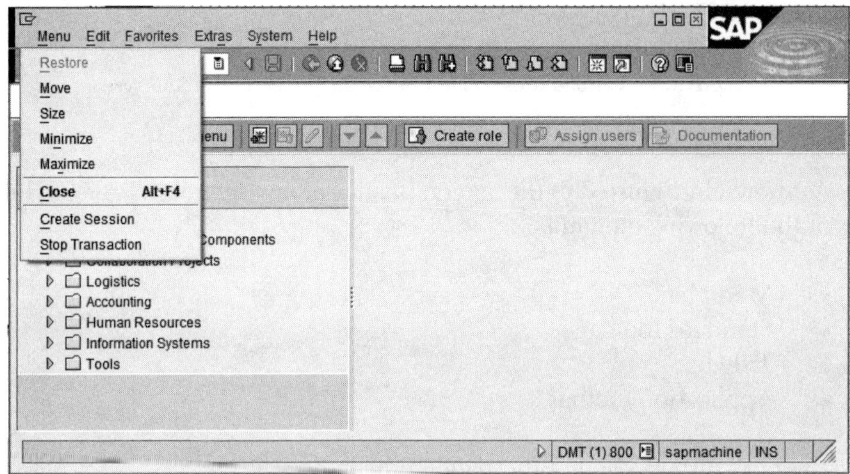

FIGURE 3.8 **Selecting the stop transaction option**

Select the desired option from the drop-down list to perform the required task.

Table 3.1 describes the default menu options:

Option	Description
System	Contains the functions that affect the working of the SAP system as a whole, such as creating a session or user profile and logging off.
Help	Provides online help.

TABLE 3.1 Default menu options

Table 3.2 describes the standard menu options available for all SAP applications:

Option	Description
<Object>	Contains the functions that affect the object as a whole, such as `Display`, `Change`, `Print`, or `Exit`. (Components of a program or application are considered as objects in SAP.) It is named after the object currently in use, such as `Material`.
Edit	Allows you to edit the current object by providing various options, such as `Select` and `Copy`. The `Cancel` option allows you to terminate a task without saving the changes.
Goto	Allows you to navigate through screens in the current task. It also contains the `Back` option, which helps navigate one level back in the system hierarchy. Before going back, the system checks the data you have entered on the current screen and displays a dialog box if it detects a problem.

TABLE 3.2 Standard menu options

Additional menu options for any specific SAP module functionality are given in Table 3.3:

Option	Description
Extras	Allows you to use additional functions to create or modify the current application.
Environment	Allows you to display additional information about the current application.
View	Displays the application or object in different views.
Settings	Sets user-specific transaction parameters.
Utilities	Performs object-independent processing, such as the delete, copy, and print functions.

TABLE 3.3 Additional menu options

The Standard Toolbar

The standard toolbar is an important element of SAP GUI. It is located below the menu bar and provides a range of icons with general SAP GUI functions and a command field to enter a transaction code. Various types of icons are found in the standard toolbar. These icons give access to common functions, such as `Save`, `Back`, `Exit`, and `Cancel`, as well as navigation help functions. The command field used to enter the transaction code is located to the right of the `Enter` ( ) icon.

By default, the `Command` field remains closed. To display the command field, click the `arrow` ( ) icon located to the left of the `Save` ( ) icon, as shown in Figure 3.9:

FIGURE 3.9 **Displaying the arrow button to open the command field**

When you click the `arrow` ( ) icon, the command field expands, where the desired transaction code can be entered. Figure 3.10 shows the expanded command field:

FIGURE 3.10 **Expanded command field**

Figure 3.10 shows the command field where the transaction code for a particular application is entered, such as the `SE38` transaction code, which opens the ABAP Editor.

> **Note:** A transaction code is a parameter of four alphanumeric characters used to identify a transaction in the R/3 system. In SAP R/3, every function has a transaction code associated with it. To call a transaction, enter the transaction code in the command field at the upper-left corner of your R/3 window and click the

Continued

Enter button or press the `ENTER` key. Use `/N` before the transaction code to end the current task and start another corresponding to the transaction code entered. For instance, `/NS000` ends the current task with the transaction code `S000`. The `S000` transaction code is used for the initial screen of SAP. Transaction code is not case-sensitive, which means you can enter the transaction code either in lowercase or uppercase. Using certain transaction code for navigating to certain screens depends on your system's authorization. If you want to find the transaction code for a particular function, select the `Status` option in the `System` menu bar. You can find the required transaction code in the transaction field of the status bar.

The SAP icons displayed on the standard toolbar provide quick access to commonly used SAP functions. If a function is not available for use on a particular screen, its corresponding icon appears gray on the toolbar. Table 3.4 describes the various icons of the standard toolbar of the SAP R/3 system,which perform different tasks according to the user's requirements.

Icon	Control Name	Keyboard Shortcut	Description
	Enter	ENTER	Confirms the data that the user has selected or entered on the screen. It works in the same manner as that of the ENTER key, but does not save the work.
	Save	CTRL+ S	Saves the changes or data in the SAP system.
	Back	F3	Navigates to the previous screen or menu level.
	Exit	SHIFT+ F3	Exits from the current menu or system task.
	Cancel	F12	Cancels the data entered in the current system task.

TABLE 3.4 Standard toolbar icons

Continued

Icon	Control Name	Keyboard Shortcut	Description
	Print	CTRL+ P	Prints a document.
	Find	CTRL+ F	Searches the open document or display screen for words and alphanumeric combinations.
	Find Next	CTRL+ G	Finds the next instance of a previously searched item.
	First Page	CTRL +PAGE UP	Enables to navigate to the first page.
	Previous Page	PAGE UP	Enables to scroll one page up.
	Next Page	PAGE DOWN	Enables to scroll one page down.
	Last Page	CTRL+ PAGE DOWN	Enables to scroll to the last page.
	Help	F1	Provides help on the field where the cursor is positioned.
	Create New Session	None	Creates a new SAP session.
	Customized Local Layout	ALT+ F12	Modifies the layout and settings of the SAP system.

TABLE 3.4 Standard toolbar icons

The Title Bar

The title bar displays the title of the opened screen in the SAP system. Figure 3.11 shows the title of the `SAP Easy Access` screen in the title bar:

SAP Easy Access

FIGURE 3.11 **The title bar**

In Figure 3.11, the title bar displays the title of the first screen of the SAP system, i.e., SAP Easy Access. Moreover, the title bar is a part of the screen header and lies between the standard toolbar and application toolbar (shown previously in Figure 3.6).

The Application Toolbar

The application toolbar contains various icons and buttons that help you to create and maintain the applications in the SAP system. These icons and buttons are application-specific, as different applications have different requirements and functionalities. The application toolbar is located just below the title bar. Figure 3.12 shows the application toolbar:

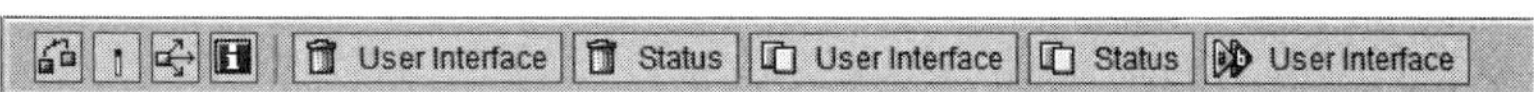

FIGURE 3.12 **The application toolbar**

The Screen Body

The area between the screen header and the status bar is known as the screen body (see Figure 3.2). It acts as a primary window where the user actually performs the task. Every transaction screen contains a screen body, and different applications have different screen bodies.

A screen body has several entry fields and a work area. In the entry field, you can enter, change, or display information to accomplish your system task. SAP R/3 has the following three field types:

- **Required fields**—Specifies that data must be filled by a user.
- **Default fields**—Contain predefined data. However, the predefined data can be overwritten depending on the system task or your SAP profile.
- **Optional field**—May or may not contain data that has to be filled by the user, depending upon the task requirement.

Figure 3.13 shows examples of the preceding fields within the screen body of an SAP screen:

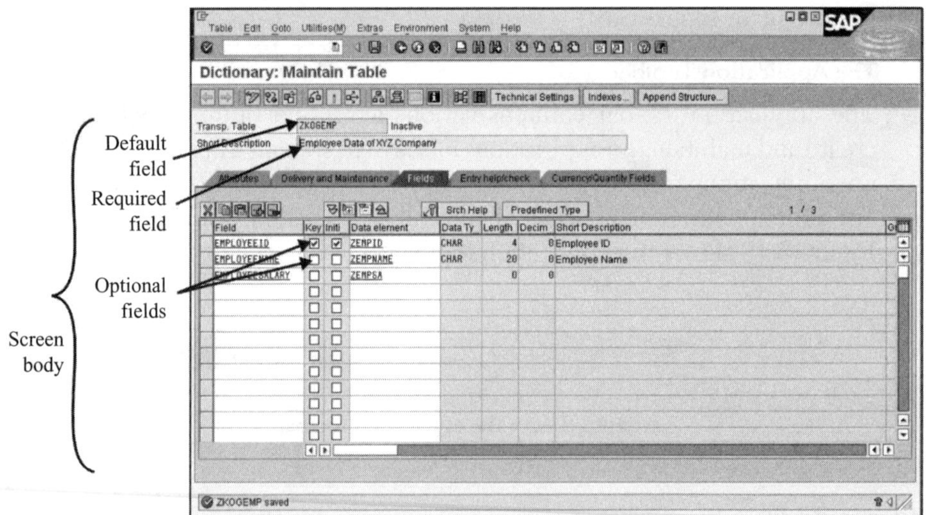

FIGURE 3.13 **Required, default, and optional fields in the screen body**

In Figure 3.13, you can see that the `Transp.Table` field is the default field, the `Short Description` field is the required field, and the `Keys` and the `Initial Values` check boxes are optional fields.

The Status Bar

The SAP status bar provides information about applications and programs being executed in the SAP system. The information may include messages about the status of executing a program, opening a transaction, or error messages. Figure 3.14 shows the SAP status bar:

FIGURE 3.14 **The SAP status bar**

In Figure 3.14, you can see that the system messages are defined on the left-hand side of the status bar. Note that the messages are flashed once and then displayed in the status bar. Table 3.5 describes the status messages with their icons:

Icon	Message Indicating	Example
	Error	Make an entry in all required fields
	Informative	Document 90006078 has been saved
	Warning	Enter PO number

TABLE 3.5 Status message with icons

The right side of the status bar contains three fields: system information, host application server name, and the mode of writing, i.e., the insert mode (INS) or the overwrite mode (OVR).

The system information includes the server name, the session number, the client number, and the `Status Information` icon. In Figure 3.10, DMT (1) 800 shows the server name as DMT, session number as 1, and the client number as 800. The status information includes the name of the host application server (in this case, it is sapmachine) and the mode of writing. In our case, the mode of writing is INS.

At times, you may find that the status bar is closed on your computer, as shown in Figure 3.15:

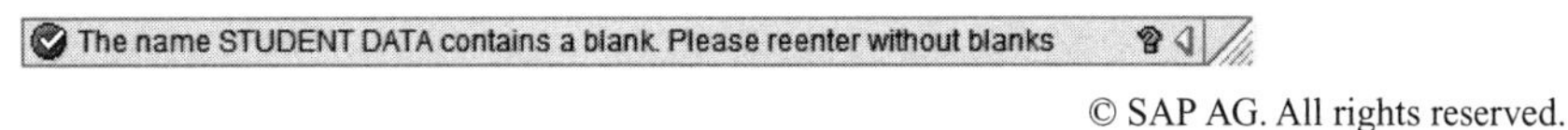

FIGURE 3.15 **Closed status bar**

To display the status bar, click the arrow at the right corner of the screen. Figure 3.16 shows the opened status bar of the SAP system:

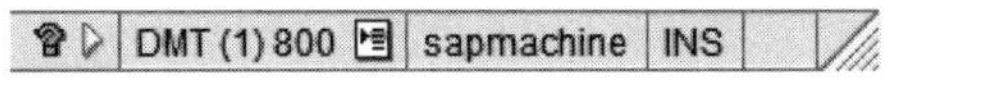

FIGURE 3.16 **Opened status bar**

The `Status Information` (icon) icon displays the current information of various elements such as Transaction, Response Time, and Interpretation Time, as shown in Figure 3.17:

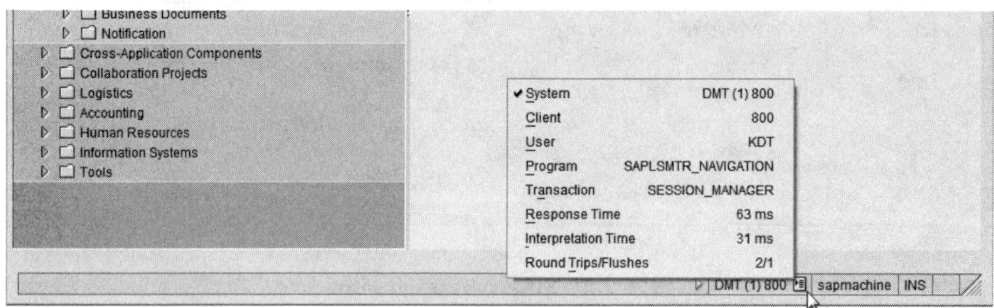

FIGURE 3.17 **Options to change the information on the status bar**

Figure 3.17 shows the status bar and various options available within the `Status Information` (icon) icon.

CUSTOMIZING THE SAP GUI

You can customize the layout and settings of the SAP system by modifying the color, text size, and window size of the screens that open in the system. For this purpose, you use the `Customized Local Layout` (icon) icon that appears in all SAP R/3 system screens. This icon is used to customize the SAP GUI settings according to the requirements of the user. Figure 3.18 shows the `Customized Local Layout` icon:

FIGURE 3.18 **Customized local layout icon on the standard toolbar**

When you click the ( ) icon, a drop-down menu appears (see Figure 3.19). You can use the selections of this drop-down menu to:

- Change the SAP R/3 window colors and text font
- Set the default size of the SAP R/3 windows
- Change the behavior of the cursor positioning in fields and set the auto-tabbing function
- Hide or display the standard toolbar, the application toolbar, and the status toolbar
- Use the clipboard to transfer information from the SAP R/3 window to other Windows applications
- Affirm the position of the cursor and status bar
- Change the display time in the status bar
- Create SAP GUI shortcuts on the desktop
- Display or hide the grid lines in a list

In this case, we select the `New Visual Design` option from the drop-down menu, as shown in Figure 3.19:

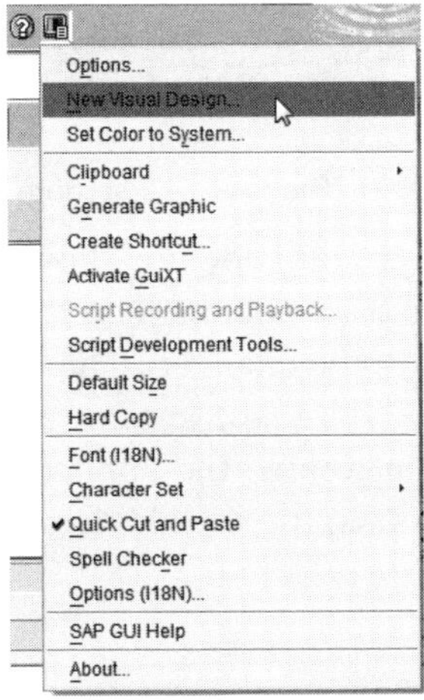

FIGURE 3.19 **The drop-down menu of the customized local layout icon**

The SAP GUI Settings dialog box appears. Now, select the Color Settings tab in it. This dialog box allows you to make changes in the SAP Easy Access screen. Figure 3.20 shows the SAP GUI Settings dialog box:

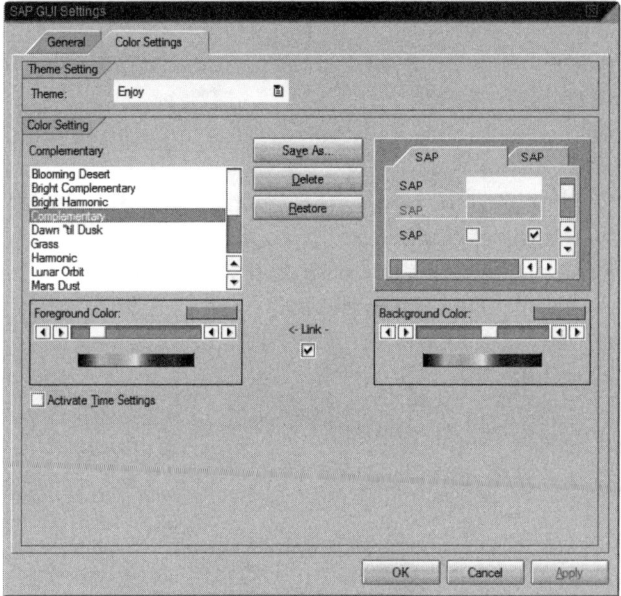

FIGURE 3.20 **The SAP GUI settings dialog box**

The SAP GUI Settings dialog box shown in Figure 3.20 helps to change the color settings of the SAP system. The foreground and background colors of the SAP system can also be changed. The time settings can also be activated by checking the Activate Time Settings check box.

Similarly, you can customize the appearance of the folders, transactions, and location of the folders in the mySAP ERP system, depending on the user's requirements.

MANAGING FAVORITES

As stated earlier, the SAP user menu contains the Favorites folder, which is used to store a list of frequently used transaction codes or web addresses.

These favorites are similar to the favorites or bookmarks added in an Internet browser. They allow users to organize transactions, web pages, applications, or documents within a personalized menu. In other words, it is a shortcut to use transactions, files, and web addresses on the `SAP Easy Access` screen. Instead of searching for the transaction in folders or remembering and typing in the transaction code, double-click the item in the `Favorites` folder. You can perform the following tasks in the `Favorites` folder:

- Add an item, such as a transaction code
- Insert a folder
- Make changes to the inserted folder and added items
- Rename the inserted folder and added items

Now, let's discuss the various types of services and actions performed within the `Favorites` folder.

To perform actions in the `Favorites` folders, click the `Favorites` menu on the menu bar and select an option, such as `Add` or `Move`, as shown in Figure 3.21:

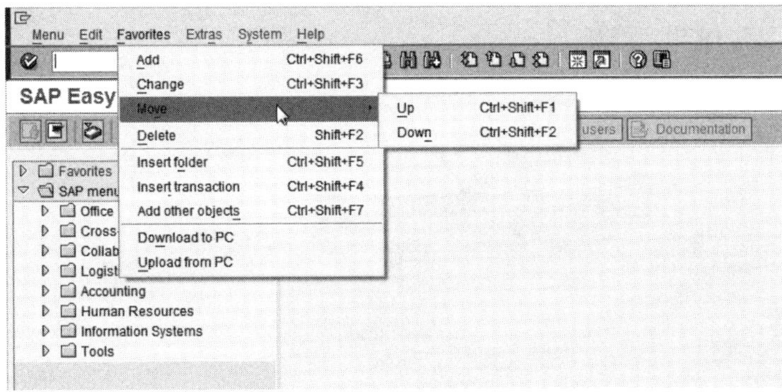

FIGURE 3.21 **The favorites menu on the menu bar**

As shown in Figure 3.21, the drop-down menu is displayed when the `Favorites` menu is clicked.

Table 3.6 shows the options in the `Favorites` menu to create and manage the `Favorites` folder and their links:

Option	Description
Add	Adds a transaction to the folders.
Change	Renames folders and links.
Move	Changes the sequence of folders and links.
Delete	Deletes folders and links.
Insert folder	Creates a new folder in the `Favorites` folder.
Insert transaction	Adds a transaction to the current folder by using transaction code.
Add other objects	Adds web links, mail systems, and other destination to folders.
Download to PC	Downloads the `Favorites` folder to a personal computer or to an external storage site.
Upload from PC	Uploads the `Favorites` folder from your personal computer or an external web site to the SAP system.

TABLE 3.6 Options in the favorites menu

The application toolbar provides several icons to manage the `Favorites` folder, as shown in Figure 3.22:

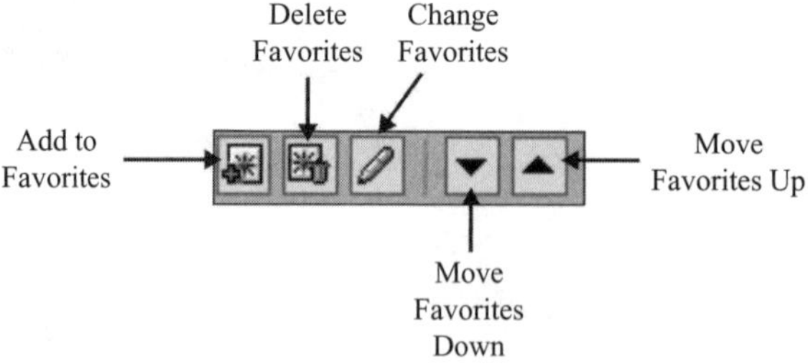

FIGURE 3.22 **Icons to manage the favorites folder**

Managing the `Favorites` folder involves the following actions:

- Adding an item
- Inserting transactions
- Inserting folders

- Moving favorites and folders
- Renaming favorites and folders
- Deleting favorites and folders
- Adding a web address

Now, let's discuss these functionalities, one by one.

Adding an Item

At times, you might need to add an item from the SAP menu to create a favorites list in the `Favorites` folder. An item can be added to the favorites list through any of the following means:

- **Using the drag-and-drop method**—Select a menu item from the SAP menu and drag-and-drop the item inside the `Favorites` folder.
- **Using the Favorites menu**—Select a menu item from the SAP menu and add it to the `Favorites` folder by selecting `Favorites` > `Add`.

Inserting Transactions

You can use the `Favorites` folder to insert a transaction by using the `Manual Entry of a Transaction` dialog box. Perform the following steps to insert a transaction in the `Favorites` folder:

1. Right-click the `Favorites` folder and select the `Insert transaction` option from the displayed context menu, as shown in Figure 3.23:

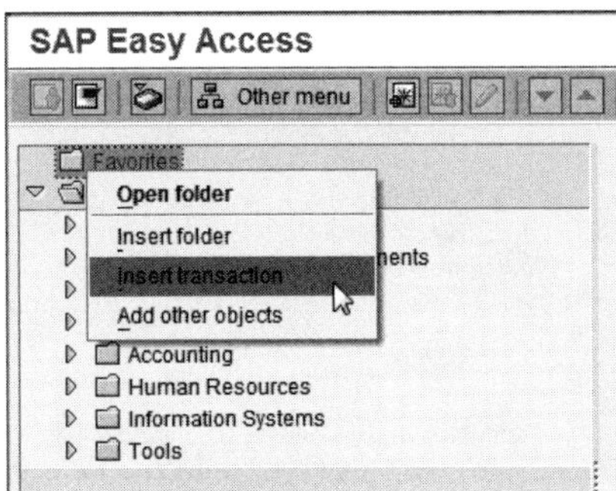

FIGURE 3.23 **Selecting the insert transaction option**

The Manual Entry of a Transaction dialog box appears, as shown in Figure 3.24.

> **Note:** The Manual entry of a transaction dialog box can also be opened by selecting Favorites > Insert transaction.

2. Enter a transaction code in the Transaction code field of the Manual Entry of a transaction dialog box. For example, the transaction code SE38 is entered in the Transaction code field. Next, click the Continue (✔) icon, as shown in Figure 3.24:

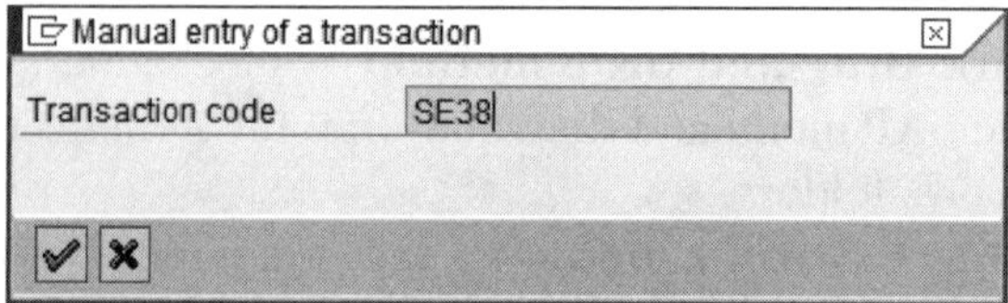

FIGURE 3.24 **Manual entry of a transaction dialog box**

Figure 3.25 shows the transaction code SE38 – ABAP Editor as a favorite in the Favorites folder:

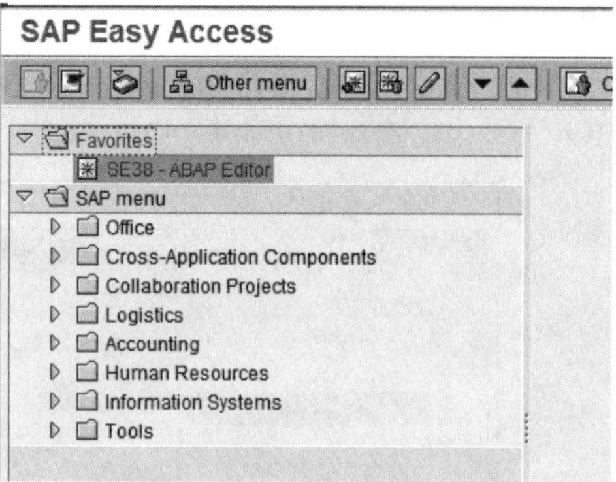

FIGURE 3.25 **Inserting a favorite in the favorites folder**

Inserting Folders

As already discussed, the Favorites folder reduces the number of clicks that are required to open a transaction or a link to perform a task. We can also create different folders inside the `Favorites` folder to simplify the task of categorizing favorites. Perform the following steps to insert a folder inside the `Favorites` folder:

1. Right–click the `Favorites` folder and select the `Insert folder` option (see Figure 3.23). The `Create a Folder in the Favorites List` dialog box opens.
2. Enter a folder name, for instance, SAP User Folder, in the `Folder` name field, as shown in Figure 3.26:

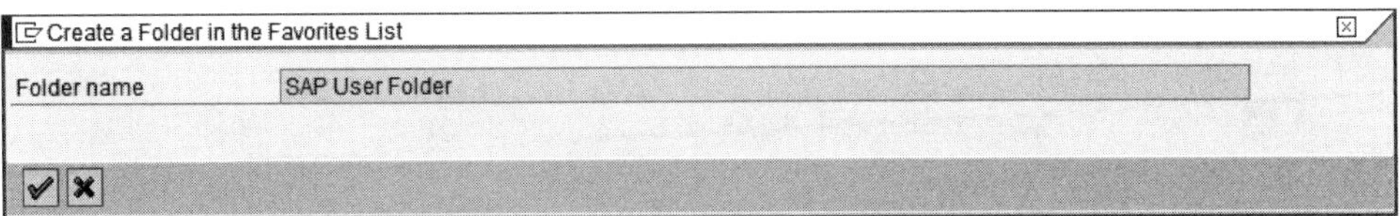

FIGURE 3.26 **Entering a folder in the favorites list dialog box**

3. Click the `Continue` (✔) icon or press the ENTER key to complete the process.

Figure 3.27 shows a folder, called `SAP User Folder`, created inside the `Favorites` folder:

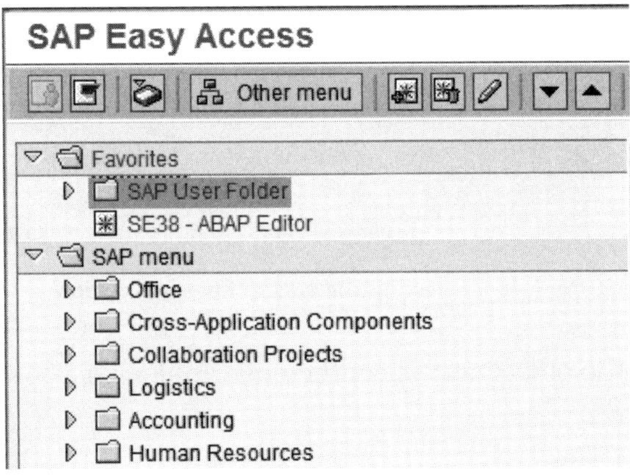

FIGURE 3.27 **The SAP user folder added in the favorites folder**

Moving Favorites and Folders

To perform certain activities, favorites and subfolders in the `Favorites` folder often need to be moved from their original location to some other location in the `Favorites` folder. Perform the following steps to add a particular object to the favorites list and then move it to a different location:

1. Select a particular object from the SAP menu. For example, the `SE80 – Object Navigator` is selected in Figure 3.28:

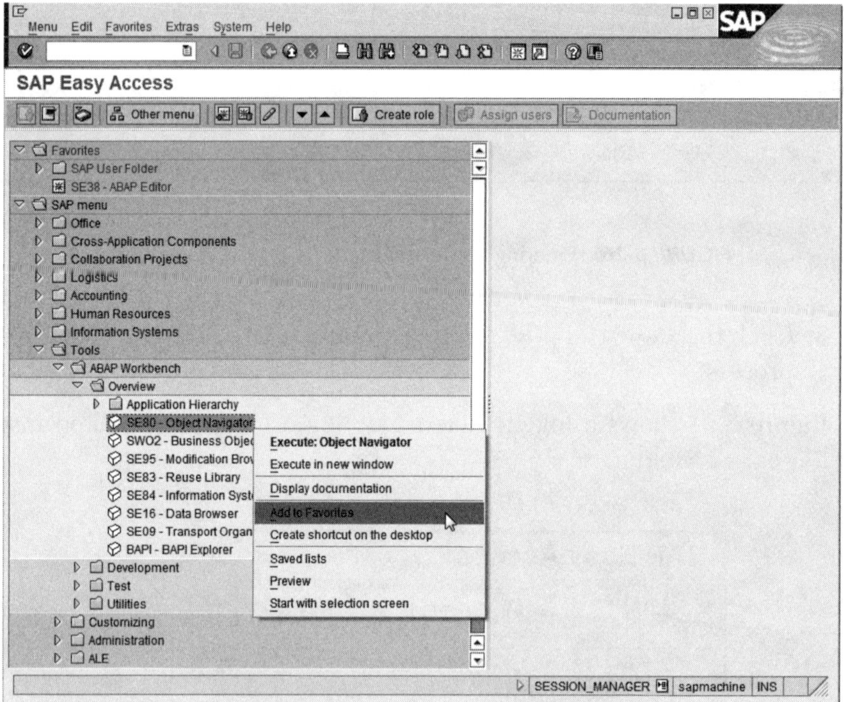

FIGURE 3.28 **Selecting the add to favorites option**

2. Right-click the object and select the `Add to Favorites` option, as shown in Figure 3.28.

A favorite of Object Navigator is added in the favorites list, as shown in Figure 3.29:

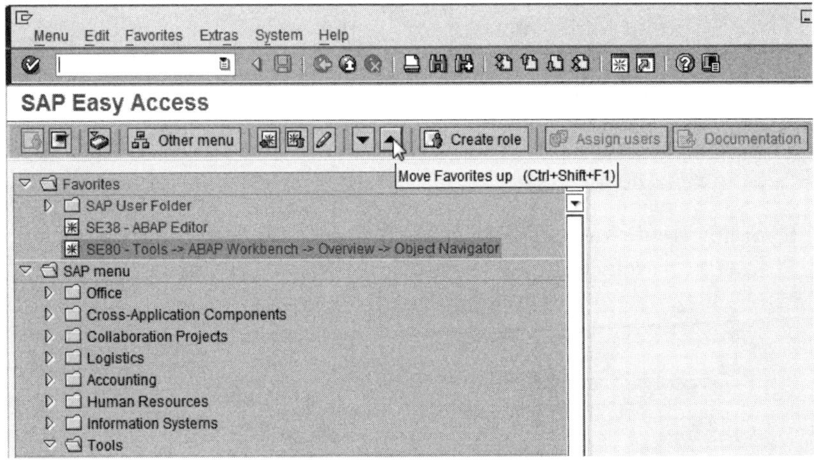

FIGURE 3.29 **A favorite added in the favorites folder**

3. Click the `Move favorites up` icon (see Figure 3.29). The `Object Navigator` favorite will move upward inside the `Favorites` folder hierarchy, as shown in Figure 3.30:

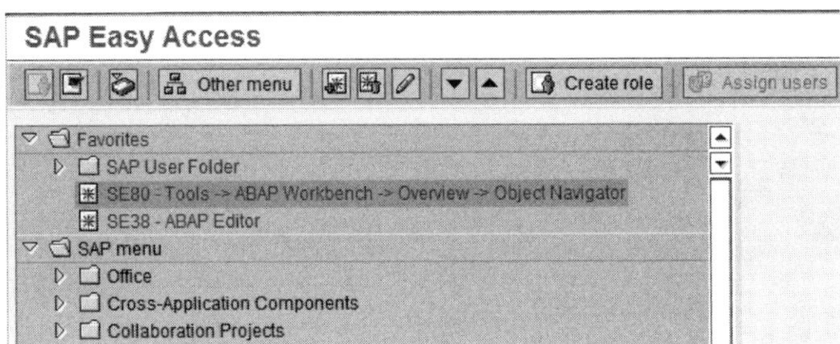

FIGURE 3.30 **Moving a favorite**

> **Note:** You can also use the drag-and-drop method to move a favorite or folder inside the `Favorites` folder. In such cases, we first select the favorite or folder and then drag-and-drop the favorite or folder to the desired position in the `Favorites` folder. The favorite or folder now appears at the desired location.

Renaming Favorites and Folders

A folder can be renamed to meet the user's requirements. Perform the following steps to rename a favorite:

1. Select the favorite or folder. In this case, a link to the `Object Navigator` favorite is selected (see Figure 3.31).
2. Click the `Favorites` menu and select the `Change` option, as shown in Figure 3.31:

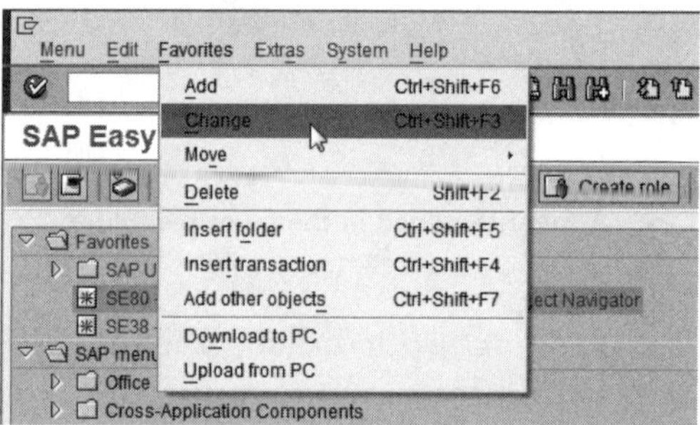

FIGURE 3.31 **Selecting the change option**

The `Change a Favorite` dialog box appears, as shown in Figure 3.32:

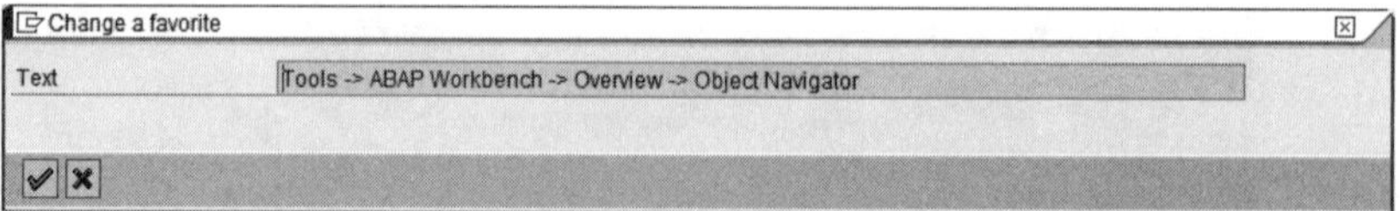

FIGURE 3.32 **The change a favorite dialog box**

Note: An alternative way to open the `Change a favorite` dialog box is by right-clicking the name of a favorite in the `Favorites` folder and then selecting the `Change a Favorite` option from the context menu.

3. Enter new text for the favorite in the `Text` field of the `Change a Favorite` dialog box. In this case, we have entered the text "Tools: Object Navigator" in the `Text` field, as shown in Figure 3.33:

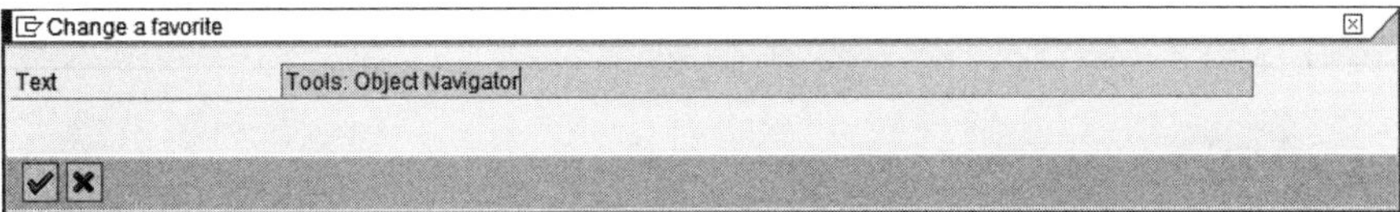

FIGURE 3.33 **Entering new text for the favorite**

4. Click the `Continue` (✔) icon in the `Change a Favorite` dialog box or press the ENTER key.

A new name is assigned to the specific favorite, as shown in Figure 3.34:

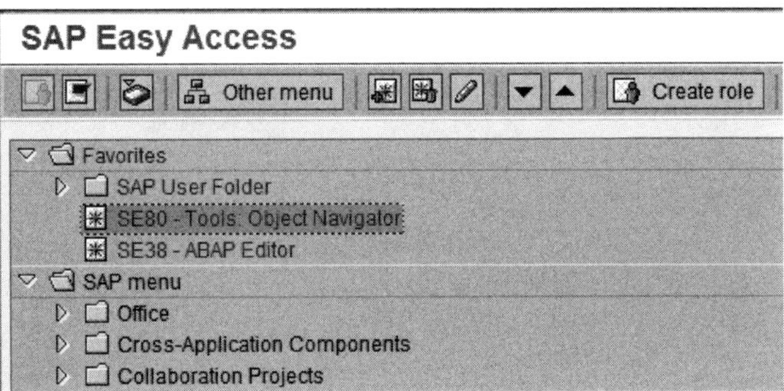

FIGURE 3.34 **A favorite renamed**

Deleting Favorites and Folders

The favorites and the folders created inside the `Favorites` folder can also be deleted, as the user wants. To delete an existing favorite or a folder from the `Favorites` folder, select the favorite or folder that has to be deleted and then select `Favorites>Delete` in the `SAP Easy Access` screen (see Figure 3.30)

> **Note:** An alternative way to delete existing favorites or folders is by right-clicking the name of a favorite or folder in the `Favorites` folder and then selecting the `Delete Favorite` option from the opened context menu.

Adding a Web Address

To include a frequently used web document or web link while you are working on another task, add the address of the web link in the `Favorites` menu. Perform the following steps to add a web address inside the `Favorites` folder:

1. Right-click the `Favorites` folder and select the `Add Other Objects` option (see Figure 3.23) from the context menu. The `Add Additional Objects` dialog box appears, as shown in Figure 3.35:

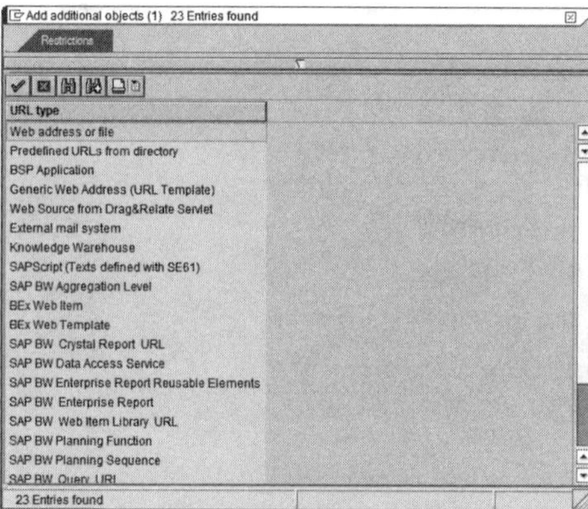

FIGURE 3.35 **The add additional objects dialog box**

2. Select the `Web address or file` option (see Figure 3.35). Click the `Copy` (✔) icon or press the `ENTER` key. The `Change Web Address or Path` dialog box opens (see Figure 3.36):

Change Web address or path

Text	sap help
Web address or file	help.sap.com
Continuation	

FIGURE 3.36 **The change web address or path dialog box**

3. In the `Change Web Address or Path` dialog box, enter the web address or the location of a file in the `Text` and `Web Address` or `File` fields, respectively. For example, in our case, sap help is entered in the `Text` field and help.sap.com is entered in the `Web Address or File` field, as shown in Figure 3.36:

> **Note:** You can add an object, such as a web page link, a data file, or an application program, such as a microsoft Excel file or a directory, on the hard disk.

4. Finally, click the `Continue` (✔) icon (see Figure 3.36) or press the `ENTER` key.

A URL is added to the `Favorites` folder, as shown in Figure 3.37:

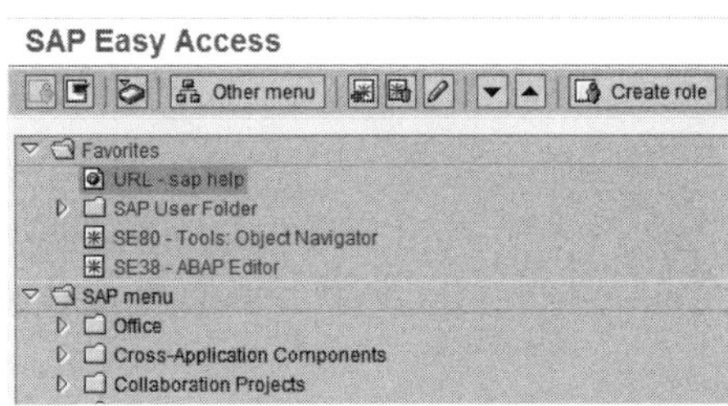

FIGURE 3.37 **A URL added to the favorites folder**

Now, let's discuss how to handle SAP sessions, in particular how to create and end a session and how to manage one session while working with another session.

HANDLING SAP SESSIONS

A session is an instance of an SAP system on the user screen. Multiple sessions or multiple instances allow users to work on multiple screens simultaneously. A maximum of six sessions can be opened at one time, and you can perform either different tasks or the same task in each of the sessions. You can also navigate from one session to another open session and close any open session without logging off of the system.

> **Note:** A record can be modified by only one user at a time in a session. Multiple write access to the same record is denied.

Handling one or more SAP sessions involves the following operations:

- Creating a new session
- Displaying a list of all sessions
- Ending a session

Now, let's discuss each operation in detail, one by one.

Creating a New Session

Every session you open is a new and independent session. An operation on one session (for example, closing it) does not change the status of the other sessions.

Note: If multiple sessions are opened simultaneously in the SAP R/3 system, the speed and performance of the system decrease. For this reason, the system administrator limits the number of sessions you can create to six.

You can create a session from any screen of the SAP system by selecting the `Create Session` option in the `System` menu, as shown in Figure 3.38:

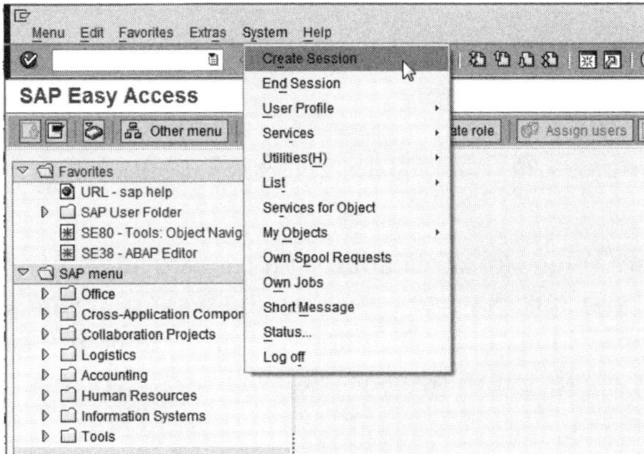

FIGURE 3.38 **Creating a Session**

Note: Another way of creating a new session from a screen of the SAP system is by clicking the `Create Session` () icon on the standard toolbar. When you create a new session, it automatically becomes the active session, while other open sessions are deactivated. This session continues to remain the active session unless you open another session. Each session has a number that is displayed in the status bar, within parentheses, next to the system name. Figure 3.39 shows three opened sessions and the number of active sessions in the status bar:

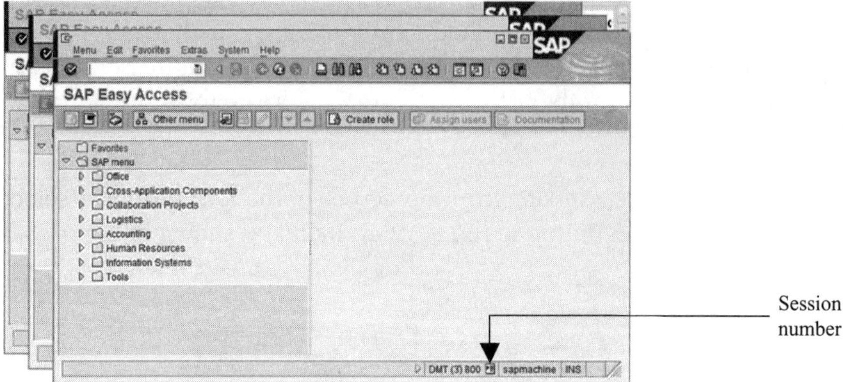

FIGURE 3.39 **Showing the new session number**

Similar to any Windows application, you can activate any session from the multiple opened sessions. Navigating among the sessions is similar to navigating among active applications in the Windows environment. You can activate any session either by clicking it or by using the ALT and TAB keys.

Displaying a List of All Sessions

To display the list of all the opened sessions within the SAP system, enter the `/o` system command in the command field. The `Overview of Sessions` dialog box appears, as shown in Figure 3.40:

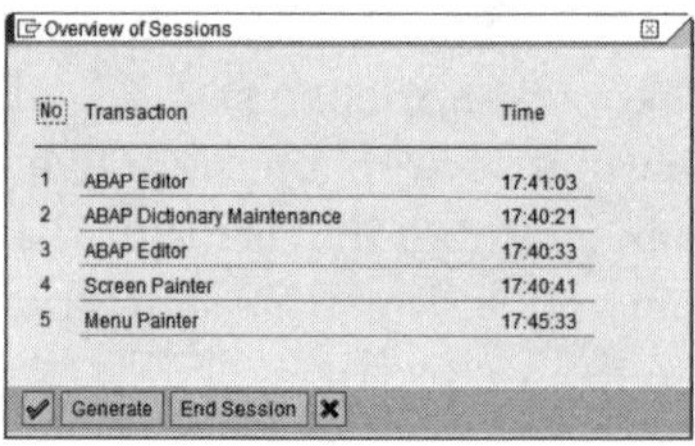

FIGURE 3.40 **The overview of sessions dialog box**

In Figure 3.40, you can see that five sessions are currently opened in the SAP system. These sessions are running the ABAP Editor, ABAP Dictionary Maintenance, ABAP Editor, Screen Painter, and Menu Painter transactions. In the Overview of Sessions dialog box, the Generate button is used to generate a new session (with the SAP Easy Access screen), and the End Session button is used to end a session that is selected from the list in the Overview of Sessions dialog box. Moreover, the Continue (✔) icon is used to close the Overview of Sessions dialog box, and the Cancel (✖) or (☒) icon is used to close the Overview of Sessions dialog box.

Ending a Session

As a best practice, you must end a session after you have finished using it because each session uses system resources, which affects the efficiency and working of the SAP R/3 system.

> **Note:** You must save useful data before ending a session, as a SAP R/3 system does not prompt you to save data.

You can choose any one of the following ways to end a session:

- Selecting System > End session, as shown in Figure 3.41:

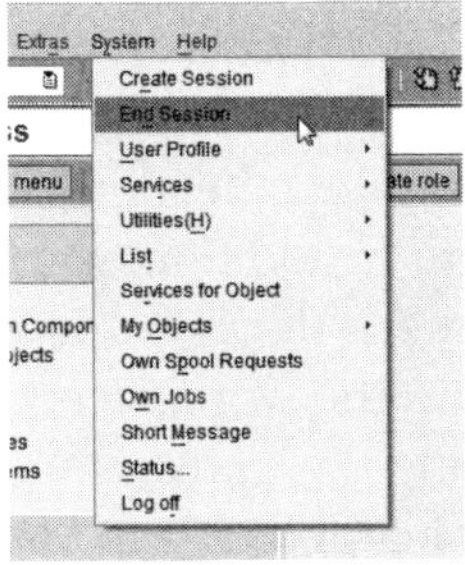

FIGURE 3.41 **Selecting the end session option**

- Clicking the `Exit` ( ) icon.
- Clicking the `Close` ( ) icon at the upper-right corner of the screen.
- Selecting the `Close` option from the drop-down menu of the ( ) icon, which is present at the upper-left corner of the SAP GUI window.
- Entering the `/i` system command in the command field of the session that you to close.
- Entering the `/i` system command followed by a session number in the command field to close a particular session specified by number. For example, the `/i5` command is used to close the fifth session.

Moreover, to close all the sessions simultaneously, perform either of the following actions:

- Enter the `/nend` system command in the command field; you are prompted to confirm that you want to close all the sessions.
- Enter the `/nex` system command in the command field; all the sessions are closed without prompting.

SUMMARY

In this chapter, you have learned about the first screen of the SAP R/3 system, SAP Easy Access. In addition, you have learned how to work with the SAP R/3 system by using various commands, tools, and facilities. This chapter also explains the SAP GUI by exploring the screen header (containing various toolbars) the screen body, and the status bar. In addition, you have learned to customize the layout and settings of the screens displayed in the SAP system. Further, you have learned to navigate within the workplace menu and manage favorites by adding, modifying, and deleting the items, such as transactions, web address, and folders. Finally, you have learned how to handle one or more sessions and navigate from one session to another.

Chapter 4

Understanding ABAP Workbench

If you need information on:	*See page:*
Overview of ABAP Workbench	90
Exploring the ABAP Workbench Tools	91
Describing Package Builder	112
Testing Tools in ABAP Workbench	114
Describing Web Services	117
Describing XSLT Editor	120

ABAP Workbench is a graphical programming environment in the SAP R/3 system to develop different applications by using the ABAP language. It provides different tools, such as `ABAP Dictionary`, `ABAP Editor`, and `Screen Painter`, to create ABAP applications. Using these tools, you can perform different tasks, such as defining data structures in `ABAP Dictionary`, developing data programs in `ABAP Editor`, and designing interfaces in `Screen Painter` and `Menu Painter`. Besides these tasks, you can also create user-defined reports, transactions, and enhancements within ABAP Workbench. Moreover, all the tools of ABAP Workbench are integrated, which means one tool recognizes the objects created by the other tools.

This chapter introduces you to ABAP Workbench. You explore the tools available in ABAP Workbench, such as `ABAP Dictionary`, `ABAP Editor`, `Screen Painter`, and `Menu Painter`. This chapter also describes the role of Package Builder to create packages for development objects. In addition, you explore the testing tools of ABAP Workbench, such as `ABAP Debugger` and

`Performance Analysis`, which are used to debug the ABAP program code and trace program performance. You also learn about web services and how ABAP Workbench helps publish, search, and call the web services. Finally, you explore the `eXtensible Stylesheet Language Transformation (XSLT) Editor` tool of ABAP Workbench, which is used to define XSL transformations.

OVERVIEW OF ABAP WORKBENCH

ABAP Workbench provides a set of tools and libraries to design, implement, test, and maintain the transactions and reports written in the ABAP language. Some examples of these tools are `ABAP Dictionary`, `Object Navigator`, and `ABAP Editor`. By using these tools of ABAP Workbench, you can create ABAP programs, user interfaces, web services, and access database information. You can use ABAP Workbench to implement additional functionality in ABAP applications in the form of programs, reports, screens, or menus, if the functions of a standard SAP system are not sufficient to meet your requirements.

All the tools provided by ABAP Workbench are integrated with each other. For instance, assume that you write a program in ABAP Editor that uses a user defined table, ZStudentData, which is already defined in `ABAP Dictionary`. Now, just by double-clicking the name of this table (ZStudentData), you receive the entire structure of this table in ABAP Editor. The integrated environment of ABAP Workbench provides the `Object Navigator` tool, which helps you to manage application development and understand the relationship between the objects of a program. You learn more about the `Object Navigator` tool later in the chapter.

Note: An ABAP application is created as a transaction or a report. A transaction represents an end-user application, which retrieves data from users and performs the relevant actions. For instance, an application that creates purchase orders is a transaction. In contrast, a report may be defined as an application that requires less or no user interaction. A monthly report of raw materials imported by a company is an example of a report.

EXPLORING THE ABAP WORKBENCH TOOLS

The ABAP Workbench tools are used to write ABAP code, design the screens, and create user interfaces. Figure 4.1 shows different tools provided by ABAP Workbench:

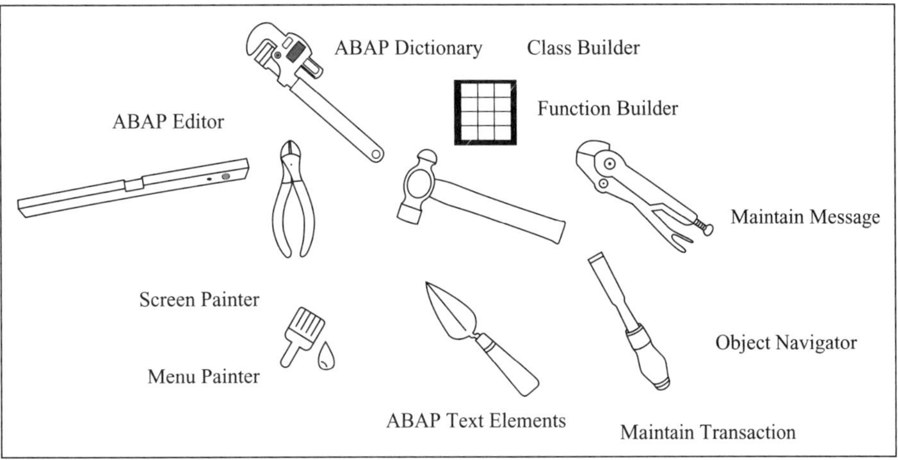

FIGURE 4.1 **ABAP workbench tools**

As shown in Figure 4.1, the following are different tools provided by ABAP Workbench:

- `ABAP Dictionary`
- `ABAP Editor`
- `Class Builder`
- `Function Builder`
- `Screen Painter`
- `Menu Painter`
- `Object Navigator`
- `Maintain Message`
- `ABAP Text Elements`
- `Maintain Transaction`

Now, let's discuss each tool in detail.

ABAP Dictionary

ABAP Dictionary is one of the important tools of ABAP Workbench. It is used to create and manage data definitions without redundancies. ABAP Dictionary always provides the updated information of an object to all the system components. The presence and role of ABAP Dictionary ensures that data stored in an SAP system is consistent and secure.

The data definitions stored in ABAP Dictionary allow you to create various objects, such as tables and views. The objects stored in ABAP Dictionary are logically related to each other in the context of an application. ABAP Dictionary also stores some standard functions that help you modify the properties of a field on a screen. For instance, you can assign an input help to a field or restrict the range to accept data from a field.

To open the initial screen of ABAP Dictionary, either select `SAP Menu>Tools>ABAP Workbench>Development>ABAP Dictionary` in the `SAP Easy Access` screen or simply enter the `SE11` transaction code in the `Command` field present on the standard toolbar and press the ENTER key. Figure 4.2 shows the initial screen of ABAP Dictionary:

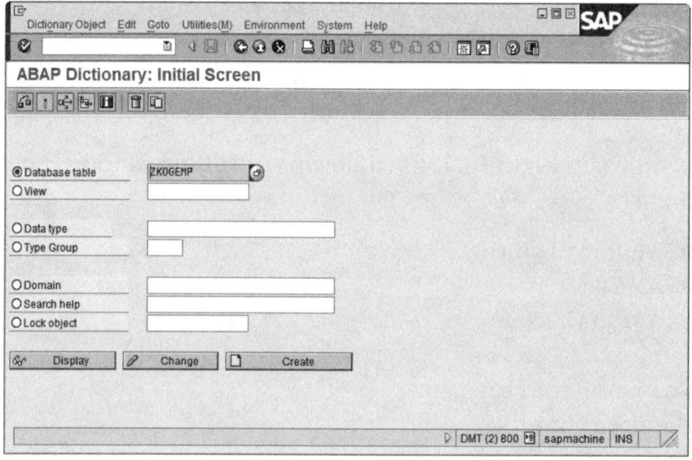

FIGURE 4.2 **Displaying the initial screen of ABAP dictionary**

As shown in Figure 4.2, the initial screen of ABAP Dictionary provides the following object types:

- **Database table**—Creates table definitions in ABAP Dictionary, independent of any database. The created table definition can then be used to create a table (with the same table structure) in the database.
- **View**—Creates view definitions in ABAP Dictionary. A view is a virtual table that does not store the data physically. It has a logical structure that represents or points to the data from one or more database tables. From the created view definition, you can create a view (with the same view structure) in the database.
- **Data type**—Creates a definition of a user-defined type in ABAP Dictionary. The created definition of a user-defined type can then be used in a program to define data types and data objects.
- **Type group**—Creates groups of data types in ABAP Dictionary.
- **Domain**—Creates domains in ABAP Dictionary. A domain is used to describe the technical attributes of a field, such as a range of values and the type of data that are acceptable in a field.
- **Search help**—Creates a help document (F4 help) or called input help for fields. A help document related to a field provides you help to enter a set of valid values in the field.
- **Lock object**—Creates a local or lock object that helps synchronize the access of multiple users simultaneously. This is because an SAP system does not allow multiple users to access an object simultaneously. In such a situation, ABAP Dictionary allows you to create a lock or local object.

Note that when you perform any change in ABAP Dictionary, the change is also reflected in the related ABAP program or screen. ABAP Dictionary also facilitates easy navigation between development objects and dictionary definitions. For example, when you double-click the name of a dictionary object in a program, the SAP system displays the definition of that object in ABAP Dictionary. If you make any changes to the dictionary objects, they are automatically reflected in the program, and the program refers to the changed objects when it is executed. Note that ABAP programs are interpreted by the interpreter, and it is not necessary to recompile the reference of changed dictionary objects.

ABAP Editor

ABAP Editor is used to create ABAP programs by writing code. You can use the ABAP Editor to define the class methods, function modules, screen flow logic, type groups, and logical databases for the ABAP programs. To open the initial screen of ABAP Editor, either select `SAP Menu>Tools>ABAP Workbench>Development>ABAP Editor` in the `SAP Easy Access` screen or simply enter the `SE38` transaction code in the `Command` field present on the standard toolbar, and press the `ENTER` key. Figure 4.3 shows the initial screen of ABAP Editor:

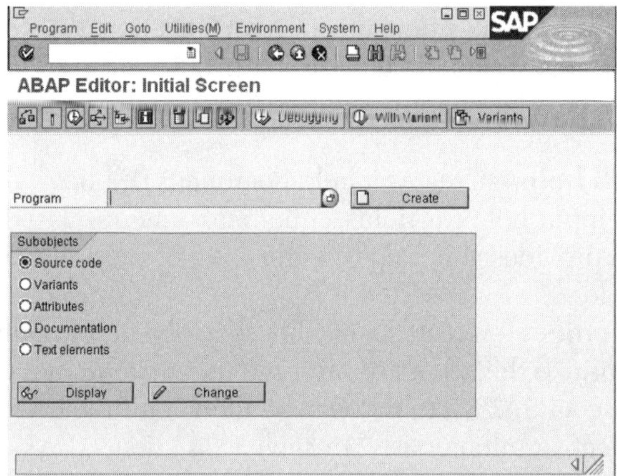

FIGURE 4.3 **Displaying the initial screen of ABAP Editor**

ABAP Editor is available in three different modes for the front-end and back-end purposes. These modes of ABAP Editor can be accessed from the `ABAP Editor` tab in the `User-Specific Settings` dialog box. You can open the `User-Specific Settings` dialog box by selecting Utilities>Settings in the initial screen of ABAP Editor. Figure 4.4 shows the three modes of ABAP Editor in the `User-Specific Settings` dialog box:

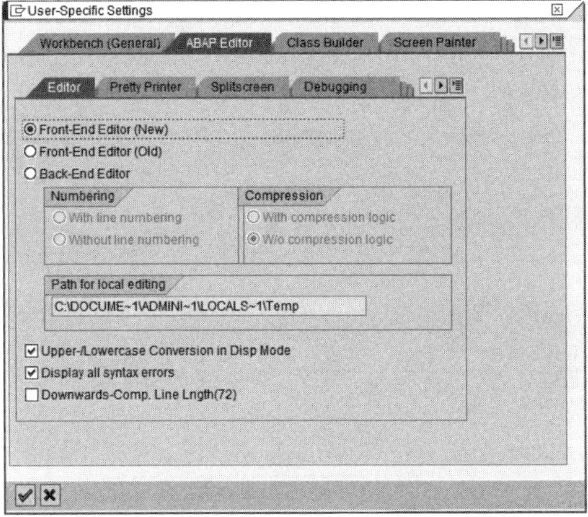

FIGURE 4.4 **Displaying the three modes of ABAP Editor**

As shown in Figure 4.4, the following are the three modes of ABAP Editor:

- `Front-End Editor (New)`
- `Front-End Editor (Old)`
- `Back-End Editor`

> **Note:** Click the `Transfer` icon to apply the desired mode of ABAP Editor and close the `User-Specific Settings` dialog box to use the editor.

Now, let's discuss these modes of ABAP Editor in detail, one by one.

Front-End Editor (New)

`Front-End Editor(New)` is the latest programming tool to create applications in an SAP system. It provides various new features, such as code hints, syntax highlighting, and auto-completion of language structures and elements. When you work in `Front-End Editor (New)`, the source code of your program is loaded in the front end of the SAP system and can be edited easily. Note that `Front-End Editor (New)` is used in situations when editing the source code does not require communication with the back end of the SAP system. Using

Front-End Editor (New), you can modify the development objects, such as ABAP programs, method implementations, function module implementations, and screen flow logic.

Figure 4.5 shows the Front-End Editor (New) screen:

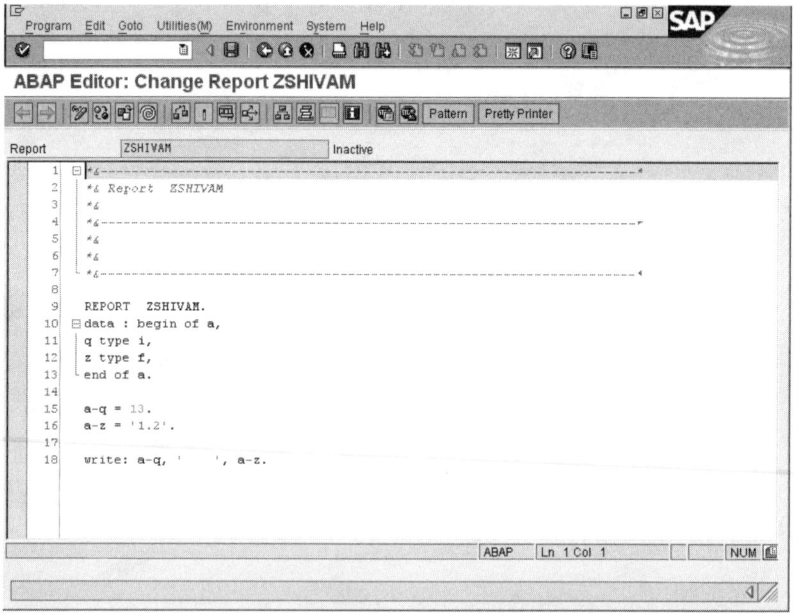

FIGURE 4.5 **Displaying the appearance of** Front-End Editor (New)

Front-End Editor (New) supports various formatting functions, such as automatic code indentation, smart tabs, automatic insertion of brackets, and mistyping correction, which speed up the development process. In addition, Front-End Editor (New) offers significantly improved functionalities over the two classical modes of the ABAP Editor, Front-End Editor (Old) and Back-End Editor.

Front-End Editor (Old)

As stated earlier, Front-End Editor (New) is used to edit the source code of the development objects. The classic mode of Front-End Editor (Old) is also used to edit the development objects, such as ABAP programs, function modules, and type groups. The source code of a program in

`Front-End Editor (Old)` appears in plain text. Figure 4.6 shows the appearance of `Front-End Editor (Old)`:

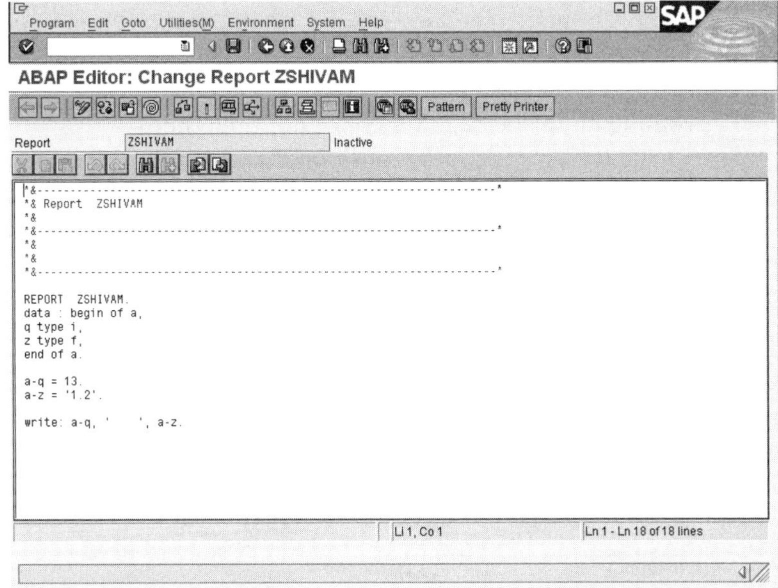

FIGURE 4.6 **Displaying the appearance of** `Front-End Editor (Old)`

When you edit the source code of a program in `Front-End Editor (Old)` the functions required for editing do not communicate with the back end of the SAP system. You can perform the following activities when you work with `Front-End Editor (Old)`:

- Performing local scrolling in an SAP window
- Performing cut, copy, and paste for selected text areas
- Dragging any text and dropping at the desired location
- Using the context menu to access editor functions
- Using the Find and Replace facility
- Using the context menu to navigate to a selected line
- Using the context menu to access the buffer and block operations
- Inserting comments on text blocks
- Working with blocks and clipboards
- Using navigation functions (forward navigation)

- Showing the syntax check, error messages, and warnings in a separate window
- Highlighting the comment lines
- Using the automatic line feed feature when the maximum line width is reached
- Using the Insert statement
- Performing undo and redo functions multiple times
- Displaying the current cursor position
- Using Pretty Printer to standardize the layout
- Importing and exporting the local files

Back-End Editor

`Back-End Editor`, another classic editor, allows users to edit ABAP code. This editor is line-based and is used to perform normal editor functions, such as cut, copy, and paste. For this, however, you must first select a block of lines. Figure 4.7 shows the line-based mode of `Back-End Editor`:

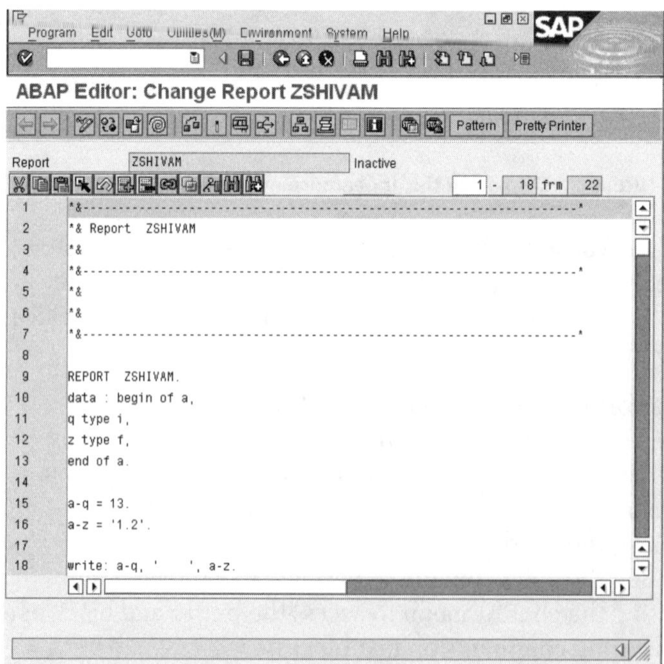

FIGURE 4.7 **Displaying** `Back-End Editor`

When you need to write a very long program, especially in the Wide Access Network (WAN) environment, `Back-End Editor` can produce better performance than `Front-End Editor`. Moreover, `Back-End Editor` allows you to edit any development object based on ABAP Editor. You can perform the following activities when you work with `Back-End Editor`:

- Navigating the functions (forward navigation)
- Selecting the block selection easily
- Using the Compression logic feature
- Using the Line Numbering feature
- Using the functions, such as Find and Replace
- Highlighting the comment lines in color
- Using the Insert Statement function
- Including the expansion
- Using the Single-step Undo function
- Converting a normal text block into the comment lines
- Using Pretty Printer to standardize the layout
- Checking the syntax of code that has the possibility of raising an error
- Uploading or downloading the local files

Class Builder

Class Builder is a tool of ABAP Workbench used to create, define, change, and test the global ABAP classes and interfaces. ABAP classes and interfaces are object types defined in Repository Browser. These classes and interfaces are stored in a central class library and are available to all the objects in an SAP system. This class library is used to display all the existing classes and interfaces by using Class Browser. Class Browser, an integral part of Class Builder, is used to display and maintain the existing global object types from the class library. Class Browser can be started either from Class Builder or simply by entering the `CLABAP` transaction code in the `Command` field. You can perform the following actions by using the Class Builder tool:

- Displaying an overview of global object types and their relationships in Class Browser
- Maintaining the already existing global classes or interfaces easily
- Creating new global classes and interfaces
- Implementing inheritance between two or more global classes

- Creating compound interfaces
- Creating and specifying the attributes, methods, and events of global classes and interfaces
- Defining internal types in classes
- Implementing the methods
- Redefining the already existing methods
- Maintaining local auxiliary classes as well
- Testing classes or interfaces in a simulated runtime environment

To open the initial screen of Class Builder, either select SAP Menu>Tools>ABAP Workbench>Development>Class Builder in the SAP Easy Access screen or enter the SE24 transaction code in the Command field and press the ENTER key. You can display the contents of the class library as well as edit a class by using the initial screen of Class Builder. Figure 4.8 shows the intial screen of Class Builder:

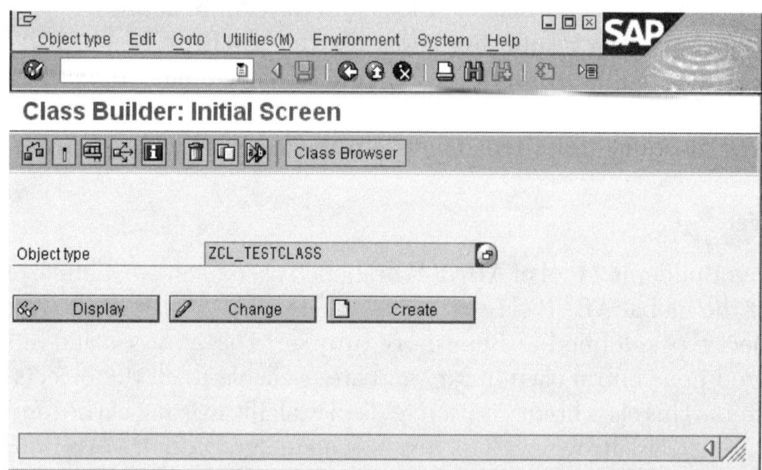

FIGURE 4.8 **Displaying the initial screen of Class Builder**

In Figure 4.8, you need to specify the name of a class or interface in the Object type field. Note that the Object type name can be up to 30 characters long. In our case, ZCL_TESTCLASS is the name of a class, specified in the Object type field. Now, you can click either the Display, Change, or Create button to perform a particular task. The Create button is used to create a new object type; however, the Display and Change buttons are used to display and modify the content of an already existing object type, respectively.

Function Builder

Function Builder plays an important role in defining and maintaining the ABAP functional modules. Function modules are procedures or routines defined in an ABAP program. They are stored in function groups, which act as containers for function modules that are logically related to each other. The Function Builder tool is used to create a function group and function module. Function modules can accept the values of input parameters from users or take default values for these parameters. In addition, function modules support exception handling. As a result, exceptions can be caught if executing the function modules causes errors. Moreover, you can test the function modules by using Function Builder. An SAP system contains several predefined function modules, such as CALCULATE_EXCHANGE_RATE and CHANGEDOCUMENT_READ_HEADERS, which can be called from any ABAP program.

To open the initial screen of Function Builder, either select SAP Menu>Tools>ABAP Workbench>Development>Function Builder in the SAP Easy Access screen or enter the SE37 transaction code in the Command field and press the ENTER key. Figure 4.9 shows the initial screen of Function Builder:

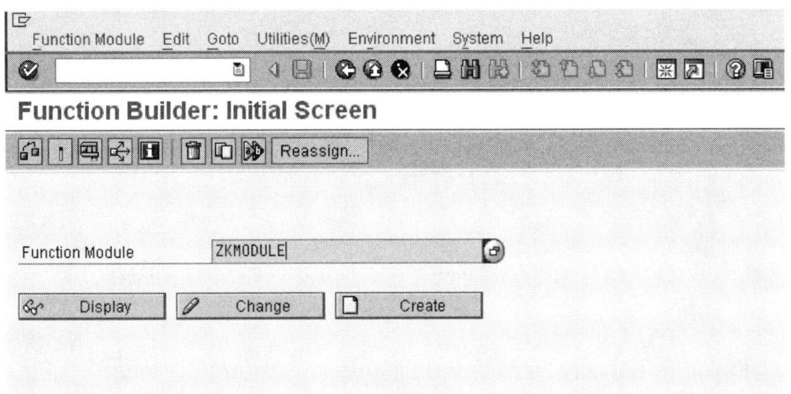

FIGURE 4.9 **Showing the initial screen of function builder**

Enter a name for the function module you are creating in the `Function Module` field of the initial screen of Function Builder. In our case, we have entered ZKMODULE, as shown in Figure 4.9. Click the `Create` button to create the given function module. Alternatively, click the `Display` button to display and the `Change` button to change the content of an already existing function module.

Screen Painter

Screen Painter is used to design and manage screens and their elements. It facilitates users to create GUI screens for transactions. To open the initial screen of Screen Painter, either select `SAP Menu > Tools > ABAP Workbench > Development > User Interface > Screen Painter` in the `SAP Easy Access` screen or enter the `SE51` transaction in the `Command` field and press the `ENTER` key. Figure 4.10 shows the initial screen of Screen Painter:

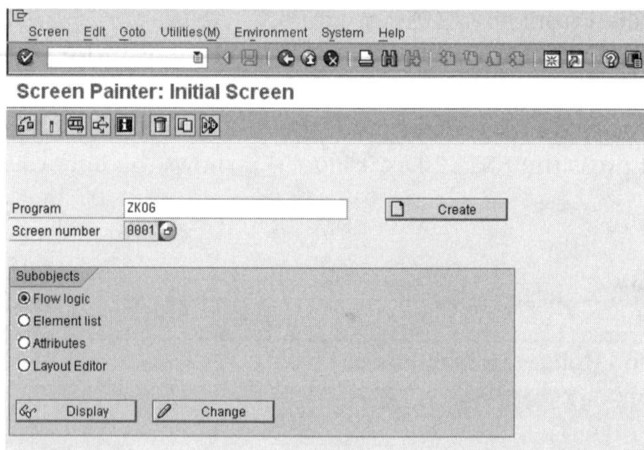

FIGURE 4.10 **Sharing the initial screen of screen painter**

In the initial screen of Screen Painter, you provide a name of the program for which the screen has to be created and a number associated with that screen. For example, ZKOG is the program name and 0001 is the screen number, as shown in Figure 4.10. Now, click the `Create` button to create the screen for the given program. Click the `Display` and `Change` buttons to display and modify the screen for the given program, respectively. Note that on the initial screen of Screen Painter, you also need to select any one of the listed subobjects. Table 4.1 describes the listed subobjects in the initial screen of Screen Painter:

Subobjects	Description
Layout Editor	Manages a screen's layout. The screen layout describes both the screen elements and their layout.
Element List	Manages the ABAP Dictionary or program fields for a screen, and assigns a program field to the `OK_CODE` (a predefined field name) field in Screen Painter. Screen elements include I/O fields, text fields, check boxes, radio buttons, buttons, and other controls.
Attributes	Manage screen's attributes. Screen attributes determine the type of a screen and the program to which the screen belongs.
Flow Logic	Manage screen's flow logic. The flow logic controls the flow of execution of a program.

TABLE 4.1 A list of subobjects on the initial screen of screen painter

Layout Editor of Screen Printer is used to design the layout for a screen. It is available in two modes, Graphical mode (available only on Microsoft Windows platforms) and Alphanumeric mode. Both modes provide the same functionalities, but in a different way. That is, in the graphical mode, you use a drag-and-drop interface similar to a drawing tool, while in the alphanumeric mode, you use the keyboard and menus.

Menu Painter

Menu Painter is used to design user interfaces for ABAP programs. The main components of Menu Painter are GUI status, menu bars, menu lists, F-key settings, functions, and titles. In other words, using Menu Painter, you can create custom menus in SAP. However, to use Menu Painter, you must understand the term GUI status. This status consists of a menu bar, a standard toolbar, an application toolbar, and a collection of function keys. The GUI status differs from the GUI title, which includes the SAP title bar, as shown in Figure 4.11:

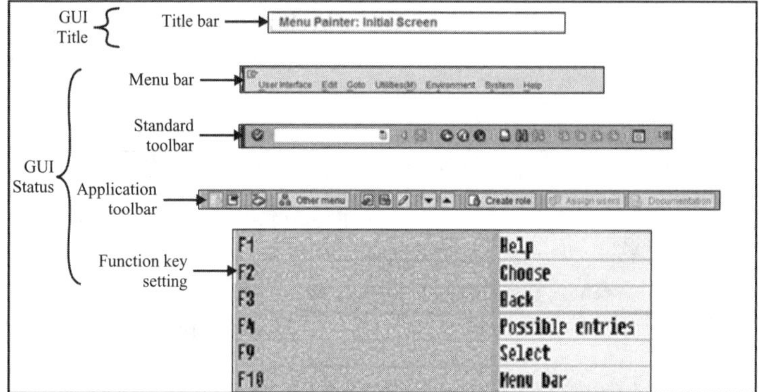

FIGURE 4.11 **Showing the components of menu painter**

To open the initial screen of Menu Painter, either select `SAP Menu>Tools>ABAP Workbench>Development>User Interface>Menu Painter` in the `SAP Easy Access` screen or enter the `SE41` transaction code in the `Command` field and press the `ENTER` key. Figure 4.12 shows the initial screen of Menu Painter:

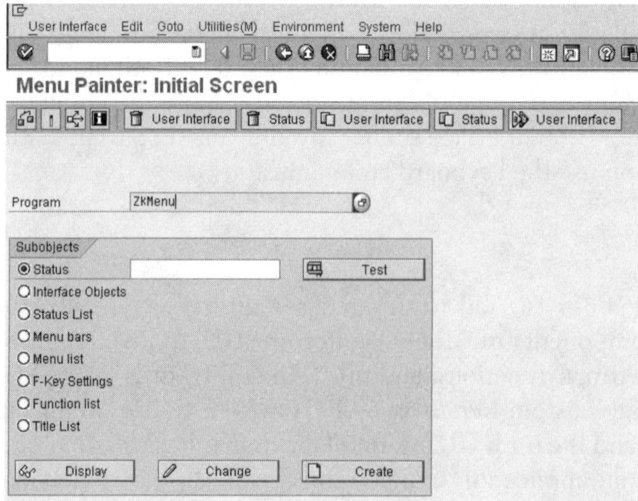

FIGURE 4.12 **Displaying the the initial screen of menu painter**

As shown in Figure 4.12, the initial screen of Menu Painter contains a program name, ZKMenu, in the `Program` field. The `Create` button is used to create the program with the given name, and the `Display` and `Change` buttons are used to display and modify the contents of the given program, respectively. The `Test` button is used to test the specified program. Note that before using the `Display` and `Change` buttons, you must specify one of the following subobjects, as given in Table 4.2:

Subobjects	Description
Status	Opens the Menu Painter work area
Interface Objects	Displays all the user interface objects for the current program
Status List	Displays a list of all the available GUI statuses for the current program
Menu Bars	Displays a list of menu bars that are sorted by status
Menu List	Displays a list of all the menus
F-Key Settings	Displays a list of function key settings
Function List	Displays a list of the function codes
Title List	Displays a list of all GUI titles for the current program

TABLE 4.2 A list of subobjects for the initial screen of menu painter

Object Navigator

Object Navigator is another important tool of ABAP Workbench. It helps create objects in an SAP system and navigate from one object to another. It acts as the central area of ABAP Workbench, where you can access any object of an SAP system. In addition, Object Navigator integrates the programming of various SAP objects in ABAP Workbench. In other words, you can create any SAP object by using Object Navigator, which would then be reflected in all the tools of ABAP Workbench. Object Navigator was also available in the earlier versions of SAP, but it was called Object Browser in Release 3.*x* and Repository Browser in Release 4.*x*. When you create an object or a component of an object in Object Navigator, the object is stored in the repository of SAP and is called a development object or a repository object. Development or repository objects are arranged in a list format, also called an object list. When you open an application, ABAP Workbench automatically opens the application in the development tool with which that object has been created.

Object Navigator is a central area of ABAP Workbench, from where you can open various browers for various development processes, including

- `Multipurpose Internet Mail Extension Files (MIME) Repository`—Displays all directories that store MIME objects, downloaded or imported from external sources in an SAP system.
- `Repository Browser`—Displays repository objects in the form of object lists on the basis of their searching category. The searching category for the repository objects can be a package, program, or class.
- `Repository Information System`—Displays the information of all the repository objects. Unlike the Repository Browser, the Repository Information System is not dependent on the selection of repository objects.
- `Tag Browser`—Displays tags for web applications.
- `Transport Organizer`—Displays the output of a user request sent to it.
- `Test Repository`—Displays the result after testing repository objects.

To open the Object Navigator screen, either select SAP menu > Tools > ABAP Workbench > Overview > Object Navigator in the `SAP Easy Access` screen or enter the `SE80` transaction code in the `Command` field and press the ENTER key. Figure 4.13 shows the Object Navigator screen:

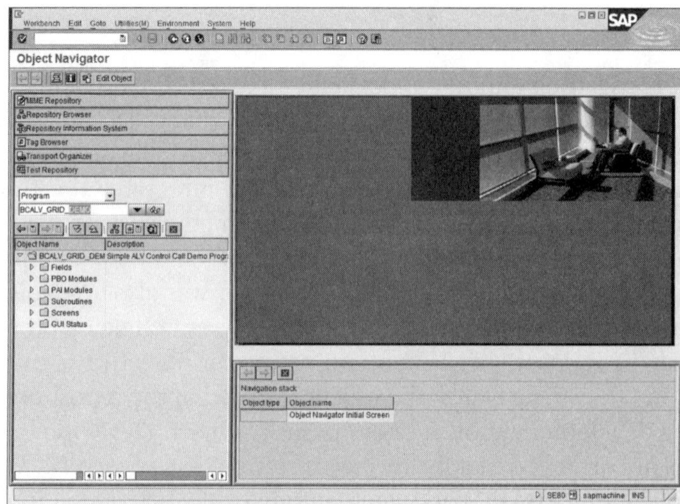

FIGURE 4.13 **Displaying the object navigator screen**

The Object Navigator screen acts as a common interface to access any application or object in an SAP system.

Object Navigator Interface

The following user interface areas appear when a user accesses ABAP Workbench through Object Navigator:

- **Navigation area**—Contains different browsers that allow you to display the development objects and open the tools associated with these objects to modify them.
- **Tools area**—Contains necessary tools to edit a development object.
- **Integrated window**—Displays the result after syntax check-ups, navigation stack, and worklist.
- **Additional dialog box**—Appears when you open an object in a new session.

Figure 4.14 shows the different areas of Object Navigator:

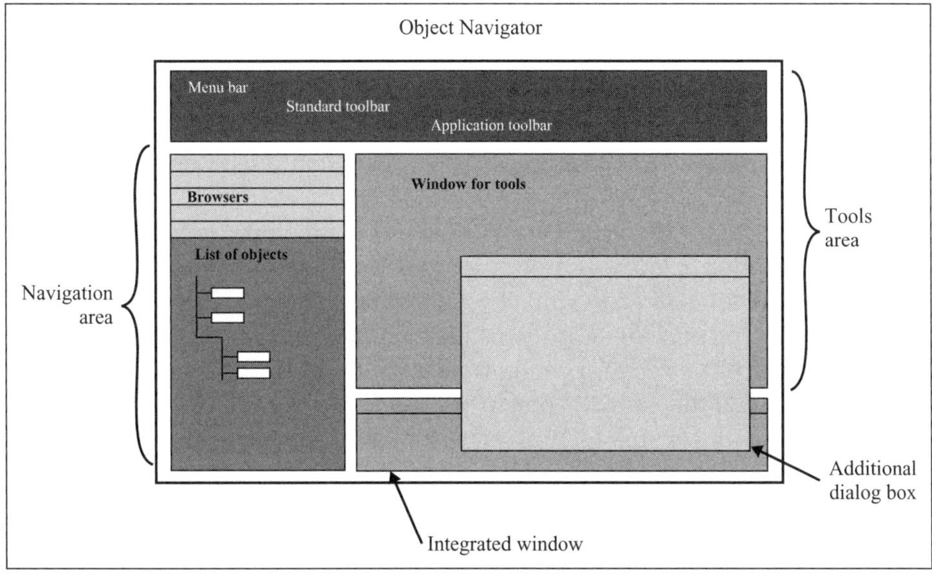

FIGURE 4.14 **Displaying the different areas of object navigator**

As shown in Figure 4.14, the two main areas of Object Navigator are the Navigation area and Tools area. The Navigation area is used to display the lists of development objects in a hierarchical order. The Tools area provides a window to open a development object. These areas are not interconnected, meaning that any change in one area is not reflected in the other area. Moreover, in both areas, you can select functions from a context menu. The options available in the context menu are different for the different development objects.

Object Navigator facilitates users to perform the following tasks:

- Select a browser and navigate in the object list
- Use the tools for development objects
- Navigate from one window to another window
- Perform syntax checks in the Integrated window
- Open an object in a new session using an Additional dialog box

As stated earlier, development objects are displayed in Repository Browser of Object Navigator in the form of object lists. An object list arranges the development objects in hierarchical order on the basis of a specified category. In Object Navigator, you can display the development objects by selecting a category from the folowing:

- **Application Hierarchy Tool**—Displays a list of applications in hierarchical order in an SAP system.
- **Package**—Displays a list of all development objects in a package.
- **Program**—Displays a list of elements of an ABAP program.
- **Function group**—Displays a list of function modules and their elements, related to a function group.
- **Class/interface**—Displays a list of all the components of a global class or interface. It also displays a list of superclasses of a class and the methods that are redefined in the class.
- **Internet service**—Displays a list of all elements of an Internet service, which includes service description, themes, Hypertext Markup Language (HTML) templates, and MIME objects.
- **Business Server Pages (BSP) application**—Displays a list of elements of a BSP application.
- **Local objects**—Displays a list of local objects created in a program. All displayed local objects belong to the $TMP

package and cannot be transported from one computer to another. In an SAP system, local objects are created for the temporary purpose of testing a program. However, you can assign a local object to a package to transport.

- **Inactive objects**—Displays a list of all inactive objects, including local and transportable objects.

Message Maintenance

Messages help an SAP system communicate with the users. For example, error messages display if the users make invalid entries on a screen, making the users aware that a wrong entry has been made. These messages are displayed by using a message class. Each message class has an ID and usually contains a set of messages. A message contains a single text line and may contain placeholders for variables.

To open the initial screen of Message Maintenance, either select `SAP Menu > Tools > ABAP Workbench > Development > Programming Environment > Messages` in the `SAP Easy Access` screen or enter the `SE91` transaction code in the `Command` field and press the `ENTER` key. Figure 4.15 shows the initial screen of Message Maintenance:

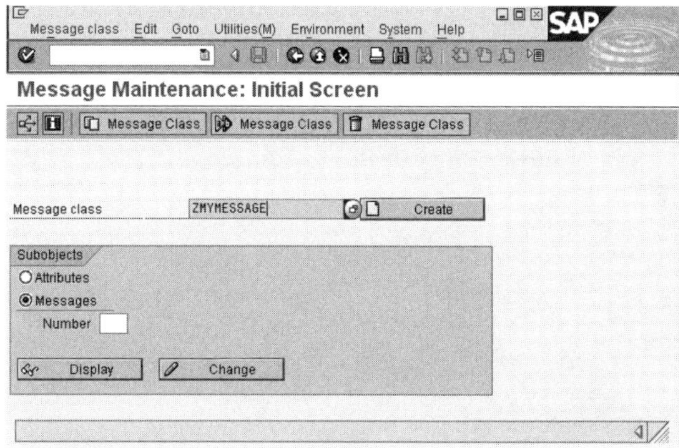

FIGURE 4.15 **Showing the initial screen of message maintenance**

After you have created a message, you can use it in a program with the help of the `MESSAGE` statement.

ABAP Text Elements

The text elements of program texts in different languages can be maintained easily with the help of a tool known as Text Elements. The text, which is displayed by a program on a screen, is called a text element. Creation, maintenance, and translation of the text elements can be done with the help of the Text Element Maintenance tool. The following are the various types of text elements:

- **Text symbols**—Used by the Write statement.
- **List and column headers**—Appear in an ABAP list.
- **Selection texts**—Appear on selection screens.

The place where the text elements are stored is known as a Text Pool. You can change the text element without changing the source code of the program. A user can also design some standard text elements to use them in other programs.

The initial screen of Text Elements can be started either from the `SAP Easy Access` screen, or from Repository Browser. To open the screen to create text elements in ABAP, either select `SAP Menu > Tools > ABAP Workbench > Develop-ment > Programming Environment > Text Elements` in the `SAP Easy Access` screen or enter the `SE32` transaction code in the `Command` field and press the `ENTER` key. Figure 4.16 shows the SAP screen to create a text element:

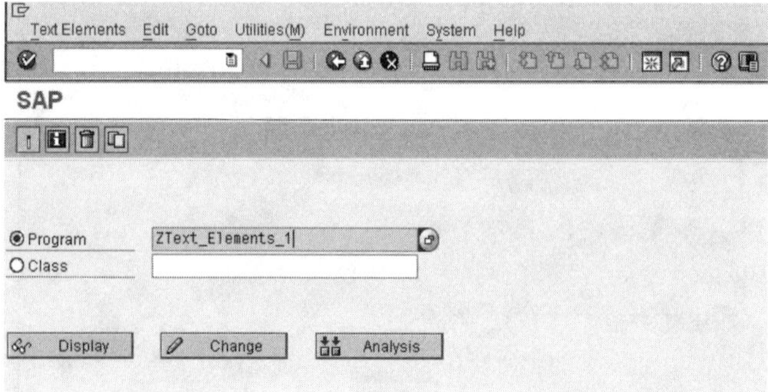

FIGURE 4.16 **Displaying the screen of the text elements**

In Figure 4.16, notice that the SAP screen contains the `Program` field, where you enter the name of an ABAP text element. For instance, `ZText_`

Elements_1 is entered in the Program field (see Figure 4.15). You then click either the Create button to create the text element or the Display button to display and edit the already maintained text elements in the display mode or the Change button.

> **Note:** In Figure 4.16, you'll notice there is a text field next to the Class radio button. This text field accepts the name of an object type (a class or interface). The name can consist of alphanumeric characters with the special characters underscore (_) and forward slash (/). However, the name must not begin with a digit.

Maintain Transaction

Maintain Transaction is an ABAP Workbench tool used to create and manage user-defined transactions. To open the Maintain Transaction screen, either select SAP Menu > Tools > ABAP Workbench > Development > Other Tools > Transactions in the SAP Easy Access screen or enter the SE93 transaction code in the Command field and press the ENTER key. Figure 4.17 shows the Maintain Transaction screen:

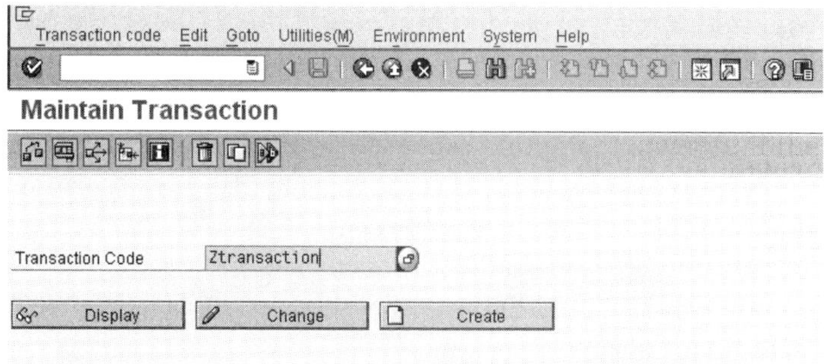

FIGURE 4.17 **Displaying the maintain transaction screen**

In Figure 4.17, you can see that the Maintain Transaction screen contains a transaction code name, Ztransaction, in the Transaction Code field. You can either click the Create button to create a user-defined transaction code or the Display and Change buttons to display and modify the contents of the given transaction code, respectively. In the Maintain

`Transaction` screen, you can create the transaction code for various types of transactions. Table 4.3 lists various types of transactions:

Transaction Type	Description
Dialog Transaction	Assigns a transaction code to a dialog program.
Report Transaction	Assigns a transaction code to either an executable program or a report.
Object-Oriented Transaction	Assigns a transaction code to a method of a class in ABAP objects.
Variant Transaction	Executes the dialog transaction with the transaction variant. In Variant Transaction, you can assign default values to the input fields of screens, change the attributes of screen elements, and hide entire screens.
Parameter Transaction	Fills the parameters in the input fields of dialog transactions.

TABLE 4.3 A list of transaction types

DESCRIBING PACKAGE BUILDER

Package Builder is a tool used to implement the concept of a package in ABAP Workbench. A package is a type of development object that acts as a container to store development objects, such as function modules, screens, menus, and transactions. Package Builder, provided by the SAP system, is used to develop and manage the development classes. Package Builder is also used to transfer existing development objects to other existing packages.

Package Builder is started by entering the `SPACKAGE` or `SE21` transaction code in the `Command` field and pressing the `ENTER` key. Figure 4.18 shows the initial screen of Package Builder:

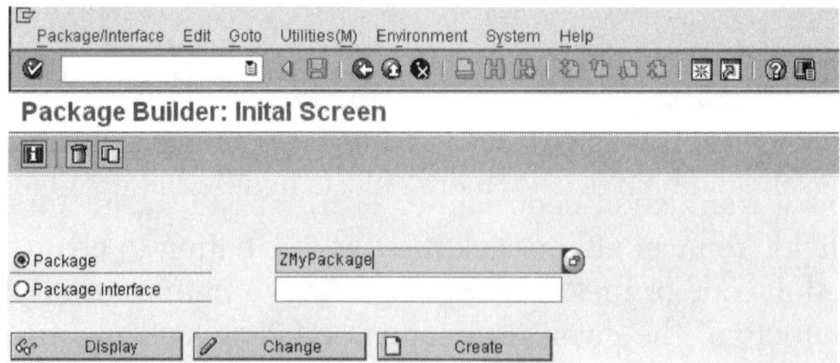

FIGURE 4.18 **Displaying the initial screen of package builder**

Some common tasks that are performed by using the Package Builder tool are:

- Creating packages and subpackages
- Specifying a package hierarchy
- Defining package interfaces for potential users
- Adding the elements to package interfaces
- Defining user access for user packages
- Restricting the use of interfaces to selected users
- Creating structure packages and defining filter package interfaces

Types of Packages

Package Builder creates two types of packages: provider (server) packages and user (client) packages. The provider package provides development elements, such as function modules, BAPIs, classes, ABAP programs, and types, to other packages by using one or more interfaces. A provider package can also be a user package, utilizing the services of other packages. In the case of a user package, you define user access for the visible elements of another package allotted to the interface.

Tasks Performed by Provider Packages

The provider package performs two tasks: creating a package and defining a package hierarchy. The main purpose of these tasks is to assign and create a structure for the packages. In the package hierarchy, there are various levels, and the top level is constructed with the help of structure packages that contain several other main packages. In addition, each main package has associated subpackages. You can find the total number of subpackages in a main package and display the levels up to which these subpackages are nested in the main package. Package interfaces are designed to provide easy access to the package elements from outside the package.

The second task is to help access the content of one package from other packages with the help of package interfaces. In other words, the package interfaces help define development objects in different packages.

Tasks Performed by User Packages

Similar to provider packages, the user package provides a structure for packages. In this case, the top level in the package hierarchy is also formed by structure packages, which generally contain main packages, and then the associated subpackages are created within the main packages.

TESTING TOOLS IN ABAP WORKBENCH

In ABAP Workbench, testing tools are used to check or test the code entered by the user. The following testing tools are used in ABAP Workbench:

- **ABAP Debugger**—Executes the ABAP program line by line or section by section.
- **ABAP Runtime Analysis**—Shows the overall duration consumed in the processing of the source code.
- **Performance Analysis**—Displays the performance of the system while accessing databases, performing locking activities, and making remote calls to reports and transactions.

Now, let's discuss these testing tools in detail, one by one.

ABAP Debugger

ABAP Debugger enables step-by-step processing of the source code of ABAP programs. ABAP Debugger interrupts the processing of an ABAP program at each step, which allows users to check the processing logic of the ABAP program. Apart from checking the processing logic, users can use ABAP Debugger to check the outcome of the individual statements used in the ABAP program. It also helps the user understand the flow of logic of the programs and displaying the data objects. You can start ABAP Debugger by doing either of the following:

- Setting a breakpoint and then running the ABAP program
- Running the ABAP program directly in debugging mode

Setting a Breakpoint and Then Running the ABAP Program

A breakpoint can be set in an ABAP program (in active mode) either by selecting `Utilities > Breakpoint > Set/Delete` or by using the `BREAK` statement directly. In addition to this, the breakpoint can also be set in the ABAP program by clicking the `Set/Delete Session Breakpoint` icon. After setting the breakpoint, the ABAP program is directly executed either by clicking the `Direct Processing` icon or by pressing the F8 key.

Running the ABAP Program in Debugging Mode

An ABAP program can be executed directly in debugging mode through any of the following ways:

- Writing the /h system command in the Command field and pressing the ENTER key. The debugging mode is switched on.
- Setting the breakpoints at the key statements.

ABAP Runtime Analysis

Runtime Analysis, another tool of ABAP Workbench, is used to trace the time duration and performance of the ABAP source code. To open the initial screen of ABAP Runtime Analysis, either select SAP Menu > Tools > ABAP Workbench > Test > Runtime Analysis in the SAP Easy Access screen or enter the SE30 transaction code in the Command field and press the ENTER key. Figure 4.19 shows the initial screen of ABAP Runtime Analysis:

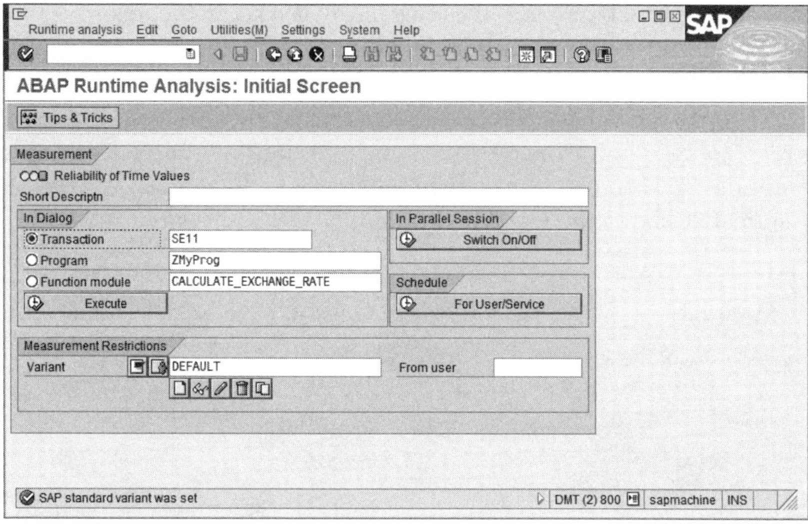

FIGURE 4.19 **Displaying the initial screen of ABAP runtime analysis**

The ABAP Runtime Analysis screen allows you to display the following:

- The execution time of each statement in a program.
- The tables accessed at run time.

- The execution time of all the statements. You can also group the statements based on the type of command.
- The execution time of each statement in the order in which they have been executed.
- The level of nesting of statements within subroutines.

With large applications, it is suggested that users analyze the entire application at the end. Now you can carry out the analysis and display, and interpret the results by doing the runtime analysis of programs with the help of the Runtime Analysis tool. Runtime Analysis also makes it possible to analyze the Web Dynpro ABAP and Business Server Pages (BSP) applications.

Performance Analysis

Performance Analysis, another tool of ABAP Workbench, performs a wide range of functions used to supervise and examine the performance of the system while accessing databases, performing locking activities, and remotely calling reports and transactions. It also uses the trace file, which keeps the record of the database accesses, reports or transactions, and then displays the performance log as a list. The Performance Analysis tool also helps analyze a trace file individually.

To open the Performance Analysis screen, either select `SAP Menu>Tools>ABAP Workbench>Test>SQL Trace` in the `SAP Easy Access` screen or enter the `ST05` transaction code in the `Command` field and press the `ENTER` key. Figure 4.20 shows the `Performance Analysis` screen:

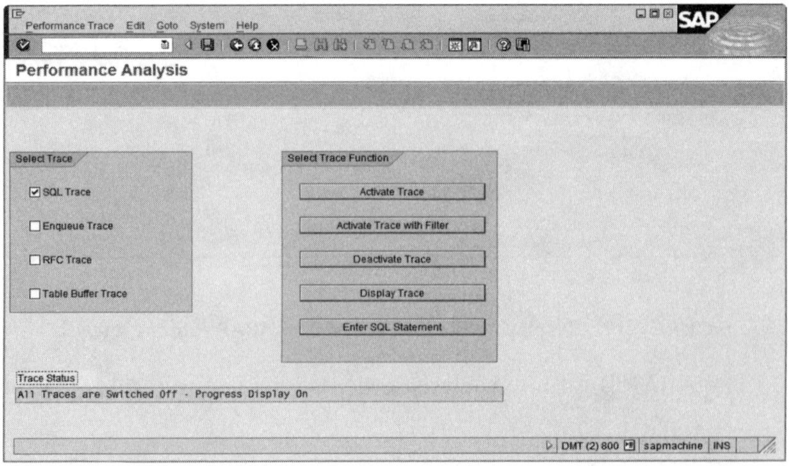

FIGURE 4.20 **Displaying the screen of performance analysis**

In Figure 4.20, the following types of traces are available in the `Performance Analysis` screen:

- **SQL Trace**—Keeps track of the various database accesses of reports and transactions.
- **Enqueue Trace**—Monitors the locking system.
- **RFC Trace**—Provides information about the remote function calls.
- **Table Buffer Trace**—Monitors the database calls of reports and transactions made through the table buffer.

DESCRIBING WEB SERVICES

A web service is defined as an independent and self-sustained unit of a software application hosted on the Internet. These self-sustained units of the software application collectively implement specific functionalities to execute the business logic of the application. You can use a web service to implement various functionalities, such as preparing the pay slips for the employees of an organization, calculating the income tax, and sending a price query to a material provider.

Web services solve the problem of integrating diverse computer applications that have been developed independently and run on a variety of software and hardware platforms. They allow applications to expose business operations to other applications, regardless of their implementation, by using the following standards:

- **Extensible Markup Language (XML)**—Represents the common markup language for communication.
- **Simple Object Access Protocol (SOAP)**—Specifies the common message format to exchange information.
- **Web Service Description Language (WSDL)**—Represents the common service specification format.
- **Universal Description, Discovery, and Integration (UDDI)**—Specifies a platform-independent framework to describe services, discover businesses, and integrate business services by using the Internet.

In addition to a common message format and markup language, there must be a general format that all service providers can use to specify service details, such as the service type, the service parameters, and the method of accessing the service.

The development and deployment of web services is governed by a standardization committee. Some enhanced standards, such as security standards or additional protocols, are continuously being updated and integrated into Web Service Framework by SAP. In the SAP system, ABAP Workbench provides an environment where you can publish a web service easily as well as call the web service. ABAP Workbench enables SAP Web Application Builder to act as a platform for web services, Internet Transactions Services (ITS) based web applications, and Business Service Pages (BSP) applications.

Web Application Builder for ITS

Web Application Builder acts as the platform to develop ITS based web applications. It also allows you to create web development objects, such as service files, HTML templates, and MIME objects. These web development objects are created as Repository objects, which are published on an ITS server. You can perform the following actions by using Web Application Builder for ITS:

- Create the Internet services for existing SAP transactions.
- Create and edit HTML templates for the screens of a transaction. An HTML template contains HTML and HTMLBusiness statements.
- Create objects for JavaScript files, which include MIME objects (icons, graphical images, and Java applets), to improve the layout.
- Create language-specific text.
- Create language-specific MIME objects.
- Execute a web application.

> **Note:** To open a Web application by logging on to a SAP system, the Internet Transaction Server (ITS) requires a relevant Internet service.

Note that Web Application Builder neither provides the syntax check facility for HTML or HTMLBusiness, nor does it provide debugger connections for HTMLBusiness.

Web Application Builder for BSP

Release 6.10 of the SAP system introduced another independent platform known as Web Application Builder, which is used to develop web applications based on the mySAP.com application server. web Application Builder is fully integrated into Object Navigator (SE80). New types of web applications are developed by Web Application Builder, popularly known as BSP applications. The following actions are supported by Web Application Builder for BSP:

- Creating BSP applications and their pages
- Editing the layout of BSPs by using HTML and the scripting languages such as ABAP and JavaScript
- Declaring the page-based data storage parameters related to the page
- Implementing the event handlers by using ABAP
- Defining page flow by using navigation requests
- Integrating the MIME Repository to store MIME objects
- Creating and defining themes for the layout adjustments
- Implementing the layout by using external tools

Note: MIME Repository is a logical container that stores MIME objects, such as graphical images, icons, and style sheets, in an SAP system. All the objects stored in MIME Repository are arranged in a hierarchical order and can be displayed in a browser.

BSP Applications

A BSP application is an SAP application created by some external tools, such as Adobe GoLive, Dreamweaver, and Microsoft FrontPage 2000. The two main components of a BSP application are BSPs and MIME objects.

The user interface of a BSP application includes:

- Static websites
- Dynamically generated websites that are BSPs or templates that contain server-side scripting
- Various MIME objects, such as pictures, icons, sound files, and style sheets, that are part of a typical web application

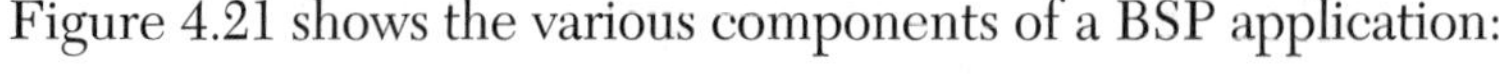

Figure 4.21 shows the various components of a BSP application:

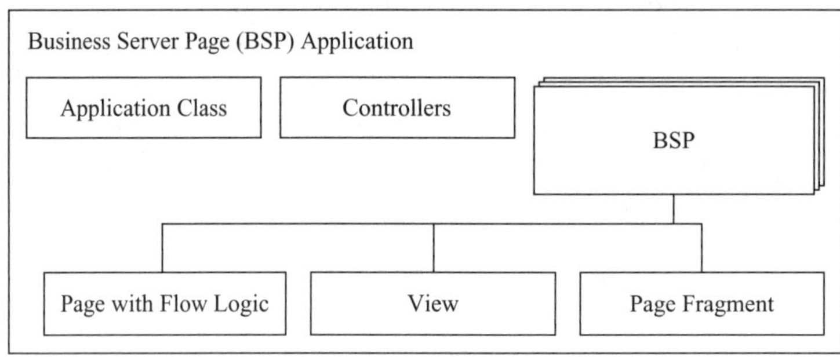

FIGURE 4.21 **Showing the structure of a BSP application**

In Figure 4.21, you can see that the structure of a BSP application contains one or more controllers and BSPs (including the elements, such as application classes, MIME objects, and themes).

> **Note:** BSPs can have different characteristics, such as a page with flow logic, a view, and a page fragment.

DESCRIBING XSLT EDITOR

Extensible Stylesheet Language Transformations (XSLT) XSLT Editor is a development tool, integrated in to ABAP Workbench, that is used to define Extensible Stylesheet Language (XSL) transformations. XSL transformations are executed on the Application server. Using XSLT Editor, the XML documents can be transformed into either XML or HTML documents, or ABAP data structures. Note that an XSLT program must be a repository object to define the transformation rules.

To call XSLT Editor, start Object Navigator by using the `SE80` transaction, select the package in Repository Browser, and double-click the required XSLT program under XSLT Transformations. XSLT Editor helps perform the following operations:

- Creating XSLT programs to define transformation rules
- Editing the source text by using Tag Browsers (XSLT, HTML, WML, or XHTML)

- Checking and activating XSLT programs
- Testing XSL transformations
- Creating breakpoints to debug XSL transformations

SUMMARY

In this chapter, you have learned about ABAP Workbench, which is a programming environment for ABAP applications. The text also explained the tools available in ABAP Workbench, such as ABAP Dictionary, ABAP Editor, Screen Painter, and Menu Painter. In addition, the chapter described the role of Package Builder and explained the testing tools of ABAP Workbench, such as ABAP Debugger and Runtime Analysis, which are used to test and check the ABAP code written by users. Further, you also learned about web services and that ABAP Workbench offers an environment where you can publish, search, or call the web services. Finally, the chapter described XSLT Editor, which is a development tool to define XSL transformations.

Chapter 5

ABAP Dictionary

If you need information on:	*See page:*
Overview of ABAP Dictionary	124
Exploring Domains	125
Exploring Data Types	138
Exploring Type Groups	145
Exploring Database Tables	146
Exploring Views	180
Exploring Search Helps	212
Exploring Lock Objects	215

ABAP Dictionary, a tool of ABAP Workbench, is used to store the description of data definitions. Using ABAP Dictionary, you can create and maintain user-defined types, such as data elements, structures, and table types, which are used in ABAP programs to declare their respective objects. In addition, ABAP Dictionary is used to create and maintain database objects, such as tables and views. ABAP Dictionary also provides several services that support program development. For example, you can set or release locks while executing database objects, define an input help (F4 help), or attach a field help (F1 help) with a field on a screen.

ABAP Dictionary is integrated completely in the development and runtime environments of the SAP system. This means any changes made to a data definition are reflected in all the related ABAP programs, function modules, menus, and screens. In addition, ABAP Dictionary ensures data integrity and manages all the data definitions without redundancy.

In this chapter, you learn about ABAP Dictionary, which acts as a storage medium for the data of an SAP system. This chapter also discusses domains, which are used to define the characteristics of fields, such as data type and value range. Next, you learn about data elements, which are used to assign a description to a field in a database table. You also learn about different kinds of tables used in ABAP Dictionary and how to create them. This chapter also describes foreign keys used to relate tables, and different kinds of table fields and views. Next, you learn about search helps, which help view the possible set of values for a field. The chapter concludes with a discussion of the Lock Object, used to synchronize simultaneous access to the same data records by multiple users.

OVERVIEW OF ABAP DICTIONARY

ABAP Dictionary is a central storage area for the description of various types of repository objects in an SAP system. The repository objects include database tables, views, data types, type groups, domains, search helps, and lock objects. You can access the repository objects in an SAP system from the initial screen of ABAP Dictionary. The initial screen of ABAP Dictionary can be opened from the `SAP Easy Access` screen, by entering the `SE11` transaction in the `Command` field on the standard toolbar and then pressing the `ENTER` key, or by clicking the `Enter` (✓) icon. Figure 5.1 displays the initial screen of ABAP Dictionary:

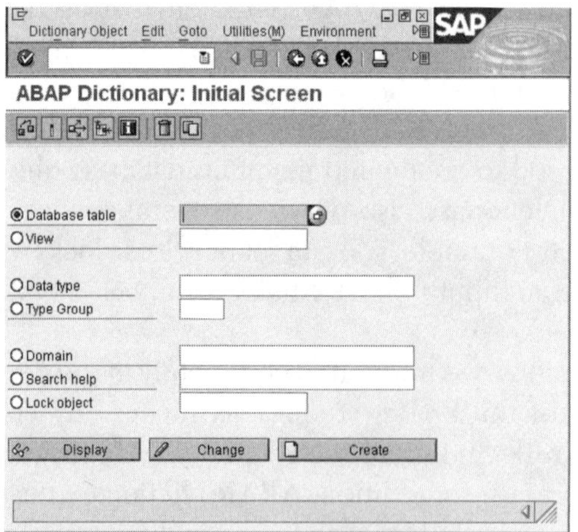

FIGURE 5.1 **The initial screen of ABAP dictionary**

Table 5.1 lists the ABAP Dictionary repository objects with their descriptions:

ABAP Dictionary Repository Object	Description
Domain	Describes the technical attributes of a field, such as the data type of the field or a fixed range of values accepted by the field.
Data Type	Creates user-defined data types, such as data elements, structures, and tables.
Type Group	Creates a group of data types in ABAP Dictionary.
Database Table	Helps design tables. Note that the name of the table should begin with either the letter Y or Z, and its length can be up to 16 characters, including Y and Z.
View	Retrieves data from database tables. A view acts as a virtual table because it does not store the data physically.
Search Help	Defines input help (F4 helps) for the fields of a database table. Input help provides a set of valid values that you can enter for a field.
Lock Object	Synchronizes simultaneous access of the same set of data records by multiple users.

TABLE 5.1 Descriptions of the ABAP dictionary repository objects

Now, let's explore each of these objects in detail.

EXPLORING DOMAINS

A domain is used to define a data type, length, and value range for a table field. The fields of a table and the fields of a structure that uses a domain automatically get the value range as defined in the domain. In other words, the relationship between the field and the domain is defined by the data element of the field. If you make any changes in a domain, the attributes of the fields related to that domain change accordingly. You can link any number of data elements with a single domain. Figure 5.2 displays the relationship between a data element and a domain:

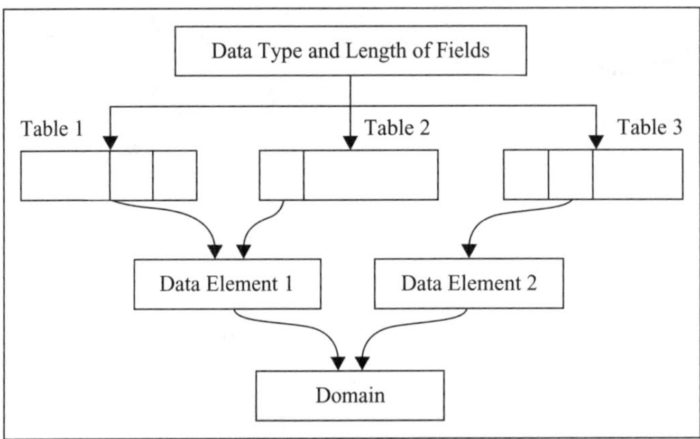

FIGURE 5.2 **Flowchart showing the relationship between domain, data elements, and tables**

You can also set a filter to check the values entered in a field. For this, you need to create a table called the Value table which checks every field value against some specified criteria mentioned in the Value table. In addition, a conversion routine can be assigned to a domain, which converts field values from display format to internal format (as discussed later in this chapter) for the fields referring to a domain.

Now, let's discuss the following topics in the context of domains:

- Describing fixed values for domains
- Exploring conversion routines for domains
- Creating a domain
- Modifying the existing domain
- Deleting a domain

Describing Fixed Values for Domains

You can assign certain fixed values specifying a value range, such as data type and length, to a domain. These fixed values are used as an input check for the fields on a screen; that is, they provide a set of data for users to select among. Fixed values also act as the source of input help (F4) provided to the fields in case no input (F1) help is maintained for the fields. Fixed values can be defined by specifying either single values or the lower and upper limits for the fields. In addition to this, you can also assign a short text to the fixed values assigned. These short descriptions can be viewed when the input help for the field is called. Some data types for which the fixed values can be defined are `CHAR`, `NUMC`, `DEC`, `INT1`, `INT2`, and `INT4`.

Sometimes you need to specify a large number of fixed values. In such cases, you can store these values in the Value table, which are used to verify the fields against the values contained in the fields of some other table.

Exploring Conversion Routines for Domains

The data entered in an SAP system is not stored in the original format in the SAP database; however, it needs to be in a format compatible with the SAP database. One example of this is the FTIME screen field, which stores the time of login in the HHH:MM (hours:minutes) format. Now, let's suppose that a user enters a login time as 2:45 in the screen field. When this value of the screen field is stored in the SAP database, it is converted to an integer number, such as 165 minutes (2 hours and 45 minutes). However, when you retrieve this data, it is again displayed in its original format, HHH:MM (hours:minutes). The conversion of values from one format to another is performed by the conversion routine assigned to a domain, which in turn is related to the screen field.

Conversion routines are defined by a five-place name and are stored as a group of two function modules, `CONVERSION_EXIT_xxxxx_INPUT` and `CONVERSION_EXIT_xxxxx_OUTPUT`.

The INPUT function module converts the contents of a screen field from the display format to the SAP internal format, and the OUTPUT function module converts the content from the SAP internal format to the display format.

> **Note:** The `CONVERSION_EXIT_xxxxx_INPUT` and `CONVERSION_EXIT_xxxxx_OUTPUT` function modules have a fixed naming convention.

Creating a Domain

Domains are created to define the technical characteristics of a field.

Perform the following steps to create a domain in ABAP Dictionary:

1. Select the `Domain` radio button on the initial screen of ABAP Dictionary, as shown in Figure 5.3:

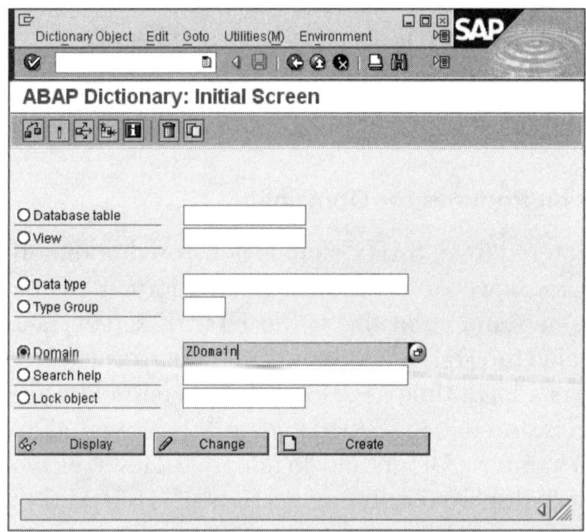

FIGURE 5.3 **Creating a domain**

2. Enter the name of the domain to be created. In our case, we enter the name as `ZDomain` (see Figure 5.3).
3. Click the `Create` button (Figure 5.3).

The `Dictionary: Maintain Domain` screen appears, as shown in Figure 5.4.

4. In the `Dictionary: Maintain Domain` screen, enter a short description for the domain in the `Short Description` field. In our case, we have entered the short description as Domain storing Toy Descriptions. In the `Format` group box, enter CHAR and 30 in the `Data Type` and `No. Characters` fields, respectively. In addition, specify the value 30 in the `Output Length` field of the `Output Characteristics` group box, as shown in Figure 5.4:

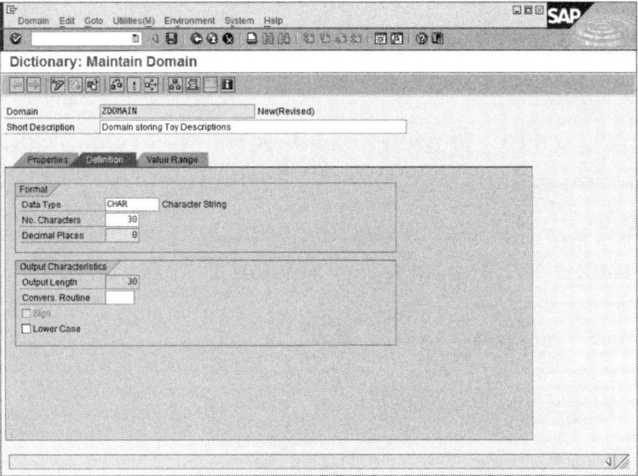

FIGURE 5.4 **Screen for domain maintenance**

5. Select the `Value Range` tab. The screen containing the options related to the `Value Range` tab appears (see Figure 5.5). Enter the values in the `Single Vals` section, as shown in Figure 5.5:

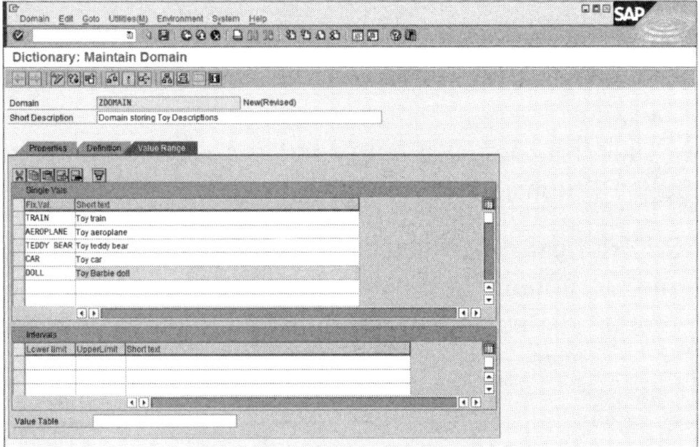

FIGURE 5.5 **The maintenance screen for the value range tab**

Note: It is not mandatory to define a value range for a domain.

The screen shown in Figure 5.5 displays the fixed values along with their short description under the `Single Vals` section.

6. Click the `Save` (💾) icon to save the domain. The `Create Object Directory Entry` dialog box appears, as shown in Figure 5.6:

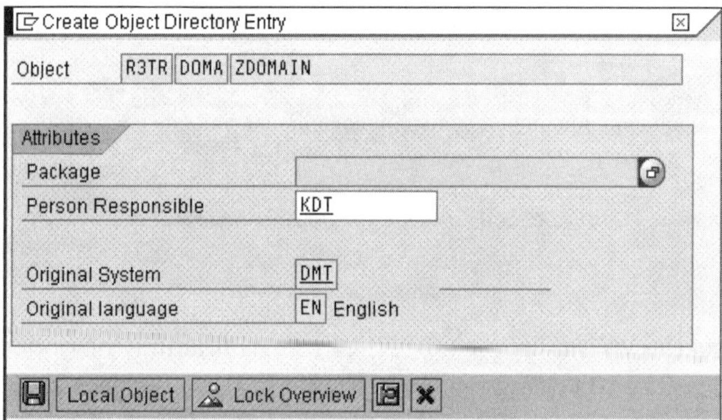

FIGURE 5.6 **The create object directory entry dialog box**

7. Click the `Local Object` button in the `Create Object Directory Entry` dialog box.
8. Finally, click the `Check` (icon) and `Activate` (icon) icons to check the syntax of the `ZDOMAIN` domain and activate it, respectively.

The `ZDOMAIN` domain is now activated and ready to be used with any number of fields. It must be noted that the domain is saved as a local object, which means that it cannot be shared among multiple SAP servers.

Note: You can make repository objects accessible over a network by storing them in a package.

Perform the following steps to create a package:

1. Open Object Navigator by entering the `SE80` transaction code on the `SAP Easy Access` screen.
2. Select `Package` as the object type and enter a name for the package to be created. In this case, we have named the package as `ZKOG_PCKG`, as shown in Figure 5.7:

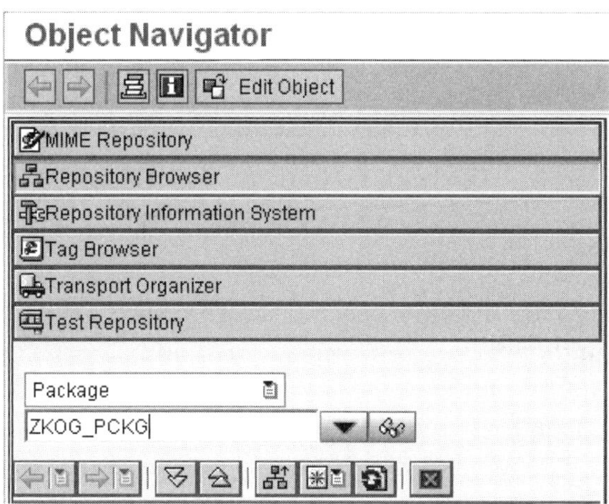

FIGURE 5.7 **Creating a package**

3. Click the `Display` ( ) icon.

The `Create Object` dialog box appears, as shown in Figure 5.8:

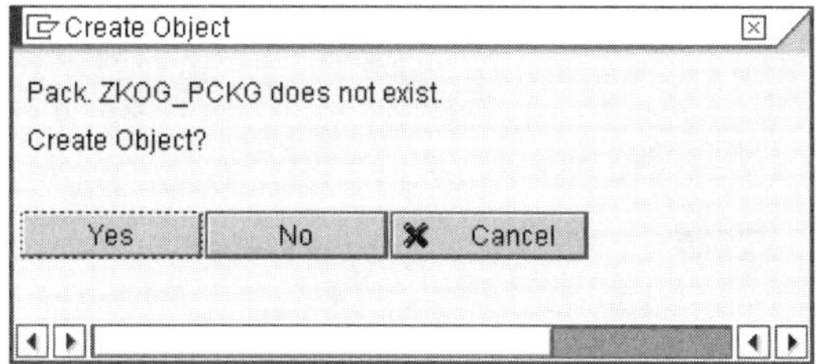

FIGURE 5.8 **Creating an object**

4. Click the `Yes` button to create the package.

The `Package Builder: Create Package` dialog box appears, as shown in Figure 5.9:

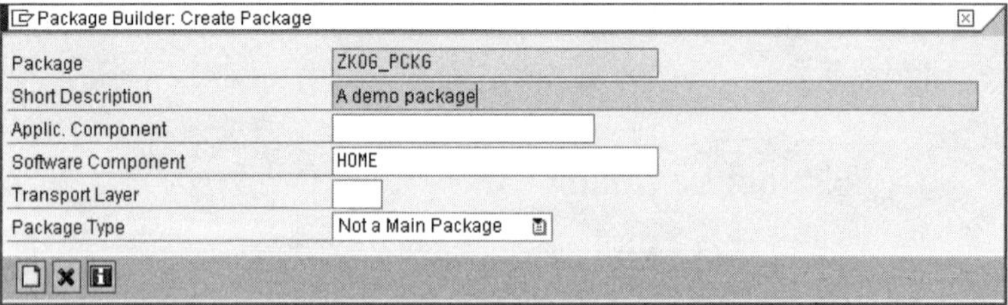

FIGURE 5.9 **Creating a package**

5. Enter the text, A demo package, in the `Short Description` field and HOME in the `Software Component` field.
6. Select "Not a Main Package" as the type of the package and then click the `Save` (▢) icon to save the package (see Figure 5.9).

The `Prompt for Local Workbench Request` dialog box appears, as shown in Figure 5.10:

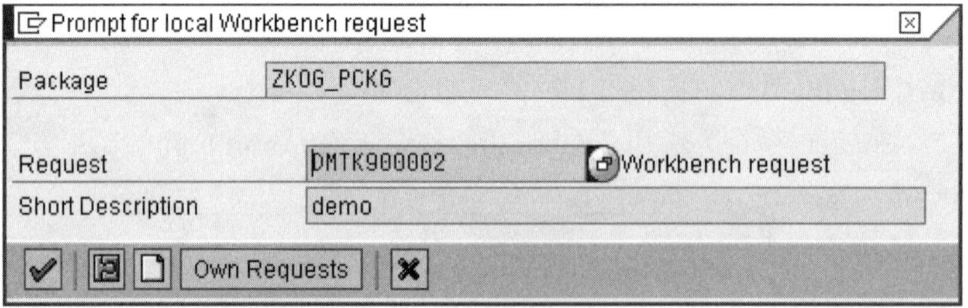

FIGURE 5.10 **Displaying the request number**

The screen shown in Figure 5.10 displays the name and description of the package, along with the automatically generated workbench request number.

7. Click the `Continue` (✔) icon (Figure 5.10).

The `Object Navigator` screen with the package name, `ZKOG_PCKG`, appears, as shown in Figure 5.11:

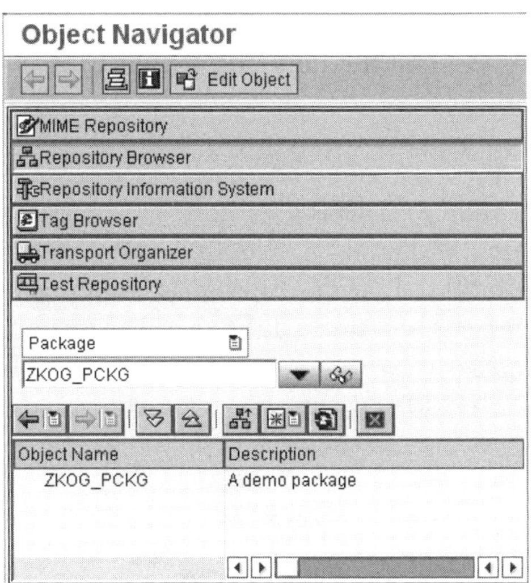

FIGURE 5.11 **Showing the created package**

The `ZKOG_PCKG` package is now created and can be used for storing repository objects.

Note: Hereafter, we will save all the repository objects in this package. The repository objects can be saved in a package by providing the name of the package in the `Package` field (Figure 5.6) and then clicking the `Save` (💾) icon. In addition, any repository object created in the forthcoming chapters will also be saved in this package.

Modifying the Existing Domain

You can modify the characteristics of an already created domain. The attributes, such as data type, number of characters, and number of decimal places, can be modified by making changes in the relevant fields in the `Dictionary: Maintain Domain` screen (shown previously in Figure 5.4). The changes are reflected in all the database tables that contain any field related to the modified domain.

You can modify an existing domain by performing the following steps:

1. Select the `Domain` radio button on the initial screen of ABAP Dictionary, and enter the name of the domain that has to be modified. In our case, we enter the name as `ZDomain` and click the `Change` button (Figure 5.3).

The `Dictionary: Maintain Domain` screen appears (see Figure 5.4).

2. In the `Dictionary: Maintain Domain` screen, you can modify the short description for the domain in the `Short Description` field. In our case, we have entered the short description as Creating a Domain. In the `Format` group box, change the values of the `Data Type` and `No. Characters` fields to "CHAR" and "40", respectively. In addition, specify the value 40 in the `Output Length` field of the `Output Characteristics` group box, as shown in Figure 5.12:

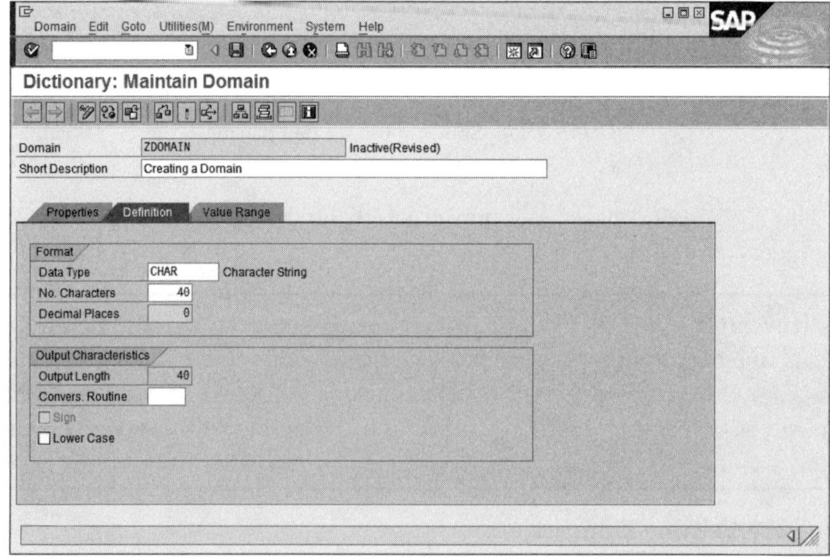

FIGURE 5.12 **Modifying the description and other field values of a domain**

3. In the `Dictionary: Maintain Domain` screen, select the `Value Range` tab and modify the values in the `Single Vals` section, as shown in Figure 5.13:

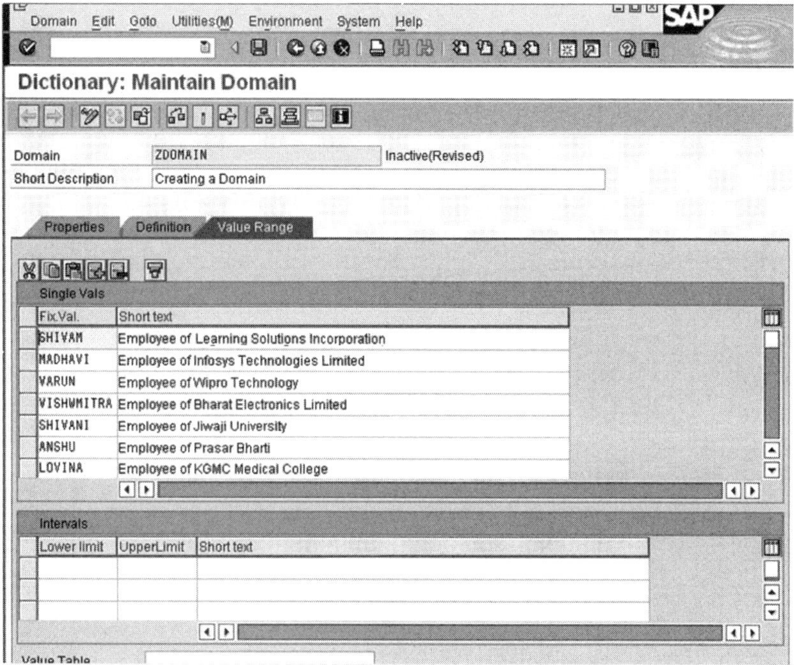

FIGURE 5.13 **Modifying the range of values of a domain**

4. Finally, click the `Save` icon to save the domain, and click the `Check` and `Activate` icons to check the syntax of the `ZDOMAIN` domain and activate it, respectively.

You should note that sometimes when you modify a domain related to a database table, the modification can affect that database table. This is because the modification in a domain attribute can also affect the attributes of the database table, such as data type of fields, number of characters to be displayed in a field, output attributes, and value table.

Perform the following steps to view the database tables related to a specific domain after modifying the domain:

1. Select the `Domain` radio button on the initial screen of ABAP Dictionary. Enter the name of the domain whose attributes need to be changed (in this case, `ZMYDOMAIN`), in the `Domain` field and click the `Display` button.

The `Dictionary: Maintain Domain` screen appears.

2. In the `Dictionary: Maintain Domain` screen, click the `Where-Used List` (icon) icon.

The `Where-Used List Domain` dialog box appears, as shown in Figure 5.14:

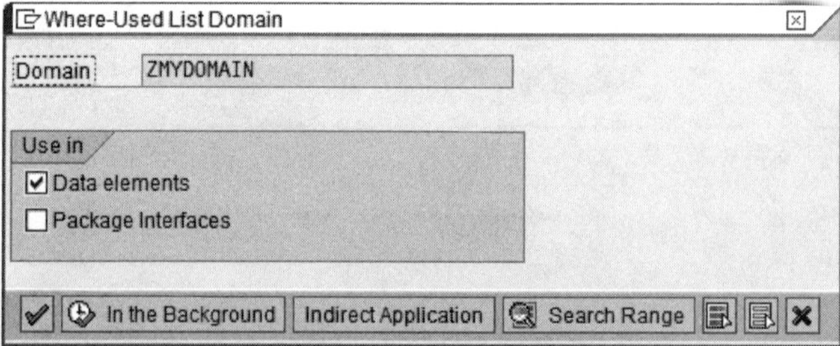

FIGURE 5.14 **The where-used list domain dialog box**

3. In the `Where-Used List Domain` dialog box, click the `Indirect Application` button (Figure 5.14).

The `Where-Used List Domain` dialog box displays the information related to the domain, as shown in Figure 5.15:

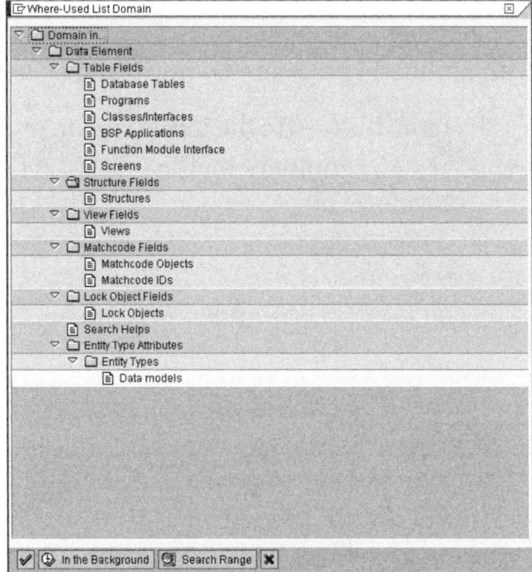

FIGURE 5.15 **Selecting database tables**

4. Select the `Database Tables` option from the `Table Fields` folder and then click the `Continue` (✔) icon (see Figure 5.15).

The `Where-used Domain ZMYDOMAIN in Database tables (2 Hits)` screen appears, displaying the names of dependent database tables using the domain.

Figure 5.16 displays a list of the database tables that are related to the `ZMYDOMAIN` domain.

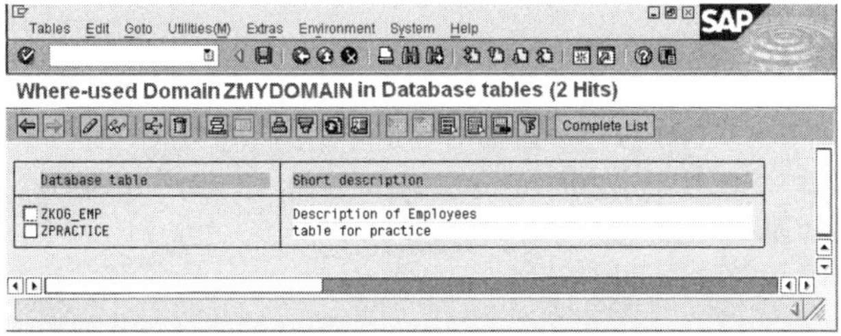

FIGURE 5.16 **List of tables**

Deleting a Domain

You can also delete an existing domain by performing the following steps:

1. Select the `Domain` radio button on the initial screen of ABAP Dictionary and then enter the name of the domain that needs to be deleted.
2. Click the `Delete` (🗑) icon. The `Delete Domain` dialog box, which is followed by the name of the domain, appears. The `Delete Domain` dialog box contains three buttons, `Yes`, `No`, and `Cancel`.
3. Click the `Yes` button to delete the selected domain.

EXPLORING DATA TYPES

A data type is a repository object of ABAP Dictionary used to create user-defined data types, such as data elements, structures, and tables. User-defined data types are the type definitions in ABAP Dictionary and can be used in an ABAP program with the `TYPE` clause. The following are the three different kinds of data types:

- Data elements
- Structures
- Table types

Data Elements

Data elements describe individual fields of a table in a database and are used to specify the types of columns in the database. The following are the two different kinds of data elements:

- **Elementary types**—Refer to data types that have semantic attributes, such as built-in data type, length, and number of decimal places. These data types can be assigned to a data element in either of the following ways:
  - **Assigning a predefined ABAP Dictionary type**—Specifies that the data element can be assigned with the predefined ABAP Dictionary types, such as `CHAR` and `NUMC`. Apart from this, you can also assign the length to the selected data type.

  - **Assigning a domain**—Specifies that the data element being created inherits the technical characteristics related to the elementary types from a predefined domain. You can use a domain with any number of data elements.

- **Reference types**—Refer to single fields that contain references to global classes and interfaces from the ABAP class library.

After creating a data element, you can also assign documentation and text information to it. The documentation of a data element is the description of the data element, which serves as an online aid to the user. The documentation entered for a data element is displayed when the user selects F1 help on fields referring to that data element. If there is no documentation for the data element, only the short text of the data element appears when the F1 key is pressed.

The documentation status is used to determine whether or not the documentation for the data element has been written. In addition to this, the documentation status also explains whether the documentation is required or not.

Table 5.2 lists the description of the different kinds of possible status entries:

Documentation Status	Description
Object Requires Documentation	Shows whether or not documentation already exists. If it does not exist, it should be written.
Object Is not Used in Any Screens	Shows that the documentation does not exist and is not required, because this data element is not used with any of the existing fields.
Object Explained Sufficiently by Short Text	Means that the short text provided for the data element is sufficient to explain the purpose for its creation. In this case, the documentation does not exist and is not required.
Documentation Is Postponed Temporarily	Means that the data element requires documentation. In this case, the documentation has not yet been written.

TABLE 5.2 Possible documentation status

Field Labels

Field labels are used to assign text information to data elements. You already know that a field is assigned to a data element. The text information related to the data element is referred to by the field and is displayed on the screen in place of the field name. If a field label is not assigned to a data element, the text entered in the short description field of the data element acts as the default field label for that field. The following are the two types of field labels:

- **Short, medium, and long fields**—Refer to keywords used to define the lengths of different fields.
- **Header fields**—Refer to information displayed above a column. The length of the header field must not exceed the length assigned to the data element.

Creating a Data Element

Perform the following steps to create a data element in ABAP Dictionary:

1. Open the initial screen of ABAP Dictionary by entering the `SE11` transaction code in the `Command` field and click the `Enter` (✓) icon or press the ENTER key.
2. Select the `Data type` radio button and enter a name for the data type, as shown in Figure 5.17:

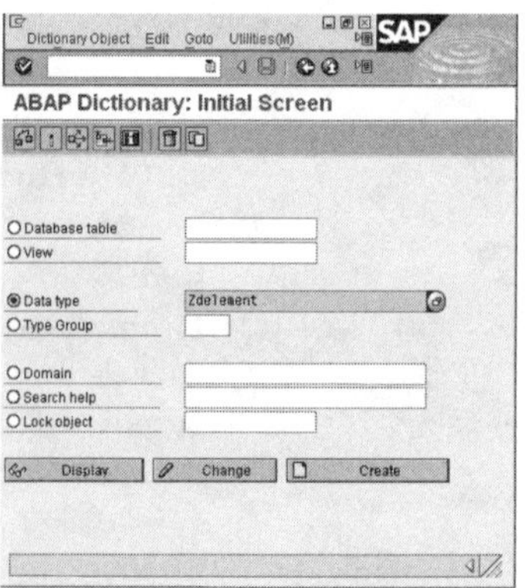

FIGURE 5.17 **Initial screen of ABAP dictionary**

In Figure 5.17, we enter the name of the data type as Zdelement.

3. Click the `Create` (Create) button. The `Create Type ZDELEMENT` dialog box appears, as shown in Figure 5.18:

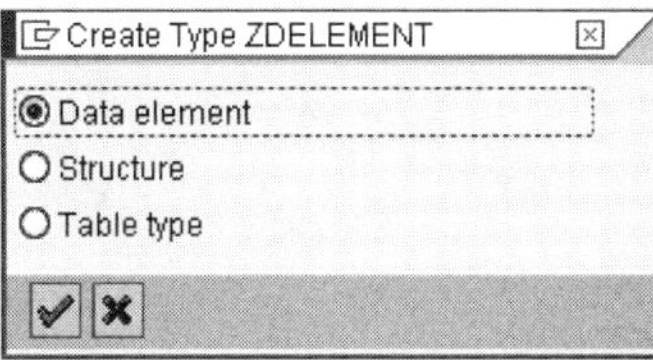

FIGURE 5.18 **The create type dialog box**

4. Select the `Data element` radio button and click the `Continue` ( ) icon.

The `Dictionary: Maintain Data Element` screen appears, as shown in Figure 5.19:

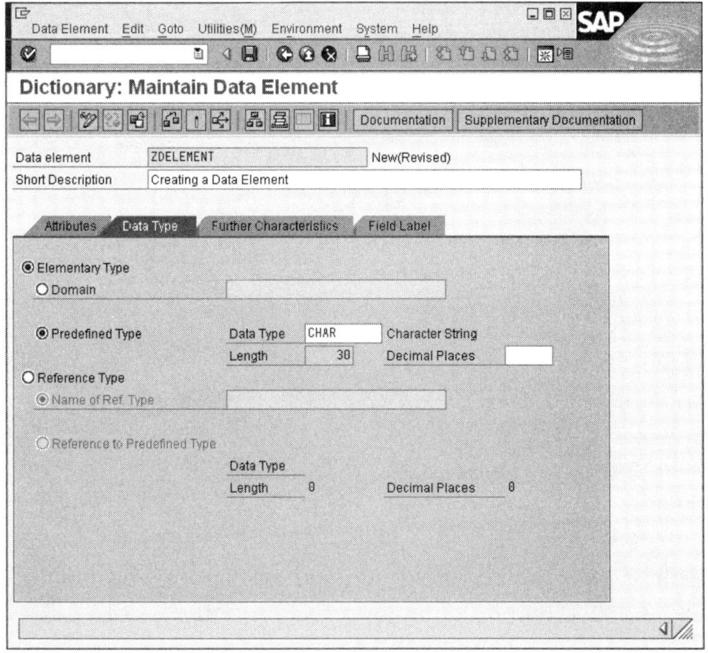

FIGURE 5.19 **The dictionary: maintain data element screen**

5. Enter a short description for the data element in the `Short Description` field. In this case, we have entered Creating a Data Element.
6. Select the `Elementary Type` and `Predefined Type` radio buttons, as shown in Figure 5.19.
7. Enter `CHAR` in the `Data Type` field and 30 in the `Length` field.

> **Note:** Sometimes the technical attributes of a data element are defined within a domain. In such cases, you only need to select the `Domain` radio button and enter the domain name in the corresponding field to access the data element.

8. Select the `Field Label` tab, which provides the options to define the text information related to the data element created, as shown in Figure 5.20:

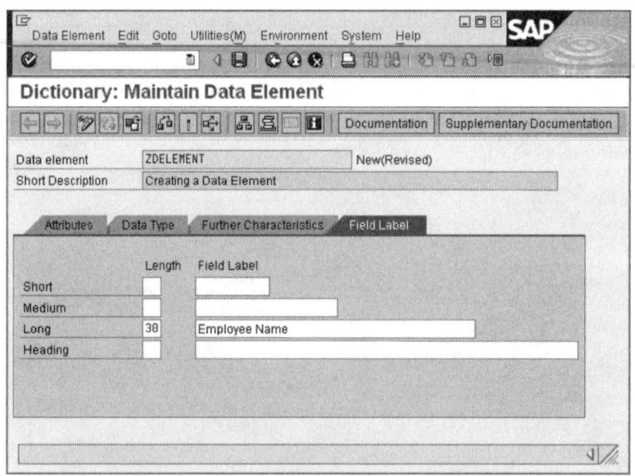

FIGURE 5.20 **The field label tab**

9. Enter a name for the field and specify the desired length for it. In this case, we have entered Employee Name in the `Field Label` column and 30 in the `Length` column of the `Long` field.

10. Click the Save (icon) icon to save the created data element in a package. In our case, we save the created data element in the ZKOG_PCKG package.
11. Now, select Go To > Documentation > Change from the Dictionary: Maintain Data Element screen (see Figure 5.20) to define the documentation for the data element.

The Change Data element: ZDELEMENT Language EN screen appears, as shown in Figure 5.21:

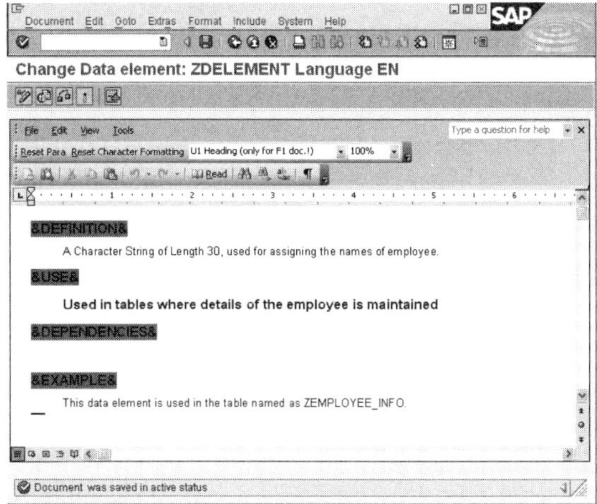

FIGURE 5.21 **Documentation for the data element**

12. Enter the documentation related to the data element under the &DEFINITION&, &USE&, &DEPENDENCIES&, and &EXAMPLE& headings, as shown in Figure 5.21.
13. Click the Save Active (icon) icon to save the documentation.
14. Click the Back (icon) icon to navigate to the maintenance screen of the data element (Figure 5.20).
15. Click the Check (icon) icon and then click the Activate (icon) icon.

The documentation for the data element is now activated and can be displayed by pressing the F1 key.

Structures

A structure is a data type in ABAP Dictionary composed of several components, including data elements, table types, and database tables. Structures are very similar to database tables, but a structure neither has a primary key nor technical characteristics associated with it. Structures are used when you want to define the same work area in multiple programs. For example, you use structures when you want to write records to a sequential file using one program and then read the same set of records by using another program. Notice that both programs must recognize the layout of the records being read and written. For this, you define the records layout in ABAP Dictionary with the help of structures. This defined structure can be included in both the programs with the help of the `TABLES` statement.

A structure can be nested within another structure. Note that whenever a structure is created in ABAP Dictionary, each of its components must be assigned a name and a data type. The structures created in ABAP Dictionary can be referred to in an ABAP program with the `TYPE` clause.

Table Types

A table type is a data type in ABAP Dictionary that describes the structure and functional attributes of an internal table. An internal table is a temporary table that exists only during the runtime of an ABAP program. In an internal table, all the records have the same structure and key. The record of the internal table is discarded when the execution of the program ends.

> **Note:** You learn more about internal tables in Chapter 7.

A table type is defined by the following attributes:

- **Row or line type**—Defines the structure and data type attributes of a line of an internal table.
- **Options**—Defines the access mode (used to manage and access data) in an internal table.
- **Key**—Defines the key definition and key category of an internal table.

Figure 5.22 shows the attributes of the TABTYPE table type in ABAP Dictionary:

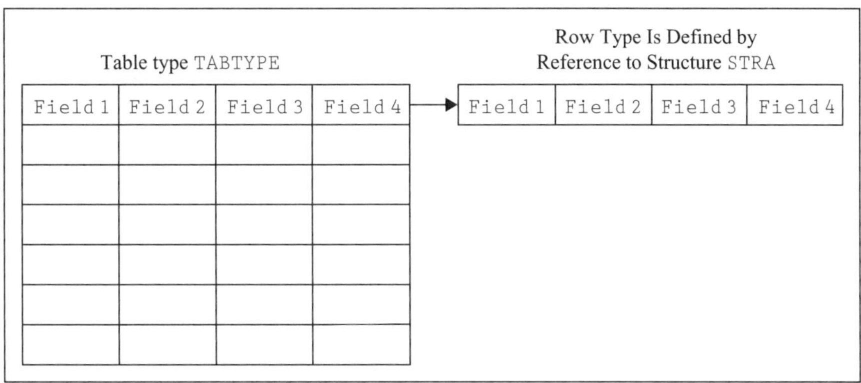

FIGURE 5.22 **Creation of a table type**

In Figure 5.22, STRA represents the row type of the TABTYPE table type. It is related to the Field 1, Field 2, Field 3, and Field 4 fields of the TABTYPE table type. The TABTYPE table type can be used in an ABAP program by using the following syntax:

```
DATA <name> TYPE TABTYPE
```

In the preceding syntax, the <name> expression is the name of the internal table to be created in an ABAP program. The internal table is similar to the TABTYPE table type created in ABAP Dictionary.

EXPLORING TYPE GROUPS

Type groups, another repository object of ABAP Dictionary, allow you to define data types directly in ABAP Dictionary, instead of defining them in an ABAP program. The name of a type group in ABAP Dictionary must have a maximum length of five characters. Every data type name defined in a type group must begin with the name of the type group followed by an underscore sign. These defined data types can be used in an ABAP program with the help of the TYPE-POOLS statement.

To create a type group, select the Type Group radio button in the initial screen of ABAP Dictionary (see Figure 5.17), enter the name of the type group, and click the Create button. Then, enter the following code snippet in the maintenance screen of the ZTYPE type group:

```
TYPE-POOL ZTYPE.
TYPES: ZTYPE_NAME(30) TYPE c,
       ZTYPE_AGE(3) TYPE i.
```

In this code snippet, two data types are created. The declared type group (that is, ZTYPE), can be used in an ABAP program, as shown in the following code snippet:

```
REPORT ZSHIVAM.
TYPE-POOLS ZTYPE.
DATA: NAME TYPE ZTYPE_NAME,
      AGE TYPE ZTYPE_AGE.
```

In the preceding code snippet, the ZTYPE type group is included in the ZSHIVAM program with the TYPE-POOLS statement. Therefore, the data types in the ZTYPE type group can be used in the ZSHIVAM program with the help of the DATA statement.

EXPLORING DATABASE TABLES

In ABAP Dictionary, tables can be defined independent of the database. When a table is activated in ABAP Dictionary, similar copy (that is, definition) of its fields is created in the database as well. In other words, the tables defined in ABAP Dictionary are translated automatically into the format that is compatible with the database because the definition of the table depends on the database used by the SAP system.

In ABAP Dictionary, a table definition consists of the following components:

- **Fields**—Store information.
- **Foreign keys**—Define the relationships between tables.
- **Technical settings**—Specify the settings of the table, such as data class and size category.
- **Indexes**—Helps retrieve the rows within a table.

Figure 5.23 displays the definition of the table in a database as compared to its definition in ABAP Dictionary:

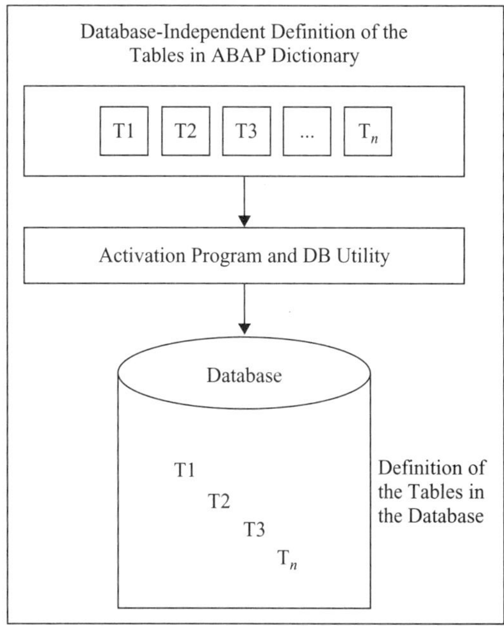

FIGURE 5.23 **Database-independent table definition**

A table can contain one or more fields, each defined with its data type and length. The large amount of data stored in a table is distributed among the several fields defined in the table.

In the next sections, we discuss the following topics in the context of database tables in ABAP Dictionary:

- Types of tables
- Types of table fields
- Technical settings of a table
- Creating tables
- Relating tables by using foreign keys

Types of Tables

In ABAP Dictionary, you can create three types of tables with different characteristics:

- Transparent tables
- Pooled tables
- Cluster tables

Apart from these, you can create some special table types, such as table pools (also called just pools) and table clusters. These two special table types are used to store information about other tables, such as internal control information, which includes screen sequences, program parameters, temporary data, and continuous texts (such as documentation). The tables assigned to a table pool or table cluster are referred to as pooled tables and cluster tables, respectively.

Transparent Tables

A transparent table forms a one-to-one relationship with the table definition in the database. Transparent tables are used to hold the application data, which represents master data or transaction data used by an application. An example of master data is the table of vendors (also called vendor master data) or the table of customers (also called customer data). An example of transaction data is an order placed by a customer or an order placed with a vendor.

Pooled Tables

A pooled table in ABAP Dictionary forms a many-to-one relationship with the table definition in the SAP database. It means that for a single table defined in the database, there are many tables in ABAP Dictionary. The names of the tables in ABAP Dictionary must differ from those of the tables stored in the database.

All pooled tables are stored in the SAP database in a single table, called a table pool, which is a database table with a special structure that can store the data of multiple pooled tables.

The table pool definition consists of two key fields (`Tabname` and `Varkey`) and a long argument field (`Vardata`). Table 5.3 lists the descriptions of fields in a table pool:

Field	Data Type	Meaning
Tabname	CHAR(10)	Holds the name of a pooled table.
Varkey	CHAR (*n*)	Stores the entries of the key fields of a pooled table as a string. The maximum length of the string is specified by the *n* variable.
Dataln	INT2(5)	Stores the length of a string in `Vardata`.
Vardata	RAW (*n*)	Holds the entries from all the data fields of a pooled table as a string, where the maximum length of the string is determined by the database system being used.

TABLE 5.3 Fields of a table pool and their data types

The length of the name of a pooled table must not exceed 10 characters. `Varkey` is a character field, so all the key fields of a pooled table must have character data types, such as `CHAR`, `NUMC`, and `CLNT`. The total length of all the key fields or all the data fields of pooled tables must not exceed the length assigned to the `Vardata` or `Varkey` field.

Figure 5.24 displays the relationship between table pools and pooled tables:

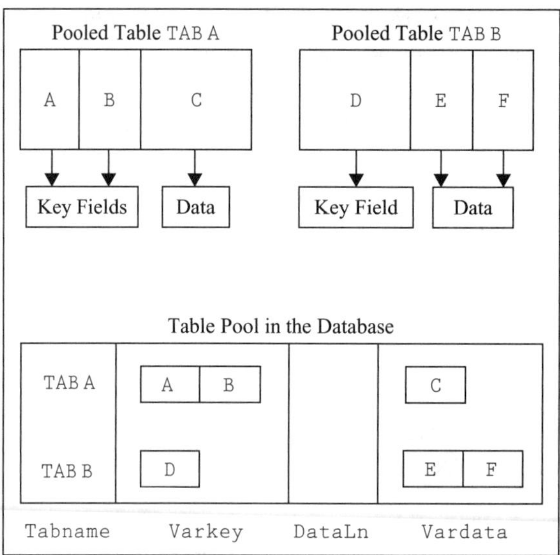

FIGURE 5.24 **Relationship between the table pool and pooled tables**

In Figure 5.24, you can see two pooled tables, `TAB A` and `TAB B`. The `TAB A` table consists of two key fields, `A` and `B`, which hold values in the fields as `C`. The `TAB B` table consists of a key field called `D` and the data are `E` and `F`. Notice that both pooled tables are stored in a table pool in the database.

Cluster Tables

Similar to a pooled table, a cluster table also forms many-to-one relationships with table definitions in the SAP database. Cluster tables are stored in a single table in the SAP database, called the table cluster. Cluster tables are used when the constituent tables have a common primary key. The data from these common primary key fields can be accessed simultaneously. The data contained in the rows that have the common primary key can be combined into a single row in the table cluster.

Table 5.4 lists the description of fields in a table cluster:

Field	Data Type	Meaning
CLKEY1	*	Denotes the first key field.
CLKEY2	*	Denotes the first key field.
CLKEYn	*	Denotes the *n*th key field.
Pageno	INT2(5)	Denotes the number of continuation records.
Timestamp	CHAR(14)	Describes time stamps.
Pagelg	INT2(5)	Denotes that the length of the associated string is stored as the Vardata type.
Vardata	RAW (*n*)	Contains the entries from the data fields of the assigned cluster tables.

TABLE 5.4 Fields and data types in a table cluster

Now, let's try to understand the concept of table clusters with the help of Figure 5.25:

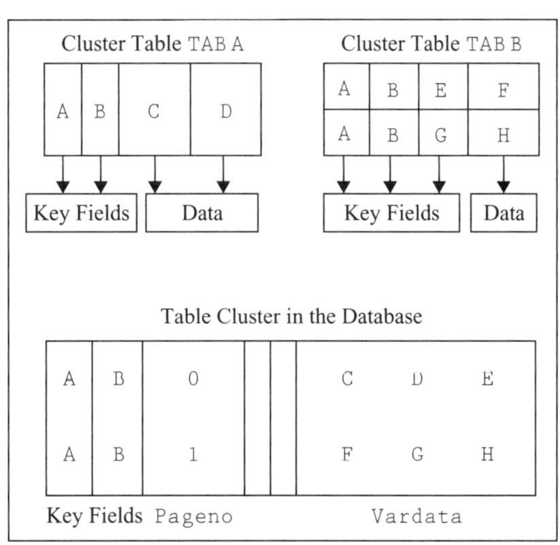

FIGURE 5.25 **Table cluster and cluster tables**

Figure 5.25 shows two cluster tables, `TAB A` and `TAB B`. The `TAB A` table consists of two key fields, `A` and `B`, which hold the data, `C` and `D`, respectively. The `TAB B` table consists of key fields `A`, `B`, `E`, and `G` with the data `F` and `H`. Now, the data from both these tables, `TAB A` and `TAB B`, is stored in the `Vardata` field of the table cluster.

Types of Table Fields

A table consists of many fields, and each field contains many elements. Table 5.5 lists the different elements that can be defined for a field:

Elements	Description
Field name	Represents the name given to a field, which can contain a maximum of 16 characters. The field name may be composed of digits, letters, and underscores; however, it must begin with a letter.
Key flag	Determines whether or not a field belongs to a key field.
Field type	Assigns a data type to a field.
Field length	Represents the number of characters that can be entered in a field.
Decimal places	Defines the number of digits permissible after the decimal point. This element is used only for numeric data types.
Short text	Explains the meaning of the corresponding field.

TABLE 5.5 Different elements of table fields

There are two types of table fields:

- Currency field
- Quantity field

Currency Field

The currency field is composed of two subfields: the currency field and the currency key field. The field that holds the numeric amount is known as the currency field, and the one that holds the currency type is known as the currency key field. For instance, if you need to store the value 1000 rupees, 1000 is stored in the currency field and rupees is stored in the currency key field. The data type of the currency field must be `CURR` and must be linked to a currency key field of the `CUKY` data type holding a currency key, such as `USD` (US dollars), `CAD` (Canadian dollars), or `ITL` (Italian lira). The currency key field acts as the reference field for the currency field.

Figure 5.26 shows the relationship between the currency field and the reference key field:

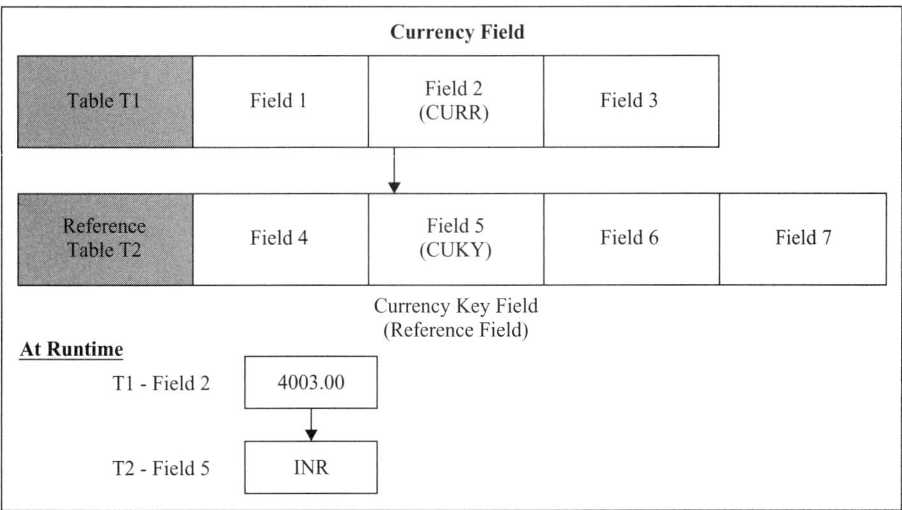

FIGURE 5.26 **Relationship between the currency field and the reference key field**

In Figure 5.26, there are two tables, T1 and T2. The T2 table acts as the reference table for the T1 table. Field 2 in the T1 table is of the type `CURR` (currency field) and Field 5 in the T2 table is of the type `CUKY` (Currency key table). The value entered in Field 2 shows the numeric amount, whereas Field 5 is used to show currency key type. In Figure 5.26, T1 - Field 2 = 4003.00 shows the amount, and T1 - Field 2 = INR shows the type of the currency.

Quantity Field

The quantity field contains a numeric value for a measurement such as length, temperature, weight, or current. These numeric measurements are supported by the units of measure field, such as inches, degree Celsius, kilograms, or kilovolts. The quantity fields have `QUAN` as the data type and must be linked to a reference field that has a `UNIT` data type.

Technical Settings of a Table

You can define technical settings for a table while declaring it. Table 5.6 lists the description of the important data parameters related to the technical settings of a table:

Data Parameters	Description
Data Class	Defines the physical area (that is, tablespace) of the SAP database in which a table must be created.
Size category	Defines the size of a table based on the number of records that can be entered in the table.
Buffering permission	Defines whether or not a table can be buffered.
Buffering type	Defines the buffering type for a table. The buffering type can be full, single-record, or generic.
Logging	Defines whether the changes made to the entries of a table should be logged. If logging is switched on, any change made to a table record is recorded in a log table.

TABLE 5.6 Description of the data parameters

Now, we will discuss the following topics in detail with regard to the technical settings for a table:

- Data class
- Size category
- Table buffering

Data Class

The data class is used to specify the physical area where the tables are stored in a database. This physical area in the database is also known as tablespace or `DBspace`. Each data class corresponds to a physical area in which all the tables assigned to this data class are stored. Table 5.7 lists the types of a data class:

Data Class Type	Description
APPL0 (master data)	Stores master data. An example of master data is the data contained in an address file, such as the name, address, and telephone number. APPLO is seldom changed.
APPL1 (transaction data)	Stores the transaction data. An example of transaction data is the goods in a warehouse, which change after each purchase order.
APPL2 (organizational data)	Stores organizational data, such as a table with country codes. APPL2 is a data class, which represents the customized data that is defined when the SAP system is installed and seldom changed.

TABLE 5.7 Types of data class

Figure 5.27 displays the different types of data that is stored in tables:

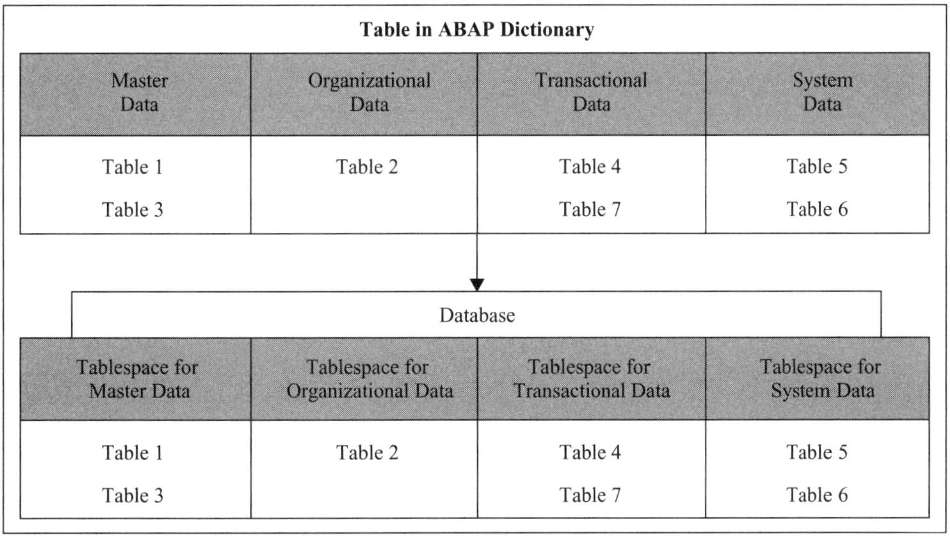

Table in ABAP Dictionary

Master Data	Organizational Data	Transactional Data	System Data
Table 1	Table 2	Table 4	Table 5
Table 3		Table 7	Table 6

Database

Tablespace for Master Data	Tablespace for Organizational Data	Tablespace for Transactional Data	Tablespace for System Data
Table 1	Table 2	Table 4	Table 5
Table 3		Table 7	Table 6

FIGURE 5.27 **Types of data classes**

Figure 5.27 shows that the tables related to a specific data are stored in their respective tablespaces. For instance, the tables for the organizational data are stored in the organizational data tablespace.

Size Category

You can assign a size for a database table by using the size category on the `ABAP Dictionary: Maintain Technical Settings` screen. The value in the size category technical setting can be a numeric value between 0 to 8. Each size category defines a possible number of records that you can maintain for a table. In addition, each size category is assigned with a certain fixed memory size in the database. The memory size allocated to the size category depends on the type of database system being used. Figure 5.28 shows the technical settings related to the size category:

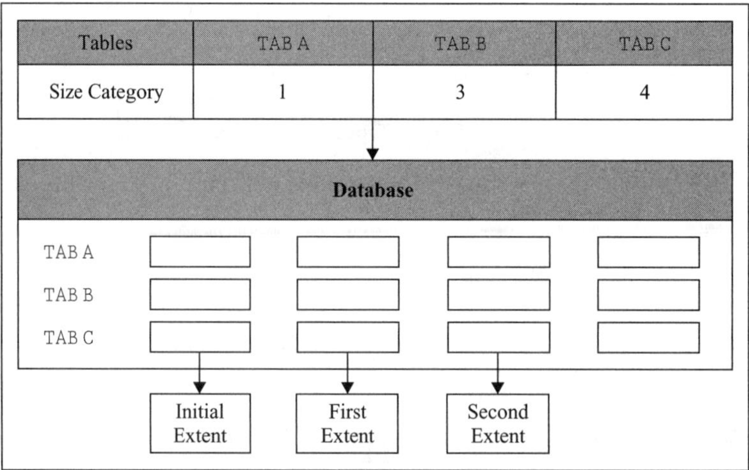

FIGURE 5.28 **Defining size category for a table**

Figure 5.28 shows three different tables, `TAB A`, `TAB B`, and `TAB C`, with different size categories 1, 3, and 4, respectively. Whenever a table is created, an initial space is automatically allotted to it.

Table Buffering

Sometimes, you need to access a particular set of records more frequently than others. Accessing records directly from a database table can be very time-consuming. To overcome this drawback, the frequently accessed records of a table can be placed in a buffer from which they can be accessed easily by a SAP system, improving performance.

You can define whether or not certain records need to be buffered from the `ABAP Dictionary: Maintain Technical Settings` screen. Note that only the transparent tables and the pooled tables can be buffered.

Table 5.8 lists various buffering permissions for a table:

Buffering	Description
Buffering Not Permitted	Specifies that either the application program always need the most recent data from the table or the table is changed frequently. Therefore, in this case, buffering is not required.
Buffering Permitted	Specifies that although buffering is permitted from the business and technical points of view, it is not activated.
But Not Activated	Table buffering is deactivated because it is not possible to find the type of field values that exist in a customer system. However, depending on your requirements, you can activate it on a customer system.
Buffering Activated	Specifies that the table is buffered. In this case, you must specify the buffering type.

TABLE 5.8 Buffering permissions for tables

Whenever a table record is accessed, it is loaded into the buffer of the application server. Table 5.9 lists three types of buffering:

Buffering Type	Description
Full buffering	Specifies that all the records of the table are loaded into the buffer when one record of the table is accessed.
Generic buffering	Specifies that when a record of the table is accessed, all the records having this record in the generic key fields (part of the table key that is left-justified, identified by specifying a number of key fields) are loaded into the buffer.
Single-record buffering	Specifies that only the accessed records of a table are loaded into the buffer.

TABLE 5.9 Types of buffering

Now, let's explain how to create a table in ABAP Dictionary.

Creating Tables

Tables in an SAP system can be created with the help of the ABAP Dictionary tool.

Perform the following broad-level steps to create a table:

1. Create and configure table fields
2. Create data elements
3. Define the technical settings of a table
4. Define the enhancement category

Creating and Configuring Table Fields

Perform the following steps to create and configure the table fields of a table:

1. Open the initial screen of ABAP Dictionary, select the `Database table` radio button, and enter a name for the table to be created. In our case, we have entered the name ZKOG_EMP, as shown in Figure 5.29:

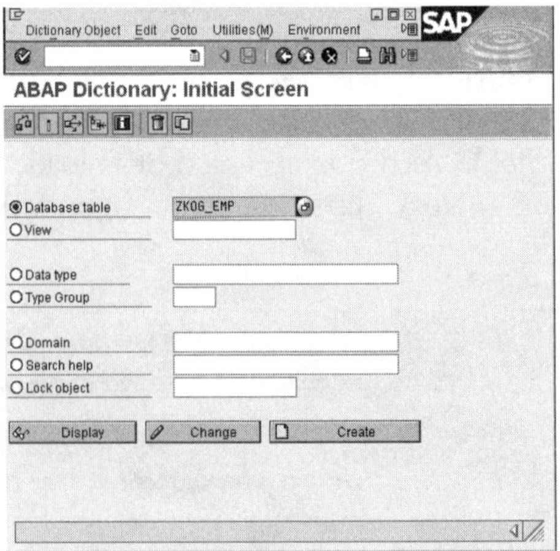

FIGURE 5.29 **Creating a table**

2. Click the `Create` (Create) button.

The `Dictionary: Maintain Table` screen appears, as shown in Figure 5.30:

FIGURE 5.30 **Maintenance screen for the table**

Notice that in the `Dictionary: Maintain Table` screen, the `Delivery and Maintenance` tab is selected by default.

3. Enter an explanatory short text in the `Short Description` field. In Figure 5.30, the short text is entered as Description of Employees.
4. Click the `Search Help` ( ) icon beside the `Delivery Class` field.

The `Delivery class (1) 7 Entries found` dialog box appears, as shown in Figure 5.31:

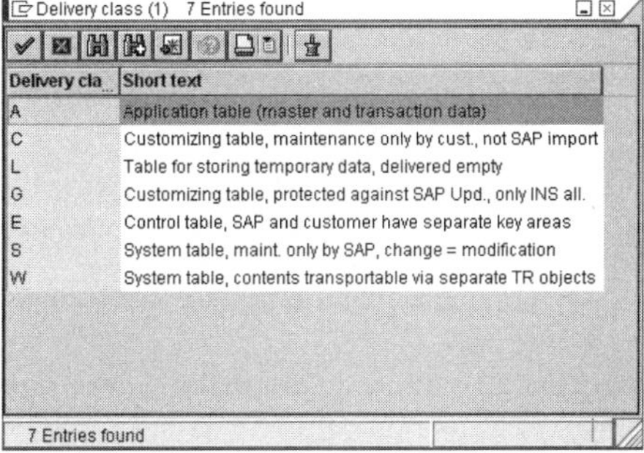

Delivery class (1) 7 Entries found
Delivery cla
Short text
A
Application table (master and transaction data)
C
Customizing table, maintenance only by cust., not SAP import
L
Table for storing temporary data, delivered empty
G
Customizing table, protected against SAP Upd., only INS all.
E
Control table, SAP and customer have separate key areas
S
System table, maint. only by SAP, change = modification
W
System table, contents transportable via separate TR objects
7 Entries found

FIGURE 5.31 **Showing the delivery class dialog box**

5. Select an option from the displayed list and click the `Copy` (✔) icon (see Figure 5.31). In our case, we have selected A [Application table (master and transaction data)] option.
6. Now, select the `Display/Maintenance Allowed` option from the `Data Browser/Table View Maintenance drop-down` menu, as shown in Figure 5.32:

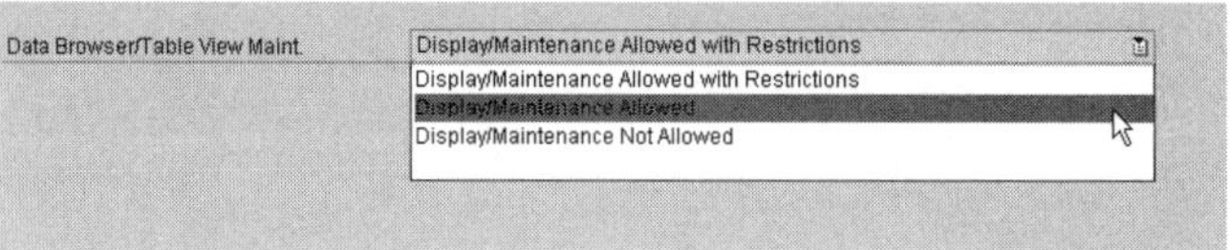

FIGURE 5.32 **Entering value for table maintenance**

The `Dictionary: Maintenance Table` screen appears, as shown in Figure 5.33:

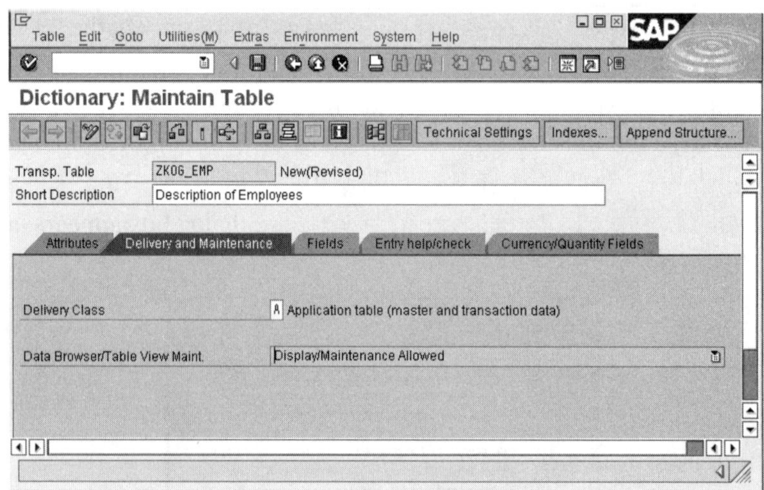

FIGURE 5.33 **Showing the maintenance screen**

7. Select the `Fields` (Fields) tab. The screen containing the options related to the `Fields` tab is shown in Figure 5.34.

8. Enter the names of table fields in the `Field` column. A field name may contain letters, digits, and underscores, but it must always begin with a letter and must not be longer than 16 characters. Select the `Key` column if you want the field to be a part of the table key. In our case, we have created two fields, `KEMPCODE` and `KEMPNAME`.

Creating Data Elements

The fields that are to be created must also have data elements because they take the attributes, such as data type, length, decimal places, and short text, from the defined data element. If no suitable data type is already present, you need to create a data element.

Perform the following steps to create a data element:

1. Enter the names for the data elements in the `Data element` column. In our case, we have assigned the names, `ZECODE` and `ZENAME`, to the `KEMPCODE` and `KEMPNAME` fields, respectively, as shown in Figure 5.34:

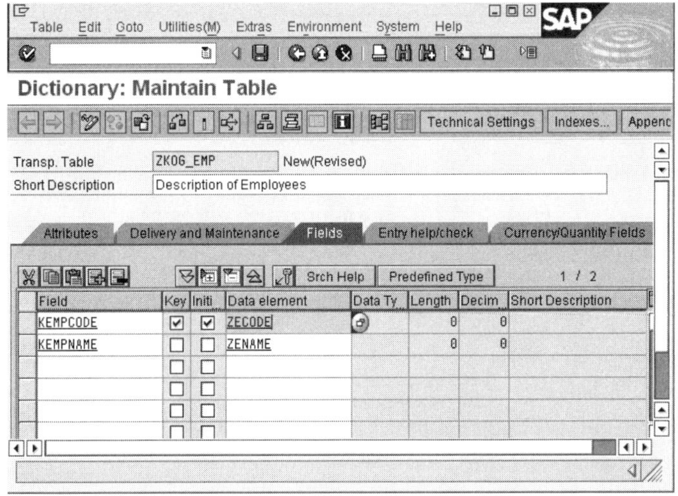

FIGURE 5.34 **The data element for the KEMPCODE field**

2. Now, double-click `ZECODE` to create the data element (see Figure 5.34).

The `Exit Processing` dialog box appears (see Figure 5.35).

3. Click the `Yes` button, as shown in Figure 5.35:

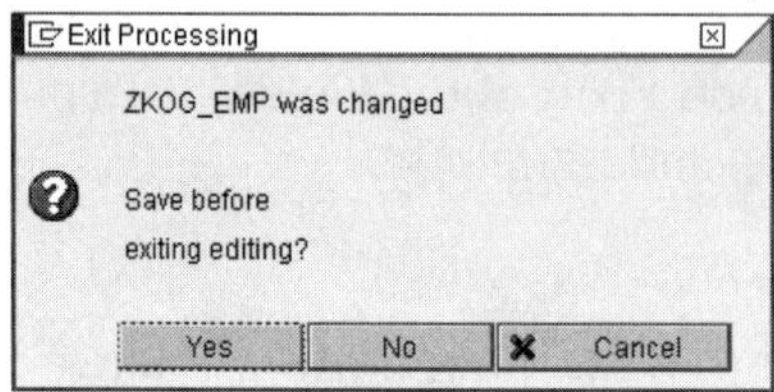

FIGURE 5.35 **Saving the data element**

The `Information` dialog box appears, specifying that the table created should be client-specific.

4. Click the `Continue` (✔) icon, as shown in the Figure 5.36:

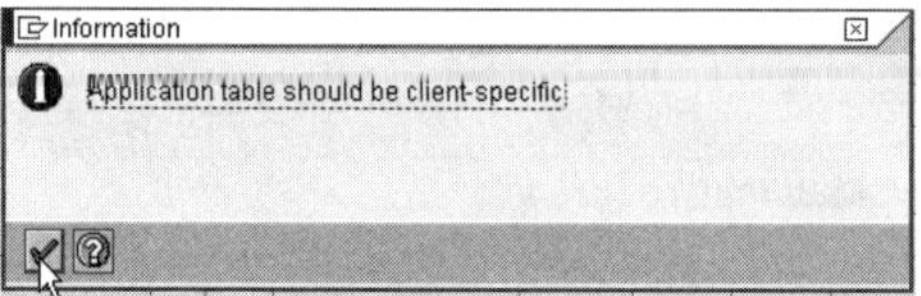

FIGURE 5.36 **The information dialog box**

The `Create Data Element dialog` box appears, as shown in Figure 5.37:

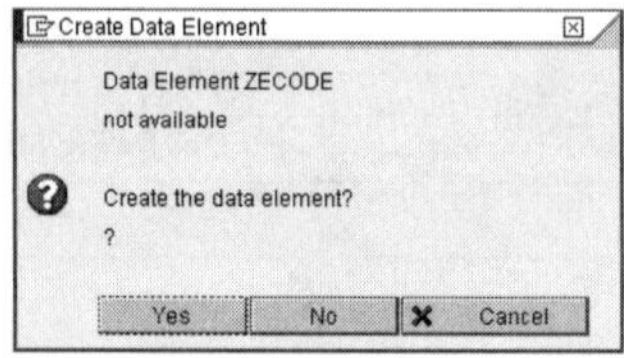

FIGURE 5.37 **Creating data element**

5. Click the `Yes` button on the `Create Data Element` dialog box.

The `Dictionary: Maintain Data Element` screen, also known as the maintenance screen for the data element, appears, as shown in Figure 5.38:

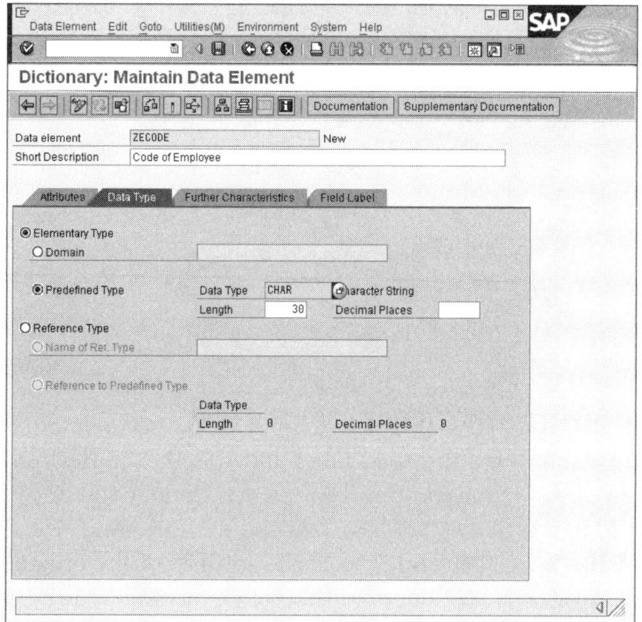

FIGURE 5.38 **Maintaining the data element**

6. Enter a short description, i.e., Code of Employee, in the `Short Description` field. If a field label for the data element is not defined, this short description acts as the description for the field when the field is displayed on the screen.
7. Select the data type for the data element as `CHAR` by clicking the `Search Help` ( ) icon. Enter the desired length in the `Length` field (see Figure 5.38).
8. Select the `Field Label` tab. The screen containing the options related to the field label appears, as shown in Figure 5.39:

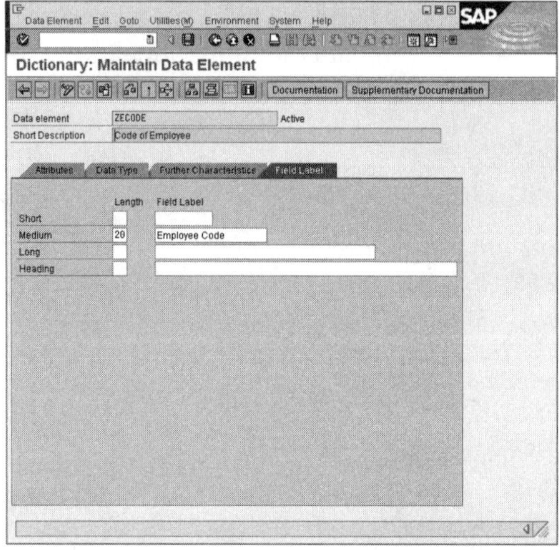

FIGURE 5.39 **Field label**

9. Enter a name for the field label and specify the desired length for it. In Figure 5.39, we have entered Employee Code in the `Field Label` column and 20 in the `Length` column for the `Medium` field.
10. Click the `Save` (💾) icon to save the settings of the created data element.
11. Click the `Back` (◀) icon and then click the `Activate` (▯) icon. The data element is activated.

Now, let's define the attributes for the ZENAME data element of the `KEMPNAME` field.

12. Double-click the ZENAME data element (Figure 5.34).

The `Create Data Element` dialog box appears, as shown in Figure 5.40:

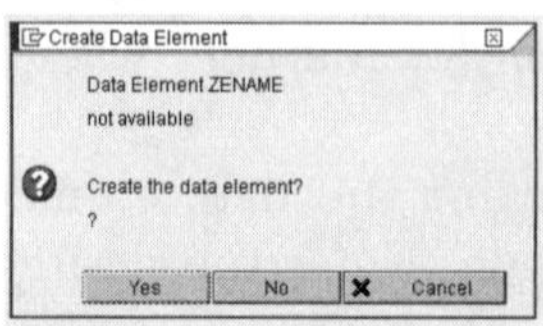

FIGURE 5.40 **Creating data element**

13. Click the `Yes` button (see Figure 5.40).

The `Dictionary: Maintain Data Element` screen appears, as shown in Figure 5.41:

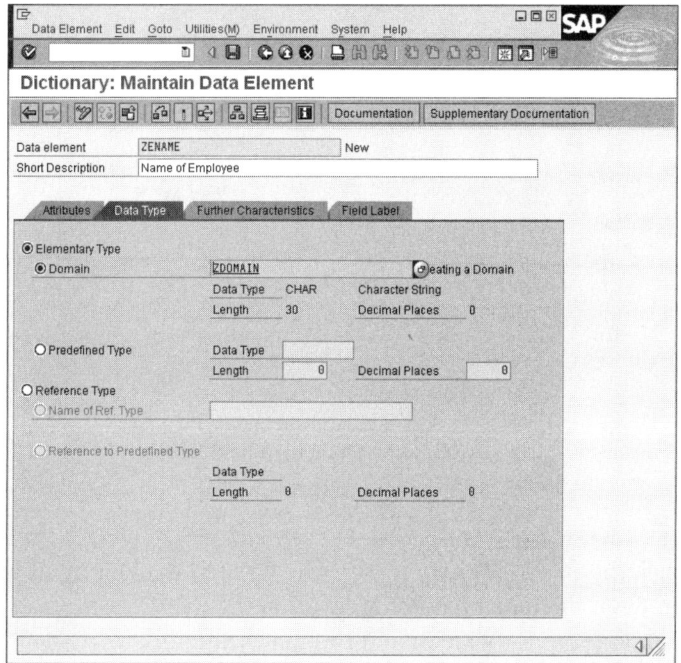

FIGURE 5.41 **Creating data element**

14. Select the `Domain` radio button under the `Elementary type` field and enter the name of the domain. In Figure 5.41, we have entered the name of the predefined domain, that is, ZDOMAIN, as shown in Figure 5.41. If the domain has not been defined earlier, double-click the name of the domain and define its attributes.
15. Select the `Field Label` tab. The maintenance screen containing the fields corresponding to the `Field Label` tab appears, as shown in Figure 5.42:

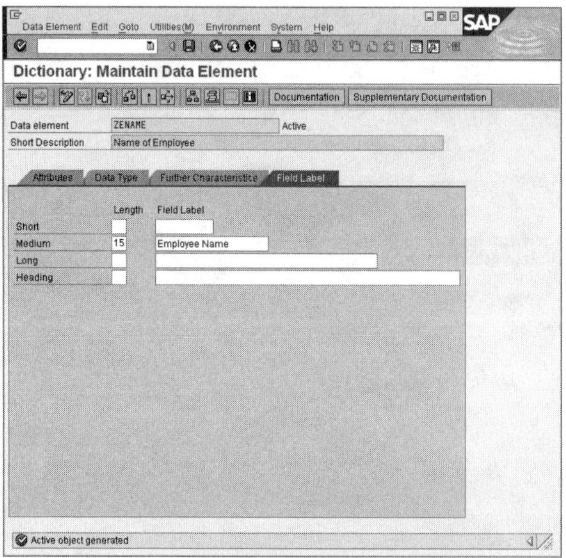

FIGURE 5.42 **Defining a field label**

16. Click the `Save` icon to save the created data element in a package. In our case, the data element is saved in the `ZKOG_PCKG` package.
17. Click the `Back` icon and then click the `Activate` icon. The data element, `ZENAME`, is activated.

Defining the Technical Settings of a Table

Now, let's learn how to define the technical settings related to the `ZKOG_EMP` table.

1. Click the `Technical Settings` (Technical Settings) button (previously shown in Figure 5.34).

The `Dictionary:Maintain Technical Settings` screen appears, as shown in Figure 5.43:

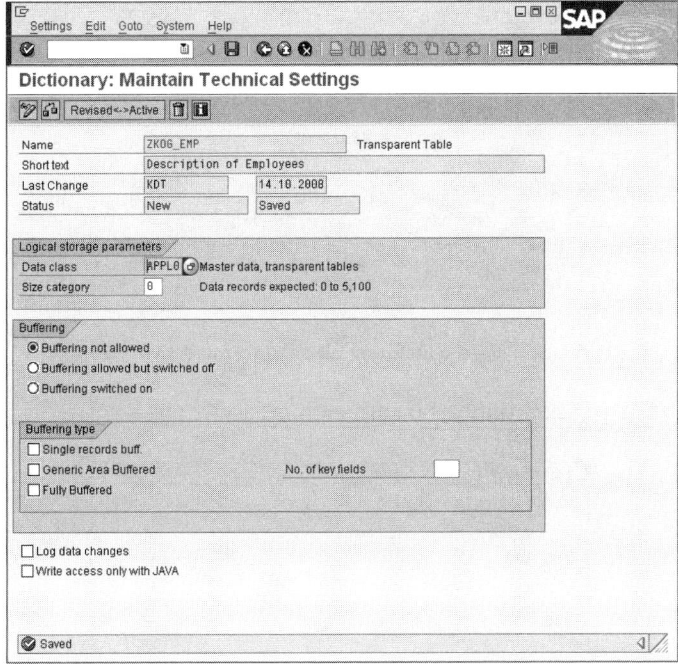

FIGURE 5.43 **Maintaining technical settings**

2. Set the `Data` class as `APPLO` and `Size category` as 0, as shown in Figure 5.43.
3. Click the `Save` ( ) icon to save the technical settings of the table.
4. Click the `Back` ( ) icon to go back to the `Dictionary: Maintain Table` screen (Figure 5.34).

Defining the Enhancement Category

Next, we define an enhancement category for the table to enhance the structures and tables created in ABAP Dictionary:

1. In the `Dictionary: Maintain Table` screen, select Extras>Enhancement Category to define the enhancement category, as shown in Figure 5.44:

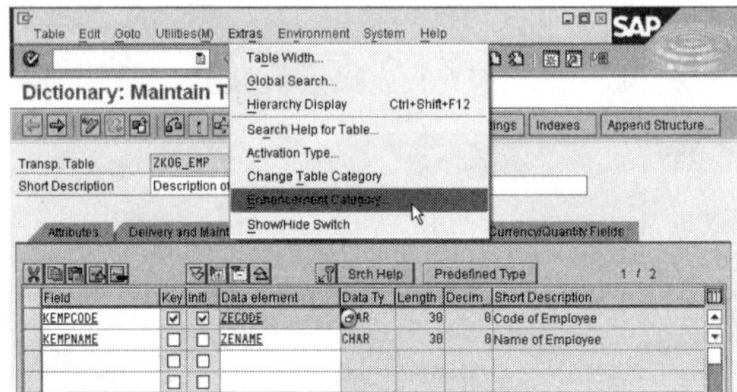

FIGURE 5.44 **Defining an enhancement category**

The `Information` dialog box appears, as shown in Figure 5.45:

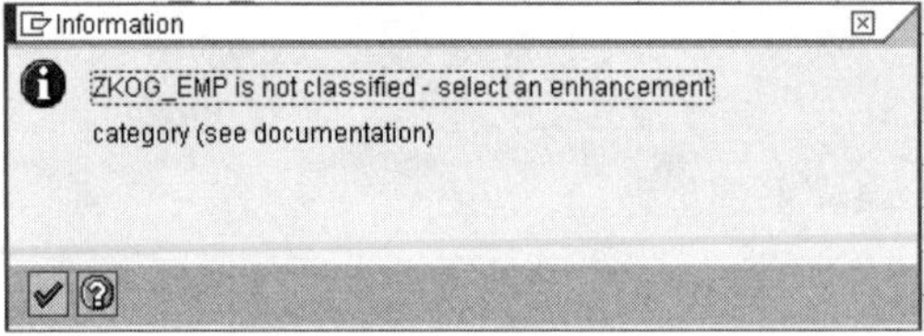

FIGURE 5.45 **Displaying the information dialog box**

2. Click the `Continue` (✔) icon.

The `Maintain Enhancement Category for ZKOG_EMP` dialog box appears, as shown in Figure 5.46:

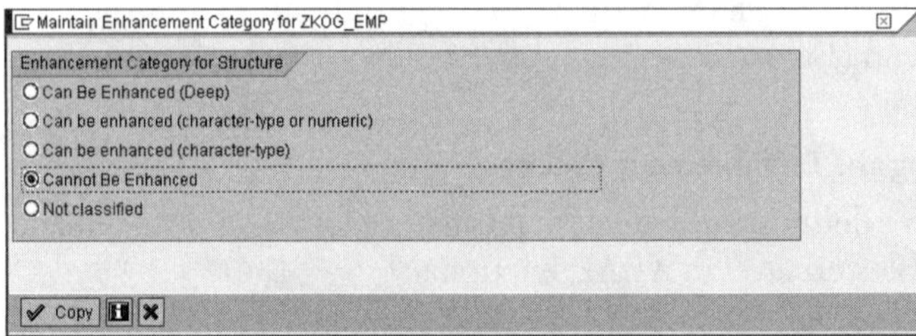

FIGURE 5.46 **Selecting an enhancement category**

3. Select the `Cannot be Enhanced` radio button for the enhancement category.

Table 5.10 lists the description of the different possible enhancement categories:

Enhancement Category	Description
Can Be Enhanced (Deep)	The table can be enhanced to contain components with any data type.
Can Be Enhanced (Character-Type or Numeric-Type)	Specifies that a table can contain only the character or numeric data types.
Can Be Enhanced (Character-Type)	Specifies that a table can contain only the character data types.
Cannot Be Enhanced	Specifies that a table cannot be enhanced.
Not Classified	Specifies that the table does not have any enhancement category.

TABLE 5.10 Enhancement categories for a table

4. Click the `Copy` (Copy) button (see Figure 5.46).
5. Click the `Save` icon, the `Check` icon, and then the `Activate` icon. The maintenance screen for the table appears, displaying the status as Active, as shown in Figure 5.47:

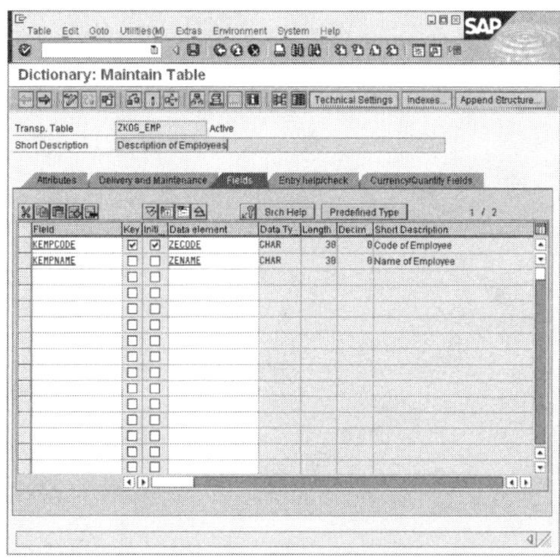

FIGURE 5.47 **Active version of the table**

6. Select Utilities > Table Contents > Create Entries, as shown in Figure 5.48:

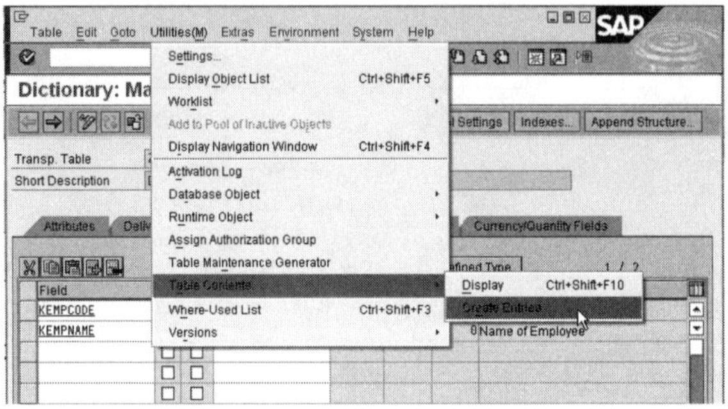

FIGURE 5.48 **Creating entries in table**

The `Table ZKOG_EMP Insert` screen appears, as shown in Figure 5.49:

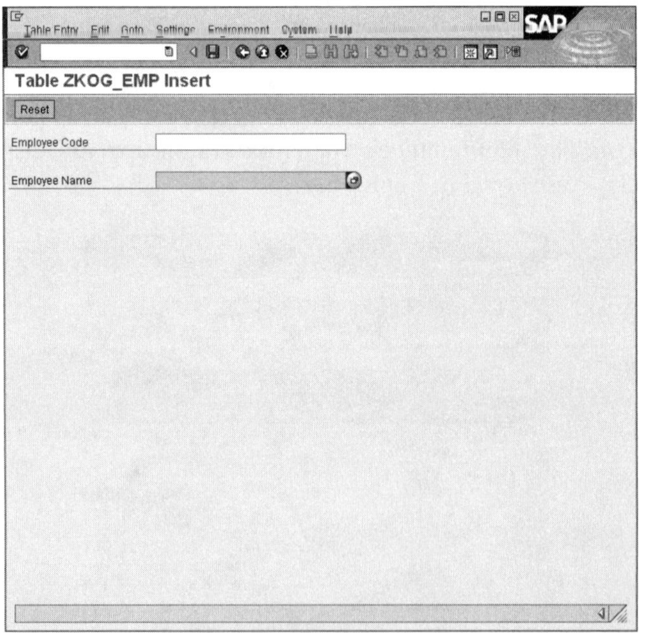

FIGURE 5.49 **Entering values into a table**

7. Click the Search Help ( ) icon beside the Employee Name field. The screen containing the predefined value range for the ZDOMAIN domain appears, as shown in Figure 5.50:

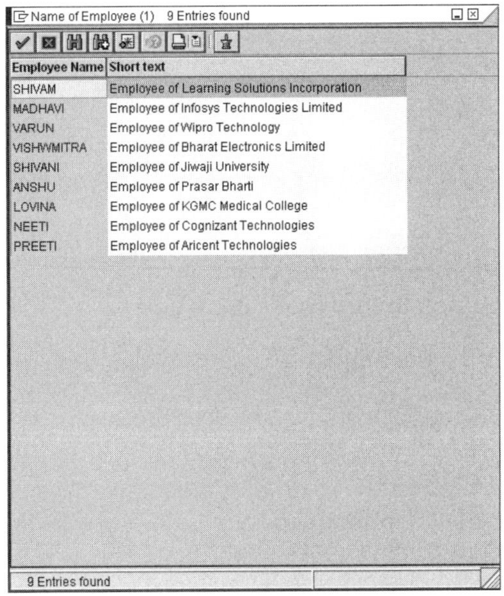

FIGURE 5.50 **Valid set of values**

Note: You cannot enter any values other than those defined in the value range for the ZDOMAIN domain. The KEMPNAME field is assigned with the ZENAME data element, which is further assigned with an elementary data type called ZDOMAIN.

8. Select SHIVAM and click the Copy ( ) icon.
9. Assign an employee code, say, KSI-0079, to the selected name, that is, SHIVAM, and click the Save ( ) icon.

Figure 5.51 shows the entry of the employee code for the employee name SHIVAM:

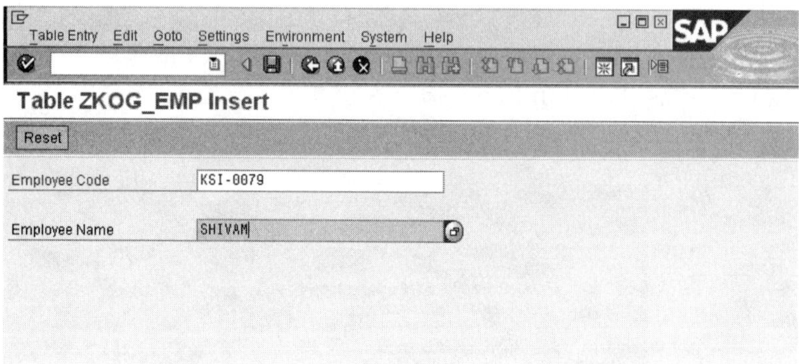

FIGURE 5.51 **First entry of the table**

10. Click the `Reset` button (see Figure 5.51).

Similarly, maintain the employee codes for the remaining employees.

11. Click the `Back` ( ) icon to go back to the `Dictionary: Maintain Table` screen.
12. Select `Utilities (M) > Table Contents > Display` to display all the entries, as shown in Figure 5.52:

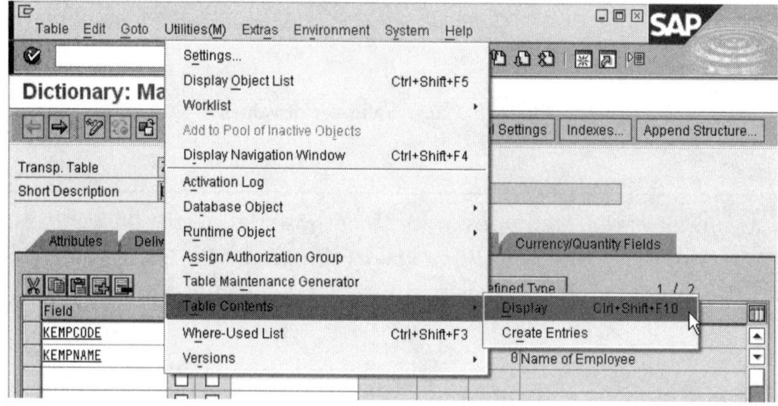

FIGURE 5.52 **Displaying the contents of the table**

The selection screen for `Data Browser: Table ZKOG_EMP` appears, as shown in Figure 5.53:

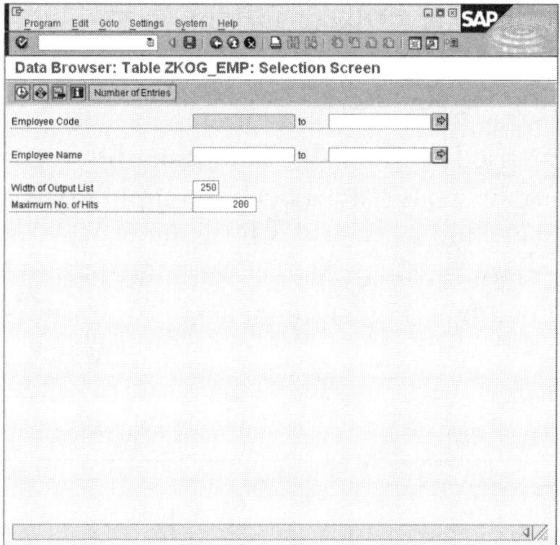

FIGURE 5.53 **Showing the selection screen for the table**

13. Click the `Execute` ( ) icon to display all the entries made in the table, as shown in Figure 5.53.

The `Data Browser: Table ZKOG_EMP Select Entries` screen appears, as shown in Figure 5.54:

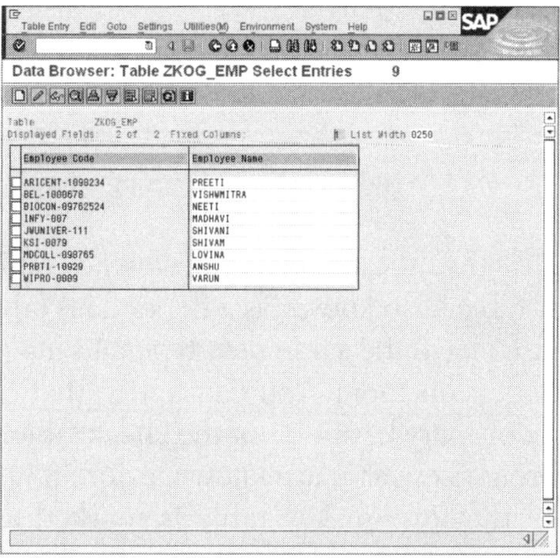

FIGURE 5.54 **Showing the contents maintained in the table**

Figure 5.54 displays all the records of the ZKOG_EMP table.

Relating Tables by Using Foreign Keys

Foreign keys are used to establish relationships between various tables in ABAP Dictionary. You can create value checks for input fields with the help of foreign keys. A foreign key links two tables by assigning the foreign key fields of one table to the primary key fields of another table. Figure 5.55 shows the process of field assignment by using a foreign key:

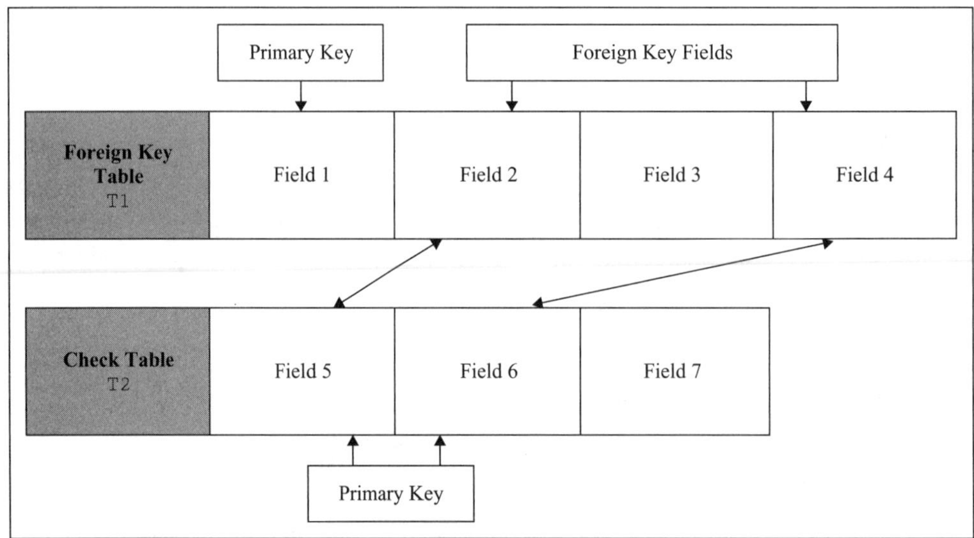

FIGURE 5.55 **Field assignment by using a foreign key**

In Figure 5.55, the T1 table is the foreign key table, whereas the T2 table refers to a check table, also known as a dependent table. The pair of fields for the two tables must have the same data type and length so that a relationship can be created between them. You can notice that fields of the foreign key table relate to the primary key fields of the check table. In our case, Field 2 and Field 4 of the foreign key table are known as foreign key fields.

A field from the foreign key table is marked as the check field. This check field is required to perform the value checks for the data entered in the input fields, which means that whenever an entry is made in the check field of the foreign key table, a check is always performed to validate whether the check table contains a record with the specified key. If the entered value matches with the value specified in the check table, the SAP system accepts the value; otherwise, the system rejects the value. Figure 5.56 shows how the check is performed between the foreign key table (`T1`) and the check table (`T2`):

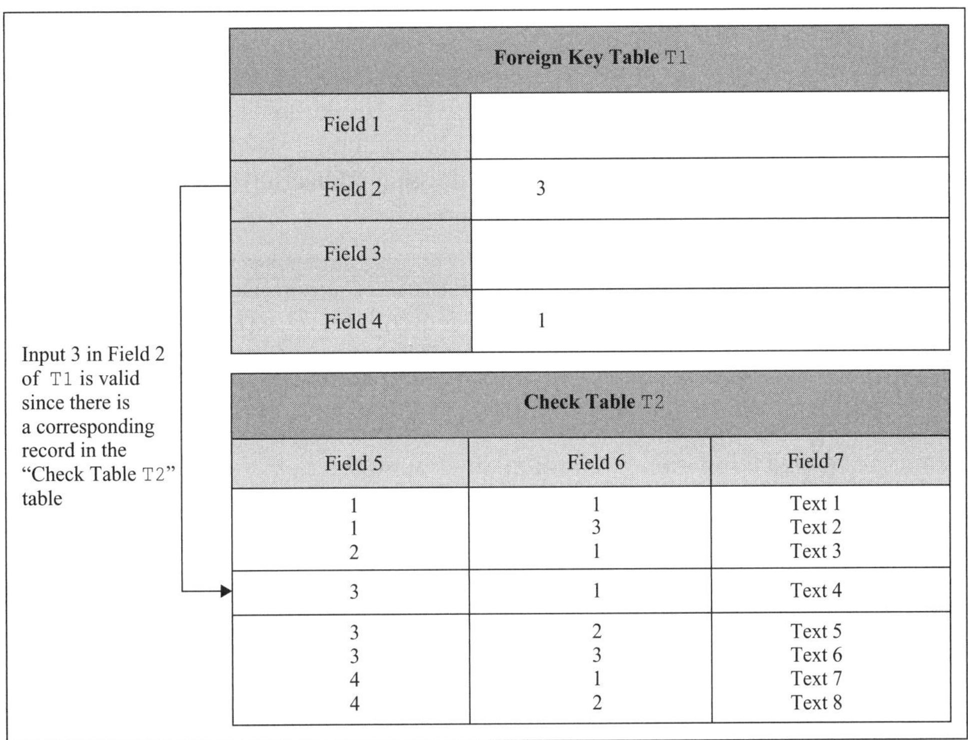

FIGURE 5.56 **The check field and the value check**

In Figure 5.56, Field 2 = 3 and Field 4 = 1 are accepted because the T2 check table contains a similar record in the key fields Field 5 = 3 and Field 6 = 1. The SAP system rejects other values apart from those specified in the check table.

Now, let's discuss the following topics in the context of foreign keys:

- Triggering foreign keys
- Exploring compound foreign keys
- Describing generic and constant foreign keys
- Exploring the cardinality of a foreign key
- Describing the foreign key field type

Triggering Foreign Keys

A foreign key is triggered as soon as you enter a value in a foreign key table. A `SELECT` statement is used to initiate this triggering. The `SELECT` statement checks for the matching rows in the check table; if the specified rows are not found in the check table, a standard message indicating that the value entered is invalid is displayed.

> **Note:** The foreign key field and the check table field must have the same domain name. This ensures that the fields being compared are compatible in data type and length.

Apart from the `SELECT` statement, a foreign key can also be triggered with the help of a function key, button, or a menu item.

Exploring Compound Foreign Keys

A compound foreign key is a foreign key consisting of two or more fields. In this case, a check is made to compare the two fields in the foreign key table against the two fields in the check table. An entry made in the foreign key fields is valid only when a corresponding value for that entry exists in the check table fields.

The field on which the compound foreign key is defined is known as the check field. A check field must not be blank. If a check field is blank, the compound foreign key is not triggered.

Describing Generic and Constant Foreign Keys

As already discussed, whenever a foreign key is created, all the primary key fields of the check table must be included in the foreign key relationship. However, in some cases, you may not want to perform a check against all these fields. In such situations, you can use generic foreign keys. In a generic foreign key, some fields can be excluded from being assigned to the key fields of the check table. The check can be performed only against the remaining key fields. Apart from this, you can assign a constant value to a key field of the check table. This allows you to check the entries against a constant value in the key field of the check table.

Figure 5.57 shows the Generic and Constant foreign keys:

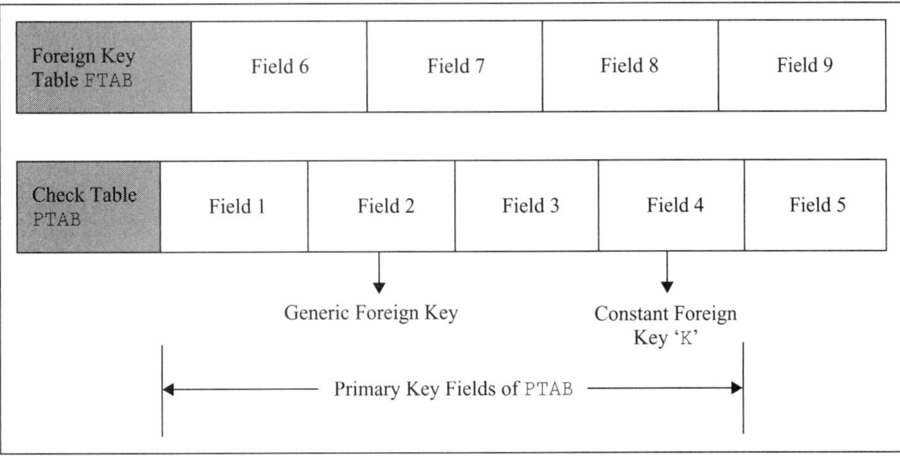

FIGURE 5.57 **Generic and constant foreign keys**

As shown in Figure 5.57, the Generic and Constant foreign keys are excluded from the foreign key relationship. The two tables used are FTAB (foreign key table) and PTAB (check table). In Figure 5.57, a foreign key relationship is established between Field 6 and Field 1 and between Field 8 and Field 3. Apart from this, Field 2 acts as the Generic key and Field 4 acts as the Constant key; therefore, both these fields are excluded from the foreign key relationship.

Let's look at how to perform a check of valid values entered by a user in different fields. Figure 5.58 shows the process of performing the check:

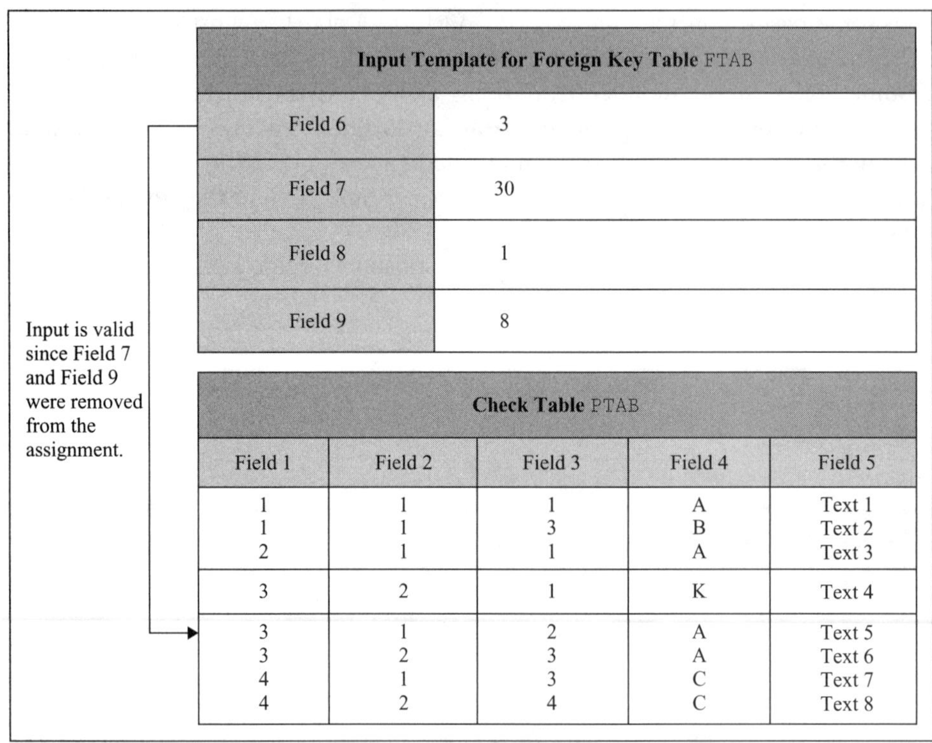

Field 1	Field 2	Field 3	Field 4	Field 5
1	1	1	A	Text 1
1	1	3	B	Text 2
2	1	1	A	Text 3
3	2	1	K	Text 4
3	1	2	A	Text 5
3	2	3	A	Text 6
4	1	3	C	Text 7
4	2	4	C	Text 8

FIGURE 5.58 **Performing a check on the values in the fields of the check table**

Figure 5.58 shows that the values entered for Field 7 and Field 9 (see Figure 5.57) are meaningless when checked against the check table. If an entry, say 3, is made in Field 6 and another entry, say 1, is made in Field 8, the SAP system accepts these entries. Notice that Field 2 and Field 4 are not included in the check.

Exploring the Cardinality of a Foreign Key

Cardinality describes the foreign key relationship with regard to the number of possible dependent records (records of the foreign key table) or referenced records (records of the check table). Cardinality is expressed as the $n{:}m$ relationship. Table 5.11 lists the possible values for the n variable:

Value	Description
1	Specifies that a check table has only one record for each record of the foreign key table.
C	Specifies that the foreign key table may contain records that do not correspond to any record of the check table.

TABLE 5.11 Possible values of the *n* variable

Table 5.12 lists the description of the possible values of the *m* variable:

Value	Description
1	Specifies that only one dependent record exists for each record in the check table.
C	Specifies that at the most, only one dependent record exists for each record of the check table.
N	Specifies that at least one dependent record exists for each record of the check table.
CN	Specifies that any number of dependent records may exist for each record of the check table.

TABLE 5.12 Possible values of the *m* variable

Describing the Foreign Key Field Type

The foreign key field type is used to describe the meaning of the foreign key field in the foreign key table. Table 5.13 describes different types of foreign key fields:

Foreign Key Field Type	Description
No key fields/candidates	Specifies that the foreign key fields are not part of the primary key fields of the foreign table. They also do not uniquely identify a record of the foreign key table (key candidates).

TABLE 5.13 Types of foreign key fields

Continued

Foreign Key Field Type	Description
Key fields/candidates	Specifies that the foreign key fields are either a part of the primary key fields of the foreign key table or uniquely identify a record of the foreign key table (key candidates).
Key fields of a text table	Specifies that the foreign key table acts as the text table for the check table.

TABLE 5.13 Types of foreign key fields

EXPLORING VIEWS

ABAP Dictionary provides a repository object, known as a view, to facilitate viewing data stored in multiple database tables. A view acts similarly to a virtual table that is, a table that does not have any physical existence. A view is created by combining the data of one or more tables (called base tables) containing information about an application object. Before creating a view, you need to define a structure for the tables and fields that are to be contained in the view. Note that if you change the data in the base tables of a view, the view itself also reflects the change. Using views, you can represent a subset of the data contained in a table or you can join multiple tables into a single virtual table. Moreover, views take up very little space in a database. This is because the database contains only the definition of the view, not a copy of the data displayed by the view.

Figure 5.59 shows that the viewed data is distributed among multiple tables:

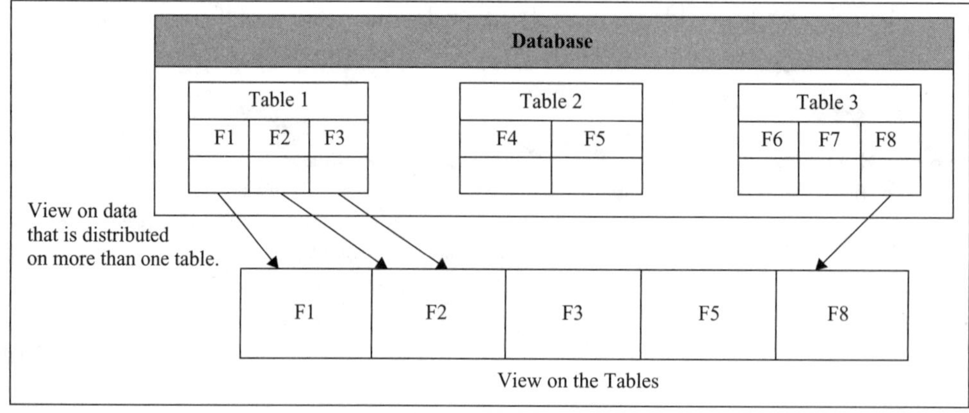

FIGURE 5.59 **Distribution of a view**

Figure 5.59 shows that the selected data from Tables 1, 2, and 3 are displayed with the help of the view object. To extract data from a view, you can either mask out one or more fields from the table (projection) or include only certain entries of a table in the view (selection). In more complicated views, data is extracted from multiple tables, where each individual table is linked to another table with a relational join operation.

Now, let's explain the following topics in the context of views:

- Relating database tables using relational operators
- Creating different types of views
- Deleting views

Relating Database Tables Using Relational Operators

Join, projection, and selection operators are the relational operators provided by SAP. These operators are used to establish relationships between different database tables. Suppose that there are two tables, `TAB A` and `TAB B`. `TAB A` has two entries and `TAB B` has four entries. Figure 5.60 shows the cross-product of both these tables:

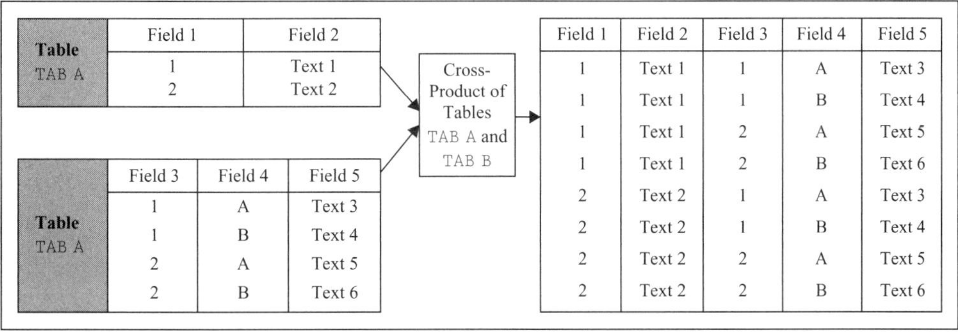

FIGURE 5.60 **The tables and the table entries**

Figure 5.60 shows the output of cross-multiplication of the records of the `TAB A` and `TAB B` tables. Now, we will see how this output varies when we apply different relational operators on the tables.

Now, let's learn how to implement the following relational operators on two or more tables:

- Join condition
- Projection condition
- Selection condition

Join Condition

The join condition is applied on tables to retrieve only the desired records in their cross-product. Figure 5.61 shows the result of applying the join condition between the TAB A and TAB B tables:

Join Condition: TAB A – Field 1 = TAB B – Field 3

Field 1	Field 2	~~Field 3~~	Field 4	Field 5
1	Text 1	~~1~~	A	Text 3
1	Text 1	1	D	Text 4
2	Text 2	~~1~~	B	Text 4
2	Text 2	~~2~~	A	Text 5
2	Text 2	~~2~~	B	Text 6

Reduce the cross-product by all records in which the entry in Field 1 is not the same as the entry in Field 3.

FIGURE 5.61 **Join condition**

In Figure 5.61, you can see that a join condition, TAB A–Field 1 = TAB B–Field 3, is applied to the TAB A and TAB B tables. The join condition removes all the records for which the entry in Field 1 is not the same as that in Field 3 (scored through in the figure).

Projection Condition

You can select the fields that you want to display in a view object. The condition to select only a specific set of fields is known as projection. Figure 5.62 shows how the projection condition can be applied to the output obtained after applying the join condition:

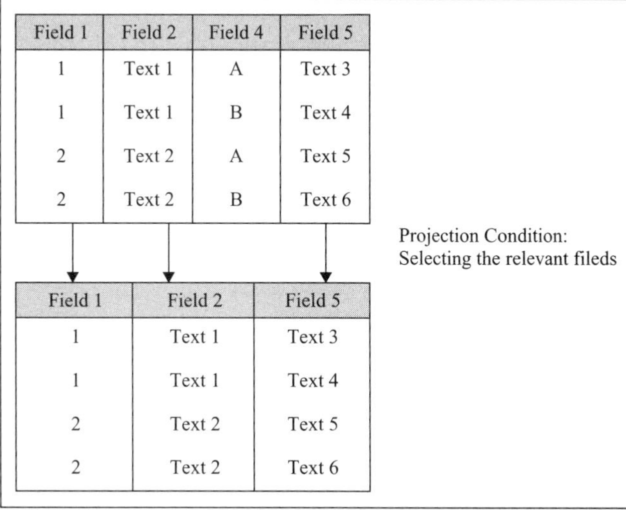

FIGURE 5.62 **Projection relational operator**

Selection Condition

A selection condition is used to filter the desired data from database tables by applying certain conditions. The selection condition uses logical operators, such as `AND` and `OR`, to filter the data. Figure 5.63 shows how to apply the selection condition on the output obtained after applying the join condition on the database tables:

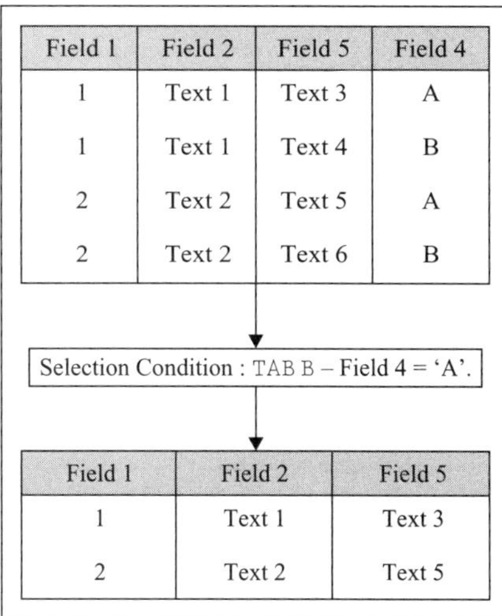

FIGURE 5.63 **Selection condition**

In Figure 5.63, notice that a selection condition is defined as `TAB B`–Field 4 = 'A'. This selection condition shows that only the records corresponding to Field 4 = 'A' are selected and displayed.

Creating Different Types of Views

As learned earlier, views are virtual tables that do not store data physically but store the data in database tables. In this section, you learn how to create the following types of views:

- Database views
- Projection views
- Maintenance views
- Help views

Let's explain these views in detail, one by one.

Database Views

As you know, data related to an application object is distributed among multiple tables by using database views. Database views use the inner join condition to join the data of different tables. You can create a database view when you want to view logically connected data from multiple tables simultaneously. You can also view the data of the database view with an ABAP program. The ABAP program retrieves the data from the database view with a database interface. Figure 5.64 shows the example of a database view:

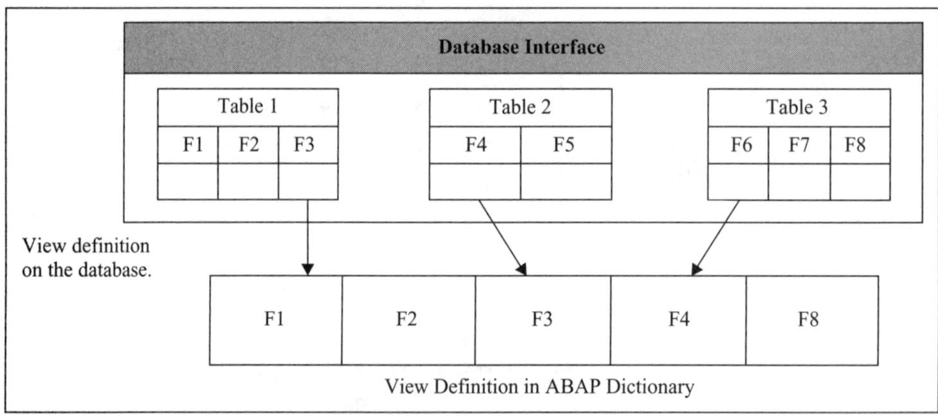

FIGURE 5.64 **Database view**

Figure 5.64 shows that the data is read from different fields distributed among multiple tables.

A database view can include an entire table. Figure 5.65 displays all the fields of a table that are included in the view:

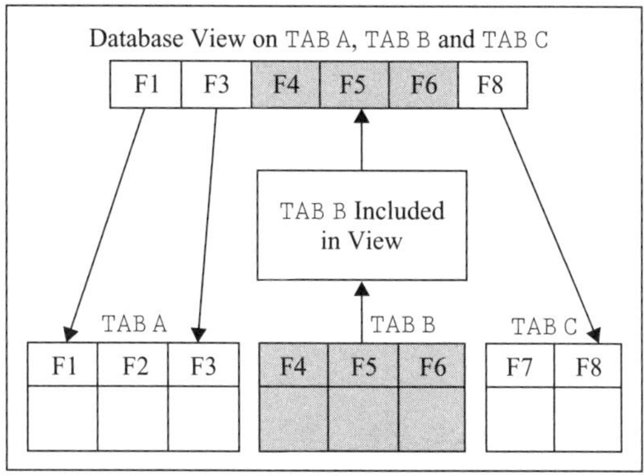

FIGURE 5.65 **Table inclusion**

In Figure 5.65, all the fields of the `TAB B` table are included in the database view. Apart from this, the fields of the `TAB A` and `TAB C` tables are also used in the view. The database view is updated automatically if any change, such as addition or deletion, is made in the existing fields.

Perform the following steps to create a database view:

1. Select the `View` radio button from the initial screen of ABAP Dictionary. Enter the name of the view to be created and click the `Create` button. In our case, we enter the name as `ZDVIEW`, as shown in Figure 5.66:

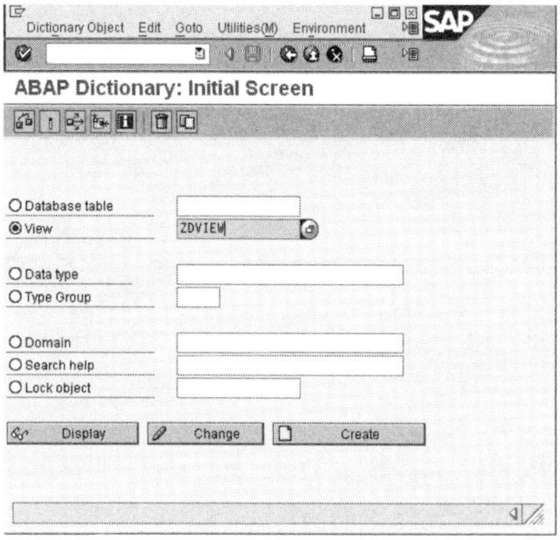

FIGURE 5.66 **Entering the name of the view**

The Choose View Type dialog box appears, as shown in Figure 5.67.

2. Select a view in the Choose View Type dialog box. In our case, we have selected Database view, as shown in Figure 5.67:

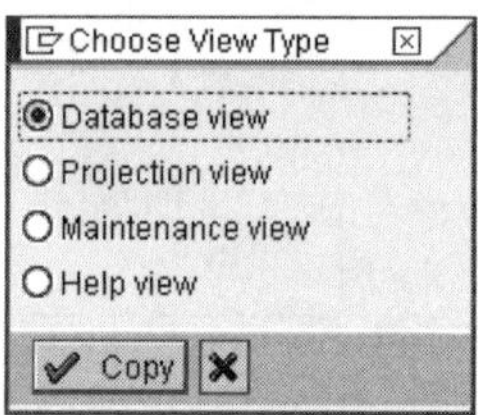

FIGURE 5.67 **Selecting a view**

3. Click the Copy (Copy) button. The Dictionary: Maintain View screen for the selected view type appears, as shown in Figure 5.68.
4. Enter a short description of the view in the Short Description field, such as Creating Database View, as shown in Figure 5.68:

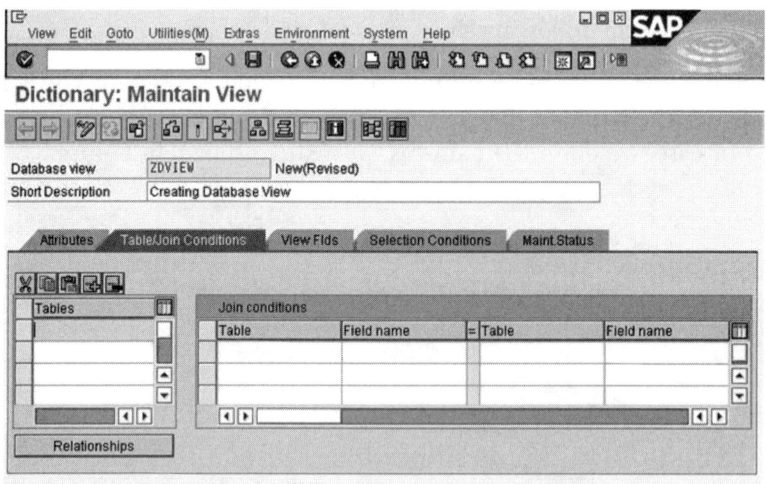

FIGURE 5.68 **Showing the maintenance screen for the selected view**

5. Enter the names of the tables, to be included in the view, in the Tables field of the Table/Join Conditions tab page.

In this case, we use the ZSTUDENT_DATA and ZSUBJECT_DATA tables, which are user-defined database tables. These two tables are linked with a foreign key. The ZSTUDENT_DATA table contains nine fields: STUDENTID, STUDENTNAME, SUBJECTCODE, MARKS, ADDRESS, CITY, CLASS, MONTHLYFEES, and YEARLYFEES. The ZSUBJECT_DATA table contains two fields, SUBJECTCODE and SUBJECTNAME. The ZSTUDENT_DATA table acts as the foreign key table, and the SUBJECTCODE field acts as the foreign key field. The ZSUBJECT_DATA table acts as the check table and the SUBJECTCODE field of this table is the primary key of the table used to define the foreign key relationship between the two tables.

Note: You can include only transparent tables in a database view.

6. Enter the name of the table containing the foreign key, that is, ZSTUDENT_DATA, in the Tables column and click the Relationships (Relationships) button to define a join condition, as shown in Figure 5.69:

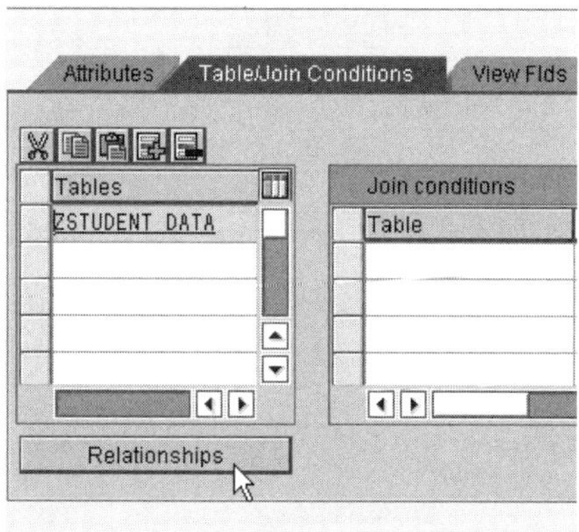

FIGURE 5.69 **An entry in the tables column**

The Relationships of Table ZSTUDENT_DATA dialog box appears (see Figure 5.70).

7. In the `Relationships of Table ZSTUDENT_DATA` dialog box, select the given check box that is displayed in respect to the `ZSTUDENT_DATA` table. The `ZSTUDENT_DATA` table has a field, which acts as a foreign key field; and the `ZSUBJECT_DATA` table has a field, which acts as a primary key field. Click the `Copy` (Copy) button, as shown in Figure 5.70:

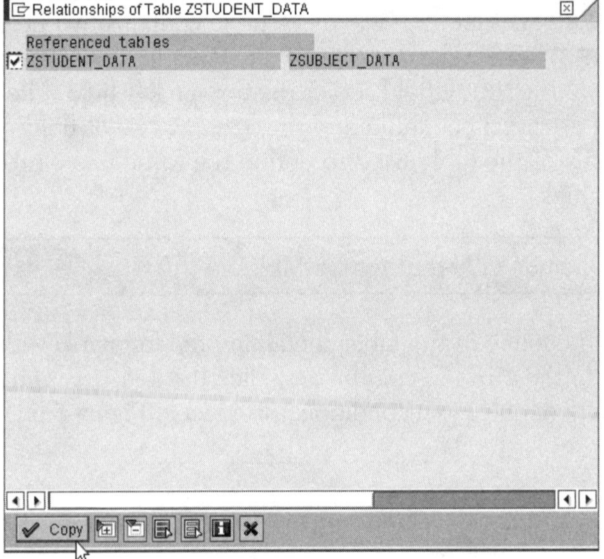

FIGURE 5.70 **Copying the join conditions**

The fields of tables that are related in a join condition are displayed, as shown in Figure 5.71:

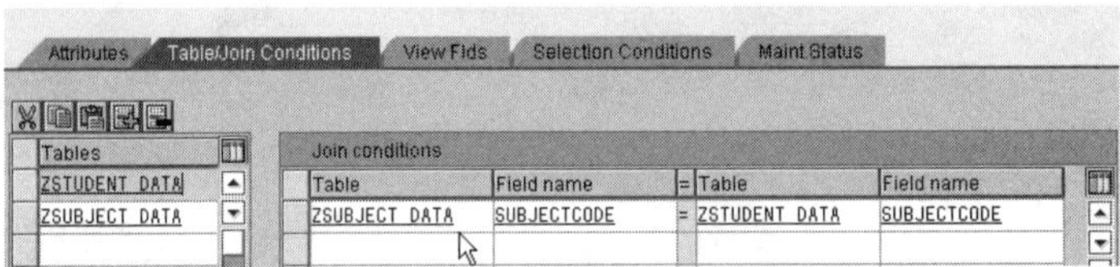

FIGURE 5.71 **Join conditions**

8. Now, select the `View Flds` (View Flds) tab to select the fields that you want to copy to the view.

The screen showing the fields related to the View Flds tab appears.

9. Click the Table fields (Table fields) button, as shown in Figure 5.72:

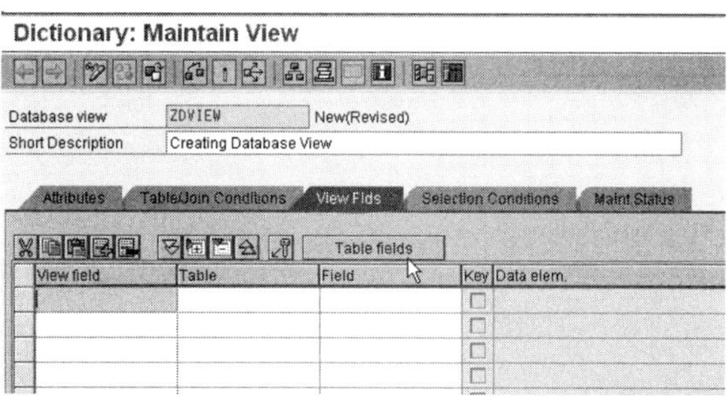

FIGURE 5.72 **Showing the view flds tab page**

The Base Tables dialog box, which displays all the tables contained in the view, appears, as shown in Figure 5.73.

10. Select all the tables, one at a time, and click the Choose (Choose) button (see Figure 5.73):

FIGURE 5.73 **Showing all the tables present in the view**

The Field Selection from Table ZSTUDENT_DATA dialog box appears, displaying all the fields used in the table (see Figure 5.74).

11. Select the fields that you want to include in the view and click the Copy button, as shown in Figure 5.74:

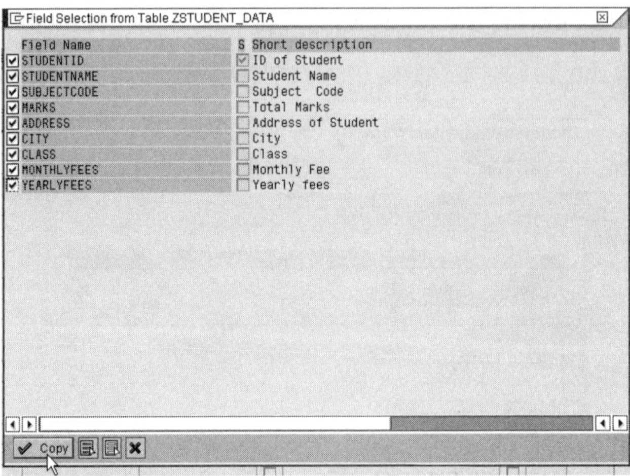

FIGURE 5.74 **Showing the selection of fields**

All the selected fields are displayed. Repeat step 5 for the second table, ZSUBJECT_DATA; however, do not select the fields that are already selected for the ZSTUDENT_DATA table. Finally, the maintenance screen displaying all the selected fields appears, as shown in Figure 5.75:

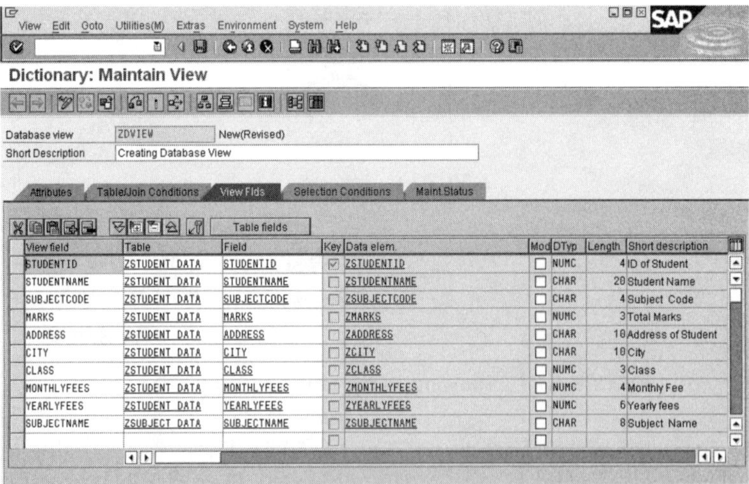

View field	Table	Field	Key	Data elem.	Mod	DTyp	Length	Short description
STUDENTID	ZSTUDENT_DATA	STUDENTID	☑	ZSTUDENTID	☐	NUMC	4	ID of Student
STUDENTNAME	ZSTUDENT_DATA	STUDENTNAME	☐	ZSTUDENTNAME	☐	CHAR	20	Student Name
SUBJECTCODE	ZSTUDENT_DATA	SUBJECTCODE	☐	ZSUBJECTCODE	☐	CHAR	4	Subject Code
MARKS	ZSTUDENT_DATA	MARKS	☐	ZMARKS	☐	NUMC	3	Total Marks
ADDRESS	ZSTUDENT_DATA	ADDRESS	☐	ZADDRESS	☐	CHAR	10	Address of Student
CITY	ZSTUDENT_DATA	CITY	☐	ZCITY	☐	CHAR	10	City
CLASS	ZSTUDENT_DATA	CLASS	☐	ZCLASS	☐	NUMC	3	Class
MONTHLYFEES	ZSTUDENT_DATA	MONTHLYFEES	☐	ZMONTHLYFEES	☐	NUMC	4	Monthly Fee
YEARLYFEES	ZSTUDENT_DATA	YEARLYFEES	☐	ZYEARLYFEES	☐	NUMC	6	Yearly fees
SUBJECTNAME	ZSUBJECT_DATA	SUBJECTNAME	☐	ZSUBJECTNAME	☐	CHAR	8	Subject Name

FIGURE 5.75 **Fields copied in the view**

> **Note:** If you want to insert restrictions for the data records to be displayed with the view, select the `Selection Conditions` (Selection Conditions) tab. In this case, we do not define any selection condition.

12. Select the `Maint. Status` (Maint.Status) tab to define the value for the `Data Browser/Table View Maint.` field. In this case, we have selected the value as the `Display/Maintenance Allowed with Restrictions` option, as shown in Figure 5.76:

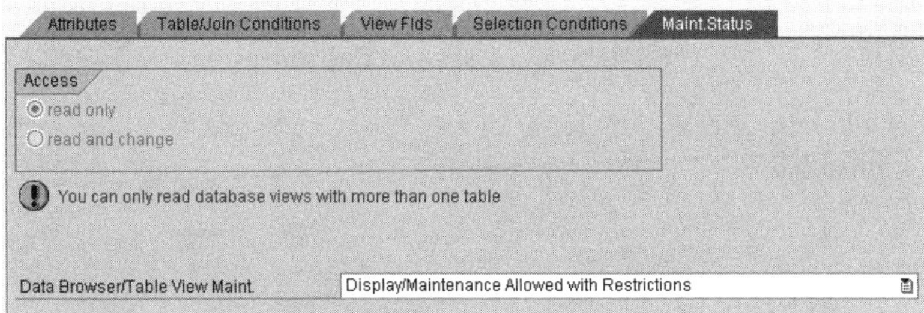

FIGURE 5.76 **Showing the maintenance status for database view**

13. Click the `Save` () icon to save all the settings related to the database view in the ZKOG_PCKG package.

> **Note:** You can maintain technical settings, such as Buffering and Buffering Type, by selecting Goto>Technical Settings.

14. Click the `Back` () icon and then the `Activate` () icon to activate the database view.

> **Note:** When the Activate icon is clicked, a log, known as the activation log, is written. The activation log can be displayed by selecting Utilities>Activation log from the maintenance screen of the table.

15. Now, select `Utilities(M)>Contents(H)` to view the content regarding the tables used in the view, as shown in Figure 5.77:

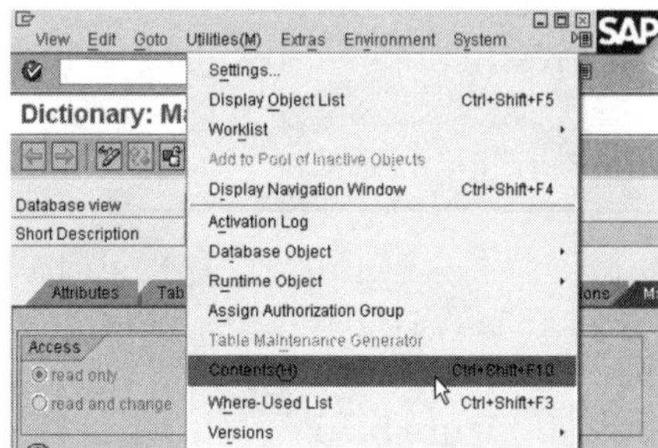

FIGURE 5.77 **Displaying the content**

The selection screen for `Data Browser: Table ZDVIEW` appears, as shown in Figure 5.78:

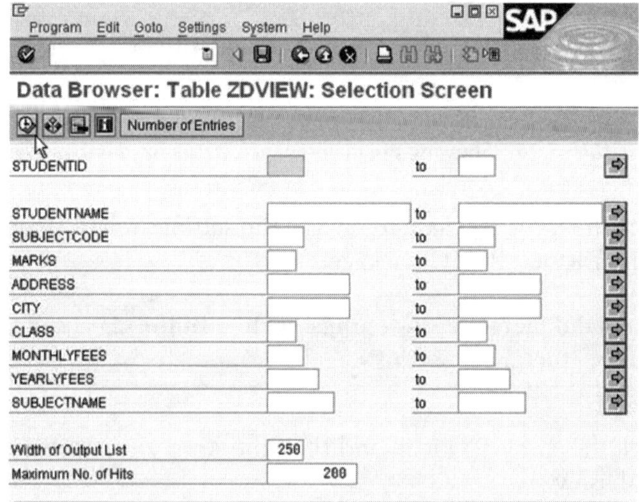

FIGURE 5.78 **The selection screen for database view**

16. Click the `Execute` (icon) icon on the application toolbar.

The `Data Browser: Table ZDVIEW Select Entries` screen appears, displaying the output of the database view, as shown in Figure 5.79:

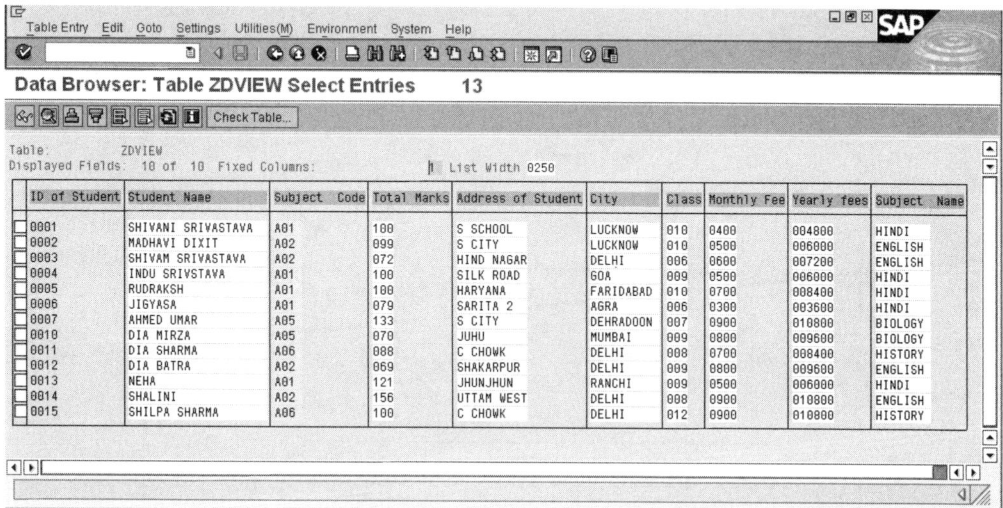

ID of Student	Student Name	Subject Code	Total Marks	Address of Student	City	Class	Monthly Fee	Yearly fees	Subject Name
0001	SHIVANI SRIVASTAVA	A01	100	S SCHOOL	LUCKNOW	010	0400	004800	HINDI
0002	MADHAVI DIXIT	A02	099	S CITY	LUCKNOW	010	0500	006000	ENGLISH
0003	SHIVAM SRIVASTAVA	A02	072	HIND NAGAR	DELHI	006	0600	007200	ENGLISH
0004	INDU SRIVSTAVA	A01	100	SILK ROAD	GOA	009	0500	006000	HINDI
0005	RUDRAKSH	A01	100	HARYANA	FARIDABAD	010	0700	008400	HINDI
0006	JIGYASA	A01	079	SARITA 2	AGRA	006	0300	003600	HINDI
0007	AHMED UMAR	A05	133	S CITY	DEHRADOON	007	0900	010800	BIOLOGY
0010	DIA MIRZA	A05	070	JUHU	MUMBAI	009	0800	009600	BIOLOGY
0011	DIA SHARMA	A06	088	C CHOWK	DELHI	008	0700	008400	HISTORY
0012	DIA BATRA	A02	069	SHAKARPUR	DELHI	009	0800	009600	ENGLISH
0013	NEHA	A01	121	JHUNJHUN	RANCHI	009	0500	006000	HINDI
0014	SHALINI	A02	156	UTTAM WEST	DELHI	008	0900	010800	ENGLISH
0015	SHILPA SHARMA	A06	100	C CHOWK	DELHI	012	0900	010800	HISTORY

FIGURE 5.79 **Output of the database view**

Now, let's learn how to create a projection view for the database table.

Projection Views

Projection views are special views used to mask certain fields in a table, displaying only the selected fields. You cannot define any selection conditions in a projection view. Apart from transparent database tables, pooled and cluster tables can be accessed with the help of a projection view. Figure 5.80 shows how to apply a projection view on a database table:

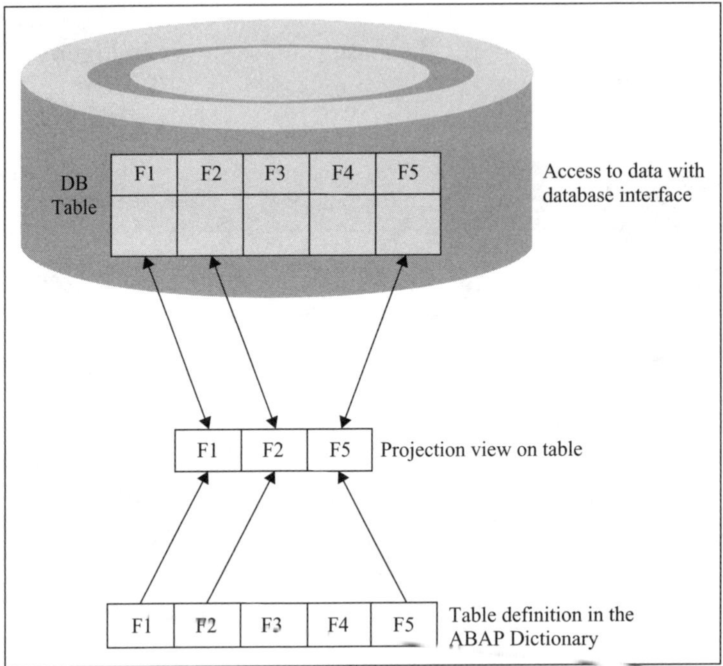

FIGURE 5.80 **Projection view**

Figure 5.80 shows that only the selected fields, such as F1, F2, and F5, of a database table are displayed in the projection view. Note that only one table can be viewed in a projection view.

Perform the following steps to create a projection view:

1. Select the `View` radio button on the initial screen of ABAP Dictionary. Enter the name of the view to be created and then click the `Create` button. In our case, we have entered the name of the view as `ZPVIEW`.

The `Choose View Type` dialog box appears.

2. Select the appropriate view to be created. In our case, we have selected the `Projection view` radio button, as shown in Figure 5.81:

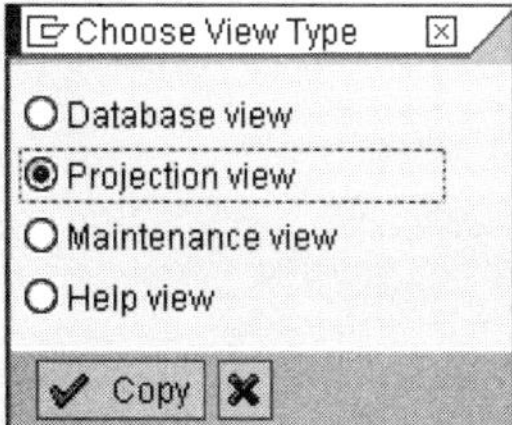

FIGURE 5.81 **Selecting the view type**

3. Click the `Copy` (Copy) button.

The `Dictionary: Maintain View` screen appears (see Figure 5.82).

4. Enter a short description in the `Short Description` field, such as Creating Projection View, as shown in Figure 5.82:

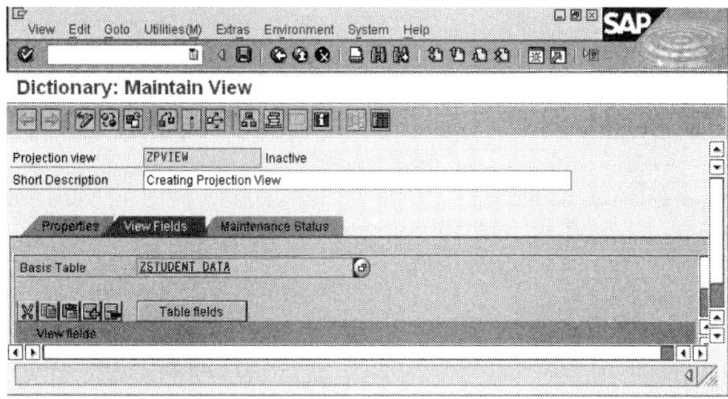

FIGURE 5.82 **Showing the maintenance screen for the projection view**

5. Enter the name of the table to be used in the projection view in the `Basis Table` field. In this case, we have entered the name of the basis table as `ZSTUDENT_DATA`.
6. Click the `Table fields` button to include the fields of the `ZSTUDENT_DATA` table in the projection view.

The `Field Selection from Table ZSTUDENT_DATA` screen appears (Figure 5.83).

7. Select the fields that you want to include in the projection view, as shown in Figure 5.83:

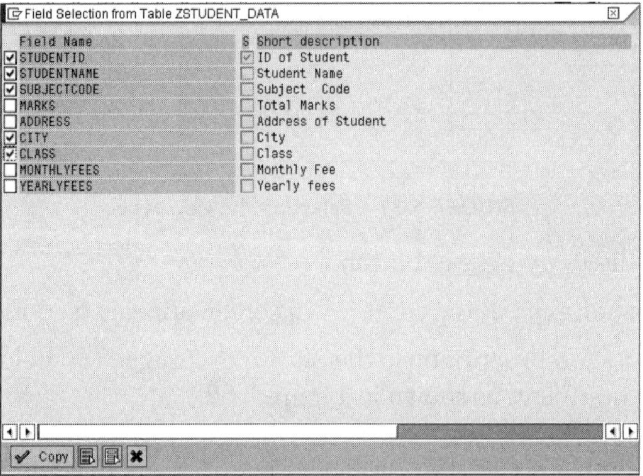

FIGURE 5.83 **Selecting fields for projection view**

In this case, we have selected the `STUDENTID`, `STUDENTNAME`, `SUBJECTCODE`, `CITY`, and `CLASS` fields.

8. Click the `Copy` (Copy) button. All the selected fields for the projection view are displayed on the maintenance screen, as shown in Figure 5.84:

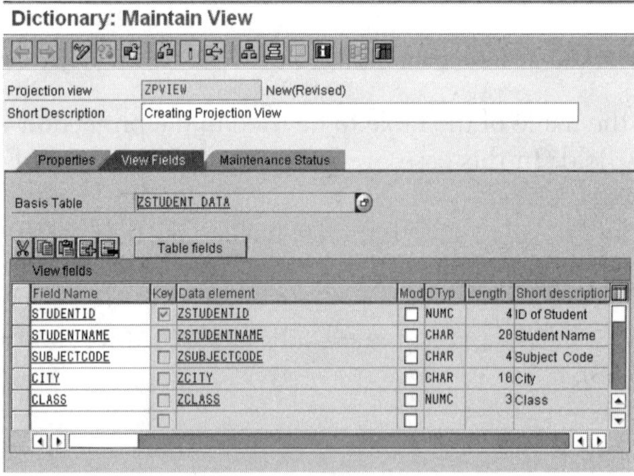

FIGURE 5.84 **Fields used for projection views**

9. Select the `Maintenance Status` (Maintenance Status) tab to define an access method. Select the `read only` radio button, as shown in Figure 5.85:

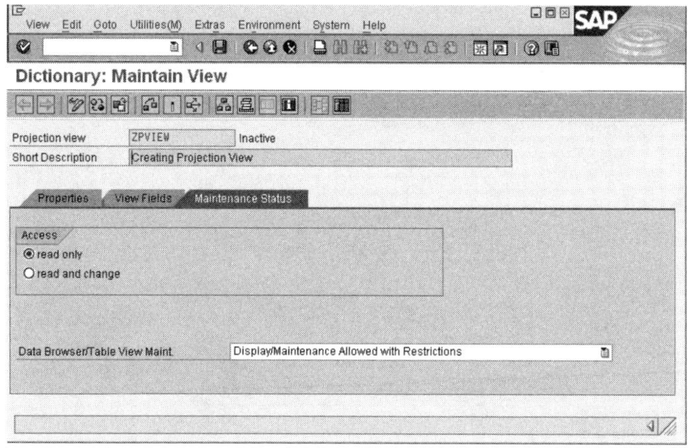

FIGURE 5.85 **Defining the maintenance status for projection view**

10. Select the `Display/Maintenance Allowed with Restrictions` option from the `Data Browser/Table View Maint.` drop-down menu (see Figure 5.85).
11. Finally, click the `Save` () icon and then click the `Activate` () icon.
12. In the `Dictionary: Maintain View` screen, select `Utilities (M) > Contents` (see Figure 5.85).

This action displays the selection screen for `Data Browser: Table ZPVIEW`, as shown in Figure 5.86:

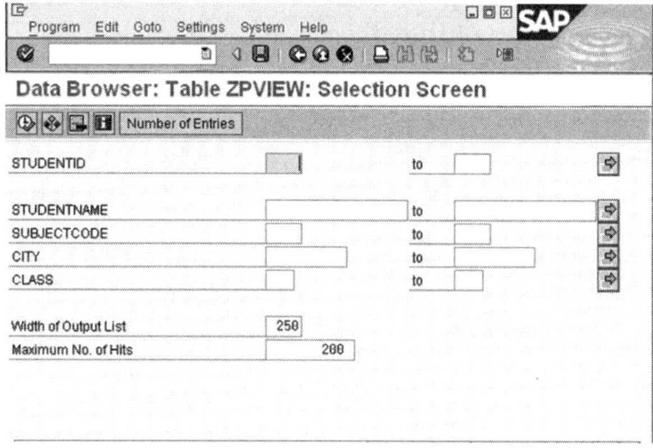

FIGURE 5.86 **The selection screen**

13. Click the `Execute` (icon) icon. The output of the projection view appears, as shown in Figure 5.87:

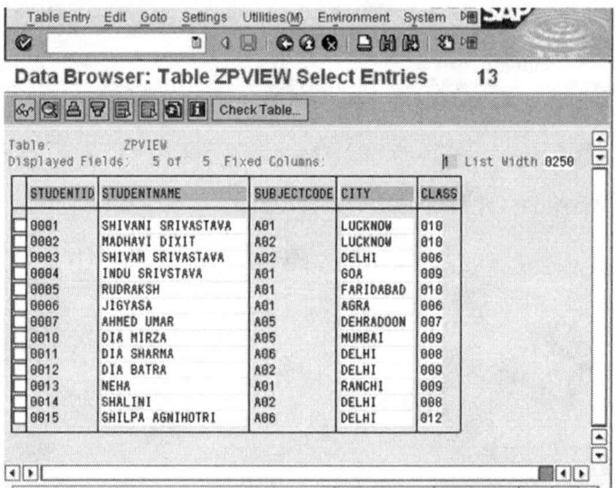

FIGURE 5.87 **Output of the projection view**

Now, let's learn how to create a maintenance view.

Maintenance Views

Multiple tables of a database can be combined to form a logical unit, but only if they are connected to each other by foreign keys. This logical unit can act as an application object. You can use a maintenance view to display and modify the data stored in an application object. Every maintenance view has a maintenance status associated with it, which determines the operations that have to be performed on the data of the associated tables.

> **Note:** A foreign key relationship must exist between the tables used in a maintenance view. The foreign key relationship is used to define the join conditions for the maintenance view.

Figure 5.88 displays the maintenance view defined for three tables:

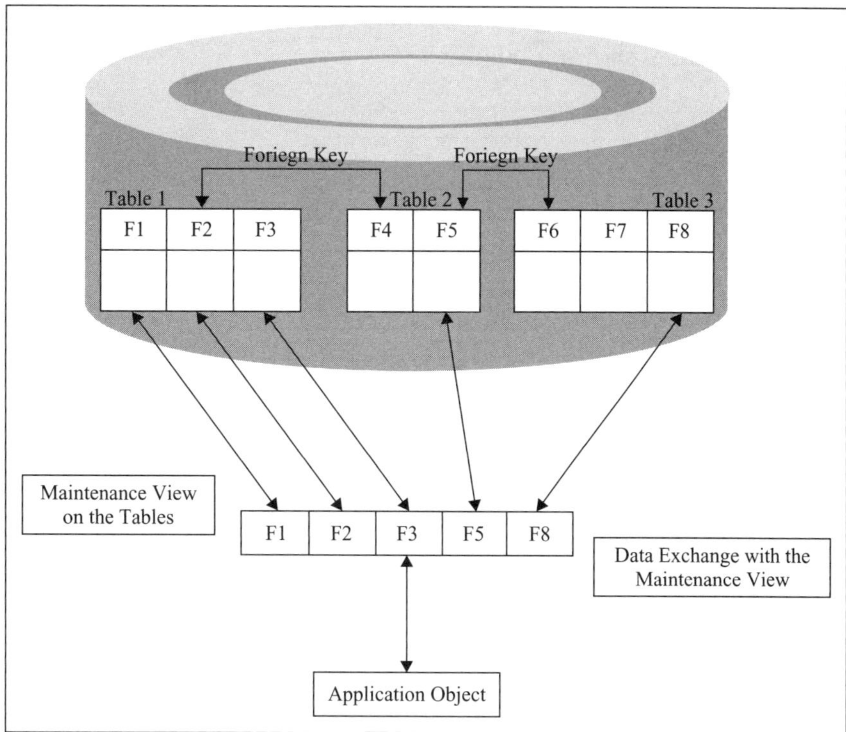

FIGURE 5.88 **Showing the maintenance view**

Figure 5.88 shows three tables: Table 1, Table 2, and Table 3. The F2 field of Table 1 is connected to the F4 field of Table 2 with a foreign key. Similarly, the F5 field of Table 2 is connected to the F6 field of Table 3 with a foreign key. The maintenance view is implemented on the three tables and is used to extract data from the F1, F2, F3, F5, and F8 fields.

Perform the following steps to create a maintenance view:

1. Select the `View` radio button from the initial screen of ABAP Dictionary. Enter the name of the view to be created and click the `Create` button. In this case, we have entered the name of the view as ZMVIEW.

The `Choose View Type` dialog box appears (see Figure 5.89).

2. Select the Maintenance view radio button, in the Choose View Type dialog box, as shown in Figure 5.89:

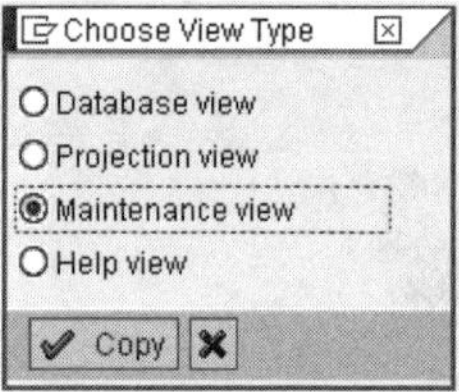

FIGURE 5.89 **Selecting type of the view**

3. Click the Copy (Copy) button.

The Dictionary: Maintain View screen appears.

4. Enter a short description in the Short Description field, such as Creating Maintenance View, as shown in Figure 5.90:

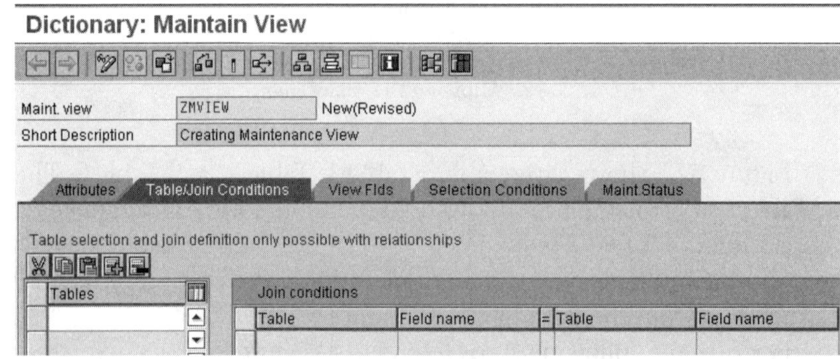

FIGURE 5.90 **Maintenance screen**

5. Enter the name of the primary table of the view under the Tables column in the Tables/Join Conditions tab page. In this case, we have entered the name of the primary table as ZSTUDENT_DATA, as shown in Figure 5.91:

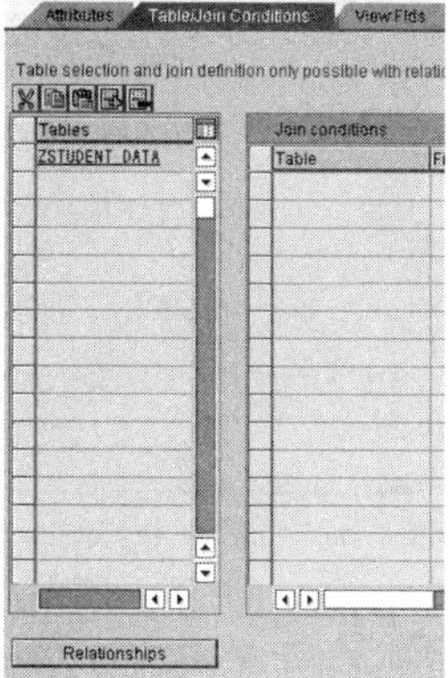

FIGURE 5.91 **Primary table**

Note that in a maintenance view, only those tables that are linked to the primary table (indirectly) with a foreign key can be viewed.

6. Place the cursor on the name of the primary table and click the `Relationships` button.

The `Relationships of Table ZSTUDENT_DATA` dialog box appears, as shown in Figure 5.92:

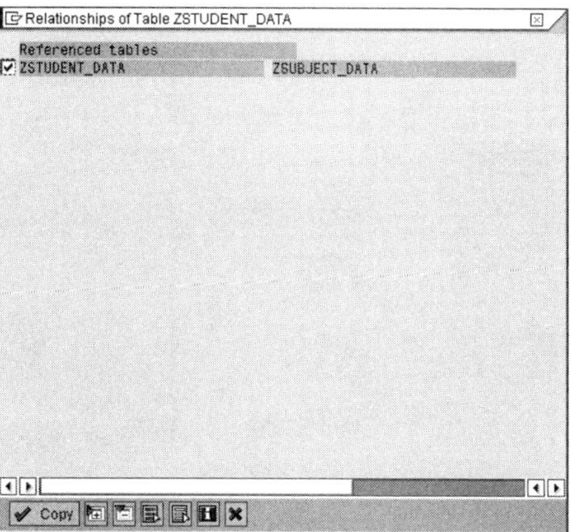

FIGURE 5.92 **Relationships between tables**

7. Select the ZSTUDENT_DATA check box (see Figure 5.92).
8. Click the Copy (Copy) button. The secondary table, that is, ZSUBJECT_DATA, is now included in the maintenance view.

> **Note:** You can also include more secondary tables associated with the mentioned secondary table, that is, ZSUBJECT_DATA. This can be done by first placing the cursor on the name of that secondary table and then clicking the Relationships button.

Figure 5.93 displays the name of the primary and secondary tables in the maintenance screen:

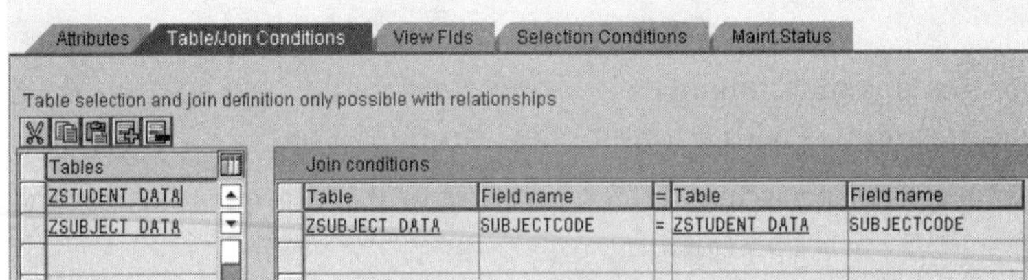

FIGURE 5.93 **Primary table and secondary table**

9. Select the View Flds (View Flds) tab to copy the fields used in the view.
10. Click the Table fields (Table fields) button. The names of the tables appear in a dialog box, as shown in Figure 5.94:

FIGURE 5.94 **Name of the tables**

11. Click the name of the tables, one at a time, and then click the `Choose` (Copy) button.

Note: All the key fields related to the primary table (`ZSTUDENT_DATA`, in our case) must be included in the maintenance view. In addition to this, all the key fields of the secondary tables that are not included in the foreign key relationship must also be included in the view.

The `Field Selection from Table ZSTUDENT_DATA` dialog box appears.

12. Select the check boxes associated with the fields that are to be included in the view. Finally, click the `Copy` (Copy) pushbutton, as shown in Figure 5.95:

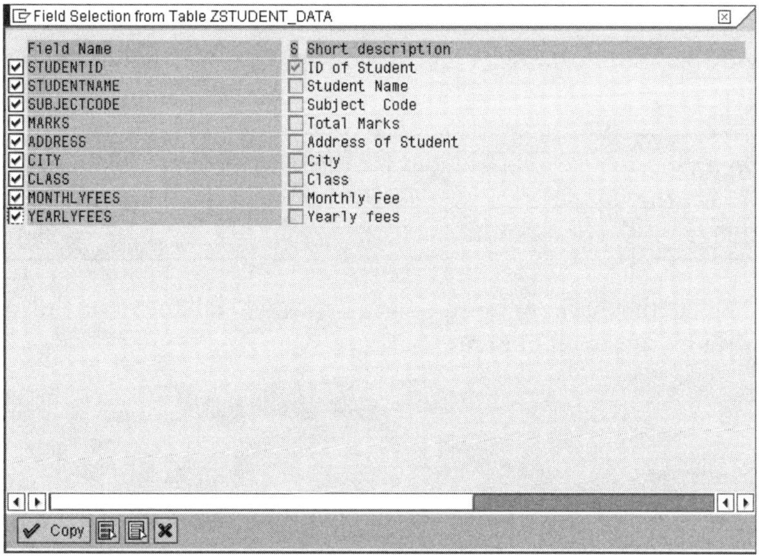

Field Selection from Table ZSTUDENT_DATA

Field Name	S	Short description
STUDENTID		ID of Student
STUDENTNAME		Student Name
SUBJECTCODE		Subject Code
MARKS		Total Marks
ADDRESS		Address of Student
CITY		City
CLASS		Class
MONTHLYFEES		Monthly Fee
YEARLYFEES		Yearly fees

Copy

FIGURE 5.95 **Selecting fields for a view**

13. Repeat the same procedure for the secondary table, that is, `ZSUBJECT_DATA`. Select all the fields except those that are already selected and then click the `Copy` (Copy) button, as shown in Figure 5.96:

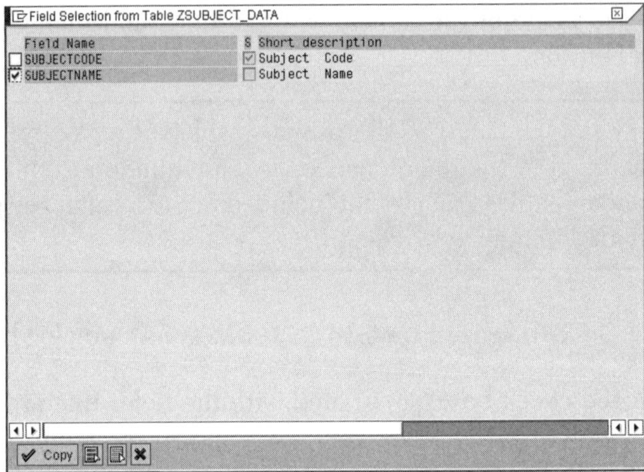

FIGURE 5.96 **Selecting fields from the secondary table**

Figure 5.96 shows the selection of the `SUBJECTNAME` field from the secondary table.

> **Note:** If you want to insert restrictions for the data records to be displayed with the view, select the `Selection Conditions` (Selection Conditions) tab. In this case, we do not define any selection condition.

14. Select the `Maintenance Status` (Maint.Status) tab to define the maintenance status, as shown in Figure 5.97:

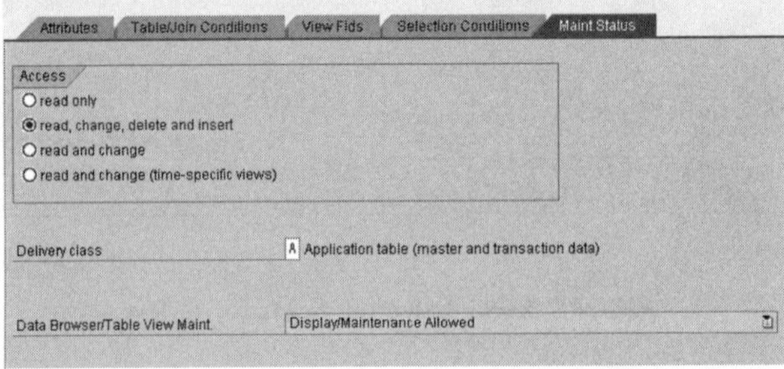

FIGURE 5.97 **Defining maintenance status**

15. Click the `Save` (icon) icon and save the view in the `ZKOG_PCKG` package. Now, click the `Activate` (icon) icon.

16. Select `Utilities(M)>Table Maintenance Generator` to generate a maintenance dialog box, as shown in Figure 5.98:

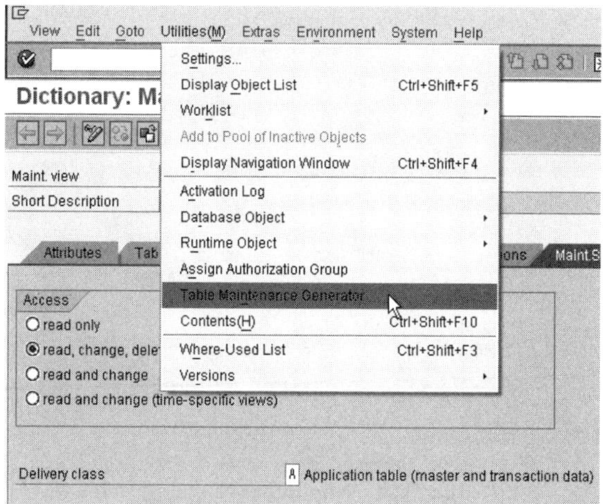

FIGURE 5.98 **Generating a maintenance dialog box**

The `Generate Table Maintenance Dialog: Generation Environment` screen appears, as shown in Figure 5.99:

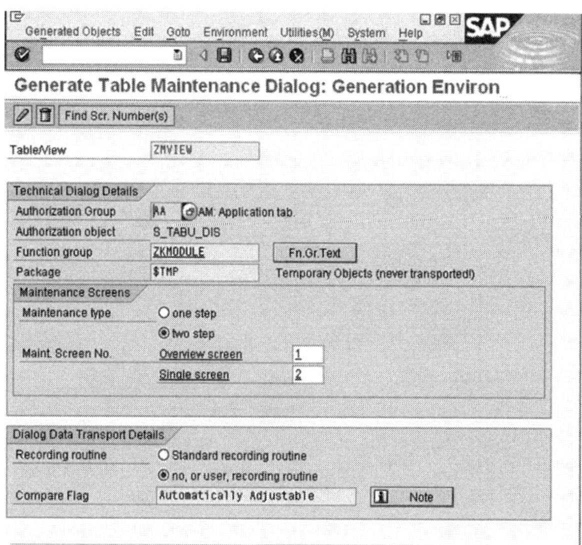

FIGURE 5.99 **The generate table maintenance dialog: generation environment screen**

Table 5.14 describes the functions of different maintenance dialog fields that appear in Figure 5.99:

Field	Description
Authorization Group	Shows that the user is responsible for maintaining the content of the table/view.
Function Group	Shows the function group in which the tables/view-specific maintenance dialog components are generated.
Maintenance Type	Contains two radio buttons, one step and two step, to maintain the settings of the screen (see Figure 5.99).
Maint. Screen No.	Shows the internal number of each maintenance screen.
Recording Routine	Shows the table/view contents that can be transported in the SAP system.

TABLE 5.14 Maintenance dialog fields

17. Enter AA as the authorization group, ZKMODULE as the function module, and select the `two step` radio button as the maintenance type (see Figure 5.99).
18. Finally, click the `Save` (💾) icon to save the settings for the maintenance dialog. Now, click the `Back` button to return to the screen shown in Figure 5.98.
19. Select `Utilities > Contents (H)`. The `Display View "Creating Maintenance View": Overview` screen appears, as shown in Figure 5.100:

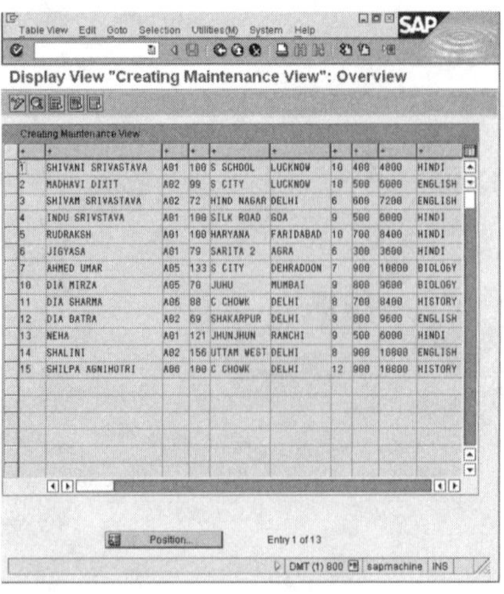

FIGURE 5.100 **Showing the display overview screen**

The screen in Figure 5.100 is shown in the display mode. Now, let's look how to change an existing entry in a field.

20. Select the entry for a field that you want to change and select the `Display>Change` () icon.

The `Information` dialog box appears, as shown in Figure 5.101:

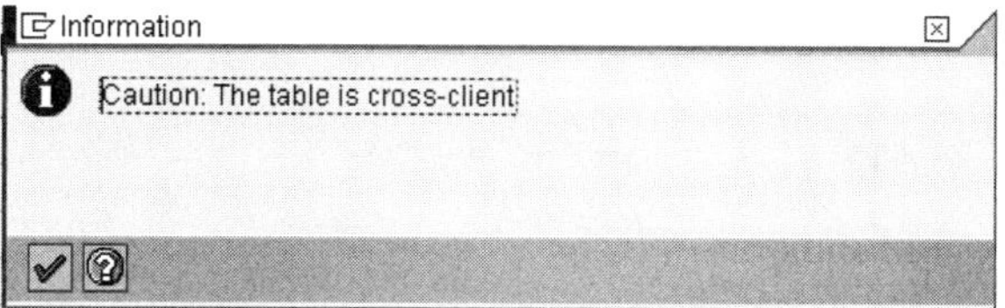

FIGURE 5.101 **Showing the information dialog box**

21. Click the `Continue` () icon to continue.

The `Change View "Creating Maintenance View" Overview` screen appears, as shown in Figure 5.102:

Change View "Creating Maintenance View": Overview

New Entries

Creating Maintenance View

+	+	+	+	+	+	+	+	+	+
1	SHIVANI SRIVASTAVA	A01	100	S SCHOOL	LUCKNOW	10	400	4800	HINDI
2	MADHAVI DIXIT	A02	99	S CITY	LUCKNOW	10	500	6000	ENGLISH
3	SHIVAM SRIVASTAVA	A02	72	HIND NAGAR	DELHI	6	600	7200	ENGLISH
4	INDU SRIVSTAVA	A01	100	SILK ROAD	GOA	9	500	6000	HINDI
5	RUDRAKSH	A01	100	HARYANA	FARIDABAD	10	700	8400	HINDI
6	JIGYASA	A01	79	SARITA 2	AGRA	6	300	3600	HINDI
7	AHMED UMAR	A05	133	S CITY	DEHRADOON	7	900	10800	BIOLOGY
10	DIA MIRZA	A05	70	JUHU	MUMBAI	9	000	9600	BIOLOGY
11	DIA SHARMA	A06	88	C CHOWK	DELHI	8	700	8400	HISTORY
12	DIA BATRA	A02	69	SHAKARPUR	DELHI	9	800	9600	ENGLISH
13	NEHA	A01	121	JHUNJHUN	RANCHI	9	500	6000	HINDI
14	SHALINI	A02	156	UTTAM WEST	DELHI	8	900	10800	ENGLISH
15	SHILPA SHARMA	A06	100	C CHOWK	DELHI	12	900	10800	HISTORY

FIGURE 5.102 **Showing the change view overview screen**

22. Change the name "SHILPA AGNIHOTRI" to "SHILPA SHARMA", as shown in Figure 5.102. Finally, click the `Save` icon to save the changes.

Help Views

Help views are created when you want to use an outer join to obtain data from database tables. This view is generally used to create a Search Help object; that is, to provide input helps (F4) for different fields. In Search Help, these views act as selection methods. These selection methods can be either a table or a view, which means that data can be selected from either a table or a view. Note that a table is used as a selection method in a help view only if you need to use an outer join to retrieve the data. Figure 5.103 shows how to apply a Help view on a database table:

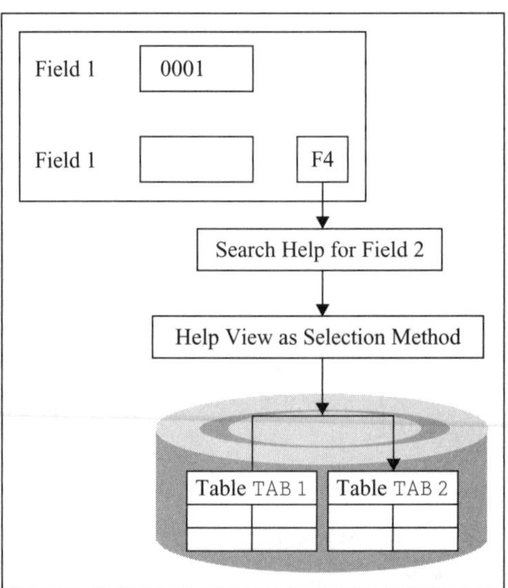

FIGURE 5.103 **Implementing the help view on database tables**

Figure 5.103 shows the method of implementing the Help view. In Figure 5.103, we have selected the Help view as the selection method for Field 2.
Perform the following steps to create a Help view:

1. Select the `View` radio button from the initial screen of ABAP Dictionary. Enter the name of the view to be created (in this case, the `ZHVIEW`) and click the `Create` button.

The `Choose View Type` dialog box appears.

2. Select the `Help view` radio button on the `Choose View Type` dialog box, as shown in Figure 5.104:

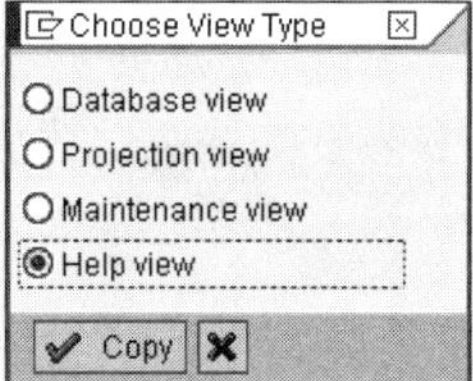

FIGURE 5.104 **Selecting the type of the view**

3. Click the `Copy` (Copy) button.

The `Dictionary: Maintain View` screen appears, as shown in Figure 5.105:

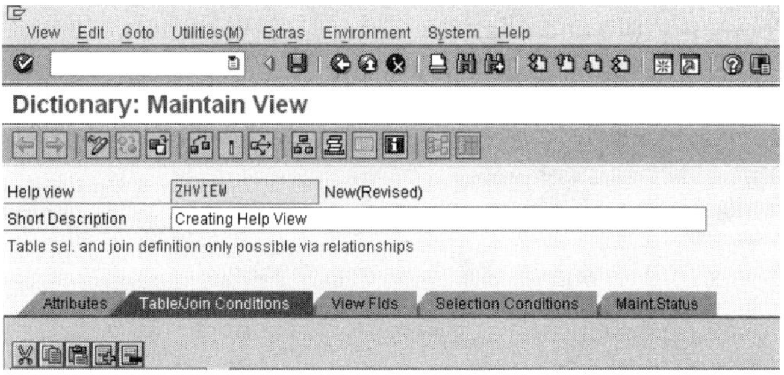

FIGURE 5.105 **Description for the help view**

4. Enter a short description in the `Short Description` field, such as Creating Help View.
5. Click the `Save` icon to save the view in the `ZKOG_PCKG` package.
6. Now, enter the name of the primary table to be used in the view under the `Tables` column in the `Tables/Join Conditions` tab page. The table that is linked with this primary table with the help of a foreign key, that is, `ZSTUDENT_DATA`, is included in the view created.
7. Position the cursor on the name of the primary table and click the `Relationship` button. When you click this button, you see the screen, that was previously shown in Figure 5.92. In Figure 5.92, we selected the check box showing the name of the primary table. Now, click the `Copy` (Copy) button. The respective join condition appears on the screen for the `Table/Join Conditions` tab page, as shown in Figure 5.106:

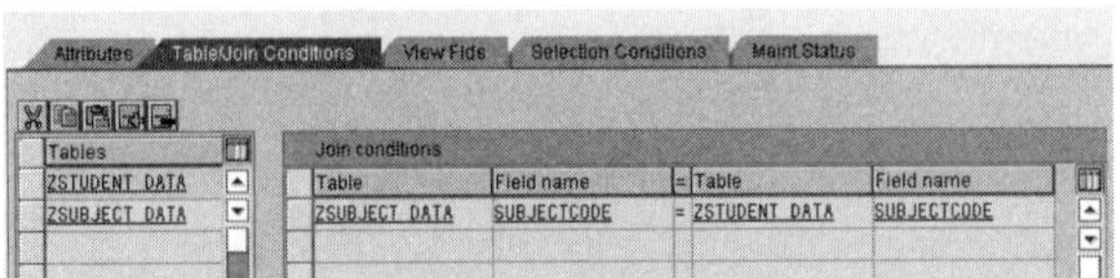

Tables
ZSTUDENT DATA
ZSUBJECT DATA

Join conditions

Table	Field name	=	Table	Field name
ZSUBJECT DATA	SUBJECTCODE	=	ZSTUDENT DATA	SUBJECTCODE

FIGURE 5.106 **The screen showing the join conditions**

8. Select the `View Flds` tab to select the fields that you want to include in the view. Note that the key fields of the primary table are copied automatically to the view as proposals.
9. Select the `Table Fields` (Table fields) button. When you click this button, a list of the tables contained in this view is displayed.
10. Select any table and click the `Copy` (✔ Copy) button. Repeat the same for all the tables. Figure 5.107 shows the screen containing the fields included in the view:

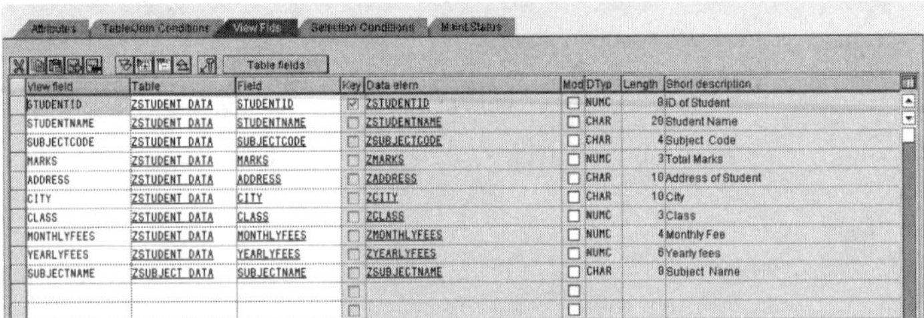

View field	Table	Field	Key	Data elem	Mod	DTyp	Length	Short description
STUDENTID	ZSTUDENT DATA	STUDENTID	☑	ZSTUDENTID	☐	NUMC	8	ID of Student
STUDENTNAME	ZSTUDENT DATA	STUDENTNAME	☐	ZSTUDENTNAME	☐	CHAR	20	Student Name
SUBJECTCODE	ZSTUDENT DATA	SUBJECTCODE	☐	ZSUBJECTCODE	☐	CHAR	4	Subject Code
MARKS	ZSTUDENT DATA	MARKS	☐	ZMARKS	☐	NUMC	3	Total Marks
ADDRESS	ZSTUDENT DATA	ADDRESS	☐	ZADDRESS	☐	CHAR	18	Address of Student
CITY	ZSTUDENT DATA	CITY	☐	ZCITY	☐	CHAR	10	City
CLASS	ZSTUDENT DATA	CLASS	☐	ZCLASS	☐	NUMC	3	Class
MONTHLYFEES	ZSTUDENT DATA	MONTHLYFEES	☐	ZMONTHLYFEES	☐	NUMC	4	Monthly Fee
YEARLYFEES	ZSTUDENT DATA	YEARLYFEES	☐	ZYEARLYFEES	☐	NUMC	6	Yearly fees
SUBJECTNAME	ZSUBJECT DATA	SUBJECTNAME	☐	ZSUBJECTNAME	☐	CHAR	8	Subject Name

FIGURE 5.107 **Fields included in the view**

In Figure 5.107, you see all the fields that are selected for the Help view.

11. Select the `Maint. Status` (Maint.Status) tab to set the access method, as shown in Figure 5.108:

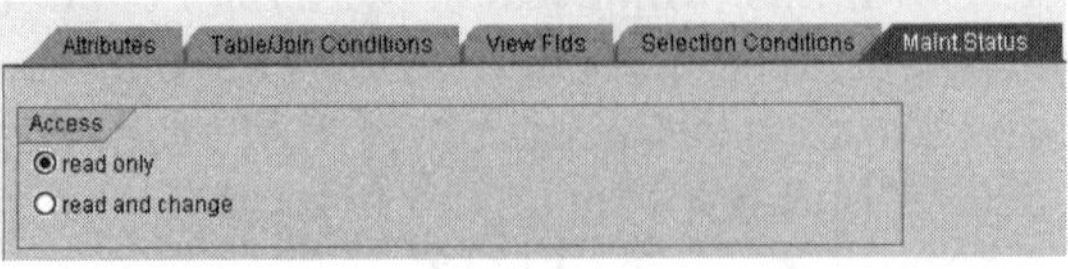

FIGURE 5.108 **The access method**

12. In the `Access` group box of the `Maint. Status` tab, select the `read only` radio button.

13. Now, click the `Activate` (icon) icon from the application toolbar. The created Help view is now activated and can be used as a selection method for Search Help.

You can restrict the set of data records that can be selected in a view by defining a selection condition. These conditions can be placed on different entries under the `Selection Condition` tab. Table 5.15 shows the description of the entries on the `Selection Conditions` tab:

Entry	Description
Table	Shows the name of the base table from which the field is taken.
Field name	Shows the name of the field for which the selection condition is formulated.
Operator	Defines the operators used to compare the field contents, and the comparison value. You can find the set of valid operators in the F4 help.
Comparison value	Shows the constant value by which the field value can be compared.
AND/OR	Shows the link between two lines of the selection condition.

TABLE 5.15 Description of the entries on the selection condition tab

Deleting Views

A view can be deleted if it is no longer in use.

Perform the following steps to delete a view:

1. Select the `View` radio button and enter the name of the view in the initial screen of ABAP Dictionary. Select the `Where-used list` (icon) icon to find the database tables associated with this view.
2. Select the `Delete` (icon) icon to delete the selected view. A dialog box appears, prompting you to confirm the delete request.
3. Confirm the delete request by clicking the `Yes` button. Consequently, the view is deleted from ABAP Dictionary and from the database being used by the SAP system.

EXPLORING SEARCH HELPS

Search Helps, another repository object of ABAP Dictionary, are used to display all the possible values for a field in the form of a list. This list is also known as a hit list. You can select the values that are to be entered in the fields from this hit list. The following are the three types of Search Help objects provided by ABAP Dictionary:

- Elementary Search Help
- Collective Search Help
- Append Search Help

Elementary Search Help

The elementary Search Help is used to define an input help. This input help allows you to perform the following functions:

- Defining the source from where the data displayed in the hit list is retrieved (the selection method)
- Defining the Search Help parameters; that is, information related to the value selection
- Defining the dialog steps to be executed in the input help

The data in a hit list can be retrieved from a single database table, multiple tables, or a client-specific table.

The interface of Search Help defines the context data that can be used in the input help and the data that can be returned to the input template. This interface consists of parameters that define the fields of the selection method. Table 5.16 lists the descriptions of different kinds of interface parameters:

Search Help Parameter	Description
Import parameter	Used when the context information from the processed input template is copied to the Search Help process.
Export parameter	Used when the values from a hit list have to be returned to the input template.

TABLE 5.16 Types of parameters

Note that the parameters of Search Help must be assigned to a data element.

Collective Search Help

The collective Search Help is a combination of several elementary Search Helps. This Search Help is used to define alternative Search Help paths. A collective Search Help is a collection of several elementary Search Helps; therefore, you can transfer the values between various elementary Search Helps and the input templates by using the collective Search Help in the input help. Consequently, a collective Search Help also has an interface to transfer the values of the associated fields.

Now, let's explain the following topics in the context of the structure of collective Search Helps:

- Interface of the collective Search Help
- Assigned Search Helps

Interface of the Collective Search Help

Similar to the elementary Search Help, the collective Search Help uses an interface for both the import and the export parameters. Data is exchanged between the screen template and the parameters of the assigned elementary Search Helps by using this interface. Figure 5.109 shows the exchange of data in a collective Search Help:

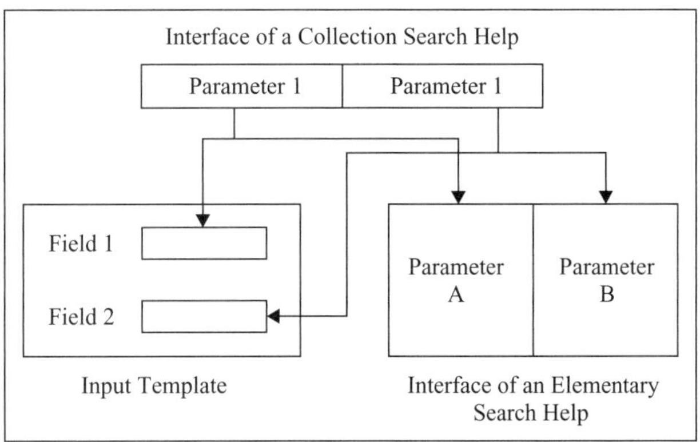

FIGURE 5.109 **The exchange of data in a collective search help**

Figure 5.109 shows how data is exchanged between a screen template and the parameters of the elementary Search Helps.

Assigned Search Helps

The assigned Search Help is a type of collective Search Help that does not include all the parameters of an elementary Search Help. Figure 5.110 shows the interface of the collective Search Help:

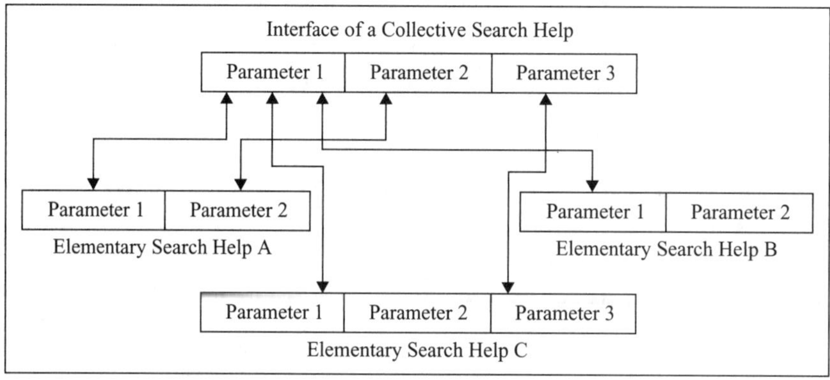

FIGURE 5.110 **Interface of a collective search help**

In Figure 5.110, you can see that certain parameters, such as Parameter 2 of the elementary Search Help B and Parameter 2 of the elementary Search Help C, are not included in the interface of the collective Search Help.

Append Search Help

You can enhance the features of the collective Search Help by appending further elementary Search Helps (also known as search parts) to it. This kind of search help is known as an append search help. The appended elementary Search Helps can also be enhanced by appending further Search Helps to them. Figure 5.111 shows the structure of an append Search Help:

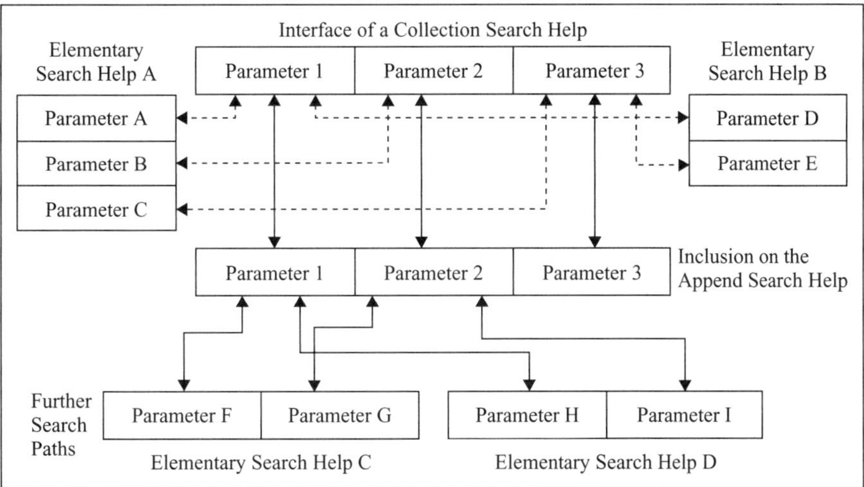

FIGURE 5.111 **The append search help structure**

Figure 5.111 shows the assignment of further search paths that is, the addition of elementary Search Helps, to an existing collective Search Help. You can see that the `Append search help` is appended to the collective Search Help. This appended Search Help is enhanced with the addition of two more Search Helps, C and D.

EXPLORING LOCK OBJECTS

Lock Object is a feature offered by ABAP Dictionary that helps multiple users to access the same set of data records synchronously. Data records are accessed with the help of specific programs. Consequently, any inconsistency at the time that data is inserted or changed in a table can be avoided by using lock objects. Figure 5.112 shows the simultaneous access to stored data in a database with the help of programs:

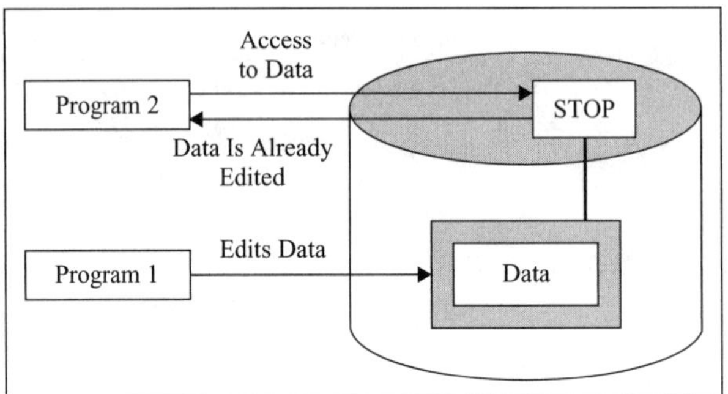

FIGURE 5.112 **Showing simultaneous access to data**

Simultaneous access is implemented with the help of a lock mechanism containing the function modules. These function modules are generated automatically from the definition of the Lock Objects in ABAP Dictionary, and they are used to set and release the Lock Objects when interactive transactions are performed.

The tables whose data records you want to lock must be defined in a Lock Object, along with their key fields. First, a primary table is selected, and then the foreign key relationships are used to add secondary tables to a Lock Object, as shown in Figure 5.113:

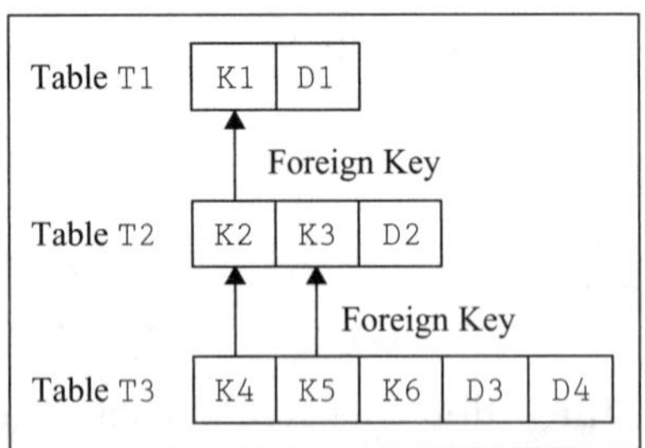

FIGURE 5.113 **Structure of lock objects**

Figure 5.113 shows the implementation of Lock Objects in tables `T1`, `T2`, and `T3`, which are related to each other with a foreign key.

Now, let's explain the following topics in the context of Lock Objects:

- Describing lock arguments
- Exploring the Lock mode and the Lock table
- Describing the Lock mechanism
- Creating Lock Objects

Describing Lock Arguments

The key fields of a table included in a Lock Object are called lock arguments. The function modules, generated after a Lock Object is created, use these lock arguments as their input parameters. These lock arguments are used to set and remove the locks generated by the Lock Object definition. Figure 5.114 shows the lock arguments containing the key fields of different tables:

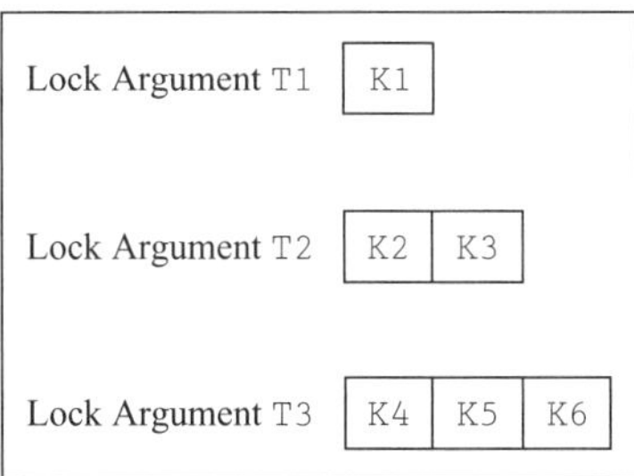

FIGURE 5.114 **Lock arguments**

Figure 5.114 shows that the lock arguments of the `T1`, `T2`, and `T3` tables consist of the key fields.

A Lock Object can be placed simultaneously on the records of multiple tables. However, in case only one table is involved in the Lock Object, the primary key field of this table acts as its lock argument.

Figure 5.115 shows the entries locked in a table:

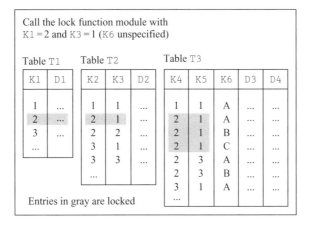

Call the lock function module with
`K1` = 2 and `K3` = 1 (`K6` unspecified)

Table `T1`

K1	D1
1	...
2	...
3	...
...	

Table `T2`

K2	K3	D2
1	1	...
2	1	...
2	2	...
3	1	...
3	3	...
...		

Table `T3`

K4	K5	K6	D3	D4
1	1	A	...	...
2	1	A	...	...
2	1	B	...	...
2	1	C	...	...
2	3	A	...	...
2	3	B	...	...
3	1	A	...	...
...				

Entries in gray are locked

FIGURE 5.115 **Entries locked in the table**

In Figure 5.115, you see that the key fields of the `T1`, `T2`, and `T3` tables are used as lock arguments. These lock arguments, that is, the key fields, are used as values for some of the fields in the function module called to set and release the lock. The function module used for the Lock Object is called whenever the value of the `K1` field is 2 and the value of the `K3` field is 1.

Exploring the Lock Mode and the Lock Table

A lock mode controls whether several users can access data records simultaneously. A lock mode can be assigned separately for each table in a Lock Object. When the lock is set, the corresponding lock entry is stored in the lock table associated with the table. A lock table is stored in the main memory of the enqueue server, which records the current locks in the SAP system. The lock table is used to manage locks and stores the record of the owner, type of lock mode used, name of the lock, and key fields of the table. Every time an enqueue server receives a request regarding a lock, the SAP system checks the table to determine whether the request is clashing with an existing lock. If it is clashing, then the request is rejected; otherwise, the new lock request is added to the lock table. Note that locks created in the lock table are not set at the database level. The structures for the entries in the lock table are shown in Figure 5.116:

Owner_1	Owner_2	Backup ID	Elementary		
			Lock Mode	Name	Argument
■ Owner ID ■ Cumulation Counter	■ Owner ID ■ Cumulation Counter	■ Backup ID ■ Flag	■ X, E, S or O	■ Name of Locked Table	■ Locked Argument
⋮	⋮	⋮	⋮		

FIGURE 5.116 **Structure of the lock table entries**

Figure 5.116 shows that the structure of the lock entry contains various fields. Table 5.17 lists the descriptions of these fields.

Field		Content and Meaning
Owner_1		Contains the Owner ID and the cumulation counter. The Owner ID contains the computer name, the work process, and a timestamp. It is also used to identify the SAP Logical Unit of Work (LUW), whereas the cumulation counter specifies the frequency of setting the associated elementary lock.
Owner_2		Contains the Owner ID and the cumulation counter. The Owner ID contains the computer name, the work process, and a timestamp. It is also used to identify the SAP LUW, whereas the cumulation counter specifies the frequency of setting the associated elementary lock.
Backup ID		Contains the Backup ID (an index indicating where the lock entry is stored in the backup file) and Flag. The value 0 of Flag indicates that no backup is present for the lock, whereas the value 1 indicates that backup is present for the lock.
Elementary Lock	Lock Mode	Specifies the following lock modes: ▪ S (Shared lock) ▪ O (Optimistic lock) ▪ E (Exclusive lock) ▪ X (Exclusive lock, extended exclusive lock, cannot be cumulated)
	Name	Contains the name of the database table in which fields are to be locked.
	Argument	Contains the locked fields in a database table.

TABLE 5.17 Description of the lock entry fields

As mentioned previously, every Lock Object has a lock mode associated with it. Further, the lock mode describes the type of lock. Table 5.18 lists the descriptions of different kinds of lock modes:

Type of Lock	Lock Mode	Description
Shared lock	S (Shared)	Allows several users (transactions) to access the locked data at the same time in the display mode. A request for another shared lock is accepted, even if it comes from another user.
Exclusive lock	E (Exclusive)	Protects the locked object against all types of locks from other transactions. Only the same lock owner can reset the lock (accumulate).
Exclusive but not cumulative lock	X (eXclusive non-cumulative)	Specifies that locks can be requested several times from the same transaction and are processed successively. In contrast, exclusive but not cumulative locks can be called only once from the same transaction.
Optimistic lock	O (Optimistic)	Behaves like shared locks initially and can be converted into exclusive locks.

TABLE 5.18 Descriptions of lock modes

Describing the Lock Mechanism

A lock mechanism is used to synchronize the access of several programs to the same set of data. The following are the two main functions accomplished with the lock mechanism:

- A program can communicate to other programs about data records that it is just reading or changing.
- A program can prevent itself from reading data that has just been changed by another program.

A logical condition is defined for the data records to be locked. When a lock is set, this logical condition is entered in a lock table. The condition remains effective until the program deletes it or the execution of the program is complete. All the locks set by the program are removed at the end of the program execution. When accessing the data records, the records just edited by other programs can be identified by an entry in the lock table. Figure 5.117 shows the lock mechanism:

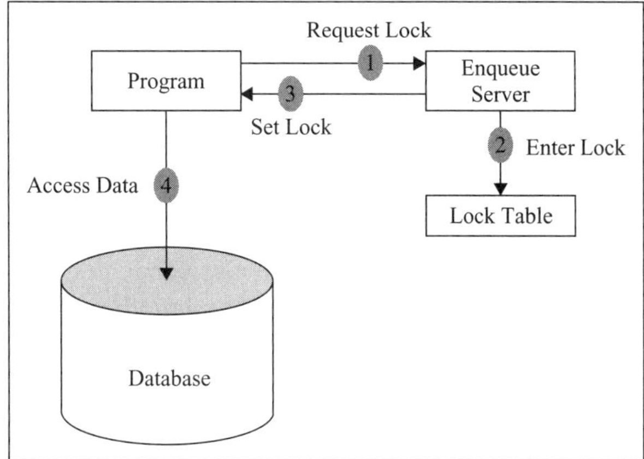

FIGURE 5.117 **Lock mechanism**

In Figure 5.117, a lock request is first generated by a program. Then this lock request goes to the enqueue server; and finally, the lock is created in the lock table. The enqueue server sets the lock, and the program is ready to access the data, with the Lock Object activated for the table.

A Lock Object must be defined in ABAP Dictionary. Whenever the Lock Object is activated, two function modules, `ENQUEUE_<lockobjectname>` and `DEQUEUE_<lockobjectname>`, are generated. The `ENQUEUE_<lockobjectname>` function module is called when data records are to be locked. When this function module is called, the values of the key fields that specify the records to be locked are passed to all the tables in the Lock Object. A generic lock is generated if a value is not passed to all the key fields. Depending on the lock mode, the SAP system decides whether the request for a lock made by another program is accepted or rejected.

Figure 5.118 shows the function module used to lock a table:

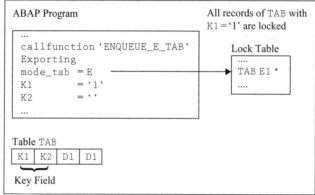

ABAP Program

```
...
callfunction 'ENQUEUE_E_TAB'
Exporting
mode_tab  = E
K1        = '1'
K2        = ' '
...
```

All records of TAB with K1 = '1' are locked

Lock Table

```
....
TAB E1 *
....
```

Table TAB

K1	K2	D1	D1

Key Field

FIGURE 5.118 **The function module used for locking**

You can see that ENQUEUE_E_TAB is used to lock the table containing the field value of K1 as 1. The lock mode is assigned as E (exclusive lock). The locked records can be unlocked by calling the DEQUEUE_<lockobjectname> function module. The key values and the lock mode used to set the lock must be passed to the DEQUEUE_<lockobjectname> function module.

Creating Lock Objects

Perform the following steps to create a Lock Object:

1. Select the `Lock Object` radio button from the initial screen of ABAP Dictionary, as shown in Figure 5.119:

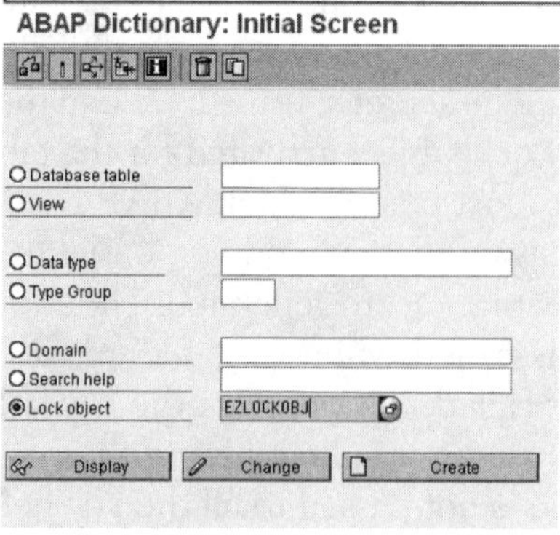

FIGURE 5.119 **The initial screen of ABAP dictionary**

2. Enter the name of the Lock Object to be created, such as `EZLOCKOBJ` (see Figure 5.119).

> **Note:** The name of the Lock Object always starts with the letters EZ.

3. Now, click the `Create` button.

The `Dictionary: Maintain Lock Object` screen appears, as shown in Figure 5.120:

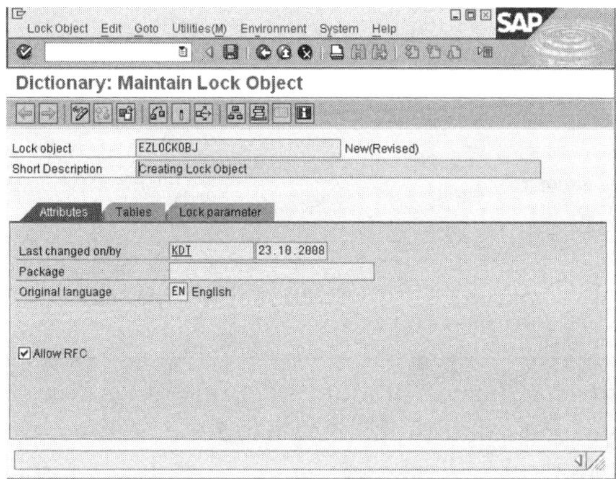

FIGURE 5.120 **The maintenance screen for the lock object**

4. Enter Creating Lock Object in the `Short Description` field and check the `Allow RFC` check box (see Figure 5.120).

> **Note:** RFC stands for Remote Function Call. When this check box is selected, the generated function modules can be called from a remote client.

5. Select the `Tables` (Tables) tab. The screen containing the options related to the `Tables` tab appears (see Figure 5.121).
6. Enter the name of the table to be locked in the `Name` field. Now, enter `ZSHIVAM` in the `Name` field. Select the `Exclusive, not cumulative` option in the `Lock Mode` field, as shown in Figure 5.121:

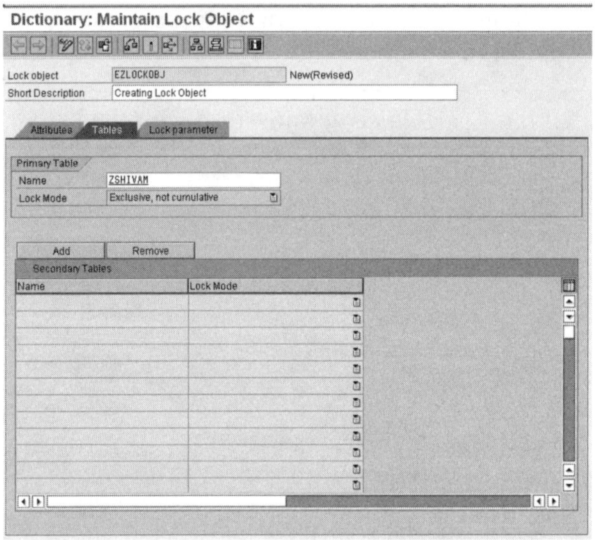

FIGURE 5.121 **Fields for the tables tab**

> **Note:** You can also lock records in more than one table. For this, click the `Add` (Add) button. A list of all the tables that are linked with the primary table specified in the `Name` field is displayed. Select the table whose records you want to lock. The primary table lock mode is copied as a lock mode. You can change this setting as required; for example, you can assign the lock mode separately for each table. Similarly, you can add a table linked with an added secondary table. To do this, place the cursor on the names of the secondary tables and click the `Add` button.

7. Click the `Save` (💾) icon to save the Lock Object in the `ZKOG_PCKG package`.
8. Select the `Lock parameter` (Lock parameter) tab. The screen containing the options related to the `Lock parameter` tab appears (see Figure 5.122). On this screen, you can set whether or not you want to include the lock parameters in the generated function module. This can be done by selecting the `W (flag)` check box. If this check box is selected, two parameters, `S` and `X_S`, are inserted in the lock parameter. These two parameters are used to copy the keys to be locked or to control the lock behavior when the initial value of the key field is passed. If you do not want the lock parameter in

the generated function module, you can deselect the `W(flag)` check box. Figure 5.122 displays the `Lock paramater tab` page:

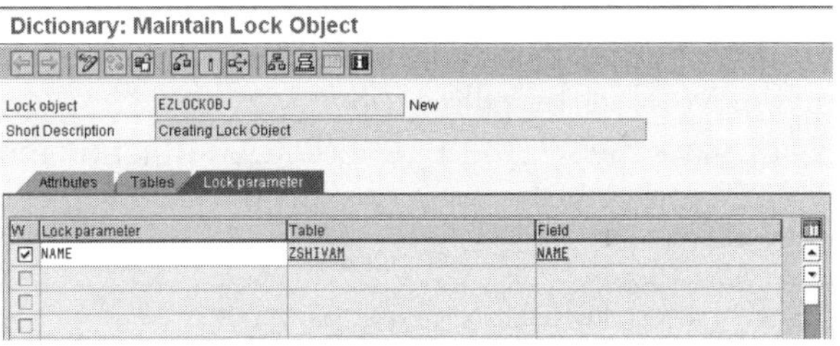

FIGURE 5.122 **Lock parameter**

In Figure 5.122, note that the lock paramater appears by default. The lock parameter is the key field of the `ZSHIVAM` table, that is, `NAME`. In addition to this, the `W(flag)` check box is already checked by default. This flag enables the lock parameters to be specified in the generated function modules. In this case, it is left unchanged.

9. Click the `Activate` (icon) icon to activate the lock. When the activation process is complete, two function modules, `ENQUEUE_<lockobjectname>` and `DEQUEUE_<lockobject>`, are generated from the definition of the Lock Object.
10. Call the generated function modules to set and release the Lock Objects. In this case, we call the function module '`ENQUEUE_EZLOCKOBJ`' by either clicking the `Pattern` (Pattern) button on the application toolbar of the `ABAP Editor` screen or pressing the Ctrl+F6 key. Figure 5.123 displays the function module together with different parameters:

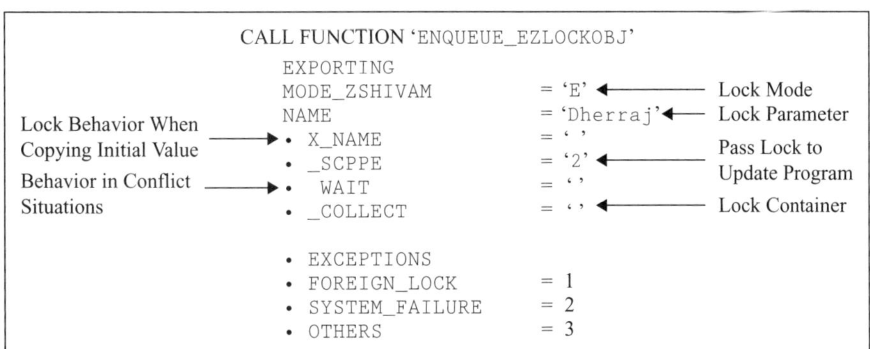

CALL FUNCTION 'ENQUEUE_EZLOCKOBJ'
EXPORTING
MODE_ZSHIVAM = 'E'
Lock Mode
NAME = 'Dherraj'
Lock Parameter
Lock Behavior When Copying Initial Value
• X_NAME = ' '
• _SCPPE = '2'
Pass Lock to Update Program
Behavior in Conflict Situations
• WAIT = ' '
• _COLLECT = ' '
Lock Container
• EXCEPTIONS
• FOREIGN_LOCK = 1
• SYSTEM_FAILURE = 2
• OTHERS = 3

FIGURE 5.123 **Function module for setting the lock**

When the ENQUEUE_EZLOCKOBJ function module is called, the name Dherraj is locked exclusively in the ZSHIVAM table. This lock is sent to the update program (_SCOPE = '2'). If there is a lock conflict, another attempt is made to set the lock after a certain period of time (specified by _WAIT = 'X').

You can remove a lock by calling the DEQUEUE_EZLOCKOBJ function module. Figure 5.124 displays the DEQUEUE_EZLOCKOBJ function module with different parameters:

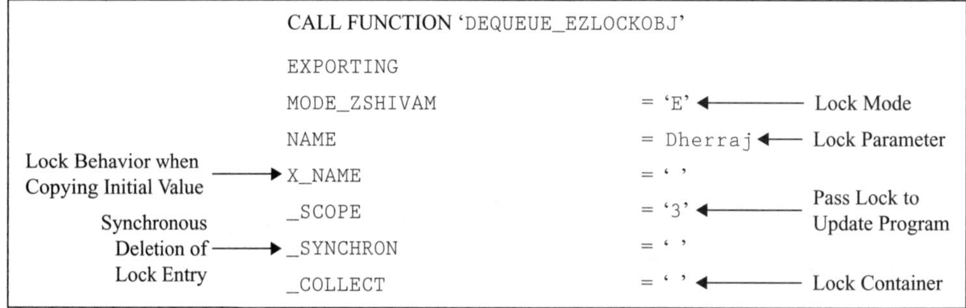

FIGURE 5.124 **Releasing a function module**

The existing exclusive lock entry for the Name field, that is, Dherraj, is deleted from the ZSHIVAM table. The request to delete the lock entries is passed to the update program (_SCOPE = '3').

SUMMARY

In this chapter, you have learned about various repository objects of ABAP Dictionary, such as Domain, Data Type, Type Group, Database Table, Views, Search Help, and Lock Objects. Apart from creating and maintaining these objects, you have learned how to perform various types of functions on the data stored in an SAP system with these objects. This chapter has also discussed how to store these objects in a package to make them transferrable among multiple SAP servers.

Chapter 6

ABAP Programming in ABAP Editor

If you need information on:	*See page:*
Structure of an ABAP Program	228
ABAP Editor	231
Inserting Comments into ABAP Programs	239
Exploring Types and Objects	241
Variables in ABAP	248
Assignment Statements	259
Formatting Options	268
Exploring System Variables	278
Dynamic Assignment	278
Describing Flow Control Statements	279

ABAP is a fourth-generation programming language used to develop ABAP programs, such as user dialogs and reports. The ABAP language provides a collection of ABAP statements, such as `DATA` and `TABLES`, to create programs. ABAP programs are created to process data within the dialog steps of an application. An ABAP program is not a single sequential unit of ABAP statements but a collection of various processing blocks that may occur in any order in the source code of the program. A processing block represents a single module of a program. It can be called either from outside an ABAP program or from another processing block in the same ABAP program.

ABAP programs are created by using the `ABAP Editor` tool of `ABAP Workbench`. Through ABAP Editor, you can create various types of programs, such as executable programs, module pools, and subroutine pools. The source code of an ABAP program can contain declaring and assigning statements, such as MOVE and WRITE TO, and commented text. Moreover, ABAP programs can be created using various formatting statements, such as FORMAT and COLORS, so that you can get the output of a program in a user-defined format.

In this chapter, you learn about the structure of an ABAP program. You also learn about the ABAP Editor tool, which is used to create, display, and modify ABAP programs. Next, you learn to add comments in an ABAP program. This chapter also describes data types and data objects, and explores how to declare variables in programs. In addition, the chapter describes various groups of types in the ABAP language. You also learn about the various kinds of assignment statements, such as MOVE, MOVE-CORRESPONDING, WRITE TO, and CLEAR. Next, you learn about the different formatting options, such as the FORMAT, WRITE, and COLORS statements, available in ABAP. Finally, you learn about the flow of control statements, such as IF, CASE, and loop construction.

STRUCTURE OF AN ABAP PROGRAM

The structure of an ABAP program includes the following:

- Introductory program part
- Global declaration part
- Processing blocks (consisting of different functions, such as procedures, dialog box, and event blocks)

Figure 6.1 shows the structure of an ABAP program:

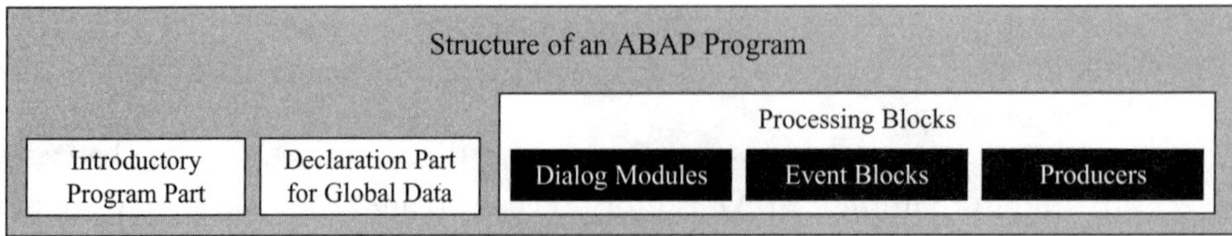

FIGURE 6.1 **Structure of an ABAP program**

The processing blocks in the ABAP program structure consist of dialog modules, event blocks, and procedures.

Now, let's disscuss each part of the structure of an ABAP program in detail.

Introductory Program Part

Every ABAP program begins with an introductory statement, such as `REPORT`, `PROGRAM`, or `FUNCTION-POOL`. Each program has a type, such as executable program, module pool program, or function group program, associated to it. The introductory statement of an ABAP program depends on the type of the ABAP program. Table 6.1 shows the introductory statements for different types of programs:

Introductory Statement	Description of the Program Type
REPORT	Represents an executable program.
PROGRAM	Represents a modue pool program and subroutines.
FUNCTION-POOL	Represents a function group.
CLASS-POOL	Represents a class pool program.
INTERFACE-POOL	Represents an interface pool program.
TYPE-POOL	Defines the type group.

TABLE 6.1 Introductory statement

When a program is created, the SAP system automatically generates the most appropriate introductory statement for that program. Since the introductory statement depends on the type of the program created, the introductory statement must be assigned manually to the type of the program defined in the program properties.

Declaration Part for Global Data, Class Definitions, and Selection Screens

You always declare global data, classes, and selection screens after the introductory program part of an ABAP program. The declaration of these objects includes:

- **Global data**—Defines global data in an ABAP program. Global data is specified by declaration statements, such as `TYPES`, `TABLES`, and `DATA`. The global data defined in a program is visible in all the internal processing blocks of the program.
- **Selection screens**—Represent special screens that are generated by using ABAP statements instead of Screen Painter. These screens allow you to enter either a single value for one or more fields or a selection criterion.
- **Local class definitions**—Contains the definitions of local classes in an ABAP program. Local class definitions are created with the help of the `CLASS DEFINITION` statement. The local classes are a part of the ABAP Objects, which are object-oriented extensions of ABAP.

Note: You learn more about ABAP Objects in Appendix A.

Processing Blocks

Another part of an ABAP program structure is the processing block. A processing block is a set of ABAP statements that represents a module of an ABAP program. As we know, ABAP programs are created to process data within the dialog steps of an application. This means an ABAP program is divided into numerous separate sections, which are interlinked in the respect of an application and are assigned to the respective dialog steps. In other words, we can say that ABAP programs have modular structure, where each module is represented by a processing block.

The types of processing blocks used in an ABAP program are as follows:

- Dialog modules
- Event blocks
- Procedures, including methods, subroutines, and function modules

Dialog modules and procedures are enclosed within ABAP statements such as `MODULE...ENDMODULE` and `FUNCTION...ENDFUNCTION`.

Event blocks are processed when events are triggered either by performing user actions on selection screens and lists or by the running environment of ABAP. A event block is introduced within ABAP statements, such as `START-OF-SELECTION` and `AT USER-COMMAND`. It is created within a processing block, which starts with an ABAP statement, such as `WRITE` and `NEW-PAGE`. Note that an event block is terminated implicitly with the beginning of the next processing block, which is introduced by using another ABAP statement. In an ABAP program, all ABAP statements, except declarative statements, are a part of a processing block. In addition, ABAP statements placed between the declaration of global data and a processing block are assigned automatically to the `START-OF-SELECTION` processing block.

Because dialog modules and event blocks can be used outside an ABAP program, a processing block can be called from outside the associated ABAP program. In addition, the processing block can be called by using an ABAP command, such as `CALL METHOD`, `CALL TRANSACTION`, `SUBMIT`, or `LEAVE TO`. Note that procedures are called by using ABAP statements in an ABAP program.

Note: Declarative statements are used to define the data types or data objects in an ABAP program. Some examples of declarative statements are `DATA`, `TABLES`, and `TYPES`. You learn more about these statements later in the chapter.

ABAP EDITOR

ABAP Editor is used to create, display, and modify ABAP programs. The initial screen of the ABAP Editor can be displayed either from the `SAP Easy Access` screen or by entering the `SE38` transaction code in the Command field (present on the standard toolbar) and pressing the ENTER key. Figure 6.2 shows the initial screen of ABAP Editor:

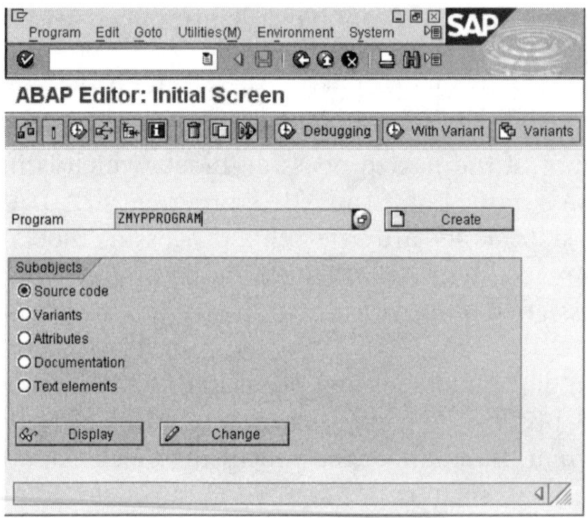

FIGURE 6.2 **Initial screen of ABAP editor**

In the `Program` text field of the initial screen, you can enter the name of the program to be created, displayed, or changed. Figure 6.2 shows `ZMYPROGRAM` as the name of a program in the Program field.

In ABAP programs,the naming conventions are as follows:

- The length of the name of an ABAP program can be from 1 to 30 characters.
- Symbols (. , ( ) ' " = * % -) and accented characters or German umlauts (à, é, ø, ä, ß, and so on) cannot be used while naming an ABAP program.

The `Subobjects` group box of the initial screen of ABAP Editor contains the `Source code`, `Variants`, `Attributes`, `Documentation`, and `Text elements` radio buttons. Table 6.2 describes these radio buttons of the `Subobjects` group box:

Radio Button	Description
Source code	Navigates to the program editor, where the source code can be written or edited. The program editor contains options to process, check, and save ABAP programs, as well as help and display functions for the source code.
Variants	Navigates to the variant maintenance tool, where you can define the fixed values of the input fields on the selection screen of a report. In addition to this, you can also edit, display, save, copy, print, and delete variants.
Attributes	Navigates to the program attributes screen, where you can maintain important program attributes, such as program type, program class, database used, authorizations, and runtime parameters. These attributes must be defined before entering the program code in ABAP Editor.
Documentation	Specifies a description of a program, explaining what it does and when it is used. You can also describe prerequisites of running a program, such as tables that must be maintained and programs that must be run. Moreover, you can also specify the examples that explain the report functions and other possible settings, such as output, integration, and activities.
Text elements	Maintains the text elements, such as title and headers, selection texts, and numbered texts, of an ABAP program.

TABLE 6.2 Options provided in the subobjects group box

Note: A variant is a set of values entered in a selection screen, which is often used in a program. When you use an ABAP program in which selection screens are defined, numerous input fields are displayed where you enter a set of values. If you use the same set of values for the same program again and again, you can create a variant of the values stored in the selection set to reuse in the selection screen. A variant is created by using the variant maintenance tool, which is accessed through ABAP Editor (`SE38`).

The `Create` button in the `ABAP Editor: Initial Screen` (see Figure 6.2) is used to create an ABAP program. The `Display` and `Change` buttons, however, are used to view or modify ABAP programs, respectively. When you enter the name of a new program in the `Program` field of `ABAP Editor: Initial Screen` and click the `Create` pushbutton, the `ABAP: Program Attributes` dialog box appears, as shown in Figure 6.3:

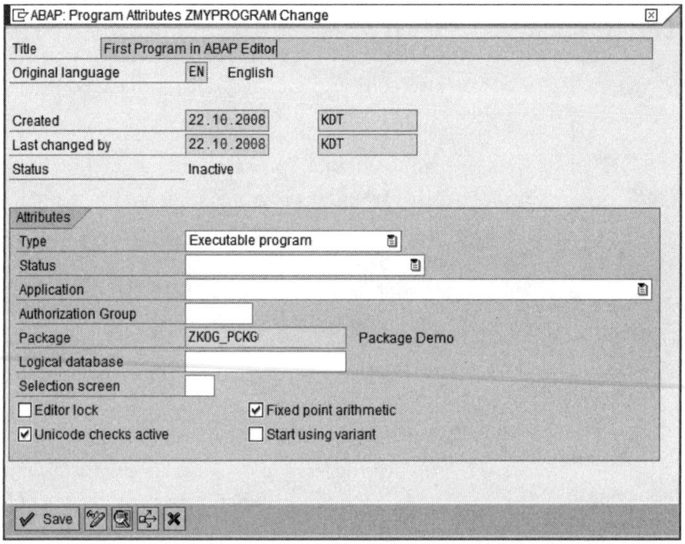

FIGURE 6.3 **The ABAP: program attributes dialog box**

Figure 6.3 shows the `ABAP: Program Attributes` dialog box, where you specify the values for the attributes of an ABAP program. In the `ABAP: Program Attributes` dialog box, you must specify the values in the following fields:

- `Title`—Describes the function of a program; that is, a short description about the program.
- `Original Language`—Contains the logon language of a user. This field is populated automatically by the SAP system.
- `Type`—Specifies the type of program.
- `Status`—Specifies whether the program is an SAP Standard Production Program, System Program, or Customer Production Program.

- `Application`—Contains the application to be used in an ABAP program, such as Financial Accounting. This field is optional.
- `Authorization Group`—Specifies the name of a program group. A program group is a collection of programs used for authorization checks.
- `Logical Database`—Defines the logical database used by an executable program (report) to read data. This field is applicable only to executable programs.
- `Selection Screen`—Specifies the selection screen based on the selection criteria of the logical database, and the `PARAMETERS` and `SELECT-OPTIONS` statements used in an ABAP program. This field is also applicable to executable programs.

The `ABAP: Program Attributes` dialog box also contains some check boxes, which implement additional features of `ABAP Editor` in an ABAP program. These check boxes are:

- `Editor lock`—Prevents other users from changing the attributes, text elements, and documentation of an ABAP program. Note that only the user who has worked on the program most recently can release the lock by clearing this check box.
- `Fixed point arithmetic`—Rounds off the value of the type `P` field according to the number of decimal places specified.
- `Start using variant`—Allows other users to start your program by using a variant. This field is also applicable to executable programs.
- `Unicode checks active`—Checks the program in the unicode format.

> **Note:** You can modify the values of the attributes of an ABAP program by using the `ABAP: Program Attributes` dialog box again. However, you navigate to the `ABAP: Program Attributes` dialog box by selecting the `Attributes` radio button in the `Subobjects` group box and clicking the `Change` button.

Now, let's learn about the different types of ABAP programs.

Types of ABAP Programs

Each ABAP program has a program type that determines whether a program can be executed. An ABAP program can be executed by either entering the program name in the intial screen of ABAP Editor or using a transaction code in the `Command` field. The `Type` field of ABAP Editor is used to specify the type of a program. The program types that can be selected are:

- Executable programs
- Module pools
- Subroutine pools
- Include programs

Besides the preceding program types, some other types of ABAP programs exist that are not created by ABAP Editor. Instead, ABAP Workbench provides specific tools to create and maintain these programs. These program types are:

- Function pools
- Class pools
- Interface pools

Now, let's discuss each program type in detail.

Defining Executable Programs

Executable programs are often called report programs because the source code of an executable program starts with the `REPORT` statement. These programs are created by processing the data stored in an SAP database. Executable programs cannot only retrieve the data from the database but also modify the data stored in the database. Executable programs can contain almost every kind of processing block, such as dialog modules, methods, and event blocks, except function modules and local classes. You do not need user-defined screens to control the executable programs. This is because the runtime environment of ABAP can call the processing blocks, screens, selection screens, and lists of executable programs automatically in a predefined sequence. Users can enter data on screens or selection screens, and then data is retrieved from the database and processed accordingly. Finally, an output list is displayed on the basis of processed data.

Executable programs can be started by entering the program name or a transaction code. Note that if a transaction code is assigned to an executable program, the program can be started by using the transaction code instead of the program name. Moreover, executable programs can be linked to a logical database that contains subroutines. These subroutines are then called by a virtual system program in a predefined sequence.

Note: Subroutines are used to make certain reporting functions reusable.

Defining Module Pools

A module pool is a program used to display data in and add functionality to a screen, such as a button, radio button, group box, or menu bar. You can write the screen flow logic using a module pool program; a subroutine is not used for this purpose. ABAP Editor is used to create module pool programs, which always start with the `PROGRAM` statement. A module pool is started using a transaction code, which is linked to a program and the initial screen of the program. Note that for a module pool program, you must define your own screens, including selection screens, by using Screen Painter. As a best practice, use a module pool program to write dialog-oriented programs using a large number of screens. Note that the flow logic of these screens determines the flow of the program.

Defining Subroutine Pools

A subroutine pool is a program that contains a collection of subroutines and local or global classes and interfaces that must be called externally in other ABAP programs. Prior to SAP release 6.0, a subroutine pool was used only to store and expose subroutines. However, with SAP release 6.0 and later, you can also call a subroutine pool program through the transaction code, which is attached with the public methods of local or global classes of this program. In ABAP Editor, a subroutine pool is created by using the `PROGRAM` statement.

Defining Include Programs

Include programs are not complete programs because they do not have a memory and cannot be executed, unlike other stand-alone programs. Alternatively, include programs act as a library of ABAP source code. Include programs are used to organize a program code into small units, which can be inserted in other ABAP programs. In other words, include programs are code snippets that can be reused in other programs. You can use these resuable code snippets with the help of the `INCLUDE` statement.

Defining Function Pools

Function pools, called function groups, are programs that contain function modules. A function pool program is created by using the `FUNCTION-POOL` statement. Each function pool contains global data, such as data objects, subroutines, or screens, which are shared by all the function modules of the function pool. Function modules are special ABAP procedures or routines that can be called in any ABAP program. Function Builder, a tool of ABAP Workbench, is used to create and manage the function pools (i.e., function groups) and function modules.

Defining Class Pools

A class pool is a special ABAP program used to store global classes and interfaces. All the ABAP programs can access these global classes and interfaces. A class pool is created by using the `CLASS-POOL` statement or by using `Class Builder`, a tool provided by ABAP Workbench. The class pool type of programs do not contain any screens or processing blocks. However, class pools contain methods that can be executed to implement the program logic.

Defining Interface Pools

Interface pools are programs that store global interfaces. An interface pool acts as a container that can store exactly one global interface. You can use an interface pool to implement the methods, which are defined in an interface of a class. To perform this, you must create reference variables of the interface type. Moreover, interface pools are maintained by using the `Class Builder` tool of ABAP Workbench.

Now, let's discuss how to write an ABAP program by following the syntax conventions.

ABAP Syntax

Every statement provided in the ABAP programming language has a predined syntax associated with it. Apart from this syntax, certain conventions need to be followed while writing the syntax for the statements. Table 6.3 describes these conventions:

Term	Description
Statement	Specifies that ABAP statements and clauses are given in uppercase. It is not mandatory to use the ABAP keywords in uppercase; for instance, the `WRITE` keyword also can be `Write` or `write`.

Continued

Term	Description
Operand	Specifies that the operands used in the statement are in lowercase.
[ ]	Specifies that the element enclosed in the square brackets is optional.
|	Specifies that there are elements on both sides of this symbol, and you can use either element in a program.
( )	Specifies that parentheses is a part of the syntax of a statement and must be used while using the statement.
,	Separates one or more variables that you need to specify in a statement.
f1, f2	Represents variables indicated with indices. You can list as many variables in a program as you want.
....	Represents the rest of the code in a program besides the syntax of ABAP statements.

TABLE 6.3 Description of conventions

INSERTING COMMENTS INTO ABAP PROGRAMS

Comments are texts written between the statements of ABAP programs to document the program and to remind programmers about the purpose of using various statements. In an ABAP program, you can use the following ways to insert comments:

- **Line Comment**—Insert an asterisk at the leftmost column of a line; the entire line becomes a comment and is therefore not executed.
- **Partial Comment**—Insert a double quotation mark in the middle of a line of code so that everything to the right of the quote mark in the line of code becomes a comment.

> **Note:** You can convert a block of ABAP statements into comments by pressing the CTRL + < key combination. In addition, you can delete comments by first selecting the block and then pressing the CTRL + > key combination.

As a best practice, always include some comments, such as the date on which the program is created, description of the program created, and the name of the author, at the begining of a program.

Figure 6.4 displays the comments included at the start of the `ZMYPROGRAM` program:

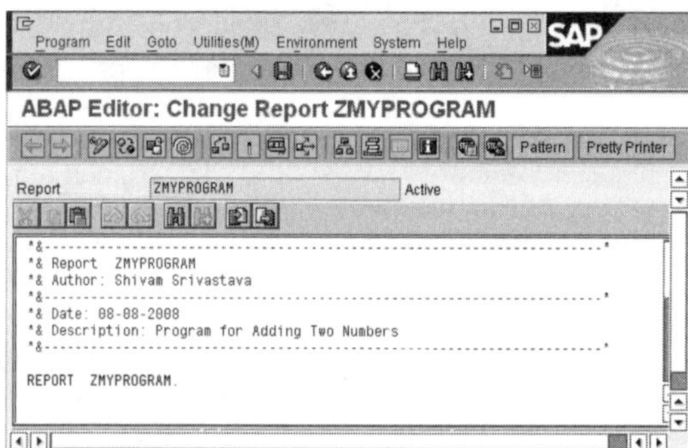

FIGURE 6.4 **Commenting the entire line**

The comments in Figure 6.4 give information about the name of the author, the date on which the program is created, and the description related to the program.

Figure 6.5 shows how line comments, partial comments, and block comments can be inserted in a program:

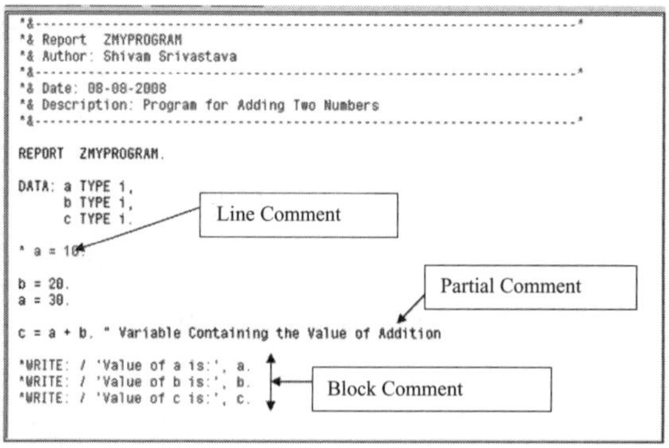

```
*&---------------------------------------------------------------------*
*& Report  ZMYPROGRAM
*& Author: Shivam Srivastava
*&---------------------------------------------------------------------*
*& Date: 08-08-2008
*& Description: Program for Adding Two Numbers
*&---------------------------------------------------------------------*

REPORT  ZMYPROGRAM.

DATA: a TYPE i,
      b TYPE i,
      c TYPE i.

* a = 10.

b = 20.
a = 30.

c = a + b. " Variable Containing the Value of Addition

*WRITE: / 'Value of a is:', a.
*WRITE: / 'Value of b is:', b.
*WRITE: / 'Value of c is:', c.
```

Line Comment

Partial Comment

Block Comment

FIGURE 6.5 **Commenting partial code of an ABAP program**

In Figure 6.5, the value 10 assigned to the variable a is ignored by the SAP system, because it is commented by using an asterisk. Note that the lines commented are ignored by the SAP system whenever the `ZMYPROGRAM` is executed.

EXPLORING TYPES AND OBJECTS

A type gives description of the technical attributes of the objects associated with that type. The objects are instances of types. Types and objects used in ABAP form a hierarchy as shown in Figure 6.6:

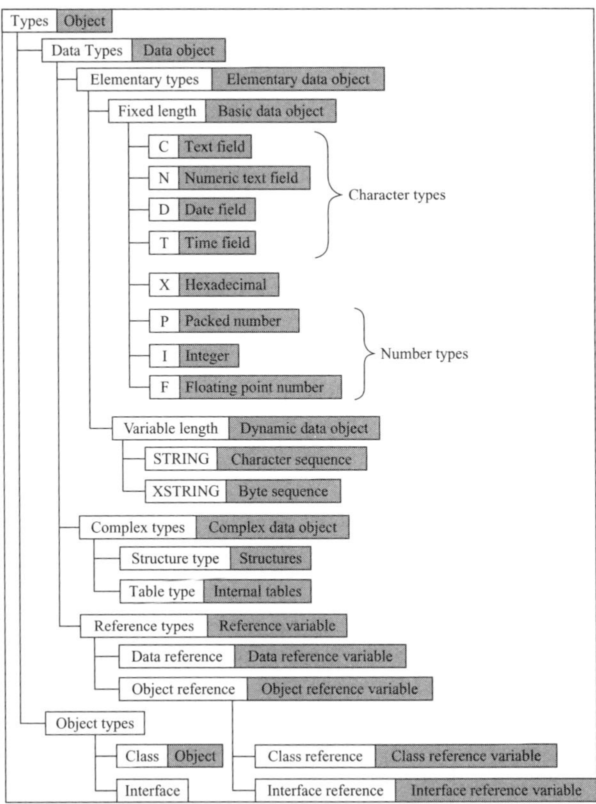

FIGURE 6.6 **Hierarchy of ABAP types and ABAP objects**

In Figure 6.6, notice that the types are categorized as data types and object types.

Data Types

Data types describe data objects. ABAP provides predefined data types that can be used in an ABAP program. Apart from the predefined data types, data types can be customized either locally in a program or globally in the SAP R/3 Repository. The following are three kinds of data types:

- Elementary types
- Complex types
- Reference types

Describing Elementary Types

Elementary types are the smallest undivided unit of predefined data types. These elementary types are already defined in the SAP system and are visible in all ABAP programs. ABAP programs use these predefined elementary types to define local data types (structures) and data objects (fields) used in a program.

> **Note:** You can also create your own elementary data types with the help of the `TYPES` statement.

The following are two types of predefined elementary data types, which can be used in an ABAP program:

- Fixed-length
- Variable-length

These types are not derived from other types. The main difference between the fixed- and variable-length types is that the memory space required by the data objects of variable-length data types can change dynamically at runtime.

Now, let's discuss each of these data types in detail.

The Fixed Length Data Type

As the name suggests, the length of the fixed length data types are fixed at runtime. The fixed-length data types are:

- Character types
- Hexadecimal types
- Numeric types

Table 6.4 shows the values of various parameters related to fixed-length data types:

Data Type	Initial Field Length (in bytes)	Valid Field Length (in bytes)	Initial Value	Description
Numeric Types				
I	4	4	0	Specifies an integer (whole number)
F	8	8	0	Represents a floating point number
P	8	1-16	0	Specifies a packed number
Character Types				
C	1	1-65535	'..........'	Denotes a text field (alphanumeric characters)
D	8	8	'00000000'	Specifies a date field (Format:YYYYMMDD)
N	1	1-65535	'0....0'	Specifies a numeric text field (numeric characters)
T	6	6	'000000'	Specifies a time field (Format:HHMMSS)
Hexadecimal Types				
X	1	1-65535	X'0.....0'	Specifies a hexadecimal field

TABLE 6.4 Fixed-length data types

The Variable-Length Data Type

A variable-length data type is used for data objects whose length cannot be fixed, as the length varies according to the specified data. The variable-length data type is of two types, `STRING` and `XSTRING described in Table 6.5.`

Variable Length Data Type	Description
STRING	Specifies a sequence of characters with variable lengths. A string can contain any number of alphanumeric characters. The length of the string can be calculated by multiplying the number of characters with the length required for the internal representation of a single character.
XSTRING	Represents a string used for byte strings of a hexadecimal type. A byte string has a variable string and can contain any number of bytes. The length of a byte string is same as the number of bytes.

TABLE 6.5 Variable-length data types

Describing Complex Types

A complex type is a combination of other types. There are no predefined complex data types in ABAP. However, complex types are created by users either in an ABAP program or in ABAP Dictionary. Complex types allow you to manage and process semantically related data under a common name. Complex types include the following:

- Structure types
- Table types

Now, let's discuss each of these types in detail.

Structure Types

A structure, also called a structure type, is a sequence of other data types defined in ABAP Dictionary, such as elementary types, structures, table types, and database tables. A structure type comprises a collection of components (also called fields), where each component has a name and data type. When you create a structure in your program, a component of the structure can refer to an elementary type, another structure, or a table type. In addition, you can nest a structure up to any level. You can use the `TYPE` clause in an ABAP program to refer to a structure directly. Moreover, structures can be used to define the data for screens and parameter types in function modules.

Table Types

A table type is another kind of complex data type that helps create complex data objects, such as internal tables. Internal tables consist of a series of lines, where all the lines have the same data type. You use internal tables when you need to use structured data within a program. Table 6.6 shows the parameters according to which internal tables are characterized:

Parameter	Description
Line or row type	Specifies that a row of an internal table can be of the elementary type, complex type, or reference type.
Key	Specifies a field or a group of fields as a key of an internal table that identifies the table rows. A key contains the fields of elementary types. Keys can be of two types, unique and non-unique.
Access method	Describes how ABAP programs access individual table entries. The three types of access are unsorted types, sorted index tables, and hashed tables.

TABLE 6.6 Parameters of an internal table

Describing Reference Data Types

Reference types are data types used to describe data objects containing references (pointers) to other objects, such as data objects and objects created in the ABAP Objects language. To use references, you need to define the references in your program.

Object Types

The objects in ABAP Objects (object-oriented extensions of the ABAP language) are described with the help of object types. These object types are as follows:

- **Classes**—Contains the description of an object. In addition, a class defines the data types and functions that an object contains.

- **Interfaces**—Contains the description of an object, similar to a class. However, interfaces partially describe the aspects of an object. An interface contains several data types and functions that can be used in classes.
- **Functions**—Describes the behavior of an object. Functions can access any attributes of a class.

> **Note:** To learn more about ABAP Objects, refer to Appendix A.

All the other data types, as shown in Figure 6.4, can be used in ABAP Objects. Depending on your needs, object types are declared in a program or in the SAP R/3 Repository.

Now, let's explore the two types of objects that can be created from ABAP types.

Objects in ABAP

The objects in ABAP are created with the help of ABAP data types (see Figure 6.6).

Describing Data Objects

Data objects are fields that hold the data used by ABAP programs at runtime. Data objects exist only untill a program is being executed. For example, if a user wants to read data from a database table or a sequential file, the data must first be read into the data object. The following are types kinds of data objects:

- **Literal**—Specifies an unnamed data object in a program having a fixed character string or a number. Literals can be a character or a numeric type, such as 45, 'Hello', '238', and 68.92. They are not created by declarative statements but have fixed technical attributes, such as field length, number of decimal places, and data type.
- **Named data object**—Specifies a named data object that is declared either statically or dynamically at runtime. Similar to a literal, the technical attributes of named data objects, such as length, number of decimal places, and the data type, are always

fixed. A named data object is assigned a name with which you can address the data object from ABAP programs. Text symbols, variables, constants, and interface work areas are examples of named data objects.

- **Predefined data object**—Specifies an already available data object in the SAP system at runtime. A predefined data object does not need to be declared explicitly.
- **Dynamic or anonymous data object**—Specifies an unnamed data object, which is created dynamically in a program and used with a data reference variable.

Note: A dynamic data object is created during the execution of a program. It is referenced by a data reference variable and the following syntax of the *CREATE DATA* statement:

```
CREATE DATA <datarefvar> {TYPE data_type}|{LIKE
data_object}.
```

In the preceding syntax, `<datarefvar>` represents a data reference variable that points to a data object created in the internal session of the current ABAP program. Note that the data object does not have its own name. You can refer this data object by using the `<datarefvar>` data reference variable.

Describing Objects

An ABAP Object is an instance of a class; for example, Car is a class and Honda City is its object. Similar to other programming languages, ABAP Objects also provide the basic features of object-oriented programming; that is, encapsulation, inheritance, and polymorphism. An ABAP Object contains methods, events, and data. A class can contain numerous objects; however, each object has its own identity and attributes.

VARIABLES IN ABAP

Variables are named data objects used to store values within the allotted memory area of a program. As the name suggests, users can change the content of variables with the help of ABAP statements. Table 6.7 shows the statements used to declare a variable statically:

Statement	Description
DATA	Declares the variable whose lifetime is linked to the context of the declaration.
STATICS	Declares the variables that can be used in subroutines, function modules, and static methods.
CLASS-DATA	Declares variables within the classes.
PARAMETERS	Declares the elementary data objects that are linked to input fields on a selection screen.
SELECT-OPTIONS	Declares the internal tables that are linked to input fields on a selection screen.
RANGES	Declares internal tables with the same structure as defined in the `SELECT-OPTIONS` statement, provided the declared internal table is not linked to a selection screen.

TABLE 6.7 Statements used to declare variables statically

Apart from declaring the variables statically, you can also declare the variables dynamically; that is, whenever you call procedures, such as subroutines. For example, the variables declared in the `FORM` statement (also known as formal parameters) inherit the technical characteristics, such as the data type and length of the parameters defined with the `PERFORM` statement (also known as actual parameters). In addition to this, the values of the actual parameters are assigned to the formal parameters.

Now, let's discuss the `DATA` and the `PARAMETERS` statements in detail.

The `DATA` Statement

The `DATA` statement is used to declare variables in an ABAP program. Variables defined by the `DATA` statement have a predefined or user-defined data type. The following syntax shows how to use the `DATA` statement:

```
DATA <f> ... [TYPE <type>|LIKE <obj>]... [VALUE <val>].
```

Table 6.8 describes the clauses that can be used in the DATA statement:

Clause	Description
<f>	Specifies the name of a variable. The name of the variable can be up to 30 characters long.
TYPE <type>	Specifies that the type of <f> variable. Any data type with fully specified technical attributes is known as <type>.The possible <type> allotted to a variable can be a nongeneric predefined ABAP type (D, F, I, T, STRING, XSTRING) or any existing local data type in a program (the TYPES statement is used to define local data types in a program) or an ABAP Dictionary data type.
LIKE <obj>	Shows that the declared variable name <f> inherits the same technical attributes as an existing data object, <obj>. Predefined data objects that do not need to be declared separately are represented by <obj>.
VALUE <val>	Specifies the initial value of the <f> variable. In case you define an elementary fixed-length variable, the DATA statement automatically populates the value of the variable with the type-specific initial value, as listed in Table 6.5. Other possible values for <val> can be a literal, constant, or an explicit clause, such as IS INITIAL.

TABLE 6.8 Description of the clauses of the DATA statement

The following conventions are used while naming a variable in an ABAP program:

- You cannot use special characters such as "+" and "," to name variables.
- The name of the predefined data objects cannot be changed.

- The name of the variable cannot be the same as any ABAP keyword or clause.
- The name of the variables must convey the meaning of the variable without the need for further comments.
- Hyphens are reserved to represent the components of structures. Therefore, avoid using hyphens in variable names.
- The underscore character can be used to separate compound words.

The following code snippet shows how to define variables by using the `DATA` statement:

```
DATA d1(2) TYPE C.
DATA d2 LIKE d1.
DATA min_value TYPE I VALUE 10.
```

In the previous code snippet, `d1` is a variable of `C` type, `d2` is a variable of `d1` type, and `min_value` is a variable of `I` type. The following code snippet demonstrates another way to declare variables:

```
*-------------------------------------------------------*
*/ Structure Declarations
*/
TYPES: BEGIN OF number,
       Number_1 TYPE I,
       Number_2 TYPE p DECIMALS 2,
       End of number.
*-------------------------------------------------------*
*/Data Declarations
*/
DATA:           n_number TYPE number,
      Num LIKE n_number-Number_1,
      Date LIKE SY-DATUM,
      Year TYPE i.
*-------------------------------------------------------*
```

In the preceding code snippet, variables are declared with reference to the internal type, named number, in a program. Another variable, `Num`, is declared similar to the component of the existing data object `n_number`. The third variable, `Date`, refers to the `SY-DATUM` variable and the `Year` variable has a reference to the predefined ABAP type `I`.

Listing 6.1 shows the incorrect access of a variable defined with the help of the `DATA` statement:

```
Report ZNAMEDISPLAY.
*/ accessing a variable
DATA name1(7) VALUE 'shivam'.
WRITE: name1, name2.
DATA name2(10) value 'srivastava'.
```

LISTING 6.1 **Accessing a variable incorrectly**

In Listing 6.1, notice that the `name2` variable accesses the `WRITE` statement before the definition of the variable. On checking Listing 6.1 in ABAP Editor, a syntax error is generated, as shown in Figure 6.7:

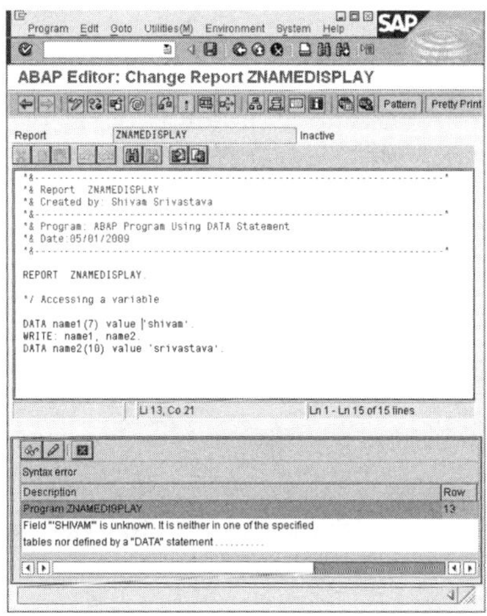

FIGURE 6.7 **Showing a syntax error in the SAP system**

In Figure 6.7, notice the syntactical error, which can be removed by moving the definition of the `name2` variable before the `WRITE` statement, that is accessing it.

Apart from the `DATA` statement, you can use the `PARAMETERS` statement to define the variables (or parameters) in an ABAP program. Now, let's discuss the `PARAMETERS` statement in detail.

The `PARAMETERS` Statement

The `PARAMETERS` statement is used to enter the values of the variables on both the standard selection screen as well as user-defined selection screens. These variables (also known as parameters) are defined with the help of the `PARAMETERS` statement. Each parameter defined with the `PARAMETERS` statement appears as an input field on the relevant selection screen. The `PARAMETERS` statement is used to enter single values in the input fields. The flow of the program can be controlled with the help of parameters. The syntax of the `PARAMETERS` statement is

```
PARAMETERS <p> [(<length>)] [TYPE <type>|LIKE <obj>]
[DECIMALS <d>].
```

In the preceding syntax, the use of the `TYPE` or `LIKE` clause is optional, but the data must be of the `C` type with length 1.

Table 6.9 describes the clauses used in the `PARAMETERS` statement:

Clause	Description
`<p>`	Represents the name of a parameter. The maximum length for naming parameters is 8 instead of 30, as in the `DATA` statement.
`<length>`	Specifies the length of a variable.
TYPE `<type>`	Specifies a data type with fully specified technical attributes. The possible `<type>` allotted to a variable can be a predefined ABAP type (`D, I, T, STRING, XSTRING`) or an ABAP Dictionary data type. The `TYPE` keyword shows that the declared parameter name `<p>` inherits the same technical attributes as that of an existing data type `<type>`.

Continued

Clause	Description
LIKE <obj>	Specifies a predefined data object that is already present and need not be declared separately, such as system variables. Fields used to provide information about the current state of the SAP system are known as system variables. The `LIKE` keyword specifies that the declared parameter name <p> inherits the same technical attributes as that of the existing data object <obj>.
DECIMALS <d>	Specifies the number of decimal places for numeric values.

TABLE 6.9 Clauses of the PARAMETERS statement

Note: The `TYPE` and `LIKE` clauses are used in ABAP statements for various purposes, some of which are:

- Defining local types in a program
- Declaring data objects
- Creating dynamic data objects
- Specifying the type of formal parameters in subroutines
- Specifying the type of formal parameters in methods
- Specifying the type of field symbols

Listing 6.2 shows how to declare variable using the `PARAMETERS` statement:

```
REPORT ZPARAMETERDISPLAY.
*-------------------------------------------------*
*/Creating Parameters
*/
PARAMETERS: NAME(10) TYPE C,
CLASS TYPE I,
SCORE TYPE P DECIMALS 2,
CONNECT TYPE MARA-MATNR.
*-------------------------------------------------*
```

LISTING 6.2 **Using the PARAMETERS statement**

In Listing 6.2, four parameters are created and displayed on the standard selection screen. The parameters are:

- `NAME`—Represents a parameter of 10 characters
- `CLASS`—Specifies a parameter of integer type with the default size in bytes
- `SCORE`—Represents a packed type parameter, with values up to two decimal places
- `CONNECT`—Refers to the `MARA-MATNR` type of ABAP Dictionary

Figure 6.8 shows the output of Listing 6.2:

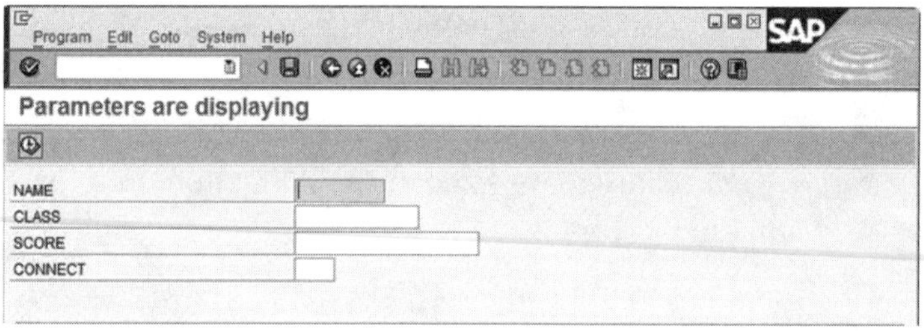

FIGURE 6.8 **Output of the PARAMETERS statement**

Apart from the clauses shown in Table 6.10, you can also define check boxes and radio buttons on the standard selection screen by using the `PARAMETERS` statement.

Defining Check Boxes by Using the `PARAMETERS` Statement

The `PARAMETERS` statement can also be used to define a check box on the standard selection screen. The following syntax is used to create a check box:

```
PARAMETERS <p> ...... AS CHECKBOX......
```

The parameter field name `<p>` is used to create a check box. The field name has a `C` type and 1 as the length, by default. The ' ' and X are valid values used in place of the `<p>` parameter field.

Listing 6.3 shows how to display a field with a check box by using the `PARAMETERS` statement:

```
REPORT ZCHECKBOXDISPLAY.
*----------------------------------------------------*
*/Creating Checkboxes Using PARAMETERS Statement
*/
PARAMETERS: BA AS CHECKBOX,
BCom AS CHECKBOX,
BSc AS CHECKBOX,
MA AS CHECKBOX,
MCom AS CHECKBOX,
MSc AS CHECKBOX DEFAULT 'X'.
*----------------------------------------------------*
```

LISTING 6.3 **Creating check boxes**

In Listing 6.3, the `PARAMETERS` statement is used to create six check boxes: `BA`, `BCom`, `BSc`, `MA`, `MCom`, and `MSc`. The `MSc` check box is set as the default. Figure 6.9 shows the output of Listing 6.3:

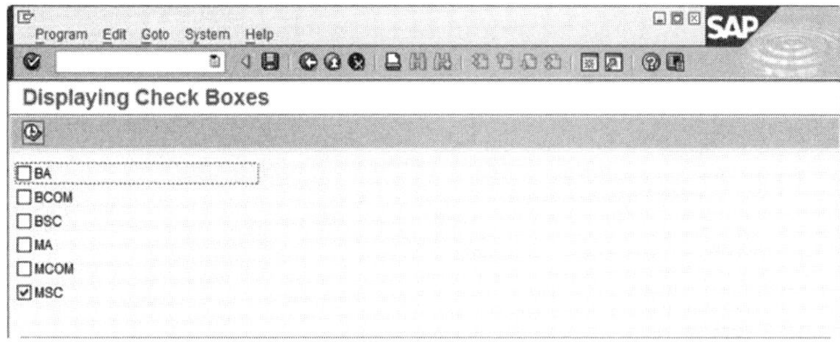

FIGURE 6.9 **Check boxes on the standard selection screen**

Defining Radio Buttons by Using the `PARAMETERS` Statement

The `PARAMETERS` statement is also used to define radio buttons on a standard selection screen. The syntax to create radio buttons is:

```
PARAMETERS <p> ...... RADIOBUTTON GROUP <radi>......
```

In the preceding syntax, a parameter `<p>` is created with type `C` and length 1. The parameter `<p>` is also assigned to a group `<radi>`. The RAD1 group is assigned with at least two parameters. Only one parameter per group can have the default value of X, assigned by using the DEFAULT clause. If the DEFAULT clause is not used, the first parameter of each group is set to zero. When the user clicks a radio button on the selection screen, the respective parameter is assigned the value X, while all the other parameters of the same group are assigned the value ' '. Listing 6.4 shows the creation of radio buttons:

```
REPORT ZRADIO_BUTTON_DISPLAY.
*-------------------------------------------------------*
*/Creating Radiobuttons
*/
PARAMETERS: FEMALE RADIOBUTTON GROUP RAD1,
MALE RADIOBUTTON GROUP RAD1 DEFAULT 'X'.
*-------------------------------------------------------*
```

LISTING 6.4 **Creating radio buttons**

In Listing 6.4, the PARAMETERS statement is used to create two radio buttons, FEMALE and MALE. The MALE radio button is set as the default.

Figure 6.10 shows the output of Listing 6.4:

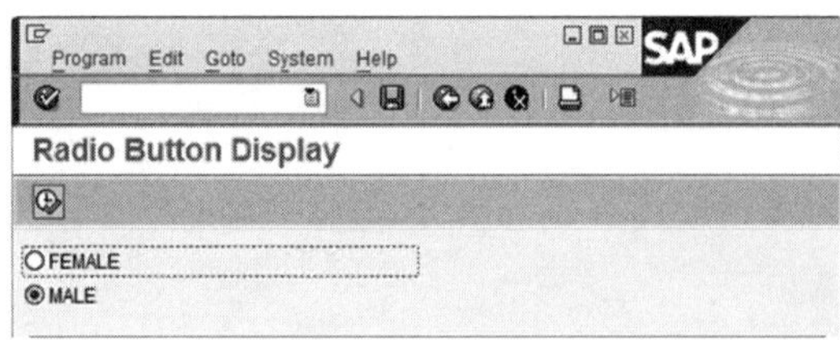

FIGURE 6.10 **Radio buttons display**

Constants in ABAP

Constants are named data objects created statically by using declarative statements. In a program, a constant is declared by assigning a value to it, which is stored in the program's memory area. The value assigned to a constant cannot be changed during the execution of the program. When the value of the constant is changed, a syntax or runtime error may occur. These named data objects are declared with the help of the CONSTANTS statement.

The syntax of the CONSTANTS statement is:

```
CONSTANTS <f> ... [TYPE <type>|LIKE <obj>]...
[VALUE <val>].
```

Notice that the syntax of the CONSTANTS statement is similar to the DATA statement.

> **Note:** You must use the VALUE clause in the CONSTANTS statement. The VALUE clause is used to assign an initial value to the constant during its declaration. This VALUE clause is optional with the DATA statement.

Constants cannot be defined for STRINGS, internal tables, references, and structures containing internal tables.

Table 6.10 describes the clauses used in the CONSTANTS statement:

Clause	Description
<f>	Specifies a name for the constant.
TYPE <type>	Represents a constant named <f>, which inherits the same technical attributes as the existing data type <type>. Any data type with fully specified technical attributes is known as a <type>.
LIKE <obj>	Specifies that the constant name <f> inherits the same technical attributes as an existing data object <obj>.
VALUE <val>	Assigns an initial value to the declared constant name <f>. If you define an elementary fixed-length variable, the CONSTANTS statement automatically populates the value of the variable with the type-specific initial value, as listed in Table 6.5. The other possible <val> values can be a literal, constant, or an explicit clause, such as IS INITIAL.

TABLE 6.10 Description of clauses

The following code snippet shows how to define constants by using the CONSTANTS statement:

```
CONSTANTS: abc TYPE P DECIMALS 5 VALUE '1.23456',
                    def TYPE C VALUE IS INITAIL.
```

In the preceding code snippet, you see constants that are declared with the CONSTANTS statement. The declared constants refer to elementary data types; therefore, the elementary data types are also called elementary constants.

The following code snippet shows how to define complex constants:

```
*-----------------------------------------------------------*
*/Defining a complex constant
*/
CONSTANTS: BEGIN OF EMPLOYEE,
               Name(20) TYPE c VALUE 'SHIVAM SRIVASTAVA',
               Company(50) TYPE c VALUE 'Software Solutions
               Incorporation',
               City(10) TYPE c VALUE 'New Delhi',
               Pincode(8) TYPE i VALUE '110002',
           END OF EMPLOYEE.
*-----------------------------------------------------------*
```

In the preceding code snippet, EMPLOYEE is a complex constant that is composed of the Name, Company, City, and Pincode fields.

The TABLES Statement

The TABLES statement is used to create a structure having the same name as a database table, view, or structure defined in ABAP Dictionary. This statement actually defines a table work area, which is a kind of interface work area, used to create in the shared area of a program.

> **Note:** An interface work area is a special named data object used to pass data between:
>
> - Screens and ABAP programs

Continued

- Logical databases and ABAP programs
- ABAP programs and external subroutines

The syntax of the TABLES statement is:

```
TABLES <dbtab>.
```

In the preceding syntax, <dbtab> represents a structure with the same data type and name of a database table, a view, or a structure from ABAP Dictionary. Prior to SAP release 4.0, the TABLES statement was necessary to include a database table in an ABAP program. Nowadays, SAP systems use Open SQL statements, which do not require the TABLES statement in the program. However, the TABLES statement is still used to define input and output fields on a screen with reference to database tables, views, or structures.

ASSIGNMENT STATEMENTS

Assignment statements are used to assign the values of data objects to a variable in an ABAP program. The four different types of assignment statements are:

- MOVE
- MOVE-CORRESPONDING
- WRITE TO
- CLEAR

Now, let's discuss each statement in detail.

The MOVE Statement

The MOVE statement is used to assign the value of a data object to another data object; that is, to transfer the content of one field to another. The following syntax shows how to use the MOVE statement:

```
MOVE <f1> TO <f2>.
```

In this syntax, <f1> is the data object whose data has to be transferred to another data object, <f2>. The equivalent statement for the MOVE statement is

`<f2> = <f1>`. The `MOVE` statement assigns the value of one data object to another, but the value of the original data object remains unchanged. It is not necessary for `<f1>` to be a data object; it can be a literal, text symbol, or constant.

You can use the `MOVE` statement to assign values to multiple data objects, such as `<f4> = <f3> = <f2> = <f1>`. The following syntax shows how to use the `MOVE` statement for multiple assignments:

```
MOVE <f1> TO <f2>.
MOVE <f2> TO <f3>.
MOVE <f3> TO <f4>.
```

In this syntax, you see that the content of `<f1>` is transferred to `<f2>`, the content of `<f2>` is transferred to `<f3>`, and, finally, the content of `<f3>` is transferred to `<f4>`. To make the transfer of values possible, the data types and data objects must be compatible. The following points must be remembered regarding the compatibility of data types and data objects:

- If the data objects `<f1>` and `<f2>` are fully compatible (that is, their data types, field length, and the number of decimal places are the same), the content of the source field `<f1>` is transferred byte by byte into the target field `<f2>`, without any calculation. In such cases, the working of the `MOVE` statement is most efficient.
- If the data objects are incompatible (that is, if the two fields are of the same type but of different lengths), the content of the source field is converted so that the source field is compatible with the data type of the target field `<f2>`. This transfer happens only if a conversion rule exists between the data types `<f1>` and `<f2>`.
- If the data types are not compatible and no conversion rule exists, transfer of values does not take place.

In the case of `MOVE` statements, if values have to be transferred between noncompatible data objects, the value of the source object always is converted into the data type of the target object. The type of conversion performed in `MOVE` statements is valid for all the different kinds of value assignments.

> **Note:** If you try to assign values between two data types for which no conversion rule exists, a syntax error or runtime error occurs.

Table 6.11 shows the conversion rules that exist between different data types:

Type of Source Field	Type of Target Field	Conversion Rule
C	P	Specifies that the source field may contain numbers, a single decimal point, or an optional sign, which can be trailing or leading. In addition to this, blanks can appear on either side of the value. Any blank value is converted to zero.
C	D	Specifies that the source field should contain a valid date in the YYYYMMDD format. If the source field does not contain a valid date format, no error occurs; however, an invalid value is assigned to the target field.
C	T	Specifies that the source field should contain a valid time in the HHMMSS format. If the source field does not contain a valid time format, no error occurs; however, an invalid value is assigned to the target field.
C	N	Specifies that the source field is scanned from left to right and only the digits 0-9 are transferred to the target field (right-justified). In addition, values on the left are padded with zeroes.
C	X	Specifies that the source field contains a hexadecimal-character string and that the valid characters are 0, 1, 2, 3, 4, 5, 6, 7, 8, 9, A, B, C, D, E, F. Note that this character string is packed as a hexadecimal number padded with zeroes or truncated on the right.

Continued

Type of Source Field	Type of Target Field	Conversion Rule
P	C	Specifies that the value in the target field is right-justified in the target field, with the rightmost byte reserved for the trailing sign.
P	D	Specifies that the value in the source field is interpreted as the number of days and stored internally in the YYYYMMDD format.
P	T	Specifies that the value in the source field is interpreted as the number of seconds since midnight converted to 24-hour clock time, and stored internally in the HHMMSS format.
D	P	Specifies that the value in the source field is converted to a number representing the number of days.
T	p	Specifies that the value in the source field is converted to a number representing the number of seconds since midnight.

TABLE 6.11 Conversion rules

Listing 6.5 shows the use of the MOVE statement:

```
REPORT ZMOVE_DEMO.
*-----------------------------------------------------*
*/ Data Declarations
*/
DATA: Number_1(10) TYPE c,
      Number_2 TYPE p DECIMALS 2,
      Number_3 TYPE i.
*-----------------------------------------------------*
Number_1 = 100.
*----------------------------------------------------**
/MOVE statement */
MOVE '5.75' TO Number_2.
```

Continued

```
*------------------------------------------------------------*
Number_3 = Number_1.
WRITE: 'Number_1 =',Number_1.
WRITE: / 'Number_2 =',Number_2.
WRITE: / 'Number_3 =',Number_3.
```

LISTING 6.5 **Using the MOVE statement**

In Listing 6.5, `Number_1`, `Number_2`, and `Number_3` are data objects of data type `C`, `P`, and `I`, respectively. The length of the `Number_1` data object is 10. `Number_1` data object stores 100, `Number_2` data object stores 5.75, and `Number_3` data object stores the value of `Number_1` data object that is, 100. Note that the values in the `Number_1` and `Number_3` data objects are assigned directly, while the value of the `Number_2` data object is assigned by using the `MOVE` statement.

Figure 6.11 shows the output of Listing 6.5:

```
Number_1 =       100
Number_2 =             5.75
Number_3 =        100
```


FIGURE 6.11 **Output of the MOVE statement**

The `MOVE-CORRESPONDING` Statement

The `MOVE-CORRESPONDING` statement is used to assign values between the components of two or more structures. The syntax of the `MOVE-CORRESPONDING` statement is

```
MOVE-CORRESPONDING <struct1> TO <struct2>.
```

When you execute the `MOVE-CORRESPONDING` statement, the content of the components of the `<struct1>` structure is copied to the components of the structure `<struct2>`, which contains identical names. In addition to this, the syntax is actually broken down into a set of `MOVE` statements, one for each pair of fields which have identical names. The following is the equivalent syntax of the `MOVE-CORRESPONDING` statement:

```
MOVE STRUCT1-<Ci> TO STRUCT-<Ci>.
```

Listing 6.6 shows the working of the `MOVE-CORRESPONDING` statement.

```
REPORT ZMOVE_DEMO.
*---------------------------------------------------*
*/ Data Declarations
*/
DATA: BEGIN OF ADDRESS,
        FNAME(20) TYPE c VALUE 'Shivam',
        LNAME(20) TYPE c VALUE 'Srivastava',
        CITY(20) TYPE c VALUE 'Lucknow',
      END OF ADDRESS.
*---------------------------*
*/ Data Declarations
*/
DATA: BEGIN OF NAME,
        LNAME(20) TYPE c,
        FNAME(20) TYPE c,
      END OF NAME.
*-------------------------**/ MOVE-CORRESPONDING statement
MOVE-CORRESPONDING Address TO Name.
*---------------------------*
WRITE:/  NAME-LNAME,
         NAME-FNAME.
```

LISTING 6.6 **Using the MOVE-CORRESPONDING statement**

Listing 6.6 shows that the values of `NAME-LNAME` and `NAME-FNAME` are set to SRIVASTAVA and SHIVAM, respectively. Figure 6.12 shows the output of Listing 6.6:

FIGURE 6.12 **Output of the MOVE-CORRESPONDING statement**

The `WRITE TO` Statement

The `WRITE TO` statement is an assignment statement that converts the content of the source field into a field of type `C`. The syntax of the `WRITE TO` statement is

```
WRITE <f1> TO <f2> [<option>].
```

In the preceding syntax, the `WRITE TO` statement converts the content of the data object `<f1>` to type `C` and places the string into the `<f2>` variable. Listing 6.7 shows the use of the `WRITE TO` statement:

```
REPORT ZWRITE_DEMO.
*----------------------------*
*/ Data Declarations
*/
DATA: Name(10) TYPE C VALUE 'SHIVAM',
TEXT(10).
*----------------------------*
*/Using WRITE TO statement to show source and target names
*/
WRITE :'Source name is :', Name.WRITE: Name TO TEXT.
WRITE: /'Target name is :', TEXT.
*-----------------------------*
```

LISTING 6.7 **Using the WRITE TO statement**

In Listing 6.7, the `Name` variable is of type `C`. The `WRITE TO` statement assigns the content of the source structure, that is, `Name`, to the target structure, that is, `TEXT`. The `WRITE TO` statement displays the content of both the source and target structure. Figure 6.13 shows the source name and the target name as SHIVAM:

```
Source name is : SHIVAM
Target name is : SHIVAM
```


FIGURE 6.13 **Output of the WRITE TO statement**

> **Note:** The data type of <f1> must be convertible into a character field. If <f1> is not convertible into a character field, a syntax or runtime error occurs. The content of the data object <f1> remains unchanged. The content of the <f2> data object always is regarded as a character string. Therefore, you must not use a target field with a numeric data type (F, I, or P). If you use a numeric target field, the SAP system displays a syntax error.

The CLEAR Statement

The CLEAR statement is used to reset the value of a data object. Resetting the values of the data objects depends on the data type of the data objects. For example, data objects of type I are set to zero and data objects of type C are set to null. The following is the syntax of the CLEAR statement:

```
CLEAR <f>.
```

In this syntax, <f> is either a field or a field string. If <f> is a field, the CLEAR statement resets the value of the field to its initial value. The initial value of the field depends on the data type of the field. If <f> is a field string, the CLEAR statement resets each of the individual fields in the header line of the field string to their respective initial values:

Table 6.12 shows the result of the CLEAR statement for the data object of the different data types:

Data Type	Description of CLEAR Statement Impact
Elementary Data Type	Resets the values to initial values and not to the start value, which is set using the VALUE parameter of the DATA statement.
Reference	Resets a reference variable to its initial value so that it does not point to any object.
Structure	Resets the individual components of a structure to their respective initial values.
Internal Table	Deletes the entire content of the internal table.

TABLE 6.12 **Impact of the CLEAR statement on different data types**

Note: You cannot use the CLEAR statement to reset a constant.

Listing 6.8 shows the working of the CLEAR statement:

```
REPORT ZCLEAR.
*-----------------------------------------*
*/ Data Declarations
*/
DATA number TYPE I VALUE '80'.
*-----------------------------------------*
WRITE number.
*-----------------------------------------**
/Using CLEAR statement
CLEAR number.
WRITE / number.
*---------------------------------------*
```

LISTING 6.8 **The CLEAR Statement**

In Listing 6.8, the CLEAR statement resets the content of a field from 80 to its initial value, 0. Figure 6.14 shows the output of Listing 6.8:

```
80
 0
```


FIGURE 6.14 **Output of the CLEAR statement**

FORMATTING OPTIONS

ABAP offers various types of formatting options to format the output of programs. For example, you can create a list that includes various items in different colors or formatting styles. ABAP offers the following statements to perform the formatting:

- The `WRITE` statement
- The `FORMAT` statement

Now, let's discuss each of these statements in detail.

The `WRITE` Statement

The `WRITE` statement is a formatting statement used to display data on a screen. There are different formatting options for the `WRITE` statement. The syntax of the `WRITE` statement is:

```
WRITE <format> <f> <options>.
```

In the preceding syntax, `<format>` represents the output format specification, which can be a forward slash (/) that indicates display of the output starting from a new line. In addition to the forward slash, the format specification includes a column number and column length. For example, the `WRITE/04(6)` statement shows that a new line begins with column 4 and the column length is 6, whereas the `WRITE 20` statement shows the current line with column 20. The `<f>` parameter can represent a data variable, text literal, or numbered text.

Table 6.13 describes various clauses used in the `WRITE` statement for formatting:

Clause	Description
`LEFT-JUSTIFIED`	Specifies that the output is left-justified.
`CENTERED`	Specifies that the output is centered.
`RIGHT-JUSTIFIED`	Specifies that the output is right-justified.
`UNDER <g>`	Specifies that the output starts directly under field <g>.
`NO-GAP`	Specifies that the blank after field <f> is rejected.
`USING EDIT MASK <m>`	Specifies the specification of the format template <m>.
`USING NO EDIT MASK`	Specifies that the format template specified in the ABAP Dictionary is deactivated.
`NO-ZERO`	Specifies that if a field contains only zeroes, they are replaced by blanks.

TABLE 6.13 Clauses representing various formatting options for all data types

Table 6.14 shows the formatting options for numeric type fields only:

Formatting Option	Function
`NO-SIGN`	Specifies that no leading sign is displayed on the screen.
`EXPONENT <e>`	Specifies that in type F, fields (i.e., floating point type fields), the exponent is defined in <e>.
`ROUND <r>`	Specifies that type P fields (i.e., packed numeric type fields) are first multiplied by 10**(-r) and then rounded off to an integer value.
`CURRENCY <c>`	Specifies that the formatting is done according to the currency <c> value that is stored in the TCURX database table.
`UNIT <u>`	Specifies that the number of decimal places is fixed according to the <u> unit as specified in the T006 database table for type P, (that is, packed type fields).
`DECIMALS <d>`	Specifies that the number of digits <d> must be displayed after the decimal point.

TABLE 6.14 Formatting options for numeric type fields

Table 6.15 lists different formatting options for the date fields and examples:

Formatting Option	Example
DD/MM/YY	13/01/85
MM/DD/YY	01/13/85
DD/MM/YYYY	13/01/1985
MM/DD/YYYY	01/13/1985
DDMMYY	130185
MMDDYY	011385
YYMMDD	850113

TABLE 6.15 Different formatting options for date fields and examples

Note: In Table 6.15, all the examples are given in the context of the date January 13, 1985. Here, DD stands for the date in two figures, MM stands for the month in two figures, YY stands for the year in two figures, and YYYY stands for the year in four figures.

Table 6.16 shows some examples of ABAP code that implements the formatting options along with the output:

ABAP Coding	Screen Output
DATA: g(6) TYPE c VALUE 'Shivam',	Shivam Srivastava
f(10) TYPE c VALUE 'Srivastava'.	Shivam
WRITE: g,f.	Srivastava
WRITE:/10 g,	ShivamSrivastava
/ f UNDER g.	
WRITE:/ g NO-GAP, f.	
DATA time TYPE t VALUE '123456'.	
WRITE: time,	123456
/(8) time USING EDIT MASK '__:__:__'.	12:34:56

Continued

ABAP Coding	Screen Output
WRITE: '000321',	000321
/ '000321' NO-ZERO.	321
DATA float TYPE f VALUE '12345 6789.0'.	
WRITE float EXPONENT 3.	123456.789000000000E+03
DATA pack TYPE p VALUE '123.456'DECIMALS 3.	123.46
WRITE pack DECIMALS 2.	12,345.600
WRITE: /pack ROUND -2,	1,234.560
/ pack ROUND -1,	12.346
/ pack ROUND 1,	1.235
/ packROUND 2.	
WRITE: SY-DATUM,	27.06.1995
/ SY-DATUMYYMMDD.	950627

TABLE 6.16 Examples of formatting options and their output

The FORMAT Statement

Different types of syntaxes are available for specific actions performed with the FORMAT statement. Table 6.17 shows the different variations in these syntaxes:

FORMAT Statement	Description
FORMAT <option1> [ON|OFF] <option2> [ON|OFF].......	Specifies that the formatting options are set statically in a program. The option mentioned in the <option> expression is applicable to all output untill the formatting option is turned off by using the OFF clause, as indicated in the statement. Note that the ON or OFF clause is optional.
FORMAT <option1> = <var1> <option2> = <var2>	Specifies that the formatting options are set dynamically at runtime. The variables var1, var2, ... are interpreted as numbers and should be declared with the data type as I. If the content in the var1 and var2 variables is zero, the variable has the same effect as the OFF clause. If the numbers in the var1 and var2

Continued

FORMAT Statement	Description
	variables are not equal to zero, either the color is shown according to the numbers stored in the variables or the variables have the same effect as that of the ON clause. Note that the formatting options are all set to their default values whenever they are used for the new event.
FORMAT RESET	Sets all the formatting options to off.

TABLE 6.17 FORMAT statement syntaxes

Using the FORMAT Statement Clauses

The FORMAT statement is also used to display the output in a colored format. The following syntax is used to set colors in a program:

```
FORMAT COLOR <num> [ON] INTENSIFIED [ON|OFF] INVERSE [ON|OFF].
```

The following syntax is used to set colors at runtime:

```
FORMAT COLOR = <const> INTENSIFIED = <int> INVERSE = <inv>.
```

In both syntaxes, the COLOR clause is used to set the background color of a line. In addition, the use of the INVERSE ON clause allows the SAP system to change the foreground color of a line instead of the background color. The <num> expression represents a color number or color specification. Table 6.18 lists the different possible values of the <num> and <const> expressions:

Color Number for the <num> Expression	Color Specification for the <num> Expression	Color Number for the <const> Expression	Color	Use of Color
OFF	COL_BACKGROUND	0	Depends on the GUI	Used for background
1	COL_HEADING	1	Gray-blue	Used for headers

Continued

Color Number for the <num> Expression	Color Specification for the <num> Expression	Color Number for the <const> Expression	Color	Use of Color
2	COL_NORMAL	2	Light gray	Used for list bodies
3	COL_TOTAL	3	Yellow	Used for data total
4	COL_KEY	4	Blue-green	Used for key columns
5	COL_POSITIVE	5	Green	Used for a positive threshold value
6	COL_NEGATIVE	6	Red	Used for a negative threshold value
7	COL_GROUP	7	Violet	Used for control levels

TABLE 6.18 Values of the <num> and <const> expressions

The INTENSIFIED clause in the FORMAT statement is used to set the intensity of the background color. The default setting is INTENSIFIED ON. The use of the COLOR OFF setting changes the foreground color instead of the background color.

The INVERSE clause is used to determine whether or not the background or foreground color is set with the COLOR clause.

Listing 6.9 shows various types of colors in a list:

```
REPORT ZCOLOR_DISPLAY_DEMO.
*-----------------------------------*
*/ Data Declarations
*/
DATA i TYPE i VALUE 0.
```

Continued

```
DATA col(15) TYPE c.
*-------------------------------------*
*/ While Loop
*/
WHILE i < 8.
CASE i.
WHEN 0.
col = 'COL_BACKGROUND '.
WHEN 1.
      col = 'COL_HEADING '.
WHEN 2.
      col = 'COL_NORMAL '.
WHEN 3.
      col = 'COL_TOTAL '.
WHEN 4.
      col = 'COL_KEY '.
WHEN 5.
      col = 'COL_POSITIVE '.
WHEN 6.
      col = 'COL_NEGATIVE '.
WHEN 7.
      col = 'COL_GROUP '.
ENDCASE.
*-------------------------------------*
*/FORMAT Statement
*/
FORMAT INTENSIFIED COLOR = i.
WRITE: /(4) i, AT 7 SY-VLINE,
col,       SY-VLINE,
col INTENSIFIED OFF, SY-VLINE,
col INVERSE.
i = i + 1.
ENDWHILE.
*--------------------------------*
```

LISTING 6.9 **Displaying various colors**

Listing 6.9 shows the use of the `COLOR` statement. Figure 6.15 shows the output of Listing 6.9:

In Figure 6.15, observe the different possibilities of colors that can be assigned to a list by using the INTENSIFIED and INVERSE clauses of the FORMAT statement. The INTENSIFIED clause is used to set the intensity of the background color.

0	COL_BACKGROUND	COL_BACKGROUND	
1	COL_HEADING	COL_HEADING	COL_HEADING
2	COL_NORMAL	COL_NORMAL	COL_NORMAL
3	COL_TOTAL	COL_TOTAL	COL_TOTAL
4	COL_KEY	COL_KEY	COL_KEY
5	COL_POSITIVE	COL_POSITIVE	COL_POSITIVE
6	COL_NEGATIVE	COL_NEGATIVE	COL_NEGATIVE
7	COL_GROUP	COL_GROUP	COL_GROUP

FIGURE 6.15 **Output of the COLORS clause in the list**

Enabling Fields for INPUT

You can enable output fields in a list as input-enabled fields (accepting input data from users) using the FORMAT statement. The value of these fields can be modified by the user. You can print out the changes that you have made in interactive lists or process them later by using the READ LINE statement. Note that the variables that accept input data from users do not change. The following syntax of the FORMAT statement is used to create input-enabled fields:

```
FORMAT INPUT [ON|OFF].
```

The syntax to make the output fields input-enabled at runtime is:

```
FORMAT INPUT = i.
```

The ON clause (or i unequal to zero) is used to format the subsequent output as input-enabled fields. The background and foreground colors of the input-enabled fields are different as compared to the remaining list. The foreground color of an input field is changed by the INTENSIFIED clause. You can also make horizontal lines input-enabled by formatting them as input fields. Listing 6.10 shows the use of the FORMAT statement to specify the various formatting options:

```
REPORT ZFORMATTING_DEMO.
WRITE 'Please enter the following details'.
WRITE /'Enter name here' INPUT ON.
ULINE.
WRITE 'Enter salary in the given field'.
*/Using FORMAT INPUT ON statement to make the output fields
input-enabled
FORMAT INPUT ON INTENSIFIED OFF.
ULINE.
```

LISTING 6.10 **Using the FORMAT statement to specify various formatting options**

In this listing, the INPUT ON clause is used with the WRITE statement to create an input field that accepts data from users. The FORMAT statement is used with the INTENSIFIED OFF clause so that the foreground color of the first input field is different from the other one. Figure 6.16 shows the output of Listing 6.10:

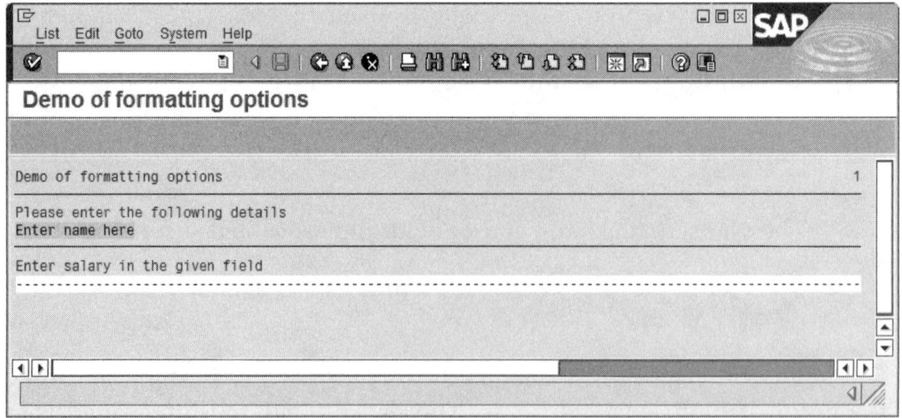

FIGURE 6.16 **Input fields in lists**

In Figure 6.16, note that the text "Enter name here" is an input field displayed in a different color. You can enter the value in the input field by deleting the existing characters in the fields. For instance, we have entered a name, Vineet Kaushal, in the "Enter name here" field and 35000 in place of the dotted lines (- - - - -) field, as shown in Figure 6.17:

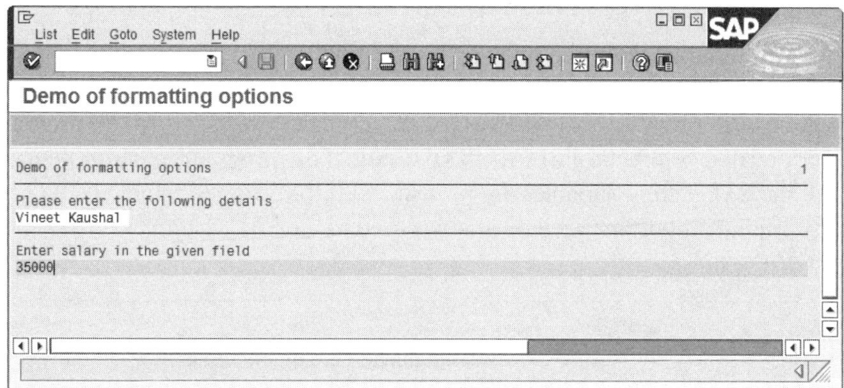

FIGURE 6.17 **Input fields**

Displaying Fields as Hotspots

The FORMAT statement can also be used to specify a field as a hotspot field, a special area on the output screen that triggers an event when a user clicks the field. The following syntax of the FORMAT statement is used to create a hotspot field:

```
FORMAT HOTSPOT [ON|OFF].
```

If you want to designate existing fields as hotspots, the following option of the FORMAT statement must be used:

```
FORMAT HOTSPOT = h.
```

The ON clause in the FORMAT statement is used to declare a field as a hotspot field. You cannot use the HOTSPOT clause if INPUT ON (as discussed in the "Enabling Fields for INPUT" section) is set because the cursor cannot be positioned on an input field by using HOTSPOT ON. In addition, you cannot format the horizontal lines created with the ULINE clause and blank lines created with the SKIP clause as hotspots.

EXPLORING SYSTEM VARIABLES

System variables store the information relation to the SAP R/3 system in an ABAP Dictionary structure named SYST. The SAP R/3 system makes system variables available within your program. These variables are available to existing ABAP programs, and are updated automatically by the SAP system if the program's environment changes. All the SAP system variables are prefixed with the string SY. Table 6.19 describes a list of some important system variables used in the SAP system:

System Variable	Description
SY-INDEX	Denotes the number of a loop pass.
SY-PAGENO	Denotes the current page number.
SY-TABIX	Denotes the current line index of an internal table
SY-DBCNT	Denotes the total number of processed lines of an internal table.
SY-LSIND	Denotes a list index.
SY-MANDT	Denotes the client number from logon.
SY-LANGU	Denotes the current language.

TABLE 6.19 Describing system variables

DYNAMIC ASSIGNMENT

Data objects are accessed dynamically in ABAP programs by using field symbols and data references. Unlike static access to a data object, where you need to specify the name of the data object, you can represent dynamic data objects by using field symbols.

Field symbols are symbolic names for fields, which do not reserve space for a field physically but act as pointers to other fields. Any data object can be pointed by a field symbol. The data object referenced by a field symbol is assigned after it has been declared in a program.

Before using a field symbol in a program, you must assign a field to the field symbol. This implies that whenever a field symbol is addressed in a program, you are actually addressing the field that is assigned to the field symbol.

> **Note:** Field symbols are similar to the dereferenced pointers in the C language (that is, pointers to which the content operator * is applied).

The operations performed on field symbols are actually applied to the fields assigned to them. For example, a `MOVE` statement assigned between two field symbols assigns the content of the source field symbol to the target field symbol.

Field symbols can be created either with or without type specifications. If the type is not assigned to a field symbol, it inherits all the technical attributes of the field assigned to it. If the type is specified, the SAP system checks whether a match exists between the assigned field and the field symbol. The following syntax is used to declare a field symbol:

```
FIELD-SYMBOLS <f> [typing].
```

The angular brackets (shown as < >) are used to identify the field symbols in a program.

When a data object is assigned to a field symbol, the field symbol inherits all the technical attributes of the data object. Therefore, the data type of the field symbol is actually the data type of the data object assigned to the field symbol.

Now, let's discuss the flow control statements of a processing block in an ABAP program.

DESCRIBING FLOW CONTROL STATEMENTS

Occasionally, ABAP programs use some conditions or loops to control the flow of execution of the ABAP program. Various conditions and loops can be implemented in programs by using the standard keywords, such as `IF`, `CASE`, `DO`, and `WHILE`.

As already discussed, the structure of an ABAP program is made up of processing blocks. In this section, you learn about controlling the flow of a program within a processing block. This is regarded as an internal control of an ABAP program as opposed to the external control provided by events in the ABAP runtime environment. According to the principles of structured programming, the internal flow of a processing block can be controlled by using control structures. The control structures divide the processing blocks into smaller statement blocks for easier processing of an ABAP program. Figure 6.18 shows the flow control statements that a processing block may contain:

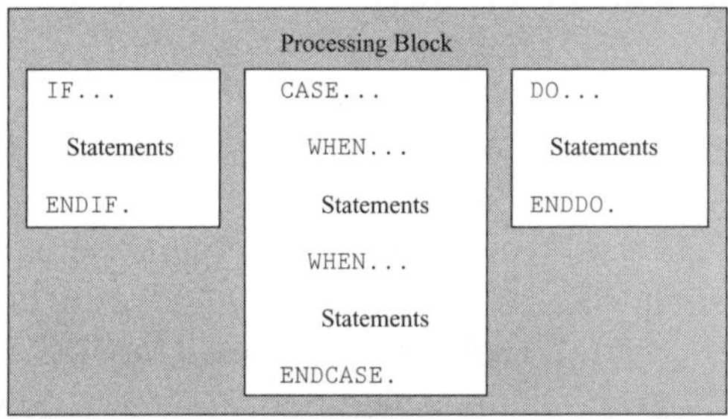

FIGURE 6.18 **Flow control statements**

The processing block of the ABAP program consists of several statements, some of which are:

- `IF...ENDIF`
- `CASE...ENDCASE`
- `DO...ENDDO`

Now, let's discuss each control statement in detail.

The `IF...ENDIF` Control Statement

`IF...ENDIF` is a control statement used to specify one or more conditions. You can also nest the `IF` control structures in an ABAP program. The following syntax is used for the `IF...ENDIF` statement:

```
IF <condition1>.
     <statement block>.
ELSEIF <condition2>
     <statement block>.
ELSEIF <condition3>
```

Continued

```
        <statement block>.
........
ELSE.
         <statement block>.
ENDIF.
```

In this syntax, the execution of the processing block is based on the result of one or more logical conditions associated with the processing block.

Table 6.20 shows the description of the clauses used in the `IF...ENDIF` control statement:

Clauses	Descriptions
condition1	Represents a logical condition that evaluates a true or false condition.
condition2	Shows the second condition specified in the ELSEIF statement, which is executed when the IF statement condition turns out to be false.
ENDIF	Shows the end of the IF statement block.

TABLE 6.20 Description of the clauses

The following guidelines must be kept in mind while constructing the `IF...ENDIF` control structure:

- Each `IF` statement must end with a matching `ENDIF` statement. The `ELSE` and `ELSEIF` statements are optional.
- You can use parentheses, but each parenthesis should be separated by a space. For example, `IF (a1 = a2) or (a3 = a4)` is correct, and `IF (s1 = s2) or (w1 = w2)` is incorrect.
- Variables can be compared with blanks and zeroes by using the `IS INITIAL` clause. For example, `IF f1 IS INITIAL` will be true if `f1` is of type `C` and blank. If `f1` is of any other data type, the statement is true if `f1` contains zeroes.

- To fulfill a negation condition, `NOT` must precede the logical expression, as shown in the following examples:
  - `IF NOT f1 IS INITIAL` is correct
  - `IF f1 IS NOT INITIAL` is incorrect
- Variables can be compared against null values by using the `IS NULL` clause. For example, `IF f1 IS NULL`.

Table 6.21 shows various types of comparison operators for different operands:

Comparison	Alternate Forms	True When
a1 = a2	EQ	a1 equals a2
a1 <> a2	NE or ><	a1 does not equal a2
a1 > a2	GT	a1 is greater than a2
a1 < a2	LT	a1 is less than a2
a1 > = a2	GE or =>	a1 is greater than or equal to a2
a1 < = a2	LE or = <	a1 is less than or equal to a2
a1 between a2 and a3	N/A	a1 lies between a2 and a3 (inclusive)
Not a1 between a2 and a3	N/A	a1 lies outside the range of a2 to a3 (inclusive)

TABLE 6.21 Comparison operators

In Table 6.21, a1, a2, and a3 can be variables, literals, or field strings. Automatic conversion is performed in case of variables or literals, if the data type or length of the variables or the literals does not match. Similarly, automatic type adjustment is performed for either one or both of the values while comparing two values of different data types. The type of conversion is decided by the data type and the preference order of the data type. The order of preference of the data types is given as follows:

- If one field is of type `C`, the other type is automatically converted to the `F` type.

- If one field is of type P, the other is converted to the P type.
- If one field is of type I, the other is converted to the I type.
- If one field is of type D, the other is converted to the D type. However, the C and N types are not converted, but compared directly.
- If one field is of type T, the other is converted to the T type. However, the C and N types are not converted, but compared directly.
- If one field is of type N and other is of type C or X, both are converted to the type P.
- If one field is of the type C and the other is of type X, the X type is converted to the C type.

> **Note:** Field strings are C type variables.

Listing 6.11 shows an example of the IF...ELSE...ENDIF statement:

```
REPORT ZIF_DEMO.
*-----------------------------------------------*
*/ Data Declarations
*/
DATA RESULT TYPE I Value 45.
*-----------------------------------------------*
*/IF Condition
IF RESULT < 0.
WRITE / 'Result is less than zero'.
ELSE.
WRITE / 'Result is either equal to or greater than zero'.
ENDIF.
*-----------------------------------------------*
```

LISTING 6.11 **Using the IF...ELSE...ENDIF statement**

In Listing 6.11, RESULT is a variable of type I, storing the value 45. The IF statement compares the value of the RESULT variable with zero. If the value of RESULT is less than zero, the output displayed is Result is less than zero; otherwise, the output is Result is either equal or greater than zero. Figure 6.19 shows the output of Listing 6.11:

```
Result is either equal or greater than zero
```


FIGURE 6.19 **Result of the IF statement**

Using the ELSEIF Statement

The ELSEIF statement is used to avoid nesting of the IF statement, because the nesting of the IF statements can make the code difficult to understand. Listing 6.12 shows how to use the ELSEIF statement:

```
REPORT ZIF_DEMO.
*-------------------------------------------*
*/ Data Declarations
*/
DATA RESULT TYPE I Value 45.
*-------------------------------------------*
*/IF and ELSEIF Statements

IF RESULT < 0.
WRITE / 'Result is less than zero'.
ELSEIF RESULT < 50.
WRITE / 'Result is less than fifty'.
ELSE.
WRITE /   'Result is either equal to or greater than zero'.
ENDIF.
*----------------------------------------*
```

LISTING 6.12 **Using the ELSEIF Statement**

In Listing 6.12, RESULT is a variable of type I, storing the value 45. The IF statement checks whether the value of the RESULT variable is less than zero. If the value of RESULT is less than zero, the output displayed is Result is less `than zero`; if the value of `RESULT` is less than fifty, the output displayed is `Result is less than fifty`, else the output displayed is `Result is either equal or greater than zero`. Figure 6.20 shows the output of Listing 6.12:

```
Result is less than fifty
```


FIGURE 6.20 **Output of the ELSEIF statement**

Working with Character String Operations

In ABAP, you can perform many operations on character strings. The operations, such as comparing the content and pattern of two character strings, can be performed easily with the help of some predefined operators. Table 6.22 shows noteworthy operators for string:

Operator	Description	True When	Case-Sensitive	Trailing Blanks Ignored
a1 CO a2	a1 Contains Only a2	a1 is solely composed of the characters in a2	Yes	No
a1 CN a2	NOT a1 Contains Only a2	a1 contains characters that are not in a2	Yes	No
a1 CA a2	a1 Contains Any a2	a1 contains at least one character of a2	Yes	No
a1 NA a2	NOT a1 Contains Any a2	a1 does not contain any character of a2	Yes	No
a1 CS a2	a1 Contains a String a2	a1 contains the character string a2	No	Yes
a1 NS a2	NOT a1 Contains a String a2	a1 does not contain the character string a2	No	Yes

Continued

Operator	Description	True When	Case-Sensitive	Trailing Blanks Ignored
a1 CP a2	a1 Contains a Pattern a2	a1 contains the pattern in a2	No	Yes
a1 NP a2	NOT a1 Contains a Pattern a2	a1 does not contain the pattern in a2	No	Yes

TABLE 6.22 Noteworthy string operators

Listing 6.13 shows how character string operations are performed using the `IF...ELSEIF...ENDIF` statement:

```
REPORT demo_flow_control_if.
*---------------------------------------*
*/ Data Declarations
*/
DATA: text1(30) TYPE c VALUE 'This is the first text',
      text2(30) TYPE c VALUE 'This is the second text',
      text3(30) TYPE c VALUE 'This is the third text',
      string(5) TYPE c VALUE 'eco'.
*---------------------------------------*
*/Using IF..ELSEIF..ENDIF statement
IF text1 CS string.
WRITE / 'Condition 1 is fulfilled'.

ELSEIF text2 CS string.
WRITE / 'Condition 2 is fulfilled'.

ELSEIF text3 CS string.
WRITE / 'Condition 3 is fulfilled'.

ELSE.
WRITE / 'No condition is fulfilled'.
ENDIF.
*-------------------------------------------*
```

LISTING 6.13 **String operations using the IF...ELSEIF...ENDIF statement**

In Listing 6.13, the second logical expression (text2 CS string) is true because the string, eco, occurs in text2. Figure 6.21 shows the output of Listing 6.13:

```
Condition 2 is fulfilled
```


FIGURE 6.21 **Output of the IF..ELSEIF...ENDIF statement**

The CASE Control Statement

The CASE control statement is used when you need to compare two or more numbers. The syntax of the CASE statement is:

```
CASE <f> .
WHEN <fij> [ OR <fij> OR.. ... ..].
      <statement block>
      WHEN <fij> [ OR <fij> OR.. ... ..].
      <statement block>
WHEN... ..
WHEN OTHERS.
      <statement block>
ENDCASE.
```

In the preceding syntax, the statement block following a WHEN clause is executed if the content of the fields shown in the <f> expression is similar to one of the fields <fij>. After executing all the conditions specified in the WHEN statement, the program continues to process the remaining statements after the ENDCASE statement. The WHEN OTHERS clause is executed in a program when the value of the <f> field does not match with any value specified in the <fij> fields of the WHEN clause.

Consider the following key points while constructing the CASE... WHEN...ENDCASE statement:

- If the WHEN OTHERS clause is omitted in a program and the value of the <f> field does not match with any value specified in the

<fij> fields, the program continues to process the remaining statements after the ENDCASE statement.

- No logical expressions can be used for the <f> field.
- The field strings used in the CASE...WHEN...ENDCASE statement are treated as type C variables.

There is a difference between the CASE and IF...ELSE control statement. In the IF...ELSE statement, you can use the complex expression in the <conditions> clause, but in the CASE statement, you can only give a single value in the <f> field. Listing 6.14 shows an example of the CASE statement:

```
REPORT demo_flow_control_case.
*-------------------------------------------------------*
*/ DATA Declaration
*/
DATA: a1    TYPE c VALUE 'X',
a2    TYPE c VALUE 'Y',
a3    TYPE c VALUE 'Z',
string    TYPE c VALUE 'A'.
*--------------------------------------------------------*
*/ CASE Control Statement
CASE string.
WHEN a1 OR a2.
WRITE: / 'String is', a1, 'OR', a2.
WHEN a3.
WRITE: / 'String is', a3.
WHEN OTHERS.
WRITE: / 'String is not', a1, a2, a3.
ENDCASE.
*-----------------------------------------------------*
```

LISTING 6.14 **Using the CASE statement**

Listing 6.14 defines three variables (a1, a2, and a3) with their corresponding values. Note that none of the values of the string variables matches the WHEN condition. In such a situation, the statement block with WHEN OTHERS is executed and the corresponding values of the a1, a2, and a3 variables are displayed. Figure 6.22 shows the output of Listing 6.14:

```
String is not X Y Z
```


FIGURE 6.22 **Output of the CASE statement**

Looping

A statement block is executed repeatedly in a program by using loops in the program. The loops are categorized into two types:

- Unconditional loops by using the `DO` statement.
- Conditional loops by using the `WHILE` statement

Now, let's discuss each in detail.

Unconditional Loops Using the DO Statement

Unconditional loops repeatedly execute several statements without specifying any condition. The `DO` statement implements unconditional loops by executing a set of statements (statement block) several times unconditionally. The syntax of the `DO` statement is:

```
DO [n TIMES] [VARYING <f> FROM <fi> NEXT <f2>].
<statement block>
ENDDO.
```

Table 6.23 shows the clauses used in the syntax of the `DO` statement:

Clause	Description
`TIMES`	Imposes a restriction on the number of loop passes, represented by n. It is necessary that the value of n is not negative or 0. If it is so, the statements in the loop are not executed. If the `TIMES` clause is not used, at least any one of the two statements (`EXIT` or `STOP`) should be used to avoid endless loops.
`VARYING`	Shows that new values of the `<f>` variable can be assigned in each loop pass.

TABLE 6.23 Clauses in the DO statement

> **Note:** The DO Statement can be nested as well as combined with other loop forms.

Listing 6.15 shows an example of the DO statement:

```
REPORT demo_do.
*----------------------------------------------------*
*/Using DO Statement
*/
DO.
WRITE / SY-INDEX.
IF SY-INDEX = 3.
EXIT.
ENDIF.
ENDDO.
*----------------------------------------------------*
```

LISTING 6.15 **Using the DO statement**

In Listing 6.15, the process passes through the loop three times and then leaves the DO loop when the value of the SY-INDEX system variable becomes 3. Figure 6.23 shows the output of Listing 6.15:

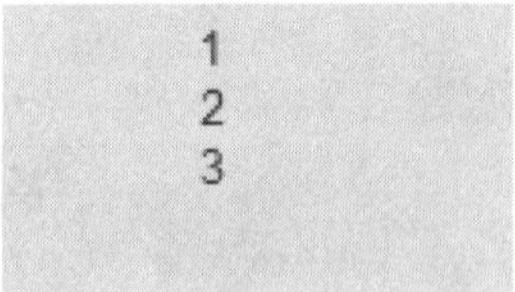

```
1
2
3
```


FIGURE 6.23 **Output of the DO statement**

Listing 6.16 shows the nesting of the DO statement:

```
*--------------------------------------*
*/ Nested DO Statement
DO 2 TIMES.
WRITE SY-INDEX.
SKIP.
  DO 3 TIMES.
WRITE / SY-INDEX.
ENDDO.
SKIP.
ENDDO.
*--------------------------------------*
```

LISTING 6.16 **Nested DO statement**

Listing 6.16 shows a nesting of the `DO` loop. The outer `DO` loop is processed twice. The inner `DO` loop is processed three times each time the outer `DO` loop is processed. That is, the inner `DO` loop is processed six times in this case. The `SY-INDEX` system variable is used to store the value of the number of loops passed. Figure 6.24 shows the output of Listing 6.16:

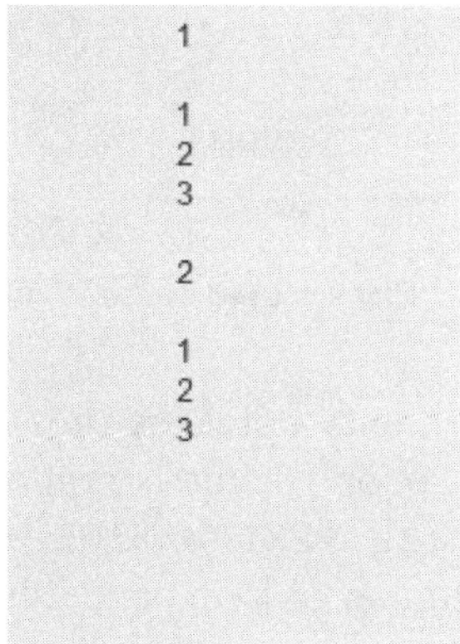

FIGURE 6.24 **Output of the nested DO loop**

Conditional Loops Using the WHILE Statement

Conditional loops execute several statements only after certain conditions are fulfilled. This can be accomplished with the WHILE statement. The WHILE statement allows you to execute a block of statements so long as the condition mentioned in the WHILE statement evaluates to true. The syntax of the WHILE statement is:

```
WHILE <condition> [VARY <f> FROM <f1> NEXT <f2>]
[statement_block]
ENDWHILE.
```

Table 6.24 describes the clauses used in the syntax of the WHILE statement:

Clause	Description
<condition>	Represents a logical expression.
[statement block]	Specifies a set of statements executed when the condition specified in the WHILE statement is true.
[VARY <f> FROM <f1> NEXT <f2>]	Specifies the condition to be verified, as specified in the <f> field. The range of values for <f> is specified from the <f1> field to the <f2> field.

TABLE 6.24 Clauses used in the WHILE statement

The block of statements between the WHILE and ENDWHILE control statements is executed so long as the condition is evaluated to true or until a termination statement, such as EXIT or STOP, is reached. The SY-INDEX system variable contains the number of loop passes, including the current loop pass.

You can nest the WHILE loop any number of times and combine the nested WHILE loop with other loop forms. Listing 6.17 shows an example of the WHILE statement:

```
REPORT ZWHILE_DEMO.
*-------------------------------------*
*/ Data Declarations
*/
DATA: LENGTH TYPE I VALUE 0,
VAR1 TYPE I VALUE 0,
TEXT1(50) TYPE C VALUE 'Calculating the Length of the Text
String'.
*-------------------------------------*
VAR1 = STRLEN( TEXT1 ).
*-------------------------------------*
*/Using WHILE statement
WHILE TEXT1 NE SPACE.
WRITE TEXT1(1).
LENGTH = SY-INDEX.
SHIFT TEXT1.
ENDWHILE.
*-------------------------------------*
WRITE: / 'STRLEN: ', VAR1.
WRITE: / 'Length of string:', LENGTH.
```

LISTING 6.17 **Using the WHILE statement**

Listing 6.17 shows a `WHILE` loop used to determine the length of a character string. This is done by shifting the string one position to the left each time the loop is processed. This loop is processed until it contains only blanks. Figure 6.25 displays the result of Listing 6.17:

```
C a l c u l a t i n g  t h e  L e n g t h  o f  t h e  T e x t  S t r i n g
STRLEN:          41
Length of string:          41
```


FIGURE 6.25 **Displaying the result of the WHILE loop**

Terminating Loops

A loop can be terminated prematurely with the help of two types of termination statements provided by ABAP. The two types of termination statements are:

- Statements that apply to a loop, such as CONTINUE, CHECK, and EXIT.
- Statements that apply to an entire processing block, such as STOP and REJECT.

The CONTINUE statement can be used only in a loop statement. On the other hand, the CHECK and EXIT statements are context-sensitive. When used in the loop, the CHECK and EXIT statements are responsible for the execution of the loop itself. However, outside the loop, the statements terminate the entire processing block, such as a subroutine, dialog module, or event block, in which they occur. CONTINUE, CHECK, and EXIT can be used in looping statements, such as DO, WHILE, LOOP, and SELECT.

A loop can be terminated conditionally or unconditionally. Now, let's learn about each of the two possible cases in detail.

Terminating a Loop Pass Unconditionally

The CONTINUE statement is used in a statement block of the loop to terminate a single loop pass immediately and unconditionally. As soon as the CONTINUE statement is executed, the execution of the remaining statements in the current processing block is stopped and the next loop pass is started. Listing 6.18 shows the working of the CONTINUE statement:

```
REPORT demo_continue.
DO 4 TIMES.
IF SY-INDEX = 2.
*/Using CONTINUE statement after which the statements are not
evaluated
CONTINUE.
ENDIF.
WRITE / SY-INDEX.
ENDDO.
```

LISTING 6.18 **Using the CONTINUE statement**

Listing 6.18 shows that a loop is executed four times but a condition is inserted with the value of the SY-INDEX system variable equal to 2. The specified condition is true for the second loop pass, so the WRITE statement is not executed. The CONTINUE statement ignores the statements in the current statement block and continues with the next loop pass. Figure 6.26 shows the output of Listing 6.18:

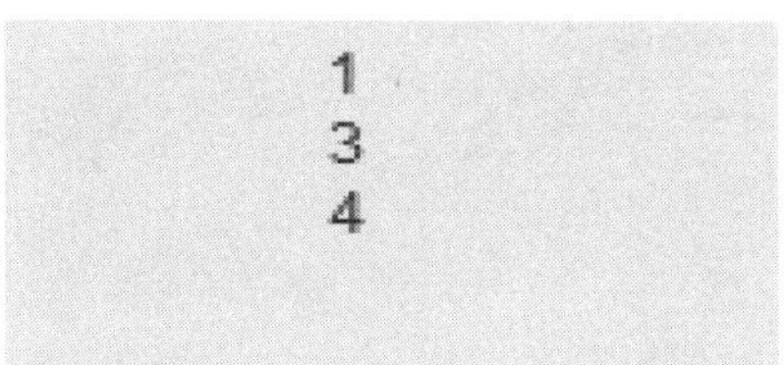

FIGURE 6.26 **Output of the CONTINUE statement**

Apart from the CONTINUE statement, the EXIT statement is used to terminate an entire loop immediately and unconditionally. As soon as the EXIT statement is executed, the loop is terminated and the statements following the structure of the loop are processed. If the EXIT statement is used in a nested loop, only the current loop is executed after the EXIT statement is executed. Listing 6.19 shows the working of the EXIT statement:

```
REPORT demo_exit.
*----------------------------------------*
*/ DO Loop
*/
DO 3 TIMES.
IF SY-INDEX = 2.
EXIT.                      " EXIT Statement
ENDIF.
WRITE SY-INDEX.
ENDDO.
*----------------------------------------*
```

LISTING 6.19 **Using the EXIT statement**

In Listing 6.19, the DO loop is terminated in the second loop pass and the WRITE statement is not executed. Figure 6.27 shows the output of Listing 6.19:

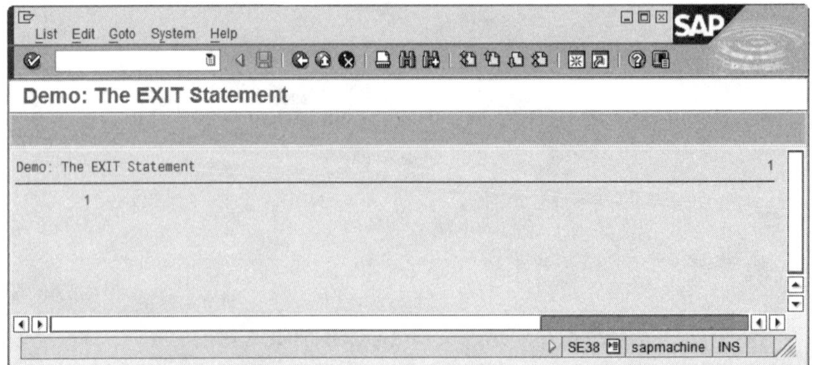

FIGURE 6.27 **Output of the EXIT statement**

Terminating a Loop Pass Conditionally

The CHECK statement terminates a loop pass based on a condition. If the condition specified in the CHECK statement is evaluated to false, the remaining statements in the statement block, after the CHECK statement, are ignored and the next loop pass starts. The condition specified in the CHECK statement can be any logical expression. Listing 6.20 shows the working of the CHECK statement:

```
REPORT demo_check.
*-----------------------------------------------*
*/DO statement using the CHECK statement
*/
DO 4 TIMES.
CHECK SY-INDEX BETWEEN 2 and 3.
WRITE / SY-INDEX.
ENDDO.
*-----------------------------------------------*
```

LISTING 6.20 **Using the CHECK statement**

In Listing 6.20, you see that the first and fourth loop passes are terminated without the execution of the `WRITE` statement because the value of the `SY-INDEX` system variable does not lie between 2 and 3. Figure 6.28 shows the output of Listing 6.20:

```
2
3
```


FIGURE 6.28 **Output of the CHECK statement**

SUMMARY

In this chapter, you have learned about the ABAP program structure, its various components, and ABAP Editor, which is an ABAP Workbench tool used to develop ABAP programs. Next, you have learned about the programs created in ABAP Editor. You have also learned to use the various options present on the initial screen of ABAP Editor and add comments to a program. In addition, you have learned about types and objects in an ABAP program. This chapter also discusses the various statements used to define data in ABAP programs. Further, you have learned about various kinds of assignment statements, such as `MOVE`, `MOVE-CORRESPONDING`, `WRITE TO`, and `CLEAR`. Next, you have learned about the different formatting options available in ABAP, such as the `FORMAT` and `WRITE` statements. Moreover, you have learned about the flow control statements, such as the `IF` and `CASE` statements. Finally, you have learned to work with loops.

Chapter 7 Internal Tables

If you need information on:	See page:
Overview of Internal Tables	300
Data Types of an Internal Table	303
Types of Internal Tables	303
Creating Internal Tables	305
Performing Operations on an Entire Internal Table	316
Operations on Individual Lines	335
Control Break Processing	392

An internal table is a temporary table that contains the records of an ABAP program while it is being executed. Consequently, an internal table exists only during the runtime of an SAP program. In addition, internal tables are used to process large volumes of data by using the ABAP language. You must declare an internal table in an ABAP program when you need to retrieve data from database tables.

Similar to any other table, data in an internal table is stored in rows and columns, where each row is called a line and each column is called a field. In an internal table, all the records have the same structure and key. The individual records of an internal table are accessed with an index or a key. Because an internal table exists till the associated program is being executed, the records of the internal table are discarded when the execution of the program is terminated.

In this chapter, you learn about internal tables, types of internal tables, and the data types of internal tables. You also learn how to create internal tables and perform operations on them, such as moving, clearing, and refreshing internal tables. In addition, you learn how to insert, modify, and delete the data stored in internal tables. The chapter concludes with a description of control break processing statements, such as `AT FIRST. . .AT LAST` and `AT NEW. . .AT END OF`, which are used in loops to retrieve data from internal tables and prepare reports based on the retrieved data.

OVERVIEW OF INTERNAL TABLES

As you learned previously, an internal table consists of one or more rows of the same structure. However, unlike a database table, an internal table does not hold data after the execution of the program has completed. Therefore, internal tables are used as temporary storage areas or temporary buffers where data can be modified as required. These tables occupy memory only at runtime and not at the time of their declaration.

Internal tables provide a means by which data from one or more database tables can be processed within a program. The size of an internal table or the number of lines it contains is not fixed. The size of an internal table changes according to the requirement of the program associated with the internal table.

Internal tables are used to perform calculations on the data stored in the fields of database tables and re-organize the data according to the requirements. For example, users can retrieve or read certain type of data from a database table and store the data in an internal table. Users can then perform operations on the data stored in the internal table, such as calculating the sum of the data or generating a ranked list from the table.

Internal tables are also used to reorganize the content of database tables according to the requirements of a program. For example, suppose the user wants to create a list of phone numbers of different customers from one or several large customer tables. To do this, the user first creates an internal table, selects the relevant data from the customer tables, and then places the data in the internal table. Now, users can access and use the internal table directly to retrieve the desired information, instead of writing a time-consuming database query to perform each operation during the runtime of the program.

Internal tables can also act as data types and data objects. A data type is the abstract description of a data object. Therefore, when an internal table acts as a data type, the corresponding data objects are also represented as internal tables that can be declared either in a program or in the ABAP Dictionary.

An internal table is accessed by using the concept of a work area. A work area is a temporary memory space that helps you in reading and modifying the data of an internal table, line by line. The work area must have the same structure as that of the associated internal table. The structure of an internal table consists of two basic parts; i.e., a body and a header line. A header line acts as an implicit work area of an internal table. Note that creating a header line for an internal table is optional, which means an internal table can be created with or without a header line. When an internal table is created with a header line, the SAP system automatically creates a work area with the same name as that of the name of the internal table, and of the same data type as that of the lines of the table. However, when an internal table is created without a header line, the SAP system does not create a work area for the table implicitly. In this case, the user has to create the work area explicitly.

You can create an internal table in the following two ways:

- Creating the internal table as a data type and then creating a data object that refers to that data type
- Creating the internal table data object directly

A data type is defined as an internal table by using the `TYPES` statement with the `OCCURS` clause. A data object is defined as an internal table either by using the `DATA` statement along with the `OCCURS` clause or by referring to another internal table by using the `TYPE` or `LIKE` clause. A data object with a data type defined as an internal table is the actual internal table with which the user works.

An internal table can have any number of rows or lines of the same data type, which can be elementary or structured. Some examples of elementary data types are `C`, `I`, and `N` (predefined data types). Here, `C` stands for characters, `I` for integers, and `N` for numeric characters. Examples of structured data types are field strings and internal tables themselves. A user can access a particular line or row of an internal table by specifying a single field or a combination of fields to identify the line.

In an internal table based on the relational model of the SAP R/3 system, the required minimum number of fields to identify a row or line is known as a key and the fields that define the key are called key fields. The following categories of keys can be defined in the fields of an internal table:

- **Standard key**—Defines those fields of the internal table whose data types are not numeric, such as `Float`, `Integers`, and `Packed` (`F`, `I`, and `P`, respectively), and the internal table itself.
- **Self-defined or user-defined key**—Defined by a user by using the `READ` statement.

The definition of an internal table consists of a body and an optional header line. The body holds the rows (that are similar in structure) of the internal table. The header line is a field string with the same structure as a row of the body, but it can hold only a single row. Header lines are buffers used to hold a record before it is added to or retrieved from an internal table.

The `OCCURS` clause is used to define the body of an internal table by declaring the fields for the table. When the `OCCURS` clause is used, you can specify a numeric constant, *n*, to determine additional default memory if required. The default size of memory that is used by the `OCCUR 0` clause is 8 KB.

As stated earlier, an internal table can be created with or without using a header line. To create an internal table with a header line, use either the `BEGIN OF` clause before the `OCCURS` clause or the `WITH HEADER LINE` clause after the `OCCURS` clause in the definition of the internal table. However, to create an internal table without a header line, use the `OCCURS` clause without the `BEGIN OF` and `WITH HEADER LINE` clauses. Figure 7.1 shows the structure of an internal table with and without a header line:

```
REPORT ZITAB_DEMO.
DATA:BEGIN OF IT1 OCCURS 10.
  F1,
  F2,
  F3,
  END OF IT1.
```
An internal table with header line

```
DATA IT2 LIKE ZTXLFA1 OCCURS 100.
```
An internal table without header line

```
DATA IT3 LIKE ZTXLFA1 OCCURS 100 WITH HEADER LINE.
```
An internal table again has a header line

FIGURE 7.1 **Creating an internal table with and without a header line**

> **Note:** As a best practice, avoid creating an internal table with a header line inside nested structures or internal tables, as it may lead to confusion.

DATA TYPES OF AN INTERNAL TABLE

An internal table is one of the complex types in the ABAP language (the other being the structure). The data type of an internal table is fully defined by three parameters:

- **Line type or row type**—Defines the attributes of the individual fields of an internal table by specifying any ABAP data type. The data type can be an element, a structure, or an internal table itself.
- **Key type**—Identifies the rows of an internal table. As already stated, two kinds of keys can be defined for an internal table: standard keys and self-defined keys (also called user-defined keys). A key that is defined for an internal table can be either unique or non-unique. When a key in an internal table is defined as unique, the table cannot have duplicate entries; however, this is not so in the case of the non-unique key. If the row type of an internal table is a structure, the standard key is defined on the fields that have the character data type. However, if the row type is an element, the entire row or line of the internal table uses a key, which is also the default key of the table. However, an internal table whose row type is also an internal table has an empty default key. In the case of a user-defined key, the fields of the internal table can neither be internal tables themselves nor contain internal tables. Internal tables with user-defined keys are also called key tables.
- **Table type**—Determines how ABAP accesses individual table entries by using the assigned key or index number.

TYPES OF INTERNAL TABLES

Internal tables can be categorized into three types: standard tables, sorted tables, and hashed tables. In addition, internal tables can be categorized on the basis of their definition, as a fully specified or generic type. A fully specified table type determines how the SAP system accesses the entries of the table based on performing key-based operations. This table type performs a linear search in standard tables, a binary search in sorted tables, and a hash algorithm search in hashed tables. However, in the generic table type, the tables are searched on the basis of indexes.

Figure 7.2 shows the hierarchy of the different types of internal tables:

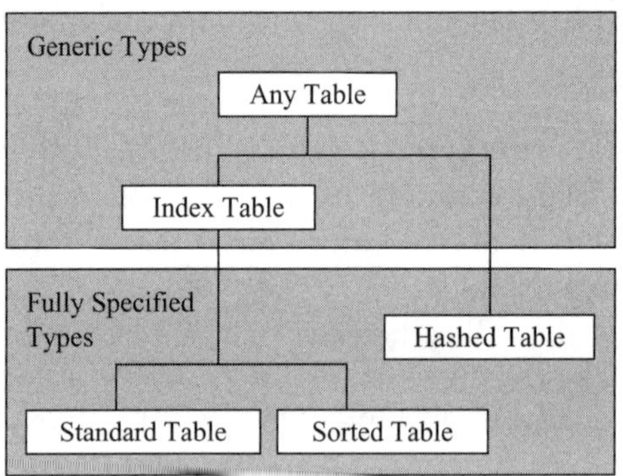

FIGURE 7.2 **Hierarchy of table types**

Let's now describe these table types in detail.

Standard Tables

Standard tables have a linear index, which manages the table as a treelike structure. The records of a standard table are accessed by using a table index or key. Standard tables always have a non-unique key. Therefore, the SAP system does not need to check the table's existing entries when new entries are added to the table. You can use standard tables when individual table entries need to be addressed on the basis of indexes, because this is the quickest way to access a table. A standard table can be populated by using the `APPEND` statement and its entries can be read, modified, and deleted by specifying the index number in the relevant ABAP statement.

Sorted Tables

Sorted tables also have internal indexes, similar to standard tables, and are sorted with a key. You can access the records of a sorted table by using a table index or key. In this case, a key also is defined as either unique or non-unique. Sorted and standard tables use indexes and are therefore also called index tables. In sorted tables, records entered are sorted automatically. These tables are populated by using the `INSERT` statement according to the sort sequence defined in the table key. As a result, whenever a user tries to add a nonsequential entry to the table, it is recognized easily. Sorted tables are used in particular situations, such as when you want to perform partial sequential processing of code. In case of partial sequential processing of code, the code is written in a loop and the beginning of the table key is specified in the `WHERE` clause.

Hashed Tables

These tables have no linear index and are accessed only by the keys. The SAP system accesses the entries of a hashed table by using a hash algorithm. While defining a hashed table, the key of the hashed table must be defined as unique. Hashed tables are selected when the user wants to perform operations based on the key and not the index. Hashed tables are useful when you want to create and use an internal table that resembles a database table, or if you want to process large volumes of data.

As stated earlier, the data type of an internal table is fully specified by its line type, key, and table type. However, it is not necessary to specify the data type of an internal table fully. Instead, you can specify a generic construction for the table by leaving the key or line type unspecified. Generic internal tables cannot be used to declare data objects.

CREATING INTERNAL TABLES

As stated earlier, internal tables can be declared as data types or data objects in ABAP. When internal tables are declared as data types, either in programs or in the ABAP Dictionary, they are used to define data objects. The minimum size of an internal table is 256 bytes. Unlike other ABAP data objects, you do not need to specify the memory required for an internal table, because, at runtime, rows are inserted and deleted dynamically by using statements, such as `INSERT`, `MODIFY`, and `DELETE`.

Let's now explore how to create internal tables as data types and data objects.

Creating Internal Tables as Data Types

You can create an internal table as a local data type (a data type used only in the context of the current program) by using the TYPES statement. This statement uses the TYPE or LIKE clause to refer to an existing table. The syntax to create an internal table as a local data type is:

```
TYPES <internal_tab> TYPE|LIKE <internal_tab_type> OF
<line_type_itab> [WITH <key>]
      [INITIAL SIZE <size_number>].
```

In the preceding syntax, a data type has not been specified after the TYPE or LIKE clause. However, a type constructor has been specified after these clauses. The type constructor is shown in the following part of the preceding syntax:

```
<internal_tab_type> OF <line_type_itab> [WITH <key>]
```

The various expressions used with the TYPES statement are as follows:

- <internal_tab_type>—Specifies a table type for an internal table <internal_tab>. Table 7.1 describes the table types:

Table Type	Description
Index Table	Creates a generic table type with index access
Any Table	Creates a fully generic table type
Standard Table or Table	Creates a standard table
Sorted Table	Creates a sorted table
Hashed Table	Creates a hashed table

TABLE 7.1 List of table types

- <line_type_itab>—Specifies the type for a line of an internal table. In the TYPES statement, you can use the TYPE clause to specify the line type of an internal table as a data type and the LIKE clause to specify the line type as a data object. When you specify a line type in an internal table, the data type can be a predefined ABAP type, a local type declared in a program, or a data type from the ABAP Dictionary. If any of the generic element types, such as C, N, P, or X, is specified as a line type, the attributes (such as the length of the field and a range of numbers) that are left unspecified are populated automatically with default values.

- <key>—Specifies the type of key for the internal table <t>, as given in the following syntax:

```
[UNIQUE|NON-UNIQUE] KEY col1 ... coln
```

In internal tables with a structured line type, col1, col2, col3...col*n* are key fields, which are not of an internal table data type or references to such data types.

Besides specifying the key fields individually, you can specify the entire line (including all the fields) of an internal table as a table key. The following syntax is used to define the entire line as a key of an internal table:

```
[UNIQUE|NON-UNIQUE] KEY table_line
```

An internal table must have any of the following elementary line types, C, D, F, I, N, P, T, and X (where C is character, D is decimal, F is float, I is integer, N is numeric characters, P is packed, T is time, and X is hexadecimal), to define the entire line as a key. However, if the user tries to define the entire line as a key in an internal table whose line type is itself an internal table, a syntax error occurs. In addition, if an internal table has a structured line type, the entire line can be specified as a key; however, it is often inappropriate because this affects the efficiency of the SAP system. You can also define a default key for an internal table by using the following syntax:

```
[UNIQUE|NON-UNIQUE] DEFAULT KEY
```

In the preceding syntax, the DEFAULT KEY clause is used to define the fields of an internal table as key fields.

If an internal table has a structured line type, the default key contains all nonnumeric columns, which are neither internal tables themselves nor the references of internal tables. If the table has an elementary line type, the entire line is the default key. The default key of an internal table, whose line type is an internal table, is empty.

Specifying a key for an internal table is optional and if the user does not specify a key, the SAP system defines a table type with an arbitrary key. The optional clause (UNIQUE or NON-UNIQUE) determines if the key is unique or non-unique; that is, whether the table can accept duplicate entries. If the user does not specify the UNIQUE or NON-UNIQUE clause with the key field of an internal table, the internal table is generic. However, if you specify the type of the table simultaneously, there are two limitations. First, you cannot use the UNIQUE clause for standard tables because the SAP system always generates the NON-UNIQUE clause automatically; second, you always must specify the UNIQUE clause while creating a hashed table.

- INITIAL SIZE <size_number>—Creates an internal table object by allocating an initial amount of memory to it. Use the following syntax to allocate initial memory to an internal table:

```
INITIAL SIZE <size_number>
```

In the preceding syntax, the INITIAL SIZE clause reserves a memory space for size_number table lines. Whenever an internal table object is declared, the size of the table does not belong to the data type of the table. Note that much less memory is consumed when an internal table is populated for the first time.

Examples of the TYPES Statement

This section provides examples of the TYPES statement along with their clauses and expressions, such as TYPE, LIKE, <internal_tab_type>, and <line_type_itab>.

Listing 7.1 shows how to declare a table type with the help of the TYPES statement:

```
REPORT ZINTERNAL_TABLE_DEMO.
*/declaring table type by using the TYPES statement

TYPES: BEGIN OF DataLine,
              S_ID TYPE C,
```

Continued

```
            S_Name(20) TYPE C,
            S_Salary TYPE I,
        END OF DataLine.
TYPES MyTable TYPE SORTED TABLE OF DataLine WITH UNIQUE
KEY S_ID.
WRITE:/'MyTable is an internal table. It is a sorted type
of table with a unique key defined on the S_ID field.'.
```

LISTING 7.1 **Declaring a table type with the TYPES statement**

In Listing 7.1, MyTable is a sorted internal table with DataLine as its line type. This table is created with a unique key in the `S_ID` field.

Note that in the mySAP ERP system, you write the source code of any ABAP program in ABAP Editor. Perform the following steps to write the code specified in Listing 7.1 in ABAP Editor:

1. Open the ABAP Editor by either navigating the SAP menu or executing the `SE38` transaction code. The initial screen of ABAP Editor appears.
2. In the initial screen of ABAP Editor, enter a name for the program, select the `Source code` radio button in the `Subobjects` group box, and click the `Create` button to create a new program, as shown in Figure 7.3:

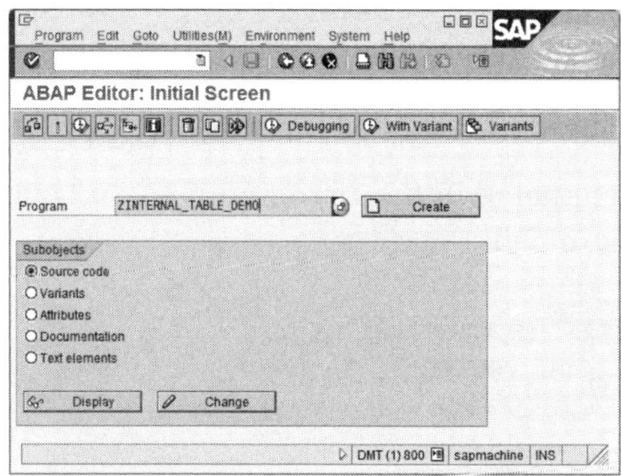

FIGURE 7.3 **Creating a new program**

The `ABAP: Program Attributes` dialog box appears.

3. In the ABAP: Program Attributes dialog box, enter a short description for the program in the Title field, select the Executable program option from the Type drop-down menu in the Attributes group box, as shown in Figure 7.4:

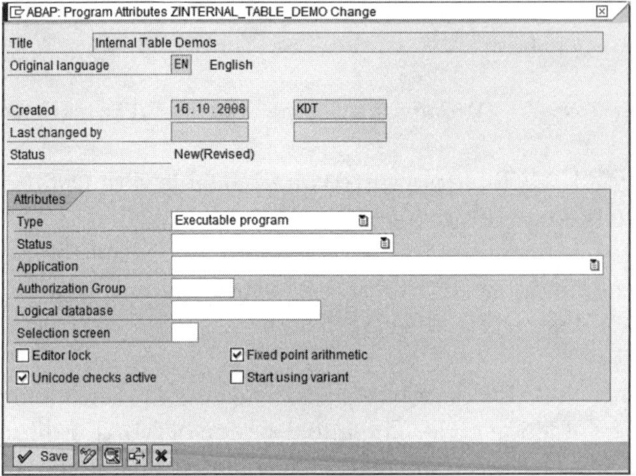

FIGURE 7.4 **The ABAP: Program attributes dialog box**

4. Now, click the Save (✔ Save) button in the ABAP: Program Attributes dialog box or press the ENTER key (see Figure 7.4). The Create Object Directory Entry dialog box appears.
5. In the Create Object Directory Entry dialog box, enter ZKOG_PCKG as the package name in the Package field and click the Save ()icon, as shown in Figure 7.5:

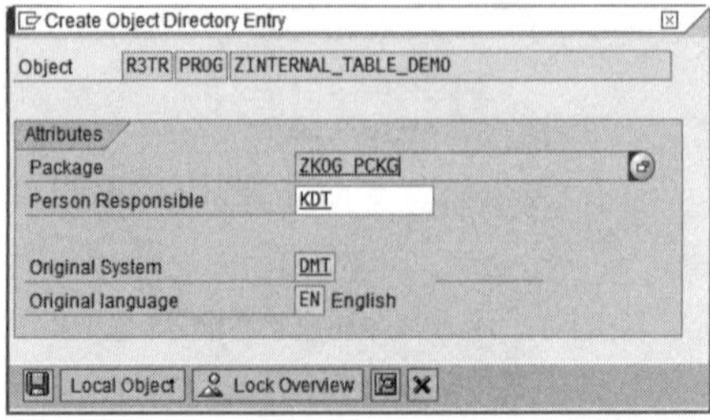

FIGURE 7.5 **Create object directory entry dialog box**

The ABAPEditor: Change Report screen appears, as shown in Figure 7.6:

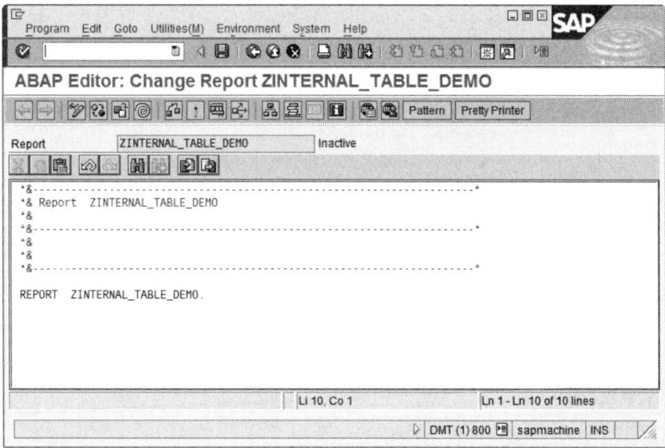

FIGURE 7.6 **ABAP editor: change report screen**

6. Write the code given in Listing 7.1 in the ABAP Editor: Change Report screen, as shown in Figure 7.7:

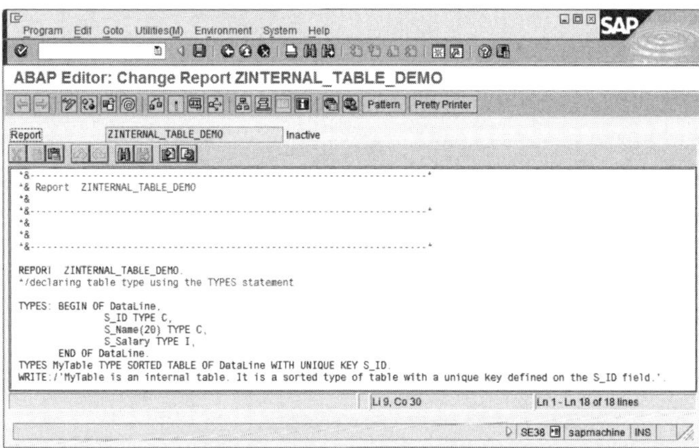

FIGURE 7.7 **Adding code in the ABAP editor: change report screen**

7. Click the Save (💾) icon or press the CTRL + S key combination to save the changes in the program.

8. Next, click the `Check` icon or press the CTRL + F2 key combination to check and remove syntax errors or warnings (if any) in the program.
9. Next, click the `Activate` icon or press the CTRL + F3 key combination to activate the program, as shown in Figure 7.8:

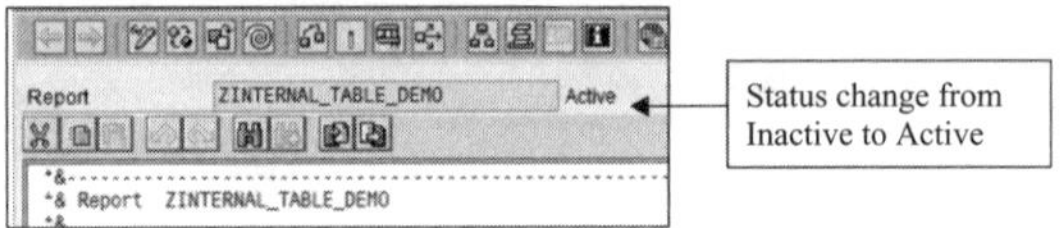

FIGURE 7.8 **Activating a program**

10. Now, click the `Direct Processing` icon or press the F8 key to execute the program.

Figure 7.9 shows the output of Listing 7.1:

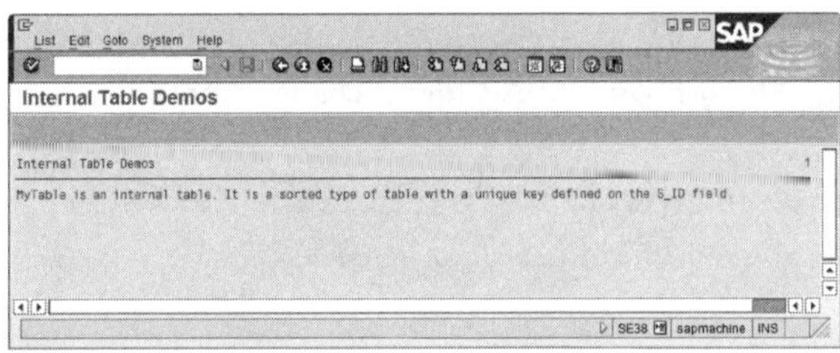

FIGURE 7.9 **Output of the ZINTERNAL_TABLE_DEMO program**

> **Note:** The preceding steps need to be performed to display the output for all the programs created in this chapter.

Listing 7.2 is another example of how to declare the table type for an internal table by using the `TYPES` statement:

```
Report ZTYPES_DEMO

*/declaring a hashed table type by using the TYPES
statement

TYPES VectorTab TYPE HASHED TABLE OF I WITH UNIQUE KEY
table_line.
```

Continued

```
TYPES: BEGIN OF LINE,
                 S_ID TYPE C,
                 S_Name(20) TYPE C,
                 S_Salary TYPE I,
           END OF LINE.
*/declaring a sorted table type by using the TYPES
statement
TYPES MyTable TYPE SORTED TABLE OF LINE WITH UNIQUE KEY
S_ID.
TYPES: BEGIN OF line2,
                 Myfield TYPE c,
                 tableX TYPE VectorTab,
                 tableY TYPE MyTable,
           END OF line2.
TYPES MyTable2 TYPE STANDARD TABLE OF line2
WITH DEFAULT KEY.
```

LISTING 7.2 **Creating three internal tables by using the TYPES statement**

In Listing 7.2, the `TYPES` statement is used to create three internal tables: `VectorTab`, `MyTable`, and `MyTable2`. The `VectorTab` table is a hashed table, which is defined by using Type I as its line type and table_line as its unique key. `MyTable` is a sorted table with `LINE` as its line type and the `S_ID` field as its unique key. `MyTable2` is a standard table, having a default key, with `line2` as its line type. Note that the key in `MyTable2` is non-unique, as the table is a standard table.

Now, let's learn how to create an internal table as a data object.

Creating Internal Tables as Data Objects

You can create an internal table as a data object by using the `DATA` statement. In this section, you first learn how to create a new internal table object and then to create a table object from an existing table object.

Creating a New Internal Table Object

The `DATA` statement is used to construct a new internal table, as shown in the following syntax:

```
DATA <internal_tab> TYPE|LIKE <internal_tab_type> OF <line_
type_itab> WITH <key>
          [INITIAL SIZE <size_number>]
          [WITH HEADER LINE].
```

In the preceding syntax, the `TYPE` clause is used to define the `<internal_tab_type>` table type, the `<line_type_itab>` line type, and the `<key>` keyfield of the `<internal_tab>` internal table. You can only create fully specified table types but not generic table types. In addition, a key must be specified as unique or non-unique. Listing 7.3 shows how to create a new internal table object:

```
Report ZINTERNAL_TABLE_DEMO
DATA MyTable TYPE HASHED TABLE OF MARA WITH UNIQUE KEY
MANDT MATNR.
```

LISTING 7.3 **Creating a new internal table**

In Listing 7.3, `MyTable` is a hashed table with `MARA` as its line type that corresponds to the `MARA` table in the ABAP Dictionary. In addition, `MyTable` has a unique key with the `MANDT` and `MATNR` fields. `MyTable` can be regarded as an internal template for the `MARA` database table.

The `WITH HEADER LINE` clause is used to create the header line of an internal table. This clause, which is optional, is used to declare an extra data object with the same name and line type as that of the internal table. The extra data object declared by the `WITH HEADER LINE` clause is known as the header line of the internal table and is used as a work area while working with an internal table.

Creating an Internal Table Object from an Existing Table Object

Internal tables are created either as new tables or from existing tables. The following is the syntax of the `DATA` statement used to create an internal table from an existing table type:

```
DATA <internal_tab> TYPE <internal_tab_type>|LIKE <obj>
[WITH HEADER LINE].
```

In the preceding syntax, the `DATA` statement creates an internal table either from an existing internal table object or from an existing internal table type by using the `TYPE` clause. The `WITH HEADER LINE` clause, which is optional, is used to create the header line of the internal table. While using internal tables with header lines, it is mandatory for the header line and the body of the table to have the same name. If a user wants to specify the complete body of an internal table with a header line, brackets must be placed after the table name (`<internal_tab>[]`); otherwise, ABAP interprets the name as the name of the header line and not the body. Listing 7.4 shows how to represent the body of an internal table:

```
REPORT ZINTERNAL_TABLE_DEMO.
TYPES VectorTab TYPE SORTED TABLE OF I WITH UNIQUE KEY
TABLE LINE.

DATA: TABLEX TYPE VectorTab,
      TABLEY LIKE TABLEX WITH HEADER LINE.

*/Table without body
MOVE TABLEX TO TABLEY. "1: will produce syntax error!

*/Table with body
MOVE TABLEX TO TABLEY[]. "2: error free line
```

LISTING 7.4 **Using square brackets to represent the body of an internal table**

In Listing 7.4, VectorTab is a sorted table type, which has `I` as its line type and `TABLE LINE` as its unique key. The `TABLEX` object is created by referring to the VectorTab table type. The `TABLEY` object has the same data type as the `TABLEX` object. In addition, the `TABLEY` object has a header line.

The `MOVE` statement is used two times (marked 1 and 2), as shown in Listing 7.4. The line marked 1 generates a syntax error since square brackets [] are not used with the `TABLEX` internal table. However, the line marked 2 does not generate a syntax error because square brackets [] are used to represent the body of the TABLEX table.

> **Note:** To learn more about the `MOVE` statement, refer to the "Moving and Assigning Internal Tables" section of this chapter.

You can resolve the error generated at the line marked 1 in Listing 7.4 by using internal tables without header lines, as shown in the following code snippet:

```
REPORT ZINTERNAL_TABLE_DEMO.
...
DATA: TABLEX TYPE VectorTab,
       TableY LIKE TABLEX. "1: will not produce syntax
       error
MOVE TABLEX TO TABLEY.
...
```

PERFORMING OPERATIONS ON AN ENTIRE INTERNAL TABLE

You can access an internal table as a single data object (including all its lines) or its individual lines to perform operations such as insertion, deletion, and sorting. In this section, we perform the following operations by treating the body of an internal table as a single data object:

- Moving and assigning internal tables
- Clearing internal tables
- Refreshing internal tables
- Releasing memory of internal tables
- Comparing internal tables
- Performing the sort operation in internal tables
- Determining the attributes of internal tables

Moving and Assigning Internal Tables

Similar to other data objects, internal tables are also used as operands in the `MOVE` statement, as shown in the following syntax:

```
MOVE <internal_tab1> TO <internal_tab2>.
```

The preceding syntax is equivalent to the following syntax, in which one internal table is assigned to another:

```
<internal_tab2> = <internal_tab1>.
```

In this syntax, both operands, `internal_tab1` and `internal_tab2`, must be either compatible or convertible. In both cases, the entire content of the `<internal_tab1>` internal table is assigned to the `<internal_tab2>` internal table. In this process, the original content of the target table (`<internal_tab2>`) is overwritten.

When internal tables are created with header lines, the names of the header line and the body of the internal table are the same. When the `MOVE` statement is used to assign one internal table to another, square brackets (`[]`) are used after the table name to represent the entire body of the internal table. Listing 7.5 shows how to assign and move the content of one internal table into another internal table:

```
REPORT ZINTERNAL_TABLE_DEMO.
*/Creating two internal tables-Tab1 and Tab2
DATA: BEGIN OF line OCCURS 0,
                 Name(10) TYPE c,
                 Salary TYPE I,
           END OF line.

DATA: Tab1 LIKE TABLE OF line,
      Tab2 LIKE TABLE OF line.

*/Appending a line into Tab1

line-Name = 'Shilpa'.
line-Salary = 10000.
APPEND line TO Tab1.

*/Moving a line from Tab1 to Tab2

MOVE Tab1[] TO Tab2.

LOOP AT Tab2 INTO line.
     WRITE: / line-Name, line-Salary.
ENDLOOP.
```

LISTING 7.5 **Assigning and moving the content of one internal table to another**

In Listing 7.5, two standard tables, Tab1 and Tab2, are created with the line type of the LINE structure. Note that Tab1 contains a header line. This table is first populated by using the APPEND statement, line by line, and then its entire content is moved to Tab2 by using the MOVE statement. Figure 7.10 shows the output of Listing 7.5:

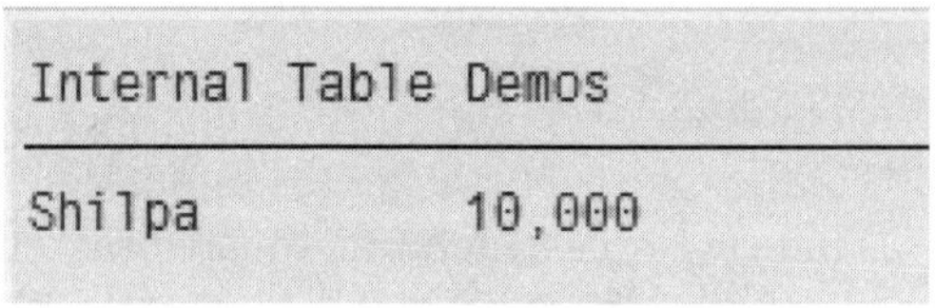

```
Internal Table Demos
--------------------------------
Shilpa          10,000
```


FIGURE 7.10 **Moving the content between two standard tables**

Listing 7.6 assigns the content of a hashed table to a sorted table.

```
REPORT ZINTERNAL_TABLE_DEMO.
DATA: TABLEF TYPE SORTED TABLE OF F
          WITH NON-UNIQUE KEY table_line,
      TABLEI TYPE HASHED TABLE OF I
          WITH UNIQUE KEY table_line,
      Var1 TYPE F.

*/Inserting three lines into TABLEI

DO 3 TIMES.
   INSERT sy-index INTO TABLE TABLEI.
ENDDO.
*/Assigning the data of TABLEI into TABLEF

TABLEF = TABLEI.
LOOP AT TABLEF INTO Var1.
   WRITE: / Var1.
ENDLOOP.
```

LISTING 7.6 **Assigning the content of one table to another**

Listing 7.6 contains two tables, TABLEF and TABLEI. TABLEF is a sorted table with a non-unique key and is of line type F, while TABLEI is a hashed table with a unique key and is of line type I. When you execute Listing 7.6, the content of TABLEF is overwritten by the content of TABLEI, as shown in Figure 7.11:

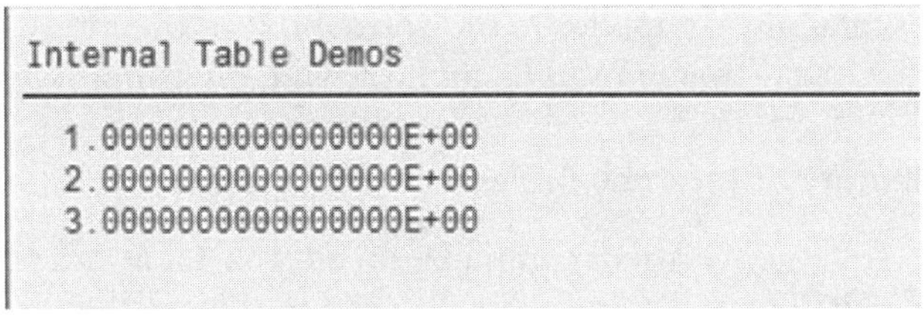

```
Internal Table Demos

  1.0000000000000000E+00
  2.0000000000000000E+00
  3.0000000000000000E+00
```


FIGURE 7.11 **Displaying the overwritten data**

Note that when a user assigns an unsorted table (TABLEI) to a sorted table (TABLEF), the entire content of the unsorted table is sorted automatically by the key of the sorted table.

Initializing Internal Tables

Similar to all data objects, an internal table can be initialized by using the CLEAR statement. The syntax to initialize an internal table is:

```
CLEAR <internal_tab>.
```

This syntax restores the original state of the <internal_tab> internal table. The original state is the state immediately after the creation of the internal table; i.e., when the internal table contains no lines. However, the memory allocated to the internal table remains unchanged until the memory is released manually by the user. The following syntax is used to clear the entire body of an internal table:

```
CLEAR <internal_tab>[].
```

Refreshing Internal Tables

The REFRESH statement is used to ensure that an internal table is initialized. The following syntax shows the use of the REFRESH statement:

```
REFRESH <internal_tab>.
```

This syntax always applies to the entire body of the internal table. Note that the memory space being used by an internal table is not released.

Releasing the Memory of Internal Tables

The FREE statement is used to initialize an internal table and release the memory allocated to it. The following syntax is used to release the memory allocated to an internal table:

```
FREE <internal_tab>.
```

Similar to the REFRESH statement, the FREE statement works only on the body of the table and not on its work area. The name of an internal table can be referenced even after using the FREE statement because even after the memory allocated to the internal table is released, the internal table continues to occupy the memory required for its header. However, when the internal table is populated again, the SAP system allocates new memory to the table.

> **Note:** The memory space initially allocated to an internal table is 256 bytes.

Listing 7.7 shows how the memory of the EmployeeDataTable internal table is released by using the REFRESH and FREE statements:

```
REPORT ZINTERNAL_TABLE_DEMO.

DATA: BEGIN OF LINE,
COL1(10) Type C,
COL2(20) Type C,
END OF LINE.
```

Continued

```
DATA EmployeeDataTable LIKE TABLE OF LINE.
LINE-COL1 = 'Emp_ID'.
LINE-COL2 = 'Emp_Name'.
*/Appending a line into EmployeeDataTable table

APPEND LINE TO EmployeeDataTable.

*/Refreshing the data of EmployeeDataTable table

REFRESH EmployeeDataTable.

*/Checking whether EmployeeDataTable table is empty or not,
if it is empty then it is released by the FREE statement

IF EmployeeDataTable IS INITIAL.
WRITE 'Employee table is empty'.
FREE EmployeeDataTable.
ENDIF.
```

LISTING 7.7 **Using the REFRESH and FREE statements with internal tables**

In Listing 7.7, `EmployeeDataTable` is an internal table that is populated and then initialized with the `REFRESH` statement. The `IF` statement is used to check whether EmployeeDataTable is empty. If the table is empty, its memory is released by using the `FREE` statement and a message is displayed stating that the table is empty, as shown in Figure 7.12:

FIGURE 7.12 **Displaying the message "Employee table is empty"**

Comparing Internal Tables

Internal tables are also used as operands in a logical expression in ABAP. Consider the following syntax:

```
.... <internal_tab1> <operator> <internal_tab2> ...
```

In this syntax, the `<operator>` expression stands for an operator from among the comparison operators `EQ`, =, `NE`, <>, ><, `GE`, >=, `LE`, <=, `GT`, >, `LT`, and <.

Note that two internal tables are compared based on the number of lines they contain. If two internal tables contain the same number of lines, they are compared line by line and component by component. If the components of an internal table line are internal tables themselves, they are compared recursively. Listing 7.8 shows the comparison of two tables on the basis of the number of lines they contain:

```
REPORT ZCOMPARE_TABLES_DEMO.

DATA: BEGIN OF LINE,
NumCol1 TYPE I,
NumCol2 TYPE I,
END OF LINE.

*/creating two tables Table1 and Table2

DATA: Table1 LIKE TABLE OF LINE,
Table2 LIKE TABLE OF LINE.

*/appending four lines in Table1

DO 4 TIMES.
LINE-NumCol1 = SY-INDEX.
LINE-NumCol2 = SY-INDEX ** 2.
  APPEND LINE TO Table1.
ENDDO.

*/Moving the data of Table1 into Table2
```

Continued

```
MOVE Table1 TO Table2.

*/appending a new line into Table2
LINE-NumCOL1 = 100.
LINE-NumCOL2 = 30.
APPEND LINE TO Table2.
IF Table1 LT Table2.
WRITE / 'Table1 is less than Table2'.
ENDIF.

*/appending the same line into Table1

APPEND LINE TO Table1.
IF Table1 EQ Table2.
WRITE / 'Table1 is equal to Table2'.
ENDIF.
*/appending a new line into Table1

LINE-NumCOL1 = 33.
LINE-NumCOL2 = 33.
APPEND LINE TO Table1.
IF Table1 GT Table2.
WRITE / 'Table1 is greater than Table2'.
ENDIF.

*/appending the same line two times into Table2

APPEND LINE TO Table2.
APPEND LINE TO Table2.
IF Table1 LE Table2.
WRITE / 'Table1 is less than or equal to Table2'.
ENDIF.

*/appending a new line into Table1

LINE-NumCOL1 = 20. LINE-NumCOL2 = 80.
APPEND LINE TO Table1.
```

Continued

```
IF Table1 NE Table2.
WRITE / 'Table1 is not equal to Table2'.
ENDIF.

*/appending a new line into Table2

LINE-NumCOL1 = 70. LINE-NumCOL2 = 30.
APPEND LINE TO Table2.
IF Table1 LT Table2.
WRITE / 'Table1 is less than Table2'.
ENDIF.
```

LISTING 7.8 **Comparing two tables on the basis of the number of lines**

In Listing 7.8, we create two internal tables of the standard type, Table1 and Table2. Table1 is populated initially with four lines and then its content is moved to Table2. Next, Table1 and Table2 are appended by one or two lines simultaneously and both are compared by using comparison operators, such as `GT`, `EQ`, and `LE`. Figure 7.13 shows the output of Listing 7.8:

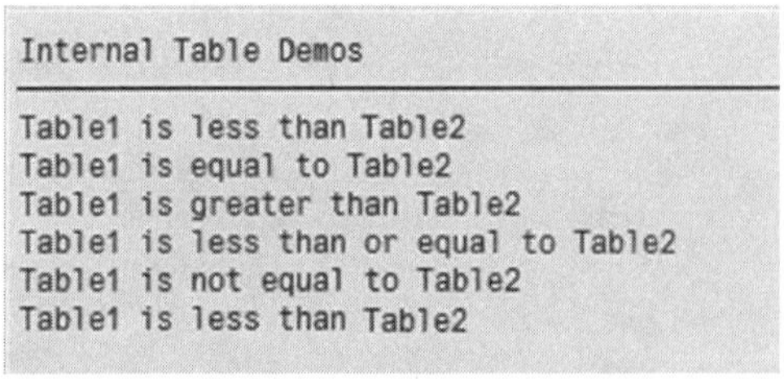

```
Internal Table Demos

Table1 is less than Table2
Table1 is equal to Table2
Table1 is greater than Table2
Table1 is less than or equal to Table2
Table1 is not equal to Table2
Table1 is less than Table2
```


FIGURE 7.13 **Result of comparing two tables**

In Figure 7.13, the first message shows that Table1 is less than Table2. Because Table1 originally had four lines and its data was moved to Table2, Table2 also contains four lines. Now, one line is appended to Table2, making a total of five lines in Table2. Therefore, when the comparison operator `LT` compares the number of lines in Table1 with Table2, it returns the first message.

Now, we append the same line to Table1 and the second comparison operator EQ checks whether the number of lines in both tables is equal. Another line is appended to Table1 and the third comparison operator, GT, checks whether the number of lines in Table1 is greater than those in Table2. The same line is now appended twice in Table2 and the fourth comparison operator, LE, checks whether the number of lines in Table1 is less than or equal to those in Table2. After appending one more line to Table1, the next operator, NE, checks to verify if the number of lines in Table1 is not equal to Table2. Finally, one more line is appended to Table2 and the last operator, LT, checks whether the number of lines in Table1 is less than the number of lines in Table2.

Performing the Sort Operation in Internal Tables

The SORT statement is used to perform the sort operation in an internal table. However, for this to work, the internal table must be of the standard or hashed type. The syntax of the SORT statement used to sort a standard or hashed table by using its key is:

```
SORT <internal_tab> [ASCENDING|DESCENDING] [AS TEXT]
[STABLE].
```

In this syntax, the SORT statement sorts the <internal_tab> internal table in ascending order by using the key of the table. The SORT statement does not apply to the header line of the internal table. The sort order depends on the sequence of fields in the standard key of an internal table. In this case, the default key consists of nonnumeric fields of the lines of the table in the sequence they occur. The ASCENDING or DESCENDING clause is used in the SORT statement to specify the direction of sort operation, which can be either in ascending or descending order. However, the default direction in the SORT statement is ascending.

The larger the sort key is, the greater the time taken by the SAP system to sort the table. If the sort key contains an internal table, the sorting process may slow down considerably.

You cannot sort a sorted table by using the SORT statement. The SAP R/3 system always maintains these tables automatically by their sort order. If an internal table is recognizable statically as a sorted table, using the SORT statement in the table generates a syntax error. However, if the table is a generic sorted table, the SORT statement generates a runtime error under the following three conditions:

- The specified key is not the same as the table key of the sorted table.
- Sorting is done in descending order or in the direction opposite to that of the sorted table.
- Sorting is done by using the AS TEXT clause.

In other words, the SORT statement is allowed only for generic internal tables, if it does not violate the internal sort order.

An internal table with a structured line type can also be sorted by specifying a key in the SORT statement that is different from the default key of the table. The following syntax of the SORT statement shows how to sort an internal table by specifying a different key for the table:

```
SORT <internal tab> [ASCENDING|DESCENDING] [AS TEXT]
[STABLE]
   BY <internal_tab_field 1> [ASCENDING|DESCENDING] [AS
   TEXT]
   ... <internal_tab_field n> [ASCENDING|DESCENDING] [AS
   TEXT].
```

In this syntax, the <internal_tab> internal table is sorted by the key fields specified in the <internal_tab_field 1>...<internal_tab_field n> expressions instead of by the table key. The number of key fields for the sort operation is limited to 250, and the sort order depends on the sequence of the <internal_tab_field 1>, <internal_tab_field 2>, and <internal_tab_field 3>...<internal_tab_field n> key fields. If the sort order is specified before the BY clause, the sort order applies to all the fields of an internal table. However, if the sort order is specified after the name of the field of the table, the sort order applies only to that field. The default sort order is ascending.

You can specify a key field for the sort operation dynamically by specifying the <internal_tab_field> field instead of using a collection of the <internal_tab_field 1>, <internal_tab_field 2>, <internal_

`tab_field 3>...<internal_tab_field n>` fields. In such a case, the `<internal_tab_field>` field is treated as the key field of the table for the sort operation. Note that if the sort operation is applied to an empty field, the sort operation for this field is ignored. Moreover, if the `<internal_tab_field>` field contains an invalid field name, a runtime error occurs.

Besides using the `ASCENDING` or `DESCENDING` clause in the `SORT` statement, the user can also specify either the entire sort field or each sort field alphabetically by using the `AS TEXT` clause, as shown in the following syntax:

```
SORT <internal_tab> ... AS TEXT ...
```

If you do not use the `AS TEXT` clause, strings are sorted according to the sequence specified by the SAP system. If you use the `AS TEXT` clause, the SAP system sorts the character fields alphabetically. This saves the time that otherwise would have been consumed in converting strings in to a format that can be sorted. Such a conversion is necessary only if you either want to sort an internal table alphabetically and then use it in a binary search or want to construct an alphabetical index for database tables in the user program.

> **Note:** Using the `AS TEXT` clause in the `SORT` statement only affects the sort fields of the data type `C`. However, if the `AS TEXT` clause is applied to a single sort field, then the field must be of the `C` type.

The `STABLE` clause is used along with the `SORT` statement to perform a stable sort. The stable sort is a sort in which the relative sequence of lines, which generally is changed by a sort, remains unchanged. The following syntax shows how to use the `STABLE` clause with the `SORT` statement:

```
SORT <internal_tab> ... STABLE.
```

Note that a stable sort takes longer to execute than an unstable sort.

Now, let's consider some examples of how the sort operation is performed in internal tables.

Examples of the Sort Operation in Internal Tables

In this section, we consider different examples of performing the sort operation in internal tables by using the `SORT` statement along with specific clauses, such as `AS TEXT`, `STABLE`, and `DESCENDING`.

Listing 7.9 shows how to sort an internal table by using the `SORT` statement with the `AS TEXT`, `STABLE`, and `DESCENDING` clauses:

```
REPORT ZINTERNAL_TABLE_DEMO.
DATA: BEGIN OF LINE,
ID(10) Type C,
Name(20) Type C,
Salary Type I,
END OF LINE.
DATA EmployeeDataTable LIKE STANDARD TABLE OF LINE WITH
NON-UNIQUE KEY ID.

*/Appending the lines into EmployeeDataTable

LINE-ID = 'A02'. LINE-NAME = 'Vineet'.
LINE-Salary = 25000.
APPEND LINE TO EmployeeDataTable.
LINE-ID = 'B03'. LINE-NAME = 'Charu'.
LINE-Salary = 25000.
APPEND LINE TO EmployeeDataTable.
LINE-ID = 'C01'. LINE-NAME = 'Vandana'.
LINE-Salary = 8000.
APPEND LINE TO EmployeeDataTable.
LINE-ID = 'A01'. LINE-NAME = 'Ashish'.
LINE-Salary = 12000.
APPEND LINE TO EmployeeDataTable.
LINE-ID = 'D02'. LINE-NAME = 'Shilpa'.
LINE-Salary = 8000.
APPEND LINE TO EmployeeDataTable.

*/Showing the default order of lines
```

Continued

```
WRITE: / 'By Default Lines'.
PERFORM LOOP_AT_EmployeeDataTable.

*/Showing the stable order of lines

WRITE: / 'Stable Lines'.
SORT EmployeeDataTable STABLE.
PERFORM LOOP_AT_EmployeeDataTable.

*/Showing the lines sorted in descending order of
employee name

WRITE: / 'Lines Sorted-Descending by Name'.
SORT EmployeeDataTable DESCENDING BY Name.
PERFORM LOOP_AT_EmployeeDataTable.

*/Showing the lines sorted in ascending order of employee
salary

WRITE: / 'Lines Sorted-Ascending by Salary'.
SORT EmployeeDataTable ASCENDING BY SALARY.
PERFORM LOOP_AT_EmployeeDataTable.

FORM LOOP_AT_EmployeeDataTable.
  LOOP AT EmployeeDataTable INTO LINE.
    WRITE: / LINE-ID, LINE-NAME, LINE-Salary.
  ENDLOOP.
  SKIP.
ENDFORM.
```

LISTING 7.9 **Using the AS TEXT, STABLE, and DESCENDING clauses with the SORT statement**

In Listing 7.9, EmployeeDataTable is an internal standard table with five lines. This table is sorted four times: by the default order, by using the `STABLE` statement, in descending order of the `Name` field, and finally in ascending order of the `Salary` field. The result of these sorts is shown in Figure 7.14:

```
Internal Table Demos
--------------------------------------------------------------
By Default Lines
A02        Vineet                   25,000
B03        Charu                    25,000
C01        Vandana                   8,000
A01        Ashish                   12,000
D02        Shilpa                    8,000

Stable Lines
A01        Ashish                   12,000
A02        Vineet                   25,000
B03        Charu                    25,000
C01        Vandana                   8,000
D02        Shilpa                    8,000

Lines Sorted-Descending by Name
A02        Vineet                   25,000
C01        Vandana                   8,000
D02        Shilpa                    8,000
B03        Charu                    25,000
A01        Ashish                   12,000

Lines Sorted-Ascending by Salary
C01        Vandana                   8,000
D02        Shilpa                    8,000
A01        Ashish                   12,000
A02        Vineet                   25,000
B03        Charu                    25,000
```


FIGURE 7.14 **Sorting of an internal table in different ways**

Let's consider another example of sorting, in which an internal table is sorted in the default order, by specifying a key field, and by specifying the `AS TEXT` clause. Listing 7.10 shows an example of sorting by using the key field and the `AS TEXT` clause:

```
REPORT ZINTERNAL_TABLE_DEMO.
DATA: BEGIN OF LINE,
      TEXT(10),
      XTEXT(160) TYPE X,
END OF LINE.

DATA NameTable LIKE HASHED TABLE OF LINE WITH UNIQUE KEY
TEXT.
*/Inserting lines into NameTable

LINE-TEXT = 'Shivam'.
```

Continued

```
CONVERT TEXT LINE-TEXT INTO SORTABLE CODE
LINE-XTEXT.
INSERT LINE INTO TABLE NameTable.

LINE-TEXT = 'Mehtab'.
CONVERT TEXT LINE-TEXT INTO SORTABLE CODE
LINE-XTEXT.
INSERT LINE INTO TABLE NameTable.

LINE-TEXT = 'Ramneek'.
CONVERT TEXT LINE-TEXT INTO SORTABLE CODE
LINE-XTEXT.
INSERT LINE INTO TABLE NameTable.

LINE-TEXT = 'Charu'.
CONVERT TEXT LINE-TEXT INTO SORTABLE CODE
LINE-XTEXT.
INSERT LINE INTO TABLE NameTable.

LINE-TEXT = 'Mehtab'.
CONVERT TEXT LINE-TEXT INTO SORTABLE CODE
LINE-XTEXT.
INSERT LINE INTO TABLE NameTable.

*/Used to show the default order of lines

WRITE: 'Team Members Name (By Default)'.
SORT NameTable.
PERFORM LOOP_AT_NameTable.

*/Used to show the lines sorted by XTEXT

WRITE: /'Team Members Name (Sort by XTEXT)'.
SORT NameTable BY XTEXT.
PERFORM LOOP_AT_NameTable.

*/Used to show the lines sorted by TEXT
```

Continued

```
WRITE: 'Team Members Name (Sort by TEXT)'.
SORT NameTable AS TEXT.
PERFORM LOOP_AT_NameTable.

FORM LOOP_AT_NameTable.
  LOOP AT NameTable INTO LINE.
    WRITE / LINE-TEXT.
  ENDLOOP.
  SKIP.
ENDFORM.
```

LISTING 7.10 **An alphabetical sorting by using the key field and the AS TEXT clause**

In Listing 7.10, NameTable is an internal table that contains a column with character data and another column with the corresponding binary data, which can be sorted alphabetically. NameTable is sorted three times: in the default order, in hexadecimal order, and in alphabetical text order. The default order of the sort is specified by the `BY DEFAULT` clause, hexadecimal order of sort is specified by the `XTEXT` field, and the alphabetical sort is specified by the `TEXT` field. Figure 7.15 shows the result of these three types of sorting:

```
Team Members Name (By Default)
Charu
Mehtab
Ramneek
Shivam

Team Members Name (Sort by XTEXT)
Charu
Mehtab
Ramneek
Shivam

Team Members Name (Sort by TEXT)
Charu
Mehtab
Ramneek
Shivam
```


FIGURE 7.15 **Alphabetical sorting of an internal table**

In Figure 7.15, you can see that the team members' names are sorted alphabetically three times: in the default order, in hexadecimal order, and, finally, by using the AS TEXT clause.

Determining the Attributes of Internal Tables

The DESCRIBE TABLE statement is used to determine attributes of an internal table that are not available statically at runtime, such as the initial size, current size, and table type. The following syntax shows the use of the DESCRIBE TABLE statement:

```
DESCRIBE TABLE <internal_tab> [LINES <l>] [OCCURS <n>]
[KIND <k>].
```

In this syntax, the LINES clause is used to specify the number of populated lines in the <l> expression, the OCCURS clause is used to specify the value of the INITIAL SIZE clause of the internal table in the <n> expression, and the KIND clause is used to specify the table type of the internal table in the <k> expression. Note that the table type specified by T is a standard table. If it is specified by S, it is a sorted table, and if it is specified by H, it is a hashed table. Listing 7.11 shows how to determine the attributes of an internal table by using the DESCRIBE TABLE statement.

```
REPORT ZDESCRIBE_TABLE_DEMO.

DATA: BEGIN OF LINE,
         COL_1_A TYPE I,
         COL_1_B TYPE I,
      END OF LINE.
DATA Table1 LIKE HASHED TABLE OF LINE WITH UNIQUE KEY
COL_1_A
                              INITIAL SIZE 50.
DATA: Col_2_A TYPE I,
      Col_2_B TYPE I,
      Col_2_C TYPE C.
```

Continued

```
*/ The DESCRIBE TABLE statement is used to show its initial
size and current size of Table1 before filling the lines
in it.

DESCRIBE TABLE Table1 LINES Col_2_B OCCURS Col_2_A KIND
Col_2_C.
WRITE: / Col_2_B, Col_2_A, Col_2_C.
DO 500 TIMES.
  LINE-Col_1_A = SY-INDEX.
  LINE-Col_1_B = SY-INDEX ** 3.
INSERT LINE INTO TABLE Table1.
ENDDO.

*/ The DESCRIBE TABLE statement is used to show its initial
size and current size of Table1 after filling the lines in
it.

DESCRIBE TABLE Table1 LINES Col_2_B OCCURS Col_2_A KIND
Col_2_C.
WRITE: / Col_2_B, Col_2_A, Col_2_C.
```

LISTING 7.11 **Using the DESCRIBE TABLE statement**

In Listing 7.11, we create Table1 as a hashed table with `LINE` as its line type and `COL_1_A` as its unique key. The initial size of Table1 is declared 50; however, the table is populated with 500 records or lines. The `DESCRIBE TABLE` statement is used to show the number of records and the size of Table1 before and after filling records in it. Figure 7.16 shows the output of Listing 7.11.

```
  0      50  H
500      50  H
```


FIGURE 7.16 **Displaying the initial and current size of an internal table**

> **Note:** The number of lines in an internal table can be changed by filling lines within it. However, the initial size of the table remains the same.

Now, let's discuss the operations that can be performed on the individual lines of an internal table, such as reading, modifying, and deleting the lines of the table.

OPERATIONS ON INDIVIDUAL LINES

As already discussed, various operations can be performed on internal tables (where an internal table is treated as a single data object), such as moving or refreshing data, comparing the records of two or more tables, and determining the attributes of a table. You can also perform DML operations on single or individual lines of an internal table. All these operations involve internal tables as a whole. However, you can perform operations on single or individual lines of an internal table as well. These operations include insertion, modification, and deletion of records, and reading and searching of records within the internal tables.

However, to perform these operations on the lines of an internal table, the user must be familiar with the following two ways of accessing a single table entry:

- **Using the work area**—Acts as a data object for an internal table so that table entries written in the internal table can be sent to the user's program and vice versa. In other words, a work area is an interface between the entries of a table and a user's program. When a user reads or fetches the data from an internal table, the data overwrites the current content of the work area, after which the new data can be used in the user's program. In addition, the data can be written back into an internal table by moving the data from a program to a work area. The header line of an internal table is also used as a work area. Moreover, the work area must be convertible to the line type of the internal table, which means the data type of a work area must be compatible with the line type of a table entry.
- **Using a field symbol**—Acts as a variable that contains an entire line of an internal table. If you access an internal table by using a field symbol, you do not need to copy the data into a work area. When a line is assigned to a field symbol, the changes made in the field symbol are also reflected in the line assigned to it. Moreover, the field symbol must have the same type as the line type of the internal table.

Figure 7.17 shows how to access the data of an internal table by using a work area or a field symbol:

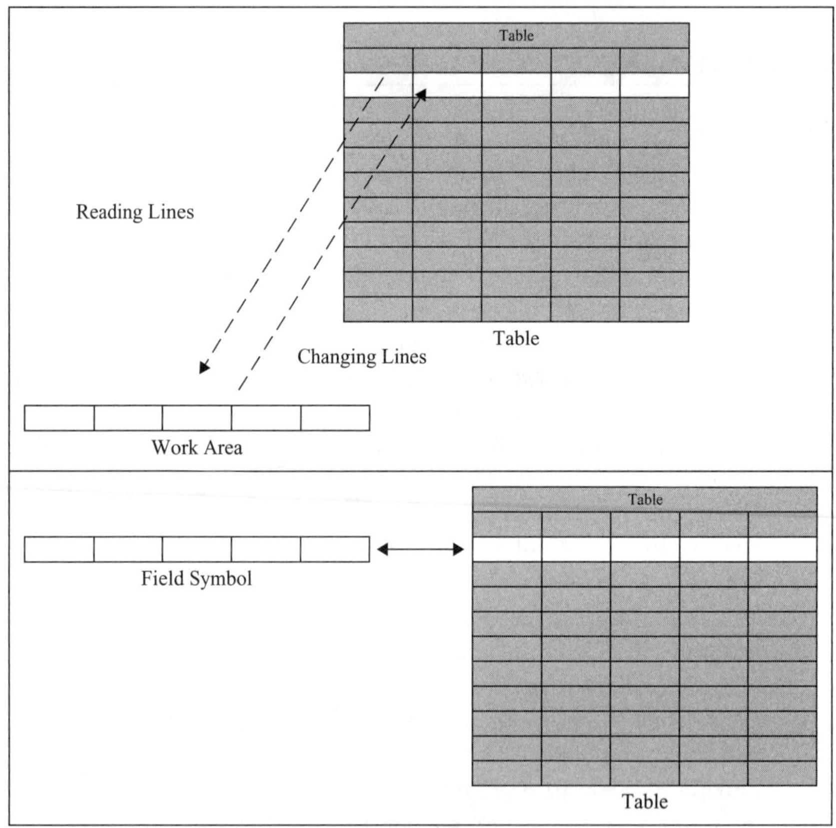

FIGURE 7.17 **Accessing data by using a work area and a field symbol**

Various operations that can be performed on individual lines of an internal table include the following:

- Inserting lines into tables
- Inserting summarized lines
- Appending lines
- Reading lines of tables

- Changing lines of tables
- Deleting lines
- Searching table entries or lines
- Maintaining internal tables

Now, let's perform each operation, one by one.

Inserting Lines in Internal Tables

The INSERT statement is used to insert a single line or a group of lines into an internal table. The following is the syntax to add a single line to an internal table:

```
INSERT [work_area_itab INTO|INITIAL LINE INTO] internal_tab
[INDEX index_number].
```

In this syntax, the INSERT statement inserts a new line in the internal_tab internal table. A new line can be inserted by using either the work_area_itab INTO expression or the INITIAL LINE INTO clause before the internal_tab parameter. When the work_area_itab INTO expression is used, the new line is taken from the work_area_itab work area and inserted into the internal_tab table. The INITIAL LINE INTO clause is used to insert an initial line in the internal_tab table. However, when neither the work_area_itab INTO expression nor the INITIAL LINE INTO clause is used to insert a line, the line is taken from the header line of the internal_tab table.

When a new line is inserted in an internal table by using the INDEX clause, the index number of the lines after the inserted line is incremented by 1. If an internal table contains <index_number>-1 lines, the new line is added at the end of the table. When the SAP system successfully adds a line to an internal table, the SY-SUBRC variable is set to 0. However, if an internal table has less than <index_number> - 1 lines, the new line cannot be inserted and the SY-SUBRC variable is set to 4. Note that without the INDEX clause, the INSERT statement can be used only in a loop and the new line can be inserted only before the current line.

Standard or sorted internal tables have a non-unique key, which means that these tables can have duplicate entries. However, a runtime error occurs if the user attempts to add a duplicate entry to a sorted table with a unique key.

Similarly, a runtime error occurs if the user violates the sort order of a sorted table by appending lines to the table.

The following is the syntax to add multiple lines to an internal table:

```
INSERT LINES OF <internal_tab1> [FROM <n1>] [TO <n 2>] INTO
TABLE <internal_tab2>.
```

In this syntax, <internal_tab1> and <internal_tab2> are internal tables with a compatible line type. The SAP system inserts the lines of the <internal_tab1> table, one-by-one, into the <internal_tab2> table by following the same rules as when inserting single lines in an internal table. If the <internal_tab1> internal table is an index table, the user can append the first and last lines of the table by specifying them in the <n1> and the <n2> expressions, respectively.

The following is the syntax to insert multiple lines from one internal table to another by using a line index:

```
INSERT LINES OF <internal_tab1> INTO <internal_tab2> [INDEX
<index_number>].
```

In this syntax, the lines of the <internal_tab1> internal table are inserted into the <internal_tab2> internal table, one-by-one, by following the same rules as when inserting a single line into an internal table. The <internal_tab1> internal table can be any type of internal table. In addition, the line type of the <internal_tab1> table must be compatible and convertible with the line type of the <internal_tab2> table.

The following is the syntax to insert the lines of an index table into another index table:

```
INSERT LINES OF <internal_tab1> [FROM <n1>] [TO <n2>] INTO
<internal_tab2>
[INDEX <index_number>].
```

In this syntax, the <n1> and the <n2> expressions specify the indexes of the first and last lines, respectively, of the <internal_tab1> internal table that the user wants to insert into the <internal_tab2> internal table.

Now, let's consider some examples of how to insert lines to an internal table.

Examples of Line Insertion

In this section, we discuss some examples of how lines are inserted to an internal table by using the `INSERT` statement.

Listing 7.12 shows how to insert lines in a sorted internal table:

```
Report ZINTERNAL_TABLE_DEMO

*/Inserting lines into a standard table EmployeeDataTable
by using INSERT statement

DATA: BEGIN OF LINE,
ID Type I,
Name(10) Type C,
City(10) Type C,
Salary Type P DECIMALS 2,
END OF LINE.
DATA EmployeeDataTable LIKE STANDARD TABLE OF LINE WITH
NON-UNIQUE KEY ID.

LINE-ID = 400. LINE-NAME = 'Vineet'. LINE-City = 'Delhi'.
LINE-Salary = '25000.67'.
INSERT LINE INTO TABLE EmployeeDataTable.

LINE-ID = 500. LINE-NAME = 'Charu'. LINE-City = 'Delhi'.
LINE-Salary = '25000.00'.
INSERT LINE INTO TABLE EmployeeDataTable.
LINE-ID = 100. LINE-NAME = 'Vandana'. LINE-City =
'Mumbai'. LINE-Salary = '8000.78'.
INSERT LINE INTO TABLE EmployeeDataTable.
LINE-ID = 300. LINE-NAME = 'Ashish'. LINE-City =
'Jaipur'. LINE-Salary = '12000.90'.
INSERT LINE INTO TABLE EmployeeDataTable.
```

Continued

```
LINE-ID = 200. LINE-NAME = 'Shilpa'. LINE-City =
'Banglore'. LINE-Salary = '8000.50'.
INSERT LINE INTO TABLE EmployeeDataTable.
LOOP AT EmployeeDataTable INTO LINE.
   WRITE: / LINE-ID, LINE-Name, LINE-City,
   LINE-Salary.
ENDLOOP.
```

LISTING 7.12 **Inserting lines in a sorted table**

In Listing 7.12, `EmployeeDataTable` is a standard internal table with `LINE` as its line type and a non-unique key defined on its ID field. Figure 7.18 shows the entries in `EmployeeDataTable`:

400	Vineet	Delhi	25,000.67
500	Charu	Delhi	25,000.00
100	Vandana	Mumbai	8,000.78
300	Ashish	Jaipur	12,000.90
200	Shilpa	Banglore	8,000.50

FIGURE 7.18 **Displaying the entries of EmployeeDataTable**

Listing 7.13 shows the insertion of lines from a standard table to a sorted table:

```
REPORT ZINTERNAL_TABLE_DEMO.

DATA: BEGIN OF LINE,
COLA TYPE I,
COLB TYPE I,
END OF LINE.

*/Creating two internal tables-Table1 and Table2
DATA: Table1 LIKE STANDARD TABLE OF LINE,
      Table2 LIKE SORTED TABLE OF LINE
           WITH NON-UNIQUE KEY COLA COLB.

*/Table1 and Table2 are populated with three lines
```

Continued

```
*/Table1 contains square of SY-INDEX system variable

DO 3 TIMES.
  LINE-COLA = SY-INDEX. LINE-COLB = SY-INDEX ** 2.
  APPEND LINE TO Table1.
  LINE-COLA = SY-INDEX. LINE-COLB = SY-INDEX ** 3.
  APPEND LINE TO Table2.
ENDDO.

*/Inserting the lines of Table1 into Table2

INSERT LINES OF Table1 INTO TABLE Table2.

LOOP AT Table2 INTO LINE.
  WRITE: / SY-TABIX, LINE-COLA, LINE-COLB.
ENDLOOP.
```

LISTING 7.13 **Inserting lines of a standard table in a sorted table**

In Listing 7.13, two internal tables, Table1 and Table2, are created with the same line type but with different table types. The table type of Table1 is standard and the table type of Table2 is sorted. Each table has two columns, `COLA and COLB`, and is populated with three lines. Table1 stores the values of the `SY-INDEX` variable in `COLA` (1, 2, 3) and the square of the values of the `SY-INDEX` variable in `COLB` (1, 4, 9). Table2 stores the values of the `SY-INDEX` variable in `COLA` (1, 2, 3) and the cube of the values of the `SY-INDEX` variable in `COLB` (1, 8, 27).

Now the lines in Table1 are inserted in Table2, as shown in Figure 7.19:

1	1	1
2	1	1
3	2	4
4	2	8
5	3	9
6	3	27

FIGURE 7.19 **Inserting the lines of one internal table into another**

Figure 7.19 displays the square and cube of the values of the SY-INDEX variable.

Listing 7.14 shows how to insert the lines of an index table into another index table by using a line index:

```
REPORT ZINTERNAL_TABLE_DEMO.
DATA: BEGIN OF LINE,
COLA TYPE I,
COLB TYPE I,
END OF LINE.
DATA: Table1 LIKE STANDARD TABLE OF LINE.
*/Appending three lines into the table
DO 3 TIMES.
  LINE-COLA = SY-INDEX ** 2.LINE-COLB = SY-INDEX ** 3.
  APPEND LINE TO Table1.
  ENDDO.
*/Inserting a line into Table1 at the index number 2
LINE COLA = 11. LINE-COLB = 22.
INSERT LINE INTO Table1 INDEX 2.
*/Inserting the first line into Table1 at the index
number 1
INSERT INITIAL LINE INTO Table1 INDEX 1.

LOOP AT Table1 INTO LINE.
  WRITE: / SY-TABIX, LINE-COLA, LINE-COLB.
ENDLOOP.
```

LISTING 7.14 **Using a line index to insert the lines of an index table into another index table**

In Listing 7.14, Table1 is a standard internal table, initially populated with three lines. The COLA field of Table1 contains the square of the values of the SY-INDEX variable (1, 4, 9) and the COLB field of Table1 contains the cube of the values of the SY-INDEX variable (1, 8, 27). A new line is inserted at index number 2, so that the original line is shifted to index number 3, and so on. Now, we insert an initial line at index 1, so that the rest of the lines are shifted once again to their next places.

Figure 7.20 shows the output of Listing 7.14:

1	0	0
2	1	1
3	11	22
4	4	8
5	9	27

FIGURE 7.20 **Inserting lines by using the line index**

Listing 7.15 shows how to insert the lines of one internal table into another internal table by using line index in a loop construction:

```
REPORT ZINTERNAL_TABLE_DEMO.

DATA: BEGIN OF LINE,
COLA TYPE I,
COLB TYPE I,
END OF LINE.
DATA: Table1 LIKE STANDARD TABLE OF LINE.
DO 3 TIMES.
  LINE-COLA = SY-INDEX. LINE-COLB = SY-INDEX ** 2.
  APPEND LINE TO Table1.
  ENDDO.
*/Using a line index in a table
LOOP AT Table1 INTO LINE.
  LINE-COLA = 100 + SY-TABIX. LINE-COLB = 10 + SY-TABIX.
  INSERT LINE INTO Table1.
ENDLOOP.

LOOP AT Table1 INTO LINE.
  WRITE: / SY-TABIX, LINE-COLA, LINE-COLB.
ENDLOOP.
```

LISTING 7.15 **Using the line index in a loop construction**

In Listing 7.15, Table1 is a standard internal table that contains the COLA and the COLB fields. Initially, Table1 is populated with three lines, in which the COLA field contains the value of the SY-INDEX variable (1, 2, 3) and the COLB field contains the square of the values of the SY-INDEX variable (1, 4, 9). Now, we insert a new line before each of the previously stored lines in Table1. This means Table1 has a total of six lines. The new lines store the addition of 100 to the corresponding values of the SY-TABIX variable in the COLA field and the addition of 10 to the corresponding values of the SY-TABIX variable in the COLB field.

Therefore, the COLA field of Table1 has the values 101, 1, 103, 2, 105, and 3, and the COLB field of Table1 has the values 11, 1, 13, 4, 15, and 9.

Figure 7.21 shows the output of Listing 7.15:

```
1      101      11
2        1       1
3      103      13
4        2       4
5      105      15
6        3       9
```


FIGURE 7.21 **Inserting lines by using a line index in a loop construction**

Listing 7.16 shows how to insert the lines of one standard table before the lines of another standard table by using an index number:

```
REPORT ZINTERNAL_TABLE_DEMO.
DATA: BEGIN OF LINE,
COLA TYPE I,
COLB TYPE I,
END OF LINE.
*/Creating two internal tables-Table1 and Table2
DATA: Table1 LIKE STANDARD TABLE OF LINE, Table2 LIKE
Table1.
*/Each table is populated with three lines
DO 3 TIMES.
```

Continued

```
  LINE-COLA = SY-INDEX + 10. LINE-COLB = SY-INDEX * 10.
  APPEND LINE TO Table1.
  LINE-COLA = SY-INDEX + 100. LINE-COLB = SY-INDEX * 100.
  APPEND LINE TO Table2.
  ENDDO.
*/Inserting the data of Table1 before the data of Table2
INSERT LINES OF Table1 INTO Table2 INDEX 1.
LOOP AT Table2 INTO LINE.
  WRITE: / SY-TABIX, LINE-COLA, LINE-COLB.
ENDLOOP.
```

LISTING 7.16 **Inserting the lines of one table before the lines of another table**

In Listing 7.16, there are two internal tables, Table1 and Table2. Each table has two columns, `COLA` and `COLB`, and is populated with three lines. Table1 stores the addition of 10 to the values of the `SY-INDEX` variable in `COLA` (11, 12, 13) and the multiplication of 10 with the values of the `SY-INDEX` variable in `COLB` (10, 20, 30). Table2 stores the addition of 100 to the values of the `SY-INDEX` variable in `COLA` (101, 102, 103) and the multiplication of 100 with the values of the `SY-INDEX` variable in `COLB` (100, 200, 300). Finally, Table1 is inserted completely before the first line of Table2, as shown in Figure 7.22:

```
1     11     10
2     12     20
3     13     30
4    101    100
5    102    200
6    103    300
```


FIGURE 7.22 **Inserting data of a table before the first line of another table**

In Figure 7.22, the first three lines show the addition to and the multiplication of 10 with the corresponding values of the SY-INDEX variable and the last three lines show the addition and multiplication of 100 with the corresponding values of the SY-INDEX variable.

Inserting Summarized Lines in Internal Tables

In ABAP, the COLLECT statement is used to summarize the data of internal tables. The syntax to summarize the entries of an internal table is as follows:

```
COLLECT <work_area_itab> INTO <internal_tab>.
```

In this syntax, the <internal_tab> expression is an internal table and the <work_area_itab> expression is a work area. All the fields of an internal table that are not part of the key of the table should be of numeric type. In other words, the fields that are not part of the table key should be of either F, I, or P type. The user specifies the line to be added in a work area that is compatible with the line type.

When we use the COLLECT statement to add a new line or record in an internal table, the SAP system checks whether the line with the same key value already exists in the table. If no such line exists, the COLLECT statement inserts the line in the internal table. However, if a line having the same key value is found in the table, the COLLECT statement adds the content of numeric fields in the work area with the content of numeric fields in the existing entry of the table.

> **Note:** The user should use the COLLECT statement only to create summarized tables. Using other statements to insert table entries may result in duplicate entries in an internal table.

Listing 7.17 shows the use of the COLLECT statement.

```
REPORT ZINTERNAL_TABLE_DEMO.

*/Creating an internal table with three fields, where Field1
and Field2 would be act as non-unique key
```

Continued

```
DATA: BEGIN OF LINE,
        Field1(3) TYPE C,
        Field2(2) TYPE N,
        Field3 TYPE I,
      END OF LINE.

DATA MyTable LIKE SORTED TABLE OF LINE
WITH NON-UNIQUE KEY Field1 Field2.

*/ The COLLECT statement used to summarize the values of
table fields, on the basis of key fields

LINE-Field1 = 'ABC'. LINE-Field2 = '10'.
LINE-Field3 = 100.
COLLECT LINE INTO MyTable.

LINE-Field1 = 'XYZ'. LINE-Field2 = '70'.
LINE-Field3 = 600.
COLLECT LINE INTO MyTable.

LINE-Field1 = 'ABC'. LINE-Field2 = '10'.
LINE-Field3 = 300.
COLLECT LINE INTO MyTable.

LOOP AT MyTable INTO LINE.
  WRITE: / SY-TABIX, LINE-Field1, LINE-Field2,
  LINE-Field3.
ENDLOOP.
```

LISTING 7.17 **Using of the COLLECT statement**

In Listing 7.17, MyTable is a sorted internal table containing three fields: `Field1`, `Field2`, and `Field3`. The MyTable table has `LINE` as its line type and a combination of the `Field1` and `Field2` fields as its unique key. The `COLLECT` statement is used three times to populate MyTable. The first two `COLLECT` statements are used to populate the ABC and XYZ values in `Field1`, the 10 and 70 values in `Field2`, and the 100 and 600 numbers in `Field3`. The third or last `COLLECT` statement is used to add 300 in `Field3`, where the values in Field1 and Field2 are ABC and 10, respectively. Figure 7.23 shows the output of the MyTable table:

```
Internal Table Demos
--------------------------------------------
        1  ABC 10         400
        2  XYZ 70         600
```


FIGURE 7.23 **Result of the COLLECT statement**

In Figure 7.23, Field3 shows the number 400 after adding the numbers 100 and 300, where the value of Field1 is ABC and the value of Field2 is 10.

Appending Lines to Internal Tables

The APPEND statement is used to add a single row or line to an existing internal table. This statement copies a single line from a work area and inserts it after the last existing line in an internal table. The work area can be either a header line or any other field string with the same structure as a line of an internal table. The following is the syntax of the APPEND statement used to append a single line in an internal table:

```
APPEND <record_for_itab> TO <internal_tab>.
```

In this syntax, the <record_for_itab> expression can be represented by the <work_area_itab> work area, which is convertible to a line type or by the INITIAL LINE clause. If the user uses a <work_area_itab> work area, the SAP system adds a new line to the <internal_tab> internal table and populates it with the content of the work area. The INITIAL LINE clause appends a blank line that contains the initial value for each field of the table structure. After each APPEND statement, the SY-TABIX variable contains the index number of the appended line.

Appending lines to standard and sorted tables with a non-unique key works regardless of whether the lines with the same key already exist in the table. In other words, duplicate entries may occur. However, a runtime error occurs if the user attempts to add a duplicate entry to a sorted table with a unique key or if the user violates the sort order of a sorted table by appending the lines to it.

The user can also append the entries of an internal table to another internal table by using the following syntax of the APPEND statement:

```
APPEND LINES OF <internal_tab1> TO <internal_tab2>.
```

In this syntax, the <internal_tab1> and <internal_tab2> expressions are two internal tables. The lines of the < internal_tab1> table are appended to the <internal_tab2> table. The <internal_tab1> table can be of any type, but its line type must be convertible to the line type of the <internal_tab2> table.

The following syntax is used to append the lines of one index table to another index table:

```
APPEND LINES OF <internal_tab1> [FROM <n1>] [TO <n2>] TO
<internal_tab2>.
```

In this syntax, the <n1> and <n2> expressions are the indexes of the first and last lines, respectively, of the <internal_tab1> table, which the user wants to append to the <internal_tab2> table.

When the user appends several lines to a sorted table, the unique key (if defined) must not violate the sort order; otherwise, a runtime error will occur.

The APPEND statement is also used to create ranked lists in standard tables. To do this, create an empty table and then use the following syntax of the APPEND statement:

```
APPEND <work_area_itab> TO <internal_tab> SORTED BY
<internal_tab_field>.
```

In this syntax, the new line added by using the APPEND statement cannot be appended at the end of the <internal_tab> table. Instead, the table is sorted by the <internal_tab_field> field in descending order. The <work_area_itab> work area must be compatible with the line type of the <internal_tab> table.

Note that if you select the table type as a sorted table, you cannot use the SORTED BY clause.

Using the APPEND Statement

Listing 7.18 shows the use of the APPEND statement in the DO loop:

```
REPORT ZINTERNAL_TABLE_DEMO.
*/Creating an internal table
DATA: BEGIN OF ROW,
         COLA TYPE C,
         COLB TYPE I,
       END OF ROW.

DATA MyTable LIKE TABLE OF ROW.
*/Using APPEND statement in the DO loop
DO 3 TIMES.
  APPEND INITIAL LINE TO MyTable.
  ROW-COLA = SY-INDEX. ROW-COLB = SY-INDEX ** 2.
  APPEND ROW TO MyTable.
ENDDO.

LOOP AT MyTable INTO ROW.
  WRITE: / ROW-COLA, ROW-COLB.
ENDLOOP.
```

LISTING 7.18 **Using the APPEND statement in the DO loop**

In Listing 7.18, we create the MyTable internal table with ROW as its line type, and COLA and COLB as its two columns. MyTable is populated with six lines by using the DO loop. Each time the loop is processed, an initialized line is appended to the MyTable table and the work area of the table is populated with the values of the SY-INDEX variable (in the COLA field) and the square of the values of the SY-INDEX variable (in the COLB field). Figure 7.24 shows the output of Listing 7.18:

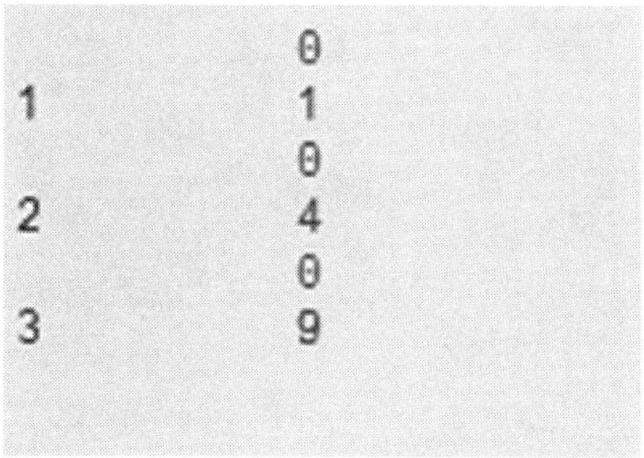

```
        0
1       1
        0
2       4
        0
3       9
```


FIGURE 7.24 **The result of the APPEND statement**

Listing 7.19 shows how to append the lines of one table with that of another table.

```
REPORT ZAPPEND_TABLE_DEMO.
*/Appending one table by another table
DATA: BEGIN OF Record1,
        ID(3) TYPE C,
        Name(10) TYPE C,
        Marks TYPE I,
      END OF Record1,
      Stud1 LIKE TABLE OF Record1.

DATA: BEGIN OF Record2,
        ColumnA(1) TYPE C,
        ColumnB LIKE Stud1,
      END OF Record2,
      Stud2 LIKE TABLE OF Record2.

Record1-ID = 'A01'. Record1-Name = 'Vidhi'.
Record1-Marks = 50.
APPEND Record1 TO Stud1.
```

Continued

```
Record1-ID = 'C05'. Record1-Name = 'Anshit'.
Record1-Marks = 30.
APPEND Record1 TO Stud1.
Record2-ColumnA = 'A'. Record2-ColumnB = Stud1.
APPEND Record2 TO Stud2.

REFRESH Stud1.

Record1-ID = 'R03'. Record1-Name = 'Mansi'.
Record1-Marks = 80.
APPEND Record1 TO Stud1.
Record1-ID = 'D07'. Record1-Name = 'Rajat'.
Record1-Marks = 96.
APPEND Record1 TO Stud1.

Record2-ColumnA = 'B'. Record2-ColumnB = Stud1.
APPEND Record2 TO Stud2.

LOOP AT Stud2 INTO Record2.
  WRITE: / Record2-ColumnA.
  LOOP AT Record2-ColumnB INTO Record1.
  WRITE: / Record1-ID, Record1-Name, Record1-Marks.
  ENDLOOP.
ENDLOOP.
```

LISTING 7.19 **Appending the lines of one table with another table**

In Listing 7.19, two internal tables, Stud1 and Stud2, are created. The line types of the Stud1 and Stud2 tables are `Record1` and `Record2`, respectively. The `Record1` line type contains the `ID`, `Name`, and `Marks` fields, while the `Record2` line type contains the `ColumnA` and `ColumnB` fields. The data types of the `ID`, `Name`, `Marks`, and `ColumnA` fields are elementary, while the data type of the `ColumnB` field is itself an internal table—that is, Stud1. The `APPEND` statement is used to populate the Stud1 and Stud2 tables by using their respective line types. Furthermore, the `REFRESH` statement is used to refresh the data of the Stud1 table. Figure 7.25 shows the lines stored in the Stud2 table by using the table in a loop:

```
A
A01 Vidhi         50
C05 Anshit        30
B
R03 Mansi         80
D07 Rajat         96
```


FIGURE 7.25 **The result of appending the lines of one table to another table**

Listing 7.20 shows how to append specific lines of one table to another:

```
REPORT ZAPPEND_TABLE_DEMO.
*/Creating two internal tables
DATA: BEGIN OF LINE,
COLA TYPE C,
COLB TYPE I,
END OF LINE.

DATA: Table1 LIKE TABLE OF LINE, Table2 LIKE Table1.
*/Inserting lines into the internal tables

DO 3 TIMES.
  LINE-COLA = SY-INDEX. LINE-COLB = SY-INDEX ** 2.
  APPEND LINE TO Table1.
  LINE-COLA = SY-INDEX. LINE-COLB = SY-INDEX ** 3.
  APPEND LINE TO Table2.
  ENDDO.
*/Appending the lines of Table2 to Table1
APPEND LINES OF Table2 FROM 2 TO 3 TO Table1.
*/Displaying the lines of Table1
LOOP AT Table1 INTO LINE.
  WRITE: / LINE-COLA, LINE-COLB.
ENDLOOP.
```

LISTING 7.20 **Appending specific lines of one index table to another table**

In Listing 7.20, two internal tables, Table1 and Table2, are created with the LINE line type. Each table has two columns, COLA and COLB, and is populated with three lines. Table1 stores the values of the SY-INDEX variable in COLA (1, 2, 3) and the square of the values of the SY-INDEX variable in COLB (1, 4, 9). Table2 stores the values of the SY-INDEX variable in COLA (1, 2, 3) and the cube of the values of the SY-INDEX variable in COLB (1, 8, 27). The last two lines of Table2 are then appended to Table1, as shown in Figure 7.26:

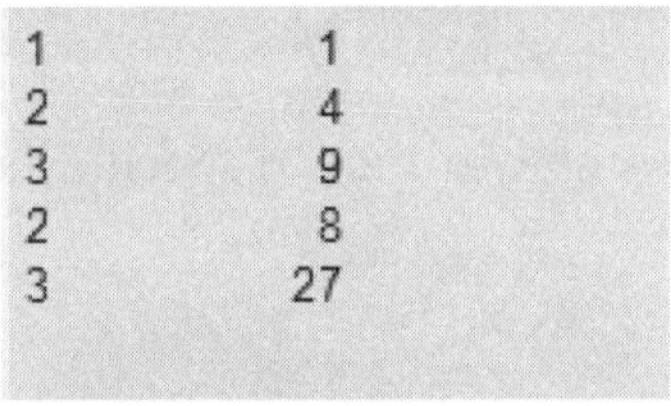

1	1
2	4
3	9
2	8
3	27

FIGURE 7.26 **Appending the last two lines from a table to another table**

Listing 7.21 shows how to use the APPEND statement with the SORTED BY clause.

```
REPORT ZAPPEND_TABLE_DEMO.

*/Creating an internal table with the initial size 2

DATA: BEGIN OF ROW,
        COL1 TYPE I,
        COL2 TYPE I,
        COL3 TYPE I,
      END OF ROW.
DATA MyTable LIKE TABLE OF ROW INITIAL SIZE 2.
*/Appending the lines in the table, by the SORTED BY clause,
so that the table is sorted by COL2 field in descending
order.
```

Continued

```
ROW-COL1 = 1. ROW-COL2 = 10. ROW-COL3 = 100.
APPEND ROW TO MyTable SORTED BY COL2.

ROW-COL1 = 2. ROW-COL2 = 20. ROW-COL3 = 200.
APPEND ROW TO MyTable SORTED BY COL2.

ROW-COL1 = 3. ROW-COL2 = 30. ROW-COL3 = 300.
APPEND ROW TO MyTable SORTED BY COL2.

ROW-COL1 = 4. ROW-COL2 = 40. ROW-COL3 = 400.
APPEND ROW TO MyTable SORTED BY COL2.

ROW-COL1 = 5. ROW-COL2 = 50. ROW-COL3 = 500.
APPEND ROW TO MyTable SORTED BY COL2.

LOOP AT MyTable INTO ROW.
  WRITE: / ROW-COL1, ROW-COL2, ROW-COL3.
ENDLOOP.
```

LISTING 7.21 **Using the APPEND statement with the SORTED BY clause**

In Listing 7.21, MyTable is an internal table with three columns: `COL1`, `COL2`, and `COL3`. In this table, we append five lines by using the `APPEND` statement and sort the lines in descending order by using the `SORTED BY` clause with the `COL2` field. However, the last three lines of MyTable are skipped because we have specified the initial size of the table as 2 by using the `INITIAL SIZE` clause. As a result, only two lines with the largest values in the `COL2` field of MyTable are displayed, as shown in Figure 7.27:

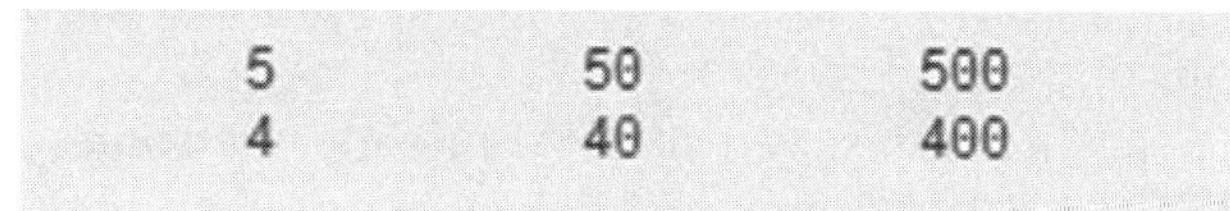

FIGURE 7.27 **Using the APPEND statement with the SORTED BY clause**

Reading the Lines of Internal Tables

In ABAP, you can read the lines of a table by using the following syntax of the READ TABLE statement:

```
READ TABLE <internal_tab> <key> <result>.
```

In this syntax, you have to specify a key for the table. Remember that you must specify the line by using the key, not the index. The key is specified in the <key> expression and the <result> expression is used to specify an additional processing option for the line to be retrieved.

Now, let's learn how to specify a key in the <key> expression and a processing option in the <result> expression.

Specifying a Key in the <key> Expression

In the <key> expression, you can specify either a table key or a different key. A table key is required to search an internal table and is specified by using the READ TABLE statement. The syntax to use the READ TABLE statement is as follows:

```
READ TABLE <internal_tab> FROM <work_area_itab>.
```

or

```
READ TABLE <internal_tab> WITH TABLE KEY <k1> = <f1> ...
<kn> = <fn>.
```

In the first syntax, the <work_area_itab> expression represents a work area that is compatible with the line type of the <internal_tab> table. The values in the key fields of this table are taken from the corresponding components of the work area.

In the second syntax, you need to provide the values of each key field explicitly. If the name of any key field is not known until the execution of the program, you can specify it as the content of the <ni> field by using the (<ni>) = <fi> form. If the data types of the <f1>, <f2>. . . <fn> fields are not compatible with the corresponding key fields, the SAP system converts them to a compatible type automatically.

You can specify a search key, but not a table key, within the READ statement by using the WITH KEY clause, as shown in the following syntax:

```
READ TABLE <internal_tab> WITH KEY = <internal_tab_
field>.
```

or

```
READ TABLE <internal_tab> WITH KEY <internal_tab_key1> =
<internal_tab_field1> ...
<internal_tab_key n> = <internal_tab_field n>.
```

In the first syntax, the entire line of the internal table is used as a search key. The content of the entire line of the table is compared with the content of the <internal_tab_field> field. If the values of the <internal_tab_field> field are not compatible with the line type of the table, these values are converted according to the line type of the table. The search key allows you to find entries in internal tables that do not have a structured line type; that is, where the line is a single field or an internal table type.

In the second syntax, the search key is specified by using the <internal_tab_key 1>...<internal_tab_key *n*> table fields. If the data types of the <internal_tab_field 1>...<internal_tab_field *n*> fields are not compatible with the components in the internal table, the SAP system first converts them into compatible forms and then performs the read operation.

Specifying a Processing Option in the <result> Expression

You can specify a work area or a field symbol in the <result> expression. The following syntax of the READ statement is used to specify a work area or field symbol by using the COMPARING or TRANSPORTING clause:

```
READ TABLE <internal_tab> <key> INTO <work_area_itab>
[COMPARING <f1> <f2> ...
                              |ALL FIELDS]
                  [TRANSPORTING <f1> <f2> ...
                                     |ALL FIELDS
                                     |NO FIELDS].
```

If the COMPARING or TRANSPORTING clause is not used, the content of the table line must be convertible into the data type of the <work_area_itab> work area, and if the clause is specified, the line type and work area must be compatible. You must always use a work area that is compatible with the line type of the relevant internal table.

When the COMPARING clause is used, the specified table fields <f1>, <f2>....<fn> of the structured line type are compared with the corresponding fields of the work area before being transported. If the ALL FIELDS clause is specified, the SAP system compares all the components. When the SAP system finds an entry on the basis of a key, the value of the SY-SUBRC variable is set to 0. In addition, the value of the SY-SUBRC variable is set to 2 or 4 if the content of the compared fields is not the same or if the SAP system cannot find an entry. However, the SAP system copies the entry into the target work area whenever it finds an entry, regardless of the result of the comparison.

The TRANSPORTING clause is used to specify the table fields of the structured line type that need to be transported into the work area. If the ALL FIELDS clause is specified without using the TRANSPORTING clause, the content of all the fields is transported. However, the NO FIELDS clause is specified, no content is transported.

In both clauses (COMPARING and TRANSPORTING), you can dynamically specify a field <fi> as the content of the <ni> field in the <ni> form. When the READ TABLE statement is executed, the <ni> field is ignored if it is empty.

You can assign a table line or table entry to a field symbol, taken from an internal table, by using the following syntax:

```
READ TABLE <internal_tab> <key> ASSIGNING <internal_tab_
fieldsymbol>.
```

In this syntax, a table entry from the <internal_tab> table is assigned to the <internal_tab_fieldsymbol> field symbol by using the ASSIGNING clause in the READ TABLE statement. The data type of the field symbol must be compatible with the line type of the table.

Examples of Reading Lines from Tables

In this section, we consider some examples to read one of more lines from internal tables by using the READ statement.

Listing 7.22 shows how to read lines by using the READ TABLE statement and the COMPARING clause:

```
REPORT ZREADLINES_DEMO.
*/Creating an internal table
DATA: BEGIN OF RECORD,
COLA TYPE I,
COLB TYPE I,
END OF RECORD.
DATA MyTable LIKE HASHED TABLE OF RECORD WITH UNIQUE KEY
COLA.
*/Filling the internal table with four lines
DO 4 TIMES.
  RECORD-COLA = SY-INDEX.
  RECORD-COLB = SY-INDEX ** 3.
INSERT RECORD INTO TABLE MyTable.
ENDDO.
*/Reading the lines of the internal table, on the basis COLA
but not on COLB, as COLA is unique key of the table

RECORD-COLA = 3. RECORD-COLB = 64.

READ TABLE MyTable FROM RECORD INTO RECORD COMPARING
COLB.

WRITE: 'SY-SUBRC =', SY-SUBRC.
SKIP.
WRITE: / RECORD-COLA, RECORD-COLB.
```

LISTING 7.22 **Using the COMPARING clause in the READ TABLE statement**

In Listing 7.22, MyTable is an internal table of the hashed table type, with RECORD as the work area and COLA as the unique key. Initially, MyTable is populated with four lines, where the COLA field contains the values of the SY-INDEX variable and the COLB field contains the cube of the values of the SY-INDEX variable. The RECORD work area is populated with 3 and 64 as values for the COLA and COLB fields, respectively. The READ statement reads the line of the table after comparing the value of the COLA key field with the value in the RECORD work area by using the COMPARING clause, and then copies the content of the read line in the work area. Figure 7.28 shows the content of the RECORD work area:

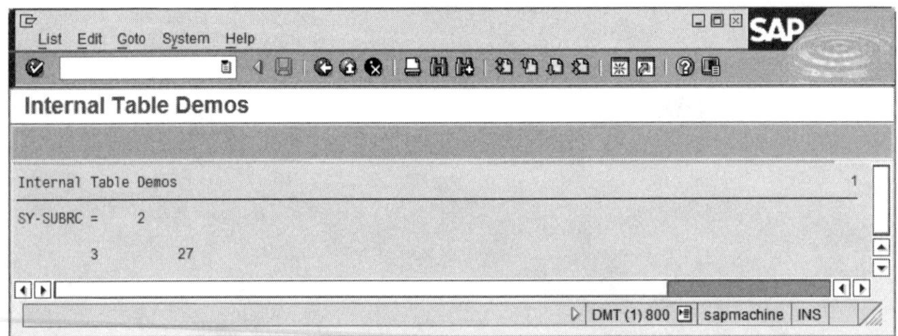

FIGURE 7.28 **The result of using the COMPARING clause**

In Figure 7.28, the value of the SY-SUBRC variable is displayed as 2 because when the value in the COLA field is 3, the value in the COLB field is not 64, but 27.

Listing 7.23 shows how to read lines from a sorted table by using the TRANSPORTING clause:

```
REPORT ZREADLINES_DEMO.
DATA: BEGIN OF LINE,
COLA TYPE I,
COLB TYPE I,
END OF LINE.
DATA MyTable LIKE Sorted TABLE OF LINE WITH UNIQUE KEY
COLA.
```

Continued

```
DO 4 TIMES.
  LINE-COLA = SY-INDEX.
  LINE-COLB = SY-INDEX ** 2.
INSERT LINE INTO TABLE MyTable.
ENDDO.

CLEAR LINE.
*/ Using the TRANSPORTING clause to transport the table
fields into the work area
READ TABLE MyTable WITH TABLE KEY COLA = 3
                 INTO LINE TRANSPORTING COLB.
WRITE: 'SY-SUBRC =', SY-SUBRC,
       / 'SY-TABIX =', SY-TABIX.
SKIP.
WRITE: / LINE-COLA, LINE-COLB.
```

LISTING 7.23 **Reading lines by using the TRANSPORTING clause**

In Listing 7.23, MyTable is a sorted table with the `LINE` line type, initially populated with four lines. In MyTable, the `COLA` field contains the values of the `SY-INDEX` variable and the `COLB` field contains the square of the values of the `SY-INDEX` variable. The `READ` statement reads the line of the table in which the `COLA` field has the same value as that in the work area and copies the line to the work area. Only the content of the `COLB` field is copied to the `LINE` work area. The value of the `SY-SUBRC` variable is 0 and that of the `SY-TABIX` variable is 3, because MyTable is an index table. Figure 7.29 shows the output of Listing 7.23:

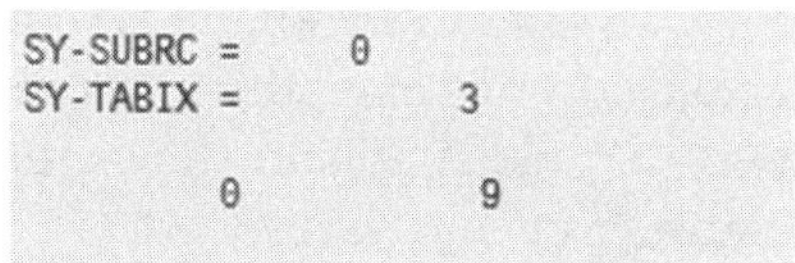

FIGURE 7.29 **The result of using the TRANSPORTING clause**

Listing 7.24 shows how to read lines by using a search key other than a table key:

```
REPORT ZREADLINES_DEMO.
DATA: BEGIN OF LINE,
COLA TYPE I,
COLB TYPE I,
END OF LINE.
DATA MyTable LIKE Sorted TABLE OF LINE WITH UNIQUE KEY
COLA.
DO 4 TIMES.
  LINE-COLA = SY-INDEX.
  LINE-COLB = SY-INDEX ** 2.
INSERT LINE INTO TABLE MyTable.
ENDDO.
*/ Using the TRANSPORTING NO FIELDS clause, so that no
fields are transported
READ TABLE MyTable WITH KEY COLB = 16 TRANSPORTING NO
FIELDS.

WRITE: 'SY-SUBRC =', SY-SUBRC,
       / 'SY-TABIX =', SY-TABIX.
```

LISTING 7.24 **Reading lines of tables by using a search key different from a table key**

In Listing 7.24, MyTable is a sorted table with the `LINE` line type, initially populated with four lines. In MyTable, the `COLA` field contains the values of the `SY-INDEX` variable and the `COLB` field contains the square of the values of the `SY-INDEX` variable. The `COLA` field is the table key of the MyTable table. However, the `READ` statement reads the line of the table on the basis of another key, which is defined in the `COLB` field. The result of the operation performed by the `READ` statement is represented by the `SY-SUBRC` and `SY-TABIX` variables. In this case, the `READ` statement successfully finds the line where the `COLB` field is 16 and shows the values of the `SY-SUBRC` and `SY-TABIX` variables as 0 and 4, respectively, as shown in Figure 7.30:

```
SY-SUBRC =      0
SY-TABIX =           4
```


FIGURE 7.30 **Reading table lines by using a different key**

Listing 7.25 shows how to read the lines of tables by using field symbols:

```
REPORT ZREADLINES_DEMO.
DATA: BEGIN OF LINE,
COLA TYPE I,
COLB TYPE I,
END OF LINE.
DATA MyTable LIKE Hashed TABLE OF LINE WITH UNIQUE KEY
COLA.
*/Declaring a field symbol
FIELD-SYMBOLS <MyField> LIKE LINE OF MyTable.
DO 4 TIMES.
LINE-COLA = SY-INDEX.
LINE-COLB = SY-INDEX ** 2.
INSERT LINE INTO TABLE MyTable.
ENDDO.
*/Reading a table with field symbol

READ TABLE MyTable WITH TABLE KEY COLA = 3 ASSIGNING
<MyField>.

<MyField>-COLB = 80.
LOOP AT MyTable INTO LINE.
  WRITE: / LINE-COLA, LINE-COLB.
ENDLOOP.
```

LISTING 7.25 **Reading lines of tables by using field symbols**

In Listing 7.25, MyTable is a hashed table with the `LINE` line type and the `COLA` and `COLB` fields. Initially, MyTable is populated with four lines, where the `COLA` field contains the values 1, 2, 3, and 4, while the `COLB` field contains the values 1, 4, 9, and 16. The `READ` statement reads the line of the table in which the value of the `COLA` field is 3 and assigns it to the `<MyField>` field symbol. In Listing 7.25, the value 80 is assigned to the `COL2` field of the `<MyField>` field symbol, which changes the value of the corresponding table field. Figure 7.31 shows the changed value of the COLB field when the value of the COLA field is 3:

1	1
2	4
3	80
4	16

FIGURE 7.31 **Assigning a value by using a field symbol**

In Figure 7.31, the value of the COLB field in the third line changes from 9 to 80.

Modifying the Lines of Internal Tables

In ABAP, the MODIFY statement is used to modify the content of one or more records stored in an internal table. To modify the content of a single record of an internal table, you must specify a table key in the MODIFY statement. Similarly, to modify the content of multiple rows, you must specify conditions within the MODIFY statement.

Besides the MODIFY statement, the WRITE TO statement is used to change the content of the lines of an internal table.

Modifying the lines of an internal table involves the following operations:

- Modify a line by using a table key
- Modify lines by using a condition

Now, let's discuss each in detail.

Modifying a Line by Using a Table Key

The MODIFY statement modifies a single line of an internal table. The following syntax shows the use of the MODIFY statement:

```
MODIFY TABLE <internal_tab> FROM <work_area_itab>
[TRANSPORTING <f1> <f2> ...].
```

In this syntax, <internal_tab> represents an internal table, <work_area_itab> represents the work area of the <internal_tab> table, and <f1> <f2>...<fn> represent non-key fields of the <work_area_itab> work area. The MODIFY statement is used to modify the content of a line of the <internal_tab> table with the help of the <work_area_itab> work area. The <work_area_itab> work area must be compatible with the line type of the <internal_tab> table. It is used for two purposes: first, to find the line that the user wants to change, and second, to insert a new line in the table.

The TRANSPORTING clause is used to specify the non-key fields that can be assigned to the table line. The SAP system searches the internal table for the line whose table key corresponds to the key fields in the <work_area_itab> work area. If a line is retrieved successfully in the specified internal table, the content of the non-key fields of the work area is copied to the corresponding fields of the line and the value of the SY-SUBRC variable is set to 0; otherwise, the value of the SY-SUBRC variable is set to 4. If the table has a non-unique key and the SAP system finds duplicate entries, it modifies the first entry.

Use the following syntax of the MODIFY statement to change lines in tables by using their indexes is as follows:

```
MODIFY <internal_tab> FROM <work_area_itab> [INDEX <index_
number>] [TRANSPORTING <f1> <f2> ... ].
```

In this syntax, the work area <work_area_itab> specified in the FROM clause replaces the existing line in the <internal_tab> internal table. The work area must be convertible into the line type of the internal table.

If the INDEX option is used, the content of the work area overwrites the content of the line with the <index_number> index; if the operation is successful, the value of the SY-SUBRC variable is set to 0. However, if the internal table contains fewer lines than the <index_number> index, no line is changed and the value of the SY-SUBRC variable is set to 4.

The MODIFY statement can be used within a loop construction, only when the INDEX clause is not used.

Modifying Multiple Lines by Using a Condition

The MODIFY statement can also modify one or more lines by specifying a condition in the WHERE clause. The following syntax is used to specify a condition in the WHERE clause of the MODIFY statement:

```
MODIFY <internal_tab> FROM <work_area_itab> TRANSPORTING
<f1> <f2> ... WHERE <cond>.
```

In this syntax, the MODIFY statement processes all the lines that meet the logical condition <cond>. The logical condition can be a combination of one or more comparisons. The <work_area_itab> work area, which is specified in the FROM clause, replaces a line in the <internal_tab> internal table. If any line is modified in an internal table, the SAP system sets the value of the SY-SUBRC variable to 0; otherwise the value is set to 4.

Now, let's consider some examples of how lines are modified in an internal table.

Examples of Changing Lines

In this section, we consider some examples that show how to change one or more lines of an internal table by using the MODIFY statement.

Listing 7.26 shows how to modify lines by specifying a unique key:

```
REPORT ZMODIFYLINES_DEMO.

*/Creating an internal table

DATA: BEGIN OF LINE,
COLA TYPE I,
COLB TYPE I,
END OF LINE.
DATA MyTable LIKE Hashed TABLE OF LINE WITH UNIQUE
KEY COLA.
```

Continued

```
*/Filling the table with four lines

DO 4 TIMES.
  LINE-COLA = SY-INDEX.
  LINE-COLB = SY-INDEX ** 2.
INSERT LINE INTO TABLE MyTable.
ENDDO.
*/Modifying a particular line of the table

LINE-COLA = 3. LINE-COLB = 80.
MODIFY TABLE MyTable FROM LINE.

LOOP AT MyTable INTO LINE.
  WRITE: / LINE-COLA, LINE-COLB.
ENDLOOP.
```

LISTING 7.26 **Modifying the lines of a table by specifying a unique key**

In Listing 7.26, MyTable is a hashed table with the LINE line type and the COLA and COLB fields. Initially, MyTable is populated with four lines, where the COLA field contains the values 1, 2, 3, and 4, and the COLB field contains the values 1, 4, 9, and 16. The MODIFY statement is used to change the value of the COLB field to 80 when the value of the COLA key field is 3, as shown in Figure 7.32:

```
1    1
2    4
3   80
4   16
```


FIGURE 7.32 **Modifying table lines by using a unique key**

Listing 7.27 shows how to modify lines by specifying a condition:

```
REPORT ZMODIFYLINES_DEMO.
*/Creating an internal table

DATA: BEGIN OF LINE,
COLA TYPE I,
COLB TYPE I,
END OF LINE.
DATA MyTable LIKE Hashed TABLE OF LINE WITH UNIQUE KEY
COLA.
*/Filling the table with six lines

DO 6 TIMES.
  LINE-COLA = SY-INDEX.
  LINE-COLB = SY-INDEX ** 2.
INSERT LINE INTO TABLE MyTable.
ENDDO.
*/Modifying a particular line of the table, on the basis
of a condition

LINE-COLB = 80.
MODIFY MyTable FROM LINE TRANSPORTING COLB
WHERE (COLB > 2) AND (COLA < 5).

LOOP AT MyTable INTO LINE.
  WRITE: / LINE-COLA, LINE-COLB.
ENDLOOP.
```

LISTING 7.27 **Modifying the lines of a table by specifying a condition**

In Listing 7.27, MyTable is a hashed table with the `LINE` line type and the `COLA` and `COLB` fields. Initially, MyTable is populated with six lines, where the `COLA` contains the values 1, 2, 3, 4, 5, and 6, and the `COLB` contains the values 1, 4, 9, 16, 25, and 36. The `MODIFY` statement is used to change the lines of the table where the value of `COLB` is greater than 2 and less than 5. Figure 7.33 shows the output of Listing 7.27:

1	1
2	80
3	80
4	80
5	25
6	36

FIGURE 7.33 **Modifying table lines by using a condition**

Listing 7.28 shows how to modify the lines of a sorted table by using the TRANSPORTING clause:

```
REPORT ZMODIFYLINES_DEMO.
*/Creating an internal table with five lines
DATA NAME(4) VALUE 'COLB'.

DATA: BEGIN OF LINE,
          COLA TYPE I,
          COLB TYPE I,
       END OF LINE.

DATA MyTable LIKE SORTED TABLE OF LINE WITH UNIQUE KEY
COLA.

DO 5 TIMES.
  LINE-COLA = SY-INDEX.
  LINE-COLB = SY-INDEX ** 3.
  APPEND LINE TO MyTable.
ENDDO.
*/Modifying the value of the line, at the index 4, by using
TRANSPORTING clause

LINE-COLB = 100.
MODIFY MyTable FROM LINE INDEX 4 TRANSPORTING (NAME).
```

Continued

```
*/Modifying the value of the line, at the index 2, without
using TRANSPORTING clause

LINE-COLA = 2.
LINE-COLB = 200.
MODIFY MyTable FROM LINE INDEX 2.

LOOP AT MyTable INTO LINE.
  WRITE: / SY-TABIX, LINE-COLA, LINE-COLB.
ENDLOOP.
```

LISTING 7.28 **Modifying the lines of a sorted table by using the TRANSPORTING clause**

In Listing 7.28, MyTable is a sorted table with `LINE` as its line type and the `COLA` and `COLB` fields. Initially, MyTable is populated with five lines, where the `COLA` field contains the values 1, 2, 3, 4, and 5, and the `COLB` field contains the values 1, 8, 27, 64, and 125. The `MODIFY` statement is used to change the value of the `COLB` field at the specified `INDEX` numbers 2 and 4. The value of the `COLB` field at `INDEX` 2 is changed from 8 to 200, whereas at `INDEX` 4, the value is changed from 64 to 100. Figure 7.34 shows the modified values in the `COLB` field of MyTable:

```
1    1      1
2    2    200
3    3     27
4    4    100
5    5    125
```


FIGURE 7.34 **Modified values of a sorted table**

A runtime error occurs if the `INDEX` number and the `LINE-COLA` value do not match because the key fields of sorted tables cannot be changed. Figure 7.35 shows the runtime error screen if the value of the `LINE-COLA` variable is 2 while that of `INDEX` is 3:

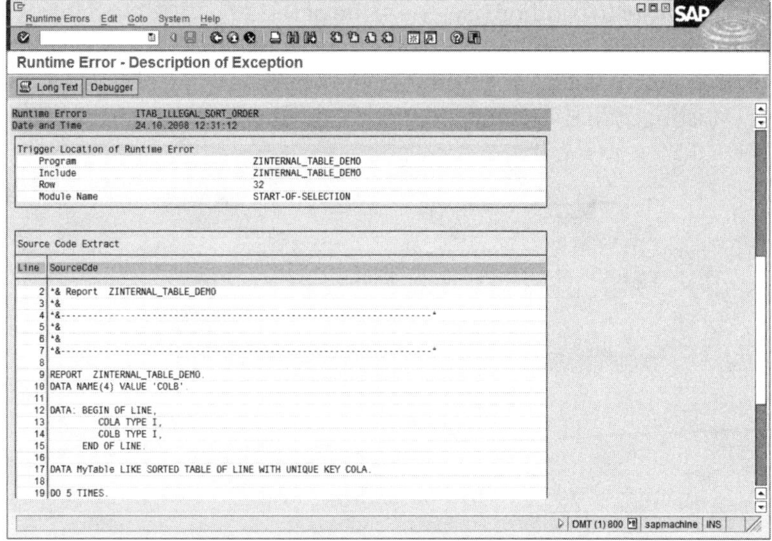

FIGURE 7.35 **Displaying a runtime error when the INDEX and LINE-COLA do not match**

In Figure 7.35, you can see the runtime error screen, which shows the details of the generated exception, such as the name of the program, date, time, and line.

Using the `WRITE TO` Statement

Besides the `MODIFY` statement, you can use the `WRITE TO` statement to modify the lines of an internal table. The syntax to use the `WRITE TO` statement to modify table lines is:

```
WRITE <f> TO <internal_tab> INDEX <index_number>.
```

In this syntax, the `WRITE TO` statement converts the content of the `<f>` field to the `C` data type and transfers the resulting character string to the line with the <index_number> index. If the operation is successful, the value of the `SY-SUBRC` variable is set to 0; otherwise, the value of the SY-SUBRC variable is set to 4. Note that the data type of the <f> field must be able to be converted into a character field; if not, a syntax or runtime error occurs.

Listing 7.29 shows how to modify the lines of an internal table by using the WRITE TO statement:

```
REPORT ZWRITELINE_DEMO.
*/Creating an internal table with three lines
DATA series(100).

DATA SeriesStore LIKE TABLE OF series.

series = '1,2,3,4,5,6...'.

APPEND series TO SeriesStore.
series = '100,200,300,400,500,600...'.

APPEND series TO SeriesStore.

series = 'A,B,C,D,E...'.

APPEND series TO SeriesStore.
*/Changing the second line of the table with WRITE
statement

WRITE 'Continueeee...' TO SeriesStore+16 INDEX 2.

LOOP AT SeriesStore INTO series.

   WRITE / series.

ENDLOOP.
```

LISTING 7.29 **Using the WRITE TO statement**

In Listing 7.29, SeriesStore is an internal table created with the elementary type C field of 100 characters. SeriesStore is populated with three series of lines, in which the first series is 1, 2, 3, 4, 5, 6…, the second series is 100, 200, 300, 400, 500, 600…, and the third series is A, B, C, D, E…. After populating the SeriesStore table with these lines, we change the second line by using the `WRITE TO` statement. As a result, the numbers after 400 are replaced by the `Continueeee...` string in the second series, as shown in Figure 7.36:

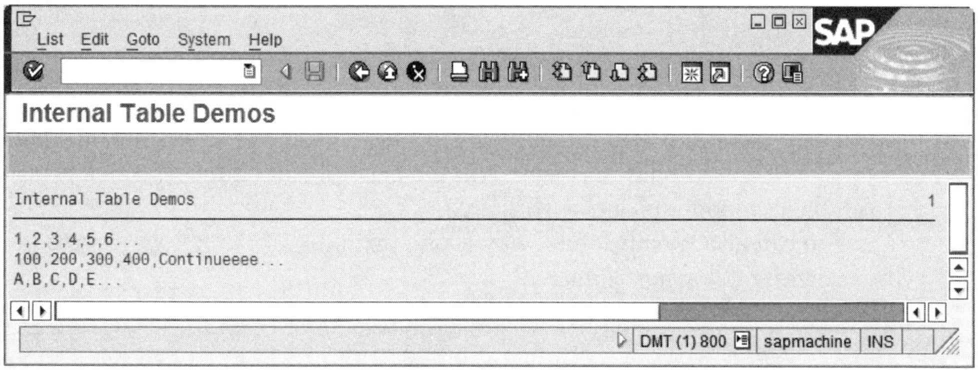

FIGURE 7.36 **Modifying a series by using the WRITE TO statement**

In Figure 7.36, notice that the `Continueeee...` string has replaced the values 500 and 600 from the second series.

Deleting Lines

The `DELETE` statement is used to delete one or more records from an internal table. The records of an internal table are deleted either by specifying a table key or condition or by finding duplicate entries. If an internal table has a non-unique key and contains duplicate entries, the first entry from the table is deleted.

Various operations that can be performed using the `DELETE` statement include:

- Deleting a line by specifying a table key
- Deleting a line by using the `INDEX` clause
- Deleting multiple lines by specifying a condition
- Deleting multiple lines by using an index or condition
- Deleting duplicate entries

Now, let's discuss each operation in detail.

Deleting a Line by Specifying a Table Key

The syntax to use the DELETE statement to delete a record or line from an internal table is as follows:

```
DELETE TABLE <internal_tab> FROM <work_area_itab>.
```

In this syntax, the <work_area_itab> expression is a work area, which must be compatible with the line type of the <internal_tab> internal table. The delete operation is performed on the basis of a default key, which is taken from the components of the work area.

You can also specify a table key explicitly in the DELETE TABLE statement by using the following syntax:

```
DELETE TABLE <internal_tab> WITH TABLE KEY <k1> = <f1> ...
<kn> = <fn>.
```

In this syntax, <f1>, <f2>....<fn> are the fields of an internal table and <k1>, <k2>....<kn> are the key fields of the table. The DELETE statement is used to delete the records or lines of the <internal_tab> table based on the expressions <k1> = <f1>, <k2> = <f2>...<kn> = <fn>. Moreover, if the data types of the <f1>, <f2>....<fn> fields are not compatible with the <k1>, <k2>...<kn> key fields, the SAP system automatically converts them into the compatible format.

Deleting a Line by Using the INDEX Clause

Use the following syntax to delete the records of an internal table based on its index:

```
DELETE <internal_tab> [INDEX <index_number>].
```

In this syntax, the DELETE statement is used to delete a line from the <internal_tab> table by specifying the <index_number> index with the INDEX clause. If the line is deleted successfully, the index of the subsequent lines in the table is reduced by 1 and the value of the SY-SUBRC variable is set to 0. However, if the delete operation is unsuccessful, the value of the SY-SUBRC variable is set to 4. In other words, when the table does not contain the line of the given <index_number> index number, the value of the SY-SUBRC variable is set to 4.

Note: Without the INDEX clause, you can use the DELETE statement only in a loop construction. In this case, the user deletes the current loop line and the <index_number> index is set implicitly to the value of the SY-TABIX variable.

Deleting Multiple Lines by Specifying a Condition

The DELETE statement is also used to delete one or more lines by specifying a condition in the WHERE clause. The syntax of the DELETE statement used to delete multiple lines based on specific conditions is:

```
DELETE <internal_tab> WHERE <cond>.
```

In this syntax, all the lines that satisfy the <cond> logical condition are deleted from the <internal_tab> table. The logical condition can consist of more than one comparison. In each comparison, the first operand must be a component of the line structure. If the lines of the table are not structured, the first operand can be the expression TABLE LINE. The comparison then applies to the entire line. If at least one line is deleted, the SAP system sets the value of the SY-SUBRC variable to 0; otherwise, the value is set to 4.

Deleting Multiple Lines by Using an Index or Condition

To delete one or more lines from an internal table, you can specify a condition in the WHERE clause or an index within the DELETE statement. The following syntax of the DELETE statement is used to delete multiple lines from an internal table, on the basis of either their line index or by the conditions specified in the WHERE clause:

```
DELETE <internal_tab> [FROM <n1>] [TO <n2>] [WHERE
<condition>].
```

In this syntax, the use of the FROM, TO, and WHERE clauses is optional in the DELETE statement. Apart from using the WHERE clause in the DELETE statement, the user can specify the lines that have to be deleted by specifying the index within the FROM and TO clauses. The SAP system deletes all the lines of the <internal_tab> internal table whose indexes lie between the <n1> and <n2> expressions. The task of deleting lines from an internal table by specifying an index between the FROM and TO clauses is similar to the task of deleting lines by specifying a condition in the WHERE clause.

Note that if the FROM clause is not specified, the SAP system deletes lines from the first line onwards; and if the TO clause is not specified, the SAP system deletes lines up to the last line (including the last line).

Deleting Duplicate Entries

The syntax to use the DELETE statement to delete adjacent duplicate lines or entries of an internal table is:

```
DELETE ADJACENT DUPLICATE ENTRIES FROM <internal_tab>
                    [COMPARING <f1> <f2> ...
                                     |ALL FIELDS].
```

In this syntax, the SAP system deletes all adjacent duplicate entries from the <internal_tab> internal table.

An internal table can have duplicate entries if it fulfills any of the following criteria:

- The content of the key fields of the table is identical in one or more lines when the COMPARING clause is not used.
- The content of the specified <f1> <f2>... fields of the table is identical in one or more lines when the COMPARING clause is used.
- The content of all fields of the table is identical in one or more lines when the COMPARING ALL FIELDS clause is used.

Examples Showing Deletion of Lines

Listing 7.30 shows how to delete a line by specifying a table key:

```
REPORT ZDELETELINES_DEMO.

*/Creating an internal table with four lines

DATA: BEGIN OF LINE,
COLA TYPE I,
COLB TYPE I,
END OF LINE.

DATA MyTable LIKE HASHED TABLE OF LINE WITH UNIQUE KEY
COLA.

DO 4 TIMES.
LINE-COLA = SY-INDEX.
LINE-COLB = SY-INDEX ** 2.
INSERT LINE INTO TABLE MyTable.
ENDDO.

*/Deleting the first and third lines from the internal
table

LINE-COLA = 1.

DELETE TABLE Mytable: FROM LINE,
WITH TABLE KEY COLA = 3.

LOOP AT MyTable INTO LINE.
WRITE: / LINE-COLA, LINE-COLB.
ENDLOOP.
```

LISTING 7.30 **Deleting a line by a table key**

In Listing 7.30, MyTable is a hashed table with two fields, `COLA` and `COLB`. Initially, MyTable is populated with four lines, where the `COLA` contains the values 1, 2, 3, and 4, while the `COLB` contains the values 1, 4, 9, and 16. The

DELETE statement is used to delete the lines from MyTable where the value of the COLA key field is 1 or 3.

After deletion, the COLA field of MyTable contains the values 2 and 4, as shown in Figure 7.37:

FIGURE 7.37 **Deleting lines by using a table key**

Listing 7.31 shows how to delete lines from an internal table by specifying a condition that uses the > and < comparison operators in the DELETE statement:

```
REPORT ZDELETELINES_DEMO.

*/Creating an internal table with six lines

DATA: BEGIN OF LINE,
COLA TYPE I,
COLB TYPE I,
END OF LINE.

DATA MyTable LIKE HASHED TABLE OF LINE WITH UNIQUE KEY
COLA.

DO 6 TIMES.
LINE-COLA = SY-INDEX.
LINE-COLB = SY-INDEX ** 3.
INSERT LINE INTO TABLE MyTable.
ENDDO.
```

Continued

```
*/Deleting the lines of the internal table, on the basis of
a condition by using comparison operators

DELETE MyTable WHERE (COLB > 8) AND (COLA < 5).
LOOP AT MyTable INTO LINE.
WRITE: / LINE-COLA, LINE-COLB.
ENDLOOP.
```

LISTING 7.31 **Deleting lines by specifying a condition in the DELETE statement**

In Listing 7.31, MyTable is a hashed table with two fields, `COLA` and `COLB`. Initially, MyTable is populated with six lines, where the `COLA` field contains the values 1, 2, 3, 4, 5, and 6, and the `COLB` field contains the values 1, 8, 27, 64, 125, and 216. The `DELETE` statement deletes the lines of MyTable in which the values of the `COLB` field are greater than 8 and the `COLA` field values are less than 5. Figure 7.38 shows the remaining lines of MyTable, after the deletion:

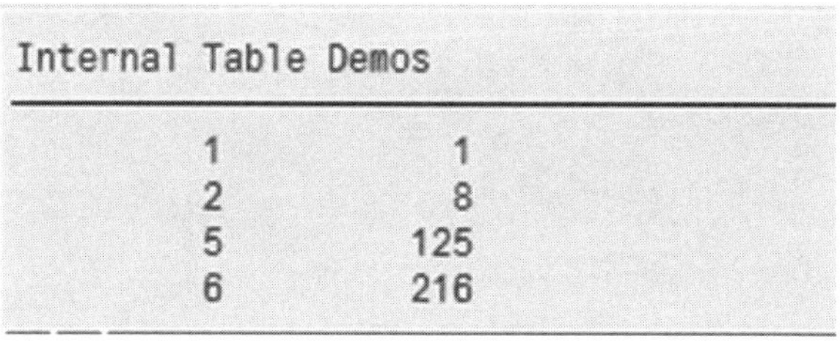

```
Internal Table Demos
----------------------------------------
        1          1
        2          8
        5        125
        6        216
```


FIGURE 7.38 **Deleting lines by specifying a condition**

Listing 7.32 shows how to delete duplicate lines of a table.

```
REPORT ZDELETELINES_DEMO.
*/Creating an internal table with seven lines
DATA OFF TYPE I.

DATA: BEGIN OF LINE,
```

Continued

```
COL1 TYPE I,
COL2 TYPE C,
END OF LINE.

DATA INTERNAL_TAB LIKE STANDARD TABLE OF LINE
       WITH NON-UNIQUE KEY COL2.

LINE-COL1 = 1. LINE-COL2 = 'A'. APPEND LINE TO
INTERNAL_TAB.
LINE-COL1 = 1. LINE-COL2 = 'A'. APPEND LINE TO
INTERNAL_TAB.
LINE-COL1 = 1. LINE-COL2 = 'B'. APPEND LINE TO
INTERNAL_TAB.
LINE-COL1 = 2. LINE-COL2 = 'B'. APPEND LINE TO
INTERNAL_TAB.
LINE-COL1 = 3. LINE-COL2 = 'B'. APPEND LINE TO
INTERNAL_TAB.
LINE-COL1 = 4. LINE-COL2 = 'B'. APPEND LINE TO
INTERNAL_TAB.
LINE-COL1 = 5. LINE-COL2 = 'A'. APPEND LINE TO
INTERNAL_TAB.

*/Deleting the adjacent duplicate entries on the basis of
all fields

OFF = 0. PERFORM LIST.

DELETE ADJACENT DUPLICATES FROM INTERNAL_TAB COMPARING ALL
FIELDS.

*/Deleting the adjacent duplicate entries on the basis of
COL1 field
```

Continued

```
OFF = 14. PERFORM LIST.

DELETE ADJACENT DUPLICATES FROM INTERNAL_TAB COMPARING
COL1.

*/Deleting the adjacent duplicate entries on the basis of
any individual field

OFF = 28. PERFORM LIST.

DELETE ADJACENT DUPLICATES FROM INTERNAL_TAB.
OFF = 42. PERFORM LIST.

FORM LIST.
  SKIP TO LINE 3.
  LOOP AT INTERNAL_TAB INTO LINE.
    WRITE: AT /OFF LINE-COL1, LINE-COL2.
  ENDLOOP.
ENDFORM.
```

LISTING 7.32 **Deleting duplicate lines of a table**

In Listing 7.32, a standard table is created and populated with data. The first DELETE statement deletes the second line from the INTERNAL_TAB internal table because this line has the same content as the first line. The second DELETE statement deletes the second line from the remaining lines stored in the table because the content of the COL1 field is the same as that of the first line. The third DELETE statement deletes the third and fourth lines from the remaining lines of the table because the content of the COL2 default key field is the same as that of the second line. Although the content of the default key is the same for the first and the fifth lines, the fifth line is not deleted because it is not adjacent to the first line. Figure 7.39 shows the output of Listing 7.32:

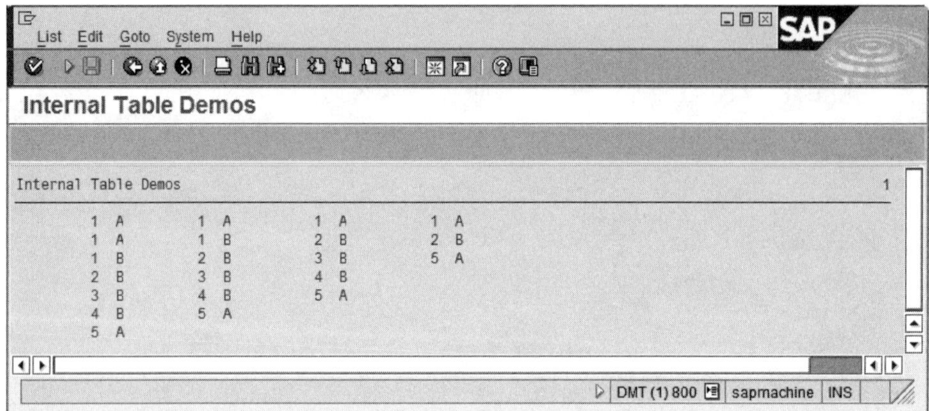

FIGURE 7.39 **Deleting duplicate lines**

Listing 7.33 shows how to delete the lines of an internal table by using the INDEX clause in the DELETE statement:

```
REPORT ZDELETELINES_DEMO.
*/Creating an internal table with six lines
DATA: BEGIN OF LINE,
        COLA TYPE I,
        COLB TYPE I,
       END OF LINE.
DATA MyTable LIKE SORTED TABLE OF LINE WITH UNIQUE KEY
COLA.
DO 6 TIMES.
  LINE-COLA = SY-INDEX.
  LINE-COLB = SY-INDEX ** 3.
  APPEND LINE TO MyTable.
ENDDO.
*/Deleting the lines specified at index number 2, 3, and
5
DELETE Mytable INDEX: 2, 3, 5.
WRITE: 'SY-SUBRC =', SY-SUBRC.
```

Continued

```
SKIP.
LOOP AT MyTable INTO LINE.
  WRITE: / SY-TABIX, LINE-COLA, LINE-COLB.
ENDLOOP.
```

LISTING 7.33 **Deleting lines by using the INDEX clause**

In Listing 7.33, MyTable is a sorted table with the `LINE` line type, initially populated with six lines. The `COLA` field of MyTable contains the values of the `SY-INDEX` variable and the `COLB` field of MyTable contains the cube of the values of the `SY-INDEX` variable. The `DELETE` statement is used to delete the lines of this table at the specified `INDEX` numbers, i.e., 2, 3, and 5. The value of the `SY-SUBRC` variable is set to 4 as the third delete operation, which deletes the line at the index number 5, fails. This is because `INDEX 2` deletes the second line, `INDEX 3` deletes the fourth line (because the fourth line shifts to the third place when the second line is deleted), but `INDEX 5` has no line to delete. In other words, the third delete operation fails because the table now has only four lines. Figure 7.40 shows the output of Listing 7.33:

```
Internal Table Demos
------------------------------------
SY-SUBRC =     4

         1        1        1
         2        3       27
         3        5      125
         4        6      216
```


FIGURE 7.40 **Deleting lines by using the INDEX clause**

Listing 7.34 shows how to delete the lines from an internal table by using the `DELETE` statement in a loop construction:

```
REPORT ZDELETELINES_DEMO.
*/Creating an internal table with ten lines
DATA: BEGIN OF LINE,
           COLA TYPE I,
           COLB TYPE I,
      END OF LINE.
```

Continued

```
DATA MyTable LIKE TABLE OF LINE.
DO 10 TIMES.
  LINE-COLA = SY-INDEX.
  LINE-COLB = SY-INDEX ** 2.
  APPEND LINE TO MyTable.
ENDDO.
*/Deleting the lines of the table, in which the value of
COLA is less than 4
LOOP AT MyTable INTO LINE.
   IF LINE-COLA < 4.
     DELETE MyTable.
   ENDIF.
ENDLOOP.
LOOP AT MyTable INTO LINE.
   WRITE: / SY-TABIX, LINE-COLA, LINE-COLB.
ENDLOOP.
```

LISTING 7.34 **Deleting lines by using the DELETE statement in a loop construction**

In Listing 7.34, MyTable is an internal table with the `LINE` line type, initially populated with 10 lines. The `COLA` field of MyTable contains the values of the `SY-INDEX` variable, and the `COLB` field of MyTable contains the square of the values of the `SY-INDEX` variable. The `DELETE` statement is used in a loop construction to delete the lines from MyTable where the value of the `COLA` field is less than 4. Figure 7.41 shows the lines of MyTable after deleting the lines of the table by using the `DELETE` statement in a loop construction:

```
1     4     16
2     5     25
3     6     36
4     7     49
5     8     64
6     9     81
7    10    100
```


FIGURE 7.41 **Deleting lines by using a loop construction**

Listing 7.35 shows how to delete lines from an internal table based on an index and a condition:

```
REPORT ZDELETELINES_DEMO.
*/Creating an internal table with ten lines
DATA: BEGIN OF LINE,
COLA TYPE I,
COLB TYPE I,
END OF LINE.
DATA MyTable LIKE TABLE OF LINE.
DO 10 TIMES.
  LINE-COLA = SY-INDEX.
  LINE-COLB = SY-INDEX ** 3.
  APPEND LINE TO MyTable.
ENDDO.
*/Deleting the lines of the table on the basis of a range
and a condition
DELETE MyTable FROM 3 TO 6 WHERE COLB > 8.
LOOP AT MyTable INTO LINE.
  WRITE: / LINE-COLA, LINE-COLB.
ENDLOOP.
```

LISTING 7.35 **Deleting lines by specifying an index with a condition in the DELETE statement**

In Listing 7.35, MyTable is an internal table with the `LINE` line type, initially populated with 10 lines. The `COLA` field of MyTable contains the values of the `SY-INDEX` variable, and the `COLB` field of MyTable contains the cube of the values of the `SY-INDEX` variable. The `DELETE` statement is used to delete a range of lines from the third line to the sixth line. In addition, the value of the `COLB` field is greater than 8. Figure 7.42 shows the output of Listing 7.35:

```
 1        1
 2        8
 7      343
 8      512
 9      729
10    1,000
```


FIGURE 7.42 **Deleting lines by specifying an index and a condition**

In Figure 7.42, you see that the records corresponding to the values 3 to 6 in the COLA field are deleted.

Searching Table Entries

Besides operations such as inserting, modifying, and deleting lines, you can perform a search operation in internal tables. The SEARCH...FOR statement is used to search for character strings in index tables. The BINARY SEARCH clause is used with the READ statement to perform a binary search in standard tables.

Now, let's learn how to search character strings and perform binary searches in index tables.

Finding Character Strings in Index Tables

The SEARCH...FOR statement is used to find a character string in the records of an index table. The syntax of the SEARCH...FOR statement is:

```
SEARCH <internal_tab> FOR <text_string> <options>.
```

In this syntax, the <internal_tab> expression represents an indexed internal table and the <text_string> expression represents a character string. The <text_string> string is searched within the records of the <internal_tab> table. If the SAP system finds the <text_string> string, the value of the SY-SUBRC system variable is set to 0, and the value of the SY-TABIX system variable is set to the index of the record in the table in which the string is found. On the contrary, if the string is not found in any record of the table, the value of the SY-SUBRC variable is set to 4.

In the <options> expression, you can use any of the following clauses to search entries in internal tables:

- ABBREVIATED—Searches the <internal_tab> table for an abbreviated word in the <text_string> expression. In the <internal_tab> table, the abbreviated characters can be separated by using other characters, such as, and ;. Note that the first character of the word stored in the <text_string> expression and the first character of a record of the internal table must be the same.

- STARTING AT <internal_tab_line>—Searches the <text_string> string that starts from the <internal_tab_line> line in the <internal_tab> table. However, the <internal_tab_line> expression can also be a variable.
- ENDING AT <internal_tab_line>—Searches the <text_string> string up to the <internal_tab_line> line of the <internal_tab> table. The <internal_tab_line> expression can also be a variable.
- AND MARK—Searches the <text_string> string in the <internal_tab> table. If the specified string is found in the table, all the characters in the search string (and those characters when the ABBREVIATED clause is used) are converted to uppercase.

Listing 7.36 shows how to search for a string in an index table by using the AND MARK clause in the SEARCH...FOR statement:

```
REPORT ZSEARCHLINES_DEMO.

*/Creating an internal table with ten lines

DATA: BEGIN OF line,
         ID(4) TYPE c,
         Name(20) TYPE c,
      END OF line.

DATA MyTable LIKE SORTED TABLE OF line WITH UNIQUE KEY
ID.
DATA num(2) TYPE n.
DO 10 TIMES.
   line-ID = sy-index.
   num = sy-index.
   CONCATENATE 'Line number ' num INTO line-Name.
   APPEND line TO MyTable.
ENDDO.
LOOP AT MyTable INTO LINE.
```

Continued

```
    WRITE: / LINE-ID, LINE-Name.
ENDLOOP.
*/Searching a particular line within the table

SEARCH MyTable FOR 'Number04' AND MARK.

WRITE: /'''Number04'' found at line', (1) sy-tabix,
        'with offset', (1) sy-fdpos.
SKIP.

READ TABLE MyTable INTO line INDEX sy-tabix.
WRITE: / line-ID, line-Name.
```

LISTING 7.36 **Using the SEARCH. . .FOR statement to find a character string in an index table**

In Listing 7.36, MyTable is a sorted table containing 10 lines. The `SEARCH` statement is used to find the line that contains the string text `Number04`. The value of the `SY-FDPOS` variable is set to 9, because it contains the offset position of the string in the table line. When the search string is found, all the characters in the search string are converted to uppercase because of the `AND MARK` clause. Figure 7.43 shows the output of Listing 7.36:

```
Internal Table Demos
------------------------------------------
  1  Line number01
  2  Line number02
  3  Line number03
  4  Line number04
  5  Line number05
  6  Line number06
  7  Line number07
  8  Line number08
  9  Line number09
 10  Line number10
'Number04' found at line 4 with offset 9

  4  Line NUMBER04
```


FIGURE 7.43 **Searching with the AND MARK option**

In Figure 7.43, notice that the string Number04 is found at the fourth line.

Binary Search in Standard Tables

The BINARY SEARCH clause is used in the READ statement to search for the records of a standard table based on a key other than the default key.

The following syntax shows the use of the BINARY SEARCH clause in the READ statement:

```
READ TABLE <internal_tab> WITH KEY <k1> = <f1>...<kn> =
<fn> <result>
BINARY SEARCH.
```

When the BINARY SEARCH clause is used to search the records of internal tables, the tables must be of the standard type and must be sorted in ascending order by specifying a search key. Listing 7.37 shows a binary search in a standard table:

```
REPORT ZBINARYSEARCH_DEMO.

*/Creating an internal table with three lines
DATA: BEGIN OF LINE,
        COLA TYPE I,
        COLB TYPE I,
      END OF LINE.
DATA MYTABLE LIKE STANDARD TABLE OF LINE.

DO 3 TIMES.
 LINE-COLA = SY-INDEX.
 LINE-COLB = SY-INDEX ** 2.
 APPEND LINE TO MYTABLE.
ENDDO.

SORT MYTABLE BY COLB.

*/Performing binary search on the basis of a key value
```

Continued

```
READ TABLE MYTABLE WITH KEY COLB = 4 INTO LINE BINARY
SEARCH.

WRITE: 'SY-SUBRC =', SY-SUBRC.
```

LISTING 7.37 **Performing a binary search in a standard table**

In Listing 7.37, MYTABLE is a standard internal table, initially populated with three lines. The COLA field of MYTABLE contains the values of the SY-INDEX variable (1, 2, 3), and the COLB field of MYTABLE contains the square of the values of the SY-INDEX variable (1, 4, 9). The SORT statement is used to sort the contents of MYTABLE according to the values in the COLB field. The READ statement uses a binary search to find the line in the table where the value of COLB is 4. Figure 7.44 displays the output of Listing 7.37:

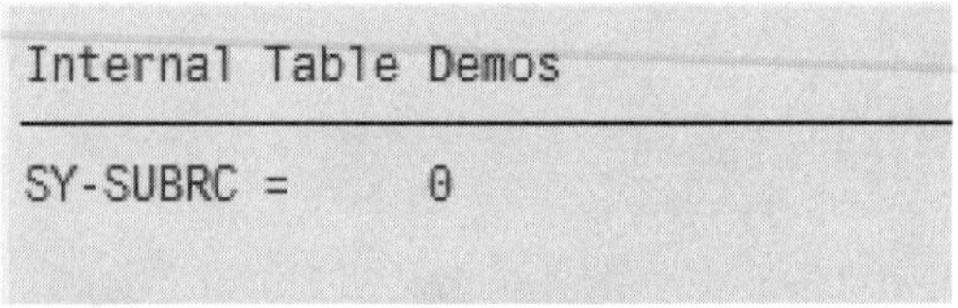

```
Internal Table Demos
--------------------
SY-SUBRC =      0
```


FIGURE 7.44 **The result of a binary search**

In Figure 7.44, the value of the SY-SUBRC variable is shown as 0, which means that a line has been searched successfully based on a binary search, where the value of the COLB field in MYTABLE is 4.

Maintaining Internal Tables

ABAP provides various statements to maintain internal tables. Table 7.2 shows a list of ABAP statements used to maintain internal tables with and without header lines:

Statement for Internal Tables Without Header Lines	Statement for Internal Tables With Header Lines
INSERT <work_area_itab> INTO TABLE <internal_tab>.	INSERT TABLE <internal_tab>.
COLLECT <work_area_itab> INTO<internal_tab>.	COLLECT <internal_tab>.
READ TABLE <internal_tab>... INTO <work_area_itab>.	READ TABLE <internal_tab>...
MODIFY TABLE <internal_tab> FROM <work_area_itab>...	MODIFY TABLE <internal_tab>...
MODIFY <internal tab> FROM <work_area_tab>...WHERE...	MODIFY <internal_tab>... WHERE...
DELETE TABLE <internal_tab> FROM <work_area_itab>.	DELETE TABLE <internal_tab>.
LOOP AT <internal_tab> INTO <work_area_itab> ...	LOOP AT <internal_tab> ...

TABLE 7.2 Operations for all table types (Standard, Sorted, and Hashed)

Table 7.3 lists ABAP statements in which the header lines and work areas are the same/different for indexed internal tables:

Statement for Internal Tables Without Header Lines	Statement for Internal Tables With Header Lines
APPEND <work_area_itab> TO <internal_tab>.	APPEND <internal_tab>.
INSERT <work_area_itab> INTO <internal_tab> ...	INSERT <internal_tab> ...
MODIFY <internal_tab> FROM <work_area_itab> ...	MODIFY <internal_tab> ...

TABLE 7.3 Operations for index tables

> **Note:** The fact that a table and its header line have the same name can cause confusion in operations involving entire internal tables. To avoid such confusion, the user should use internal tables with differently named work areas.

Now, let's discuss control break processing statements, such as `AT FIRST`, `AT LAST`, `AT NEW`, `AT END OF`, and `ON CHANGE OF`, which are used in loops and help retrieve data from internal tables and prepare a report from the retrieved data.

CONTROL BREAK PROCESSING

Sometimes a user may want to display summarized data, such as, the sum of data, at the top or bottom of the report or the subtotals of data in the body of the report. In such cases, users can read the data from internal tables by using control break statements in the loops. Control break statements are used within the body of a loop construction and are executed when a specific condition within the loop is met. Control break statements include the following:

- The `AT FIRST` and `AT LAST` statements
- The `AT NEW` and `AT END OF` statements
- The `SUM` statement
- The `ON CHANGE OF` statement

Now, let's discuss each statement in detail.

The `AT FIRST` and `AT LAST` Statements

The `AT FIRST...ENDAT` and `AT LAST...ENDAT` statements are used to control code execution when the loop construction containing the code is processed for the first and last time, respectively. The following syntax shows the use of the `AT FIRST` and `AT LAST` statements:

```
LOOP AT <internal_tab>.
.....
    AT FIRST.
.......
    ENDAT.
AT LAST.
.......
```

Continued

```
    ENDAT.
.......
ENDLOOP.
```

In the preceding syntax, `<internal_tab>` is the name of an internal table. The dotted lines (...) represent any number of lines of code (even zero).

The AT FIRST and AT LAST statements are used only in the loop, not in the SELECT statement. These statements can be used in any sequence, meaning that it is not necessary that the AT FIRST statement should be written before the AT LAST statement. There is no limitation on the number of times the statements appear inside the loop. In other words, the user can use any number of AT FIRST and AT LAST statements inside the loop. However, remember that nesting of these statements is not allowed; that is, the user cannot nest the AT FIRST statement inside the AT LAST...ENDAT pair. As soon as the processing of a loop starts, the execution of the AT FIRST...ENDAT statement also starts, and when the loop is processed for the last time, the AT LAST...ENDAT statement is executed. Moreover, if there are more than one occurrence of the AT FIRST...ENDAT statement, all the occurrences are executed at the time the loop starts processing. Similarly, in the case of the AT LAST...ENDAT statement, all the occurrences of the statement are executed when the loop is processed for the last time.

The AT FIRST...ENDAT statement is used to initialize a loop for processing, displaying the total sum of the data at the top of a report and information in the heading section of a report.

The AT LAST...ENDAT statement is used to terminate the processing of a loop, displaying the total sum of data at the bottom of a report and information in the footer section of a report.

Listing 7.38 shows the working of the AT FIRST and AT LAST statements:

```
REPORT ZCONTROL_BREAK_PROS_DEMO.
TABLES: LFA1.
DATA IT1 LIKE LFA1 OCCURS 25 WITH HEADER LINE.
SELECT * FROM LFA1 UP TO 25 ROWS INTO TABLE IT1 WHERE
LAND1 = 'DE'.
LOOP AT IT1.
```

Continued

```
*/Using AT FIRST statement
AT FIRST.
        WRITE: / 'Client',
12 'Account Number',
27 'Country Key',
59 'Name1'.
ULINE.
ENDAT.

WRITE:/ IT1-MANDT,
       12 IT1-LIFNR,
       27 IT1-LAND1,
       59 IT1-NAME1.
*/Using AT LAST statement
       AT LAST.

        WRITE:/ '******',
             12 '*************',
             27 '**********',
             59 '******************************'.

ENDAT.
ENDLOOP.
```

LISTING 7.38 **Using the AT FIRST and AT LAST statements**

In Listing 7.38, the `TABLES` statement is used to create a work area having the same structure as that of the LFA1 table. The `DATA` statement is used to define the IT1 internal table with a structure similar to that of the LFA1 database table. The `SELECT` statement is used to fill the IT1 table with 25 records of the LFA1 table, where the `LAND1` field of the LFA1 table is DE. The `AT FIRST` statement is used to show the title of the fields of the IT1 table and the `AT LAST` statement is used to show the asterisk (*) character at the end, after displaying all the records. Figure 7.45 shows the output of Listing 7.38:

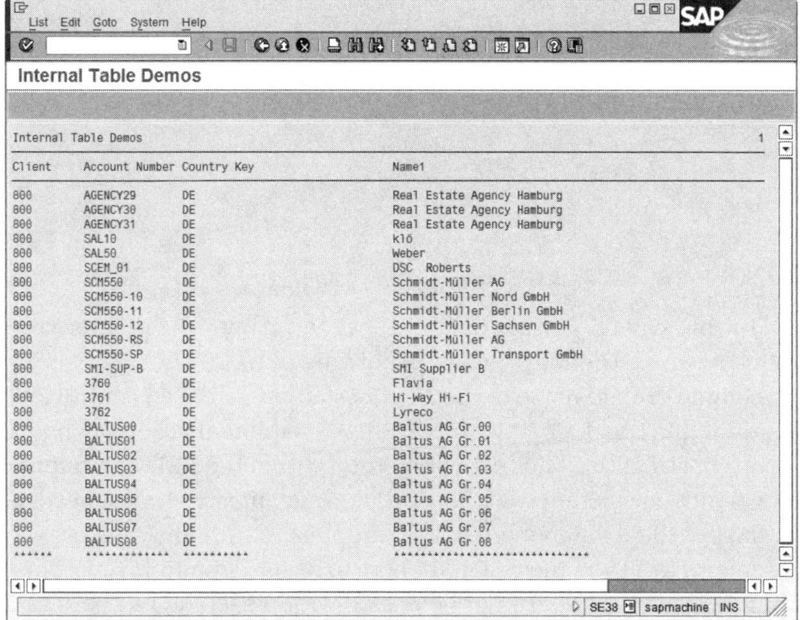

FIGURE 7.45 **Output showing the use of control break statements**

In Figure 7.45, you can see that the column titles are shown at the top of the records and the asterisk (*) character is used at the bottom of the records.

The `AT NEW` and `AT END OF` Statements

The `AT NEW...ENDAT` and `AT END OF...ENDAT` statements are used to detect any change when one loop passes to the next value in a field of an internal table. These statements help execute the code at the beginning and end of a group of lines of an internal table. The following syntax shows how to use the `AT NEW...ENDAT` and `AT END OF...ENDAT` statements:

```
SORT BY Col_name.
   LOOP AT <internal_tab>.
```

Continued

```
.....
   AT NEW Col_name.
      .......
      ENDAT.
   AT END OF Col_name.
      .......
      ENDAT.
.......
ENDLOOP.
```

In this syntax, `<internal_tab>` is the name of the internal table. The dotted lines (....) denote the number of lines of code. The `Col_name` expression is a column or field name of the `AT NEW` statement, called control level. The `AT NEW...ENDAT` and `AT END OF...ENDAT` statements can only be used within a loop construction. They cannot be used within the `SELECT` statement. These statements can also appear in any order, which means it is not necessary for the `AT NEW...ENDAT` statement to always appear before the `AT END OF...ENDAT` statement. In a loop, these statements can be used multiple times for execution. These statements also cannot be nested within each other.

Whenever the value in the `Col_name` control level component changes, the lines of code in the `AT NEW...ENDAT` statement are executed. This block (lines of code) is also executed during passing the first loop or if any fields to the left of the `Col_name` control level component change. Between the `AT NEW` and the `ENDAT` statements, the numeric fields to the right of the `Col_name` control level component are set to zero, while the non-numeric fields are populated with the asterisk (*) character.

Listing 7.39 shows how to use the `AT NEW...ENDAT` statements:

```
REPORT ZCONTROL_BREAK_PROS_DEMO.
*/Using AT NEW and ENDAT statements
DATA : BEGIN OF ROW OCCURS 0,
FIELD1,
FIELD2,
END OF ROW.
ROW = '1A'.
```

Continued

```
APPEND ROW.
ROW = '1B'.
APPEND ROW.

ROW = '2B'.
APPEND ROW.

ROW = '3A'.
APPEND ROW.

ROW = '2A'.
APPEND ROW.

ROW = '1C'.
APPEND ROW.

ROW = '3B'.
APPEND ROW.

ROW = '3C'.
APPEND ROW.

ROW = '2C'.
APPEND ROW.

ROW = '2A'.
APPEND ROW.

ROW = '1C'.
APPEND ROW.

SORT ROW BY FIELD1.
LOOP AT ROW.
 AT NEW FIELD1.
     WRITE: / ROW-FIELD1, ROW-FIELD2.
ENDAT.
```

Continued

```
ENDLOOP.
SORT ROW BY FIELD2.
LOOP AT ROW.
AT NEW FIELD2.
   WRITE: / ROW-FIELD1, ROW-FIELD2.
ENDAT.
ENDLOOP.
```

LISTING 7.39 **Using the AT NEW...ENDAT statements**

In Listing 7.39, the `Field1` field is sorted. The `AT FIRST` statement is triggered for the first time through a loop and each time, there is a change in the `Field1` field. Now, the internal table is sorted again by the `Field2` field. The `AT NEW` statement is triggered each time there is a change in the value of the `Field1` or `Field2` field, because a control level is triggered whenever the value of the `Field2` field or of a field before `Field2` changes. Figure 7.46 shows the output of Listing 7.39:

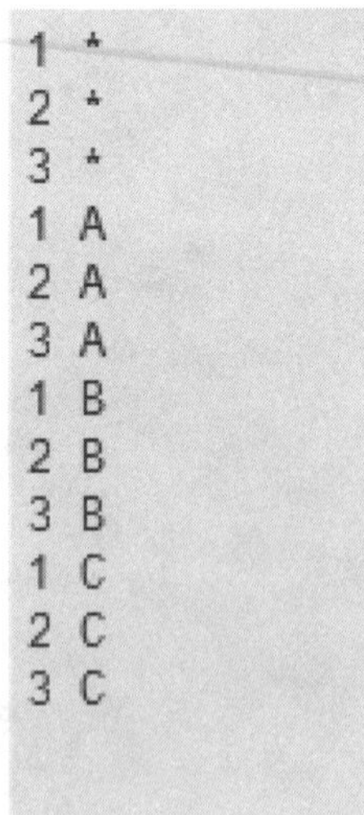

1 *
2 *
3 *
1 A
2 A
3 A
1 B
2 B
3 B
1 C
2 C
3 C

FIGURE 7.46 **Result of the AT NEW statement**

In Figure 7.46, the first five records are shown in numerical order and the last five records are shown in alphabetical order.

The lines of code between the AT END OF...ENDAT pair of statements is executed under the following conditions:

- When there is a change in the value of the Col_name control level
- When there is a change in a field before the Col_name control level
- When the SAP system finds the last row of the table

Listing 7.40 shows the use of the AT END OF statement:

```
REPORT ZCONTROL_BREAK_PROS_DEMO.
*/Using at end and ENDAT statements
DATA : BEGIN OF ROW OCCURS 0,
FIELD1,
FIELD2,
END OF ROW.
ROW = '1A'.
APPEND ROW.

ROW = '4B'.
APPEND ROW.

ROW = '2C'.
APPEND ROW.

ROW = '5D'.
APPEND ROW.

ROW = '3E'.
APPEND ROW.

SORT ROW BY FIELD1.
LOOP AT ROW.
  AT NEW FIELD1.
  WRITE: /'Start', ROW-FIELD1.
```

Continued

```
    ENDAT.
    WRITE: /4 ROW-FIELD1.
AT END OF FIELD1.
WRITE:/ 'Stop', ROW-FIELD1.
ENDAT.
ENDLOOP.
```

LISTING 7.40 **Using the AT END OF statement**

In Listing 7.40, `Field1` is a control level and is sorted twice. The `AT NEW` statement is triggered each time the value in the `Field1` control level changes. The `AT END OF` statement executes when there is a change in the value of the `Field1` control level and reads the next or last row. Figure 7.47 shows the output of Listing 7.40:

```
Start 1
   1
Stop 1
Start 2
   2
Stop 2
Start 3
   3
Stop 3
Start 4
   4
Stop 4
Start 5
   5
```


FIGURE 7.47 **Sorting by using the AT NEW and AT END statements**

In Figure 7.47, the loop shows the message `Start` five times, along with the field number. However, the message `Stop` is displayed only four times because it appears only after the execution of the `AT END OF` statement. The last execution of this statement breaks the loop without displaying the `STOP` message.

The SUM Statement

The SUM statement is used to calculate the total of the values stored in the rows of a control level. The syntax to use the SUM statement is as follows:

```
AT FIRST/LAST/NEW/END OF.
....
SUM.
...
ENDAT.
```

In this syntax, the SUM statement is used to calculate the total of the values stored in a control-level component. Listing 7.41 illustrates the working of the SUM statement.

```
REPORT ZCONTROL_BREAK_PROS_DEMO.
DATA: BEGIN OF ROW OCCURS 0,
           FIELD1,
           FIELD2 TYPE I,
           FIELD3 TYPE I,
      END OF ROW.

ROW-FIELD1 = 'P'.
ROW-FIELD2 = 100.
ROW-FIELD3 = 11.
APPEND ROW.

ROW-FIELD1 = 'Q'.
ROW-FIELD2 = 300.
ROW-FIELD3 = 33.
APPEND ROW.

ROW-FIELD1 = 'R'.
ROW-FIELD2 = 200.
ROW-FIELD3 = 22.
APPEND ROW.
```

Continued

```
ROW-FIELD1 = 'Q'.
ROW-FIELD2 = 500.
ROW-FIELD3 = 55.
APPEND ROW.

SORT ROW BY FIELD1.
LOOP AT ROW.
*/Using the At new...Sum...Endat statement

AT NEW FIELD1.
SUM.
WRITE:/ 'Total=', ROW-FIELD1, ROW-FIELD2, ROW-FIELD3.
ENDAT.
WRITE:/ ROW-FIELD2, ROW-FIELD3.
ENDLOOP.
```

LISTING 7.41 **Using the SUM statement**

In Listing 7.41, the `SUM` statement is used to get the total of the values of the `Field2` and `Field3` fields based on the changes in the values of `Field1`. Figure 7.48 shows the output of Listing 7.41:

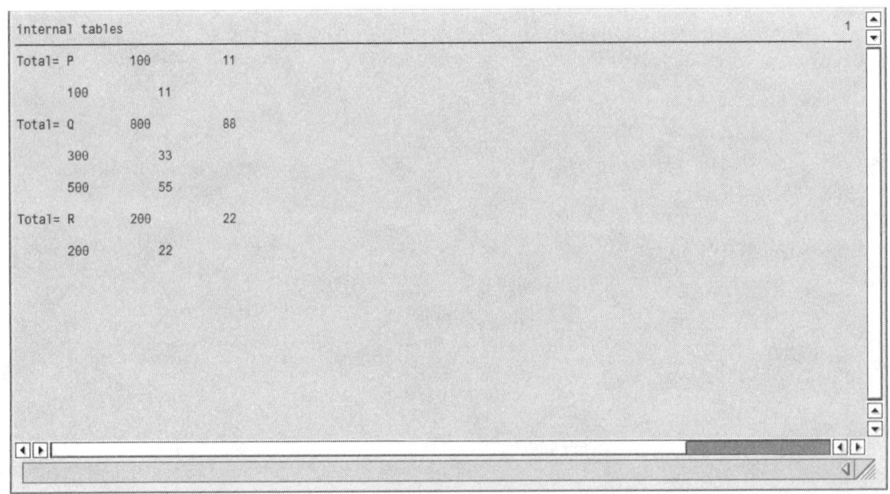

FIGURE 7.48 **Displaying the Sum of the values at the top**

In Figure 7.48, you see that the total value is shown at the top of each record where the values of the `Field1` field are P, Q, and R.

The `ON CHANGE OF` Statement

The functionality of the `ON CHANGE OF...ENDON` statement is similar to that of the `AT NEW` statement. The syntax to use the `ON CHANGE OF...ENDON` statement is as follows:

```
ON CHANGE OF V1 [OR V2...]
- - - - -
[ELSE.
- - - ]
ENDON.
```

In this syntax, `V1` and `V2` are variable or field string names. The dotted line (...) represents the conditions specified on the variables or field string names, and the dashed lines (- - -) denote any number of lines of code, or the lines of code between the `ON CHANGE OF...ENDON` pair of statements are executed if the value of any of the variables (`V1`, `V2`, and so on) changes. However, if no change is detected in the values of these variables and the `ELSE` clause is specified, the lines of code following the `ELSE` clause are executed.

The `ON CHANGE OF` statement can be executed by a change in one or more fields named after the `OF` clause and separated by the `OR` clause. These fields can be elementary fields or field strings. When the `ON CHANGE OF` statement is used within a loop, a change in a field to the left of the control level does not execute a control break statement. When the `ON CHANGE OF` statement is used in a loop, the values of the fields to the right side of the statement still contain their original values. The `ON CHANGE OF` statement can be used along with the `SUM` statement. The `SUM` statement finds the sum of all numeric fields except the fields that appear after the `OF` clause.

The use of the `ON CHANGE OF` statement is similar to that of the `AT NEW` statement, but there are few differences between the two as well. Table 7.4 lists the differences between the `AT NEW...ENDAT` and `ON CHANGE OF...ENDON` statements:

Parameter	ON CHANGE OF **Statement**	AT NEW **Statement**
Loop construction	Can be used in any kind of loop construction, beside AT LOOP... ENDLOOP, such as SELECT... ENDSELECT, CASE...ENDCASE, DO...ENDDO, and WHILE... ENDWHILE, and even inside GET events. In addition, the ON CHANGE OF statement can be used outside a loop construction.	Can only be used inside the AT LOOP... ENDLOOP statements. Note that the AT NEW statement is used with internal tables only.
WHERE Expression	Can be used in a loop along with the <internal_tab>WHERE... expression.	Cannot be used in the loop along with the <internal_tab> WHERE... expression.
ELSE Clause	Can be used between the ON CHANGE OF and ENDON statements.	Cannot be used between the AT NEW and ENDAT statements.

TABLE 7.4 Comparing the AT NEW. . .ENDAT and ON CHANGE OF. . .ENDON Statements

Now, let's consider some examples to show the use of the ON CHANGE OF statement and the difference between the ON CHANGE OF and AT NEW statements.

Listing 7.42 shows the working of the ON CHANGE OF statement:

```
REPORT ZCONTROL_BREAK_PROS_DEMO.
DATA: BEGIN OF ROW OCCURS 8,
FIELD1 TYPE I,
FIELD2,
FIELD3 TYPE I,
FIELD4,
END OF ROW.
ROW-FIELD1 = 10.
ROW-FIELD2 = 'A'.
```

Continued

```
ROW-FIELD3 = 111.
ROW-FIELD4 = 'P'.
APPEND ROW.

ROW-FIELD1 = 40.
ROW-FIELD2 = 'A'.
ROW-FIELD3 = 333.
ROW-FIELD4 = 'Q'.
APPEND ROW.

ROW-FIELD1 = 30.
ROW-FIELD2 = 'B'.
ROW-FIELD3 = 222.
ROW-FIELD4 = 'R'.
APPEND ROW.

ROW-FIELD1 = 40.
ROW-FIELD2 = 'B'.
ROW-FIELD3 = 444.
ROW-FIELD4 = 'S'.
APPEND ROW.

*/Using the On change of statements
LOOP AT ROW.
ON CHANGE OF ROW-FIELD2.
       WRITE: / ROW-FIELD1, ROW-FIELD2, ROW-FIELD3,
       ROW-FIELD4.
       ENDON.
ENDLOOP.
WRITE: /'Loop Ends'.

LOOP AT ROW.
AT FIRST.
WRITE: / 'Loop Resets'.
ENDAT.
ON CHANGE OF ROW-FIELD2.
```

Continued

```
    WRITE: / ROW-FIELD1, ROW-FIELD2, ROW-FIELD3,
    ROW-FIELD4.
ELSE.
WRITE: / 'On Change Of - Row Not Triggered',
SY-TABIX.
ENDON.
ENDLOOP.

WRITE: /'Loop Finishes'.
```

LISTING 7.42 **Using the ON CHANGE OF statement**

In Listing 7.42, ROW is an internal table and `FIELD1, FIELD2, FIELD3`,and `FIELD4` are its fields. This table is populated initially with four lines, where `FIELD1` stores 10, 140, 30, and 40; `FIELD2` stores A, A, B, and B; `FIELD3` stores 111, 333, 222, and 444; and `FIELD4` stores P, Q, R, and S. When the first loop is processed, it displays the values of all the fields only when there is a change in the values of `FIELD2`. The `WRITE` statement is then used to display the message Loop Ends. Finally, another loop starts along with displaying the message Loop Resets. It is processed by showing the values of all the fields only when there is a change in the values of `FIELD2`; otherwise, the message "`On Change Of - Row Not Triggered`" appears. Finally, this loop displays the message Loop Finishes. Figure 7.49 shows the output of Listing 7.42:

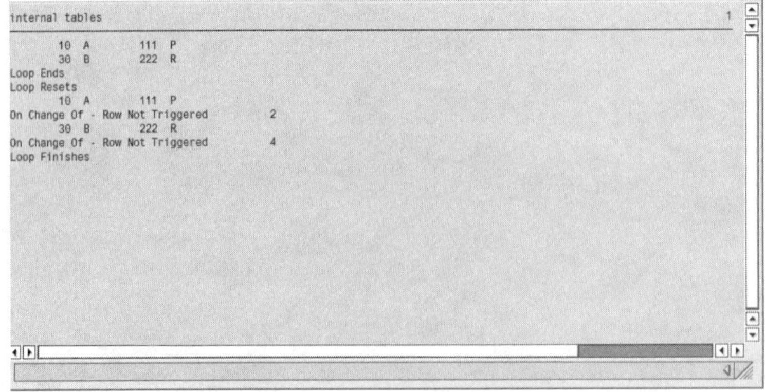

FIGURE 7.49 **Result of the ON CHANGE OF statement**

Listing 7.43 shows the difference between the `AT NEW...ENDAT` and `ON CHANGE OF...ENDON` statements:

```
REPORT ZCONTROL_BREAK_PROS_DEMO.

* Difference between the AT NEW...ENDAT and ON CHANGE OF...
ENDON statements
DATA : BEGIN OF ROW OCCURS 0,
FIELD1,
FIELD2,
END OF ROW.
ROW = '1A'.

APPEND ROW.
ROW = '1B'.

APPEND ROW.

ROW = '2B'.
APPEND ROW.

ROW = '3A'.

APPEND ROW.
ROW = '2A'.

APPEND ROW.
ROW = '1C'.

APPEND ROW.
ROW = '3B'.

APPEND ROW.
ROW = '3C'.

APPEND ROW.
```

Continued

```
ROW = '2C'.

APPEND ROW.
ROW = '2A'.

APPEND ROW.
ROW = '1C'.

APPEND ROW.
SORT ROW BY FIELD1.
WRITE:' AT NEW statement with Field1'.

LOOP AT ROW.
*the AT NEW statement with Field1
AT NEW FIELD1.
WRITE: / ROW-FIELD1, ROW-FIELD2.
ENDAT.

ENDLOOP.

WRITE:/'__________________________________________'.
WRITE:/' ON CHANGE OF statement with Field1'.

LOOP AT ROW.
*the ON CHANGE OF statement with Field1
ON CHANGE OF ROW-FIELD1.
    WRITE: / ROW-FIELD1, ROW-FIELD2.
ENDON.

ENDLOOP.
SORT ROW BY FIELD2.
WRITE:/'__________________________________________'.
WRITE:/' AT NEW statement with Field2'.

LOOP AT ROW.
*the AT NEW statement with Field2
```

Continued

```
AT NEW FIELD2.

WRITE: / ROW-FIELD1, ROW-FIELD2.
ENDAT.
ENDLOOP.
WRITE:/'__________________________________________'.

WRITE:/' ON CHANGE OF statement with Field2'.

LOOP AT ROW.
*the ON CHANGE OF statement with Field2

ON CHANGE OF ROW-FIELD2.
WRITE: / ROW-FIELD1, ROW-FIELD2.
ENDON.
ENDLOOP.
```

LISTING 7.43 **Showing the difference between the AT NEW. . .ENDAT and ON CHANGE OF. . .ENDON statements**

In Listing 7.43, ROW is an internal table and FIELD1 and FIELD2 are its fields. These fields are populated by various records, where FIELD1 stores numbers while FIELD2 stores characters. FIELD1 is sorted by the SORT statement and then used with the AT NEW statement in the AT LOOP. . .ENDAT statement. In addition, sorted FIELD1 is used with the ON CHANGE OF statement. Next, FIELD2 is sorted by the SORT statement and then used with the AT NEW and ON CHANGE OF statements.

In the output of Listing 7.43, you see that there is not much difference between the AT NEW and ON CHANGE OF statements when these statements are used with FIELD1, except that in case of AT NEW statement, characters are shown in the form of the asterisk (*) symbol. However, the values of the AT NEW and ON CHANGE OF statements are different if these statements are used with FIELD2. The difference is that the AT NEW statement shows the values when any change occurs in the FIELD2 or FIELD1 field. However, the ON CHANGE OF statement shows the values any change that occured only in the FIELD2 field. Figure 7.50 shows the output of Listing 7.43:

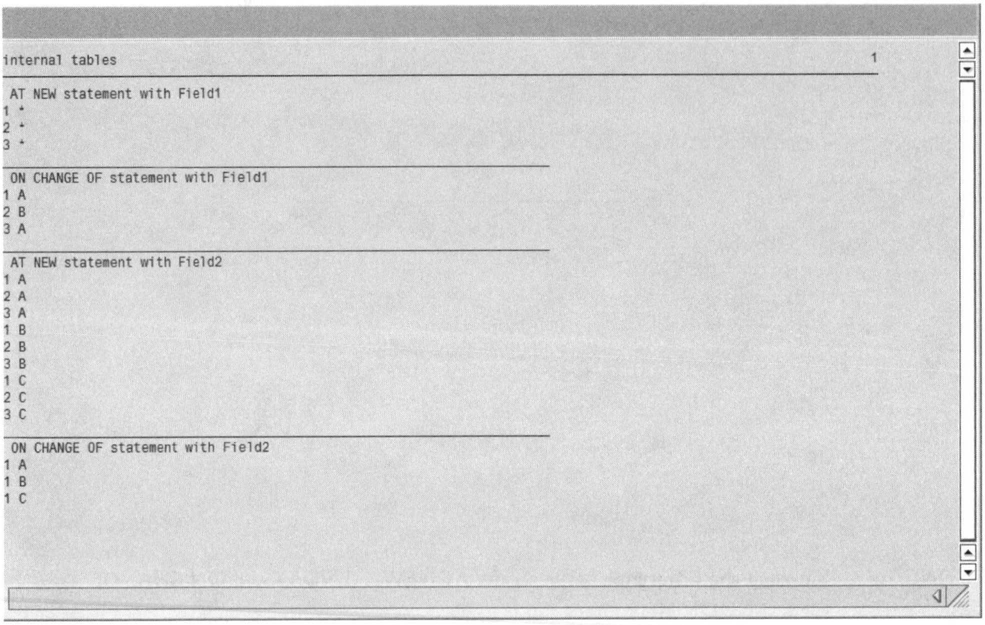

```
internal tables                                                    1

 AT NEW statement with Field1
1 *
2 *
3 *

 ON CHANGE OF statement with Field1
1 A
2 B
3 A

 AT NEW statement with Field2
1 A
2 A
3 A
1 B
2 B
3 B
1 C
2 C
3 C

 ON CHANGE OF statement with Field2
1 A
1 B
1 C
```


FIGURE 7.50 **Showing the difference between ON CHANGE OF and AT NEW statements**

SUMMARY

In this chapter, you have learned about internal tables, which are temporary tables created at runtime. In addition, you have learned about the data types of an internal table and the various types of internal tables, such as generic tables (any tables and index tables) and fully specified tables (standard tables, sorted tables, and hashed tables). You have also learned how to create internal tables by using the `TYPES` and `DATA` statements and perform functions on them, such as assigning, clearing, refreshing, and sorting internal tables, releasing the memory of internal tables, and comparing two tables. You have also learned about various operations, such as insertion, modification, and deletion of lines in an internal table, by using the `INSERT`, `READ`, `MODIFY`, and `DELETE` statements. Finally, you have learned about control break processing statements, such as `AT FIRST`, `AT NEW`, and `AT LAST`.

In the next chapter, you learn how ABAP programs access data in the SAP system through Open SQL statements, such as `INSERT`, `DELETE`, `UPDATE`, and `MODIFY`.

Chapter 8

Accessing Data in the SAP System

If you need information on:	*See page:*
Accessing Database Tables	412
Reading Data Using the SELECT Statement	416
Subqueries	465
Inserting Data into a Database Table	471
Updating Data in a Database Table	477
Deleting the Data from a Database Table	483
Modifying the Lines of Database Tables	488
Using Cursors to Read Data	490
Committing Database Changes	494

ABAP programs need to access various types of databases to ensure data persistency and implement the business logic of SAP applications. Data persistency means storing data at permanent places so that we can access it as and when required. The SAP system is equipped with a central relational database system (Database Dictionary), which is used to implement the concept of data persistency. A relational database is accessed by using Structured Query Language (SQL), which is a standardized language used to work with databases. A SAP system uses Open SQL statements, a subset of standard SQL, to access and maintain its central relational database. The Open SQL statements consist of a set of ABAP statements used to perform various operations, such as reading, inserting, deleting, and updating data in a database. Using Open SQL statements ensures that the SQL statements in ABAP programs can interoperate between various types of databases. Besides Open SQL statements, which include ABAP code elements, another category of standard SQL statements, Native SQL statements, contain only database manipulation statements. Database tables that are not administered by the ABAP Dictionary can be accessed by using Native SQL.

In this chapter, you learn how database tables are accessed by ABAP programs in an SAP system. You also learn how data is read from database tables by using subqueries and the `SELECT` statement and its various clauses, such as `INTO`, `WHERE`, and `GROUP BY`. Next, you learn how database operations, such as insert, update, and delete, are performed by using the `INSERT`, `UPDATE`, and `DELETE` statements, respectively. You also learn how cursors are used to read data from database tables. Finally, you learn how the `COMMIT WORK` and `ROLLBACK WORK` statements are used to save or revert the final changes made in a database, respectively.

ACCESSING DATABASE TABLES

In a relational database model, data is represented in the form of tables. We know that a table is a two-dimensional matrix consisting of rows or records (also known as lines in SAP) and columns (known as fields in SAP). Programmers generally use standard SQL, which is compatible with all databases, to access database tables. However, standard SQL statements do not ensure interoperability between different types of databases. As a result, SAP uses Open SQL statements, which are interoperable and compatible with all types of databases.

Each work process in the SAP R/3 system has a common database interface. The database interface converts all the database requests into the respective standard SQL statements to interact with the database tables stored in the ABAP Dictionary. Figure 8.1 shows a representation of how a database interface interacts with the components of an SAP R/3 system:

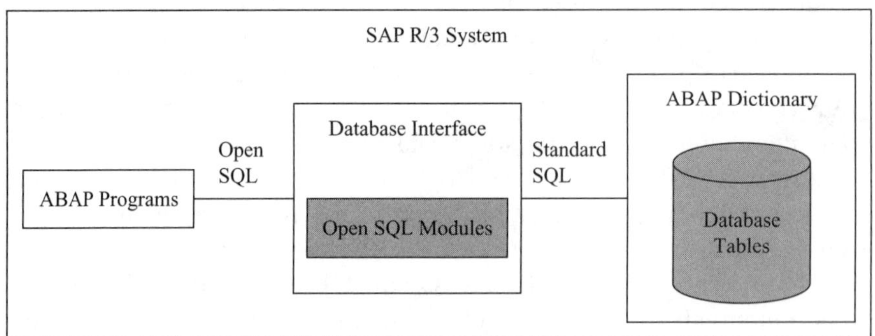

FIGURE 8.1 **Database interface in the SAP R/3 system**

As learned previously, in the SAP R/3 system, the ABAP programs communicate with the database by using the database interface. The ABAP Dictionary, which stores the database tables, uses the Open SQL statements to create and change database tables. The ABAP Dictionary allows users to create and administer database tables. It contains metadescriptions of all database tables in the SAP R/3 system.

In an SAP R/3 system, data from a database can be accessed by an ABAP program by using the following types of statements:

- Open SQL
- Native SQL

Now, let's discuss these statements in detail.

Open SQL

Open SQL, a subset of Standard SQL, consists of a set of ABAP statements that perform operations on the databases in a SAP R/3 system. It provides a uniform syntax and semantics for all the database systems supported by SAP. Consequently, ABAP programs that use Open SQL statements can work in any SAP R/3 system, regardless of the database system being used. Open SQL statements can work with database tables that have been created in the ABAP Dictionary. When an ABAP program using Open SQL statements is executed, the SAP Basis component of the SAP R/3 system converts the Open SQL statements into Native SQL statements to access the database.

Note: To learn more about the SAP Basis component, refer to Chapter 1.

The Open SQL statements consist of the Data Manipulation Language (DML), which is a part of Standard SQL. In other words, Open SQL statements allow you to read (i.e., to `SELECT`) and change (i.e., to `INSERT`, `UPDATE`, or `DELETE`) data.

In the ABAP Dictionary, you can combine columns of different database tables with a database view. In Open SQL statements, views are manipulated in the same way as database tables. Therefore, any references to database tables in the following sections apply to views as well.

Table 8.1 lists the commonly used Open SQL statements:

Statement	Description
`SELECT`	Reads data from database tables
`INSERT`	Adds lines to database tables
`UPDATE`	Changes the contents of lines of database tables
`MODIFY`	Inserts new lines into database tables or changes the content of existing lines
`DELETE`	Deletes lines from database tables
`OPEN CURSOR`	Reads lines of database tables using the cursor
`FETCH`	
`CLOSE CURSOR`	

TABLE 8.1 Commonly used open SQL statements

Whenever a user logs in and accesses an SAP database, the user must specify a client. If a database operation is initiated by the user after logon, the SAP system generates a return code specifying whether the operation has been successful.

Now, let's explore automatic client-handling and return code in an SAP system.

Automatic Client-Handling

A single SAP R/3 system can manage the application data of different business processes, such as creating sales and delivery orders in a company. Each of these commercially separate business processes in the SAP R/3 system is called a client, which is assigned with a unique number for identification. When a user logs on to an SAP R/3 system, the user has to specify a client. As a result, every database table in SAP is structured to include the clients of an SAP system. Consequently, when you create a database table in SAP, the first column, `MANDT`, is created automatically to store client-related data.

By default, Open SQL statements use the automatic client-handling feature, which always accesses the current client. The `MANDT` column cannot be manipulated by using the `WHERE` clause of an Open SQL statement if the automatic client-handling feature is turned on. If you try to manipulate the `MANDT` column, the SAP system returns an error either during the syntax check or at runtime. You can, however, manipulate the `MANDT` field after disabling the automatic client-handling feature. The automatic client-handling feature can be disabled by using the `CLIENT SPECIFIED` clause.

Return Code Used in Open SQL

As stated earlier, return code specifies the status of executing a database operation. The status is specified by the following two system variables:

- SY-SUBRC—Specifies whether or not the database operation has been successful. If the SY-SUBRC system variable returns 0, it specifies that the database operation has been successful. Consequently, any value other than 0 signifies an unsuccessful operation.
- SY-DBCNT—Specifies the number of database lines processed after an Open SQL statement has been executed.

Native SQL

Unlike Open SQL, which includes ABAP code elements, Native SQL contains only database manipulation statements. Database tables that are not administered by the ABAP Dictionary can be accessed by using Native SQL. A Native SQL statement is used within the EXEC SQL and ENDEXEC statements, as shown in the following syntax:

```
EXEC SQL [PERFORMING <form>].
<Native SQL statement>
ENDEXEC.
```

In this syntax, note that we have not used a period (.) after the Native SQL statement. Moreover, unlike in ABAP syntax, inverted commas (") and asterisks (*) in Native SQL statements do not convert a line of code into a comment. In addition, you must know whether the table and field names are case-sensitive in the specified database.

The data stored in log columns with types LCHR and LRAW and declared in the ABAP Dictionary can be manipulated by using Open SQL statements. If you use Native SQL statements to access log columns with types LCHR and LRAW, the results might be incorrect. In addition, Native SQL does not support the automatic-client handling feature, unlike Open SQL.

You can use Native SQL statements to perform the following tasks:

- Transfer the values of ABAP fields to database tables
- Read or retrieve the values from database tables and process them in ABAP programs
- Access the tables that are not declared in the ABAP Dictionary

Some disadvantages of Native SQL are as follows:

- The code written between the `EXEC` and `ENDEXEC` statements is not checked for syntax errors.
- An ABAP program that contains the database-specific SQL statements is not compatible with different database systems.
- The automatic client-handling feature for client-dependent tables is not supported by Native SQL.

> **Note:** An ABAP program contains database-specific SQL statements that do not run under different database systems. If you need to use your ABAP program on more than one database platform, you must use only Open SQL statements.

READING DATA USING THE `SELECT` STATEMENT

In Open SQL, the `SELECT` statement and its various clauses are used to read data from database tables. The syntax to use the `SELECT` statement to read the data from database tables is:

```
SELECT      <selected_result>
INTO        <target_area>
FROM        <source_database_tab>
[WHERE      <where_condition>]
[GROUP BY   <fields>]
[HAVING     <having_condition>]
[ORDER BY   <fields>].
```

In this syntax, we have used various clauses, such as `WHERE`, `GROUP BY`, and `ORDER BY`, in the `SELECT` statement.

Table 8.2 describes the various clauses of the `SELECT` statement:

Clause	Description
SELECT <selected_result>	Defines the structure of data that you want to read from database tables. The structure of the data can be read by specifying the number of lines, column names, and whether duplicate entries are acceptable.
INTO <target_area>	Specifies the target area, where the data has to be sent after being read from the source database table.
FROM <source_database_tab>	Specifies the database table or view from which data is to be read. The FROM clause can also be placed before the INTO clause in a SELECT statement.
WHERE <where_condition>	Specifies the condition based on which data is read from database tables.
GROUP BY <fields>	Groups a selected set of lines into a set of summarized lines, by using the values of one or more columns listed in the <fields> parameter.
HAVING <having_condition>	Sets logical conditions for the lines to be combined by using the GROUP BY clause.
ORDER BY <fields>	Defines a sequence of <fields> parameters for the lines of the result set generated after executing the SELECT statement.

TABLE 8.2 Clauses used within the SELECT statement

Now, let's discuss all these clauses in detail.

The SELECT Clause

In Open SQL, the SELECT clause is used to define the structure of the result set that the user wants to read from a database. The SELECT clause can be divided into two parts, lines and columns, as shown in the following syntax:

```
SELECT <database_tab_lines> <database_tab_columns> ...
```

In this syntax, the <database_tab_lines> expression specifies whether the user wants to read one or more lines and the <database_tab_columns> expression defines the column selection.

You can use the SELECT statement to read any of the following from a database table:

- A single line
- Multiple lines

- A single column
- All columns
- Aggregate data
- Dynamic data

Now, let's explore these in detail, one by one.

Reading a Single Line

The SELECT statement can read a single entry from the database table by using the following syntax:

```
SELECT SINGLE <database_tab_columns> ... WHERE ...
```

In this syntax, the SINGLE clause is used to read a single entry from a database table, and the WHERE clause is used to specify a condition for the selection. For example, you can specify a condition in the WHERE clause by writing the values for the primary key fields of a table. If the WHERE clause does not contain all the key fields of the table, a warning is generated and the SELECT statement reads the first entry according to the key fields that are specified. The result of such a query is either an elementary field or a flat structure, depending on the number of columns specified in the <database_tab_columns> expression. If the system finds a line with the corresponding key, the value of the SY-SUBRC system variable is set to 0; otherwise, it is set to 4.

Listing 8.1 shows how to read a single line:

```
REPORT ZDATA_ACCESS.

*/Reading the data using SELECT statement

DATA LINE TYPE KNA1.
SELECT SINGLE KUNNR LAND1 NAME1 ORT01 ADRNR
INTO CORRESPONDING FIELDS OF LINE
FROM KNA1
WHERE KUNNR EQ '0000000515'.
IF SY-SUBRC EQ 0.
   WRITE: / LINE-KUNNR, LINE-LAND1, LINE-NAME1, LINE-ORT01,
   LINE-ADRNR.
ENDIF.
```

LISTING 8.1 **Reading a single line from a database table**

In Listing 8.1, the SINGLE clause is used in the SELECT statement, which reads a single entry from the KNA1 database table, where the value of the KUNNR field is equal to 0000000515. The columns specified in the `SELECT` clause are transferred to the corresponding components of the structure `LINE`.

> **Note:** All the source code in this chapter uses some standard tables of the SAP R/3 system. Table 8.3 lists these standard tables:

Table Name	Description
MAKT	Material descriptions
MAKV	Material cost distribution
MAKZ	Material cost distribution equivalence numbers
MNA1	General data in customer master
MAKT	Short document: material movement
MARA	General material data

TABLE 8.3 Some standard tables in the SAP R/3 system

Perform the following steps to create an ABAP program to read a single line from a database (by using the code of Listing 8.1):

1. Open the initial screen of ABAP Editor either by navigating through the SAP menu or by executing the `SE38` transaction code.
2. On the initial screen of ABAP Editor, enter a name for the program, such as, `ZDATA_ACCESS`. Select the `Source code` radio button in the `Subobjects` group box and then click the `Create` button to create a new program, as shown in Figure 8.2:

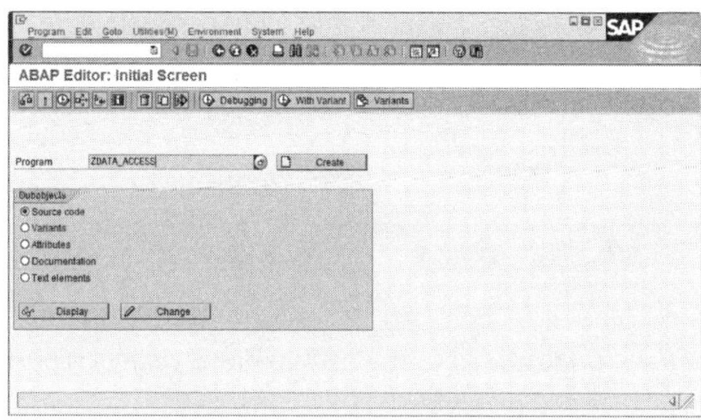

FIGURE 8.2 **Creating a new program**

The `ABAP: Program Attributes` dialog box appear.

3. In the `ABAP: Program Attributes` dialog box, enter a short description for the program in the `Title` field. Select `Executable program` as the attributes type, as shown in Figure 8.3:

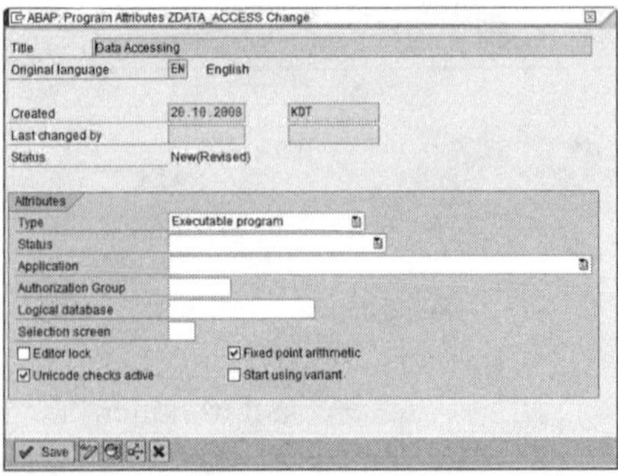

FIGURE 8.3 **The ABAP: program attributes screen**

4. Click the `Save` button (see Figure 8.3) or press the `ENTER` key. The `Create Object Directory Entry` dialog box appears.
5. In the `Create Object Directory Entry` dialog box, enter the package name, ZKOG_PCKG, beside the `Package` field, and then click the `Save` (💾) icon.

The `ABAP Editor: Change Report` screen appears, as shown in Figure 8.4:

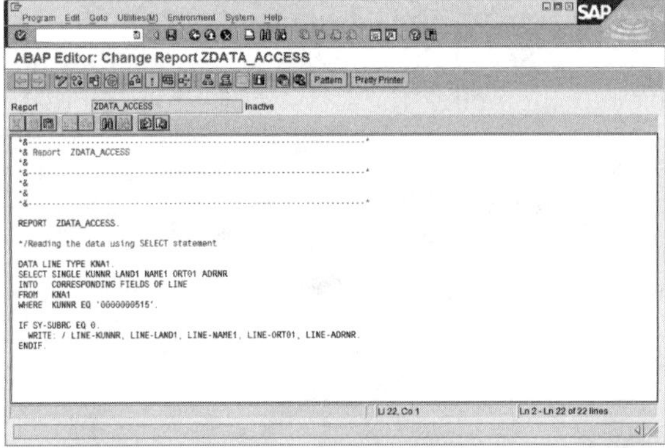

FIGURE 8.4 **Code added to the ABAP editor: change report screen**

6. Write the code, as given in Listing 8.1, in the `ABAP Editor: Change Report` screen (see Figure 8.4).
7. Click the `Save` (icon) icon or press the CTRL+S key combination to save the current changes in the program.
8. Click the `Check` (icon) icon or press the CTRL+F2 key combination to check and remove the syntax error or warning (if any) in the program. After removing the syntax errors from the program, click the `Activate` (icon) icon or press the CTRL+F3 key combination to activate the program.
9. Click the `Direct Processing` (icon) or press the F8 key to display the output of the program. Figure 8.5 shows the output:

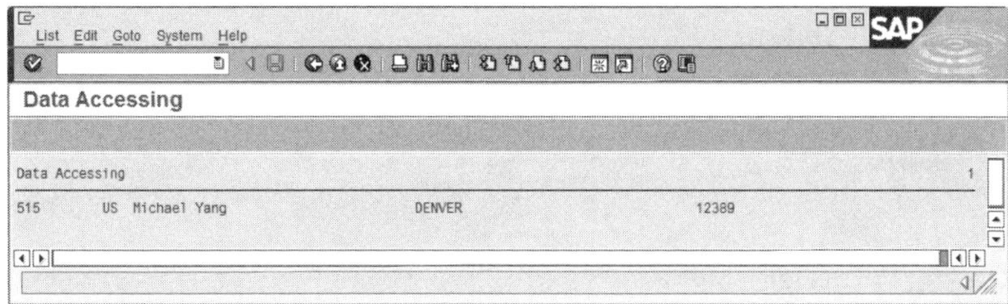

FIGURE 8.5 **Reading a single entry**

> **Note:** Follow all the steps that have been previously described to generate and view the results of all the programs given in this chapter.

Reading Several Lines

The `SELECT` statement is used to read several entries of a database table by using the following syntax:

```
SELECT [DISTINCT] <database_tab_columns> INTO <target_area>
... WHERE ...
```

In this syntax, the `DISTINCT` clause is used to ensure that no duplicate entries are read. If the `DISTINCT` clause is not used, the SAP system reads all the lines that satisfy the `WHERE` condition. The target area of the `INTO` clause can be an internal table with a line type compatible with the `<database_tab_columns>` expression. If the target area is a flat structure, the `ENDSELECT` statement must be included at the end of the SELECT statement. The following syntax shows how to use the ENDSELECT statement along with the SELECT statement:

```
SELECT [DISTINCT] <database_tab_columns> INTO <target_area>
... WHERE ...
   ...
ENDSELECT.
```

The SELECT...ENDSELECT statement, shown in the preceding code snippet, searches the records based on the condition specified in the WHERE clause. Each of these records is copied into a structure variable and then processed in the SAP system. The following code snippet shows how to use the SELECT... ENDSELECT statement:

```
SELECT * FROM KNA1 INTO cust_nm WHERE NAME1 = 'Roger Zahn'.
  WRITE cust_nm-ORT01.
ENDSELECT.
```

Reading Particular Columns

The following syntax of the SELECT statement is used to read single columns from a database table:

```
SELECT <database_tab_lines> <dbtab_col1> [AS <dbtab_col_
alias1>] <dbtab_col2> [AS
<dbtab_col_alias1>] ...
```

In this syntax, <dbtab_col 1>, <dbtab_col 2>...<dbtab_col n> stands for column names and the AS clause is used to assign the alias names <dbtab_col_alias1>, <dbtab_col_alias2>...<dbtab_col_alias n> corresponding to these columns. An alias name can be used in the following situations:

- When one database table is referred to in the FROM clause more than once. In this situation, using the alias name ensures that each column referred to in the FROM clause is considered unique.
- When the full names of columns are specified in the SELECT statement. The full name of a column is required when a column specified in the SELECT statement exists in two or more database tables.

The AS clause is used to specify an alias name, <dbtab_col_alias i>, for each column, <dbtab_col i>. The specified alias is used instead of the real name of the column in the INTO and ORDER BY clauses. Listing 8.2 shows how to read the data of the columns specified in the SELECT statement:

```
REPORT ZDATA_ACCESS.
*/Reading the data of a particular column of a table, containing
multiple lines
DATA: MyTable TYPE STANDARD TABLE OF KNA1,
   KOG LIKE LINE OF MyTable.
SELECT KUNNR LAND1 NAME1 ORT01 ADRNR
INTO CORRESPONDING FIELDS OF TABLE MyTable
FROM KNA1
WHERE LAND1 NE 'US'.
IF SY-SUBRC EQ 0.
   LOOP AT MyTable INTO KOG.
            WRITE: / KOG-KUNNR, KOG-LAND1, KOG-NAME1,
            KOG-ORT01, KOG-ADRNR.
   ENDLOOP.
ENDIF.
```

LISTING 8.2 **Reading data of the columns by using the SELECT statement**

In Listing 8.2, MyTable is an internal table that contains the KOG work area and the same column names as the column names of the KNA1 database table. The SELECT statement reads all the lines of the KNA1 database table that satisfy the condition specified in the WHERE clause. The columns specified in the SELECT statement are then transferred to the corresponding columns of the KOG work area. Figure 8.6 displays the values of the columns stored in the KOG work area of the MyTable table:

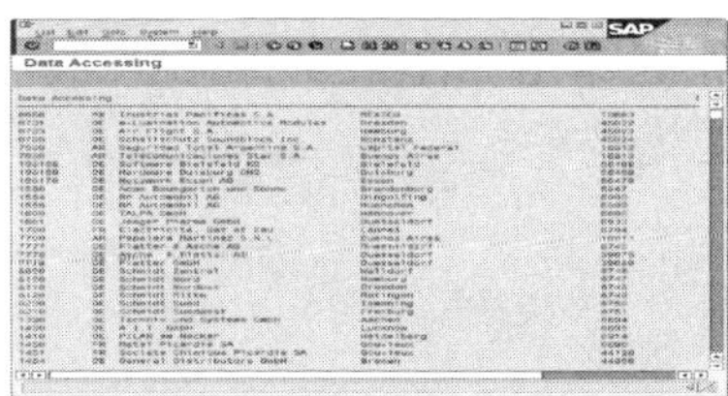

FIGURE 8.6 **Reading particular fields from a table**

Reading All Columns

The syntax of the SELECT statement to read all the columns of a database table is:

```
SELECT <database_tab_lines> * ...
```

In this syntax, the asterisk (*) symbol is used to specify all the columns of a database table.

Listing 8.3 shows how to read the data from all the columns of a database table:

```
REPORT ZDATA_ACCESS.
*/Reading all the columns of a table
DATA KOG TYPE KNA1.
SELECT *
INTO CORRESPONDING FIELDS OF KOG
FROM KNA1
WHERE LAND1 EQ 'BR'.
  WRITE: / SY-DBCNT,
KOG-KUNNR, KOG-LAND1, KOG-NAME1, KOG-ORT01, KOG-ADRNR.
ENDSELECT.
```

LISTING 8.3 **Reading data from all the columns of a database table**

In Listing 8.3, the SELECT statement reads all the lines of the KNA1 database table, where the value of the LAND1 field is BR. All the columns of the KNA1 table are then transferred to the corresponding columns of the KOG work area. Figure 8.7 shows the output of Listing 8.3:

1	484	BR	Marcelo da Silva	Sao Paolo - Consolacao	12260
2	407856	BR	Equity Avaliacoes S/C Ltda (GI 4th	Rio de Janeiro	46514
3	BR-S50A00	BR	Motor Market Ltda	São Paulo	11819
4	BR-S50B00	BR	Cliente isento de ICMS e IPI	São Paulo	12085
5	BR-S50Z00	BR	Cliente na Zona Franca de Manaus	MANAUS	12591
6	CLIE-7100	BR	Centro Rio de Janeiro	Rio de Janeiro	11647
7	CLIE00-20	BR	Cliente Nacional / Cobrança Boleto	São Paulo	11681
8	CLIE00-21	BR	Cliente Nacional / Cobrança Duplica	São Paulo	11682
9	RJ00-CLI	BR	SAP Brasil - Filial Rio de Janeiro	RIO DE JANEIRO	34447

FIGURE 8.7 **Reading the data from the columns of a table**

> **Note:** As a best practice, specify only the required columns in the SELECT statement to reduce the time that data takes to process.

Reading Aggregate Data for Columns

The syntax to use the SELECT statement to read aggregate data of a column from a database table is:

```
SELECT <database_tab_lines> <agg>( [DISTINCT] <s1> )
[AS <a 1>]
<agg>( [DISTINCT] <s2> ) [AS <a 2>] ...
```

In this syntax, the <s1> <s2>. . .<s n > expressions stand for field labels. The <agg> expression represents one of the following aggregate functions:

- **MAX**—Returns the maximum value of the <s i> columns.
- **MIN**—Returns the minimum value of the <s i> columns.
- **AVG**—Returns the average value of the <s i> columns.
- **SUM**—Returns the sum of the values of the <s i> columns.
- **COUNT**—Counts the total lines of the database table.
- **COUNT** (DISTINCT <s i>)—Returns the number of different values in the <s i> columns.
- **COUNT(*)**—Returns the total number of lines in the result set of the SELECT statement.

The DISTINCT clause ensures that no duplicate values are used to calculate the aggregate of the data. The aggregate functions AVG and SUM are used only with numeric fields. If you use the MAX, MIN, and SUM functions, ensure that the data type of the corresponding columns must be of the ABAP Dictionary type, such as I and F. When the aggregate function is AVG, the ABAP Dictionary type must be FLTP, and when the aggregate function is COUNT, the ABAP Dictionary type must be INT4.

It is to be noted that null values are not used for calculation. If all the lines in a selection contain the null value in the corresponding fields, the result of the calculation also turns out to be null. In ABAP, the null value is interpreted as zero (depending on the data type of the field).

The AS clause is used to define an alternative column name (also called an alias), <a i>, for each aggregate expression. An alias column name is preferred over the actual column name because it helps simplify the query. The field names specified in the SELECT clause for aggregate functions are also included in the GROUP BY clause.

Now, let's consider an example. Assume that the ITEM database table contains two columns and 10 lines, as shown in Table 8.4:

COL_1	COL_2
1	3
2	1
3	5
4	7
5	2
6	3
7	1
8	9
9	4
10	3

TABLE 8.4 The ITEM table

The following code snippet is used to apply an aggregate function on the data stored in Table 8.4:

```
DATA RESULT TYPE P DECIMALS 2.
SELECT <agg>( [DISTINCT] COL_2 )
        INTO RESULT
        FROM ITEM.
WRITE RESULT.
```

This code snippet generates the result based on different combinations that the aggregate expression <agg> forms with the DISTINCT clause, as shown in Table 8.5:

Aggregate Expression	DISTINCT	Result
MAX	No	9.00
MAX	Yes	9.00
MIN	No	1.00
MIN	Yes	1.00
AVG	No	3.80
AVG	Yes	4.43
SUM	No	38.00
SUM	Yes	31.00
COUNT	Yes	7.00
COUNT(*)	---	10.00

TABLE 8.5 Result of aggregate expressions and the DISTINCT clause

Note: The DISTINCT clause does not work with the COUNT(*) aggregate expression.

Specifying Columns Dynamically

You can also use the SELECT statement to specify the columns of an internal table dynamically. The internal table can either be empty or contain columns names or aggregate expressions. If the internal table is empty, the SAP system reads all columns. The following syntax is used to specify the columns dynamically:

```
SELECT <database_tab_lines> (<internal_tab>) ...
```

This syntax shows that the name of the internal table, <internal_tab>, is written inside the parentheses (). Note that the line type of the <internal_tab> table must be the C type (storing character data), with a maximum length of 72 characters.

Listing 8.4 shows how to read columns that are specified dynamically:

```
REPORT ZDATA_ACCESS.
*/Specify and Reading the columns dynamically
DATA: MyTable TYPE STANDARD TABLE OF KNA1,
```

Continued

```
    KOG LIKE LINE OF MyTable.
DATA: LINE(200) TYPE C,
      LIST LIKE TABLE OF LINE(200).
LINE = ' Land1 ORT01 '.
APPEND LINE TO LIST.
SELECT DISTINCT (LIST)
       INTO CORRESPONDING FIELDS OF TABLE MyTable
       FROM KNA1.
LOOP AT MyTable INTO KOG.
 WRITE: / KOG-Land1, KOG-ORT01.
ENDLOOP.
```

LISTING 8.4 **Specifying and reading columns dynamically**

In Listing 8.4, MyTable is an internal table that retrieves data from the columns of the KNA1 database table. The `DISTINCT` clause in the `SELECT` statement is used to remove the lines with the same content in both the columns. Figure 8.8 shows the values of the `Land1` and `ORT01` fields of the KNA1 table after removing the duplicate entries:

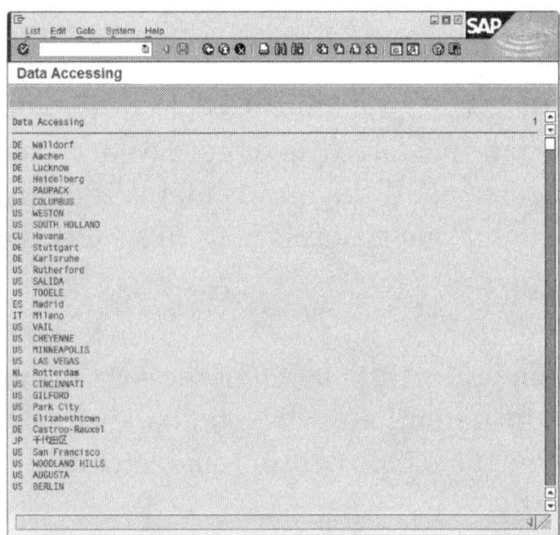

FIGURE 8.8 **Displaying the result after using the DISTINCT clause in the SELECT statement**

The `INTO` Clause

The `INTO` clause, in the `SELECT` statement, is used to define the target area. The target area is a variable that contains the field names whose data type is compatible with the field names specified in the SELECT statement. The SELECT statement uses the following specifications to determine the data type of the target area:

- **The** <database_tab_lines> **specification**—Determines the target area, such as a flat or a tabular structure.
- **The** <database_tab_cols> **specification**—Determines the structure or the line type of the target area.

The target area is flat when a single line is selected, and it can be either tabular or flat if multiple lines are selected. Note that if the target area is flat, it must be specified in the SELECT...ENDSELECT loop construction.

When you specify all the columns of a database table in the SELECT statement, the target area is either a structure type or a type that can be converted into a structure. However, if you specify the names of columns individually in the SELECT statement, the target area can be a component of a structure or a field. The elementary type of fields in the SELECT statement must be compatible with the corresponding elementary components of the target area.

The following syntax of the INTO clause is used to read the data from database table and send it to a work area:

```
SELECT ... INTO [CORRESPONDING FIELDS OF] <work_area> ...
```

In this syntax, <work_area> represents a work area. The use of the CORRESPONDING FIELDS clause is optional after the INTO clause. The CORRESPONDING FIELDS clause is used to limit the amount of data being read from the result set of the SELECT statement and transferred into an ABAP program. Note that the CORRESPONDING FIELDS clause does not limit the amount of data being read from a database table.

When an asterisk (*) symbol is used in the SELECT statement to specify all columns of a database table, the data is transferred into the <work_area> from left to right according to the structure of the database table. However, when individual columns or aggregate expressions are used in the SELECT statement, the columns are transferred into the work area from left to right according to the structure of the work area. Note that when the data is retrieved from a database table into the <work_area>, the values of the components of <work_area> are overwritten. However, the values of the components of <work_area> are not affected by the SELECT statement.

If the user uses the asterisk (*) symbol to read all the columns of a single database table in the SELECT statement, the INTO clause can be kept empty.

The SELECT statement then writes the data by default into the table work area with the same name as the database table. Note that you must declare this table work area by using the TABLES statement.

You can also specify an internal table in the INTO clause in case you have to retrieve a large number of lines from a database table. The following syntax of the INTO clause is used for reading several lines of a database table and placing them into an internal table:

```
SELECT ... INTO|APPENDING [CORRESPONDING FIELDS OF]
TABLE <internal_tab>
                    [PACKAGE SIZE <n>] ...
```

In this syntax, the <internal_tab> internal table is populated with all the lines of the selection. The APPENDING clause is another option that you can use instead of the INTO clause. The main difference between the INTO and the APPENDING clause is related to the existing lines in the <internal_tab> table. When you use the INTO clause, all the existing lines in the <internal_tab> table are deleted. When you use the APPENDING clause, new lines are added to the existing internal table, <internal_tab>. Fields in the internal table that are not affected by the selection are populated with initial values.

The PACKAGE SIZE clause is used to write the selected lines into the <internal_tab> internal table in the form of packets, but not all at once. You can define packets of <n> lines that are written one after the other into the internal table. If you use the INTO clause, each packet replaces the preceding one. If you use the APPENDING clause, the packets are inserted one after the other.

> **Note:** The PACKAGE SIZE clause is used only in the SELECT ... ENDSELECT loop, because outside the SELECT statement, the content of the internal table is undetermined.

When the names of the fields of a database table or aggregate functions are specified in the SELECT statement, the INTO clause can also specify the name of fields individually. The following syntax is used to specify the field names in the INTO clause:

```
SELECT ... INTO (<f1>, <f 2>, ...). ...
```

In this syntax, <f1> and <f2> represent the names of fields.

Examples of Using the `INTO` Clause

Listing 8.5 shows a flat structure as a target area in the `INTO` clause:

```
REPORT ZDATA_ACCESS.
*/An example of INTO clause, where KOG is a flat structure acts
as a target area
DATA KOG TYPE MARA.
SELECT *
INTO KOG
FROM MARA.
   WRITE: / KOG-MATNR, KOG-ERSDA, KOG-ERNAM, KOG-MTART,
KOG-MBRSH.
ENDSELECT.
```

LISTING 8.5 **Showing a flat structure as a target area**

In Listing 8.5, KOG is a flat structure of the same data type as the target area (a database table named `MARA`) of the `SELECT` statement. The individual components of the KOG structure are specified within the `WRITE` statement. Figure 8.9 shows the values of the `MATNR`, `ERSDA`, `ERNAM`, `MTART`, and `MBRSH` fields of the `MARA` table:

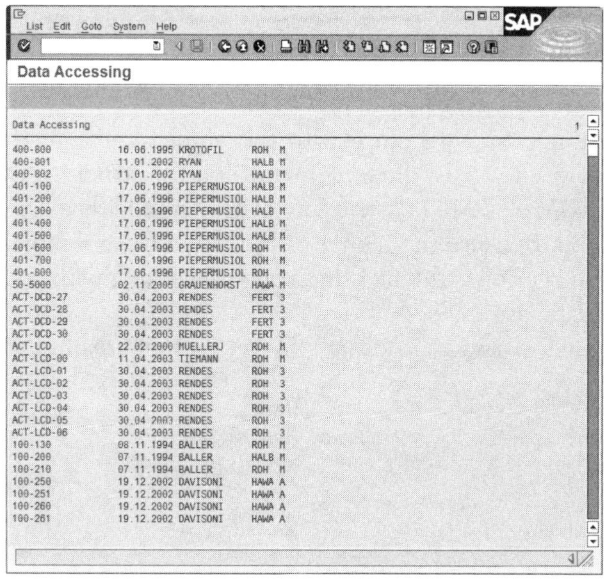

FIGURE 8.9 **Displaying the result of the INTO clause**

Listing 8.6 shows how to specify the same name for a data object and a database table:

```
REPORT ZDATA_ACCESS.
*/The name of data object and of database are same.
DATA MARA TYPE MARA.
SELECT *
FROM MARA.
   WRITE:  /  MARA-MATNR,  MARA-ERSDA,  MARA-ERNAM,
   MARA-MTART, MARA-MBRSH.
ENDSELECT.
```

LISTING 8.6 **Using the same name for an ABAP data object and a database table**

The code given in Listing 8.6 displays a warning, when executed, as shown in Figure 8.10:

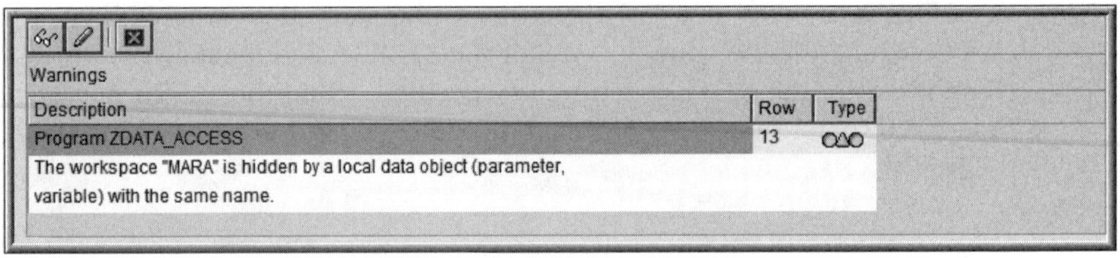

Warnings

Description	Row	Type
Program ZDATA_ACCESS	13	
The workspace "MARA" is hidden by a local data object (parameter, variable) with the same name.		

FIGURE 8.10 **The warning generated when the structure and the database table have the same name**

In Listing 8.6, a structure with the name similar to the MARA table is created. In other words, the table name and the structure name are the same; that is, MARA. The MARA structure is used implicitly as the target area in the `SELECT` loop. Because the names of the structure and table are the same, the SAP system overlooks the fact that you are working with an ABAP data object and not a database table.

Listing 8.7 shows an internal table as a target area in the `INTO` clause:

```
REPORT ZDATA_ACCESS.
*/An internal table-MyTable- acts as a target area
DATA: BEGIN OF KOG,
        MATNR TYPE MAKV-MATNR,
WERKS TYPE MAKV-WERKS,
```

Continued

```
CSPLIT TYPE MAKV-CSPLIT,
KTEXT TYPE MAKV-KTEXT,
END OF KOG,
MyTable LIKE SORTED TABLE OF KOG
            WITH NON-UNIQUE KEY MATNR.
SELECT MATNR WERKS CSPLIT KTEXT
INTO CORRESPONDING FIELDS OF TABLE MyTable
FROM MAKV.
IF SY-SUBRC EQ 0.

LOOP AT MyTable INTO KOG.
   WRITE: / sy-Tabix, KOG-MATNR, KOG-WERKS, KOG-CSPLIT,
   KOG-KTEXT.
ENDLOOP.
ENDIF.
```

LISTING 8.7 **Internal table as a target area**

In Listing 8.7, MyTable is a sorted internal table with the KOG line type. MyTable contains the four fields with the same names and data types as the database table MAKV. The `CORRESPONDING FIELDS` clause is used to place the columns from the `SELECT` clause into the corresponding fields of MyTable. Figure 8.11 shows the output of Listing 8.7:

```
 1  CH_4200            1100 0010 FeKoAuft HaPr,2 KuPr
 2  CPF10051           3100 0001 Schema ICE
 3  PA-300             1100 0001 Cost Distribution
 4  PQR-100            3100 001  PQR BK 100
 5  T-COP              1000 0001 Pumpe(Kuppelprodukt)
 6  T-FF100            1100 0001 T-FF100 + T-FF300
 7  T-FV100            1100 0001 T-Fv100
 8  T-FV100            3100 0001 T-Fv100
 9  T-MC               1000 0001 Aufteilung
10  T-MCA              1000 1
11  T-MCA              1000 2
12  Y-300              1100 0001 Y-300 and P-300
13  Y-300              3100 0001 co-product
14  Y-300B             1100 PI01 PI apportionment
15  Z-300              1100 0001 Cost distribution
16  Z-300              3100 0001 Cost distribution
```


FIGURE 8.11 **The CORRESPONDING FIELDS clause is placing fields in an internal table**

Listing 8.8 shows how data is read in packets and placed into internal tables by using the `INTO` clause:

```
REPORT ZDATA_ACCESS.
*/Reading the data in packets and keeping them into an
   Internal Table
DATA: KOG TYPE KNA1,
    MyTable TYPE SORTED TABLE OF KNA1
            WITH UNIQUE KEY KUNNR.
SELECT KUNNR NAME1 ORT01 FROM KNA1
INTO CORRESPONDING FIELDS OF TABLE MyTable
      PACKAGE SIZE 10.
   WRITE: / 'Total lines found : ', SY-DBCNT.
LOOP AT MyTable INTO KOG.
   WRITE: / sy-Tabix, KOG-KUNNR, KOG-NAME1, KOG-ORT01.
ENDLOOP.
   SKIP 1.
ENDSELECT.
```

LISTING 8.8 **Reading and placing data in packets into an internal table**

Listing 8.8 shows that the data is read in the packet format. The package size is specified as 10, so that a group of 10 lines are read from the `KNA1` database table, which are then placed in the MyTable internal table of the KOG structure type. The values stored in the corresponding components of the KOG type are displayed as shown in Figure 8.12:

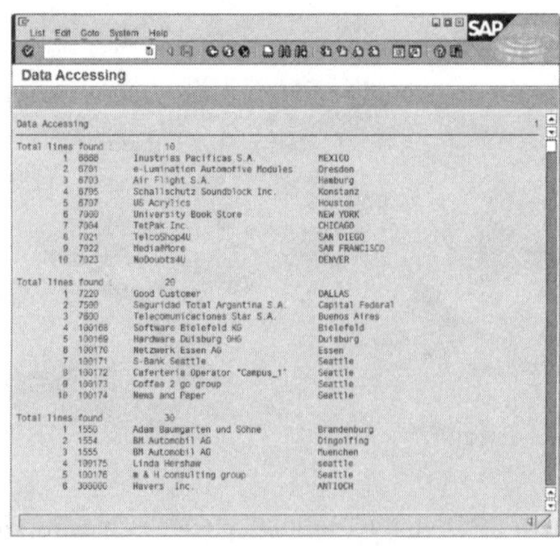

FIGURE 8.12 **Result of the INTO clause**

In Listing 8.8, if the APPENDING clause is used instead of the INTO clause, the output is as it appears in Figure 8.13:

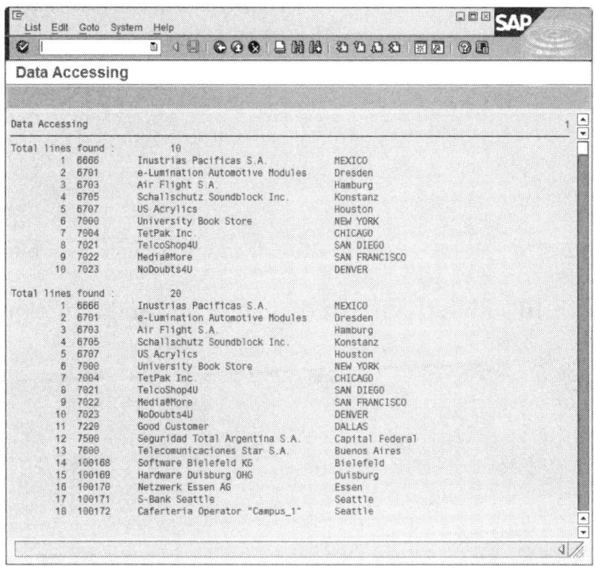

FIGURE 8.13 **Displaying the result of using the APPENDING clause**

In Figure 8.13, you can see that the result of the APPENDING clause is different from the result of the INTO clause (see Figure 8.12). In the case of the INTO clause, 10 records are inserted in MyTable and then displayed. However, in the case of the APPENDING clause, 10 records are added each time and appended at the end of the previous records in MyTable and then displayed.

Listing 8.9 shows how single fields are specified as a target area by using the INTO clause:

```
REPORT ZDATA_ACCESS.
*/Specifying individual fields in target area
DATA: AVERAGE TYPE P DECIMALS 2,
      SUM TYPE P DECIMALS 2.
SELECT AVG( MENGE ) SUM( MENGE )
INTO (AVERAGE, SUM)
FROM MARI.
WRITE: / 'Average:', AVERAGE,
       / 'Sum :', SUM.
```

LISTING 8.9 **Specifying single fields as target areas**

In Listing 8.9, the `SELECT` clause contains two aggregate expressions to calculate the average and sum of the `MENGE` field from the MARI database table. The target fields are called `AVERAGE` and `SUM`. Figure 8.14 shows the average and sum of the values stored in the `MENGE` field:

```
Average:        154,631.67
Sum    :  1,478,278,810.01
```


FIGURE 8.14 **Result of the AVERAGE and SUM aggregate functions**

Listing 8.10 shows the usage of an alias in the `INTO` clause:

```
REPORT ZDATA_ACCESS.
*/Creating and Using aliases-MAXI and MINI
DATA: BEGIN OF LINE,
MAXI TYPE P decimals 4,
      MINI TYPE p decimals 4,
      END OF LINE.
SELECT MAX( MENGE ) AS MAXI MIN( MENGE ) AS MINI
INTO CORRESPONDING FIELDS OF LINE
FROM MARI.
WRITE: / 'Maximum value:', LINE-MAXI,
     / 'Minimum value:', LINE-MINI.
```

LISTING 8.10 **Using aliases**

In Listing 8.10, the `SELECT` clause contains two aggregate expressions to calculate the maximum and minimum values of the `MENGE` field of the `MARI` database table. A structure `LINE` is used as the target area and the names of the structure components are used as aliases in the `SELECT` clause. Figure 8.15 shows the maximum and minimum values of the `MENGE` field of the MARI database table:

```
Maximum value: 644,000,000.0000
Minimum value:           0.0000
```


FIGURE 8.15 **The maximum and minimum values of a field**

The FROM Clause

The FROM clause of the SELECT statement determines the source area, which are database tables from which data needs to be retrieved. You can specify either a single table or multiple tables, linked by using inner or outer joins, in the FROM clause. The syntax to use the FROM clause is:

```
SELECT... FROM <database_tab> <options>...
```

In this syntax, the FROM clause is followed by the name of the <database_tab> database table and the <options> expression. The <options> expression represents any clause that can be used to control access to the database.

In the SELECT statement, the name of a database table can be specified statically or dynamically. In addition, you can specify and use the alias names (alternative names) of these tables. The following syntax is used to specify the name of a database table statically:

```
SELECT... FROM <database_tab> [AS <database_tab_alias>]
<options> ...
```

In this syntax, <database_tab> represents a database table that must exist in the ABAP Dictionary. The AS clause is used to assign the <database_tab_alias> alias to the <database_tab> table. Using aliases helps eliminate the ambiguities when you use more than one database table or when a single database table is used more than once in a join expression.

The following syntax is used to specify the name of a database table dynamically:

```
SELECT... FROM (<database_tab>) <options> ...
```

The <database_tab> expression represents the name of a database table in uppercase. When the name of a database table is specified dynamically, you cannot use an empty INTO clause to read all the columns of the database table. It is also not possible to use alternative or alias table names.

The following tasks can be performed by using the FROM clause with the SELECT statement:

- Using JOIN (INNER or OUTER)
- Client-handling

- Disabling data buffering
- Restricting number of lines

Now, let's discuss these tasks in detail, one by one.

Using JOIN (INNER or OUTER)

Sometimes you need to retrieve the data of two or more database tables, such as while creating a report. In such a situation, you can join the tables. To join two or more database tables, you use the JOIN clause in the SELECT statement. In Open SQL, two kinds of joins can be used to join two or more tables, INNER and LEFT OUTER. The following syntax shows how to use the INNER or LEFT OUTER clause to read data from more than one table:

```
... [(] {database_tab_left [AS database_tab_alias_left]}
| join
              {[INNER] JOIN}|{LEFT [OUTER] JOIN}
              {database_tab_right [AS database_tab_alias_right]
              ON <join_cond>}
[)]
  ....]
```

In this syntax, a join expression contains a left-side table and a right-side table that are joined by using either [INNER] JOIN or LEFT [OUTER] JOIN. As specified in the syntax, a join expression can be an inner join (INNER) or an outer join (LEFT OUTER). Furthermore, a join expression is used in parentheses ().

The inner join is used to join two database tables such that a single result set is obtained. This result set is based on the matching records of the left-side and the right-side tables specified in the join expression. The data in this result set contains all the combinations of rows whose columns meet the <join_cond> condition. The following syntax shows how to implement an inner join:

```
SELECT...
...
FROM <database_tab_left> [AS <database_tab_alias_left>]
[INNER] JOIN <database_tab_right> [AS <database_tab_alias_
right>] ON <join_cond>
...
```

In this syntax, <database_tab_left> and <database_tab_right> are database tables that can be specified statically or dynamically. You can also use alias names of the database tables. The use of the INNER clause is optional; however, the JOIN clause is mandatory if you want specify a join expression.

A join expression links the lines of <database_tab_left> with those of <database_tab_right> that meet the <join_cond> condition. The syntax of the <join_cond> condition is similar to that of the WHERE clause, where one or more conditions are combined by using the AND operator. Each comparison must contain a column from the right-hand table, <database_tab_right>. Moreover, you can specify columns that have the same name in the <database_tab_left> and <database_tab_right> tables on both sides of a comparison operator.

The LEFT OUTER join is used to display all the records of the left database table and only the matching records of the right database table. The syntax to use the LEFT OUTER join is:

```
SELECT...
...
FROM <database_tab_left> [AS <database_tab_alias_left>] LEFT
[OUTER] JOIN
<database_tab_right> [AS <database_tab_alias_right>] ON
<join_cond>
<options> ...
```

In this syntax, the <database_tab_left> and <database_tab_right> are database tables. The use of the OUTER clause is optional. The tables are linked by using the LEFT JOIN or LEFT OUTER JOIN clause and specifying the <join_cond> condition, similar to the inner join. The final selection includes all the lines of the <database_tab_left> table, but matching lines of the <database_tab_right> table. However, the lines of the <database_tab_right> table, which do not match the corresponding lines of the <database_tab_left> table, contain null values.

In the INNER join, all the combinations of matching records of the two database tables are selected. However, in the LEFT OUTER join, all the records of the left-hand database table are selected along with the matching records of the right-hand database table.

In the LEFT OUTER join, the following restrictions apply to the <join_cond> condition:

- Use either the `EQ` or = relational operator.
- Specify at least one comparison between the columns of the `<database_tab_left>` and `<database_tab_right>` database tables.
- Include the columns of the `<database_tab_right>` table in the `<join_cond>` condition when these columns are used in comparisons.

Note: Including the name of the columns of the `<database_tab_right>` table is not necessary in the `WHERE clause`.

Note that the previous restrictions do not apply while working with an `INNER` join.

Client-Handling

As already mentioned, you can switch off automatic client-handling in Open SQL statements by using a special clause, `CLIENT SPECIFIED`. In the `SELECT` statement, the `CLIENT SPECIFIED` clause comes after the table specified in the `FROM` clause, as shown in the following syntax:

```
SELECT ... FROM <database_tab> CLIENT SPECIFIED ...
```

In this syntax, the `CLIENT SPECIFIED` clause allows you to manipulate the fields of the specified client in the individual clauses of the `SELECT` statement.

Disabling Data Buffering

One of the important features of the `SELECT` statement in Open SQL is that it always retrieves or reads the data from the buffer area in the database interface of the current application server. This means that the `SELECT` statement does not retrieve the data from the database table directly. However, you can disable data buffering of a table by using the `BYPASSING BUFFER` clause, as shown in the following syntax:

```
SELECT ... FROM <database_tab> BYPASSING BUFFER ...
```

The `BYPASSING BUFFER` clause ensures that the data being read or retrieved directly from the database tables is the updated one.

Note: Buffering of the data is preferred when the data does not change frequently because it improves the performance of the SAP R/3 system.

Restricting the Number of Lines

The SELECT statement can be used to specify a number (fixed or absolute) up to which the rows or lines of a database table can be retrieved or selected, as shown in the following syntax:

```
SELECT ... FROM <database_tab> UP TO <n> ROWS ...
```

In this syntax, the <n> expression represents either a positive number or zero. If <n> is a positive integer, the SAP system can retrieve the <n> lines from a <database_tab> database table. If <n> is zero, the SAP system retrieves all lines from the table that meet the selection criteria.

Now, let's consider some examples of using the FROM clause.

Examples of Using the FROM Clause

Listing 8.11 shows how to specify a database table statically:

```
REPORT ZDATA_ACCESS.
*/Specifying a database table statically
DATA KOG TYPE MAKV.
SELECT *
INTO KOG
FROM MAKV UP TO 6 ROWS.
WRITE: / KOG-MATNR, KOG-WERKS, KOG-CSPLIT, KOG-KTEXT.
ENDSELECT.
```

LISTING 8.11 **Specifying a database table statically**

The code given in Listing 8.11 reads six lines from the MAKV database table and places them into the KOG structure. The MATNR, WERKS, CSPLIT, and KTEXT components of the KOG structure are displayed, as shown in Figure 8.16:

```
CH_4200       1100 0010 FeKoAuft HaPr,2 KuPr
CPF10051      3100 0001 Schema ICE
PA-300        1100 0001 Cost Distribution
PQR-100       3100 001  PQR BK 100
T-COP         1000 0001 Pumpe(Kuppelprodukt)
T-FF100       1100 0001 T-FF100 + T-FF300
```


FIGURE 8.16 **Reading lines from a table**

Listing 8.12 shows how to switch off automatic client-handling by using the `CLIENT SPECIFIED` clause:

```
REPORT ZDATA_ACCESS.
*/Using the CLIENT SPECIFIED clause
DATA KOG TYPE MARI.
DATA name(10) TYPE c VALUE 'MARI'.
SELECT *
    INTO KOG
    FROM (name) CLIENT SPECIFIED
    WHERE MANDT = '800' and USNAM = 'BUROW'.
        WRITE: / KOG-MBLNR, KOG-MATNR, KOG-BWART, KOG-USNAM.
ENDSELECT.
```

LISTING 8.12 **Using the CLIENT SPECIFIED clause**

In Listing 8.12, automatic client-handling is switched off by using the `CLIENT SPECIFIED` clause. The KOG structure contains the data of the MARI database table, where the value of the `MANDT` field is 800 and that of the `USNAM` field is BUROW. The identical components of the KOG structure are displayed. Figure 8.17 shows the output of Listing 8.12:

```
49000020   103-100          501  BUROW
49000020   103-200          501  BUROW
49000020   100-300          501  BUROW
49000020   103-400          501  BUROW
49000020   100-500          501  BUROW
49000020   100-700          501  BUROW
49000023   100-600          501  BUROW
49000033   100-300          501  BUROW
49000033   100-500          501  BUROW
49000033   100-600          501  BUROW
49000033   100-700          501  BUROW
49000033   103-100          501  BUROW
49000033   103-200          501  BUROW
49000033   103-400          501  BUROW
```


FIGURE 8.17 **Displaying the result when a client is specified manually**

Listing 8.13 shows how two database tables are joined by using the INNER join:

```
REPORT ZDATA_ACCESS.
*/Using INNER join in between two tables
DATA: BEGIN OF KOG,
            MATNR TYPE MARA-MATNR,
            ERNAM TYPE MARA-ERNAM,
MAKTX TYPE MAKT-MAKTX,
END OF KOG,
MYTABLE LIKE SORTED TABLE OF KOG
               WITH UNIQUE KEY MATNR ERNAM MAKTX.
SELECT MR~MATNR MR~ERNAM MK~MAKTX
    INTO CORRESPONDING FIELDS OF TABLE MYTABLE
    FROM ( MARA AS MR
    INNER JOIN MAKT AS MK ON MK~MATNR = MR~MATNR )
WHERE MR~ERNAM = 'RUDISILL'.
WRITE: 'Material Number', ' ', 'Created by', ' ', 'Material
Description'.
skip.
LOOP AT MYTABLE INTO KOG.
    AT NEW MATNR.
            WRITE: / KOG-MATNR.
ENDAT.
    WRITE: KOG-ERNAM, KOG-MAKTX.
ENDLOOP.
```

LISTING 8.13 **Joining two database tables by using the INNER join**

In Listing 8.13, the ERNAM field of the MARA table and the MAKTX field of the MAKT table are joined by the INNER JOIN based on the MATNR field of both the tables. An alias name is assigned to each table; for instance, MR is an alias name of the MARA table and MK is an alias name of the MAKT table. Listing 8.13 creates a list of material numbers and their descriptions, where the value of the ERNAM field is RUDISILL (the ERNAM field contains the name of the person who has created the material). Figure 8.18 shows the list of material numbers created by RUDISILL:

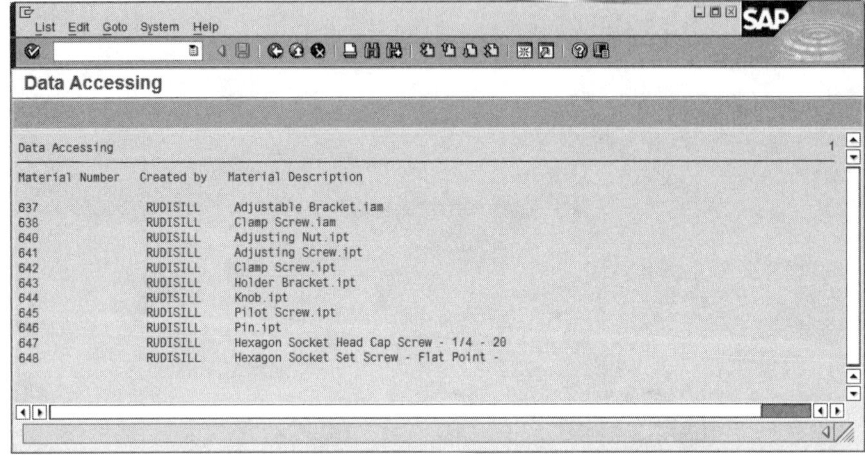

FIGURE 8.18 **Displaying the result of using the INNER join**

Listing 8.14 shows how two database tables are joined by using the `LEFT OUTER` join:

```
REPORT ZDATA_ACCESS.
*/Using LEFT OUTER join in between two tables
DATA: BEGIN OF KOG,
        MATNR TYPE MARA-MATNR,
        ERNAM TYPE MARA-ERNAM,
          SPRAS TYPE MAKT-SPRAS,
END OF KOG,
MyTable LIKE SORTED TABLE OF KOG
WITH NON-UNIQUE KEY MATNR.
SELECT MR~MATNR MR~ERNAM MK~SPRAS
    INTO CORRESPONDING FIELDS OF TABLE MyTable
    FROM MARA AS MR
LEFT OUTER JOIN MAKT AS MK ON MR~MATNR = MK~MATNR AND MK~SPRAS =
'J'.
LOOP AT MyTable INTO KOG.
    WRITE: / KOG-MATNR, KOG-ERNAM, KOG-SPRAS.
ENDLOOP.
```

LISTING 8.14 **Joining two database tables by using the LEFT OUTER join**

In Listing 8.14, the `ERNAM` field of the MARA table and the `SPRAS` field of the MAKT table are joined by the `LEFT OUTER JOIN` based on the `MATNR` field of both the tables, where the value in the `SPRAS` field of the MAKT table is J. An alias name is assigned to each table; MR for the MARA table and MK for the MAKT table. Figure 8.19 shows the result of the `LEFT OUTER` join:

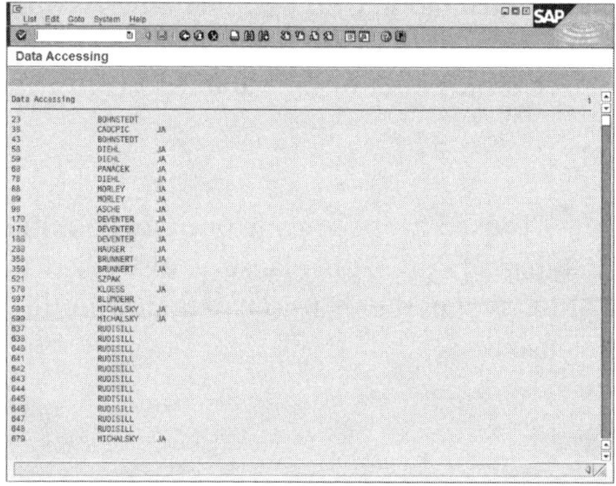

FIGURE 8.19 **Displaying the result of using the LEFT OUTER join**

Now, replace the `LEFT OUTER` join with the `INNER` join in Listing 8.14. The output is shown in Figure 8.20:

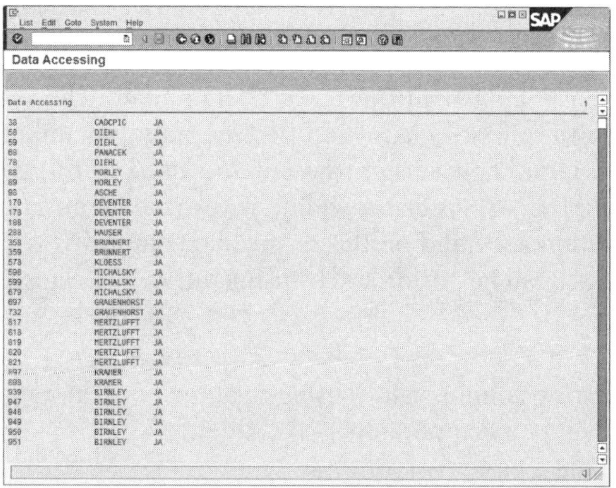

FIGURE 8.20 **Displaying the result when the LEFT OUTER join is changed to the INNER join**

You can see that the result displayed in Figure 8.20 differs from the result displayed in Figure 8.19. The INNER join shows all the combinations of the matching records of the MARA and MAKT database tables, where their MATNR fields have equal values, and the SPRAS field of the MAKT table contains the value J. However, in the case of the LEFT OUTER join, all the records of the MARA table are shown along with the matching records of the MAKT table, where the MATNR fields of both the tables have the same value and the SPRAS field of the MAKT table contains the value J.

The WHERE Clause

The WHERE clause is used to specify one or more conditions to read or retrieve data from a database table. This clause is also used in the OPEN CURSOR, UPDATE, and DELETE statements (discussed later in this chapter). The syntax of the WHERE clause is:

```
SELECT ... WHERE <where_condition> ...
```

In this syntax, the <where_condition> expression represents one or more conditions. The conditions may include the use of one or more comparison operators, such as >, <, and ==, or some special expressions, such as GT, LT, and EQ. You can also combine multiple conditions into a single condition using the logical operators, such as AND, OR, and NOT. Moreover, the conditions may also be specified dynamically.

The column names included in the conditions, specified by using the WHERE clause, can also appear in the SELECT statement. The result of a condition specified in the WHERE clause can be true, false, or unknown. The result of a condition is unknown when the column used in the condition has a null value. Using the WHERE clause, a line is retrieved from a database table only if the condition specified on the respective columns is true for the line. The following tasks can be performed by using the WHERE clause within the SELECT statement:

- Comparing column values using relational operators
- Specifying range operators
- Matching a pattern
- Specifying a list
- Checking subqueries

- Checking selection tables
- Checking null values
- Specifying negating conditions
- Specifying linking conditions
- Specifying dynamic conditions
- Specifying tabular conditions

Now, let's discuss these tasks in detail, one by one.

Comparing Column Values by Using Relational Operators

The syntax to compare the value of a column of any data type with another value is:

```
SELECT ... WHERE <s> <operator> <f> ...
```

In this syntax, the <s> expression represents a column of one of the database tables named in the FROM clause. The <f> expression represents a column in a database table specified in the FROM clause, a data object, or a scalar subquery.

Table 8.6 describes a list of relational operators and their meanings:

Operator	Meaning
EQ	Equal to
=	Equal to
NE	Not equal to
<>	Not equal to
><	Not equal to
LT	Less than
<	Less than
LE	Less than or equal to
<=	Less than or equal to
GT	Greater than
>	Greater than
GE	Greater than or equal to
>=	Greater than or equal to

TABLE 8.6 Relational operators and their meanings

The values of the operands can be converted to other data types, if necessary. The conversion may be dependent on the platform and code page.

Specifying Range Operators

The following syntax is used to determine whether the value of a column lies within a specified range of values:

```
SELECT ... WHERE <s> [NOT ] BETWEEN <f 1> AND <f 2> ...
```

The condition is evaluated to true if the value of the `<s>` column lies between the data objects `<f1>` and `<f2>` in the case of the `BETWEEN` range operator and does not lie between the values of the data objects `<f1>` and `<f2>` in the case of the `NOT BETWEEN` range operator. You cannot use the `BETWEEN` clause in the `ON` condition of the `FROM` clause.

Matching a Pattern

The syntax to determine whether the value of a column matches a pattern is:

```
SELECT ... WHERE <s> [NOT ] LIKE <f> [ESCAPE <h>] ...
```

In this syntax, the condition is true if the value of the `<s>` column matches or does not match the pattern specified in the data object `<f>`. The data type of the column must be alphanumeric. The `<f>` data object must be of the `C` type.

You can use the following wildcard characters in the `<f>` data object:

- % for a sequence of characters (including spaces)
- _ for a single character

For example, ABC_EFG% matches the strings ABCxEFGxyz and ABCxEFG but does not match ABCEFGxyz. If you want to use two wildcard characters explicitly in the comparison, use the `ESCAPE` clause to specify an escape symbol in the `<h>` expression. If the `ESCAPE` clause is preceded by the `<h>` expression, the wildcards and the escape symbol itself lose their usual function within the pattern `<f>`. The use of _ and % corresponds to Standard SQL usage; however, the logical expressions can use the other wildcard characters (+ and *) in an ABAP program.

Note: You cannot use the LIKE clause in the ON condition of the FROM clause.

Specifying a List

The syntax to find out whether the value of a column is stored in a list of values is:

```
SELECT ... WHERE <s> [NOT ] IN (<f 1>, ......, <f n>) ...
```

The condition is true if the value of the <s> column exists in the list <f1> ... <fn> in the case of the IN clause, or does not exist in the list <f1> ... <fn> in the case of the NOT IN clause.

Checking Subqueries

The following syntax is used to find whether the value of a column is stored in a scalar subquery:

```
SELECT ... WHERE <s> [NOT ] IN <subquery> ...
```

The condition is true if the value of <s> is stored in the result set of the <subquery> scalar subquery in the case of the IN clause, or not stored in the result set of the <subquery> scalar subquery in the case of the NOT IN clause.

The following syntax is used to find whether the selection of a subquery contains any lines:

```
SELECT ... WHERE [ NOT ] EXISTS <subquery> ...
```

This condition is evaluated to true if the result set of the <subquery> subquery contains at least one record in the case of the EXISTS clause, and no record in the case of the NOT EXISTS clause. The subquery does not have to be scalar.

Checking Selection Tables

The following syntax is used to find whether or not the value of a column satisfies the conditions in a selection table:

```
SELECT ... WHERE <s> [NOT ] IN <seltab> ...
```

This syntax uses two operators, IN and NOT IN. The IN operator validates that the value specified in the <s> column matches with the values of the <seltab> expression. The NOT IN operator validates that the value specified in the <s> column does not match with the values stored in the <seltab> expression. The <seltab> expression can be either a real selection table or a RANGES table.

Checking Null Values

The following syntax is used to ascertain whether the value of a column is null:

```
SELECT ... WHERE <s> IS [NOT ] NULL ...
```

This syntax uses two operators, IS NULL and IS NOT NULL. The IS NULL operator validates that the value specified in the <s> column is null. Alternatively, the IS NOT NULL operator validates that the value specified in the <s> column is not null.

Specifying Negating Conditions

The syntax to negate the result of a WHERE clause is:

```
SELECT ... WHERE NOT <cond> ...
```

The condition is true if the <cond> condition specified by the WHERE clause is evaluated to false, and vice versa. The result of an unknown condition remains unknown when negated.

Specifying Linking Conditions

At times, you might need to specify more than one condition in a WHERE clause. In such cases, you can use the AND and OR operators in the WHERE clause, as shown in the following syntax:

```
SELECT ... WHERE <cond 1> AND <cond 2> ...
SELECT ... WHERE <cond 1> OR <cond 2> ...
```

This syntax demonstrates two WHERE clauses; the first WHERE clause uses the AND operator and the second WHERE clause uses the OR operator. The AND operator returns true if the <cond1> and <cond2> conditions are true, whereas the OR operator returns true if one or both the conditions are true.

When NOT, AND, and OR operators are used simultaneously, the priority level of the NOT operator is higher than that of the AND operator and AND takes priority over OR. However, parentheses () can be used to control the processing sequence.

Specifying Dynamic Conditions

The syntax used to specify a condition dynamically is:

```
SELECT ... WHERE (<internal_tab>) ...
```

In this syntax, the <internal_tab> expression represents an internal table with line type C and a maximum length of 72 characters. In this code, you may use only literals for an internal table, not the names of data objects. The internal table can also be left empty.

Use the following syntax if you want to specify only a part of the condition dynamically:

```
SELECT ... WHERE <cond> AND (<internal_tab>) ...
```

You cannot link a static and a dynamic condition by using the OR operator.

> **Note:** Dynamic conditions are specified in the WHERE clause of the SELECT statement.

Specifying Tabular Conditions

The WHERE clause of the SELECT statement has a special variant that allows you to derive conditions from the lines and columns of an internal table, as shown in the following syntax:

```
SELECT ... FOR ALL ENTRIES IN <internal_tab> WHERE
<cond> ...
```

In this syntax, the <internal_tab> expression represents an internal table and the <cond> expression represents one or more conditions of the WHERE clause. The <cond> conditions accept the fields of internal tables as operands. You can use the FOR ALL ENTRIES clause to compare the records or lines of a database table against all lines of the internal table. Consequently, the SAP system selects the lines from the database table that satisfy the condition for each line of the internal table. The result set of the preceding `SELECT` statement consists of the matching records of both the internal table and the database table. Duplicate lines are eliminated automatically from the result set. If the `<internal_tab>` internal table is empty, the `FOR ALL ENTRIES` clause is discarded and all the entries are retrieved or read from the database table.

The internal table `<internal_tab>` must have a structured line type, and each field that occurs in the condition `<cond>` must be compatible with the column of the database with which it is compared. The fields of an internal table cannot be compared by using the `LIKE`, `BETWEEN`, and `IN` operators.

You can use the `FOR ALL ENTRIES` clause to replace nested select loops by operations on internal tables. Using the `FOR ALL ENTRIES` clause can improve the performance significantly for large sets of selected data.

Examples of Using the `WHERE` Clause

In this section, we consider some examples of using the `WHERE` clause to specify various conditions on the `ZSTUDENT_DATA` table, which is a user-defined table. The `ZSTUDENT_DATA` table contains the `STUDENTID`, `STUDENTNAME`, `SUBJECTCODE`, `MARKS`, `ADDRESS`, `CITY`, `CLASS`, `MONTHLYFEES`, and `YEARLYFEES` fields. The records of the `ZSTUDENT_DATA` table are shown in Figure 8.21:

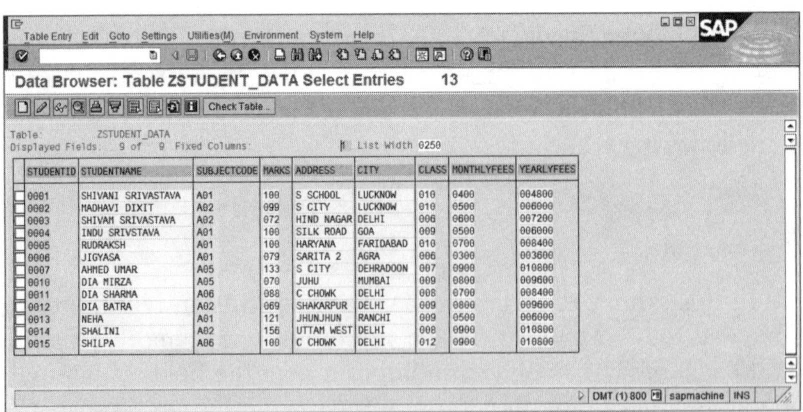

STUDENTID	STUDENTNAME	SUBJECTCODE	MARKS	ADDRESS	CITY	CLASS	MONTHLYFEES	YEARLYFEES
0001	SHIVANI SRIVASTAVA	A01	100	S SCHOOL	LUCKNOW	010	0400	004800
0002	MADHAVI DIXIT	A02	099	S CITY	LUCKNOW	010	0500	006000
0003	SHIVAM SRIVASTAVA	A02	072	HIND NAGAR	DELHI	006	0600	007200
0004	INDU SRIVSTAVA	A01	100	SILK ROAD	GOA	009	0500	006000
0005	RUDRAKSH	A01	100	HARYANA	FARIDABAD	010	0700	008400
0006	JIGYASA	A01	079	SARITA 2	AGRA	006	0300	003600
0007	AHMED UMAR	A05	133	S CITY	DEHRADOON	007	0900	010800
0010	DIA MIRZA	A05	070	JUHU	MUMBAI	009	0800	009600
0011	DIA SHARMA	A06	088	C CHOWK	DELHI	008	0700	008400
0012	DIA BATRA	A02	069	SHAKARPUR	DELHI	009	0800	009600
0013	NEHA	A01	121	JHUNJHUN	RANCHI	009	0500	006000
0014	SHALINI	A02	156	UTTAM WEST	DELHI	008	0900	010800
0015	SHILPA	A06	100	C CHOWK	DELHI	012	0900	010800

FIGURE 8.21 **Displaying the data of the ZSTUDENT_DATA table**

Table 8.7 lists various conditions that can be specified with the `WHERE` clause on the ZSTUDENT_DATA table:

Condition	Description
`TABLES: ZSTUDENT_DATA.` `SELECT * FROM ZSTUDENT_DATA WHERE CITY = 'DELHI'.` `ENDSELECT.`	Demonstrates the use of a simple `WHERE` clause. The condition specified in the `WHERE` clause is evaluated to true if the `CITY` field has the value DELHI.
`TABLES: ZSTUDENT_DATA.` `SELECT * FROM ZSTUDENT_DATA WHERE YEARLYFEES GE 8000.` `ENDSELECT.`	Shows the use of the `GE` operator with the `WHERE` clause. The condition specified in the `WHERE` clause is evaluated to true if the `YEARLYFEES` field contains numbers greater than or equal to 8000.
`TABLES: ZSTUDENT_DATA.` `SELECT * FROM ZSTUDENT_DATA WHERE ADDRESS NE 'C CHOWK'.` `ENDSELECT.`	Illustrates the use of the `NE` operator with the `WHERE` clause. The condition specified in the `WHERE` clause is evaluated to true if the `ADDRESS` field does not contain the string C CHOWK.
`TABLES: ZSTUDENT_DATA.` `SELECT * FROM ZSTUDENT_DATA WHERE MONTHLYFEES BETWEEN 500 AND 800.` `ENDSELECT.`	Exhibits the use of the `BETWEEN` range operator with the `WHERE` clause. The condition specified in the `WHERE` clause is evaluated to true if the field `MONTHLYFEES` contains numbers between 500 and 800.
`TABLES: ZSTUDENT_DATA.` `SELECT * FROM ZSTUDENT_DATA WHERE YEARLYFEES NOT BETWEEN 6000 AND 10000.` `ENDSELECT.`	Demonstrates the use of the `NOT BETWEEN` range operator with the `WHERE` clause. The condition specified in the `WHERE` clause is evaluated to true if the field `YEARLYFEES` contains numbers not between 6000 and 10000.
`TABLES: ZSTUDENT_DATA.SELECT * FROM ZSTUDENT_DATA WHERE STUDENTID NOT BETWEEN '0003' AND '0010'.` `ENDSELECT.`	Shows the use of the `NOT BETWEEN` range operator with the `WHERE` clause. The condition specified in the `WHERE` clause is evaluated to true if the field `STUDENTID` is four characters long and its values do not lie between 0003 and 0010.

Continued

Condition	Description

`TABLES: ZSTUDENT_DATA.`
`SELECT * FROM ZSTUDENT_DATA WHERE`
`STUDENTNAME LIKE '%SRIVASTAVA'.`
`ENDSELECT.`
	Illustrates the use of the LIKE operator with the WHERE clause. The condition specified in the WHERE clause is evaluated to true if the field STUDENTNAME contains a string containing the pattern SRIVASTAVA at the end of a student's name.

`TABLES: ZSTUDENT_DATA.`
`SELECT * FROM ZSTUDENT_DATA WHERE`
`CITY NOT LIKE '_A%'.`
`ENDSELECT.`
	Demonstrates the use of the NOT LIKE operator with the WHERE clause. The condition specified in the WHERE clause is evaluated to true if the field City contains a value whose second character is not A.

`TABLES: ZSTUDENT_DATA.`
`SELECT * FROM ZSTUDENT_DATA WHERE`
`STUDENTNAME LIKE 'DIA#%'`
`ESCAPE '#'.`
`ENDSELECT.`
	Demonstrates the use of the LIKE operator with the WHERE clause to search according to the specified characters. The condition specified in the WHERE clause is evaluated to true if the values contained in the field STUDENTNAME begin with DIA.

`TABLES: ZSTUDENT_DATA.`
`SELECT * FROM ZSTUDENT_DATA WHERE`
`CITY IN ('AGRA', 'MUMBAI',`
`'LUCKNOW').`
`ENDSELECT.`
	Shows the use of the IN operator with the WHERE clause. The condition specified in the WHERE clause is evaluated to true if the column CITY contains one of the values AGRA, MUMBAI, or LUCKNOW.

`TABLES: ZSTUDENT_DATA.`
`SELECT * FROM ZSTUDENT_DATA WHERE`
`CITY NOT IN ('DELHI', 'GOA').`
`ENDSELECT.`
	Demonstrates the use of the NOT IN operator with the WHERE clause. The condition specified in the WHERE clause is evaluated to true if the column CITY does not contain the values DELHI or GOA.

`TABLES: ZSTUDENT_DATA.`
`SELECT * FROM ZSTUDENT_DATA WHERE`
`( SUBJECTCODE = 'A01' OR`
`SUBJECTCODE = 'A02' ) AND NOT ( CITY`
`= 'DELHI' OR CITY = 'LUCKNOW' ).`
`ENDSELECT.`
	Exemplifies the use of the OR, AND, and NOT operators with the WHERE clause. The condition specified in the WHERE clause is evaluated to true if the field SUBJECTCODE contains the value A01 or A02 and the field CITY contains neither DELHI nor LUCKNOW.

TABLE 8.7 Examples of the WHERE clause

We have explored various examples of using different operators with the WHERE clause. Now, let's consider an example of using dynamic conditions, as shown in Listing 8.15:

```
REPORT ZDATA_ACCESS.

*/Specifying a condition dynamically
DATA: CITYDATA(72) TYPE C,
      CITYDETAIL LIKE TABLE OF CITYDATA.
PARAMETERS: CITY_A(10) TYPE C, CITY_B(10) TYPE C.
DATA KOG TYPE KNA1-ORT01.
CONCATENATE 'ORT01 = ''' CITY_A '''' INTO CITYDATA.
APPEND CITYDATA TO CITYDETAIL.
CONCATENATE 'OR ORT01 = ''' CITY_B '''' INTO CITYDATA.
APPEND CITYDATA TO CITYDETAIL.
CONCATENATE 'OR ORT01 = ''' 'GERA' '''' INTO CITYDATA.
APPEND CITYDATA TO CITYDETAIL.
LOOP AT CITYDETAIL INTO CITYDATA.
      WRITE CITYDATA.
ENDLOOP.
SKIP.
SELECT ORT01 INTO KOG FROM KNA1 WHERE (CITYDETAIL).
   WRITE / KOG.
ENDSELECT.
```

LISTING 8.15 **An example of dynamic conditions**

In Listing 8.15, CITYDATA is a variable of C type and CITYDETAIL is a variable of type CITYDATA. The value of CITYDATA is appended to CITYDETAIL.

Figure 8.22 shows the output of Listing 8.15, displaying two text fields, CITY_A and CITY_B:

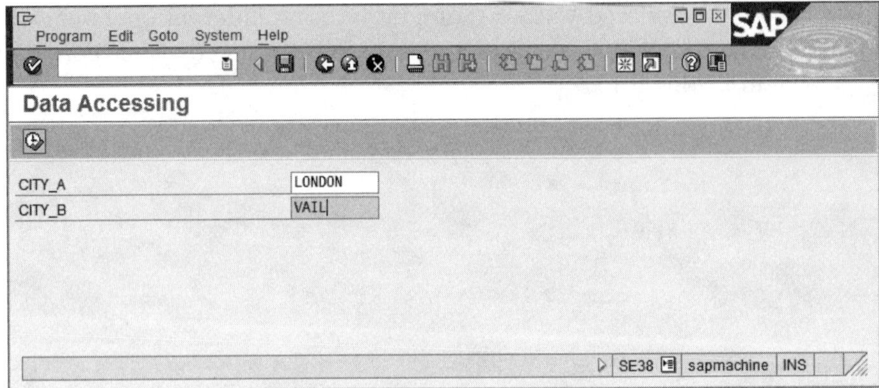

FIGURE 8.22 **Displaying the CITY_A and CITY_B text fields**

You can enter the data dynamically by entering the values in the `CITY_A` and `CITY_B` text fields. For instance, enter LONDON and VAIL in the `CITY_A` and `CITY_B` fields, respectively, and then click the Execute (icon) icon , as shown in Figure 8.22. The resultant output is shown in Figure 8.23:

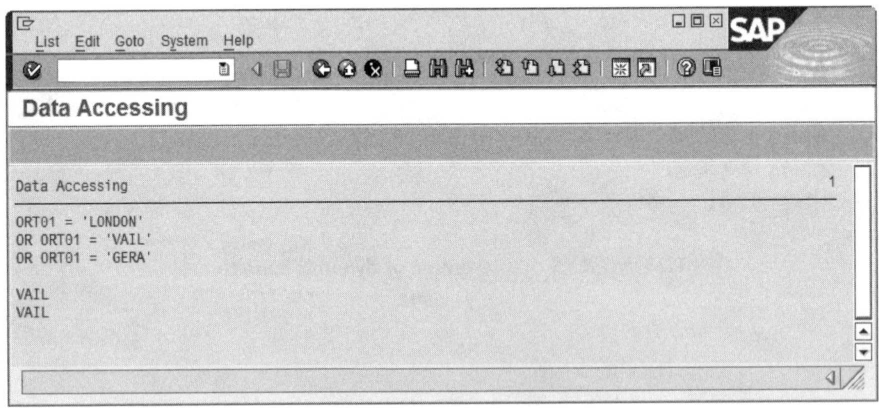

FIGURE 8.23 **Result of dynamic conditions**

Now, let's consider some examples of how to specify a tabular condition in a `WHERE` clause.

Listing 8.16 shows the first example of specifying a tabular condition:

```
REPORT ZDATA_ACCESS.

*/Specifying a tabular condition
DATA: BEGIN OF RECORD,
      KUNNR TYPE KNA1-KUNNR,
      LAND1 TYPE KNA1-LAND1,
      NAME1 TYPE KNA1-NAME1,
      ORT01 TYPE KNA1-ORT01,
   END OF RECORD,
   MYTABLE LIKE TABLE OF RECORD.
RECORD-LAND1 = 'FR'.
RECORD-ORT01 = 'Paris'.
APPEND RECORD TO MYTABLE.
RECORD-LAND1 = 'GB'.
RECORD-ORT01 = 'London'.
APPEND RECORD TO MYTABLE.
SELECT KUNNR LAND1 NAME1 ORT01
INTO CORRESPONDING FIELDS OF RECORD
FROM KNA1
FOR ALL ENTRIES IN MYTABLE
WHERE LAND1 = MYTABLE-LAND1 AND ORT01 = MYTABLE-ORT01.
  WRITE: / RECORD-KUNNR, RECORD-LAND1, RECORD-NAME1, RECORD-
  ORT01.
ENDSELECT.
```

LISTING 8.16 **Example of specifying a tabular condition**

In Listing 8.16, the following tabular conditions are specified:

- The `LAND1` column contains FR and the `ORT01` column contains Paris.
- The `LAND1` column contains GB and the `ORT01` column contains London.

Figure 8.24 shows the result after specifying the tabular conditions:

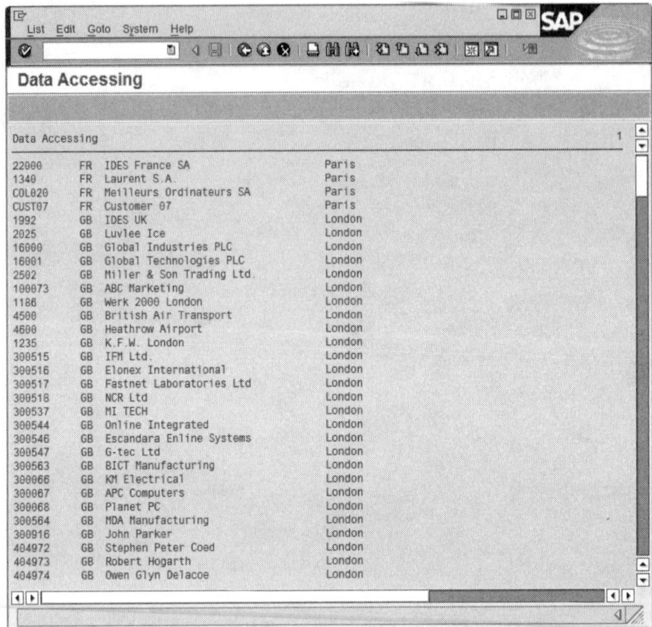

FIGURE 8.24 **Displaying results after specifying the tabular conditions**

Listing 8.17 shows another example of specifying a tabular condition:

```
REPORT ZDATA_ACCESS.

*/Specifying and using tabular condition

DATA: TABLE_A TYPE TABLE OF MARA,
      TABLE_B TYPE SORTED TABLE OF MAKT
                        WITH UNIQUE KEY TABLE LINE,
    KOG LIKE LINE OF TABLE_B.
SELECT MATNR ERNAM
INTO CORRESPONDING FIELDS OF TABLE TABLE_A
FROM MARA
WHERE ERNAM = 'RUDISILL'.
SELECT MATNR MAKTX
```

Continued

```
INTO CORRESPONDING FIELDS OF TABLE TABLE_B
FROM MAKT
FOR ALL ENTRIES IN TABLE_A
WHERE MATNR = TABLE_A-MATNR.
WRITE: 'Material Number', ' ', 'Material
Description'.
skip.
LOOP AT TABLE_B INTO KOG.
   AT NEW MATNR.
       WRITE: / KOG-MATNR.
   ENDAT.
WRITE: KOG-MAKTX.
ENDLOOP.
```

LISTING 8.17 **Specifying a tabular condition**

In Listing 8.17, the data of the MAKT database table is selected on the basis of the corresponding fields of the MARA table, where the value of the `ERNAM` field is RUDISILL. Figure 8.25 shows the output of Listing 8.17:

Material Number	Material Description
637	Adjustable Bracket.iam
638	Clamp Screw.iam
640	Adjusting Nut.ipt
641	Adjusting Screw.ipt
642	Clamp Screw.ipt
643	Holder Bracket.ipt
644	Knob.ipt
645	Pilot Screw.ipt
646	Pin.ipt
647	Hexagon Socket Head Cap Screw - 1/4 - 20
648	Hexagon Socket Set Screw - Flat Point -

FIGURE 8.25 **Displaying results from multiple tables after specifying conditions**

The `GROUP BY` Clause

The `GROUP BY` clause collects several lines from a database table into a single line. It allows you to categorize and summarize the lincs of a database table on the basis of a single column or group of columns. Note that the columns used in the `GROUP BY` clause cannot be specified for aggregate functions in the `SELECT` statement. However, the columns that are not used in the `GROUP BY` clause can be included in the `SELECT` statement for aggregate functions.

You can specify the columns in the GROUP BY clause either statically or dynamically.

Now, let's explore these two ways of specifying columns in the GROUP BY clause, one by one.

Specifying Columns Statically

The following syntax is used to specify the columns in the GROUP BY clause statically:

```
SELECT <database_tab_lines> <s1> [AS <a 1>] <s 2>
[AS <a 2>] ...
        <agg> <sm> [AS <a m>] <agg> <s n> [AS <a n>] ...
...
GROUP BY <s1> <s 2>....
```

In this syntax, <s1>, <s2>...<sn> represents column names of a database table; <a1>, <a2>...<an> represent alias names for these column names; the <agg> expression represents aggregate functions; and <am> and <an> represent alias names for the columns that are involved in aggregate functions.

To use the GROUP BY clause, you must specify all the relevant columns in the SELECT statement. You should include only those column names in the GROUP BY clause whose values are repeated in the table. The alias names of the columns, specified in the SELECT statement, are not allowed in the GROUP BY clause.

All columns of the SELECT clause that are not listed in the GROUP BY clause must be included in aggregate functions. This defines how the values stored in these columns are calculated when the lines are summarized.

Specifying Columns Dynamically

The following syntax is used to specify the columns in the GROUP BY clause dynamically:

```
... GROUP BY (<internal_tab>) ...
```

In this syntax, <internal_tab> represents an internal table with line type C and a maximum length of 72 characters.

Now, let's consider an example of using the GROUP BY clause, as shown in Listing 8.18:

```
REPORT ZDATA_ACCESS.

*/Using GROUP BY Clause
DATA: MATNR TYPE MARI-MATNR,
      MINIMUM TYPE P DECIMALS 2,
      MAXIMUM TYPE P DECIMALS 2.
SELECT MATNR MIN( MENGE ) MAX( MENGE )
INTO (MATNR, MINIMUM, MAXIMUM)
FROM MARI
GROUP BY MATNR.
  WRITE: / MATNR, MINIMUM, MAXIMUM.
ENDSELECT.
```

LISTING 8.18 **An example of using the GROUP BY clause**

In Listing 8.18, the data of the MARI database table is grouped based on the values of the `MATNR` field because the `MATNR` field is used in the `GROUP BY` clause. The minimum and maximum values of the `MENGE` field for each group are then obtained and placed in the summarized line, as shown in Figure 8.26:

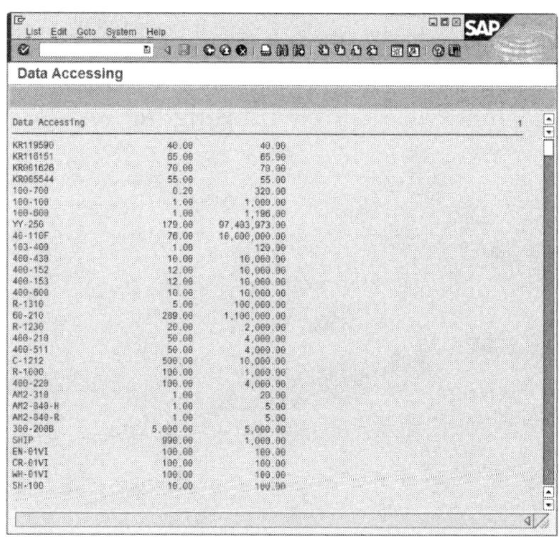

FIGURE 8.26 **Showing the usage of the GROUP BY clause**

The HAVING Clause

The HAVING clause is used to restrict the output to selected groups based on specified conditions. The HAVING clause can be used only in conjunction with the GROUP BY clause. The syntax to select lines is:

```
SELECT <database_tab_lines> <s1> [AS <a1>] <s2> [AS <a2>]
...
       <agg> <sm> [AS <am>] <agg> <sn> [AS <an>] ...
. . .
GROUP BY <s1> <s2> ....
HAVING <cond>.
```

In this syntax, the HAVING clause is used after the GROUP BY clause to specify one or more conditions in the <cond> expression. The fields specified in the conditions of the HAVING clause should be the same as those used in the SELECT clause. If you use an invalid column, a runtime error occurs.

You can also specify the aggregate expressions in the HAVING clause for the columns that do not appear in the GROUP BY clause. However, you cannot use aggregate expressions in the conditions specified in the WHERE clause. Moreover, in the HAVING clause, similar to the WHERE clause, the conditions can be specified in the form of an internal table with line type C and a length of 72 characters.

Listing 8.19 shows an example of using the HAVING clause:

```
REPORT ZDATA_ACCESS.

*/Using GROUP BY with HAVING Clause

DATA KOG TYPE MARI.
SELECT ZEILE
INTO KOG-ZEILE
FROM MARI
WHERE USNAM = 'BUROW'
GROUP BY ZEILE
HAVING SUM( MENGE ) > 10.
    WRITE: / KOG-ZEILE.
ENDSELECT.
```

LISTING 8.19 **Example of using the HAVING clause**

In Listing 8.19, the data of the MARI table is displayed only when:

- The value in the `USNAM` field is BUROW
- The data is grouped by the values of the `ZEILE` field
- The sum of the values in the `MENGE` field is greater than 10

Figure 8.27 shows the data of the MARI table after using the `GROUP BY` and `HAVING` clauses:

```
005
004
002
006
001
007
003
```


FIGURE 8.27 **Displaying results after using the GROUP BY and HAVING clauses**

The `ORDER BY` Clause

The `ORDER BY` clause sorts the result set according to the content of its columns. You can sort the selection by any column (not necessarily the primary key) and specify the columns either statically or dynamically.

The syntax to sort the selection set in ascending order by the primary key is:

```
SELECT <database_tab_lines> *
...
... ORDER BY PRIMARY KEY.
```

The sorting method, shown in this syntax, is possible only if you use an asterisk (*) in the `SELECT` clause to select all the columns. Moreover, it works only if you specify a single database table in the `FROM` clause. You cannot use views or joins because neither has a defined primary key.

The following syntax is used to sort the lines in the selection by specifying one or more columns in the `ORDER BY` clause:

```
SELECT ...
... ORDER BY <s1> [ASCENDING|DESCENDING]
<s2> [ASCENDING|DESCENDING] ...
```

This syntax shows that the lines are sorted by the <s1>, <s2>,. . . columns in the ORDER BY clause in either ASCENDING or DESCENDING order. The default is the ascending order. The sort order depends on the sequence in which you list the columns.

You can use either the names of the columns specified in the SELECT clause or their alias names. By using alias names for aggregate expressions, you can use them as sort fields.

The syntax to specify the columns in the ORDER BY clause dynamically is:

```
SELECT . . .
. . .
ORDER BY (<internal_tab>).
```

In this syntax, <internal_tab> is an internal table, with line type C and a maximum length of 72 characters, containing the column names <s1>, <s2>, . . . <sn>.

Listing 8.20 shows an example of using the ORDER BY clause:

```
REPORT ZDATA_ACCESS.

*/Using ORDER BY with DESCENDING Clause

DATA: BEGIN OF KOG,
USNAM TYPE MARI-USNAM,
MAX TYPE I,
END OF KOG.
SELECT USNAM MAX( MENGE ) AS MAXI
INTO CORRESPONDING FIELDS OF KOG
FROM MARI
GROUP BY USNAM
ORDER BY USNAM DESCENDING.
WRITE: / KOG-USNAM, '|', KOG-MAXI.
ENDSELECT.
```

LISTING 8.20 **Example of using the ORDER BY clause**

In Listing 8.20, the lines of the MARI database table are grouped on the basis of the USNAM field. The SAP system finds the maximum value of the MENGE field for each group. The ORDER BY clause is then used to sort the USNAM field in descending order. It is to be noted that an alias, MAXI, is created to store the maximum value of the MENGE field. Figure 8.28 shows the output of Listing 8.20:

List Edit Goto System Help

Data Accessing

Data Accessing 1

ZUERKER	10
ZIMMERMANNV	10
WONGY	99,000
WINTHER	3
WINKEL	50
WILDEO	116
WF-SM-1	1
WETTENGL	5,000
WESTERNHAGEN	2
WESTERMANN	3,750
WESSENDORF	100
WENIG	232
WEIS	100
WEINERJ	10
WEINBRECHT	100,000
WEIMANN	30
VELILLA	100
VDLINGEN	1,000,000
VANDIJK	16,000
VANDERBECK	10,970
VAN DIJK	5,000
UHLE	42
THYS	10,000
THOMPSON	200,000
THOMAS	100
THOMA	10,970
THIELE	20,000
TENNITY	1,000,000
STROBELJ	2,000
STEVENSK	1,000
STEVENS	1,000

FIGURE 8.28 **Displaying results after using the ORDER BY clause**

SUBQUERIES

A subquery is a type of the SELECT statement used within the WHERE clause of another SELECT statement, that is, a SELECT statement nested inside another SELECT statement. In this kind of nesting, the outer SELECT statement forms an outer query, while the inner SELECT statement forms an inner query or subquery. The following syntax is used to implement a subquery:

```
(SELECT <result>
FROM <source>
[WHERE <sql_condition>]
[GROUP BY <group_fields>]
[HAVING <group_condition>])
```

In this syntax, you can see that a subquery is provided in the parentheses (). A subquery can use all the clauses of the SELECT statement except the INTO and ORDER BY clauses. Also note that a subquery cannot be used in the ON condition of the FROM clause. The level of nesting of subqueries is fixed to 10, which means that the WHERE and the HAVING clauses of a SELECT statement can have 10 levels of nested SELECT statements. When a nested subquery in the WHERE clause uses the fields from the outer query, it is known as a correlated query.

A subquery can be specified by using the following logical expressions in the <sql_condition> condition of the WHERE clause:

- **Using the ALL, ANY, or SOME clause along with relational operators**—The syntax to specify the ALL, ANY, or SOME clause is:

```
. . . col operator [ALL|ANY|SOME] subquery . . .
```

In this syntax, operator stands for a relational operator, such as =, <=, and >=. The result set can have single or multiple lines. The ALL clause is used when the comparison is evaluated to true for all the lines of a subquery, while the ANY or SOME clause is used when the comparison is evaluated to true for at least one line of the subquery. The equality operator (= or EQ), in conjunction with the ANY or SOME clause, has the same effect as the IN operator to check a value.

If the result set of the subquery contains only one line, the comparison can be carried out without the specification of the ALL, ANY, or SOME clause. However, if the result set for the subquery contains multiple lines, an unhandled exception occurs when the statement is executed.

- **Using the EXISTS or NOT EXISTS clause**—The syntax to specify the EXISTS or NOT EXISTS clause is:

```
... [NOT] EXISTS subquery ...
```

In this syntax, the EXISTS or NOT EXISTS clause is used when the result set of the subquery contains at least one line or no lines.

- **Using the IN or NOT IN clause**—The syntax to specify the IN or NOT IN clause is:

```
... col [NOT] IN subquery ...
```

In this syntax, the `IN` or `NOT IN` clause is used to check whether or not the value for the `col` column is stored in the subquery.

Examples of Subqueries

Listing 8.21 shows an example when the result set of a subquery contains only one line:

```
REPORT ZDATA_ACCESS.

*/Creating subquery by using equal to (=) operator

DATA: Tab1 TYPE TABLE OF MAKZ,
      KOG LIKE LINE OF Tab1.
SELECT * INTO TABLE Tab1 FROM MAKZ
  WHERE MATNR = ( select MATNR
                  FROM MAKV
                  WHERE MATNR = 'T-COP').
LOOP AT Tab1 INTO KOG.
  WRITE: / KOG-MATNR, KOG-WERKS, KOG-KUPPL, KOG-DATUB.
ENDLOOP.
```

LISTING 8.21 **The result set of a subquery containing one line**

In Listing 8.21, the subquery returns a single line to the outer query, where the `MATNR` field of the value of the MAKV table is T-COP. Consequently, the outer query displays all the lines of the MAKZ table, where the value of the `MATNR` field is T-COP, as shown in Figure 8.29:

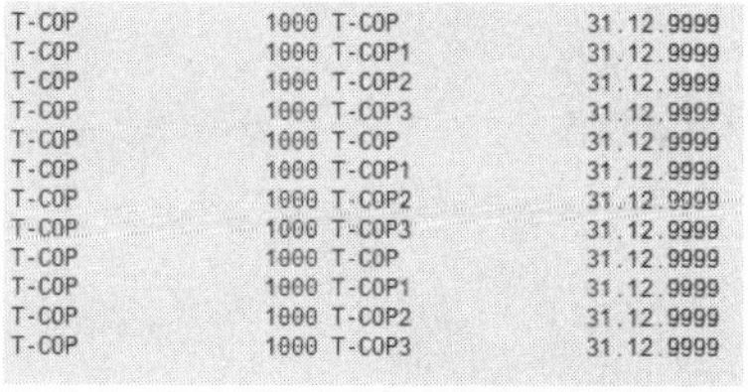

```
T-COP       1000 T-COP        31.12.9999
T-COP       1000 T-COP1       31.12.9999
T-COP       1000 T-COP2       31.12.9999
T-COP       1000 T-COP3       31.12.9999
T-COP       1000 T-COP        31.12.9999
T-COP       1000 T-COP1       31.12.9999
T-COP       1000 T-COP2       31.12.9999
T-COP       1000 T-COP3       31.12.9999
T-COP       1000 T-COP        31.12.9999
T-COP       1000 T-COP1       31.12.9999
T-COP       1000 T-COP2       31.12.9999
T-COP       1000 T-COP3       31.12.9999
```


FIGURE 8.29 **Displaying result set when the subquery returns a single line**

Listing 8.22 shows a correlated subquery:

```
REPORT ZDATA_ACCESS.

*/Creating a subquery by using EXISTS keyword

DATA: Tab1 TYPE TABLE OF MAKZ,
      KOG LIKE LINE OF Tab1.
SELECT * INTO TABLE Tab1 FROM MAKZ
   WHERE EXISTS ( select *
                  FROM MAKV
                  WHERE MATNR = 'T-COP').
LOOP AT Tab1 INTO KOG.
  WRITE: / KOG-MATNR, KOG-WERKS, KOG-KUPPL, KOG-DATUB.

ENDLOOP.
```

LISTING 8.22 **A correlated subquery**

Listing 8.22 shows that the outer query contains the `EXISTS` keyword in the `WHERE` clause, according to which only those records of the MAKZ table for which the `MATNR` field of the MAKV table contains the value T-COP are displayed, as shown in Figure 8.30:

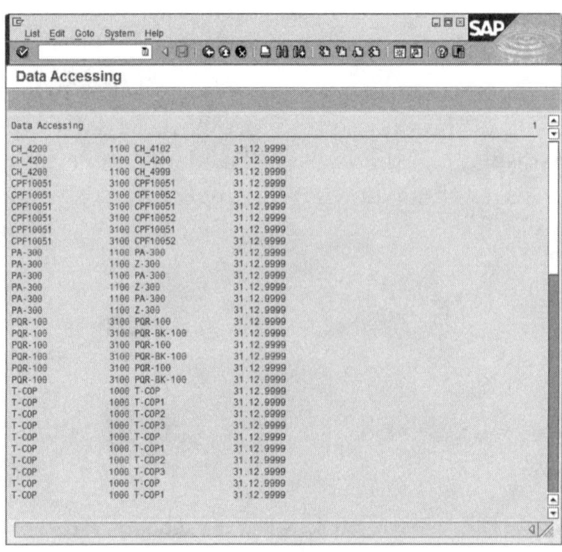

FIGURE 8.30 **Displaying the result of the correlated subquery**

Listing 8.23 shows an example when the outer query contains the `NOT IN` operator:

```
REPORT ZDATA_ACCESS.

*/Creating a subquery by using NOT IN

DATA: Tab1 TYPE TABLE OF MAKZ,
      KOG LIKE LINE OF Tab1.
SELECT * INTO TABLE Tab1 FROM MAKZ
    WHERE MATNR NOT IN (select MATNR
           FROM MAKV
           WHERE MATNR = 'T-COP' OR MATNR = 'PA-300').
LOOP AT Tab1 INTO KOG.
 WRITE: / KOG-MATNR, KOG-WERKS, KOG-KUPPL, KOG-DATUB.

ENDLOOP.
```

LISTING 8.23 **Example of an outer query containing the NOT IN operator**

Listing 8.23 shows that the outer query contains the `NOT IN` operator in the `WHERE` clause. As a result, the outer query displays all the records of the MAKZ table where the value of the `MATNR` field of the MAKV table is not T-COP or PA-300. Figure 8.31 shows the output of Listing 8.23:

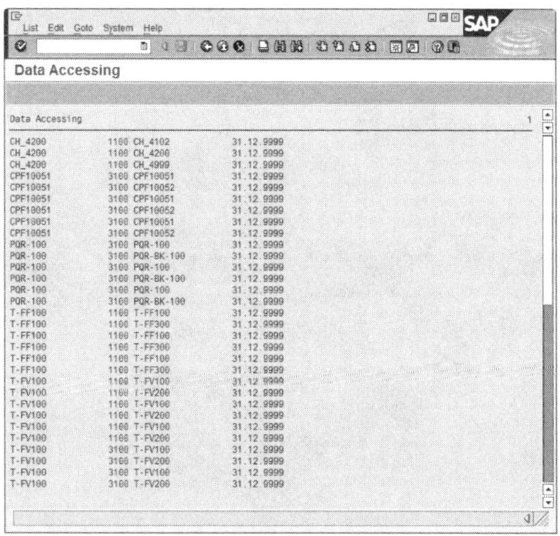

FIGURE 8.31 **Displaying the result of a subquery when the outer query contains the NOT IN operator**

Listing 8.24 shows an example of a subquery containing an aggregate function:

```
REPORT ZDATA_ACCESS.

*/Subquery on the basis of an aggregate function
Tables: MARI.
DATA: MARI_TAB TYPE TABLE OF MARI,
      KOG LIKE LINE OF MARI_TAB.
SELECT *
  INTO TABLE MARI_TAB FROM MARI
  WHERE MENGE > (select avg( MENGE ) FROM MARI
                WHERE USNAM = 'SCHMITTV').
LOOP AT MARI_TAB INTO KOG.
  WRITE: / KOG-MBLNR, KOG-ZEILE, KOG-USNAM, KOG-MENGE.

ENDLOOP.
```

LISTING 8.24 **Example of a subquery containing an aggregate function**

In Listing 8.24, the outer query shows all the records of the MARI table, where the values of the `MENGE` field are greater than their average value, and the value in the `USNAM` field is SCHMITTV. Figure 8.32 shows the result of Listing 8.24:

```
49001782  001 SCHMITTV    10,000,000.000
49001782  002 SCHMITTV    10,000,000.000
49001782  003 SCHMITTV    10,000,000.000
49001782  004 SCHMITTV    10,000,000.000
49001782  005 SCHMITTV    10,000,000.000
49001782  006 SCHMITTV    10,000,000.000
49001782  007 SCHMITTV    10,000,000.000
49001782  008 SCHMITTV    10,000,000.000
49001782  009 SCHMITTV    10,000,000.000
49001782  010 SCHMITTV    10,000,000.000
49001782  011 SCHMITTV    10,000,000.000
49001782  012 SCHMITTV    10,000,000.000
49001782  013 SCHMITTV    10,000,000.000
49001782  014 SCHMITTV    10,000,000.000
49001782  015 SCHMITTV    10,000,000.000
49001782  016 SCHMITTV    10,000,000.000
49001782  017 SCHMITTV    10,000,000.000
49001782  018 SCHMITTV    10,000,000.000
49001782  020 SCHMITTV    10,000,000.000
49001782  021 SCHMITTV    10,000,000.000
49001782  024 SCHMITTV    10,000,000.000
49001782  025 SCHMITTV    10,000,000.000
49001782  027 SCHMITTV    10,000,000.000
49001782  028 SCHMITTV    10,000,000.000
49001782  029 SCHMITTV    10,000,000.000
49001782  030 SCHMITTV    10,000,000.000
49001782  031 SCHMITTV    10,000,000.000
49001782  032 SCHMITTV    10,000,000.000
49001782  033 SCHMITTV    10,000,000.000
49001782  034 SCHMITTV    10,000,000.000
49001782  035 SCHMITTV    10,000,000.000
50005970  002 BOLLINGER    4,725,933.000
50006100  002 BOLLINGER    4,974,667.000
50006187  002 BOLLINGER    5,223,400.000
50005661  003 BOLLINGER  644,000,000.000
50005661  004 BOLLINGER    5,150,000.000
50005738  001 BOLLINGER  140,486,500.000
50005739  001 BOLLINGER   21,285,833.000
50005740  001 BOLLINGER   97,403,973.000
50005742  002 BOLLINGER   53,667,000.000
```


FIGURE 8.32 **Displaying the result when an aggregate function is used in a subquery**

INSERTING DATA INTO A DATABASE TABLE

In Open SQL, the INSERT statement is used to insert one or more lines into a database table. The following syntax shows the use of the INSERT statement:

```
INSERT INTO <target_database_tab> <database_tab_lines>.
```

In this syntax, <target_database_tab> represents a database table and <database_tab_lines> represents the lines that have to be inserted in the table. You can specify the <target_database_tab> database table either statically or dynamically.

The syntax to specify a database table statically is:

```
INSERT INTO <target_database_tab> [CLIENT SPECIFIED]
<database_tab_lines>.
```

The syntax to specify a database table dynamically is:

```
INSERT INTO <target_database_tab>) [CLIENT SPECIFIED]
<database_tab_lines>.
```

In both syntaxes, the <target_database_tab> expression represents the name of a database table defined in the ABAP Dictionary. The CLIENT SPECIFIED clause is used to disable automatic client-handling feature of Open SQL.

The syntax to insert a row of a single line into a database table is:

```
INSERT INTO <target_database_tab> VALUES <work_area>.
```

In this syntax, <work_area> is a work area created for the <target_database_tab> database table. The <work_area> work area has the same length and alignment as the line structure of the <target_database_tab> table.

If the database table does not contain a line with the same primary key as specified in the work area, the operation is completed successfully and the value of the SY-SUBRC variable is set to 0. Otherwise, the line is not inserted and the value of the SY-SUBRC variable is set to 4. The syntax to insert lines individually by using the INSERT statement is:

```
INSERT <target_database_tab> FROM <work_area >.
```

In this syntax, the FROM clause is used instead of the VALUES clause, allowing you to insert data without using the INTO clause. Another way to write the INSERT statement is as follows:

```
INSERT <target_database_tab>.
```

In this syntax, the INSERT statement inserts a line into the <target_database_tab> database table by using a table work area. The table work area is defined by using the TABLES statement. Note that the name of the table work area is the same as that of the database table. Note that in this case, you cannot specify the name of a data base table dynamically.

The following syntax is used to insert several lines into a database table:

```
INSERT <target_database_tab> FROM TABLE <internal_tab>
[ACCEPTING DUPLICATE KEYS].
```

In this syntax, lines from the <internal_tab> internal table are transferred to a database table, <target_database_tab>. The value of the SY-SUBRC variable is set to zero when all the lines have been transferred successfully. However, a runtime error occurs if it fails to transfer one or more lines because of duplicate entries in the same fields. This runtime error can be prevented by using the ACCEPTING DUPLICATE KEYS clause. When the ACCEPTING DUPLICATE KEYS clause is used, the lines that can cause runtime errors are discarded and the value of the SY-SUBRC variable is set to 4.

Note: The SY-DBCNT system variable displays the number of lines that are inserted into the database table.

Note: Use an internal table with the INSERT statement to insert a large number of lines into a database table rather than inserting one line at a time.

Examples of Data Insertion

In this section, all the listings use the ZEMPLOYEE_DATA table, which is a user-defined database table created in the ABAP Dictionary. The ZEMPLOYEE_DATA table initially has 10 lines, as shown in Figure 8.33:

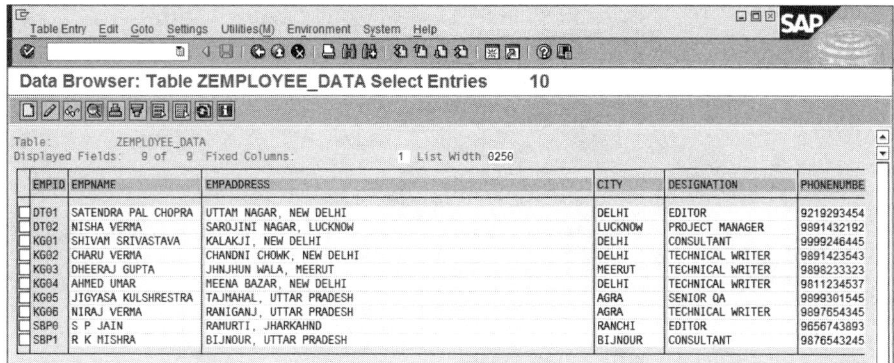

EMPID	EMPNAME	EMPADDRESS	CITY	DESIGNATION	PHONENUMBE
DT01	SATENDRA PAL CHOPRA	UTTAM NAGAR, NEW DELHI	DELHI	EDITOR	9219293454
DT02	NISHA VERMA	SAROJINI NAGAR, LUCKNOW	LUCKNOW	PROJECT MANAGER	9891432192
KG01	SHIVAM SRIVASTAVA	KALAKJI, NEW DELHI	DELHI	CONSULTANT	9999246445
KG02	CHARU VERMA	CHANDNI CHOWK, NEW DELHI	DELHI	TECHNICAL WRITER	9891423543
KG03	DHEERAJ GUPTA	JHNJHUN WALA, MEERUT	MEERUT	TECHNICAL WRITER	9898233323
KG04	AHMED UMAR	MEENA BAZAR, NEW DELHI	DELHI	TECHNICAL WRITER	9811234537
KG05	JIGYASA KULSHRESTRA	TAJMAHAL, UTTAR PRADESH	AGRA	SENIOR QA	9899301545
KG06	NIRAJ VERMA	RANIGANJ, UTTAR PRADESH	AGRA	TECHNICAL WRITER	9897654345
SBP0	S P JAIN	RAMURTI, JHARKAHND	RANCHI	EDITOR	9656743893
SBP1	R K MISHRA	BIJNOUR, UTTAR PRADESH	BIJNOUR	CONSULTANT	9876543245

FIGURE 8.33 **Displaying the lines stored in the ZEMPLOYEE_DATA table**

Now, let's insert some lines into the ZEMPLOYEE_DATA table, as shown in Listing 8.25:

```
REPORT ZINSERT_DATA.

*/Inserting three lines into the ZINSERT_DATA table

TABLES ZEMPLOYEE_DATA.
DATA KOG TYPE ZEMPLOYEE_DATA.
KOG-EMPID = 'KG07'.
KOG-EMPNAME = 'MEHTAB ALAM'.
KOG-EMPADDRESS = 'MUKHNANDAN VIHAR, PATNA'.
KOG-CITY = 'PATNA'.
KOG-DESIGNATION = 'TECHNICAL WRITER'.
KOG-PHONENUMBER = '9981145622'.
KOG-SALARY = 13000.
KOG-JOININGDATE = '20062006'.
KOG-MAILID = 'MEHTAB.ALAM@YAHOO.COM'.
INSERT INTO ZEMPLOYEE_DATA VALUES KOG.
KOG-EMPID = 'KG08'.
KOG-EMPNAME = 'VIKASH SUMAN'.
KOG-EMPADDRESS = 'BHARATPUR, PATNA'.
```

Continued

```
KOG-CITY = 'PATNA'.
KOG-DESIGNATION = 'TECHNICAL WRITER'.
KOG-PHONENUMBER = '9981718812'.
KOG-SALARY = 13000.
KOG-JOININGDATE = '20062006'.
KOG-MAILID = 'VIKASH.SUMAN@YAHOO.COM'.
INSERT ZEMPLOYEE_DATA FROM KOG.
KOG-EMPID = 'KG09'.
KOG-EMPNAME = 'RAM KUMAR'.
KOG-EMPADDRESS = 'CHANDAN NAGAR, PATNA'.
KOG-CITY = 'PATNA'.
KOG-DESIGNATION = 'TECHNICAL WRITER'.
KOG-PHONENUMBER = '9911424281'.
KOG-SALARY = 13500.
KOG-JOININGDATE = '20060723'.
KOG-MAILID = 'RAM.KUMAR@YAHOO.COM'.
INSERT ZEMPLOYEE_DATA.
```

LISTING 8.25 **Inserting Lines in the ZEMPLOYEE_DATA table**

Listing 8.25 shows the insertion of three lines into the KOG work area, which are then inserted into the table `ZEMPLOYEE_DATA`. It must be noted that each line is first inserted in the work area and then into the table. This process is repeated for each individual insertion. In this case, this process is repeated three times because we have inserted three lines in the `ZEMPLOYEE_DATA` table. As shown in Listing 8.25, any of the following syntaxes can be used to insert lines into a table:

```
INSERT INTO ZEMPLOYEE_DATA VALUES KOG.
```

or

```
INSERT ZEMPLOYEE_DATA FROM KOG.
```

or

```
INSERT ZEMPLOYEE_DATA
```

Listing 8.25 shows the application of all these. three syntaxes to insert lines into the `ZEMPLOYEE_DATA` table.

Figure 8.34 shows the output of Listing 8.25:

EMPID	EMPNAME	EMPADDRESS	CITY	DESIGNATION	PHONE
DT01	SATENDRA PAL CHOPRA	UTTAM NAGAR, NEW DELHI	DELHI	EDITOR	92192
DT02	NISHA VERMA	SAROJINI NAGAR, LUCKNOW	LUCKNOW	PROJECT MANAGER	98914
KG01	SHIVAM SRIVASTAVA	KALAKJI, NEW DELHI	DELHI	CONSULTANT	99992
KG02	CHARU VERMA	CHANDNI CHOWK, NEW DELHI	DELHI	TECHNICAL WRITER	98914
KG03	DHEERAJ GUPTA	JHNJHUN WALA, MEERUT	MEERUT	TECHNICAL WRITER	98982
KG04	AHMED UMAR	MEENA BAZAR, NEW DELHI	DELHI	TECHNICAL WRITER	98112
KG05	JIGYASA KULSHRESTRA	TAJMAHAL, UTTAR PRADESH	AGRA	SENIOR QA	98993
KG06	NIRAJ VERMA	RANIGANJ, UTTAR PRADESH	AGRA	TECHNICAL WRITER	98976
KG07	MEHTAB ALAM	MUKHNANDAN VIHAR, PATNA	PATNA	TECHNICAL WRITER	99811
KG08	VIKASH SUMAN	BHARATPUR, PATNA	PATNA	TECHNICAL WRITER	99817
KG09	RAM KUMAR	CHANDAN NAGAR, PATNA	PATNA	TECHNICAL WRITER	99114
SBP0	S P JAIN	RAMURTI, JHARKAHND	RANCHI	EDITOR	96567
SBP1	R K MISHRA	BIJNOUR, UTTAR PRADESH	BIJNOUR	CONSULTANT	98765

FIGURE 8.34 **Displaying three more lines inserted into the ZEMPLOYEE_DATA table**

In Figure 8.34, you can see that the lines corresponding to the values MEHTAB ALAM, VIKASH SUMAN, and RAM KUMAR in the `EMPNAME` field are added to the `ZEMPLOYEE_DATA` table.

Listing 8.26 shows how to transfer data from an internal table to a database table:

```
REPORT ZDATA_ACCESS.
*/Inserting two lines into the ZEMPLOYEE_DATA table with the
help of an internal table-MYTABLE
DATA: MYTABLE TYPE HASHED TABLE OF ZEMPLOYEE_DATA
WITH UNIQUE KEY EMPID,
KOG LIKE LINE OF MYTABLE.

KOG-EMPID = 'KG10'.
KOG-EMPNAME = 'SHARJEEL AHMAD'.
KOG-EMPADDRESS = 'JAMUNA NAGAR, PATNA'.
KOG-CITY = 'PATNA'.
KOG-DESIGNATION = 'QUALITY ANALYSIS MANAGER'.
KOG-PHONENUMBER = '9981148113'.
KOG-SALARY = 30000.
KOG-JOININGDATE = '20070506'.
KOG-MAILID = 'SHARJEEL.AHMAD@YAHOO.COM'.
INSERT KOG INTO TABLE MYTABLE.
INSERT INTO ZEMPLOYEE_DATA VALUES KOG.
```

Continued

```
KOG-EMPID = 'KG11'.
KOG-EMPNAME = 'ASHISH CHAUHAN'.
KOG-EMPADDRESS = 'MAHROLI, DELHI'.
KOG-CITY = 'DELHI'.
KOG-DESIGNATION = 'TECHNICAL WRITER'.
KOG-PHONENUMBER = '9911343421'.
KOG-SALARY = 13000.
KOG-JOININGDATE = '20081001'.
KOG-MAILID = 'ASHISH.CHAUHAN@YAHOO.COM'.
INSERT KOG INTO TABLE MYTABLE.

INSERT ZEMPLOYEE_DATA FROM TABLE MYTABLE ACCEPTING DUPLICATE
KEYS.

IF SY-SUBRC = 0.
...
ELSEIF SY-SUBRC = 4.
...
ENDIF.
```

LISTING 8.26 **Transferring data from an internal table to a database table**

Listing 8.26 inserts two lines together into the KOG work area, which are then inserted into the `MYTABLE` internal table. Finally, the content of the `MYTABLE` internal table is inserted into the `ZEMPLOYEE_DATA` database table. The value of the `SY-SUBRC` variable is checked with the help of the `IF...ELSEIF` construct to verify whether the operation has been successful. Figure 8.35 shows the result of Listing 8.26:

Employee ID	Employee Name	Employee Address	City	Employee Desigation	Employe
DT01	SATENDRA PAL CHOPRA	UTTAM NAGAR, NEW DELHI	DELHI	EDITOR	9219293
DT02	NISHA VERMA	SAROJINI NAGAR, LUCKNOW	LUCKNOW	PROJECT MANAGER	9891432
KG01	SHIVAM SRIVASTAVA	KALAKJI, NEW DELHI	DELHI	CONSULTANT	9999246
KG02	CHARU VERMA	CHANDNI CHOWK, NEW DELHI	DELHI	TECHNICAL WRITER	9891423
KG03	DHEERAJ GUPTA	JHNJHUN WALA, MEERUT	MEERUT	TECHNICAL WRITER	9898233
KG04	AHMED UMAR	MEENA BAZAR, NEW DELHI	DELHI	TECHNICAL WRITER	9811234
KG05	JIGYASA KULSHRESTRA	TAJMAHAL, UTTAR PRADESH	AGRA	SENIOR QA	9899301
KG06	NIRAJ VERMA	RANIGANJ, UTTAR PRADESH	AGRA	TECHNICAL WRITER	9897654
KG07	MEHTAB ALAM	MUKHNANDAN VIHAR, PATNA	PATNA	TECHNICAL WRITER	0998114
KG08	VIKASH SUMAN	BHARATPUR, PATNA	PATNA	TECHNICAL WRITER	0998171
KG09	RAM KUMAR	CHANDAN NAGAR, PATNA	PATNA	TECHNICAL WRITER	9911424
KG10	SHARJEEL AHMAD	JAMUNA NAGAR, PATNA	PATNA	QUALITY ANALYSIS MAN	9981148
KG11	ASHISH CHAUHAN	MAHROLI, DELHI	DELHI	TECHNICAL WRITER	0991134
SBP0	S P JAIN	RAMURTI, JHARKAHND	RANCHI	EDITOR	9656743
SBP1	R K MISHRA	BIJNOUR, UTTAR PRADESH	BIJNOUR	CONSULTANT	9876543

FIGURE 8.35 **Displaying two more lines inserted in the ZEMPLOYEE_DATA table**

In Figure 8.35, you can see that the lines corresponding to the values "SHARJEEL AHMAD" and "ASHISH CHAUHAN" in the Employee Name field are newly added in the ZEMPLOYEE_DATA table.

UPDATING DATA IN A DATABASE TABLE

The UPDATE statement of Open SQL used to update the data in a database table is:

```
UPDATE <target_database_tab> <database_tab_lines>.
```

In this syntax, <target_database_tab> represents a database table and <database_tab_lines> represents the lines that have to be updated in the table. You can specify a database table either statically or dynamically.

The syntax to update a database table, which is specified statically, is:

```
UPDATE <target_database_tab> [CLIENT SPECIFIED] <database_
tab_lines>.
```

The syntax to update a database table, which is specified dynamically, is:

```
UPDATE (<target_database_tab>) [CLIENT SPECIFIED] <database_
tab_lines>.
```

In both syntaxes, the <target_database_tab> field contains the name of a database table defined in the ABAP Dictionary. The CLIENT SPECIFIED clause is used to disable the automatic client-handling feature of Open SQL.

The following syntax is used to change certain columns in the database table:

```
UPDATE <target_database_tab> SET <si> ... [WHERE <cond>].
```

In this syntax, the WHERE clause is used to specify a condition on the basis of which the table lines are updated. If you do not specify a WHERE clause, all the lines are changed. The <s1>, <s2>. . .<sn> expressions are different

SET statements that can be replaced by any one of the expressions listed in Table 8.8:

Expression	Description
<s i> = <f>	Sets the value of the <si> column to the value <f> for all lines of the result set
<s i> = <s i> + <f>	Sets the value of the <si> column, which is increased by the value of <f> for all lines of result set
<s i> = <s i> - <f>	Sets the value of the <si> column, which is decreased by the value of <f> for all lines of result set

TABLE 8.8 Three different expressions of the SET statement

In Table 8.8, <s i> stands for the <s 1>, <s 2>...<s n> field names, and <f> represents a data object or a column of the database table.

Note: If you use the SET statements, you cannot specify the database table dynamically.

The syntax is used to overwrite a single line in a database table with the content of a work area:

```
UPDATE <target_database_tab> FROM <work_area> .
```

The content of the work area, <work_area>, overwrites the content of a line in the <target_database_tab> database table that has the same primary key. The work area <work_area> must be a data object with at least the same length and alignment as the line structure of the database table. The data is placed in the database table according to the line structure of the table and regardless of the structure of the work area. It is a good idea to define the work area with reference to the structure of the database table.

If the database table contains a line with the same primary key as specified in the work area, the operation is completed successfully and the value of the SY-SUBRC variable is set to 0; otherwise, the line is not inserted and the value of the SY-SUBRC variable is set to 4.

A shortened form of using the UPDATE statement is as follows:

```
TABLES <target_database_tab>
UPDATE <target_database_tab>.
```

In this syntax, the content of the <target_database_tab> database table is updated or overwritten by the content of a table work area defined by using the TABLES statement. Note that the name of the table work area and the name of the database table must be the same. However, it is not possible to specify the name of the database table dynamically.

The following is the syntax used to overwrite several lines in a database table with the content of an internal table:

```
UPDATE <target_database_tab> FROM TABLE <internal_tab>.
```

This syntax shows that the content of the internal table <internal_tab> overwrites the lines in the <target_database_tab> database table on the basis of the same key.

Sometimes, a record of an internal table may not get updated in the database table because the database table does not contain the corresponding record. In such situations, the entire operation of updating records is not terminated and the system continues to process the next record of the internal table.

If all the lines of the internal table are processed, the value of the SY-SUBRC variable is set to 0; otherwise, it is set to 4. If the internal table is empty, the values of the SY-SUBRC and SY-DBCNT variables are set to 0.

As a best practice, use an internal table in cases where you need to update a large number of lines in a database table.

Examples of Updating Data in Tables

Listing 8.27 shows how to update the values of columns in a table:

```
REPORT ZDATA_ACCESS.

*/Updating the values of EMPADDRESS and CITY are updated where
EMPID is KG01
UPDATE ZEMPLOYEE_DATA SET EMPADDRESS = 'SAROJINI NAGAR,
LUCKNOW' CITY = 'LUCKNOW'
WHERE EMPID = 'KG01'.
```

LISTING 8.27 **Updating the values of two columns of a table**

In Listing 8.27, the value of the `EMPADDRESS` and `CITY` fields are updated. The value of the `EMPADDRESS` field is set to SAROJINI NAGAR, LUCKNOW and that of the `CITY` field is set to LUCKNOW. The value of the `EMPID` field is KG01. Figure 8.36 shows the updated record, where the value of the `EMPID` field is KG01:

Employee ID	Employee Name	Employee Address	City	Employee Desigation	Employee
DT01	SATENDRA PAL CHOPRA	UTTAM NAGAR, NEW DELHI	DELHI	EDITOR	92192934
DT02	NISHA VERMA	SAROJINI NAGAR, LUCKNOW	LUCKNOW	PROJECT MANAGER	98914321
KG01	SHIVAM SRIVASTAVA	SAROJINI NAGAR, LUCKNOW	LUCKNOW	CONSULTANT	99992464
KG02	CHARU VERMA	CHANDNI CHOWK, NEW DELHI	DELHI	TECHNICAL WRITER	98914235
KG03	DHEERAJ GUPTA	JHNJHUN WALA, MEERUT	MEERUT	TECHNICAL WRITER	98982333
KG04	AHMED UMAR	MEENA BAZAR, NEW DELHI	DELHI	TECHNICAL WRITER	98112345
KG05	JIGYASA KULSHRESTRA	TAJMAHAL, UTTAR PRADESH	AGRA	SENIOR QA	98993015
KG06	NIRAJ VERMA	RANIGANJ, UTTAR PRADESH	AGRA	TECHNICAL WRITER	98976543
KG07	MEHTAB ALAM	MUKHNANDAN VIHAR, PATNA	PATNA	TECHNICAL WRITER	09981145
KG08	VIKASH SUMAN	BHARATPUR, PATNA	PATNA	TECHNICAL WRITER	09981718
KG09	RAM KUMAR	CHANDAN NAGAR, PATNA	PATNA	TECHNICAL WRITER	99114242
KG10	SHARJEEL AHMAD	JAMUNA NAGAR, PATNA	PATNA	QUALITY ANALYSIS MAN	99811481
KG11	ASHISH CHAUHAN	MAHROLI, DELHI	DELHI	TECHNICAL WRITER	09911343
SBP0	S P JAIN	RAMURTI, JHARKAHND	RANCHI	EDITOR	96567438
SBP1	R K MISHRA	BIJNOUR, UTTAR PRADESH	BIJNOUR	CONSULTANT	98765432

FIGURE 8.36 **Displaying the updated record where EMPID is KG01**

Listing 8.28 shows how to update the field values by using the `MOVE` and `UPDATE` statements:

```
REPORT ZDATA_ACCESS.

*/Updating the records of a table by using the MOVE statement

TABLES ZEMPLOYEE_DATA.
DATA KOG TYPE ZEMPLOYEE_DATA.
MOVE 'SBPO' TO KOG-EMPID.
MOVE 'A K SINHA' TO KOG-EMPNAME.
MOVE 'SAROJINI NAGAR, DELHI' TO KOG-EMPADDRESS.
MOVE 'DELHI' TO KOG-CITY.
UPDATE ZEMPLOYEE_DATA FROM KOG.
MOVE 'DT02' TO ZEMPLOYEE_DATA-EMPID.
MOVE 'SOMYA SRIVASTAVA' TO ZEMPLOYEE_DATA-EMPNAME.
MOVE 'SITA RAM BAZAR, DELHI' TO ZEMPLOYEE_DATA-EMPADDRESS.
MOVE 'DELHI' TO ZEMPLOYEE_DATA-CITY.
UPDATE ZEMPLOYEE_DATA.
```

LISTING 8.28 **Using the MOVE and UPDATE statements**

In Listing 8.28, the values in the EMPNAME, EMPADDRESS, and CITY fields of the ZEMPLOYEE_DATA table are updated by the MOVE statement. The value of the EMPNAME field is updated to "SOMYA SRIVASTAVA", that of the EMPADDRESS field to "SITA RAM BAZAR, DELHI", and that of the CITY field to "DELHI", where EMPID is "DT02". In addition, the value of the EMPNAME field is updated to "A K SINHA", that of the EMPADDRESS field to "SAROJINI NAGAR, DELHI", and that of the CITY field to "DELHI", where EMPID is "SBP0". Figure 8.37 shows the updated records for the EMPID field:

Employee ID	Employee Name	Employee Address	City	Employee Desigation	Employee
DT01	SATENDRA PAL CHOPRA	UTTAM NAGAR, NEW DELHI	DELHI	EDITOR	921929345
DT02	SOMYA SRIVASTAVA	SITA RAM BAZAR, DELHI	DELHI		000000000
KG01	SHIVAM SRIVASTAVA	SAROJINI NAGAR, LUCKNOW	LUCKNOW	CONSULTANT	999924644
KG02	CHARU VERMA	CHANDNI CHOWK, NEW DELHI	DELHI	TECHNICAL WRITER	989142354
KG03	DHEERAJ GUPTA	JHNJHUN WALA, MEERUT	MEERUT	TECHNICAL WRITER	989823332
KG04	AHMED UMAR	MEENA BAZAR, NEW DELHI	DELHI	TECHNICAL WRITER	981123453
KG05	JIGYASA KULSHRESTRA	TAJMAHAL, UTTAR PRADESH	AGRA	SENIOR QA	989930154
KG06	NIRAJ VERMA	RANIGANJ, UTTAR PRADESH	AGRA	TECHNICAL WRITER	989765434
KG07	MEHTAB ALAM	MUKHNANDAN VIHAR, PATNA	PATNA	TECHNICAL WRITER	099811456
KG08	VIKASH SUMAN	BHARATPUR, PATNA	PATNA	TECHNICAL WRITER	099817188
KG09	RAM KUMAR	CHANDAN NAGAR, PATNA	PATNA	TECHNICAL WRITER	991142428
KG10	SHARJEEL AHMAD	JAMUNA NAGAR, PATNA	PATNA	QUALITY ANALYSIS MAN	998114811
KG11	ASHISH CHAUHAN	MAHROLI, DELHI	DELHI	TECHNICAL WRITER	099113434
SBP0	A K SINHA	SAROJINI NAGAR, DELHI	DELHI		000000000
SBP1	R K MISHRA	BIJNOUR, UTTAR PRADESH	BIJNOUR	CONSULTANT	987654324

FIGURE 8.37 **Displaying updated records for employee ID DT02 and SBP0**

In Figure 8.37, you can see the updated values in the record, where Employee ID is DT02 or SBP0. It must be noted that when values are updated in the specified fields of the ZEMPLOYEE_DATA table, the other fields whose values are not specified in the MOVE statement remain blank.

Listing 8.29 shows how a database table is updated by using the lines of a hashed internal table:

```
REPORT ZDATA_ACCESS.

*/Updating the values of a table, using a hashed table

DATA: MYTABLE TYPE HASHED TABLE OF ZEMPLOYEE_DATA
WITH UNIQUE KEY EMPID,
KOG LIKE LINE OF MYTABLE.
KOG-EMPID = 'KG07'.
KOG-EMPNAME = 'MANISHA TAHEEM'.
KOG-EMPADDRESS = 'MAYUR VIHAR, DELHI'.
```

Continued

```
KOG-CITY = 'DELHI'.
KOG-DESIGNATION = 'HR MANAGER'.
KOG-PHONENUMBER = '9981145622'.
KOG-SALARY = 30000.
KOG-JOININGDATE = '20080101'.
KOG-MAILID = 'MANISHA.TAHEEM@YAHOO.COM'.
INSERT KOG INTO TABLE MYTABLE.
KOG-EMPID = 'KG08'.
KOG-EMPNAME = 'RAMNEEK KAUR'.
KOG-EMPADDRESS = 'NANKANA SAHIB, AMRITSAR'.
KOG-CITY = 'AMRITSAR'.
KOG-DESIGNATION = 'TECHNICAL WRITER'.
KOG-PHONENUMBER = '9986022198'.
KOG-SALARY = 10000.
KOG-JOININGDATE = '20080911'.
KOG-MAILID = 'RAMNEEK.KAUR@GMAIL.COM'.

INSERT KOG INTO TABLE MYTABLE.

UPDATE ZEMPLOYEE_DATA FROM TABLE MYTABLE.
```

LISTING 8.29 **Updating a database table by using a hashed internal table**

In Listing 8.29, two lines of the ZEMPLOYEE_DATA table are updated. First, we insert two lines together into the KOG work area, which are then inserted into the MYTABLE internal table. Finally, the content of the MYTABLE internal table modifies the lines of the ZEMPLOYEE_DATA database table, where EMPID is KG07 or KG08. Figure 8.38 shows the result of Listing 8.29:

Employee ID	Employee Name	Employee Address	City	Employee Desigation	Employee P
DT01	SATENDRA PAL CHOPRA	UTTAM NAGAR, NEW DELHI	DELHI	EDITOR	9219293454
DT02	SOMYA SRIVASTAVA	SITA RAM BAZAR, DELHI	DELHI		0000000000
KG01	SHIVAM SRIVASTAVA	SAROJINI NAGAR, LUCKNOW	LUCKNOW	CONSULTANT	9999246445
KG02	CHARU VERMA	CHANDNI CHOWK, NEW DELHI	DELHI	TECHNICAL WRITER	9891423543
KG03	DHEERAJ GUPTA	JHNJHUN WALA, MEERUT	MEERUT	TECHNICAL WRITER	9898233323
KG04	AHMED UMAR	MEENA BAZAR, NEW DELHI	DELHI	TECHNICAL WRITER	9811234537
KG05	JIGYASA KULSHRESTRA	TAJMAHAL, UTTAR PRADESH	AGRA	SENIOR QA	9899301545
KG06	NIRAJ VERMA	RANIGANJ, UTTAR PRADESH	AGRA	TECHNICAL WRITER	9897654345
KG07	MANISHA TAHEEM	MAYUR VIHAR, DELHI	DELHI	HR MANAGER	9981145622
KG08	RAMNEEK KAUR	NANKANA SAHIB, AMRITSAR	AMRITSAR	TECHNICAL WRITER	9986022198
KG09	RAM KUMAR	CHANDAN NAGAR, PATNA	PATNA	TECHNICAL WRITER	9911424281
KG10	SHARJEEL AHMAD	JAMUNA NAGAR, PATNA	PATNA	QUALITY ANALYSIS MAN	9981148113
KG11	ASHISH CHAUHAN	MAHROLI, DELHI	DELHI	TECHNICAL WRITER	0991134342
SBP0	A K SINHA	SAROJINI NAGAR, DELHI	DELHI		0000000000
SBP1	R K MISHRA	BIJNOUR, UTTAR PRADESH	BIJNOUR	CONSULTANT	9876543245

FIGURE 8.38 **Displaying the two updated lines in the ZEMPLOYEE_DATA table**

DELETING THE DATA FROM A DATABASE TABLE

In Open SQL, the `DELETE` statement is used to delete one or more lines from a database table. The following syntax shows the use of the `DELETE` statement:

```
DELETE [FROM] <target_database_tab> <database_tab_lines>.
```

In the preceding syntax, `<target_database_tab>` represents a database table and `<database_tab_lines>` represents the lines that have to be deleted from the table. You can specify the `<target_database_tab>` database table either statically or dynamically.

The following syntax is used to specify the database table statically:

```
DELETE [FROM] <target_database_tab> [CLIENT SPECIFIED]
<database_tab_lines>.
```

The following syntax is used to specify the database table dynamically:

```
DELETE [FROM] (<target_database_tab>) [CLIENT SPECIFIED]
<database_tab_lines>.
```

In both syntaxes, the `<target_database_tab>` expression represents the name of a database table defined in the ABAP Dictionary. The `CLIENT SPECIFIED` clause is used to disable the automatic client-handling feature of Open SQL.

The following syntax is used to select the lines to be deleted by using a condition:

```
DELETE FROM <target_database_tab> WHERE <cond> .
```

This syntax deletes all the lines from the `<target_database_tab>` database table that satisfy the conditions in the `WHERE` clause. The `FROM` clause must occur between the `DELETE` clause and the name of the `<target_database_tab>` table.

Listing 8.30 shows an example of deleting a single record from a database table:

```
REPORT ZDATA_ACCESS.

*/Deleting a record from the ZEMPLOYEE_DATA table, where EMPID
is KG08
TABLES: ZEMPLOYEE_DATA.
DELETE FROM ZEMPLOYEE_DATA WHERE EMPID = 'KG08'.
```

LISTING 8.30 **Deleting a single record from a database table**

In Listing 8.30, a single line is deleted from the ZEMPLOYEE_DATA table, where the value of the EMPID field is KG08. Figure 8.39 shows the deletion of the specified record from the ZEMPLOYEE_DATA table:

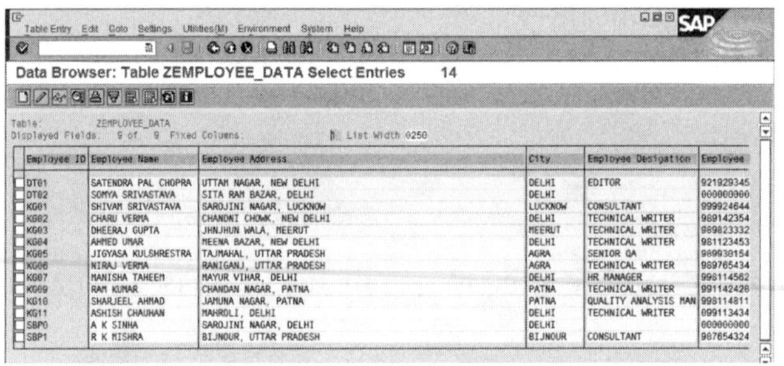

Employee ID	Employed Name	Employed Address	City	Employee Desigation	Employee
DT01	SATENDRA PAL CHOPRA	UTTAM NAGAR, NEW DELHI	DELHI	EDITOR	921929345
DT02	SOMYA SRIVASTAVA	SITA RAM BAZAR, DELHI	DELHI		000000000
KG01	SHIVAM SRIVASTAVA	SAROJINI NAGAR, LUCKNOW	LUCKNOW	CONSULTANT	999924644
KG02	CHARU VERMA	CHANDNI CHOWK, NEW DELHI	DELHI	TECHNICAL WRITER	989142354
KG03	DHEERAJ GUPTA	JHNJHUN WALA, MEERUT	MEERUT	TECHNICAL WRITER	989823332
KG04	AHMED UMAR	MEENA BAZAR, NEW DELHI	DELHI	TECHNICAL WRITER	981123453
KG05	JIGYASA KULSHRESTRA	TAJMAHAL, UTTAR PRADESH	AGRA	SENIOR QA	989930154
KG06	NIRAJ VERMA	RANIGANJ, UTTAR PRADESH	AGRA	TECHNICAL WRITER	989765434
KG07	MANISHA TAHEEM	MAYUR VIHAR, DELHI	DELHI	HR MANAGER	998114562
KG09	RAM KUMAR	CHANDAN NAGAR, PATNA	PATNA	TECHNICAL WRITER	991142428
KG10	SHARJEEL AHMAD	JAMUNA NAGAR, PATNA	PATNA	QUALITY ANALYSIS MAN	998114811
KG11	ASHISH CHAUHAN	MAHROLI, DELHI	DELHI	TECHNICAL WRITER	099113434
SBP0	A K SINHA	SAROJINI NAGAR, DELHI	DELHI		000000000
SBP1	R K MISHRA	BIJNOUR, UTTAR PRADESH	BIJNOUR	CONSULTANT	987654324

FIGURE 8.39 **Showing the deletion of a record from the ZEMPLOYEE_DATA table**

Instead of using a WHERE clause, you can also use the following syntax to delete the lines by using a work area:

```
DELETE <target_database_tab> FROM <work_area> .
```

This syntax deletes the line with the same primary key as that of the <work_area> work area. The FROM clause must not occur between the <target_database_tab> database table and <work_area> and between the DELETE clause and the <target_database_tab> database table. The <work_area> work area has the same length and alignment as the line structure of the <target_database_tab> table. Another way to use the DELETE statement is as follows:

```
TABLES <target_database_tab>.
DELETE <target_database_tab>.
```

In this syntax, the DELETE statement deletes one or more lines from the <target_database_tab> database table by using a table work area. The table work area is defined by using the TABLES statement. Note that the name of the table work area and the database table must be the same. It is not possible to specify the name of the database table dynamically.

The following syntax is used to delete several lines from a database table by using an internal table:

```
DELETE <target_database_tab> FROM TABLE internal_tab
<work_area>.
```

This syntax deletes all lines from the <target_database_tab> database table that have the same primary key in the <internal_tab> internal table. Sometimes, a record of an internal table may not be deleted from the database table because the database table does not contain the matching record. In such situations, the operation of deleting the records is not terminated and the SAP system continues to process the next record of the internal table.

If all the lines from the internal table have been processed, the value of the SY-SUBRC variable is set to 0; otherwise, it is set to 4. If the internal table is empty, the values of the SY-SUBRC and SY-DBCNT variables are set to 0.

As a best practice, use an internal table where you need to delete a large number of lines from a database table.

Examples of Deleting Data

Listing 8.31 shows the delete operation by using the WHERE clause:

```
REPORT ZDATA_ACCESS.

*/Deleting records from the ZEMPLOYEE_DATA table, where EMPID
is DT02 and CITY is
DELHI

TABLES: ZEMPLOYEE_DATA.
DELETE FROM ZEMPLOYEE_DATA WHERE EMPID = 'DT02' AND
CITY = 'DELHI'.
```

LISTING 8.31 **Using the WHERE clause to specify a condition for the delete operation**

In Listing 8.31, the `DELETE` statement is used to delete all the lines from the `ZEMPLOYEE_DATA` table, where the value of the Employee ID field is DT02 and the value of the `City` field is "DELHI". Figure 8.40 shows that the specified record has been deleted:

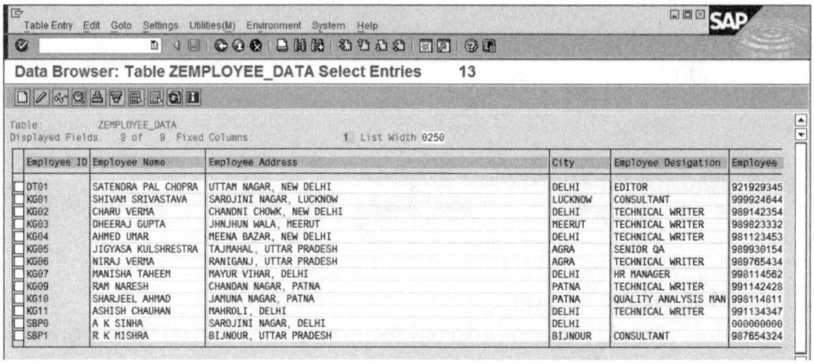

Table Entry Edit Goto Settings Utilities(M) Environment System Help

Data Browser: Table ZEMPLOYEE_DATA Select Entries 13

Table: ZEMPLOYEE_DATA
Displayed Fields: 9 of 9 Fixed Columns: 1 List Width 0250

Employee ID	Employee Name	Employee Address	City	Employee Desigation	Employee
DT01	SATENDRA PAL CHOPRA	UTTAM NAGAR, NEW DELHI	DELHI	EDITOR	921929345
KG01	SHIVAM SRIVASTAVA	SAROJINI NAGAR, LUCKNOW	LUCKNOW	CONSULTANT	999924644
KG02	CHARU VERMA	CHANDNI CHOWK, NEW DELHI	DELHI	TECHNICAL WRITER	989142354
KG03	DHEERAJ GUPTA	JHNJHUN WALA, MEERUT	MEERUT	TECHNICAL WRITER	989823332
KG04	AHMED UMAR	MEENA BAZAR, NEW DELHI	DELHI	TECHNICAL WRITER	981123453
KG05	JIGYASA KULSHRESTRA	TAJMAHAL, UTTAR PRADESH	AGRA	SENIOR QA	989930154
KG06	NIRAJ VERMA	RANIGANJ, UTTAR PRADESH	AGRA	TECHNICAL WRITER	989765434
KG07	MANISHA TAHEEM	MAYUR VIHAR, DELHI	DELHI	HR MANAGER	998114562
KG09	RAM NARESH	CHANDAN NAGAR, PATNA	PATNA	TECHNICAL WRITER	991142428
KG10	SHARJEEL AHMAD	JAMUNA NAGAR, PATNA	PATNA	QUALITY ANALYSIS MAN	998114811
KG11	ASHISH CHAUHAN	MAHROLI, DELHI	DELHI	TECHNICAL WRITER	991134347
SBP0	A K SINHA	SAROJINI NAGAR, DELHI	DELHI		000000000
SBP1	R K MISHRA	BIJNOUR, UTTAR PRADESH	BIJNOUR	CONSULTANT	987654324

FIGURE 8.40 **Deleting the record where EMPID is DT02 and city is DELHI**

Listing 8.32 shows the deletion of records or lines by using the `MOVE` and `DELETE` statements:

```
REPORT ZDATA_ACCESS.

*/Deleting the records using the MOVE and DELETE statements
TABLES ZEMPLOYEE_DATA.
DATA: BEGIN OF KOG,
EMPID TYPE ZEMPLOYEE_DATA-EMPID, CITY TYPE ZEMPLOYEE_
DATA-CITY,
END OF KOG.

MOVE 'SBP0' TO KOG-EMPID.
MOVE 'DELHI' TO KOG-CITY.
DELETE ZEMPLOYEE_DATA FROM KOG.

MOVE 'KG11' TO ZEMPLOYEE_DATA-EMPID.
MOVE 'DELHI' TO ZEMPLOYEE_DATA-CITY.
DELETE ZEMPLOYEE_DATA.
```

LISTING 8.32 **Deleting the records by using the MOVE and DELETE statements**

In Listing 8.32, records where the values of the Employee ID and `City` are SBP0 and DELHI, respectively, or the values of Employee ID and `City` are KG11 and DELHI, respectively, are deleted from the `ZEMPLOYEE_DATA` table. Figure 8.41 shows that records with Employee ID SBP0 and KG11 are deleted:

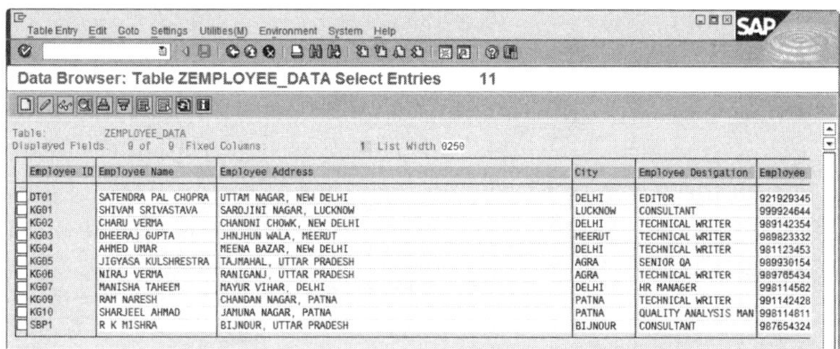

Employee ID	Employee Name	Employee Address	City	Employee Desigation	Employee
DT01	SATENDRA PAL CHOPRA	UTTAM NAGAR, NEW DELHI	DELHI	EDITOR	921929345
KG01	SHIVAM SRIVASTAVA	SAROJINI NAGAR, LUCKNOW	LUCKNOW	CONSULTANT	999924644
KG02	CHARU VERMA	CHANDNI CHOWK, NEW DELHI	DELHI	TECHNICAL WRITER	989142354
KG03	DHEERAJ GUPTA	JHNJHUN WALA, MEERUT	MEERUT	TECHNICAL WRITER	989823332
KG04	AHMED UMAR	MEENA BAZAR, NEW DELHI	DELHI	TECHNICAL WRITER	981123453
KG05	JIGYASA KULSHRESTRA	TAJMAHAL, UTTAR PRADESH	AGRA	SENIOR QA	989930154
KG06	NIRAJ VERMA	RANIGANJ, UTTAR PRADESH	AGRA	TECHNICAL WRITER	989765434
KG07	MANISHA TAHEEM	MAYUR VIHAR, DELHI	DELHI	HR MANAGER	998114562
KG09	RAM NARESH	CHANDAN NAGAR, PATNA	PATNA	TECHNICAL WRITER	991142428
KG10	SHARJEEL AHMAD	JAMUNA NAGAR, PATNA	PATNA	QUALITY ANALYSIS MAN	998114811
SBP1	R K MISHRA	BIJNOUR, UTTAR PRADESH	BIJNOUR	CONSULTANT	987654324

FIGURE 8.41 **Deleting records by using the MOVE and DELETE statements**

Listing 8.33 shows the deletion of records from a database table by using an internal table:

```
REPORT ZDATA_ACCESS.

*/Deleting a record from the ZEMPLOYEE_DATA table, with the help
of an internal table-MYTABLE

DATA: MYTABLE TYPE HASHED TABLE OF ZEMPLOYEE_DATA
WITH UNIQUE KEY EMPID,
KOG LIKE LINE OF MYTABLE.
KOG-EMPID = 'KG07'.
KOG-EMPNAME = 'MANISHA TAHEEM'.
KOG-EMPADDRESS = 'MAYUR VIHAR, DELHI'.
KOG-CITY = 'DELHI'.
KOG-DESIGNATION = 'HR MANAGER'.
KOG-PHONENUMBER = '9981145622'.
KOG-SALARY = 30000.
```

Continued

```
KOG-JOININGDATE = '20080101'.
KOG-MAILID = 'MANISHA.TAHEEM@YAHOO.COM'.

INSERT KOG INTO TABLE MYTABLE.

DELETE ZEMPLOYEE_DATA FROM TABLE MYTABLE.
```

LISTING 8.33 **Deleting the records by using an internal table**

Listing 8.33 shows the deletion of a line from the ZEMPLOYEE_DATA table. First, a line is inserted into the KOG work area and then it is inserted into the MYTABLE internal table. Finally, the content of the MYTABLE table deletes the lines of the ZEMPLOYEE_DATA database table where the value of Employee ID is KG07. Figure 8.42 shows the output of Listing 8.33:

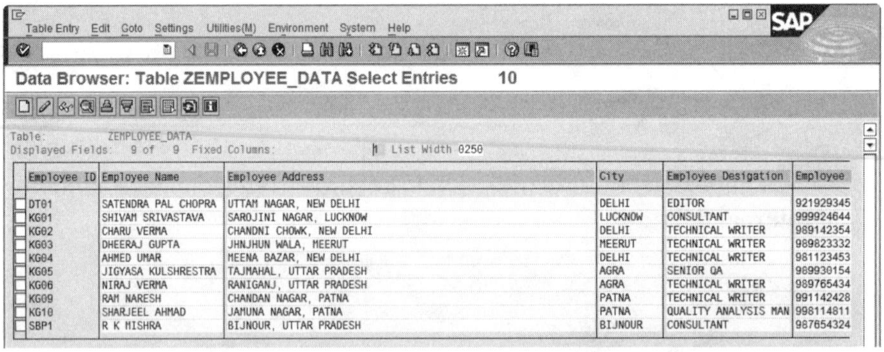

Employee ID	Employee Name	Employee Address	City	Employee Desigation	Employee
DT01	SATENDRA PAL CHOPRA	UTTAM NAGAR, NEW DELHI	DELHI	EDITOR	921929345
KG01	SHIVAM SRIVASTAVA	SAROJINI NAGAR, LUCKNOW	LUCKNOW	CONSULTANT	999924644
KG02	CHARU VERMA	CHANDNI CHOWK, NEW DELHI	DELHI	TECHNICAL WRITER	989142354
KG03	DHEERAJ GUPTA	JHNJHUN WALA, MEERUT	MEERUT	TECHNICAL WRITER	989823332
KG04	AHMED UMAR	MEENA BAZAR, NEW DELHI	DELHI	TECHNICAL WRITER	981123453
KG05	JIGYASA KULSHRESTRA	TAJMAHAL, UTTAR PRADESH	AGRA	SENIOR QA	989930154
KG06	NIRAJ VERMA	RANIGANJ, UTTAR PRADESH	AGRA	TECHNICAL WRITER	989765434
KG09	RAM NARESH	CHANDAN NAGAR, PATNA	PATNA	TECHNICAL WRITER	991142428
KG10	SHARJEEL AHMAD	JAMUNA NAGAR, PATNA	PATNA	QUALITY ANALYSIS MAN	998114811
SBP1	R K MISHRA	BIJNOUR, UTTAR PRADESH	BIJNOUR	CONSULTANT	987654324

FIGURE 8.42 **Deleting two lines from the ZEmployee_Data table**

In Figure 8.42, notice that there is no line with Employee ID KG07.

MODIFYING THE LINES OF DATABASE TABLES

The MODIFY statement is used to insert new lines or update the values of existing lines within a database table. If the key specified in the MODIFY statement is not present in any existing line of the database table, the MODIFY statement works as an INSERT statement; that is, the line is inserted. If the key specified in the MODIFY statement is present in an existing line of the database table, the MODIFY statement works as an UPDATE statement; that is, the line is updated. The following syntax of the MODIFY statement is used to insert or update one or more lines into a database table:

```
MODIFY <target_database_tab> <database_tab_lines>.
```

In this syntax, <target_database_tab> represents a database table and <database_tab_lines> represents the lines that have to be inserted or updated in the table.

> **Note:** For performance reasons, you should use the MODIFY statement only if you cannot distinguish between the INSERT and UPDATE statements in an ABAP program.

You can specify the <target_database_tab> database table either statically or dynamically.

The following is the syntax used to specify the database table statically:

```
MODIFY <target_database_tab> [CLIENT SPECIFIED] <database_
tab_lines>.
```

The following syntax is used to specify the database table dynamically:

```
MODIFY (<target_database_tab>) [CLIENT SPECIFIED] <database_
tab_lines>.
```

In both syntaxes, the <target_database_tab> expression represents the name of a database table defined in the ABAP Dictionary. The CLIENT SPECIFIED clause is used to disable the automatic client-handling feature of Open SQL.

The following syntax is used to insert or change a single line in a database table:

```
MODIFY <target_database_tab> FROM <work_area>.
```

In this syntax, <work_area> is a work area created for the <target_database_tab> database table. If the database table does not contain a line with the same primary key as specified in the work area, a new line is inserted.

If the database table contains a line with the same primary key as specified in the work area, the existing line is overwritten. The value of the SY-SUBRC system variable is always set to 0.

The preceding syntax can also be written in the following way:

```
MODIFY <target_database_tab>.
```

In this syntax, the MODIFY statement inserts or updates one or more lines in the <target_database_tab> database table by using a table work area. The table work area is defined by using the TABLES statement. Note that the name of the table work area and that of the database table must be the same. However, you cannot specify the name of the database table dynamically.

The following syntax is used to insert or update several lines in a database table by using an internal table:

```
MODIFY <target_database_tab> FROM TABLE <internal_tab>.
```

This syntax is used to insert lines from the <internal_tab> internal table to the <target_database_tab> database table. Note that the lines inserted do not exist in the <target_database_tab> database table. However, matching lines of an internal table with the database table are overwritten.

Now, let's explore the concept of cursors, which are used to read data from database tables.

USING CURSORS TO READ DATA

Cursors are similar to data objects or variables used to retrieve the data from the result set obtained by using the SELECT statement. For this, you must open a cursor by using the OPEN CURSOR statement. Then retrieve the data from the result set by using the FETCH NEXT CURSOR statement. Finally, close the cursor by using the CLOSE CURSOR statement. Therefore, we can say that using a cursor to read data involves the following processes:

- Opening and closing cursors
- Retrieving data

Now, let's discuss each process in detail.

Opening and Closing Cursors

The following syntax is used to open a cursor for a `SELECT` statement:

```
OPEN CURSOR [WITH HOLD] <c> FOR SELECT <result>
                                   FROM <source>
                                   [WHERE <condition>]
                                   [GROUP BY <fields>]
                                   [HAVING <cond>]
                                   [ORDER BY <fields>].
```

In this syntax, the `OPEN CURSOR` statement is used to open the `<c>` cursor. You can use all the clauses of the `SELECT` statement (other than the `INTO` clause) to select one or more lines. However, you cannot specify the names of the columns individually in the `SELECT` statement and the columns cannot contain aggregate expressions.

You can open more than one cursor in a parallel way for a single database table. Moreover, an already opened cursor cannot be reopened. The `CLOSE CURSOR` statement is used to close a cursor. The following syntax shows the use of the `CLOSE CURSOR` statement:

```
CLOSE CURSOR <c>.
```

This syntax is used to close all cursors that are no longer required, because only a limited number of cursors can be opened simultaneously.

The `WITH HOLD` clause in the `OPEN CURSOR` statement allows you to prevent a cursor from closing when a database is committed in Native SQL. However, the `WITH HOLD` clause cannot be specified when the cursor is opened for a secondary database connection.

Retrieving Data

The `FETCH NEXT CURSOR` statement is used to retrieve data from a database table.

The following syntax is used to read the data into a target area in an ABAP program by using the `FETCH NEXT CURSOR` statement:

```
FETCH NEXT CURSOR <c> INTO <target>.
```

In this syntax, the FETCH NEXT CURSOR statement inserts a line of the database table into a target area, which is a variable. After the FETCH NEXT CURSOR statement retrieves the data, the cursor moves to the next line of the database table. The value of the SY-SUBRC system variable is set to 0 until all the lines of the selection have been read; otherwise, it is set to 4. Moreover, after the FETCH NEXT CURSOR statement is executed, the SY-DBCNT system variable is updated to reflect the number of lines that have been read.

Listing 8.34 shows an example of reading data using cursors:

```
REPORT ZDATA_ACCESS.

*/Declaring Cursors-c1 and c2

DATA: c1 TYPE cursor,
      c2 TYPE cursor.

DATA: work_area1 TYPE MARA,
      work_area2 TYPE MARA.

DATA: flag1(1) TYPE c,
      flag2(1) TYPE c.

*/Opening Cursors-c1 and c2
OPEN CURSOR: c1 FOR SELECT MATNR ERSDA ERNAM
                    FROM MARA
                    where ERNAM = 'RUDISILL',
             c2 FOR SELECT LAEDA AENAM
                    FROM MARA
                    WHERE ERNAM = 'RUDISILL'.
DO.
  IF flag1 NE 'X'.
*/Using the c1 cursor to fetch the data
  FETCH NEXT CURSOR c1 INTO CORRESPONDING FIELDS OF work_
  area1.
```

Continued

```
        IF sy-subrc <> 0.
*/Closing the c1 cursor
        CLOSE CURSOR c1.
        flag1 = 'X'.
ELSE.
        WRITE: / work_area1-MATNR, work_area1-ERSDA, work_
        area1-ERNAM.
ENDIF.
ENDIF.

IF flag2 NE 'X'.
*/Using the c2 cursor to fetch the data
        FETCH NEXT CURSOR c2 INTO CORRESPONDING FIELDS OF work_
        area2.
        IF sy-subrc <> 0.
*/Closing the c2 cursor
        CLOSE CURSOR c2.
        flag2 = 'X'.
ELSE.
        WRITE: / work_area2-LAEDA, work_area2-AENAM.
ENDIF.
ENDIF.
    IF flag1 = 'X' AND flag2 = 'X'.
EXIT.
ENDIF.
ENDDO.
```

LISTING 8.34 **Reading data by using cursors**

In Listing 8.34, cursors are used to read data from the MARA table. The `DATA` statement defines two variables, `c1` and `c2`, which are used as cursors in the listing. The `DATA` statement also defines two work areas, `work_area1` and `work_area2`, which have the type similar to the fields of the MARA table. The `OPEN CURSOR` statement is used to open the `c1` and `c2` cursors. A `DO` loop is initiated, so that the required data is retrieved from the database table and stored in the work areas. The retrieved values finally are displayed on the output screen. The value of the `SY-SUBRC` system variable remains 0 until all the values are read. As soon as all the values are read, the value of the SY-SUBRC system variable is set to 4. Figure 8.43 shows the output of Listing 8.34:

```
637                30.07.2002 RUDISILL
23.01.2003 I021066
638                30.07.2002 RUDISILL
23.01.2003 I021066
640                30.07.2002 RUDISILL
23.01.2003 I021066
641                30.07.2002 RUDISILL
23.01.2003 I021066
642                30.07.2002 RUDISILL
23.01.2003 I021066
643                31.07.2002 RUDISILL
23.01.2003 I021066
644                31.07.2002 RUDISILL
23.01.2003 I021066
645                31.07.2002 RUDISILL
23.01.2003 I021066
646                31.07.2002 RUDISILL
23.01.2003 I021066
647                31.07.2002 RUDISILL
23.01.2003 I021066
648                31.07.2002 RUDISILL
23.01.2003 I021066
```


FIGURE 8.43 **Using cursors to retrieve data**

Now, let's learn how to save and undo the changes made by the DML operations by using the COMMIT and ROLLBACK statements, respectively.

COMMITTING DATABASE CHANGES

In Open SQL, the COMMIT WORK statement is used to save database updates and the ROLLBACK WORK statement is used to undo the database updates performed. The COMMIT WORK statement is declared by using the following syntax:

```
COMMIT WORK.
```

The syntax to use the ROLLBACK WORK statement to undo database updates is:

```
ROLLBACK WORK.
```

Note that the COMMIT WORK statement always concludes a database Logical Unit of Work (LUW) and starts a new one. However, the ROLLBACK WORK statement always reverts the changes to the initial position of the database LUW.

SUMMARY

In this chapter, you have learned about the two types of SQL statements, Open SQL and Native SQL. You also have learned how to perform DML operations on the data stored in a database table, defined in the ABAP Dictionary, by using the INSERT, UPDATE, MODIFY, and DELETE Open SQL statements. Next, you have learned how to use cursors to read data from database tables. You also have learned how to use the COMMIT WORK and ROLLBACK WORK statements to confirm or revert the final changes made in a database.

Chapter 9

Modularization Techniques

If you need information on:	*See page:*
Working with Subroutines	498
Function Modules	526
Source Code Modules	543

Modularization techniques enhance the readability and understandability of large ABAP programs. At times, it becomes difficult to enhance and debug the source code of a lengthy ABAP program. The ABAP language simplifies the debugging process by offering various modularization techniques, such as subroutines, function modules, and source code modules. Modularization techniques help to remove redundancy that occurs when an ABAP program contains the same or similar blocks of statements or the same function is used multiple times. Modularization techniques also improve the structure of an ABAP program and make it easy to read, maintain, and update.

In this chapter, you learn about three modularization techniques: subroutines, function modules, and source code modules. We start the chapter by discussing subroutines, which are modularization units in a program. In addition, you learn how to pass the values to the parameters of these subroutines and terminate them. Next, we discuss function modules that encapsulate the processing logic of a program into the form of a function. Finally, you learn about source code modules, which are collections of ABAP statements that are not required to be included in an ABAP program.

Now, let's begin our discussion with subroutines and learn how to work with them.

WORKING WITH SUBROUTINES

A subroutine is a mini-program that consists of a sequence of statements. Subroutines are used to prevent redundancy of the statements in an ABAP program. A subroutine is defined with the help of the `FORM` statement that signifies the start of the subroutine. Within a subroutine, you can define variables, execute ABAP statements to calculate results, and display the calculated result on the screen. You can end the subroutine with the help of the `ENDFORM` statement. The length of the name of a subroutine is limited to 30 characters. Subroutines defined in an ABAP program can be called either in the same ABAP program or from any other ABAP program with the `PERFORM` statement (you learn about `PERFORM` statements later in this chapter).

> **Note:** Subroutines cannot be nested. As a best practice, specify the subroutine definition at the end of an ABAP program.

The following syntax shows how to define a subroutine by using the `FORM` statement:

```
FORM sub_name [USING         prm1 TYPE type
                             prm2 LIKE field
                             . . . .
                             VALUE(prm3) TYPE type
                             VALUE (prm4) LIKE field
                             . . . . . ]
 [CHANGING { {VALUE(prm1)}|{prm1 [{TYPE type}|{LIKE field}]}
                {VALUE(prm2)}|{prm2  [ {TYPE  type}|{LIKE
                field}]}
                . . . .
 } ]
 . . . . . .
 ENDFORM.
```

In this syntax, the `sub_name` expression denotes the name of the subroutine, while the `USING` and `CHANGING` clauses define the parameter interface.

Programs for subroutines are written in the ABAP Editor tool of ABAP Workbench. Perform the following steps to create a subroutine program in ABAP Editor:

1. Select `SAP menu>Tools>ABAP Workbench>Development>SE38-ABAP Editor` to start the initial screen of ABAP Editor.

> **Note:** You can also simply enter the `SE38` transaction in the command field and click the `Enter` (icon) icon or press the ENTER key to start the initial screen of ABAP Editor.

The initial screen of ABAP Editor appears, as shown in Figure 9.1:

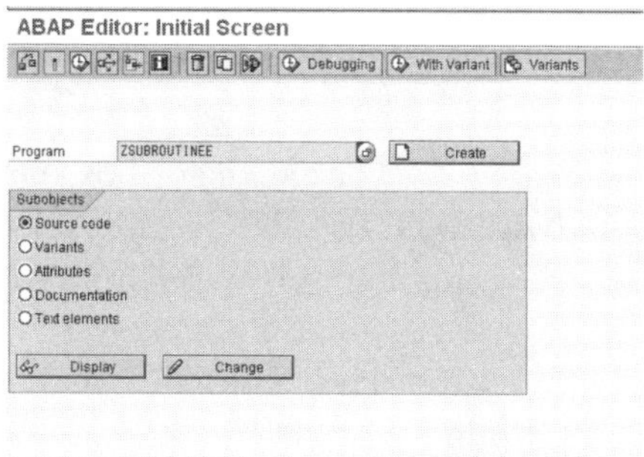

FIGURE 9.1 **Displaying the initial screen of ABAP editor**

2. Enter the name of the program in the `Program` field as "ZSUBROUTINEE".

> **Note:** You will notice that the `Source code` radio button under the Subobjects group box is already selected by default. You can select any of the radio buttons depending on the purpose. To learn more about these radio buttons, please refer to Chapter 6.

3. Click the `Create` button.

The `ABAP: Program Attributes ZSUBROUTINE1 Change` dialog box appears, as shown in Figure 9.2:

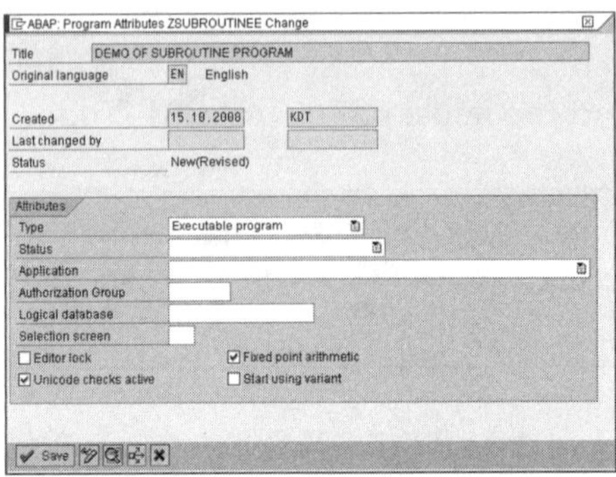

FIGURE 9.2 **Displaying the ABAP: program attributes dialog box**

4. In the `ABAP Program Attributes` dialog box, enter the title of the program as "DEMO OF SUBROUTINE PROGRAM", select the Type of the program as `Executable program`, and select the `Unicode checks active` check box to make the program compatible.
5. Now, click the `Save` button. The `Create Object Directory Entry` dialog box appears, as shown in Figure 9.3:

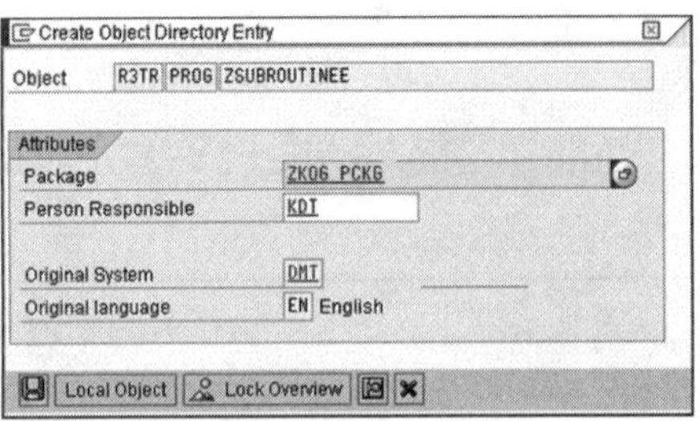

FIGURE 9.3 **Entering the package name**

6. Enter the package name in the `Package` field as ZKOG_PCKG, as shown in Figure 9.3.
7. Click the `Save` (💾) icon. The `Prompt for local Workbench request` dialog box appears, as shown in Figure 9.4:

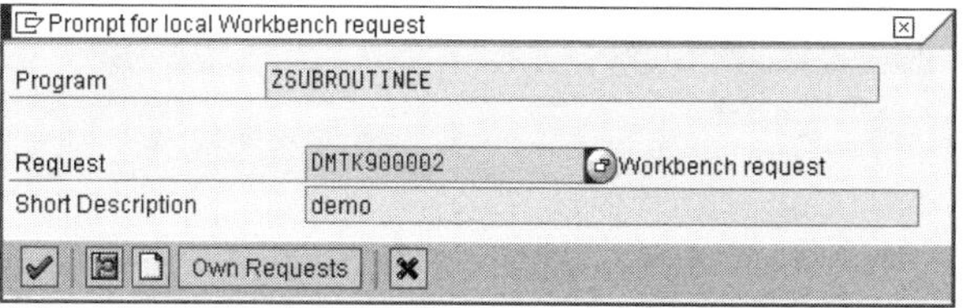

FIGURE 9.4 **Saving the program in a package**

8. Click the `Continue` (✔) icon. The `ABAP Editor: Change Report ZSUBROUTINE` screen appears, as shown in Figure 9.5:

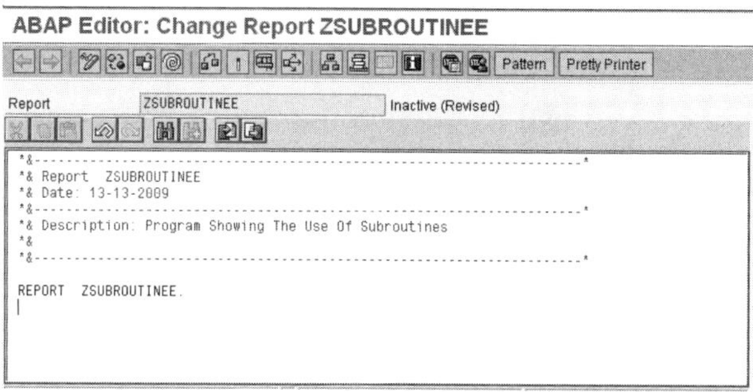

FIGURE 9.5 **Displaying the ABAP editor screen**

In Figure 9.5, notice the generated program name, i.e., ZSUBROUITNEE appears with the `REPORT` statement. In the `ABAP Editor: Change Report ZSUBROUTINE` screen, we have added some comments regarding the date and description of the program.

9. Enter the code of an ABAP program. For instance, we have inserted the code for creating a subroutine in Figure 9.6:

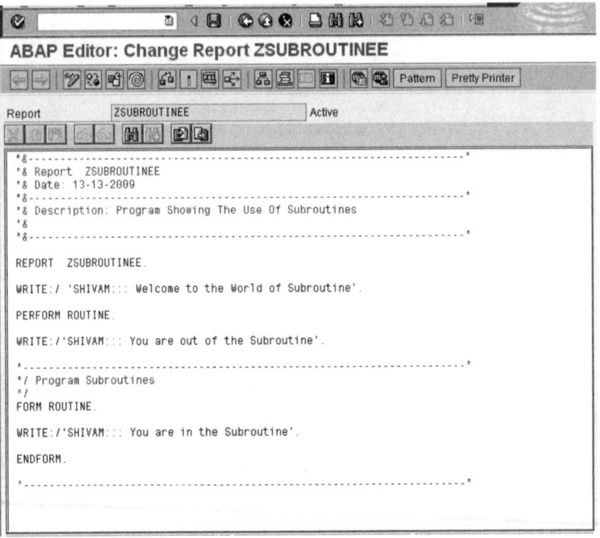
```
*&---------------------------------------------------------------------*
*& Report  ZSUBROUTINEE
*& Date: 13-13-2009
*&---------------------------------------------------------------------*
*& Description: Program Showing The Use Of Subroutines
*&
*&---------------------------------------------------------------------*

REPORT  ZSUBROUTINEE.

WRITE:/ 'SHIVAM::: Welcome to the World of Subroutine'.

PERFORM ROUTINE.

WRITE:/'SHIVAM::: You are out of the Subroutine'.

*---------------------------------------------------------------------*
*/ Program Subroutines
*/
FORM ROUTINE.

WRITE:/'SHIVAM::: You are in the Subroutine'.

ENDFORM.
*---------------------------------------------------------------------*
```


FIGURE 9.6 **The screen showing the subroutine program**

10. Click the `Save` icon, click the `Check` icon, and then click the `Activate` icon.
11. Click the `Direct Processing` icon to see the output of the program. Figure 9.7 shows the output of the program ZSUBROUTINEE:

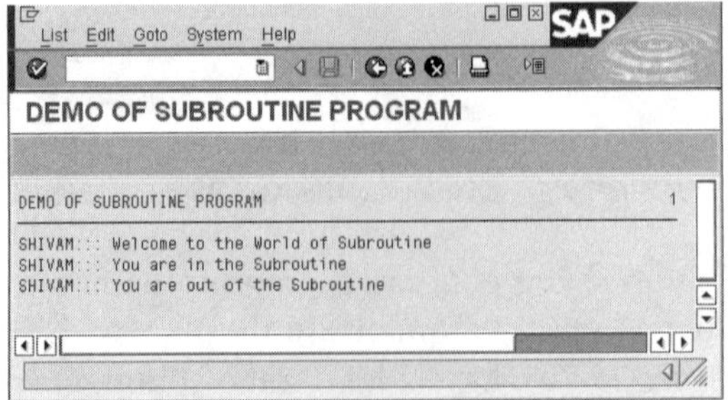

FIGURE 9.7 **Displaying the output of the subroutine program**

In the following sections, we learn to:

- Work with formal and actual parameters
- Handle data in subroutines
- Make internal and external calls
- Pass parameters to subroutines
- Terminate subroutines

Now, let's discuss each in detail.

Working with Formal and Actual Parameters

In subroutines, parameters are defined by using the `FORM` and `PERFORM` statements. When you define the parameters by using the `FORM` statement, the parameters are said to be formal parameters. The parameters defined by using the `PERFORM` statement are called actual parameters. `USING` and `CHANGING` are additional clauses in the `FORM` statement, which are used to include or change the type or field of formal parameters by using `TYPE` and `LIKE` clauses, respectively. Each clause, whether it is `USING` or `CHANGING`, is followed by one or more formal parameters. Formal parameters behave as dynamic local data inside a subroutine. Formal parameters hide the global data objects that have the same name as the formal parameters.

Whenever the subroutine is called, all the formal parameters must be populated with the values of the actual parameters. At the end of the subroutine, the values in the formal parameters are passed back to the corresponding actual parameters. The syntax to define formal parameters is:

```
FORM sub_name USING prm1[{TYPE type}|{LIKE field}]
                     prm2[{TYPE type}|{LIKE field}]
                     . . . .
          CHANGING     prm1[{TYPE type}|{LIKE field}]
                     prm2[{TYPE type}|{LIKE field}]
                     . . . .
```

In this syntax, `sub_name` represents the name of a subroutine, `prm1` and `prm2` represent formal parameters, and `field` represents the name of a predefined field. You do not need to allocate memory space to formal parameters because only the address of the actual parameters is transferred to the formal parameters. If the value of the formal parameter is changed, the content of the actual parameter in the calling program also changes. The USING clause is used for the documentation of those parameters that do not change in the subroutine (also known as input parameters), and the CHANGING clause is used for the documentation of those parameters that change in the subroutine (also known as output parameters). It is possible that the values of the actual parameters change during the processing of the subroutine. This change in the values of the actual parameters can be prevented with the help of different clauses, such as USING VALUE and CHANGING VALUE, used in the FORM statement. The values of the actual parameters can be prevented from changing in the following ways:

- **Passing values using input parameters**—Input parameters are used to pass data to subroutines. They are specified after the USING VALUE clause in the FORM statement. The following syntax shows how to define input parameters:

```
FORM sub_name USING VALUE(prm1) [{TYPE type}|{LIKE field}]
                    VALUE(prm2) [{TYPE type}|{LIKE field}]
                    . . . . . .
```

- **Passing values using output parameters**—Output parameters are used to pass data from subroutines. The output parameters are specified after the CHANGING VALUE clause in the FORM statement. The following syntax shows how to define output parameters:

```
FORM subr CHANGING VALUE(prm1) [{TYPE type}|{LIKE field}]
                   VALUE(prm2) [{TYPE type}|{LIKE field}]
                   . . . . . .
```

Handling Data in Subroutines

A subroutine handles the data of a program by adopting any of the following methods:

- Using global data of a program
- Using data types and data objects in subroutines

Using Global Data of a Program

A subroutine defined in a program can access all the global data of that program. The values stored in global data can be modified by executing a subroutine. To avoid the change in the values of global data, you must use the parameter interface. With the help of parameter interface, a subroutine can perform complex operations on its own data and pass the data back to the actual parameters without affecting the global data of the associated program.

The values in the global objects in a subroutine can be prevented from changing through the use of the LOCAL statement. The following is the syntax of the LOCAL statement:

```
LOCAL f.
```

The LOCAL statement should be used in between the FORM and ENDFORM statements. Note that you cannot declare the table work area already defined by the TABLES statement with another TABLES statement inside a subroutine. If you want to use the table work area locally and preserve the contents of the table work area outside the subroutine, you must use the LOCAL statement. Listing 9.1 shows an example of the LOCAL statement:

```
REPORT ZMYSUBROUTINE1.
*-------------------------------------------*
*/ Tables Used in the Program
*/
TABLES MARA.
*-------------------------------------------*

PERFORM routine1.
```

Continued

```
WRITE: / MARA-MTART, MARA-MBRSH.

PERFORM routine2.

WRITE: / MARA-MTART, MARA-MBRSH.
*-----------------------------------------------------*
*/ Definition of Subroutine
*/
FORM routine1.

      MARA-MTART = 'HALB'.
      MARA-MBRSH = 'M'.
      WRITE: / MARA-MTART, MARA-MBRSH.

ENDFORM.
*-----------------------------------------------------*
*/ Definition of Subroutine
*/
FORM routine2.

      LOCAL MARA.
      MARA-MTART = 'HAWA'.
      MARA-MBRSH = '1'.
      WRITE: / MARA-MTART,
      MARA-MBRSH.

ENDFORM.
*-----------------------------------------------------*
```

LISTING 9.1 **Using the LOCAL statement in subroutines**

In Listing 9.1, notice that when the first subroutine, `routine1`, is called, the values of the `MTART` (MATERIAL TYPE) and `MBRSH` (INDUSTRY SECTOR) fields are displayed. When `routine2` is called, the `LOCAL` statement is used. The `LOCAL` statement is used to preserve the values of the global data objects. In our case, the global data object is a table named MARA. Any changes made to the fields of this table (MARA) in the `routine2` definition are not reflected outside the definition of routine2. Figure 9.8 shows the effect of the `LOCAL` statement in a subroutine:

HALB M
HALB M
HAWA 1
HALB M

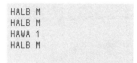

FIGURE 9.8 **Displaying the effect of the LOCAL statement**

Using Data Types and Data Objects in a Subroutine

Data declaration is done in procedures such as subroutines, function modules, and source code modules, to create local data types and data objects that are visible only within that procedure. The following are the two types of local data types and data objects:

- Dynamic data types and data objects
- Static data types and data objects

Dynamic Data Types and Data Objects

Dynamic data types and data objects are declared in a subroutine with the help of the `TYPES` and `DATA` statements. Dynamic data types and data objects exist only when a subroutine is running, and they are deleted when the subroutines end and recreated each time the subroutine is called.

Every subroutine has its own local namespace. A user cannot address the global data type or the data object from within the subroutine whose names are used to declare the names of the local data type or data object. Local data types or data objects hide the global data types declared or data objects that have the same name. The global data types and the data objects can be prevented from being hidden by assigning different names to the local data types and the data objects. Listing 9.2 shows how to use the dynamic data types and data objects:

```
Report ZMYSUBROUTINE2.
*-------------------------------------------*
*/ Defining Data
*/
```

Continued

```
TYPES numbers(10) TYPE c.
DATA digits TYPE numbers.
*-----------------------------------------------------*
digits = '987654321'.
WRITE:/ 'The sequence of the digits is ::', digits.

PERFORM subroutine.

WRITE:/ 'The sequence of the digits is ::', digits.
*-----------------------------------------------------*
*/ Definition of Subroutine
*/

FORM subroutine.

TYPES alphabet(7) TYPE c.
DATA name TYPE alphabet.

name = 'SHIVANI'.
WRITE:/ 'The name of the candidate is::', name.
ENDFORM.
*-----------------------------------------------------*
```

LISTING 9.2 **Using dynamic data types and data objects in a subroutine**

In Listing 9.2, a data type named `numbers` is created with the help of the `TYPES` statement. A global data object named `digits` with the data type as numbers is declared. A value has been assigned to the `digits` data object and is displayed on the output screen. The subroutine named `subroutine` is called; a local data type, `alphabet`, and a local data object, `name`, with the type `alphabet` is declared inside the subroutine. These local data types and the data objects hide the global data type and data object. Note that the global definitions are valid again after the subroutine has been executed. Figure 9.9 shows the output of Listing 9.2:

```
The sequence of the digits is :: 987654321
The name of the candidate is:: SHIVANI
The sequence of the digits is :: 987654321
```


FIGURE 9.9 **Displaying the dynamic data types and data objects**

Static Data Types and Data Objects

The data types and data objects defined in a subroutine are known as either static data types and static data objects or local data types and local data objects. Use the `STATICS` statement if you want to ensure that the values in the local data objects do not change after exiting the subroutine. This statement declares a data object that is globally defined, but is only locally visible from the subroutine in which it is defined. Listing 9.3 shows the use of the `STATICS` statement in a subroutine:

```
Report ZMYSUBROUTINE3.

PERFORM subroutine1.
PERFORM subroutine1.
SKIP 2.
PERFORM subroutine2.
PERFORM subroutine2.
*-----------------------------------------------------*
*/ Definition of Subroutine
*/
FORM subroutine1.

TYPES alphabets(7) TYPE c.
DATA name TYPE alphabets value 'MEHER'.
WRITE name.
name = '786'.
WRITE name.

ENDFORM.
```

Continued

```
*-----------------------------------------------*
*/ Definition of Subroutine
*/
FORM subroutine2.

TYPES alphabets(7) TYPE c.
STATICS name TYPE alphabets VALUE 'SHIVAM'.
WRITE name.
name = 'MADHAVI'.
WRITE name.

ENDFORM.
*-----------------------------------------------*
```

LISTING 9.3 **Using the STATICS statement in subroutines**

Listing 9.3 shows that two similar subroutines, `subroutine1` and `subrouitne2`, are defined. In `subroutine2`, the `STATICS` statement is used instead of the `DATA` statement to declare a data object, `name`. Each time `subroutine1` is called, the name `data object` is initialized, but `subroutine1` maintains the original value for `subroutine2`. The `VALUE` clause in the `STATICS` statement works only when `subroutine2` is called for the first time. Figure 9.10 shows the output of Listing 9.3:

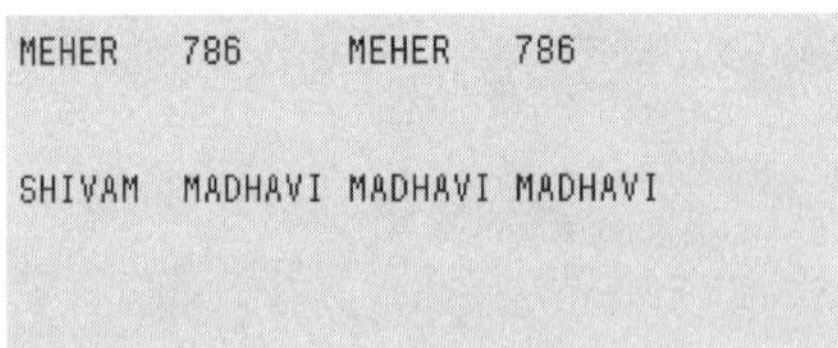

MEHER 786 MEHER 786
SHIVAM MADHAVI MADHAVI MADHAVI

FIGURE 9.10 **Displaying the static data types and data objects**

Using Local Field Symbols

When a field symbol is defined within a subroutine, it is called a local field symbol. This is because a local field symbol does not have its scope and cannot be used outside the subroutine definition. A local field symbol is defined in a subroutine by using the `FIELD-SYMBOLS` statement. The following are some rules that apply to local field symbols:

- Addressing the local field symbols outside a subroutine is not possible.
- Whenever a subroutine is called, no field is assigned to a local field symbol.
- The names of the local field symbols can be the same as the names of the global field symbols (field symbols defined outside the subroutine).

Within a subroutine, local copies of the global data objects can be created on the local stack. The following syntax creates local copies of the global data object by using local field symbols and the ASSIGN statement:

```
ASSIGN LOCAL COPY OF field TO <fs>.
```

In this syntax, the ASSIGN statement helps an SAP system place the copy of the specified global data object, represented by the field expression, on the local stack.

In a subroutine, you can access and change the copy of the global data object without changing the original value of the global data object. You can access the copy of the global data object by writing the field symbol in the <fs> expression. The LOCAL COPY OF clause can be used with all the variants of the ASSIGN statement except ASSIGN COMPONENT. Table 9.1 shows different syntaxes of the ASSIGN statement:

Variation	Description
ASSIGN LOCAL COPY OF INITIAL field TO <fs>	Creates an initialized copy of the field global data object on the stack without transporting the field content.
ASSIGN LOCAL COPY OF INITIAL LINE OF itab TO <fs>	Creates an initial copy of the lines of a global internal table, itab, on the stack.
ASSIGN LOCAL COPY OF INITIAL LINE OF (field) TO <fs>	Creates an initial copy of the lines of a global internal table, itab, on the stack. The internal table is specified dynamically, similar to the contents of the global data object field.

TABLE 9.1 Variations of the ASSIGN statement

Listing 9.4 shows how to use the ASSIGN statement to declare local field symbols in a program:

```
Report: ZMYSUBROUTINE4.
*-------------------------------------------------------*
*/ Defining the Data
*/
DATA name(10) TYPE c VALUE 'MADHAVI1'.
*-------------------------------------------------------*

PERFORM assignment.
Write / name.

*-------------------------------------------------------*
*/ Definition of Subroutine
*/
FORM assignment.

      FIELD-SYMBOLS <fs> TYPE ANY.
      ASSIGN LOCAL COPY OF name TO <fs>.
      Write / <fs>.
      <fs> = 'MADHAVI2'.
      Write / <fs>.
      ASSIGN name to <fs>.
      Write / <fs>.
      <fs> = 'MADHAVI3'.

ENDFORM.
*-------------------------------------------------------*
```

LISTING 9.4 **Using the ASSIGN statement to declare local field symbols**

In Listing 9.4, the name data object is assigned to the <fs> local field symbol in the assignment subroutine. A copy of the name data object is placed on the local data stack. This local copy can only be read and changed by addressing the field symbol represented by the <fs> expression in the ASSIGN statement. The global data object is not affected by the operations on the local copy. If the data object is assigned to the field symbol without using the LOCAL

COPY OF clause, the field symbol points directly to the global data object. Now, if you perform any operations on the global data object, it affects the global field. Figure 9.11 shows the output of Listing 9.4:

```
MADHAVI1
MADHAVI2
MADHAVI1
MADHAVI3
```


FIGURE 9.11 **Displaying the output of the local field symbol**

Making Internal and External Calls

The subroutines created in ABAP can be called only by using the PERFORM statement. The subroutines created in ABAP programs are of two types, internal subroutines and external subroutines. Internal subroutines are defined in the same program in which they are called, and external subroutines are defined in one program and called in another program. The PERFORM statement is used to call the internal as well as external subroutines. Therefore, depending on the type of the subroutines, the call can be divided into the following two categories:

- Internal calls
- External calls

Internal Calls

In this type of subroutine call, the definition of the subroutine as well as the calling procedure exists in the same ABAP program. The call is made with the help of the PERFORM statement. The following syntax is used for the PERFORM statement:

```
PERFORM sub_name    [USING      prm1 prm2 . . . . . ]
                    [CHANGING     prm1 prm2. . . . ]
```

In this syntax, the `sub_name` expression represents the name of the subroutine, and `prm1` and `prm2` represent the actual parameters. All the global data of the calling program can be accessed by the internal subroutine. The clauses used in the `PERFORM` statement are the same as those used with the `FORM` statement. Listing 9.5 shows how to use the `PERFORM` statement while making an internal call in a program:

```
Report ZMYSUBROUTINE5.
*-----------------------------------------------------*
*/ Variables Used
Data: number1      type i,
          number2     type i,
          number3     type i.
*-----------------------------------------------------*

number1 = 2.
number2 = 2.

PERFORM multiply.

number1 = 5.
number2 = 5.

PERFORM multiply.
*-----------------------------------------------------*
*/ Definition of Subroutine
*/
FORM multiply.
  number3 = number1 * number2.
PERFORM output.
ENDFORM.
*-----------------------------------------------------*
*/ Definition of Subroutine
*/
FORM output.
```

Continued

```
    WRITE: / 'Multiplication of', number1, 'and', number2, 'is',
    number3.
ENDFORM.
*-------------------------------------------------------------*
```

LISTING 9.5 **Using the PERFORM statement in an internal call**

In Listing 9.5, the two subroutines, named `multiply` and `output`, are defined at the end of the program. The `multiply` subroutine is called by the program, which in turn calls the `output` subroutine. The subroutines have access to the `number1`, `number2`, and `multiply` global data objects. Figure 9.12 shows the multiplication of the two numbers:

```
Multiplication of          2  and          2  is          4
Multiplication of          5  and          5  is         25
```


FIGURE 9.12 **Displaying the multiplication of number1 and number2**

External Calls

In the external call of a subroutine, a subroutine is defined in one program and is called in another program. Sometimes, you might also have a separate ABAP program, which consists of only subroutines. Note that the name of the ABAP program that needs to be called must be known. The following syntax is used to make external calls:

```
PERFORM sub_name (prog) [USING    prm1 prm2 . . . ]
                 [CHANGING prm1 prm2 . . . ] [IF FOUND].
```

In this syntax, the name of the ABAP program is represented by the `(prog)` expression, which is defined statically. The `IF FOUND` clause is used to prevent the runtime error, which may occur if the ABAP program `(prog)` does not contain a subroutine named `sub_name`. If the mentioned subroutine, `sub_name`, is not found, the SAP system ignores the `PERFORM` statement. Listing 9.6 shows the use of the `PERFORM` statement in an external call:

```
Report ZMYSUBROUTINE7.
PERFORM systemdata.
*-----------------------------------------------------*
*/ Definition of Subroutine
*/
FORM systemdata.
      WRITE: / 'Program started by:', sy-uname,
             / 'On host:', sy-host,
             / 'Date:', sy-datum.

ENDFORM.
*-----------------------------------------------------*
```

LISTING 9.6 **Using the PERFORM statement in an external call**

In Listing 9.6, the information related to an SAP system, such as the system user name, host information, and the system date on which the program is created, is displayed with the help of a subroutine named `systemdata`. Figure 9.13 shows the output of Listing 9.6:

```
Program started by: KDT
On host: sapmachine
Date: 14.10.2008
```


FIGURE 9.13 **Displaying the output of system data**

Now, the `systemdata` subroutine can also be called from some other program. Listing 9.7 shows how an external call is made:

```
REPORT ZEXTERNALSUB.
PERFORM systemdata (ZSUBROUTINE8) IF FOUND.
```

LISTING 9.7 **Calling a subroutine externally**

In case of an external call, we give the name of the subroutine to be called, i.e., `systemdata`, and the name of the ABAP program, `ZSUBROUTINE8`, which contains the definition of the called subroutine. The output of Listing 9.7 appears, as shown in Figure 9.13.

In addition to the external call of the subroutine, you can specify the name of the program in which the subroutine occurs dynamically at runtime, as shown in the following syntax:

```
PERFORM sub_name [IN PROGRAM (fprog)] [USING      prm1
prm2 . . . ]
                                [CHANGING prm1 prm2 . . . ]
                                    [IF FOUND].
```

In this syntax, the sub_name expression represents the name of the subroutine and the (fprog) expression shows the name of the external program containing the subroutine.

Apart from the internal and external call of the subroutine, a user can also call a subroutine from a list of subroutines. The following syntax shows how to call a subroutine from a list of subroutines:

```
PERFORM <idx> OF <subr1> <subr2> . . . . . <subrn>.
```

In this syntax, the SAP system calls a subroutine from the subroutine list represented by the <subr1>, <subr2>, and <subrn> expressions. The position of the called subroutine in the subroutine list is denoted by the <idx> expression. The <idx> expression can be a literal or a variable. Listing 9.8 shows how to call subroutines from a list:

```
Report ZMYSUBROUTINE8.
DO 3 TIMES.
PERFORM SY-INDEX OF first second third.
ENDDO.
*-----------------------------------------------*
*/ Definition of Subroutine
*/
FORM first.
WRITE / 'Shivam Srivastava Worked in Infosys Technologies'.
ENDFORM.
*-----------------------------------------------*
```

Continued

```
*/ Definition of Subroutine
*/

FORM second.
WRITE / 'K C Srivastava is Working in Scooters India Ltd'.
ENDFORM.
*-------------------------------------------------*
*/ Definition of Subroutine
*/
FORM third.
WRITE / 'Indu Bala Srivastava Worked in Avadh Rubber Ltd'.
ENDFORM.
*-------------------------------------------------*
```

LISTING 9.8 **Calling subroutines from a subroutine list**

In Listing 9.8, the three subroutines, named `first`, `second`, and `third`, are called consecutively from the subroutine list. Figure 9.14 shows the output of Listing 9.8:

```
Shivam Srivastava Worked in Infosys Technologies
K C Srivastava is Working in Scooters India Limited
Indu Bala Worked in Avadh Rubber Ltd
```


FIGURE 9.14 **Calling a subroutine from a list**

Passing Parameters to Subroutines

If a subroutine contains a parameter interface, you must provide values to all the formal parameters. The sequence of the actual parameters is essential whenever the values are passed. Consequently, the value of the first actual parameter in the list of parameters is passed to the first formal parameter, the value of the second actual parameter is passed to the second formal parameter, and so on.

The technical attributes of the actual parameters must be compatible with the type specified for the corresponding formal parameter. Actual parameters can be any data objects or field symbols of the calling program. The following are the three methods to pass parameters to a subroutine:

- Passing by reference
- Passing by value
- Passing by value and result

Table 9.2 shows different kinds of additions that can be used in the `FORM` statement to identify the type of method used in an ABAP program:

Addition	Name of the Method	Description
USING `prm` OR CHANGING `prm`	Pass by reference	Shows that the parameters are passed by reference. The pass by reference method is very effective because it passes a pointer to the original memory location of the passed variable.
USINGVALUE `(prm)`	Pass by value	Shows that the parameters are passed by value. This method ensures that no change is made to the memory of the passed variable. A new memory location is allocated to the passed variable within a subroutine, which becomes freed as soon as the subroutine ends.
CHANGING VALUE (v1)	Pass by value and result	Shows that the parameters are passed by value and result. This method is similar to the pass by value method, but the content of the new memory location is copied back into the original memory.

TABLE 9.2 Additions used in the FORM statement

Note: The following points must be kept in mind to avoid errors while passing parameters:

- The `PERFORM` and `FORM` statements must contain the same number of parameters.

Continued

- The way in which the PERFORM and FORM statements are coded may differ.
- You cannot use the VALUE clause on the PERFORM statement.
- The USING clause must always be used before the CHANGING clause.
- You can use the USING and CHANGING clause only once in a statement.

The Pass by Reference Method

In the pass by reference method of passing parameters, no new memory location is allocated for the value. Instead, a pointer to the original memory location is passed. If the value of the variable is changed within a subroutine, the original memory location is changed immediately. Listing 9.9 shows how to use this method:

```
Report ZMYSUBROUTINE9.
*-----------------------------------------------*
*/ Defining Variable
*/
DATA: pmname(35) VALUE 'RUDRAKSH BATRA'.
*-----------------------------------------------*

WRITE: 'NAME OF PROJECT MANAGER IS:::', pmname.

PERFORM routine USING pmname.
WRITE:/ pmname1.

*-----------------------------------------------*
*/ Subroutine Definition
*/
FORM routine USING pmname1.

pmname1 = 'NAME OF TEAM MEMBER IS::: SHIVAM'.
ENDFORM.
*-----------------------------------------------*
```

LISTING 9.9 **The pass by reference method**

In Listing 9.9, a memory location is allocated to the `pmname` variable. Now, let's assume that the assigned memory location is 2000. When a subroutine named `routine` is called, the `USING VALUE` clause on the `FORM` statement causes the `pmname` variable to be passed by reference. Therefore, `pmname1` acts as a pointer to the memory location 2000. The assignment to the variable `pmname1`, changes the contents of the memory location 2000 to "NAME OF TEAM MEMBER IS::: SHIVAM", which previously was "RUDRAKSH BATRA". Figure 9.15 shows the output of Listing 9.9:

```
NAME OF PROJECT MANAGER IS::: RUDRAKSH BATRA
NAME OF TEAM MEMBER IS::: SHIVAM
```


FIGURE 9.15 **Displaying the output of the pass by reference method**

Pass by Value Method

In the pass by value method of passing parameters, a new memory location is allocated for the value being passed. A new memory location is allocated when the subroutine is called and is released when the execution of the subroutine is completed. Therefore, any references made to the parameter are actually the references made to the unique memory area allocated, which are valid only within the subroutine. The original value of the variable remains unchanged even if you change the value of the parameter. Listing 9.10 demonstrates the pass by value method:

```
Report ZMYSUBROUTINE10.
*------------------------------------------------------*
*/ Defining Variable
DATA: kogemp(36) value 'SHIVAM SRIVASTAVA'.
*------------------------------------------------------*

PERFORM routine USING kogemp.
WRITE:/ 'NAME OF EMPLOYEE IS:::',kogemp.
```

Continued

```
*-------------------------------------------------------*
*/ Definition of Subroutine
*/
FORM routine USING VALUE(kogemp1).
kogemp1 = 'NAME OF EMPLOYEE IS::: DHEERAJ GUPTA'.
WRITE:/ kogemp1.
ENDFORM.
*-------------------------------------------------------*
```

LISTING 9.10 **The pass by value method**

In Listing 9.10, you see that a memory location is allocated to the `kogemp` variable. When the `routine` subroutine is called, the `USING VALUE (kogemp1)` clause on the `FORM` statement causes the `kogemp` variable to be passed by value. Therefore, the `kogemp1` variable refers to a new memory location that is independent of the memory location used by the `kogemp` variable. Moreover, the content of the memory location for the `kogemp` variable remains unchanged. Figure 9.16 shows the output of Listing 9.10:

```
NAME OF EMPLOYEE IS::: DHEERAJ GUPTA
NAME OF EMPLOYEE IS::: SHIVAM SRIVASTAVA
```


FIGURE 9.16 **Displaying the output of the pass by value method**

The Pass by Value and Result Method

In the pass by value and result method, a new memory location is allocated to the variable passed. In addition to this, an independent copy of the variable is maintained at the new memory location. The value at this new memory location is freed when the subroutine ends. When the `ENDFORM` statement is executed, the value in the new memory location is copied to the original memory location. Listing 9.11 shows how to use this method:

```
Report ZOURSUBROUTINE.
*-----------------------------------------------------*
*/ Defining Variable
*/
DATA: kogemp(40) value 'Satendra Pal Chopra'.
*-----------------------------------------------------*

PERFORM Routine USING kogemp.
WRITE:/ 'HEAD OF ACHEIVERS TEAM IS:::', kogemp.
*-----------------------------------------------------*
*/ Definition of Subroutine
FORM Routine CHANGING value(kogemp1).
Kogemp1 = 'NAME OF FORMATTER IS::: NIRMAL KUMAR'.
ENDFORM.
*-----------------------------------------------------*
```

LISTING 9.11 **The pass by value and result method**

In Listing 9.11, a memory location is allocated to the `kogemp` variable. When the `Routine` subroutine is called, the `CHANGING VALUE (kogemp1)` clause on the `FORM` statement causes the `kogemp` variable to be passed by value and result. Therefore, the `kogemp1` variable refers to a new memory location that is independent of `kogemp`. In Listing 9.11, the value of `kogemp` is copied automatically to the memory location of `kogemp1`. In addition, the content of the memory location for `kogemp1` is changed. The `(Kogemp1 = 'NAME OF FORMATTER IS::: NIRMAL KUMAR')` line of Listing 9.11 copies the value of the `kogemp1` variable back to the `kogemp` variable, and the value in the `kogemp1` variable is now freed. Figure 9.17 shows the output of Listing 9.11:

```
NAME OF FORMATTER IS::: NIRMAL KUMAR
```


FIGURE 9.17 **Displaying the output of the pass by value and result method**

Terminating Subroutines by Using EXIT and CHECK Statements

Under normal conditions, the subroutine ends when the ABAP program encounters the ENDFORM statement. However, the subroutine can also be terminated by using the EXIT or CHECK statements at any time. If a subroutine is ended with the EXIT or CHECK statement, the current values of the output parameters (CHANGING parameters passed by value) are returned to the corresponding actual parameter.

The EXIT statement is used to terminate a subroutine without any condition. After exiting from the subroutine, the SAP system continues the processing of the ABAP program, executing the statements after the PERFORM statement. Listing 9.12 shows how to use the EXIT statement in a subroutine:

```
Report ZMYLIBRARY.
PERFORM LIBRARY.
WRITE / 'THANKING YOU FOR VISITING SHIVAM LIBRARY'.
*----------------------------------------------------*
*/ Definition of Subroutine
*/
FORM LIBRARY.
WRITE / 'MY LIBRARY HAS SAP BOOKS '.
WRITE / 'MY LIBRARY HAS ASP.NET BOOKS'.
WRITE / 'MY LIBRARY HAS JAVA BOOKS'.
EXIT.
WRITE 'MY LIBRARY does not have novels '.
ENDFORM.
*----------------------------------------------------*
```

LISTING 9.12 **The EXIT statement in a subroutine**

In Listing 9.12, a subroutine named LIBRARY is defined. This subroutine is ended when the third WRITE statement is executed. Figure 9.18 shows the output of Listing 9.12:

```
MY LIBRARY HAS SAP BOOKS
MY LIBRARY HAS ASP.NET BOOKS
MY LIBRARY HAS JAVA BOOKS
THANKING YOU FOR VISITING SHIVAM LIBRARY
```


FIGURE 9.18 **Showing the function of the EXIT statement**

The CHECK statement is used to terminate a subroutine conditionally. The subroutine is ended when the condition specified in the CHECK statement evaluates to false. When the subroutine ends, the program continues to execute the statements following the PERFORM statement. Listing 9.13 shows how to use the CHECK statement in a program:

```
Report ZMYCHECK.
*-----------------------------------------------*
*/ Defining Variable
*/
DATA: Number1 TYPE I,
      Number2 TYPE I,
      R TYPE P DECIMALS 2.
*-----------------------------------------------*
Number1 = 3.
Number2 = 4.
PERFORM DIVISION USING Number1 Number2 CHANGING R.
Number1 = 5.
Number2 = 0.
PERFORM DIVISION USING Number1 Number2 CHANGING R.
Number1 = 2.
Number2 = 3.
```

Continued

```
PERFORM DIVISION USING Number1 Number2 CHANGING R.
*-----------------------------------------------*
*/ Definition of Subroutine
*/
FORM DIVISION USING Number1 Number2 CHANGING R.
CHECK Number2 NE 0.
R = Number1 / Number2.
WRITE: / Number1, '/', Number2, '=', R.
ENDFORM.
*-----------------------------------------------*
```

LISTING 9.13 **The CHECK statement in a subroutine**

In Listing 9.13, the SAP system terminates the execution of the DIVISION subroutine during the second call of the DIVISION subroutine. It is because during the second call, the value of NUMBER2 is zero, and the condition checked by the CHECK statement evaluates to false. Figure 9.19 shows the output of Listing 9.13:

```
3 /          4 =          0.75
2 /          3 =          0.67
```


FIGURE 9.19 **Showing the functioning of the CHECK statement**

> **Note:** The EXIT and CHECK statements function differently in loops and subroutines.

FUNCTION MODULES

Function modules are ABAP routines that are administered in a central function library. Function modules are assigned to a function pool, also called function group. A function group is a container where all the function modules are connected logically to each other. Function modules apply across applications and are available throughout the SAP system. In other words, function modules are used in remote communication between SAP R/3 systems or between an SAP R/3 system and a non-SAP R/3 system. Function modules also support exception handling and help update databases.

Function groups and function modules are not defined in the source code of a program. Instead, function modules are created with the help of an ABAP Workbench tool known as Function Builder. Moreover, Function Builder can also be used to test function modules without including them in an ABAP program.

Function modules encapsulate program code and provide an interface for data exchange, similar to subroutines. Function modules must belong to a pool called a function group. Some of the features of function modules are:

- A fixed interface is provided by a function module to exchange data between the function module and an ABAP program. Due to this interface, you can pass input and output parameters easily to and from the function module.
- No data can be exchanged between the calling program and function module by using the shared memory area because function modules always use their own memory.
- A function module can be called in an ABAP program by using the `CALL FUNCTION` statement.

Use of function modules within an ABAP program can be determined by the function module interface parameters. Table 9.3 describes the interface parameters used for function modules:

Interface Parameter	Description
Import	Transfers the values of the parameters from the calling program to the function module. The contents of the import parameter cannot be overwritten at runtime.
Export	Transfers the values of the parameters from the function module back to the calling program.
Changing	Acts as both the import and export parameters simultaneously. The original value of a changing parameter is transferred from the calling program to the function module. The initial value of the changing

Continued

Interface Parameter	Description
	parameter can be changed by the function module and can be returned back to the calling program.
Tables	Specifies the names of the internal tables that can be imported and exported. The content of the internal tables is transferred from the calling program to the function module. The content of the internal tables can also be altered by the function module and returned to the calling program. Remember that table parameters are passed by reference.
Exceptions	Show the error situations that occur within a function module. These parameters are primarily used by the calling program to identify any error in the function module.

TABLE 9.3 Interface parameters of function modules

Creating Function Modules

As learned earlier, Function Builder is a tool of ABAP Workbench, which is used to create, test, and administer function modules in an integrated environment. The initial screen of the Function Builder can be started from the initial screen, i.e., `SAP Easy Access`, by selecting `SAP Menu>Tools>Development>Function Builder`, as shown in Figure 9.20:

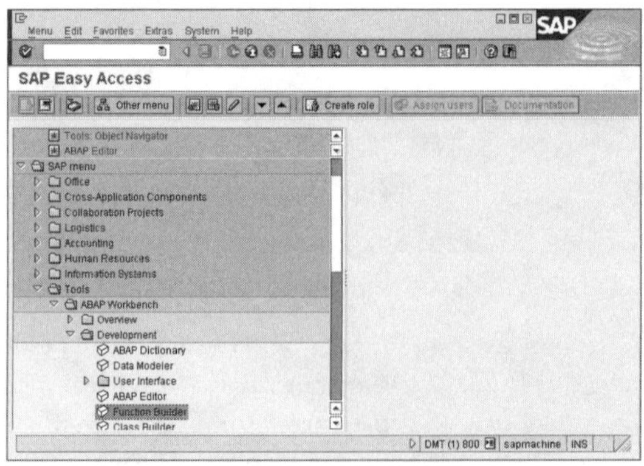

FIGURE 9.20 **Accessing function builder**

> **Note:** An alternative way to access Function Builder is to enter the `SE37` transaction code in the `Command` field.

Figure 9.21 shows the initial screen of Function Builder:

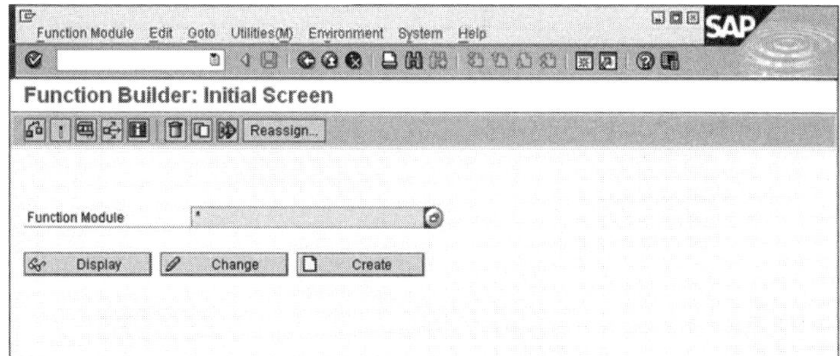

FIGURE 9.21 **The initial screen of function builder**

You can create a function module in the SAP R/3 system by performing the following steps:

1. Before creating a function module, a function group is created that actually holds the created function module. Function groups are created from the initial screen of the function builder. To create a function group, select `Go To>Function Groups>Create Group`, as shown in Figure 9.22:

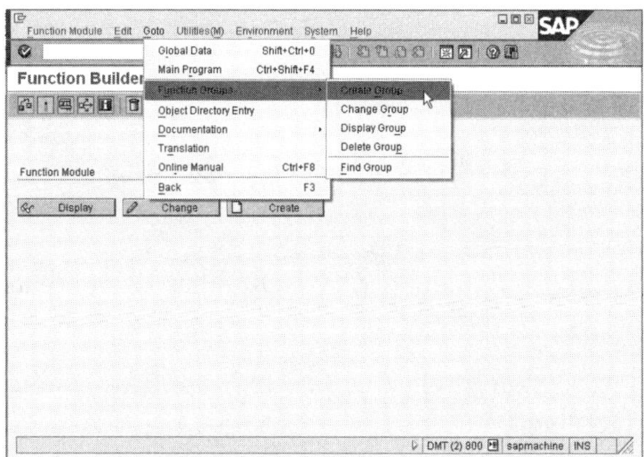

FIGURE 9.22 **Creating a function group**

The `Create Function Group` dialog box appears.

2. Enter the name of the function group that you want to create in the `Function group` field, and a short description in the `Short text` field. Finally, click the `Save` button, as shown in Figure 9.23:

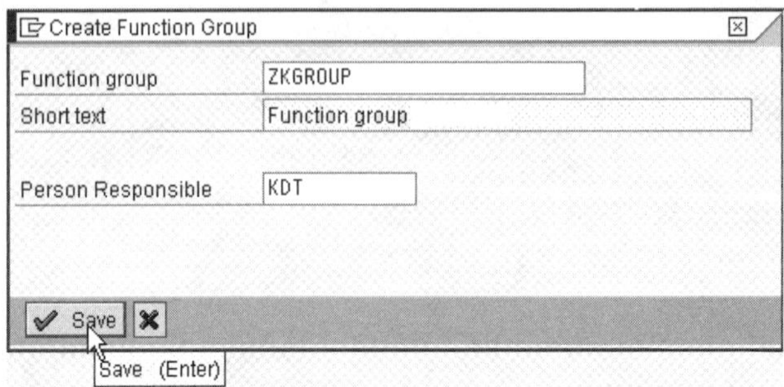

FIGURE 9.23 **Creating a function group**

The `Create Object Directory Entry` dialog box appears.

3. In the `Create Object Directory Entry` dialog box, enter ZKOG_PCKG as the name of the package in the `Package` field. Click the `Save` (💾) icon.

A confirmation message appears on the status bar of the initial screen, as shown in Figure 9.24:

FIGURE 9.24 **Confirmation message**

Now, a function group named ZKGROUP has been created and saved in the SAP system.

4. Start a new session by clicking the `Create New Session` (▣) icon on the standard toolbar.

5. Enter the `SE80` transaction in the command field and press the `ENTER` key. The `Object Navigator` screen appears (Figure 9.25). The initial screen of Object Navigator appears where you select the Function Group option from the drop-down menu, as shown in Figure 9.25:

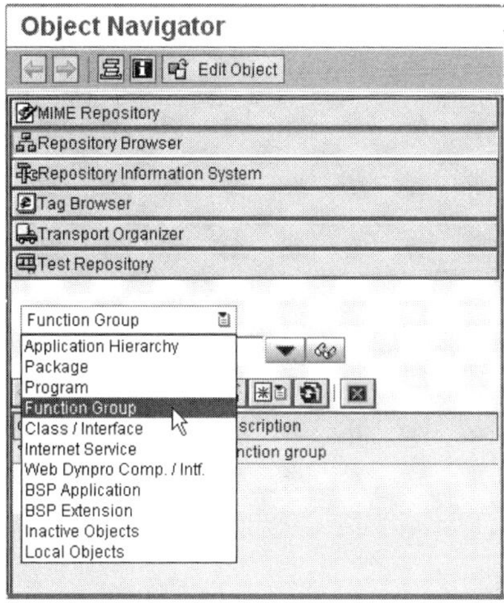

FIGURE 9.25 **Selecting the function group**

6. Enter `ZKGROUP` as the name of the function group in the next field below the `Function Group` field, as shown in Figure 9.26:

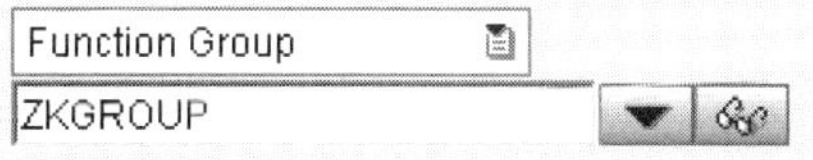

FIGURE 9.26 **Entering the name of the function group**

7. Press the ENTER key. The name of the function group `(ZKGROUP)` appears in the Object Name column, and the respective description of the function module appears under the Description column, as shown in Figure 9.27:

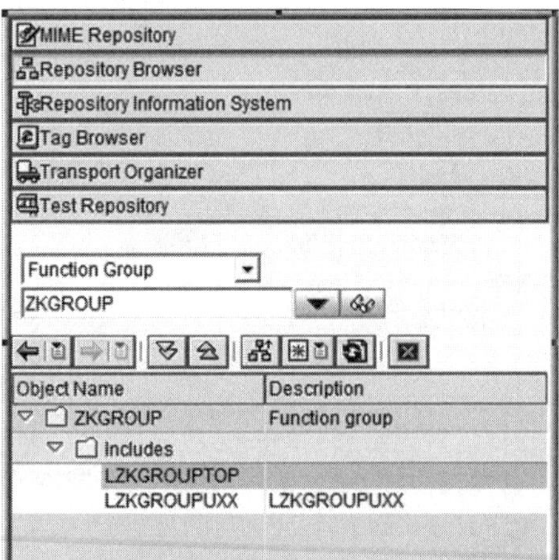

FIGURE 9.27 **Viewing the function group**

> **Note:** When you create a function group in an SAP system, the system automatically generates a main program and its subsequent include programs. The name of the main program always contains the prefix `SAPL`, and is followed by the name of the function group. Therefore, in our case, the main program is `SAPLZKGROUP` and the include programs are `LZKGROUPTOP` and `LZKGROUPUXX`. In Figure 9.27, you can see the `Includes` folder in Object Navigator that contains the `LZKGROUPTOP` and `LZKGROUPUXX` include programs.

8. Right-click the name of the function group and select the Activate option from the drop-down menu to activate the function group, as shown in Figure 9.28:

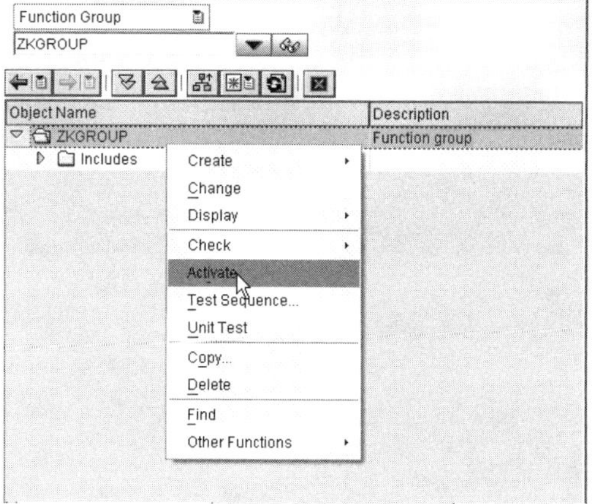

FIGURE 9.28 **Activating the function group**

The `Inactive Objects for KDT` dialog box appears.

9. Click the `Continue` (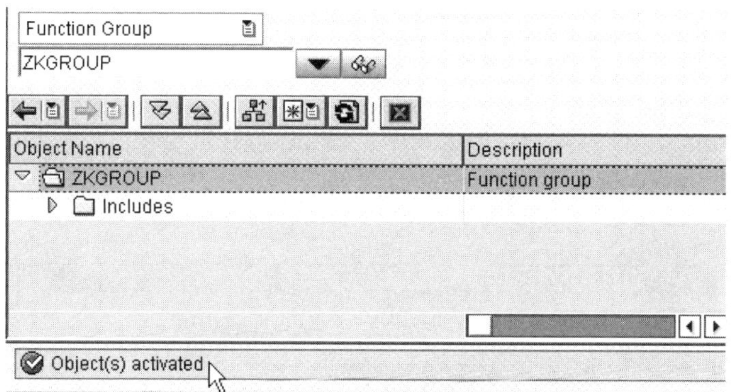) icon. A message appears on the status bar, which states that the created function module is activated, as shown in Figure 9.29:

FIGURE 9.29 **Function group activated**

10. Start a new session by clicking the `Create New Session` (▣) icon on the standard toolbar. Enter the `SE37` transaction in the `Command` field. The initial screen of Function Builder appears, as shown in Figure 9.30:

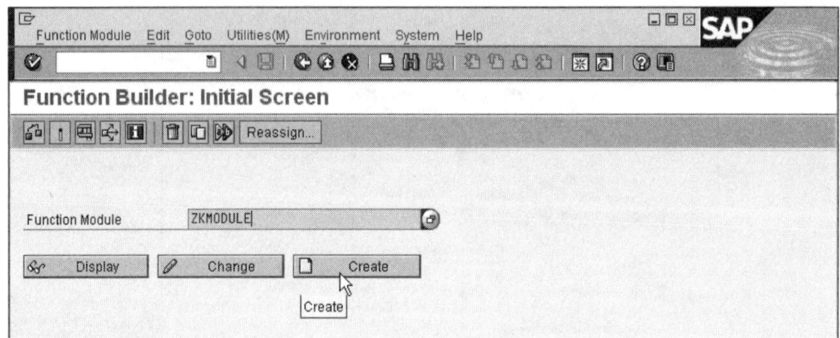

FIGURE 9.30 **The initial screen of function builder**

11. Enter the name of a function module in the `Function Module` field. In this case, we enter the name of the function module as ZKMODULE and click the `Create` button.

The `Create Function Module` dialog box appears (Figure 9.31).

12. In the `Create Function Module` dialog box, enter the name of a function group in the `Function group` field. In addition, enter a description for the function module in the `Short text` field. In this case, the function group is ZKGROUP and the description is Function module. Finally, click the `Save` button, as shown in Figure 9.31:

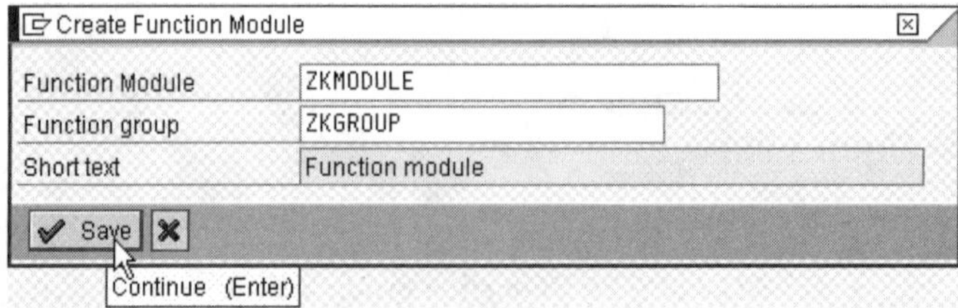

FIGURE 9.31 **Displaying the name of the function group and short description**

The `Information` dialog box appears, as shown in Figure 9.32:

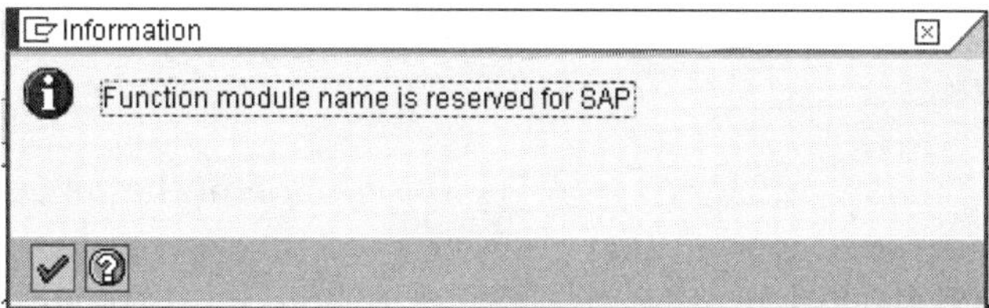

FIGURE 9.32 **Displaying the information dialog box**

13. Click the `Continue` (✔) icon:

The `Function Builder: Change ZKMODULE` screen appears, as shown in Figure 9.33:

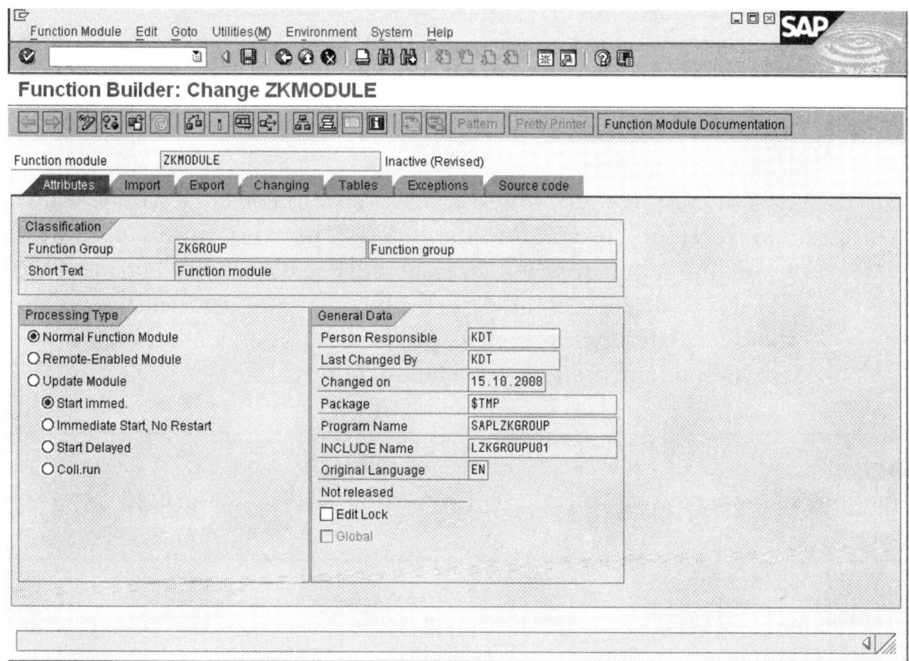

FIGURE 9.33 **Displaying the function module**

On this screen, you set the various subobjects, such as `Attributes`, `Import`, `Export`, `Changing`, `Tables`, `Exceptions`, and `the Source code`. These subobjects are known as interface parameters for the function module (see Figure 9.33).

14. Click the `Attributes` tab. The description of the function group, which was assigned earlier, that is, `Function module for kogent`, appears automatically in the `Short Text` field. You can also change the description and can provide a new description to the function module created. The processing type of the function module is selected as `Normal Function Module`. To call a function module from a program running in another SAP system, select the `Remote-Enabled Module` radio button.

> **Note:** The `Remote-Enabled Module` radio button is selected when the function module that you have to use in your program exists on a different system. In an SAP system, such function modules are invoked by using the Remote Function Call (RFC) interface system. The RFC interface system enables a function call between SAP systems or between an SAP system and an external system (a non-SAP system).

15. Click the `Import` tab, where you set the variables that can be transferred from the calling program to the function module. In this case, we define two import parameters, as `NUMBER1` and `NUMBER2`, with `Type` as TYPE and `Associated Type` as I (refers to the integer type). You can also define some other associated types, such as predefined data element, any predefined structure, or any predefined database tables.

> **Note:** To get the list of the associated types, click the `Search Help` (icon) icon, which appears when you place the cursor in the `Associated` type field (see Figure 9.34).

Figure 9.34 shows the screen displaying the different parameters related to the `Import` tab:

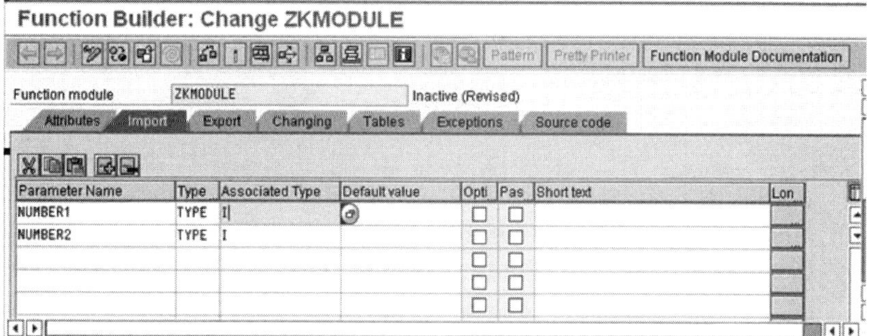

FIGURE 9.34 **Displaying the parameters on the import tab**

16. Click the `Export` tab, where you set the variables whose values are transferred from the function module to the calling program. In this case, we define a parameter named `OPERATION` with the `Type` specification as TYPE and the `Associated Type` as I (refers to integer type). Figure 9.35 shows the different parameters related to the `Export` tab:

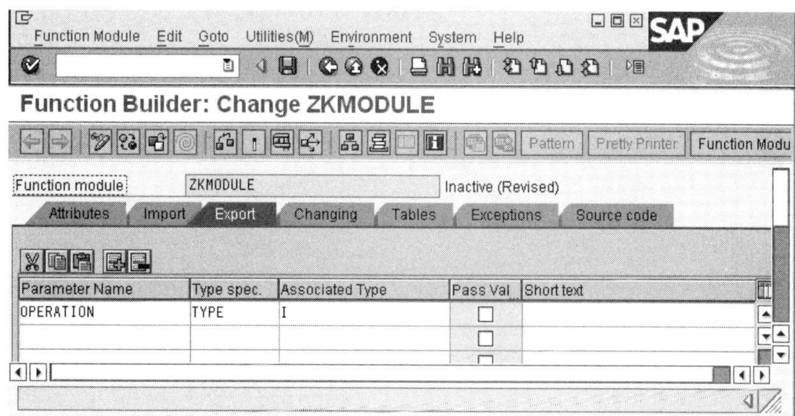

FIGURE 9.35 **Displaying the parameters on the export tab**

> **Note:** You can also define some other associated types, such as predefined data element, a predefined structure, or a predefined database table by clicking the `search help` (🔍) icon.

17. Click the `Changing` tab, where you define the variables that act as import and export parameters simultaneously.
18. Click the `Tables` tab to define the internal tables that can be either exported or imported. The content of the internal table is shifted from the calling program to the function module. In this function module, we do not use the `TABLES` subobject.
19. Click the `Exceptions` tab, where different parameters are defined. These parameters are used to determine any kind of error occurred in the function module.
20. Click the `Source code` tab, where the program for the function module is actually written, as shown in Figure 9.36:

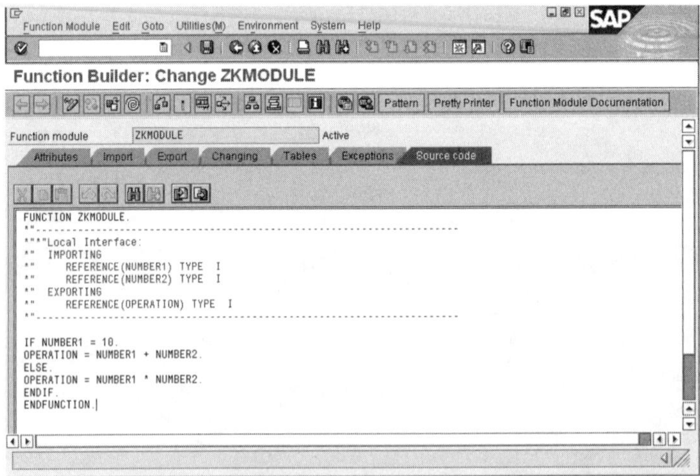

FIGURE 9.36 **Displaying the source code for the function module**

21. Click the `Check` (🔲) icon to find whether there is any error in the function module, and then click the `Activate` (🔲) icon to activate the source code.

22. Click the `Direct processing` (icon) icon to test whether the function module is working properly. The initial screen of Test Function Module appears, as shown in Figure 9.37:

Test Function Module: Initial Screen

Debugging | Test data directory

Test for function group ZKGROUP
Function module ZKMODULE
Uppercase/Lowercase

Import parameters	Value
NUMBER1	10
NUMBER2	20

FIGURE 9.37 **Displaying the screen where values are entered**

23. Enter the values for the import parameters, `NUMBER1` and `NUMBER2`. In this case, we enter 10 as the value for `NUMBER1` and 20 as the value for `NUMBER2`. Now, according to the condition given in the source code (see Figure 9.36), if `NUMBER1` = 10, 30 is assigned as the value of the `OPERATION` export parameter.
24. Click the `Execute` (icon) icon to execute the created function module. Figure 9.38 shows the result screen of Test Function Module, displaying the value of the export parameter `OPERATION`:

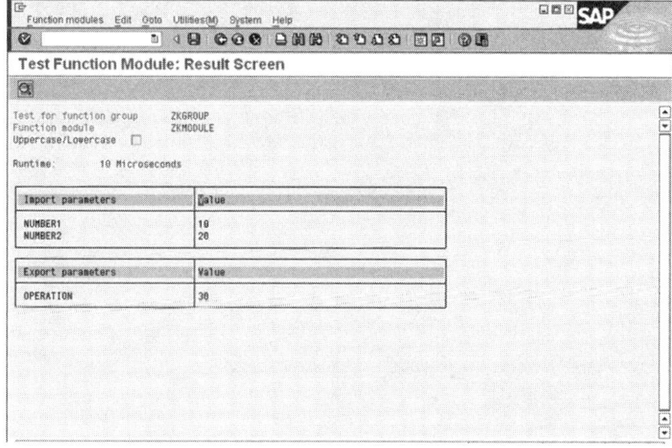

FIGURE 9.38 **Showing the function module test screen**

Now, let's learn how to use the created function module in this ABAP program example.

Calling Function Modules from ABAP Programs

The function modules created by using the Function Builder tool of ABAP Workbench can be called from ABAP programs. For this, you can call the generated function module by clicking the `Pattern` (Pattern) button on the application toolbar. Let's suppose that an executable type program, ZKOGFUN, is created in ABAP Editor. In this program, we define a function module named ZKMODULE. To call a function module, you need to create variables. In this case, we use two variables because the ZKMODULE function module consists of the two input variables, `NUMBER1` and `NUMBER2`, and an output variable, `OPERATION`. In this case, we use the `PARAMETERS` statement to assign values to variables. Values assigned to the variables are transferred from the function module to the calling program. A third variable, `NUM3`, is defined with the `DATA` statement so that the result from the function module can be passed to the calling program. The `NUM3` variable holds the value of the result. Perform the following steps to call a function module within an ABAP program:

1. Create an executable program type in ABAP Editor. In this case, we create a program named ZKOGFUN. Figure 9.39 shows the `ABAP Editor: Change Report ZKOGFUN` screen, containing the statements for this program:

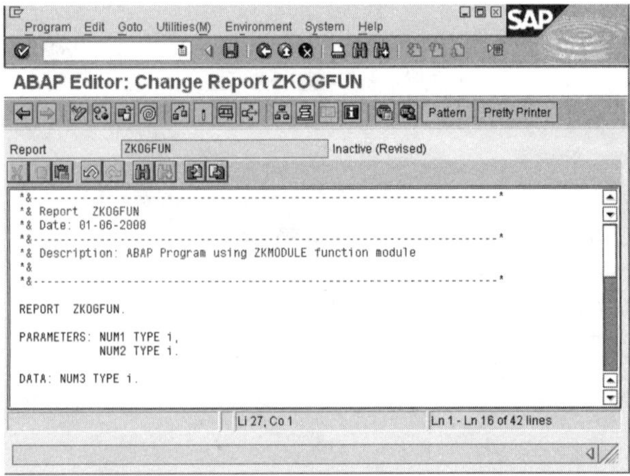

FIGURE 9.39 **Displaying the ABAP editor screen**

2. Click the `Pattern` button on the application toolbar, as shown in Figure 9.40:

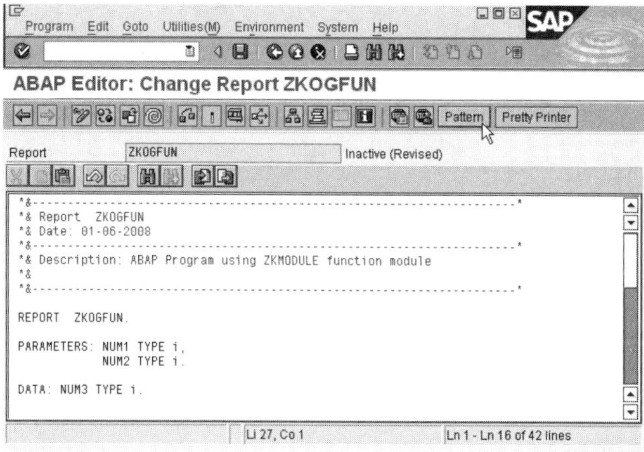

FIGURE 9.40 **Clicking the pattern button**

The `Ins. Statement` dialog box appears, as shown in Figure 9.41.

3. Enter the name of the function module to be included in the ABAP program. In this case, we enter ZKMODULE in the `CALL FUNCTION` field and click the `Continue` icon, as shown in Figure 9.41:

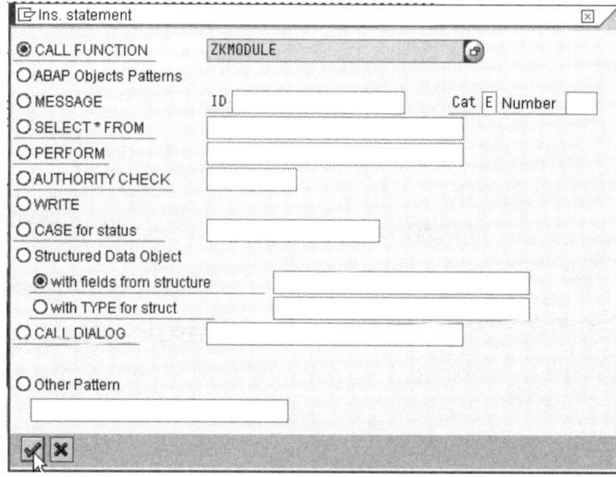

FIGURE 9.41 **Calling the function module**

The function module ZKMODULE is included in the program ZKOGFUN.

4. Write the code for the ZKOGFUN program in the ABAP Editor, as shown in Figure 9.42:

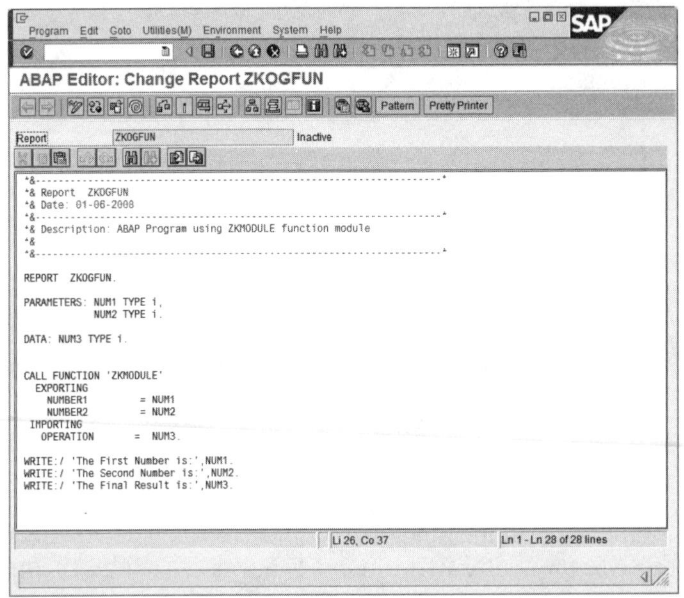

FIGURE 9.42 **Displaying the ABAP program using the function module**

In Figure 9.42, you see in the ZKOGFUN program that `NUMBER1` and `NUMBER2` are `EXPORTING` parameters that are assigned with the values of the `NUM1` and `NUM2` variables. Now, assign the value of the `NUM3` variable to the `IMPORTING` parameter, `OPERATION`.

5. Finally, click the `Save` (💾) icon to save the created program, the `Check` icon to check for any errors, and the `Activate` icon to activate the program.

Figure 9.43 shows the output of the program, where you need to enter the values for the variables:

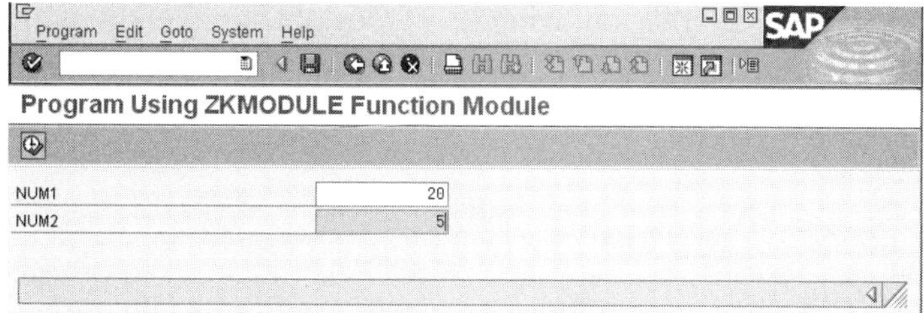

FIGURE 9.43 **Showing the values assigned to the variables**

6. Enter the values for the variables `NUMBER1` and `NUMBER2`. In our case, we enter the values as 20 and 5, respectively, as shown in Figure 9.43.
7. Click the `Execute` ( ) icon; the output corresponding to the values entered in the `NUM1` and `NUM2` fields appears, as shown in Figure 9.44:

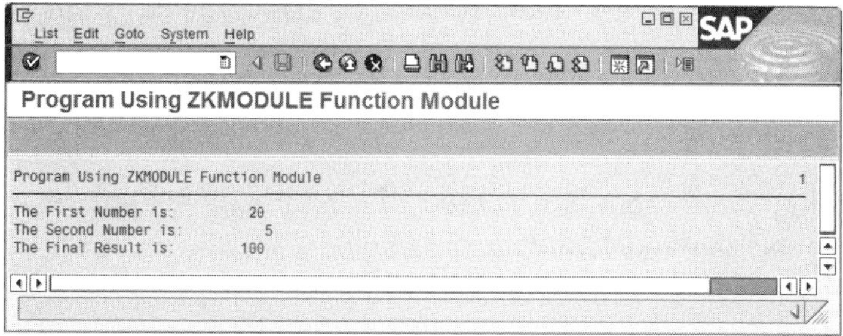

FIGURE 9.44 **Output screen**

SOURCE CODE MODULES

Source code modules are used to modularize your source code. Modularizing a source code means placing a sequence of ABAP statements in a module. The modularized source code can be called in a program depending on the user's requirements. Source code modules enhance the readability and understandability of ABAP programs. They also help to minimize data redundancy by avoiding repeated occurrence of the same set of statements. It must be noted that source code modules do not modularize tasks and functions.

ABAP provides the following two types of source code modules:

- Macros
- Include programs

Macros

A macro is a set of statements that can be used more than once in the ABAP program. For example, a macro can be useful for long calculations or for writing complex WRITE statements. A macro can be used only in that program in which it is created. You can define a macro within the DEFINE...END-OF-DEFINITION statement. The following syntax defines a macro:

```
DEFINE macro.
   statements
END-OF-DEFINITION.
```

A macro must be defined prior to its call in the ABAP program. Execute the following statement to use a macro:

```
macro [prm1 prm2... prm9].
```

When a program is executed, the SAP system replaces the macro by appropriate statements and the placeholders &1, &2, ..., &9 by the parameters prm1, prm2, ..., prm9.

A macro can be used within macros; however, a macro cannot call itself. Listing 9.14 shows an example of a nested macro:

```
REPORT ZMYMACRO.
*-----------------------------------------------------------*
*/ Defining Variables
*/
DATA: Finally TYPE i,
              number1      TYPE i VALUE 5,
              number2      TYPE i VALUE 10.
*-----------------------------------------------------------*

DEFINE operation.
```

Continued

```
                    finally = &1 &2 &3.
                    output &1 &2 &3 finally.
END-OF-DEFINITION.

DEFINE output.
        write: / 'The final of &1 &2 &3 is', &4.
END-OF-DEFINITION.
operation 10 * 3.
operation 20 ** 2.
  operation number2 - number1.
```

LISTING 9.14 **Nesting of a macro**

In Listing 9.14, two macros, `operation` and `output`, are defined. The `output` macro is nested within the `operation` macro. The `operation` macro is executed three times with different parameters. When the program is executed, the SAP system replaces the `operation` macro with the statements defined inside the macro and replaces each placeholder, `&1`, `&2`, and `&3`, by the parameters defined in the macro. Figure 9.45 shows the output of Listing 9.14:

```
The final of 10 * 3 is          30
The final of 20 ** 2 is         400
The final of NUMBER2 - NUMBER1 is          5
```


FIGURE 9.45 **Use a macro**

Include Programs

Include programs are global repository objects used to modularize the source code. They allow you to use the same source code in different programs. Include programs also allow you to manage complex programs in an orderly way. To use an include program in another program, use the following syntax of the `INCLUDE` statement:

```
INCLUDE <incl>.
```

The INCLUDE statement has the same effect as copying the source code of the include program <incl> into another program. An include program cannot run independently; it must be built into other programs. You can nest include programs.

The following restrictions must be considered while writing the source code for include programs:

- Include programs cannot call themselves
- Include programs must contain complete statements

Perform the following steps to create and use an include program:

1. Create the program to be included in ABAP Editor. Remember to set the Type of the program to INCLUDE program, as shown in Figure 9.46:

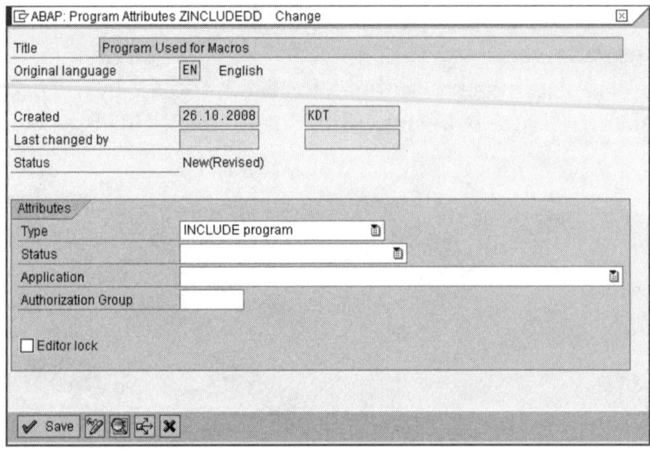

FIGURE 9.46 **Defining the attributes**

2. Click the Save (Save) button and save the program in a package named ZKOG_PCKG. Listing 9.15 shows the content of the program to be included in ABAP Editor:

```
PROGRAM ZINCLUDED.
WRITE:     / 'Program started by::', SY-UNAME,
            / 'On host:', SY-HOST,
            / 'Date:', SY-DATUM,
            / 'Time:' SY-UZEIT.
```

LISTING 9.15 **Program to be included**

3. Create another program where the program ZINCLUDED has to be used. In this case, we have created another program named ZINCLUDING and assigned a type for the program, such as `Executable program`. Now, the coding for the ZINCLUDING program includes the ZINCLUDED program with the help of the `INCLUDE` statement, as shown in Listing 9.16:

```
REPORT ZINCLUDING.
INCLUDE ZINCLUDED.
```

LISTING 9.16 **Coding for the program ZINCLUDING**

In Listing 9.16, notice that the program named ZINCLUDED is called with the help of the `Include` statement. Figure 9.47 shows the output of Listing 9.16:

```
Program started by:: KDT
On host: sapmachine
Date: 15.10.2008
```


FIGURE 9.47 **Displaying the output of an INCLUDE program**

SUMMARY

In this chapter, you have learned about the different types of modularization techniques, including subroutines, which acts like a mini-program consisting of sequence of statements, function modules, and source code modules. Function modules encapsulate program code, and source code modules are used to modularize source code.

Chapter 10 ABAP User Dialogs

If you need information on:	*See page:*
Introducing Dialog Programming	550
Screen Painter	552
Menu Painter	599
Working with Selection Screens	620

ABAP user dialogs are user-defined screens that are created by using ABAP statements and enable users to interact with ABAP programs. Some examples of ABAP user dialogs are screens, selection screens, modal dialog boxes, lists, and messages. The process of creating these user dialogs programmatically is called dialog programming. In dialog programming, you can create and design screens according to user requirements. Dialog programming involves specifying a certain sequence of screens that are processed by the SAP system one after the other. A dialog program is started by using a transaction code.

Screens are dynamic ABAP programs that contain various data objects or fields. These data objects are linked with their respective input or output fields that appear on the screen itself. When a screen is processed, the SAP system automatically passes the data from the screen fields to the data objects in the associated ABAP program. You use the Screen Painter and Menu Painter tools of ABAP Workbench to design screens or menus for the screens, respectively. The Screen Painter tool is also used to define the flow logic of a screen.

Besides screens, which are dynamic ABAP programs, you can also use dialog programming to create another kind of user dialog called a selection screen. A selection screen is different from the other general type of screens, which are designed with the help of ABAP Workbench tools such as Screen Painter and Menu Painter. A selection screen is created by using ABAP statements, such as `PARAMETERS` and `SELECTION-SCREEN` statements, and is designed to accept data from users. Selection screens allow you to define various selection criteria required by a program. Using a selection screen, you can create a list containing data from a very large database table. In other words, a selection screen presents an input template to users that allows them to enter selections and reduces the amount of data that has to be read from a database.

In this chapter, you learn about dialog programming. You also explore Screen Painter, which is an ABAP Workbench tool to design screens for user interaction. In addition, you learn about different UI elements of Screen Painter. Finally, you learn to define, call, and process selection screens.

INTRODUCING DIALOG PROGRAMMING

Dialog programming involves using a certain sequence of screens that are processed by the SAP system one after the other. With the help of dialog programming, a user can create a customized interface. A user cannot start a dialog program directly; instead, transaction codes are used to start a dialog program.

After a dialog program is executed, the user enters the required values in the fields displayed on the screen. The screen is then processed depending on the user action, such as clicking an icon or selecting a menu entry. Subsequently, another screen appears, depending on the flow logic of the screens. The flow logic is processed, according to the user input or any kind of request is made by the user on that particular screen. To understand the concept of flow logic, let's consider an example. Suppose that a travel agent wants to book a railway ticket. The user inserts the related data on the screen. After entering the related data, one of the following two screens is displayed:

- **Availability**—Specifies that berths are available for reservation
- **Unavailability**—Specifies that berths are not available for reservation

In this example, if the Availability screen appears, the user can enter the passenger details and book the ticket in the next screen. Alternatively, the user might be prompted to log out if the Unavailability screen is displayed.

Screens can be designed for the following three types of programs:

- Executable type programs (Type `1`)
- Module pool type programs (Type `M`)
- Function groups (Type `F`)

There is no limit to the number of screens that can be designed for an ABAP program. The screens of an ABAP program can be combined to form a screen sequence.

A screen consists of the following:

- Screen elements, such as buttons, text fields, tabstrips, and table controls
- Flow logic events, such as the `process before output` (`PBO`), `process after input` (`PAI`), `process on help request` (`POH`), and `process on value (POV)` events

The events related to the flow logic are processed only after the user enters the required input. You can call a single screen or a screen sequence by using transaction codes or the `CALL SCREEN` statement in the corresponding ABAP program. Screens and screen sequences can be called from inside or outside the corresponding ABAP program. When you call a screen or screen sequence, the screen flow logic takes control of the ABAP program execution. Figure 10.1 shows a screen located between the ABAP program and the GUI status:

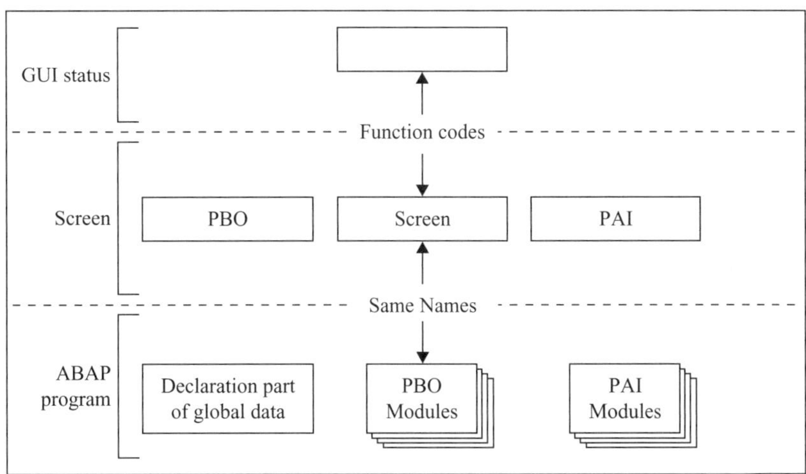

FIGURE 10.1 **Screen located between the ABAP program and the GUI status**

In Figure 10.1, the screen consists of the `PAI` and `PBO` events. Various modules related to the `PAI` and `PBO` events are defined in the ABAP program, provided that the names of the modules used in the ABAP program are the same as those declared inside screen events. The ABAP program consists of data objects and definitions related to these modules. In addition, function code is assigned to the button screen element.

Screens are dynamic ABAP programs that contain numerous data objects or fields. These data objects are linked with the corresponding input/output fields that appear on the screen itself. When a screen is processed, the SAP system automatically passes the data from the screen fields to the data objects in the associated ABAP program. A screen also has a GUI status, which is created by using the Menu Painter tool of ABAP Workbench. A GUI status provides a range of functions related to a particular screen, where each function has a corresponding function code. There are three types of GUI status:

- **Dialog status**—Consists of a menu bar, a toolbar, an application toolbar, and the function key settings
- **Dialog box**—Contains a toolbar and provides the standard function codes of the toolbar and function keys
- **Context menus**—Contains a context menu

SCREEN PAINTER

Screen Painter, a tool of ABAP Workbench, is used to create screens containing fields and graphical elements. The flow logic (that is, the order in which the screens are called) is also defined in Screen Painter. The screens created in an ABAP program are sometimes called dynpros, which is an abbreviated form of dynamic programming. Dynpros refers to the combination of the screen and the flow logic. You can perform the following tasks by using the Screen Painter tool:

- Designing new screens for programs written in the ABAP Editor tool
- Examining the existing screens
- Designing new layouts for existing screens

You can open the initial screen of Screen Painter from the `SAP Easy Access` screen by selecting `SAP menu>Tools>ABAP Workbench>Development>User Interface>Screen Painter`, as shown in Figure 10.2:

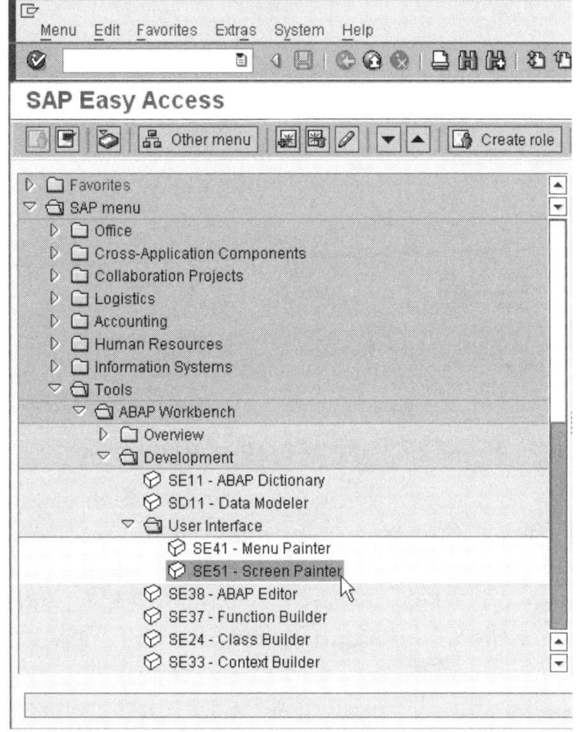

FIGURE 10.2 **Opening screen painter**

> **Note:** You can also open Screen Painter directly by entering the `SE51` transaction code in the `Command` field and either pressing the ENTER key or clicking the `Continue` (✔) icon.

The initial screen of Screen Painter appears, as shown in Figure 10.3:

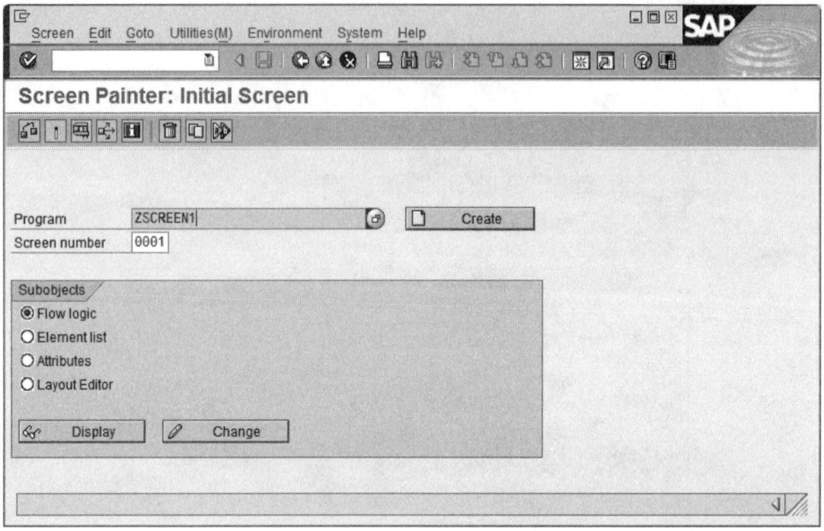

***FIGURE 10.3* Initial screen of screen painter**

In Figure 10.3, notice the `Program` field, which contains the name of the program for which the screen has to be created or changed. In the `Screen number` field, you can enter the number of the screen (which is of a four-digit number), such as 0001. Now, depending on the choice and requirements, you can click either the `Create` button (for creating a new screen), the `Display` button (for opening the existing screen in the display mode), or the `Change` button (for changing the existing screen). Apart from these, there are four subobjects present on the initial screen.

Table 10.1 shows the explanation of the subobjects on the initial screen of Screen Painter:

Subobject	**Description**
Flow logic	Maintains the flow of the program associated with a screen
Elements list	Maintains the program fields for a screen and assigns a program field to the `OK_CODE` field in Screen Painter

Continued

Subobject	Description
Attributes	Includes the program associated with a screen and declares the screen type
Layout editor	Designs a screen layout, which defines the screen elements, such as check boxes and radio buttons

TABLE 10.1 Subobjects on the initial screen of screen painter

Learning About Attributes

The attributes related to a screen can be defined on the screen by selecting the corresponding radio button (except the Layout Editor) present on the initial screen of Screen Painter. Figure 10.4 shows the screen on which the attributes related to a screen are designed and maintained:

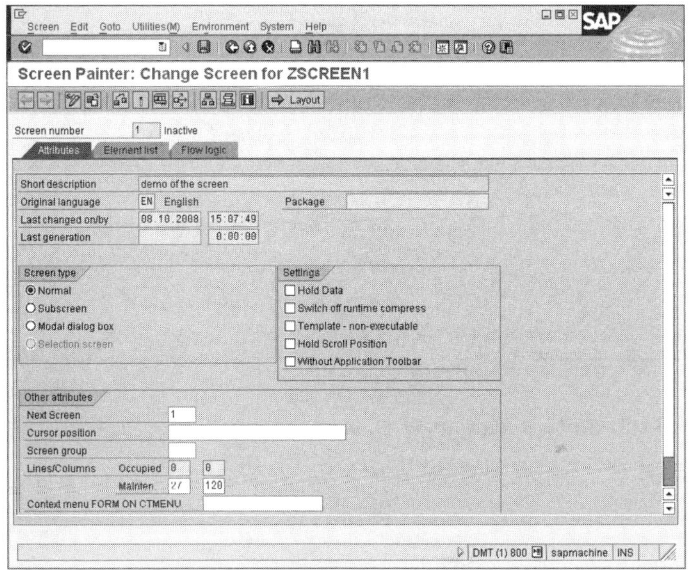

FIGURE 10.4 **Screen of attributes defined**

Figure 10.4 shows three tabs, `Attributes`, `Element list`, and `Flow Logic`. By default, the `Attributes` tab is selected and you can make changes to the various attributes under this tab. Note that the `Attributes` tab contains various fields and group boxes, such as `Short description`, `Screen type`, and `Settings`.

Table 10.2 shows the description of the various fields that appear in the `Attributes` tab:

Attribute	Description
Screen number	Assigns a number to a particular screen, composed of four digits.
Short description	Describes the purpose of a screen that you are designing.
Original language	Informs about the maintenance language of the screen. The language is set automatically by the SAP system. This language is similar to the language used by the program for which the screen is being designed.
Package	Denotes the package to which the screen belongs.
Last changed or Last generated	Displays the date and time when the screen was last changed or generated.

TABLE 10.2 Fields present on the attributes tab of the screen

> **Note:** All screen numbers greater than 9000 are reserved for SAP customers. The number 1000 is also reserved for table screens and selection screens.

The screen type can also be defined by selecting one of the radio buttons in the `Screen type` group box, as shown in Figure 10.5:

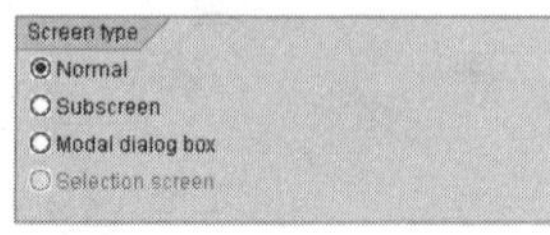

FIGURE 10.5 **Defining the screen type**

Table 10.3 shows the description of different types of screens that you can design for a program:

Screen Type	Description
Normal	Defines the screen as a normal screen. This option is set by default.
Subscreen	Designs a subscreen.
Modal dialog box	Describes a specialized interface to display lists in a dialog box.
Selection screen	Defines a screen that asks for the values of the database selection criteria before a report is initiated.

TABLE 10.3 Types of screens

Apart from the types of screens, you can apply other settings to the screens by using the `Settings` group box (see Figure 10.4).

Table 10.4 shows the settings of the `Settings` group box:

Setting	Description
Hold data	Holds entries created at runtime and displays them if a user calls the screen again. The supported functions are `Hold data`, `Set data`, and `Delete data`.
Switch off runtime compress	Specifies that the SAP system does not compress a screen at runtime.
Template - non-executable	Specifies that a screen is created as a template but is not executed. If this attribute is set for a screen, the screen cannot be activated and executed. In addition, the screen is not included in the screen consistency checks during the extended program check.
Hold scroll position	Specifies that the SAP system restores the vertical or horizontal scroll positions when a user navigates to the original screen.
Without application toolbar	Hides the application toolbar.

TABLE 10.4 Type of settings

The `Other attributes` group box contains the fields to define additional features, such as `Cursor position` and `Screen group`, related to a screen. Figure 10.6 shows the set of fields present on the `Other attributes` group box:

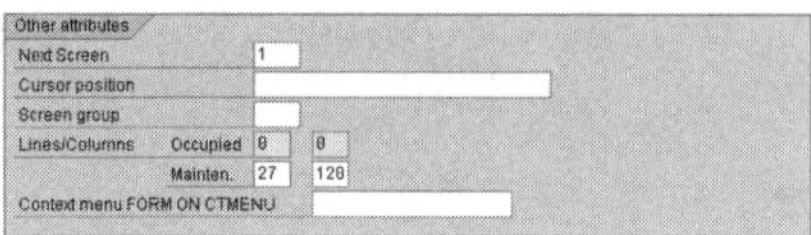

FIGURE 10.6 **The other attributes group box**

Table 10.5 shows the description of the fields present on the `Other attributes` group box:

Attribute	Description
Next screen	Specifies the screen number of the next screen to be displayed.
Cursor position	Specifies the position of the cursor, if you want to position the cursor at a desired field rather than on the first field (which is the default position). To do so, you need to enter the name of the desired field on which the cursor needs to be positioned.
Screen group	Defines a string of up to four characters, which denotes the name of the screen group. Using this string, several screens can be assigned to define a screen group so that any changes made to the screens in the screen group are consistent.
Lines/columns used	Defines the size of the screen area currently engaged by the screen elements.
Lines/columns maint.	Defines the size of the screen to be displayed in the rows/columns format for maintenance.

TABLE 10.5 Other attributes tab fields

> **Note:** The `Element list` tab is used to assign and maintain the screen elements of a screen. The `Element list` tab is rarely used, since the screen elements on a screen can be easily assigned and managed by using the `Layout` button (see Figure 10.4).

Flow Logic

The flow logic of a screen determines the procedural part of the screen. The language in which you write the program of the flow logic of a screen has syntax similar to that of an ABAP program, but is not part of the ABAP language. In fact, the language is sometimes known as screen language. The flow logic of a screen is displayed by selecting the `Flow Logic` tab on the Screen Painter screen (opened in the change mode while creating a screen), as shown in Figure 10.7:

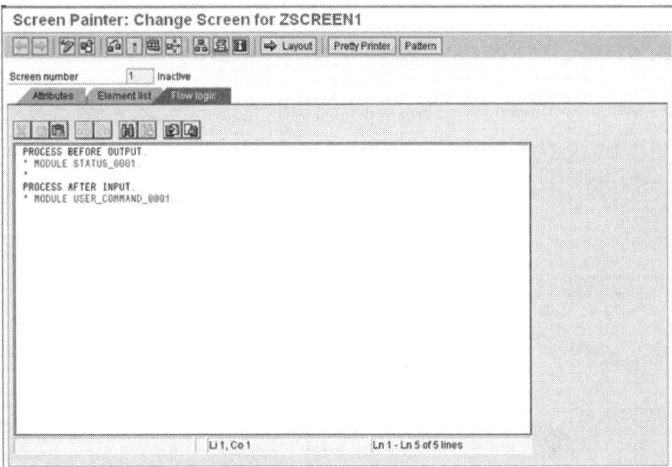

FIGURE 10.7 **Selecting the flow logic tab for writing flow logic of screens**

In Figure 10.7, you see the flow logic editor by selecting the `Flow Logic` tab. In this editor, you write the processing blocks of code for screens along with some predefined events.

Table 10.6 describes the predefined events that are used in the flow logic of a screen:

Event	Description
PROCESS BEFORE OUTPUT (PBO)	Triggered after the processing of the PROCESS AFTER INPUT(PAI) event of the previous screen and before displaying the current screen. A screen is displayed after the PBO event is processed.
PROCESS AFTER INPUT (PAI)	Triggered when a user selects a function on a screen. When this event is triggered, the SAP system either calls the next screen or continues the task from the point on the screen where this event is triggered.
PROCESS ON HELP-REQUEST (POH)	Triggered when a user requests fields help (F1).
PROCESS ON VALUE-(POV) REQUEST	Triggered when a user wants to view the possible set of values (F4) for a field.

TABLE 10.6 Events descriptions

Apart from the events, you can use predefined keywords with the events, as described in Table 10.7:

Keywords	Descriptions
CALL	Calls a subscreen
CHAIN	Starts a processing chain
ENDCHAIN	Ends a processing chain
ENDLOOP	Stops the processing of a loop
FIELD	Specifies a field that can be combined with the MODULE and SELECT keywords
LOOP	Starts the processing of a loop
MODIFY	Modifies a table
MODULE	Identifies the processing module

Continued

Keywords	Descriptions
`ON`	Checks the individual conditions for all the fields of a screen, which are specified in the current chain
`PROCESS`	Defines the processing event
`SELECT`	Performs a check for an entry against a table
`VALUES`	Determines the allowed input values

TABLE 10.7 List of keywords

Learning About the Layout Editor

A layout editor is used to define the layout of the screen being created. The layout editor contains two modes:

- Graphical layout editor
- Alphanumeric fullscreen editor

The preceding two modes are the same except for one difference: they use different interfaces. In the case of graphical modes, you use the drag-and-drop interface, similar to a drawing tool. The graphical mode works on three platforms, Microsoft Windows 95, Microsoft Windows NT, and nix/Motif platforms. In the case of alphanumeric modes, the keyboard and menus are used.

Let's discuss each of these two modes in detail.

Graphical Layout Editor

The Graphical layout editor provides a user-friendly environment as well as an easy technique for designing screens. You can access the Graphical layout editor by opening the initial screen of Screen Painter or using the Repository Browser. Perform the following steps to open the Graphical layout editor from the initial screen of Screen Painter:

1. In the initial screen of Screen Painter, enter the name of the program and the screen number for which the screen has to be designed. In this case,

the name of the Program is ZSCREEN1 and the screen number is 0001, as shown in Figure 10.3.

2. Select Utilities (M) > Settings, as shown in Figure 10.8:

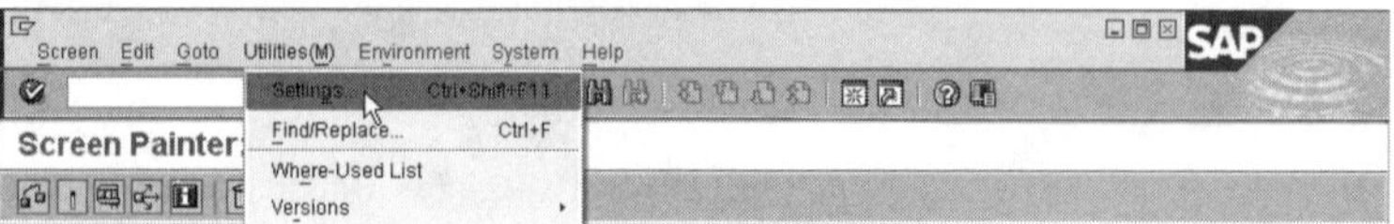

FIGURE 10.8 **The settings option**

The User-Specific Settings dialog box appears, as shown in Figure 10.9:

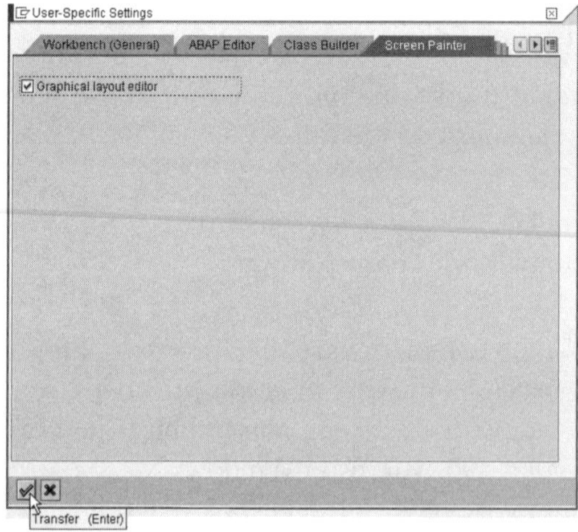

FIGURE 10.9 **User-Specific settings dialog box**

3. In the User-Specific Settings dialog box, select the Graphical layout editor check box and click the Transfer (Enter) icon (see Figure 10.9).

The User-Specific Settings dialog box disappears and the initial screen of Screen Painter appears again.

4. Now, click the Create button to create a new screen or click the Change button to change an existing screen. In this case, the Create button is clicked because a new screen has to be designed. You now see the Change screen for ZSCREEN1.

5. Click the `Layout` (⇨ Layout) button on the application toolbar to start the Graphical layout editor.

Finally, you see the `Graphical layout editor` screen, as shown in Figure 10.10:

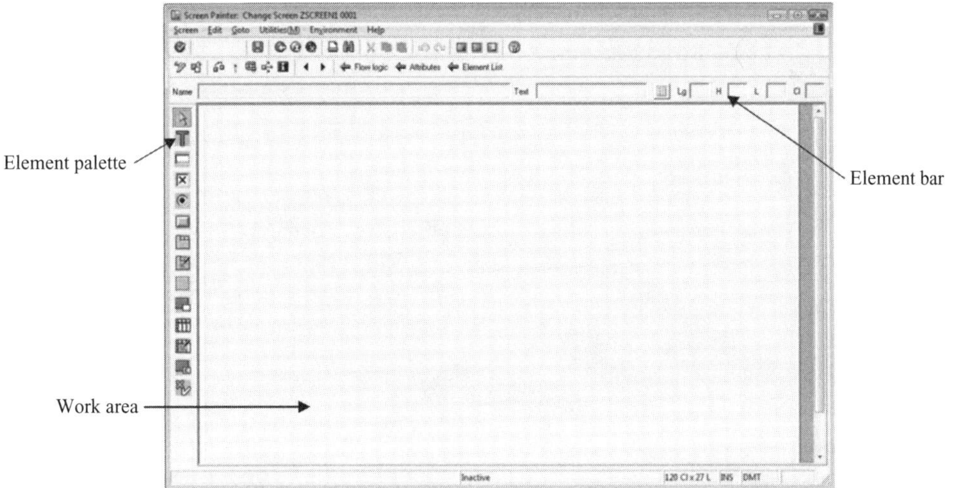

FIGURE 10.10 **The graphical layout editor screen**

Table 10.8 shows the descriptions of the three main areas of the `Graphical layout editor` screen:

Main Area	Description
Element palette	Creates screen elements. The elements from the palette can be selected and dropped onto the screen at the desired place.
Work area	Shows the area of the Graphical layout editor where the screen is designed.
Element bar	Shows a screen element when it is selected by a user. This bar consists of the essential attributes of the screen element. The displayed attributes can also be changed in the corresponding fields.

TABLE 10.8 Descriptions of the main areas

The element palette consists of different screen elements, such as text fields, check boxes, and radio buttons.

Table 10.9 shows the descriptions of the various screen elements on the element palette:

Picture	Name of Screen Element	Description
	Reset	Resets the settings defined for a screen element.
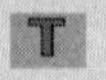	Text field	Provides labels for other screen elements. Text elements are only display elements; that is, they are used mainly to display the text assigned to the other screen elements. You cannot modify the text field at runtime after defining it. The text elements appear on the screen but at a fixed position assigned by the user.
	Input/output field	Helps enter and display data.
	Check box	Permits a user to create multiple selections from a number of options.
	Radio button	Permits a user to create single selection from a number of options. If a user selects any one option among the group of radio buttons, then the other radio buttons in the group automatically get deselected. It is necessary to define the radio buttons in a group to make the selection mutually exclusive.
	Button	Triggers a particular action or function. When a user selects a button, the function code related to the button is passed to the underlying ABAP program. The control of the program automatically returns to the work process on the application server that processes the PAI module.
	Tabstrip control	Combines several components of an application on a single screen. Tabstrip controls are complex graphical elements.

Continued

Picture	Name of Screen Element	Description
	Tabstrip (with wizard)	Helps create a working tabstrip control by following a certain sequence of steps.
	Box	Groups a set of elements that logically belong together, such as a radio button group.
	Subscreen area	Displays the screens at runtime. A subscreen area does not include any other screen elements on the element palette.
	Table control	Displays the data in a tabular pattern. The table controls are also complex graphical elements.
	Table control wizard	Helps create a working table control by following a certain sequence of steps.
	Custom control	Implants one or more controls within a screen area.
	Status icon	Displays the current status of an application in the status bar.

TABLE 10.9 Explaining the screen elements

Note: The text assigned to a label must not begin with an underscore or a question mark. However, if the text consists of several words, combine the words by placing an underscore between them. The underscores used to separate the words allow the SAP system to recognize these words as a single unit.

Alphanumeric Fullscreen Editor

The Alphanumeric fullscreen editor also provides an easy way of designing the screens. This mode of the layout editor helps create screens on all platforms. The initial screen of the Alphanumeric fullscreen editor can be started from the initial screen of Screen Painter. Perform the following steps to start the initial screen of the Alphanumeric fullscreen editor:

1. Enter the name of the program screen number of the screen that has to be designed. In our case, the name of the `Program` is ZSCREEN1 and the screen number is 0001, as shown in Figure 10.3.
2. Select `Utilities(M)>Settings` (see Figure 10.8) to open the project in the Alphanumeric fullscreen editor.
3. Clear the `Graphic layout editor` check box if it is selected, and click the `Transfer (Enter)` icon, as shown in Figure 10.11:

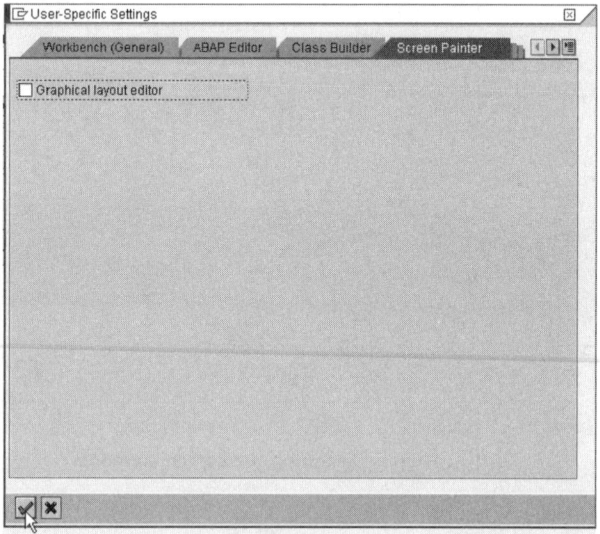

FIGURE 10.11 **Clearing the graphical layout editor check box**

The initial screen of Screen Painter appears again.

4. Click the `Create` button to create a new screen, or click the `Change` button to change the existing screen. In this case, the `Create` button is clicked because a new screen has to be designed. You now see the `Change` screen for ZSCREEN1.
5. Click the `Layout` button on the application toolbar to start the Graphical layout editor.
6. Finally, you see an Alphanumeric fullscreen editor screen on which certain fields related to flight information are designed, as shown in Figure 10.12:

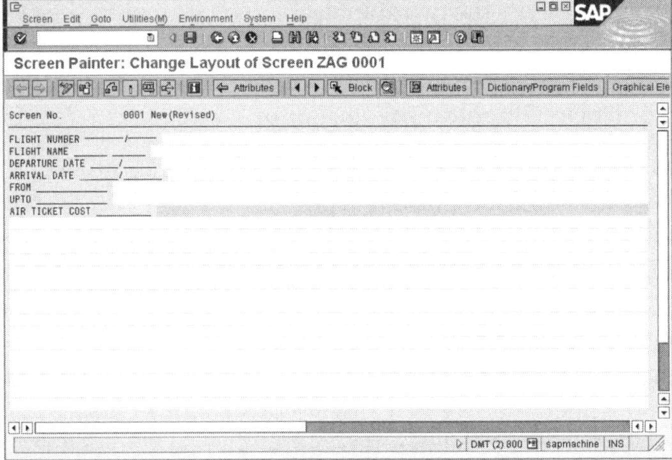

FIGURE 10.12 **The alphanumeric fullscreen editor screen**

The only differences between the two mentioned modes are only the method of creating the screen elements and how the screen elements are displayed on the screen. In the graphical layout mode, the screen elements are selected from the element palette. However, in the alphanumeric mode, select `Edit>Create Element>Text Field` (or any other screen element), as shown in Figure 10.13:

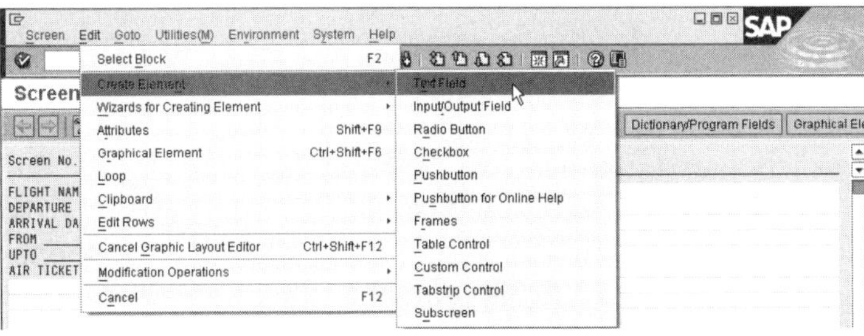

FIGURE 10.13 **Creating screen elements in the alphanumeric fullscreen editor**

> **Note:** In this book, we focus mainly on the graphical layout mode and design the screen by using this mode because it is easier to use than the alphanumeric mode.

Now, let's discuss the two graphical screen elements, the tabstrip, and table controls.

The Tabstrip Control in Graphical Layout Editor

The tabstrip control is a screen element that contains two or more tab pages. Each tab page has a tab title and a page area where other screen elements are stored. When the area that a tabstrip control occupies is not sufficient to display all of the tab titles, a scrollbar appears to allow you to view the titles that are not displayed. In addition, there is a button displaying a list of all tab titles.

You can use a tabstrip control in an application to place a number of screens belonging to the application on a single screen. A tab page in tabstrip control actually acts as a subscreen with a button (displayed as a tab title) assigned to the subscreen. When you want to use the tabstrip control, you need to define both the tabstrip area and the tab titles in the screen layout. The tabstrip area has a unique name, position, length, and height. You can also specify whether the tabstrip area can be resized vertically or horizontally when a user resizes the window. When you define a tabstrip area, it contains two tab titles by default. If you want to create a new tab title, simply create buttons in the row containing the tab titles. This is because tab titles have the same attributes as buttons. Each tab title contains a name, a text, and a function code, and it can also contain icons and dynamic texts.

Creating a Tabstrip Control

In this section, we create a program to design a screen, which contains two tabs, `Material` and `Vendor`. Apart from these two tabs, the screen contains two buttons, `Display` and `Exit`. Under the `Material` tab, some fields of the MARA dictionary table (General material data) are displayed on the screen; however, under the `Vendor` tab, some fields of the LFA1 dictionary table (Vendor related data) are displayed on the screen. Now, suppose that a user accesses the `Material` tab and enters a value into a field, where the cursor is positioned by default. After entering the value, the user clicks the `Display` button. The values of all fields related to that entered value are displayed. If the user clicks the `Exit` button, the processing stops and the `SAP Easy Access` screen is displayed. Perform the following steps to create a tabstrip control:

1. Create a program in ABAP Editor. Assign the type of the program as module pool by entering the `SE38` transaction code in the `Command` field present on the standard toolbar of the `SAP Easy Access` screen. The initial screen of ABAP Editor opens.

2. Write the name of the program for which the tabstrip has to be created in the `Program` field of ABAP Editor. In this case, the name of the program is ZKTABSTRIP. Click the `Create` pushbutton, as shown in Figure 10.14:

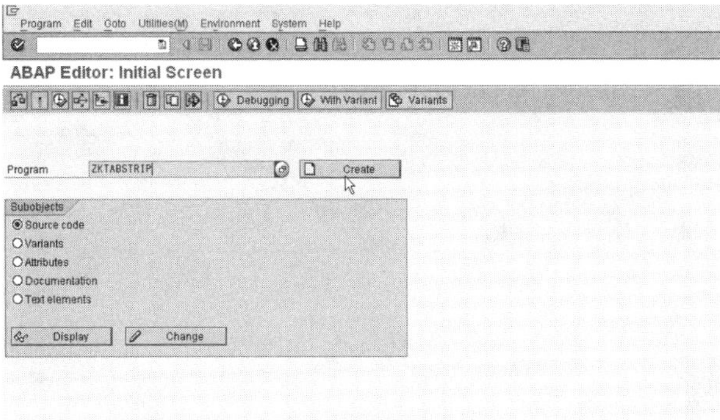

FIGURE 10.14 **The ABAP editor initial screen**

The `ABAP Program Attributes ZKTABSTRIP Change` dialog box appears.

3. In the `ABAP Program Attributes ZKTABSTRIP Change` dialog box, enter a description for the program in the `Title` field. In this case, the title is assigned as Demo Of Tabstrip. Then, select `Module Pool` as the type of program, as shown in Figure 10.15:

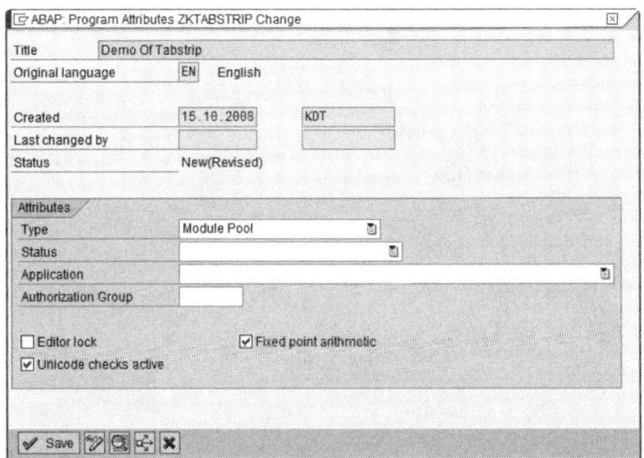

FIGURE 10.15 **The ABAP program attributes dialog box**

4. Finally, click the `Save` (Save) button, as shown in Figure 10.15, and save the tabstrip in the package named ZKOG_PCKG. The screen where the program is actually written after designing the tabstrip control is displayed, as shown in Figure 10.16:

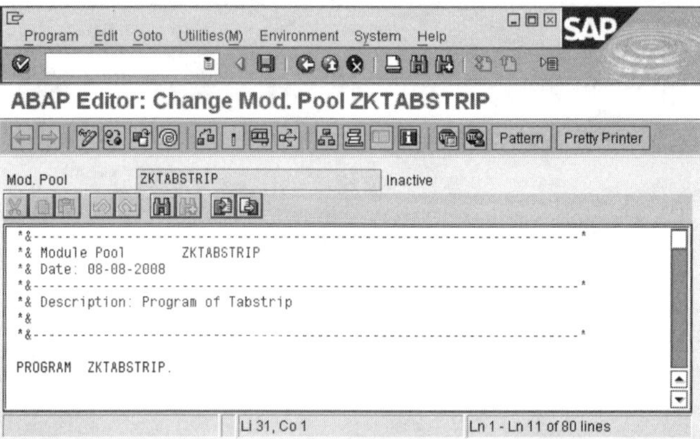

FIGURE 10.16 **The screen showing the written program**

5. Navigate to the initial screen of Screen Painter by entering the `/nSE51` transaction code in the `Command` field. Enter the name ZKTABSTRIP in the `Program` field, and the number 0001 in the `Screen number` field of Screen Painter. Click the `Create` button. The `Screen Painter: Change Screen for ZKTABSTRIP` screen appears, as shown in Figure 10.17:

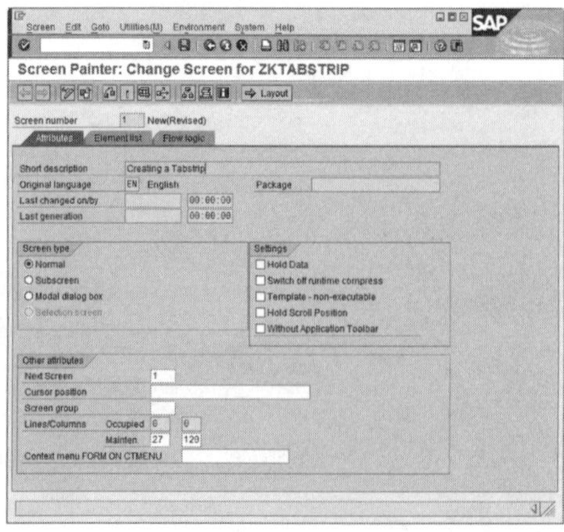

FIGURE 10.17 **Fields related to the attributes tab**

In the `Screen Painter: Change Screen for ZKTABTSRIP` screen, enter a short description of the tabstrip being created and ensure that the screen type is selected as normal.

6. Click the `Save` (💾) icon on the standard toolbar to save the settings. Click the `Check` () icon to check for any errors and, finally, activate the settings by clicking the `Activate` () icon.

> **Note:** For each click on the icons mentioned, you see a corresponding message in the status bar of the screen.

7. Click the `Layout` button to design the tabstrip control for the program. You see a screen on which you design the tabstrip with the help of various screen elements. To design the tabstrip control, select the `Tabstrip Control` screen element from the element palette, as shown in Figure 10.18:

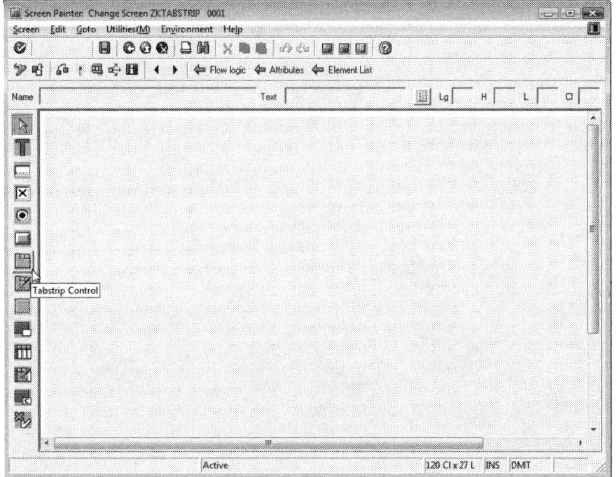

***FIGURE 10.18* The tabstrip control screen element**

8. Select and drag the tabstrip control screen element and drop it on the work area. Expand the tabstrip control element with the help of an arrow that appears on the screen as you position the cursor on any corner. Figure 10.19 shows the tabstrip in the work area:

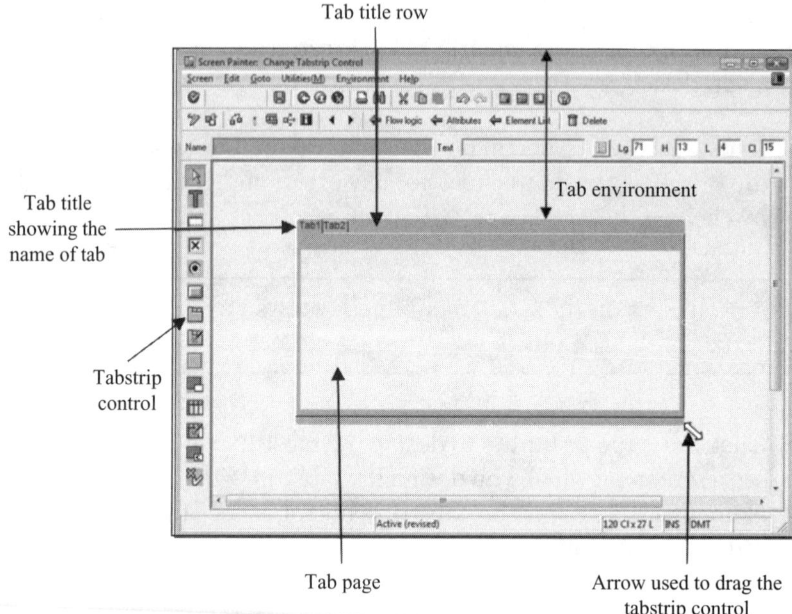

FIGURE 10.19 **The change tabstrip control screen**

9. Double-click the `Quad arrow` (), as shown in Figure 10.20:

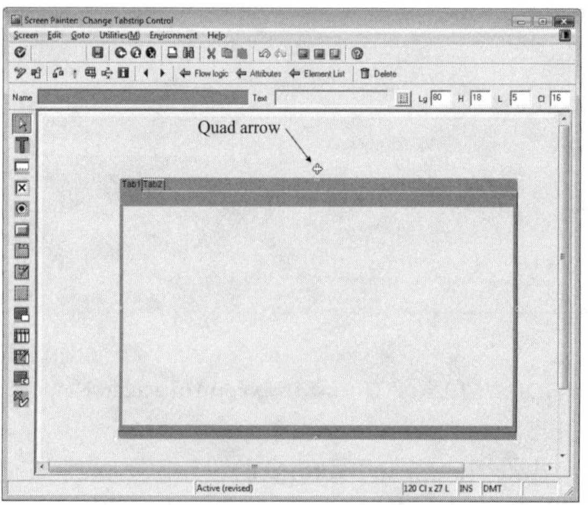

FIGURE 10.20 **Double-clicking the symbol**

The `Screen Painter: Attributes` dialog box appears.

10. Enter the name of the tabstrip in the `Name` field and set the number of tabs you want to present on the tabstrip control. In this case, the name of the tabstrip control is KTABSTRIP and the number of tabs is two in the `Tab Title` field. Figure 10.21 shows the attributes screen related to the tabstrip:

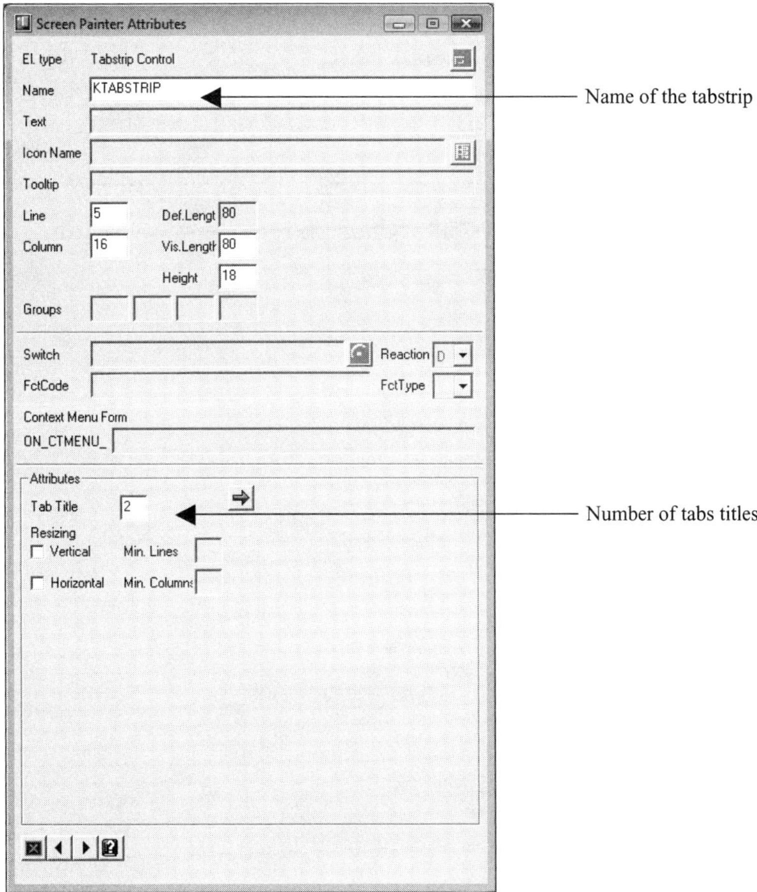

FIGURE 10.21 **Defining the attributes of the tabstrip control**

11. Double-click `Tab1` (a button) and assign the attributes to Tab1; enter the name of the Tab1 in the `Name` field, the text to be displayed on Tab1 in the `Text` field, the function code related to Tab1 in the `FctCode` field, and

the name of the reference field (that is, the name of the subscreen) in the `Ref. Field` field.

> **Note:** You define a function code in the `FctCode` field. Function codes are defined for screen elements, such as buttons, tab titles in the tabstrip controls, and input/output fields. Whenever a user selects a button or tab title, the function code related to the selected screen element is placed in the `OK-Code` screen field. A screen field is a variable in the working memory of a screen. Screen fields are linked with the input and output fields of a screen using the `OK-Code` field. In addition, the `FctCode` field is related with the reference field, which is used to signify the name of the subscreen corresponding to the selected tab title, since the reference field creates a link to another screen element.

Figure 10.22 shows the attributes dialog box of the `Tab1` button:

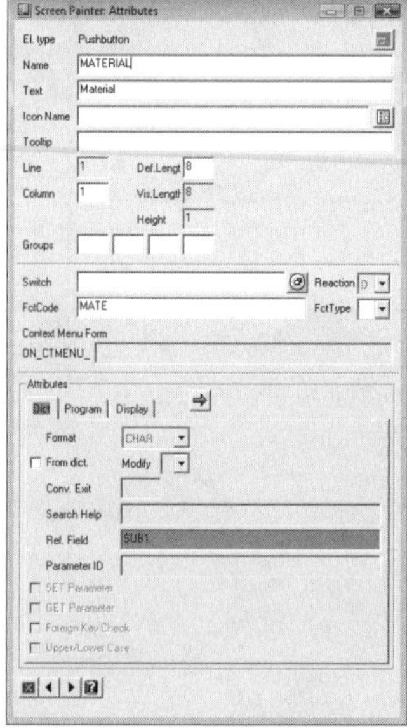

FIGURE 10.22 **Attributes of Tab1**

In this case, the name of Tab1 is specified as Material, text as Material, the function code as MATE, and the reference field as SUB1 (see Figure 10.22). Similarly, for the second tab, the name of the Tab2 is specified as VENDOR, the text as Vendor, the function code as VEND, and the reference field as SUB2 (the name of the subscreen related to this tab). Figure 10.23 shows the tabstrip control with the specified names:

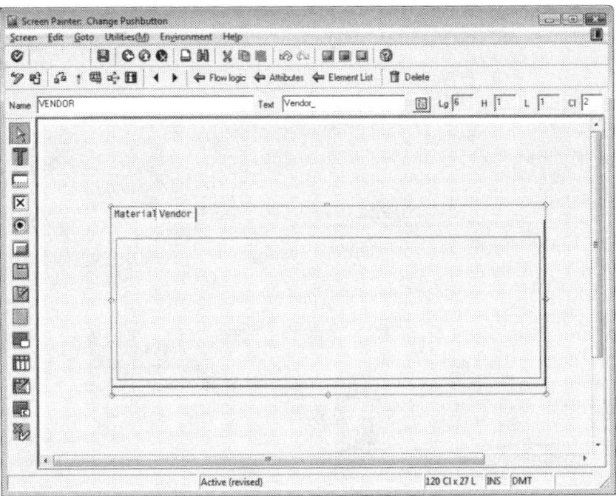

FIGURE 10.23 **The tabstrip control with specified names**

12. Click the `Material` tab, and assign a subscreen area to the `Material` tab by selecting the `Subscreen Area` screen element from the element palette and dropping it under the `Material` tab on the work area. Expand the `Subscreen Area` screen element to the entire length of work area under the `Material` tab by selecting the arrow shown at the bottom right corner of the subscreen. Figure 10.24 shows the subscreen on the tabstrip control:

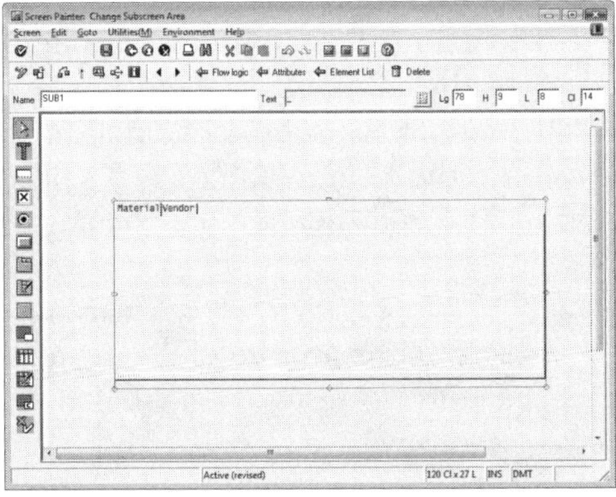

FIGURE 10.24 **The subscreen of the material tab on the tabstrip control**

13. Double-click inside the subscreen area. The `Screen Painter: Attributes` dialog box appears, as shown in Figure 10.25:

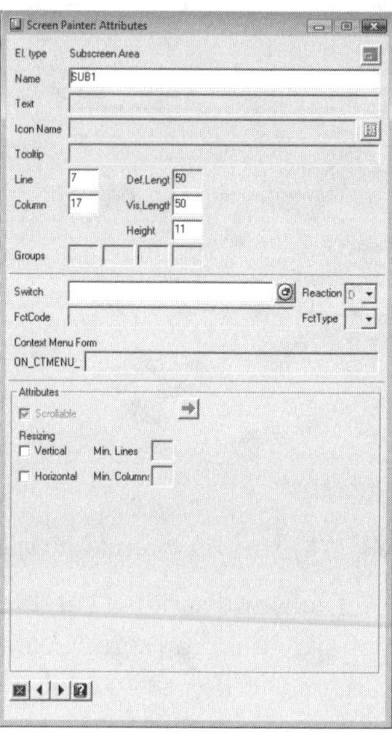

FIGURE 10.25 **The attribute dialog box related to the subscreen**

In Figure 10.25, notice that the name of the subscreen area is already populated in the `Name` field. The name of the subscreen is populated because you have already declared it in the `Ref.Field` field (see Figure 10.22). Similarly, assign the `Name` attribute to the subscreen area for the `Vendor` tab. Repeat the same procedure for the `Vendor` tab by first selecting the subscreen area from the element palette and then double-clicking the area inside the subscreen area.

Note: A text box has been selected from the screen palette to describe the designed tabstrip control. It is not mandatory to use a text field screen element when creating a tabstrip program. However, we have used it in this case to provide an interactive interface to the designed tabstrip control.

Now, perform the following steps to use a text field screen element in the current program:

1. Select the `Text Field` screen element from the element palette and drop it on the window (see Figure 10.24).
2. Double-click the screen element to define the attributes of the text box. The `Screen Painter: Attributes` dialog box appears, as shown in Figure 10.26:

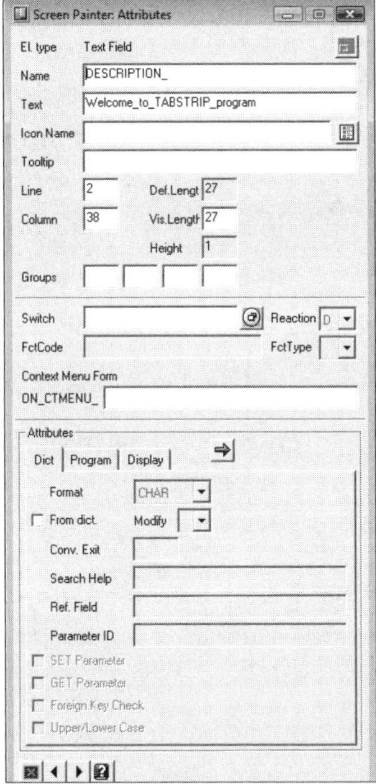

FIGURE 10.26 **Description of attributes in the screen painter: attributes dialog box**

3. Enter the values in the `Name` and `Text` fields of the `Screen Painter: Attributes` dialog box. For instance, we have entered "DESCRIPTION_" and "Welcome_to_TABSTRIP_program", respectively (see Figure 10.26).

Click `Close` (■) icon, so that the screen of Screen Painter displays the text field, as shown in Figure 10.27:

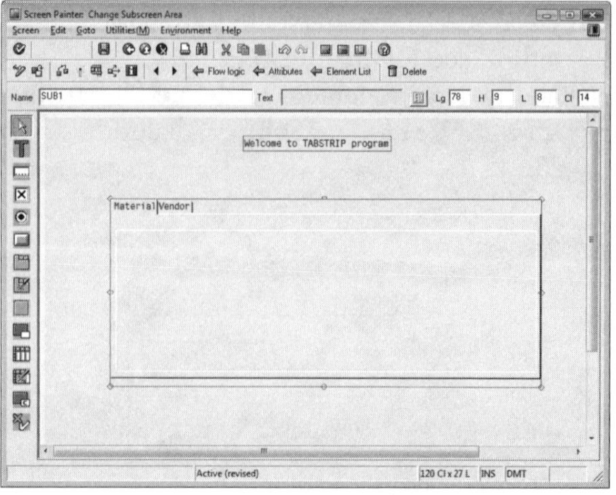

FIGURE 10.27 **The text field on the screen**

Let's now assign two buttons, Display and Exit.

4. Select a `Pushbutton` screen element from the element palette and drop it on the screen, as shown in Figure 10.28:

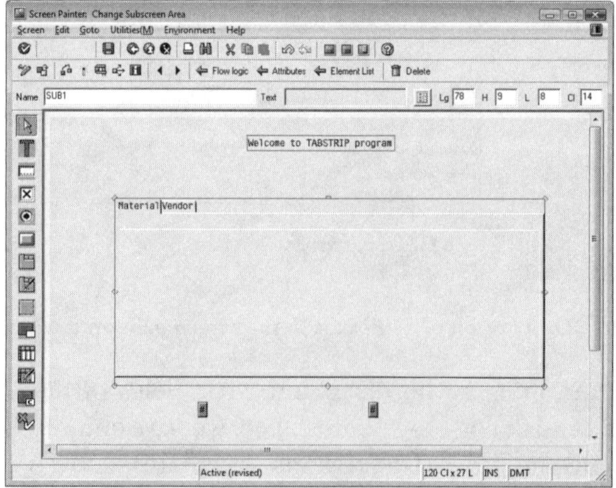

FIGURE 10.28 **Pushbuttons on the screen**

5. Double-click the respective buttons to define the attributes related to the buttons, such as name, text, and function code. The `Screen Painter: Attributes` dialog box opens in respect to a button, as shown in Figure 10.29:

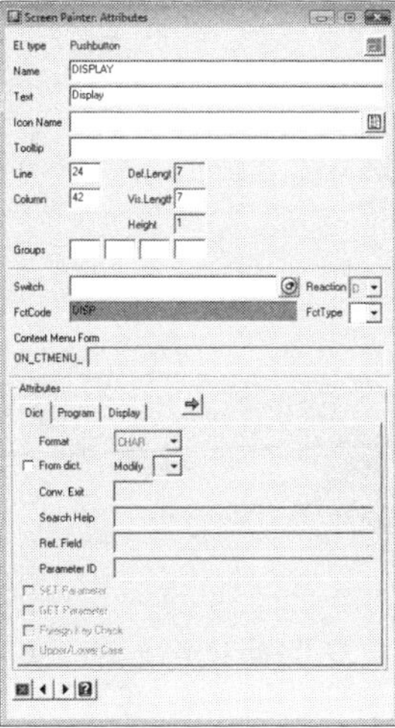

FIGURE 10.29 **Attributes of the display button**

Similarly, we add another button called `Exit`. For this button, EXIT is assigned as the value of the `Name` field, the `Text` field, and the `FctCode` field. Figure 10.30 shows two buttons, `Display` and `Exit`, on the `Screen Painter` screen:

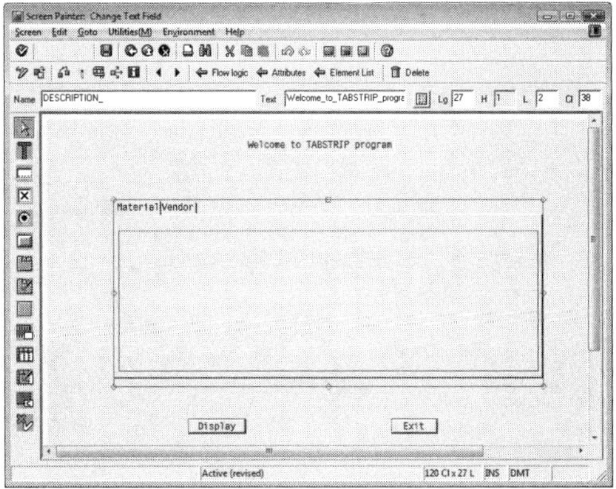

FIGURE 10.30 **Buttons on the screen painter screen**

6. Finally, save, check, and activate the layout designed for the tabstrip control.
7. Now, navigate to the initial screen of Screen Painter by clicking the `Back` () icon on the standard toolbar. We now design the subscreen area. Enter the screen number as 0002 and click the `Create` button, as shown in Figure 10.31:

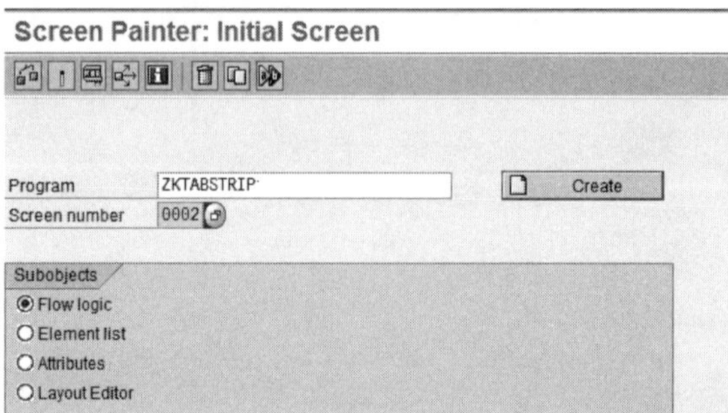

FIGURE 10.31 **Designing the subscreen area**

8. Now, provide a description for the subscreen, such as Designing the Subscreen Area, and select the `Subscreen` radio button under the `Screen type` group box, as shown in Figure 10.32:

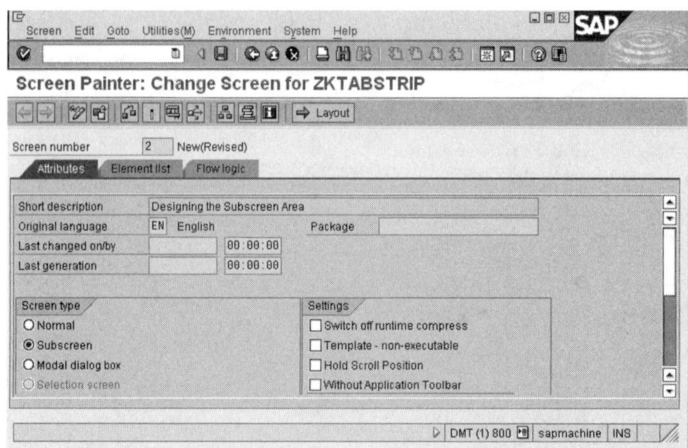

FIGURE 10.32 **Screen type tab**

9. Click the `Layout` button to design the screen related to the subscreen area. Click the `Dictionary/Program Fields Windows` (icon) icon. The `Screen Painter: Dict,/Program Fields` screen appears. Write the name of the table in the `Table/Field Name` field and click the `Get from the Dictionary` button. Now, select the fields that you want to display on the screen and, finally, click the `Ok` (icon) icon, as shown in Figure 10.33:

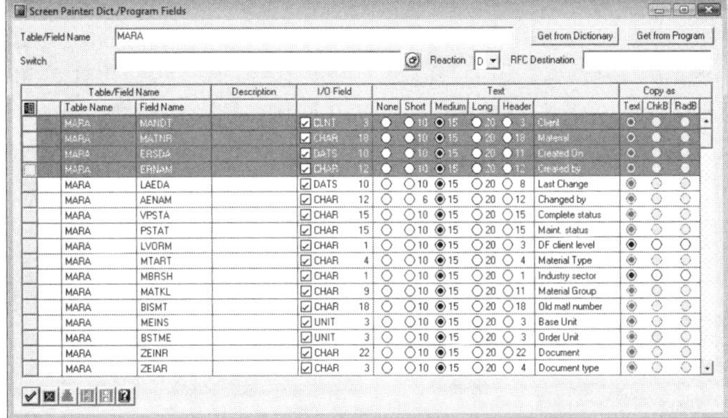

FIGURE 10.33 **Selecting fields from the MARA table**

10. Place the selected fields on the screen and click the `Save` (icon), `Check` (icon), and `Activate` (icon) icons, as shown in Figure 10.34:

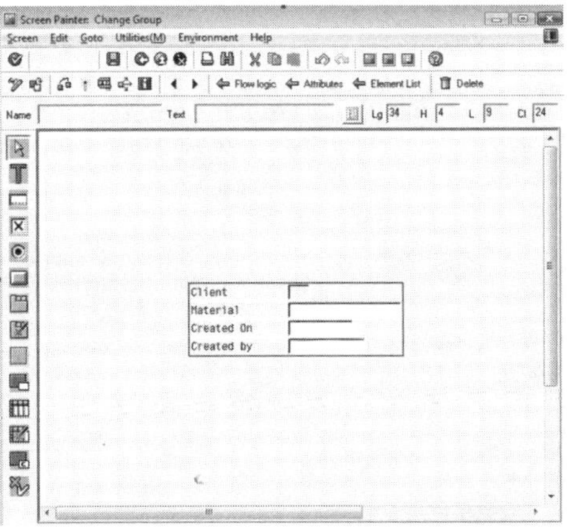

FIGURE 10.34 **Designing the subscreen 0002**

11. Navigate to the initial screen of Screen Painter by using the `Back` (icon) icon to design subscreen number 0003.
12. On the initial screen, enter the screen number as 0003 in the screen number field and click the `Create` button. The `Screen Painter: Change Screen for ZKTABSTRIP` screen appears.
13. In the `Screen Painter: Change Screen for ZKTABSTRIP` screen, enter a short description for your screen and select the `Subscreen` radio button under the `Screen type` group box.
14. Click the `Layout` button on the screen to design the screen numbered as 0003. On the next screen, click the `Dictionary/Program Fields Windows` (icon) icon. Write the name of the table in the `Table/Field Name` field of the `Screen Painter: Dict,/Program Fields` screen. In this case, we enter the name of the table as LFA1. Select the fields that you want to display on the screen and then click the `Get from Dictionary` button. Figure 10.35 displays the selected fields from the table LFA1:

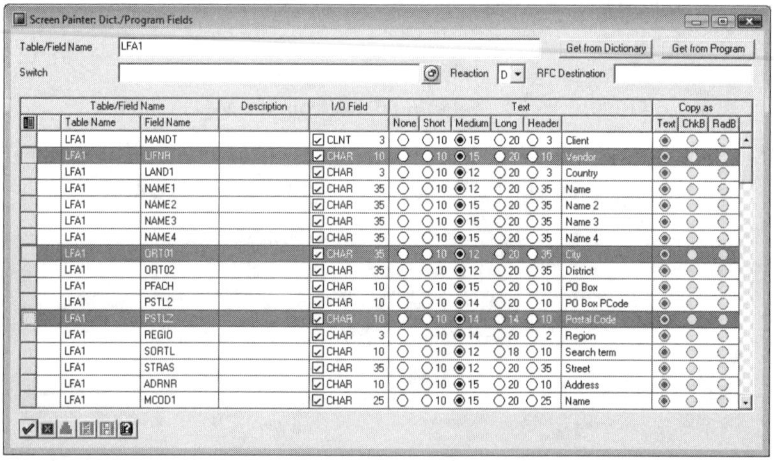

Screen Painter: Dict./Program Fields

Table/Field Name: LFA1 | Get from Dictionary | Get from Program

Switch | Reaction: D | RFC Destination

Table Name	Field Name	Description	I/O Field		None	Short	Medium	Long	Header	Text	Copy as Text	ChkB	RadB
LFA1	MANDT		CLNT	3		10	15	20	3	Client			
LFA1	LIFNR		CHAR	10		10	15	20	10	Vendor			
LFA1	LAND1		CHAR	3		10	12	20	3	Country			
LFA1	NAME1		CHAR	35		10	12	20	35	Name			
LFA1	NAME2		CHAR	35		10	15	20	35	Name 2			
LFA1	NAME3		CHAR	35		10	15	20	35	Name 3			
LFA1	NAME4		CHAR	35		10	15	20	35	Name 4			
LFA1	ORT01		CHAR	35		10	12	20	35	City			
LFA1	ORT02		CHAR	35		10	12	20	35	District			
LFA1	PFACH		CHAR	10		10	15	20	10	PO Box			
LFA1	PSTL2		CHAR	10		10	14	20	10	PO Box PCode			
LFA1	PSTLZ		CHAR	10		10	14	14	10	Postal Code			
LFA1	REGIO		CHAR	3		10	14	20	2	Region			
LFA1	SORTL		CHAR	10		10	12	18	10	Search term			
LFA1	STRAS		CHAR	35		10	12	20	35	Street			
LFA1	ADRNR		CHAR	10		10	15	20	10	Address			
LFA1	MCOD1		CHAR	25		10	15	20	25	Name			

FIGURE 10.35 **Selected fields of table LFA1**

15. Finally, click the `Continue` (icon) icon (see Figure 10.35).
16. Place the selected fields on the screen, as shown in Figure 10.36:

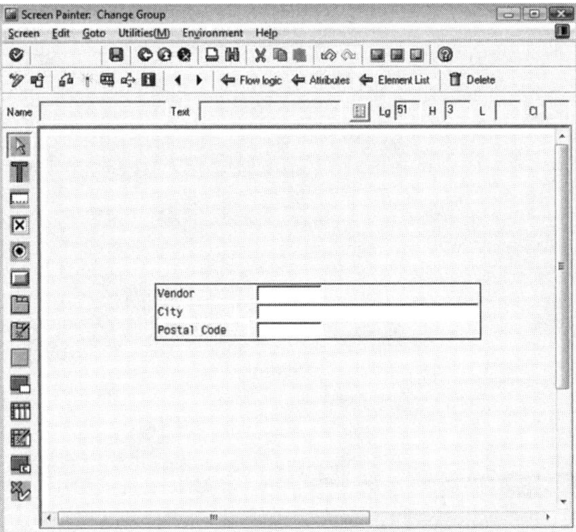

FIGURE 10.36 **Selected fields from the LFA1 table**

17. Click the `Save`, `Check`, and `Activate` icons. When the screen is activated, navigate to the `Screen Painter: Change Screen for ZKTABSTRIP` screen by clicking the `Back` (◉) icon. Figure 10.37 shows the screen containing the flow logic for the designed tabstrip:

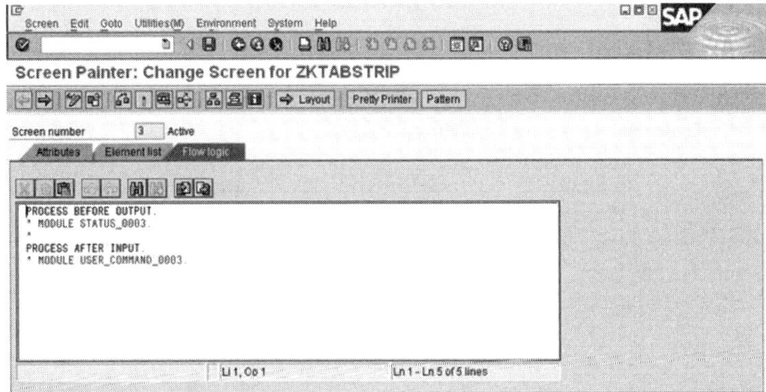

FIGURE 10.37 **The screen after activating the layout of subscreen 0003**

18. Click the `Back` icon to navigate to the initial screen of Screen Painter. Write the screen number as 0001 in the initial screen of Screen Painter. Click the `Change` button. Delete `MODULE STATUS_0001` and `MODULE USER_COMMAND_0001`, and write the statements as shown in Figure 10.38, so that the designed subscreens 0002 and 0003 can be called in a program:

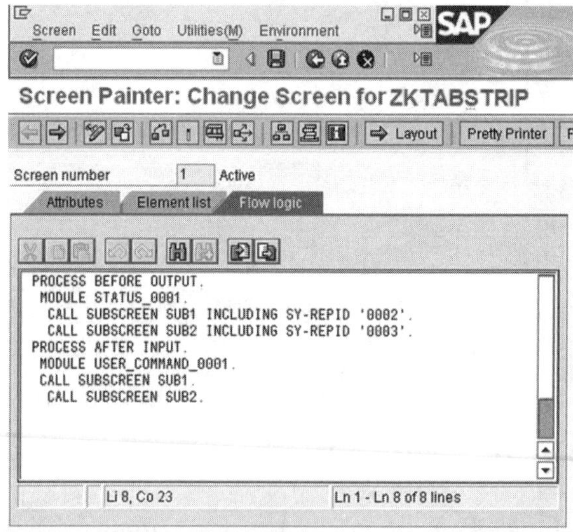

FIGURE 10.38 **Flow logic for the subscreens 0002 and 0003**

19. Double-click `MODULE USER_COMMAND_0001`. A dialog box appears showing that the PAI module does not exist. Click the `Yes` button to create the object, as shown in Figure 10.39:

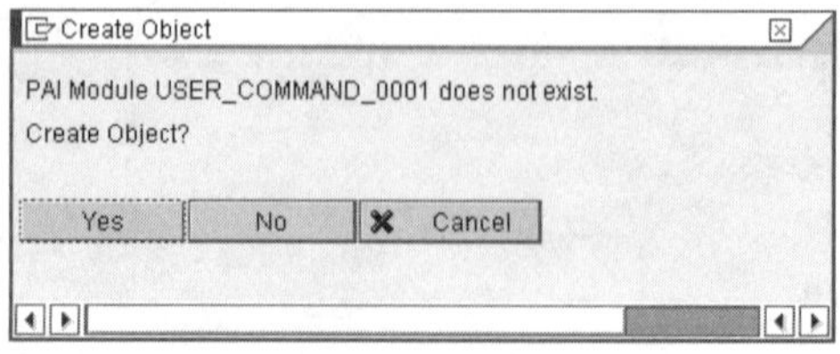

FIGURE 10.39 **Creating the object**

20. Select the name of the program as ZKTABSTRIP to create the PAI module and click the `Continue` (☑) icon, as shown in Figure 10.40:

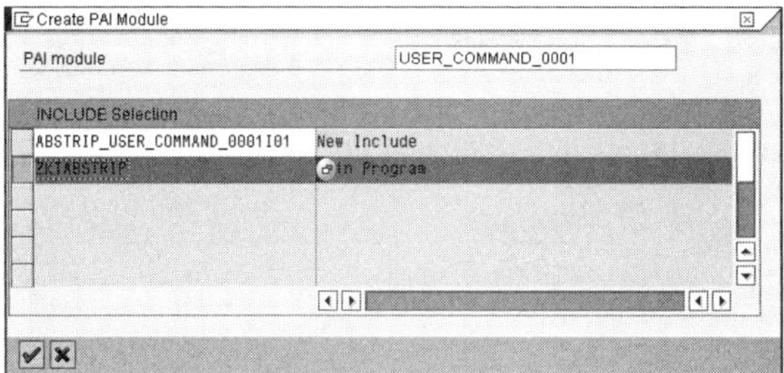

FIGURE 10.40 **Creating the PAI module**

The `ABAP Editor` screen appears, where you write the statements for the tabstrip program, as shown in Figure 10.41.

21. Click the `Save` (💾) icon, as shown in Figure 10.41:

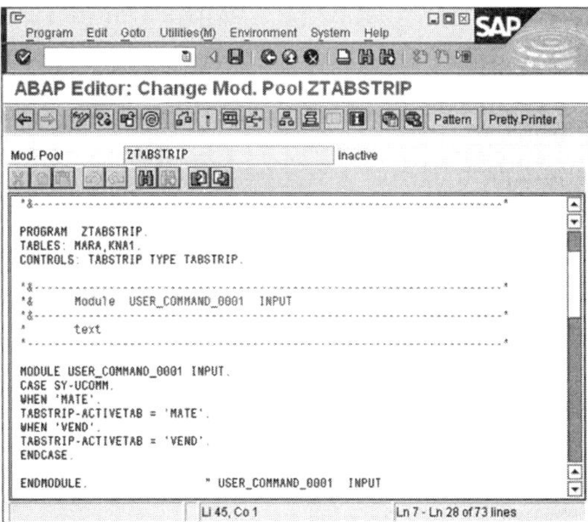

FIGURE 10.41 **The program related to subscreen 0001**

22. Click the `Back` (⊙) icon to navigate to the initial screen of Screen Painter (see Figure 10.31). On this screen, write the screen number as 0002 and click the `Change` pushbutton to observe the flow logic related to the subscreen number 0002. Uncomment `MODULE USER_COMMAND_0002` in the PAI event. Now, double-click this module to open the `ABAP Editor` screen, where you enter the sequence of statements for this module, as shown in Figure 10.42:

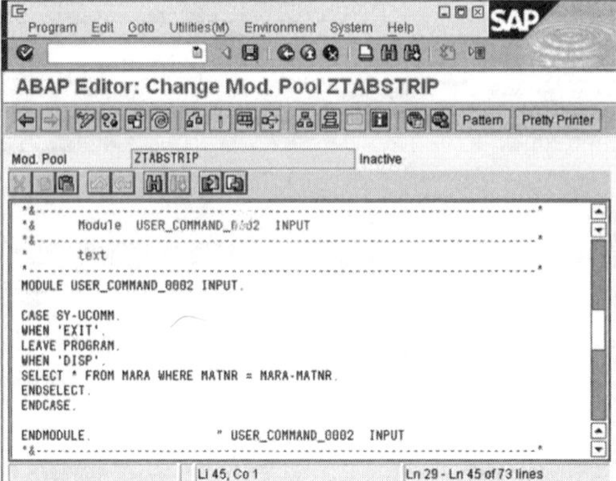

FIGURE 10.42 **The program related to subscreen 0002**

23. Click the `Back` icon to navigate to the initial screen of Screen Painter (see Figure 10.31). Now, on this screen, enter the screen number as 0003 and click the `Change` button to see the flow logic related to screen number 0003. Uncomment `MODULE USER_COMMAND_0003` in the PAI event. Double-click this module to display the `ABAP Editor` screen, where you enter the sequence of statements for this module, as shown in Figure 10.43:

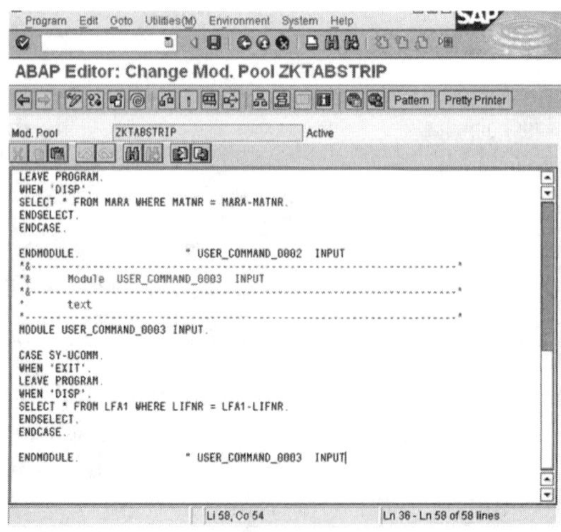

FIGURE 10.43 **The program related to subscreen 0003**

24. Finally, click the `Save`, `Check`, and `Activate` icons.

Because this is a module pool type program, this program is not executed directly; rather, a separate transaction code must be created for this program.

25. Enter the `SE93` transaction code in the `Command` field of the `SAP Easy Access` screen, or directly enter `/nSE93` in the `Command` field of any opened screen. The `Maintain Transaction` screen opens, where you write the transaction code. This transaction code is used to run the ZKTABSTRIP program. In this case, let's enter "ZTRANSACTION" as the transaction code. Click the `Create` button, as shown in Figure 10.44:

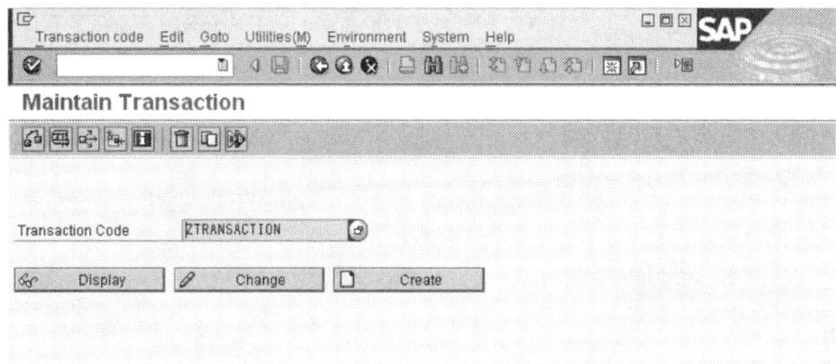

FIGURE 10.44 **The maintenance transaction screen**

The `Create Transaction` dialog box appears, as shown in Figure 10.45.

26. In the `Create Transaction` dialog box, enter a short description, such as "TRANSACTION CODE FOR ZKTABSTRIP", in the `Short` text field, and select the `Program and screen (dialog transaction)` radio button. Finally, click the `Continue` (☑) icon, as shown in Figure 10.45:

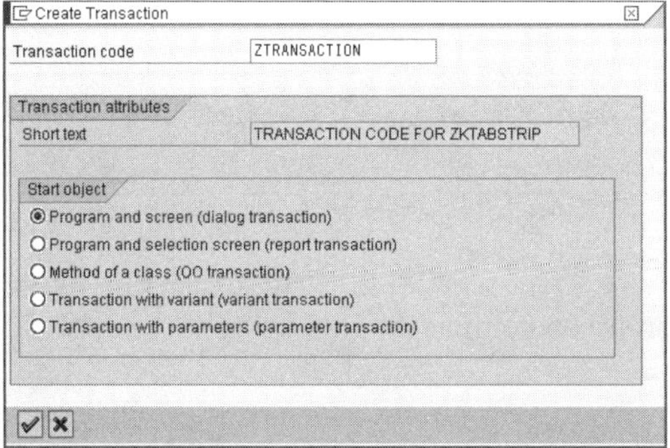

FIGURE 10.45 **The create transaction screen**

The `Create Dialog Transaction` screen appears.

27. In the `Create Dialog Transaction` screen, enter the name of the program for which the transaction code has been designed. Give the screen number as 0001 and check the `SAP GUI for Windows` check box, as shown in Figure 10.46:

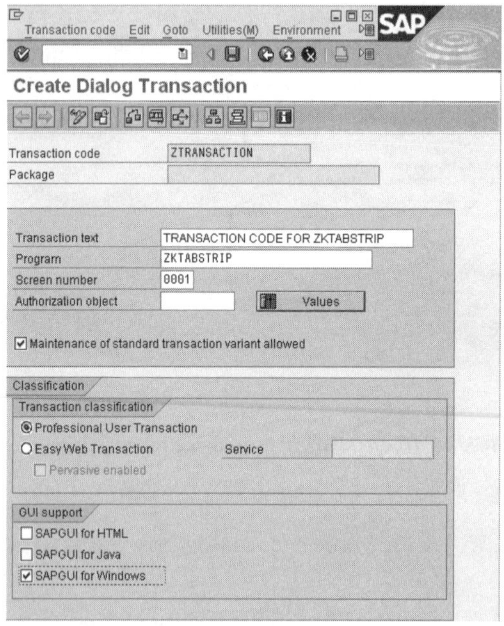

FIGURE 10.46 **Creating the transaction code for the ZKTABSTRIP tabstrip control**

> **Note:** We select the SAP GUI for Windows check box because we are using the SAPGUI software application on Microsoft Windows, not with Java or HTML.

28. Click the `Save`, `Check`, and `Test` icons to test the transaction (see Figure 10.46). An SAP screen containing the highlighted `Material` tab appears, as shown in Figure 10.47:

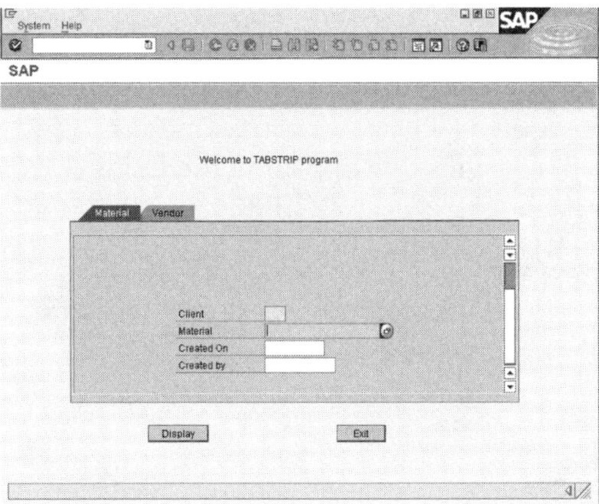

FIGURE 10.47 **The output screen**

29. Enter the name of the material in the `Material` field. In case you do not know the name of the material, you can search for possible values with the help of the `Search Help` (icon) icon. Click this icon to open the Material Number screen. Click the `Continue` (icon) icon and select any value from the list, as shown in Figure 10.48:

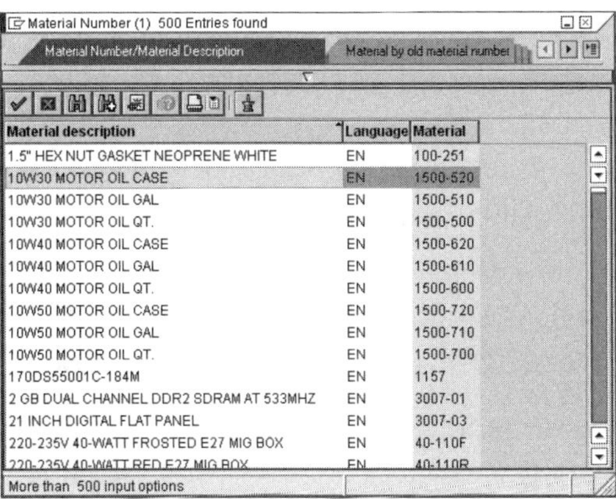

FIGURE 10.48 **The material number screen**

In this case, we have selected 1500-520.

30. Click the `Display` button. The output—consisting of the values in the remaining fields, such as `Client`, `Created on`, and `Created by`—is displayed. The values that appear in the fields correspond to the value that you enter in the `Material` field. Figure 10.49 shows the output screen of the TABSTRIP control:

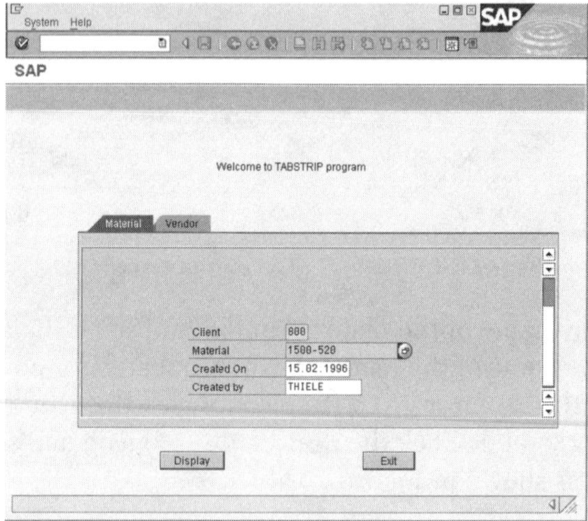

FIGURE 10.49 **Output screen of the TABSTRIP control**

Repeat the same steps for the Vendor tab. You can navigate to the `SAP Easy Access` screen by clicking the `Exit` pushbutton.

Now, let's learn how to create a table control.

Creating a Table Control by Using Graphical Layout Editor

A table control is a complex graphical screen element used to display data in a tabular form. The data can be entered, displayed, and modified easily by using table controls. There are different functions that the table control provides during its definition and runtime. Fixed columns and column headers are examples of the functions provided by the table control during its definition. During runtime, the table control provides other functions, such as vertical scrolling, horizontal scrolling, selecting any row or column, movable columns, and column width, which can be modified. A table control is processed by using a loop. Figure 10.50 shows the table control:

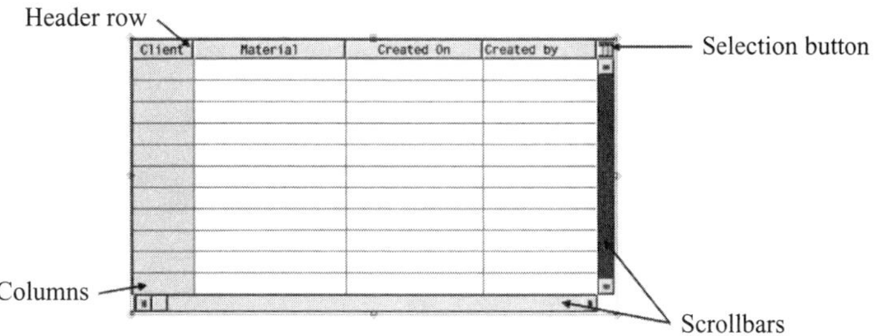

FIGURE 10.50 **The table control**

The table control shows two scrollbars, vertical and horizontal. A table title shows the title of the table program, settings button, a selection column (which is used to make selections), and the header line, which consists of various columns showing the description of different fields. The columns shown in Figure 10.50 are obtained from the MARA table.

Creating a Table Control Program

We now create a table control program containing information related to material, such as material number, created by, created on, and client number. This information of the material can be retrieved from the MARA database table. Perform the following steps to create a table control program:

1. Create a module pool type program in ABAP Editor by using the `SE38` transaction, and save, check, and activate the program. In this case, the name of the module type program is ZKTABLECONTROL.
2. Open the initial screen of Screen Painter by using the `SE51` transaction code. Enter the ZKTABLECONTROL program name in the `Program` field, and assign a screen number (i.e, 0001) to the `Screen number` field. Click the `Create` button, as shown in Figure 10.51:

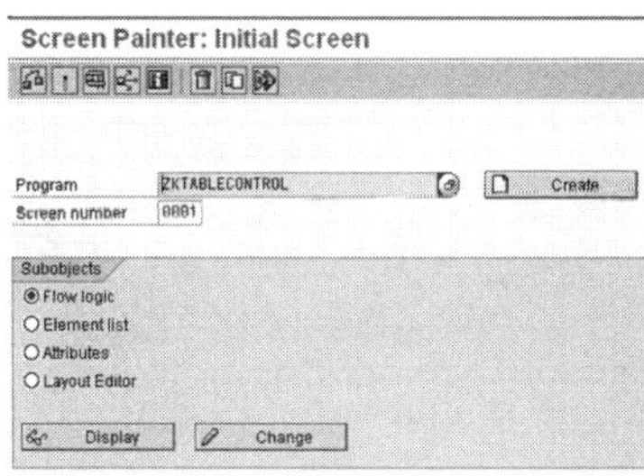

FIGURE 10.51 **The create button on the initial screen of screen painter**

The `Screen Painter: Change Screen for ZKTABLECONTROL` screen appears.

3. Enter a short description and click the `Layout` button to design the table control. In this case, the short description is Table Control, as shown in Figure 10.52:

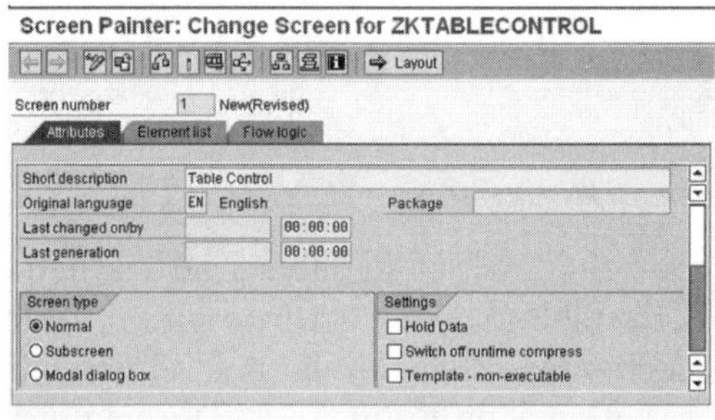

FIGURE 10.52 **The change screen for the ZKTABLECONTROL program**

The `Graphical layout editor` screen appears.

4. Select the `Table control` element from the element palette and place it on the work area. Now, expand the table control element to the desired size with the help of resizing arrows that appears at every corner of the table control element. Figure 10.53 shows the `Table control` screen element on the `Graphical layout editor` screen:

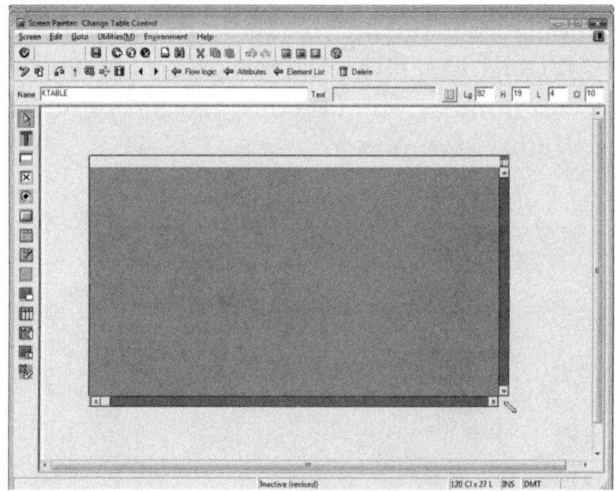

FIGURE 10.53 **The table control screen element**

5. Now, double-click the `Quad` arrow (). Figure 10.54 shows the `Screen Painter: Attributes` dialog box, where you specify different attributes for the table control screen element:

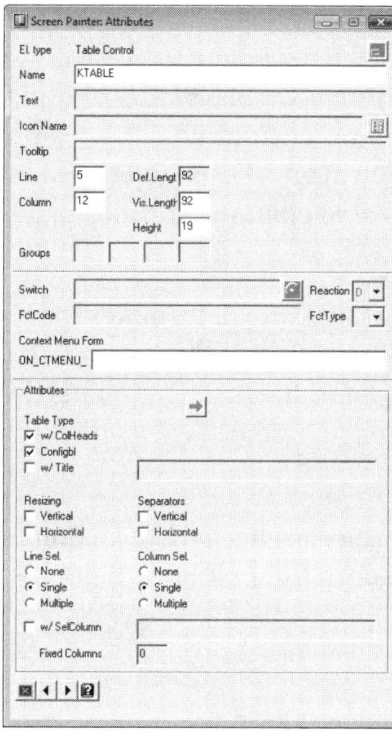

FIGURE 10.54 **The screen painter: attributes dialog box for table control**

Table 10.10 shows the description of different check boxes under the `Table Type` attribute:

Table Type	Description
With column headers	Controls the naming of the columns in a table control
Configurability	Specifies how the user can save the changes made to the column sequence and width
With title line	Determines whether or not the table control can have a title as a top line

TABLE 10.10 Table type attribute

The Resizing attribute in the Screen Painter: Attributes dialog box for a table control consists of two check boxes, Vertical and Horizontal. These check boxes are used to resize a window of a table control manually.

In the Separators attribute, the following two options are available:

- **Vertical separator**—Displays vertical separator lines between all the table columns at runtime
- **Horizontal separator**—Displays horizontal separator lines between all the table columns at runtime

The Line Selection attribute determines the numbers of lines in a table that can be selected simultaneously. If the Single radio button is set, only one line can be selected at a time. If the Multiple radio button is selected, any number of lines can be selected at a time.

Apart from this, you can check the selection column to add another column containing buttons before the first table field.

6. In the Screen Painter: Attributes dialog box, click the Close ( ) icon. Now, navigate to the Screen Painter: Change Table Control screen, as shown in Figure 10.53.
7. In the Screen Painter: Change Table Control screen, click the Dictionary/Program Fields ( ) icon and write the name of the table in the Table/Field Name field (see Figure 10.33). In this case, we have entered the name of the table as MARA because we want to retrieve data related to materials, such as material number, material type, and material description.
8. Click the Get from Dictionary button and select the MANDT, MATNR, ERSDA, and ERNAM fields (see Figure 10.33).
9. Click the Continue icon. A set of fields appears. Place this set in the work area of the table control, as shown in Figure 10.55:

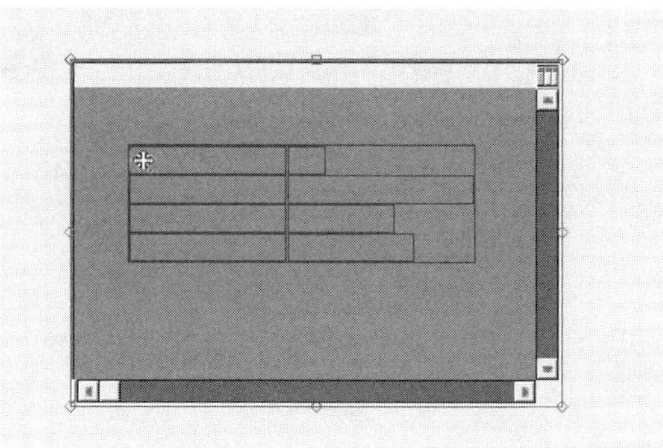

FIGURE 10.55 **Placing the set of fields from the MARA table**

10. Finally, click the `Save`, `Check`, and `Activate` icons to activate the layout of the table control. Now, click the `Back` icon to navigate to the `Flow logic` screen and write the statements used to call the table control. The change screen for ZKTABLECONTROL of Screen Painter appears, as shown in Figure 10.56:

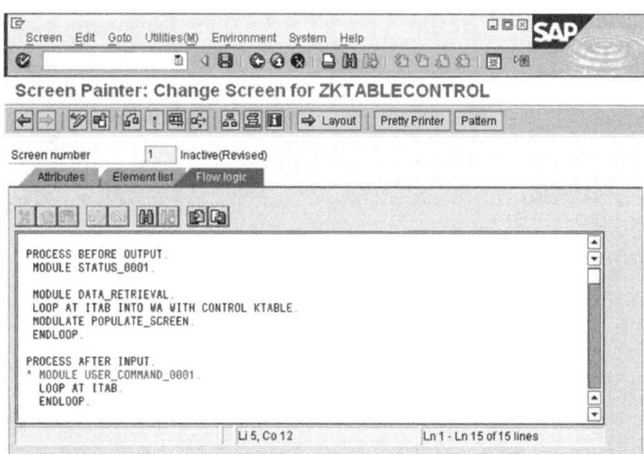

FIGURE 10.56 **Statements for the flow logic of the ZKTABLECONTROL table control**

11. Double-click the `MODULE DATA_RETRIEVAL` statement. The `Create Object` dialog box appears. Click the `Yes` button, as shown in Figure 10.57:

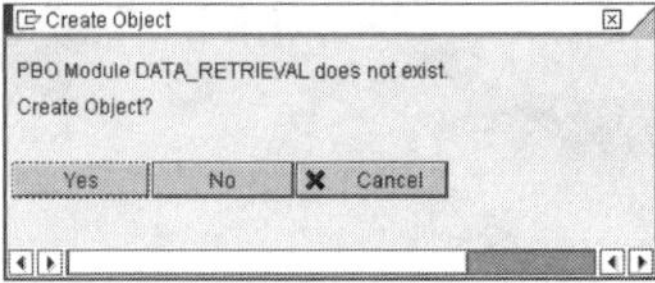

FIGURE 10.57 **The create object dialog box**

12. The `Create PBO Module` dialog box appears. Click the name of the program and then click the `Continue` (✔) icon, as shown in Figure 10.58:

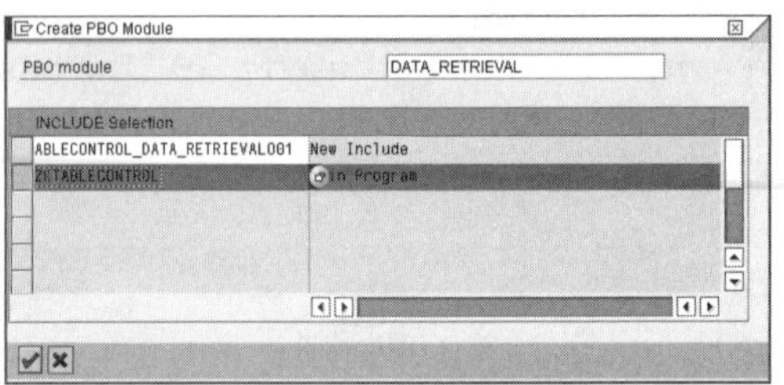

FIGURE 10.58 **Creating the PBO module dialog box**

13. The `Exit Screen Painter` dialog box appears. Click the `Yes` button, as shown in Figure 10.59:

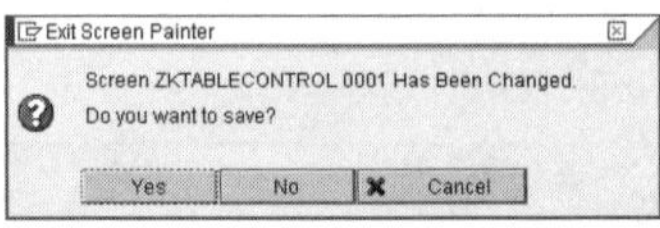

FIGURE 10.59 **Dialog asking to save the screen number 0001**

14. Now, in the `ABAP Editor` screen, write the ABAP code, along with the `SELECT` query for the `MODULE DATA_RETRIEVAL OUTPUT` statement, as shown in Figure 10.60:

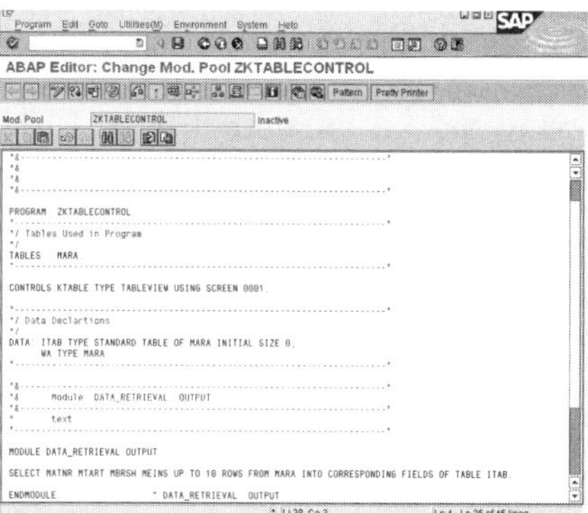

FIGURE 10.60 **Sequence of steps of ABAP code**

15. Save, check, and activate the program. Now, click the `Back` icon to navigate to the `Screen Painter: Change Screen for ZKTABLECONTROL` screen. Double-click the module written as `MODULATE POPULATE_SCREEN` (see Figure 10.56). The `Create Object` dialog box appears, as shown in Figure 10.61:

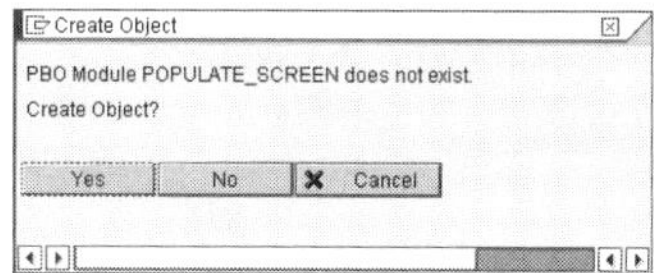

FIGURE 10.61 **Creating an object for the PBO module**

16. Click the `Yes` button. The `Create PBO Module` dialog box appears. Select the name of the program and click the `Continue` icon, as shown in Figure 10.62:

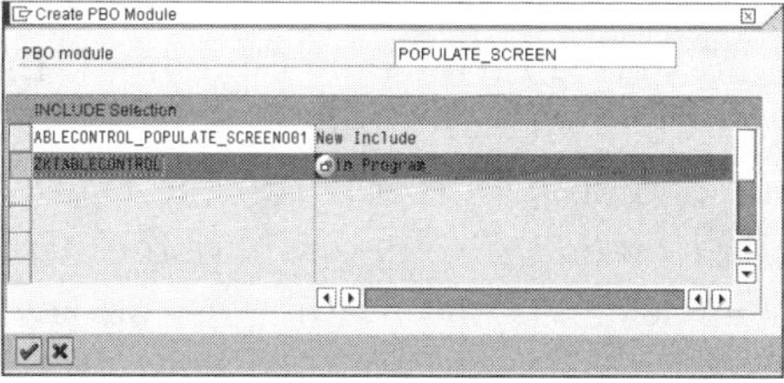

FIGURE 10.62 **Creating the PBO module**

The ABAP Editor screen appears again.

17. Add the following code at the end of the existing code in ABAP Editor:

```
MODULE POPULATE_SCREEN OUTPUT.
MOVE-CORRESPONDING WA TO MARA.
ENDMODULE.
```

Figure 10.63 shows the ABAP Editor screen after adding the previous code snippet:

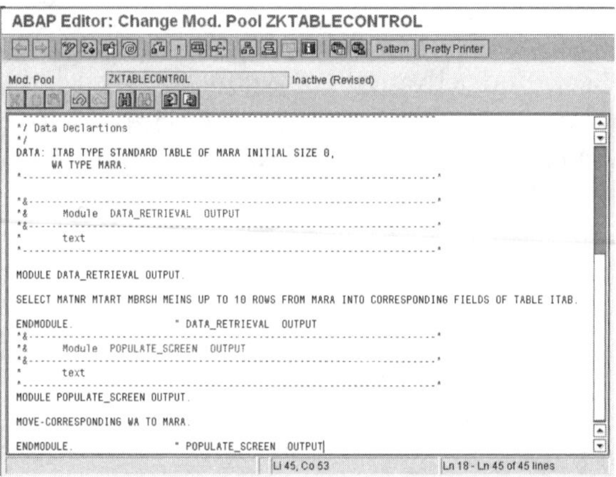

FIGURE 10.63 **The ABAP editor screen**

18. Finally, save, check, and activate the program.
19. Create a transaction code for the ZKTABLECONTROL program in the same way as for the tabstrip control program. In this case, ZKTABLE is the transaction code created for the ZKTABLECONTROL table control program (the module pool type). Test the transaction by either selecting the Test (icon) icon on the screen, where the attributes for the transaction code have been designed, or entering the transaction code in the Command field of the SAP Easy Access screen. Figure 10.64 shows the output screen of the table control:

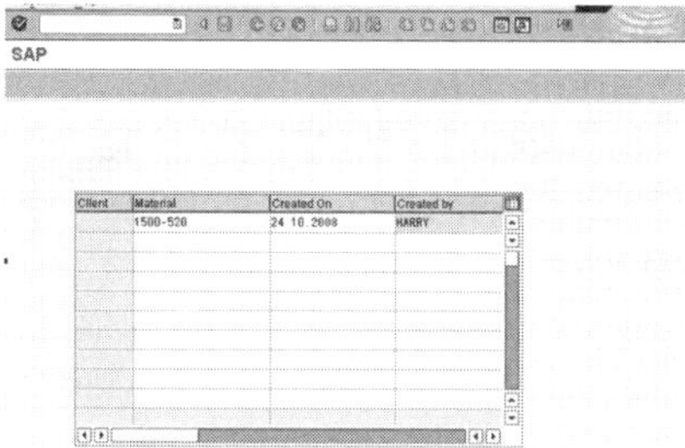

FIGURE 10.64 **The output screen of the table control**

Now, let's learn how to create user interfaces for our screen with the help of another tool of ABAP Workbench: Menu Painter.

MENU PAINTER

Menu Painter is an ABAP Workbench tool, which helps in creating the user interfaces for ABAP programs. As already known, ABAP programs consist of a variety of functions, which are classified further into subcategories. These functions in the ABAP programs are handled with Menu Painter. A user interface generally consists of menu bars, an application toolbar, a standard toolbar, and some function keys. The combination of all these elements is known as the GUI Status. However, the description of the user interface is displayed in the title bar.

The initial screen of Menu Painter is opened from the `SAP Easy Access` screen by selecting `SAP menu>Tools>ABAP Workbench>Development>User Interface>Menu Painter`, as shown in Figure 10.65:

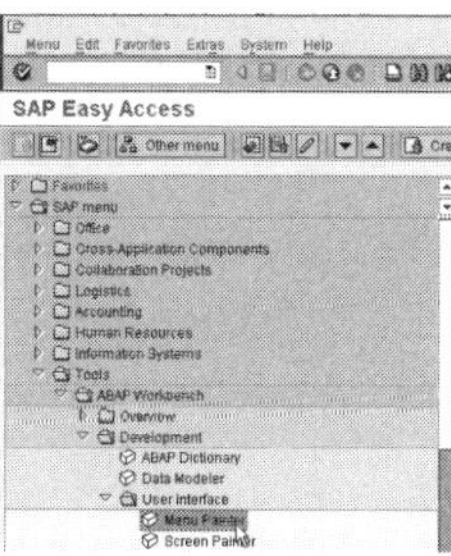

FIGURE 10.65 **The menu painter screen**

The initial screen can also be opened directly by entering the `SE41` transaction code in the `Command` field and then pressing the ENTER key. On the initial screen, notice a field known as `Program`, where you write the name of the program for which the user interface has to be created. This program is of the executable type and is created already in ABAP Editor.

Apart from the program field, various subobjects, displayed as radio buttons, are present on the initial screen. Table 10.11 describes these subobjects:

Subobject	Description
Status	Opens the Menu Painter work area
Interface objects	Shows all the user interface objects, such as the status object, menu bars, menu lists, function key settings, function lists, and title of the current program
Status list	Displays the list of the status objects, such as the menu bar, application toolbar, and function key settings
Menu bar	Shows the list of all the menu bars
Menu list	Displays the list of all the created menus on the program interface screen
F-Key settings	Displays the list of all the function key settings
Function list	Displays the list of all the function codes used for the function code on the program interface screen
Title list	Shows the title of the current program on the program interface screen

TABLE 10.11 Subobjects on the initial screen

Working with Menu Painter

Now, let's create a program that implements different user interfaces. Before creating the programs for the interfaces, we must create a program of the executable type in ABAP Editor. Perform the following steps to design the user interface for a program:

1. Open the initial screen of ABAP Editor by using the `SE38` transaction code.
2. In the initial screen of ABAP Editor, enter a name for the program, for example, ZMENU_PAINTERR, as shown in Figure 10.66:

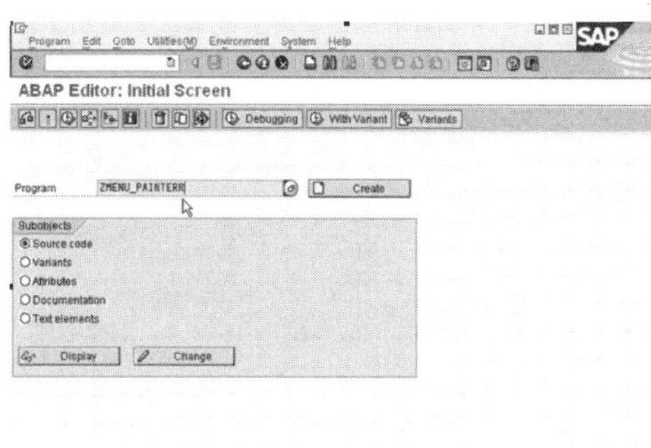

FIGURE 10.66 **The initial screen of the ABAP editor**

3. Click the `Create` button. The `ABAP: Program Attributes ZMENU_ PAINTERR Change` dialog box appears. Enter the title of the program, such as Program for Menu Painter, assign the type of the program as `Executable program`, and then click the `Save` button, as shown in Figure 10.67:

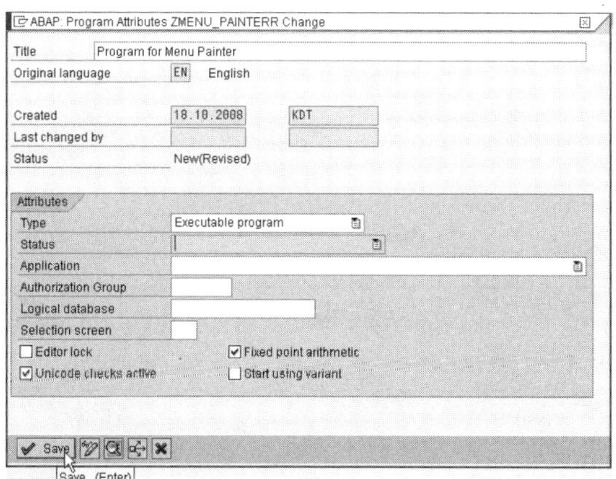

FIGURE 10.67 **The attributes dialog box**

The Create Object Directory Entry dialog box appears.

4. In the Create Object Directory Entry dialog box, enter the package name, ZKOG_PCKG, beside the Package field, and then click the Save (💾) icon. Finally, the screen of ABAP Editor appears containing the source code related to Menu Painter, as shown in Figure 10.68:

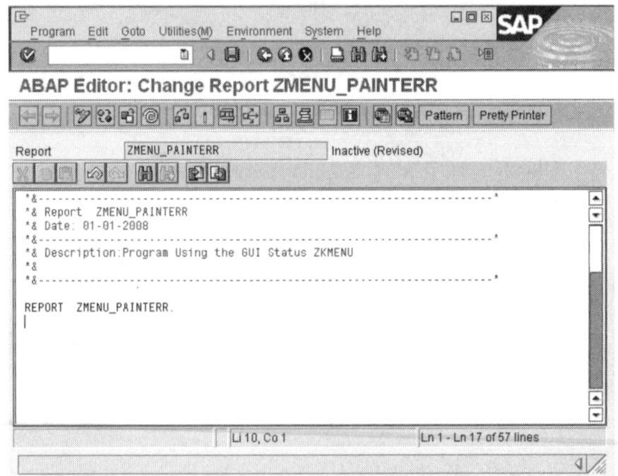

FIGURE 10.68 **The screen where the source code is written**

5. Open another session by clicking the New Session (▣) icon on the standard toolbar, as shown in Figure 10.69:

FIGURE 10.69 **The new session icon**

Note: You can also start a new session by entering the /n transaction code in the Command field and either pressing the ENTER key or clicking the (✔) icon.

6. Open the initial screen of Menu Painter by using the SE41 transaction code.
7. In the initial screen of Menu Painter, enter the program name, ZMENU_PAINTERR. Select the Status radio button in the Subobjects group

box, and enter a name for the status, for example, ZKMENU. Now, click the `Create` button, as shown in Figure 10.70:

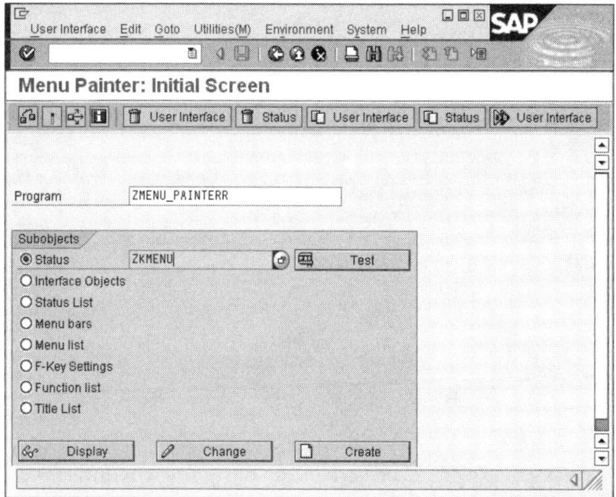

FIGURE 10.70 **Entering the name of the status**

The screen in which you enter the short description for the status that you created appears. In this case, the description is Status for Menu Painter.

8. Click the `Continue` icon, as shown in Figure 10.71:

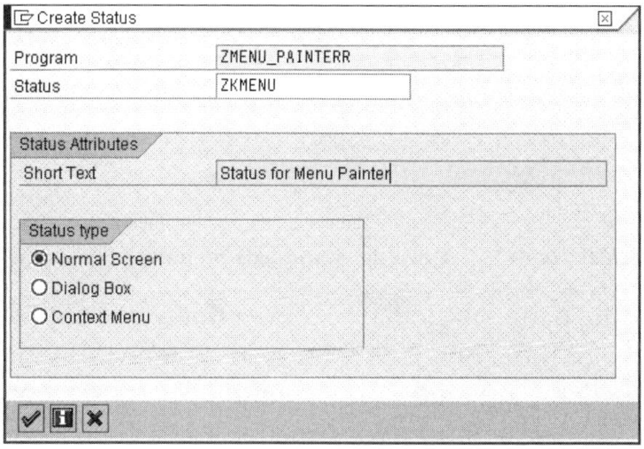

Create Status
Program ZMENU_PAINTERR
Status ZKMENU
Status Attributes
Short Text Status for Menu Painter
Status type
Normal Screen
Dialog Box
Context Menu

FIGURE 10.71 **Create status screen**

Finally, the `Maintain Status ZKMENU of Interface ZMENU_PAINTERR` screen appears, where you can maintain the interface of the program manually. The interface includes the menu bar, application toolbar, and function keys, as shown in Figure 10.72:

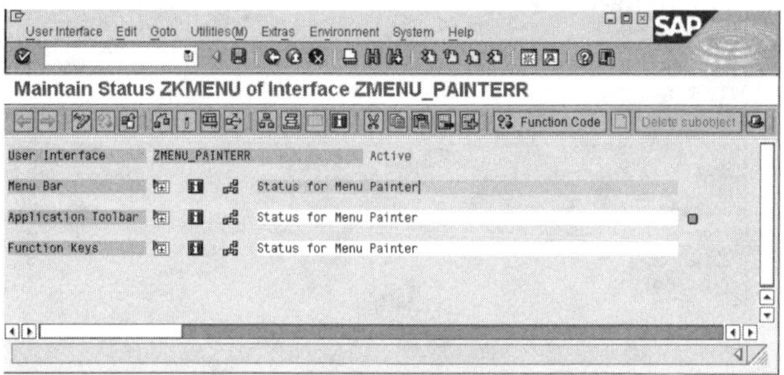

FIGURE 10.72 **The screen for designing the interface**

9. Click the `Expand Subtree` ( ) icon adjacent to the `Menu Bar` title under `User Interface`, as shown in Figure 10.73:

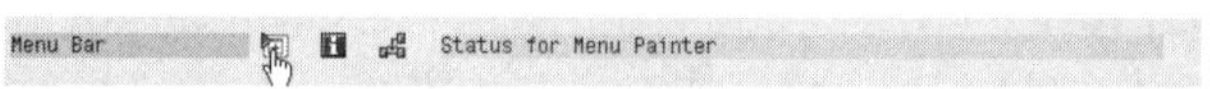

FIGURE 10.73 **Expanding the subtree icon adjacent to the menu bar**

A `Display Standards menu` appears for the menu bar, as shown in Figure 10.74:

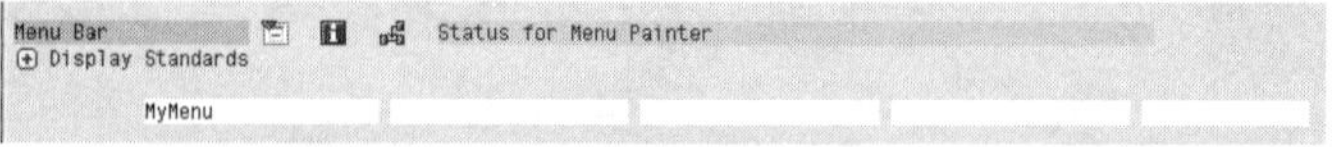

FIGURE 10.74 **The display standards menu for the menu bar**

10. Specify the name of the menu option that you want to create. In this case, the name of the menu is MyMenu (see Figure 10.74).
11. Double-click the name of the menu (that is, MyMenu). Now, enter the text of various menu options in the `Text` field and the corresponding transaction codes in the `Code` field. In this case, menu options are Display

ABAP Editor, Move to Dictionary, and Exit; and the transaction codes are `TC01`, `TC02`, and `TC03`, respectively. Figure 10.75 shows the menu options with the corresponding transaction codes:

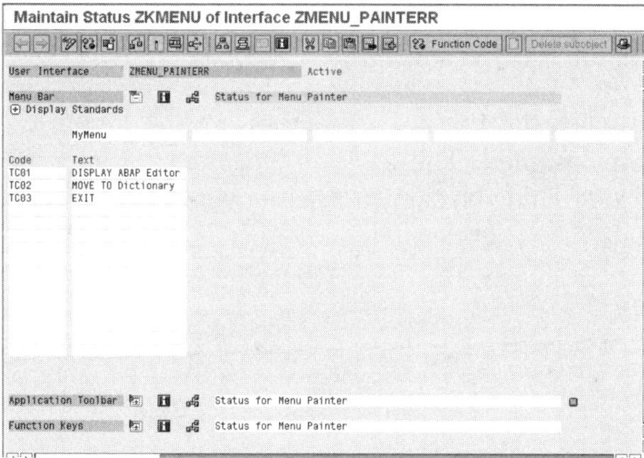

FIGURE 10.75 **The screen showing options related to the MyMenu menu**

12. Finally, click the `Save` () icon. A message stating that the designed menu bar has been saved appears on the status bar, as shown in Figure 10.76:

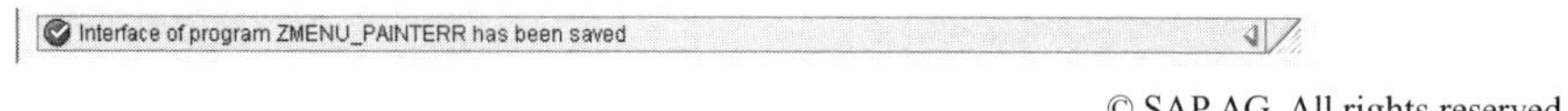

FIGURE 10.76 **The confirmation message on the status bar**

13. Click the `Check` () icon to check for any syntax errors that may have occurred while creating the menu bar. If there are no errors, a message confirming no syntax errors is displayed, as shown in Figure 10.77:

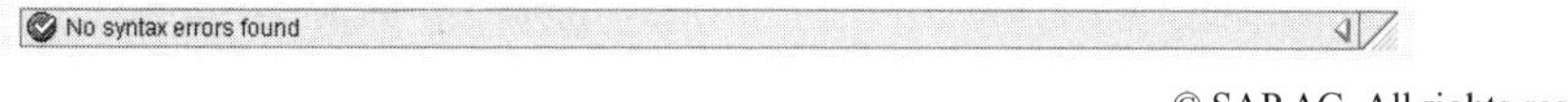

FIGURE 10.77 **The message confirming error-free creation of the menu bar**

14. Click the `Activate` () icon to activate the menu bar.

Note: If the name of the program is not visible, use the scroll bar to search for the name of the program.

Again, a message is displayed on the status bar, which confirms that the interface for the program is activated.

15. Finally, click the `Direct Processing` (▦) icon to check whether the menu is designed. The `Status Simulation for Interface ZMENU_PAINTERR` dialog box appears, as shown in Figure 10.78:

FIGURE 10.78 **The status simulation dialog box**

16. Click the `Execute` button (see Figure 10.78). The `Test Screen SAPMSEUA 8998` dialog box appears, where you can specify the window coordinates, as shown in Figure 10.79:

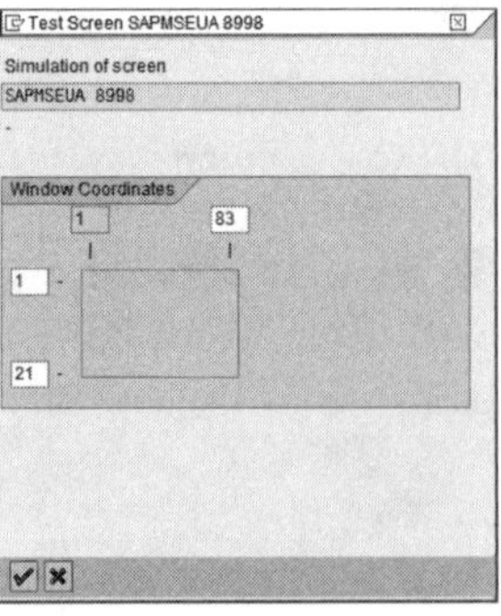

FIGURE 10.79 **Setting window coordinates**

17. Finally, click the `Continue` (☑) icon (see Figure 10.79).

The output screen where the MyMenu menu bar and the suboptions appear is shown in Figure 10.80:

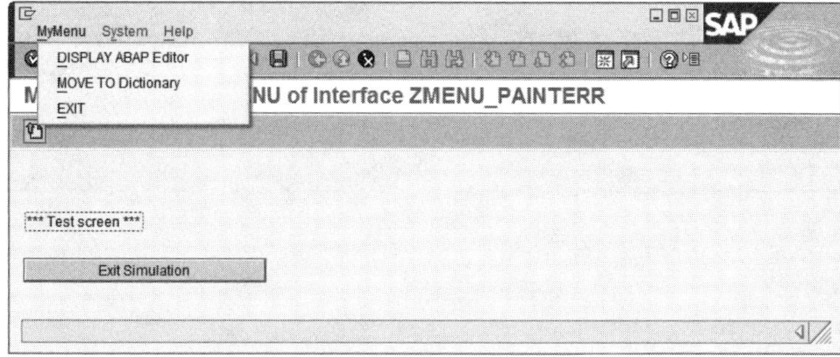

FIGURE 10.80 **The designed MyMenu menu and its suboptions**

18. Now, click the `Exit Simulation` button shown on the screen (see Figure 10.80) to design the application toolbar.

Now, we design an application toolbar for our screen.

19. Click the `Expand Subtree` ( ) icon, which is adjacent to the Application toolbar, in the `Maintain Status ZKMENU of Interface ZMENU_PAINTERR` screen. Figure 10.81 shows the `Expand Subtree` icon:

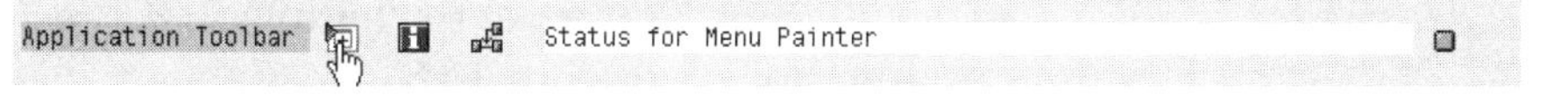

FIGURE 10.81 **Displaying the expand subtree icon**

This action displays a tabular format to define various functions for your application toolbar. You can create a maximum of seven functions, as shown in Figure 10.82:

Application Toolbar Status for Menu Painter

Items 1 - 7							
Items 8 - 14							
Items 15 - 21							
Items 22 - 28							
Items 29 - 35							

FIGURE 10.82 **Tabular representation of the application toolbar**

> **Note:** The (▣) icon (see Figure 10.82) signifies that the attributes related to the application toolbar are in the hidden mode. When you click the (▣) icon, the `Application Toolbar Attributes` dialog box opens, as shown in Figure 10.83.

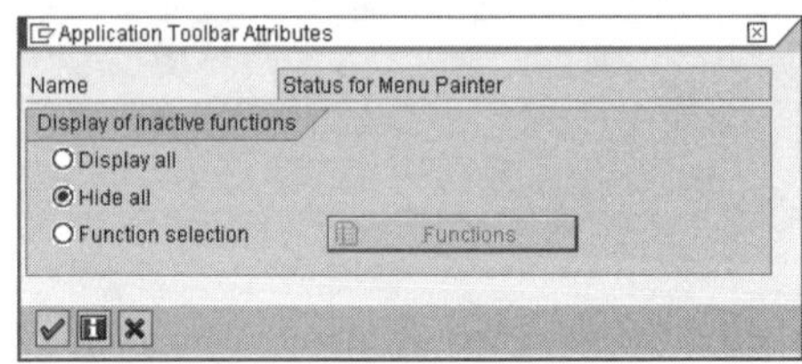

FIGURE 10.83 **Screen showing the attributes of application toolbar**

> In the `Application Toolbar Attributes` dialog box, you can change the attributes of the application toolbar.

To design the application toolbar, let's suppose that an icon, such as `RETURN`, is designed. A short description must be written for the buttons in the respective columns provided for the item list 1-7. Figure 10.84 shows how a short text related to the `RETURN` icon is written in the application toolbar:

Application Toolbar Status for Menu Painter

Items 1 - 7	RETURN						
Items 8 - 14							
Items 15 - 21							
Items 22 - 28							
Items 29 - 35							

FIGURE 10.84 **The screen showing the creation of the RETURN icon on the application toolbar**

20. Double-click the `RETURN` text. The `Enter Function Text` dialog box appears, which displays the `RETURN` text in the `Function` field. Select the

Static Text radio button in the Choose Text Type group box. Click the Continue (✔) icon, as shown in Figure 10.85:

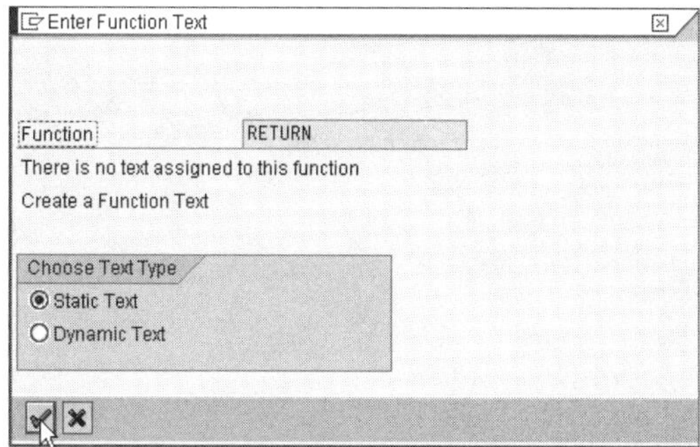

FIGURE 10.85 **The enter function text dialog box**

The Enter Function Text dialog box opens another screen to assign a function text to the RETURN function.

21. In the Enter Function Text dialog box, RETURN is displayed in the Function Code field. Enter a function text; for instance, we have entered "MOVE BACK TO MENU PAINTER" in the Function Text field. Specify an icon name with the help of the Search Help ( ) icon. Click the Continue (✔) icon, as shown in Figure 10.86:

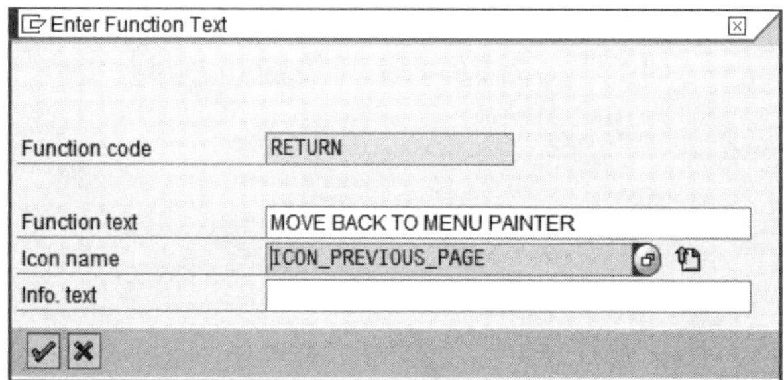

FIGURE 10.86 **The dialog box for entering function text for the RETURN function**

The Assign Function to Function Key dialog box appears, where you assign a key to a function, as shown in Figure 10.87.

22. Select a key in the `Assign Function to Function Key` dialog box. In this case, we have selected the F7 key for the `RETURN` function on the application toolbar. Click the `Continue` (☑) icon, as shown in Figure 10.87:

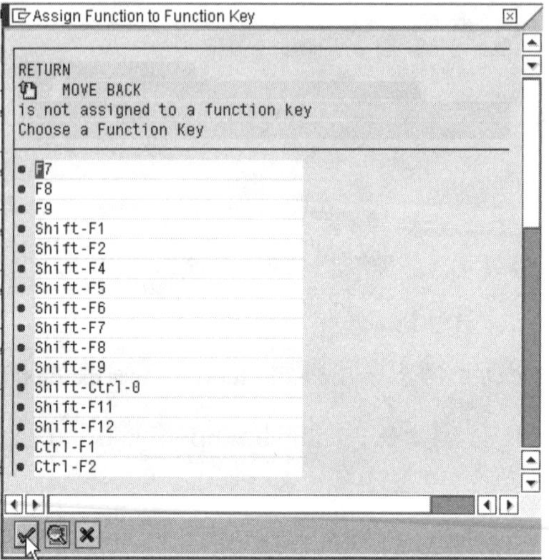

FIGURE 10.87 **Selecting a key**

The `Function Attributes` dialog box appears, where you can specify a text for your icon; however, it is an optional step.

23. In the `Function Attributes` dialog box, click the `Continue` (☑) icon, as shown in Figure 10.88:

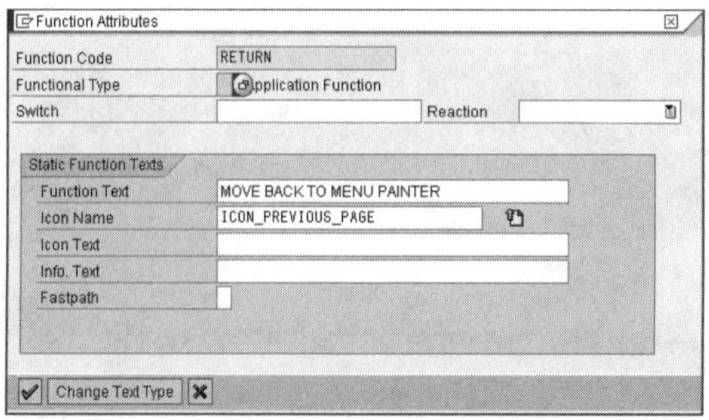

FIGURE 10.88 **The dialog box showing the function attributes**

The RETURN (icon) icon is finally seen on the Maintain Status ZKMENU of Interface ZMENU_PAINTERR screen, as shown in Figure 10.89:

Application Toolbar Status for Menu Painter

Items 1 - 7	RETURN						
Items 8 - 14							
Items 15 - 21							
Items 22 - 28							
Items 29 - 35							

FIGURE 10.89 **Maintaining status ZKMENU of the interface ZMENU_PAINTERR screen**

24. Finally, click the Save (icon) icon, Check (icon) icon, and Activate (icon) icon to activate the settings. Now, click the Execute icon to check whether the application toolbar consists of the RETURN (icon) icon. The Maintain Status ZKMENU of Interface ZMENU_PAINTERR screen appears, as shown in Figure 10.90:

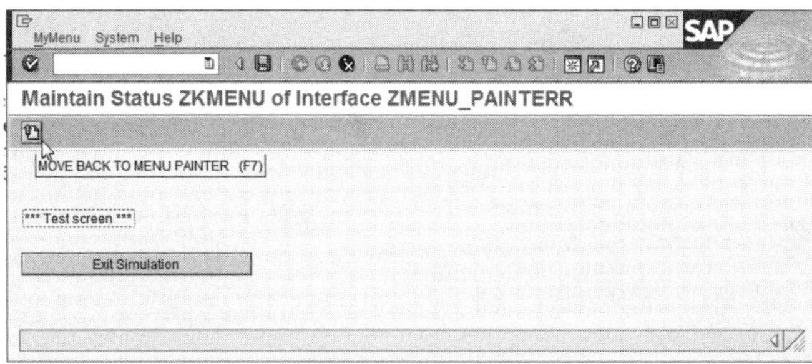

FIGURE 10.90 **The output screen of maintain status ZKMENU of interface ZMENU_PAINTERR screen**

In Figure 10.90, you see the RETURN (icon) icon with the screen tip text, MOVE BACK TO MENU PAINTER (F7).

Now, let's learn how to change the text or the function key of an icon present on the standard toolbar. Note that you cannot create new functions for the standard toolbar, but you can modify the existing one. Perform the following steps to change the function text of the `Enter` and `Save` icons of the standard toolbar:

1. In the `Maintain Status ZKMENU of Interface ZMENU_PAINTERR` screen (see Figure 10.78), click the `Expand Subtree` icon beside the text `Function Keys`, as shown in Figure 10.91:

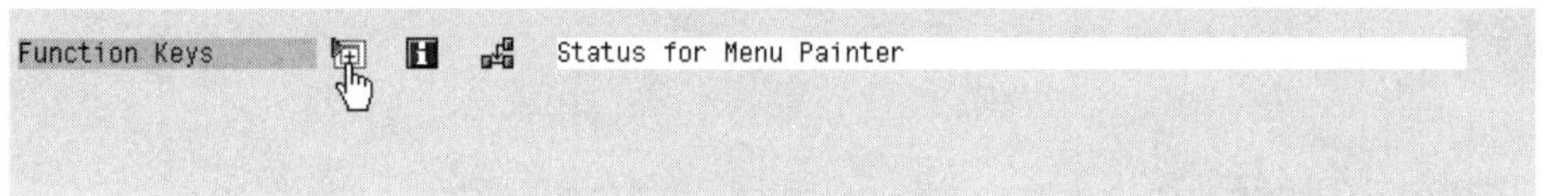

FIGURE 10.91 **Expanding the function keys**

The `Maintain Status ZKMENU of Interface ZMENU_PAINTERR` screen displays all the icons of the functions on the standard toolbar, as shown in Figure 10.92:

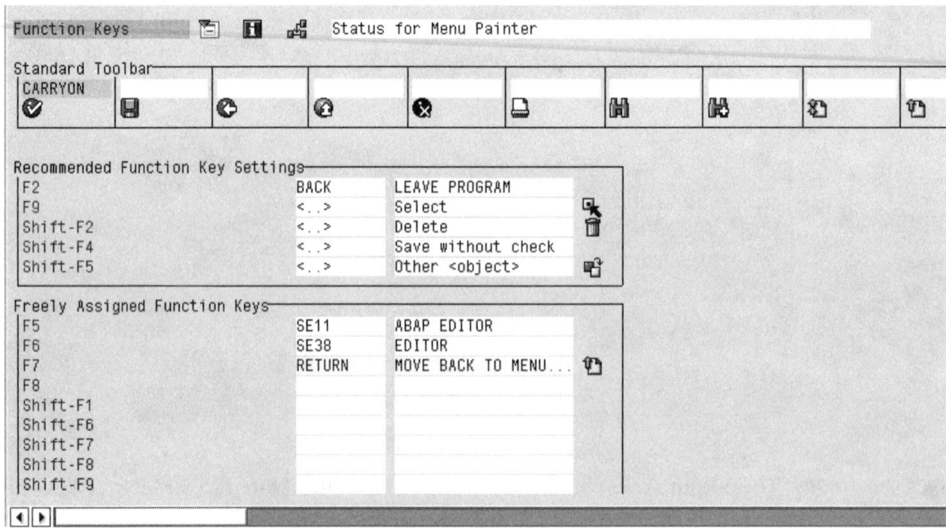

FIGURE 10.92 **The screen showing the list of all function keys**

2. In the `Maintain Status ZKMENU of Interface ZMENU_PAINTERR` screen, write text, such as CARRYON, in the space provided at the top of

the Enter ( ) icon (see Figure 10.92). Now, double-click the CARRYON text. The Enter Function Text dialog box appears. CARRYON appears in the Function field of the Enter Function Text dialog box.

3. Select the Static Text radio button in the Choose Text Type group box and click the Enter ( ) icon, as shown in Figure 10.93:

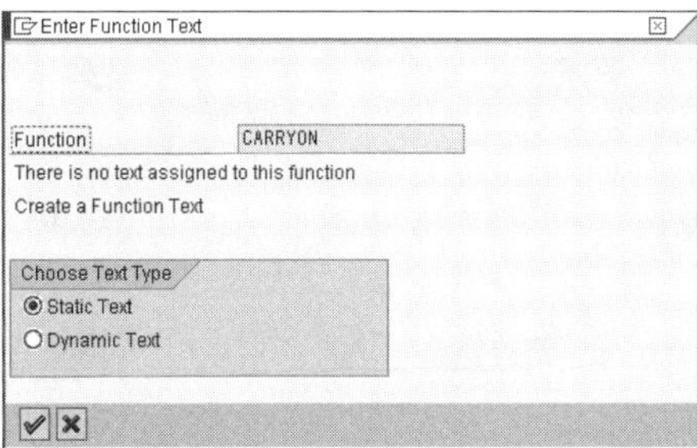

FIGURE 10.93 **The dialog box to enter the function text**

The Enter Function Text dialog box opens the next screen to assign a function text to the CARRYON function.

4. In the Enter Function Text dialog box, CARRYON is displayed in the Function Code field. Enter a function text; for instance, we have entered CONTINUE in the Function Text field. Click the Continue ( ) icon, as shown in Figure 10.94:

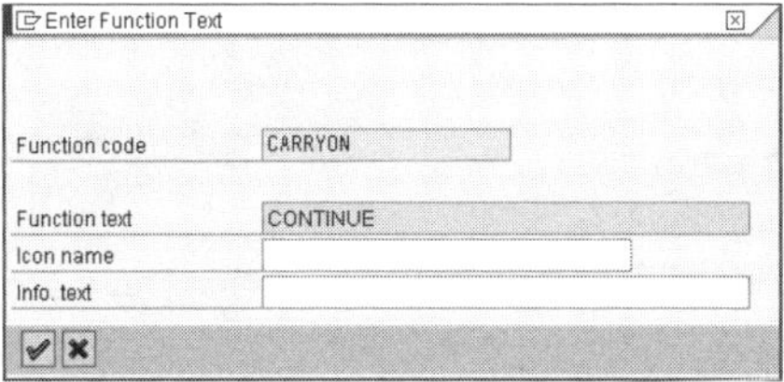

FIGURE 10.94 **The dialog box where the function key text is assigned**

The Function Attributes dialog box appears.

5. In the `Function Attributes` dialog box, you can assign the attributes related to an icon or function on the standard toolbar. Click the `Continue` icon, as shown in Figure 10.95:

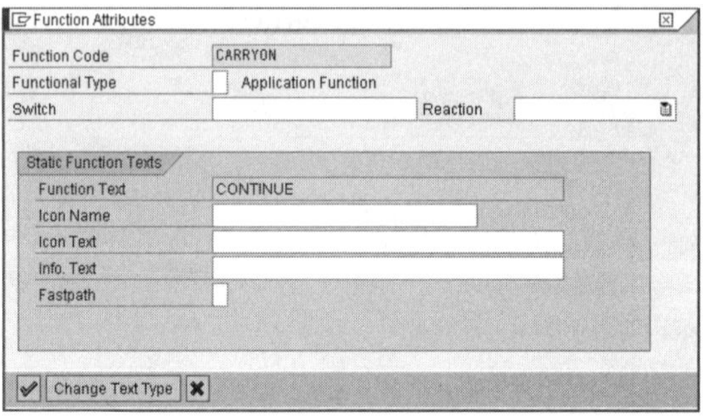

FIGURE 10.95 **The function attributes dialog box**

Similarly, perform steps 1-5 to assign a different function text to the `Save` icon. The STORE function text is assigned to the `Save` icon, as shown in Figure 10.96:

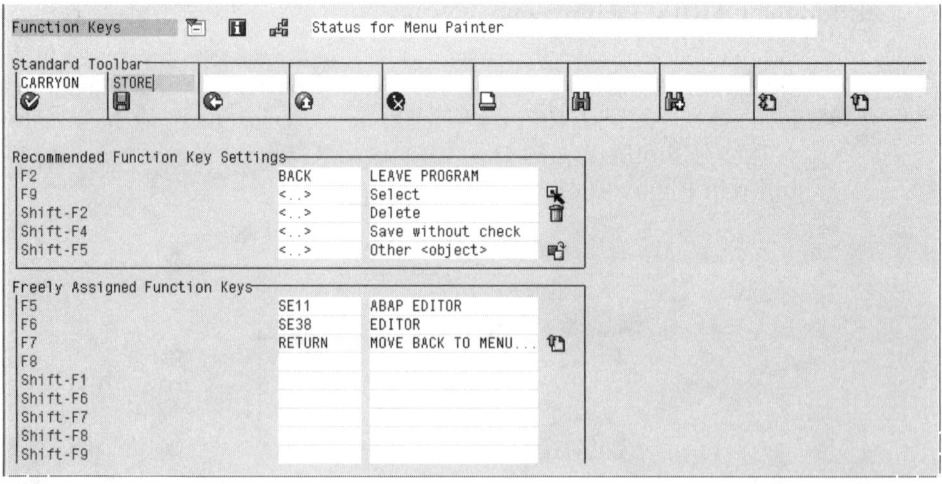

FIGURE 10.96 **Assigning a function code to the save function key**

6. Double-click the function code (that is, STORE). The `Function Attributes` dialog box appears, where you assign the function text to the function key, such as ACCUMULATE. Click the `Continue` icon, as shown in Figure 10.97:

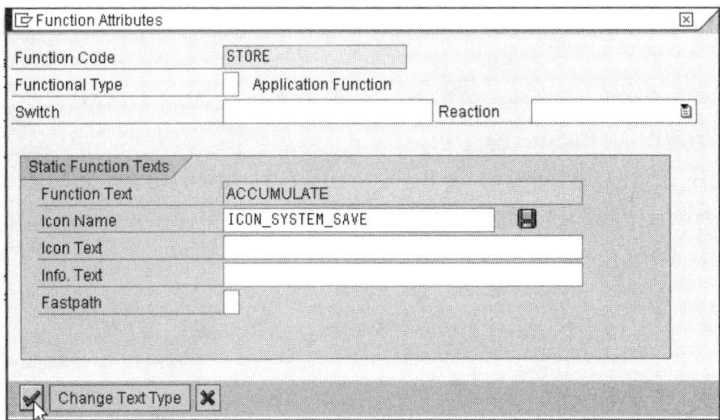

FIGURE 10.97 **The dialog box showing the function attributes of the save function key**

7. Finally, save all the settings by clicking the `Save` (💾) icon on the standard toolbar. Check for any errors by clicking the `Check` icon and activate the settings by clicking the `Activate` icon on the application toolbar.

Figure 10.98 shows the `Enter` and `Save` icons on the standard toolbar, with their associated descriptions:

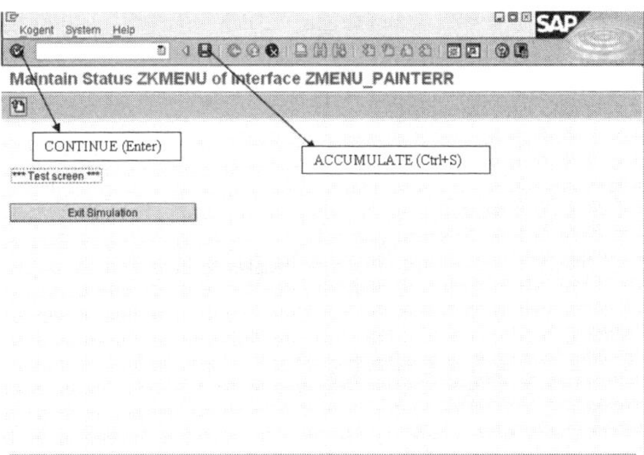

FIGURE 10.98 **Function keys and their descriptions**

Note that the description related to an icon appears whenever a user places the cursor on the icon.

Next, we explain how to design a title bar for a screen. Perform the following steps to design a user-defined title bar for a screen:

1. Open the initial screen of Menu Painter by using the `SE41` transaction code.
2. In the initial screen of Menu Painter, enter ZMENU_PAINTERR as the program name in the `Program` field. Select the `Title List` radio button in the `Subobjects` group box and enter ZMENU in the given field for the `Title List` field. Now, click the `Create` button, as shown in Figure 10.99:

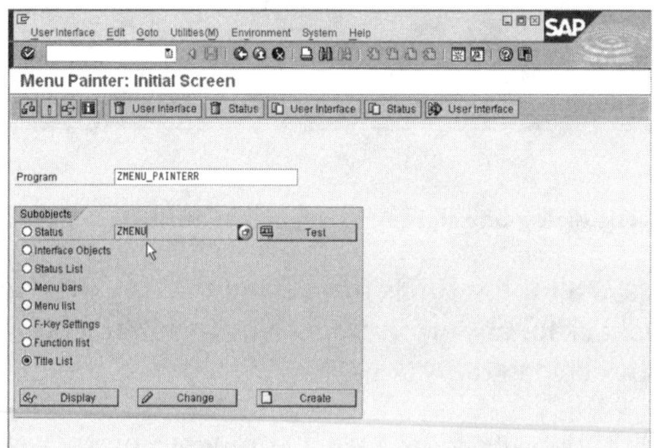

FIGURE 10.99 **Selecting the title list radio button**

The `Create Title` dialog box appears.

3. In the `Create Title` dialog box, enter a title code and title description in the `Title Code` and `Title` fields, respectively. In this case, we have entered ZMENU_PAINTERR and USER INTERFACE in these fields. Click the `Transfer` (☑) icon, as shown in Figure 10.100:

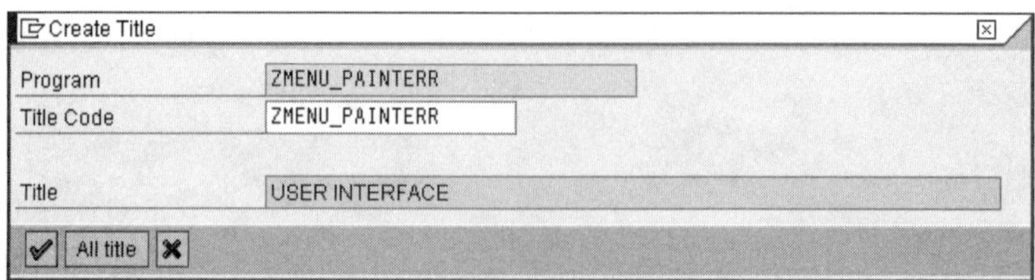

FIGURE 10.100 **Dialog box for creating title**

The `Status Simulation for Interface ZMENU_PAINTERR` dialog box appears.

4. In the `Status Simulation for Interface` dialog box, enter the `Title Code` (see Figure 10.100) in the `Title` field. In this case, we have entered ZMENU_PAINTERR in the `Title` field. Click the `Execute` button, as shown in Figure 10.101:

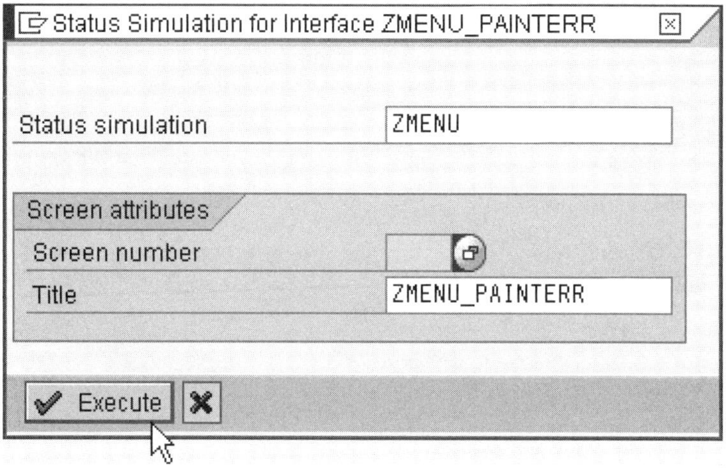

Status Simulation for Interface ZMENU_PAINTERR
Status simulation ZMENU
Screen attributes
Screen number
Title ZMENU_PAINTERR
Execute

FIGURE 10.101 **The screen attributes dialog box**

The `Test Screen SAPMSEUA 8998` dialog box appears, where you set the coordinates for the window, as shown in Figure 10.102:

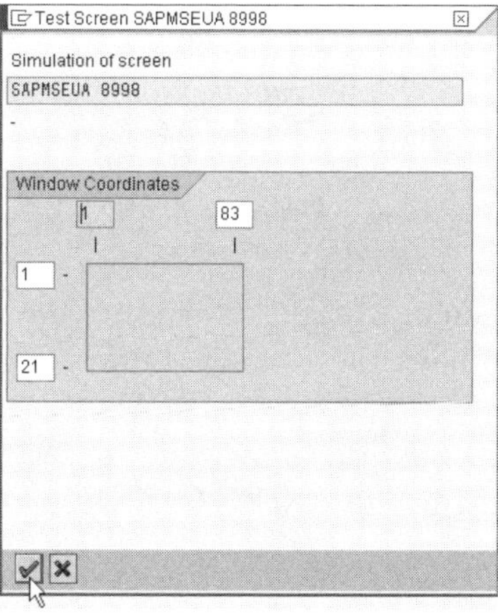

FIGURE 10.102 **The test screen**

5. In the `Test Screen SAPMSEUA 8998` dialog box, click the `Continue` (✔) icon (Figure 10.102).

The output is shown in a screen titled `USER INTERFACE`, as shown in Figure 10.103:

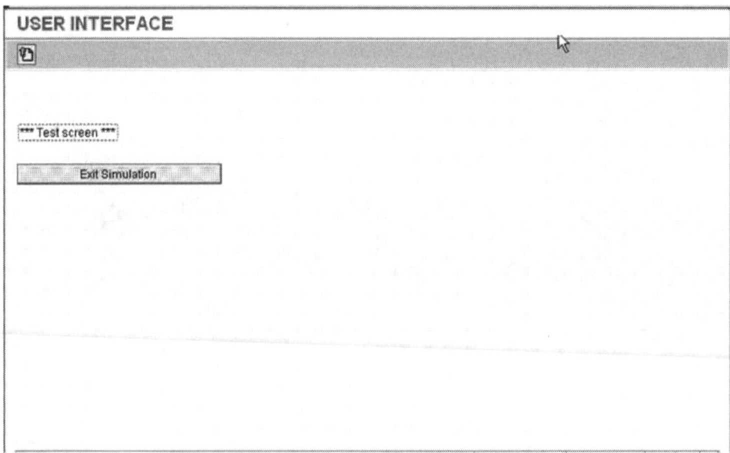

FIGURE 10.103 **The output screen**

Next, we design an ABAP program that creates a screen for ZMENU.

1. Open the initial screen of ABAP Editor by using the `SE38` transaction code.
2. In the initial screen of ABAP Editor, enter the program name as ZMENU_PAINTERR and click the `Change` button. The `ABAP Editor: Change Report ZMENU_PAINTERR` screen appears.
3. In the `ABAP Editor: Change Report ZMENU_PAINTERR` screen, write the ABAP code for the ZMENU_PAINTERR program, as shown in Figure 10.104:

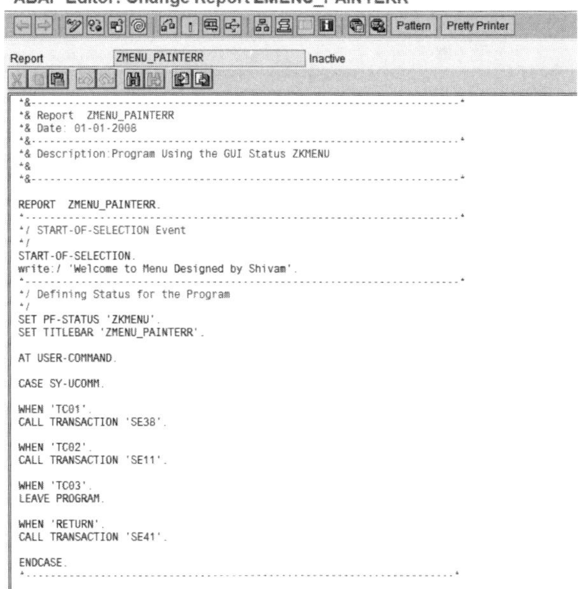

ABAP Editor: Change Report ZMENU_PAINTERR

Report ZMENU_PAINTERR Inactive

```
*&---------------------------------------------------------------------*
*& Report  ZMENU_PAINTERR
*& Date: 01-01-2008
*&---------------------------------------------------------------------*
*& Description:Program Using the GUI Status ZKMENU
*&
*&---------------------------------------------------------------------*

REPORT  ZMENU_PAINTERR.
*----------------------------------------------------------------------*
*/ START-OF-SELECTION Event
*/
START-OF-SELECTION.
write:/ 'Welcome to Menu Designed by Shivam'.
*----------------------------------------------------------------------*
*/ Defining Status for the Program
*/
SET PF-STATUS 'ZKMENU'.
SET TITLEBAR 'ZMENU_PAINTERR'.

AT USER-COMMAND.

CASE SY-UCOMM.

WHEN 'TC01'.
CALL TRANSACTION 'SE38'.

WHEN 'TC02'.
CALL TRANSACTION 'SE11'.

WHEN 'TC03'.
LEAVE PROGRAM.

WHEN 'RETURN'.
CALL TRANSACTION 'SE41'.

ENDCASE.
*----------------------------------------------------------------------*
```


FIGURE 10.104 **The editor screen showing the program**

4. Finally, activate the program by clicking the `Save` (icon) icon, the `Check` (icon) icon, and the `Activate` (icon) icon. Now, click the `Execute` (icon) icon to execute the program. Figure 10.105 shows the final output screen of the ZMENU_PAINTERR program designed for the interface:

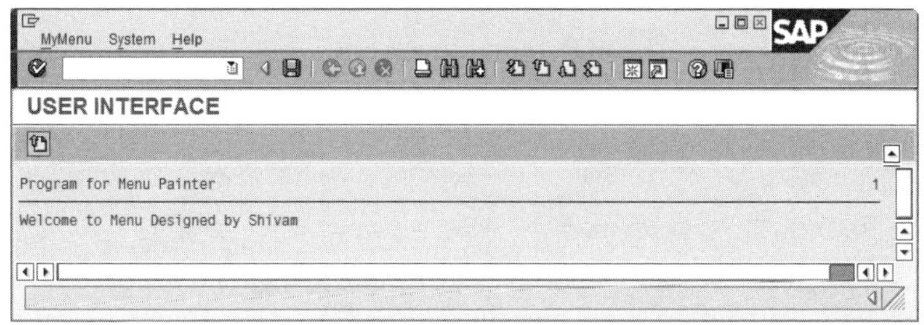

FIGURE 10.105 **The final output screen of the ZMENU_PAINTERR program**

WORKING WITH SELECTION SCREENS

A selection screen is one of the four types of user dialogs. The selection screen is different from the other general type of screens, which are designed with the help of ABAP Workbench tools such as Screen Painter and Menu Painter. The selection screens are designed whenever a user wants to design a screen meant only for accepting data input. You can either enter a single value or complex criteria for a field on the selection screen. The single value entered in a field is used primarily to control the flow of a program. The complex criteria, on the other hand, are used to restrict the amount of data read from the SAP database.

The selection screen can be defined with ABAP statements. Working on a selection screen involves the following:

- Defining a selection screen
- Calling a selection screen
- Processing a selection screen

Now, let's discuss each topic in detail, one by one.

Defining a Selection Screen

The selection screen can be defined with the following three ABAP statements:

- The `PARAMETERS` statement
- The `SELECT-OPTIONS` statement
- The `SELECTION-SCREEN` statement

The `PARAMETERS` Statement

The `PARAMETERS` statement is used to define a single field on a selection screen. The variables defined by using the `PARAMETERS` statement accept only single values. The most important function of the selection screen is to minimize the data to be read from database tables. Consequently, this function cannot be implemented by the selection screen defined in the `PARAMETERS` statement. Therefore, to implement the specified function, ABAP provides the selection criteria. A selection criterion helps a user handle complex selections. The selection criterion can be linked to the columns of databases tables and to internal fields in a program. A selection table can contain more than one selection criterion. The selection criteria are based on special internal tables known as selection tables.

The SELECT-OPTIONS Statement

The SELECT-OPTIONS statement is used to create a user interface that determines how a selection screen is displayed by entering the values of the fields of the selection table. The following syntax is used for the SELECT-OPTIONS statement:

```
SELECT-OPTIONS <selection_tab> FOR <fld>.
```

In this syntax, <selection_tab> represents an object of an internal table of the standard table type, which has a standard key and a header line. The <fld> expression represents a column of a database table or an internal field in the corresponding program. When the SELECT-OPTIONS statement is executed, an internal table (or a selection table in this context) containing four components, SIGN, OPTION, LOW, and HIGH, is created. These components correspond to the fields of a database table or an internal field in the corresponding program. Table 10.12 explains these four components:

Component	Description
SIGN	Specifies whether the result of the row condition needs to be included for each row. The data type of the SIGN component is C, with length 1. The possible values of the SIGN component are I (Inclusive) and E (Exclusive).
OPTION	Specifies the option for comparison operators, such as EQ (equal to), NE (not equal to), and GT (greater than). If the HIGH component is populated, you can use the BT (between) and NB (not between) operators only.
LOW	Determines the lower limit for a selection range.
HIGH	Determines the upper limit for a selection range.

TABLE 10.12 Description of the components

As already discussed, selection screens are created with statements written in ABAP Editor. The following steps are performed to create a selection screen:

1. Open the initial screen of ABAP Editor from the initial screen of `SAP Easy Access` or by using the `SE38` transaction code.
2. On the initial screen of ABAP Editor, enter the name of the program to be created. In this case, we enter the name of the program as ZSELECTIONSCREEN, as shown in Figure 10.106:

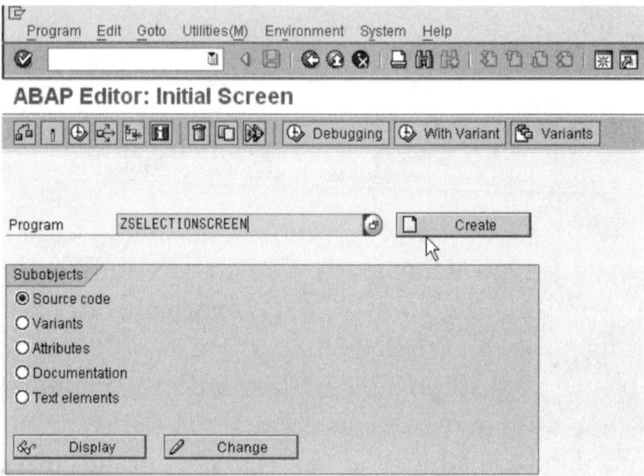

FIGURE 10.106 **Initial screen of ABAP editor**

3. Click the `Create` button. The `ABAP Program Attributes ZSELECTION SCREEN Change` dialog box appears. In this dialog box, enter the title of the program and select the type of program to be created. In this case, we enter the title as Demo Of Selection Screen and select `Executable Program` as the type of the program, as shown in Figure 10.107:

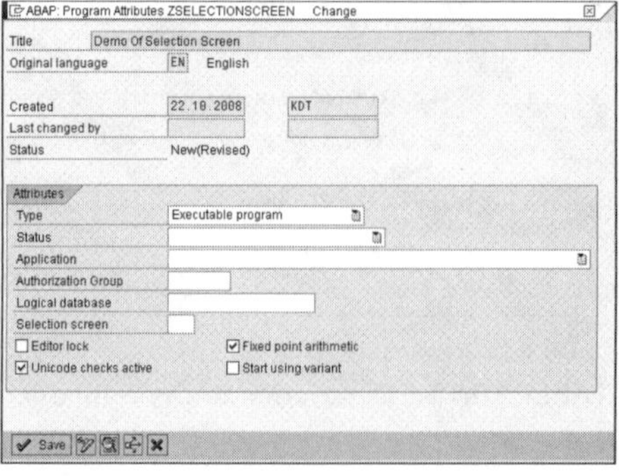

FIGURE 10.107 **Defining the program attributes**

4. Click the `Save` (Save) button. The `Create Object Directory Entry` dialog box appears.
5. In the `Create Object Directory Entry` dialog box, enter the name of the package as ZKOG_PCKG and click the `Save` () icon. The `Prompt for the local Workbench request` dialog box appears. Click the `Continue` () icon. The screen on which the statements to create a selection screen are written appears, as shown in Figure 10.108:

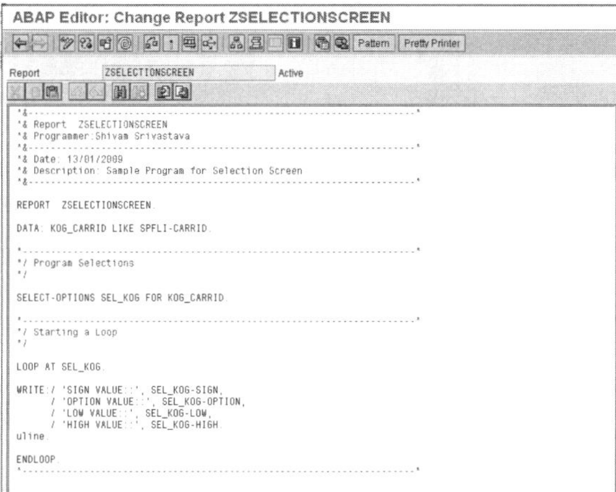

FIGURE 10.108 **The screen showing the creation of the selection screen**

6. Finally, click the `Save` (), `Check` (), and `Activate` () icons.

In this example, we create a selection table named SEL_KOG, which is similar to a data object named KOG_CARRID.

7. Now, click the `Direct Processing` () icon. The standard selection screen appears, as shown in Figure 10.109:

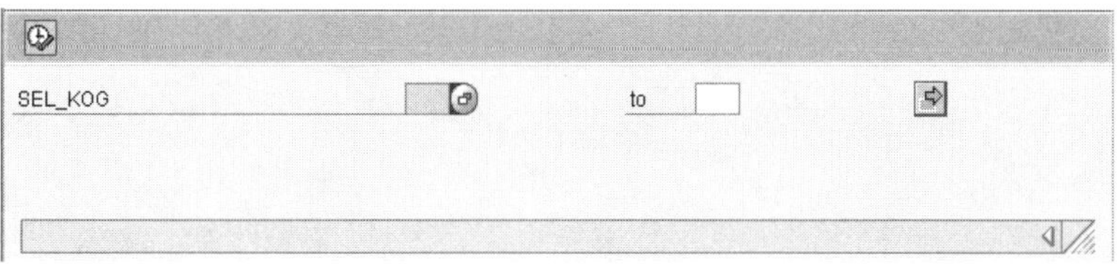

FIGURE 10.109 **The selection screen**

This screen contains an input field (SEL_KOG) and a `Multiple Selection` ( ) icon. The value entered by a user in the first input field is copied into the SEL_KOG-LOW field of the selection table. Similarly, the value entered in the second input field is copied into the SEL_KOG-HIGH field of the selection table.

8. Now, let's suppose that we enter the first field as AA and click the `Execute` ( ) icon, as shown in Figure 10.110:

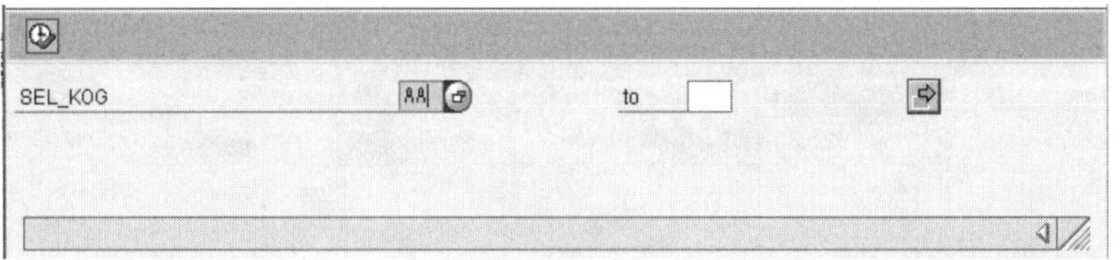

FIGURE 10.110 **The selection screen containing input fields and the maintain selection icon**

The output is shown in Figure 10.111:

FIGURE 10.111 **Output of the selection screen**

Note that the second field is left blank, which means that it is a single field comparison. Therefore, in this case, the default settings for the `SIGN` and `OPTION` components are I and EQ, respectively.

9. Enter the value for the second field, such as BB, as shown in Figure 10.112:

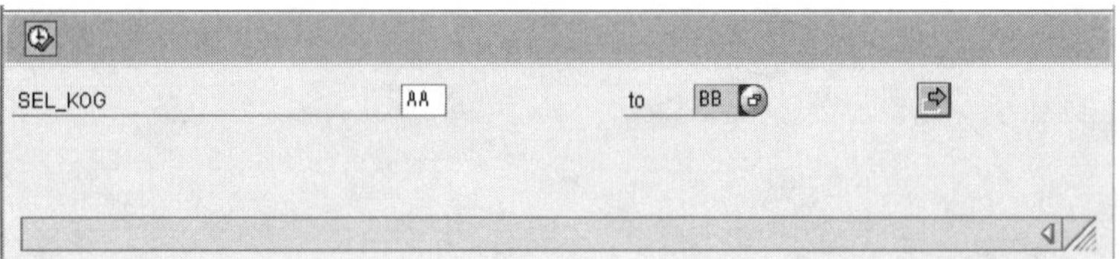

FIGURE 10.112 **The screen showing second field value**

In this case, the default settings for the `SIGN` and `OPTION` components are `I` and `BT`, respectively.

10. Click the `Execute` () icon that appears in Figure 10.112. Figure 10.113 displays the output corresponding to the changes made:

```
Demo Of Selection Screen                                   1

SIGN VALUE:: I
OPTION VALUE:: BT
LOW VALUE:: AA
HIGH VALUE:: BB
```


FIGURE 10.113 **Output of the selection screen**

11. To set a complex selection pattern, click the `Maintain Selection` ( ) icon (see Figure 10.110) without writing any values in the input fields. The `Multiple Selection for SEL_KOG` dialog box appears, where you can define `Select Single Values`, `Select Ranges`, `Exclude Single Values`, and `Exclude Ranges`. In this case, we define all the options one by one. Figure 10.114 shows how to define the Select Single Values:

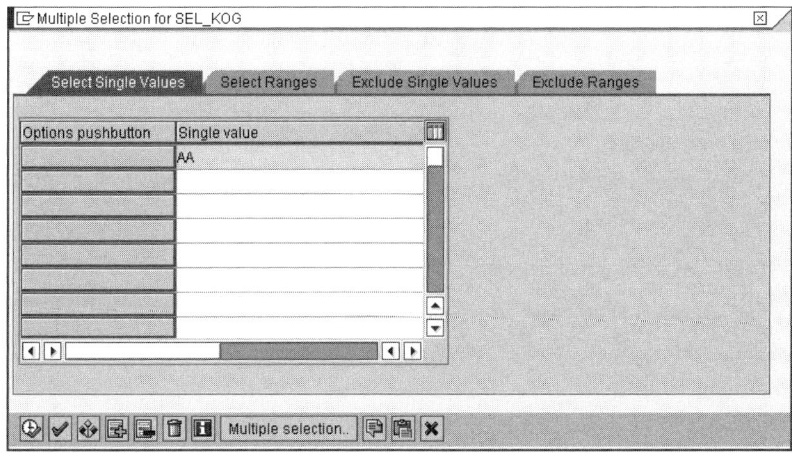

FIGURE 10.114 **Defining single values**

Note: The Select Single Values tab is activated by default.

12. Select the `Select Ranges` tab and define the lower limit and upper limit. In this case, we enter the lower range as DL and JL and the upper range as NG and SQ, as shown in Figure 10.115:

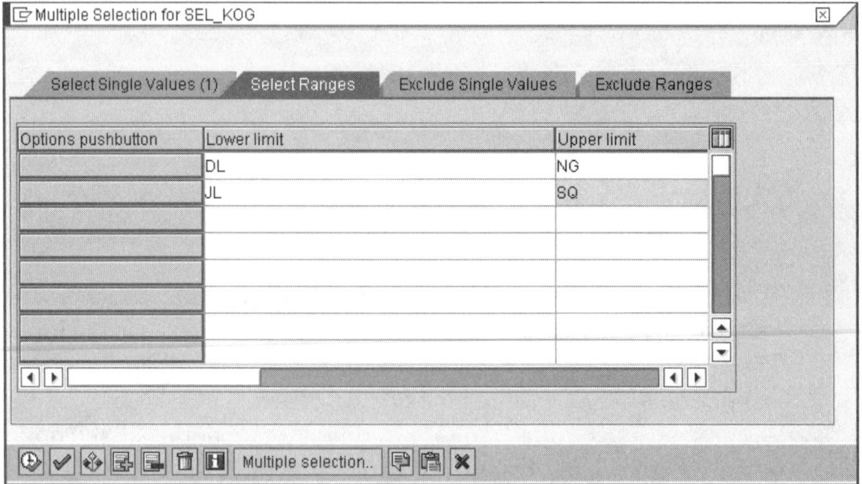

FIGURE 10.115 **Maintaining complex selection criteria**

13. Finally, click the `Copy` (⊕) icon. The initial selection screen appears (see Figure 10.110).
14. Click the `Execute` (⊕) icon; the output appears as shown in Figure 10.116:

Note: In our case, the value set for the `SIGN` component is I, since the values are included in the selection.

```
Demo Of Selection Screen                                                    1
--------------------------------------------------------------------------------
SIGN VALUE:: I
OPTION VALUE:: EQ
LOW VALUE:: AA
HIGH VALUE::
--------------------------------------------------------------------------------
SIGN VALUE:: I
OPTION VALUE:: BT
LOW VALUE:: DL
HIGH VALUE:: NG
--------------------------------------------------------------------------------
SIGN VALUE:: I
OPTION VALUE:: BT
LOW VALUE:: JL
HIGH VALUE:: SQ
--------------------------------------------------------------------------------
```


FIGURE 10.116 **Output of the complex selection criteria**

Apart from this, you can also set the values for `Exclude Single Values` and `Exclude Ranges` for the selection. In this case, if the values of these two tabs are set, the value of the `SIGN` component is set to `E`.

Further, the value of the `SIGN` and `OPTION` fields can also be set explicitly. This can be done on the selection screen, which you see after executing the program (see Figure 10.110). When you double-click the input field or press the F2 key on this screen, the `Maintain Selection Options` dialog box appears. You can explicitly select any of the options, such as `Single Value`, `Greater than or Equal to`, or `Less than or Equal to`, in this dialog box. In this case, we select the `Greater than` operator for the `OPTION` field. Notice that the value I for the `SIGN` field is activated already.

15. Now, click the `Continue` (☑) icon, as shown in Figure 10.117:

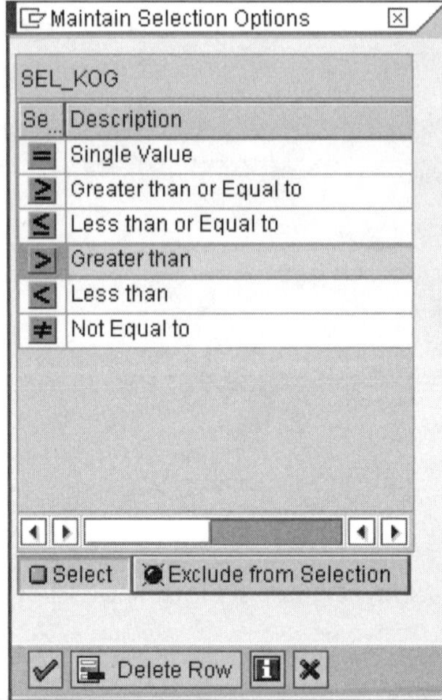

FIGURE 10.117 **Maintaining selection screen options**

> **Note:** You can also switch between I and E for the `SIGN` field with the help of the (Exclude from Selection) button (see Figure 10.117).

A selection screen, having the greater than (>) symbol for the input field, appears. In this case, we enter the value AG as the value in the input field, as shown in Figure 10.118:

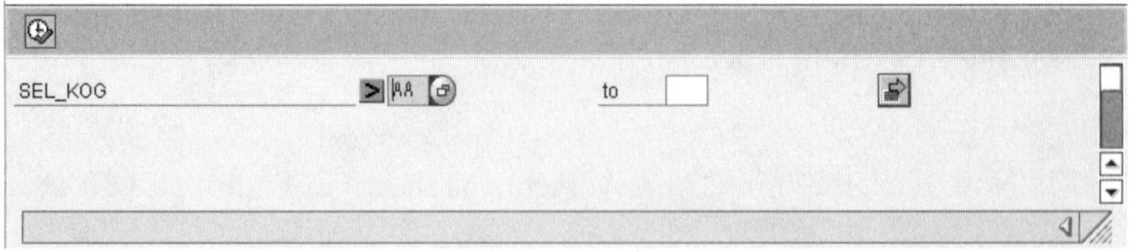

FIGURE 10.118 **Value in the input field**

16. Click the `Execute` (icon) icon; the output appears as shown in Figure 10.119:

```
Demo Of Selection Screen                                    1

SIGN VALUE:: I
OPTION VALUE:: GT
LOW VALUE:: AA
HIGH VALUE::
```


FIGURE 10.119 **The screen showing the value set for the OPTION field**

In this figure, the values of the fields of the SEL_KOG internal table are set. Notice that the lower limit is set as AA and the upper limit is left blank. The fields of the internal table display the respective values in the fields when you click the `Execute` icon.

The `SELECTION-SCREEN` Statement

The selection screen defined by the `PARAMETERS` and `SELECT-OPTIONS` statements has a standard layout, in which the parameters appear line by line on the screen. However, you can also customize the layout with the help of various formatting options provided by the `SELECTION-SCREEN` statement. You can perform various formatting options, such as setting the layout of parameters, setting the selection criteria for parameters, setting the display of comments, and setting underlines on the selection screen, by using the `SELECTION-SCREEN` statement.

The layout designed by a user can be viewed only if the selection screen is called. Standard selection screens are called automatically in a program. Apart from these standard selection screens, you can also define a user-defined selection screen that otherwise cannot be called directly. The user-defined screens are called by using the `CALL SELECTION-SCREEN` statement. These user-defined selection screens contain a screen number other than 1000. You can perform the following actions by using the `SELECTION-SCREEN` statement:

- Assigning blank lines, underlines, and comments
- Assigning several elements in a single line
- Assigning blocks of elements

Now, let's discuss each task in detail.

Assigning Blank Lines, Underlines, and Comments

You can set blank lines, underlines, and comments for the designed selection screen. The following syntax is used to place blank lines on a selection screen:

```
SELECTION-SCREEN SKIP [<n>].
```

This syntax generates `<n>` blank lines on the selection screen. The value of n can be any number between 1 and 9. If you want to place a single blank line on a selection screen, you can omit the `<n>` expression.

The following syntax is used to generate underlines on the selection screen:

```
SELECTION-SCREEN ULINE [/] [pos|POS_LOW|POS_HIGH](len)[MODIF
ID <key>].
```

Table 10.13 describes the clauses that are used in the `SELECTION-SCREEN` statement to assign several elements in a single line:

Clauses	Description
ULINE	Denotes that an underline has to be placed on the selection screen, which begins at a predefined location.
[/] [pos|POS_LOW|POS_HIGH](len)	Places an underline, which begins at the `pos` position in the current line, and continues for `(len)` length of characters. If several elements exist in one line, you can also assign `(len)` without `pos`. If `[pos|POS_LOW|POS_HIGH](len)` is not used, an underline is generated following the current line. The length of the underline is same as the current line. A slash (/) produces a line feed, which means the cursor is placed in the next line.
MODIF ID <key>	Modifies the underline preceding the call of the selection screen.

TABLE 10.13 Clauses in the statement

> **Note:** You can also use the `POS_LOW` and `POS_HIGH` clauses to mark the position of the two input fields of a selection criterion.

Apart from placing blank lines and generating underlines, you can also place comments on the selection screen. The following syntax is used to place comments on a selection screen:

```
SELECTION-SCREEN COMMENT [/] [pos|POS_LOW|POS_HIGH]
(len) <comm> [FOR FIELD <f>]
[MODIF ID <key>].
```

Table 10.14 shows the description of the clauses in the syntax used for placing comments:

Clause	Description
COMMENT	Denotes that a comment has to be placed on the selection screen.
<comm>	Represents a comment that is declared by a text or field symbol.
[/] [pos|POS_LOW|POS_HIGH](len)	Places a comment of length `(len)` that begins at the `pos` position in the current line. If you do not use the slash symbol (/), the comment is written on the current line
FOR FIELD <f>	Assigns a field label to the comment.
MODIF ID <key>	Modifies the comment before the selection screen is called.

TABLE 10.14 Clauses in the statement

Listing 10.1 shows how to use the three syntaxes:

```
REPORT ZKCOMMENT.
*-----------------------------------------------------*
*/ Program Selections
```

Continued

```
*/
SELECTION-SCREEN COMMENT /2(50) TEXT-001 MODIF ID SG1.
SELECTION-SCREEN SKIP 1.
SELECTION-SCREEN ULINE /1(55).
SELECTION-SCREEN COMMENT /10(30) COMM1.
SELECTION-SCREEN ULINE /1(55).
PARAMETERS: R1 RADIOBUTTON GROUP RAD1,
R2 RADIOBUTTON GROUP RAD1, R3 RADIOBUTTON GROUP RAD1.
SELECTION-SCREEN ULINE /1(55).
SELECTION-SCREEN COMMENT /10(30) COMM2.
SELECTION-SCREEN ULINE /1(55).
PARAMETERS: S1 RADIOBUTTON GROUP RAD2,
S2 RADIOBUTTON GROUP RAD2,
S3 RADIOBUTTON GROUP RAD2.
SELECTION-SCREEN ULINE /1(55).
*------------------------------------------------------*
*/ Initialization Section-Default Parameter value
*/
INITIALIZATION.
COMM1 = 'Group 1 of Radio buttons'.
COMM2 = ' Group 2 of Radio buttons '.
*------------------------------------------------------*
*/ Loop for the Selection Screen
*/
LOOP AT SCREEN.
IF SCREEN-GROUP1 = 'SG1'.
SCREEN-INTENSIFIED = '1'.
MODIFY SCREEN.
ENDIF.
ENDLOOP.
*------------------------------------------------------*
```

LISTING 10.1 **Generating comments on the selection screen**

In Listing 10.1, `TEXT-001` is a text symbol that stores the text, `Creating Blank Lines, Underlines, and Comments on Selection Screen`. The `SELECTION-SCREEN ULINE` statement is used for underline and the `SELECTION-SCREEN COMMENT` statement is used for comments. `COMM1` and `COMM2` are comment variables that store the Group 1 of radio buttons and Group 2 of radio buttons texts, respectively. These comment variables display their values in underlines. `R1`, `R2`, and `R3` are three radio buttons in the Group RAD 1 for radio buttons and `S1`, `S2`, and `S3` are radio buttons for Group RAD 2. Figure 10.120 shows the output of Listing 10.1:

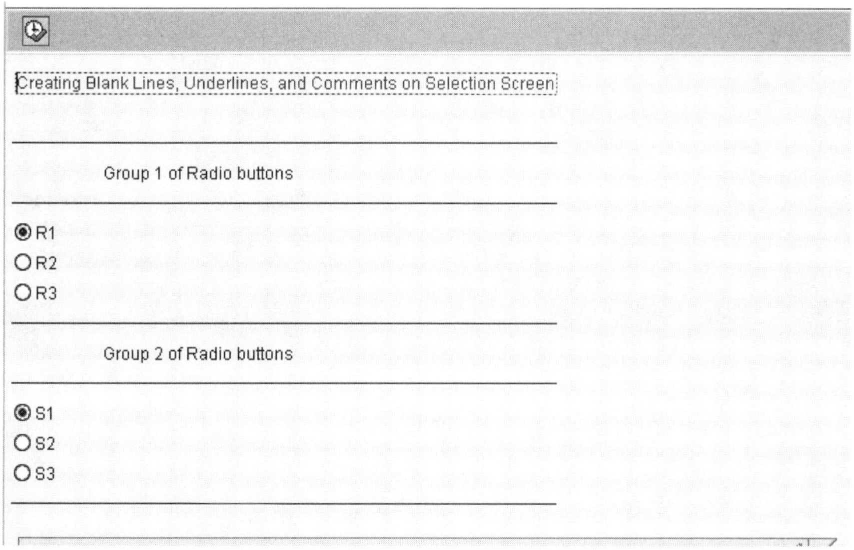

FIGURE 10.120 **The user-defined selection screen**

Note: Listing 10.1 uses a text symbol, TEXT-001. A text symbol is created by using either the `SE32` (ABAP Text Elements) transaction code or the `SE38` (ABAP Editor) transaction code. Perform the following steps to create a text symbol for a program:

1. Open the initial screen of ABAP Editor by using the `SE38` transaction code.
2. In the initial screen of ABAP Editor, enter the program name as ZKCOMMENT, and click the `Create` button. The ABAP Editor opens in the change mode.

Continued

3. Select GoTo > Text Elements > Text Symbols from the change screen of ABAP Editor. The ABAP Text Elements: Change Text Symbols Language English screen appears, as shown in Figure 10.121.
4. In the ABAP Text Elements: Change Text Symbols Language English screen, the Program field contains the ZKCOMMENT program name. Enter a symbol, for instance 001, in the Sym field and a description, Creating Blank lines, Underlines, and Comments on Selection Screen, in the Text field. Figure 10.121 shows the ABAP Text Elements: Change Text Symbols Language English screen:

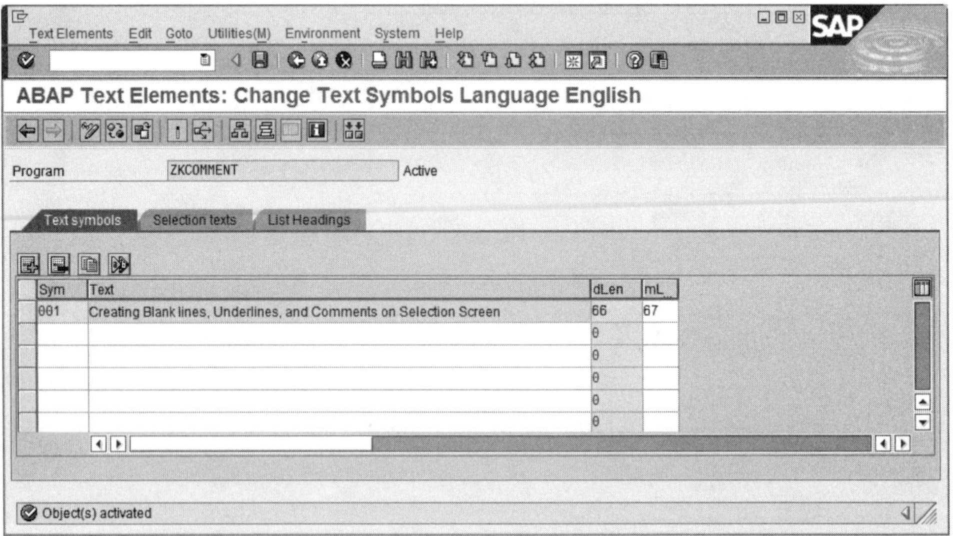

FIGURE 10.121 **The screen used to create text symbols**

5. Save and activate the created text symbol. After the text symbol is activated, it is now ready to be used by the ZKCOMMENT program.

Assigning Several Elements in a Single Line

You can set various text fields in a single line on a selection screen. Use the following syntax to create various text fields in a single line:

```
SELECTION-SCREEN BEGIN OF LINE.
 ...
SELECTION-SCREEN END OF LINE.
```

Note: In the preceding syntax, you cannot display the selection text and use a slash (/) in the formatting option `<pos(len)>`.

In the `SELECTION-SCREEN` statement, the`<pos(len)>`expression represents the position of an element. However, `<pos>` can be omitted within the syntax.

Use the following syntax to determine the current position of an element in a line:

```
SELECTION-SCREEN POSITION <pos>.
```

In this syntax, the `<pos>` expression can have the `POS_LOW` or `POS_HIGH` constants to determine the position of the input fields of a selection criterion.

Note: The `POSITION` clause is used only between the `BEGIN OF LINE` and `END OF LINE` statements.

Listing 10.2 shows how several elements can be assigned to a single line on a selection screen:

```
REPORT ZKELEMENT.
*-------------------------------------------------------*
*/ Table Used in the Program
*/
TABLES: MARA.
*-------------------------------------------------------*
*/ Program Selections
*/
SELECTION-SCREEN BEGIN OF LINE.

  SELECTION-SCREEN COMMENT 1(10) TEXT-001.
```

Continued

```
   PARAMETERS: P1(10), P2(20).
SELECTION-SCREEN END OF LINE.

SELECTION-SCREEN SKIP 2.
SELECT-OPTIONS NUMBER FOR MARA-MATNR.

SELECTION-SCREEN BEGIN OF LINE.
   SELECTION-SCREEN POSITION POS_LOW.
   SELECTION-SCREEN POSITION POS_HIGH.

SELECTION-SCREEN END OF LINE.
*----------------------------------------------------*
```

LISTING 10.2 **Elements assigned on a selection screen**

In Listing 10.2, `TEXT-001` is a text symbol that stores the text Name. The `PARAMETERS` clause is used to display two fields named `P1` and `P2`. A field name, `NUMBER`, is assigned to the `MATNR` column of the MARA table. The `POS_LOW` and `POS_HIGH` constants are used to specify the lowest and highest value limits with respect to the `MATNR` column. Figure 10.122 shows the output of Listing 10.2:

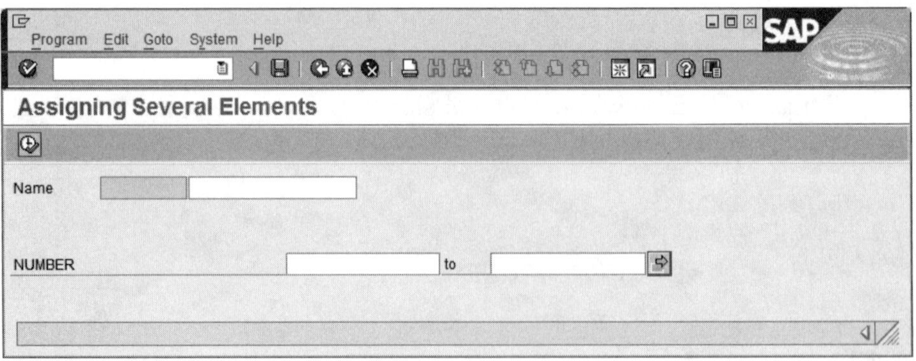

FIGURE 10.122 **Assigning several elements**

In Figure 10.122, two fields corresponding to the text Name are displayed on the selection screen. In addition to these fields, two more fields corresponding to the NUMBER text are placed at different locations on the selection screen.

Assigning Blocks of Elements

On a selection screen, you can also combine different fields in a block, as shown in the following syntax:

```
SELECTION-SCREEN BEGIN OF BLOCK <block>
     [WITH FRAME [TITLE <title>]
     [NO INTERVALS].
  ...
SELECTION-SCREEN END OF BLOCK <block>.
```

The block of elements can be assigned on the selection screen with the help of different clauses of the SELECTION-SCREEN statement. Table 10.15 describes the clauses in the syntax used for the block of elements:

Clause	Description
`<block>`	Defines the name of the block.
WITH FRAME	Defines a frame around the block. A maximum of five different blocks can be framed.
TITLE `<title>`	Assigns a title to each block frame. The title can be a text symbol or a field with a maximum length of eight characters.
NO INTERVALS	Retains the selection criteria of selection screens, which are integrated as subscreen dynpros.

TABLE 10.15 Clauses in the statement

Listing 10.3 shows how to assign a block of elements:

```
REPORT ZKBLOCK.
*---------------------------------------------------*
*/ Program Selections
*/
```

Continued

```
SELECTION-SCREEN BEGIN OF BLOCK RADIO WITH FRAME.
   PARAMETERS R1 RADIOBUTTON GROUP GR1.
   PARAMETERS R2 RADIOBUTTON GROUP GR1.
   PARAMETERS R3 RADIOBUTTON GROUP GR1.

SELECTION-SCREEN END OF BLOCK RADIO.
*-----------------------------------------------------------*
```

LISTING 10.3 **Assigning a block of elements**

In Listing 10.3, the `SELECTION-SCREEN BEGIN` and `SELECTION-SCREEN END` statements are used to create the `RADIO` block. A frame is created using the `WITH FRAME` clause. The frame contains three radio buttons, `R1`, `R2`, and `R3`, which belong to a radio button group, GR1. Figure 10.123 shows the output of Listing 10.3:

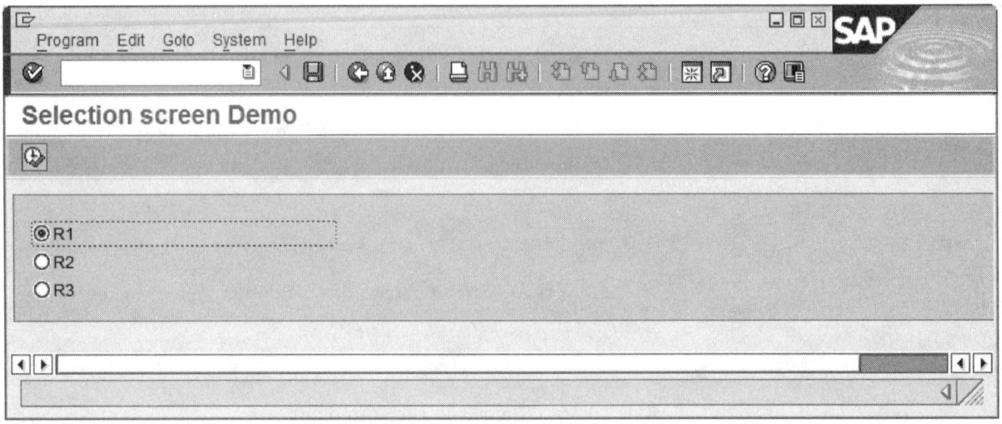

Program Edit Goto System Help

Selection screen Demo

R1
R2
R3

FIGURE 10.123 **Output containing the block of elements on a selection screen**

Calling a Selection Screen

Calling a selection screen depends on whether you have created a user-defined selection screen or a standard selection screen. As already discussed, a standard selection screen is called automatically; however, in the case of user-defined selection screens, they are called by using the `CALL SELECTION-SCREEN` statement. The syntax of the `CALL SELECTION-SCREEN` statement is:

```
CALL SELECTION-SCREEN <numb> [STARTING AT <x1> <y 1>] [ENDING
AT <x2> <y 2>].
```

Table 10.16 describes the clauses used in the syntax of the `CALL SELECTION-SCREEN` statement:

Clause	Description
<numb>	Denotes the number of the user-defined selection screens
STARTING AT	Displays the user-defined selection screen as a modal dialog box
ENDING AT	Displays the user-defined selection screen as a modal dialog box

TABLE 10.16 Clauses in the CALL SELECTION-SCREEN statement

The user-defined selection screen can also be defined as a modal dialog box by using the `AS WINDOW` clause while declaring the user-defined selection screen, as shown in the following syntax:

```
SELECTION-SCREEN BEGIN OF SCREEN <numb> [TITLE <title>] [AS
WINDOW].
 .........................
SELECTION-SCREEN END OF SCREEN <numb>.
```

As a best practice, use the modal dialog box for the selection screen because the error and warnings messages that appear during the processing of the selection screen are displayed in the modal dialog boxes. The `SY-SUBRC` system variable holds two possible values after the processing of the selection screen is complete:

- `SY-SUBRC` is equal to zero if you click the `Execute` icon on the selection screen.
- `SY-SUBRC` is equal to four if you select the `Cancel` icon on the selection screen.

Listing 10.4 shows how to call the standard selection screen and user-defined selection screen.

```
REPORT ZKCALLING.
*-----------------------------------------------------------*
*/ Program Selections
*/

SELECTION-SCREEN BEGIN OF BLOCK BOX1 WITH FRAME
TITLE T1.

   PARAMETERS: PUR_NUM TYPE EKPO-EBELN,
               IT_NUM TYPE EKPO-EBELP.

SELECTION-SCREEN END OF BLOCK BOX1.
*-----------------------------------------------------------*
*/ Program Selections
*/
SELECTION-SCREEN BEGIN OF SCREEN 500 AS WINDOW.

SELECTION-SCREEN INCLUDE BLOCKS BOX1.
SELECTION-SCREEN BEGIN OF BLOCK BOX2
                    WITH FRAME TITLE T2.

PARAMETERS: COM_CODE LIKE EKPO-BUKRS,
            PLANT LIKE EKPO-WERKS.

SELECTION-SCREEN END OF BLOCK BOX2.
SELECTION-SCREEN END OF SCREEN 500.
*-----------------------------------------------------------*
*/ Initialization Section-Parameters with default Value
*/

INITIALIZATION.
T1 = 'Purchasing Document Item'.
```

Continued

```
*-----------------------------------------------------*
*/ Start of Selection- Processing of Main Program Begins
*/

START-OF-SELECTION.
T1 = 'Purchase and Item Number'.
T2 = 'Company Code and Plant'.
CALL SELECTION-SCREEN 500 STARTING AT 10 10.
T1 = ' Purchase and Item Number '.
CALL SELECTION-SCREEN 1000 STARTING AT 10 10.
*-----------------------------------------------------*
```

LISTING 10.4 **Calling selection screen**

In Listing 10.3, the standard and user-defined selection screens are defined. In this case, the screen number allotted to the user-defined selection screen is 500. This user-defined selection screen is displayed as a modal dialog box because of the `AS WINDOW` clause. Moreover, the user-defined selection screen also contains the `BOX1` block of the standard selection screen. The title of the block of the standard selection screen is defined in the `INITIALIZATION` event, whereas the title for the block of the user-defined selection screen is defined in the `START-OF-SELECTION` event.

The output of Listing 10.4 is shown in Figure 10.124:

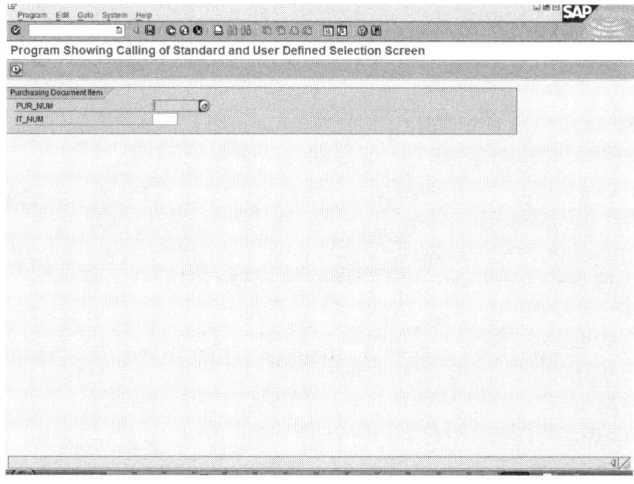

FIGURE 10.124 **The standard selection screen**

In Figure 10.124, you see the `Purchasing Document Item` group box containing two parameters, `PUR_NUM` and `IT_NUM`. Click the Execute (⊕) icon on the screen (see Figure 10.124). The user-defined selection screen numbered as 500 is displayed as a modal dialog box, as shown in Figure 10.125:

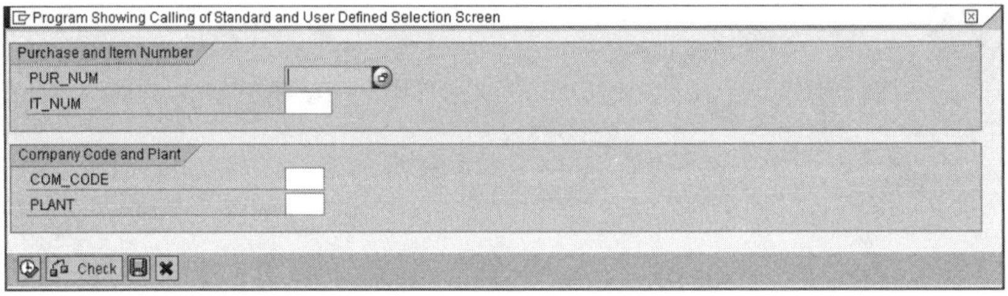

Program Showing Calling of Standard and User Defined Selection Screen
Purchase and Item Number
PUR_NUM
IT_NUM
Company Code and Plant
COM_CODE
PLANT
Check

FIGURE 10.125 **The user-defined selection screen**

The `Program Showing Calling of Standard and User Defined Selection Screen` screen includes two group boxes, `Purchase and Item Number` and `Company Code and Plant`. The `Purchase and Item Number` group box contains PUR_NUM and IT_NUM fields. The `Company Code and Plant` group box contains COM_CODE and PLANT fields.

Again, click the `Execute` (⊕) icon (see Figure 10.125). A standard selection screen is called again. However, this time, the standard selection screen is called as a modal dialog box because of the `AT STARTING` clause. There is no provision to define the standard selection screen as a modal dialog box. Figure 10.126 displays a selection screen in the form of a modal dialog box:

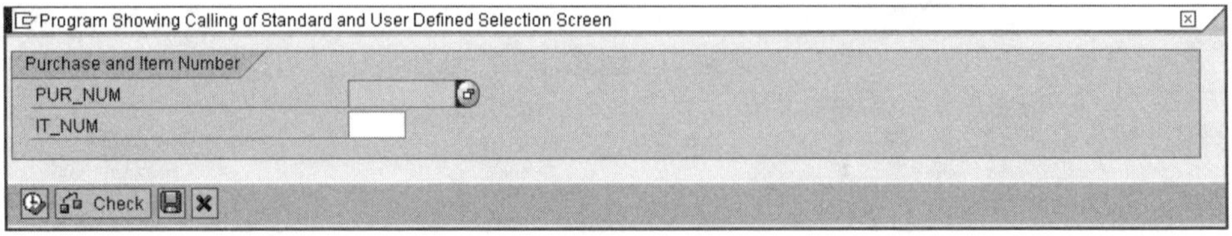

Program Showing Calling of Standard and User Defined Selection Screen
Purchase and Item Number
PUR_NUM
IT_NUM
Check

FIGURE 10.126 **Output after calling the standard selection screen as a modal dialog box**

In Figure 10.126, you see the `Program Showing Calling of Standard and User Defined Selection Screen` modal dialog box that contains the `Purchase and Item Number` group box and the PUR_NUM and IT_NUM fields.

Processing Selection Screens

As already mentioned, you design a selection screen only when you want the screen to accept input values. The processing of selection screens is handled totally by the ABAP runtime environment. The ABAP runtime environment provides different selection screen events, such as `AT SELECTION-SCREEN OUTPUT`, which are used by ABAP programmers to modify the selection screen before display. In addition, the ABAP runtime environment includes other events used to handle the selection screen after a user has executed different actions on the selection screen, such as:

- `AT SELECTION-SCREEN.`
- `AT SELECTION-SCREEN ON <field>.`
- `AT SELECTION-SCREEN ON BLOCK <block>.`
- `AT SELECTION-SCREEN ON RADIOBUTTON GROUP <radi>.`
- `AT SELECTION-SCREEN ON <seltab>.`

Programmers do not have access to the flow logic of the selection screen; that is, no dialog modules can be defined for selection screens. Different event blocks can be defined by a programmer in an ABAP program corresponding to a selection screen event. The most basic selection screen event is the `AT SELECTON SCREEN` event, which is used when the ABAP runtime environment passes all the data from the selection screen to the ABAP program for further processing. On the other hand, other selection screen events are used to change the selection screen before display and specially check the input entered by a user.

The events related to a selection screen occur during the processing of the standard and user-defined selection screens. The processing of the selection screens occurs after the `INITIALIZATION` event is executed with the `AT SELECTION SCREEN OUTPUT` clause. The `SY-DYNNR` system variable contains the number of the active selection screens and helps determine the currently processing selection screen.

SUMMARY

In this chapter, you have learned about dialog programming, which consists of screens. A screen consists of different kinds of screen elements and flow logic related to the screens. The flow logic actually manages the sequence in which the screens have to be executed. These screens are designed with the help of a tool called Screen Painter. Further, you have learned how to create complex graphical elements such as tabstrip and table controls. Next, you have learned how to create the GUI Status, which includes a menu bar, an application toolbar, and function keys related to the screen. The GUI Status is created by using a tool called Menu Painter. You have also learned how to create screens used to accept user input—that is, the selection screen. You have also learned to define standard selection screens and user-defined selection screens. The method to call the defined selection screens is also discussed in detail. Finally, you have learned about the different events used to process the selection screen.

Chapter 11

The BDC and LSMW Tools

If you need information on:	*See page:*
The Data Transfer Techniques	646
Data Transfer Methods	649
Data Transfer by Using the BDCDATA Structure	652
The Legacy System Migration Workbench Tool	697

At times, you might need to transfer legacy data files from one SAP system to another or from a non-SAP system to an SAP system. Batch Data Communication (BDC) and Legacy System Migration Workbench (LSMW) are two migration tools used to transfer data in the SAP system. BDC uses some methods, such as the session and call transaction methods, to transfer data from one SAP system to another or from a non-SAP system to an SAP system. It is used to transfer data through SAP transactions. This means when you use the BDC tool for data transfer, the sequence of steps is the same as when you use standard SAP transaction screens to upload data. The only difference is that you can use different options for foreground and background processing.

The LSMW tool, on the other hand, is used to migrate legacy data from a non-SAP system to an SAP system. It provides various options, such as batch input, direct input, BAPIs, and IDocs to import legacy data into an SAP system. Some examples of legacy data are text files, Microsoft Excel sheets, and Comma Separated Values (CSV) files. The LSMW tool converts the legacy data into batch input files automatically. However, if you use the BDC tool, you have to write your batch input file manually, line by line. The BDC tool provides a collection of batch input functions so that you can write your own batch input file. On the other hand, the LSMW tool opens a wizard by which you can create batch input files. Note that a wizard can handle only some specific formats of files, such as Excel and CSV files, but not all file formats. You need to use the BDC method to transfer files not supported by LSMW.

In this chapter, you learn about BDC and LSMW. The chapter starts by explaining various techniques to transfer external data into an SAP system. Next, the chapter explores various data transfer methods. Then, you learn how to transfer external data into an SAP system by using BDCDATA structure. Finally, we discuss the BDC and LSMW tools in detail.

THE DATA TRANSFER TECHNIQUES

Data can be uploaded into an SAP system with some predefined standard data transfer techniques. Depending on the requirements of the user, the data can be transferred directly, through a batch input session, or by using the BAPI technique. The following are the three types of standard data transfer techniques employed:

- The batch input technique
- The direct input technique
- The BAPI technique

The Batch Input Technique

In the batch input technique, data is transferred through a batch input session. For this, a batch input session first is created by the data transfer program (also known as the batch input program). This batch input session holds all the transferable data related to a transaction. This data is then processed and transferred to the SAP system.

The following are some of the benefits of the batch input technique:

- Facilitates transfer of large sets of data from a non-SAP system to an SAP system or between two SAP systems.
- Allows periodic data transfer at regular intervals, such as hourly or monthly.
- Needs less monitoring as compared to other techniques. Only a periodic check made by the system administrator is sufficient to ensure that all the batch input sessions are running properly.

Figure 11.1 shows the sequence of steps required to process the batch input technique:

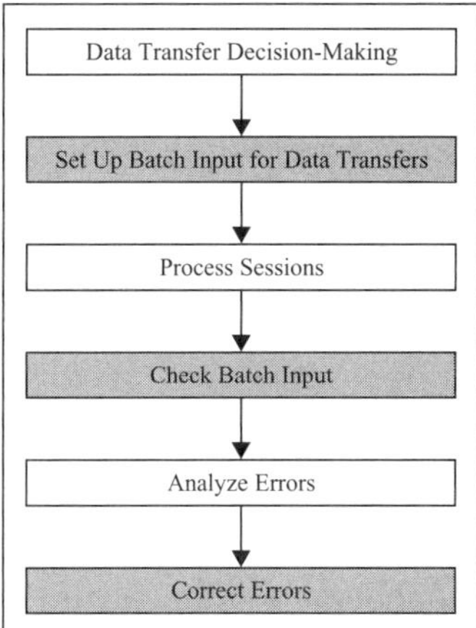

FIGURE 11.1 **Process flow in the batch input technique**

Now, let's discuss each of these steps in detail.

Data Transfer Decision-Making

The batch input process begins only after the decision to transfer data related to a transaction from an external source to an SAP system is made. The external source from where the data is transferred can be a legacy system or any other external system. For example, the data related to the customers in the older versions of SAP systems can be transferred to a new SAP system with the batch input process.

Set Up Batch Input for Data Transfers

The data related to a transation can be entered in an SAP system either all at once or in small chunks at regular intervals. The manner in which data is transferred can be set with the help of customization settings in the SAP customization system.

Process Sessions

The data to be transfered in an SAP system is maintained in the batch input session. Running any batch input session means executing the transactions stored in the sessions and finally transferring the data into an SAP system. Usually, the SAP system automatically executes the batch input sessions; however, the data can also be processed with the `SM35` transaction code. A batch input session is processed in the following three modes:

- **Process/foreground mode**—Specifies that you can interactively correct the incorrect transactions.
- **Background mode**—Specifies that you want to process the session in the background.
- **Display errors-only mode**—Specifies that transactions that are not yet processed and do not have any errors can be run non-interactively. If an error occurs in a transaction, the processing of the session stops and the screen on which the error has occurred is displayed.

Check Batch Input

The system administrator checks whether all the batch input sessions are running successfully. This check can be performed with the help of the `SM35` transaction code provided by SAP.

Analyze Errors

In the Analyze Errors step, the system administrator analyzes the errors that have occurred while processing the transactions.

Correct Errors

After analyzing the errors, they need to be corrected, which is done by the combined effort of the system administrator and the department associated with the data transfer. The batch input system ensures that the processed transactions in a session are not executed again.

The Direct Input Technique

In the direct input technique of data transfer, the data to be transferred into an SAP system is stored in a data transfer file. This data transfer file is then checked to verify whether it meets certain criteria for data transfer, such as the format of data being transferred. If the criteria assigned by the SAP system are met, the data is transferred directly into the SAP system and the database of the SAP system is updated. The following are the two ways in which the direct input technique can be triggered:

- **Starting the program directly**—In this case, the system does not generate an error log. Moreover, it is not possible to restart the system if an error occurs.
- **Processing the data in the background**—In this case, if any logical error occurs during the processing of data, or the program performing the data transfer ends abruptly, the processing of data can be restarted in the background. In background processing, the input file is not stored on the application server.

In the direct input technique of data transfer, the load on the SAP system is reduced because no data can be transferred twice in the SAP system.

The BAPI Technique

A `BAPI` is a set of standard programming interfaces that provide access to the different business processes and data used in a business application system, such as SAP. Apart from accessing different business processes running within a business application system, BAPIs define their own interfaces. These interfaces are implemented outside the SAP system in such a way that they can be called from different external systems or applications developed by different customers.

DATA TRANSFER METHODS

In an SAP system, various methods and techniques are used to transfer data. In this section, we explore certain predefined methods that facilitate easy transfer of data in an SAP system:

- The direct input method
- The call transaction method
- The batch input with sessions method

The Direct Input Method

The direct input method generally is used when you need to transfer a large amount of data directly into an SAP system. In this method, a number of function modules are called to transfer data directly to the database of an SAP system. These function modules also make relevant checks to avoid any kind of errors during data transfer. If an error occurs, the error is fixed with the help of a restart mechanism. However, to activate this mechanism, direct input programs must be executed in the background. Table 11.1 lists some predefined direct input programs:

Direct Input Programs	Application
RFBIBL00	Designed for finance (FI) applications
RMDATIND	Designed for material management (MM) applications
RVAFSS00	Designed for sales and distribution (SD) applications
RAALTD11	Designed for asset management (AM) applications
RKEVEXT0	Designed for controlling (CO) applications

TABLE 11.1 Direct input programs

The Call Transaction Method

In the call transaction method, an ABAP program is created to transfer data. This ABAP program uses an ABAP statement, `CALL TRANSACTION USING`, to run an SAP transaction. In this method, the data to be transferred does not need to be stored in a session for later processing. Instead, the entire processing takes place directly with the ABAP program. The call transaction method transfers data quicker than the batch input with session method, which we discuss next.

The Batch Input with Session Method

In the batch input with session method, an ABAP program first reads the external data that is to be transferred to an SAP system. This data is then stored in a batch input session (also known as a session) created by the ABAP program. This session uses SAP transactions to record all the actions required to transfer data into an SAP system. The transactions in the generated sessions are executed whenever the session is processed.

A session can be monitored easily with the batch input management function. You can start the batch input management function by selecting `System>Services>Batch Input` from the `SAP Easy Access` screen.

Table 11.2 lists the differences between the call transaction method and the batch input with session method:

Parameter	Call Transaction Method	Batch Input with Session Method
Data processing	The data is processed synchronously.	The data is processed asynchronously.
Data transfer	The data from an individual transaction is transferred each time the `CALL TRANSACTION USING` statement is called.	The data can be transferred from many transactions at a time.
Data update in the SAP database	The data can be updated in the database of the SAP system both synchronously and asynchronously.	The data can be updated in the database of the SAP system synchronously.
Processing log	No processing log is created for the batch input to be transferred.	A batch input processing log is generated for a session.

TABLE 11.2 Comparing the call transaction and batch input with session method

DATA TRANSFER BY USING THE BDCDATA STRUCTURE

The data to be transferred in an SAP system is first processed by a call transaction or a batch input session method. For this, you must first create an internal table. This internal table must be structured according to the predefined ABAP Dictionary structure named BDCDATA. The internal table stores the data that has to be transferred to an SAP system and all the actions needed to process the required transactions. The following syntax shows how to declare an internal table in an ABAP program:

```
DATA: <bdc_internal_tab> LIKE BDCDATA OCCURS <occurs-parameter>
WITH HEADER LINE.
```

In this syntax, the `<bdc_internal_tab>` expression shows the name of the internal table. BDCDATA represents the predefined ABAP Dictionary structure of the internal table. This BDCDATA structure consists of five fields: PROGRAM, DYNPRO, DYNBEGIN, FNAM, and FVAL.

> **Note:** To learn more about internal tables, refer to Chapter 7.

Table 11.3 shows the BDCDATA structure with technical characteristics:

Field Name	Type	Length	Short Text
PROGRAM	CHAR	40	BDC module pool
DYNPRO	NUMC	4	BDC screen number
DYNBEGIN	CHAR	1	BDC screen start
FNAM	CHAR	132	BDC field name
FVAL	CHAR	132	BDC field content

TABLE 11.3 Structure of BDCDATA

Now, let's explore using the BDC tool to transfer data to an SAP system.

THE BDC TOOL

The BDC tool is the oldest batch input tool used to upload data into an SAP system. Note that the transfer of data is not bidirectional; that is, the data can only be transferred into an SAP system, not from the SAP system. The BDC tool works through an ABAP program and is based on the principle of simulating user input for transactional screens. This means that a model of all the data for different types of screens is created. The input is provided in the form of a text file, also known as a flat file. The created BDC program reads the flat file and formats the input data screen by screen into an internal table whose structure is similar to the structure of `BDCDATA`. The transaction is then started and processed in the background by using an internal table. Figure 11.2 shows how the data is transferred by using the BDC tool:

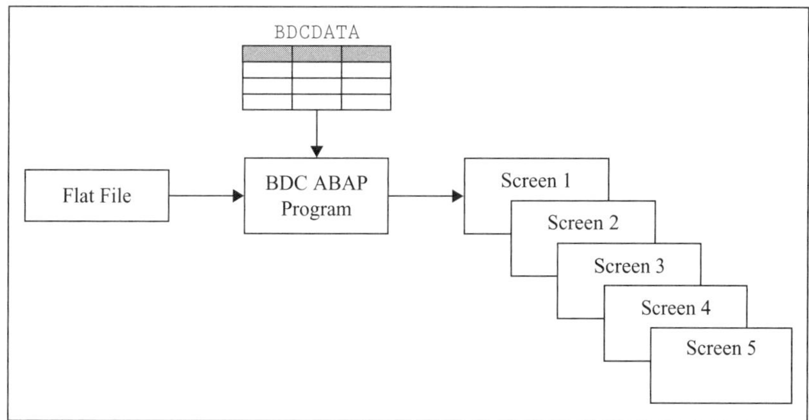

FIGURE 11.2 **BDC method**

The BDC tool can be run either by using the call transaction method or by using the batch input session method. Now, let's learn how to create a BDC program by using the call transaction method.

Creating a BDC Program by Using the Call Transaction Method

In the call transaction method, we transfer data related to a material, such as the name of the material, material number, and description of a material, into an SAP system. For this, we first create a flat file, which holds the data to be transferred to an SAP system. The flat file is then uploaded into the internal table, which is then mapped into the `BDCDATA` structure. Now, by using the `CALL TRANSACTION USING` statement in the ABAP program, the data is transferred from a non-SAP system to an SAP system in a particular transaction. In this case, the transaction related to material is MM01.

Perform the following steps to enable data transfer:

1. Open the initial screen of the batch input recorder from the `SAP Easy Access` screen by selecting `System>Services>Batch Input>Recorder`, as shown in Figure 11.3:

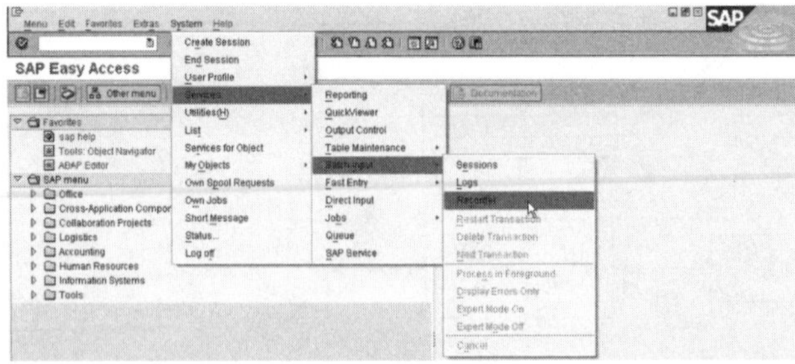

FIGURE 11.3 **Starting the transaction recorder screen**

> **Note:** An alternate way to start the initial screen of the batch input recorder is by entering the `SHDB` transaction code in the `Command` field on the standard toolbar and pressing the ENTER key or clicking the `Enter` ( ) icon, as shown in Figure 11.4.

FIGURE 11.4 **The transaction code in the command field**

The `Transaction Recorder` screen appears, as shown in Figure 11.5:

Recording	CreatedBy	Date	Time	Transact	Screens
FL_IDES	D027220	26.09.2006	11:59:40	130	650
MT_IDES	D046387	04.05.2006	11:34:29	15	105
KLON	GWOSDZIK	21.04.2005	16:09:44	1	2
ZIFM_PA30_1	HENLEY	10.05.2002	16:45:47	1	2
Z_BELMER01	CORRALES	14.02.2002	21:34:37	1	4
DAN	MCNULTY	12.02.2002	16:24:48	1	21
TEST1	BONIN	18.01.2000	16:47:50	1	5

FIGURE 11.5 **The initial screen of the transaction recorder**

Figure 11.5 shows the recording screen, where you record the transactions related to the material data. The screen displays an overview of the previously created recordings by different users.

2. Click the `New recording` button.

The `Create Recording` dialog box appears, as shown in Figure 11.6:

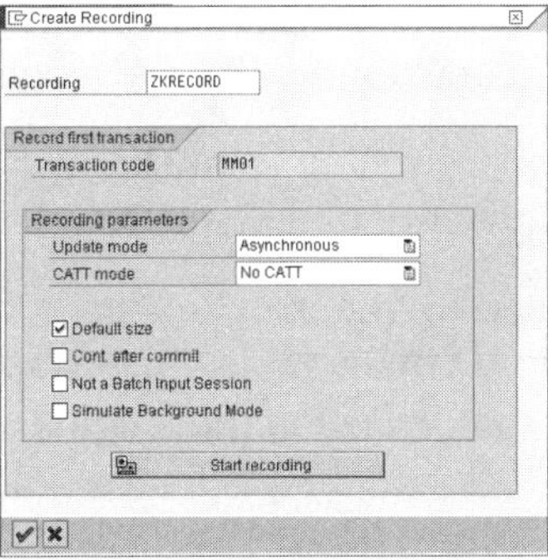

FIGURE 11.6 **The create recording dialog box**

3. Enter the name of the recording, say, ZKRECORD, in the `Recording field` and the transaction, MM01, in the `Transaction code` field. Click the `Start recording` button.

The `Create Material (Initial Screen)`screen appears, as shown in Figure 11.7:

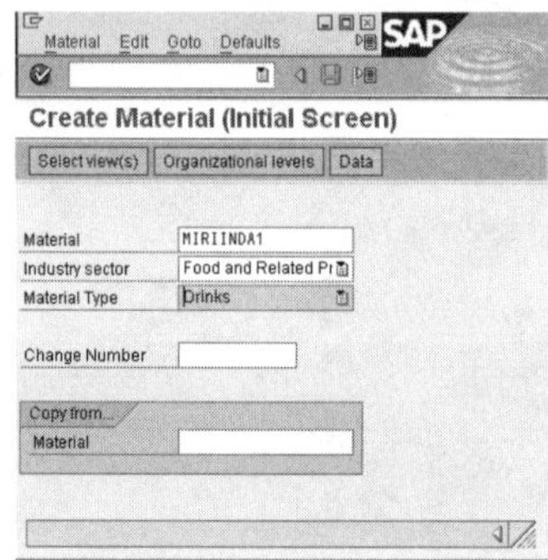

FIGURE 11.7 **The create material initial screen**

4. Enter the name of the material to be created in the `Material` field, say, MIRIINDA1.

The information related to the `Material` field, such as name, type, and length, is stored in the MARA table. In this case, the name of this field is MATNR, the type is character, the and the length is 18.

5. Select the appropriate sector from the drop-down list in the `Industry sector` field. In this case, we have selected Food and Related Products.

The information related to `Industry sector` field, such as name, type, and length, is stored in the MARA table. In this case, the name of this field is MBRSH, the type is character, and the length is 1.

6. Select the appropriate sector from the drop-down list in the `Material Type` field. In this case, we have selected Drinks as the material type.

The information related to the `Material Type` field, such as name, type, and length, is stored in the MARA table. In this case, the name for the `Material Type` field is MTART, the type is character, and the length is 4.

> **Note:** To view the information related to a particular field, place the cursor in that field and press the F1 key. A documentation for that field appears. Now, either press the F9 key or click the `Technical Information` ( ) icon to view the technical information related to that field.

7. Click the `Select view(s)` button (see Figure 11.7).

The `Select View(s)` dialog box appears, as shown in Figure 11.8:

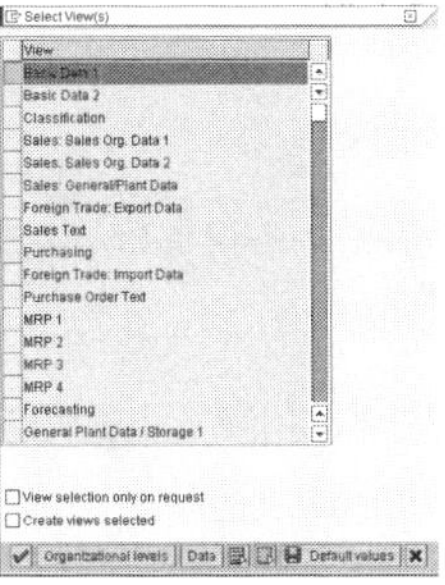

FIGURE 11.8 **The select views screen**

8. Select the `Basic Data1` option and click the `Continue` ( ) icon (see Figure 11.8).

The Create Material MIRIINDA (Drinks) screen appears, as shown in Figure 11.9:

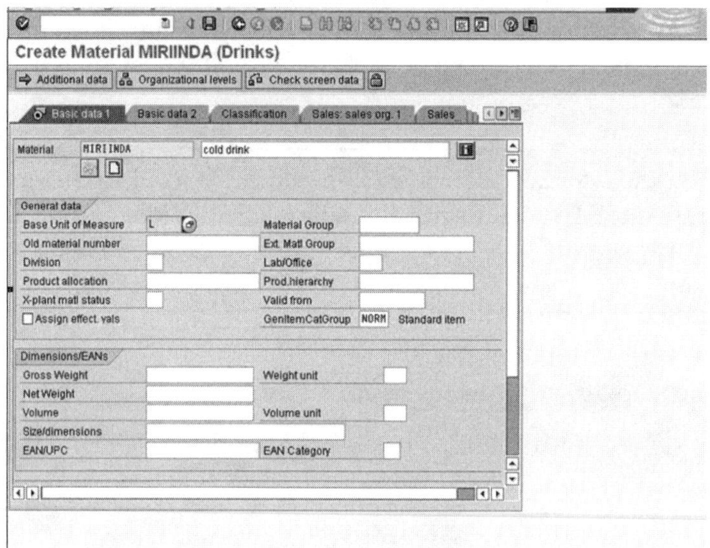

FIGURE 11.9 **The create material MIRIINDA (Drinks) screen**

9. Enter the description related to the MIRIINDA material in the text box beside the Material field. In this case, we have entered cold drink, as shown in Figure 11.9.

The information related to the description of the material, such as name, type, and length, is stored in the MAKTX table. In this case, the name of this field is MAKT, the type is character, and the length is 1.

10. Select the unit as L in the Base Unit of Measure field by clicking the Search help () icon (see Figure 11.9).

The information related to the description of the Base Unit of Measure, such as name, type, and length, is stored in the MARA table. In this this case, the name of this field is MEINS, the type is character, and the length is 3.

> **Note:** The number of fields that can be handled at a time is actually decided by the number of views that we select in the `Select View(s)` screen, as shown in Figure 11.8. In this case, we have selected Basic Data 1, so a maximum of five fields can be handled at a time.

11. Click the `Save` () icon (see Figure 11.9).

In the status bar, a message `Recording running` appears followed by the message `Recording complete; transaction has been transferred`.

The `Transaction Recorder: Change Recording ZKRECORD` screen appears.

12. Click the `Save` () icon on the Standard toolbar to save the information displayed in the screen, as shown in Figure 11.10:

Transaction Recorder: Change Recording ZKRECORD

Record Process

	Program	Screen	St	Field name	Field value
1			T	MM01	
2	SAPLMGMM	0060	X		
3				BDC_CURSOR	RMMG1-MATNR
4				BDC_OKCODE	=AUSW
5				RMMG1-MATNR	MIRIINDA
6				RMMG1-MBRSH	F
7				RMMG1-MTART	FGTR
8	SAPLMGMM	0070	X		
9				BDC_CURSOR	MSICHTAUSW-DYTXT(01)
10				BDC_OKCODE	=ENTR
11				MSICHTAUSW-KZSEL(01)	X
12	SAPLMGMM	0060	X		
13				BDC_CURSOR	RMMG1-MATNR
14				BDC_OKCODE	=AUSW
15				RMMG1-MATNR	MIRIINDA1
16				RMMG1-MBRSH	F
17				RMMG1-MTART	FGTR
18	SAPLMGMM	0070	X		
19				BDC_CURSOR	MSICHTAUSW-DYTXT(01)

FIGURE 11.10 **The transaction recorder: change recording ZKRECORD screen**

A message `Recording complete; transaction has been transferred` appears in the status bar. In addition to this, you see five different columns, `Program`, `Screen`, `Status`, `Field name`, and `Field value`.

13. Click the `Back` () icon (see Figure 11.10).

The `Transaction Recorder: Recording Overview` screen appears, as shown in Figure 11.11:

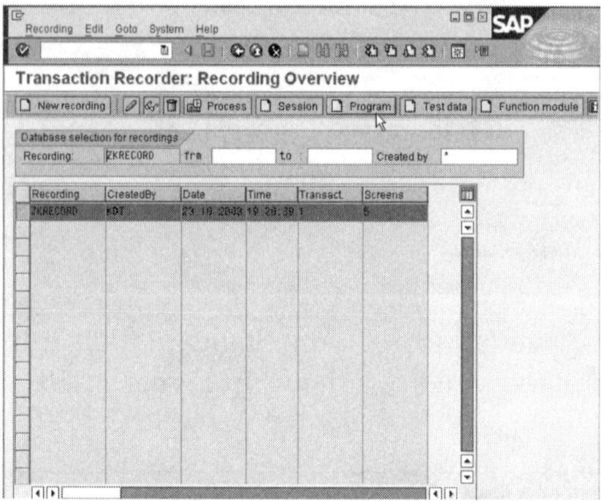

FIGURE 11.11 **The transaction recorder: recording overview screen**

14. Select the name of the recording (that is, ZKRECORD) and click the `Program` button, as shown in Figure 11.11.

The `Generate Program for Recording ZKRECORD` dialog box appears, as shown in Figure 11.12:

Generate Program for Recording ZKRECORD

Program Name ZKPROGRAM

Field contents
Read from file
Transfer from recording

Test data
Create
File name

FIGURE 11.12 **Creating a program**

15. Enter the name of the program, say, ZKPROGRAM, in the `Program Name` field, select the `Transfer from recording` radio button, and click the `Continue` (✔) icon (see Figure 11.12).

The `ABAP: Program Attributes ZKPROGRAM` dialog box appears, as shown in Figure 11.13:

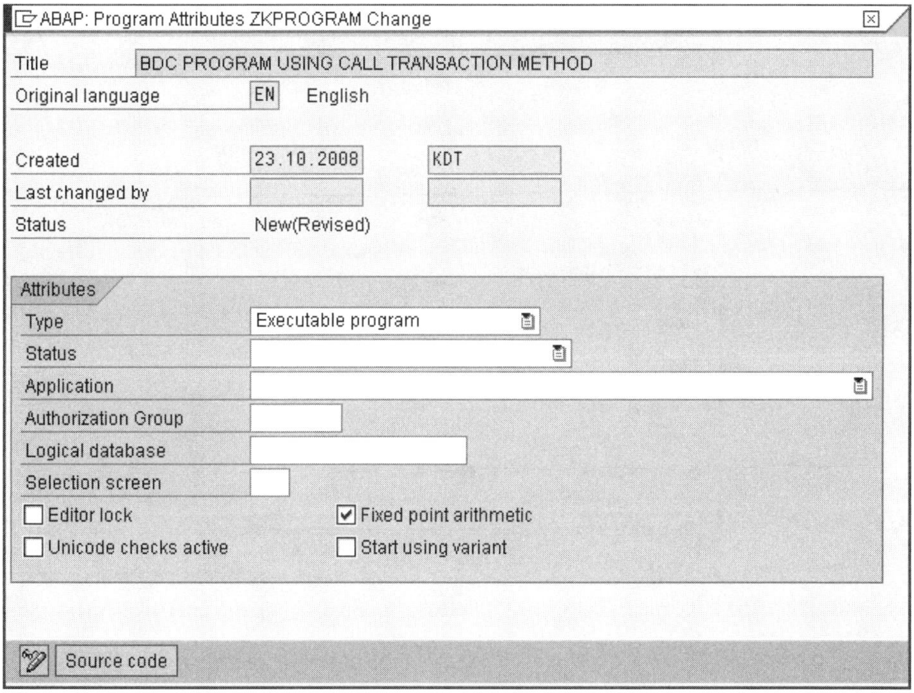

FIGURE 11.13 **The attributes dialog box related to the program**

16. Enter the title as BDC PROGRAM USING CALL TRANSACTION METHOD in the `Title` field and select the type as Executable program in the `Type` field (see Figure 11.13).
17. Click the `Source code` button and save the program in the package named ZKOG_PCKG.

The `ABAP Editor: Change Report ZKPROGRAM` screen appears, as shown in Figure 11.14:

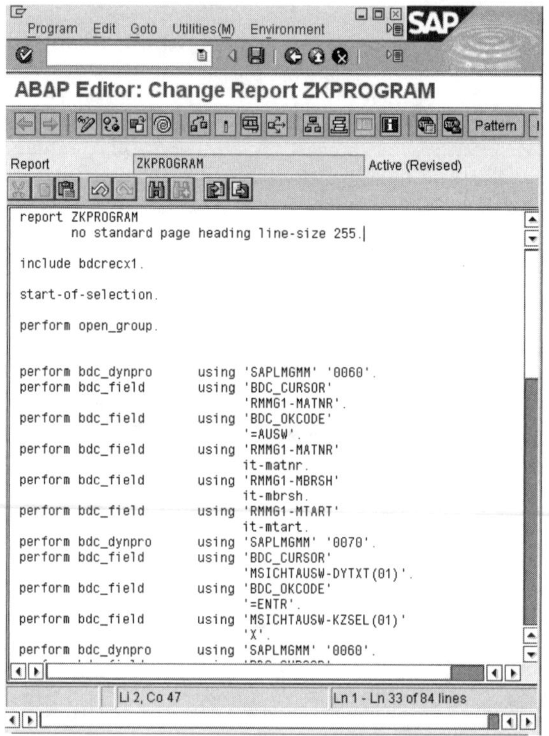

FIGURE 11.14 **Diaplaying the ABAP editor screen**

In Figure 11.14, some predefined statements appear for the data transfer program.

18. Double-click the included structure, named bdcrecx1, as shown in Figure 11.14.

The `ABAP Editor: Display Include BDCRECX1` screen appears, displaying different statements of the included structure, as shown in Figure 11.15:

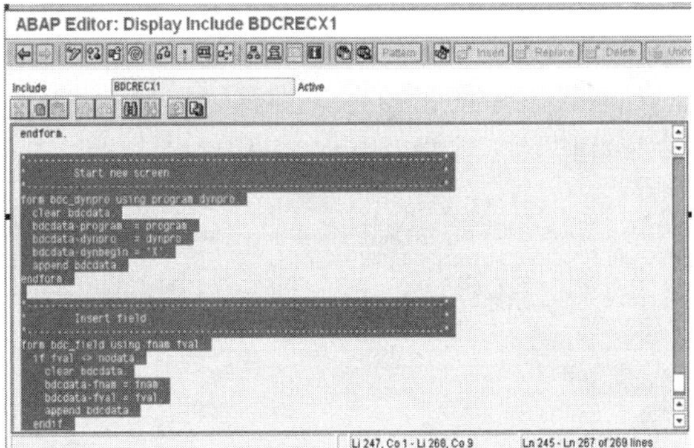

FIGURE 11.15 **Listing of the BDCREX1 structure**

19. Scroll down to the end of the page and copy two subroutines, named `form bdc_dynpro` using program dynpro and `form bdc_field` using fnam fval, as shown in Figure 11.15.
20. Click the `Back` (icon) icon (see Figure 11.15) to return to Figure 11.14.
21. Paste the copied subroutines at the end of the ZKPROGRAM program. Note that when the ZKPROGRAM program is executed by performing this action, every screen appears with the automatically populated values that have to be transferred to the SAP system, as shown in Figure 11.16:

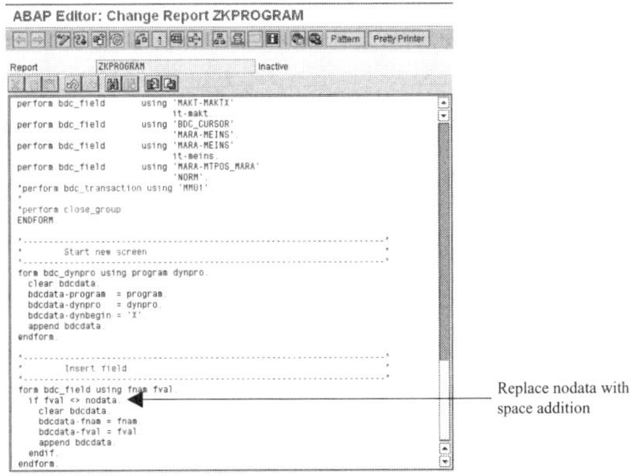

FIGURE 11.16 **Subroutines in the program**

22. Replace nodata in `form bdc_field` using fnam fval with the space addition, as shown in Figure 11.16.

The next screen appears, as shown in Figure 11.17:

```
perform bdc_field       using 'MARA-MEINS'
                              'L'.
perform bdc_field       using 'MARA-MTPOS_MARA'
                              'NORM'.
perform bdc_transaction using 'MM01'.

perform close_group.

*----------------------------------------------------------------*
*        Start new screen                                        *
*----------------------------------------------------------------*
form bdc_dynpro using program dynpro.
  clear bdcdata.
  bdcdata-program  = program.
  bdcdata-dynpro   = dynpro.
  bdcdata-dynbegin = 'X'.
  append bdcdata.
endform.

*----------------------------------------------------------------*
*        Insert field                                            *
*----------------------------------------------------------------*
form bdc_field using fnam fval.
  if fval <> space.
    clear bdcdata.
    bdcdata-fnam = fnam.
    bdcdata-fval = fval.
    append bdcdata.
  endif.
endform.
```


FIGURE 11.17 **The screen with changes**

23. Put an asterisk (*) before the statements that you do not want to execute. A statement preceded by an asterisk is treated as a comment and, therefore, is not executed (see Figure 11.18). In this case, we put an asterisk before the following statements:

    - `include bdcrecx1`
    - `start-of-selection`
    - `perform open_group`
    - `perform bdc_transaction using MM01`
    - `perform close_group`

24. Declare an internal table named IT, containing five fields and a `BDCDATA` structure, as shown in Figure 11.18:

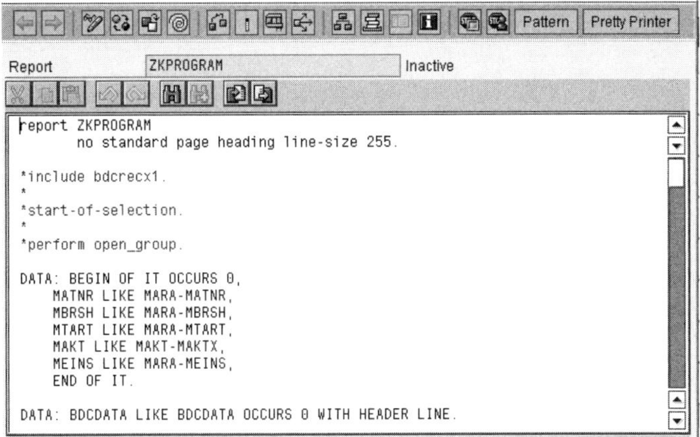

FIGURE 11.18 **Defining an internal table and declaring the BDCDATA structure**

25. Click the `Pattern` button (see Figure 11.18).

The `Ins. statement` dialog box appears, as shown in Figure 11.19:

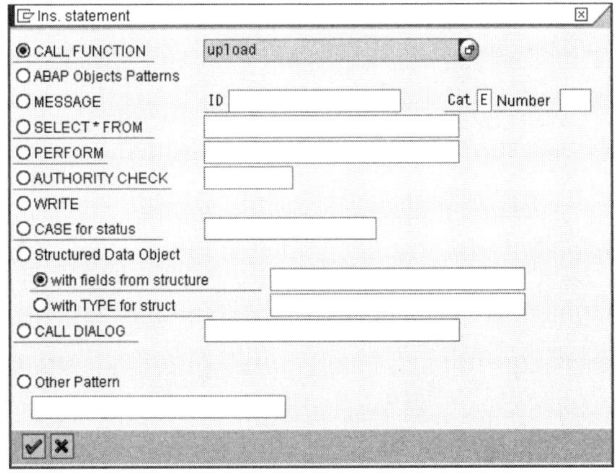

FIGURE 11.19 **Calling the function module**

26. Enter the name of the function module (that is, upload) in the `CALL FUNCTION` field and click the `Continue` (✔) icon (see Figure 11.19).

The `Information` dialog box appears, as shown in Figure 11.20:

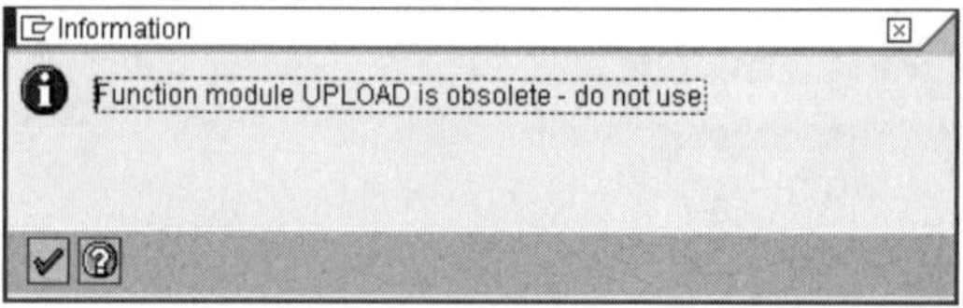

FIGURE 11.20 **The information dialog box**

27. Click the `Continue` (✔) icon (Figure 11.20).

The definition of the `UPLOAD` function module containing various options is displayed on the `ABAP Editor` screen, as shown in Figure 11.21:

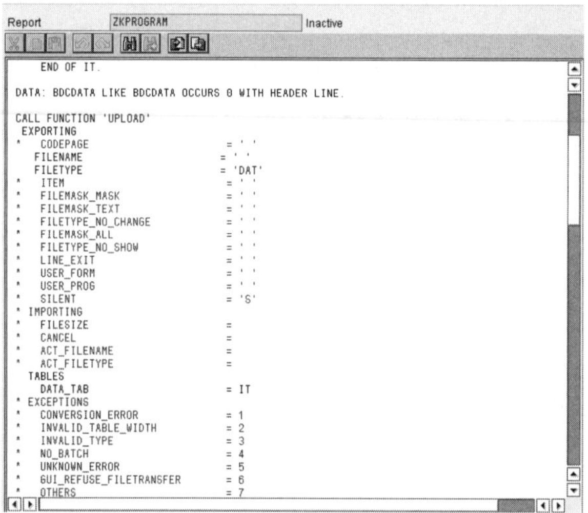

FIGURE 11.21 **Changes in the UPLOAD function**

28. Now, delete the asterisk (*) symbol from the `EXPORTING`, `FILENAME`, and `FILETYPE` options.

The `EXPORTING` option is uncommented to export the data from the external file to the internal table. The type of file that will be exported in this case is DAT, as shown in Figure 11.21.

29. Now, enter the following code snippet after the definition of the `UPLOAD` function module:

```
LOOP AT IT.
REFRESH BDCDATA.
PERFORM MAPPING.
CALL TRANSACTION 'MM01' USING BDCDATA MODE 'A'.
ENDLOOP.
```

Figure 11.22 shows the insertion of preceding code snippet after the definition of the `UPLOAD` function module:

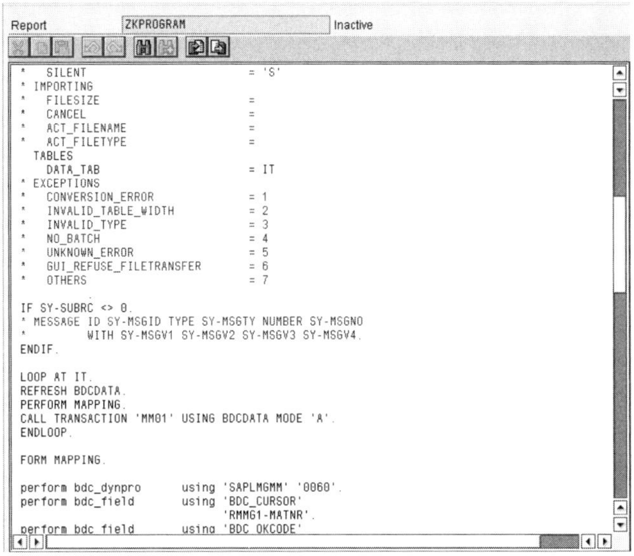

```
Report    ZKPROGRAM    Inactive

*   SILENT                       = 'S'
* IMPORTING
*   FILESIZE                     =
*   CANCEL                       =
*   ACT_FILENAME                 =
*   ACT_FILETYPE                 =
  TABLES
    DATA_TAB                     = IT
* EXCEPTIONS
*   CONVERSION_ERROR             = 1
*   INVALID_TABLE_WIDTH          = 2
*   INVALID_TYPE                 = 3
*   NO_BATCH                     = 4
*   UNKNOWN_ERROR                = 5
*   GUI_REFUSE_FILETRANSFER      = 6
*   OTHERS                       = 7
          .
IF SY-SUBRC <> 0.
* MESSAGE ID SY-MSGID TYPE SY-MSGTY NUMBER SY-MSGNO
*         WITH SY-MSGV1 SY-MSGV2 SY-MSGV3 SY-MSGV4.
ENDIF.

LOOP AT IT.
REFRESH BDCDATA.
PERFORM MAPPING.
CALL TRANSACTION 'MM01' USING BDCDATA MODE 'A'.
ENDLOOP.

FORM MAPPING.

perform bdc_dynpro      using 'SAPLMGMM' '0060'.
perform bdc_field       using 'BDC_CURSOR'
                              'RMMG1-MATNR'.
perform bdc_field       using 'BDC_OKCODE'
```


FIGURE 11.22 **Displaying code insertion after the UPLOAD function module**

30. Now, in the definition of the subroutine named MAPPING, replace all the content, such as MIRIINDA, F, FGTR, cold drink, and L, with the corresponding fields of the internal tables; that is, it-matnr, it-mbrsh, it-mtart, it-makt, and it-meins, respectively, as shown in Figure 11.23:

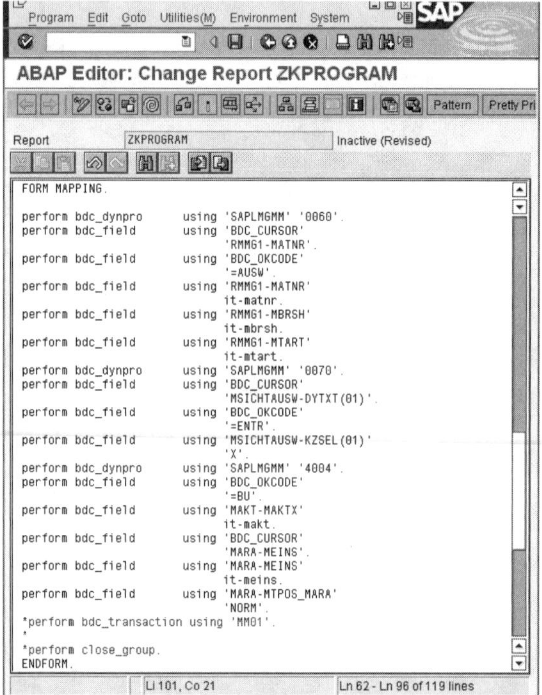

FIGURE 11.23 **Listing of a BDC program by using the call transaction method**

The content is replaced so that the data can be mapped from the flat file to the BDCDATA structure.

31. Click the `Save` (icon) icon, the `Check` (icon) icon, and the `Activate` (icon) icon (see Figure 11.23).
32. Click the `Direct Processing` (icon) icon.

The system now asks for the file name that is to be transferred into the SAP system, as shown in Figure 11.24:

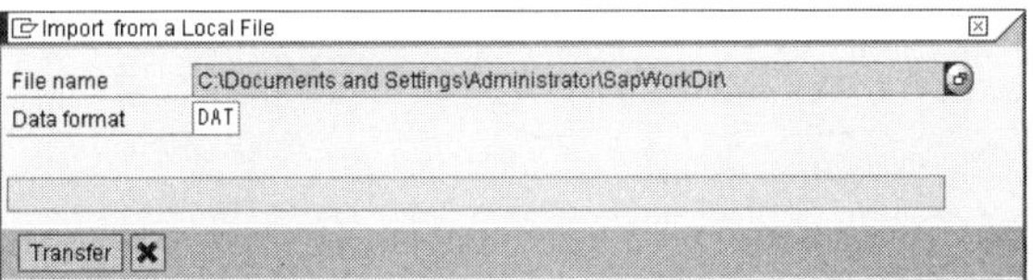

FIGURE 11.24 **The import from a local file screen**

In Figure 11.24, we need to enter the name of the file containing the data that has to be transferred to the SAP system. For this, we first create a file in a notepad.

33. Create a notepad file and save it at a particular location so that it can be uploaded easily. Figure 11.25 displays the notepad file:

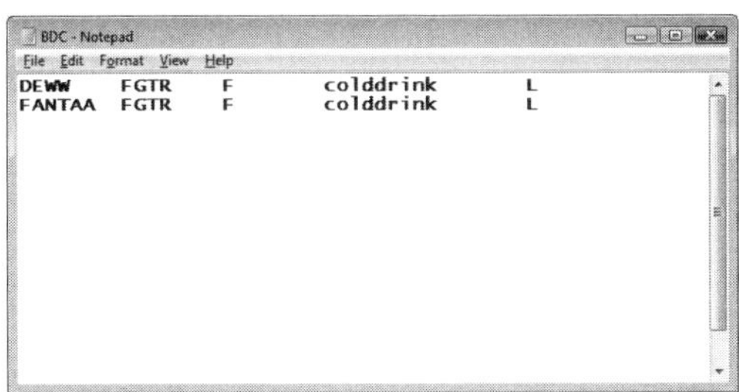

FIGURE 11.25 **The notepad file**

In the opened notepad file, we define the properties of two materials, DEWW and FANTAA, specifying the Industry sector as FGTR, Drinks as F, Material Description as colddrink, and the Basic unit of Measure as L.

34. Save this file. In this case, the file is saved as BDC on the desktop.
35. Now, click the `Search Help` ( ) icon, as shown in Figure 11.24.

The `Open` dialog box appears, as shown in Figure 11.26:

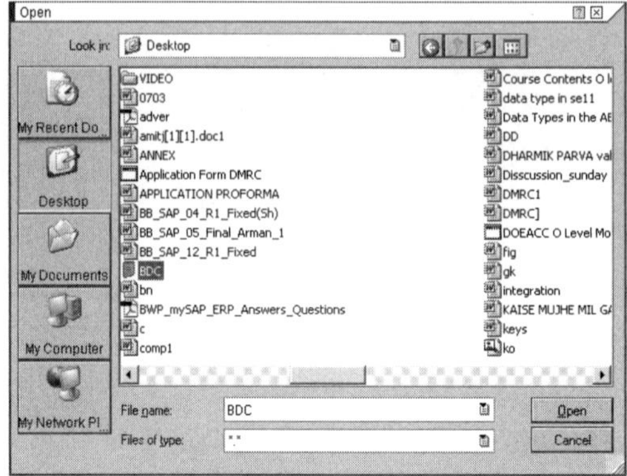

FIGURE 11.26 **Importing a file**

36. Select the name of the file from the stored location, as shown in Figure 11.26.
37. Click the `Open` button.

The `Import from a Local File` dialog box appears, with the address of the file in the `File name` field, as shown in Figure 11.27:

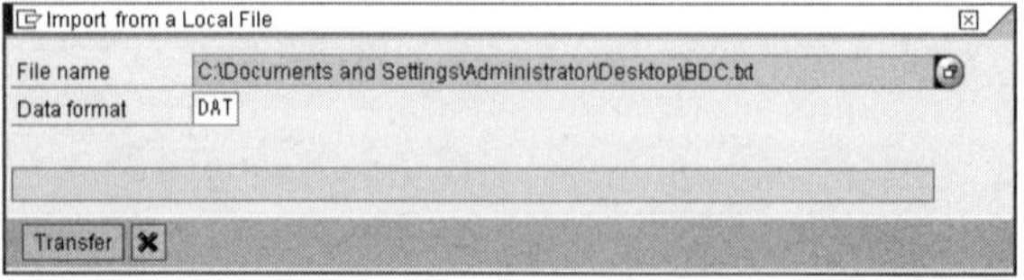

FIGURE 11.27 **Importing the BDC named text file**

38. Click the `Transfer` button (see Figure 11.27).

The `Create Material (Initial Screen)` screen appears, as shown in Figure 11.28:

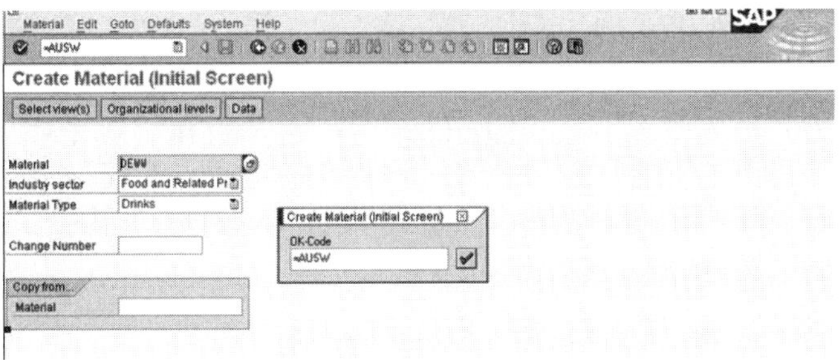

FIGURE 11.28 **The initial material screen**

In the `Create Material (Initial Screen)` screen, the first data entry of the notepad file (that is, DEWW, FGTR, F, colddrink, and L), gets transferred automatically to the respective fields, as shown in Figure 11.29. In addition, the `Create Material (Initial Screen)` dialog box showing the OK-Code for the screen is also displayed.

> **Note:** Whenever a user selects a function code (a sequence of 20 characters that can be assigned to the specific control elements of a user interface), the SAP system copies the function code into a field called the `OK-Code`.

39. Click the `Continue` (✔) icon in the the `Create Material (Initial Screen)` dialog box (see Figure 11.28).

The OK-Code value for the `Select View` dialog box (see Figure 11.8) is displayed, as shown in Figure 11.29:

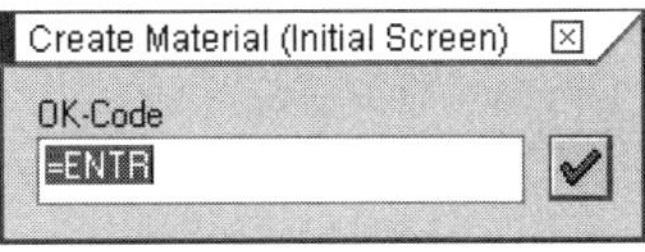

FIGURE 11.29 **OK-Code field**

40. Click the `Continue` (✔) icon.

The `Create Material MIRIINDA1 (Drinks)` screen appears, as shown in Figure 11.9.

41. Enter the description related to the material DEWW in the `Description` field and L in the `Basic unit of measure` field. Click the `Save` (💾) icon and then click the `Back` (◀) icon to perform the same sequence of steps for the second entry made in the notepad file; that is, FANTAA.

> **Note:** When you click the `Back` (◀) icon after saving the DEWW data, a message, such as `Material DEWW is created`, appears in the status bar.

42. To check whether or not the material has been created, open a new session by entering the `SE11` transaction code in the `Command` field. Figure 11.30 displays the initial screen of the ABAP Dictionary:

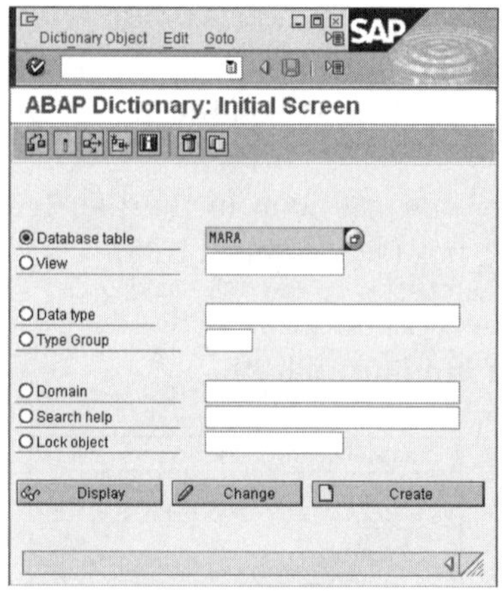

FIGURE 11.30 **The ABAP dictionary screen**

43. Enter MARA as the name of the table corresponding to the the data related to material, and click the `Display` button, as shown in Figure 11.30. The `Dictionary: Display table` screen appears, as shown in Figure 11.31:

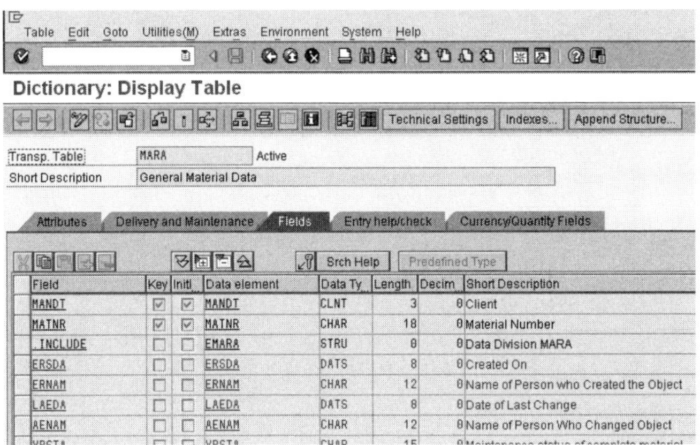

FIGURE 11.31 **Displaying the data fields of the MARA table**

44. Select `Utilities>Table Contents>Display`, as shown in Figure 11.32:

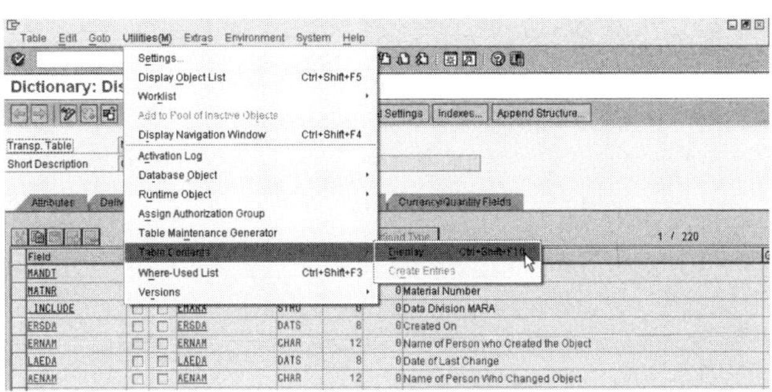

FIGURE 11.32 **Displaying the contents of MARA**

The `Data Browser:Table MARA: Selection Screen` screen appears, displaying all the contents related to the selected table, as shown in Figure 11.33:

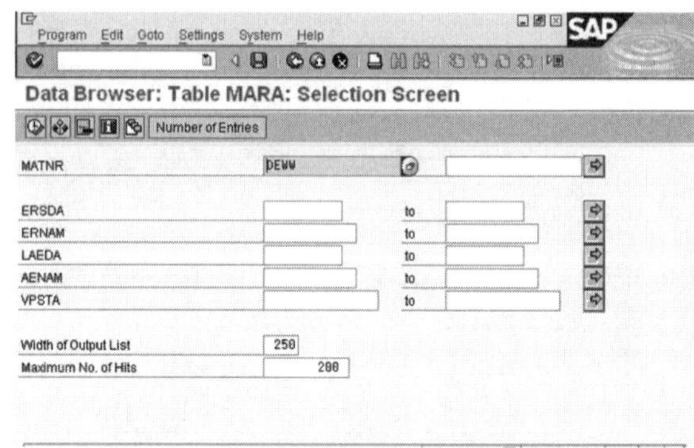

FIGURE 11.33 **The screen for displaying the content of MARA**

45. Enter the data to be searched in the MATNR field (that is, DEWW and FANTAA), and click the `Execute` (⊕) icon (see Figure 11.33).

Figure 11.34 shows that the DEWW data has been transferred from a non-SAP system to an SAP system:

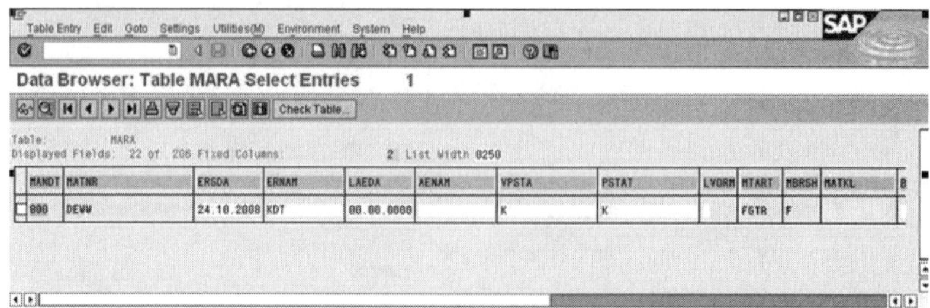

FIGURE 11.34 **The screen showing the transferred DEWW material in the SAP system**

Note: You can follow the same procedure to transfer the FANTAA data as well.

Transferring Data by Using the Batch Input with Session Method of BDC

The batch input with session method of BDC is used to transfer data to a transaction with the help of a session. In this case, we transfer data to ABAP Dictionary (transaction code `SE11`). The data is transferred to the ZSUBJECT_DATA database table. Perform the following steps to learn the procedure of data transfer:

1. Start the initial screen of the batch input recorder by using the `SHDB` transaction code. The `Transaction Recorder: Recording Overview` screen appears, displaying a list of all the previously generated recordings, as shown in Figure 11.35:

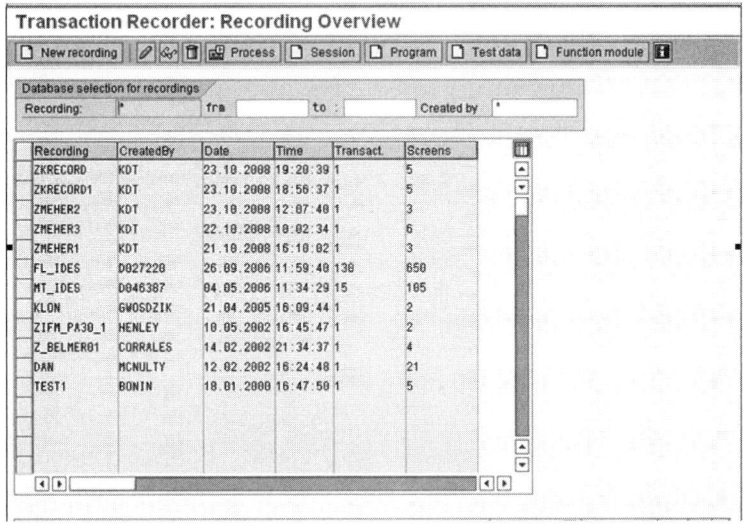

FIGURE 11.35 **The initial screen of recording**

2. Click the `New recording` button, as shown in Figure 11.35.

The Create Recording dialog box appears, as shown in Figure 11.36:

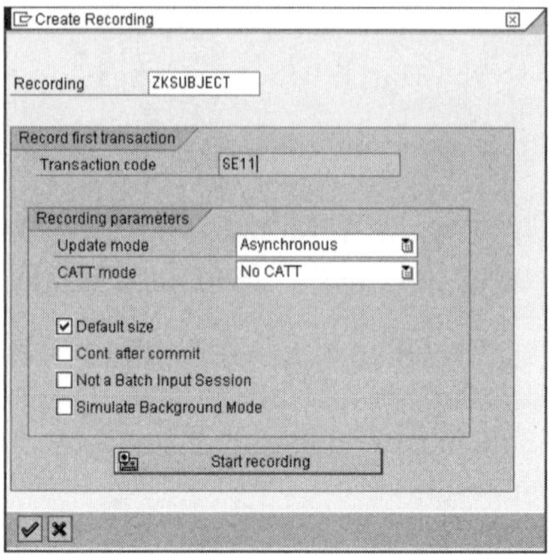

FIGURE 11.36 **Creating the recording screen**

3. Enter the name of the recording, say, ZKSUBJECT, and transaction code as SE11. Click the Start recording button, as shown in Figure 11.36.

The initial screen of the ABAP Dictionary appears.

4. Enter the name of the table as ZSubject_Data in the Database table field and then click the Change pushbutton. A message, Recording is running, appears in the status bar. The Dictionary: Maintain Table screen appears, as shown in Figure 11.37:

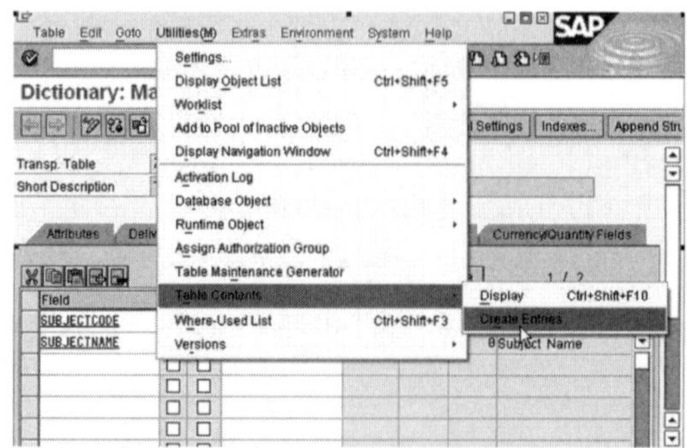

FIGURE 11.37 **Creating an entry**

5. Click Utilities (M)>Table Contents>Create Entries to create an entry in the ZSubject_Data table (see Figure 11.37).

The Table ZSUBJECT_DATA Insert screen appears, as shown in Figure 11.38:

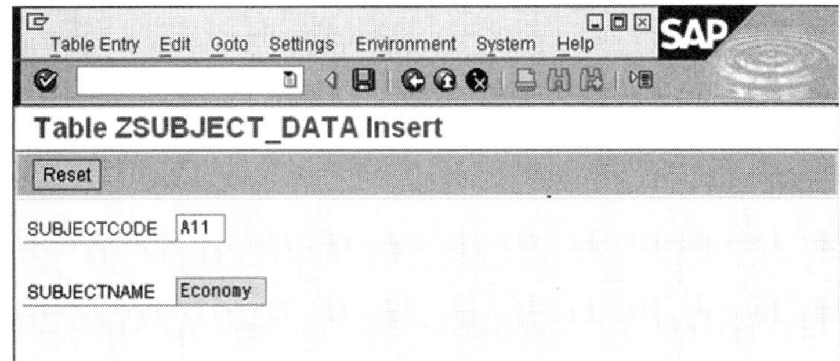

FIGURE 11.38 **Making an entry in the table ZSUBJECT_DATA**

6. Enter A11 in the SUBJECTCODE field and Economy in the SUBJECTNAME field. Click the Save (💾) icon (see Figure 11.38).
7. Click the Back (◀) icon (see Figure 11.38).

The Transaction Recorder: Change Recording ZKSUBJECT screen appears, as shown in Figure 11.39:

	Program	Screen	St	Field name	Field value
1			T	SE11	
2	SAPMSRD0	0102	X		
3				BDC_CURSOR	RSRD1-TBMA_VAL
4				BDC_OKCODE	=EDIT
5				RSRD1-TBMA	X
6				RSRD1-TBMA_VAL	ZSubject_Data
7	SAPLSD41	2200	X		
8				BDC_CURSOR	DD02D-DDTEXT
9				BDC_OKCODE	=TDED
10				DD02D-DDTEXT	Table Containing Subject Code with Subject Name
11				BDC_SUBSCR	SAPLSD41 2201TS_SCREEN
12	SAPLSP01	0300	X		
13				BDC_OKCODE	=CANC
14	SAPLSD41	2200	X		
15				BDC_CURSOR	DD02D-DDTEXT
16				BDC_OKCODE	=WB_SAVE
17				DD02D-DDTEXT	Table Containing Subject Code with Subject Name
18				BDC_SUBSCR	SAPLSD41 2201TS_SCREEN

FIGURE 11.39 **The recording screen**

Figure 11.39 shows the description of the screen, such as the screen name in the `Program` column, the number associated with each screen under the `Screen` column, the status under the `Status` column, and the value of each field under the `Field value` column.

8. Click the `Save` (💾) icon to save this recording (see Figure 11.39).

The message `Recording was saved` appears on the Status bar.

9. Click the `Back` (◀) icon (see Figure 11.39).

The `Transaction Recorder: Recording Overview` screen appears, as shown in Figure 11.40:

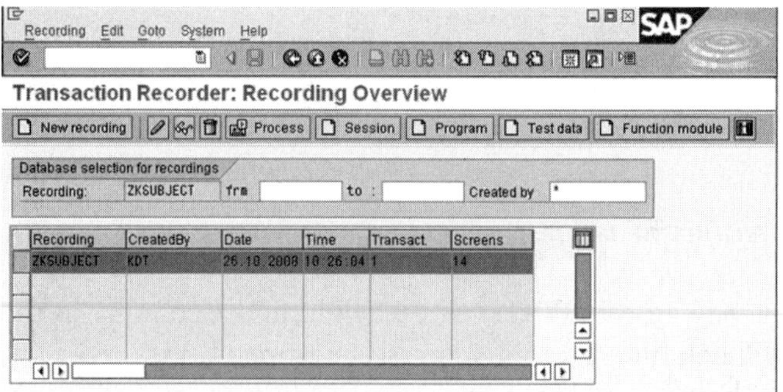

FIGURE 11.40 **Overview of the created recording**

10. Select the created recording (that is, ZKSUBJECT) and then click the `Program` button, as shown in Figure 11.40.

The `Generate Program for Recording ZKRECORD` dialog box appears, as shown in Figure 11.41:

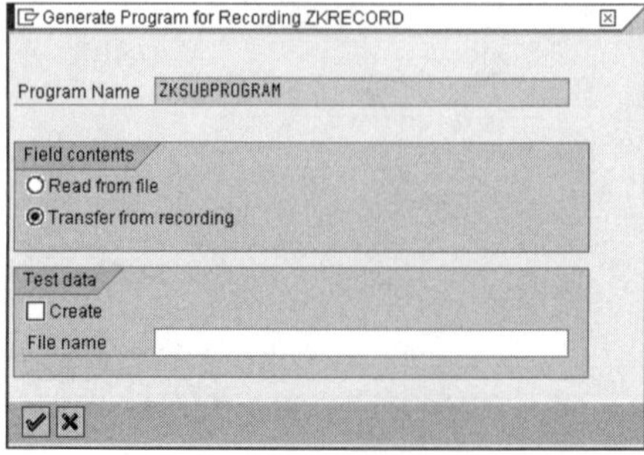

FIGURE 11.41 **The generate program for recording ZKRECORD**

11. Enter the name of the program, ZKSUBPROGRAM, in the `Program Name` field and select the `Transfer from recording` radio button. Click the `Continue` (☑) icon (see Figure 11.41).

The `ABAP: Program Attributes ZKSUBPROGRAM Change` dialog box appears, as shown in Figure 11.42:

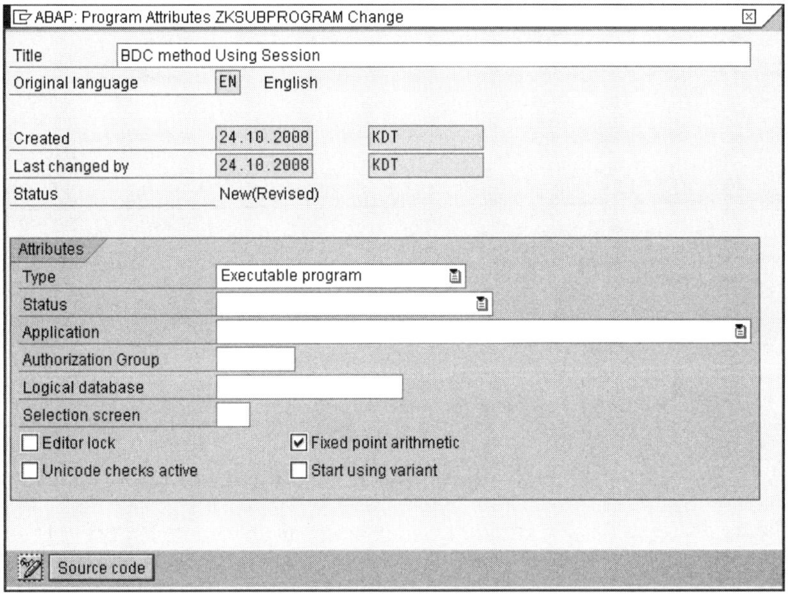

FIGURE 11.42 **The attributes screen related to the BDC program**

Figure 11.42 displays the screen where you assign the attributes related to the ZKSUBPROGRAM program.

12. Enter `BDC method Using Session` in the `Title` field and `Executable program` in the `Type` field.
13. Click the `Source code` button and save the program in a package. In this case, we have saved the program in a ZKOG_PCKG package.

The `ABAP Editor Change` screen appears.

Repeat steps 12 to 20 used in the BDC method by using the call transaction method. Note that when the internal table is declared, it includes only two fields because we transfer the data related to only two fields of the ZSUBJECT_DATA table. Figure 11.43 shows the internal table and BDCDATA structure:

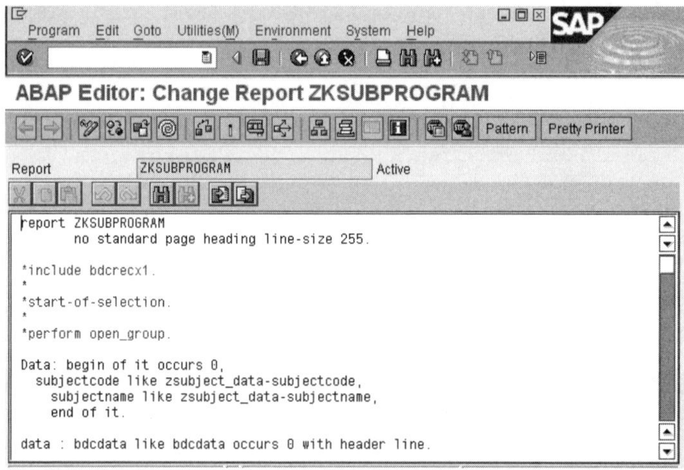

FIGURE 11.43 **Including the internal table and BDCDATA structure**

14. Click the `Pattern` button in ABAP Editor (see Figure 11.43).

The `Ins. statement` dialog box appears, as shown in Figure 11.44:

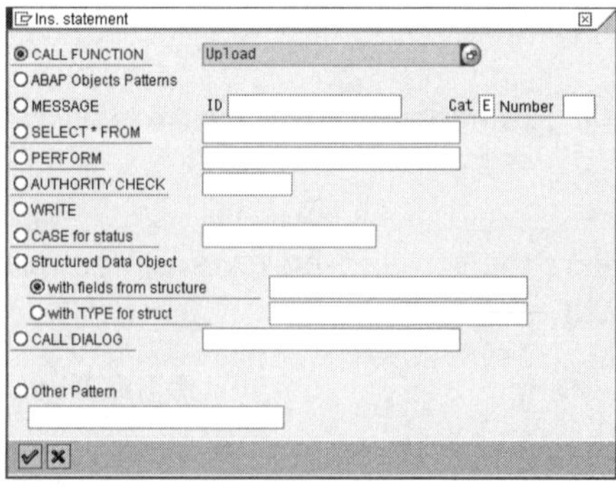

FIGURE 11.44 **Uploading function module**

15. Enter the name of the function module, Upload, which is to be uploaded in the ZKSUBPROGRAM program (Figure 11.44).

The definition regarding the `UPLOAD` function module appears in the code, as shown in Figure 11.45:

FIGURE 11.45 **The UPLOAD function module**

16. Uncomment the `EXPORTING`, `FILENAME`, and `FILETYPE` parameters by deleting the asterisk symbol. Write the name of the internal table in the `DATA_TAB` parameter (see Figure 11.45).
17. Click the `Pattern` button.

The `Ins. statement` screen appears again, as shown in Figure 11.44. Now, we include a function module named BDC_OPEN_GROUP, which is used to create a new session. Figure 11.46 shows the definition of the BDC_OPEN_GROUP function module in the editor screen:

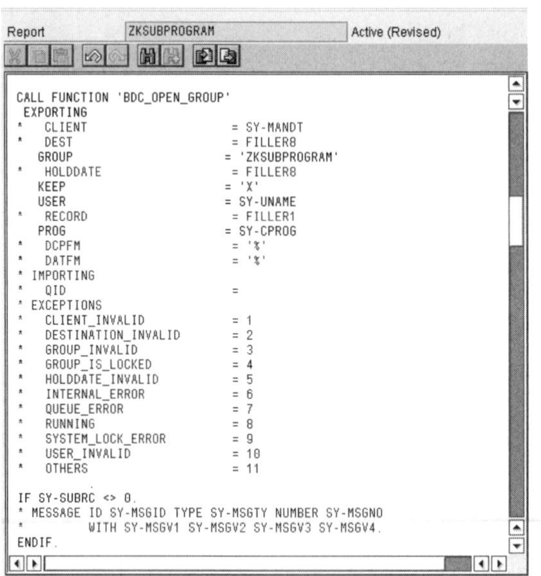

FIGURE 11.46 **The BDC_OPEN_GROUP function module**

18. Now, uncomment the `EXPORTING`, `GROUP`, `KEEP`, `USER`, and `PROG` parameters. Enter the name of the program, ZKSUBPROGRAM, for the `GROUP` parameter, X for the `KEEP` parameter, `SY-UNAME` for the `USER` parameter, and SY-CPROG for the `PROG` parameter, as shown in Figure 11.46.
19. Start a loop for the created internal table named IT to transfer the data one by one in an SAP system. Now, call a function named `BDC_INSERT` after writing the `PERFORM` statement by clicking the `Pattern` button on the application toolbar. Write the function name `BDC_INSERT` in the `CALL FUNCTION` field. The `BDC_INSERT` function module inserts the `SE11` transaction code to the batch input session. Figure 11.47 shows the definition of the `BDC_INSERT` function module:

```
IF SY-SUBRC <> 0.
* MESSAGE ID SY-MSGID TYPE SY-MSGTY NUMBER SY-MSGNO
*         WITH SY-MSGV1 SY-MSGV2 SY-MSGV3 SY-MSGV4.
ENDIF.

LOOP AT IT.
REFRESH BDCDATA.
PERFORM MAPPING.
CALL FUNCTION 'BDC_INSERT'
 EXPORTING
   TCODE                  = 'SE11'
*   POST_LOCAL            = NOVBLOCAL
*   PRINTING              = NOPRINT
*   SIMUBATCH             = ' '
*   CTUPARAMS             = ' '
  TABLES
   DYNPROTAB              = BDCDATA
* EXCEPTIONS
*   INTERNAL_ERROR        = 1
*   NOT_OPEN              = 2
*   QUEUE_ERROR           = 3
*   TCODE_INVALID         = 4
*   PRINTING_INVALID      = 5
*   POSTING_INVALID       = 6
*   OTHERS                = 7

IF SY-SUBRC <> 0.
* MESSAGE ID SY-MSGID TYPE SY-MSGTY NUMBER SY-MSGNO
*         WITH SY-MSGV1 SY-MSGV2 SY-MSGV3 SY-MSGV4.
ENDIF.
ENDLOOP.
```


FIGURE 11.47 **The function BDC_INSERT is called**

20. In the definition of the `BDC_INSERT` function module, uncomment the `EXPORTING`, `TCODE`, `TABLES`, and `DYNPROTAB` parameters and include the function module named `BDC_CLOSE_GROUP`.

Figure 11.48 shows the code with the definition of the `BDC_CLOSE_GROUP` function module:

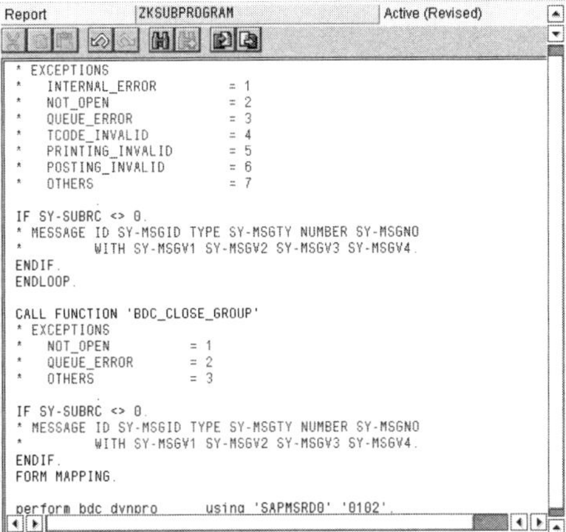

```
* EXCEPTIONS
*   INTERNAL_ERROR        = 1
*   NOT_OPEN              = 2
*   QUEUE_ERROR           = 3
*   TCODE_INVALID         = 4
*   PRINTING_INVALID      = 5
*   POSTING_INVALID       = 6
*   OTHERS                = 7

IF SY-SUBRC <> 0.
* MESSAGE ID SY-MSGID TYPE SY-MSGTY NUMBER SY-MSGNO
*         WITH SY-MSGV1 SY-MSGV2 SY-MSGV3 SY-MSGV4.
ENDIF.
ENDLOOP.

CALL FUNCTION 'BDC_CLOSE_GROUP'
* EXCEPTIONS
*   NOT_OPEN         = 1
*   QUEUE_ERROR      = 2
*   OTHERS           = 3

IF SY-SUBRC <> 0.
* MESSAGE ID SY-MSGID TYPE SY-MSGTY NUMBER SY-MSGNO
*         WITH SY-MSGV1 SY-MSGV2 SY-MSGV3 SY-MSGV4.
ENDIF.
FORM MAPPING.

perform bdc_dynpro      using 'SAPMSRD0' '0102'.
```


FIGURE 11.48 **The BDC_CLOSE_GROUP function module**

21. Now, type FORM MAPPING after the `ENDIF` statement, as shown in Figure 11.48. In the figure, FORM represents a type of statement and MAPPING represents the subroutine name. Write the `ENDFORM` statement in the `ABAP Editor: Change Report ZKSUBPROGRAM` screen, at the place shown in Figure 11.17.
22. Replace values A11 and Economy with the respective internal table fields named `it-subjectcode` and `it-subjectname` inside the definition of FORM MAPPING, as shown in Figure 11.49:

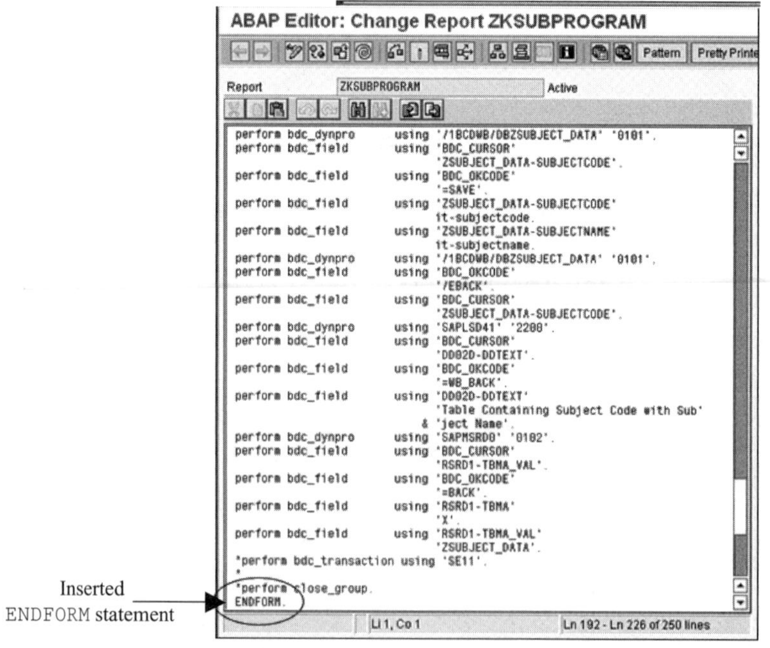

FIGURE 11.49 **Changing the content with the respective field names of the internal table**

23. Click the `Save` (💾) icon, the `Check` icon, and the `Activate` icon to activate the program.
24. Now, create a notepad file and store it in a particular location.

In this case, we create a notepad file session and store it on the desktop. This file contains data related to the subject code and subject name. The content of this file has to be transferred into the SAP system. Figure 11.50 shows the data contained in the session file:

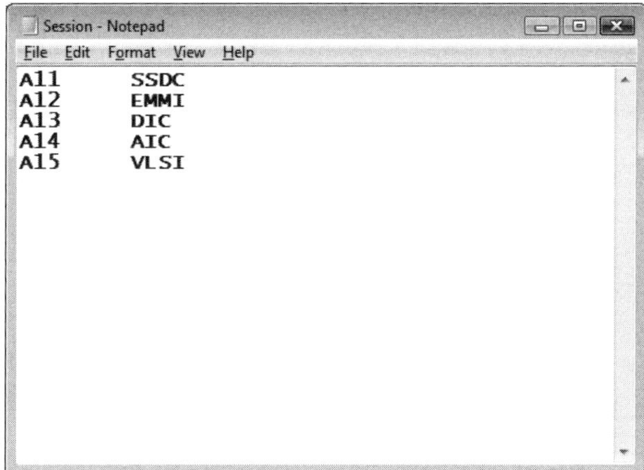

FIGURE 11.50 **The notepad file**

The session file consists of five subject names with their corresponding subject codes.

25. Click the `Direct Processing` (icon) icon (see Figure 11.49).

The `Import from a Local File` dialog box appears, as shown in Figure 11.51:

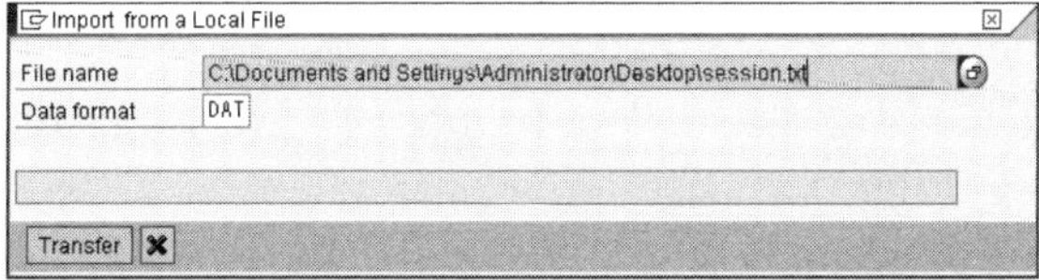

FIGURE 11.51 **Import from a local file**

26. Enter the location of the notepad file that is to be transferred into the SAP system and click the `Transfer` button (see Figure 11.51).

The message `Byte transferred` appears in the status bar.

27. Execute the transaction in a new session to check whether the batch input session has been created. Figure 11.52 shows the `Batch Input: Session Overview` screen, which displays the ZKSUBPROGRAM session name:

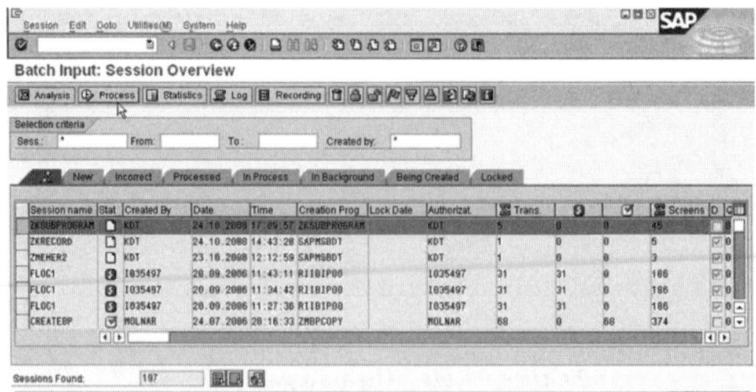

FIGURE 11.52 **The batch input session overview screen**

Figure 11.52 shows the transaction details, such as the name of the user under the `Created By` column, date on which the program was created under the `Date` column, the time at which the session was created under the `Time` column, and authorization information under the `Authorization` column.

28. Select the name of the session. In this case, we select ZKSUBPROGRAM, as shown in Figure 11.52.
29. Click the `Process` pushbutton (see Figure 11.52).

The `Process Session ZKSUBPROGRAM` dialog box appears, as shown in Figure 11.53:

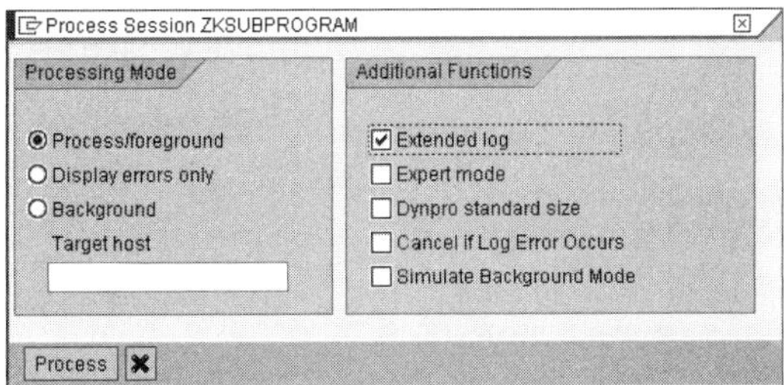

FIGURE 11.53 **Processing the created session**

30. Select the `Process/foreground` radio button and the `Extended log` check box. Click the `Process` button, as shown in Figure 11.53.

The initial screen of the ABAP Dictionary appears, as shown in Figure 11.54:

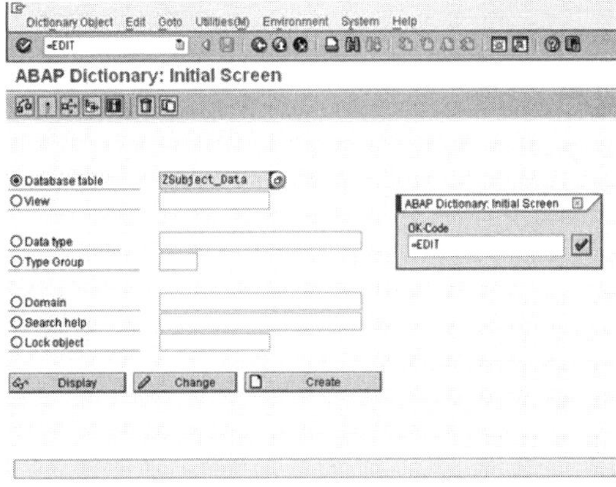

FIGURE 11.54 **The initial screen of the ABAP dictionary**

In the initial screen of ABAP Dictionary, the name of the table, ZSubject_Data, automatically appears in the `Database table` field. The associated OK-Code field (=EDIT) for the screen also appears.

31. Click the `Continue` (☑) icon.

The `Dictionary: Maintain Table` screen appears, as shown in Figure 11.55:

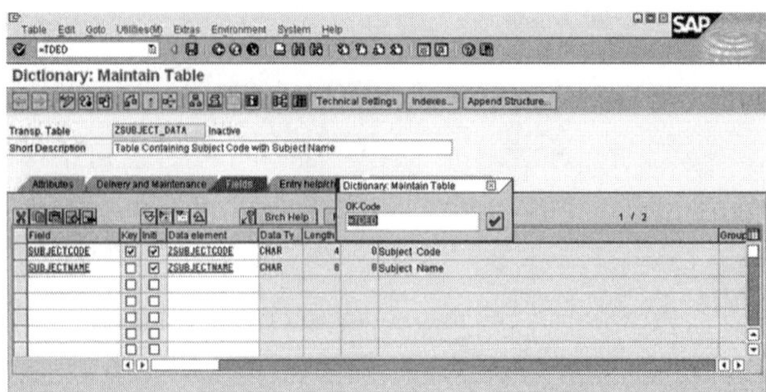

FIGURE **11.55 The screen showing the fields of the table**

Figure 11.55 displays the short description related to the ZSUBJECT_DATA table.

32. Click the `Continue` (☑) icon.

The `Call Data Browser` dialog box appears asking whether you want to save the ZSUBJECT_DATA table. Figure 11.56 displays the `Call Data Browser` dialog box:

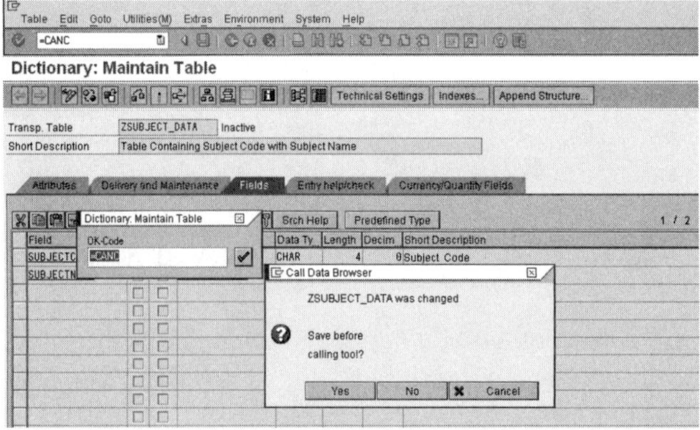

FIGURE 11.56 **The Ok-Code field for the maintain table**

The value of the OK-Code for the screen, =CANC, also appears (see Figure 11.56).

33. Click the `Continue` (☑) icon.

The `Dictionary: Maintain Table` screen appears, as shown in Figure 11.57:

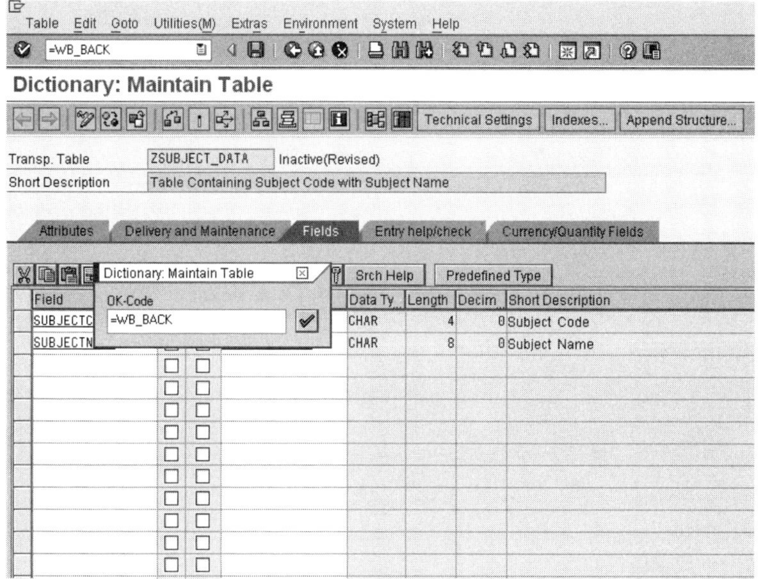

FIGURE 11.57 **The screen after saving with different OK-Code fields**

The value of the OK-Code for the screen, WB_BACK, is displayed.

34. Click the `Continue` (☑) icon.

The value of the OK-Code for the screen, =CANC, appears, as shown in Figure 11.56.

35. Click the `Continue` (☑) icon.

The `Dictionary: Maintain Table` dialog box appears, as shown in Figure 11.58:

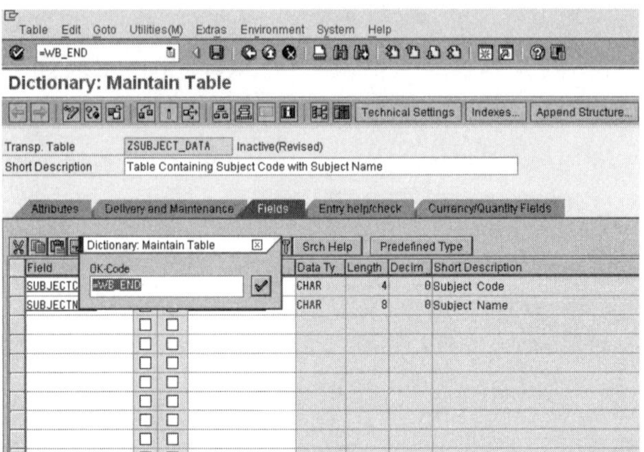

FIGURE 11.58 **The Ok-Code field**

36. Click the `Continue` (✔) icon.

The `Call Data Browser` dialog box appears, as shown in Figure 11.56.

37. Click the `Continue` (✔) icon for the screen containing the `OK-Code` field as =CANC (see Figure 11.56).

Now, the `Dictionary: Maintain Table` screen appears, as shown in Figure 11.59:

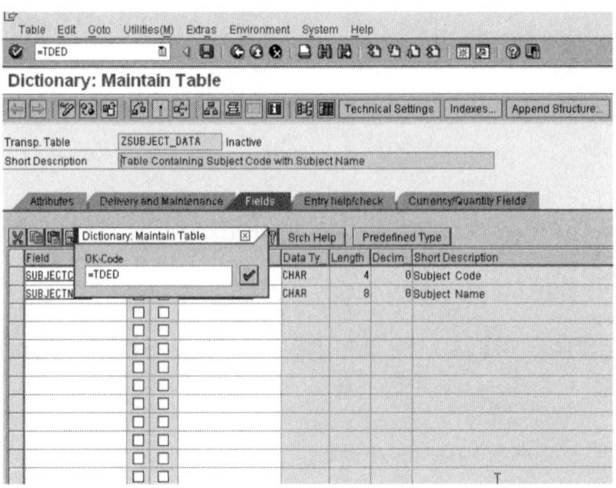

FIGURE 11.59 **The screen showing the Ok-Code (=TDED)**

In Figure 11.59, the `OK-Code` field for the screen appears as =TDED.

38. Click the `Continue` (☑) icon.

The `Call Data Browser` dialog box appears, as shown in Figure 11.60:

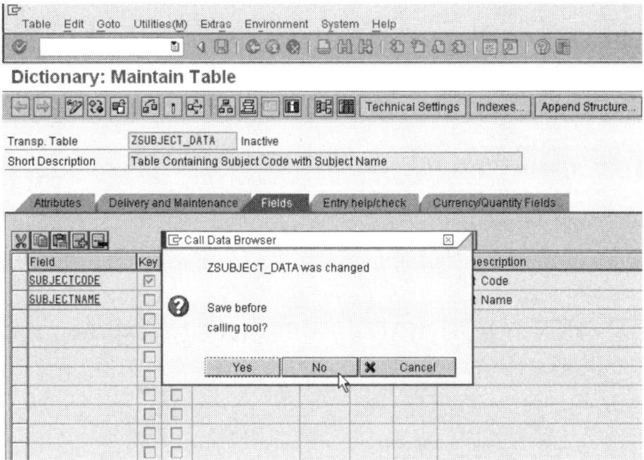

FIGURE 11.60 **The call data browser screen**

A dialog box appears asking whether or not you want to save the ZSUBJECT_DATA table.

39. Click the `No` button, because we do not want to save the table (see Figure 11.60).

The `Table ZSUBJECT_DATA Insert` screen appears along with its `OK-Code` field, as shown in Figure 11.61:

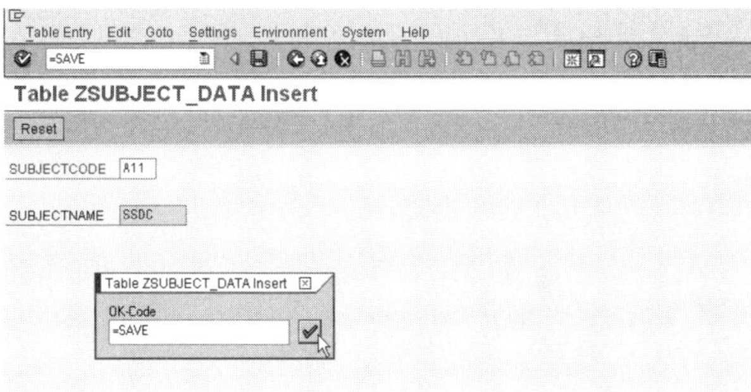

FIGURE 11.61 **Inserting first data from the notepad file into the database table**

In Figure 11.61, you see that the first entries related to the subject code and subject name are picked from the session notepad file and are inserted into the ZSUBJECT_DATA table.

40. Click the `Continue` (✔) icon for the `OK-Code` field (=SAVE).

The message `Database record successfully created` appears in the status bar, as shown in Figure 11.62:

FIGURE 11.62 **Status bar**

The value of OK-Code, /EBACK, is displayed, as shown in Figure 11.63:

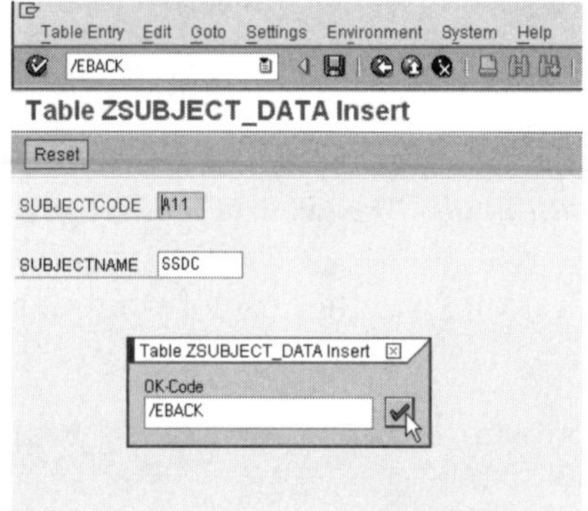

FIGURE 11.63 **The screen showing the Ok-Code as /EBACK**

41. Click the `Continue` (✔) icon.

The value of OK-Code for the screen, =WB_BACK, appears, as shown in Figure 11.57.

42. Click the `Continue` (✔) icon.

The `Exit Processing` dialog box appears asking whether you want to save the ZSUBJECT_DATA table, as shown in Figure 11.64:

FIGURE 11.64 **The exit processing dialog box**

43. Click the `No` button (see Figure 11.64).

The Initial screen of the ABAP Dictionary appears, as shown in Figure 11.65:

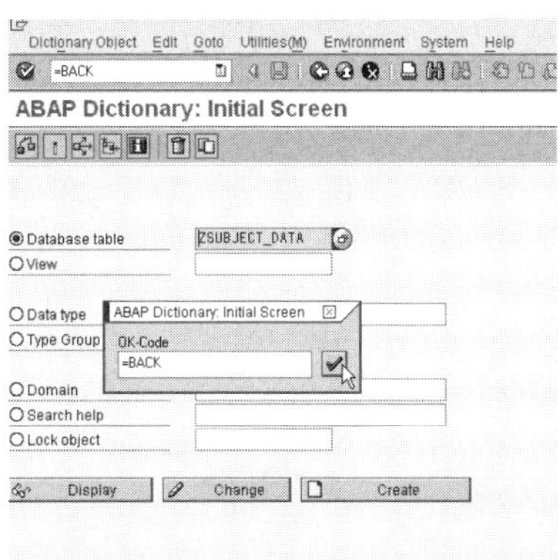

FIGURE 11.65 **The ABAP dictionary initial screen**

In the `OK-Code` field, the value, =BACK, for the screen is displayed.

44. Click the `Continue` (✔) icon.
45. Now, repeat Steps 30 to 43 to transfer all the records mentioned in the session notepad file into the SAP system.

An information dialog box appears after the successful transfer of the data from the notepad file to the ZSUBJECT_DATA table, as shown in Figure 11.66:

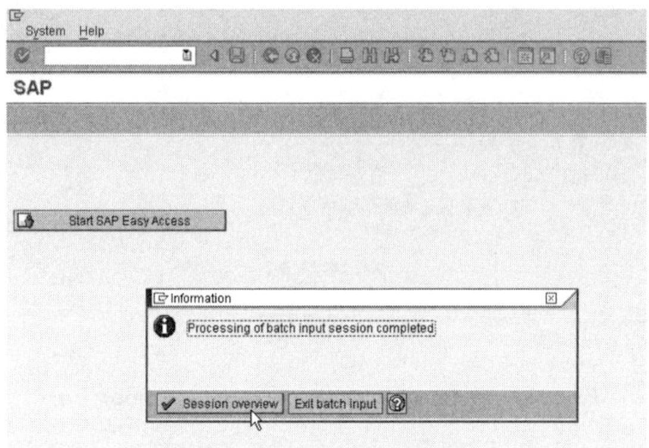

FIGURE 11.66 **Information dialog box**

46. Click the `Session overview` button to view the generated session, as shown in Figure 11.66.

The `Batch Input: Session Overview` screen appears, as shown in Figure 11.67:

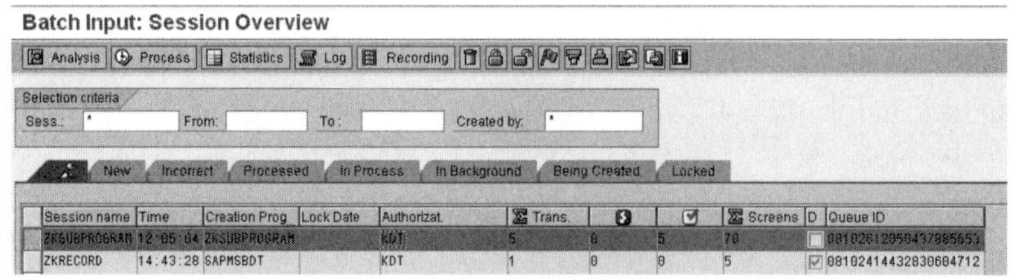

FIGURE 11.67 **Session overview**

Figure 11.67 displays the information related to the processed session, such as the session name, the time at which the session was processed, the name of the authorized user, the total number of transactions involved, the number of transactions processed, and the total number of screens required to process the session.

47. Now, to check whether the transactions were made in the ZSUBJECT_DATA table, open a new session and then start the ABAP Dictionary by using the SE11 transaction code. Figure 11.68 displays the initial screen of the ABAP Dictionary:

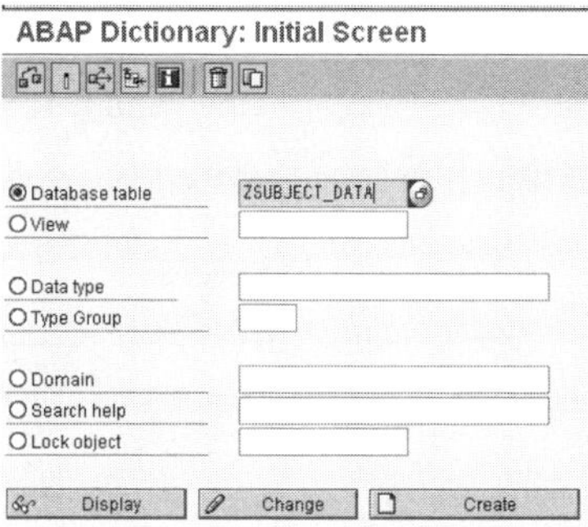

FIGURE 11.68 **The ABAP dictionary initial screen**

48. Enter ZSUBJECT_DATA in the Database table field and click the Change button, as shown in Figure 11.68.

The Dictionary: Maintain Table screen appears, displaying the SUBJECTCODE and SUBJECTNAME fields of the ZSUBJECT_DATA table, as shown in Figure 11.69:

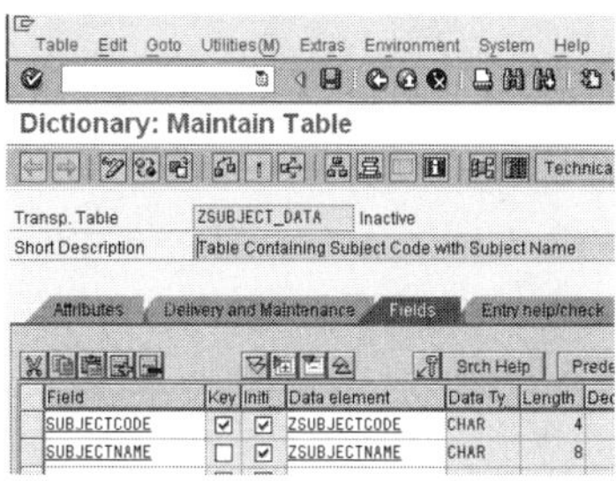

FIGURE 11.69 **Fields of the database table**

49. Select `Utilities(M)>Table Contents>Display`, as shown in Figure 11.70:

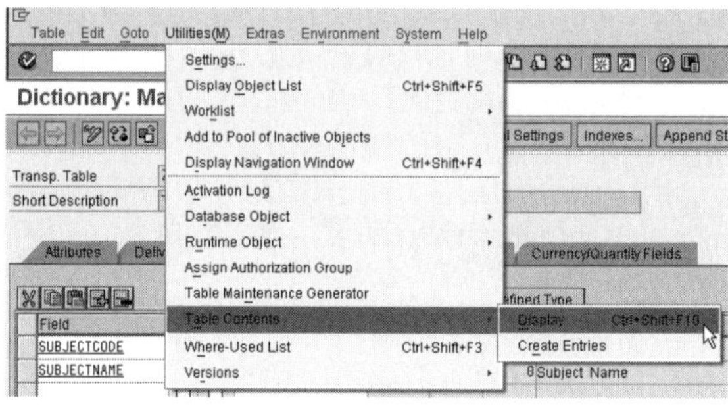

FIGURE 11.70 **Displaying the contents of ZSUBJECT_DATA**

This action is used to display the contents of the ZSUBJECT_DATA table, to check whether the data from the notepad file has been transferred to the SAP system. The selection screen of Data Browser for the ZSUBJECT_DATA table appears, as shown in Figure 11.71:

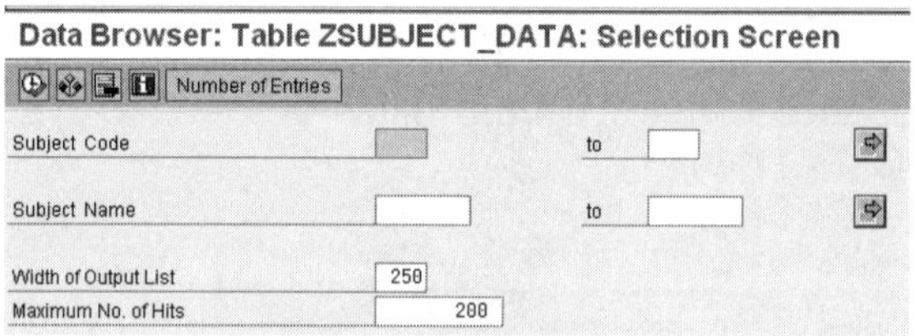

FIGURE 11.71 **The selection screen**

50. Click the `Execute` (icon) icon (see Figure 11.71).

The `Data Browser: Table ZSUBJECT_DATA Select Entries` screen appears, as shown in Figure 11.72:

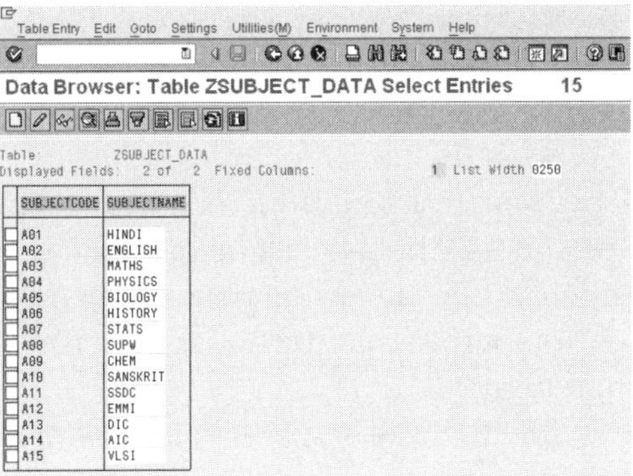

FIGURE 11.72 **Data in table**

In Figure 11.72, you can see that the data of the notepad file has been transferred to the ZSUBJECT_DATA table.

Now, let's learn about another technique of transferring data into an SAP system: LSMW.

THE LSMW TOOL

Legacy System Migration Workbench (LSMW) is a tool used to transfer data from a legacy system to an SAP system. The data can be transferred either all at once or periodically at regular intervals. The LSMW tool, a cross-application component of the SAP system, first reads the legacy data from the spreadsheet tables or sequential files and then converts it to a format supported by the target system. Finally, the converted data is imported in the database used by the SAP system. Use the LSMW transaction code to access the LSMW interface.

You must consider the following points before you start working with the LSMW tool:

- LSMW is used only after the SAP system has been installed and application customization has been completed.

- The data in the legacy system is analyzed.
- The transactions required to transfer the data into an SAP system must be identified.
- You must process the identified transactions in the SAP system manually by using test data from the legacy system.
- The source and SAP fields must be mapped to each other.
- You must define the conversion rule, which uses the field content of the source structure and is then converted into the target structure fields.
- You must define the way in which data is extracted from the legacy system.
- You can either use any of the standard import techniques or generate a recording of the transaction with the batch input recording method.

As no prior knowledge of programming is required to work with LSMW, this tool can be employed by functional consultants directly, whereas the BDC tool can be used only by technical people because it requires programming knowledge. With the help of LSMW, you can transfer new records as well as update the existing records in an SAP system.

Now, let's learn how to update a customer's master record with LSMW by using the batch input recording method.

Updating Records by Using the Batch Input Recording Method

Sometimes, to cater to the needs of different customers in a more efficient manner, the data related to the customer master records of all the customers are linked. In terms of SAP, the linking of the customer data implies that we only change the data of the sales office, sales group, and customer group related to the customer master records.

Perform the following steps to update a customer master record by using the batch input recording method of LSMW:

1. Start the initial screen of the LSMW tool by entering `LSMW` transaction code in the Command field of the `SAP Easy Access` screen, as shown in Figure 11.73:

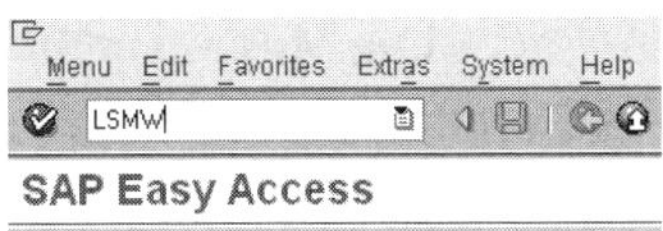

FIGURE 11.73 **Starting LSMW**

2. Press the ENTER key or click the `Continue` ( ) icon.

The `Legacy System Migration Workbench` screen appears, as shown in Figure 11.74:

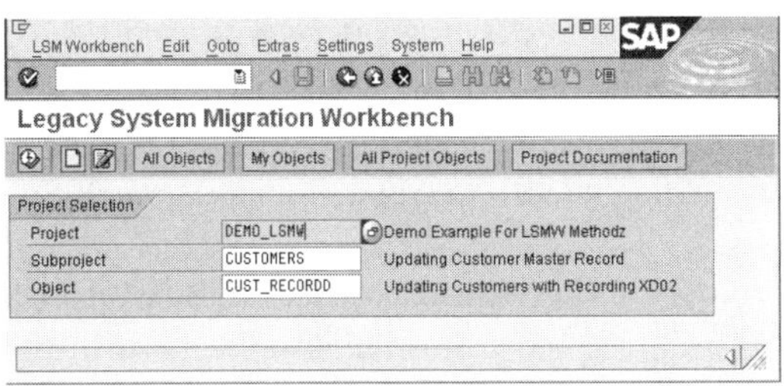

FIGURE 11.74 **Legacy system migration workbench screen**

In Figure 11.74, notice that three structures named `Project`, `Subproject`, and `Object` are provided.

We create a project named DEMO_LSMW next.

3. Enter DEMO_LSMW in the `Project` field and click the `Create Entry` ( ) icon, as shown in Figure 11.74.

The `Create project` dialog box appears, as shown in Figure 11.75:

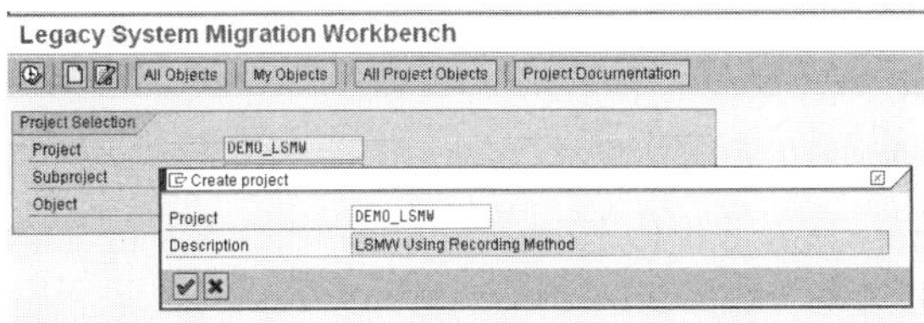

FIGURE 11.75 **Creating a project**

4. Enter LSMW Using Recording Method in the `Description` field and click the `Continue` (✔) icon (see Figure 11.75).

The `Create Subproject` dialog box appears, as shown in Figure 11.76:

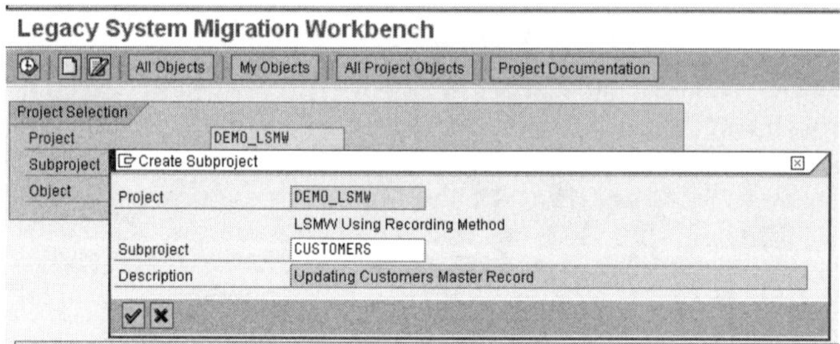

FIGURE 11.76 **Create the subproject screen**

5. Enter the name of the subproject as CUSTOMERS in the `Subproject` field, enter Updating Customer Master Record in the `Description` field, and click the `Continue` (✔) icon (see Figure 11.76).

The `Create Object` dialog box appears, as shown in Figure 11.77:

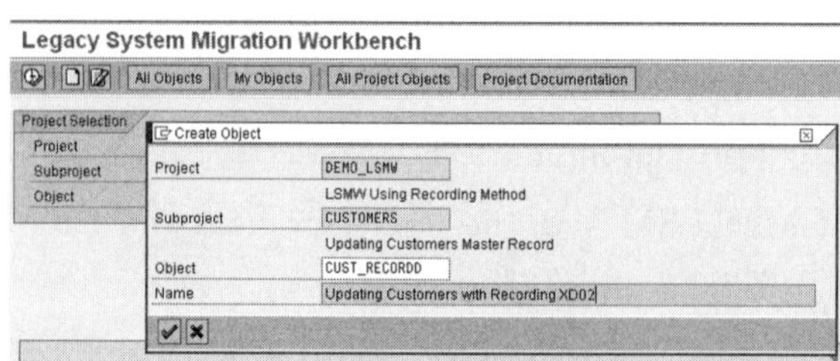

FIGURE 11.77 **Create object screen**

6. Enter the name of the object as CUST_RECORD and the description Updating Customers with Recording XD02 in the `Object` and `Name` fields, respectively. Click the `Continue` (✔) icon.

The initial screen of the LSMW appears, displaying the values in all the fields, as shown in Figure 11.78:

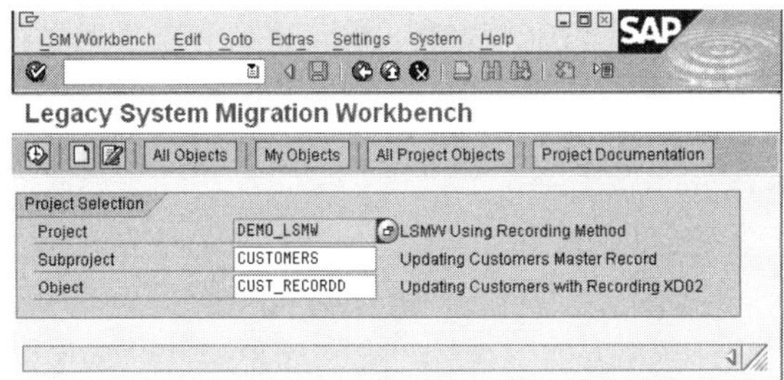

FIGURE 11.78 **The initial screen of the LSMW**

7. Click the `Execute` (icon) icon (Figure 11.78).

The `LSM Workbench: DEMO_LSMW, CUSTOMERS, CUST_RECORDD: Updating Customers with Recording XD02` screen appears, as shown in Figure 11.79:

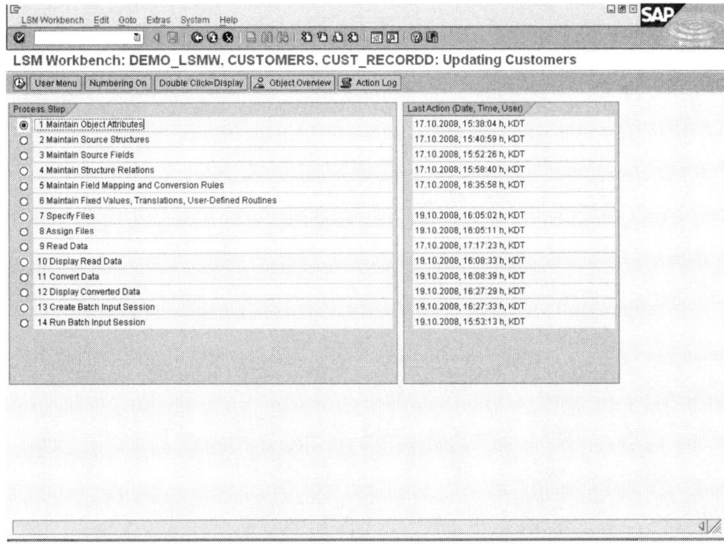

FIGURE 11.79 **The LSMW wizard**

In Figure 11.79, the screen contains a sequence of process steps that you can execute to transfer data. When one process step is executed, the cursor automatically points at the next process step. Note that this screen is also referred to as the LSMW wizard.

> **Note:** The process steps depend on the settings of the User menu. These settings can be altered by clicking the `User Menu` button. The number related to each step can also be displayed by clicking the `Numbering Off` button or can be hidden by clicking the `Numbers On` button. Each step can be executed either by double-clicking the row or by clicking the `Execute` (⊕) icon. The `Double Click=Change` (Double Click=Change) button displays the steps in change mode; whereas the `Double Click=Display` (Double Click=Display) button displays the steps in display mode.

Executing the First Process Step

The name of the first process step of the LSMW wizard is Maintain Object Attributes. In this step, an object attribute, such as object type and import method, is defined. Perform the following steps to execute the Maintain Object Attributes process step:

1. Double-click the Maintain Object Attributes process step. The `LSM Workbench: Change Object Attributes` screen appears, as shown in Figure 11.80:

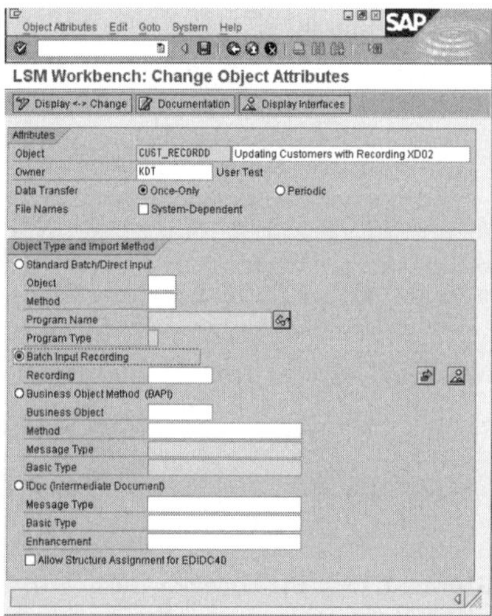

FIGURE 11.80 Batch input recording

Figure 11.80 shows the import methods in the form of radio buttons: `Standard Batch/Direct Input`, `Batch Input Recording`, `Business Object Method (BAPI)`, and `IDoc (Intermediate Document)`. You can select any of these radio buttons according to your requirements. In this case, we have selected the `Batch Input Recording` radio button.

2. Select the `Batch Input Recording` radio button and then click the `Recording: Overview` (icon) icon to record the R/3 transaction (see Figure 11.80).

The `Recordings of Project 'DEMO_LSMW': Overview` screen appears, as shown in Figure 11.81:

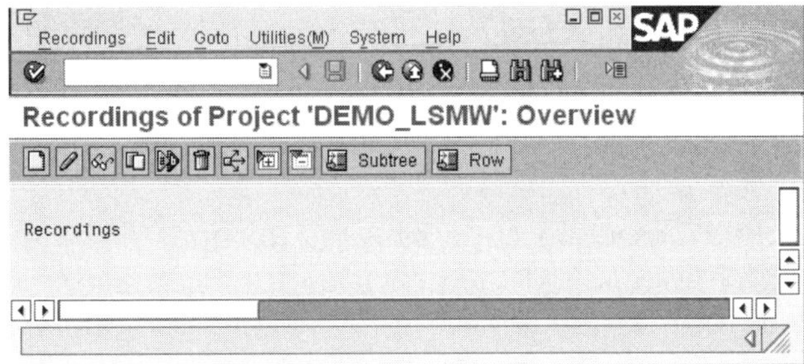

FIGURE 11.81 **Creating recording**

3. Click the `Create Recording` (icon) icon to create a recording of a transaction in the SAP system, as shown in Figure 11.81.

The `Create Recording` dialog box appears, as shown in Figure 11.82:

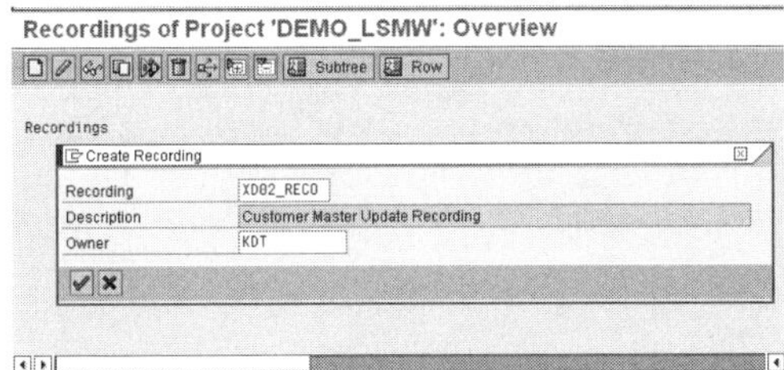

FIGURE 11.82 **Recording of the project**

4. Enter the XD02_RECO and Customer Master Update Recording in the `Recording` and `Description` fields, respectively. Click the `Continue` (✅) icon.

The `Transaction Code` dialog box appears, as shown in Figure 11.83:

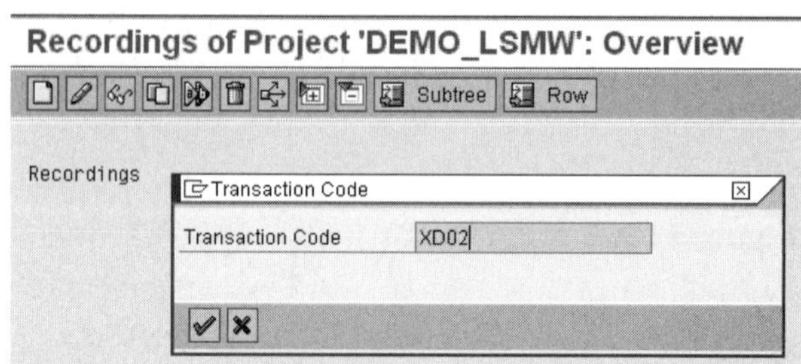

FIGURE 11.83 **Entering transaction code**

5. Enter the transaction code as `XD02` to update the existing customer in the SAP system and then click the `Continue` (✅) icon, as shown in Figure 11.83.

The initial screen of Customer Change appears, as shown in Figure 11.84:

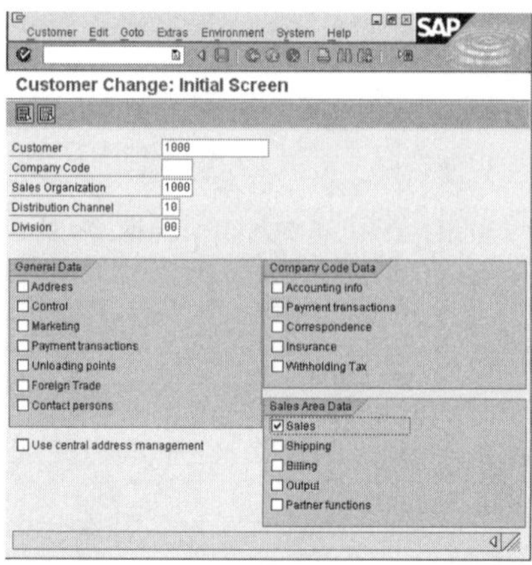

FIGURE 11.84 **The customer change screen**

6. Enter the details of the existing customer—say, Customer number as 1000, Sales Organization as 1000, Distribution Channel as 10, and Division as 00 (see Figure 11.84). Select the `Sales` check box and press the ENTER key.

The message `Recording running` appears in the status bar, and then the `Customer Change: Sales Sales Area` screen appears, as shown in Figure 11.85:

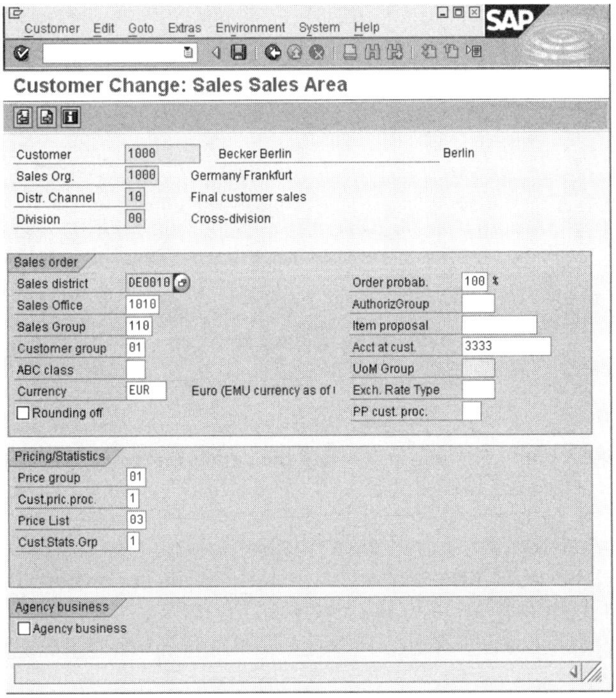

FIGURE 11.85 **Performing transaction recording for transaction XD02**

Figure 11.85 displays the information related to the customer sales area.

7. Click the `Save` (💾) icon and then click the `Back` (◀) icon.

The `Create Recording` screen appears, as shown in Figure 11.86:

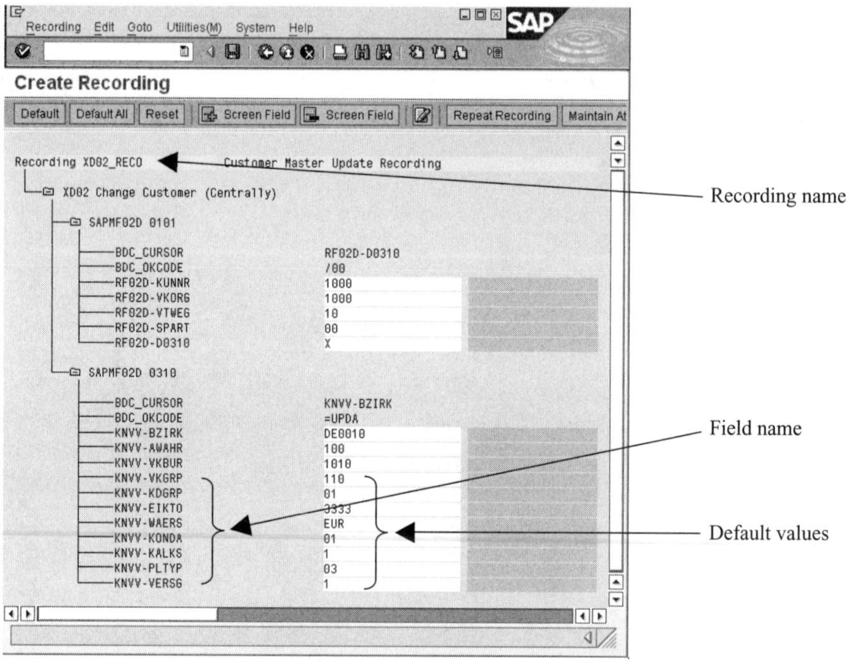

FIGURE 11.86 **The screen showing the details regarding the recording**

The `Create Recording` screen displays the name of the recording created (that is, XD02_RECO) along with the field names and their default values, such as BDC_CURSOR, BDC_OKCODE, RF02D-KUNNR, and RF02D-VKORG. On this screen, you can also delete the fields not needed in the recording by clicking the `Remove Screen field` (Screen Field) button.

As shown in Figure 11.86, the field names are shown in a technical format. You can replace these technical names with the descriptive names by double-clicking the field. In this case, we change the technical names of the required fields.

8. Double-click the field whose name you want to change. In our case, we double-click the `RF02D-KUNNR` field.

The `Create Recording` dialog box appears, as shown in Figure 11.87:

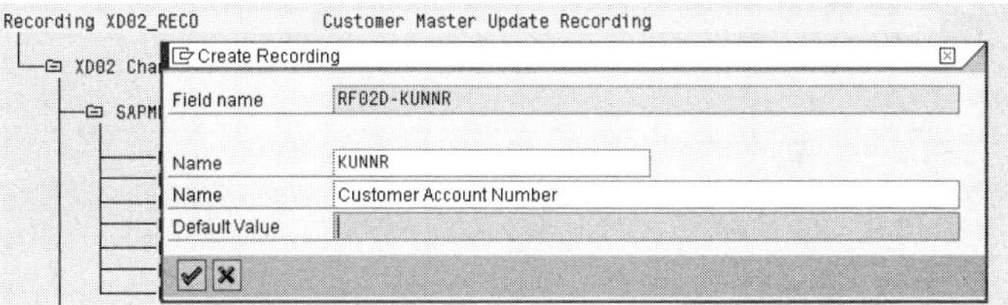

FIGURE 11.87 **Changing the details regarding the fields**

9. Enter the name of the field (that is, KUNNR) in the `Name` field and the description related to this field (that is, Customer Account Number), in the second `Name` field. Similarly, we change the technical names of all these fields by following the same procedure mentioned for the field RF02D-KUNNR. After all the changes are made, the `Create Recording` screen appears, as shown in Figure 11.88:

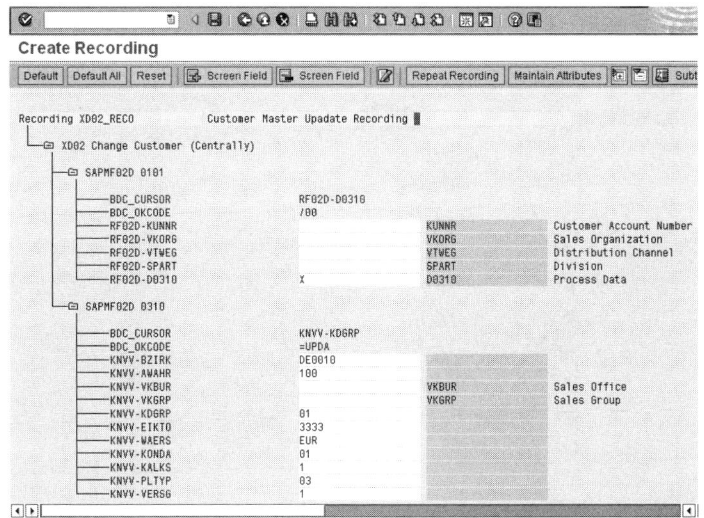

FIGURE 11.88 **The screen showing the changes**

10. Click the `Save` (💾) icon and then click the `Back` (◎) icon.

The `Recordings of Project DEMO_LSMW: Overview` screen appears, as shown in Figure 11.89:

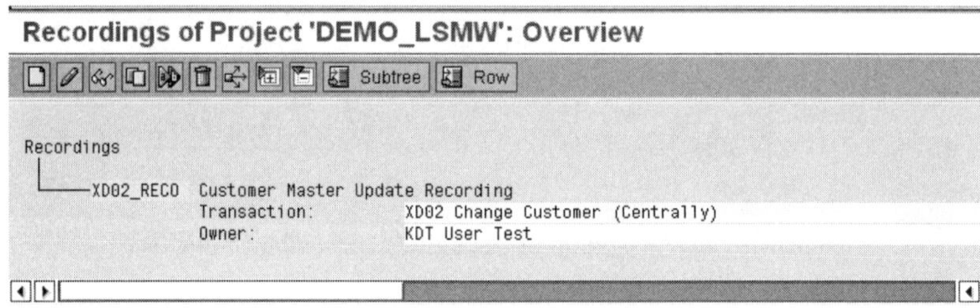

FIGURE 11.89 **Recording overview**

Figure 11.89 displays the details of the created recording, XD02_REC.

11. Click the `Back` (◎) icon.

The `LSM Workbench: Change Object Attributes` screen appears, as shown in Figure 11.90:

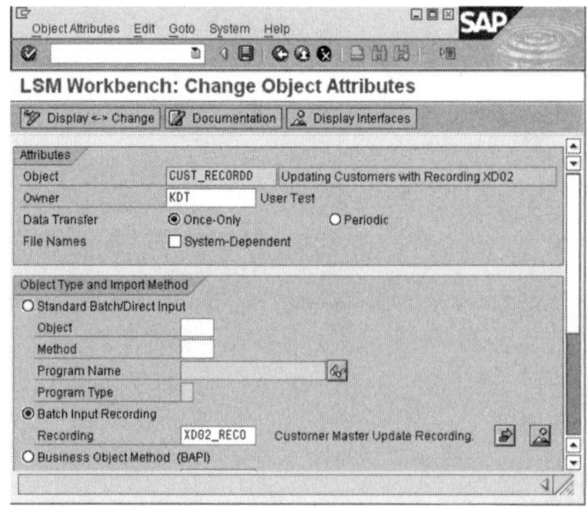

FIGURE 11.90 **The change object attributes screen**

12. Enter the name of the created recording as XD02_RECO in the `Recording` field, as shown in Figure 11.90.
13. Click the `Save` (💾) icon and then click the `Back` (◉) icon.

The cursor is shifted automatically to the next step in the `LSM Workbench: DEMO_LSMW, CUSTOMERS, CUST_RECORDD: Updating Customers with Recording XD02` screen.

Executing the Second Process Step

The second process step of the LSMW wizard is Maintain Source Structures. In this process step, a source structure is defined. Execute this step by double-clicking it.

> **Note:** Now, you see only 14 steps on the screen, because we want to import the data with the help of the recording method, which means that the steps related to the Standard Batch/Direct Input, Direct input, and IDoc methods have been hidden.

The `LSM Workbench: Change Source Structures` screen appears, as shown in Figure 11.91:

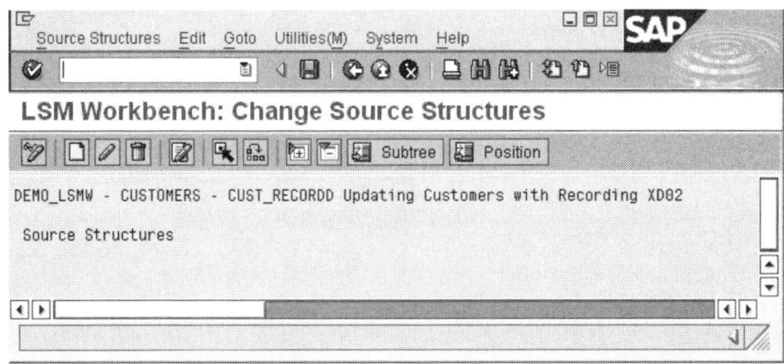

FIGURE 11.91 **The LSM workbench: change source structures screen**

In the `LSM Workbench: Change Source Structures` screen, we create a source structure for the method, as shown in the following steps:

1. Click the Create a Structure (▢) icon (see Figure 11.91).

The Create Source Structure dialog box appears, as shown in Figure 11.92:

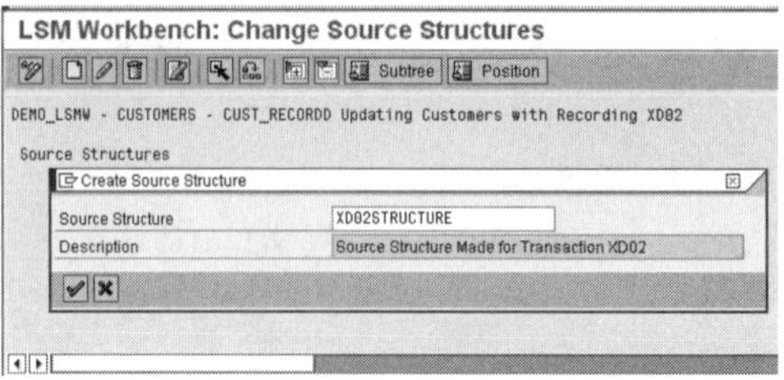

FIGURE 11.92 **The create source structure screen**

2. Enter the name of the source structure in the Source Structure field and a related description in the Description field. In this case, we enter XD02STRUCTURE in the Source Structure field and Source Structure Made for Transaction XD02 in the Description field, as shown in Figure 11.92.
3. Click the Continue (✔) icon.

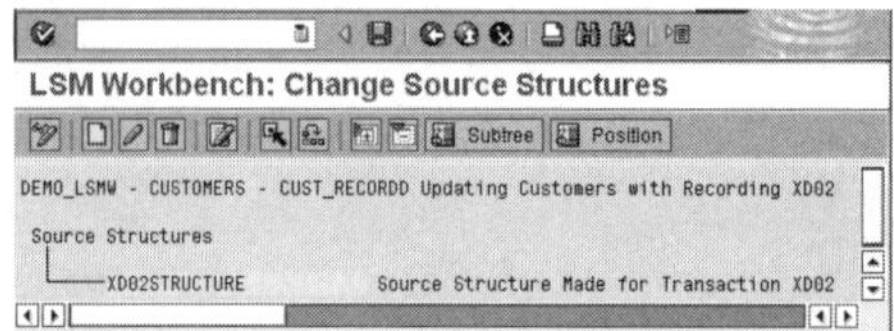

FIGURE 11.93 **Description of the source structure**

The Change Source Structures screen appears, as shown in Figure 11.93:

4. Click the Save (💾) icon and then click the Back (◀) icon.

Executing the Third Process Step

The third process step of the LSMW wizard is Maintain Source Fields. In this process step, source fields related to the source structure are defined. Execute this process step by double-clicking it.

The `LSM Workbench: Change Source Fields` screen appears, as shown in Figure 11.94:

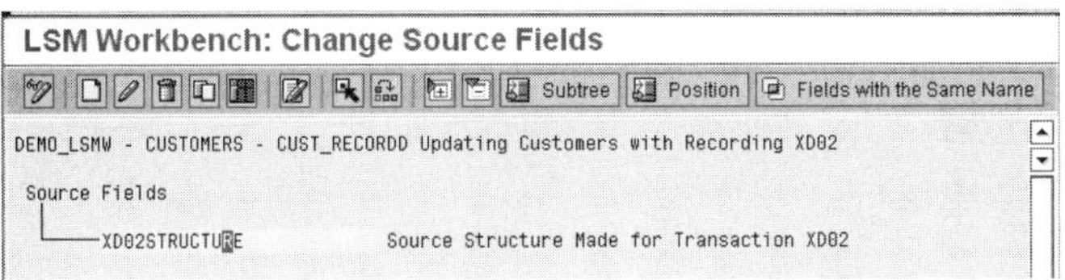

FIGURE 11.94 **The change source fields screen**

In the `LSM Workbench: Change Source Fields` screen, you need to list all the fields you want to include in the source structure To do so, perform the following steps:

1. Select the created source structure, XD02STRUCTURE, and then click the `Table Maintenance` (▦) icon, as shown in Figure 11.94.

The `Source Fields for Source Structure XD02STRUCTURE` screen appears, as shown in Figure 11.95:

Source Fields for Source Structure XD02STRUCTURE

Field Name	Type	Le..	Field description
CUSTOMER	C	10	CUSTOMER
SALESORG	C	4	SALESORG
DISTCHANNEL	C	2	DISTCHANNEL
DIVISION	C	2	DIVISION
SALESOFFICE	C	4	SALESOFFICE
SALESGROUP	C	3	SALESGROUP

FIGURE 11.95 **Maintaining source fields for the source structure**

2. Enter the values for different fields present on the screen, as shown in Figure 11.95.

In addition to this, you also need to update two fields, SALESOFFICE and SALESGROUP.

3. Click the Save (💾) icon and then click the Back (◉) icon.

The LSM Workbench: Change Source Fields screen appears, as shown in Figure 11.96:

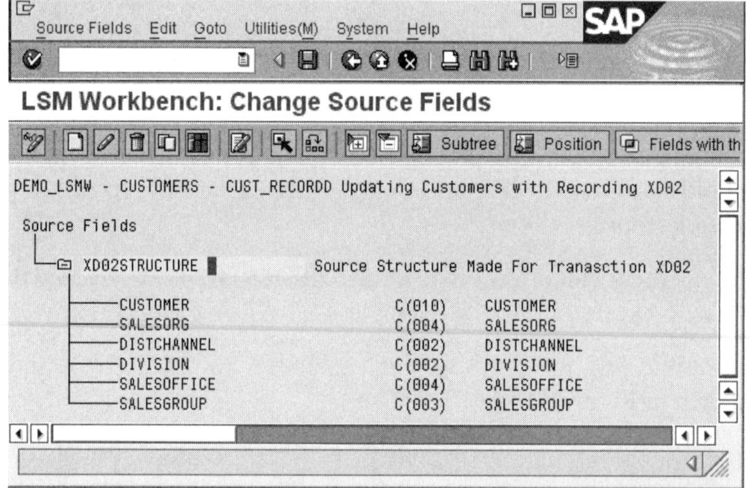

FIGURE 11.96 **Description of source fields of the source structure**

The names of the fields, along with their respective descriptions, appear on the screen.

4. Click the Save (💾) icon and then click the Back (◉) icon.

Executing the Fourth Process Step

The fourth process step of the LSMW wizard is Maintain Structure Relations. In this step, you establish the relationship between the source structure and target structure. Execute this process step by double-clicking it.

The LSM Workbench: Change Structure Relationships screens appears, as shown in Figure 11.97:

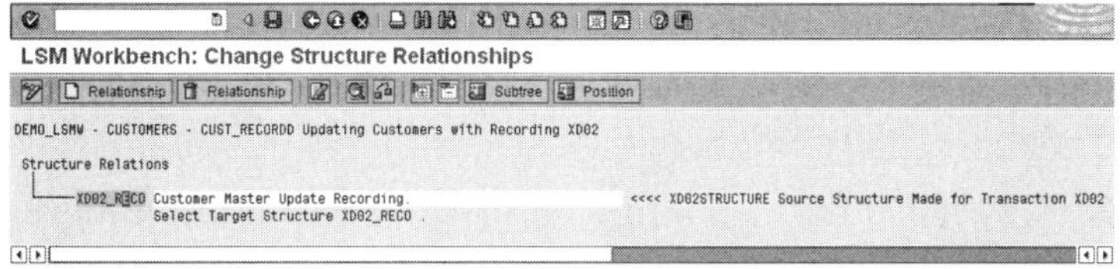

FIGURE 11.97 **Maintaining the relationship for the structure**

In this case, only one source structure and target structure is present; therefore, the relationship between them already exists by default. In case there are more source structures and target structures, select the target structure name and then click the `Relationship` button.

Then, click the `Save` (💾) icon and then click the `Back` (◀) icon.

Executing the Fifth Process Step

The fifth process step of the LSMW wizard is Maintain Field Mappings and Conversion Rules. In this step, you first assign the source stucture fields to the target structure fields and then define how the field content is to be converted. For each field of the target structure, you define the field description and assign the source structure fields, the type of rule, and the code. Execute this process step by double-clicking it.

The `LSM Workbench: Change Field Mappings and Conversion Rules` screen appears, as shown in Figure 11.98:

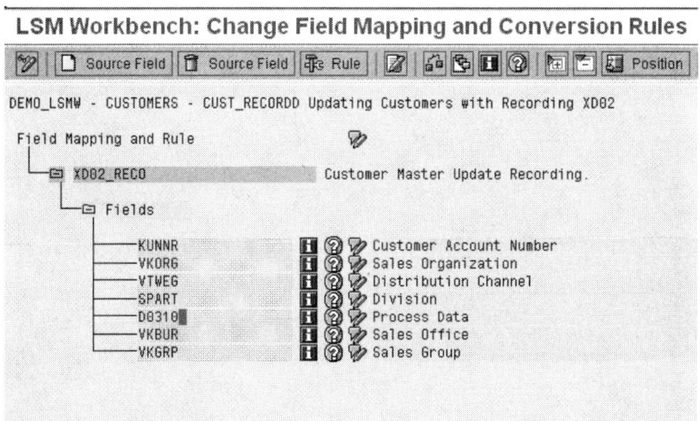

FIGURE 11.98 **The screen for entering the value of the XD02_REC_D0310 field**

On this screen, the D0310 field represents that you have selected Sales View for the customer master screen and its value should be set to X so that data conversion is not affected.

Now, perform the following steps to execute the fifth process step:

1. Click the D0310 field and then click the Constant (Constant) button present on the application toolbar.

The Value For XD02_RECO-D0310 dialog box appears, as shown in Figure 11.99:

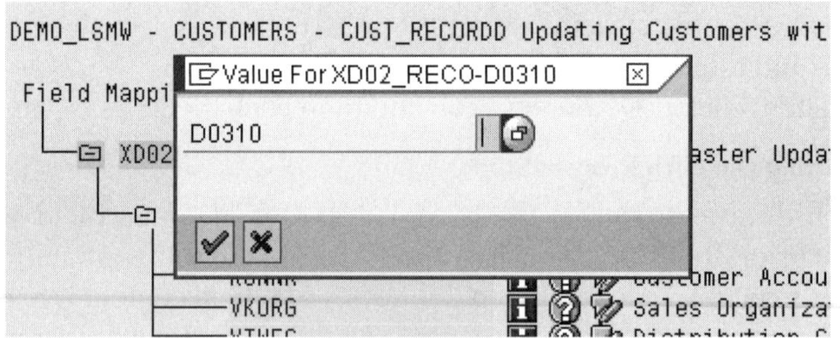

FIGURE 11.99 **The screen for entering the value**

2. Click the Search Help () icon beside the D0310 field (see Figure 11.99).

The Process data? dialog box appears, as shown in Figure 11.100:

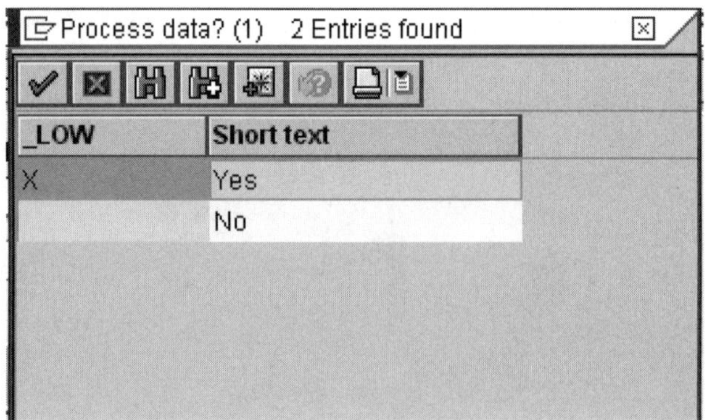

FIGURE 11.100 **The process data dialog box**

3. Select the Yes option and then click the Copy (✓) icon.

The corresponding value for the field, X, appears in the D0310 field, as shown in Figure 11.101:

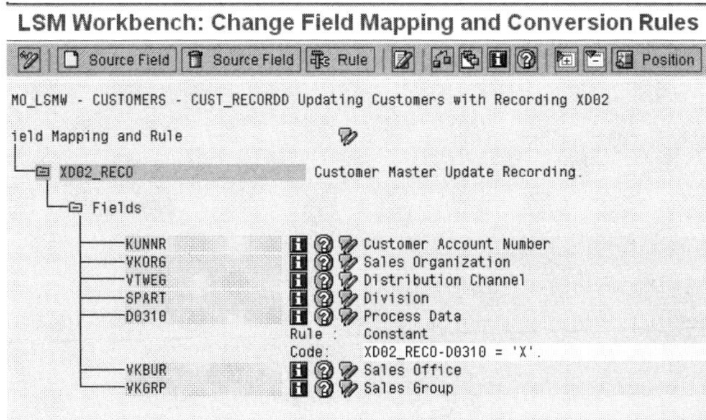

FIGURE 11.101 **Mapping of the field**

Figure 11.101 shows that the rule and the corresponding code are assigned to the D0310 field.

4. Click the KUNNR field and then click the Source Field (Source Field) button.

The XD02_RECO-KUNNR: Assign Source Field dialog box appears, as shown in Figure 11.102:

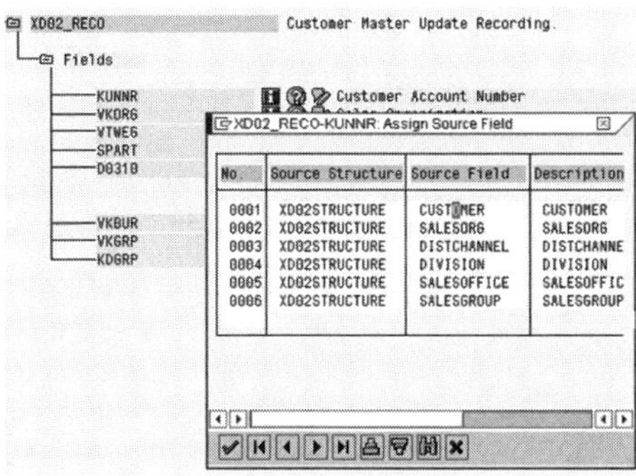

FIGURE 11.102 **The screen for assigning the source field**

5. Select the source field as CUSTOMER and then click the `Choose` (☑) icon.

Follow the same procedure for the rest of the fields, such as `VKORG`, `VTWEG`, `SPART`, `VKBUR`, and `VKGRP`, to define the code to transfer data from the fields of the source data structure to the respective fields in the target structure.

Finally, the `LSM Workbench: Change Field Mapping and Conversion Rules` screen appears, as shown in Figure 11.103:

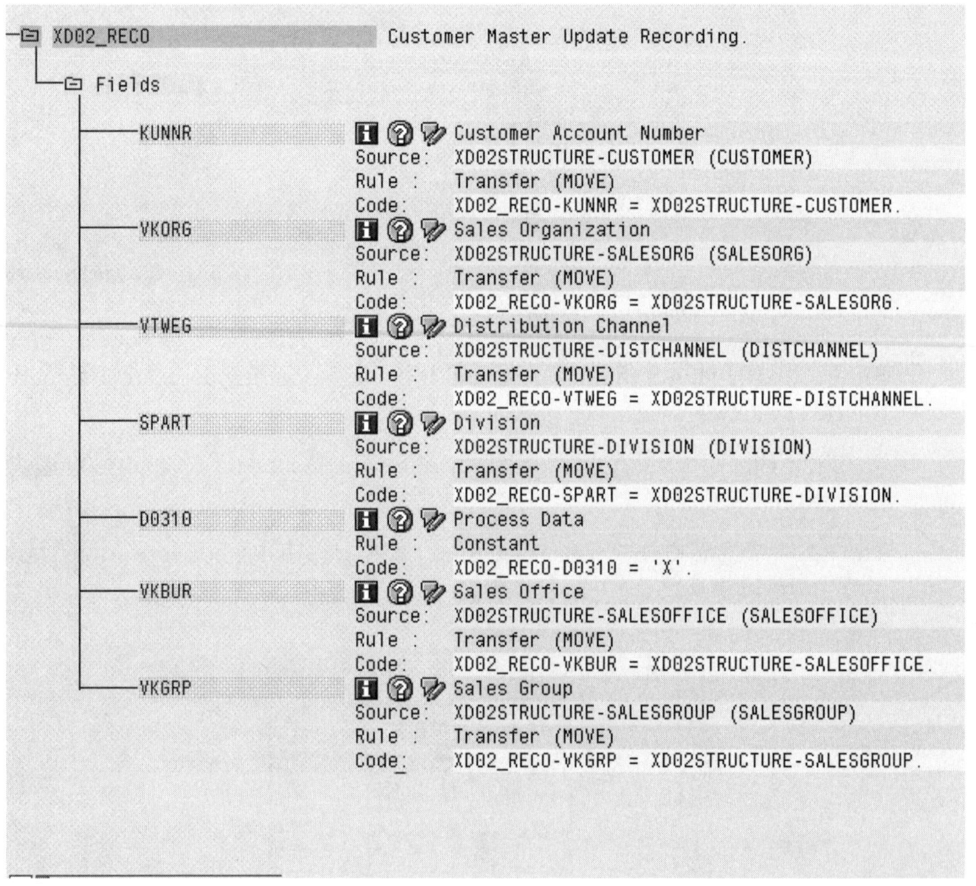

FIGURE 11.103 **Mapping the fields and defining source structures**

In Figure 11.103, note that the relations are established between the fields of the source and target structures.

6. Click the `Save` (💾) icon and then click the `Back` (⊙) icon.

Executing the Sixth Process Step

The sixth process step of the LSMW wizard is Maintain Fixed Values, Translations, User-Defined Routines. This step allows you to process the reusable rules, such as fixed values, translations, and user-defined routines related to the project. This process step also allows you to define fixed values; that is, a fixed value object is assigned to the field of the target structure. In addition, you can also define reusable translations; that is, the code to carry out field content conversion must be assigned to the target field. You can also use a user-defined routine in different objects related to a project. Execute this process step by double-clicking it.

The `LSM Workbench: Fixed Values, Translations, UserDefined Routines` screen appears, as shown in Figure 11.104:

FIGURE 11.104 **Maintaining fixed values, translations, and user-defined routines**

In this case, we do not process any reusable rules; therefore, the sixth step has been skipped. Click the `Back` (⊙) icon.

Executing the Seventh Process Step

The seventh process step of the LSMW wizard is Specify Files. In this step, the location of the file containing legacy data is specified. Execute this step by double-clicking it.

The LSM Workbench: Specify Files (Change) screen appears, as shown in Figure 11.105:

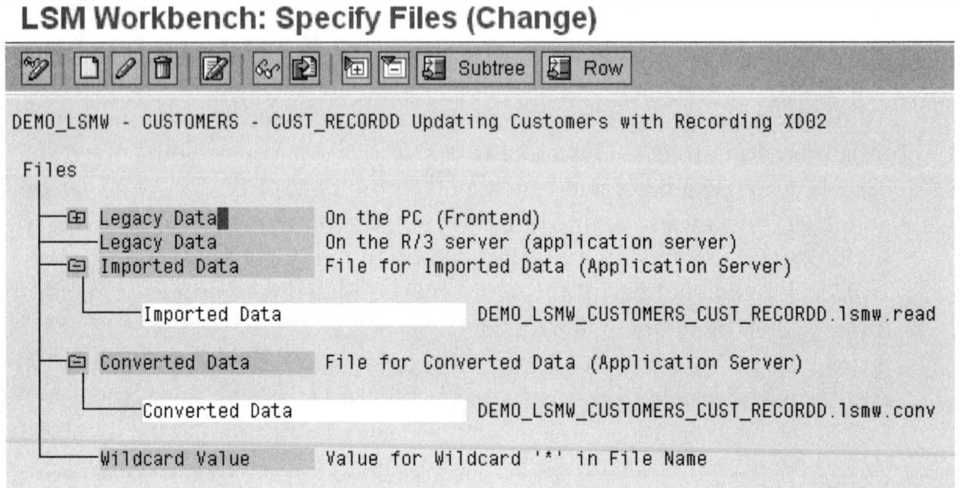

FIGURE 11.105 **Specifying the input file**

In the LSM Workbench: Specify Files (Change) screen, the layout of the input file (a notepad file) is specified. This file contains the field names of the XD02 transaction in the first line. Save this input file in the [Tab] delimited file category. Note that this file will be saved in the local drive on your computer. In this case, the file is saved at the location C:\XD02.txt.

Perform the following steps to execute the seventh process step:

1. Double-click Legacy Data on the PC (Frontend), as shown in Figure 11.105.

The File on Front End: Maintain Properties dialog box appears, as shown in Figure 11.106:

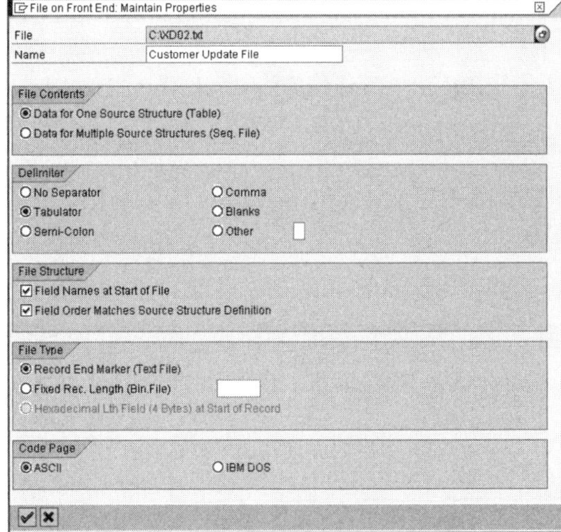

FIGURE 11.106 **Specifying the input file**

2. Select the delimiter as `Tabulator` and the file structure as `Field Names at Start of File`. Click the `Continue` (☑) icon.

The `LSM Workbench: Specify Files (Change)` screen appears, as shown in Figure 11.107:

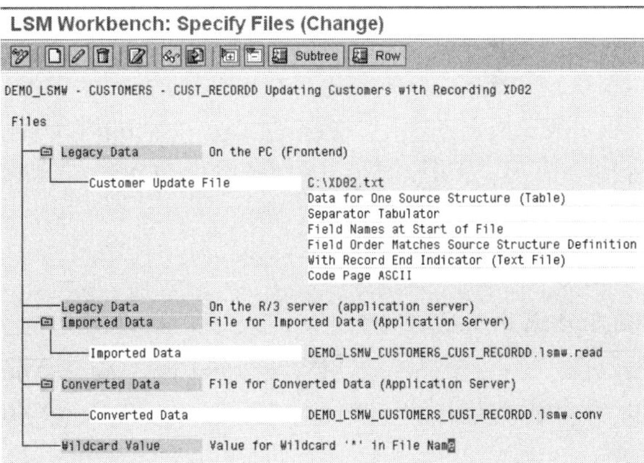

FIGURE 11.107 **Details of the input file**

All the selected attributes of the file are displayed on the screen.

3. Click the `Save` (💾) icon and then click the `Back` (◀) icon to return to the `LSM Workbench: DEMO_LSMW, CUSTOMERS, CUST_RECORDD: Updating Customers with Recording XD02` screen.
4. Create an Excel file containing data related to customers, as shown in Figure 11.108:

A	B	C	D	E	F
Customer	SalesOrg	DistChnl	Division	SalesOff	SalesGrp
1000	1000	10	00	1010	110
1005	1000	10	00	1010	110
1007	1000	10	00	1010	110
1030	1000	10	00	1010	110
1031	1000	10	00	1010	110
1171	1000	10	00	1010	110
1172	1000	10	00	1010	110
1200	1000	10	00	1010	110
1235	1000	10	00	1010	110
1280	1000	10	00	1010	110

FIGURE 11.108 **An input excel file**

Figure 11.108 shows the records of the customer that need to be updated. Now, save this Excel file as a Tab-delimited text file named XD02 on the local drive of your computer (in this case, it is C:\).

Executing the Eighth Process Step

The next process step of the LSMW wizard is Assign Files. In this step, the file name is assigned to the source structure. Execute this step by double-clicking it.

The `LSMWorkbench: Assign Files (Change)` screen appears, as shown in Figure 11.109:

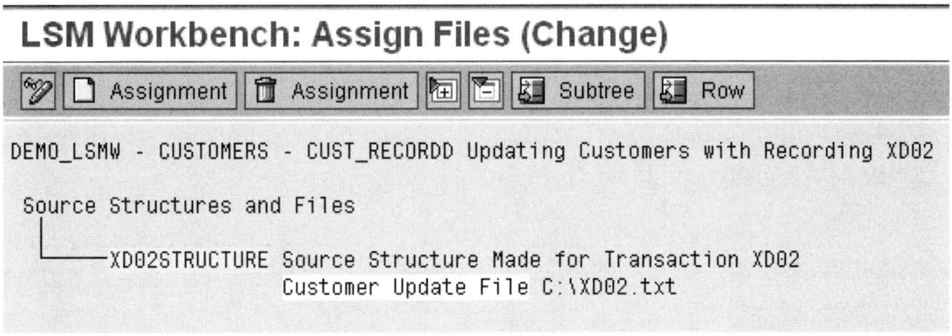

LSM Workbench: Assign Files (Change)

Assignment | Assignment | Subtree | Row

DEMO_LSMW - CUSTOMERS - CUST_RECORDD Updating Customers with Recording XD02

Source Structures and Files

XD02STRUCTURE Source Structure Made for Transaction XD02
Customer Update File C:\XD02.txt

FIGURE 11.109 **Assigning input files**

The SAP system automatically assigns the file name to the source structure. In this case, the file name is XD02.txt.

Click the `Save` () icon and then the `Back` () icon.

Executing the Ninth Process Step

The next process step of the LSMW wizard is Read Data. In this step, the data is read from the source file. Execute this step by double-clicking it.

The `LSM Workbench: Import Data For DEMO_LSMW, CUSTOMERS, CUST_RECORDD` screen appears, as shown in Figure 11.110:

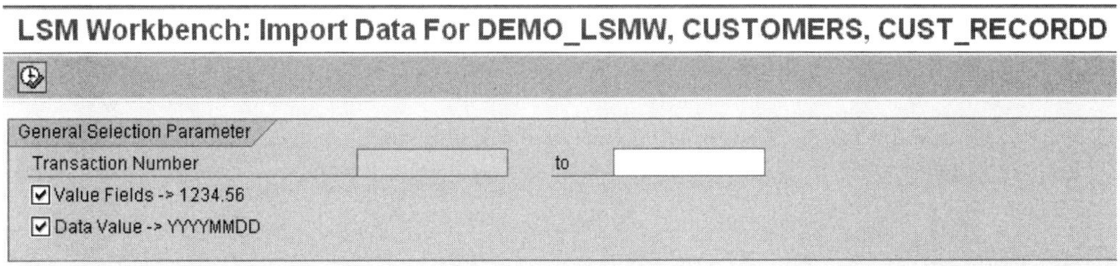

LSM Workbench: Import Data For DEMO_LSMW, CUSTOMERS, CUST_RECORDD

General Selection Parameter
Transaction Number ______ to ______
☑ Value Fields -> 1234.56
☑ Data Value -> YYYYMMDD

FIGURE 11.110 **Importing data**

In the `LSM Workbench: Import Data For DEMO_LSMW, CUSTOMERS, CUST_RECORDD`, screen LSMW reads the data from the source input file; that is, XD02.

Now, perform the following steps to execute the ninth process step:

1. Click the Execute (⊕) icon.

The LSM Workbench: Import Data For DEMO_LSMW, CUSTOMERS, CUST_RECORDD screen appears, as shown in Figure 11.111:

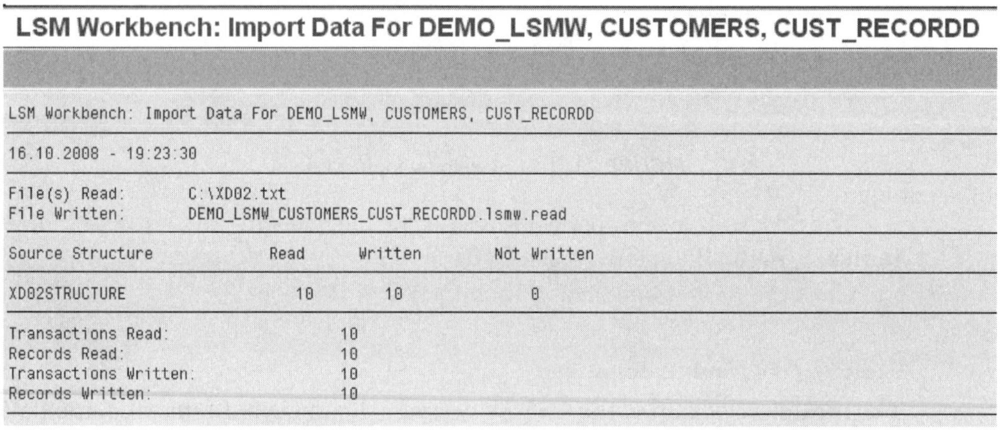

LSM Workbench: Import Data For DEMO_LSMW, CUSTOMERS, CUST_RECORDD

```
LSM Workbench: Import Data For DEMO_LSMW, CUSTOMERS, CUST_RECORDD

16.10.2008 - 19:23:30

File(s) Read:        C:\XD02.txt
File Written:        DEMO_LSMW_CUSTOMERS_CUST_RECORDD.lsmw.read

Source Structure            Read       Written          Not Written

XD02STRUCTURE                 10         10                 0

Transactions Read:                 10
Records Read:                      10
Transactions Written:              10
Records Written:                   10
```


FIGURE 11.111 **Displaying the details of the read data**

In Figure 11.111, note that the number of records maintained in the input file (XD02.txt) is read and written in the given transaction.

2. Click the Back (◉) icon twice. The LSM Workbench: DEMO_LSMW, CUSTOMERS, CUST_RECORDD: Updating Customers with Recording XD02 screen appears.

Executing the Tenth Process Step

The tenth process step of the LSMW wizard is Display Read Data. This step is used to read the converted data. Execute this step by double-clicking it.

The Display Read Data dialog box appears, as shown in Figure 11.112:

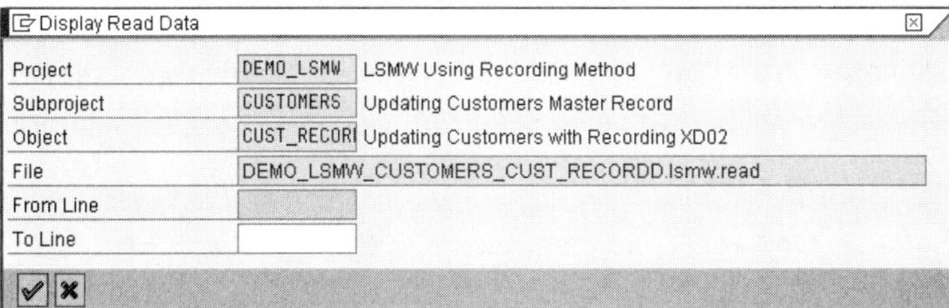

FIGURE 11.112 **Displaying the read data**

This screen allows you to provide the number of lines in the `From Line` and `To Line` fields that you want to display. If you do not enter any number in these fields, all the lines of the notepad file (XD02. txt) will be displayed. In this case, we want to display all the lines; therefore, we leave these fields blank.

Perform the following steps to execute the tenth process step:

1. Click the `Continue` (✔) icon.

The `LSM Workbench: Imported Data` screen appears, as shown in Figure 11.113:

LSM Workbench: Imported Data

Field Contents | Change Display | Display Colour Legend

File DEMO_LSMW_CUSTOMERS_CUST_RECORDD.lsmw.read

Row	Struct.	Conts.
	LSMWDEMO_LSMW CUSTOMERS	CUST_RECORDD DMT 80020081017171638KDT
1	XD02STRUCTURE	1000 10001000101011 0
2	XD02STRUCTURE	1005 10001000101011 0
3	XD02STRUCTURE	1007 10001000101011 0
4	XD02STRUCTURE	1030 10001000101011 0
5	XD02STRUCTURE	1031 10001000101011 0
6	XD02STRUCTURE	1171 10001000101011 0
7	XD02STRUCTURE	1172 10001000101011 0
8	XD02STRUCTURE	1200 10001000101011 0
9	XD02STRUCTURE	1235 10001000101011 0
10	XD02STRUCTURE	1280 10001000101011 0

FIGURE 11.113 **Imported data**

In the LSM Workbench: Imported Data screen, the details of the imported data are displayed. In addition to this, you can view the detailed description of any record by double-clicking it. Figure 11.114 shows the details of the imported data:

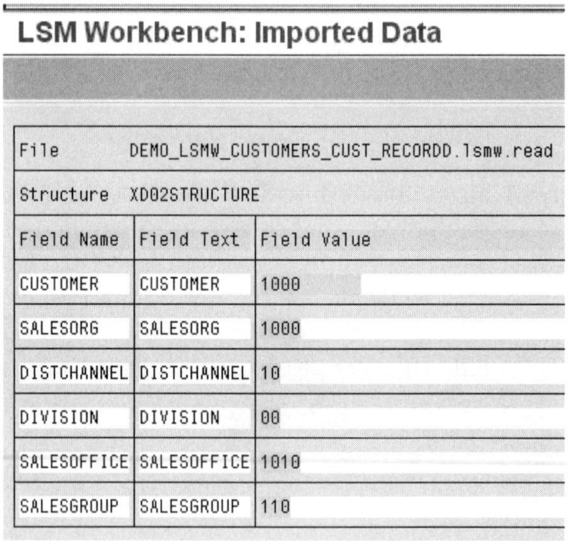

LSM Workbench: Imported Data

File DEMO_LSMW_CUSTOMERS_CUST_RECORDD.lsmw.read

Structure XD02STRUCTURE

Field Name	Field Text	Field Value
CUSTOMER	CUSTOMER	1000
SALESORG	SALESORG	1000
DISTCHANNEL	DISTCHANNEL	10
DIVISION	DIVISION	00
SALESOFFICE	SALESOFFICE	1010
SALESGROUP	SALESGROUP	110

FIGURE 11.114 **Detailed description of the data**

2. Click the Back (◙) icon twice. The LSM Workbench: DEMO_LSMW, CUSTOMERS, CUST_RECORDD: Updating Customers with Recording XD02 screen appears.

Executing the Eleventh Process Step

The eleventh process step of the LSMW wizard is Convert Data. This step is used to convert the data from the source format into the target format. Execute this step by double–clicking it.

The LSM Workbench: Convert Data For DEMO_LSMW, CUSTOMERS, CUST_RECORDD screen appears, as shown in Figure 11.115:

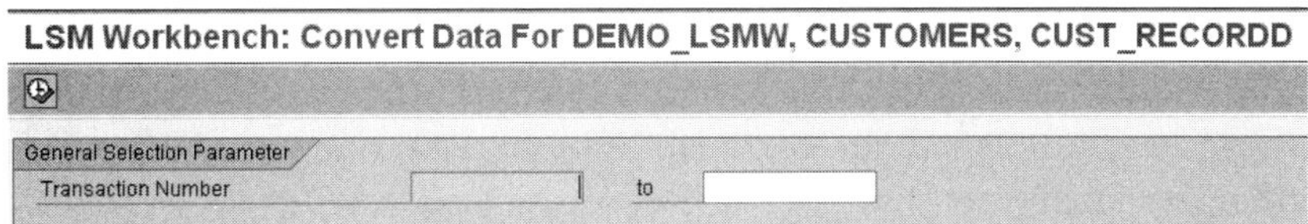

FIGURE 11.115 **Converting data**

Perform the following steps to execute the eleventh process step:

1. Click the `Execute` icon.

The `LSM Workbench: Convert Data For DEMO_LSMW, CUSTOMERS, CUST_RECORDD` screen appears, as shown in Figure 11.116:

LSM Workbench: Convert Data For DEMO_LSMW, CUSTOMERS, CUST_RECORDD

LSM Workbench: Convert Data For DEMO_LSMW, CUSTOMERS, CUST_RECORDD

16.10.2008 - 19:42:07

File Read: DEMO_LSMW_CUSTOMERS_CUST_RECORDD.lsmw.read
File Written: DEMO_LSMW_CUSTOMERS_CUST_RECORDD.lsmw.conv

Transactions Read: 10
Records Read: 10
Transactions Written: 10
Records Written: 10

FIGURE 11.116 **The screen showing the converted data**

In Figure 11.116, information, such as Transactions Read, Records Read, Transactions Written, and Records Written, is displayed.

2. Click the `Back` icon twice. The `LSM Workbench: DEMO_LSMW, CUSTOMERS, CUST_RECORDD: Updating Customers with recording XD02` screen appears.

Now, let's learn about the next process step.

Executing the Twelfth Process Step

The twelfth process step of the LSMW wizard is Display Converted Data. This step is used to display the converted source data. Execute this process step by double-clicking it.

The `Display Converted Data` dialog box appears, as shown in Figure 11.117:

Display Converted Data
Project
DEMO_LSMW
LSMW Using Recording Method
Subproject
CUSTOMERS
Updating Customers Master Record
Object
CUST_RECOR
Updating Customers with Recording XD02
File
DEMO_LSMW_CUSTOMERS_CUST_RECORDD.lsmw.conv
From Line
To Line

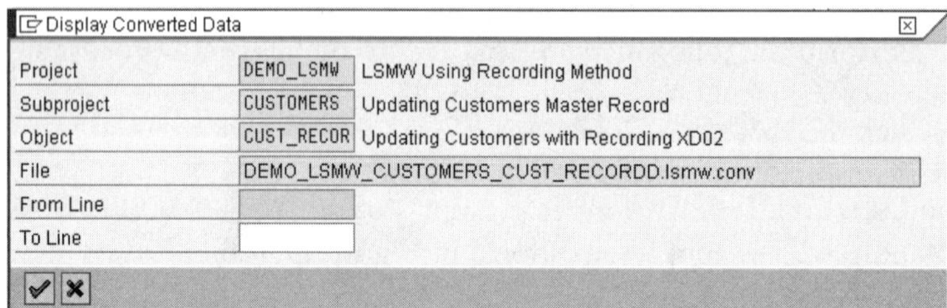

FIGURE 11.117 **Converted data**

Perform the following steps to execute the twelfth process step:

1. Click the `Continue` (✔) icon.

The `LSM Workbench: Converted Data` screen appears, as shown in Figure 11.118:

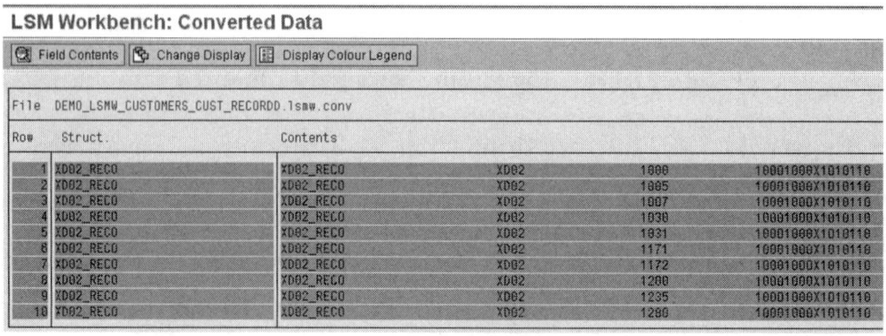

LSM Workbench: Converted Data
Field Contents
Change Display
Display Colour Legend
File DEMO_LSMW_CUSTOMERS_CUST_RECORDD.lsmw.conv
Row
Struct.
Contents
1 XD02_RECO XD02_RECO XD02 1000 10001000X1010110
2 XD02_RECO XD02_RECO XD02 1005 10001000X1010110
3 XD02_RECO XD02_RECO XD02 1007 10001000X1010110
4 XD02_RECO XD02_RECO XD02 1030 10001000X1010110
5 XD02_RECO XD02_RECO XD02 1031 10001000X1010110
6 XD02_RECO XD02_RECO XD02 1171 10001000X1010110
7 XD02_RECO XD02_RECO XD02 1172 10001000X1010110
8 XD02_RECO XD02_RECO XD02 1200 10001000X1010110
9 XD02_RECO XD02_RECO XD02 1235 10001000X1010110
10 XD02_RECO XD02_RECO XD02 1280 10001000X1010110

FIGURE 11.118 **Displaying data after conversion**

In the LSM Workbench: Converted Data screen, you can view the detailed description of any record by double-clicking it. Figure 11.119 shows the details of the converted data in the tabular format:

LSM Workbench: Converted Data

File DEMO_LSMW_CUSTOMERS_CUST_RECORDD.lsmw.conv		
Structure XD02_RECO		
Fld Name	Fld Text	FldValue
TABNAME	Table Name	XD02_RECO
TCODE	Transaction Code	XD02
KUNNR	Customer Account Number	1000
VKORG	Sales Organization	1000
VTWEG	Distribution Channel	10
SPART	Division	00
D0310	Process Data	X
VKBUR	Sales Office	1010
VKGRP	Sales Group	110

FIGURE 11.119 **Data of customer 1000**

2. Click the Back (◉) icon to navigate back to the LSMWorkbench:DEMO_LSMW, CUSTOMERS,CUST_RECORDD:Updating Customers with Recording XD02 screen.

Executing the Thirteenth Process Step

The thirteenth process step of the LSMW wizard is Create Batch Input Session. This step is used to create a batch input session. Execute this step by double-clicking it.

The `LSM Workbench: Generate Batch Input Folder` screen appears, as shown in Figure 11.120:

LSM Workbench: Generate Batch Input Folder

File Name (with Path)	DEMO_LSMW_CUSTOMERS_CUST_RECORDD.lsmw.co
Display Trans. per BI Folder	
Name of Batch Input Folder(s)	CUST_RECORDD
User ID	KDT

☐ Keep batch input folder(s)?

FIGURE 11.120 **Creating the batch input folder**

Now, perform the following steps to execute the thirteenth process step:

1. Click the `Execute` icon.

An `Information` dialog box appears, as shown in Figure 11.121:

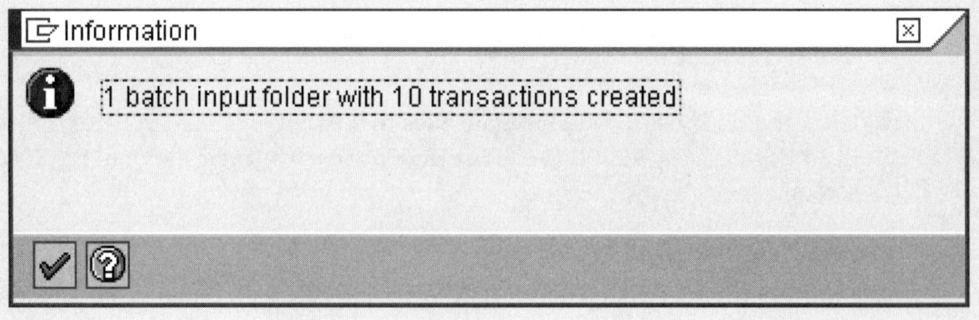
Information
1 batch input folder with 10 transactions created

FIGURE 11.121 **The information dialog box**

2. Click the `Continue` (☑) icon.

Executing the Fourteenth Process Step

The fourteenth process step of the LSMW wizard is Run Batch Input Session. This step is used to process the created batch input session. Execute this step by double-clicking it.

The `Batch Input: Session Overview` screen appears, as shown in Figure 11.122:

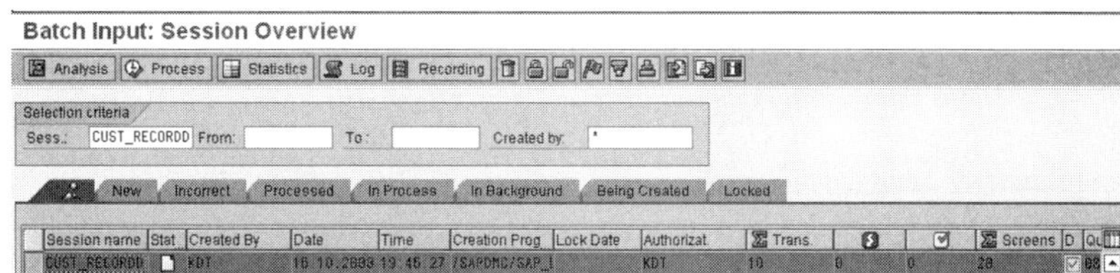

FIGURE 11.122 **Session overview**

Figure 11.122 displays information related to the CUST_RECORDD session, such as Status, Created By, Date, Time, Creation Program, Lock Date, Authorization, Total Number of Transactions, Transactions with errors, Transactions processed, Screens, Deletion Idx., and Queue ID.

1. Select the session name and click the `Process` button.

The `Process Session CUST_RECORDD` dialog box appears, as shown in Figure 11.123:

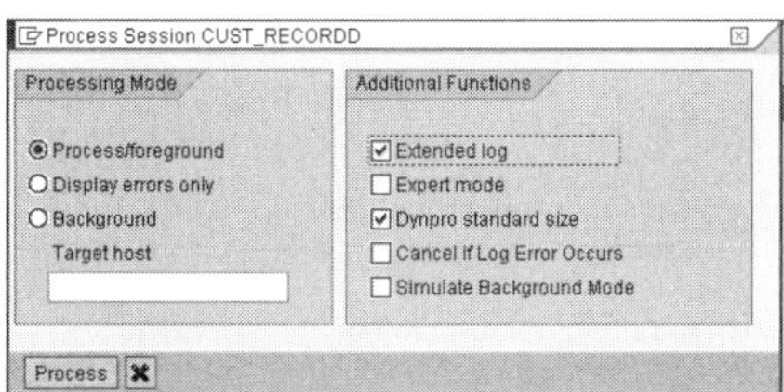

FIGURE 11.123 **Processing screen**

This screen allows you to select any additional functions required to process the CUST_RECORDD session.

2. Select the `Process/foreground` radio button, and the `Extended log` and `Dynpro standard size` check boxes. Now, click the `Process` button.

The initial screen of Customer Change appears, as shown in Figure 11.124:

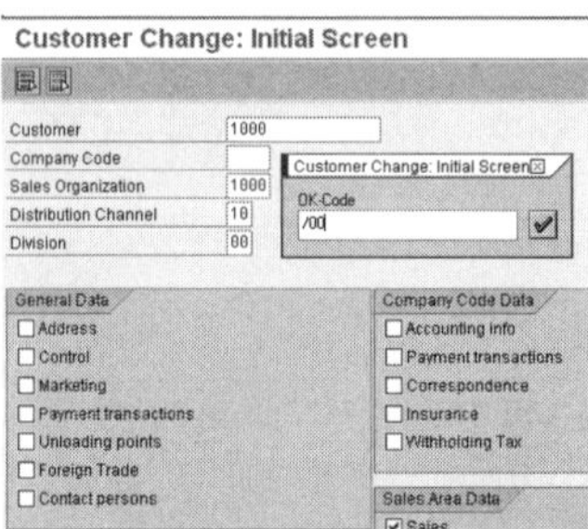

FIGURE 11.124 **Changing customer**

The OK-Code for the initial screen of Customer Change is also displayed in Figure 11.124.

3. Click the `Continue` (✔) icon.

The `Customer Change: Sales Sales Area` screen appears, as shown in Figure 11.125:

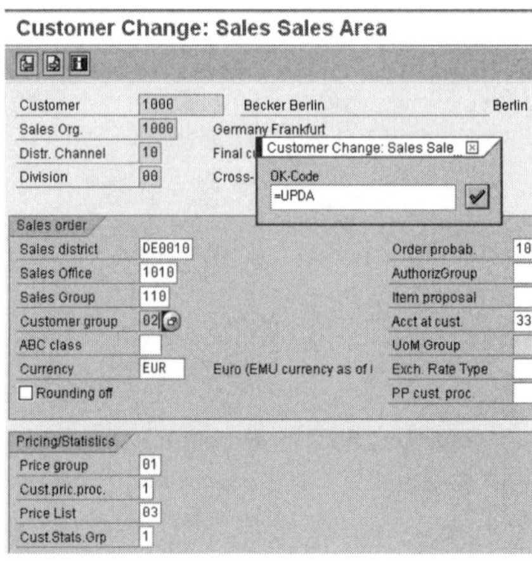

FIGURE 11.125 **Changing customer group**

4. Update the `Customer group` field from 01 to 02, as shown in Figure 11.125.

The OK-Code for the screen is displayed as =UPDA.

5. Click the `Continue` (☑) icon of the `Customer Change: Sales Sales Area` dialog box.

Customer details corresponding to the customer number 1005 are displayed, as shown in Figure 11.126:

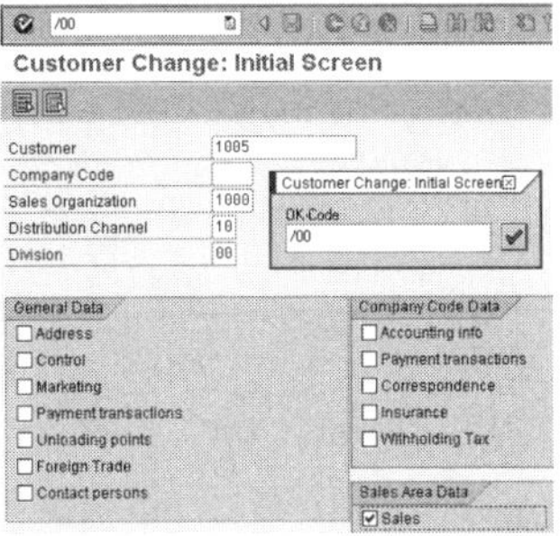

FIGURE 11.126 **Details of customer**

The OK-Code for this screen is displayed as /00.

6. Click the `Continue` (☑) icon of the `Customer Change: Initial Screen` dialog box (Figure 11.126).

The `Customer Change: Sales Sales Area` screen for customer number 1005 appears, as shown in Figure 11.127:

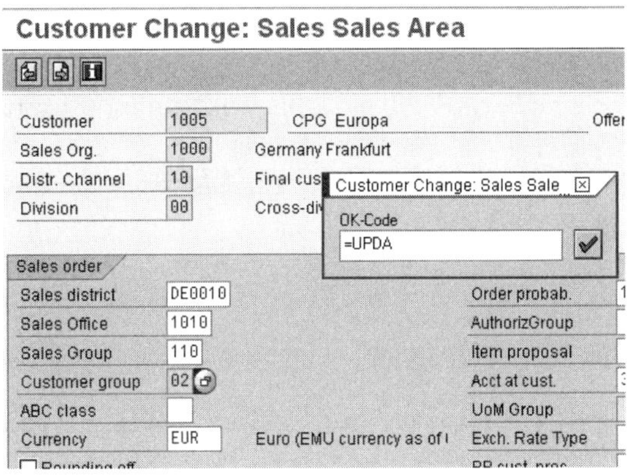

FIGURE 11.127 **The sales data screen**

In Figure 11.127, note that the OK-Code for the screen is also shown as =UPDA.

7. In `Customer Change: Sales Sales Area` screen, change the value in the `Customer group` field from 01 to 02 (see Figure 11.127).
8. Click the `Continue` (✔) icon (Figure 11.127) of the `Customer Change: Sales Sales Area` dialog box.

The initial screen of Customer Change for the next customer (that is, 1007), appears.

9. Repeat Steps 2 to 5 to update the `Customer group` field for the remaining customers as mentioned in the Excel file (see Figure 11.108).

After making the changes for the remaining customers in the `Customer group` field, an information dialog box appears, as shown in Figure 11.128:

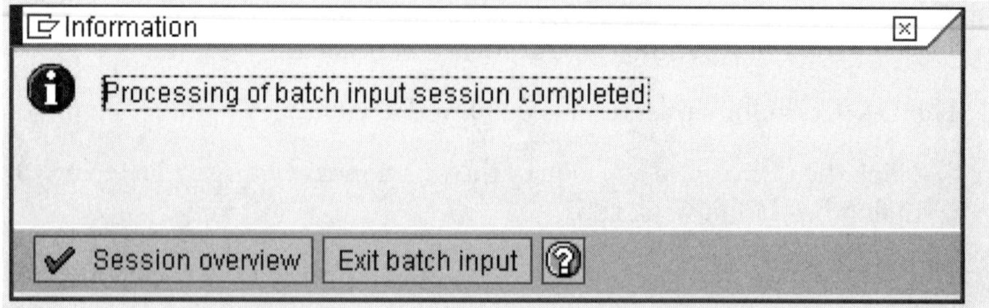

FIGURE 11.128 **The information dialog box**

10. Click the `Session overview` pushbutton (see Figure 11.128).

The `Batch Input: Session Overview` screen appears, as shown in Figure 11.129:

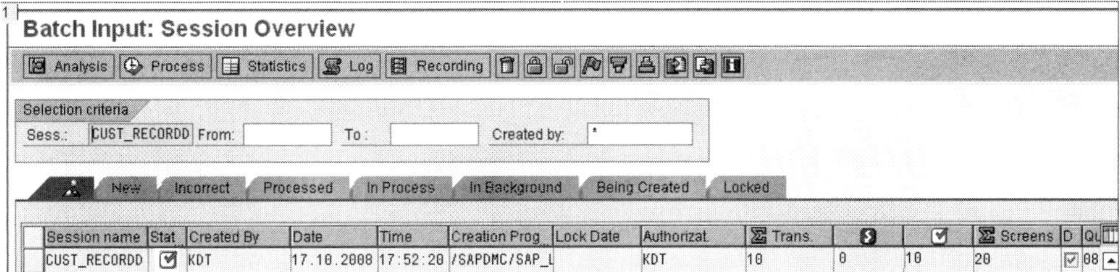

FIGURE 11.129 **Session overview**

Note that the status of the CUST_RECORDD session appears as processed, shown by a tick mark. The total number of screens involved during the processing of the session is 20. The number of transactions processed is 10. If any errors occur in processing the session, they are displayed under the `Transactions with errors` ( ) column.

After the batch input session has been executed successfully, the customer master records are updated in the SAP system. The updated customer master records can be viewed by using the `XD03` transaction code.

SUMMARY

In this chapter, you have learned about the methods of data transfer from a non-SAP system to an SAP system or between two SAP systems. You have also learned how to transfer data related to material from a non-SAP system to an SAP system by using the BDC tool. Next, you have learned how to update the customer master records by using the LSMW tool. In addition, various methods, such as the direct method, the call transaction method, and the batch input with session method, have been discussed in detail.

Chapter 12

Forms in mySAP ERP: SAPscript and SAP Smart Forms

If you need information on:	*See page:*
Exploring the SAPscript Tool	736
The SAP Smart Forms Tool	793
Comparing SAPscript and Smart Forms	808
Migrating SAPscript Forms to Smart Forms	810

A business form is used as a standard format to document various processes in a business. Examples of business forms that companies routinely maintain to record the business processes are invoices, credit memos, and delivery notes. The mySAP ERP system provides two SAP programming tools, SAPscript and SAP Smart Forms, to design, build, and print business forms. SAPscript was the only tool in versions of SAP R/3 before release 4.6 that allowed you to use built-in forms as templates to create the required business forms. SAP Smart Forms is an alternative tool used to design, build, and print business forms in an SAP system. The SAPscript tool cannot be used to print multiple forms simultaneously. To overcome this drawback, you can use the SAP Smart Forms tool, which supports mass printing. In other words, you can design and print multiple forms simultaneously by using the SAP Smart Forms tool. This tool provides the facility to print and send documents through e-mail, fax, and the Internet, and was first shipped with SAP R/3 4.6.

SAPscript has two important components, a print program and a layout set. A print program is a sequence of function modules such as `OPEN_FORM`, `START_FORM`, and `WRITE_FORM`. The print program is used to retrieve the data of a form and call the layout set objects, which are called windows. In SAPscript, an ABAP program populates the contents of a window through a function call given by the print program. SAP Smart Forms, on the other hand, has three important components: a print program manually, a layout set, and a function module. Unlike SAPscript, where you have to activate a layout set for a form manually, the layout set for the form is generated automatically in SAP Smart Forms. This automatic generation of a layout set creates a standard callable SAP function module, which reduces the time to generate the output. This is because when a print program of Smart Forms calls a form, the form itself takes over the task of generating the output (using the generated function module), without the involvement of the print program.

In this chapter, you learn about the SAPscript and SAP Smart Forms tools in detail, including the structure and components of an SAPscript form, the print programs used to print the forms, and the various function modules, control commands, and symbols used in SAPscript. This chapter also discusses the SAP Smart Forms tool and its advantages, the differences between an SAPscript form and a Smart Form, and how to migrate an SAPscript form to a Smart Form.

EXPLORING THE SAPSCRIPT TOOL

The SAPscript tool of the mySAP ERP system is used to build and manage business forms, such as invoices and purchase orders. The SAPscript tool provides numerous templates that simplify the designing of a business form. Figure 12.1 shows an example of an invoice form created by using the SAPscript tool:

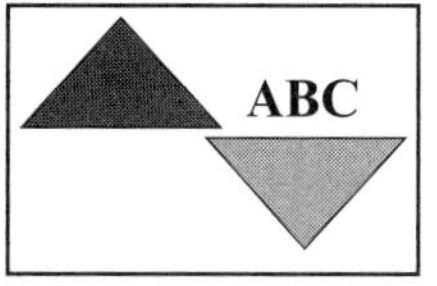

ABC Inc.
QA-23, Industrial
Sector-7,
Delhi

Phone: (450) 653-4030
Fax: (450) 653-4052
Internet: www.myabc.com

Invoice

Billing Address

157 A/B
Okhla Industrial Area
New Delhi - 110011

Information

Document Number	99992401
Document Data	05/04/2009
Purchase Order No.	Ref. 64-ABC-07
Purchase Order Date	05/04/2009
Packing List Number	b0013456
Sales Order Number	423
Payment Terms	Net 3D
Billing Date	05/04/2009
Currency	Rupees

1 of 1

Invoice Details

Item	Material Description	Quantity	Unit Price	Amount
0001	Super Performance Widget Class A-234-500	50EA	1000/1EA	50000
0002	Hi-Grade Widget Composing I-01 45-m-000 Cust. Manual No: CUST 2303	20EA	1000/1EA	20000
0003	Super Performance Widget Class B-234-500	30EA	1000/1EA	30000
			Itcms total...........	100000
			Tax amount..........	12000
			Total amount.......	$ 88000

FIGURE 12.1 Example of an invoice form in SAPscript

The mySAP ERP system comes with standard SAPscript forms that are delivered with the SAP standard client (usually referred to as client 000). Examples of standard SAPscript forms delivered with client 000 are described in Table 12.1:

Form Description	Form Name
Sales Order Confirmation	RVORDER01
Packing List	RVDELNOTE
Invoice	RVINVOICE01
Purchase Order	MEDRUCK
Prenumbered Check	F110_PRENUM_CHCK

TABLE 12.1 Examples of standard SAPscript forms

In the forthcoming sections, we describe the following:

- Components of the SAPscript tool
- Structure of an SAPscript form
- Managing tools
- Accessing PC Editor
- Accessing the Form Painter tool
- Form subobjects
- The SAPscript runtime environment
- The print program
- SAPscript function modules
- Controlling SAPscript forms
- SAPscript control commands
- SAPscript symbols

Components of the SAPscript Tool

The following is a brief description of the various components of the SAPscript tool:

- **Editor**—Edits the text in an SAPscript form. The transaction of an application automatically calls this editor if you need to maintain texts related to the application.
- **Styles and Forms**—Define and print the style and layout of SAPscript forms.
- **Composer or Form Processor**—Acts as a central output module to prepare final layout and text for an output device by including styles, various formatting options, and the respective text.
- **Programming Interface**—Allows you to include SAPscript components into ABAP programs and control the output of forms from the programs.
- **Database Tables**—Store texts, styles, and forms.

Figure 12.2 graphically represents the components of the SAPscript tool:

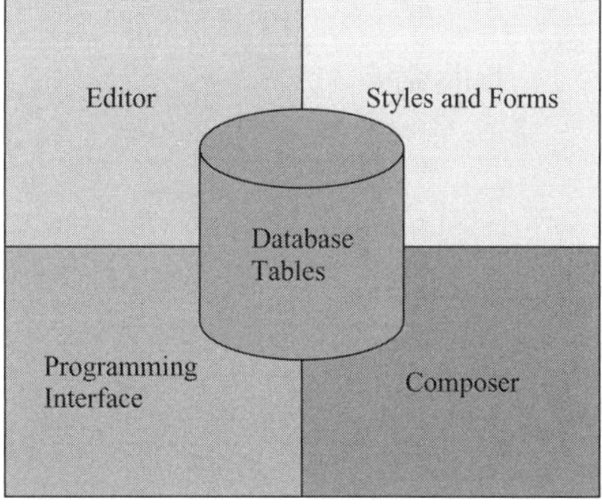

FIGURE 12.2 **Components of the SAPscript tool**

Structure of an SAPscript Form

The structure of an SAPscript form comprises two main components:

- **Content**—Can be either text (for example, the business data for an invoice) or graphics (for example, the company logo).
- **Layout**—Defined by a set of windows in which the content of the form appears.

Figure 12.3 shows the structure of an SAPscript form (an invoice):

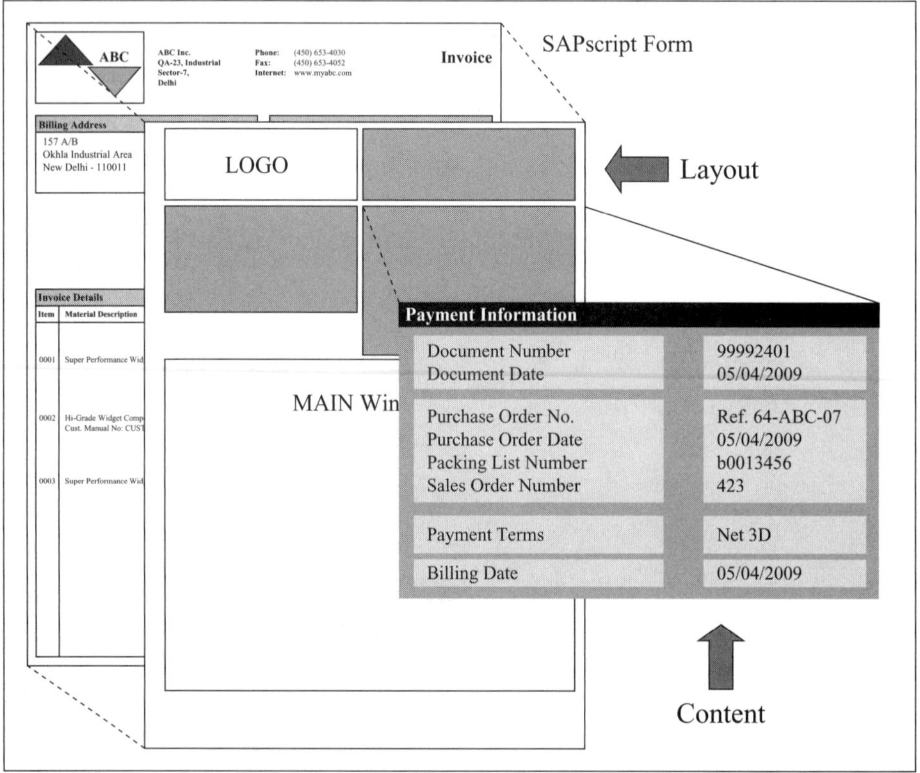

FIGURE 12.3 **Structure of an SAPscript form**

Figure 12.3 shows the layout and content of an SAPscript invoice. The layout is defined by a set of windows: the Logo window, Address window, Billing Address window, Information window, and Main window. These windows contain details of the invoice, as shown in Figure 12.4:

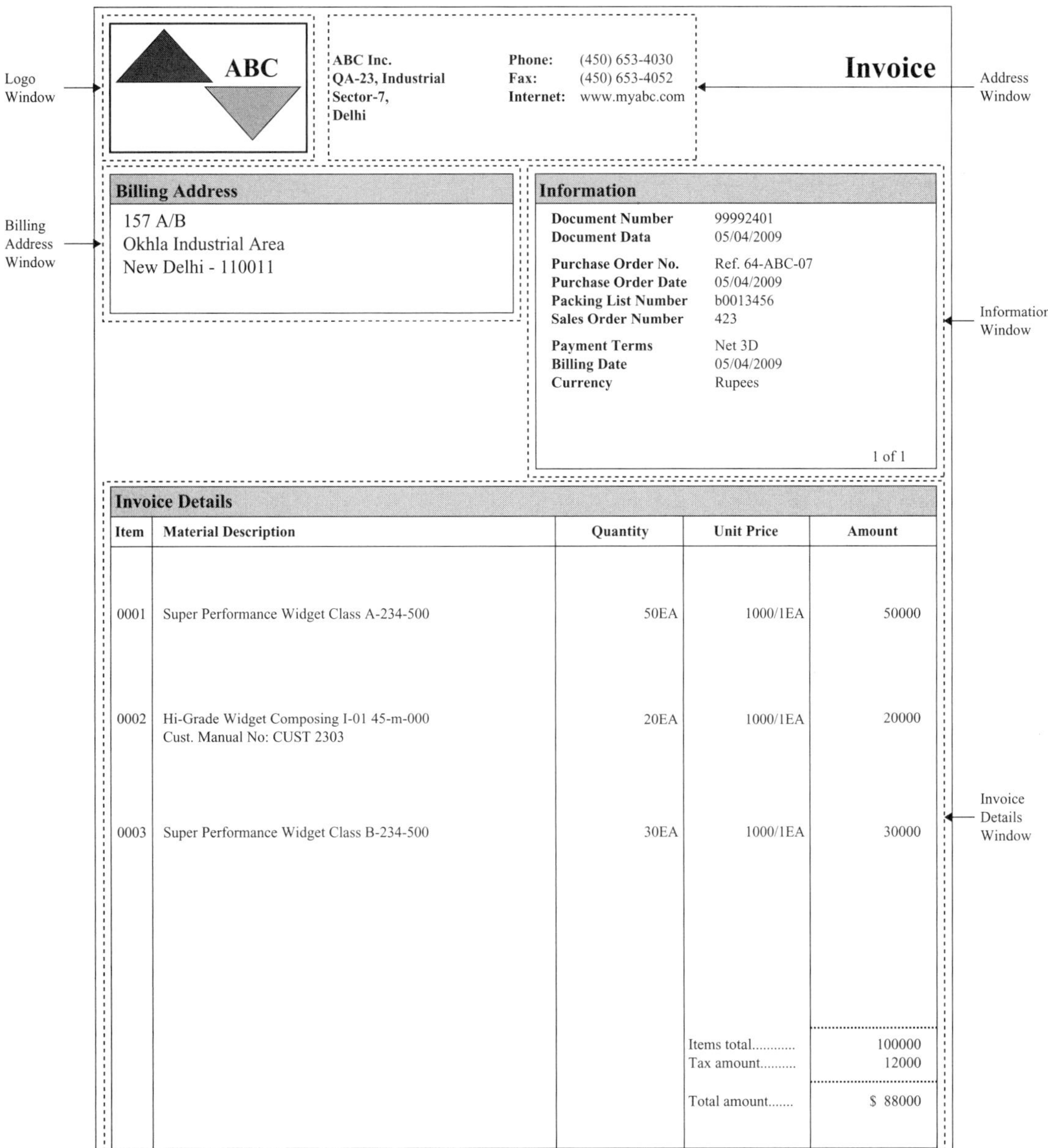

ABC

ABC Inc.
QA-23, Industrial
Sector-7,
Delhi

Phone: (450) 653-4030
Fax: (450) 653-4052
Internet: www.myabc.com

Invoice

Billing Address

157 A/B
Okhla Industrial Area
New Delhi - 110011

Information

Document Number	99992401
Document Data	05/04/2009
Purchase Order No.	Ref. 64-ABC-07
Purchase Order Date	05/04/2009
Packing List Number	b0013456
Sales Order Number	423
Payment Terms	Net 3D
Billing Date	05/04/2009
Currency	Rupees

1 of 1

Invoice Details

Item	Material Description	Quantity	Unit Price	Amount
0001	Super Performance Widget Class A-234-500	50EA	1000/1EA	50000
0002	Hi-Grade Widget Composing I-01 45-m-000 Cust. Manual No: CUST 2303	20EA	1000/1EA	20000
0003	Super Performance Widget Class B-234-500	30EA	1000/1EA	30000

Items total...........	100000
Tax amount..........	12000
Total amount.......	$ 88000

FIGURE 12.4 **Windows in an SAPscript invoice form**

Now, perform the following steps to access an SAPscript form:

1. In the `SAP Easy Access` screen, select `SAP menu > Tools > Form Printout > SAPscript`, as shown in Figure 12.5:

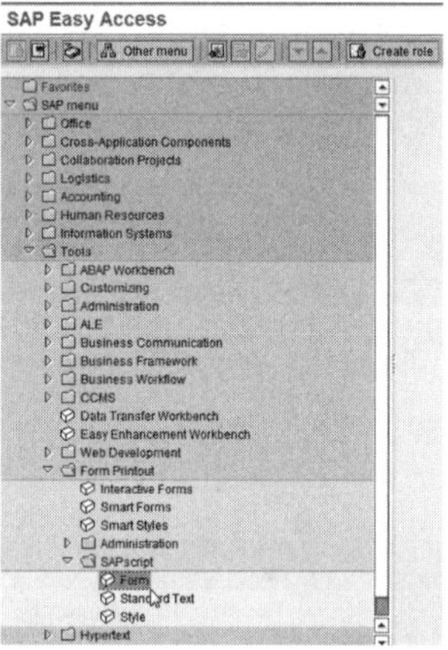

FIGURE 12.5 **Selecting the form option in the SAPscript folder**

2. Double-click the `Form` option in the `SAPscript` folder (Figure 12.5). The request screen of Form Painter appears, as shown in Figure 12.6:

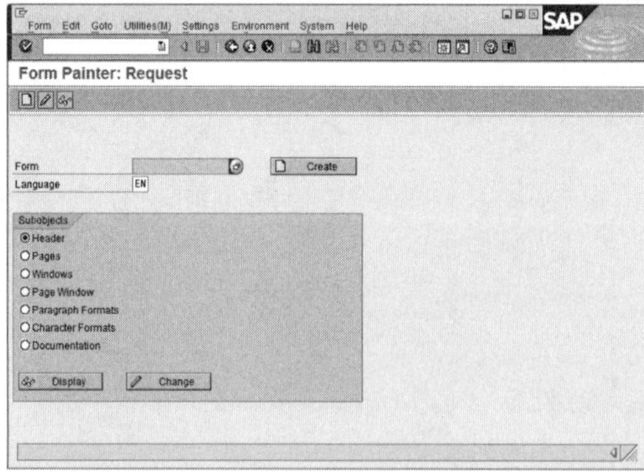

FIGURE 12.6 **The form painter: request screen**

> **Note:** An alternative way to open the `Form Painter: Request` screen is to write the `SE71` transaction code in the `Command` field and then click the `Enter` (✓) icon or press the ENTER key.

Managing Tools

The task of managing forms typically involves managing the layout and content. The SAP system provides the following tools to manage SAPscript forms:

- **PC Editor (or Graphical PC Editor)**—Manages the content of an SAPscript form. It is a graphical text-based tool.
- **Form Painter (or Graphical Form Painter)**—Manages the design and layout of an SAPscript form. It is a graphical tool.

Now, let's learn how to access and use these tools to manage the content of an SAPscript form.

Accessing PC Editor

In this section, we explain how to manage the content of an SAPscript form by using the PC Editor tool. In this case, we use the `RVORDER01` form, which is a predefined form in the mySAP ERP system.

Now, perform the following steps to display the RVORDER01 form by using the PC Editor tool:

1. In the `Form Painter: Request` screen (see Figure 12.6), enter a name for the form in the `Form` field, for example, RVORDER01. In addition, ensure that the `Language` field has EN as the default value.
2. In the `Subobjects` group box, select a radio button for any one of the following options: `Header`, `Pages`, `Windows`, `Page Window`, `Paragraph Formats`, `Character Formats`, and `Documentation`. Table 12.2 provides a brief description of these options:

Subobject	Description
Header	Contains global data of an SAPscript form, such as its page format, page orientation, or the initially used font. It also includes basic information about the form, such as its name, description, and status (that is, whether the form is active or not).
Pages	Defines the pages included in an SAPscript form. A page can have attributes, such as the name of the next page and the type of page numbering. Note that the settings of the pages of a form, which are specified by a user, are maintained throughout the form.
Windows	Represents the logical units that do not have a physical position on a page, such as an address or logo window. A window name should

Continued

Subobject	Description
	reflect the text displayed in the window (for example, the address window would contain the address of a company or an organization). Every window is assigned a window type, such as a constant window, a variable window, or a main window. Unlike other windows, the text `Continuous` appears in the main window, which signifies that this window contains several pages.
Page Window	Describes the position and size of a window on a specific page of an SAPscript form.
Paragraph Formats	Specifies the font, tab, and outline information for the paragraphs in an SAPscript form.
Character Formats	Specifies information of the font in the paragraphs of an SAPscript form.
Documentation	Consists of technical documentation about the components of an SAPscript form, such as its pages and windows.

TABLE 12.2 List of SAPscript subobjects

Note: The preceding components are discussed in detail later in this chapter.

Figure 12.7 shows the `Header` radio button selected in the `Form Painter: Request` screen:

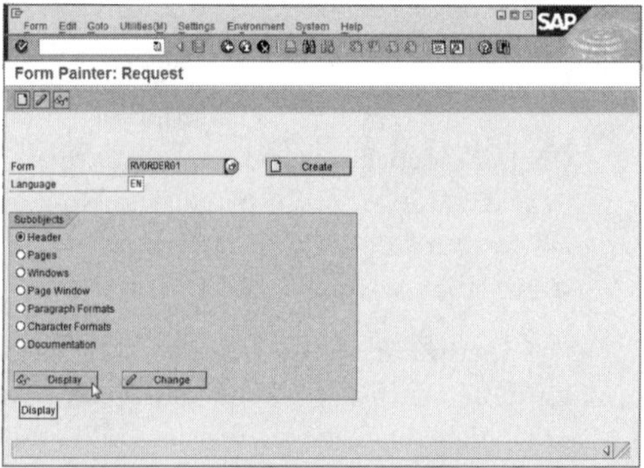

FIGURE 12.7 **Selecting the header radio button**

3. Click the `Display` or `Change` button on the `Form Painter: Request` screen. The `Display` button is used to open an SAPscript form in the display mode so that it can be read. The `Change` button is used to open the same form in the change mode so that it can be modified. In this case, we click the `Display` button (see Figure 12.7).

> **Note:** If your SAP client number is other than 000, the Information message box informs you that the `RVORDER01` form language EN is not available in client XXX. In this message, XXX stands for the client number of your SAP system.

Clicking the `Display` button displays the `Form: Display Header: RVORDER01` screen, as shown in Figure 12.8:

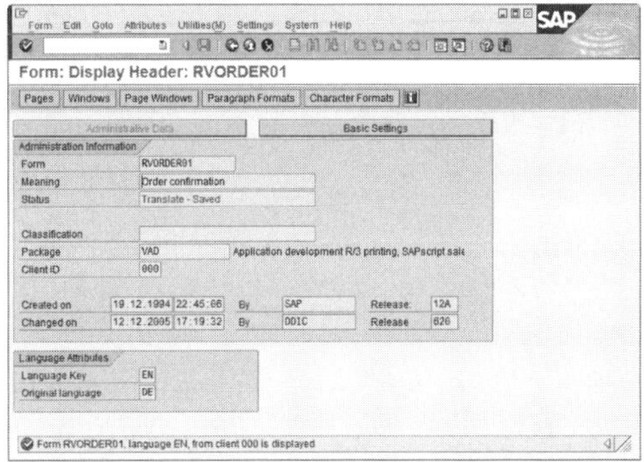

FIGURE 12.8 **The form: display header: RVORDER01 screen**

Figure 12.8 displays the information stored in the `Administrative Data` control of the `RVORDER01` form, which includes administrative information related to the form, such as the name, functionality, status, creation and modification dates, and language-related information, such as the current and original languages of the form.

The `Basic Settings` control includes page-related information, such as page orientation, format, name, and default text formatting values pertaining to the paragraph, tab stop position, and font family.

> **Note:** To know more about administrative and page-related information of a form, refer to the "Form Subobjects" section of this chapter.

Now let's learn how to activate the Form Painter tool. Remember that, unlike the PC Editor tool, which is activated by default, you need to activate the Form Painter tool to access it.

Activating the Form Painter Tool

The Form Painter tool provides the graphical layout of an SAPscript form as well as the various functionalities to manipulate the form. Before using the Form Painter tool, you need to activate it by performing the following steps:

1. Open the `Form Painter: Request` screen by either navigating through the `SAP menu` or by using the `SE71` transaction code.
2. In the `Form Painter: Request` screen, select `Settings` > `Form Painter`, as shown in Figure 12.9:

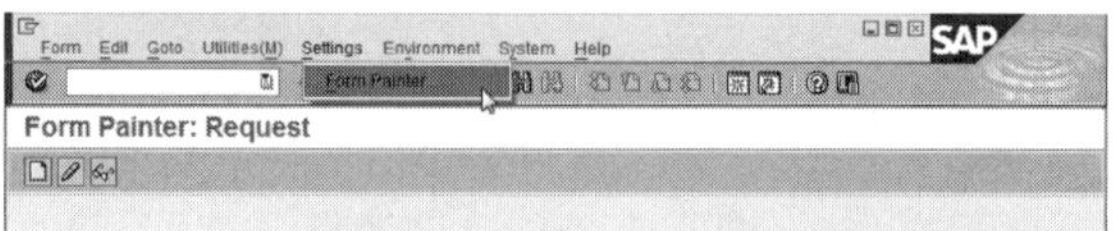

FIGURE 12.9 **Displaying the form painter option**

The `User-Specific Setting` dialog box appears.

3. In the `User-Specific Setting` dialog box, select the `Graphical Form Painter` check box in the `Form Painter` group box. In addition, ensure that the `Graphical PC editor` check box is selected by default, as shown in Figure 12.10:

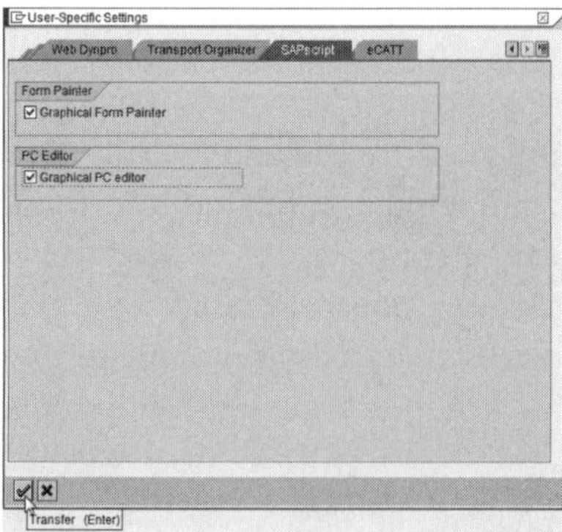

FIGURE 12.10 **The user-specific setting dialog box**

4. Click the Transfer (✔) icon or press the ENTER key to use the settings specified in the User-Specific Settings dialog box for creating an SAPscript form.

Note that the Form Painter: Request screen contains a different set of options in the Subobjects group box from those shown in Figure 12.7. Now, the Subobjects group box contains the Header, Page Layout, Paragraph Formats, Character Formats, and Documentation radio buttons.

Accessing the Form Painter Tool

Form Painter is a graphical tool used to design and set the layout of an SAPscript form. In this section, we learn how to create an invoice form after copying its basic layout structure from a standard SAPscript form, RVINVOICE01, and display its layout by accessing the Form Painter tool. Perform the following steps to do so:

1. Open the Form Painter: Request screen either by navigating the SAP menu or by using the SE71 transaction code.
2. In the Form Painter: Request screen, enter a name and language for an SAPscript form in the Form and Language fields, respectively. In this case, we have entered "RVINVOICE01" and "EN," respectively, in these fields (see Figure 12.11).
3. Select the Page Layout radio button in the Subobjects group box, as shown in Figure 12.11:

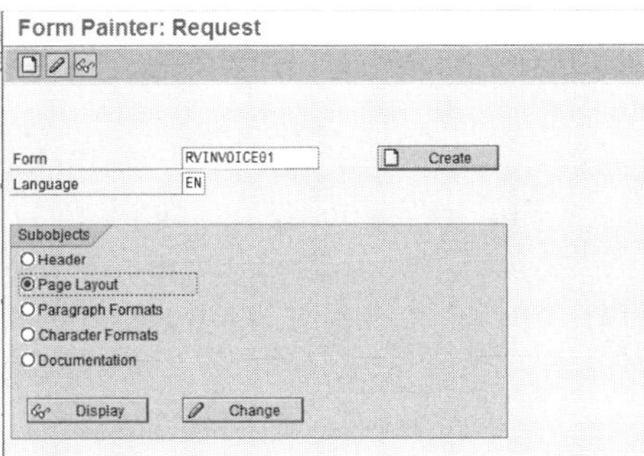

FIGURE 12.11 **Entering field values in the form painter: request screen**

4. Next, select Utilities > Copy from Client to create a copy of the RVINVOICE01 form, as shown in Figure 12.12:

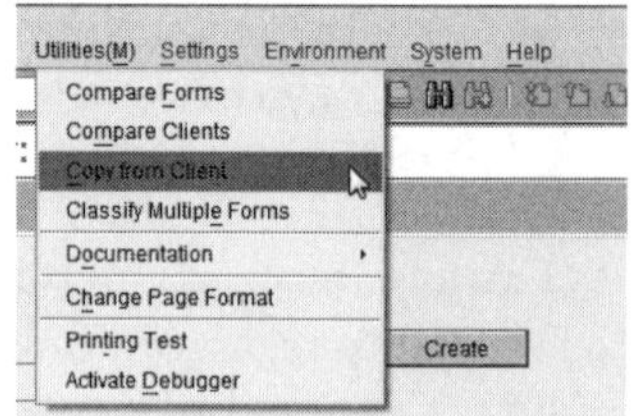

FIGURE 12.12 **Selecting the copy from client option**

The `Copy Forms Between Clients` screen appears.

5. In the `Copy Forms Between Clients` screen, enter the original name of the form, "RVINVOICE01," in the `Form Name` field, the number of the source client, "000," in the `Source Client` field, and the name of the target form, "ZINVOICE02," in the `Target Form` field. Ensure that other settings remain unchanged, as shown in Figure 12.13:

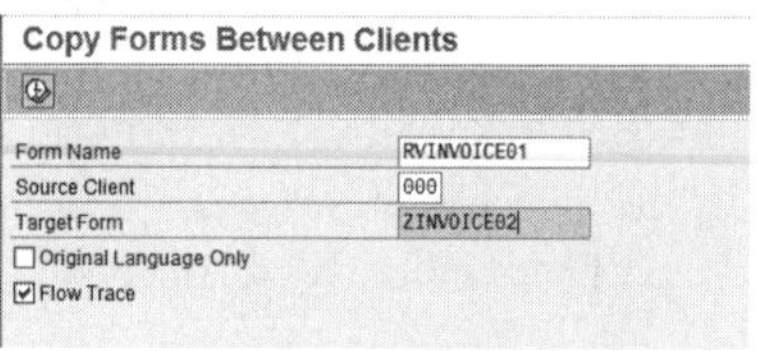

FIGURE 12.13 **Specifying the fields in the copy forms between clients screen**

6. Next, click the `Execute` () icon in the `Copy Forms Between Clients` screen (Figure 12.13). The `Create Object Directory Entry` dialog box appears.
7. In the `Create Object Directory Entry` dialog box, enter the package name, ZKOG_PCKG, in the `Package` field and click the `Save` () icon. The `Prompt for local Workbench request` dialog box appears, as shown in Figure 12.14:

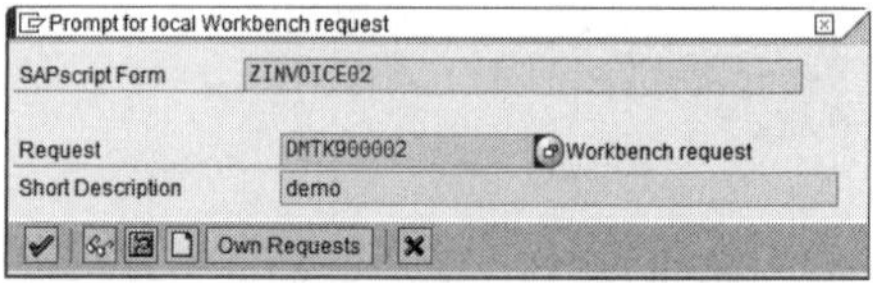

FIGURE 12.14 **The prompt for local workbench request dialog box**

8. In the `Prompt for local Workbench request` dialog box, click the `Continue` (✔) icon. The ZINVOICE02 form is copied from the RVINVOICE01 form and displayed in the `Copy Forms Between Clients` screen, as shown in Figure 12.15:

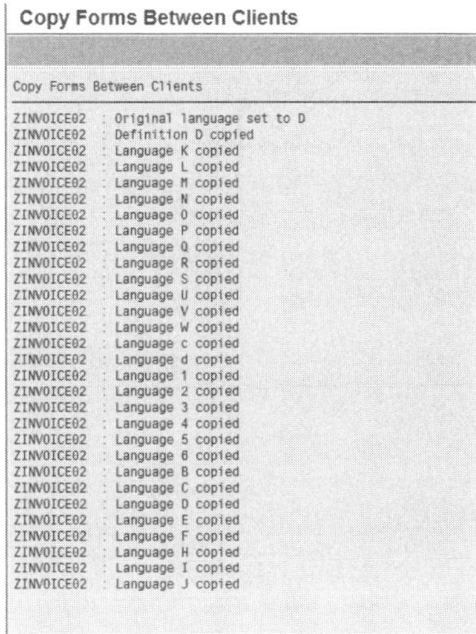

FIGURE 12.15 **Copying a form between two clients**

9. Now, click the `Back` (◀) icon twice and navigate back to the `Form Painter:Request` screen, which contains the name of the copied form (ZINVOICE02), as shown in Figure 12.16:

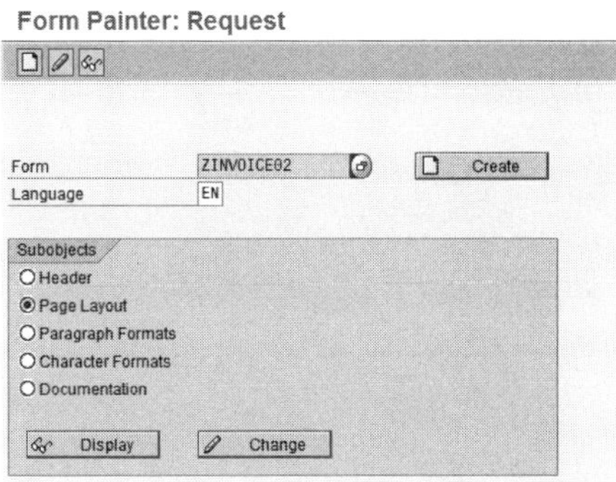

FIGURE 12.16 **Displaying the ZINVOICE02 form in the form painter: request screen**

10. Now, click the `Display` or `Change` button. In our case, we click the `Change` button (Figure 12.16). The `Form ZINVOICE02: Layout of Page FIRST` window and the `Form: Change Page Layout: ZINVOICE02` screen appear, as shown in Figure 12.17:

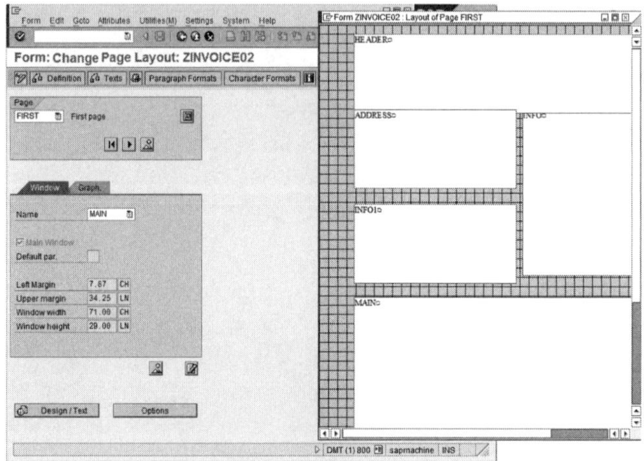

FIGURE 12.17 **The form ZINVOICE02: layout of page FIRST window**

In Figure 12.17, the `Form ZINVOICE02: Layout of Page FIRST` window shows the initial layout of the ZINVOICE02 form. The layout of the ZINVOICE02 form contains five windows: `HEADER`, `ADDRESS`, `INFO`, `INFO1`, and `MAIN`. The description of these windows can be accessed in PC Editor. For instance, select the MAIN window in the `Form ZINVOICE02: Layout of Page FIRST` window and click the `Text` icon in the `Form: Change Page Layout: ZINVOICE02` screen, as shown in Figure 12.18:

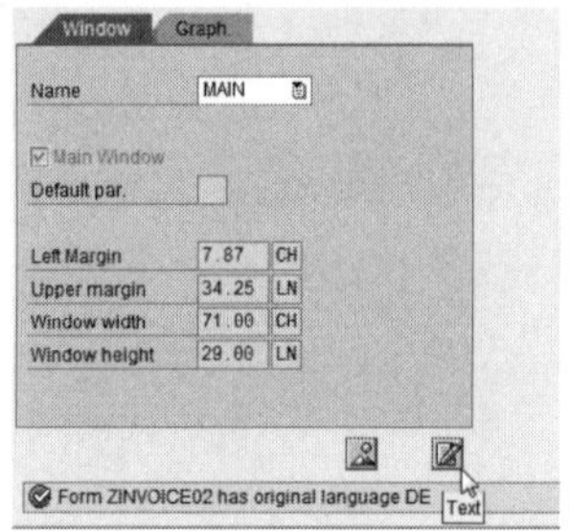

FIGURE 12.18 **Text icon in the form: change page layout: ZINVOICE02 screen**

The Window MAIN screen opens and displays a description of the main window in PC Editor, as shown in Figure 12.19:

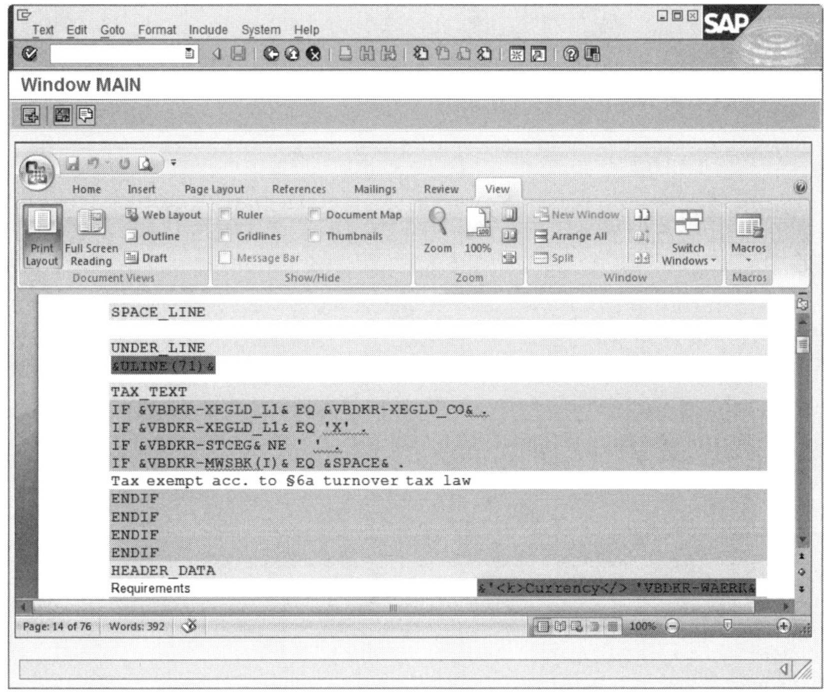

FIGURE 12.19 **Displaying text in the window MAIN screen**

You can also modify the text of the main window in PC Editor.

> **Note:** When you change the text of any window, for example, the Window MAIN, remember to click the Save (💾) icon from the standard toolbar to save the changes.

Next, let's discuss the options available in the Subobjects group box in the Form Painter: Request screen.

Form Subobjects

The Subobjects group box in the Form Painter: Request screen contains the following options (see Figure 12.16):

- `Header`
- `Page Layout`
- `Paragraph Formats`
- `Character Formats`
- `Documentation`

Now, let's discuss these options in detail.

The `Header` Option

The `Header` option or subobject is used to display or accept the information related to an SAPscript form, such as its name and language, and the font used for the text of the SAPscript form. You select the `Header` radio button in the `Form Painter: Request` screen (see Figure 12.16) and open the SAPscript form by clicking the `Display` or `Change` button. In this case, we have clicked the `Change` button, so that the header of the ZINVOICE02 form is displayed in the change mode. Figure 12.20 shows administrative and language-related information of the ZINVOICE02 form:

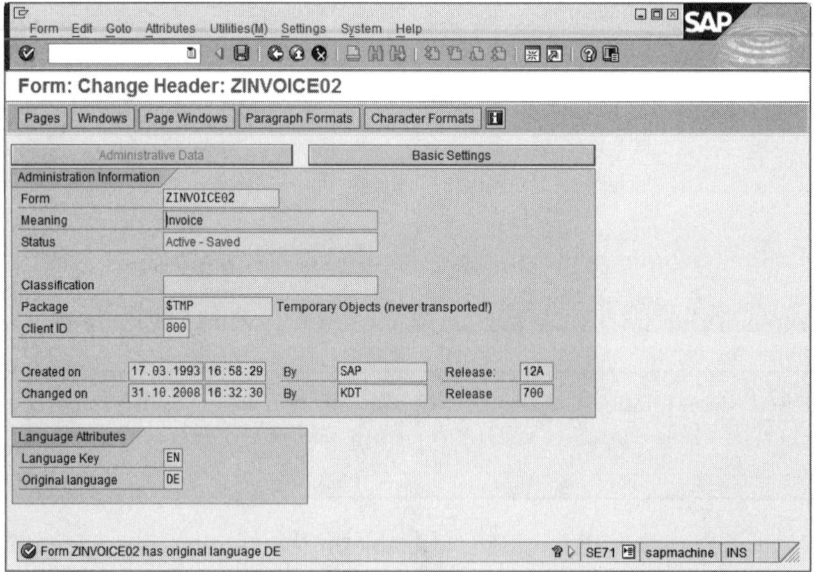

FIGURE 12.20 **Displaying administration information of an invoice form**

Figure 12.20 shows the administrative data of the ZINVOICE02 form in change mode. The `Form: Change Header: ZINVOICE02` screen has two controls, `Administrative Data` and `Basic Settings`, which are used to specify the administrative and formatting information, respectively, of a form. In the `Administrative Data` control, the `Administration Information` group box is used to specify form-related information, such as its description, client number, and the dates on which the form was created and last modified.

The `Language Attributes` group box contains the `Language Key` field representing the current language of the SAPscript form and the `Original language` field representing the language in which the form was created.

The `Basic Settings` control two group boxes, `Set up Page` and `Default Values for Text Formatting`, which are used to set the values of an SAPscript form. Figure 12.21 shows the various elements of the `Basic Settings` control of an invoice form:

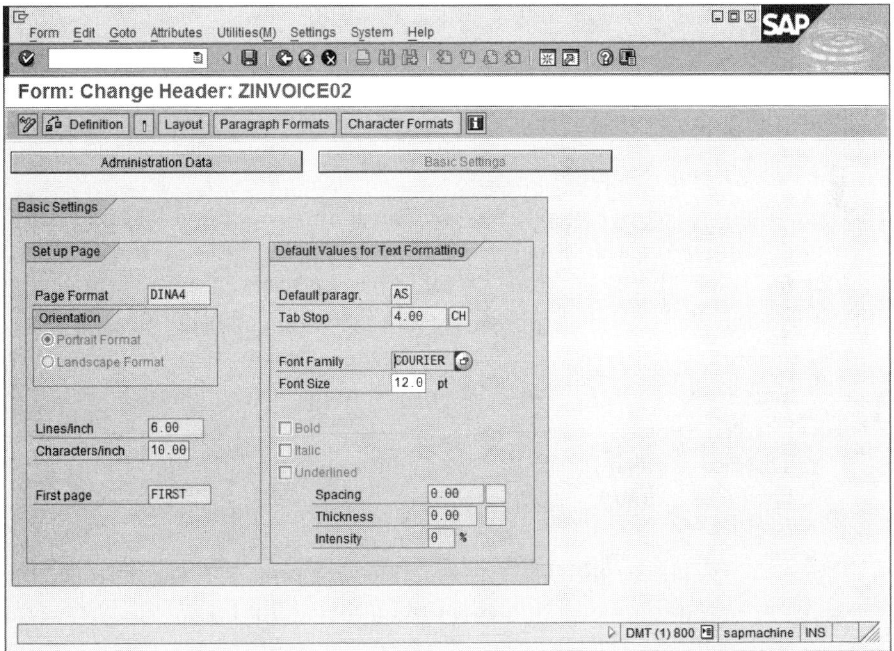

FIGURE 12.21 **The basic settings control of an invoice form**

Figure 12.21 shows that the `Basic Settings` control contains two group boxes, `Set up Page` and `Default Values for Text Formatting`. In the `Set up Page` group box, you can select the page format and orientation of an SAPscript form. For example, the page format of the SAPscript form shown in Figure 12.21 is DINA4. You can also specify values for the `Lines/Inch` and `Characters/inch` fields to set the number of lines or characters in the pages of an SAPscript form. In addition, you can specify the font family, font size, and tab position of the form. For example, the font family and font size of the form shown in Figure 12.21 are courier and 12.0 points, respectively.

> **Note:** You can navigate easily to other subobjects of an SAPscript form, such as `Layout` and `Paragraph Format`, from the screen for the `Header` subobject by selecting the corresponding button in the Application toolbar. For example, to navigate from the `Header` option to the `Page Layout` option, select the `Layout` button in the Application toolbar.

The `Page Layout` Option

Using the `Page Layout` option, you can define the individual pages and new windows needed for an SAPscript form. When you activate the Form Painter tool and select the `Page Layout` radio button in the `Subobjects` group box in the `Form Painter: Request` screen, the following interfaces appear:

- The `Form: Change Page Layout` screen (also called the `Administrative` screen)
- The `Form Layout of Page FIRST` window (also called the Design window)

Figure 12.22 shows the `Administrative` screen and the Design window, which are used to modify the layout of an SAPscript form:

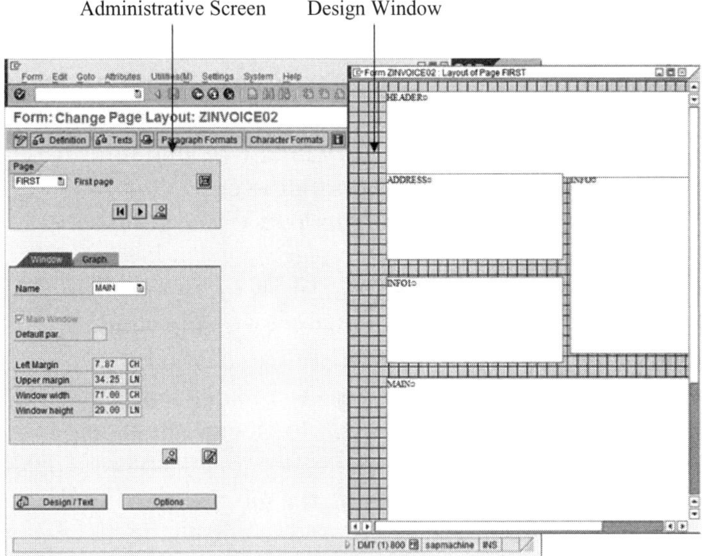

FIGURE 12.22 **The administrative screen and the design window of an SAPscript form**

In Figure 12.22, you see the `Administrative` screen, where you can enter page-related information such as page name, its windows, and their size and position on the page. In the Design window, you determine the layout of different windows of a page graphically. The SAP system always synchronizes the `Administrative` screen with the Design window and vice versa; that is, the changes made in any one of these are reflected in the other.

The `Administrative` screen and the Design window are used to determine the output areas (windows), define pages, and position the windows on the respective pages. In the `Administrative` screen, the different pages and the respective windows can be edited by specifying the values in the following areas:

- **The page area**—Specifies page-related information, such as the sequence and description of the page. Moreover, you can select Edit > Page > Create on this area to create individual pages, Edit > Page > Copy to create a page by using the copy function, Edit > Page > Rename to rename the page, and Edit > Page > Delete to delete individual pages.

- **The window area**—Specifies window-related information, such as a list of all the windows on the current page, and the text elements of the windows. You can select Edit > Windows > Create to create new windows (of the Variables or Main type) and the labels for the windows. By default, the SAP system creates a variable window (type VAR) and assigns it a default name. You can select Edit > Windows > Rename to rename a window, Edit > Windows > Change type to change the type of a window (Main or Var), Edit > Windows > Delete to delete individual windows on the current page, and Edit > Windows > Text Elements to edit the text elements of a window.
    - In addition, you can select Edit > Clipboard > Cut to Clipboard to cut individual windows and Edit > Clipboard > Copy to Clipboard to copy individual windows to the clipboard. The clipboard stores the size and position of a window as well as its text elements. You can also paste a window, including its text elements, size, and position, by selecting Edit > Clipboard > Paste From Clipboard to any page of the form. In addition, you can align all the windows by selecting Edit > Align With Grid. Remember that the main window, unlike the variable window, must always have the same width on all the pages. If a user changes the width of the main window on a page, this change is reflected on all the pages as well.

The Text (icon) icon is used to edit the text elements of a selected window in the Line Editor or WYSIWYG PC Editor (see Figure 12.19). You can switch between these two editors by selecting Go To > Change editor. For example, the text elements of the Window MAIN are displayed in Line Editor, as shown in Figure 12.23:

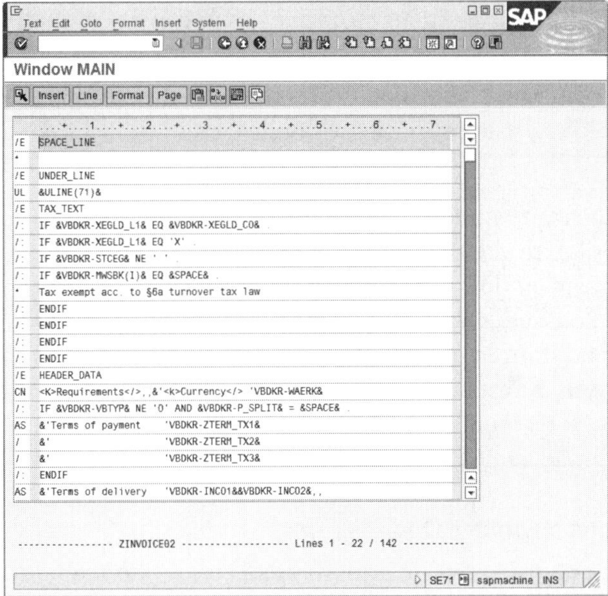

FIGURE 12.23 **Description of the window MAIN in line editor**

The text area in Line Editor consists of the ruler and the subsequent lines where you can enter text.

> **Note:** When you define the window of a form, you have to select its window type. The following are the three types of windows:
>
> - Constant windows (CONST)—Specifies the windows of the same size in all the pages of an SAPscript form.
> - Variable windows (VAR)—Represents the windows of different sizes on different pages of an SAPscript form. If the text exceeds the window size, the text is truncated, but the SAP system does not trigger a page break.

Continued

- Main windows—Contains the text body of an SAPscript form, which may span several pages. The Window MAIN controls the page break and allows you to specify the position of the text elements at the upper and lower margins of the window.

The Design window has a grid surface that allows you to align various windows of a form easily. From the `Administrative` screen, you can assign two different modes, design and text, to the Design window, by clicking the `Design/Text` (Design / Text) button. In the Design mode, you can use the mouse to position or change the size of a window. In the Text mode, however, the SAP system displays the text elements of the individual windows. You can view the text elements by using the scrolling feature of the window. However, the text is read-only.

The Paragraph Formats Option

The `Paragraph Formats` option is used to define the information needed to format text in an SAPscript form. Usually, not all formatting features are used in a form because most form paragraphs consist of only a line or word.

The font and tab attributes generally are used to specify a paragraph format in an SAPscript form. If no font is specified, the default font is used for the header of the form. Figure 12.24 shows the font attributes of a paragraph definition:

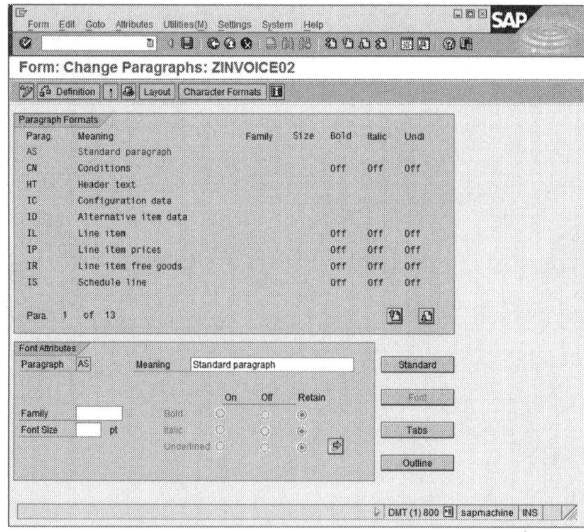

FIGURE 12.24 **Font attributes in the form: change paragraphs screen**

Using tab attributes, you can display the text data of a paragraph in the columns format.

Figure 12.25 shows the tab attributes of a paragraph definition:

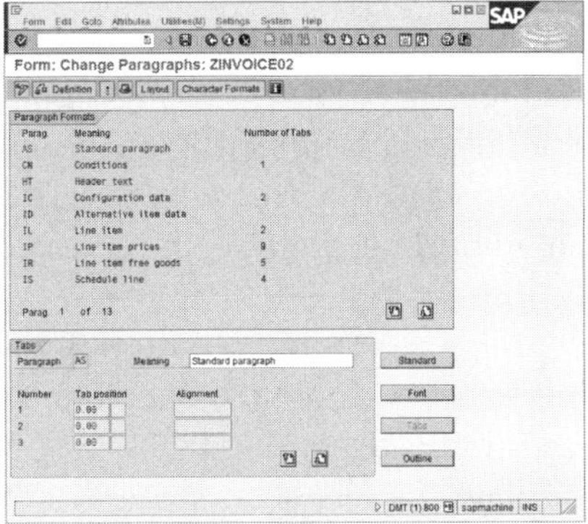

FIGURE 12.25 **Tab attributes in the form: change paragraphs screen**

In Figure 12.25, you can specify the values of the fields in the `Tabs` group box, such as meaning (or description) of a paragraph and position and alignment of tabs.

The Character Formats Option

The `Character Formats` option is used to specify the formatting options for the character data of an SAPscript form; for example, italicizing a single word in a paragraph, instead of the entire paragraph. Figure 12.26 shows the `Form: Change Character Strings: ZINVOICE02` screen, which accepts character formatting information of the ZINVOICE02 form in the change mode:

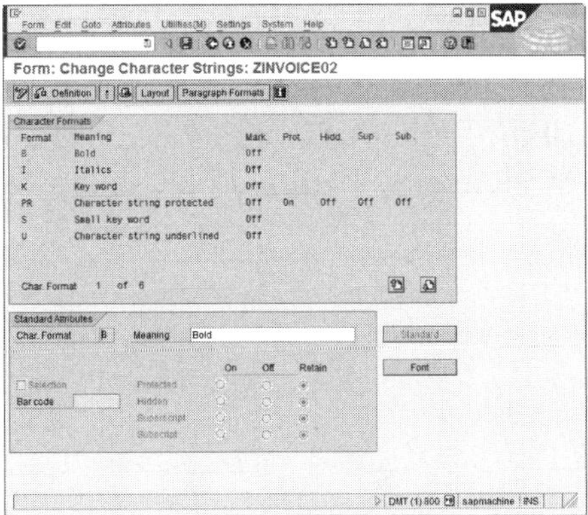

FIGURE 12.26 **Font attributes in the form: change character strings screen**

In the `Standard Attributes` group box (see Figure 12.26), you can specify a bar code format as a character format for the text. You can use PC Editor to include a character string by enclosing the name of the character string in angular brackets (< >) before the specific text and inserting a slash within angular brackets (</>) at the end of the specific text. For example, `<B>`These words are in the bold format`</B>`.

The font attributes of a character string can be accessed by clicking the `Font` button in the `Form: Change Character Strings` screen. You can specify the font attributes to underline, italicize, or bold a character string by selecting the respective radio button.

In Figure 12.26, the `Retain` radio button is used to retain the underline, italic, or bold setting in a paragraph. If a character string has no specified font, the default paragraph font is used.

Figure 12.26 displays the character string B, which changes the format to bold while retaining the Italics and Underline settings in the paragraph.

The Documentation Option

The `Documentation` option is used to create, display, or edit information about the windows and text elements required in an SAPscript form. For instance, you can create a help document corresponding to an SAPscript form, which can include the description of the program symbols used in the program or the purpose of a specific window.

In an SAP system, the documentation of a form is a form itself. This means that the documentation of a form is also language dependent and is involved in the transportation of the form. When you create a document for a form, the SAP system automatically generates a template for the form. This template contains certain sections of read-only lines; however, you can provide additional information about these sections.

In the documentation of an SAPscript form, the read-only lines represent different objects of the form; that is, general information of the form, its pages, windows, and text elements. Figure 12.27 shows the documentation of the `RVORDER01` SAPscript form in the display mode:

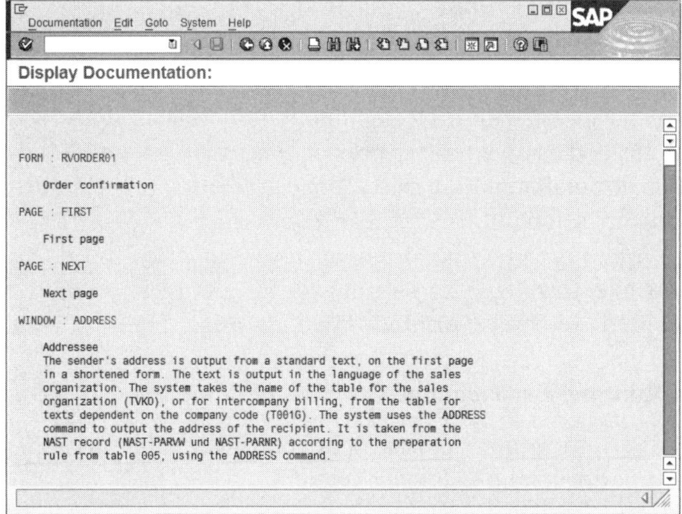

***FIGURE 12.27* The display documentation screen**

The `Display Documentation` screen displays useful information about an SAPscript form, such as its description, the windows it uses, and the text elements it contains. There is a keyword for each text element (`FORM`, `PAGE`, `WINDOW`, and `ELEMENT`) that is followed by its corresponding definition. The `FORM` keyword is followed by the name of the form, the `PAGE` keyword is followed by different page descriptions, the `WINDOW` keyword is followed by the description for different kinds of windows, and the `ELEMENT` keyword is followed by the description of text elements.

You can enhance the already-existing documentation of an SAPscript form by adding new objects to it, which become active after saving the form. When you delete the pages, windows, or text elements of an SAPscript form, the SAP system does not delete the existing documentation; it flags it as "`no longer needed *`" beside the corresponding keyword. Moreover, if you create an object with the same name later, the SAP system deletes the flag and preserves the documentation. Note that the objects flagged as "`no longer needed *`" always appear at the end of the object list but in the same sequence of objects (`FORM`, `PAGE`, `WINDOW`, and `ELEMENT`).

You can select Utilities>Documentation>Clean up to delete all sections that are flagged as no longer needed `*`. This also deletes all the read-only lines for which no documentation exists. You can also delete the entire documentation of a form by selecting `Utilities>Documentation>Delete` in the `Form Paint: Request` screen. Moreover, you can print the documentation of a form by selecting `Utilities>Documentation>Print`. However, only documented objects are printed.

The SAPscript Runtime Environment

The SAPscript runtime environment coordinates the processing of SAPscript forms. It performs the following tasks:

- Retrieving the layout and content data from an SAPscript form
- Collecting the necessary business data from the SAP R/3 database
- Generating the final SAPscript form

The resulting business form can be printed, e-mailed, faxed, or displayed on your computer. Figure 12.28 shows the SAPscript runtime environment in the SAP R/3 system:

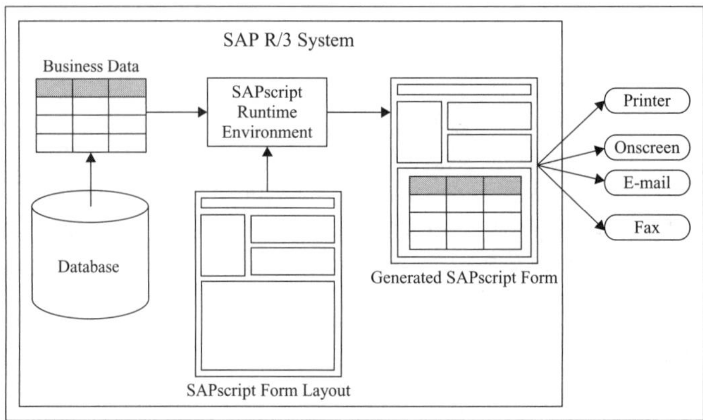

FIGURE 12.28 **SAPscript runtime environment**

Print Program

A print program is an application program (such as Report or ModulePool) used to print forms. The print program retrieves the required data from a database table, defines the order in which the elements of the text are printed, selects the form to print, selects an output device and print options, and processes and prints the form.

A print program uses the following function modules to print a form:

- `OPEN_FORM`
- `CLOSE_FORM`
- `WRITE_FORM`
- `START_FORM`
- `END_FORM`
- `CONTROL_FORM`

> **Note:** To know more about these function modules, refer to the "SAPscript Function Modules" section of this chapter.

The `OPEN_FORM` and `CLOSE_FORM` function modules are used to open and close a form, respectively; and the `START_FORM` and `END_FORM` function modules combine forms into a single spool request for printing. The `WRITE_FORM` function module determines the order in which the text elements are printed. Finally, the `CONTROL_FORM` function module transfers the control statements (for instance, `NEW-PAGE`) from an ABAP program to a form at runtime. A print program can be divided into six parts:

1. **Part 1**—Contains statements to read data from a table. The syntax to read data from a table is:

```
Tables: abc.
SELECT * FROM abc.
```

2. **Part 2**—Contains the `OPEN_FORM` function module to open a form.
3. **Part 3**—Contains the `START_FORM` function module to start a spool request for printing.
4. **Part 4**—Contains the `WRITE_FORM` function module to write the text elements of the windows of the form.

5. **Part 5**—Contains the `END_FORM` function module to end the spool request started by the START_FORM function module.
6. **Part 6**—Contains the `CLOSE_FORM` function module to close the form after displaying or printing the required data.

For example, RSTXEXP1 is a standard print program in the mySAP ERP system and corresponds to the S_EXAMPLE_1 form. Listing 12.1 shows the code of the RSTXEXP1 print program:

```
report rstxexpl.
tables: scustom, sbook, spfli.
select-options: s_id for scustom-id default 1 to 1,
              s_fli for sbook-carrid default 'LH' to 'LH'.
data customers like scustom occurs 100
              with header line.
data bookings like sbook occurs 1000
              with header line.
data connections like spfli occurs 1000
              with header line.
data: begin of sums occurs 10,
              forcuram like sbook-forcuram,
              forcurkey like sbook-forcurkey,
      end of sums.

* Get data
select * from scustom into table customers
              where id in s_id
              order by primary key.
select * from sbook into table bookings
              where customid in s_id and carrid in s_fli
              order by primary key.
select * from spfli into table connections
              for all entries in bookings
              where carrid = bookings-carrid
              and connid = bookings-connid
              order by primary key.
* Open print job
```

Continued

```
call function 'OPEN_FORM'
     exporting
                    device       = 'PRINTER'
                    form         = 'S_EXAMPLE_1'
                    dialog       = 'X'
     exceptions
                    canceled     = 1
                    device       = 2
                    form         = 3
                    options      = 4
                    unclosed     = 5
                    others       = 6.
if sy-subrc <> 0.
      write 'Error in open_form'(001).
      exit.
endif.

* Print form for all customers
loop at customers.
* Set customer address
      scustom = customers.
* Open form of respective customer
      call function 'START_FORM'
            exceptions
                     others      = 1.
if sy-subrc <> 0.
      write 'Error in start_form'(002).
      exit.
endif.

* Display column headings of main window
      call function 'WRITE_FORM'
            exporting
                  element        = 'HEADING'
                  function       = 'SET'
                  type           = 'TOP'
                  window         = 'MAIN'
            exceptions
                  others         = 1.
```

Continued

```
if sy-subrc <> 0.
      write 'Error in write_form printing top element of
      main'(003).
      exit.
endif.
* Customer bookings
      clear sums. refresh sums.
      loop at bookings
              where customid = customers-id.
      sbook = bookings.
* Get departure time
      read table connections with key carrid = bookings
                                               -carrid
                                      connid = bookings
                                               -connid.
      if sy-subrc = 0.
              spfli = connections.
      else.
              clear spfli.
      endif.
* Print position
      call function 'WRITE_FORM'
              exporting
                     element        = 'BOOKING'
                     function       = 'SET'
                     type           = 'BODY'
                     window         = 'MAIN'
              exceptions
                     others         = 1.
      if sy-subrc <> 0.
              write 'Error in write_form printing body of
              main'(004).
              exit.
      endif.
* Add current position to corresponding entry in table
  sums
      move-corresponding sbook to sums.
      collect sums.
endloop.              " at bookings
* Print sum
```

Continued

```
      loop at sums.
      move-corresponding sums to sbook.
      call function 'WRITE_FORM'
              exporting                      .
                     element          = 'SUM'
                     function         = 'SET'
                     type             = 'BODY'
                     window           = 'MAIN'
              exceptions
                     others           = 1.
      if sy-subrc <> 0.
      write 'Error in write_form printing sum of
      invoice'(005).
      exit.
endif.
      endloop.      " at sums

* Close customer form
      call function 'END_FORM'
              exceptions
                     others           = 1.
if sy-subrc <> 0.
              write 'Error in end_form'(006).
              exit.
      endif.
endloop.      " at customers

* close print job
call function 'CLOSE_FORM'
              exceptions
                     others           = 1.
if sy-subrc <> 0.
      write 'Error in close_form'(007).
      exit.
endif.
```

LISTING 12.1 **Code of the RSTXEXP1 print program**

The code given in Listing 12.1 creates an invoice form that contains company-related information, such as the flight bookings of a customer, customer address, and flight booking dates.

In Listing 12.1, the data of the form is read from a database table and populated in internal tables (for example, BOOKINGS). The `OPEN_FORM` function module is called to open the S_EXAMPLE_1 form for printing. The `WRITE_FORM` function module is used to write the `HEADING` text element in the `MAIN` window of the form. The `HEADING` text element displays the column or field names of the invoice in the `MAIN` window of the form. The `BOOKING` text element in the `MAIN` window provides information related to the bookings of the customer. The information displayed by the BOOKING text element is retrieved by using the BOOKINGS internal table in a loop. The address of the customer and company-related information are displayed by using default text elements. The `CLOSE_FORM` function module finally closes the form.

Note: The various function modules are discussed in detail later in this chapter.

Now, perform the following steps to view a print preview of the S_EXAMPLE_1 form through the RSTXEXP1 print program:

1. Open ABAP Editor by either navigating through the `SAP` menu or executing the `SE38` transaction code and entering the name of the print program, RSTXEXP1, in the specified `Program` text field, as shown in Figure 12.29:

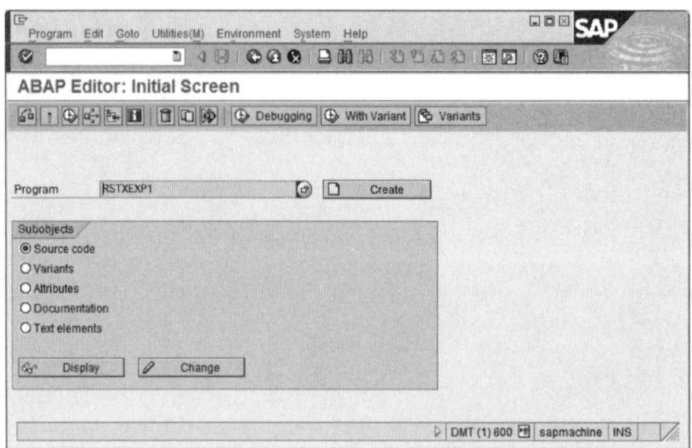

FIGURE 12.29 **Entering the program name in ABAP editor**

2. Select the `Source code` radio button in the Subobjects list and then click the `Display` button (see Figure 12.29). ABAP Editor displays the source code of the RSTXEXP1 print program, as shown in Figure 12.30:

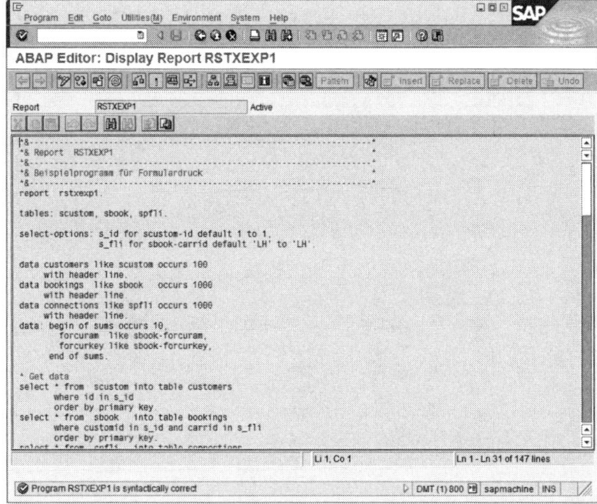

FIGURE 12.30 **Source code of the RSTXEXP1 print program**

3. Click the `Check` icon to check the source code of the program. Next, click the `Activate` icon to activate the program and the `Direct Processing` icon to process the RSTXEXP1 program (see Figure 12.30).

The `SAPscript: Sample Program for Form Printing` screen appears, as shown in Figure 12.31:

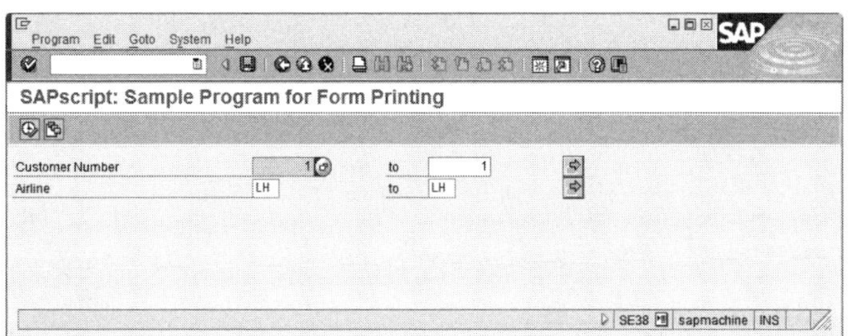

FIGURE 12.31 **The SAPscript: sample program for form printing screen**

4. Click the `Execute` icon or press the F8 key, as shown in Figure 12.31. The `Print` dialog box appears.

5. Enter the value lp01 in the `Output Device` text field of the `Print` dialog box, as shown in Figure 12.32:

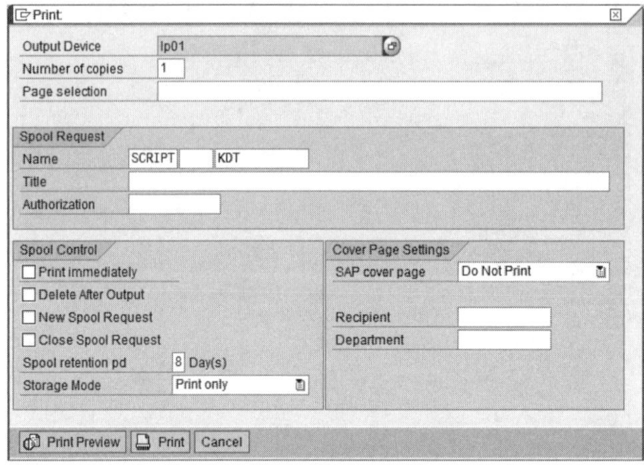

FIGURE 12.32 **The print dialog box**

6. Click the `Print Preview` button of the `Print` dialog box (see Figure 12.32) to display the print preview of the S_EXAMPLE_1 form.

Figure 12.33 shows the print preview of the S_EXAMPLE_1 SAPscript form:

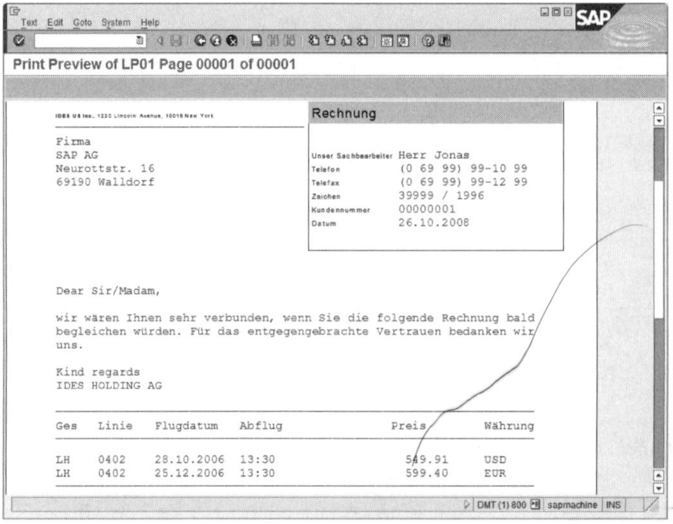

FIGURE 12.33 **Print preview of the S_EXAMPLE_1 form**

SAPscript Function Modules

Table 12.3 describes some commonly used function modules to process SAPscript forms:

Function Module	Description
OPEN_FORM	Opens a form to display or print it.
CLOSE_FORM	Closes a form.
START_FORM	Starts a new form for spooling a print request.
WRITE_FORM	Writes a text element in a form.
WRITE_FORM_LINES	Writes lines of text in a form.
END_FORM	Ends or terminates the spool request of printing the current form.
CONTROL_FORM	Sends a control statement to a form.
READ_FORM_ELEMENTS	Retrieves the elements of a form.
READ_FORM_LINES	Reads the lines of the elements of a form and stores them in an internal table.

TABLE 12.3 Commonly used function modules for SAPscript forms

Now, let's describe each function module in detail.

The `OPEN_FORM` Function Module

The `OPEN_FORM` function module opens an SAPscript form to display or print its data. It is, therefore, used before other function modules. Using the name of a form is optional with the `OPEN_FORM` function module. However, if the name of the form is omitted, the `START_FORM` function module must be used to open the form. A form must be closed by the `CLOSE_FORM` function module; otherwise, the SAP system does not print or display the form.

Note that a pair of `OPEN_FORM. . . CLOSE_FORM` function modules can be used any number of times in a program. This allows you to display or print a form for several different spool requests from one program. The following is the syntax used to call the `OPEN_FORM` function module:

```
CALL FUNCTION 'OPEN_FORM'
EXPORTING FORM = SPACE
LANGUAGE = SY-LANGU
DEVICE = 'PRINTER'
DIALOG = 'X'
OPTIONS = SPACE
APPLICATION = 'TX'
ARCHIVE_INDEX = SPACE
ARCHIVE_PARAMS = SPACE
IMPORTING LANGUAGE =
RESULT =
NEW_ARCHIVE_PARAMS =
EXCEPTIONS CANCELED =
DEVICE =
FORM =
OPTIONS =
UNCLOSED =
```

The `OPEN_FORM` function module is called by using the export parameters listed in Table 12.4:

Parameter	Description
FORM	Specifies the name of a form. The default value of this parameter is `SPACE`. If this parameter is left blank, the `START_FORM` function module must be called with a valid form name before starting a spool request for printing.
LANGUAGE	Specifies the desired language, as forms are language-dependent. The default value of this parameter is `SY-LANGU`.
DEVICE	Specifies the desired device type for the output of a form. The possible values for this parameter are `PRINTER` for the print output, `TELEX` for the telex output, `TELEFAX` for the telefax output, `ABAP` for the output as an ABAP list, and `SCREEN` for the screen output. The default value of this parameter is `PRINTER`.
DIALOG	Determines whether or not to display a dialog box before printing the form. The default value of this parameter is `X`, which displays the print parameter screen. The other possible value for this parameter is ' ', which does not display the print parameter screen.

Continued

Parameter	Description
OPTIONS	Sets several options to specify the format to print a form. The default value of this paramter is SPACE.
APPLICATION	Specifies an interface name provided by SAPscript. The default value of this parameter is TX.
ARCHIVE_INDEX	Specifies index information for the print output that needs to be archived. The default value of this parameter is SPACE.
ARCHIVE_PARAMS	Specifies a value that is interpreted by the SAP system to archive the output. The default value of this parameter is SPACE.

TABLE 12.4 Export parameters in the OPEN_FORM function module

The OPEN_FORM function module uses the import parameters listed in Table 12.5:

Parameter	Description
LANGUAGE	Specifies the language of a form.
RESULT	Contains the results of the process to specify a format to print a form.
NEW_ARCHIVE_PARAMS	Contains the results of the archive process.

TABLE 12.5 Import parameters in the OPEN_FORM function module

Calling the OPEN_FORM function module can raise exceptions when the parameters specified in Table 12.6 contain invalid values:

Parameter	Description
CANCELED	Handles the exception raised when no form is opened for output.
DEVICE	Handles the exception raised when an invalid device type is found.

Continued

Parameter	Description
FORM	Handles the exception raised when a form of the specified name is not found in an SAP system. The possible reasons for this may be that either the form does not exist or there is no active version of the form.
OPTIONS	Handles the exception raised when invalid values are specified for the formatting options while printing a form.
UNCLOSED	Handles the exception raised when an SAP system tries to open another form without closing the earlier form.

TABLE 12.6 Exception parameters in the OPEN_FORM function module

Note: In an SAP system, the searching criteria to find a form can be explained in the following way: SAPscript first searches for the form in the current client and in the specified language. If the form is not found, SAPscript tries the original language of the form. If the form is still not found, it searches for the form in client 000, first in the specified language and then in the original language of the form.

The `CLOSE_FORM` Function Module

The `CLOSE_FORM` function module closes an open form. You can use this function module to close the form; otherwise, no output appears on the printer or screen.

The syntax to call the `CLOSE_FORM` function module is:

```
CALL FUNCTION 'CLOSE_FORM'
IMPORTING RESULT =
TABLES OTFDATA = ?...
EXCEPTIONS UNOPENED =
```

In this syntax, `RESULT` is the import parameter that receives the results of formatting a form for printing. By comparing the fields of the `OPTIONS` parameter (of the `OPEN_FORM` function module) with the corresponding fields of the `RESULT` parameter, you can find out whether any changes have been made to the settings on the print control screen. OTFDATA is the table parameter, which is optional if the value of the OPTIONS parameter is X for the TDGETOTF field. This is because in this case, the SAP system returns the formatted output in the OTF format, which means that the SAP system does not produce any output to printer, screen, faxmachine, or telex. The SAP system throws the UNOPENED runtime exception if it is not able to execute the current form function because the output of the form has not yet been initialized by the OPEN_FORM function module.

Note that you can open or close one or more forms by using the OPEN_FORM and CLOSE_FORM function modules, respectively. In addition, you can combine multiple forms into one print output, but all these forms must have the same page format.

The START_FORM Function Module

The START_FORM function module is used to start a spool request to print or display a form. On the contrary, the END_FORM function module is used to stop or end the spool request for printing or displaying the form. You can use the pair of START_FORM and END_FORM function modules more than once inside the pair of the OPEN_FORM and CLOSE_FORM function modules.

You can also use the START_FORM function module to switch from one form to another. For this, you must end the spool request to print the first form by using the END_FORM function module and then use the START_FORM function module to start the the spool request to print the second form.

If you do not specify the name of a form when calling the START_FORM function module, the SAP system restarts the process of formatting the last opened form. If no form is activated after the OPEN_FORM function module is called, the SAP system raises the UNUSED exception.

The syntax to call the START_FORM function module is:

```
CALL FUNCTION 'START_FORM'
EXPORTING FORM = SPACE
LANGUAGE = SPACE
STARTPAGE = SPACE
PROGRAM = SPACE
ARCHIVE_INDEX = SPACE
IMPORTING LANGUAGE =
```

Continued

```
EXCEPTIONS FORM =
FORMAT =
UNENDED =
UNOPENED =
UNUSED =
```

The `START_FORM` function module is called by using the export parameters listed in Table 12.7:

Parameter	Description
FORM	Specifies the name of the form a user wants to print. If no form is specified, the SAP system restarts the printing operation of the last active form. The default value of this parameter is `SPACE`.
LANGUAGE	Specifies the language of a form. If the form does not exist in the specified language, the SAP system calls the form in its original language. If the form is still not found, the SAP system uses the language of the last activated form. The default value of this parameter is `SY-LANGU`.
STARTPAGE	Specifies the starting page of a form. If this parameter is not defined, the SAP system uses the start page defined in the page layout of the form. The default value of this parameter is `SPACE`.
PROGRAM	Specifies a program name that is replaced by the original program in the final output. The default value of this parameter is `SPACE`.
ARCHIVE_INDEX	Specifies the index information of the print output to be archived. The default value of this parameter is SPACE.

TABLE 12.7 Export parameters in the START_FORM function module

The `LANGUAGE` import parameter is used in the `START_FORM` function module to specify the language variant of the form being used by the SAP system.

Calling the START_FORM function module can raise exceptions in case the parameters specified in Table 12.8 contain invalid values:

Parameter	Description
FORM	Handles the exception raised when the form of the specified name is not found in an SAP system. The possible reasons may be that either the form does not exist or there is no active version of the form.
FORMAT	Handles the exception raised when the page format of one form differs from the other forms; while both the forms have the same print format.
UNENDED	Handles the exception raised when the last form is still open. The user must end the form by using the END_FORM function module or close the form by using the CLOSE_FORM function module.
UNOPENED	Handles the exception raised when the specified form is not opened by using the OPEN_FORM function module.
UNUSED	Handles the exception raised when either the FORM or LANGUAGE parameter is left blank, or when a form is opened by using the default name and language.

TABLE 12.8 Exception parameters in the START_FORM function module

The WRITE_FORM Function Module

The WRITE_FORM function module is used to write the output of an SAPscript form in the specified element and to specify a window of the output. The following syntax is used to call the WRITE_FORM function module:

```
CALL FUNCTION 'WRITE_FORM'
EXPORTING ELEMENT = SPACE
WINDOW = 'MAIN'
FUNCTION = 'SET'
TYPE = 'BODY'
IMPORTING PENDING_LINES =
```

Continued

```
EXCEPTIONS ELEMENT =
FUNCTION =
TYPE =
UNOPENED =
UNSTARTED =
WINDOW =
```

The WRITE_FORM function module is called by using the export parameters listed in Table 12.9:

Parameter	Description
ELEMENT	Specifies the name of the text element that needs to be printed in a form. The SAP system uses the default text element if you do not specify any text element. The default value of this parameter is SPACE.
WINDOW	Specifies the name of the window in which the user wants to provide the output of a text element of an SAPscript form. The default value of this parameter is MAIN.
FUNCTION	Specifies the output of a text element in the respective windows contained in a page of a form. The default value of this parameter is SET.
TYPE	Specifies the area of the MAIN window in which the user wants to provide the output of a text element. The possible values for this parameter are TOP for the header area and BOTTOM for the footer area. The default value of this parameter is BODY for the main area of the window.

TABLE 12.9 Export parameters in the WRITE_FORM function module

The PENDING_LINES import parameter of the WRITE_FORM function module contains the value X when the text lines of a form are pending for print output, which is handled by the print program.

Calling the WRITE_FORM function module can raise exceptions when the parameters specified in Table 12.10 contain invalid values:

Parameter	Description
ELEMENT	Handles the exception raised when an SAP system does not find the name of a form element. The following are possible reasons for this: ▪ The element does not exist for a specified window in the defined form. ▪ The element is specified for a window, but not defined in the form. ▪ The defined form, having the text element in the specified window, is not active.
FUNCTION	Handles the exception raised when the function specified in this parameter is unknown. The possible values for the FUNCTION export parameter are SET, APPEND, and DELETE.
TYPE	Handles the exception raised when the TYPE parameter specifies an invalid type of window. The possible values for this parameter are BODY for all windows and TOP or BOTTOM for the MAIN window.
UNOPENED	Handles the exception raised when the WRITE_FORM function module executes a form that has not been opened.
UNSTARTED	Handles the exception raised when no form is open. The following are possible reasons for this exception: ▪ The OPEN_FORM function module starts processing a form without specifying the form name in the function module. ▪ The END_FORM function module ends the processing of a form, which had been started by using the START_FORM function module. ▪ The current form has no subsequent page after populating the last page. In this case, the SAP system automatically terminates the printing of the form after this page and raises the UNSTARTED exception.

Continued

Parameter	Description
	▪ The current form does not contain any page having the MAIN window, but a text element is specified to be displayed in the MAIN window.
WINDOW	Handles the exception raised when the form window specified in the WINDOW export parameter does not exist in the current form.

TABLE 12.10 Exception parameters in the WRITE_FORM function module

The WRITE_FORM_LINES Function Module

The WRITE_FORM_LINES function module is used to insert records or lines stored in a table to a specified window of a form. The following syntax is used to call the WRITE_FORM_LINES function module:

```
CALL FUNCTION 'WRITE_FORM_LINES'
EXPORTING HEADER = ?...
WINDOW = 'MAIN'
FUNCTION = 'SET'
TYPE = 'BODY'
IMPORTING PENDING_LINES =
FROMPAGE =
TABLES LINES = ?...
EXCEPTIONS FUNCTION =
TYPE =
UNOPENED =
UNSTARTED =
WINDOW =
```

The WRITE_FORM_LINES function module is called by using the export parameters listed in Table 12.11:

Parameter	Description
HEADER	Specifies the header field of a form to be printed.
WINDOW	Specifies the name of the window where the user wants to provide the output of the form element, specified in the ELEMENT parameter. The default value of this parameter is MAIN.
FUNCTION	Specifies the output of the text element in the respective windows of the form. The default value of this parameter is SET.
TYPE	Specifies the area of the MAIN window where you want to display the output of a text element. The possible values of this parameter are TOP for the header area and BOTTOM for the footer area. The default value of this parameter is BODY for the main area of the window.

TABLE 12.11 Export parameters in the WRITE_FORM_LINES function module

The WRITE_FORM_LINES function module is called by using the import parameters listed in Table 12.12:

Parameter	Description
PENDING_LINES	Specifies the value X when the text lines of a form that is handled by the print program are pending.
FROMPAGE	Specifies the starting page of a form where printing has to begin.

TABLE 12.12 Import parameters in the WRITE_FORM_LINES function module

The WRITE_FORM_LINES function module is called by using the LINES table parameter if the name of the table containing the text lines to be printed is specified.

Calling the WRITE_FORM_LINES function module can raise exceptions when the parameters specified in Table 12.13 contain invalid values:

Parameter	Description
FUNCTION	Handles the exception raised when the function specified in the FUNCTION export parameter is unknown. The possible values of this parameter are SET, APPEND, and DELETE.
TYPE	Handles the exception raised when the type of window area specified in the TYPE export parameter is invalid. The possible values of this parameter are BODY for all windows and TOP or BOTTOM for the MAIN window.
UNOPENED	Handles the exception raised when the WRITE_FORM_LINES function module cannot be executed because the form has not yet been opened by the OPEN_FORM function module.
UNSTARTED	Handles the exception raised when no open form is found. The possible reasons for this exception are as follows: ▪ The OPEN_FORM function module starts a form without specifying the name of the form in the START_FORM function module. ▪ The END_FORM function module ends the form whose processing had not been started by using the START_FORM function module. ▪ The current form has no subsequent page after populating the last page. In this case, the SAP system automatically terminates the printing of the form after this page and raises the UNSTARTED exception. The current form does not contain any page having the MAIN window, but a text element is specified to be displayed in the MAIN window.
WINDOW	Handles the exception raised when the window of the form specified in the WINDOW parameter does not exist in the current form. This may be because a wrong window name is specified or the form containing this window is not active.

TABLE 12.13 Exception parameters in the WRITE_FORM_LINES function module

The END_FORM Function Module

The END_FORM function module ends or terminates the currently opened form and performs the required processing to terminate it. The task of the

END_FORM function module is different from that of the CLOSE_FORM function module; the CLOSE_FORM function module is used to close an SAPscript form that you want to print. The following syntax is used to call the END_FORM function module:

```
CALL FUNCTION 'END_FORM'
IMPORTING RESULT =
EXCEPTIONS UNOPENED =
```

In this syntax, the RESULT parameter contains the results of the formatting of a form before the form is printed. By comparing the corresponding fields of the OPTIONS parameter with those of the RESULT parameter, you can determine if changes have been made in the settings of the print control screen. The SAP system throws the UNOPENED runtime exception when it is not able to execute the END_FORM function module, because the form has not yet been opened by the OPEN_FORM function module.

The CONTROL_FORM Function Module

The CONTROL_FORM function module is used to pass SAPscript control statements to a form. The following syntax is used to call the CONTROL_FORM function module:

```
CALL FUNCTION 'CONTROL_FORM'
EXPORTING COMMAND = ?...
EXCEPTIONS UNOPENED =
UNSTARTED =
```

In this syntax, the COMMAND export parameter is used to enter the SAPscript statement that you want to execute in the Interchange Text Format (ITF), but without the '/:' statement paragraph attribute.

The SAP system throws the UNOPENED runtime exception when it is not able to execute the CONTROL_FORM function module because the form has not yet been opened by the OPEN_FORM function module.

The UNSTARTED exception is thrown when an SAP system cannot find a form to start. The possible reasons for this exception are as follows:

- The OPEN_FORM function module starts processing a form without specifying the name of the form in the START_FORM function module.

- The END_FORM function module ends the processing of a form whose processing was not started by using the START_FORM function module.
- The current form has no subsequent page after filling the last page. In this case, the system automatically terminates the printing of the form after this page and raises the UNSTARTED exception.
- The current form does not contain any page having the MAIN window, but a text element is specified to be displayed in the MAIN window.

The READ_FORM_ELEMENTS Function Module

The READ_FORM_ELEMENTS function module populates a table with all the text elements of a form. The following syntax is used to call the READ_FORM_ELEMENTS function module:

```
CALL FUNCTION 'READ_FORM_ELEMENTS'
EXPORTING FORM = SPACE
LANGUAGE = SPACE
TABLES ELEMENTS = ?...
EXCEPTIONS FORM =
UNOPENED =
```

The READ_FORM_ELEMENTS function module is called by using the export parameters listed in Table 12.14:

Parameter	Description
FORM	Specifies the name of the form whose list of elements need to be created. If you leave this parameter blank, the SAP system uses the current active form. The default value of this parameter is SPACE.
LANGUAGE	Specifies the desired language of a form. The default value of this parameter is SPACE.

TABLE 12.14 Export parameters in the READ_FORM_ELEMENTS function module

ELEMENTS, a table parameter of the READ_FORM_ELEMENTS function module, is used to specify the name of a table that stores the name of all windows and their respective text elements. Note that the SAP system assigns a specific number to each text element, which is the number of text lines contained by the text element. Calling the READ_FORM_ELEMENTS function module can raise exceptions when the parameters listed in Table 12.15 contain invalid values:

Parameter	Description
FORM	Handles the exception raised when a form of the specified name is not found in an SAP system. The reason for this may be that either the form does not exist or there is no active version of the form.
UNOPENED	Handles the exception raised when the specified form cannot be opened by using the OPEN_FORM function module.

TABLE 12.15 Exception parameters in the READ_FORM_ELEMENTS function module

The READ_FORM_LINES Function Module

The READ_FORM_LINES function module is used to transfer the lines of a text element of a form to an internal table. If the name of a form is not specified, the SAP system transfers the text lines of a currently opened form. However, if the name of a form is specified, the SAP system transfers the lines of the text elements of the active form to an internal table. The following syntax is used to call the READ_FORM_LINES function module:

```
CALL FUNCTION 'READ_FORM_LINES'
EXPORTING FORM = SPACE
LANGUAGE = SPACE
WINDOW = 'MAIN'
ELEMENT = SPACE
TABLES LINES = ?...
EXCEPTIONS ELEMENT =
FORM =
UNOPENED =
```

The READ_FORM_LINES function module is called by using the export parameters listed in Table 12.16:

Parameter	Description
FORM	Specifies the name of the form whose element list is to be created. If this field is left blank, the SAP system uses the currently active form. The default value of this parameter is SPACE.
LANGUAGE	Specifies the desired language of the form. The default value of this parameter is SPACE.
WINDOW	Specifies the name of the window where the text element of a form has to be read. The default value of this parameter is MAIN.
ELEMENT	Specifies the name of the element of a form whose text lines need to be read. The default value of this parameter is SPACE.

TABLE 12.16 Export parameters in the READ_FORM_LINES function module

LINES, a table parameter of the READ_FORM_LINES function module, is used to specify the name of a table that stores the text lines of the specified element of a form. Calling the READ_FORM_LINES function module can raise exceptions when the parameters specified in Table 12.17 contain invalid values:

Parameter	Description
ELEMENT	Handles the exception raised when an SAP system does not find the name of a element of a form.The possible reasons for this are as follows: ▪ The element does not exist for a specified window in the defined form. ▪ The element is specified for a specific window but not defined in the form. ▪ The defined form, having the text element in the specified window, is not active.
FORM	Handles the exception raised when a form of the specified name is not found in the SAP system. The possible reasons may be that either the form does not exist or there is no active version of the form.
UNOPENED	Handles the exception raised when the READ_FORM_LINES function module is not executed, as the form has not yet been opened by the OPEN_FORM function module.

TABLE 12.17 Exception parameters in the READ_FORM_LINES function module

Controlling the SAPscript Forms

To retrieve the output of an SAPscript form through a print program, you must always open a form using the OPEN_FORM function module and close it using the CLOSE_FORM function module. The OPEN_FORM function module initializes the SAPscript composer and opens the specified form for print output. The SAP system continuously collects data for the output of the form until the form is closed by using the CLOSE_FORM function module. If the CLOSE_FORM function module is not specified in the print program of the form, nothing is printed. The WRITE_FORM, WRITE_FORM_LINES, and CONTROL_FORM function modules are used to write data in a form. You can use these function modules any number of times and in any order after opening and before closing a form.

> **Note:** The SAPscript composer is a program that converts the format of a form's text into a printable format.

The following are some additional functions that can be performed with an SAPscript form or with the controls of the form:

- **Processing multiple print requests**—Opens and closes several forms to print. However, you cannot print multiple forms simultaneously.
- **Starting a form again**—Starts a form for printing repeatedly by using the START_FORM and END_FORM function modules.
- **Switching forms**—Switches from one form to another in a print request, but the forms must have the same page format.
- **Finding forms**—Searches for another version of the form, if the specified version is not found.

Let's explore these tasks in detail.

Multiple Print Requests

You can open and close various forms within one transaction by using the OPEN_FORM and CLOSE_FORM function modules. However, these forms cannot be opened simultaneously.

Starting a Form Again

A print program allows you to print multiple copies of one letter or form for different customers. To print several copies of a form for different customers, you must start the form every time it needs to be printed.

To start a form, you must end the form (if it is already started) and then start it again. Within one print request, you need to call the END_FORM function module to execute the final processing for the form. Next, start the form again by using the START_FORM function module, as shown in the following syntax:

```
CALL FUNCTION 'OPEN_FORM'
:
CALL FUNCTION 'START_FORM'
:
CALL FUNCTION 'END_FORM'
:
CALL FUNCTION 'START_FORM'
:
CALL FUNCTION 'END_FORM'
:
CALL FUNCTION 'CLOSE_FORM'
```

> **Note:** When you use the START_FORM and END_FORM function modules, you must not use the OPEN_FORM function module to open the form.

Switching Forms

A user can switch forms within one print request. This may be necessary if you need to customize the format of the form's output depending on customer preferences. For example, you may need to switch forms to generate the output in a different layout, depending on the geographical location of a customer. In this case, you need to switch from one form to another by using the START_FORM function module.

> **Note:** When switching forms, ensure that you use only those forms that have the same page format, such as DINA4 or LETTER page format. However, you can mix forms with different page orientations easily; that is, LANDSCAPE or PORTRAIT.

Finding Forms

The SAPscript form processor generates business forms based on SAPscript forms that act as templates for business forms. The SAPscript form processor searches for a predefined SAPscript form in the available clients. If the SAPscript form processor does not find the specified SAPscript form, it automatically searches for another version of the same form. Figure 12.34 shows how the SAPscript form processor searches for an SAPscript form in an SAP system:

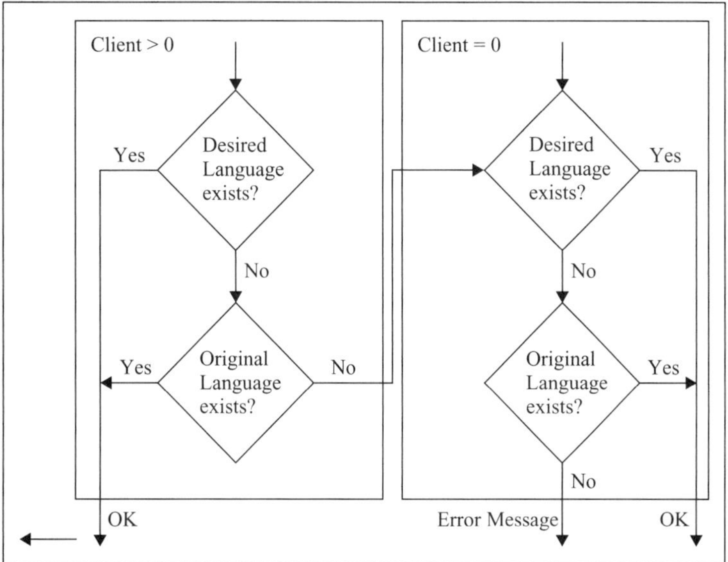

FIGURE 12.34 **Searching forms in different versions**

In Figure 12.34, note that the SAPscript form processor executes a cross-client search only if the current client does not contain the form. If the SAPscript form processor finds the form in the current client, it generates and stores it in the client that has started the search. If the request for the form is started again, the SAPscript form processor finds it in the current client.

SAPscript Control Commands

SAP control commands allow you to format the final output. These commands are passed to the SAPscript composer to process a form. Some common tasks performed by the SAPscript composer are line and page formatting, replacing symbols with their current values, and formatting the text of a form according to the specified paragraph and character formats. Table 12.18 shows a list of SAPscript control commands:

Control Command	Description
ADDRESS	Formats the text specified for the `Address` window in a form.
BOTTOM ... ENDBOTTOM	Defines the footer text in a window.
BOX, POSITION, SIZE	Specifies a box or line in a form that needs to be formatted.
CASE, ENDCASE	Specifies multiple conditions based on text printed.
DEFINE	Assigns values to text symbols in a form.
HEX, ENDHEX	Specifies hexadecimal values in a form.
IF, ENDIF	Specifies conditional text in a form.
INCLUDE	Includes other text in a form.
NEW-PAGE	Inserts a page in a form explicitly.
NEW-WINDOW	Inserts a new main window in a form.
PRINT-CONTROL	Inserts a print control character in a form.
PROTECT, ENDPROTECT	Prevents a page break in a form.
RESET	Initializes the outline paragraph in a form.
SET COUNTRY	Sets country-specific formatting in a form.
SET DATE MASK	Specifies the format of the date fields in a form.
SET SIGN	Inserts the + or - sign in a form.
SET TIME MASK	Specifies the format of the time fields in a form.
STYLE	Changes the style of the text in a form.
SUMMING	Inserts the sum of the variables in a form.
TOP	Sets the header text in the main window.

TABLE 12.18 List of SAPscript control commands

SAPscript Symbols

SAPscript symbols are used to include a program, system data, or predefined text in a form. The name of the symbol is specified by using the ampersand (&) symbol. For example, the following syntax is used for the DATE symbol:

```
&DATE&.
```

You can insert a symbol anywhere in the text of any window or page of a form. When the form is printed or displayed, SAPscript substitutes the current value of the symbol with the name of the symbol in the form.

The following four categories of SAPscript symbols are used in the SAP system:

- **System symbols**—Receive their values from SAPscript. The names and text of the system symbols are fixed. Table 12.19 describes a list of system variables:

System Symbol	Description
DATE	Displays the current date.
DAY	Displays the current day of the week.
DEVICE	Specifies an output device, such as PRINTER, SCREEN, or FAX.
HOURS	Displays the hours in the context of the current time.
MINUTES	Display the minutes in the context of the current time.
MONTH	Displays the current month.
NAME_OF_MONTH	Displays the name of the month in the context of the current date.
NEXTPAGE	Displays the next page number of a form.
PAGE	Displays the current page number of a form.
SECONDS	Displays the seconds in context with the current time.
SPACE	Inserts a blank space in a form.

Continued

System Symbol	Description
TIME	Displays the current time of day.
ULINE	Underlines text in a form.
VLINE	Displays a vertical line in a form.
YEAR	Displays the current year.

TABLE 12.19 List of system symbols used in a form

You can access system symbols by selecting `Include>Symbols>System from PC Editor for a window`. They are of the following types:

- **Program symbols**—Receive the data either from the fields of a database table or from the globally stored data in an SAP system. Note that when you print an SAPscript form, the data is retrieved directly from the fields of the database table, instead of the symbols. For instance, `&MARA-MAKTL&`, is a program symbol, in which `MARA` is the name of a standard database table and `MAKTL` is one of the fields of this table. To access a program symbol, select `Include>Symbols>Program from PC Editor for a window`.
- **Standard symbols**—Receive the data from the TTDTG table. TTDTG is a predefined table in the SAP system to store SAPscript standard symbols for word processing. You can access the TTDTG table using the `SM30` or `SE11` transaction code. Standard symbols are static text, which are assigned by a user. The `&WR&` expression can represent an example of a standard symbol to denote the With Regards text. Standard symbols are language-dependent, which means that a symbol is first translated and then inserted in the text in the defined language of a form. Standard symbols are accessed by selecting `Include>Symbols>Standard from PC Editor for a window`.
- **Text symbols**—Store user-defined text for a form. These symbols are defined locally in a text module. Text symbols can be used only in the form for which they are defined. The `DEFINE` command is used to define a text symbol by using the following syntax:

```
/: DEFINE &symbolname&='Symbol text'
```

The following examples show the use of text symbols:

```
/: DEFINE &MYSYMBOL& = '100'.
```

and

```
/: DEFINE &OBJECT&='my country'.
```

After the text is assigned to a text symbol, the text symbol can be included in the text by typing its name or by selecting `Include>Symbols>Text from PC Editor for a window.`

> **Note:** When you use any symbol in your SAPscript form, the SAP system automatically recognizes the type of the symbol. The SAP system first checks whether the symbol is a system symbol. If the symbol is not a system symbol, the SAP system checks whether the symbol is defined in the calling program. If it is so, the symbol is specified as a program symbol. Otherwise, the SAP system checks the symbol from the entries stored in the TTDTG table, and in this case the symbol is specified as a standard symbol. Finally, if a symbol neither belongs to the category of system symbols nor to the categories of program and standard symbols, it is considered a text symbol.

THE SAP SMART FORMS TOOL

The SAP Smart Forms tool was introduced with SAP R/3 4.6 to print and send documents through e-mail, the Internet, or facsimile. This tool helps develop forms, PDF files, e-mails, and documents for the Internet. The SAP Smart Forms tool provides an interface to build and maintain the layout and logic of a form. In addition to the SAP Smart Forms tool, SAP delivers a selection of forms for business processes, such as those used in Customer Relationship Management (CRM), Sales and Distribution (SD), Financial Accounting (FI), and Human Resources (HR).

In the upcoming sections, we describe the following:

- Overview of the SAP Smart Forms tool
- Smart Form components
- Explaining the Smart Forms process
- Advantages of Smart Forms
- Important objects for form development
- Creating and maintaining Smart Forms
- Style builder

Overview of the SAP Smart Forms Tool

In the earlier versions of SAP, SAPscript was the only option available to create printable documents or forms. However, implementing and maintaining SAPscript forms can be difficult because these forms are not fully integrated with the other applications in an SAP system since they make use of batch printing and spool control. Therefore, to simplify and facilitate the printing of these forms, SAP introduced a new tool called SAP Smart Forms. Introduced with SAP R/3 4.6, the SAP Smart Forms tool is fully integrated with the core applications of an SAP system, such as HR and mySAP ERP. The SAP Smart Forms tool also supports Web applications, which is a key area of expansion for most companies.

The SAP Smart Forms tool allows you to modify forms by using simple graphical tools instead of using any programming tool. This means that a user with no programming knowledge can configure these forms with data for a business process easily.

In a Smart Form, data is retrieved from static and dynamic tables, the table heading and subtotal are specified by the triggered events, and the data is then sorted before the final output. A Smart Form allows you to incorporate graphics, which can be displayed either as part of the form or as the background. You can also suppress a background graphic, if required, while taking a printout of a form.

Some examples of Smart Forms available in the mySAP ERP system are as follows:

- **SF_EXAMPLE_01**—Represents an invoice with a table output for flight booking for a customer.
- **SF_EXAMPLE_02**—Specifies an invoice similar to SF_EXAMPLE_01, but with subtotals.

- **SF_EXAMPLE_03**—Represents an invoice similar to SF_EXAMPLE_02, but one in which several customers can be selected in an application program. A form is created for each customer and then all the forms are included in a single request for the output.

SAP Smart Form Components

The basic structure of an SAP Smart Form comprises four basic components: Smart Form Builder, the Smart Form print form template, the Smart Form function module, and the Smart Form print program.

Now, let's discuss these components in detail.

Smart Form Builder

Smart Form Builder is the main interface used to build a Smart Form. It is available on the initial screen of SAP Smart Forms. You can type the `SMARTFORMS` transaction code in the `Command` field to open the initial screen of SAP Smart Forms, as shown in Figure 12.35:

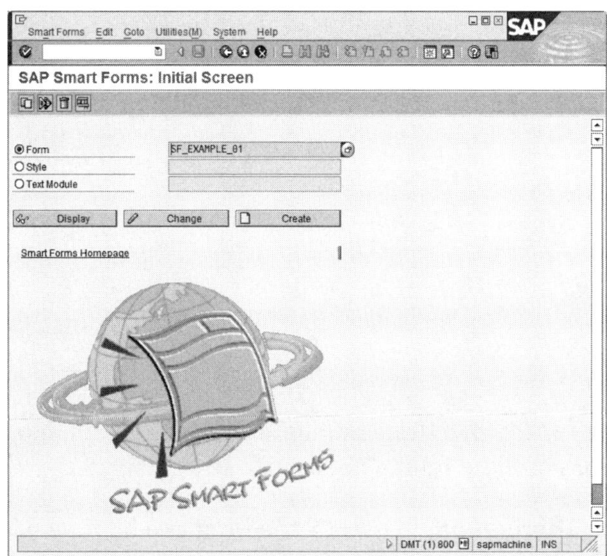

FIGURE 12.35 **The initial screen of SAP smart forms**

> **Note:** An alternative way to open the initial screen of SAP Smart Forms is by selecting `SAP menu>Tools>Forms>Smart Forms` in the `SAP Easy Access` screen.

Next, you need to enter the name of the form that you want to display, copy, or create in the initial screen of SAP Smart Forms. In this case, we click the `Display` button after entering a predefined Smart Form name in the `Form` field (see Figure 12.35). The SF_EXAMPLE_01 form appears in the `Form Builder` screen, as shown in Figure 12.36:

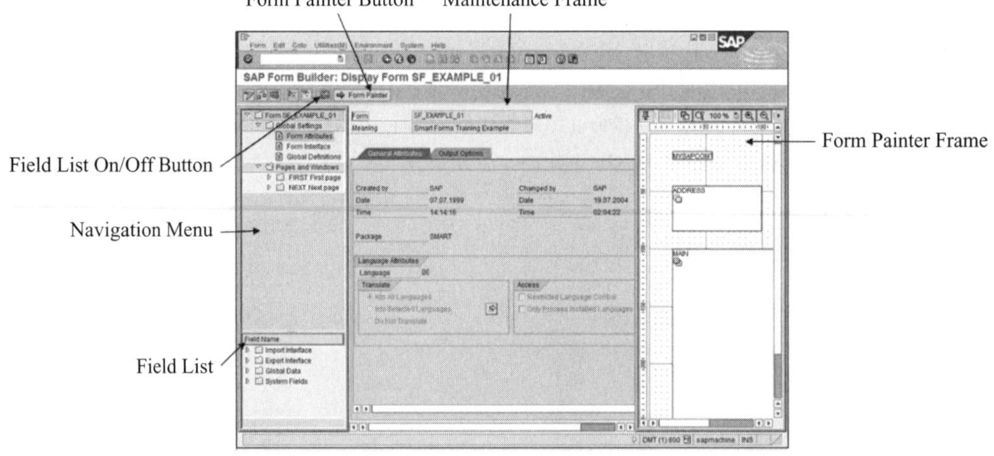

FIGURE 12.36 **The form builder screen**

Figure 12.36 shows three frames in the `Form Builder` screen. The names and positions of these frames are as follows:

- **Navigation menu**—Displays the form as a hierarchy in which each element of the form is represented by a node. The `Navigation` menu appears on the left of the screen and provides you direct access to the elements of the opened form.

- **Maintenance frame**—Maintains the attributes of the currently selected node in the navigation tree. This frame appears in the middle of the screen.
- **Field List**—Displays the data currently defined in the form. If Field List is not displayed on the `Form Builder` screen, click the `Field List On/Off` (icon) icon (see Figure 12.36).
- **Form Painter frame**—Acts as a graphical tool to design the layout of a form by using the output areas, such as the size and location of the windows. This frame appears at the right side of the screen. If the Form Painter frame is not visible on the screen, click the `Form Painter` button (see Figure 12.36).

Each frame can be resized by clicking and dragging its borders. When you select a node in the `Navigation` menu, the view in the other frames also changes. For example, when you double-click a node in the `Navigation` menu, the corresponding information related to the node is displayed in the maintenance frame. In addition, the selection of the output area in the Form Painter frame can be changed by using the drag-and-drop feature, according to the node selected in the `Navigation` menu.

In the `Navigation` menu, the form is represented as branches. The top hierarchy level of the `Navigation` menu contains the following nodes and subnodes:

- **Global Settings**—Contains the `Form Attributes`, `Form Interface`, and `Global Definitions` subnodes.
- **Pages and Windows**—Contains the `FIRST First page` and `NEXT Next page` subnodes.

You can add more subnodes under the `Pages and Windows` node, while creating a form. However, no subnode can be added to the `Global Settings` node.

The Smart Form Print Form Template

The Smart Form print form template provides a preconfigured design and layout to create a Smart Form in a printable format. It can be created by using Smart Form Builder. A Smart Form print form template contains the layout of the form, the fields required in the form, the conditions that specify how to populate the form, and some special programming instructions for printing the form. The form created by a Smart Form print form template generates the final output after using the Smart Form function modules.

The Smart Form Function Module

The Smart Form function module is a sequence of statements that are generated automatically when the Smart Form print form is activated. If you make any change in the print form of Smart Form Builder, you need to save the change and activate the form again in Smart Form Builder to get the desired output.

The Smart Form Print Program

The Smart Form print program controls the printing of a Smart Form. Generally, one Smart Form print program is associated with one type of form. For example, the purchase order Smart Form has a corresponding purchase order print program. Note that customer-specific customization performed in the Smart Form print form is more efficient than that performed in the Smart Form print program.

> **Note:** The print program of an SAPscript form is different from the print program of a Smart Form and cannot be used with a Smart Form.

Explaining the Smart Form Process

As discussed earlier, the structure of an SAP Smart Form consists of Smart Form Builder, the Smart Form print form template, the Smart Form function module, and the Smart Form print program. These components work together in the program or workflow of a Smart Form. The program flow of a Smart Form process can be explained in the following way:

- A user creates a Smart Form for an application and includes application data into the form by using a form template in the Smart Form Builder.
- After designing the form, it needs to be activated before it can be tested or made accessible to print programs.

Activating the form generates a function module that handles the processing of the form. This function module interacts with an application and creates the output according to the specified output device.

Figure 12.37 shows the program flow of a Smart Form process:

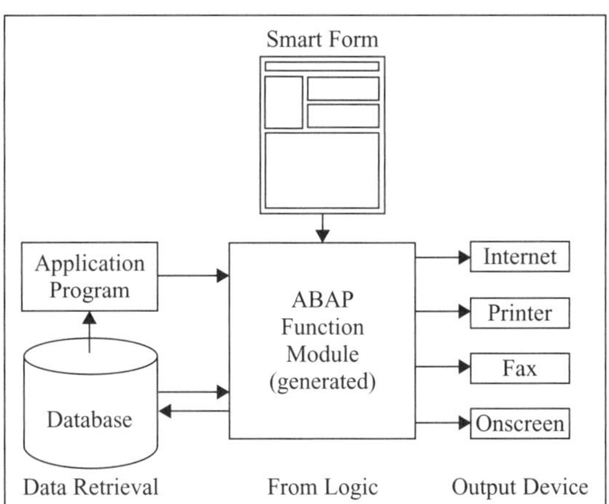

FIGURE 12.37 **The program flow of a smart form process**

In Figure 12.37, you can see that to take a printout of a Smart Form, a user requires an application program for data retrieval and a Smart Form that consists of the entire logic of the form. The application program passes the data through a function module interface to a Smart Form. When activating a Smart Form, the SAP system automatically generates a function module, which is then processed by the SAP system at runtime. The function module generated by the SAP system encapsulates all the attributes of the Smart Form. As soon as the application program calls the function module, the Smart Form uses the module interface (which corresponds to the interface of the form) to transfer previously selected table data and print the form as described in the form description. This process is also known as calling a Smart Form for printing.

Note: The description of a Smart Form includes the following:

- The layout of the form
- Individual elements, such as text, graphics, addresses, and tables
- The logic of the form, for example, to read application data from internal tables and to control the process flow

- A form interface to transfer application data into the form definition

Advantages of Smart Forms

A Smart Form has the following advantages:

- Enables you to create interactive Web forms with input fields, buttons, and radio buttons
- Enables you to create the layout and logic of a form by using graphic tools, an operation for which programming knowledge is not necessary
- Displays table structures
- Displays a colored output of the text
- Enables you to use the user-friendly and integrated Form Painter to design forms graphically
- Enables you to draw Smart Form tables by using a special control; that is, Graphical Table Painter
- Enables you to display the background graphics using templates
- Enables you to use the format of fonts and paragraphs defined in a Smart style
- Enables you to display the output in the HTML format

Important Objects for Form Development

To create a business form, the SAP Smart Forms tool uses some important objects, such as a Smart style, text module, and Smart Form template. A Smart style is a collection of paragraph and character formats. Each Smart Form uses at least one Smart style. A text module is an encapsulated text that allows a text element to be used in one or more Smart Forms. A Smart Form template is a collection of form processing logic, content, and layout, and also refers to Smart styles and text modules.

Besides the Smart style and text module objects, a Smart Form can also include a graphic object, such as company's logo or preprinted forms, scanned as background images.

Another important object is the Table Painter, which is used to create dynamic expandable tables in Smart Forms. A Smart Form template has a fixed number of rows, while a Smart Form table can have a dynamic number of rows. In the Maintenance frame of SAP Form Builder, a new type of tab, the `Table` tab, appears. In the Table tab, you can define table characteristics and turn on the Table Painter (▦) icon to specify the rows and columns of dynamically expandable tables. However, the Table Painter icon does not show the actual output, because the depth of a table row output depends dynamically on the number of records received from an application.

Creating and Maintaining Smart Forms

In this section, you learn how to create a form by using the SAP Smart Forms tool. You also learn how to add a node in the Smart Form and test the form.

We begin with creating a copy of the SF_EXAMPLE_01 form by using the SAP Smart Forms tool. The SF_EXAMPLE_01 form is a standard Smart Form available in an SAP system. Perform the following steps to create a form:

1. In the SAP menu path, select Tools>Forms>Smart Forms or use the SMARTFORMS transaction code in the Command field. The initial screen of SAP Smart Forms appears. In this screen, enter the form name, SF_EXAMPLE_01, in the Form field (see Figure 12.35).
2. Select Smart Forms>Copy or click the Copy (⧉) icon to open the Copy Form or Text dialog box, as shown in Figure 12.38:

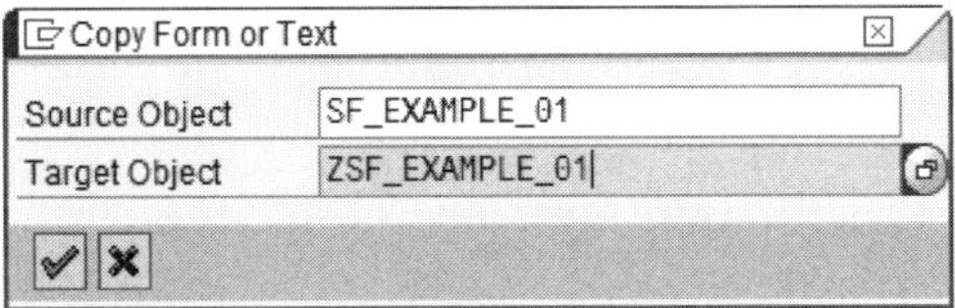

FIGURE 12.38 **The copy form or text dialog box**

3. In the Target Object field, enter a name for the new form. The name must begin with the Y or Z letter. In our case, the name of the form is ZSF_EXAMPLE_01 (see Figure 12.38).
4. Click the Continue (✔) icon or press the ENTER key in the Copy Form or Text dialog box so that the ZSF_EXAMPLE01 form is created as a copy of the predefined form SF_EXAMPLE_01. The Create Object Directory Entry dialog box appears.
5. In the Create Object Directory Entry dialog box, enter the package name, ZKOG_PCKG, in the Package field and then click the Save (💾)

icon. The name of the form is displayed in the `Form` field on the initial screen of SAP Smart Forms, as shown in Figure 12.39:

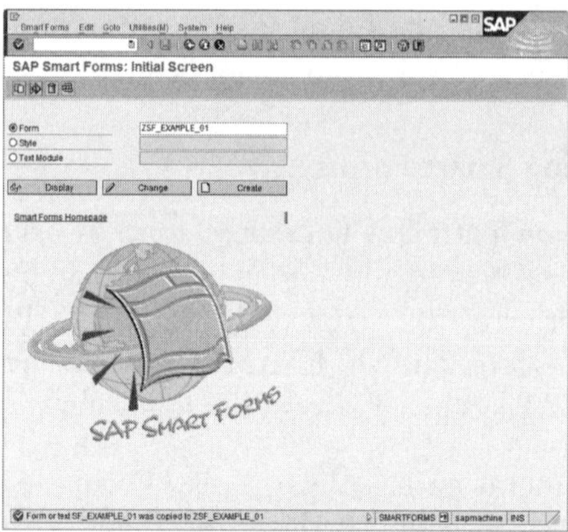

FIGURE 12.39 **Displaying the copied form in the initial screen of SAP smart forms**

6. Click the `Create` button on the initial screen of SAP Smart Forms. The ZSF_ EXAMPLE_01 form appears in Form Builder, as shown in Figure 12.40:

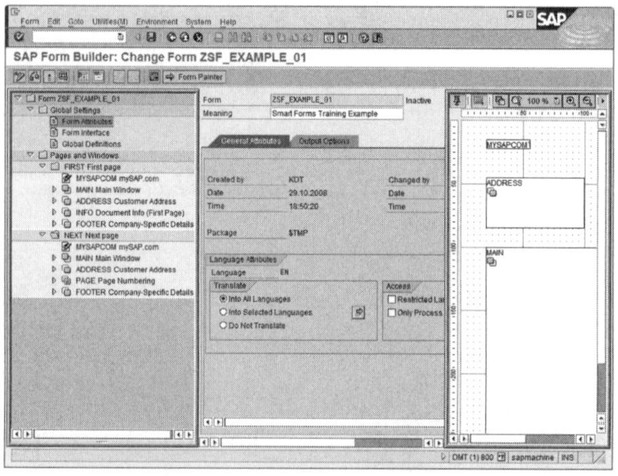

FIGURE 12.40 **The ZSF_EXAMPLE_01 form in form builder**

In Figure 12.40, the first draft page is created with a MAIN window. All the components of the new form are based on the SF_EXAMPLE_01 predefined form. You can click a node in the Navigation menu to view its content.

Nodes are created or moved by using the Navigation menu. The order of the nodes determines the order in which the output of the form is processed. In addition, the order of the output is determined by the order in which the nodes are arranged in the Navigation menu.

A node can be moved by clicking and dragging it to the desired location in the navigation tree. The attributes for each node, such as the text or the name of an image, are defined in the Form Builder's maintenance frame.

Now, performing the following steps to create a text node in the form:

1. Open a form in the change mode of the SAP Form Builder screen (see Figure 12.40). Next, right-click the Main Window option in the First Page node and select Create>Text from the context menu, as shown in Figure 12.41:

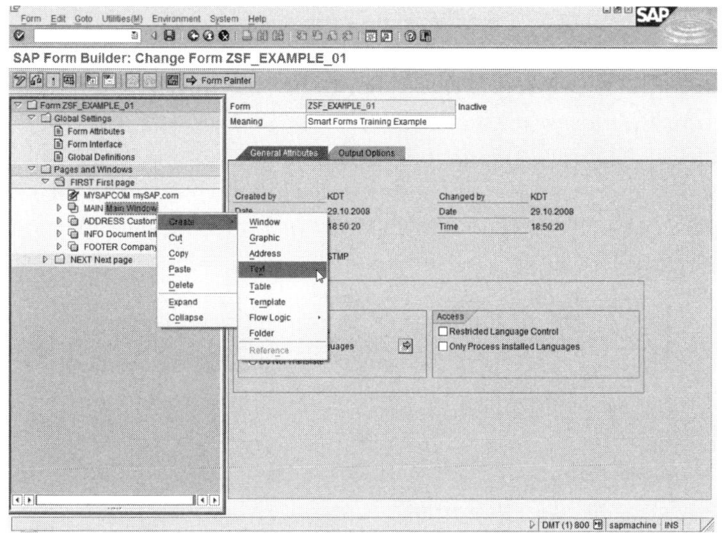

FIGURE 12.41 **Selecting a new node in the main window**

2. Modify the text in the Text field to MYTEXT and the text in the Meaning field to Text Node Demo, as shown in Figure 12.42:

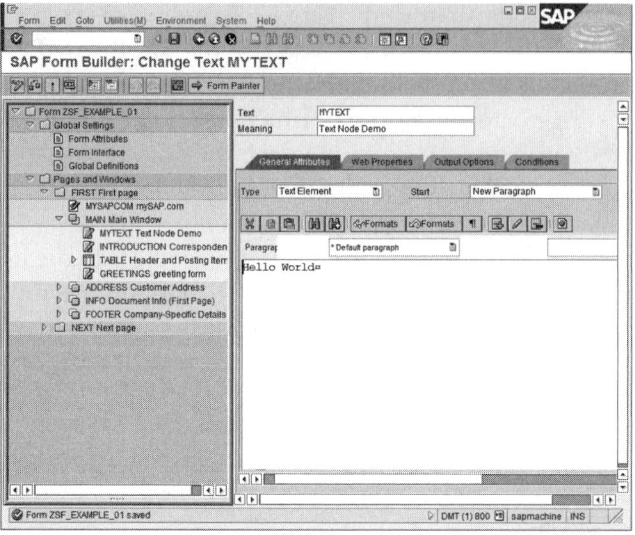

FIGURE 12.42 **Specifying the attributes of the new text node**

3. Enter the text “Hello World” in the text-editing box in the center frame of Form Builder (see Figure 12.42).
4. Click the `Save` () icon to save the node.
5. Next, activate and test the node by clicking the `Activate` () and `Test` () icons, respectively. The initial screen of Function Builder appears, as shown in Figure 12.43:

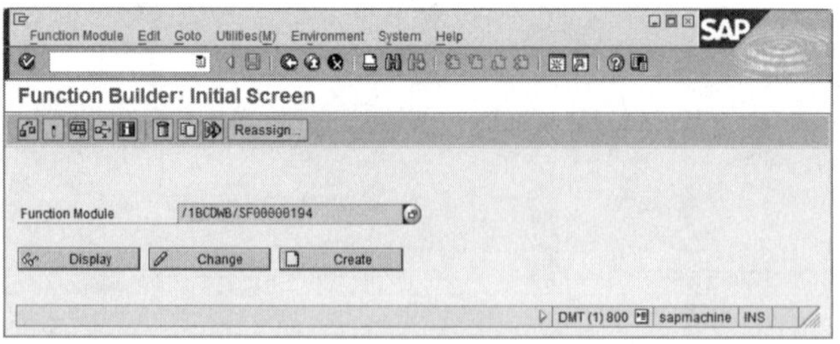

FIGURE 12.43 **The initial screen of function builder**

6. Activate and test the function module by clicking the `Activate` ( ) and `Test/Execute` ( ) icons. The parameters of the function module are displayed in the initial screen of Function Builder, as shown in Figure 12.44:

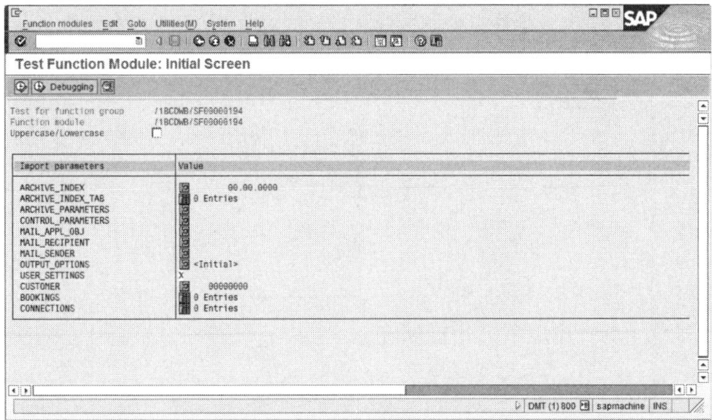

FIGURE 12.44 **Displaying the parameters in the initial screen of test function module**

7. Execute the function module by clicking the `Execute` ( ) icon (see Figure 12.44). The `Print` dialog box appears, as shown in Figure 12.45:

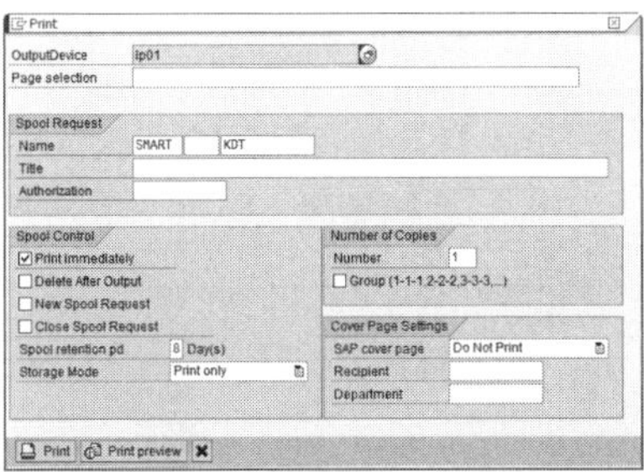

FIGURE 12.45 **The print dialog box**

8. Specify the output device as lp01 and click the `Print preview` button, as shown in Figure 12.45.

The print preview of the ZSF_EXAMPLE_01 form appears, with the text Hello World, as shown in Figure 12.46:

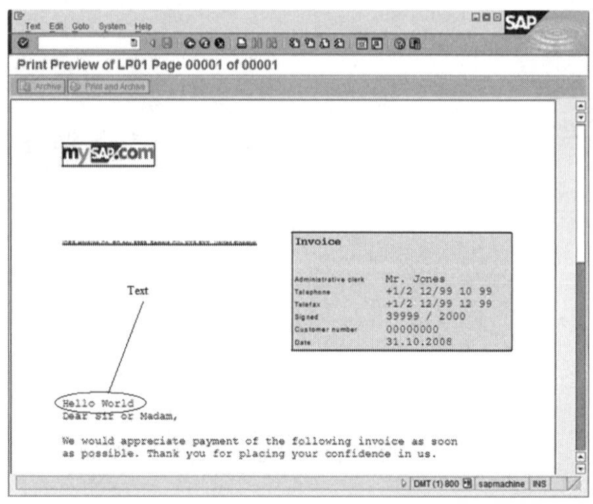

FIGURE 12.46 **Print preview of the form**

Figure 12.46 shows the print preview of the ZSF_EXAMPLE_01 form.

Style Builder

Style Builder is a tool used to define a Smart style for a Smart Form. It is available on the initial screen of Smart Styles, which is opened by using the `SMARTSTYLES` transaction code. Figure 12.47 displays the initial screen of Smart styles:

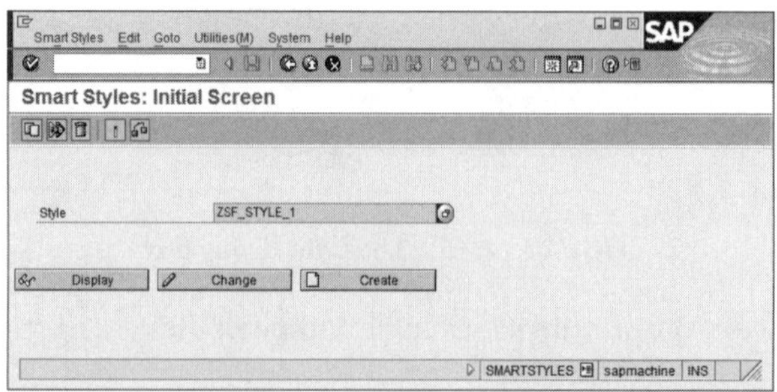

FIGURE 12.47 **The initial screen of smart styles**

In Figure 12.47, note that the initial screen of Smart Styles contains the `Style` field to specify the Smart style name that you want to create, change, or display. Now, let's enter a name for a Smart style (for example, ZSF_STYLE_1), and click the `Create` button, as shown in Figure 12.47. The ZSF_STYLE_1 Smart style appears in Style Builder (in change mode), as shown in Figure 12.48:

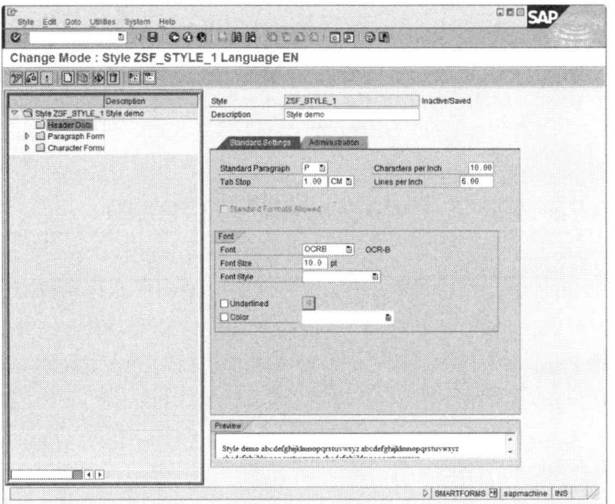

FIGURE 12.48 **The ZSF_STYLE_1 smart style in style builder**

Note: The interface of Style Builder, as shown in Figure 12.48, can also be accessed by entering the name of the Smart style in the initial screen of SAP Smart Forms and clicking the `Create` button, as shown in Figure 12.49:

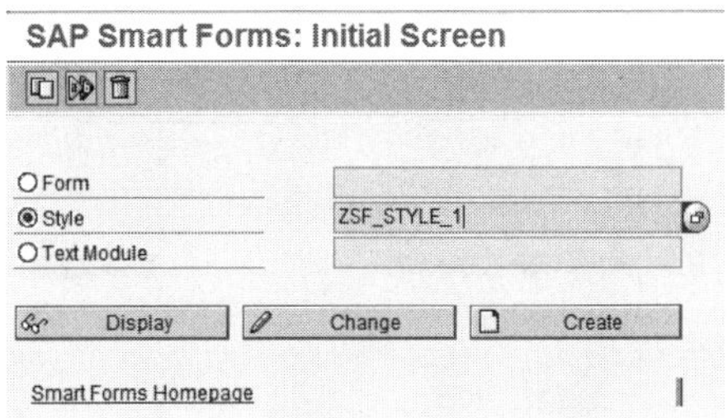

FIGURE 12.49 **Entering a smart style name in the initial screen of SAP smart forms**

Figure 12.48 shows a style tree to the left of the `Style Builder` screen, which consists of predetermined nodes (`Header Data`, `Paragraph Formats`, and `Character Form`). You can navigate between the nodes or create new nodes. On the right is a maintenance screen, where you specify various settings in a Smart style. Note that when you specify any settings in the maintenance frame, the `Preview` group box displays the preview of the specified font settings.

You must activate a Smart style in a Smart Form before using it. A Smart style is activated by clicking the `Activate` ( ) icon. During activation, the SAP system checks the Smart style for errors and, if necessary, displays an error list.

COMPARING SAPSCRIPT AND SMART FORMS

SAPscript forms and Smart Forms have various similarities, such as their use to generate business forms; there are differences between the two as well. One major difference is that SAPscript forms are client-dependent, while Smart Forms are client-independent.

SAPscript is a word processing tool that displays the data on an SAPscript form by using various text elements and a print program that stores the logic of these text elements. SAPscript forms are, therefore, designed to be driven by their specific print programs and are often called client-dependent. Figure 12.50 shows the process of creating a form by using the SAPscript tool:

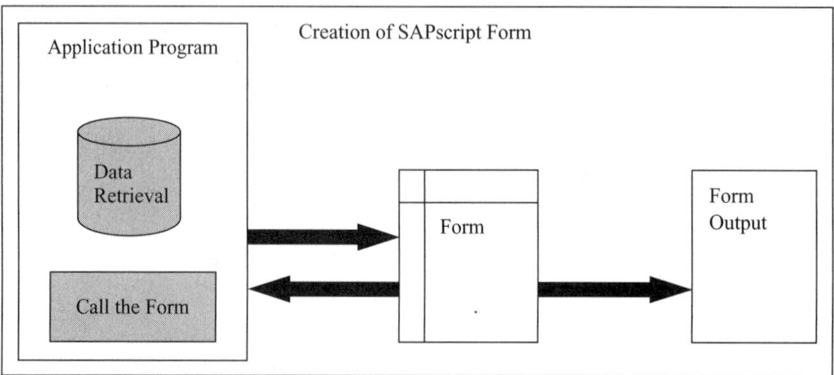

FIGURE 12.50 **The process of creating a form by using SAPscript**

A print program determines the output document, the values of the areas, and the frequency of the output, during the processing of an SAPscript form. The print program also accesses the SAP database to retrieve data that is populated in the corresponding fields of the form, which means that the SAPscript tool directs the print program to print the output.

Moreover, an SAPscript form uses a layout set that describes the layout of the individual print pages and uses text elements to supply definable output blocks, which a print program can call.

Smart Forms, on the other hand, are executed through a function module. When a print program calls a Smart Form, the form itself takes over the task of generating the output, without any intervention from the print program. Figure 12.51 shows the process of creating a form by using the SAP Smart Forms tool:

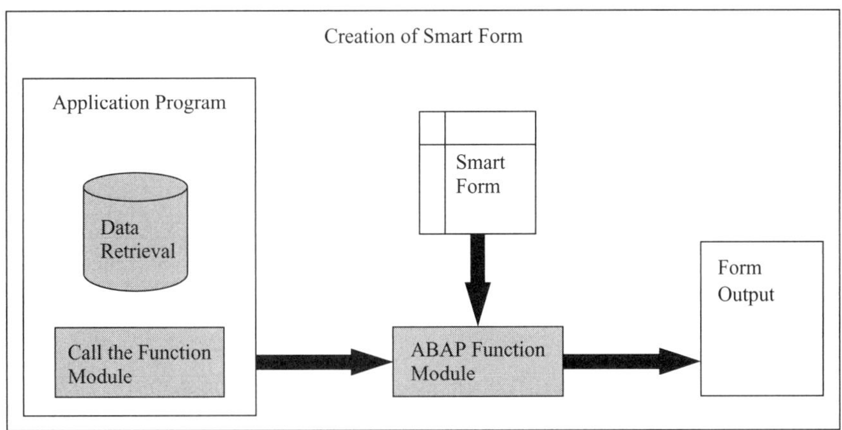

FIGURE 12.51 **The process of creating a form by using SAP smart forms**

The following tasks are performed in a Smart Form:

- Designing the form
- Activating the form and automatically generating the function modules
- Using an application program to retrieve data and call the Smart Form

In Figure 12.51, you can see that ABAP function modules use the layout of a Smart Form and an application program, which retrieves the data from different sources, to generate the output of the form.

Other differences that exist between the two types of forms are as follows:

- Smart Forms can have multiple page formats
- Smart Forms do not necessarily have a MAIN window
- Smart Forms cannot have labels
- Smart Forms can have routines
- Smart Forms generate function modules on activation

MIGRATING SAPSCRIPT FORMS TO SMART FORMS

At times, you might need to create a business form that is not provided in the built-in templates provided by Smart Form. In such situations, you can migrate an SAPscript form to a Smart Form. SAP provides a migration tool to migrate the layout and text of an SAPscript form to a Smart Form. However, remember that when you migrate an SAPscript form to a Smart Form, the SAPscript form's logic of the print program is not migrated. You can migrate an SAPscript form to a Smart Form in two ways, by individual migration and by mass migration (multiple SAPscript forms migrated simultaneously).

The SAP system performs the following actions during the migration of an SAPscript form to a Smart Form:

- Converts layout information, such as information about the pages and windows, and their attributes
- Copies language attributes and output options
- Copies the text from an SAPscript form to the Smart Form
- Displays program symbols in the text
- Converts SAPscript commands (such as `NEW-PAGE` or `IF... ENDIF`) to comment lines and displays them in the text

In the upcoming sections, we describe the following:

- Individual migration
- Mass migration
- Converting a style (that is, the conversion of an SAPscript style into a Smart style)

Individual Migration

When converting an SAPscript form to a Smart Form, you have to provide the names of the SAPscript form and Smart Form involved in the migration.

Now, perform the following steps to migrate an SAPscript form to a Smart Form:

1. Open the initial screen of SAP Smart Forms either by selecting `Tools>Forms>Smart Forms` or by using the `SMARTFORMS` transaction code in the `Command` field and entering the name ZMySmartForm in the `Form` field.
2. Select `Utilities(M)>Migration>Import SAPscript form`, as shown in Figure 12.52:

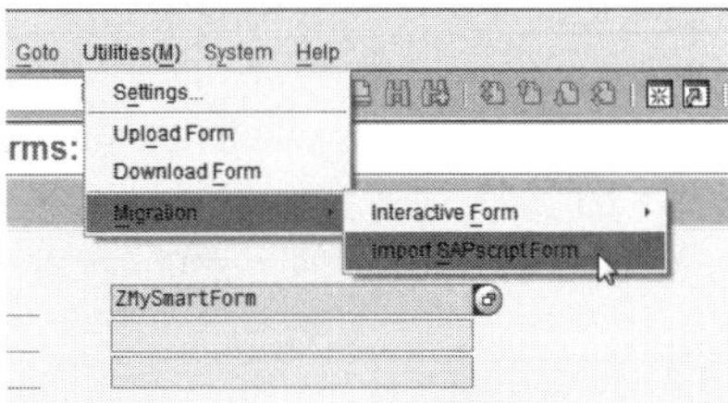

FIGURE 12.52 **Selecting the import SAPscript form option**

The `Import SAPscript Form` dialog box appears.

3. Enter the name and the language of the source SAPscript form; for example, enter S_EXAMPLE_1, as shown in Figure 12.53:

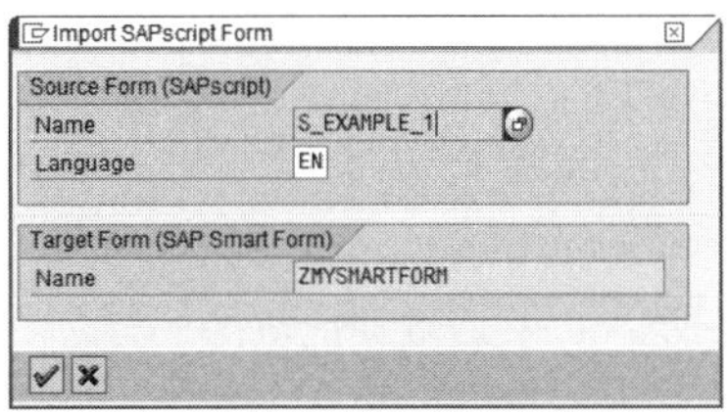

FIGURE 12.53 **The import SAPscript form dialog box**

4. Click the `Continue` (✔) icon or press the ENTER key. Form Builder opens the ZMySmartForm form in the change mode, as shown in Figure 12.54:

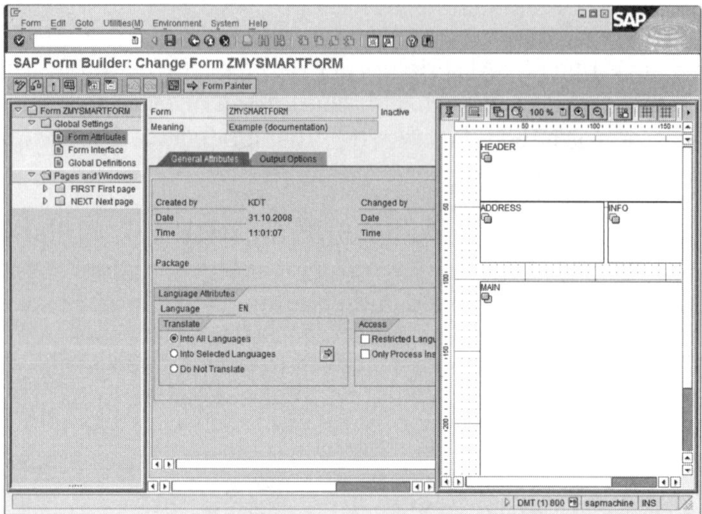

FIGURE 12.54 **Opening the ZMySmartForm form in the change mode**

> **Note:** If the SAPscript form does not exist in the selected language, a dialog box appears, where you can select one of the existing languages.

Now, you can change the design of a Smart Form, save the changes, and activate the form.

Mass Migration

To convert multiple SAPscript forms into Smart Forms, you have to provide a range of SAPscript forms.

Perform the following steps to migrate multiple SAPscript forms to Smart Forms:

1. Open the initial screen of ABAP Editor by using the `SE38` transaction code. In the initial screen of ABAP Editor, enter the program name SF_MIGRATE and click the `Display` button.
2. ABAP Editor opens the SF_MIGRATE report in the display mode, as shown in Figure 12.55:

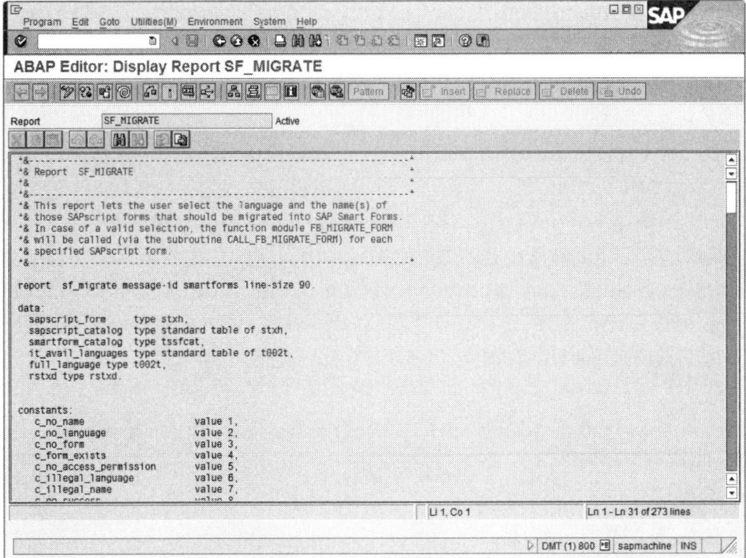

FIGURE 12.55 **The SF_MIGRATE report in display mode**

3. Activate and execute the SF_MIGRATE report by clicking the `Activate` (icon) and `Direct Processing` (icon) icons, respectively.

The `Report for migrating SAPscript forms` screen appears, as shown in Figure 12.56:

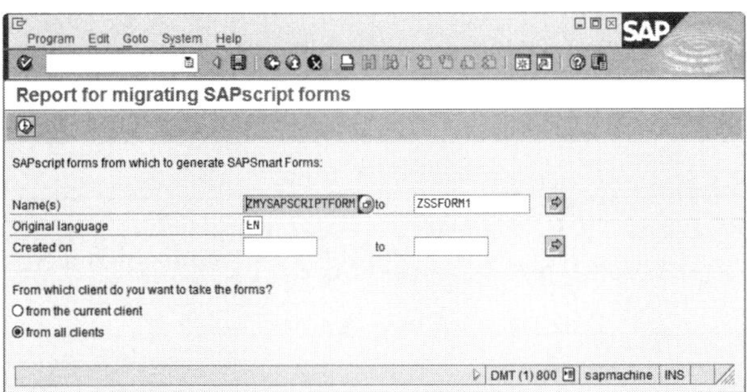

FIGURE 12.56 **The report for migrating SAPscript forms screen**

4. Enter the names and languages of the range of SAPscript forms that you want to migrate; for example, enter the range of names from ZMYSAPSCRIPTFORM to ZSSFORM1 and the language as EN (see Figure 12.56).
5. Specify the client information by selecting either the `from the current client` or `from all clients` radio button. In our case, we have selected the `from all clients` radio button, as shown in Figure 12.56.
6. Click the `Execute` (⊕) icon to complete the process. The SAP system creates Smart Forms corresponding to the names of SAPscript forms, with the extension `_SF`. Figure 12.57 shows a list of forms that were migrated and also forms that could not be migrated:

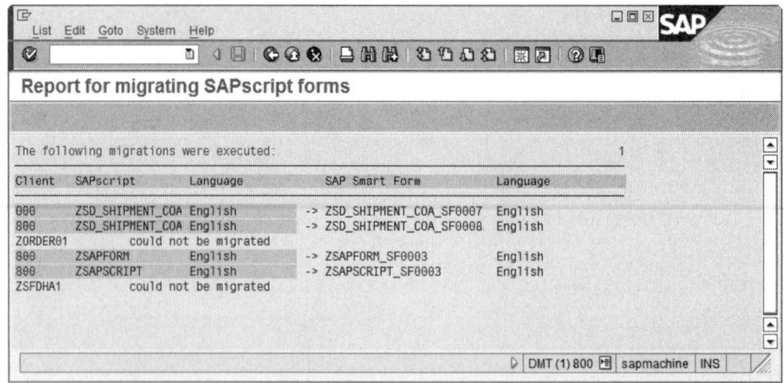

FIGURE 12.57 **List of migrated/not migrated forms**

> **Note:** Use the `SMARTFORMS` transaction code to modify a Smart Form and activate the Smart Form.

Now, let's learn how to convert an SAPscript style into a Smart style.

Converting a Style

You can also convert an SAPscript style into a Smart style and apply the converted Smart style to one or more Smart Forms. Now, let's learn how to convert an

SAPscript style (in this case, the name of the SAPscript style is YS_STYLE1) to a Smart style. Perform the following steps to do so:

1. Open the initial screen of Smart Styles by using the SMARTSTYLES transaction code and then enter the name of the Smart style that you want to create, for example, enter ZSF_STYLE_1 (see Figure 12.47).
2. Select Utilities(M) > Convert SAPscript Style, as shown in Figure 12.58:

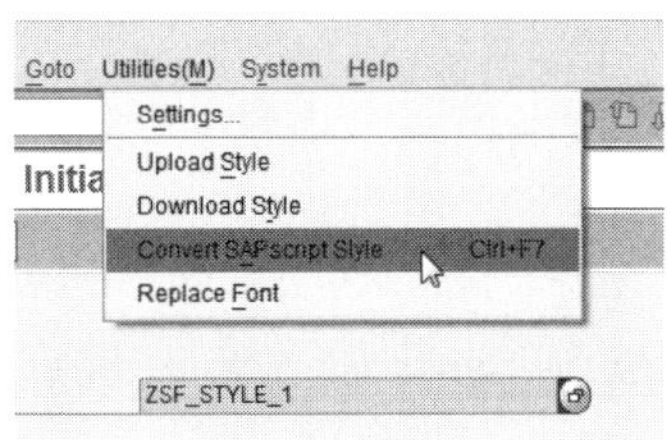

FIGURE 12.58 **Selecting the convert SAPscript style option**

The Convert SAPscript Style dialog box appears.

3. In the Convert SAPscript Style dialog box, enter the name of the SAPscript style in the From (SAPscript Style) field. For example, enter YS_STYLE1, as shown in Figure 12.59:

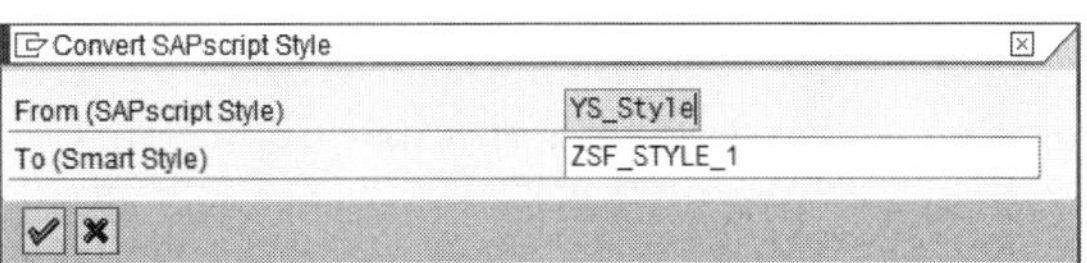

FIGURE 12.59 **The convert SAPscript style dialog box**

4. Click the Continue (✔) icon or press the ENTER key in the Convert SAPscript Style dialog box to proceed. The Create Object Directory Entry dialog box appears.
5. In the Create Object Directory Entry dialog box, enter the name of the package as ZKOG_PCKG in the Package field and then click the Save (💾) icon.

A list of the converted styles are displayed in the initial screen of Smart styles, as shown in Figure 12.60:

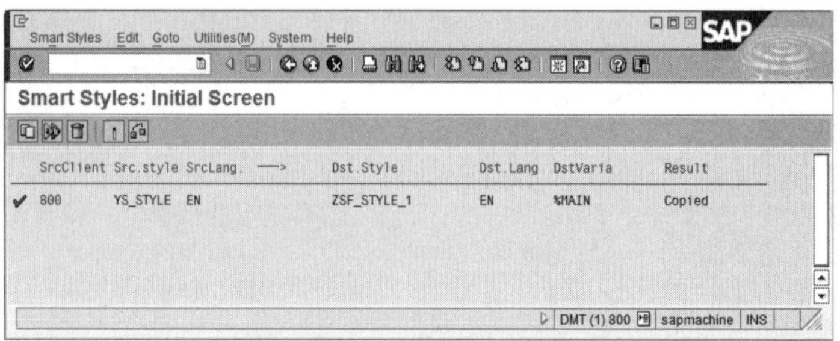

FIGURE 12.60 **Displaying the converted styles in the initial screen of smart styles**

You can click the `Back` (icon) icon from the standard toolbar to navigate to the `Smart Styles:InitialScreen` screen and then click the `Change` button to make additional changes in the converted Smart style. Note that you must activate the Smart style by using the `Activate` (icon) icon before using it to create a Smart Form.

SUMMARY

In this chapter, you have learned about the SAPscript and SAP Smart Forms tools in detail. This chapter has also discussed the structure and components of an SAPscript form, the print programs used to print the forms, and the various function modules, control commands, and symbols used in SAPscript. In addition, you have learned about the SAP Smart Forms tool and its advantages. You have also explored the differences between an SAPscript form and a Smart Form. Finally, you have learned how to migrate an SAPscript form to a Smart Form.

In the next chapter, you learn how to create a report based on database tables and explore the concepts of interactive and Application List Viewer (ALV) reports.

Chapter 13 Reports

If you need information on:	*See page:*
Working with Classical Reports	818
Interactive Reports	827
ALV Reports	839

A report, in general, is a presentation of data in a specific format and organized structure. Many DBMS include a report writer that enables you to design and generate reports. SAP is one of the software applications that support reports creation. In SAP, you can create three types of reports: classical, interactive, and ABAP List Viewer (ALV) reports. In a classical report, the output is displayed in a single list, while in an interactive report, you can view multiple lists simultaneously. ALV reports, however, allow you to perform various functions with the displayed output, such as sorting, arranging, filtering, and retrieving data. In addition, you can view the output of ALV reports either in a grid view or a list view, by using the `REUSE_ALV_GRID_DISPLAY` and `REUSE_ALV_LIST_DISPLAY` function modules, respectively.

Classical reports are simple reports, which are created by using the output data (final data that have to be displayed in a report) in the `WRITE` statement inside a loop. These reports do not contain any sub reports. Interactive reports, on the other hand, are used when you need to interact with a report. With the help of interactive reports, first, an overview list (also called a basic list) is displayed, based on which further output lists (or called secondary lists) are displayed. These secondary lists are actually sub reports, which are displayed when you click specific values of fields included in the basic list. Moreover, SAP also provides some standard reports, such as

RSCLTCOP, which is used to copy tables across clients, and RSPARAM, which is used to display instance parameters. Using these standard reports, you can create your own customized reports.

In this chapter, you learn how to create a classical report and explore the events used to create classical reports. You also learn how to create interactive reports and comprehend the events used to create an interactive report. Finally, you learn about ALV reports.

Now, let's learn about classical reports and how to create them.

WORKING WITH CLASSICAL REPORTS

As discussed earlier, a classical report displays data by using the WRITE statement inside a loop. Classical reports are normal reports and do not contain any sub report. These reports consist of only one screen/list as an output. You use various events, such as INITIALIZATON and TOP-OF-PAGE, to create a classical report. Each event has its own importance during the creation of a classical report. Each of these events is related to a specific user-action and is triggered only when the user performs that action. Table 13.1 lists the events and circumstances when these events are triggered:

Entry	Description
INITIALIZATON	Triggered before displaying the selection screen.
AT SELECTION-SCREEN	Triggered after the processing of the user input on the selection screen. This event verifies the user input prior to the execution of a program. After processing the user input, the selection screen stills remains in the active mode.
START-OF-SELECTION	Triggered only after the processing of the selection screen is over; that is, when the user clicks the Execute (⊕) icon on the selection screen.
END-OF-SELECTION	Triggered after the last statement in the START-OF-SELECTON event is executed.

Continued

Entry	Description
TOP-OF-PAGE	Triggered by the first `WRITE` statement to display the data on a new page.
END-OF-PAGE	Triggered to display the text at the end of a page in a report. Note that this event is the last event while creating a report, and should be combined with the `LINE-COUNT` clause of the `REPORT` statement.

TABLE 13.1 Description of the events

Classical reports are executable-type programs; that is, these reports always start with the `REPORT` statement. The `REPORT` statement, together with the name of the executable program, appears on the screen of ABAP Editor (where the user writes the program code) by default.

Table 13.2 describes the clauses used in the `REPORT` statement:

Clauses	Description
LINE-SIZE	Specifies the width of the output list, or, in other words, the number of characters to be displayed in the output list for printing or displaying. Note that a line can have 255 characters for displaying data, but for printing purposes, a maximum of 132 characters is allowed.
LINE-COUNT	Specifies the number of lines per page. After declaring the number of lines per page, the number of lines reserved for the footer is specified in a pair of brackets. This footer is accessed by using the `END-OF-PAGE` event.
MESSAGE-ID	Allows you to use the `MESSAGE` statement without explicitly specifying the message id.
NO STANDARD PAGE HEADING	Directs SAP not to display the standard page heading (as declared in the Title field of the attributes subobject) on every new page.

TABLE 13.2 Clauses to the REPORT statement

Apart from the events and clauses used with the REPORT statement, the SELECT-OPTIONS statement is used to create a user interface that determines how a selection screen is displayed, by entering the values of the fields of the selection table. The following syntax is used for the SELECT-OPTIONS statement:

```
SELECT-OPTIONS <selection_tab> FOR <fld>.
```

In this syntax, <selection_tab> represents an object of an internal table of the standard table type, which has a standard key and a header line. The <fld> expression represents a column of a database table or an internal field in the corresponding program. When the SELECT-OPTIONS statement is executed, an internal table (or a selection table in this context) containing four fields, SIGN, OPTION, LOW, and HIGH, are created. These fields correspond to the fields of a database table or an internal field in the corresponding program. Note that the SELECT-OPTIONS statement can only be used with the fields of a table that is defined in the TABLES statement. Table 13.3 describes the four fields of the internal table created:

Fields	Description
SIGN	Holds one of the two values, I (include) or E (exclude), depending on whether or not to include the specified values.
OPTION	Specifies the option for comparison, such as EQ (equal to), NE (not equal to), and GT (greater than).
LOW	Specifies the lower limit for a selection range.
HIGH	Specifies the upper limit for a selection range.

TABLE 13.3 Description of the fields

Creating a Classical Report

You can create a classical report by using ABAP Editor. A classical report is used to display the information stored in any database table, such as MARA, MAKT, or KNA1. This task is performed by writing a sequence of statements in ABAP Editor. Perform the following steps to create a classical report:

1. Open the initial screen of ABAP Editor by either navigating to the SAP menu or executing the `SE38` transaction code.
2. In the initial screen of ABAP Editor, enter the name of the program for the classical report, select the `Source code` radio button in the `Subobjects` group box, and click the `Create` button to create a new program, as shown in Figure 13.1:

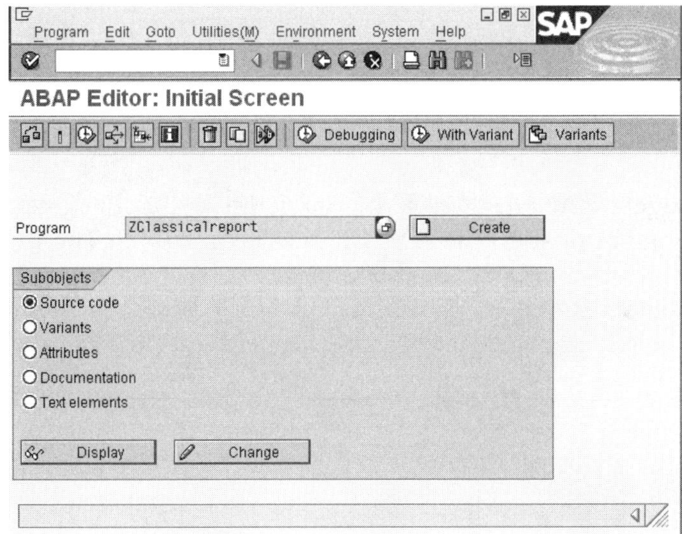

FIGURE 13.1 **Entering the name of the classical report**

The `ABAP: Program Attributes` dialog box appears (Figure 13.2).

3. In the `ABAP: Program Attributes` dialog box, enter a short description for the program in the `Title` field and select the `Executable program` option from the `Type` drop-down list in the `Attributes` group box, as shown in Figure 13.2:

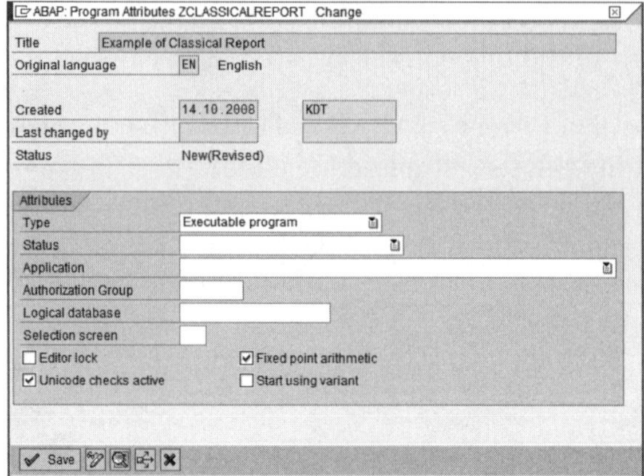

FIGURE 13.2 **Saving the attributes of ZCLASSICALREPORT**

4. Now, click the `Save` (Save) button in the `ABAP: Program Attributes` dialog box or press the ENTER key (Figure 13.2). The `Create Object Directory Entry` dialog box appears.
5. In the `Create Object Directory Entry` dialog box, enter ZKOG_PCKG as the package name in the `Package` field and click the `Save` ( ) icon.

The `ABAP Editor: Change Report ZCLASSICALREPORT` screen appears, as shown in Figure 13.3:

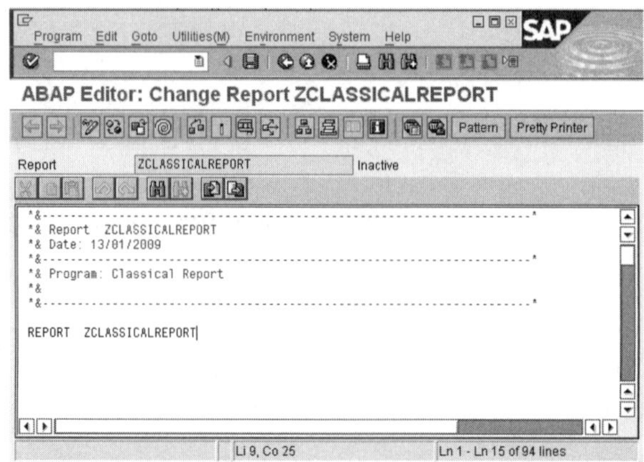

FIGURE 13.3 **ABAP editor change report screen**

6. Write the code given in Listing 13.1, in the `ABAP Editor: Change Report` screen, to generate the respective report:

```
REPORT ZCLASSICALREPORT
        LINE-SIZE 70
        LINE-COUNT 30(3)
        NO STANDARD PAGE HEADING.
*---------------------------------------------------------*
*/ Tables Used in Program
*/
Tables: MARA.
*---------------------------------------------------------*
*/ Data Definitions for the Program
*/
DATA: Begin of itab occurs 10,

      MATNR LIKE MARA-MATNR,
MBRSH LIKE MARA-MBRSH,
MEINS LIKE MARA-MEINS,
MTART LIKE MARA-MTART,

 End of itab.
*---------------------------------------------------------*
*/ Program Selections
*/
SELECT-OPTIONS: MATERIAL FOR MARA-MATNR.
*---------------------------------------------------------*
*/ INITIALIZATION Event Used for Setting the Default Values
to the Parameters
*/
INITIALIZATION.
MATERIAL-LOW = '1'.
MATERIAL-HIGH = '500'.
APPEND MATERIAL.
*---------------------------------------------------------*
*/ AT SELECTION SCREEN Event Used for Performing Parameters
Verification
*/
AT SELECTION-SCREEN.
```

Continued

```
 IF MATERIAL-LOW = ' '.
 MESSAGE I000(ZKMESSAGE).
 ELSEIF MATERIAL-HIGH = ' '.
 MESSAGE I001(ZKMESSAGE).
 ENDIF.
*----------------------------------------------------------*
*/ START-OF-SELECTION Event
*/
START-OF-SELECTION.
SELECT MATNR MBRSH MEINS MTART FROM MARA INTO CORRESPONDING
FIELDS OF itab WHERE MATNR IN MATERIAL.

LOOP AT itab.
WRITE:/ itab-MATNR UNDER 'MATERIAL',
      itab-MBRSH UNDER 'INDUSTRY',
itab-MEINS UNDER 'UNITS',
      itab-MTART UNDER 'MATERIAL TYPE'.
*----------------------------------------------------------*
*/ END-OF-SELECTION Event
*/
END-OF-SELECTION.
WRITE:/  'CLASSICAL  REPORT  CREATED  BY  SHIVAM  SRIVASTAVA'
COLOR 7.
ULINE.
SKIP.
*----------------------------------------------------------*
*/ TOP-OF-PAGE Event Used for Displaying Information at the
Top of Every Page
TOP-OF-PAGE.
WRITE:/ 25 'CLASSICAL REPORT CONTAINING THE GENERAL MATERIAL
DATA FROM THE TABLE MARA' COLOR 6.
ULINE.
WRITE:/ 'MATERIAL' COLOR 1,
       'INDUSTRY' COLOR 2,
       'UNITS' COLOR 3,
       'MATERIAL TYPE' COLOR 4.
ULINE.
END-OF-PAGE.
```

Continued

```
WRITE:/ 'PAGE NUMBER', SY-PAGNO,
     'DATE', SY-DATUM.
*----------------------------------------------------*
```

LISTING 13.1 **Code to create the classical report**

In Listing 13.1, the width of the list to be displayed is 70 characters. The `LINE-SIZE` clause of the `REPORT` statement represents that the number of lines per page has been set to 30 and 4 lines have been left for the footer. The `TABLES` statement is used to declare all the database tables that are accessed in the report. In our case, the `MARA` table is accessed. An internal table named MATERIAL is declared with the help of the `SELECT-OPTIONS` statement.

Figure 13.4 shows the screen of ABAP Editor after entering the code given in Listing 13.1:

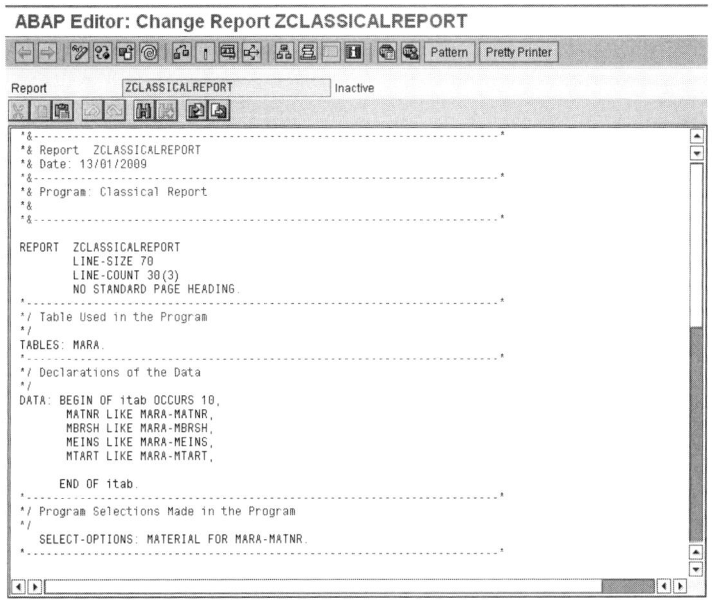

FIGURE 13.4 **Adding code in ABAP editor to create a classical report**

7. Click the `Save` (💾) icon or press the CTRL + S keys combination to save the changes in the program.

8. Next, click the `Check` () icon or press the CTRL + F2 keys combination to check and remove syntax errors or warnings (if any) in the program.
9. Next, click the `Activate` () icon or press the CTRL + F3 keys combination to activate the program.
10. Now, click the `Direct Processing` () icon or press the F8 key to execute the program.

Figure 13.5 shows the output of Listing 13.1:

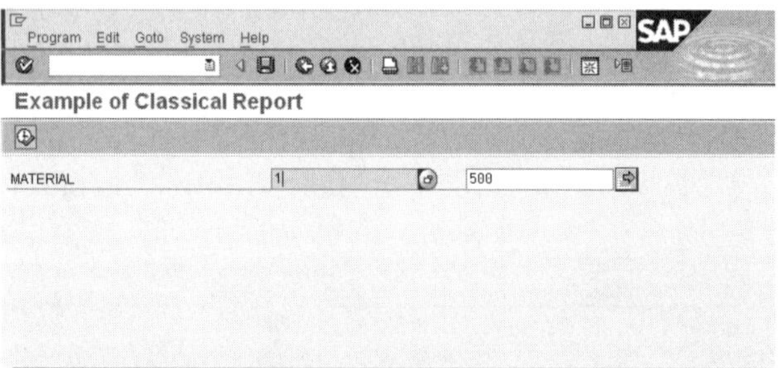

FIGURE 13.5 **The selection screen**

In Figure 13.5, the minimum (1) and maximum (500) values of the MATERIAL variable appear in the respective fields. These values are already declared in the `INITIALIZATION` event. Note that you can modify these values as per your choice.

11. If you remove the minimum value of the MATERIAL variable [that is, 1 (by default)] and then click the `Execute` () icon, an information dialog box appears, prompting you to enter a value for the lower limit of the variable. Figure 13.6 shows the information dialog box:

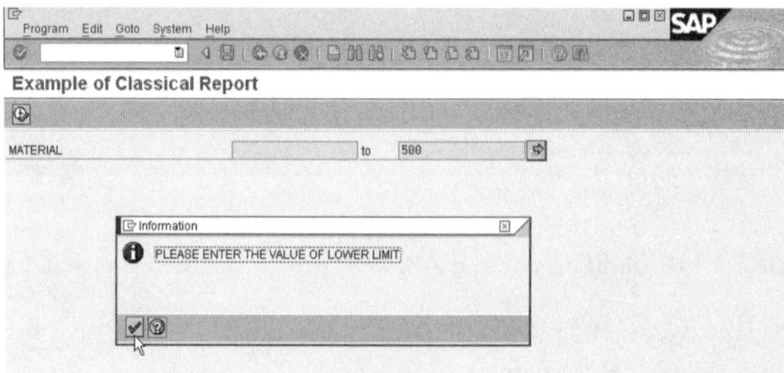

FIGURE 13.6 **Information dialog box**

12. Click the `Continue` (☑) icon. Notice that the system takes the lower limit of the variable as 1 by default. On the output screen, the data corresponding to the `MATNR`, `MBRSH`, `MEINS`, and `MTART` fields are displayed. Figure 13.7 shows the classical report created:

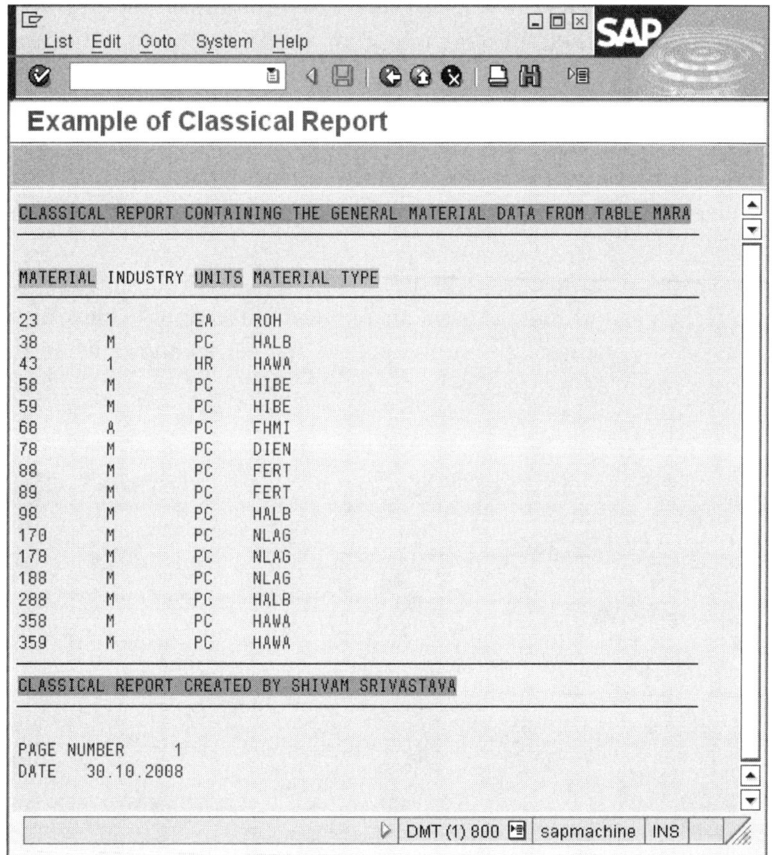

FIGURE 13.7 **A classical report retrieving material data from the MARA table**

INTERACTIVE REPORTS

Interactive reports allow you to control the retrieval of data. With the help of interactive reports, the user first displays an overview list, also known as the basic list. On the basis of the basic list, other lists are displayed according to the user requirements. These other lists or sublists (also known as secondary lists), provide a detailed description of data. For example, if the first column in an overview list of an interactive report represents the data related to material numbers, and you want to display the information of all the vendors related to a particular material number, that material number is temporarily stored at the current line and then another report or sublist containing the vendor details corresponding to the clicked material number is displayed.

Interactive reports can contain a basic list (containing the data displayed after the interactive reports are executed) and additional 19 secondary detailed lists. In other words, an interactive report can contain a maximum of 20 lists. If a user tries to generate a list numbered as 21, a runtime error occurs.

Various events are used to create an interactive report. These events are triggered only after you perform an action, such as double clicking a line in the displayed list, or pressing a function key. Table 13.4 shows when these events are triggered:

Events	Description
AT LINE-SELECTION	Triggered from a displayed list; that is, whenever the user selects the `Choose` (icon) icon or double-clicks a line in the displayed list.
AT USER-COMMAND	Triggered when the user executes a function defined within a menu of the displayed list.
AT PFn	Triggered for the predefined function keys.
TOP OF PAGE DURING LINE SELECTION	Triggered for the top of the page event defined for secondary lists.

TABLE 13.4 Description of the events

In addition to the events shown in Table 13.4, interactive reports also use the events defined in Table 13.1.

Creating an Interactive Report

In this section, you learn how to create an interactive report that accesses data-related various fields of multiple tables in the SAP database. The data and the table fields are as follows:

- Vendor master from the LFA1 table
- General material data from the MARA table
- Data related to the purchasing document header from the EKKO table
- Purchasing document item data from the EKPO table
- Material descriptions from the MAKT table

This interactive report consists of one basic list and four secondary lists. The basic list contains information related to the vendor master. The first secondary list contains information related to the purchasing document header, the second secondary list contains information related to the purchasing document item, the third secondary list contains information related to the general material description, and the fourth secondary list contains the description of the material.

> **Note:** The tables accessed by interactive reports must have at least one field in common. This is because when you double-click any particular value from a list, the corresponding values from some other table for that particular value is displayed in the subsequent list.

In this case, the `LIFNR` field is common for the LFA1 and EKKO tables. The `EBELN` field is common for the EKKO and EKPO tables. The `MATNR` field is common for the EKPO and MARA tables and the last field, `MATNR`, is common for the MARA and MAKT tables.

Perform the following steps to create an interactive report:

1. Open the initial screen of ABAP Editor by either navigating the SAP menu or entering the `SE38` transaction code. The initial screen of ABAP Editor appears (see Figure 13.8).
2. In the initial screen of ABAP Editor, enter a name for the program, select the `Source code` radio button in the `Subobjects` group box, and click the `Create` button to create a new program, as shown in Figure 13.8:

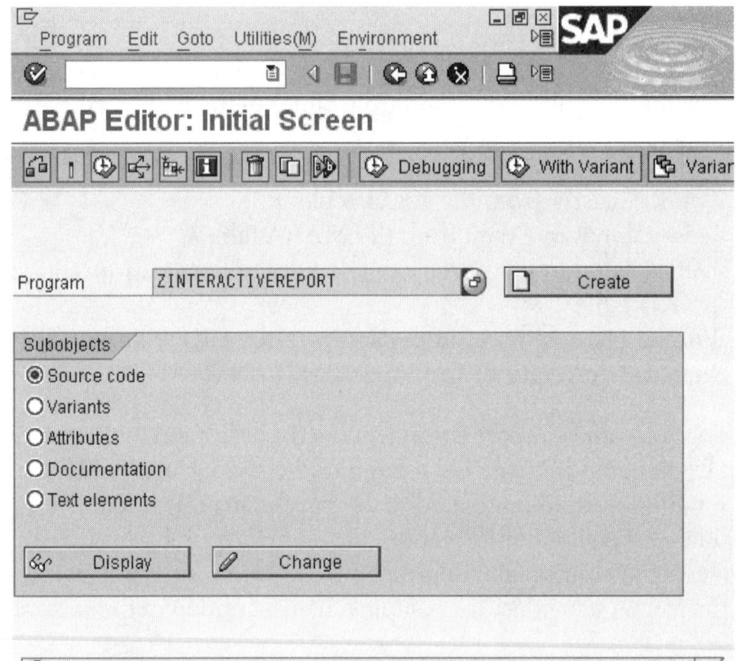

FIGURE 13.8 **Creating interactive reports**

The `ABAP: Program Attributes` dialog box appears.

3. In the `ABAP: Program Attributes` dialog box, enter a short description (Example for interactive reports) for the program in the `Title` field and select the `Executable program` option from the `Type` drop-down in the `Attributes` group box. Now, click the `Save` (Save) button in the `ABAP: Program Attributes` dialog box or press the ENTER key. The `Create Object Directory Entry` dialog box appears.
4. In the `Create Object Directory Entry` dialog box, enter ZKOG_PCKG as the package name in the `Package` field and click the `Save` icon. The `ABAP Editor: Change Report` screen appears.
5. Write the code given in Listing 13.2, in the `ABAP Editor: Change Report` screen, to generate the interactive report:

```
REPORT      ZINTERACTIVEREPORT
            LINE-SIZE 90
            LINE-COUNT 30(4)
            NO STANDARD PAGE HEADING.
*---------------------------------------------------------*
*/ Tables Used in the Program
*/
Tables: MARA, LFA1, EKPO, EKKO, MAKT.
*---------------------------------------------------------*
*/ Program Selections Used for the Program
*/
SELECT-OPTIONS: VENDOR FOR LFA1-LIFNR.
*---------------------------------------------------------*
*/ INITIALIZATION Event Used for the Default Values to the
Parameters
*/
INITIALIZATION.
VENDOR-LOW = '1'.
VENDOR-HIGH = '200'.
VENDOR-SIGN = 'I'.
APPEND VENDOR.
*---------------------------------------------------------*
*/ TOP-OF-PAGE Event Used for the Program Heading
*/
TOP-OF-PAGE.
WRITE: 'WELCOME TO INTERACTIVE REPORT: YOU SEE THE FIRST
LIST OF THE REPORT KNOWN
AS BASIC LIST' COLOR 7.
ULINE.
SKIP.
WRITE:/10 'VENDOR' COLOR 1,
       30 'NAME' COLOR 2,
       66 'LAND1' COLOR 3,
       80 'SORTL' COLOR 4.
*---------------------------------------------------------*
*/ START-OF-SELECTION Event Used for Starting Main Program
Processing
```

Continued

```
*/
START-OF-SELECTION.

SELECT * FROM LFA1 WHERE LIFNR IN VENDOR.

WRITE:/ LFA1-LIFNR UNDER 'VENDOR',
        LFA1-NAME1 UNDER 'NAME',
        LFA1-LAND1 UNDER 'LAND',
        LFA1-SORTL UNDER 'SORTL'.

HIDE LFA1-LIFNR.
CLEAR LFA1.
ENDSELECT.
*-------------------------------------------------------------*
*/ AT LINE-SELECTION Event Used for User Selection
*/
AT LINE-SELECTION.
CASE SY-LSIND.

WHEN '1'.

SELECT * FROM EKKO WHERE LIFNR = LFA1-LIFNR.
WRITE:/ EKKO-LIFNR UNDER 'VENDOR',
        EKKO-EBELN UNDER 'PURCHASE',
        EKKO-BUKRS UNDER 'COMPANY CODE',
        EKKO-BSART UNDER 'DOC TYPE'.

HIDE EKKO-EBELN.
CLEAR EKKO.
ENDSELECT.

WHEN '2'.
WRITE:/10 'PURCHASE NUMBER' COLOR 1,
       40 'MATERIAL NUMBER' COLOR 2,
       60 'DOC TYPE' COLOR 3.

SELECT * FROM EKPO WHERE EBELN = EKPO-EBELN.
```

Continued

```
WRITE:/ EKPO-EBELN UNDER 'PURCHASE',
        EKPO-BUKRS UNDER 'MATERIAL NUMBER',
        EKKO-EBELN UNDER 'DOC TYPE'.
HIDE EKPO-EBELN.
CLEAR EKPO.
ENDSELECT.

WHEN '3'.
WRITE:/10 'PURCHASE NUMBER' COLOR 1,
       30 'INDUSTRY' COLOR 2,
       40 'DOC TYPE' COLOR 3.

SELECT * FROM MARA WHERE MATNR = MARA-MATNR.
WRITE:/ MARA-MATNR UNDER 'MATERIAL NUMBER',
        MARA-MBRSH UNDER 'INDUSTRY',
        MARA-MTART UNDER 'DOC TYPE'.

HIDE MARA-MATNR.
CLEAR MARA.
ENDSELECT.

WHEN '4'.
WRITE:/10 'MATERIAL NUMBER' COLOR 1,
       30 'DESCRIPTION' COLOR 2.

SELECT * FROM MAKT WHERE MATNR = MARA-MATNR.
WRITE:/ MAKT-MATNR UNDER 'MATERIAL NUMBER',
        MAKT-MAKTX UNDER 'DESCRIPTION'.

ENDSELECT.
ENDCASE.
*------------------------------------------------------*
*/ TOP-OF-PAGE Used for Setting the Headings for the
Secondary List
*/
TOP-OF-PAGE DURING LINE-SELECTION.
CASE SY-LSIND.
```

Continued

```
WHEN '1'.
WRITE: / 'REPORT CONTAINING THE DETAILS REAGARDING PURCHASING
DOCUMENT HEADER:: FIRST SECONDARY LIST' COLOR 5.
ULINE.
SKIP.
WRITE:/10 'VENDOR' COLOR 1,
       30 'PURCHASE' COLOR 2,
       60 'COMPANY CODE' COLOR 3,
       90 'DOC TYPE' COLOR 4.

WHEN '2'.
WRITE:/ 'REPORT CONTAINING THE DETAILS REGARDING PURCHASING
DOCUMENT ITEM:: SECOND SECONDARY LIST' COLOR 5.
ULINE.
SKIP.

WHEN '3'.
WRITE:/ 'REPORT CONTAINING THE DETAILS REAGARDING PURCHASING
DOCUMENT HEADER:: THIRD SECONDARY LIST' COLOR 5.
ULINE.
SKIP.

WHEN '4'.
WRITE:/ 'REPORT CONTAINING THE DETAILS REAGARDING MATERIAL
DESCRIPTIONS::FOURTH SECONDARY LIST' COLOR 5.
ULINE.
SKIP.
ENDCASE.
*-------------------------------------------------------*
*/ END-OF-PAGE Event for Displaying the Page Number, Date
at the End of the Page
*/
END-OF-PAGE.
SKIP.
WRITE:/'PAGE NUMBER', SY-PAGNO,
       / 'DATE', SY-DATUM.
/ 'REPORT CREATED BY SHIVAM SRIVASTAVA'.
*-------------------------------------------------------*
```

LISTING 13.2 **Code to create an interactive report**

Figure 13.9 shows the screen of ABAP Editor after entering the code given in Listing 13.2:

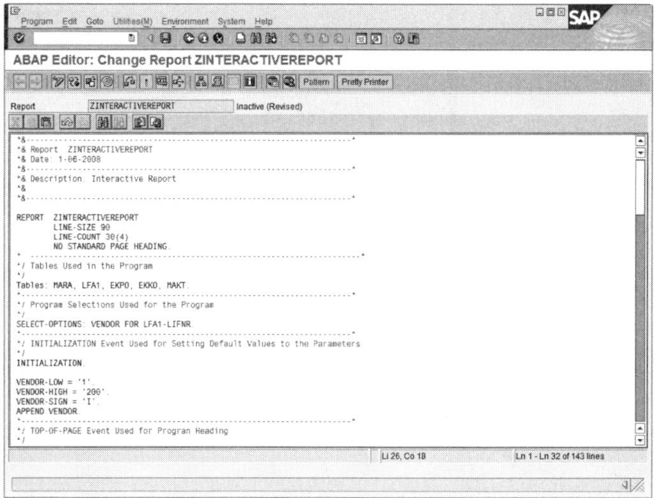

FIGURE 13.9 **The ABAP editor screen**

6. Click the `Save` (💾) icon and then click the `Check` (icon) icon. Finally, click the `Activate` (icon) icon to activate the program before executing it. Click the `Direct processing` (icon) icon to process the interactive report created. The selection screen appears, displaying the `VENDOR` field. The value for the lower limit and upper limit of the `VENDOR` field are 1 and 2000, respectively. Note that you can specify these values as per your requirement.
7. Click the `Execute` (icon) icon, as shown in Figure 13.10:

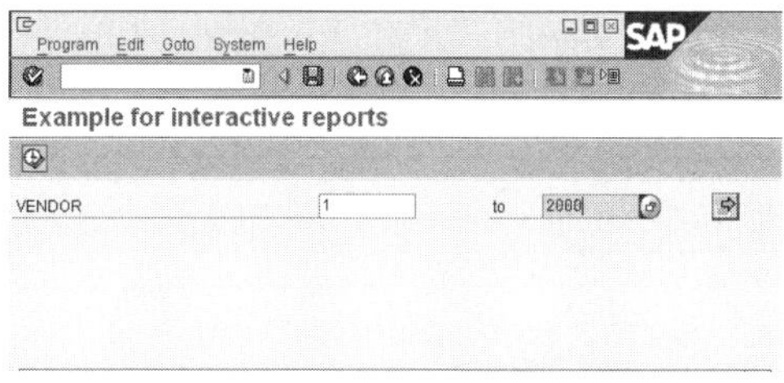

FIGURE 13.10 **Selection screen**

8. The first output screen (basic list) appears, which displays information about the vendor master from the LFA1 table, as shown in Figure 13.11:

```
List  Edit  Goto  System  Help

Example for interactive reports

WELCOME TO INTERACTIVE REPORT: YOU SEE THE FIRST LIST OF THE REPORT KNOWN AS BASIC LIST

VENDOR      NAME                                   LAND1   SORTL
1           Forks Manufacturing GmbH               DE      CPG
2           Electronic Components Distributor      US      ELECTRO
5           Safety Clean Inc.                      DE      SAFETY CLE
8           Jose Fernandez                         MX      DERPFI
10          Dupont de la Rivière                   FR      DUPONT
15          Tiedemeier Entsorgung GmbH             DE      TIEDEMEIER
25          Metropol                               DK      DERPFI
50          Central Logistics Inc.                 DE      CENTRAL LO
75          Meier Logistics GmbH                   DE      MEIER L
100         C.E.B. BERLIN                          DE      ALLGEMEIN
111         KBB Schwarze Pumpe                     DE      PUME
200         SMP                                    US      AUTO
222         Express Vendor Inc                     US      LES
300         AluCast                                US      AUTO
424         Sedona Suppliers                       US      SEDONA
500         IDES AG New GL - (InterCompany Acco    DE      IDES
603         Intercompany Resources US              CA      SERVICE PR
604         Intercompany Resources to Belgium      CA      SERVICE PR
605         Intercompany Resources Canada          CA      SERVICE PR
935         Burton's Machine Shop                  US      JTE
954         Ander Group                            US      MG
1000        C.E.B. BERLIN                          DE      ALLGEMEIN

PAGE NUMBER     1
DATE 23.10.2008
REPORT CREATED BY SHIVAM SRIVASTAVA

WELCOME TO INTERACTIVE REPORT: YOU SEE THE FIRST LIST OF THE REPORT KNOWN AS BASIC LIST

VENDOR      NAME                                   LAND1   SORTL
1001        SKF Kugelmeier KGaA                    DE      AUTO/PUMPE
```


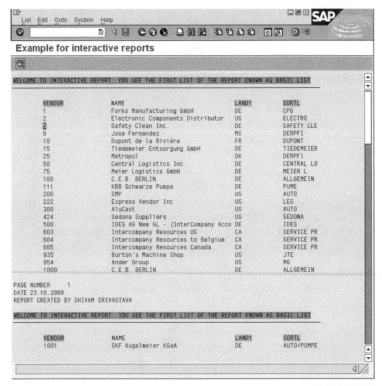

FIGURE 13.11 **The basic list containing vendor master data**

9. Double-click a particular value of a vendor from the basic list; for example, double-click 5.

> **Note:** Alternatively, you can first click 5 and then the `Choose` ( ) icon.

You can now see the corresponding values of the fields from the EKKO table. Use the HIDE statement to prevent any change in the selected value. The `HIDE` statement places the field name, that is, LFA1-LIFNR, and its content in the hidden area of the list. The `CLEAR` statement is used to clear the value of the fields stored on the output line.

Figure 13.12 shows the first secondary list corresponding to the value of the selected field; that is, 5:

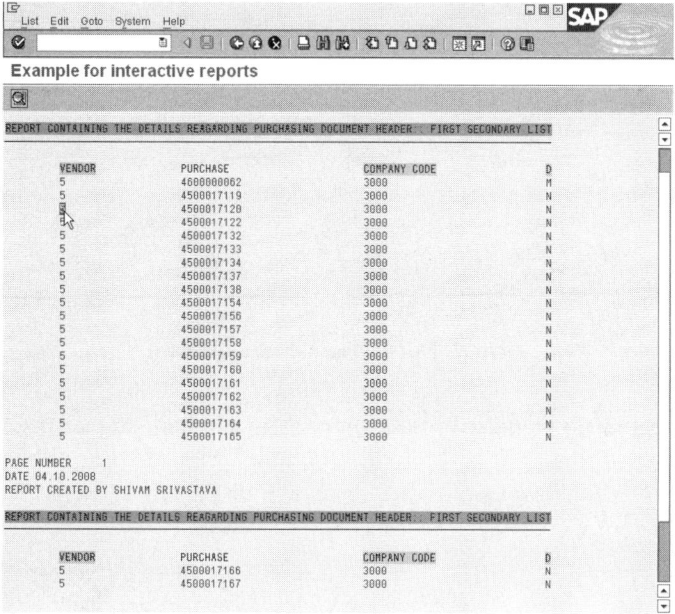

FIGURE 13.12 **First secondary list**

Now, from the first secondary list, you can retrieve the information related to the purchasing document item from the EKPO table, corresponding to the value selected from the first secondary list.

> **Note:** At times, when you double-click a particular value, you may not find any respective value from the next defined table. This is because the corresponding table might not contain any entry for the selected value.

In this case, if a user double-clicks the value 5 to see the details regarding the purchasing document item from the EKPO table, the user cannot see any details because the EKPO table does not contain any entries in the EBELN, MATNR, and EBELP fields for the selected value. Figure 13.13 shows the second secondary list containing no values:

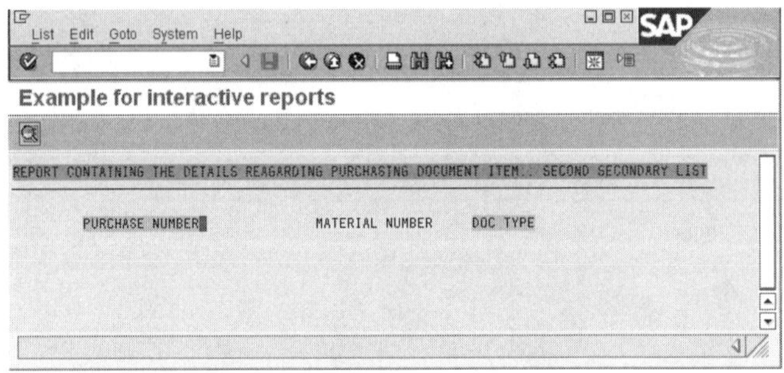

FIGURE 13.13 **Second secondary list**

Because no values can be seen on this window, you will not be able to see any value in the third and fourth secondary lists. If you double-click any title, you see the third secondary list, as shown in Figure 13.14:

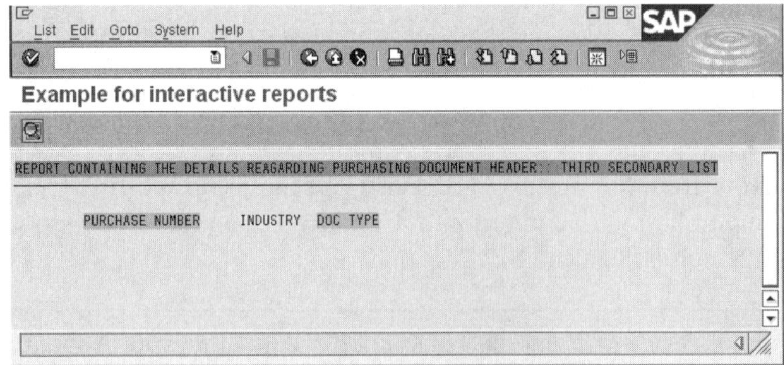

FIGURE 13.14 **Third secondary list**

Similarly, you can also see the fourth secondary list.

Comparing Classical and Interactive Reports

Although both classical and interactive reports are used to retrieve data from one or more database tables, there exist some basic differences between the two. Table 13.5 compares a classical report with an interactive report:

Classical Report	Interactive Report
Does not allow the user to interact with an SAP system	Allows the user to interact with an SAP system
Provides no control over the output after executing the report	Enables users to control the output after executing the report
Does not support drilling, which means that you cannot navigate to the next level of detail	Supports drilling, which means that the user can navigate to the next level of detail

TABLE 13.5 Comparison between classical and interactive reports

ALV REPORTS

ALV reports allow you to perform various functions dynamically, such as sorting, arranging, filtering, and retrieving data. You can use various `ALV` function modules to perform functions on the data of the report. You need to create an ALV report when you need to include the columns that store more than 255 characters in their field values in a report. Using `ALV` function modules, you can select columns for displaying, can arrange the columns as per requirements, and can also save different variants for report display. An ALV report can display up to 90 columns or more with various display options. Some features of ALV reports include:

- User friendliness
- Ability to handle events
- Use of moderate code

Table 13.6 describes various ALV function modules available in the SAP system:

Function Module	Description
REUSE_ALV_GRID_DISPLAY	Displays an ALV grid as per the parameters defined in the function call
REUSE_ALV_LIST_DISPLAY	Displays an ALV list as per the parameters defined in the function call
REUSE_ALV_COMMENTARY_WRITE	Displays the list header information
REUSE_ALV_HIERSEQ_LIST_DISPLAY	Displays two internal tables that are formatted in the hierarchical-sequential list format
REUSE_ALV_VARIANT	Displays a variant selection dialog box
REUSE_ALV_VARIANT_EXISTENCE	Checks the existence of the variant display

TABLE 13.6 Function modules for ALV reports

Now, let's learn how to create an ALV report by using the REUSE_ALV_GRID_DISPLAY function module.

Creating an ALV Report

In this section, you explore how to create an ALV report, which accesses data of the QMEL table of the SAP database. First, a structure named I_QMEL is created, which is similar to the structure of the QMEL table. A title, "AN ALV REPORT CREATED BY SHIVAM SRIVASTAVA", is then assigned to the report by using the WS-TITLE variable. Perform the following steps to create the ALV report:

1. Open the initial screen of ABAP Editor by either navigating to the SAP menu or executing the SE38 transaction code.
2. In the initial screen of ABAP Editor, enter ZALVREPORT as the name of the program, select the Source code radio button in the Subobjects group box, and click the Create pushbutton to create a new program, as shown in Figure 13.15:

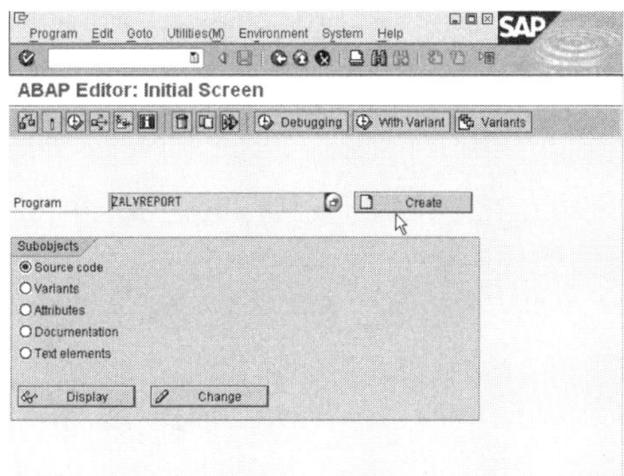

FIGURE 13.15 **The initial screen of ABAP editor**

The `ABAP: Program Attributes` dialog box appears.

3. In the `ABAP: Program Attributes` dialog box, enter a short description (Example of ALV Reports) for the program in the `Title` field and select the `Executable program` option from the `Type` drop-down list in the `Attributes` group box. Now, click the `Save` (Save) pushbutton in the `ABAP: Program Attributes` dialog box or press the ENTER key. The `Create Object Directory Entry` dialog box appears.
4. In the `Create Object Directory Entry` dialog box, enter ZKOG_PCKG as the package name in the `Package` field and click the `Save` (💾) icon. The `ABAP Editor: Change Report ZALVREPORT` screen appears (see Figure 13.16).
5. Write the following code snippet for the ALV report being created in the `ABAP Editor: Change Report ZALVREPORT` screen:

```
*----------------------------------------------------------*
*/ Data Declarations for the Program
DATA: I_QMEL LIKE QMEL OCCURS 0.
DATA: WS_TITLE type LVC_TITLE VALUE 'AN ALV REPORT CREATED
BY SHIVAM SRIVASTAVA'.
*----------------------------------------------------------*
*/ Selecting Fields from QMEL Table
*/
SELECT * FROM QMEL INTO TABLE I_QMEL
*----------------------------------------------------------*
```

Figure 13.16 shows the `ABAP Editor: Change Report ZALVREPORT` screen after inserting the preceding code snippet:

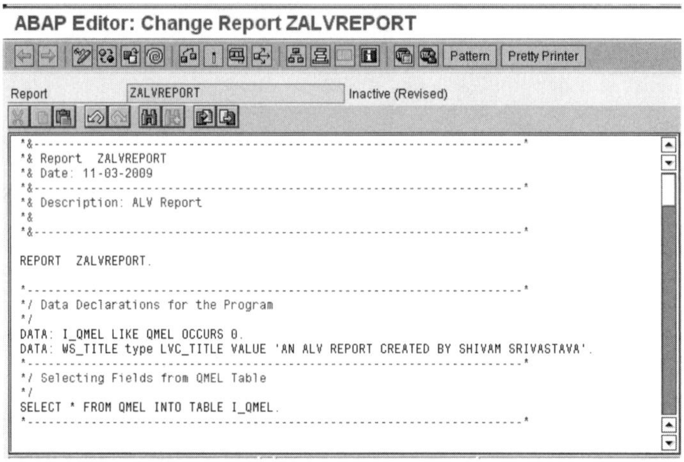

ABAP Editor: Change Report ZALVREPORT

Pattern | Pretty Printer

Report ZALVREPORT Inactive (Revised)

```
*&---------------------------------------------------------------------*
*& Report  ZALVREPORT
*& Date: 11-03-2009
*&---------------------------------------------------------------------*
*& Description: ALV Report
*&
*&---------------------------------------------------------------------*

REPORT  ZALVREPORT.

*---------------------------------------------------------------------*
*/ Data Declarations for the Program
*/
DATA: I_QMEL LIKE QMEL OCCURS 0.
DATA: WS_TITLE type LVC_TITLE VALUE 'AN ALV REPORT CREATED BY SHIVAM SRIVASTAVA'.
*---------------------------------------------------------------------*
*/ Selecting Fields from QMEL Table
*/
SELECT * FROM QMEL INTO TABLE I_QMEL.
*---------------------------------------------------------------------*
```


FIGURE 13.16 **The ABAP editor screen where the code for the ALV report is written**

6. Call the `REUSE_ALV_GRID_DISPLAY` function module by clicking the `Pattern` button present on the application toolbar. When you click the `Pattern` button, the `Ins Statement` dialog box appears, as shown in Figure 13.17:

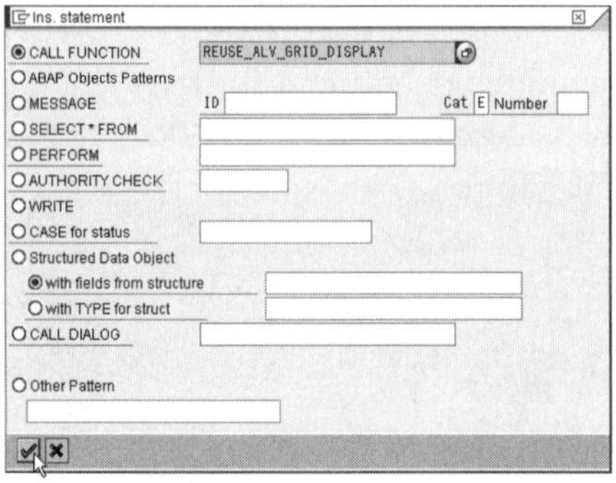

Ins. statement

- (•) CALL FUNCTION — REUSE_ALV_GRID_DISPLAY
- ( ) ABAP Objects Patterns
- ( ) MESSAGE — ID — Cat E — Number
- ( ) SELECT * FROM
- ( ) PERFORM
- ( ) AUTHORITY CHECK
- ( ) WRITE
- ( ) CASE for status
- ( ) Structured Data Object
  - (•) with fields from structure
  - ( ) with TYPE for struct
- ( ) CALL DIALOG
- ( ) Other Pattern

FIGURE 13.17 **Calling the function module**

7. In the `Ins Statement` dialog box, write the name of the function module (`REUSE_ALV_GRID_DISPLAY`) in the `CALL FUNCTION` field and click the `Continue` (✔) icon (see Figure 13.17). The code given in Listing 13.3, for the `REUSE_ALV_GRID_DISPLAY` function module, is displayed in the ABAP Editor:

```
*-------------------------------------------------------------*
*/ Data Declarations for the Program
DATA: I_QMEL LIKE QMEL OCCURS 0.
DATA: WS_TITLE type LVC_TITLE VALUE 'AN ALV REPORT CREATED
BY SHIVAM SRIVASTAVA'.
*-------------------------------------------------------------*
*/ Selecting Fields from QMEL Table
*/
SELECT * FROM QMEL INTO TABLE I_QMEL
*-------------------------------------------------------------*
*/ Calling a Function Module 'REUSE_ALV_GRID_DISPLAY'
*/
CALL FUNCTION 'REUSE_ALV_GRID_DISPLAY'
EXPORTING
*     I_INTERFACE_CHECK                 = ' '
*     I_BYPASSING_BUFFER                = ' '
*     I_BUFFER_ACTIVE                   = ' '
*     I_CALLBACK_PROGRAM                = ' '
*     I_CALLBACK_PF_STATUS_SET          = ' '
*     I_CALLBACK_USER_COMMAND           = ' '
*     I_CALLBACK_TOP_OF_PAGE            = ' '
*     I_CALLBACK_HTML_TOP_OF_PAGE       = ' '
*     I_CALLBACK_HTML_END_OF_LIST       = ' '
      I_STRUCTURE_NAME                  = 'QMEL'
*     I_BACKGROUND_ID                   = ' '
      I_GRID_TITLE                      = WS_TITLE
*     I_GRID_SETTINGS                   =
*     IS_LAYOUT                         =
*     IT_FIELDCAT                       =
*     IT_EXCLUDING                      =
```

Continued

```
*       IT_SPECIAL_GROUPS                         =
*       IT_SORT                                   =
*       IT_FILTER                                 =
*        IS_SEL_HIDE =
        I_DEFAULT                                 = 'X'
*       I_SAVE                                    = ' '
*       IS_VARIANT                                =
*       IT_EVENTS                                 =
*       IT_EVENT_EXIT                             =
*       IS_PRINT                                  =
*       IS_REPREP_ID                              =
*       I_SCREEN_START_COLUMN                     = 0
*       I_SCREEN_START_LINE                       = 0
*       I_SCREEN_END_COLUMN                       = 0
*       I_SCREEN_END_LINE                         = 0
*       I_HTML_HEIGHT_TOP                         = 0
*       I_HTML_HEIGHT_END                         = 0
*       IT_ALV_GRAPHICS                           =
*       IT_HYPERLINK                              =
*       IT_ADD_FIELDCAT                           =
*       IT_EXCEPT_QINFO                           =
*       IR_SALV_FULLSCREEN_ADAPTER                =
*       IMPORTING
*       E_EXIT_CAUSED_BY_CALLER                   =
*       ES_EXIT_CAUSED_BY_USER                    =
        TABLES
        T_OUTTAB                                  = I_QMEL
*       EXCEPTIONS
*       PROGRAM_ERROR                             = 1
*       OTHERS                                    = 2
          .
IF SY-SUBRC <> 0.
*       MESSAGE ID SY-MSGID TYPE SY-MSGTY NUMBER SY-MSGNO
*       WITH SY-MSGV1 SY-MSGV2 SY-MSGV3 SY-MSGV4.
ENDIF.
*-------------------------------------------------------*
```

LISTING 13.3 **Sequence of statements for the ALV report**

Figure 13.18 shows the code given in Listing 13.3 in the `ABAP Editor` screen:

ABAP Editor: Change Report ZALVREPORT

Pattern | Pretty Printer

Report ZALVREPORT Inactive (Revised)

```
*&---------------------------------------------------------------*
*& Report  ZALVREPORT
*& Date  11-03-2009
*&---------------------------------------------------------------*
*& Description  ALV Report
*&
*&---------------------------------------------------------------*

REPORT  ZALVREPORT.

*---------------------------------------------------------------*
*/ Data Declarations for the Program
*/
DATA: I_QMEL LIKE QMEL OCCURS 0.
DATA: WS_TITLE type LVC_TITLE VALUE 'AN ALV REPORT CREATED BY SHIVAM SRIVASTAVA'.
*---------------------------------------------------------------*
*/ Selecting Fields from QMEL Table
*/
SELECT * FROM QMEL INTO TABLE I_QMEL.
*---------------------------------------------------------------*
*/ Calling a Function Module 'REUSE_ALV_GRID_DISPLAY'
*/
CALL FUNCTION 'REUSE_ALV_GRID_DISPLAY'
 EXPORTING
*   I_INTERFACE_CHECK                 = ' '
*   I_BYPASSING_BUFFER                = ' '
*   I_BUFFER_ACTIVE                   = ' '
*   I_CALLBACK_PROGRAM                = ' '
*   I_CALLBACK_PF_STATUS_SET          = ' '
*   I_CALLBACK_USER_COMMAND           = ' '
*   I_CALLBACK_TOP_OF_PAGE            = ' '
*   I_CALLBACK_HTML_TOP_OF_PAGE       = ' '
*   I_CALLBACK_HTML_END_OF_LIST       = ' '
   I_STRUCTURE_NAME                  = 'QMEL'
*   I_BACKGROUND_ID                   = ' '
   I_GRID_TITLE                      = WS_TITLE
```


FIGURE 13.18 **The ABAP editor screen containing statements for the ALV report**

8. Click the `Save` (💾) icon and then click the `Check` icon. Finally, click the `Activate` icon to activate the program before executing it. Now, click the `Direct processing` icon to execute the created ALV report. Figure 13.19 shows the generated ALV report:

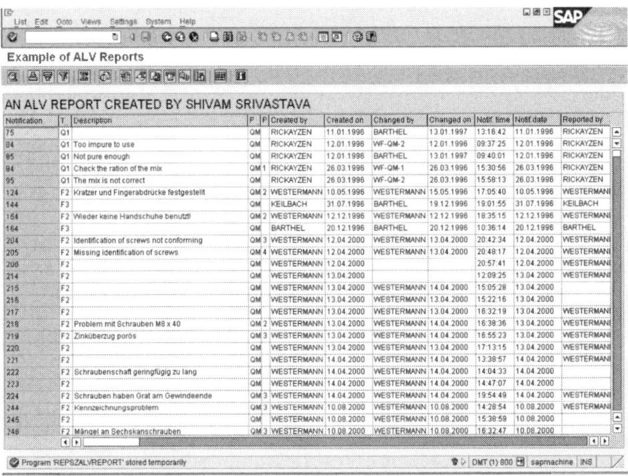

List Edit Goto Views Settings System Help

Example of ALV Reports

AN ALV REPORT CREATED BY SHIVAM SRIVASTAVA

Notification	T	Description	P	P	Created by	Created on	Changed by	Changed on	Notif. time	Notif. date	Reported by
75	Q1		QM		RICKAYZEN	11.01.1996	BARTHEL	13.01.1997	13:16:42	11.01.1996	RICKAYZEN
84	Q1	Too impure to use	QM		RICKAYZEN	12.01.1996	WF-QM-2	12.01.1996	09:37:25	12.01.1996	RICKAYZEN
85	Q1	Not pure enough	QM		RICKAYZEN	12.01.1996	BARTHEL	13.01.1997	09:40:01	12.01.1996	RICKAYZEN
94	Q1	Check the ration of the mix	QM	1	RICKAYZEN	26.03.1996	WF-QM-1	26.03.1996	15:30:56	26.03.1996	RICKAYZEN
95	Q1	The mix is not correct	QM		RICKAYZEN	26.03.1996	WF-QM-2	26.03.1996	15:58:13	26.03.1996	RICKAYZEN
124	F2	Kratzer und Fingerabdrücke festgestellt	QM	2	WESTERMANN	10.05.1996	WESTERMANN	15.05.1996	17:05:40	10.05.1996	WESTERMANN
144	F3		QM		KEILBACH	31.07.1996	BARTHEL	19.12.1996	19:01:55	31.07.1996	KEILBACH
154	F2	Wieder keine Handschuhe benutzt!	QM	2	WESTERMANN	12.12.1996	WESTERMANN	12.12.1996	18:35:15	12.12.1996	WESTERMANN
164	F3		QM		BARTHEL	20.12.1996	BARTHEL	20.12.1996	10:36:14	20.12.1996	BARTHEL
204	F2	Identification of screws not conforming	QM	3	WESTERMANN	12.04.2000	WESTERMANN	13.04.2000	20:42:34	12.04.2000	WESTERMANN
205	F2	Missing identification of screws	QM	4	WESTERMANN	12.04.2000	WESTERMANN	13.04.2000	20:48:17	12.04.2000	WESTERMANN
208	F2		QM		WESTERMANN	12.04.2000			20:57:41	12.04.2000	WESTERMANN
214	F2		QM		WESTERMANN	13.04.2000			12:09:25	13.04.2000	WESTERMANN
215	F2		QM		WESTERMANN	13.04.2000	WESTERMANN	14.04.2000	15:05:28	13.04.2000	
216	F2		QM		WESTERMANN	13.04.2000	WESTERMANN	13.04.2000	15:22:16	13.04.2000	
217	F2		QM		WESTERMANN	13.04.2000	WESTERMANN	13.04.2000	16:32:19	13.04.2000	WESTERMANN
218	F2	Problem mit Schrauben M8 x 40	QM	2	WESTERMANN	13.04.2000	WESTERMANN	14.04.2000	16:38:36	13.04.2000	WESTERMANN
219	F2	Zinküberzug porös	QM	3	WESTERMANN	13.04.2000	WESTERMANN	14.04.2000	16:55:23	13.04.2000	WESTERMANN
220	F2		QM		WESTERMANN	13.04.2000	WESTERMANN	13.04.2000	17:13:15	13.04.2000	WESTERMANN
221	F2		QM		WESTERMANN	14.04.2000	WESTERMANN	14.04.2000	13:38:57	14.04.2000	WESTERMANN
222	F2	Schraubenschaft geringfügig zu lang	QM		WESTERMANN	14.04.2000	WESTERMANN	14.04.2000	14:04:33	14.04.2000	
223	F2		QM		WESTERMANN	14.04.2000	WESTERMANN	14.04.2000	14:47:07	14.04.2000	
224	F2	Schrauben haben Grat am Gewindeende	QM	3	WESTERMANN	14.04.2000	WESTERMANN	14.04.2000	19:54:49	14.04.2000	WESTERMANN
244	F2	Kennzeichnungsproblem	QM	3	WESTERMANN	10.08.2000	WESTERMANN	10.08.2000	14:28:54	10.08.2000	WESTERMANN
245	F2		QM		WESTERMANN	10.08.2000	WESTERMANN	10.08.2000	15:38:59	10.08.2000	
246	F2	Mängel an Sechskanschrauben	QM	3	WESTERMANN	10.08.2000	WESTERMANN	10.08.2000	16:32:47	10.08.2000	

Program 'REPSZALVREPORT' stored temporarily

DMT (1) 800 sapmachine INS

FIGURE 13.19 **The generated ALV report**

In Figure 13.19, you see the required data, such as Notification and Description, corresponding to the QMEL table in grid view. You can perform various functions, such as sorting and filtering in the generated ALV report.

SUMMARY

In this chapter, you have learned about reports used to retrieve data from one or more tables in a database without making any changes in the tables. You have also learned about the different types of reports, such as classical reports, interactive reports, and ALV reports, and how to create each of them. In addition, you have learned about the different types of events used to create these reports, such as `INITIALIZATION`, `At SELECTION-SCREEN`, and `START-OF-SELECTION`. You have learned about differences between classical and interactive reports. Finally, you have explored the function modules used to create ALV reports.

Chapter 14

Business Add-Ins (BADIs)

If you need information on:	*See page:*
Concept of BADIs	848
Enhancement Framework	849
Structure of a BADI	856
Definition of BADIs	858
Implementation of BADI	870
Calling BADIs	875
Differences Between Classic and New BADIs	875
Filter-Dependent BADIs	876
Function Code Enhancements	878
Screen Enhancements	879

At times, some special functions or programs need to be predefined in a software application to enhance the functionality of the application. For example, there are many Microsoft Excel add-ins (such as converters, sorting tools, and complex table filters) to enhance the basic functionality provided by Excel. Similarly, SAP facilitates in predefining such functions by providing Business Add-Ins (BADIs). A BADI is an enhancement technique that facilitates an SAP programmer, a customer, or a specific industry to enhance or add some additional code to existing standard programs in an SAP system. You can use standard or customized logic to enhance the SAP system. A BADI must first be defined and then implemented to enhance an SAP application. While defining a BADI, an interface is created. The BADI is implemented by this interface, which in turn is implemented by one or more adaptor classes. Finally, you need to create an instance of the adaptor class and method calls in the SAP application as per the requirements to use the BADI.

In this chapter, you learn about the concept of BADIs, Enhancement Framework, enhancement concepts, different enhancement techniques in Enhancement Framework, and BADIs as one of the enhancement techniques in Enhancement Framework. Next, you learn about the structure of BADIs and how to define, implement, and call BADIs. You also learn about the filter-dependent BADIs. Finally, at the end of this chapter, you learn about different features of BADIs, such as function code enhancements (a new name adopted for the menu enhancements), and screen enhancements. Now, let's start by exploring the concept of BADIs.

CONCEPT OF BADIs

A BADI is an enhancement technique of SAP that uses ABAP objects to create predefined points in the SAP ERP components. These predefined points are then implemented by the individual industry solutions, country variants, or even by partners and customers to suite their specific requirements. SAP introduced the BADI enhancement technique with Release 4.6A; the technique was re-implemented in Release 7.0.

Prior to BADI, a technique called customer exits was used to add custom functionalities to existing standard business applications in an SAP system. Customer exits were created to add some specific programs, screens, and menus to standard applications. These exits, however, do not contain any functionality of their own, but help add further functionality. In addition, customer exits are based on a two-level structure that incudes an SAP system and a customer solution. In contrast to customer exits, however, BADIs are based on a multi-level structure that includes an SAP system, industry solutions, country-specific versions, partner solutions, and customer solutions.

The BADI technique is different from other enhancement techniques in two respects. First, enhancement techniques can be implemented only once; second, enhancement techniques can be used by multiple customers simultaneously. In addition, you can create filter BADIs, which means BADIs are defined on the basis of filtered data, which is not possible with enhancement techniques.

The concept of BADIs has been redefined in SAP Release 7.0 with the following goals:

- Enhancing the standard applications in an SAP system by adding two new elements in the ABAP language, i.e., `GET BADI` and `CALL BADI`.
- Providing more flexibility features, such as contexts and filters, for the enhancement of standard applications in an SAP system.

When a BADI is created, it contains an interface and other additional components, such as function codes for menu enhancements or screen enhancements. A BADI creation allows customers to include their own enhancements in the standard SAP application. The enhancement, interface, and generated classes are located in an appropriate application development namespace.

Now, let's explain the concept of Enhancement Framework and the use of a BADI as one of the enhancement techniques of Enhancement Framework.

ENHANCEMENT FRAMEWORK

Enhancement Framework is an enhancement concept of ABAP Workbench that integrates different elements of an SAP application to modify and enhance the development objects. Prior to Release 7.0 of SAP, Enhancement Framework was used to fulfill two goals: enhancing an SAP application by inserting user developments at predefined points in an SAP system and modifying the delivered development objects. With Release 7.0 of SAP, the aim of Enhancement Framework has changed. Now, Enhancement Framework is used to unify all possible ways to modify or enhance the SAP products; for example, repository objects, which could not be customized in earlier releases of SAP. In addition, you can replace a repository object with an object having the same name, and you can enhance a repository object at a predefined position in an SAP system.

> **Note:** Within Enhancement Framework, any explicit reference to the BADI concept prior to Release 7.0 is termed as classic BADIs. References to the BADI concept in Release 7.0 is simply termed as BADI.

It is interesting to note that, unlike modifications, you can introduce enhancements at different development levels, which are as follows:

1. Core development
2. Application development
3. Add-on development
4. Customer development

Figure 14.1 shows the enhancements at the different development levels:

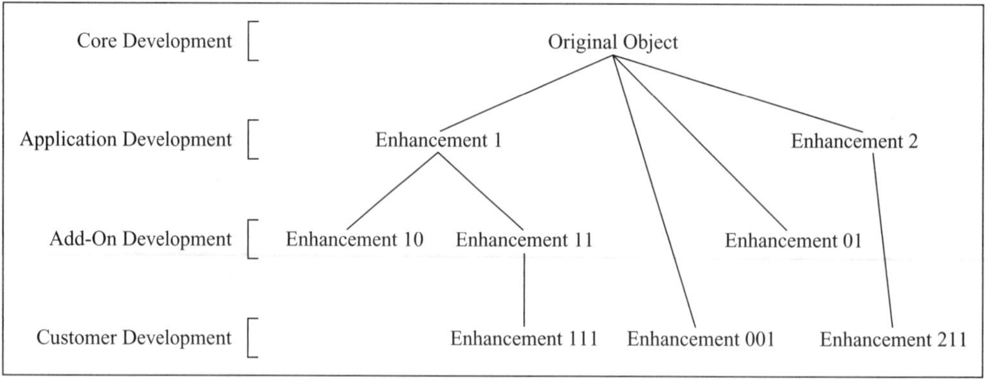

FIGURE 14.1 **Enhancements at the different development levels**

> **Note:** You can create multiple enhancement implementations or replace an enhancement implementation on different layers. However, enhancements cannot be nested.

Now, let's discuss the following topics in the context of Enhancement Framework:

- Enhancement concept
- Enhancement Builder
- Different enhancement techniques in Enhancement Framework

Overview of Enhancement

The enhancement concept enables you to integrate the following concepts to modify and enhance development objects:

- Enhancement options
- Enhancement spots
- Enhancement implementations

Enhancement Options

Enhancement options are positions in repository objects where enhancements can be made. These options are either defined explicitly (by the developers) or exist implicitly.

Enhancement Spots

Enhancement spots are points in an SAP system where enhancement options are created. An enhancement spot contains information about how an enhancement option is defined in an SAP system. One enhancement spot can be used to manage one or more enhancement options. Conversely, one enhancement option can be managed by one or more enhancement spots.

An enhancement option is created when an enhancement spot is created as a repository object at a point and processed by the relevant tool. This enhancement option can then be called at different points by calling the elements of relevant enhancement spots. The definition and the corresponding call of an element of an enhancement spot together comprise the definition of an enhancement option.

The definition of an element of an enhancement spot must be assigned to one or more simple enhancement spots. Further, enhancement spots are assigned to one or more composite enhancement spots. Simple and composite enhancement spots are repository objects that form a tree-like structure. The branches of this tree-like structure represent composite enhancement spots and leaves represent simple enhancement spots. Note that a simple enhancement spot is always assigned to an enhancement technology, such as ABAP source code enhancement or BADI; whereas composite enhancement spots are a collection or group of simple enhancement spots. Moreover, a composite enhancement spot not only contains one or more simple enhancement spots but also one or more composite enhancement spots of the relevant type. Figure 14.2 shows the grouping of simple and complex enhancement spots:

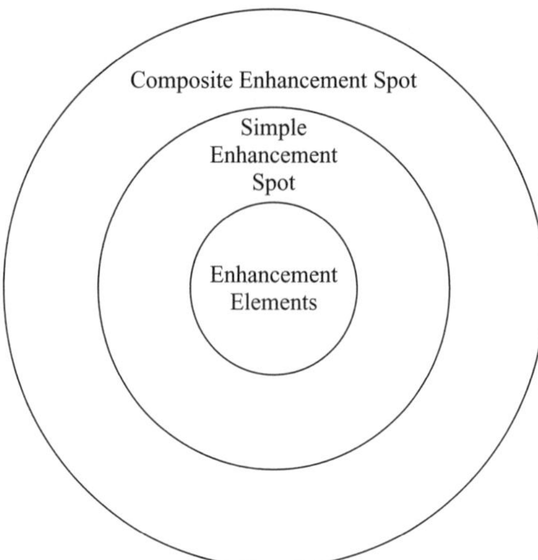

FIGURE 14.2 **Grouping of the simple and complex enhancement spots**

Enhancement spots are processed with the Enhancement Builder tool, which is integrated in the ABAP Workbench tool. Enhancement spots in Enhancement Builder indicate that enhancement options are explicit and are managed by developers.

Enhancement Implementations

Enhancement implementations manage enhancement options, both explicitly and implicitly. Similar to differentiated enhancement options and their management, we also differentiate the actual enhancement and its management in the case of enhancement implementations.

An enhancement implementation describes the enhancement of a repository object at one or more enhancement options. Note that an element of an enhancement implementation can belong to one enhancement option. However, elements of several enhancement implementations can be assigned to one enhancement option. The enhancement implementations are also divided into two categories: simple and composite. A composite enhancement implementation contains one or more simple enhancement implementations or may contain one or more composite enhancement implementations of the relevant type. An enhancement implementation is processed by using the Enhancement Builder tool.

You can manage an enhancement by assigning one or more simple enhancement implementations to an enhancement spot. However, a simple enhancement implementation belongs to only one enhancement spot. In addition, a simple enhancement implementation must be assigned to at least one composite enhancement implementation. Figure 14.3 shows the grouping of the simple and composite enhancement implementations:

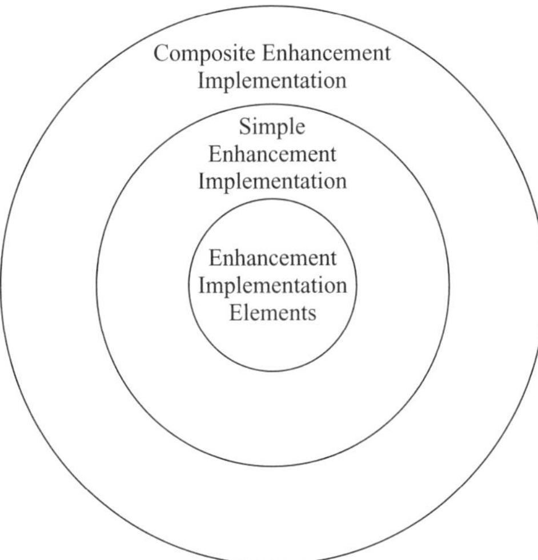

FIGURE 14.3 **Grouping of the simple and complex enhancement implementations**

Similar to simple and composite enhancement spots, simple and composite enhancement implementations are repository objects that form a tree-like structure. The branches of this tree-like structure represent composite enhancement implementations, and the leaves represent simple enhancement implementations. To implement the actual enhancement, one or more elements of an enhancement implementation are assigned to a definition of the element of an enhancement spot, which is assigned to an explicit or implicit enhancement option.

Figure 14.4 shows an overview of enhancement spots and enhancement implementations:

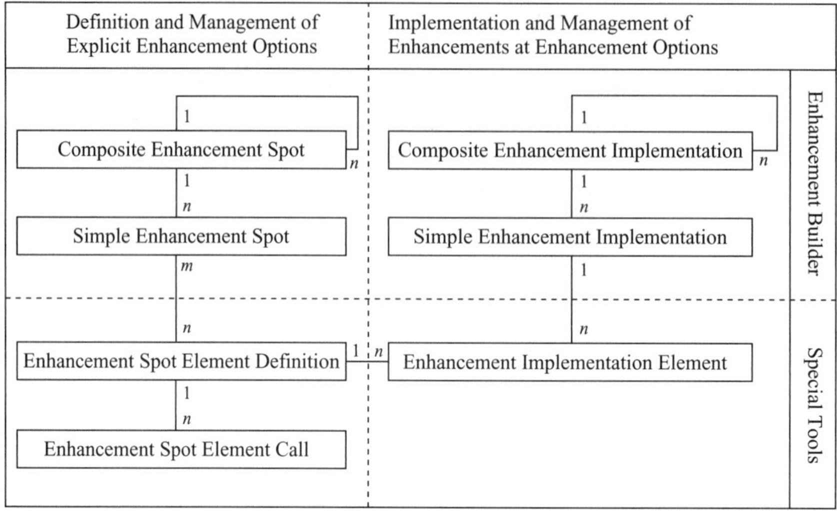

FIGURE 14.4 **Enhancement spots and enhancement implementations**

In Figure 14.4, the left part shows the common terms used for enhancement spots and the types of relationships between them. These enhancement spot terms apply only to explicit enhancement options. Moreover, no enhancement spots are required for implicit enhancement options.

The right part of the figure shows the common terms used for enhancement implementations and the types of relationships between them. However, the enhancement spot terms apply to enhancements of both explicit and implicit enhancement options.

The Enhancement Builder Tool

The Enhancement Builder tool is a collection of individual tools used to create, manage, and maintain the enhancement spots and enhancement implementations. Enhancement Builder is integrated in the ABAP Workbench tool. Moreover, the Enhancement Builder tool contains special tools for navigation and administration.

Enhancement Techniques in Enhancement Framework

The following are some enhancement techniques used in Enhancement Framework:

- **ABAP Source Code Enhancements**—Enhance the ABAP source code by using source code plug-ins. The source code plug-ins do not modify the ABAP source code; rather, they execute the enhancements using implicit and explicit enhancement options. A source code plug-in refers to an enhancement implementation element of a simple enhancement implementation. A source code plug-in is assigned to a single enhancement option. However, an enhancement option can have several source code plug-ins and enhancement implementations. A source code plug-in is created by using the Enhancement Builder tool, which defines the explicit enhancement options and implements the enhancements. The source code plug-in has a unique ID and is displayed in the ABAP Editor. The following syntax shows how to write the enhancement option:

```
ENHANCEMENT id.
...
ENDENHANCEMENT.
```

In this syntax, the enhancement is implemented between the `ENHANCEMENT` and `ENDENHANCEMENT` lines.

- **Function Module Enhancements**—Refer to various types of enhancements, which are:
  - **Source code enhancements**—Specify enhancements performed by using the ABAP source code.
  - **Parameter interface enhancements**—Specify enhancements performed by using a parameter interface. This means formal parameters are used as enhancement implementation elements using the Enhancement Builder tool.
- **Global Class Enhancements—**Refer to enhancements made to global classes and interfaces. Global class enhancements are related to the enhancement in the following areas:
  - **Enhancements to the source code of methods, local classes, and others**—Specify enhancements performed by using the ABAP source code.

- **Enhancements to the components of global classes and global interfaces**—Specify enhancements performed by inserting new attributes, methods, formal parameters to existing methods, and the implementation of an overwritten method, and a pre- or post-method for existing methods. Note that a pre-method is always executed directly before the first statement of the existing method is executed, while a post-method is executed after the execution of the last statement of the existing method, but before the `ENDMETHOD` statement. This condition is valid only if the method ends by using the `ENDMETHOD` statement.

- **BADIs**—Refer to a new enhancement technique to enhance the standard version of an SAP system. The goal behind the development of BADI was to insert some predefined points in the SAP system so that users can insert their applications to enhance the SAP system at the defined points. For example, if you need to predefine a special function in an application to carry out a particular task, SAP allows you to predefine such functions in your application. BADI is not limited to SAP applications; it can be integrated in customer applications as well, where it can be enhanced by other customer applications.

STRUCTURE OF A BADI

A BADI acts as a definition of elements of an enhancement spot. BADIs are basic requirements for the object plug-ins, which are used to enhance the functions in an ABAP program without modifying them. BADIs enable you to create enhancement options in the form of interfaces, which can be implemented later, either in the same SAP system or different SAP systems.

The definition of a BADI contains a BADI interface, a set of filters, and the settings that affect the runtime behavior later. A BADI interface can form the partial or entire interface of an object plug-in. A BADI implementation consists of a BADI implementation class that implements the BADI interface, and a condition that is imposed on the filters specified in the BADI definition.

The definition of a BADI is usually created in an SAP system. ABAP programs are then created to define the calling points for the definition of a BADI. The definition of a BADI, along with its calling points in ABAP programs, forms the explicit enhancement options in such programs. A BADI implementation is the term used in Enhancement Framework for an enhancement implementation element.

The calling points of a BADI are defined through the ABAP statements, `GET BADI` (to get objects) and `CALL BADI` (to call interface methods). These statements, in the definition of Enhancement Framework, represent the enhancement spot element calls of the explicit enhancement option.

Figure 14.5 shows the object types in the structure of a BADI:

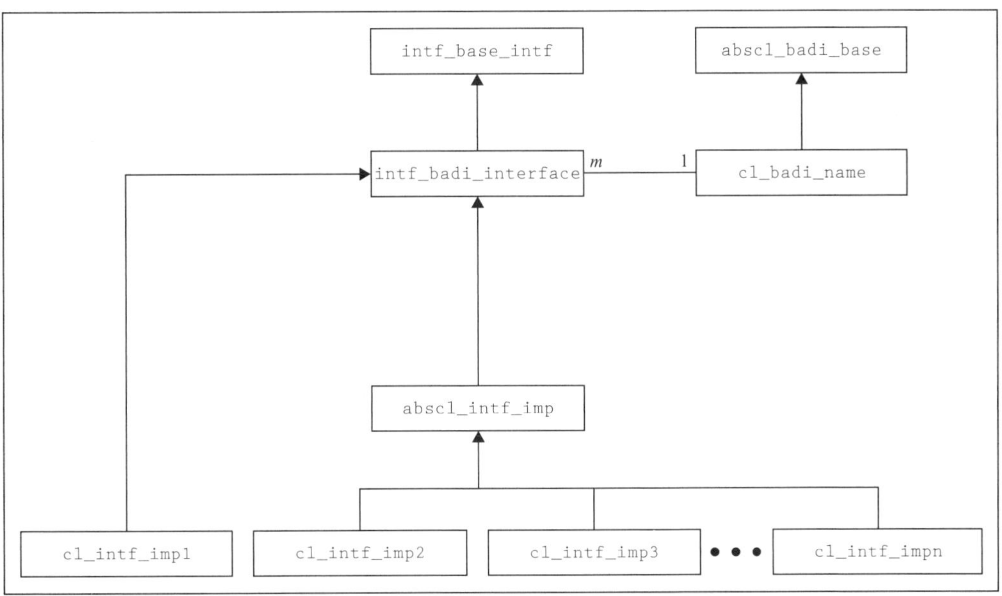

FIGURE 14.5 **Structure of a BADI**

In Figure 14.5, notice that the name of the BADI is `cl_badi_name`. A class with the same name, `cl_badi_name`, is created in the Enhancement Builder tool. This class is the final subclass of the `abscl_badi_base` abstract global class. Note that the BADI class forms the template for the BADI object but cannot be used directly.

The name of the BADI interface, for which the `cl_badi_name` class is defined, is `intf_base_intf` and contains the predefined tag interface, `intf_badi_interface`. The BADI interface must not contain any variable attributes. If the BADI interface is used multiple times in different contexts, it must not contain any methods with exporting or returning parameters.

The BADI implementation classes (`cl_intf_impl`, `cl_intf_imp2`, `cl_intf_impl3 ...`, `cl_intf_impn`) also implement the BADI `interface intf_base_intf`. There are no limitations with regard to the classes to be implemented, provided they implement the BADI interface only. A BADI implementation class can even implement two different BADI interfaces with the help of an abstract class. In Figure 14.5, the `abscl_intf_imp` abstract class is displayed, which is the partial implementation of the BADI interfaces. In addition, the actual BADI implementation classes are inherited from the `abscl_intf_imp` abstract class.

> **Note:** The BADI class is not a BADI implementation class and does not implement the BADI interface, but merely contains references to the actual object plug-ins (objects of BADI implementation classes).

DEFINITION OF BADIs

The definition of a BADI contains the name of a BADI, an interface of BADI, and some filter conditions. A filter consists of a filter name, a condition, and a data type (for example, `integer` or `string`). When you create the definition of a BADI, you must use a suitable prefix (for instance `BADI_`) when you specify the name of the BADI. In addition, you also define BADI properties, Instance Generation Mode, and Multiple Use at the runtime of a program. These properties are handled by using the `GET BADI` and `CALL BADI` statements. The Instance Generation Mode property controls the instantiation of an object plug-in when the `GET BADI` statement is executed. You can specify any of the following values for the Instance Generation Mode property:

- **Newly created instantiation**—Creates a new object plug-in every time the `GET BADI` statement is executed.
- **Reused instantiation**—Reuses an object plug-in more than once.
- **Context-dependent instantiation**—Controls the creation of an object plug-in by specifying a context for the `GET BADI` statement. You can reuse a BADI if the `GET BADI` statement needs to be used

for a different purpose (other than creating a new object plug-in) in the same context. A context is defined as an instance of a class that implements the `if_badi_context` tag interface.

Note that the first two values are used for context-free BADIs.

The Multiple Use property is used to decide the number of BADI implementations that can be selected. You can select zero, one, or an arbitrary number of implementations when a BADI object is initialized by using the `GET BADI` statement. The `CX_BADI_MULTIPLY_IMPLEMENTED` exception is raised when several implementations are selected in the `GET BADI` statement for a BADI. In addition, the `CX_BADI_NOT_IMPLEMENTED` exception is raised when no implementation is found in a BADI definition.

Note that in the standard version of the SAP system, a BADI is provided for a single use, but it can be used multiple times as well. In the case of multiple use of a BADI, the methods defined in the BADI must not contain any `EXPORTING` or `RETURNING` parameters but can have `CHANGING` parameters. The `EXPORTING` or `RETURNING` parameter cannot be used because a single definition of a BADI cannot return values to multiple implementations of a BADI. However, the `CHANGING` parameter is allowed because changes in the values are made by calling the methods of BADI implementations.

The following are some other properties that can also be assigned to a BADI:

- **An optional fallback BADI implementation class**—Specifies that a BADI implementation with some filter conditions or a standard implementation is not found.
- **Whether or not the BADI is internal**—Specifies that an internal BADI is essentially implemented inside the SAP system and not accessible to external systems.
- **Whether the BADI is a function code or screen enhancement**—Specifies that a BADI defined as a function code enhancement must not have any filters, must not be defined for multiple use, and must not be assigned to any switch.

Now, let's move on to discuss the following topics in the context of the definition of BADIs:

- Defining a BADI
- Displaying, changing, or deleting a BADI definition

Defining a BADI

Enhancement Builder, one of the tools of ABAP Workbench, is used to create and mange the definition of a BADI. You can access the Enhancement Builder tool by using the `SE18` transaction code. Enhancement Builder manages the definition of classic as well as new BADI. When you have to display the definition of an existing BADI, the Enhancement Builder tool analyzes whether the BADI is a classic BADI or a new BADI and then opens the BADI in the respective tool. In case of a new BADI, Enhancement Builder opens the enhancement spot editor.

Note: Creating classic BADIs is no longer supported.

Perform the following steps to create a new BADI definition in the Enhancement Builder tool:

1. In the `SAP` menu, select `Tools>ABAP Workbench>Utilities>Business Add-Ins>Definition`, as shown in Figure 14.6:

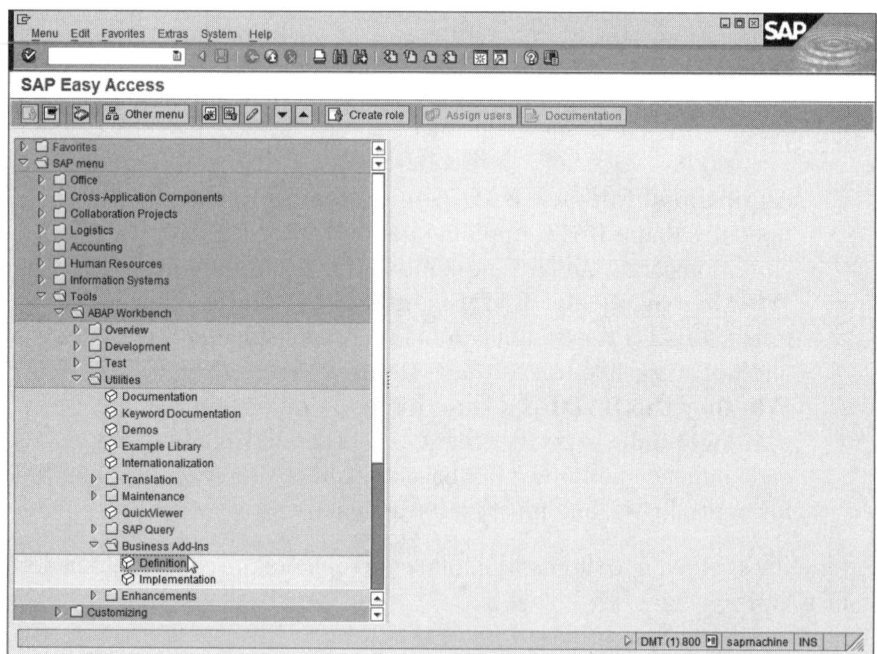

FIGURE 14.6 **Selecting the definition option**

The initial screen for definitions opens in the BADI builder, as shown in Figure 14.7:

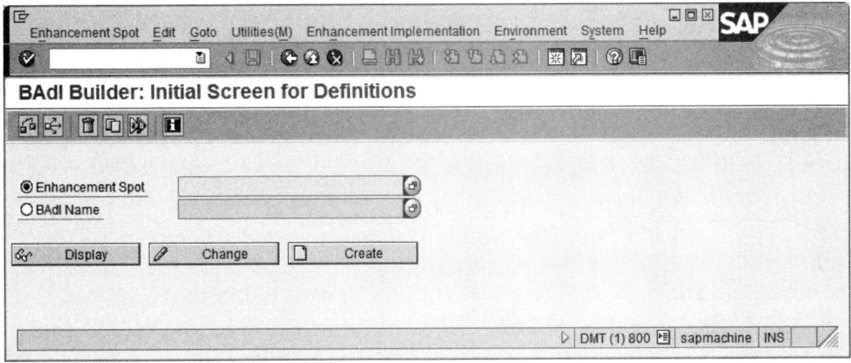

FIGURE 14.7 **The initial screen for definitions**

> **Note:** An alternative way to open the initial screen for definitions is by using the `SE18` transaction code.

2. In the initial screen for definitions, enter a name for a new `enhancement spot`. In this case, we have entered the name as ZKOG_ESPOT, as shown in Figure 14.8:

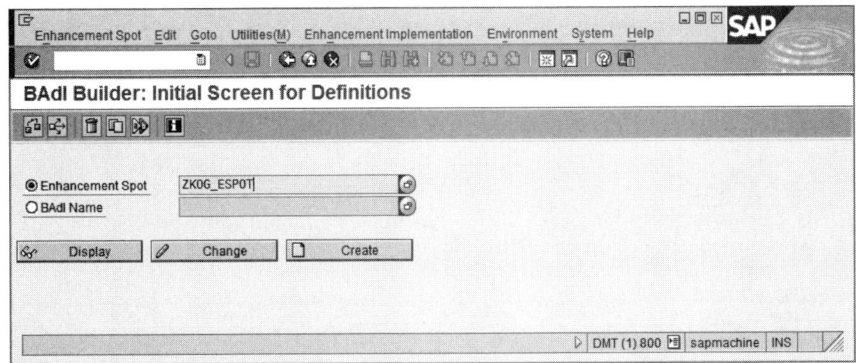

FIGURE 14.8 **Specifying an enhancement spot**

3. Click the `Create` button (see Figure 14.8).

The `Create Enhancement Spot` dialog box appears, as shown in Figure 14.9:

Create Enhancement Spot

Enhancement Spot	ZKOG_ESPOT
Short Text	This is the creation of simple enhancement spot
Technology	BADI Definition
Composite Enhancement Spot	

FIGURE 14.9 **The create enhancement spot dialog box**

4. Enter a short description to create a new enhancement spot in the `Short Text` field. Ensure that the `Enhancement Spot` field and the `Technology` field are populated automatically, and then click the `Continue` (✔) icon, as shown in Figure 14.9. The `Create Object Directory Entry` dialog box appears.
5. In the `Create Object Directory Entry` dialog box, enter the package name ZKOG_PCKG in the `Package` field and click the `Save` (💾) icon. The ZKOG_ESPOT enhancement spot is opened in the `Change` mode of Enhancement Builder, as shown in Figure 14.10:

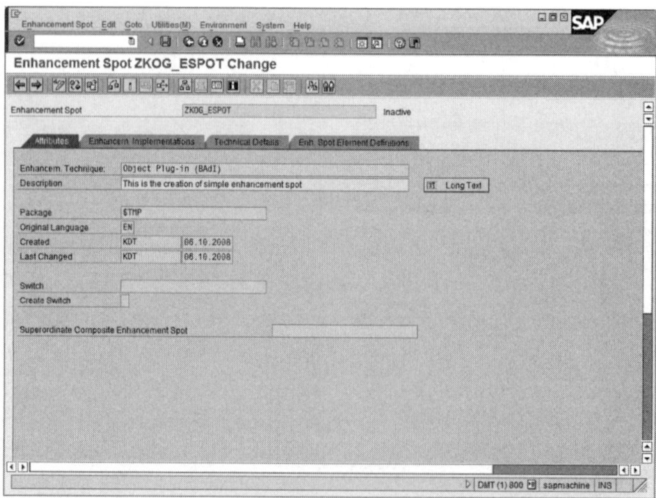

FIGURE 14.10 **The ZKOG_ESPOT enhancement spot**

6. Select the `Enh. Spot Element Definitions` tab, as shown in Figure 14.10. The `Enh. Spot Element Definitions` tab page appears, as shown in Figure 14.11:

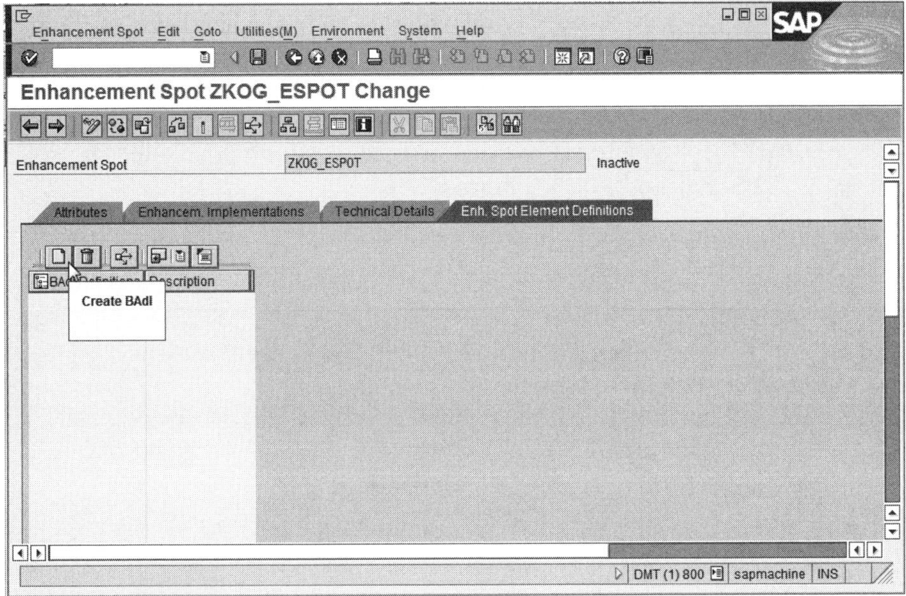

FIGURE 14.11 **The enh. spot element definitions tab page**

7. Click the `Create BADI` () icon; see Figure 14.11.

The `Create BADI Definition` dialog box opens, as shown in Figure 14.12:

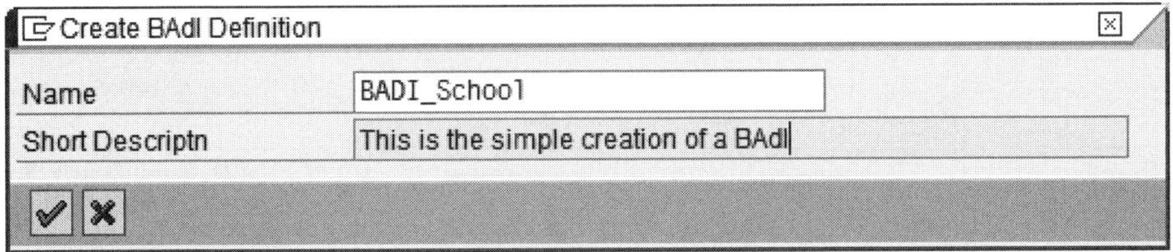

FIGURE 14.12 **The create BADI definition dialog box**

8. In the `Create BADI Definition` dialog box, enter a name and a description for the BADI definition in the `Name` and `Short Description` fields, respectively. Click the `Continue` (✅) icon, as shown in Figure 14.12.

The definition of a BADI is created in the Enhancement Builder tool, as shown in Figure 14.13. Perform the following on the right-hand side of the page:

a. Enter the usability by selecting the Multiple Use check box (optional)
b. Enter the instance creation mode
c. Enter the attribute for internal SAP BADIs (only SAP internal use)
d. Enter a Fallback Class (optional)

9. Double-click the `Interface` node, as shown in Figure 14.13:

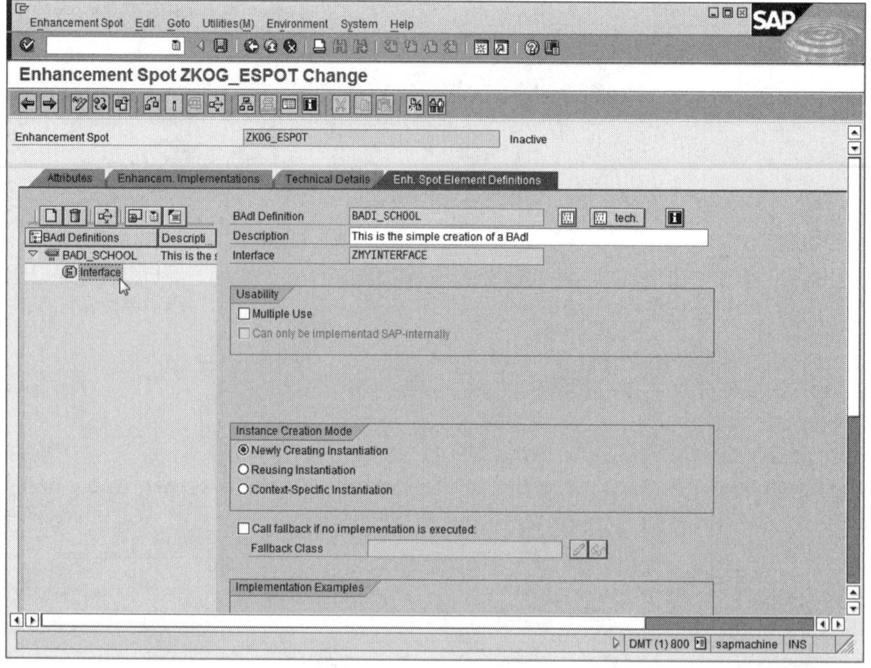

FIGURE 14.13 **A BADI is created in the enhancement builder tool**

The tab page, storing the information about the interface of the BADI definition, appears, as shown in Figure 14.14:

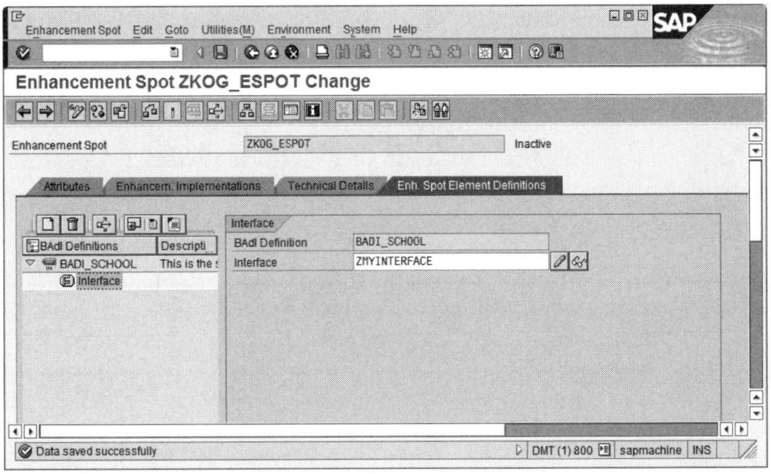

FIGURE 14.14 **Information about the interface of the BADI definition**

10. Enter the name of an interface in the `Interface` text field. In this case, we have specified the interface name as ZMYINTERFACE (see Figure 14.14). Click the `Change` (✎) icon, so that you can define methods to this interface, in the `Class Builder` tool. Figure 14.15 shows the screen of the `Class Builder` tool to define methods for the ZMYINTERFACE interface:

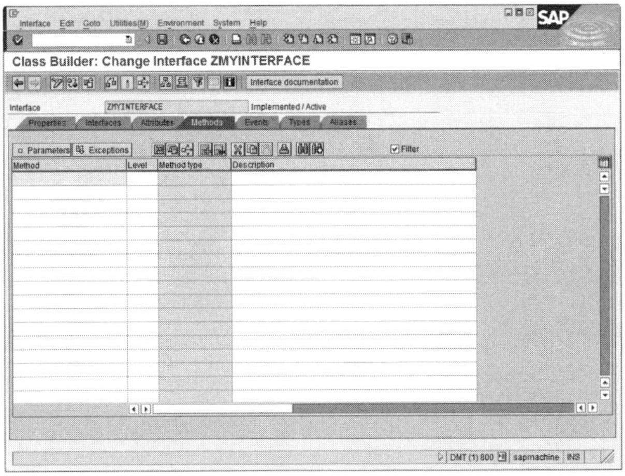

FIGURE 14.15 **The screen of the class builder tool**

You can assign a method to the interface and define a parameter with the attributes in the `Class Builder` tool. Use the `Save` ( ) and `Activate` ( ) icons to activate the interface and navigate back to the BADI definition. The method created for the interface appears in the BADI screen.

Note that when the methods are created in the BADI interface, the corresponding executing class (the Adapter class) is also generated, which further implements the interface methods.

> **Note:** Steps 11 to 14, which follow, are optional. Users can follow these steps according to their requirement of the BADI definition.

11. You can create a filter by selecting the `Create Filter` option from the context menu, which is displayed when the BADI definition is selected in the `Navigation` menu of the created BADI definitions, as shown in Figure 14.16:

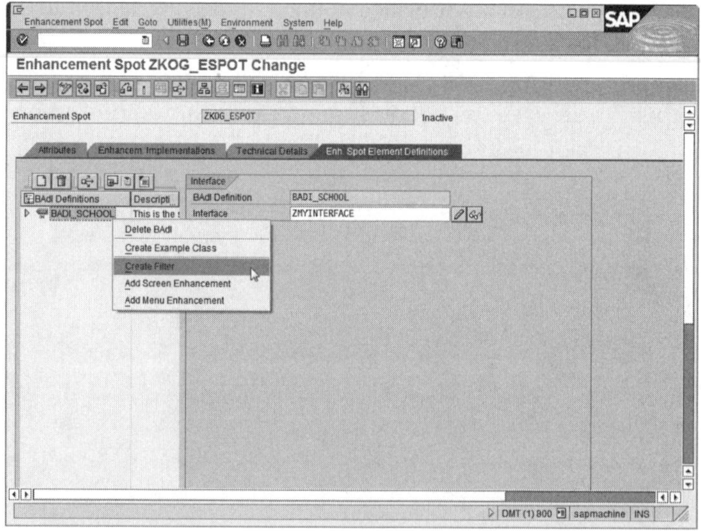

FIGURE 14.16 **Selecting the create filter option**

The previous action displays the `Create Filter for BADI` dialog box, as shown in Figure 14.17:

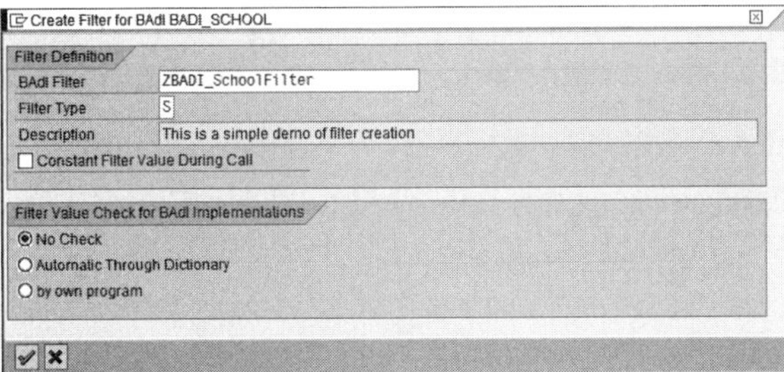

FIGURE 14.17 **The create filter for BADI dialog box**

In the `Create Filter for BADI` dialog box, enter a filter name, filter type, and description. In this case, the filter name is ZBADI_SchoolFilter, the filter type is S, and the description is This is a simple demo of filter creation (see Figure 14.17).

If you select the `Constant Filter Value During Call` check box, you can specify only a constant value for the respective filter when using the `GET BADI` statement. Click the `Continue` (✔) icon (see Figure 14.17).

12. Select the `Add Screen Enhancement` option (see Figure 14.16) to create the BADI as a screen enhancement. The `Add Subscreen to BADI` dialog box, as shown in Figure 14.18:

Add Subscreen to BAdI BADI_SCHOOL
Calling Program
Screen number
Subscreen Area
Description
Dflt value
DEFAULT VALUES
Default Program
Default Dynpro
0

FIGURE 14.18 **The add subscreen to BADI dialog box**

Enter the values for the `Calling Program`, `Screen number`, `Subscreen Area`, and `Description` fields. If you select the `Dflt value` check box, you have to specify a screen of a program that is used if no active implementation is found at runtime. Click the `Continue` (✔) icon. Note that when the BADI is created as a screen enhancement, it must not be of the multiple use type.

13. Select the `Add Menu Enhancement` option (see Figure 14.16) to create the BADI as a function code enhancement. The `Create Fcode Enhancement for BADI` dialog box, as shown in Figure 14.19:

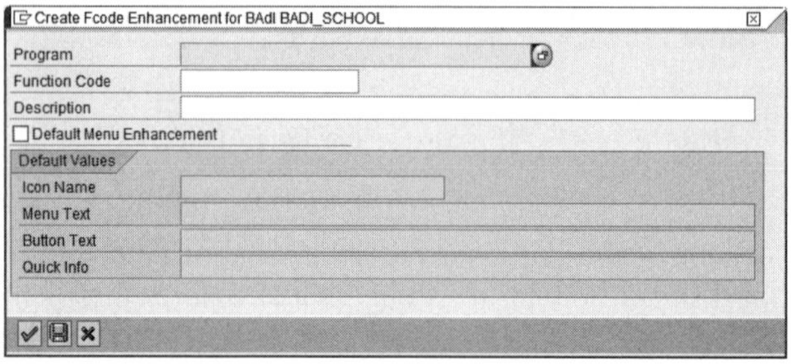

FIGURE 14.19 **The create fcode enhancement for BADI dialog box**

Enter the values for the `Program`, `Function Code`, and `Description` fields. If you select the `Default Menu Enhancement` check box, you have to specify an icon, a menu text, a button text, and quick info, which are used when no active implementation is found at runtime.

Click the `Continue` (✔) icon. Note that when the BADI is created as a function code enhancement, it must not have any filters and must not be of the multiple use type.

14. Select the `Create Example Class` option (see Figure 14.16) to create an example implementation. Figure 14.20 shows the `Create Example Implementation` dialog box:

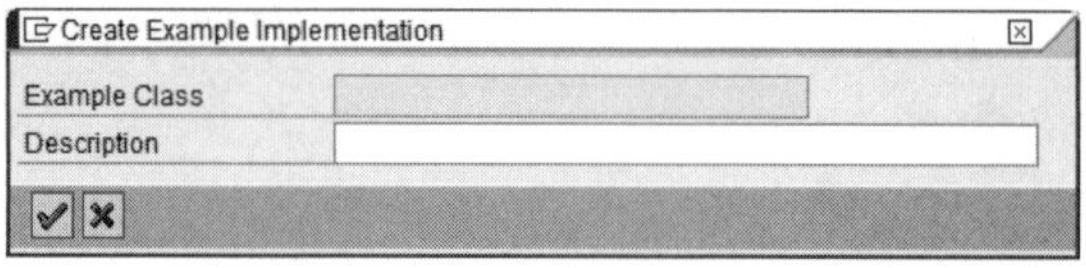

FIGURE 14.20 **The create example implementation dialog box**

Enter the name of a BADI implementation class and a description. Click the `Continue` (✔) icon.

After performing any one or more of the optional steps from 11 to 14, you must save and activate the BADI definition by using the `Save` (), `Check` (), and `Activate` () icons, in the same order.

Figure 14.21 shows the activation of the ZKOG_ESPOT enhancement spot:

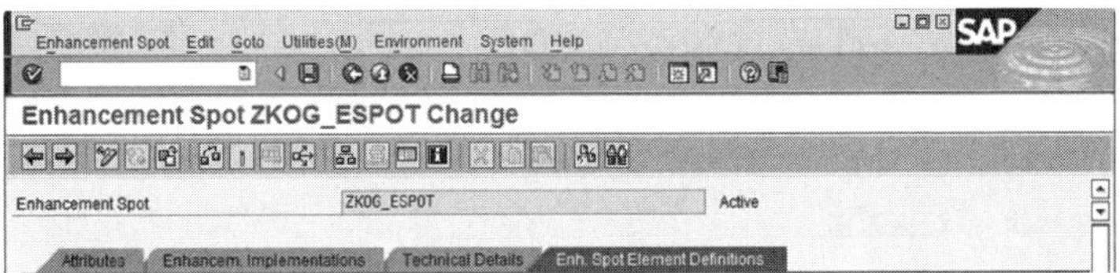

FIGURE 14.21 **Activation of the ZKOG_ESPOT enhancement spot**

Note that the activation of the ZKOG_ESPOT enhancement spot also activates the definition of the BADI_School BADI.

Displaying, Changing, or Deleting a BADI Definition

Perform the following steps to display, change, or delete the definition of a BADI:

1. Open the initial screen for a BADI by using the `SE18` transaction code or by selecting `Tools > ABAP Workbench > Utilities > Business Add-Ins > Definition` in the SAP menu.
2. Enter the name of an existing BADI definition that needs to be displayed or changed. In this case, the BADI definition name entered is BADI_School, as shown in Figure 14.22:

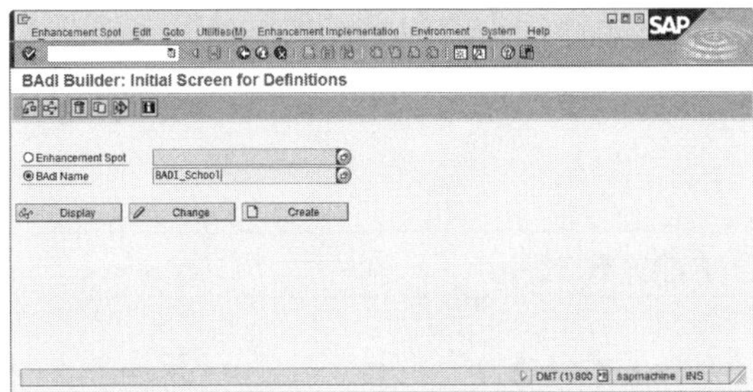

FIGURE 14.22 **The initial screen for definitions**

3. Now, click the `Display` or `Change` button to bring the selected BADI definition in the display or change mode, respectively. Moreover, in the `change` mode of the enhancement spot, click the `Delete` (🗑) icon to delete the selected BADI definition, as shown in Figure 14.23:

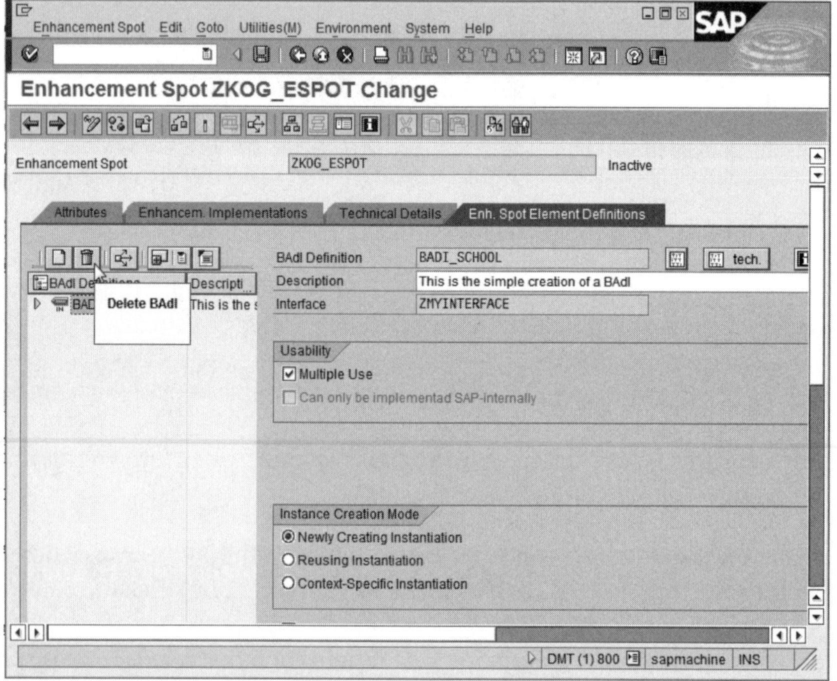

FIGURE 14.23 **Deleting a BADI definition in the change mode of the enhancement spot**

> **Note:** Click the `Save` (💾) icon to save any changes in the enhancement spot.

IMPLEMENTATION OF BADIs

The implementation of a BADI refers to the implementation of the interface and the filters defined in the BADI definition. A BADI implementation consists of an implementation class and a filter condition by which the BADI implementation is selected using the `GET BADI` statement. The BADI implementation is identified by a unique name in the enhancement concept. Perform the following steps to implement a BADI definition:

1. Open the initial screen for BADI implementation by using the `SE19` transaction code or by selecting `Tools > ABAP Workbench > Utilities > Business Add-Ins > Implementation` from the `SAP` menu. Figure 14.24 shows the initial screen for BADI implementation:

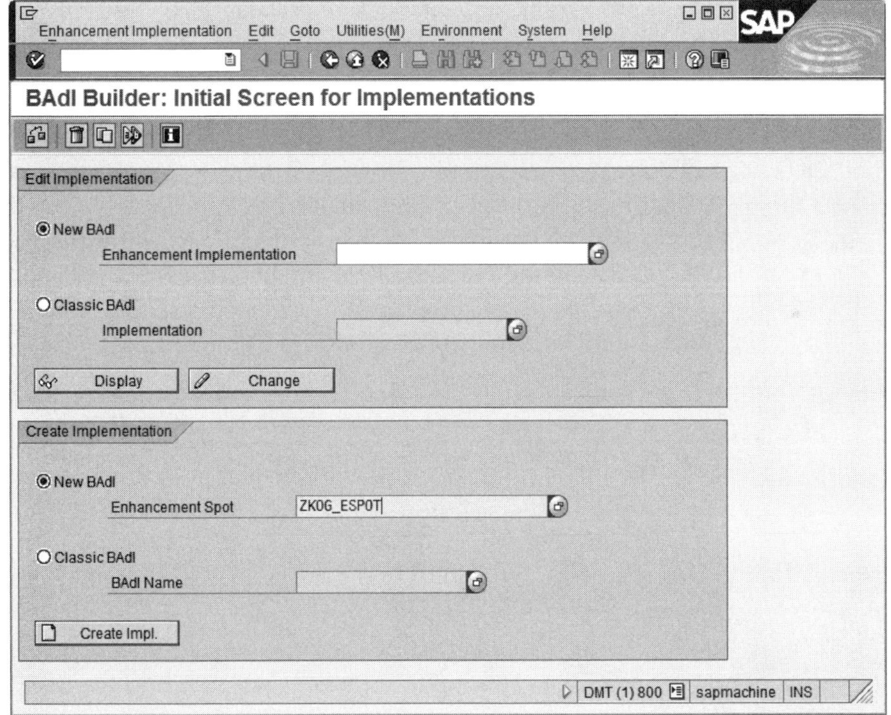

FIGURE 14.24 **The initial screen for BADI implementation**

2. In the `Create Implementation` group box, enter the name of an existing enhancement spot. In this case, the enhancement spot entered is ZKOG_ESPOT, as shown in Figure 14.24.

3. Click the `Create Impl.` button (see Figure 14.24). The `Create Enhancement Implementation` dialog box appears, as shown in Figure 14.25:

Create Enhancement Implementation

Enhancement Implementation	ZImp_KOG_ESPOT
Short Text	Demo of BADI Implementation
Composite Enhancement Implementation	

FIGURE 14.25 **The create enhancement implementation dialog box**

4. In the `Create Enhancement Implementation` dialog box, enter a name and short description for the enhancement implementation. In Figure 14.25, `Enhancement Implementation` is ZImp_KOG_ESPOT, and `Short Text` is Demo of BADI Implementation. Now, click the `Continue` (✔) icon. The `Create Object Directory Entry` dialog box appears.
5. In the `Create Object Directory Entry` dialog box, enter the package name ZKOG_PCKG in the `Package` field and click the `Save` (💾) icon. The `Enhancement Implementation` dialog box, respective to the enhancement spot implementation, is displayed, as shown in Figure 14.26:

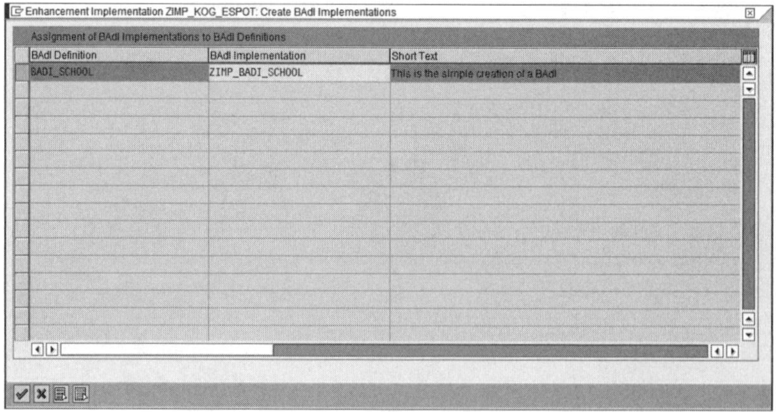

FIGURE 14.26 **The enhancement implementation dialog box**

6. In the `Enhancement Implementation` dialog box, enter a name for BADI Implementation, such as ZIMP_BADI_SCHOOL, as shown in Figure 14.26.

7. Click the `Continue` (☑) icon to display the screen for Enhancement Implementation, as shown in Figure 14.27:

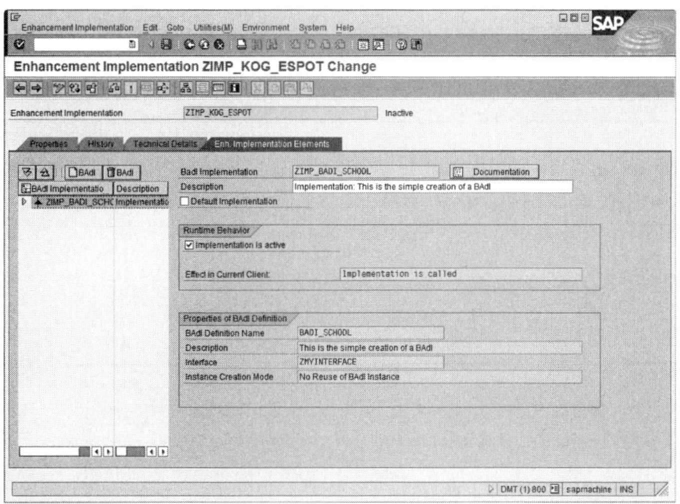

FIGURE 14.27 **The screen for enhancement implementation**

8. In the `Navigation` menu for the BADI implementation, double-click the `Implementing Class` option and provide a name for the `Implementing Class` field, as shown in Figure 14.28:

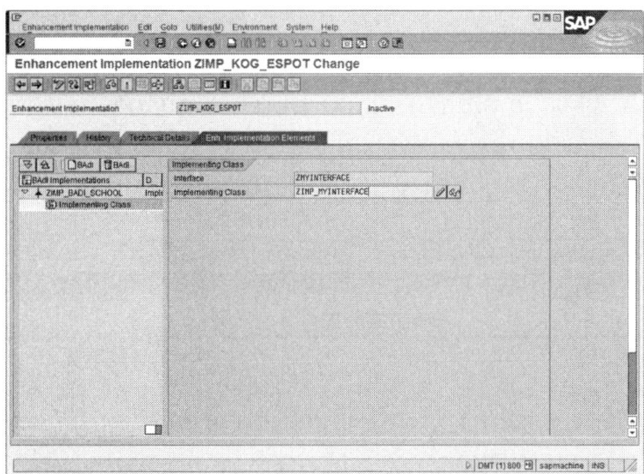

FIGURE 14.28 **Implementing a class**

In Figure 14.28, the name for `Implementing Class` is ZIMP_MYINTERFACE. Click the `Change` (✎) icon to write the methods in the Class Builder tool for the ZIMP_MYINTERFACE class.

> **Note:** The `Display` (🔍) icon is used to display the methods of the implementing class.

The `Class Builder` tool opens the implementing class in the change mode to define the methods in it. Figure 14.29 shows the `Class Builder` tool for implementing the class:

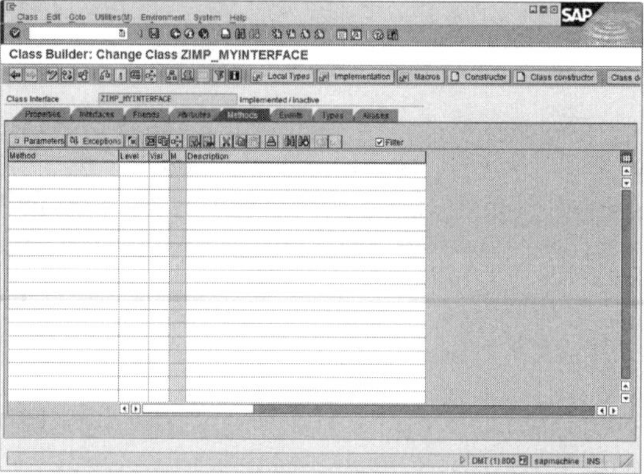

FIGURE 14.29 **The class builder tool for implementing the class**

Note that when the BADI implementation is created for the first time, the creation of the class implementation and the enhancement spot implementation is confirmed by the respective dialog boxes. For example, the creation of an implementing class is confirmed in Figure 14.30:

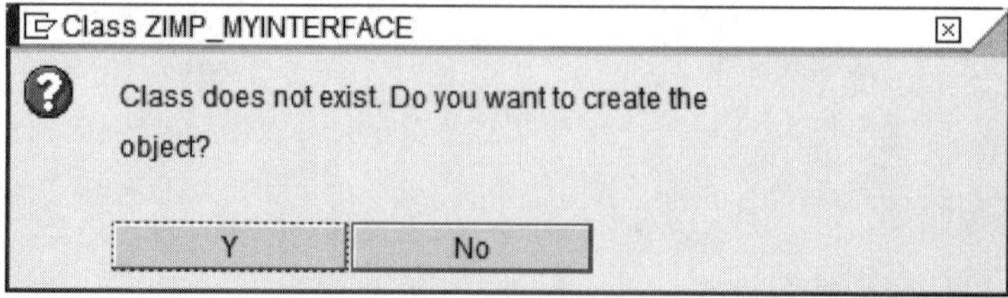

FIGURE 14.30 **Confirming the creation of the implementing class**

Click the `Y` button (see Figure 14.30) to create the implementing class.

Figure 14.31 shows the `Edit Enhancement Implementation` dialog box to save the changes in the enhancement implementation:

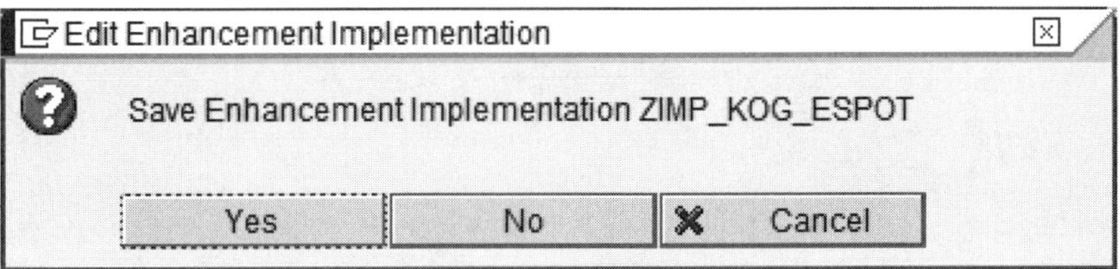

FIGURE 14.31 **Saving the enhancement implementation**

Click the `Yes` button (Figure 14.31) to save the changes in the enhancement implementation.

CALLING BADIs

In the classic BADIs, when we create a BADI definition, the enhancement management generates an adaptor class that implements the interface created in the class definition. An instance of this adaptor class is created by a factory method. The instance is used to call the methods defined in the adaptor class.

The following ABAP statements are used to call the newly created BADIs:

- `GET BADI`—Selects the BADI implementations based on the filter condition specified in the statement. The BADI implementation classes assigned to the selected implementations are instantiated and passed to a simultaneously created BADI object that serves as a handle for the implementation.
- `CALL BADI`—Uses the reference of a BADI object that passes the call of BADI methods to the BADI handler using object plug-ins.

DIFFERENCES BETWEEN CLASSIC AND NEW BADIs

Classic and new BADIs differ on various features, some of which are described in Table 14.1:

Feature	Classic BADI	New BADI
Object creation	A factory method is used to call a classic BADI object. In addition, a reference variable of the type of BADI interface is used to refer to the BADI object.	The `GET BADI` statement is used to create a new BADI object. In addition, a reference variable of the type of BADI class is used to refer to the BADI object.
Filter values	The filter values are stored in a structure and passed when the BADI methods are called.	The comparison values for the filters are used to search for implementations that are passed when the BADI object is created with the `GET BADI` statement.
BADI calling	A classic BADI can be called only once, and the call positions are registered centrally.	Multiple calls are possible, and the call positions are not registered centrally.

TABLE 14.1 Differences between classic and new BADIs

FILTER-DEPENDENT BADIs

BADIs may be implemented on the basis of a filter value. For example, if a country-specific enhancement is available in the standard version of SAP, the partner countries can implement this enhancement individually by using filters to create and activate their respective implementations. To implement a BADI on the basis of a filter value, a filter type is entered while defining an enhancement. All the methods created in the enhancement's interface have some filter value as their importing parameter. An application program then provides the filter value for the enhancement method. This method finally selects the active implementation for that value.

To define a filter-dependent BADI perform the following steps:

First, create the definition of the BADI and select the `Filter` checkbox, as shown in Figure 14.32:

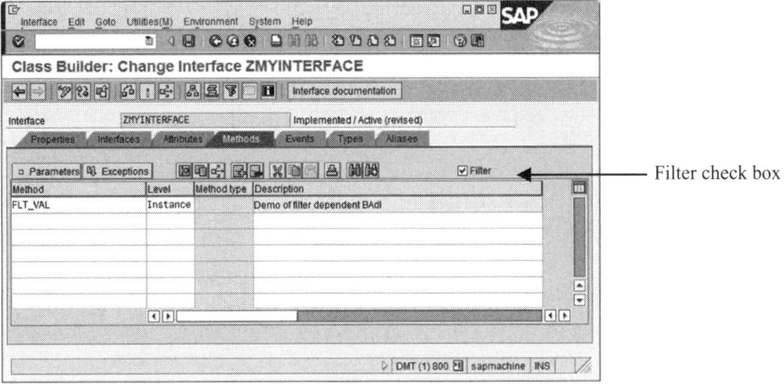

FIGURE 14.32 **Creating a filter-dependent BADI**

Next, specify the data element or structure as a filter type. A data element can be predefined or user-defined. You can use different elements as filter types, such as a country, a material, an object type, and an internal parameter. These data elements also are valid while using structures.

Now create an interface with methods. Note that for each method, the filter value must be defined as the importing parameter so that the application program can provide the filter value to the enhancement method. The enhancement method then selects the active implementation for the specified value. The filter value is always declared by using the `flt_val` parameter, and is predefined in the list of parameters.

Now, when you create an instance of the generated class in the application program and call the corresponding method at the appropriate time, the filter value is passed to the method as an export parameter.

When a filter-dependent BADI is called by using only one filter value, you can use the `SXC_EXIT_CHECK_ACTIVE` function module to check whether an active implementation for this filter value exists.

> **Note:** If the filter type is specified as Extendable, you can create implementations for filter values that do not exist any more.

FUNCTION CODE ENHANCEMENTS

Menu enhancement has been renamed function code enhancement in Release 7.0 of the SAP R/3 system.

In this release, you do not need to use the `GET BADI` and `CALL BADI` statements of ABAP; the runtime environment of SAP system automatically inserts the implementation of a function code enhancement. Function code enhancements are used for BADIs that are single-use add-ins and not filter-dependent. Nowadays, function code enhancements can be created by using a program interface.

Function code enhancements are provided to customers along with function codes. Note that at the development time, a developer creates a BADI definition that includes a specific function, which is assigned to a menu option in the appropriate menu list by using the Menu Painter tool. In addition, the developer ensures that when such a menu option is searched by the customer, the corresponding BADI method is invoked. On the customer side, function code enhancements are used by creating a new implementation, which includes the text selection for a menu option and the method to apply the implementation. This method depends on the action performed by the menu option and is implemented differently for different menu options. To create a function code enhancement, perform the following steps:

Create a BADI definition and define its interface.

Now, select the `Add Menu Enhancement` option from the context menu, which is displayed when the BADI definition is selected in the `Navigation` menu of the created BADI definitions, as shown in Figure 14.33:

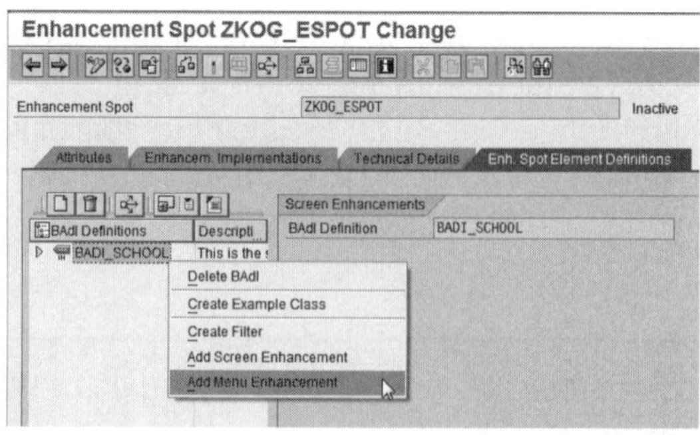

FIGURE 14.33 **Selecting the add menu enhancement option**

The `Create Fcode Enhancement for BADI` dialog box appears, as shown in Figure 14.34:

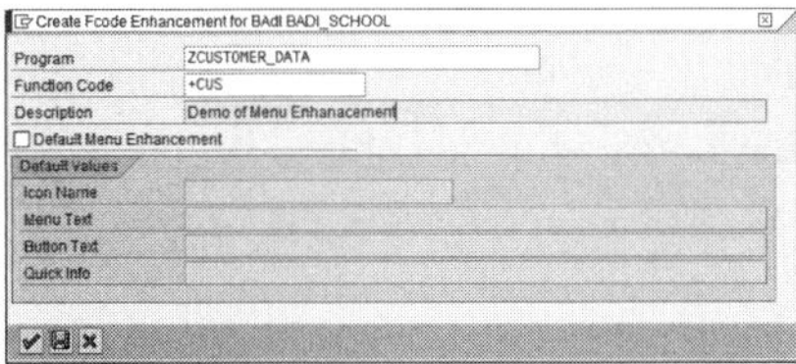

FIGURE 14.34 **The create fcode enhancement for BADI dialog box**

Enter the values in the `Program`, `Function Code`, and `Description` fields for the function code enhancements. The following code snippet shows the code to a function code enhancement:

```
(...)
case fcode.
when 'SAP'.
(...)
when '+CUS'
call method ...
```

> **Note:** Function code enhancements become visible only after the implementation has been activated and the application that calls the BADI has been executed.

SCREEN ENHANCEMENTS

Besides programs and function code enhancements, you can create screen enhancements for BADIs. However, screen enhancements are not supported for BADIs designed for multiple use. In the case of screen enhancements, the concept of a class has been adopted with the following exceptions:

- The call to the `CL_EXITHANDLER=>GET_PROG_AND_DYNP_FOR_SUBSCR` method has been replaced by the call to the

CL_ENH_BADI_RUNTIME_FUNCTIONS=>GET_PROG_AND_DYNP_FOR_SUBSCR method with the same interface.

- The PUT_DATA_TO_SCREEN and GET_DATA_FROM_SCREEN methods cannot be generated. Users can create their own BADI methods for the data transport and call these BADI methods by using the CALL BADI statement.
- Users do not need to call the CL_EXITHANDLER=>SET_INSTANCE_FOR_SUBSCREENS and CL_EXITHANDLER=>GET_INSTANCE_FOR_SUBSCREENS methods because these methods are now unnecessary because they only place the BADI reference in a temporary storage.

SUMMARY

In this chapter, you have learned about the BADIs, which are one of the enhancement techniques of Enhancement Framework. This chapter also describes Enhancement Framework, the various techniques supported by it, and the structure of BADIs. You have also learned about the definition, the implementation, and the use of the BADIs. In addition, you have learned about the differences between the classic and the new BADIs, and about filter-dependent BADIs. At the end of this chapter, the features of BADIs are explained by describing function code enhancements (previously called menu enhancements) and screen enhancements.

Appendix A: Object Orientation in ABAP

If you need information on:	*See page:*
Overview of ABAP Objects	882
Explaining the Basic Concepts of OOP in ABAP	883
Defining and Implementing a Class	887
Handling the Objects	893
Declaring and Implementing Interfaces	895
Declaring and Calling Methods	898
Declaring and Calling Constructors	901
Working with Events in ABAP Objects	902

Object orientation in ABAP (also known as ABAP Objects) is an extension of the ABAP language that provides the advantages of object-oriented programming (OOP), such as encapsulation, inheritance, and polymorphism. In other words, ABAP Objects, a part of ABAP Workbench, is a programming language used to create and execute program objects in an SAP system. It includes a virtual machine to compile and execute SAP applications. The objects created by using the ABAP Objects language are compatible with the existing programs of the ABAP language. However, the syntax-checking process is stronger in ABAP Objects programs, which ensures that ABAP Objects programs do not use the syntax construction of older programs.

Similar to earlier procedural programming languages, such as COBOL, ABAP was initially developed as a procedural language. However, ABAP has now adapted the principles of object-oriented paradigms with the introduction of ABAP Objects. The object-oriented concepts in ABAP Objects, such as class, object, inheritance, and polymorphism, are essentially the same as those of other modern object-oriented languages, such as C++ or Java.

In this appendix, you learn about the ABAP Objects as an extension of the ABAP language. We begin this appendix by providing an overview of ABAP Objects. Next, you learn the basic concepts of OOP in ABAP, such as classes, objects, encapsulation, and inheritance. You also explore how to declare and implement a class, handle an object, and declare and implement an interface. In addition, you learn how to declare and call methods and constructors in classes and interfaces. The appendix concludes with a discussion on how to define events in a class or interface that triggers the event-handler methods of other classes and interfaces.

OVERVIEW OF ABAP OBJECTS

ABAP Objects is one of the new-generation languages that have implemented object-oriented features. The concept of the ABAP Objects language has been launched with SAP R/3 Release 4.0. This concept is important from two perspectives. First, it represents the runtime environment of ABAP that indicates that SAP is based on the object-oriented approach. Second, ABAP Objects is an object-oriented extension of the ABAP language, which unites data and functions in objects. ABAP Objects are not only used in existing programs, but it is also used in new ABAP Objects programs.

Prior to SAP R/3 Release 4.0, the nearest equivalent of ABAP Objects were function modules and function groups. The actual task of executing the business logic of a program was performed by function groups. However, the function groups were not used directly; instead they were used through the function modules. For example, you have a function group for processing orders. Now, the function group contains the global data that are actually attributes of the order. In addition, the function modules of the function group represent the actions that have to be performed on the data of the function group. In this way, the entire detail related to the order processing is actually encapsulated in the function group and cannot be addressed directly, but only through the function modules.

Function groups have some limitations, in spite of being object-oriented. For instance, in an ABAP program, you cannot have multiple instances of a single function group, although multiple instances of different function groups can be created. In addition, you need to use the same data structure in all the function modules and function groups. Moreover, changing the internal data structure of a function group affects many users, and it is often difficult to predict the implications.

These limitations can be avoided by using the concept of interfaces and classes in ABAP. The use of an interface or a class ensures that the internal structure of the instance of the interface or class is hidden and can be changed later according to user requirements. The object-oriented paradigm of ABAP Objects allows you to define data and functions in classes instead of function groups. Therefore, by using the ABAP Objects language, you can create an ABAP program that can have various instances or objects of one or more classes. With the introduction of ABAP Objects, an ABAP program does not require loading a function group in the memory of an SAP system to call a function module. Alternatively, the program generates the instances or objects of a class by using the `CREATE OBJECT` statement. Each object has a unique address, which is also called the object reference of that object. You use the object reference of an object to access the object. After giving a brief overview of ABAP Objects, we explain the basic concepts of OOP in ABAP, such as objects, classes, encapsulation, and inheritance.

EXPLAINING THE BASIC CONCEPTS OF OOP IN ABAP

OOP is a problem-solving method to find solutions to problems related to programming by using real-world objects. An object in an OOP model is a collection of attributes (data) and methods (functions). Examples of objects in a business environment include customer, order, and invoice. In SAP Release 3.1 and later, the Business Object Repository (BOR) contains examples of such objects. The object model of ABAP Objects is compatible with the object model of the BOR.

In this section, we describe some fundamental concepts of OOP that also occur in ABAP Objects. These basic terms are:

- Objects
- Classes
- Interfaces
- Encapsulation

- Inheritance
- Polymorphism

Objects

An object is a pattern or instance of a class. For example, Nissan Sentra and Ford Focus are objects, and Car is their class. An object represents a real-world entity, such as a person, place, or a programming entity, such as constants, variables, and memory location. Professors, doctors, and students are examples of real-world entities, whereas hardware and software components of a computer are examples of programming entities. An object has the following three main characteristics:

- Has a state
- May or may not display a behavior
- Has a unique identity

The state of an object can be described as a set of attributes and their values. For example, an account has a set of attributes, such as Account Number, Account Type, Name, and Balance, and the values of each of these attributes. The behavior of an object refers to the changes that occur in its attributes over a period of time. For example, a washing machine is in the static state of behavior when it is switched off. However, it displays a specific behavioral change by washing the clothes when you switch it on.

Each object has a unique identity that distinguishes it from other objects. Two objects may exhibit the same behavior and may or may not have the same state, but they never have the same identity. For example, two persons have the same name, age, and gender but are not identical. The identity of an object never changes throughout its lifetime.

Objects can interact with one another by sending messages. For example, if employee and salary are two objects in a program, the employee object may send a message to the salary object to confirm the tax deduction from the salary. The object that receives the message is called a receiver, and the set of actions taken by a receiver is represented by a method.

Objects contain data and code to manipulate the data. An object can also be used as a user-defined data type with the help of a class. Objects are also called variables of the type class. After defining a class, you can create any number of objects belonging to that class. Each object is associated with the data of the type class with which it has been created.

Classes

Class is a prototype that defines the data and behavior common to all the objects of a specific type. In a class, data is represented by class attributes and the behavior of an instance of the class is provided by class methods. In other words, we can say that classes describe objects.

In the ABAP Objects language, a class is defined by writing the declaration part of the class, and if required, an implementation part of the class. A class can be of two types, global class or local class. A global class can be accessed by all the ABAP programs in an SAP system, while a local class can be accessed within the same program where the class has been defined. In the SAP system, a global class is defined by using the Class Builder tool of ABAP Workbench; however, a local class is defined in an ABAP program.

Interfaces

Interfaces, similar to classes, contain attributes and methods. However, unlike classes, interfaces do not have the implementation part. The methods defined in an interface can be implemented within the implementation of a class. Moreover, interfaces implement the polymorphism feature of OOP in the ABAP Objects language.

Encapsulation

Encapsulation is a feature of OOP that prevents access to non-essential details of a class. For example, when you switch on a television set, it displays the programs being telecast in the form of audio and video. You cannot see the actual complex process of the television, such as how the signals from the cable are being transformed into audio and video. Encapsulation is also referred to as data hiding because it hides important but unnecessary details of an object or a class from the user. Note that the encapsulated data of a class can be accessible outside the class only when the data is used in the functions of the class. However, a limited number of operations can be performed on encapsulated data by executing the functions or methods of the class.

When you use encapsulation, the visibility of the attributes and methods of a class or object are restricted to three basic levels, which are:

- **Public**—Specifies that the members (attributes and methods) of a class are accessible to all users and methods of the class, and any classes inherited from it.
- **Protected**—Specifies that all the members of a class are accessible to all the methods of the class and of classes inherited from it.
- **Private**—Specifies that all the members of a class are accessible only in the methods of the same class.

> **Note:** The three levels of visibility of attributes and methods of a class are discussed later in this chapter.

Inheritance

Inheritance is a mechanism that allows a class to inherit the properties of another class. If the *X* class inherits some properties from the *Y* class, we say that *X* has been inherited from *Y*. In this scenario, *Y* is called the superclass or base class of *X*, and *X* is called a subclass or derived class of *Y*, as shown in Figure A.1:

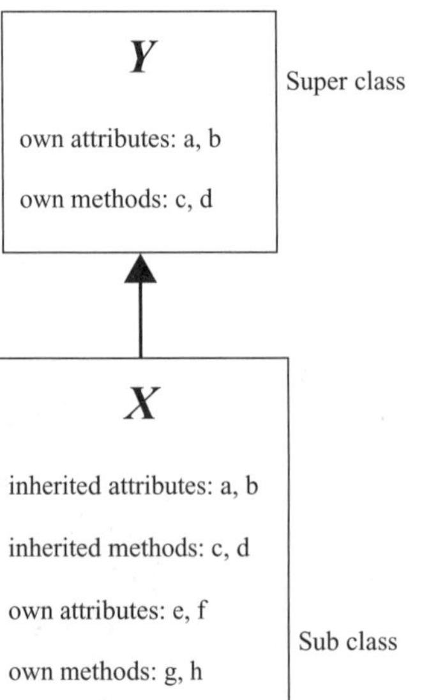

FIGURE A.1 **Showing inheritance between the X and Y classes**

The objects of the *X* class have access to attributes and methods of the *Y* class. Objects of subclass *X* can be used where objects of the corresponding superclass *Y* are required. This is because the objects of the subclass *X* share the same behavior as the objects of the superclass *Y*.

Inheritance enables you to reuse classes in multiple programs or different parts of the same program. This means that we can add additional features to an existing class without modifying it by deriving a new class from an existing class. In addition, you can define a subclass with some unique features that are different from the features already defined in the corresponding superclass. In addition to its own features, the new class contains the features of the parent class.

In the ABAP Objects language, a subclass contains the attributes and methods of its corresponding superclass, in addition to its own attributes and methods. A subclass derives all the public members (attributes and methods) of its superclass, but not the private members of the superclass. The protected members of a superclass are inherited to a subclass; however, their visibility changes to private.

Polymorphism

Polymorphism is the ability of an object to exist in different forms. The term polymorphism has been derived from the Greek words poly (many) and morphos (forms). In the context of OOP, polymorphism is the ability of a function to behave differently, depending on the context in which it is called.

In ABAP Objects, the names of methods in different classes can be identical, but the methods behave differently in different classes because the implementation of a method (that is, the body of the method) is different in different classes. This is possible in an OOP language either by using the concept of interface or by overriding the methods or by redefining the methods in each class after inheritance. In other words, you can implement polymorphism by using interfaces or overriding methods. Note that an interface enables you to implement methods with the same name in different objects, because the form of a method's name is always the same; however, the implementation of the method is specific to a particular class.

After explaining the basic concepts of OOP in ABAP, we define and implement a class in terms of ABAP Objects.

DEFINING AND IMPLEMENTING A CLASS

A class acts as a template for an object. It defines the abstract characteristics of an object, such as attributes, fields, and properties. It also defines the behaviors of objects. For example, the Car class consists of attributes that all cars possess, such as wheels and seats, and the ability in respect of speed mileage (behaviors).

In the ABAP Objects language, global classes are always stored in a class pool in the class library of the SAP repository. All the ABAP programs can access these global classes. A local class, however, is defined in a program, so that it can be accessed in the program itself but not from outside the program. When you use a class in an ABAP program, the SAP system identifies whether or not the class declared in a program is local. If the class is not a local class, the program searches for the required global class in the class pool.

Note: A class pool is like a container for a global class and contains exactly one global class. Besides a global class, a class pool can also have global types, local classes, and local interfaces to be used in the global class. In an SAP system, class pools are managed by Class Builder.

The definition of a local class contains ABAP source code between the `CLASS` and `ENDCLASS` statements. Note that a class definition includes the class declaration and, if required, the class implementation. The following syntax shows how to define a local class:

```
CLASS <class_nm> DEFINITION.
...
ENDCLASS.
```

The definition of a local class can contain various components of the class, such as attributes, methods, and events. Moreover, when you declare a method in the class declaration, the method implementation must be included in the class implementation. The following syntax shows how to implement a class:

```
CLASS <class_nm> IMPLEMENTATION.
...
ENDCLASS.
```

Note that the implementation of a class contains the implementation of all its methods.

In ABAP Objects, the structure of a class contains components; that is, attributes, methods, events, types, and constants. Each component of a class is assigned to a visibility section; that is, a public section, protected section, or private section.

Exploring the Components of a Class

The content or definition of a class includes the components of the class. All the components are declared in the declaration part of the class. These components define the attributes of the objects in a class. All of the components of a class are visible within the class.

All the components of a class can be divided into two categories, instance and static. An instance component exists separately for each object of a class. A static component, on the other hand, is shared by all the objects of a class. This means that only one static component exists for the whole class, regardless of the number of objects in the class.

Attributes

Attributes are data fields of a class that can have any ABAP data type, such as `C`, `I`, `F`, and `N`. They are declared in the class declaration. The data stored in the attributes of a class can determine the state of the objects of the class.

The attributes of a class can be divided into two categories, instance attributes and static attributes. An instance attribute defines the instance-specific state of an object. Instance-specific states are different for different objects. For instance, assume that you are the owner of a company, XYZ. Your company has to interact with other companies to supply goods manufactured in your company. Now, the name and address of all these companies are examples of instance attributes, because the name and address of one company is different from that of the others. An instance attribute is declared by using the `DATA` statement.

Static attributes define a common state of a class that is shared by all the instances of the class. For instance, if we consider the same example of the XYZ company, the terms and conditions to deal with any company regarding the supply of goods are examples of static attributes, because the terms and conditions do not differ for different companies. Note that if you change a static attribute in one object of a class, the change is visible to all the other objects of the class as well. A static attribute is declared by using the `CLASS-DATA` statement.

Methods

A method is a function or procedure of a class that represents the behavior of an object in the class. In a class definition, the methods of the class can access any attribute of the class. The definition of a method can also contain parameters, so that you can supply the values to these parameters when the methods are called, and can also receive the values back from the methods.

The definition of a method is declared in the class declaration and implemented in the implementation part of a class. The `METHOD` and `ENDMETHOD` statements are used to define the implementation part of a method. The following syntax shows how to implement a method:

```
METHOD <meth_nm>.
...
ENDMETHOD.
```

In this syntax, `<meth_nm>` represents the name of a method. Note that you can call a method by using the `CALL METHOD` statement.

Similar to other components of a class, the methods of a class can also be divided into two basic categories, instance methods and static methods. A method that can access all the attributes and trigger all the events of a class is called an instance method. An instance method is declared by using the `METHODS` statement.

Static methods of a class, on the other hand, can access only static attributes and trigger static events. They are declared by using the `CLASS-METHODS` statement.

In addition to instance and static methods, constructors are special methods that are called automatically, either while creating an object or accessing the components of a class. Constructors are again of two types, instance and static. An instance constructor is declared by using the `CONSTRUCTOR` statement. It can access all the attributes and can trigger all the events of a class. A static constructor, on the other hand, is declared by using the `CLASS_CONSTRUCTOR` statement. It can access the static attributes and static events of a class.

Events

An event is a set of outcomes that are defined in a class to trigger the event handlers in other classes. In addition, when an event is triggered, any number of event handler methods can be called. The link between a trigger and its handler method is decided dynamically at runtime.

In a normal method call, a calling program determines which method of an object or a class needs to be called, and when. However, in the case of event handling, the handler method determines the event that needs to be triggered. This is because a fixed handler method is not registered for every event.

An event of a class can trigger an event handler method of the same class by using the `RAISE EVENT` statement. In addition, for an event, the event handler method can be defined in the same or different class by using the `FOR EVENT` clause, as shown in the following syntax:

```
FOR EVENT <evt_nm> OF <class_nm>.
```

Similar to the methods of a class, an event can also have parameter interface but has only output parameters. The output parameters are passed to the event handler method by the `RAISE EVENT` statement, which receives them as input parameters. An event is linked to its handler method dynamically in a program by using the `SET HANDLER` statement.

Events are also of two types, instance events and static events. An instance event can be triggered only from an instance method. It is declared by using the `EVENTS` statement. A static event however, can be triggered only from a static method. It is declared by using the `CLASS-EVENTS` statement. Note that an event and its handler can be an object (in the case of instance events) or a class (in the case of static events). In addition, when an event is triggered, the corresponding event handler methods are executed in all the registered handling classes.

Types

In a class, you can create your own ABAP data types by using the `TYPES` statement. Types are not instance-specific and exist only once for all of the objects in a class.

Constants

Constants are static values for the attributes of a class. These values are specified at the time of declaring the attributes in a class. Constants are declared by using the `CONSTANTS` statement. Moreover, constants are not instance-specific but exist only once for all of the objects in a class.

> **Note:** All the components of a class can also be declared inside the declaration of an interface.

Next, we explain the visibility sections for the components of a class.

Visibility Sections in a Class

In a class definition, each component of the class is assigned to one of the three visibility sections, `PUBLIC SECTION`, `PROTECTED SECTION`, or `PRIVATE SECTION`, to define the external access of the component outside the class. The following syntax shows the three visibility sections in a class:

```
CLASS <class_nm> DEFINITION.
PUBLIC SECTION.
...
PROTECTED SECTION.
...
PRIVATE SECTION.
...
ENDCLASS.
```

In this syntax, `<class_nm>` represents the name of a class and the `CLASS` and `ENDCLASS` statements represent the start and end of the class definition. The three visibility sections in a class are represented by the `PUBLIC SECTION`, `PROTECTED SECTION`, and `PRIVATE SECTION` keywords.

Note that the public components of a global class may not be changed. Moreover, after defining the visibility of an attribute, you can protect it from any external change by using the `READ-ONLY` clause.

Listing A.1 shows an example of a class along with its components and visibility sections:

```
CLASS NUM_COUNT DEFINITION.
  PUBLIC SECTION.
    METHODS:SET_NUM  IMPORTING  VALUE(SET_VALUE)
            TYPE I,
            INCREMENT_NUM,
            GET_NUM  EXPORTING  VALUE(GET_VALUE)
            TYPE I.
  PRIVATE SECTION.
    DATA NUM TYPE I.
ENDCLASS.
CLASS NUM_COUNT IMPLEMENTATION.
  METHOD SET_NUM.
    NUM = SET_VALUE.
  ENDMETHOD.
  METHOD INCREMENT_NUM.
    ADD 1 TO NUM.
  ENDMETHOD.
  METHOD GET_NUM.
    GET_VALUE = NUM.
  ENDMETHOD.
ENDCLASS.
```

LISTING A.1 **Showing the components and visibility sections in a class**

In this example, `NUM_COUNT` is a class containing three public methods: `SET_NUM`, `INCREMENT_NUM`, and `GET_NUM`. Each of these methods accesses a private field, `Num`, of the I type. The `SET_NUM` method has an import parameter, `SET_VALUE`, while the `GET_NUM` method has an export parameter `GET_NUM`. Note that the methods declared in the definition of the `NUM_COUNT` class are used in the implementation of the class, but the `NUM` field is not. This is because the `NUM` field is defined in the private section of the `NUM_COUNT` class.

HANDLING THE OBJECTS

In an ABAP program, an object is accessed by using the object references, which are pointers to objects. In the ABAP Objects language, object references are stored in reference variables. In ABAP, reference variables are treated as the other elementary data objects, which means that a reference variable can be a component of a structure or an internal table, or it can refer to itself.

In ABAP Objects, the object reference can be of the type class reference or interface reference. A class reference is defined by using the TYPES or DATA statement along with the following syntax:

```
... TYPE REF TO <class_nm>
```

A class reference allows you to create an instance or object of the corresponding class and to access a component of the class, as shown in the following syntax:

```
cref->comp
```

In this syntax, cref represents class reference and comp represents a component of the class.

To create an object for a class, you need to declare a reference variable of the class. Use the following syntax to create an object of a class by using the CREATE OBJECT statement:

```
CREATE OBJECT <cref>.
```

In this syntax, <cref> represents a reference variable of a class. The CREATE OBJECT statement creates an object of a class with the <cref> class reference.

An object exists in a program until at least one reference points to it, or at least one method of the object is registered as an event handler. When no reference of the object is used in a program and none of the methods of the object is registered as event handler, the object is deleted by the automatic memory management (garbage collection) process.

DECLARING AND IMPLEMENTING INTERFACES

Similar to classes in ABAP Objects, interfaces act as data types for objects. The components of interfaces are same as the components of classes; that is, attributes, methods, events, types, and constants. However, the declaration of an interface does not include the visibility sections, unlike the declaration of classes. This is because the components defined in the declaration of an interface are always integrated in the public visibility section of the classes.

Interfaces are used when two similar classes have a method with the same name, but the functionalities of these methods are different from each other. Interfaces might appear similar to classes; however, unlike classes, the functions defined in an interface are implemented in a class to extend the scope of that class. Moreover, interfaces, along with the inheritance feature, provide a base for polymorphism, because a method defined in an interface can behave differently in different classes.

Similar to global and local classes, interfaces can be classified as global or local. A global interface can be used in any program, while a local interface can be used only in the same program in which it is declared. Similar to a class, you can create a global interface by using Class Builder. Use the `PUBLIC` clause to identify an interface as a global interface. A global interface is stored in an interface pool, which cannot contain any local type declaration. Note that the interface pool is used to either implement an interface defined in it or to create reference variables of the interface type defined in it.

You create a local interface in an ABAP program by using the following syntax:

```
INTERFACE <intf_nm>.
  DATA ...
  CLASS-DATA ...
  METHODS ...
  CLASS-METHODS ...
  ...
ENDINTERFACE.
```

In this syntax, <intf_nm> represents the name of an interface. The DATA and CLASS-DATA statements can be used to define the instance and static attributes of the interface, respectively. In addition, the METHODS and CLASS-METHODS statements can be used to define the instance and static methods of the interface, respectively.

Unlike classes, the definition of an interface does not include the implementation class. Therefore, it is not necessary to add the DEFINITION clause in the declaration of an interface. Note that all the methods of an interface are abstract. They are fully declared, including their parameter interface, but not implemented in the interface. All the classes that want to use an interface must implement all the methods of the interface; otherwise, the class becomes an abstract class.

To use an interface in a class, use the following syntax in the implementation part of the class:

```
INTERFACES <intf_nm>.
```

In this syntax, <intf_nm> represents the name of an interface. Note that this syntax must be used in the public section of the class that wants to use the <intf_nm> interface.

The following syntax is used to implement the methods of an interface inside the implementation of a class:

```
METHOD <intf_nm~imeth>.
...
ENDMETHOD.
```

In this syntax, <intf_nm~imeth> represents the fully declared name of a method of the <intf_nm> interface.

Listing A.2 shows an example to declare and implement an interface:

```
INTERFACE my_interface.
  METHODS message.
ENDINTERFACE.

CLASS num_counter DEFINITION.
  PUBLIC SECTION.
    INTERFACES my_interface.
    METHODS add_num.
  PRIVATE SECTION.
    DATA num TYPE I.
ENDCLASS.

CLASS num_counter IMPLEMENTATION.
  METHOD my_interface~message.
    WRITE: / 'The number is', num.
  ENDMETHOD.
  METHOD add_num.
    ADD 1 TO num.
  ENDMETHOD.
ENDCLASS.

CLASS car DEFINITION.
  PUBLIC SECTION.
    INTERFACES my_interface.
    METHODS speed.
  PRIVATE SECTION.
    DATA wheel TYPE I.
ENDCLASS.
CLASS car IMPLEMENTATION.
  METHOD my_interface~message.
    WRITE: / 'The number of wheels in the car is', wheel.
  ENDMETHOD.
  METHOD speed.
    ADD 10 TO wheel.
  ENDMETHOD.
ENDCLASS.
```

LISTING A.2 **Declaring and implementing an interface**

In Listing A.2, `my_interface` is the name of an interface that contains the message method. Next, two classes, `num_counter` and `car`, are defined and implemented. Both these classes implement the message method, in addition to the specific methods that define the behavior of their respective instances, such as the `add_num` and `speed` methods. Note that the `add_num` and `speed` methods are specific to the respective classes and are not related to the `my_interface` interface.

Now, let's explore how to declare, implement, and call the methods in classes and objects.

DECLARING AND CALLING METHODS

As stated earlier, methods are internal procedures in a class, which define the behavior of an object or instance of the class. In the ABAP Objects language, instance methods are declared by using the `METHODS` statement. The following syntax is used to declare an instance method:

```
METHODS method_nm IMPORTING [VALUE(]i1 i2 ... [)] TYPE type
[OPTIONAL]...
EXPORTING [VALUE(]e1 e2 ... [)] TYPE type ...
CHANGING [VALUE(]c1 c2 ... [)] TYPE type [OPTIONAL]...
RETURNING VALUE(r)
EXCEPTIONS exc1 exc2 ... .
```

Static methods are declared by using the `CLASS-METHODS` statement. The following syntax is used to declare static class methods:

```
CLASS- METHODS method_nm IMPORTING [VALUE(]i1 i2 ... [)]
TYPE type [OPTIONAL]...
EXPORTING [VALUE(]e1 e2 ... [)] TYPE type ...
CHANGING [VALUE(]c1 c2 ... [)] TYPE type [OPTIONAL]...
RETURNING VALUE(r)
EXCEPTIONS exc1 exc2 ... .
```

In this syntax, when a method (instance method or static method) is declared, its parameters are declared by using the IMPORTING (input parameter), EXPORTING (output parameter), CHANGING (input/output parameter), and RETURNING (return code) clauses. You can also define whether a parameter needs to be passed by reference or value (VALUE), the type of parameter (TYPE), and whether the parameter is optional or default, by using the OPTIONAL or DEFAULT clause, respectively. Note that, unlike function modules, the default way of passing a parameter in a method is by reference. The VALUE clause is used to pass a parameter by value. The RETURNING clause is used to return a value, which must always be passed explicitly as a value. This is suitable for methods that return a single output value. Note that you cannot use the EXPORTING or CHANGING clauses with the RETURNING clause. Moreover, the EXCEPTIONS clause is used to define exception parameters, similar to function modules, which allow users to handle errors when the method is executed.

Next, use the following syntax to implement a method in the implementation part of a class:

```
METHOD method_nm.
...
ENDMETHOD.
```

In this syntax, the method_nm expression represents the name of a method. The implementation code of a method must be written between the METHOD and ENDMETHOD statements. You should note that the implementation part of a method does not include the parameters of the method, as the parameters are defined only in the method's declaration part. The parameters declared in a method act as local variables in the implementation of the method. However, you can define additional local variables in the implementation of a method by using the DATA statement. Moreover, you can use the RAISE and MESSAGE RAISING statements in the implementation of a method to handle errors.

The following syntax is used to call a method:

```
CALL METHOD method_nm | ref->method_nm | class_nm => method_
nm EXPORTING i1 = f1 i2 =f2 ...
     IMPORTING e1 = g1 e2 =g2 ...
     CHANGING c1 = f1 c2 =f2 ...
     RECEIVING r = h
     EXCEPTIONS e1 = rc1 e2 =rc2 ...
```

In this syntax, the `CALL METHOD` statement and its parameters are used to call a method, depending on the method declaration. The following syntax is used to call a method of the same class directly by using its name, `method_nm`:

```
CALL METHOD method_nm ...
```

You can call a method from outside a class by using the following syntax:

```
CALL METHOD ref->method_nm ...
```

In this syntax, `ref` is a reference variable whose value points to an instance of a class. Outside the class, a method can be called based on the visibility of the method. The visibility of a method, however, is decided by you, when you declare a method.

Visible instance methods can also be called from outside a class by using the following syntax:

```
CALL METHOD class_nm => method_nm ...
```

In this syntax, `class_nm` is the name of the relevant class.

When a method is called, all non-optional input parameters are passed by using the `EXPORTING` or `CHANGING` clause in the `CALL METHOD` statement. You can import the output parameters by using the `IMPORTING` or `RECEIVING` clause and can handle exceptions by using the `EXCEPTIONS` clause.

The methods defined in an interface can also have parameters. Consider the following expression:

```
... Formal parameter = Actual value or parameter
```

In this expression, the interface parameters, also called formal parameters, are specified at the left side of the equals (=) sign. However, the actual values or parameter for the interface parameters are specified at the right side of the equals sign.

Note that if the call to a method contains only a single import parameter, you can use the following shortened syntax form of the method call:

```
    CALL METHOD method ( act_par ).
```

In this syntax, `act_par` represents the actual parameter, which is passed to the input parameters of the method being called.

Similarly, if the call to a method contains only import parameters, you can use the following shortened syntax form of the method call:

```
CALL METHOD method ( frm_par1 = act_par 1 frm_par2 = act_
par 2 ...).
```

In this syntax, `act_par 1`, `act_par 2,... act_par n` represent the actual parameters and `frm_par 1, frm_par 2,... frm_par n` represent formal parameters. Each actual parameter is assigned to the corresponding formal parameter.

Next, we explore how to declare and call a constructor in ABAP Objects.

DECLARING AND CALLING CONSTRUCTORS

Constructors are called automatically when you create an object or access the components of a class for the first time. However, constructors are not called by using the `CALL METHOD` statement, as in the case of a normal method call. The instance constructor of a class is the predefined instance method, called

CONSTRUCTOR. An instance constructor is always declared in the public section of a class. Use the following syntax to declare an instance constructor:

```
METHODS CONSTRUCTOR
    IMPORTING.. [VALUE(]<par 1> <par 2>...<par n>[)] TYPE type
    [OPTIONAL]..
    EXCEPTIONS.. <e 1> <e 2>...<e n>.
```

The static constructor of a class is the predefined static method, called CLASS_CONSTRUCTOR. Similar to an instance constructor, a static constructor is also declared in the public section of a class. Use the following syntax to declare a static constructor:

```
CLASS-METHODS CLASS_CONSTRUCTOR.
```

A constructor is implemented in the implementation section of a class, just like any other method. An instance constructor is called once for each instance of the class, after the object has been created in the CREATE OBJECT statement. You can pass the values to the input parameters of an instance constructor and can handle its exceptions by using the EXPORTING and EXCEPTIONS clauses.

A static constructor, however, has no parameters. A static constructor is called once for each class, before the class is accessed for the first time. Therefore, a static constructor cannot access the components of its class.

Now, let's explore another important component of a class or an interface; that is, events.

WORKING WITH EVENTS IN ABAP OBJECTS

In the ABAP Objects language, certain methods act as triggers or events that are handled or reacted by certain other methods, called handlers or handler methods. This means that handler methods are executed when associated events occur. The link between a trigger and its handler method is decided dynamically at runtime.

Triggering an Event

An event is triggered by declaring an event in the declaration part of a class or interface. The event is triggered in one of the methods of the class associated with the event. The EVENTS statement is used to declare an instance event, and the CLASS-EVENTS statement is used to declare a static method. Use the following statement to declare an instance event:

```
EVENTS <evt_nm> EXPORTING... VALUE(<e 1> <e 2>…<e n>) TYPE
type [OPTIONAL]..
```

Use the following statement to declare a static event:

```
CLASS-EVENTS <evt_nm> EXPORTING... VALUE(<e 1> <e 2>…<e n>)
TYPE type [OPTIONAL]..
```

When an event is declared, you can use the EXPORTING clause to specify the parameters that are passed to the event handler. The parameters are always passed by value. Moreover, instance events always contain the SENDER implicit parameter of the type of a reference to the class or the interface in which the event is declared.

After declaring an event in the declaration part of a class or interface, the event is executed or triggered as a method of a class by using the RAISE EVENT statement. In case of an instance event, the event can be triggered by any method in the class; however, in case of a static method, the event can be triggered by any static method. Use the following statement to trigger an event in a method:

```
RAISE EVENT <evt_nm> EXPORTING... <e 1> = <f 1> <e 2> =
<f 2>...<e n> = <f n>
```

In this syntax, <e 1>, <e 2>...<e n> represent formal parameters, which are non-optional, and <f 1>, <f 2>...<f n> represent actual parameters, corresponding to each formal parameter. Note that the ME self-reference is automatically passed to the SENDER implicit parameter.

Handling an Event

When an event is triggered, it calls its event handler. For this, you must define an event-handler method and register it for the event at runtime. An event handler method can be defined either in the same class of the event or in a different class. Use the following syntax to declare an event-handler method corresponding to an instance event of a class or interface:

```
METHODS <method_nm> FOR EVENT <evt_nm> OF <cif> IMPORTING..
<e 1> <e 2>…<e n>
```

Use the following syntax to declare an event-handler method corresponding to a static event:

```
CLASS-METHODS <method_nm> FOR EVENT <evt_nm> OF <cif>
IMPORTING.. <e 1> <e 2>…<e n>
```

In both syntaxes, `<method-nm>` represents a method and `<evt_nm>` represents an event declared in the `<cif>` class or interface. The handler method contains the formal parameters defined in the declaration of the `<evt_nm>` event. It is not necessary for an event-handler method to use all the parameters, which are passed in the `RAISE EVENT` statement. Note that when an event-handler method is declared in the same class of the event, the instances of such class or the class itself handle an event, `<evt_nm>`, which is triggered in a method.

As stated earlier, a handler method can react to an event after registering it for the event at runtime. The following syntax is used to register an event handler method:

```
SET HANDLER... <h 1> <h 2>...<h n>... [FOR]...
```

In this syntax, the `SET HANDLER` statement is used to link a list of handler methods with the corresponding triggers or events. As we know, an event can be either instance or static. The `FOR` clause is used in the `SET HANDLER` statement to register an event-handler method corresponding to an instance event.

Use the following syntax to handle an instance event by using a reference variable, `<ref>`:

```
SET HANDLER... <h 1> <h 2>…<h n>...FOR <ref>.
```

Use the following syntax to register the handler for all instances that can trigger the event:

```
SET HANDLER... <h 1> <h 2>…<h n>...FOR ALL INSTANCES.
```

In this syntax, the registration of handler methods applies even to triggering instances that have not yet been created when you register the handler.

The following syntax is used to handle a static event without using the FOR clause:

```
SET HANDLER... <h 1> <h 2>…<h n>...
```

In this syntax, the registration of handler methods applies to the entire class as well as all those classes that implement the interface that contains the static event. When a static event of an interface has to be handled by a handler method, the registration also applies to classes that are not loaded until the handler has been registered.

Handler methods are executed in the order in which they were registered. Because event handlers are registered dynamically, the order in which they would be processed is not known. In fact, all event handlers can even be executed simultaneously.

Furthermore, after the execution of the `RAISE EVENT` statement, all registered handler methods are executed before the next statement is processed (synchronous event handling). If an event-handler method itself triggers events, its handler methods are executed before the original handler method executes. An event handler can be nested to a maximum of 64 levels to avoid the possibility of falling into an infinite loop.

Appendix B Introducing Cross-Application Technologies

If you need information on:	See page:
Introducing IDoc	908
Benefits of the IDoc Interface	912
Describing the IDoc Structure	913
IDoc Runtime Components	917
ALE	919
RFC	924

A business process in a company includes a sequence of actions or functions that collectively produce a business result. Therefore, all these processes need to be integrated with each other so that exchange of data between them can be handled easily. Let's consider a real-life example to understand the concept. Suppose a customer wants to purchase an item from a vendor company. To serve the purpose, the customer places a purchase order, which is then sent to the vendor through either fax or mail. The vendor receives the purchase order and enrolls it in the sales order business process. The vendor also generates a date to deliver the order, which is sent back to the customer again through either fax or mail. The vendor then dispatches the item, along with an invoice, through a courier. When the item is delivered, the customer makes the payment for the purchased item, either by check or cash. If the payment is made through a check, the vendor deposits the check in the bank with which the vendor is maintaining an account. Finally, the funds are transferred from the customer's bank account to the vendor's bank account.

In the business process explained through this example, ensuring appropriate communication requires exchanging different kinds of documents between the business partners involved in the business process. In addition, appropriate integration of the business processes (both within a company and between different companies) is required for successful implementation of SAP. Integrating processes within a company involves interfacing with legacy systems, communicating with third-party products, and integrating business processes across distributed SAP systems. This type of integration can be achieved with the help of cross-application technologies, such as Application Link and Enabling (ALE) and Electronic Data Interchange (EDI). These two technologies use the Intermediate Document (IDoc) interface to exchange data in an SAP system.

In this appendix, you learn about IDoc, which acts as a container to store the information to be exchanged between two or more business processes. Next, you learn about SAP's proprietary technology known as ALE, which is used to integrate distributed business processes within a company. In addition, you learn about RFC, which is the standard SAP interfacing technique used for communication between SAP systems. Now, let's start our discussion with IDoc.

INTRODUCING IDoc

As already stated, IDoc is a container used to store information to be exchanged between any two processes, provided that the processes understand the syntax and semantics of the information or data being exchanged. In SAP systems, IDocs are predefined and stored in database tables. Information related to predefined IDocs can be displayed in an SAP system with the help of the `WE02` transaction code. Note that an IDoc is not a process in itself.

Whenever an IDoc is generated in an SAP system, a unique number is allocated to it. The generated number of an IDoc is unique for every client. IDocs can be used to communicate either between SAP systems or between SAP and non-SAP systems, as long as the processes understand the syntax and semantics of the information to be shared. However, IDocs depend on some standards, such as EDI, American National Standards Institute Accredited Standards Committee (ANSI ASC X12), and Electronic Data Interchange For Administration, Commerce, and Transport (EDIFACT). The size and format of the data elements in an IDoc type is derived by using any of the mentioned standards.

IDocs are also independent of the direction of data exchange, which means that the same IDoc can be used both by an inbound as well as outbound process.

This can be understood with the help of an example of the ORDERS01 IDoc (a predefined IDoc, stored in the database). The ORDERS01 IDoc is used by the Purchasing module to send a purchase order as well as by the Sales and Distribution module to accept a sales order. IDocs are stored in a text format instead of a binary format and can be viewed by using a text editor. The file format of an IDoc can be unconverted, clipboard, spreadsheet, rich text, or HTML.

In the following sections, we describe certain concepts related to IDocs, which are:

- Uses of IDoc
- Benefits of the IDoc interface
- IDoc structure
- IDoc runtime components

Exploring the Uses of IDoc

In this section, we learn about different uses of IDoc. As already learned, IDoc interface helps an SAP system communicate with other SAP systems, as well as with external applications. The following are some areas in which an IDoc can be used:

- EDI technique
- ALE technique
- Legacy system integration
- Third-party product integration
- Workflow integration
- SAP R/2 integration
- Internet and Extensible Markup Language (XML) integration
- Optical Character Recognition (OCR) integration
- Intelligent Character Recognition (ICR) integration

Now, let's discuss in detail how each of these techniques uses the IDoc interface.

EDI Technique

EDI refers to the process of electronically exchanging business documents, such as purchase orders and sales orders, between different trading partners.

These business documents are circulated in a common industry standard format, such as ANSI X12 or EDIFACT. Different kinds of applications in SAP, such as Purchasing, Sales, and Shipping, are EDI-enabled. For example, if the Purchasing application uses EDI for information exchange, a purchase order is the first application document created. Now, this purchase order is converted into an IDoc by the EDI interface layer. The generated IDoc is then transferred to the EDI subsystem, which further translates the IDoc into an industry standard format. The document is finally transfered to the respective business partners.

ALE Technique

The ALE technique facilitates the exchange of data between two SAP systems in a distributed SAP environment. Data exchange is implemented by integrating different business processes and SAP applications distributed across multiple SAP systems.

Legacy System Integration

As already discussed, IDocs are independent of sending and receiving applications. Therefore, the ALE technique can also be used to facilitate communication between an SAP system and a legacy system. Now, let's suppose that a legacy application needs to send legacy data to an SAP system. In such a situation, the legacy application first exports the desired legacy data either in an IDoc format or a proprietary format. If the proprietary format is used, a third-party translator tool is used to convert the proprietary format data into an IDoc format (discussed later in this chapter). This IDoc data can then be easily transferred to the SAP system with the help of the ALE/EDI interface layer.

Third-Party Product Integration

The products of several Complementary Software Partners (CSPs) use the IDoc interface to communicate with an SAP system. For applications such as warehouse management systems, production-planning optimizers, and transportation-planning optimizers, a standard IDoc interface has been defined. This standard interface describes different IDocs and the sequence in which these IDocs must be communicated to and from the SAP system.

Workflow Integration

A workflow specifies how to control and coordinate the sequence of steps in a business process. The following are the two situations where IDocs are used for the workflow:

- **Enabling the Form interface by the IDoc interface—** Enables an infrequent user of the SAP system to perform a task in SAP without logging on to the SAP system. The form interface keeps the complexity of the SAP system hidden from an infrequent user. For example, a form developed in Microsoft Visual Basic might act as the front end to the SAP system for an infrequent user. Whenever the form is executed, the form's data is saved in an IDoc format. The IDoc is then passed to the SAP system, where it finds a corresponding workflow process that can further process the received IDoc.
- **Enabling exchange of data between workflows in a distributed SAP environment—**Implements data exchange when one or more steps of a workflow process started in one SAP system needs to be executed in another SAP system. In such a scenario, the data required to execute the steps in the second system is made available with the help of IDocs.

SAP R/2 System

IDocs are also used to transfer information between different versions of SAP systems. For example, in some organizations, some business processes run on the SAP R/2 platform and some run on the SAP R/3 platform. In such a scenario, the communication between these business processes happens with the IDoc interface.

Internet and XML Integration

Web-based and XML applications can also be integrated into an SAP business process. This can be done by first capturing the data from these applications through an interface, i.e., a web browser. The captured data is in the HTTP format, which is then converted into an IDoc format. This conversion is performed with an SAP tool called Business Connector. The IDoc format can now be transferred to the SAP applications through the IDoc interface. In addition, you can import and export IDoc data in XML format instead of using a standard flat file.

OCR Integration

OCR is a technology that scans and interprets printed matter by using pattern recognition. You can also integrate an OCR application with SAP by using IDoc. In OCR, the documents to be transferred are first scanned to generate IDocs and then transferred to an SAP system for further processing.

ICR Integration

ICR is a technique used to encode data. A barcode system is an example of the ICR technique. The data encoded by using the barcodes can be captured and stored as an IDoc. This stored IDoc can then be passed to the SAP system for further processing.

BENEFITS OF THE IDoc INTERFACE

Benefits of using the IDoc interface include:

- Ensures that an IDoc can be integrated easily with different applications.
- Provides a proper environment for interfacing one SAP system with other SAP systems.
- Integrates an external system with an SAP system. This integration has several advantages, such as a thoroughly documented interface, independence of the application product, use of numerous testing and troubleshooting tools, and an intricate means of error handling through proper workflow.
- Acts as an open interface, which means that the IDoc interface is not dependent on the internal structure of an SAP system. As stated previously, this interface is also independent of the sending and receiving of applications.

- Ensures compatibility with different versions. In other words, you can continue using the older version of IDocs and can switch easily to work with newer versions.
- Ensures scalability of IDocs. You can easily enhance IDocs in the SAP system and create new custom IDocs with the help of the tools available in SAP, such as the IDocs editor and Segment editor. For example, data can be exchanged with a legacy system by using enhanced predefined IDocs or custom IDocs.

DESCRIBING THE IDoc STRUCTURE

IDocs are stored in the SAP database. Every IDoc has a structure associated with it. To understand what an IDoc structure is, let's consider a structure in the form of a flat file that contains employee details, as shown in Figure B.1:

Last Name (20)	First Name (20)	ID Number (15)	Date of Birth (8)	Employee Information (Occurs once, required)	
Week (1)	Worked Hours (3)	Rate of Hours (3)	Client Site (25)	Description of Work (50)	Details of Week (Multiple)
Total Hours (3)	Total Amount (10)	Monthly Summary (Occurs once)			

FIGURE B.1 **A flat file structure**

In Figure B.1, the flat file structure consists of records related to an employee, such as first and last name, date of birth, and weekly working hours. At the end of every month, a file containing the monthly report data for each employee is delivered to the external system. Now, this application is replaced by an SAP system and a standard IDoc is developed to support the process. The file structure of this application consists of the following details:

- It consists of three kinds of records containing the employee information. Each of these records summarizes the personal details as well as duration of the working hours of an employee on a weekly and monthly basis. In Figure B.1, notice the three records: Employee Information, Details of Week, and Monthly Summary.

- Each record has attributes, which suggest whether the records are optional or mandatory, the number of times a record can be repeated, the field names in the records, the data type for each field in the record, and the length of each field in the record.
- The weekly details include description of the work performed at the client site. It is not necessary that these details are always present.

The flat file structure can be represented in terms of an IDoc, as shown in Figure B.2:

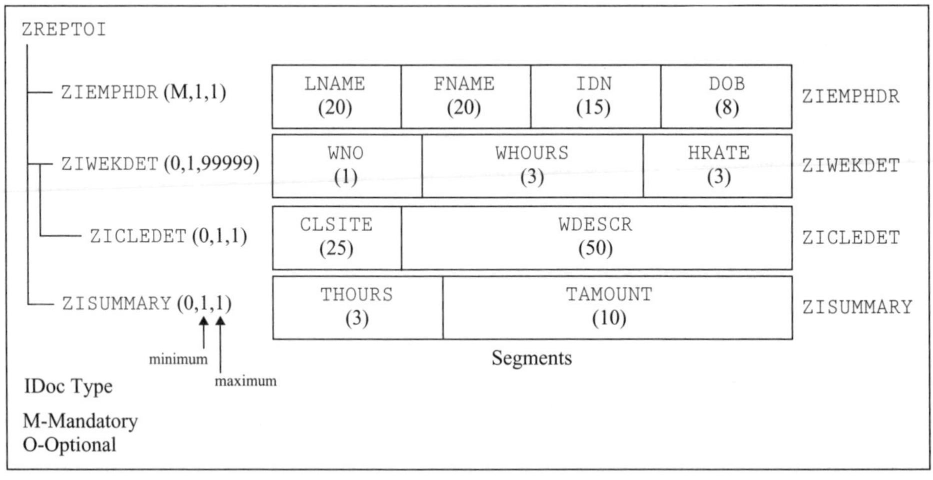

FIGURE B.2 **IDoc representation**

In Figure B.2, notice that a basic IDoc type has been created and named ZREPTO1. In this basic IDoc type, there are four segments: Z1EMPHDR, Z1WEKDET, Z1CLEDET, and Z1SUMMARY. Each segment consists of fields; for example, the Z1EMPHDR segment consists of four fields: LNAME, FNAME, IDN, and DOB; and the Z1WEKDET segment consists of three fields: WNO, WHOURS, and HRATE.

Figure B.3 shows an example of a record of an employee corresponding to the flat file structure described earlier:

Srivastava	Shivam	123-45-6789	10769	
1	30	40	ABC Tech	Consultant
2	40	50	Replicon	Software Engineer
3	30	40	DT Publications	Technical Writer
4	50	60	DSP Technology	Quality Analyst
140	7000			

FIGURE B.3 **Employee record**

Figure B.4 shows the IDoc representation of the employee record shown in Figure B.3, Shivam Srivastava:

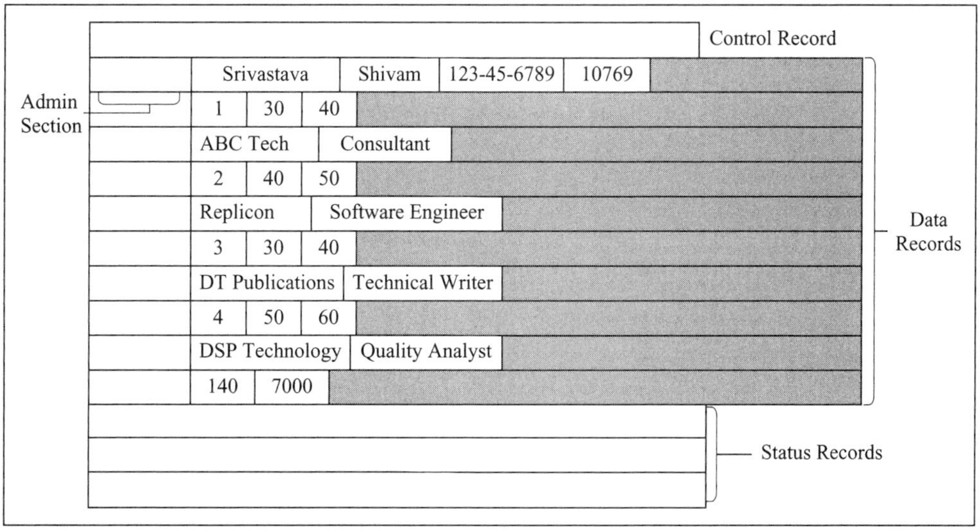

FIGURE B.4 **Employee record in the IDoc format**

The IDoc also consists of different kinds of records, such as control records, status records, and data records. The basic IDoc type is used to define the structure and format of the business documents that are exchanged between any two systems. The basic IDoc types are usually referred to as IDoc types, but there is a technical difference between the two. Basic IDoc types are obtained by adding some features to the existing IDoc types. The basic IDoc type can refer to the SAP-provided basic IDoc type or the customer-defined basic IDoc type.

> **Note:** The customer-defined basic IDoc type can also be applied to the SAP-provided basic IDoc type.

The following are the main characteristics of a basic IDoc:

- **Name—**Specifies that the name of the basic IDoc type can be 30 characters long. Note that the name of the customer IDoc types always starts with the character Z; the last two characters of the name represent the version number. In this case, the name of the basic IDoc type is `ZREPT01`. When a basic IDoc type is released (ready to be used by an SAP system) and you shift to a new version of the SAP system, any changes made in the existing basic IDoc types creates a new basic IDoc type. Therefore, `ZMPREP02` represents the improved version of this basic IDoc type. The segments involved in the older version of the basic IDoc type are never deleted.
- **List of segments—**Specifies that a combination of segments makes an IDoc structure. A segment defines the structure of the data record to be used in communication. These segments can be used in any IDoc type. For example, in Figure B.2, the segments included are `Z1EMPHDR`, `Z1WEKDET`, `Z1CLEDET`, and `ZISUMMARY`.
- **Hierarchy of segments—**Explains whether there is any parent-child relationship between the segments. A parent-child relationship denotes that the child segment does not exist without the parent segment. In Figure B.2, `Z1CLEDET` is the child of the segment `Z1WEKDET`.
- **Mandatory and optional segment—**Defines whether the segment included is mandatory or optional. In Figure B.2,

the `Z1EMPHDR` segment is the mandatory segment since no report can be generated without the employee record.

- **Minimum/maximum range for each segment**—Specifies that the segments in an IDoc are assigned with the minimum and maximum values. These values are used to determine the number of times a data record corresponding to the segment can exist in the IDoc.

IDoc RUNTIME COMPONENTS

IDoc runtime components are elements that are attached to an IDoc at the time of executing an IDoc. The structure of an IDoc is record-oriented, similar to the record structure in a flat file, as shown in Figure B.1. The following are some events that occur at runtime:

- Every IDoc is assigned with a unique number. This IDoc number binds all the records of an IDoc.
- A control record is attached to the IDoc.
- Segments of an IDoc are converted into respective data records.
- Status records are attached to an IDoc.
- Syntax rules are checked for the defined IDoc. The runtime component of an IDoc is also compared with the definition of the IDoc.

We know that there are several records in an IDoc, which are grouped under different records. As mentioned, at runtime, records such as control, data, and status are generated and attached to an IDoc. Let's now discuss each kind of record in detail.

Control Record

The control record stores the control information about an IDoc. IDoc number, sender information, receiver information, message type information, and information regarding the type of an IDoc are examples of control information. There is only one control record per IDoc. The structure of the control record is the same as for all the IDocs. This structure is defined by the SAP system with the help of the data dictionary structure known as EDI_DC40. The data of the control record is stored in the EDIDC table. The EDIDC table has a key field, IDoc number, which can be used to access the control record. The information regarding the control record that appears in an IDoc file can be viewed online with the help of the `WE61` transaction code.

Data Records

The data records of an IDoc contain the application data. As shown in Figure B.4, the data regarding the employee details, including the summary of the weekly and monthly details, constitutes the data records.

Status Records

Status records of an IDoc contain information such as status code, date, and time. This information is generated every time the IDoc is processed or an error is produced while processing. Status records are attached to an IDoc. The following are the main characteristics of status records:

- An IDoc contains many status records.
- In the case of an outbound process, the status records are generated by the EDI subsystem; in the case of an inbound process, SAP generates the status records.
- Each IDoc has a status in the form of a status code. There are predefined sets of status codes from 01 to 49, which can be defined for the outbound processes, and the status codes 50 and greater are reserved for use by the inbound processes. The following are the main characteristics of each status code:
    - Contains a description
    - Contains an attribute direction, which defines whether the status code is inbound or outbound
    - Contains a process level attribute, which defines the point of the process at which the status code must be attached
    - Contains a status group for statistical reporting
    - Defines the safety guidelines regarding the placement of IDoc

Use the `WE47` transaction code to view a list of available status codes, along with their details.

ALE

ALE is SAP technology that supports distributed, yet integrated processes across several SAP systems. A distributed process is a process where a part of the business process is carried out in one SAP system and the other part of the business process is carried out in some other SAP system. This can be understood by considering an example of a business process of SAP, such as the Sales and Distribution processes. All the sales-related activities, such as storing a sales order, calculating the delivery dates, checking for availability, performing credit checks, and calculating the price, can be carried out on one SAP system. Similarly, the shipping process, which performs the shipping-related activities such as determining the shipping point, creating deliveries, picking goods, finding the shortest route, and determining the cheapest mode of transportation, can be carried out on another SAP system. Now, these two SAP systems need to exchange data with each other to stay synchronized.

ALE ensures effective and reliable exchange of information between the distributed processes to achieve a distributed but integrated SAP system. ALE is not based on any database-replication technique; rather, it is based on the application-to-application integration technique. This technique uses messaging architecture, where messages are used to define the data to be exchanged between the processes. The data to be exchanged is stored in IDocs. Consequently, IDocs play an important role in the ALE process.

The architecture of ALE is independent of the systems taking part in communication. Therefore, communication is possible between SAP systems or even between non-SAP systems to SAP systems. The ALE technique supports guaranteed delivery of a message, which means that an application sending a message does not have to worry about any errors occurring in a network or any kind of damage to the established connection. The application that sends a message first identifies the exact receiver and then delivers the message to the identified receiver. If any error occurs in the network during the transfer of the message, the message is buffered, and the buffered message is delivered to the intended receiver after the problem is sorted out.

The SAP system also takes care of the fact that no messages are transferred twice. Any of the distributed SAP systems can be enhanced with a newer release of the SAP system, without changing the existing functionality. In addition to this, each SAP system involved in communication maintains its own set of data and applications, and is administered separately. Further, different maintenance tasks are also carried out to maintain the SAP system without affecting the partner SAP system in communication.

ALE Architecture

ALE technology supports all the technical aspects related to the generation of the IDoc format for better comprehension of the flow of data between these systems. The ALE technology implements the ALE architecture, which includes three types of processes, facilitating the exchange of data between the distributed SAP systems. The processes included are as follows:

- Outbound process
- Inbound process
- Exception handling process

Now, let's discuss each process in detail.

Outbound Process

The outbound process is used to transfer data to one or more SAP systems. Distributed systems can use outbound, inbound, or exception handling process. All the three processes always exchange three types of data, as described in Table B.1:

Data	Description
Transactional Data	Includes data regarding the sales order, purchase orders, contracts, invoices, and General/Ledger (G/L) postings.
Master Data	Includes data regarding the material master, vendor master, and employee master.
Control Data	Includes data regarding the company codes, business areas, plants, sales organization, distribution channels, and divisions.

TABLE B.1 Types of data

Figure B.5 shows the outbound process flow related to ALE:

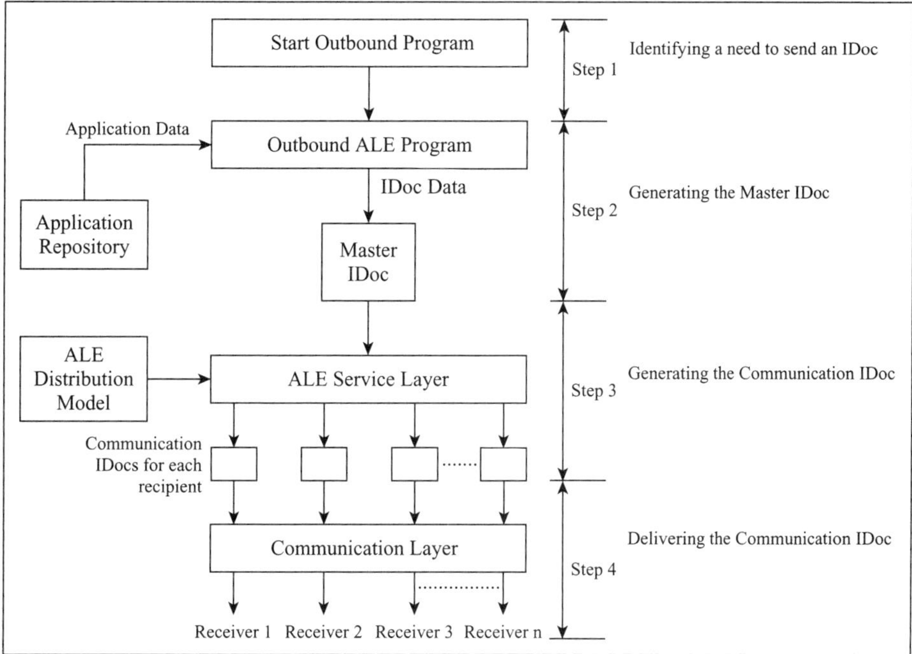

FIGURE B.5 **The outbound ALE process**

In Figure B.5, you can see that an outbound ALE process is divided into four steps:

1. Identify the need to send an IDoc
2. Generate the master IDoc
3. Generate the communication IDoc
4. Deliver the communication IDoc

Now, let's discuss each of the preceding steps in detail.

Identifying the Need to Send an IDoc

The need to send an IDoc is identified when an application document is created. When the application document is created, the outbound program starts working and prompts the ALE layer to determine if any other system requires the created material master data. If a system requires the created material master data, the

ALE layer starts sending the application data (that is, the material master data), to the system.

Generating the Master IDoc

In this step, the application document or the master data to be delivered is read from the database and then changed into the IDoc format. The changed master data is now known as the master IDoc. Note that the data of the master IDoc can be changed into the format understood by the recipient.

Generating the Communication IDoc

Separate IDocs are created from the master IDoc for each receiver that requires the data because each recipient might require a different version or subset of the master IDoc. Separate IDocs are created by the ALE service layer, as shown in Figure B.5. These separate IDocs are called communication IDocs and are stored in the database. The recipients of the IDocs are found out from the customer distribution model, which maintains a list of all the messages exchanged between any two systems.

> **Note:** The communication IDocs are stored in the database, but not the master IDoc. The master IDoc is stored in the memory buffer until all the communication IDocs are generated.

Delivering the Communication IDoc

In this step, the generated IDocs are delivered to the respective recipients by using the asynchronous communication method. Asynchronous communication allows the sending system to continue with its processing without waiting for the destination system to receive and process the IDoc.

Inbound Process

In an inbound process, an IDoc is received and a document is created in the SAP system. Similar to the outbound process, the inbound process also handles three types of data, as shown in Table B.1.

Figure B.6 shows the flow control of the inbound process of ALE:

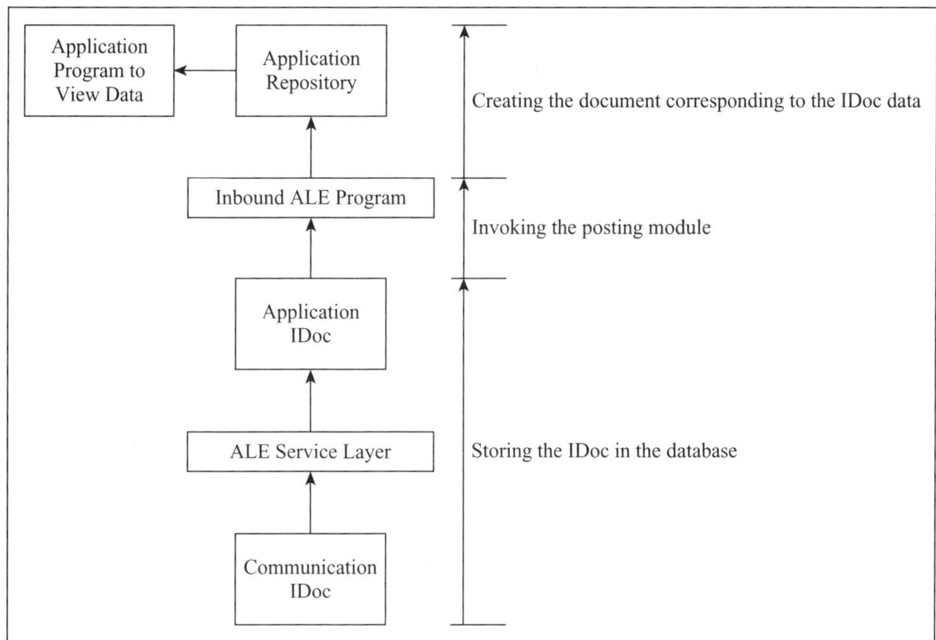

FIGURE B.6 **Inbound ALE process**

In Figure B.6, you can see that the inbound process is divided into the following three steps:

1. **Store the IDoc in the database**—When an IDoc is received, it is stored in the SAP database. The stored IDoc then undergoes a basic integrity check and a syntax check.
2. **Invoke the posting module**—After storing and checking the IDoc, the control information stored in IDoc and the configuration tables are read to determine the posting module or program. A posting program is a function module that reads data from an IDoc and creates an application document from it.
3. **Create the document corresponding to the IDoc data**—An application document is created in the SAP system on the basis of IDoc data. The result, such as the total number of read IDocs, is then logged in the IDoc.

Exception Handling Process

Exceptions can occur at any step in an outbound or inbound process. They can be of different kinds, such as the problems related to a network or the problems related to some data. The workflow determines the correct process responsible to handle the errors at runtime; and correspondingly informs the process so that the error can be rectified. The process then receives a work item that can be executed to display the error and diagnose the problem. Errors are fixed outside the workflow, and then the process can again be restarted from the point of failure.

RFC

RFC is a technique used to establish communication between the SAP systems. RFC acts as the standard SAP interface technique to ensure proper communication between the SAP systems in the SAP environment possible. RFC calls a function that is executed in a remote system. Now, let's explain the following topics in the context of RFC:

- RFC interface
- Types of RFC

RFC Interface

Communication between different SAP systems happens with the help of the RFC interface system. In other words, the RFC interface facilitates function calls between any two SAP systems or between an SAP system and an external system. The RFC interface system provides the following features:

- Provides a calling interface for each ABAP program.
- Provides the `CALL FUNCTION` statement to call a remote function module in an ABAP program. The `CALL FUNCTION` statement must include the `DESTINATION` parameter, which informs an SAP system that the called function module runs in a different system.
- Ensures that the function modules used in the RFC are in a proper format and registered as a remote function module in the required SAP system.

- Specifies that the calling program can be any ABAP program, but the called program must be a function module. If the calling program and called program are both ABAP programs, the RFC interface system provides both programs with the communication partners.

In all the SAP systems, the `CALL FUNCTION` statement executes a function module in the same system, whereas the RFC acts as an extended form of the `CALL FUNCTION` statement in a distributed environment. Any function module can be executed by using an RFC from a remote system. This is possible only by using the `DESTINATION` parameter of the `CALL FUNCTION` statement. The `DESTINATION` parameter displays an entry in the table known as RFCDES. This table is defined with the `SM59` transaction code. Whenever a function call is made, the following tasks are performed by the RFC interface:

- Converting all the data related to the parameter in the representation as needed in the remote system. This includes the conversion related to the character strings and hardware. During the conversion, all the data types are supported.
- Calling all the communication routines required to communicate with the remote system.
- Handling all kinds of communication errors. These communication errors can be brought to the notice of the caller with the `EXCEPTIONS` parameter of the `CALL FUNCTION` statement.

The RFC interface is not visible to the ABAP programmer. The processing required to call the remote programs is built into the `CALL FUNCTION` statement, whereas the processing required for being called is generated automatically for each and every function module declared as remote. The processing for the function being called is generated in the form of the RFC stub, which acts as an interface between the calling program and the function module.

The calling program must define all the parameters related to the connection while calling a function module by using the RFC interface. The definition of the connection includes information such as the type of connection, the partner program, and the target system. This definition can be maintained with the help of the `SM59` transaction code. Different kinds of connections, such as R/2 connections, ABAP connections, and TCP/IP connections, can be established.

In the case of synchronous RFCs, the destination must be defined explicitly, whereas in the case of asynchronous RFCs, a destination may or may not be specified. If a user does not define the destination for the function module, it is called by using the RFC interface in the same system.

Types of RFC

In RFC, the execution of function modules can be either synchronous or asynchronous. Consequently, RFCs are categorized as synchronous or transactional, based on the execution of the functional modules. Now, let's discuss each RFC in detail.

Synchronous RFC

When the execution of functional modules is synchronous, the respective RFC is called a synchronous RFC. Synchronous communication means that both the systems involved in the communication are available when the call is made. In other words, the receiving system also remains active when the function call is made by the sending system. This ensures faster transfer of data between the systems.

Transactional RFC

When the execution of functional modules is asynchronous, the respective RFC is called a transactional RFC (tRFC). This type of RFC was previously known as an asynchronous RFC. The called function module is executed only once in the RFC server. It is not necessary that the remote system is always available at the time when the tRFC is executed by the RFC client program. The tRFC component stores the called RFC function module with the corresponding data in the SAP database. The RFC function module is stored under a unique transactional ID. If a remote call is made and the receiving system is down, the remote call remains in the local queue. Now, it is not that the calling program waits for the receiving system to become free; instead, the program can continue with further processing. In case the receiving system does not become active within a certain amount of time, the call is then planned to be run in a batch.

GLOSSARY

ABAP

Advanced Business Application Programming (ABAP, also known as ABAP/4) is a fourth-generation programming language developed in the 1980s. It originally was used to prepare reports, which enabled large corporations to build mainframe business applications for material management and financial and management accounting. ABAP is one of the first programming languages to include the concept of logical database, which provides a high level of abstraction from the centralized database of the SAP system. Apart from the concept of logical database, you can also use SQL statements to retrieve and manipulate data from the centralized database.

ABAP Dictionary

ABAP Dictionary (accessed by transaction code `SE11`) is a tool of ABAP Workbench, which is used to create and manage data definitions, without redundancies, in the SAP system. The data definitions stored in ABAP Dictionary allow you to create various objects such as tables and views. The objects stored in ABAP Dictionary are logically related to each other in the context of an application. ABAP Dictionary always provides the updated information of an object to all the system components. The presence and role of ABAP Dictionary ensures that data stored in an SAP system is always consistent and secure.

ABAP Editor

ABAP Editor (accessed by transaction code `SE38`) a tool of ABAP Workbench, is used to create ABAP programs by writing the code of these programs using the ABAP language. In addition, ABAP Editor is also used to define the class methods, function modules, screen flow logic, type groups, and logical databases for ABAP programs.

ABAP Objects

ABAP Objects is one of the new-generation languages that have implemented the object-oriented features. The concept of the ABAP Objects language has been launched with SAP R/3 Release 4.0. This concept is important in two ways. First, it represents the runtime environment of ABAP that indicates that SAP is following an object-oriented approach. Second,

ABAP Objects is an object-oriented extension of the ABAP language, which unites the data and functions in objects. ABAP Objects is not only used for existing programs but also in new ABAP Objects programs.

ABAP user dialogs
ABAP user dialogs are user-defined screens, which are created by using ABAP statements and enable users to interact with ABAP programs. Some examples of ABAP user dialogs are screens, selection screens, modal dialog boxes, lists, and messages. The process of creating these user dialogs is called dialog programming.

ABAP Workbench
ABAP Workbench is a graphical programming environment in the SAP R/3 system used to develop different applications by using the ABAP language. It provides different tools, such as ABAP Dictionary, ABAP Editor, and Screen Painter, used to create ABAP applications. Using these tools, you can perform different tasks, such as defining data structures in ABAP Dictionary, developing data programs in ABAP Editor, and designing interfaces using the Screen Painter and Menu Painter. Besides these tasks, you can create user-defined reports, transactions, and enhancements within ABAP Workbench. Moreover, all the tools of ABAP Workbench are integrated, which implies that one tool recognizes the objects created by the other tool.

ALE
Application Link and Enabling (ALE) is an SAP technology that supports distributed yet integrated processes across several SAP systems. A distributed process is a process where one part of the business process is carried out in one SAP system, and the other part is carried out in another SAP system.

Alphanumeric fullscreen editor
The alphanumeric fullscreen editor provides an easy way of designing screens. This mode of the layout editor helps create screens on all platforms. The initial screen of the alphanumeric fullscreen editor can also be started from the initial screen of Screen Painter.

ALV reports
ALV is an acronym for ABAP List Viewer. ALV reports allow users to perform various functions with the displayed output of reports, such as sorting, arranging, filtering, and retrieving data. In addition, users can view the output of ALV reports either in a grid view or a list view.

BADI
Business Add-In (BADI) is an enhancement technique of SAP that uses ABAP Objects to create predefined points in the SAP ERP components. These predefined points are then implemented by individual industry solutions, country variants, or partners and customers to suit their specific requirements. SAP introduced the BADI enhancement technique with

SAP R/3 Release 4.6A. This technique was re-implemented in Release 7.0 of SAP.

BDC

Batch Data Communication (BDC) is a migration tool to transfer legacy data files from one SAP system or non-SAP system to other SAP systems. Some examples of data legacy files are text files, Microsoft Excel files, and Comma Separated Values (CSV) files. BDC uses methods, such as session methods and call transaction methods, to transfer the data from one SAP System to another, or from a non-SAP system to an SAP system. It is used to transfer data through SAP transactions itself. This means that when you use the BDC tool for data transfer, the sequence of steps is the same as when you use standard SAP transaction screens for data upload. The only difference is that you can use different processing modes for foreground and background processing in BDC.

Buffering permission

Buffering permission is a technical setting that defines whether or not the table can be buffered.

Buffering type

Buffering type is a technical setting that defines the buffering type for the table. The buffering type can be full, single-record, or generic.

Cardinality

Cardinality describes the foreign key relationship with regard to the number of possible dependent records (records of the foreign key table) or referenced records (records of the check table).

Class Builder

Class Builder (accessed by transaction code `SE24`) a tool of ABAP Workbench, is used to create, define, change, or test the global ABAP classes and interfaces. ABAP classes and interfaces are object types stored in a central class library and are available to all the objects in an SAP system. This class library is used to display all the existing classes and interfaces by using the Class Browser. The Class Browser is an integral part of the Class Builder that is used to display and maintain the existing global object types from the class library.

Class pool

A class pool is a special ABAP program used to store global classes and interfaces. All the ABAP programs can access these global classes and interfaces. A class pool program is created by using Class Builder, a tool provided by ABAP Workbench and the `CLASS-POOL` statement. Class pool programs do not contain any screens or processing blocks; they contain methods that can be executed to implement the program logic.

Class

A class is a prototype that defines the data and behavior common to all the objects of a specific type. In a class, data is represented by the class attributes and the behavior is provided by class methods.

Classical report

Classical reports are simple reports that are created by using the output data (final data that must be displayed in a report) in the `Write` statement inside a loop. These reports do not contain any sub reports. These reports consist of only one screen as an output. Various events, such as `INITAILIZATON` and `TOP-OF-PAGE`, are used to create a classical report. Each event has its own importance during the creation of a classical report. Each of these events is related to a specific user-action and is triggered only when the user performs that action.

Cluster table

A cluster table is a type of a table that can be created in ABAP Dictionary. This table type forms a many-to-one relationship with a table definition in the database similar to pooled table.

Collective Search Help

Collective Search Help is a type of search help that is a combination of several elementary search helps.

Compound foreign key

A compound foreign key is a key consisting of two or more fields. In a compound foreign key, a check is done to compare two fields in the foreign key table against the two fields in the check table.

Data class

A data class is a technical setting that defines a physical area of database (called a table space) where a table should be created.

Data type

A data type is a repository object of ABAP Dictionary that is used to create user-defined data types, such as data elements, structures, and tables. User-defined data types are type definitions in ABAP Dictionary and can be used in an ABAP program with the `TYPE` clause. In the SAP system there are three different kinds of data types: data elements, structures, and table types.

Database table

A database table is a repository object of ABAP Dictionary that helps in designing tables.

Database view

A database view is a type of view that is used to display distributed data, i.e., data that is distributed in different tables.

Dialog programming

Dialog programming allows users to interact with the SAP system by creating user dialogs. Dialog programming involves the use of a certain sequence of screens that are processed by the SAP system consecutively. With the help of dialog programming, a user can create a customized interface. A user cannot start the dialog program directly; instead, transaction codes are used to start a dialog program.

Dialog step
A dialog step is a procedure in which a new screen appears in the SAP R/3 system for user interaction. Dialog steps are dispatched in such a way that they navigate from one screen to another, where one screen accepts a request from the user and the other screen displays the result of the request.

Domain
A domain is a repository object of ABAP Dictionary that is used to define a value range, a data type, and the length of a table field. The value range of fields in a table or structure that uses a domain is defined automatically by the domain. If you make any changes in the domain, the attributes of the fields related to that domain also change accordingly.

Elementary search help
Elementary search help is a type of search help that is used to define the standard flow of an input help.

Encapsulation
Encapsulation is a feature of OOP that prevents access to non-essential details of a class. It is also referred to as data hiding because it hides important but unnecessary details of an object or class from the user. Note that the encapsulated data of a class is accessible outside the class only when the data is used in the functions of the class. However, a limited number of operations can be performed on encapsulated data by executing the functions or methods of the class.

ERP
An Enterprise Resource Planning (ERP) system is a system that automates and integrates all modules of the business, such as finance or sales and distribution. An ERP system is used to integrate several data sources and processes, such as manufacturing, control, and distribution of goods in an organization. This integration of several data sources is achieved by using various hardware and software components.

Executable program
Executable programs are often called report programs because the source code of an executable program starts with the `REPORT` statement. These programs are created by processing the data stored in the SAP database. Executable programs can retrieve and modify the data stored in the database. They contain every kind of processing blocks, except function modules and local classes. Executable programs can be started by entering either the program name in ABAP Editor or a transaction code in Command field.

Flow control statements
Flow control statements are the statements that are used to control the processing of

an ABAP program. Various conditions and loops can be implemented in programs by using the standard keywords, such as `IF`, `CASE`, `DO`, and `WHILE`, in the flow of the program.

Foreign key

Foreign keys are used to establish relationships between various tables in ABAP Dictionary.

Form Painter

Form Painter (also known as Graphical Form Painter) is a graphical tool that manages the design and layout of the form.

Function Builder

Function Builder (accessed by transaction code `SE37`) a tool of ABAP Workbench, is used to define and maintain ABAP functional modules. Function modules are procedures or routines defined in an ABAP program. They are stored in function groups, which act as containers for function modules that are logically related to each other. Moreover, the Function Builder tool is used to create both a function group and a function module.

Function group

A function group is a container of function modules that are connected logically to each other. It is created and maintained with the help of an ABAP Workbench tool known as Function Builder.

Function modules

Function modules are ABAP routines that are administered in a central function library. They are assigned to a function pool, called a function group. Function modules are created with the help of Function Builder, an ABAP Workbench tool.

Function pools

Function pools (also called function groups) are programs to contain function modules. A function pool program is created using the `FUNCTION-POOL` statement. Function modules are special ABAP procedures or routines that can be called in any ABAP program. Function Builder, a tool of ABAP Workbench, is used to create and manage function groups and function modules. Each function pool contains global data, such as data objects, subroutines, or screens, which are shared by all the function modules of the function pool.

Graphical Layout Editor

Graphical Layout Editor provides a user-friendly environment and an easy technique to design screens. The initial screen of Graphical Layout Editor can be started either from the initial screen of Screen Painter or from the Repository Browser.

Hashed table

Hashed tables have no linear index and are accessed only by the keys. The SAP system accesses the entries of a hashed table by using the hash algorithm. While defining a hashed table, the key of the hashed table must be defined as unique.

Help view

The Help view is a type of view that is used when you want to use an outer join to obtain data from other database tables.

IDoc

Intermediate Document (IDoc) is a container used to store information that is exchanged between any two processes, provided that the processes understand the syntax and semantics of the information or the data to be shared. In SAP systems, IDocs are predefined and stored in database tables. Information related to predefined IDocs can be displayed in the SAP system with transaction code called `WE02`. Note that an IDoc is not a process in itself. Whenever an IDoc is generated in an SAP system, a number is allocated to it that is unique for every client.

Include program

Include programs are not complete programs in themselves. These programs cannot be executed similarly to stand-alone programs that have a memory area of their own. Include programs act as a library of the ABAP source code. Include programs are used to organize a program code into smaller units, which can be inserted in other ABAP programs with the help of the `INCLUDE` statement.

Inheritance

Inheritance is a mechanism that allows a class to inherit the properties of another class. If the X class inherits the properties from the Y class, we say that the X class has been inherited from the Y class. In this scenario, Y is called a superclass or base class of X, and X is called a subclass or derived class of Y.

Interactive report

With the help of interactive reports, an overview list (called a basic list) is displayed based on which further output lists (called secondary lists) are displayed. These secondary lists are actually subreports, which are displayed when you click specific values of fields included in the basic list.

Interface pools

Interface pools are programs to store global interfaces. An interface pool can store exactly one global interface. You can use an interface by implementing the methods defined in the interface to a class, and by creating reference variables of the type of its interface. Interface pools are maintained by using the Class Builder tool of ABAP Workbench.

Interface

Interfaces, similar to classes, contain attributes and methods. However, unlike classes, interfaces do not have the implementation part. The methods defined in an interface can be implemented within the implementation of a class. Moreover, interfaces implement the polymorphism feature of OOP in the ABAP Objects language.

Internal tables

Internal tables are temporary tables that are stored in the RAM of the application server. Line-by-line memory is used to store the data that has the same structure. Internal tables exist only during the runtime of the program.

Lock object

Lock Object is a repository object of ABAP Dictionary that synchronizes simultaneous access of the same set of data records by different users.

Logging

Logging is a technical setting that defines whether the changes made to the table entries should be logged. If logging is switched on, then each change to a table record is recorded in a log table.

LSMW

Legacy System Migration Workbench (LSMW) is a migration tool to transfer legacy data files from a non-SAP system to an SAP system. Some examples of data legacy files are: text files, Microsoft Excel files, and Comma Separated Values (CSV) files. LSMW provides various options, such as batch input, direct input, BADIs, and IDocs to import data into the SAP system. The LSMW tool automatically converts data into batch input files. However, if you use the BDC tool, you have to write the batch input file yourself, line by line. The BDC tool provides a collection of Batch Input functions so that you can write your own batch input file. The LSMW tool opens a wizard with which you can create your own batch input file.

Macro

A macro is a set of statements that can be used more than once in the ABAP program. A macro can be used only in that program in which it is created. The `DEFINE...END OF DEFINITION` statement is used to define a macro in a program.

Maintenance view

Maintenance view is a type of view that is used to modify the data of an application object.

Menu Painter

Menu Painter (accessed by transaction code `SE41`) is a tool of ABAP Workbench, and is used to design user interfaces for ABAP programs. The main components of Menu Painter are status, menu bars, menu lists, F-key settings, functions, and titles. In other words, using Menu Painter, you can create custom menus in SAP GUI screens.

Modularization techniques

Modularization techniques enhance the readability and understandability of large ABAP programs. Occasionally, it becomes difficult to enhance and debug the source code of a lengthy ABAP program. ABAP language simplifies the work of developers by offering various modularization techniques, such as subroutines, function modules, and source code modules.

Module pool

A module pool is a program that is used to display the data in a screen. It is also used to add different functionalities to the screen, such as buttons, radio buttons, group boxes, and menu bars. It is used to write the screen flow logic. ABAP Editor is used to create module pool programs, which always start with the `PROGRAM` statement. A module pool is started using a transaction code, which is linked to a program and one of the screen (initial screen) of the program.

mySAP ERP

mySAP Enterprise Resource Planning (ERP) is a follow-up product of the SAP R/3 system. The mySAP ERP application is one of the applications present within the mySAP Business Suite. This suite includes mySAP ERP, mySAP Supply Chain Management (SCM), mySAP Customer Relationship Management (CRM), mySAP Supplier Relationship Management (SRM), and mySAP Product Lifestyle Management (PLM). The latest release of the mySAP ERP application is SAP ERP Central Component (ECC 6.0). The mySAP ERP categorizes the applications into three core functional areas: logistics, finance, and human resources.

Native SQL

Unlike Open SQL, which includes ABAP code elements, Native SQL contains only database manipulation statements. Database tables that are not administered by ABAP Dictionary can be accessed by using Native SQL. A Native SQL statement is used within the `EXEC SQL` and `ENDEXEC` statements.

Object Navigator

Object Navigator (accessed by transaction code `SE80`) is a tool of ABAP Workbench which is used to create objects in an SAP system and to navigate from one object to another. It acts as the central area of ABAP Workbench where any object of an SAP system can be accessed. When you create an object or a component of an object in Object Navigator, the object is stored in the Repository of the SAP system and is called a development object or a repository object. All the development or repository objects are arranged in a list format, called an object list. When you open an application, ABAP Workbench automatically opens the application in the respective development tool with the help of which the object has been created. Moreover, in Object Navigator you can open various browsers for various development processes.

Object

An object is a pattern or instance of a class. For example, a Nissan Sentra and a Ford Focus are objects and car is their class. An object represents a real-world entity, such as a person or place, or a programming entity, such as constants, variables, or memory location. Professors, doctors, and students are examples of real-world entities, whereas hardware and software components of a computer are examples of programming entities. An object has the following three main characteristics:

- Has a state
- May or may not display a behavior
- Has a unique identity

Open SQL

Open SQL, a subset of Standard SQL, consists of a set of ABAP statements that perform operations on the databases in the SAP R/3 system. It provides uniform syntax and semantics for all the database systems supported by SAP. Consequently, ABAP programs that use Open SQL statements can work in any SAP R/3 system, regardless of the database system used. Open SQL statements can work with database tables that have been created in ABAP Dictionary.

Package Builder

Package Builder (accessed by `SE21` or the `SPACKAGE` transaction code) is a tool of ABAP Workbench, and is used to implement the concept of a package in ABAP Workbench. A package is a type of development object that acts as a container to store development objects such as function modules, screens, menus, and transactions. It is also used to transfer existing development objects into other existing packages.

PC Editor

PC Editor (also known as Graphical PC Editor) is a graphical text-based tool that manages the content of an SAPscript form.

Polymorphism

Polymorphism is the ability of an object to exist in different forms. The term polymorphism derives itself from the Greek terms poly (many) and morphos (forms). In the context of OOP, polymorphism is the ability of a function to behave differently, depending on the context in which it is called.

Pooled table

A pooled table is one of the table types in ABAP Dictionary which forms a many-to-one relationship with the table definition in the database. This means that with respect to a single table in the database, there are several tables in ABAP Dictionary.

All pooled tables are stored in the SAP database in a single table, called the table pool. A table pool is a database table with a special structure that can store the data of multiple pooled tables.

Print program

A print program is an application program (such as Report or Module Pool) that is used to print forms. The print program retrieves the required data from a database table, defines the order in which the elements of the text are printed, selects the form to print, selects an output device and print options, and finally processes and prints the form.

Projection view

Projection view is a type of view that is used to suppress or mask certain fields in a table, consequently displaying only the selected fields.

Report

A report, in general, is the presentation of data, in a specific format and organized structure. Many database management systems (DBMS) include a report writer that enables you to design and generate reports. SAP is one of the software applications that supports the creation of reports. In SAP, you can create three types of reports: classical, interactive, and ABAP List Viewer (ALV) reports.

Return code

Return codes are system variables that are used in Open SQL to specify the status of executing a database operation. Some examples of return codes used in ABAP are `SY-SUBRC` and `SY-DBCNT`.

RFC

Remote Function Call (RFC) is a technique used to establish communication between SAP systems. RFC acts as the standard SAP interface technique to make proper communication between the SAP systems in the SAP environment possible. A RFC is the call of a function module that runs in different SAP systems by using a calling program (an ABAP program).

Roll area

A roll area is a memory area with a defined size that is allocated to a work process in the SAP system. It is located in the heap of the virtual address space of the work process.

Row type

A row type defines the structure and data type attributes of a line of an internal table.

SAP GUI

System Application and Products (SAP) Graphical User Interface (GUI) is the software that displays a graphical interface to enable the users to interact with an

SAP system. This software acts as a client in the three-tier architecture of an SAP system, which contains a database server, an application server, and a client. The SAP GUI can run on a variety of operating systems, such as Microsoft Windows, Apple Macintosh, and UNIX.

SAP R/1

SAP R/1 was the first financial and accounting software developed for the purpose of continuous development of other software components. Here, R stands for real-time data processing and 1 indicates single-tier architecture, which means that the three networking layers on which the SAP architecture depends (Presentation, Application, and Database), are implemented on a single system.

SAP R/2

SAP R/2, the version created immediately after SAP R/1, was introduced in 1980. It was based on a two-tier, client-server architecture, that enabled an SAP client to connect to an SAP server to access the data stored in the SAP database. SAP R/2 was implemented on mainframe databases, such as DB/2, IMS, and Adabas.

SAP R/3

SAP R/3 is based on a three-tier architecture of the client-server model. It was officially launched on July 6, 1992. It has introduced a new era of business software—from the mainframe computing architecture to the three-tier architecture consisting of the Database layer, the Application layer (business logic), and the Presentation layer. The SAP R/3 system is a customized software with predefined features that you can turn on or off according to your requirements. It integrates all the business modules of a company so that the information, once entered, can be shared across all these modules. The SAP R/3 system runs on various platforms, such as Microsoft Windows and UNIX. It also supports various relational databases of different database management systems, such as Oracle, Adabas, Informix, and Microsoft SQL Server.

SAP Smart Forms

SAP Smart Forms is a tool introduced with SAP R/3 Release 4.6 to print and send documents through e-mail, the Internet, or facsimile. This tool helps develop forms, Printable Document Format (PDF) files, e-mails, and documents for the Internet. The SAP Smart Forms tool provides an interface to build and maintain the layout and logic of a form.

SAP

SAP is the acronym for System Applications and Products in Data Processing. It is a translation of the German phrase Systeme, Anwendungen, und Produkte in der Datenverarbeitung. It was developed by SAP AG, Germany. The basic idea behind developing the SAP system was the need for a standard application software to help real-time business processing.

SAPscript

SAPscript, a tool of the SAP R/3 system, is used to build and manage business forms such as invoices and purchase orders. A SAPscript form is a template that simplifies the designing of a business form. It provides the layout and content of the form.

Screen Painter

Screen Painter (accessed by transaction code `SE51`) is a tool of ABAP Workbench, and is used to design and manage screens and their elements. It facilitates the users to create GUI screens for transactions.

Search help

Search help is a repository object of ABAP Dictionary that is used to define input helps (F4 helps) for fields.

Selection screen

A selection screen is a type of user dialog box that is different from the other general type of screens, which are designed with the help of ABAP Workbench tools, such as Screen Painter and Menu Painter. A selection screen is created by using ABAP statements, such as `PARAMETERS` and `SELECTION-SCREEN` statements, and is designed to accept data from users. Selection screens allow you to define various selection criteria required by a program. Using a selection screen, you can create a list containing data from a very large database table.

Size category

A size category is a technical setting that defines the size of a table based upon the number of records that can be entered in the table.

Smart Form Builder

Smart Form Builder is the main interface used to build a Smart Form. It is available on the initial screen of the SAP Smart Forms.

Sorted table

Sorted tables have internal indices, similar to standard tables and are sorted with the help of a key. You can access the records of a sorted table by using a table index or key. In sorted tables, a key can be defined as either unique or non-unique. Sorted and standard tables use indexes and are therefore also called index tables.

Source code module

Source code modules modularize the source code; i.e., placing a sequence of ABAP statements in a module. Source code modules help to minimize data redundancy by avoiding repeated occurrence of the same set of statements. ABAP provides two types of source code modules: macros and include programs.

Standard table

Standard tables have a linear index which manages the table as a tree-like structure. The records of a standard table are accessed by using a table index or key. Standard tables always have a non-unique key.

Style Builder

Style Builder is a tool used to define a Smart Style for a Smart Form. It is available on the initial screen of Smart Styles, which is opened by using the `SMARTSTYLES` transaction code.

Subquery

A subquery is a type of `SELECT` statement that is used within the `WHERE` clause of another `SELECT` statement, that is, a `SELECT` statement is nested inside another `SELECT` statement.

Subroutine

A subroutine is a mini-program that consists of a sequence of statements. Subroutines prevent redundancy of statements in an ABAP program. A subroutine is defined within the `FORM` and `ENDFORM` statements. Within a subroutine, you can define variables, execute ABAP statements to calculate results, and display the calculated result on the screen. Subroutines defined in an ABAP program can be called either in the same ABAP program or from any other ABAP program with the help of the `PERFORM` statement.

Subroutine pool

A subroutine pool is a program that contains a collection of subroutines that can be called externally in other ABAP programs. Besides subroutines, a subroutine pool can contain local classes and interfaces. After SAP release 6.0, subroutine pool programs also can be called through transaction codes which are attached with the public methods of local or global classes of these programs. In ABAP Editor, a subroutine pool is created by using the `PROGRAM` statement.

System variable

The SAP R/3 system information is stored in the system variables stored in the ABAP Dictionary structure named SYST. The SAP R/3 system makes the system variables available within your program. These variables are updated automatically by the system as your program's environment changes. All the system variables are prefixed with SY, such as `SY-DYNNR` and `SY-DATUM`.

Table control

The table control is a complex graphical screen element that is used to display data in a tabular form. The data can be entered, displayed, and modified easily in table controls. There are different functions that the table control provides during its definition and runtime. During its definition, functions such as fixed columns and column headers are provided by the table control. During runtime, functions, such as vertical scrolling, horizontal scrolling, selecting any row or column, movable columns, and column width, can be modified.

Table type

A table type is a data type in ABAP Dictionary that describes the structure and functional attributes of an internal table. An internal table is a temporary table that exists only during the runtime of an ABAP program. In an internal table, all the records have the same structure and key. The record of the internal table is discarded when the execution of the program is terminated.

Tabstrip control

Tabstrip control is a screen element that contains two or more tab pages. Each tab page has a tab title and a page area, where other screen elements are stored. You can use a tabstrip control in an application to place a number of screens belonging to the application on a single screen. A tab page in tabstrip control actually acts as a subscreen with a button (displayed as a tab title) assigned to the subscreen.

Transparent table

A transparent table is one of the table types in ABAP Dictionary. It forms a one-to-one relationship with the table definition in the database. Transparent tables are used to hold the application data, which represents either the master data or the transaction data used by an application.

Type group

A type group is a repository object of ABAP Dictionary that is used to create a group of data types in ABAP Dictionary.

User context

User context represents the data specifically assigned to an SAP user. The information stored in the user context can be changed by using the roll area of the memory management system in the SAP system.

View

A view is a repository object of ABAP Dictionary that is used to retrieve data from the database tables.

Web service

A web service is defined as an independent and self-sustained unit of a software application that is hosted on the Internet. These self-sustained units collectively implement specific functionalities to execute the business logic of an application. Web services allow applications to expose business operations to other applications, regardless of their implementation by using the various standards: Extensible Markup Language (XML), Simple Object Access Protocol (SOAP), Web Service Description Language (WSDL), and Universal Description, Discovery and Integration (UDDI). ABAP Workbench enables SAP Web Application Builder to act as a platform for creating and publishing Web services, Internet Transactions Services (ITS)–based Web applications, and Business Server Pages (BSP) applications.

XSLT Editor

XSLT is an acronym for eXtensible Stylesheet Language Transformation. The XSLT Editor is a development tool integrated in ABAP Workbench and used to define XSL transformations. XSL transformations are executed on the application server. Using the XSLT Editor, XML documents can be transformed into either other Extensible Markup Language(XML) or Hypertext Markup Language(HTML) documents or ABAP data structures.

INDEX

A

ABAP Debugger, 89–90, 114–115
ABAP Dictionary, 92–94, 123–125, 138, 140, 144–149, 158, 174, 180, 212, 215, 244, 258, 412, 413, 425, 652, 695
ABAP Editor, 90, 94–95, 227, 228, 231–239, 499, 605, 618, 820, 829
ABAP Objects, 245–247, 881–887, 902–905
ABAP Processor, 17–18
ABAP Runtime Analysis, 115–116
ABAP Text Elements, 110–111, 634
ABAP user dialogs, 549
ABAP Workbench service, 10
Advanced Business Application Programming (ABAP), 1, 6, 24, 114, 115, 184, 227, 416, 515, 540, 552, 650, 651, 736, 883
Alphanumeric mode, 103
ALV Reports, 839–846
Append Search Help, 214–215
`APPEND` statement, 348–352
`APPENDING` clause, 430, 435
APPL0 (master data), 155
APPL1 (transaction data), 155
APPL2 (organizational data), 155
Apple Macintosh, 55, 60
Application Layer, 11–13
Application servers, 2, 11, 12, 15
Application Toolbar, 67, 74, 607, 608
`AT FIRST` and `AT LAST` statements, 392–395
`AT LINE-SELECTION` Event, 828
`AT NEW` and `AT END OF` statements, 395–400
Attributes, 103, 133, 144, 145, 233, 303, 333–335, 555–559, 720, 803, 889
Authorization Group, 206

B

Back-End Editor, 98–99
BAPIs, 113, 645, 649
BAPIs technique, 649
Batch Data Communication (BDC), 645
Batch Input with Session Method, 651, 675
BDCDATA structure, 652, 654, 665, 680
`BEGIN OF` clause, 302
`BINARY SEARCH` clause, 386, 389
Breakpoint, 114
Buffering permission, 154, 157

Buffering type, 154, 157
Business Server Pages (BSP), 108, 116

C

CALL BADI statement, 858, 878, 880
CALL SCREEN statement, 551
CALL SELECTION-SCREEN statement, 629, 639
Call Transaction Method, 650, 653, 668
Cardinality, 178
CASE Control Statement, 287–288
CASE Statement, 288
Character formats, 744, 759, 800
CHECK Statement, 296, 525, 526
Class Browser, 99
Class Builder, 99–101, 238, 865, 866, 874
Class pools, 238
Classes, 885
Classical reports, 817, 818–827
CLEAR Statement, 266–268, 837
Client, 4, 26, 30, 55, 414, 440, 738, 789
Cluster tables, 150–152
COLLECT statement, 346–348
Collective Search Help, 213–214
Command field, 44, 64, 92, 94, 99, 100, 102, 104, 106, 111, 116, 236, 534, 570, 587, 600, 795, 811
Comments, 239–241, 630–632
COMMIT WORK statement, 494, 495
Complex types, 244
Composer or Form Processor, 739
Compound foreign keys, 176
CONTINUE Statement, 294, 295
CONTROL_FORM function module, 763, 783–784
CONVERSION_EXIT_xxxxx_INPUT, 127
CONVERSION_EXIT_xxxxx_OUTPUT, 127
CPU, 20
Currency field, 152–153

D

Data class, 154–155
Data elements, 138–139, 161–166
DATA Statement, 248–252, 313, 315, 324, 493
Data transfer methods, 649–651
Data type, 93, 125, 138, 144, 242, 244, 266, 300, 301, 305, 425
Database layer, 13
Database server, 11
Database table, 93, 125, 146, 149, 181, 412–416, 422, 437, 438, 444, 452, 461, 471–483, 488–490
Database views, 184
DBMS, 9, 13, 817
DELETE Statement, 373–375, 378, 379, 383–385, 485, 486
DESCRIBE TABLE statement, 333, 334
Dialog steps, 12, 22
Direct input method, 650
Dispatcher, 16, 22, 23, 25
DO statement, 289–291
Documentation, 139, 143, 233, 744, 760, 761
Domain, 93, 125–138
Dynamic Assignment, 278–279
Dynamic or anonymous data object, 247

E

Editor, 90, 94–99, 103, 227, 228, 231–239, 499, 555, 561–599, 605, 618, 820, 829
Element bar, 563
Element list, 103
Element Palette, 563, 564
Elementary lock, 219
Elementary Search Help, 212–213
Elementary types, 138, 242
Elements list, 554
ELSEIF statement, 284–285
END_FORM function module, 764, 775, 779, 782–783
ENDFORM statement, 498, 522, 524, 684
END-OF-PAGE event, 819
END-OF-SELECTION event, 818
Enhancement Builder, 854, 860, 862, 864
Enhancement Category, 167–173
Enhancement Framework, 849–856
Enhancement implementations, 852–854
Enhancement options, 851, 852
Enhancement spots, 851–852, 854
Enterprise Resource Planning (ERP), 2–4, 56, 738
Events, 231, 551, 643, 818, 828, 890–891, 902, 917
Exclusive but not cumulative lock, 220
Exclusive lock, 220
Executable programs, 236–237
EXIT Statement, 294, 295, 524
Export parameter, 212
External calls, 515–518

F

Favorites, 56, 72–84
FETCH NEXT CURSOR statement, 491, 492
Field list, 797
Fields, 30, 33, 125, 147, 152, 161, 174, 185, 203, 217, 218, 244, 246, 275–278, 346, 358, 365, 403, 430, 462, 506, 552, 558, 621, 629, 820
F-Key Settings, 105, 600
Flow logic, 17, 22, 103, 237, 550–552, 554, 559–561, 643
FOR ALL ENTRIES clause, 451, 452
Foreign keys, 147, 174–180
Form Painter, 743, 746–751
FORM statement, 498, 503, 519, 522, 523
FORMAT Statement, 271–278
FREE statement, 320, 321
FROM clause, 417, 437–446, 472, 483, 484
Front-End Editor (New), 95–96
Front-End Editor (Old), 96–98
Full buffering, 157
Function Builder, 101–102, 238, 527, 528, 534
Function group, 101, 108, 206, 237, 526, 529, 882
Function list, 105, 600
Function modules, 101, 216, 217, 238, 526–543, 771–786

G

Gateway, 1, 16
Generic and constant foreign keys, 176–178

Generic buffering, 157
GET BADI statement, 849, 858, 859, 875, 876
Global settings, 797
Graphical mode, 103
GROUP BY clause, 459–462

H

Hashed tables, 305
Header, 60–61, 743, 752–754
Help views, 207–211
HIDE statement, 836
HTML, 118–120

I

IF Statement, 283, 284, 321
IF...ENDIF Control Statement, 280–282
Import parameter, 212, 773, 781
Inactive objects, 109
Include programs, 237, 545–547
Indexes, 147
INNER join, 438, 439, 443, 445
Integrated window, 107, 108
Interactive reports, 827–839
Interface objects, 105, 600
Interface pools, 238
Interfaces, 246, 885, 895–898
Internal calls, 513–515
Internal tables, 267, 299
INTO clause, 428–436
ITS, 118

J

JOIN clause, 438, 439
Join condition, 182

K

Kernel and Basis services, 9–10
Key, 144, 174–180, 245, 303, 356–357, 364–365, 374

L

Layout Editor, 103, 555, 561–599
LEFT OUTER join, 439, 444–446
Legacy System Migration Workbench (LSMW), 697–733
List and column headers, 110
Lists, 817, 827–829
Literal, 246
Local objects, 108–109
LOCAL statement, 505, 506
Lock mode, 218–220
Lock object, 93, 125, 215–226
Logging, 52–53, 154
Logical view, 9–10
Looping, 289–291
LUW, 21, 219, 495

M

Macros, 544–545
Maintain transaction, 91, 111–112, 587
Maintenance, 109, 198–207, 797, 800

Maintenance type, 206
Maintenance views, 198–207
Master data, 13, 148, 155, 920
Menu bar, 61–63, 105, 600
Menu list, 105, 600
Menu Painter, 103–105, 599–619
Message maintenance, 109
Message server, 12, 14, 15, 49
Messages, 109
Microsoft Windows, 5, 37, 588
MIME, 106, 118, 119
Modularization techniques, 497
Module pools, 237
MOVE Statement, 259–263
MOVE-CORRESPONDING Statement, 263–265
mySAP Customer Relationship Management (CRM), 6
mySAP ERP, 5, 6, 27, 28, 56, 309, 735, 736, 738, 743, 764, 794
mySAP Product Lifestyle Management (PLM), 6
mySAP Supplier Relationship Management (SRM), 6
mySAP Supply Chain Management (SCM), 6

N

Named data object, 246–247, 248, 256
Native SQL, 19, 411, 415–416
Navigation area, 107
Navigation menu, 796, 797, 803

O

Object navigator, 105–109
Object types, 245–246
Objects, 125, 215–226, 246–247, 313–316, 507–510, 800–801, 882–883, 884–885, 887, 889, 893–894, 902–905
OCCURS clause, 301, 302, 333
OK_CODE, 103, 554
ON CHANGE OF statement, 403–410
Open SQL, 19, 411, 413–415, 416, 417, 438, 440, 471, 477, 483, 494
OPEN_FORM function module, 768, 771–774, 779, 782, 783, 787
Optimistic lock, 220
Options, 49, 62, 63, 74, 144, 268–278, 851

P

Package, 108, 112–113, 131–133, 501, 556
Page window, 744
Pages, 743, 755, 791, 797
Pages and windows, 797
Paragraph formats, 744, 758–759
PARAMETERS Statement, 252–258, 540, 620
Pass by reference method, 520–521
Pass by value and result method, 522–523
Pass by value method, 521–522
Passing parameters to subroutines, 518–520

Password, 30, 50–51
PERFORM statement, 248, 503, 513, 515–516, 524
Performance Analysis, 90, 114, 116–117
Pooled tables, 149–150
POSITION clause, 635
Predefined ABAP Dictionary type, 138
Predefined data object, 247, 249, 253
Presentation Components service, 10
Presentation layer, 5, 11
Private memory, 24
PROCESS AFTER INPUT (PAI), 17, 560
PROCESS BEFORE OUTPUT (PBO), 17, 560
Programming interface, 739
Projection condition, 182
Projection views, 184, 193–198

Q

Quantity field, 153–154

R

R/3 sessions, 14
READ TABLE statement, 356, 358, 359
Recording routine, 206
Reference data types, 245
REFRESH statement, 320, 321, 352
Relational operators, 181, 447
Remote Function Call (RFC), 16, 117, 223, 536
REPORT statement, 236, 501, 819, 825
Repository Browser, 99, 106, 108, 120, 561
Repository Information System, 106
Repository Objects, 13, 106, 118, 125, 226
REUSE_ALV_GRID_DISPLAY function module, 840, 842, 843
REUSE_ALV_LIST_DISPLAY function module, 817
Roll area, 24–25
ROLLBACK WORK statement, 412, 494–495
Row or line type, 144, 303

S

SAP Basis, 7, 413
SAP Easy Access screen, 30, 56–59, 66, 92, 94, 110, 115, 231, 568, 599, 698, 742
SAP ECC, 60
SAP Extended Memory, 24
SAP Graphical User Interface (GUI), 10, 37, 55, 60, 64, 70–72
SAP Logon, 28, 31–37, 42, 47–50
SAP Logon Configuration, 47, 49
SAP menu, 57–59, 75, 78, 309, 746
SAP R/1, 4
SAP R/2, 4–5, 911
SAP R/3, 5–6, 8–14, 21, 26, 67, 412, 419, 762, 882
SAP Roll Area, 24
SAP session, 46–47, 84–88
SAP shortcut, 37–47
SAP Smart Forms, 7, 26, 793–808
SAP Web Application server, 7
SAProuter string, 33
SAPscript, 26, 736, 738, 762, 771, 787, 789, 808, 810

SAPscript Control commands, 789–790
SAPscript symbols, 791–793
Screen body, 56, 67–68
Screen enhancements, 849, 879–880
Screen header, 60–61
Screen number, 102, 556, 596
Screen Painter, 39, 102–103, 552, 561, 566, 577, 593
Screen Processor, 17
Search help, 93, 125, 212–215
`SEARCH...FOR` statement, 386
`SELECT` statement, 416, 417, 423, 428, 437, 446
Selection condition, 183–184, 211
Selection screens, 229, 620–643
Selection texts, 110
`SELECTION-SCREEN` statement, 550, 629–638
`SELECT-OPTIONS` statement, 621–629
Self-defined or user-defined key, 302
Shared lock, 220
Shared memory, 16
Shortcuts, 31, 37–47
Single-record buffering, 157
Size category, 154, 156
Smart Form function module, 795, 798
Smart Form print form template, 795, 797
Smart Form print program, 795, 798
SOAP, 117
`SORT` statement, 325, 326, 329, 409
Sorted tables, 304–305
Source code, 233, 419, 497, 538, 543–547, 855
Source code module, 497, 543–547
SQL, 6, 117, 411, 413–416
Standard key, 302
Standard tables, 304, 318, 389, 419
Standard toolbar, 61, 64–66, 70
`START_FORM` function module, 775–777, 788
`START-OF-SELECTION` Event, 231, 641, 818
`STATICS` Statement, 509–510
Status, 103, 105, 139, 552, 600, 603, 918
Status bar, 56, 68–70, 605, 692
Status list, 105, 600
Structure of a BAdI, 856–858
Structure type, 244
Structures, 16, 25, 120, 144, 216, 218, 228–231, 244, 267, 652, 739, 856–858, 913
Styles and forms, 739
Subqueries, 449, 465–470
Subroutine pools, 237
Subroutines, 237, 498, 505, 518, 524, 663
`SUM` function, 425
`SUM` statement, 401–403
`SY-INDEX`, 278, 291, 341, 344, 354, 362, 383
System ID, 33, 39
System number, 33
System variables, 278, 415, 472, 791
Systems, 1, 2, 4, 28, 31, 52, 60, 62, 411, 697, 791, 910
Systems Applications and Products (SAP), 1, 4, 8, 24, 26, 28, 31, 52, 60, 84, 735, 793
`SY-SUBRC`, 337, 358, 362, 365, 375, 386, 415, 640

T

Table control, 565, 590–599
Table Maintenance Generator, 205
Table type, 138, 144–145, 245, 303, 306, 593
TABLES, 148–152, 174, 181, 258, 300, 303, 316, 364, 390, 412, 449, 479, 528
Tabstrip control, 564, 568, 571, 575, 590
Tag browser, 106, 120
Technical settings, 147, 154, 166
Test Repository, 106
Text elements, 110, 233
Text symbols, 110, 634
Title bar, 61, 66
Title field, 39, 44, 310, 569, 616, 679
Title list, 105, 600, 616
Tools area, 107, 108
TOP-OF-PAGE Event, 818, 819
Transaction code, 53, 64, 112, 236, 588, 654, 704
Transparent tables, 148
Transport Organizer, 106
Type field, 39, 100, 165, 236, 269
Type Group, 93, 125, 145–146
TYPE-POOLS, 146
TYPES Statement, 249, 306, 308–313

U

UDDI, 117
Unicode checks active check box, 500
UNIX, 5, 55
UPDATE statement, 477, 479, 480, 489
User, 13, 24, 30, 56, 65, 113, 119, 300, 302, 549, 562, 880

V

Variants, 233
View, 9–14, 63, 93, 125, 180, 184–211

W

WHERE Clause, 305, 366, 375, 446, 452, 485
Windows, 5, 13, 741, 743, 757, 797
WITH HEADER LINE clause, 302, 314
Work area, 258, 301, 335, 391, 563
Work processes, 15, 19–22
WRITE statement, 268–271
WRITE TO statement, 265–266, 364, 371–373
WRITE_FORM function module, 763, 777–780
WSDL, 117

X

XSL, 90, 120, 121
XSLT, 90, 120–121